D1773231

Quick Java Basics

Types

int	32 bits	9 digits
long	64 bits	19 digits
double	64 bits	16 places
char	16 bits	
short	16 bits	
byte	8 bits	
float	32 bits	7 places
boolean	1 bit	

if statement (See page 87)

```
if (condition)
   if_true_statement
```

if-else statement (See page 90)

```
if (condition)
   if_true_statement
else
   if_false_statement
```

while statement (See page 107)

```
while (condition)
  while_true_statement
```

switch statement (See page 152)

```
switch (test_expression)  {
  case expression1:
                    statement1
  case expression2:
                    statement2
            .....
  default:
                    default_statement
}
```

for statement (See page 159)

```
for (initialize; test; update)
   for_statement
```

do-while statement (See page 163)

```
do
  statement
while (condition) ;
```

Operator Precedence Table

Highest

Postfix Operators	[ ] . () ++ --	page 59
Unary Operators	++ (prefix) -- (prefix) + - ~ !	pages 52, 60, 141
Cast, Allocation	() new	pages 42, 106
Multiplicative	* / %	page 53
Additive	+ -	page 53
Shift	<< >> >>>	page 926
Relational	< > <= >= instanceof	page 83
Equality	== !=	page 83
Bitwise, Logical AND	&	page 925
Bitwise, Logical XOR	^	page 925
Bitwise, Logical OR			page 925
Conditional AND	&&	page 139
Conditional OR	||	page 140
Conditional	?:	page 892
Assignment	= += -= *= /= %= >>= <<= >>>= &= ^= |=	pages 40, 57

Lowest

COMPUTING WITH JAVA™: PROGRAMS, OBJECTS, GRAPHICS

ALTERNATE SECOND EDITION

Art Gittleman

California State University, Long Beach

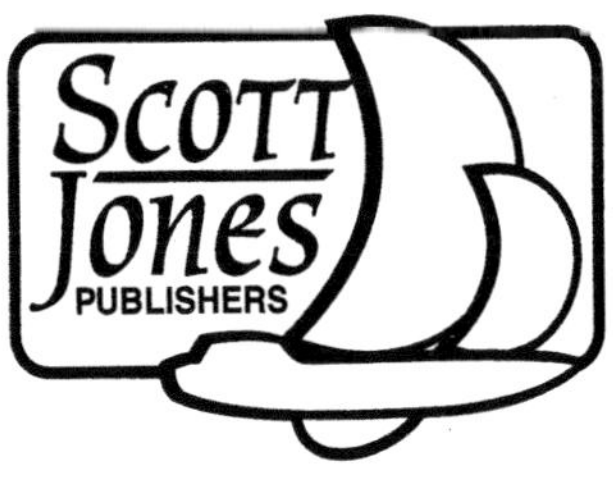

Scott/Jones, Inc.
P.O. Box 696,
El Granada, California, 94018
Voice: **650-726-2436**
Facsimile: **650-726-4693**
e-mail: **marketing@scottjonespub.com**
Web page: **//www.scottjonespub.com**

ISBN 1-57676-074-x

Computing with Java™: Programs, Objects, Graphics, Alternate Second Edition

Art Gittleman
California State University, Long Beach

XW 432

ISBN: 1-57676-074-x

The publisher wishes to acknowledge the memory and influence of James F Leisy. Thanks, Jim. We miss you.

Composition: Stephen Adams
Book Manufacturing: Von Hoffmann Graphics

Scott/Jones Publishing Company

Publisher: Richard Jones
Editorial Group: Richard Jones, Mike Needham, Denise Simon, Michelle Windell, and Patricia Miyaki
Production Management: Heather Bennett
Marketing and Sales: Victoria Judy, Page Mead, Hazel Dunlap, Donna Cross, and Michelle Windell
Business Operations: Michelle Robelet, Cathy Glenn, and Natasha Hoffmeyer

Contents

CHAPTER 8 *Arrays* 339

CHAPTER 9 *Inheritance* 399

CHAPTER 13 *Data Structures* 587

CHAPTER 14 *Collections* 627

CHAPTER 15 *Multimedia* 665

CHAPTER 16 *Networking* 711

CHAPTER 17 *Java Database Connectivity (JDBC)* 753

CHAPTER 18 *Servlets and JavaServer Pages™* 807

CHAPTER 19 *Java Beans* 845

Preface

The Alternate Second Edition of Computing with Java introduces objects early, and adds enough material so the text can be used for an entire year if desired.

Objects Early and Often

Introducing objects early helps students develop object-oriented thinking from the start. They are able to develop simpler, clearer programs, and gain a good foundation for software design. To make this approach work I use a spiral approach, presenting object-oriented programming and design in graded stages.

Chapter 1, Computing with Java, introduces the object concept and object-oriented design independently of Java. It includes a simple vending machine example. Scenarios model a simple fast food order and an ATM deposit. I begin the use of the Unified Modeling Language diagrams. The chapter starts with an introduction to computing and an overview of Java. It shows how to compile and run Java applications and applets. Students learn how program-driven applications differ from event-driven ones. As motivation, a few screen captures show a Web page containing an applet, developed fully in a later chapter, which simulates online banking.

Changes in the Alternate Second Edition: The added introduction to objects illustrated with a vending machine provides a gentle start. The lengthy code to the online banking example only appears in a later chapter.

Chapter 2, Programming with Objects, shows how a class defines an object type, and how one uses an object's services. It simulates the simple vending machine introduced in Chapter 1. After introducing arithmetic expressions it improves and extends the vending machine. The next section begins the discussion of parameter passing and presents the Swing input dialog. Using an input dialog allows students to input values without requiring any special code library. Chapter 2 concludes with an introduction to applets and events. Students like to use graphics and interact. Introducing graphics early increases interest and motivation. As they progress through this chapter students can begin to program in Java.

Changes in the Alternate Second Edition: Objects are now integrated into the chapter rather than being left to an optional section at its end. I expanded the discussion of parameter passing. Using the Swing input dialog removes the need for extra code, so the specially designed `iopack` package used in the first edition is no longer needed in the second. The last section adding graphics early is new.

Chapter 3, Software Engineering with Control Structures, introduces a minimal set of control structures to enable students to write more complex programs. I teach program development with pseudocode so students learn to program carefully with precision. Introducing the type `double` makes some examples more realistic. A debugging section provides some simple and useful techniques. The last section shows how to draw shapes again using applets.

Changes in the Alternate Second Edition: Objects are now integrated into the chapter rather than being left to an optional section at its end. The last section adding graphics early is new.

Chapter 4, More Control Structures and Types, adds additional control structures and types to make programming more convenient. It includes Math library methods. The final section presents a case study on iterated program development so student can develop larger programs in a controlled manner.

Changes in the Alternate Second Edition: Objects are now integrated into the chapter rather than being left to an optional section at its end.

Chapter 5, Object-Oriented Design and Programming, returns to object-oriented design after students have developed skill with objects using control structures. The `String` class provides a rich example for object use. I implement the QuickFood and BankAccount designs begun in Chapter 1 introducing additional UML diagrams. I amplify class design, adding both class and instance variables and methods and object composition.

Changes in the Alternate Second Edition: This is a new chapter that amplifies some of the material from the earlier chapters of the first edition, and adds additional examples. It includes additional UML diagrams. It clarifies the distinction between instance and class variables and methods. I postpone the advanced concepts in Chapter 5 of the first edition to Chapter 9.

Chapter 9, Inheritance, covers the more advanced concepts of inheritance including abstract classes and polymorphism. Carefully designed examples illustrate each feature of inheritance, so students learn one concept before moving on to the next.

Changes in the Alternate Second Edition: The first section contains several examples that illustrate each facet of inheritance. First a class extends another class without adding anything to it, showing that it inherits the state and behavior of its superclass. In the next example a subclass explicitly defines a constructor, illustrating how a subclass constructor needs to call a superclass constructor. Additional examples illustrate extending a class by adding state and behavior, and overriding behavior. The section on polymorphism includes a simple `Animal` example to make the discussion more concrete. The `Shape` example and the ATM case study now use the graphics that have been introduced earlier.

Event-driven programming

Students enjoy event-driven programming with graphics and user interfaces. Again I use a spiral approach. I introduce applets in the first three chapters as motivation and to get students started simply. Then Chapters 6, 7, and 10 cover event-driven programming gradually increasing the difficulty.

Chapter 6, Event-Driven Programming, concentrates on the simpler paint events. We start with a short introduction to HTML. Examples use fonts and color. The later sections introduce interfaces, with intuitive examples, and the Java event model, in preparation for the study of user interfaces in the next chapter.

Changes in the Alternate Second Edition: This chapter contains some material from Chapter 7 of the first edition. The `ColorChips` example replaces `Colorful` that had some complex calculations not relevant to the use of color. New simpler and more intuitive examples explain interfaces, replacing the rate change example used in the first edition. The last section contains a first look at inheritance, just enough to prepare for user interfaces in the next chapter. In this way students can do event-driven programming before taking the time needed to study of inheritance in detail, which I postpone to Chapter 9. The `Tangram` example from the former Chapter 7 has moved to Chapter 10.

Chapter 7, User Interfaces, uses high-level events to implement graphical user interfaces. The first section explains the use of a layout manager. The second section covers the `Button` and `TextField` components that generate Action events. The third section covers the `Checkbox` and `Choice` components that generate Item events. The fourth section uses the Grid and Border layouts. The next section covers the `List` and `TextArea` components and the chapter concludes with a discussion of the GridBag layout only needed in examples in the advanced chapters. High-level events come before the more complex low-level events treated in Chapter 10.

Changes in the Alternate Second Edition: The first four sections are from Chapter 8 of the first edition. The last two sections are new. The sorting example from the original chapter 8 will be found in the new chapter 8 on arrays.

Chapter 10, Window, Mouse, and Key Events, covers the low-level events that require more complex interfaces. It starts with window events. The next section develops graphical standalone applications. I chose to start graphics using applets to avoid the need to cover window handling earlier or to introduce canned code to hide the details from students. In this chapter students learn that all the graphics they used in applets can be used in standalone applications. The chapter continues with mouse and key events, and concludes with a tangram case study using low-level events.

Changes in the Alternate Second Edition: This chapter contains material from the original Chapter 9, however I put window events before mouse and key events, so that covering the first two sections to introduce graphical standalone applications is possible without covering the mouse and key events that follow. I removed the displaying of window events other than `WINDOW_CLOSING` from the `AppletFrame` example. The tangram case study includes the two sections from Chapters 7 and 9 of the first edition.

Additional Core Topics

Chapter 8, Arrays, covers arrays including arrays of arrays. It contrasts array variables, which are references, with primitive type variables, which hold values. One section discusses passing array arguments and returning array values from methods. Several examples illustrate the use of arrays, including a case study on sorting comprising the last two sections

Changes in the Alternate Second Edition: This chapter uses material from Chapter 6 of the first edition. Postponing arrays allows students to start event-driven programming earlier. The GUI part of the case study was in Chapter 8 in the first edition.

Chapter 11, Exception Handling and Input/Output, introduces exception handling. Then one section covers text file input and output and another treats binary I/O. The first section explains program arguments and applet parameters.

Changes in the Alternate Second Edition: The first three sections come from Chapter 10 of the first edition, but the sections on passing program arguments was moved to the start of the chapter in order to be available in the later sections. The section of binary I/O is new.

Advanced Java and Data Structures

The remaining chapters allow for longer courses and provide flexibility to select topics.

Chapter 12, Swing Components, covers the user interface components that supplement those provided in the AWT. Components covered include buttons, lists, toggle buttons, scroll panes, menus, dialogs, tabs, and tables. This chapter is new in the alternate second edition.

Chapter 13, Data Structures, covers recursion, linked lists, stacks, queues, vectors, enumerations, and hash tables.

Changes in the Alternate Second Edition: The first three sections are from Chapter 10 of the first edition. The sections on vectors and hash tables are new.

Chapter 14, Collections, discusses the data structures introduced with the Java 2 Platform, including sets, iterators, lists, map sorted sets, sorted maps, and algorithms. It is new in the alternate second edition.

Chapter 15, Threads and Multimedia, discusses threads and uses them in animation. Sections on images and sound precede an introduction to the Java Media Framework. The final section treats concurrent programming.

Changes in the Alternate Second Edition: The first four sections are from Chapter 11 of the first edition while the last two are new.

Chapter 16, Networking, starts with the URL which hides the details of the protocol used to communicate across the network. The next section discusses HTTP and uses the URLConnection, which hides the protocol details but allows the programmer to customize the connection as desired. At the lowest level sockets require the programmer to fully implement the communication protocol. A very simple browser and web server serve as illustrations. The last section covers remote method invocation for distributed computing.

Changes in the Alternate Second Edition: Most of this chapter is new, but it does incorporate Section 11. 5 from the first edition.

Chapter 17, Java Database Connectivity (JDBC), starts with an introduction to relational databases and Structured Query Language (SQL). The next sections show how to connect to a database and to execute queries. More advanced techniques follow including using metadata, prepared statements, and transactions. The chapter concludes with a case study using a GUI to access a database. This chapter is new in the second alternate edition.

Chapter 18, Servlets and JavaServer™ Pages, presents an introduction to Java on the server. It shows how to use servlets with the JRun servlet engine. The next section shows how input from the client in an HTML can be handled by a servlet. Server-side includes and servlet chaining add additional capabilities. Three-tiered architectures may use a servlet in the middle to communicate between a database on the backend and a client at the front. Session tracking allows the server to handle multiple request from the same client. The last section introduces JavaServer™ Pages which add script tags to a web page, and the engine creates the servlet automatically. This chapter is new in the alternate second edition.

Chapter 19, Java Beans, introduces the JavaBean™ component technology. Using an application building tool such as the BeanBox included with the Beans Development Kit, a developer can build an application from JavaBean™ with little or no coding. After showing how to use the BeanBox, the chapter goes on to show how to build beans. Next it covers the use of BeanInfo to make a bean easier to use use. The chapter concludes by showing how to use beans without the benefit of a visual building tool. This chapter is new in the alternate second edition.

Chapter 20, XML (Extensible Markup Language), covers XML, which provides platform independent data, just as Java provides platform independent code. XML focuses on the content of the document not its presentation. After describing XML syntax it covers SAX and DOM parsing, and the XSLT stylesheets used, to transform XML, perhaps to a display format such as HTML. The chapter includes with an introduction to SOAP, used to access web services. This chapter is new in the second alternate edition.

These topics provide students with the knowledge to use Java effectively both in future study in specialized areas, and in careers where such Java knowledge is in great demand.

Features

Example Programs

Examples give new concepts a concrete embodiment that facilitates learning. I include over 200 complete, fully annotated programs. I could use comments to annotate the code, but the detailed comments necessary for teaching purposes would obscure the code. For that I reason I much prefer to label significant lines and then present the extended comment in a Note immediately following the code. Each example is a complete program presented with sample output.

Exercises

The programs can be found at www.aw.com/cssupport. I provide many and varied exercises to allow the learner to assimilate concepts and techniques actively using them thoughtfully.

- **Test Your Understanding** exercises appear interspersed within the text to provide an immediate opportunity to use the ideas presented. By putting exercises in each section I target each new idea as it occurs. Answers to many of these appear at the end of the text and the answers to most of the remaining can be found on www.aw.com/cssupport. Some, labeled **Try It Yourself** encourage the learner to experiment with the examples, modifying them to better understand the principles involved.
- **Skill Builder Exercises** at the end of chapters 2–15 provide various matching, fill-in-the-blanks, and code tracking exercises to build a working knowledge of the material covered. Answers to all of these appear at the end of the text.
- **Critical thinking Exercises** at the end of chapters 2–15 provide multiple choice questions that force students to think carefully about the concepts. Answers to all appear at the end of the text.
- **Debugging Exercise.** In each of Chapters 3–15, 1 give one program with errors that are to be found and corrected if possible. The code for these challenging exercises is on www.aw.com/cssupport to encourage students to attempt them.
- **Program Modification Exercises** occur as soon we develop examples complex enough to modify fruitfully. Much of a professional programmer's work involves modifying existing code, so I believe in giving students early practice at it.

  Marked **Putting It All Together Exercises** revisit examples from previous chapters in the light of the new ideas in the current chapter.
- **Program Design Exercises** appear in quantity to provide a variety of assignments at all levels of difficulty to enable students to develop design and programming ability.

Comprehensive Content

I cover the fundamental concepts of object-oriented and event-driven programming, AND more advanced topics including Swing, Collections, threads, concurrent programming, networking, database connectivity, servlets, JavaServer Pages, JavaBeans, XML.

Students have a comprehensive one-volume reference for modern Java-based technology.

Software Engineering

I integrate software engineering throughout the text.

- **Problem Solving Methods,** Section 3.5, teaches program design with pseudocode, while 3.6 introduces debugging techniques.
- **Solving Problems with Java** sections in Chapters 4 and 8 illustrate software-engineering principles in the context of solving problems.
- **Case Studies** develop extended examples, including insertion sort and the creation of a tangram puzzle, and object-oriented design. The ATMScreen example provides a theme for the first part of the book, and results in a full object-oriented design in Chapter 9.
- **Object-Oriented Design** presents use cases, scenarios, and the Unified Modeling Language (UML) to prepare students for further study in this area of growing importance.
- **Tips and Style** The tips help the student avoid common mistakes and misconceptions while the style notes give students guidance on appropriate program formatting. I use these judiciously, hoping that students will remember and use them, rather than be overwhelmed by an overly long list.

Event-driven Programming

I present event-driven programming gradually with motivation and examples. First, starting in Chapter 6, I concentrate on graphics where painting a window does not require understanding the Java event model. Chapter 7 on user interfaces covers only high-level events such as button presses. Only in Chapter 10 do I cover the low-level more complex event handling needed for window, mouse, and key events. Instructors have a choice of how much event-driven programming to include.

Reference Material

New appeddices cover the javadoc documentation tool and list packages and classes and methods used in the text.

Using this Text

Instructors can use this text in several ways. Students with no knowledge of Java, and no prior computing background would concentrate on the first half. The first eight chapters cover software engineering, object-oriented programming, event-driven programming and basic Java constructs. Instructors may include additional material depending on the length and pace of the course. I cover Chapters 1–9 and parts of Chapters 10 and 11. Optionally, a follow-up course emphasizing Internet applications would cover the remainder of the text.

Students with additional background could proceed more rapidly over the early chapters and include selected advanced topics. Chapters 9–20 are mostly independent of one another so instructors have flexibility in choosing additional topics.

Other Options

This is the third text in my series of Java texts with Scott/Jones Publishing. A brief comparison of these texts is given below:

Computing with Java™: Programs, Objects, Graphics, Second Edition	Computing with Java™: Programs, Objects, Graphics, Alternate Second Edition	Advanced Java™ Internet Applications, Second Edition
Introductory: Control structures before objects	Introductory: Objects before control structures	Advanced course with an introductory Java prerequisite
Chapter 6–15 are identical		It contains the second-half of this text and Java 2D™, Java 3D™, Internationalization, Enterprise JavaBeans™, Security and the Java Virtual Machine, Programming Mobile Devices, Jini™ and JavaSpaces™. JSP Tags, Messaging, and Naming
	Chapters 16–20 available only in Alternate Edition	

Advanced Java only: Instructors who need a text for an advanced Java course may use my **Advanced Java™ Internet Applications, Second Edition**, 2002, Scott/Jones Inc. It contains the second half of this text and additional chapters on Java 2D™, Java 3D™, Internationalization, Enterprise JavaBeans™, Security and the Java Virtual Machine, Programming Mobile Devices, Jini™ and JavaSpaces™. JSP Tags, Messaging, and Naming.

Objects after control structures: Instructors who prefer to defer objects until the easier Java basics and control structures have been covered may use my **Computing with Java™: Programs, Objects, Graphics, Second Edition**, 2001, Scott/Jones, Inc. In this text, Chapters 2, 3 and 4 cover Java basics and control structures without using objects. Chapter 5 starts objects, and is the same as Chapter 5 of the alternate edition except that it incorporates Section 1.7 of the alternate edition. Chapters 6–15 are the same as in both editions. Chapters 16-20 are only available in the alternate edition.

Versions of Java

The latest version of the Java 2 Platform may be downloaded from Sun's Java site, `java. sun. com`. Chapter 18 requires a servlet engine. JRun from Macromedia can be downloaded from Macromedia.com. Chapter 19 requires a JavaBean development tool. The BDK (JavaBeans™ Development Kit) may be downloaded from java.sun.com. Chapter 20 requires the Java APIs for XML Processing (JAYP), which may be downloaded from java.sun.com, and the SOAP API, which may be downloaded from apache.org.

Acknowledgements

One day in 1995, Jeremy Woo-Sam, then a graduate student, gave me a copy of a whitepaper on Java. I had been saving newsgroup messages on Java until I had a chance to read them; Jeremy sparked my interest so that by Spring 1996 I was teaching Java and have spent a substantial portion of my life since then engrossed with it.

My students have been a big help to me, giving me the perspective to improve my presentation and organization of the material, and correcting many typographical errors. My colleague Sheila Foster has been an inspiration to me. Using her clear and elegant **C by Discovery**, Second Edition, Scott/Jones, Inc., 1994 (and the first edition) impressed me with the value of Notes for annotating programs, and of including exercises within each section so students can immediately test their understanding.

Richard Jones, as editor, has helped me at every step of the way with his insightful suggestions. His assistance has been invaluable. It has been a great pleasure to work with Heather Bennett, Stephen Adams, Michelle Windell, Victoria Judy and the rest of the Scott/Jones team who have done so much so well to make this book a reality.

I thank my wife and daughter for their forbearance. At least they always know where to find me (at the computer), and I answer my email fast because I am always online.

I have been fortunate to have fine reviewers who gave me careful critiques of various portions of earlier drafts. They include:

Robert P. Burton
Brigham Young University

Stephen J. Hartley
Rowan University

John L. May
Oklahoma State University, Okmulgee

Alok Mehta
Rensselaer Polytechnic Institute

Bruce A. Mielke
University of Wisconsin, Green Bay

Bill Shay
U of Wisconsin - Green Bay

Reviewers for the first edition

Ahmad Abuhejleh
University of Wisconsin, River Falls

Ijaz Awan
Savannah State University

Don Biggerstaff
Fayetteville Community College

Ken Collier
Northern Arizona University

John Connely
California Polytechnic University
San Luis Obispo

Herb Dershem
Hope College

Dan Everett
University of Georgia

Mark Harris
Appalachian State University

Norman Jacobson
University of California, Irvine

James Johnson
Valencia Junior College

Mark Lattanzi
James Madison University

Gary Lippman
California State University Hayward

Michael Milligan
Front Range Community College

Sandeep Mitra
SUNY Brockport

Hoang Nguyen
Intel Corporation/ DeAnza College

Mark Pelczarski
Elgin Community College

Chang Shyh Peng
California Lutheran University

Jon Preston
Georgia Institute of Technology

Dallan Quass
Brigham Young University

James Richards
Bemidji State University

In Hai Ro

Langston University
Dolly Samson
Weber State University

James Shaw
Texas State Techncial College

Meenu Singh
Kentucky State University

Peter Spoerri
Fairfield University

Evelyn Stiller
Plymouth State College

William Taffe
Plymouth State College

Yonglei Tao
Grand State University

Jim Thomas
Ohlone College
Jack van Luik
Mt. Hood Community College

Ray Wiseman
Indiana State University

James Wolfe
Cedarville College

Web Site

My web site for this book is at `http://www.cecs.csulb.edu/~artg/cwj/` where an errata list will be posted. Please send any typos or other errors to me directly at `artg@csulb.edu`.

CHAPTER

1 Computing with Java

OUTLINE

Introduction

Once upon a time giant digital computers filled large rooms with their thousands of vacuum tubes. They were slow beasts, but looked awesome. In the years since the 1940s when electronic digital computers were first developed, computers have dramatically decreased in size and increased their computing power. Starting as a tool for science and engineering, computers have become an essential part of our society.

Studying computing challenges us to keep up with rapid technological change. With Java we can learn the basic techniques of programming that have brought us to this point, and go forward with object-oriented, interactive, graphical, event-driven programming and networking that take us to the future.

Objectives:

- Introduce basic computing concepts.
- Survey Java's history, its features, and how it works.
- Edit, compile, and run a Java standalone application.

- Edit, compile, and run a Java applet.
- Be aware of the difference between program-driven and event-driven programming, both of which Java supports.
- Be aware of the difference between character mode and graphics mode programs, both of which Java supports.
- Be aware of the difference between procedural and object-oriented programming, both of which Java supports.
- Introduce basic computing concepts.

1.1 Introduction to Computing

Hardware

The familiar personal computer, in a typical multimedia configuration, has a keyboard, a mouse, a microphone, and a joystick to receive input from the user, and a monitor, speakers, and a printer to provide output to the user. The case contains the processor, memory, a hard disk, a floppy disk drive, a CD-ROM drive, and a modem.

The processor executes programs stored in memory, using the memory to store data needed in the computation. The hard disk and floppy disk allow us to read and write persistent data that will remain after the processor finishes executing the program that produced the data. The CD-ROM stores data in a read-only mode; we can read from a CD-ROM, but not write to it.

Software

The software consists of the programs that the computer executes. The operating system software makes it much easier for us to use the computer. It provides an interface to the hardware for us, so that each of us does not have to write programs to read input from the keyboard, write output to the screen or create files on the hard disk. An operating system can be relatively simple, providing few services, or it can be a huge program with many bells and whistles for us to use.

Programmers appreciate utility programs such as editors that allow us to create or modify programs, and compilers that translate programs from one language to another to facilitate their execution. End users run word processors, spreadsheets, games, and browsers, among many other applications. Businesses rely on computer software to serve customers and for their accounting, payroll and other management needs.

The processor executes software using its specially designed instruction set. Each instruction is fairly simple so that it may take hundreds, thousands, or millions of instructions to implement the tasks we want our software to perform. Each instruction has several parts; these parts specify the operation, `addition`, for example, that the instruction performs, and any operands that it uses, such as the numbers to add. Each memory location has a numerical address. To give the flavor of hardware execution, we describe an addition on each of two imaginary processors, called ABC and

XYZ. Inside the computer we represent both programs and data numerically. For simplicity our examples use ordinary integers rather than binary numbers.*

Imaginary Processor ABC

Processor ABC computes values in memory. Its `addition` operation uses three operands, the memory addresses of the numbers to add and the memory address of the location to store the result. Each memory address uses four digits and the addition operator, represented by the number `15`, uses two digits. A sample instruction

```
15 2500 3224 4000
```

adds the number found in memory location `2500` to the number found in location `3224`, storing the result in location `4000`.

Imaginary Processor XYZ

Processor XYZ computes values in a special location called the accumulator. Its `load`, `add`, and `store` operations each use one operand. The operand of the `load` instruction is the memory address of the number to load into the accumulator, the operand of the `add` instruction is the memory address of the number to add to the number in the accumulator, while the operand of the store instruction is the memory address of the location in which to store the number in the accumulator. Each memory address uses four digits and the operators use two digits, with `load` represented by `20`, `add` by `21`, and `store` by `22`.

On processor XYZ the computation represented by the sample processor ABC instruction `15 2500 3224 4000` is

```
20 2500
21 3224
22 4000
```

which loads the number in memory location `2500` into the accumulator, adds the number in location `3224` to the number in the accumulator, and stores the number in the accumulator (the sum) in location `4000`.

High-Level Languages

Although processors ABC and XYZ are imaginary, they illustrate the point that each processor has its own instruction set that uses numerical codes for the operators and numerical addresses for the operations. Each instruction performs one basic step such as an addition, a load, or a store. Programming using a processor's instruction set would make it difficult to accomplish any but the simplest tasks. Moreover such a program would have to be written all over again for the instruction set of a different processor. A program using processor ABC's instruction set will not run on Processor XYZ, and vice-versa.

A high-level language allows us to express the computation in a more understandable form, combining several steps into one expression, and to write a program that can

* See Appendix A for an introduction to the binary number system.

be implemented on many different types of processors. For example, we can express an addition like the one we programmed above for processors ABC and XYZ as:

```
totalSalary = baseSalary + bonus;
```

and write more complicated statements such as:

```
totalScore =
(judge1Score + judge2Score + judge3Score) * difficulty;
```

which represents the total score obtained by first adding the scores of three judges, and then multiplying that sum by a difficulty factor. We use the star, `*`, to denote multiplication.

Compilers

A compiler translates a program from one language to another. If we want to write a program in a high-level language and run it on processor ABC, we can use a compiler to translate our high-level program to an equivalent program using the instruction set of processor ABC. Each high-level statement will usually translate to several processor ABC instructions. Figure 1.1 shows this process.

Figure 1.1 Translating a high-level program

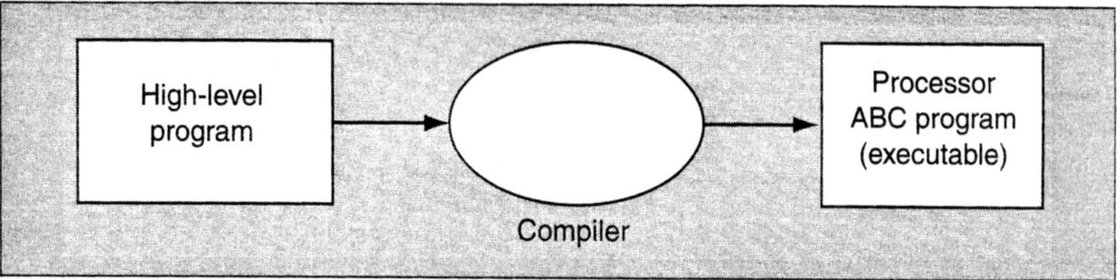

To run the same program on processor XYZ we would need another compiler that translates from the high-level language to the instruction set of processor XYZ. The high-level program is called the source code, while the translated program is called the executable code, or the binary code (reflecting its use of the binary number system to represent operators and operands.) Implementations of the C and C++ languages almost always use compilers to produce executable code for specific processors.

Compilers are indispensable tools for program developers, but end users have no desire to use them. A player of a game wants a program that will run, an executable program. The vendor of that game must provide executable versions of the game for each processor.

Interpreters

An interpreter is a program that executes the code rather than translating it to another language. For example, an interpreter would execute the statement

```
totalSalary = baseSalary + bonus;
```

by finding the values of `baseSalary` and `bonus`, adding them, and storing the result in `totalSalary`. In this example, the interpreter executes a high-level language statement. The BASIC language, used on early personal computers which had insufficient memory to support the compilation process, was typically implemented by an interpreter.

We could also use an interpreter to allow one machine to simulate the instructions of another. For example, we could write a program that executes, on processor XYZ, programs written using processor ABC's instruction set. As we shall see in the next section, Java uses a combination of compilation and interpretation, as did the first implementations of the Pascal language.

Networks

Thus far we have focused on the software and hardware for a single computer. With the advent of the Internet, computers easily communicate with other computers in the same office, the same company, or at remote sites all over the world. Many of us use email more than regular mail or the telephone. A computer may be connected by cable to other computers in a network, or use a modem to connect over telephone lines.

The Internet is a vast network of networks. We use familiar services such as email and file transfer. The World Wide Web, a rapidly growing part of the Internet, uses hypertext to create a web of links from one computer to another. Hypertext, which we discuss in Section 6.1, allows us to include images, sounds, and links to other computers, as well as formatted text and Java applets, in web pages that we display using a browser. Many use browser software as their primary access to computers.

THE BIG PICTURE

Operating system software handles the details of input, output, and files. Each hardware processor uses its own low-level instruction set. Higher level languages allow programmers to write more meaningful statements. A compiler translates a program in a high-level language to the instruction set for a specific processor. An interpreter executes the high-level code directly.

TEST YOUR UNDERSTANDING

1. Describe each component of the computer that you will be using to program in Java. What is the function of each?
2. List several software applications that you have used or would like to use. Identify each as an operating system, word processor, game, etc.
3. Translate the processor ABC instruction

   ```
   15 3500 4200 2300
   ```

   into equivalent code for processor XYZ.
4. Translate the processor XYZ code

   ```
   20  3950
   21  5600
   22  1234
   ```

into equivalent code for processor ABC.

5. What do we call the type of program that translates a program in a high-level language to an equivalent program in another language?
6. What do we call the type of program that executes another program?

1.2 Overview of Java

History

FORTRAN and COBOL were among the first high-level languages, introduced in the late 1950s. Both are still used today, FORTRAN for scientific applications and COBOL for business. Pascal, designed for teaching, introduced in the early 1970s, and its successors Modula-2 and Modula-3 influenced the design of Java. Much of Java's basic syntax is modeled after C, developed by in the early 1970s, and its successor, C++, developed beginning in the 1980s.

The C language became very popular due in part to efficiency; developer's can write C programs that perform well. The C++ language, as its name suggests, adds features to C to enable the writing of larger programs using object-oriented programming. While C is a relatively small language, C++ is large and complex. The team at Sun Microsystems who were developing what was to become Java tried at first to use C++, but found it did not meet their needs for a language to develop software for devices such as cellular phones and digital assistants. They began the development of a new language, originally called Oak, in the early 1990s coinciding with the growth of the Internet and the World Wide Web. Seeing greater opportunities for their new language in network programming they changed their focus and created Java.

Java's Features

Java's designers list its important characteristics as:

- simple, object-oriented, and familiar
- robust and secure
- architecture neutral and portable
- high performance
- interpreted, threaded, and dynamic

Simplicity and Robustness

Java gets its simplicity by omission of some of the complexities such as pointers and memory management that plague C and C++ programmers. However C and C++ programmers will find Java familiar as it borrows much of its syntax from them. We will consider Java's object-oriented features in detail in this text.

A robust program is reliable, running without crashing due to programming errors, erroneous input, or failures of external devices. By remaining simple, Java eliminates the source of many errors. It checks that data is being properly accessed, and provides exception handling to manage unexpected events. Security, especially when communicating across a network with unknown and potentially untrustworthy sources, requires careful measures that Java implements.

Architecture and Portability

Being architecture neutral means a compiled Java program will run on a variety of processors using various operating systems. A programmer can create a program, compile it, and make it available over the Internet to users all over the world who download that program and run it on many different processors and operating systems. We will explore this further when we discuss how Java works. Besides architecture neutrality, an important component of portability, Java specifies the language so as to reduce the implementation dependencies prevalent in other languages.

As Java develops it attains higher levels of performance. Its designers hope in time to match the performance of the most efficient current languages while still maintaining portability. In network applications, communications delays lessen the need for speed of code execution.

Multitasking

Multitasking operating systems allow users to switch between several applications running at the same time, for example editing one program, while downloading another from the Internet. Java threads allow a Java program to perform multiple tasks simultaneously. Animation can run while the user is entering data in a form, for example. Java can link dynamically, while the program is running, to library code it needs.

In sum, Java is a general purpose programming language well suited to interactive and network programming. Since its introduction in 1995 it has been enormously successful.

How Java Works

Java uses a compiler, but (typically) does not translate a high-level program to the machine instructions of each specific processor. The Java creators designed a machine, called the Java Virtual Machine (JVM) because it is not usually implemented in hardware. The Java compiler takes as input the high-level Java program and produces as output an equivalent program written using the instruction set of the JVM. If our processor is a JVM, we can run this program very efficiently; if not we use an interpreter to run the JVM code on our processor. Figure 1.2 shows the compilation of a Java program to a JVM program followed by the interpretation of the JVM program to produce the results on two different processors.

The Java developers call the code for the JVM byte code. The advantage of producing byte code instead of code for each different processor is that the same byte code will run anywhere that has a Java byte code interpreter. We can download a Java program which has been compiled to byte code for the JVM on one type of machine and run it on a much different type of machine. For networking, this feature of Java is invaluable. The disadvantage of producing byte code is slower execution, because

Figure 1.2 Compiling and executing a Java program

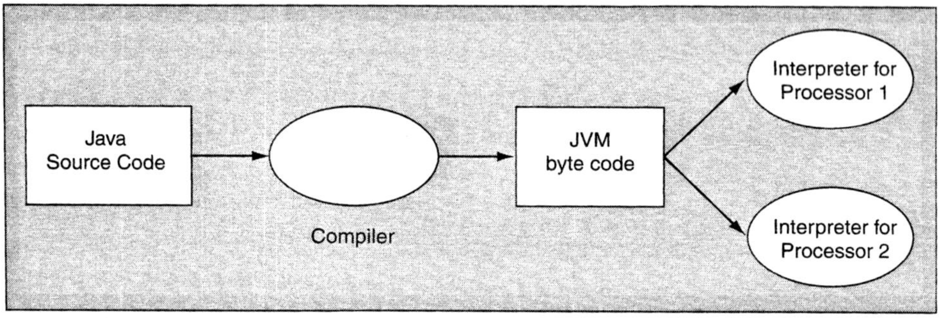

running byte code using a software interpreter is a slower process than running code for a specific processor directly on that hardware. New advances in compilation technology are reducing execution time.

THE BIG PICTURE

Java was created in the mid-1990s, basing much syntax on C and C++ and using concepts from several other languages. Its creators characterize it as simple, object-oriented, familiar, robust, secure, architecture neutral, portable, high performance, interpreted, threaded, and dynamic.

Java source compiles to byte code interpreted by a Java Virtual Machine. The byte code runs anywhere, which makes Java very popular for Internet applications in which diverse machines communicate.

TEST YOUR UNDERSTANDING

7. From what language did Java derive much of its basic syntax?
8. List Java's features as portrayed by the developers of Java.
9. The Java compiler (usually) translates Java programs to equivalent programs using the instruction set of which machine?
10. What is the advantage of translating a Java program to byte code?

1.3 Running Java Programs and Applets

Java programs fall into two main categories: applications and applets.

An application, often called a standalone application, runs on its own, whereas an applet is a small application embedded in a web page (See Section 6.1 for an introduction to the writing of web pages). A Java interpreter in the browser runs the applet when the browser loads the web page containing that applet.

Editing, Compiling, and Running a Java Application

Various vendors provide tools with which to develop Java programs. Each has its own steps used to create, compile, and run Java programs and applets.* We use the Java 2 Platform, Standard Edition, provided free by Sun Microsystems on the CDROM included with this text, (and downloadable from `http://java.sun.com/`).

Example 1.1 shows a standalone application that just displays the message "Hello World!" when we run it.

EXAMPLE 1.1 Hello.java

```
/* Displays "Hello World!"
 */

public class Hello {
  public static void main(String [] args) {
    System.out.println("Hello World!");
  }
}
```

Output

```
Hello World!
```

We will explain the elements of this program later, and just use it here as an example of how to compile and run a Java application. To enter Example 1.1, we can either use the code on the disk included with this text, or use an editor, such as Notepad included with Windows operating systems, to enter the program and save it. The file name for this program must be `Hello.java`, exactly the same as the public class name in Example 1.1, where case is important. Java considers the name `hello.java` as different from the name `Hello.java`.

To compile and run Example 1.1 using Sun's tools, we first get a command window,

- On Windows 2000 or NT 4.0 systems click on the Start button, Programs, and Command Prompt to get the console window from which to enter the compilation command.
- On Windows 95 or 98 systems click on the Start button, Programs, and MS-DOS Prompt to get the console window from which to enter the compilation command.

and then locate the directory containing the program. On the author's machine, the `Hello.java` code is in the `d:\booklr\ch1` directory, so the command

```
cd  /d  d:\booklr\ch1
```

will change to the correct directory.

* See Appendix E for instructions on using some integrated development environments.

Because we installed the Java 2 Platform in the `d:\jdk1.3` directory, the Java compiler, called `javac`, will be in the `d:\jdk1.3\bin` directory. To compile, we can use the command

```
d:\jdk1.3\bin\javac  Hello.java
```

To avoid having to type the full path, `d:\jdk1.3\bin\javac`, when compiling we can set the PATH environment variable,* which lists all the directories the system should look in for executable files. After setting the path, we can use the command

Figure 1.3 Compiling and running Example 1.1

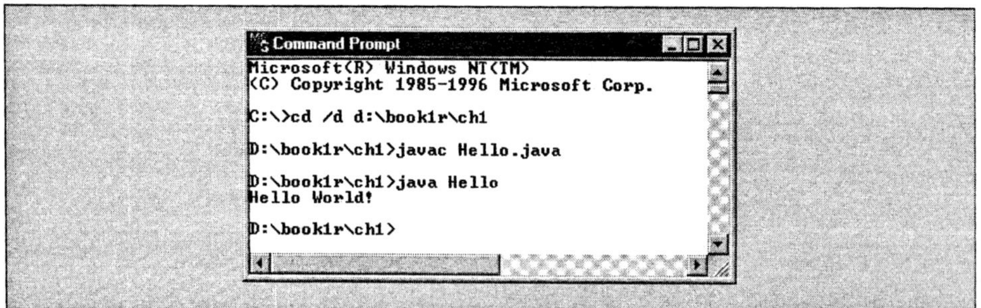
Command Prompt
Microsoft(R) Windows NT(TM)
(C) Copyright 1985-1996 Microsoft Corp.
C:\>cd /d d:\book1r\ch1
D:\book1r\ch1>javac Hello.java
D:\book1r\ch1>java Hello
Hello World!
D:\book1r\ch1>

```
javac Hello.java
```

Figure 1.3 shows the command window with the command used to compile Example 1.1.

The name `javac` represents the Java compiler which translates the Java program `Hello.java` to an equivalent byte code program, `Hello.class`, for the JVM. Files with the `.class` extension are byte code files.

Once we have compiled Example 1.1 we can execute the code. To run this program using the Standard Edition,† we enter the command `java Hello` in the console window. (Without setting the path, we would need to enter `d:\jdk1.3\bin\java Hello`.) The name `java` designates the Java interpreter that executes the byte code file `Hello.class`. The interpreter executes the method named `main`, which must be present in the program. We see that Example 1.1 does have a `main` method. Every standalone Java application must have a `main` method.

TIP

When compiling, we include the extension in the file name, as in:

```
javac Hello.java
```

* In Windows 95 and 98 we can edit the `autoexec.bat` file, adding the following line at the end `set path=c:\jdk1.3\bin;%path%` where c:`\jdk1.3` is the directory in which the JDK is installed. (Replace 1.3 by the number of the Java version used, `1.2` for version 1.2, for example.) In Windows NT 4.0 and 2000, click on the Start button, Settings, Control Panel, and the System icon. Click on the Environment tab and the Path variable. Add the directory `c:\jdk1.3\bin` to the list in the value box, where c:`\jdk1.3` is the directory in which the JDK is installed. Then click the Set button and the OK button.

† See Appendix E for instructions on running Java programs using an integrated development environment.

but when executing the byte code, we omit the extension, as in:

```
java Hello
```

Editing, Compiling, and Running a Java Applet

An applet is simply a type of Java program we can embed in a web page. We edit and compile it just as we did the Java application in Example 1.1. For our first applet we display the message "Hello World!" Example 1.2 shows the code for this applet. Do not try to understand this code now; we will explain it later.

EXAMPLE 1.2 HelloApplet.java

```
/* Displays the message "Hello World!" in
 * a browser or applet viewer window.
 */
import java.applet.Applet;
import java.awt.Graphics;

public class HelloApplet extends Applet {
  public void paint(Graphics g) {
    g.drawString("Hello World!",30,30);
  }
}
```

The World Wide Web (WWW) uses the Hypertext Markup Language (HTML) (introduced in Section 6.1) to create web pages. HTML uses tags enclosed in angle brackets, <>, to format a web page. The tags help the browser to display the page. We do not see them when we browse. A web page designer may include an applet, using an `<applet>` tag, to make the web page more interesting or useful. Example 1.2 is just a simple applet used to illustrate how applets work.

To run an applet, we create an HTML file, `HelloApplet.html`, that can be as simple as that of Figure 1.4,

Figure 1.4 An HTML file for the applet of Example 1.2

```
<applet code=HelloApplet.class width=300 height=200>
</applet>
```

which is a very simple web page containing nothing but an applet. The applet tag specifies the code file as `HelloApplet.class`, the applet width as 300 pixels and its height as 200. We obtain the `HelloApplet.class` file by compiling the `HelloApplet.java` file of Example 1.2 using the command `javac HelloApplet.java`. Once we have compiled

Figure 1.5 Browsing a web page containing an applet

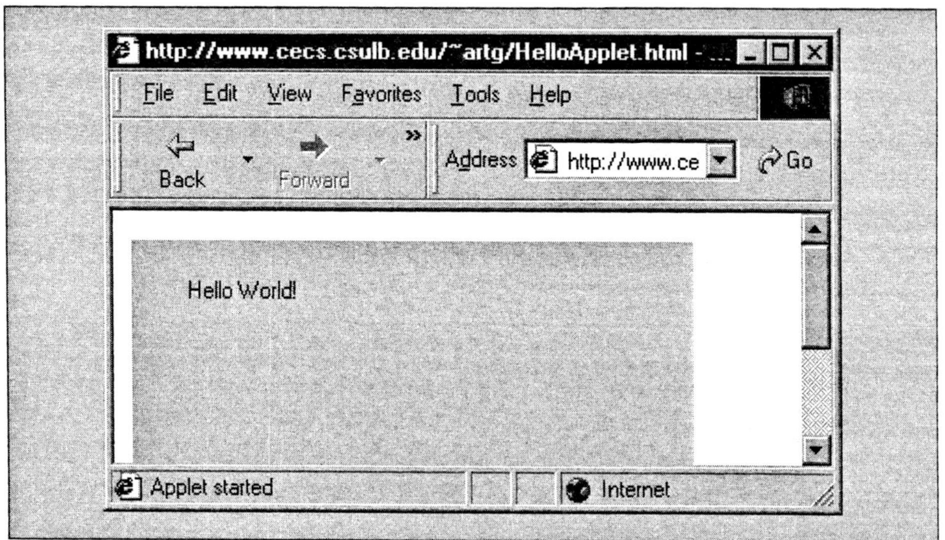

Figure 1.6 The applet of Example 1.2

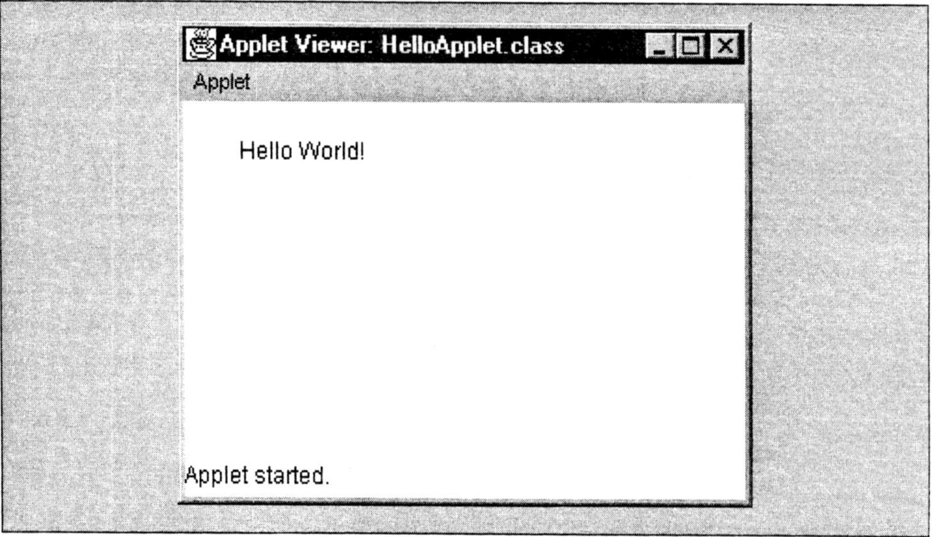

the applet code we can display the applet using a browser or applet viewer. Typically one person, the web page developer, creates a web page containing an applet, and other people use a browser to view that page. We created the web page, `HelloApplet.html`, and placed it at the site `http://www.cecs.csulb.edu/~artg/HelloApplet.html`. Entering this address in the browser will produce Figure 1.5.

Sun provides the applet viewer* tool for applet developers to test applets. The `appletviewer HelloApplet.html` command, where `HelloApplet.html` is the file shown in Figure 1.4, will run the applet of Example 1.2. Figure 1.6 shows the applet window, 300×200 pixels, in which we draw "Hello World!"

Figure 1.7 The ten numbers to be sorted in Example 1.3

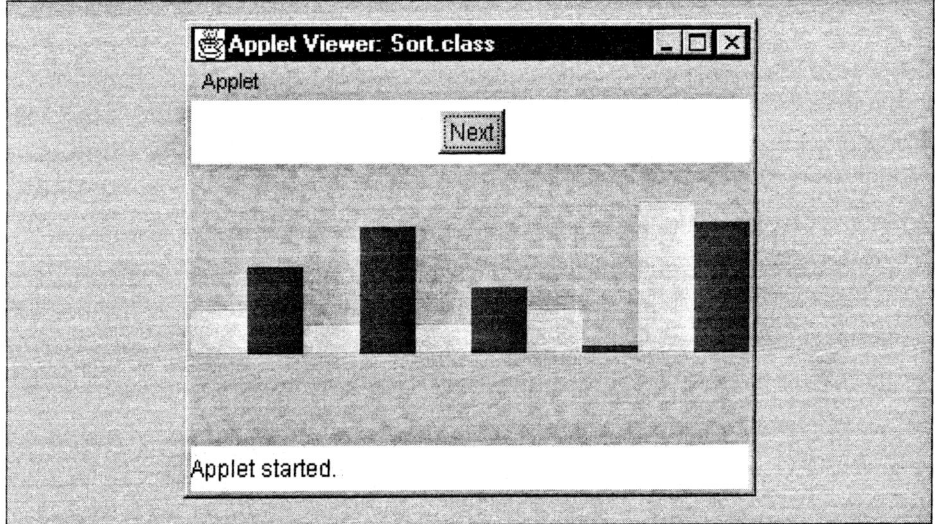

A Graphical Applet

Applets, usually embedded in web pages, typically use graphics and have a user interface. Our first applet in Example 1.2 was very simple. Example 1.3 demonstrates a graphical applet that we use in the next section to illustrate event-driven programming.

EXAMPLE 1.3 Sort.java

```
/* Generates 10 random numbers between 0 and 99,
 * displaying them in a bar chart. Inserts the next number
 * in numerical order with respect to the numbers to the left
 * of it, until all 10 numbers are ordered from smallest to
 * largest. The code is on the disk included with this text.
 */
```

After we compile the applet using the command `javac Sort.java`, we can display it using the command `appletviewer Sort.html`†, or open it in a browser. Initially the

* Using an applet viewer will ensure that the applet can be viewed. Some browsers are not configured with the latest versions of Java.The Java Plugin (See Appendix E) can be used to provide the latest Java version.

† Integrated development environments have their own applet viewers or call a browser to display applets.

display will contain a pink square with a `Sort` button in the top center. Pressing the `Sort` button displays 10 rectangles of randomly chosen heights shown in Figure 1.7.

After displaying the initial data the applet changes the label on the button to `Next`. When the user presses the `Next` button the next value, starting with the second, is inserted in numerical order with respect to the numbers to the left of it. The first

Figure 1.8 **The `Sort` applet after inserting four numbers**

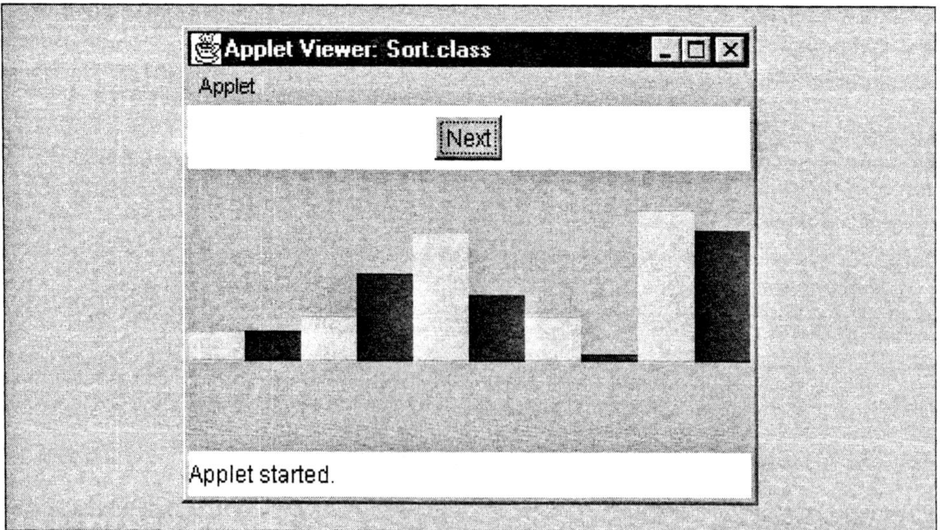

time the user presses the `Next` button, the applet will move the second bar in front of the first if it is smaller than the first. The second time the user presses the `Next` button, the applet will insert the third bar from the left in its proper place with respect to the first two, and so on. Figure 1.8 shows the applet after the user pressed the Next button four times.

THE BIG PICTURE	
Standalone applications: Run using the Java interpreter to call the `main` method.	*Applets:* Run in an HTML file displayed by a browser or tested with an applet viewer.

TEST YOUR UNDERSTANDING

TRY IT YOURSELF 11. Compile and run the `Hello.java` program of Example 1.1.

TRY IT YOURSELF 12. Compile and run the `HelloApplet.java` applet of Example 1.2.

TRY IT YOURSELF 13. Compile and run the `Sort.java` applet of Example 1.3 using the code found on the disk included with this text.

1.4 Program-Driven vs. Event-Driven Applications

Older programming languages support the program-driven style of programming in which our program executes from beginning to end following the steps of our code much as a cook follows a recipe. Java permits program-driven code, and further supports event-driven programming in which our program, like the firemen in the station, wait for an event to spur them to action.

The Character Mode

For many years computers had no graphical interfaces. Characters were the means of inputting data to the computer and getting results from it. Computer operators could enter commands from a typewriter-like console, but the most common means of input was punched cards. A programmer typed at a keypunch machine that would punch holes in the card representing the characters typed. Initially, alphabets only included uppercase letters because of the limited number of punch codes.

During these years, computers executed programs in batch mode. The computer operator put together a batch of programs, using the card reader to feed them to the computer that executed the programs one after another, printing a listing of each program and the results. When the operating system started a program, that program had control of the processor until it finished executing. We call such execution program-driven because the program continues executing the program, one statement after the other until the program ends or a fatal error occurs.

Executing such a program is like preparing a dish from a recipe. The cook is in charge, executing the steps of the recipe until the dish is complete. Figure 1.9 shows the "program" for the preparation of a simple omelet.

Figure 1.9 The "program" for preparing an omelet

Get the ingredients.
Get the cookware needed.
Crack the eggs into a bowl.
Add salt.
Beat the eggs.
Melt some butter in the frying pan.
Pour the eggs into the frying pan.
Turn the eggs over.
Add the cheese, folding the eggs over.
Serve the omelet.
Clean up.

Program-driven applications are still a very important part of computing. Preparing the payroll does not require user intervention. The payroll program takes the input regarding hours worked and rate of pay and prepares the paychecks and other payroll records. As another example, the Java compiler takes the source program as its input and produces the byte code for the JVM with no need for a graphical user interface, operating in character mode in which input and output consists of characters.

The Graphical User Interface (GUI)

With monitors and operating systems capable of displaying graphics, we can develop programs that interact with the user via a graphical user interface (GUI). The operating system responds to the user's input, conveying it to the program that passively waits for user input to request it to provide some service. We represent these user requests as events. An event-driven program includes code to respond to messages informing it about events involving its window, such as button presses or data entry.

Program-driven applications	Event-driven applications
Execute code in a step-by-step fashion like a recipe.	Wait for the user to generate an event. Include code to respond to that event.
Transform input into output, without user intervention.	Respond to user actions.
Typically use character mode.	Typically have a graphical user interface.

Example 1.3, the `Sort` program, illustrates event-driven programming. This program initially displays a window with a *`Sort`* button and a pink canvas. The program waits passively until the user presses the *`Sort`* button, at which time the operating system relays this event to the program which displays a bar chart showing ten numbers from 0 to 99 as shown in Figure 1.7. Again the `Sort` program waits passively until the user presses the *`Next`* button, at which time the operating system passes this event to the program which inserts the next bar into numerical order with respect to the bars to its left. After the user inserts the remaining nine numbers, the program disables the *`Next`* button, waiting passively until the user terminates the program.

To contrast an event-driven with a program-driven application, we rewrite Example 1.3 to create 10 numbers at random, display a list of the numbers, sort the numbers in numerical order from smallest to largest and display the resulting sorted list. The `SortCommand` program of Example 1.4 does not require a GUI. It generates its own data, performing the computation without interference, like a cook preparing an omelet, finally listing the results in the console window.

EXAMPLE 1.4 SortCommand.java

```
/* Generates 10 integers from 0 to 99 at random.
 * Sorts these numbers in order from smallest to
 * largest, displaying the sorted numbers.
 * Illustrates a program-driven application.
 * Complete code is on the disk included with this text.
 */
```

Compiling and running Example 1.4 follows the steps outlined for Example 1.1. The output will look like

```
The data to sort is {8,80,21,36,68,80,65,7,3,43}
The sorted data is {3,7,8,21,36,43,65,68,80,80}
```

although the numbers will change each time we run the program, because we generate them randomly. The console window in which the output appears may look different on different operating systems and development environments. In the Windows operating system, on an x86 type processor, the output may appear in a console window as shown in Figure 1.10.[*]

Figure 1.10 The console window for entering commands

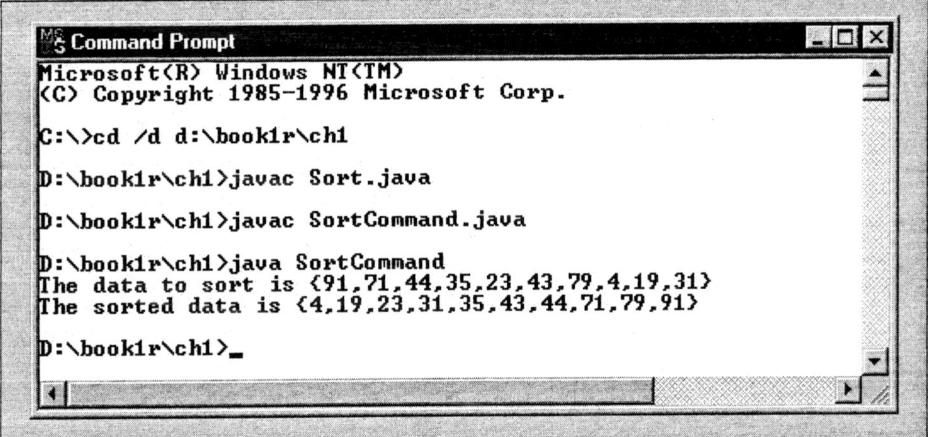

Command Prompt
Microsoft(R) Windows NT(TM)
(C) Copyright 1985-1996 Microsoft Corp.
C:\>cd /d d:\book1r\ch1
D:\book1r\ch1>javac Sort.java
D:\book1r\ch1>javac SortCommand.java
D:\book1r\ch1>java SortCommand
The data to sort is (91,71,44,35,23,43,79,4,19,31)
The sorted data is (4,19,23,31,35,43,44,71,79,91)
D:\book1r\ch1>_

TIP ☛ The command prompt window of Figure 1.10 is a character mode window. Only characters, not graphics, appear in a limited choice of fonts. By contrast, the graphics windows of Figures 1.7 and 1.8 allow us to draw shapes in various sizes and colors, text in various fonts, sizes, and colors, and to add user interface components such as buttons.

[*] On x86 based processors running Windows 95, 98, 2000, or NT, the user can change back and forth between a full screen command prompt and a command prompt window, as shown in Figure 1.10 , by hitting the Enter key while pressing the Alt key.

THE BIG PICTURE

The program-driven approach suits applications such as compilers that require no user interaction. Event-driven programs suit user interfaces whose components respond to user interactions such as pressing a button or making a selection. With the advent of more powerful computers with graphics capabilities, event-driven applications have taken a more important place in computing.

TEST YOUR UNDERSTANDING

14. Illustrate the idea of a program-driven application by writing a "program" to wash a car, in the spirit of the "program" for preparing an omelet in Figure 1.9.
15. Illustrate the idea of an event-driven application by writing a "program" for the operation of a fire station, including responses to several emergencies.

TRY IT YOURSELF

16. Compile and run the `SortCommand.java` program of Example 1.4, using the code on the disk included with this text.

1.5 Procedural vs. Object-Oriented Programming

We contrast two styles of programming, procedural and object-oriented. Java supports them both. The newer object-oriented style models our everyday intuition and, if used well, can make software more reusable and easier to maintain.

Procedural Programming

Procedural programming emphasizes the procedures used to manipulate the data. Think of a bunch of rocks that cannot do anything by themselves. We can use a throw procedure, which takes a rock and tosses it, a juggle procedure which takes three rocks (small ones) and juggles them, or a sculpt procedure that carves a rock into a sculpture.

These procedures operate on the rocks. If we call our rocks, `rock1`, `rock2`, and `rock3`, informally we might say, `"throw rock1"` or `"juggle rock1, rock2,` and `rock3"` or `"sculpt rock2"`. In a programming language notation, these commands might look like

```
throw(rock1);
juggle(rock1, rock2, rock3);
sculpt(rock2);
```

As programmers, we would spend our time writing code to implement these operations, giving much less regard to the data.

We might describe the throw procedure as

```
Pick up the rock;
if (right-handed) {
   Raise the right arm overhead;
   Pull the right arm back then step forward with the
   left foot, shifting weight to the right foot;
```

```
    Swing the right arm forward while shifting weight to the left foot,
    releasing the rock at its highest point;
    Complete the motion of the right arm;
    Return left foot to its original position;
    if (recycling) fetch rock;
}
else {
// same process with left and right reversed
}
```

When we test this procedure on some sample rocks, we find it works for rocks that fit conveniently in one hand, but requires modification for larger rocks. We may need to use two hands to lift and toss the rock. With a very heavy rock, we need to bend our knees and use other muscles to lift the rock. In addition, optionally, we may want to generate more force by throwing from a running start, but this modification only works for rocks light enough to carry.

Writing a throw procedure that covers all the variations can become a logical nightmare of choices and choices within choices. Each new modification becomes more difficult to make because the structure of the procedure gets more and more complex with each improvement.

We could name separate methods for each kind of rock, so our code would look like

```
if (the rock is a pebble)
    use the throwPebble procedure;
else if (the rock is a chunk)
    use the throwChunk procedure;
else if (the rock is a blob)
    use the throwBlob procedure;
```

Using this approach requires us to modify the code if we add a new type of rock, perhaps an artificial, low-density toy that requires yet another throwing method. We would then add

```
else if (the rock is a modelToy)
    use the modelToy procedure;
```

to our code. Similar complexities arise when we try to describe the juggle or sculpt procedures. By focusing on the data more, object-oriented programming alleviates many of these problems.

Object-Oriented Programming

Object-oriented programming combines data and procedures into an object that has its own attributes and behavior. To transform our rock example, we define a `Rock` class with operations `throw`, `juggle`, and `sculpt`. We are defining a type of object, whose operations tell us what we can ask it to do. If we have three `Rock` objects, `rock1`, `rock2`, and `rock3`, informally we can send the `throw` message to `rock1`, a `sculpt` message to `rock2`, or a `juggle` message to `rock1`, with the names, `rock2` and `rock3`, of the other rocks juggled with `rock1`. In a programming language, these invocations might look like

```
rock1.throw();
rock2.sculpt();
rock1.juggle(rock2, rock3);
```

The object invokes one of its behaviors, in contrast to the procedural approach in which a procedure operates on data.

The power of object-oriented programming shows up when we address the complexities of the operations. We can specialize the `rock` type to have several subtypes, say `pebble`, `chunk`, and `blob`. Because each is a `rock` it has all of the rock operations, but may define them differently. A `pebble` will implement its throw behavior as described above, while a `chunk`, being larger, will require using two-hands. The heavier `blob` will require bending down to lift it, and a two-handed toss without raising it over the head.

As programmers we need not worry about such distinctions, leaving each type of object to implement its own throw behavior. We can invoke

```
rock1.throw();
```

to throw our rock and it will use the correct version of the `throw` operation. For example, if `rock1` is a chunk, we will use two hands to throw it. The same invocation works if we add a `ModelToy` subtype. As programmers, we just ask the rock to throw and it will use the correct procedure depending on what type of rock it is.

Procedural programs:	Object-oriented programs:
Focus on the procedures needed to solve the problem.	Focus on the objects needed to solve the problem.
Separate functions and data.	Combine data and operations in objects.
Must check many cases to deal with different types of data.	Leave it to objects to provide the correct operations for their type.

THE BIG PICTURE

In a procedural program, expect to see a lot of logic used to test the data and do different operations depending on the type of the data.

In an object-oriented program, expect to see a type definition that defines permissible operations for objects of that type. Much of the program will consist of objects invoking one another's behaviors.

TEST YOUR UNDERSTANDING

17. A puppet show and a stage play are two types of performances. Explain which type is more analogous to procedural programming, and which to object-oriented programming.

1.6 A First Look at Everything: A User Interface Example

We show a user interface example that could be extended to provide Internet banking. It uses most of the topics, including object-oriented and event-driven programming, covered in this text.

Figure 1.11 shows the web page containing the applet of Example 1.5. The web page has instructions in its top portion with the applet below. We set up accounts for two customers who, after entering a name and PIN, can deposit to, withdraw from, or get the balance of their accounts. At each step a message instructs the user about the next step, just as an ATM machine does.

Rather than deploying Example 1.5 on our web site, we load it into the browser from our local machine, entering the path

```
d:\booklr\ch1\AtmScreen.html
```

to the web page in the address field of the browser. Figure 1.12 shows the HTML file for the web page. We will see how to write such a web page in Chapter 6. For now, we note that the tags of Figure 1.12 do not appear in the web page displayed by the browser in Figure 1.11.

EXAMPLE 1.5 **AtmScreen.java**

```
/* Illustrates event-driven object-oriented programming previewing the
 * concepts and techniques to be introduced in the rest of the text. The code is
 * on the disk included with this text.
 */
```

The applet viewer only displays Java applets. It ignores any other HTML tags. Figure 1.13 shows the web page of Figure 1.12 displayed by the applet viewer. Only the user interface of Example 1.5 appears, because the applet viewer does not display the instructions, which are not part of the applet.

1.7 An Introduction to Object-oriented Design

We introduce the object concept with an intuitive analogy to a vending machine, and present the fundamentals of object-oriented design.

Figure 1.11 Browsing AtmScreen.html

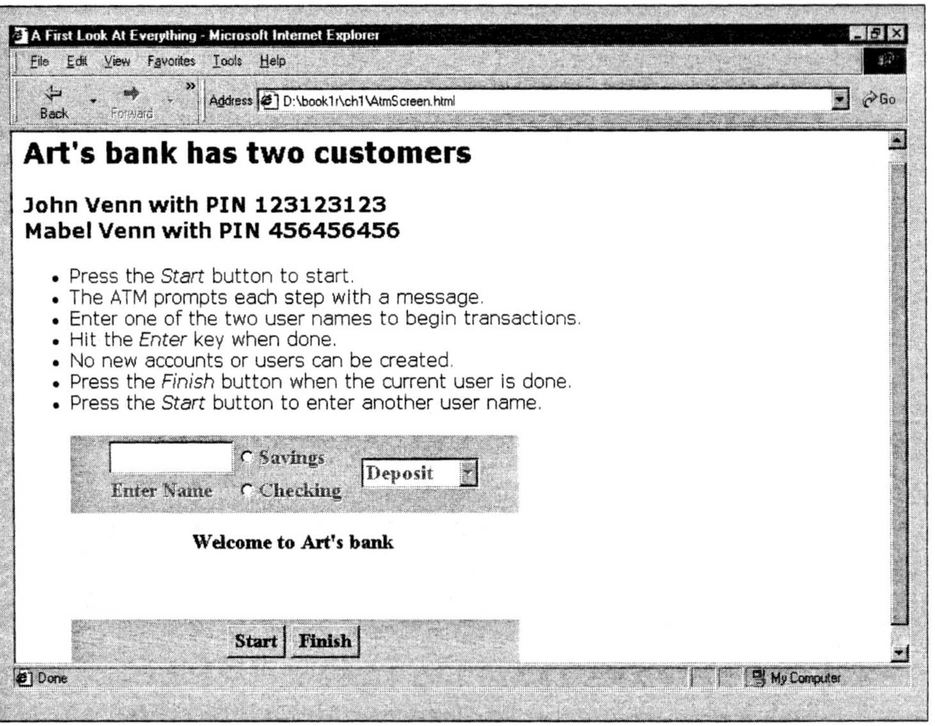

Figure 1.12 The HTML file used to run Example 1.5

```
<title> A First Look At Everything </title>
<h2> Art's bank has two customers <br>  </h2>
<h3> John Venn with PIN 123123123  <br>
     Mabel Venn with PIN 456456456   <h3><p>
<ul>
  <li> Press the <em>Start</em> button to start.
  <li> The ATM prompts each step with a message.
  <li> Enter one of the two user names to begin transactions.
  <li> Hit the Enter key when done.
  <li> No new accounts or users can be created.
  <li> Press the Finish button when the current user is done.
  <li> Press the Start button to enter another user name.
<p>
<applet code=AtmScreen.class width=400 height=200>
</applet>
```

Figure 1.13 Viewing AtmScreen.html with the applet viewer

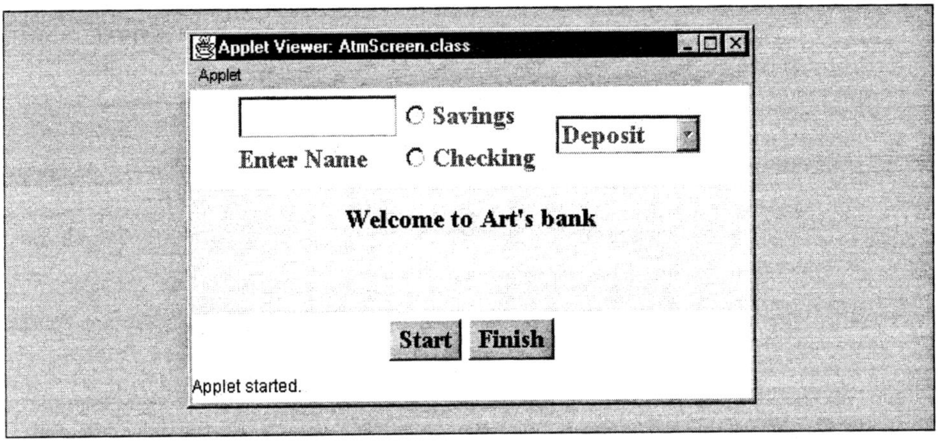

Objects

An **object** has state, behavior, and identity. We sometimes speak of our state of mind, happy, sad, angry, meaning a particular condition we are in. Humans are rather complex objects. For simplicity let us deal with inanimate objects such as vending machines, or even conceptual objects such as bank accounts or character strings.

A vending machine has a state. It may be operational or broken. It may have plenty of candy or be out of candy. It may be able or unable to provide change. Some information about its state may be public, for example a big sign may state it is out of order, or we may be able to see the number of candy bars available. Other information may be private, such as the amount of coffee available, or the amount of change.

A vending machine has behavior. It does not initiate behavior, but it does provide services that we think of as its behavior. For example, we may select coffee, or candy, or ask for a refund. Most of the vending machine's behavior is public. After all, the purpose of a vending machine is to provide services. However, there might be some private behavior, used only internally, such as filling water from a pipe when needed.

A vending machine has an identity. Another vending machine may have exactly the same state and provide the same services, but it is a different machine.

Although we do not (yet) have vending machines for programs, they do at least provide an instructive model for object-oriented programming. When we select coffee, we do not need to know the details of how the vending machine provides the coffee, whether the coffee is brewed in a big urn, whether instant coffee is mixed with hot water, or even as young children may think, whether little people in the machine make it.

As customers, we use the vending machine's services without needing to know the details of the machine's construction. The buttons or levers of the vending machine provide an interface to its behavior. Vending machine users do not have to manage the details of how to make the coffee or of how to dispense the candy.

Figure 1.14 A vending machine object

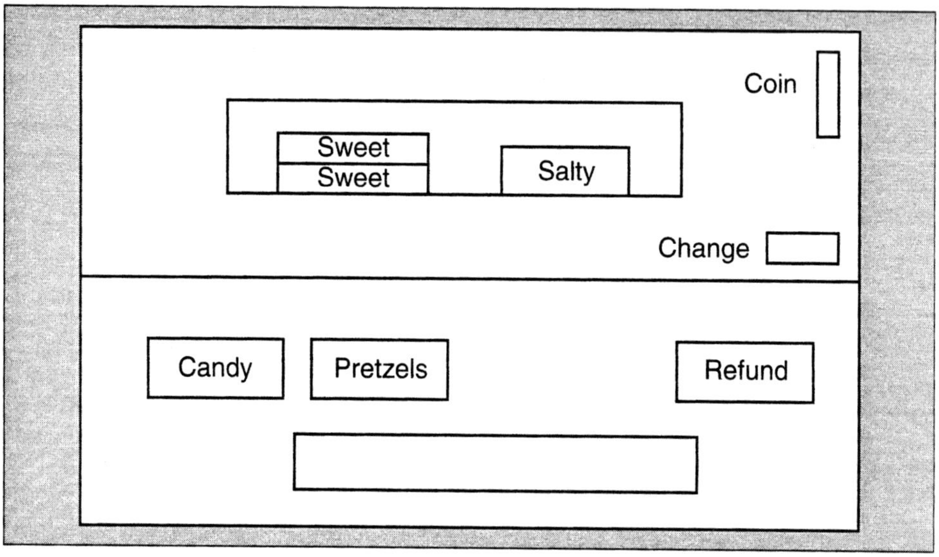

Vending machines are handy, especially when we are hungry or thirsty, but we can use Java objects to illustrate the same principles. Java libraries provide many types of objects. For example, the `String` class, has many operations for manipulating strings of characters, which we explain in Chapter 5.

Object-Oriented Design

Computer programmers must develop ever larger systems with more capabilities. They seek programming techniques that allow them to be highly productive, achieving quality programs. The procedural approach, used since the first high-level languages were introduced in the late 1950s is being challenged by object-oriented programming, an approach first discussed in the 1960s, but which became popular in the late 1980s and the 1990s.

In fiction, each story has a point of view. A single person can tell the entire story from his or her point of view, with the thoughts of the other characters never appearing. Another approach is to have each character express his or her thoughts and feelings as well as show actions. Procedural programming is programming from a single point of view, using a controller that orchestrates all the action while the data acted on is passive. Object-oriented programming puts the data inside objects that actively manage that data by providing services to other objects. Rather than having a single controller manipulating passive data, an object-oriented program lets the objects interact with each other, each meeting its responsibilities. Object-oriented programming combines the data and its operations into objects.

A Definition

Bertrand Meyer gives an example of a payroll program which produces paychecks from timecards.* Management may later want to extend this program to produce statistics or tax information. The payroll function itself may need to be changed to produce weekly checks instead of biweekly checks, for example. The procedures used to implement the original payroll program would need to be changed to make any of these modifications. Meyer notes that any of these payroll programs will manipulate the same sort of data, employee records, company regulations, etc.

Focusing on the more stable aspect of such systems, Meyer states a principle

"Ask not first what the system does:
Ask WHAT it does it to!"*

and a definition

"Object-oriented design is the method which leads to software architectures based on the objects every system or subsystem manipulates (rather than "the" function it is meant to ensure)."†

Use Cases and Scenarios

In this section we model a customer order at a fast food restaurant, showing how objects interact and call one another's services, leading to a true object-oriented simulation. We first need to identify the types of objects we will need, which we do by considering typical uses of the system, called **use cases**, and various **scenarios** which show, in a step-by-step manner, the interactions among objects that take place relating to that use case.

When designing using objects, we may start by identifying the use cases. In our example, one use case would be a customer placing an order. To better understand each use of the system we describe typical scenarios. For each use case, we develop a primary scenario showing the normal interactions, and several secondary scenarios which list the interactions that take place in more unusual or error situations.

For our restaurant example, a normal scenario, shown in Figure 1.15, would involve a customer entering the restaurant, walking up to the counter, and placing an order.

Figure 1.15 A scenario for a fast food order

```
The customer orders a burger, soda, and fries from the waiter.
The waiter asks the cook to make a burger.
The waiter serves the soda to the customer.
The waiter asks the cook to make the fries.
The cook gives the waiter the burger to serve.
The cook gives the waiter the fries to serve.
The waiter asks the customer to pay.
```

* Bertrand Meyer, *Object-Oriented Software Construction,* Second Edition, Prentice-Hall, 1997, p. 105.

* Ibid., p. 116.

† Ibid., p. 116.

From this scenario, we identify three objects, a customer, a waiter, and a cook. The scenario also shows the responsibilities of each object, and we can easily determine the information each object needs to maintain in its state. The customer has money to buy food, the waiter has cash received, and the cook has a supply of burgers and fries.

Figure 1.16 State and responsibilities for Customer, Waiter, and Cook

	Customer	Waiter	Cook
State	money	cash	burgers and fries
Responsibilities	place an order	take an order	make burgers
	pay	serve an item	make fries

An object-oriented program to simulate this use of a restaurant would create the customer, waiter, and cook objects and let them interact as the scenario indicates. In the last section we visualized objects as vending machines with buttons for their services. We depict them in Figure 1.17 more schematically as black boxes with a handle for each service. In design, a black box signifies we cannot see inside at the workings of the object but must use its services.

Figure 1.17 Objects showing only available services

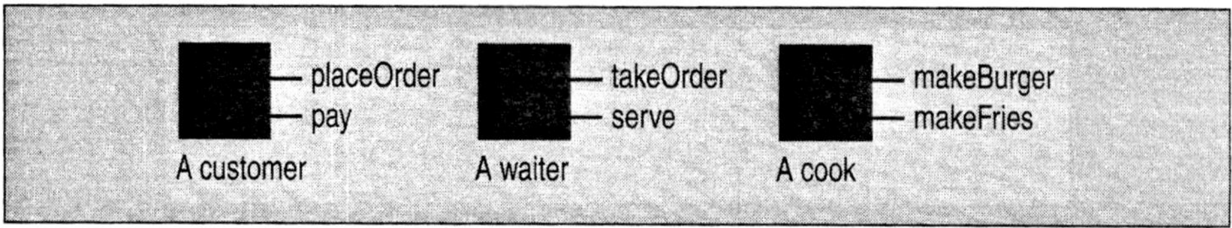

Where do we define these services and the items that make up the state of the objects? In Java, each object is an instance of a class which defines the state variables and service methods for that type of object. For example, a `Customer` class defines the state and behavior for `Customer` objects, as do the `Waiter` and `Cook` classes for `Waiter` and `Cook` objects. In the next chapter we go carefully over the coding of classes, and in Section 5.4 we write the `Customer`, `Waiter`, and `Cook` classes. First we introduce another example of analysis and design to which we shall return several times in this text.

Scenarios for an ATM system

Before getting into the details of object-oriented programming in Java, we start another design, previewing the automated teller machine simulation we design in Section 9.5. The familiar situation is that a user inserts a card into the teller machine, the teller asks the user for a personal identification number (PIN), the user enters his or her PIN, and so on until the transaction is complete. Going through complete scenarios of typical uses of the system helps us to find the objects and identify their responsibilities. Figure 1.18 shows such a scenario for a deposit transaction.

Figure 1.18 A scenario for a successful deposit

The user asks the teller to accept an ATM card.
The teller asks the user to enter a PIN.
The user asks the teller to accept a PIN.
The teller asks the user to select a transaction type.
The user asks the teller to accept a deposit.
The teller asks the user to select an account type.
The user asks the teller to accept a savings account type.
The teller asks the bank to find the bank account of the chosen
  type for the user with the specified PIN.
The bank gives the teller a reference to the account.
The teller asks the user to specify an amount.
The user asks the teller to accept an amount.
The teller asks the account to deposit the specified amount.
The teller asks the user to select another transaction, ...

Looking at the scenario of Figure 1.18, we identify four objects: user, teller, bank, and bank account. From this scenario we can identify the responsibilities of each object as shown in Figure 1.19.

Figure 1.19 Responsibilities derived from the scenario of Figure 1.18

User	Specify a PIN Select a transaction type Select an account type Specify an amount
Bank	Find a specified account
BankAccount	Deposit an amount
Teller	Accept an ATM card Accept a PIN Accept a transaction type Accept an account type Accept an amount Accept an account

By writing scenarios for other types of transactions we would find other responsibilities for our objects, and perhaps other objects. For example, an account object will have the additional responsibilities of

Withdraw an amount
Get the account balance

We will look more closely at such an account object in Chapter 5.

To implement the ATM system, we need to create `User`, `Bank`, `Account`, and `Teller` objects, that we identified using a use case and scenarios, and let them interact.

Now we are ready to see how Java lets us define and create objects, which leads us to the classification process.

Classification

Many of our everyday concepts involve a classification of objects. When we sit on a chair, we are sitting on a specific instance of the `Chair` concept. The particular chair may be hard or soft, expensive or inexpensive. It provides a service, a place to sit, and has a state, occupied or unoccupied. A lamp, an instance of the `lamp` class, is not a chair. Its service is light and its state is on or off. We use language to categorize groups of objects. Natural language is imprecise, but we all generally agree on what we call a chair or a lamp.

In Java we must be more precise, but the idea is similar. Java uses a class to define the state and behavior of a type of object. The word *class* evokes the idea of classification. To understand how to build a class to define a type of object, we focus first on the `BankAccount` class.

A `BankAccount` class must describe the components of the state and behavior for the various `BankAccount` objects we create. In Java, variables save the state of an object, and methods implement its behaviors. Informally, Figure 1.20 shows how the `BankAccount` class implements the state and behaviors for each of its instances.

Figure 1.20 Implementing `BankAccount` state and behavior

balance
    A decimal value representing the dollar amount
    of the current balance for that account.

deposit an amount
    Add the amount to the current balance.

withdraw an amount
    If the amount is not greater than the current balance,
    subtract the amount from the current balance.

getBalance
    Get the current balance.

The Unified Modeling Language

The Unified Modeling Language (UML) has become the standard for object-oriented modeling; we will use UML diagrams in this text.* The UML diagram of Figure 1.20 represents the class of all bank accounts, showing their common structure. The top section in Figure 1.21 gives the class name, the middle section lists the variables used to represent the state of an account, and the bottom section lists each

* See http://www.rational.com/uml/ for more information on the UML.

Figure 1.21 The `BankAccount` class

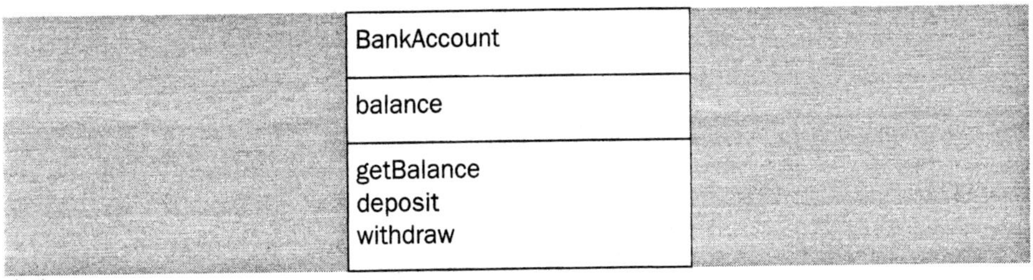

BankAccount
balance
getBalance deposit withdraw

account's operations used to provide its services. We say each bank account object is an instance of the `BankAccount` class. The class describes the state (data) and behavior (operations) each object instance possesses; it is like a pattern or template specifying the state and behavior of each of its instances.

Just as we may point to a favorite chair, confident it fully exemplifies the `Chair` concept, we create each `BankAccount` object to instantiate the `BankAccount` class. In the UML notation, objects, as pictured in Figure 1.22, also have three-part diagrams. In the top part we name the object and indicate the class that defines it, underlining both as in

`myAccount : BankAccount`

The middle section shows the balance with a specific value, for example

```
balance = 24.50
```

The `BankAccount` class specifies each account must have a `balance`. In the object itself, the balance has a specific value. This is analogous to the concept of a chair which specifies a seat and legs, contrasted with an actual chair object that has a hard seat and curved legs.

The third part of the object diagram lists the services the object provides. Each `BankAccount` object can deposit, withdraw, or get its balance.

The objects `myAccount` and `yourAccount` of Figure 1.22 are instances of the `BankAccount` class. In Chapter 5 we will write the Java code that implements the `BankAccount` class.

Figure 1.22 Two `BankAccount` objects

myAccount : BankAccount
balance = 24.50
getBalance deposit withdraw

yourAccount : BankAccount
balance = 142.11
getBalance deposit withdraw

THE BIG PICTURE

An object has state, behavior, and identity. In designing an object-oriented program, we write use cases listing the desired uses of the system. For each use case, scenarios show the steps for successful and unsuccessful interactions with the system. We identify objects and their responsibilities from these scenarios.

Just as a particular chair exemplifies the properties of the `Chair` concept, objects are instances of a class that defines their state and behavior. We define a class, to implement a type for each object, which specifies the data and implements operations for each object of that type.

The Unified Modeling Language (UML) is the standard notation for object-oriented design.

TEST YOUR UNDERSTANDING

18. Write a scenario in which the customer orders a burger, fries, and a soda, but the drink machine is broken.

19. As a start for an object-oriented program, write a scenario describing the interactions when a customer rents a car. What objects, with what responsibilities, do you identify from this scenario?

SUMMARY

- Computers composed of a processor, memory, disk drives, and various input and output devices run a variety of software from operating systems, which make computers easier to use, to sophisticated business, engineering, and personal applications that have made the computer an essential part of our lives.
- Each processor has its own instruction set which uses numerical codes to represent operations and numerical addresses to represent memory locations. High-level languages allow us to program more expressively with greater ease than were we to use the processor's instruction set directly. A compiler is a program that translates a high-level language program to an equivalent program in another language so that it can be executed more easily. An interpreter is a program that executes a program directly rather than translating it to another language.
- Java maintains many features of earlier languages, modeling its basic syntax on the C language syntax, but both simplifies and extends earlier languages in useful ways. The Java developers describe Java as simple, object-oriented, familiar, robust, secure, architecture neutral, portable, high performance, interpreted, threaded, and dynamic. Its development coincided with a rapid growth of the Internet. Java is designed to be especially useful for network programming.
- Sun implements Java using both a compiler and an interpreter. The compiler translates the Java source code to byte code, which uses an instruction set for the Java Virtual Machine. The "virtual" in the name means this machine is usually not implemented in hardware. Rather, an interpreter executes the byte code directly.

The advantage of such an approach is the byte code can be transported across networks to machines with different types of processors and it will run on any of these machines as long as there is a Java interpreter for the JVM. The disadvantage is a somewhat slower execution of code.

- Java programs fall into two main categories, applications and applets. Applications stand on their own, while applets, embedded in web pages, are viewed in a browser or applet viewer. We edit and compile applications and applets similarly, but we call the Java interpreter to execute the byte code for an application, while the browser uses its own JVM interpreter to execute the byte code for an applet.
- Program-driven applications are like the cook making an omelet; they perform one step after another maintaining control until finished. Such programs use the character mode for input and output. By contrast, event-driven programs are more like firemen waiting for a call at which point they respond as appropriate. They often use graphical user interfaces to allow users to generate events, such as button presses, to which they respond.
- Procedural programming develops procedures that act on separate data. This style of programming requires a procedure to test what type of data it is using and to modify its algorithm to support each type. By contrast, in object-oriented programming, we place the operations together with the data in an object. When we ask an object to perform an operation it uses the method defined for its particular type. Object-oriented programs require less modification to work with new types, and more closely model our understanding of the problem.
- An object has state, behavior, and identity. To design with objects we start by identifying the use cases representing the functions our system performs. For each use case we develop scenarios showing typical patterns of use. We include scenarios for the expected successful outcome and various error outcomes. From the scenarios we can identify the objects that make up the system and the responsibilities of each object that define its behavior. In Java we will use a class to define each type of object. The unified Modeling Language is the standard notation for object-oriented design.

CHAPTER

2 Programming with Objects

OUTLINE

Introduction

Java programs use objects and primitive types such as numbers. We start with the Java basics. First we have to name the objects and values we use. Then we need to create them and use them to solve our problems. We use a character string as our first object and an integer as our first primitive type.

A string is like a word or sentence, composed of various letters and other characters enclosed in quotes. For example

```
"A big car!"
```

and

```
"Do you like tomato soup?"
```

are strings.

Each object has various responsibilities that it meets. For example a Java string must provide its length, and must tell us the location of the first occurrence of a given character. For example the string "A big car!" would tell us that its length is 10, and the first occurrence of the letter 'i' is at position 3. (Java starts numbering positions at 0.)

Each primitive type has operators that operate on its values, for example, 3 + 5 = 8. The addition operator, '+,' computes the sum of the integers 3 and 5, producing the result of 8.

Figure 2.1 After pressing `Start` in Example 1.5

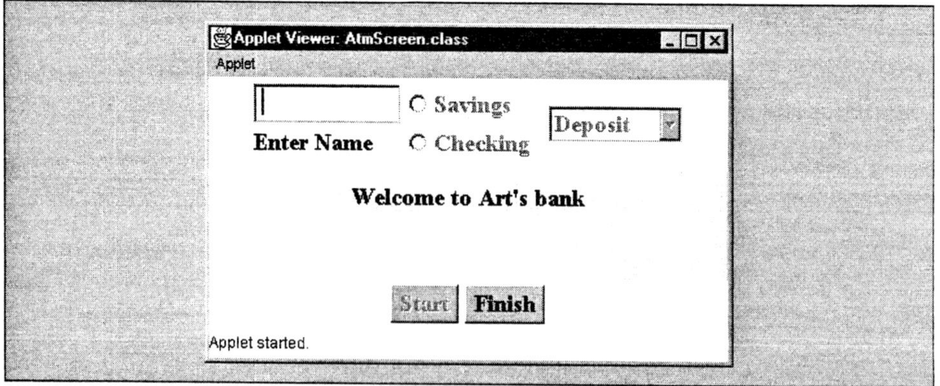

Figure 2.1 shows the `AtmScreen` of Example 1.5 just after the user pressed the `Start` button, which has become disabled. We enable the text field to allow the user enter a name. Note that the label `Enter Name` is now bold, and the cursor flashes in the text field where the user may enter the name.

The user has just pressed the `Start` button and we are starting our study of the Java constructs necessary to write such a program.

OBJECTIVES:

- Name objects and other Java entities.
- Build a class to define objects.
- Use methods to invoke object behavior.
- Use arithmetic expressions to compute values.
- Input in a dialog.
- Use an `import` statement.
- Get started with applets and events.

2.1 Names

Java is a wonderful language for doing object-oriented programming. We start in the early chapters using objects while learning the basic Java constructs. After introducing objects we learn how to name objects and other Java entities.

Object Behavior

Objects communicate by invoking each other's responsibilities. The `AtmScreen` applet shown in Figure 2.1 contains several objects. The field in the upper left corner, in which we enter the name, is a `TextField` object. A `TextField` provides methods we can use to invoke its behavior. For example we can ask a `TextField` object to `getText`, in order to retrieve the text that the user entered. To use objects we need to be able to name them and name their methods that we use. The names we use are called **identifiers. Keywords** are identifiers that are reserved for special uses.

Identifiers

Identifiers are used as names for variables and other items such as methods, which we will discuss later in this chapter. A Java identifier must start with a letter (including underscore, _, and dollar sign, $), followed by letters or digits or both. It can be of any length.

Figure 2.2 Valid and Invalid Java identifiers

Valid Identifiers

```
savings,  textLabel, rest_stop_12,  x,
I3,  _test, $soup
```

Not valid Identifiers

```
4you      // Starts with a number
x<y       // Includes an  illegal character, <
top-gun   // Includes an illegal character, -
int       // Reserved, see below
```

Unlike some programming languages (but like C and C++), Java is case-sensitive, meaning that upper- and lowercase letters are different. Thus `Finish` is a different identifier than `finish`.

Keywords

Keywords are reserved for special uses and cannot be used as identifiers. Figure 2.3 lists the Java keywords.

The Character Set

The character set defines the characters that can be used in a program. The ASCII (pronounced as′-key) character set contains 128 printing and non-printing characters shown in Appendix D. The ASCII characters include upper- and lowercase letters, digits, and punctuation. For worldwide use, a programming language must have a much

Figure 2.3 Java Keywords

abstract	do	implements	package	throw
boolean	double	import	private	throws
break	else	inner	protected	transient
byte	extends	instanceof	public	try
case	final	int	rest	var
cast	finally	interface	return	void
catch	float	long	short	volatile
char	for	native	static	while
class	future	new	super	
const	generic	null	switch	
continue	goto	operator	synchronized	
default	if	outer	this	

bigger character set to include the many characters of the various major languages. Java uses the Unicode character set which contains thousands of characters, including all the ASCII characters. We will only use the ASCII characters in this book.

THE BIG PICTURE

Valid Java identifiers start with a letter and use letters, numerals, $, and _. Keywords are reserved and may not be used as identifiers.

TEST YOUR UNDERSTANDING

1. Which of the following are valid identifiers? For each non-valid example, explain why it is not valid.

a. `Baby`	b. `_chip_eater`	c. `any.time`	d. `#noteThis`
e. `&car`	f. `GROUP`	g. `A103`	h. `76trombones`
i. `float`	j. `intNumber`	k. `$$help`	

2.2 Objects and Classes

The Java class forms the basis for all Java programs. Java classes define objects. We show how to develop a class to define a type of object. We illustrate with a simulation of a familiar simple vending machine that we introduced in Section 1.7.

Simulating a Vending Machine

To simulate a vending machine in Java we need to provide its state, behavior, and identity. Figure 2.4 shows the Java constructs we use to define vending machine objects. We introduce each briefly.

Classes

A **class** defines a type of object. The class concept in Java models familiar usage. We classify objects into categories, such as `Dog` and `Cat`. The class `Dog` describes and

Figure 2.4 Java constructs for defining objects

Java entity	Use
Class	define a type of object
instance variable	define object state
instance method	define object behavior
constructor	provide object identity

defines the properties common to all dogs. We might say that each dog is an example or an instance of the `Dog` concept.

To define a vending machine type we will create a class named `Vending1`. We use the name `Vending1`, rather than `Vending`, because as we improve it we will create other vending machine classes such as `Vending2`, and so on. The Java code for the `Vending1` class has the structure

```
public class Vending1 {

  // variables, methods, and constructors go here

  }
```

The Java style* starts class names with an uppercase character. The `public` modifier provides the most access to `Vending1` objects. We discuss modifiers more fully later in the text. The double forward slashes, //, start a comment, which is text to clarify the code. Java ignores everything from the two slashes to the end of the line. Multiple line comments start with /* and end with */, as in

```
/*  This is a multiple line
    comment.
*/
```

Variables and State

Our `Vending1` machine will be very simple. It will dispense only candy, and will accept only quarters. The number of candy bars it contains along with the number of quarters it contains will define its state. In our simulation, our machine will have a location in the computer's memory. It will store these two integers that define its state. Java uses variables to denote storage locations. Each variable has a type. To represent the state of a vending machine we will use two variables of type `int`.

Integer Variables

Integer variables hold integer values. Java always uses 32 bits to represent an integer internally as a binary (base 2) number. It allows for both positive and negative integers, which can range from –2,147,483,648 to 2,147,483,647. Following the C language,

* The Java style is not required, but reflects common usage.

`int` is the type name for integers. In Java we must declare each variable. For the `Vending1` class we declare a variable `quarters` to hold the number of quarters

```
private int quarters;
```

This declaration starts with the `private` modifier. We use `private` because we want to keep the state hidden and access the vending machine only through the services it provides. We declare a second variable, `candyBars`, to hold the number of candy bars in the vending machine. We place these declarations inside the `Vending1` class, which we are using to define vending machine objects. So far the `Vending1` class is

```
public class Vending1 {
  private int quarters;
  private int candyBars;

  // methods and constructors go here

}
```

Next we look at constructors used to create objects.

Constructors and Identity

When we create an object, we initialize its state. For example, we stock a vending machine with candy and quarters to make change. A constructor creates an object. It allocates space for its instance variables. Inside the constructor we can initialize these instance variables to desired values which represent the initial state of the object. Each object we construct has its own location in memory giving it an identity distinct from other objects, even those with the same state and behavior.

A constructor has the same name as the class, and may have formal parameters to pass data to it. It has no return value.*

The `Vending1` class has a constructor that initializes the number of candy bars and the number of quarters in the machine. Its code is

```
  public Vending1(int qStart, int cStart) {
    quarters = qStart;
    candyBars = cStart;
  }
```

Later we will use this constructor to create vending machine instances of the `Vending1` class. The constructor will create a `Vending1` object with its own identity in a separate area of memory, distinct from any other object. That memory will include space for the variables `quarters` and `candyBars` to hold the state of that particular machine.

---

* Unlike methods, a constructor does not use the keyword `void` to indicate the absence of a return value.

Methods and Behavior

Each object has a set of responsibilities that it meets. Each responsibility signifies a service that the object should provide. These services define the object's behavior. It has Java methods to implement each of them. A method may have parameters to pass data to it, and it may return a value to its caller. We specify methods using the form

```
access_modifier   returnValue  methodName(parameterList){
  // method body goes here
}
```

The method body contains the code that implements the method. The preferred Java style starts method names with a lowercase letter.

`Vending1` objects model a vending machine that allows the user to enter money and to select a candy bar. We use two methods, `enterMoney` and `selectCandy` to model this behavior. These will be **instance methods**, meaning that each object will have its own `enterMoney` and `selectCandy` methods, just as each has its own state. A user enters money into a particular vending machine and selects candy from a particular machine. The results of these operations may depend upon the state of that particular machine. For our first example we simplify as much as possible and design the vending machine to dispense only one kind of candy.

The `enterMoney` method has the form

```
public void enterMoney(int numberOfQuarters) {
  quarters = quarters + numberOfQuarters;
}
```

It has a single parameter that specifies the number of quarters that the user enters. The type `void` denotes that `enterMoney` has no return value. The `public` access makes it available to users of `Vending1` objects.

The body of the `enterMoney` method uses the `assignment` statement to update the state of the vending machine. The assignment statement

```
quarters = quarters + numberOfQuarters;
```

computes the value on the right, `quarters + numberOfQuarters`, and updates the value of the variable, `quarters`, on the left. Note that a semicolon terminates Java statements. Figure 2.5 illustrates the assignment process, assuming that the value of `quarters` initially was 10 and the value of `numberOfQuarters` is 3.

The `selectCandy` method has no parameters. In a physical vending machine, pressing the `Candy` button would cause the machine to dispense candy. In our simulation the `selectCandy` method returns a `String` object that describes the item.

A string is a sequence of characters. We enclose strings in double quotes, as for example "`house`" or "`A big car`." Later we will explore the `String` class that Java uses to represent string objects.

The `selectCandy` method has the form

Figure 2.5 The effect of an assignment statement

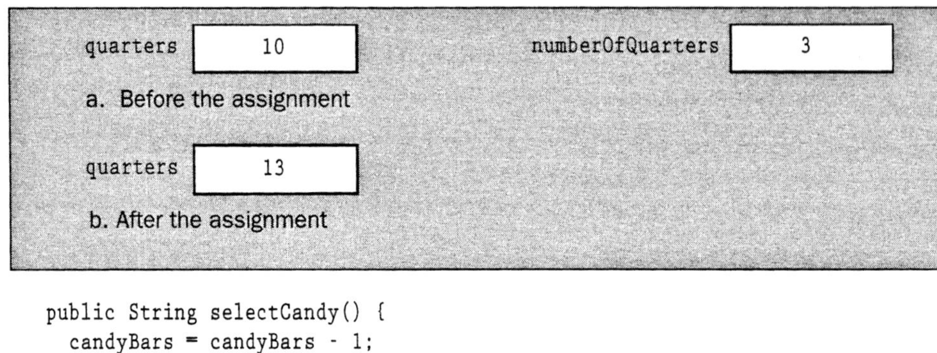


```
public String selectCandy() {
  candyBars = candyBars - 1;
  return "Candy";
}
```

The `public` access makes it available to users of `Vending1` objects. It has no parameters and it returns a value of type `String`. The body of the `selectCandy` method uses the `assignment` statement, with the = operator, to decrease the number of candy bars in the machine by one. It uses the `return` statement to return the value "`Candy`," showing that the user selected candy. In later versions of our vending machine simulation we will be more informative.

A First Look at Packages

Java organizes classes into packages. We will put all of our vending machine classes into a package named `vend`. A Java package name corresponds to a directory name in the host file system. Java style starts package names with a lowercase letter. To hold our vending machine classes we create a `vend` directory.* To place a class in the package `vend` we include the statement

```
package vend;
```

as the first line of the program. If we do not use a package, our class goes into a default package, which consists of all classes in the current directory.

We have shown how to build a `Vending1` class to define the `Vending1` type of object. We have instance variables to define the state, a constructor to create an object with its own identity, and instance methods to specify the behavior of `Vending1` objects. Example 2.1 puts all these together in the `Vending1` class.

EXAMPLE 2.1 Vending1.java

```
/* Defines the Vending1 type to simulate
 * a simple vending machine.
 */

package vend;                                        // Note 1
```

* On the author's machine the `vend` directory is located in `D:\book1a`.

```
public class Vending1 {
  private int quarters;                                          // Note 2
  private int candyBars;

  public Vending1(int qStart, int cStart) {                      // Note 3
    quarters = qStart;
    candyBars = cStart;
  }
  public void enterMoney(int numberOfQuarters) {
    quarters = quarters + numberOfQuarters;                      // Note 4
  }
  public String selectCandy() {
    candyBars = candyBars - 1;                                   // Note 5
    return "Candy";                                              // Note 6
  }
}
```

Note 1: The package statement must be the first non-comment line in the program. The package name must correspond to a directory in the file system that contains the compiled code for the classes in the package.

Note 2: We include the number of quarters in the state although this simple vending machine does not make change. We model the action of the user entering money but do not work out the details until we learn some Java statements to make choices and repeat code.

Note 3: This constructor has two parameters to specify the initial number of quarters and candy bars in the machine. We could have also included a constructor that takes no arguments and initializes a vending machine with a fixed number of quarters and candy bars. We call such a constructor, which has no parameters, a default constructor. We leave this enhancement for the exercises.

Note 4: This assignment statement updates the number of quarters in the machine. Later in the chapter we will see how to use a compound operator to abbreviate this statement.

Note 5: This assignment statement decrements the number of candy bars in the machine. Later in the chapter we will see how to use the decrement operator to abbreviate this statement. After we introduce the `if-else` statement we will only dispense candy when enough money has been deposited.

Note 6: `return "Candy"`
Our simple vending machine always indicates that it dispenses candy. Later when we learn Java control structures we will be able to create vending machines that give choices to the user.

To compile `Vending1.java`, we move to the `vend` directory containing the code and use the command

```
javac Vending1.java
```

which produces the `Vending1.class` byte code file.* The `Vending1` class defines the `Vending1` type of object. It uses Java to specify the structure of `Vending1` objects. In the next section we will show how to use this definition to simulate the creation and operation of vending machines.

THE BIG PICTURE

A Java class may be used to define a type of object. Instance variables specify the state. Instance methods specify behavior, and constructors build distinct objects with their own identity as distinct objects in memory locations.

TEST YOUR UNDERSTANDING

2. Could the following be a valid `Vending1` constructor?

```
public void Vending1() {
    quarters = 0;
    candyBars = 0;
}
```

3. Write a default constructor for the `Vending1` class. A default constructor has no arguments.
4. What state variables and methods might be appropriate in a class used to define an employee?

2.3 Using Objects

We create and use `Vending1` objects, and in so doing illustrate the concepts that apply to any objects.

Creating Objects

Given a class definition such as the `Vending1` class of Example 2.1, we can create instances of that class using an expression such as

```
new Vending1(10,15);
```

which creates a Vending1 object with 10 quarters and 15 candy bars. Figure 2.6 shows the UML notation for this object

The UML object diagram of Figure 2.6 has three parts. The top part has the form

```
object_name : Class_name
```

in which a colon separates the name of the object from its class, and the line is underlined. We do not name the object because Java names a variable that refers to it, as we shall see.

* An integrated development environment will provide a menu to compile Java code.

Figure 2.6 A `Vending1` instance

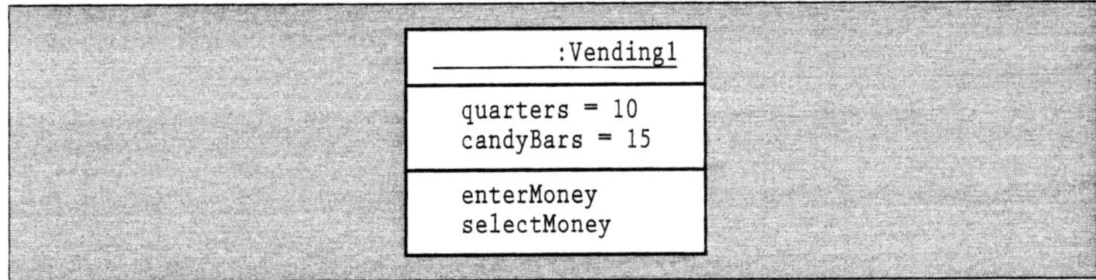

The second part of the object diagram contains the state variables showing their values for this object. The third part contains the names of the method we can invoke for this object.

Executing

```
new Vending1(20, 12);
```

will create another object which is an instance of `Vending1` and which has 20 quarters and 12 candy bars.

Reference Variables

In order to use the objects we create, we need to be able to refer to them. Variables of type `Vending1` can refer to `Vending1` instances. For example

```
Vending1 byTheDoor = new Vending1(10, 15);
```

creates a vending machine with 10 quarters and 15 candy bars, and a variable `byTheDoor` to refer to that object. Figure 2.7 diagrams this relationship. We show the reference as an arrow. This represents that the reference variable holds the address of the `Vending1` instance, which we denote using its UML diagram.

Figure 2.7 A reference variable of type `Vending1`

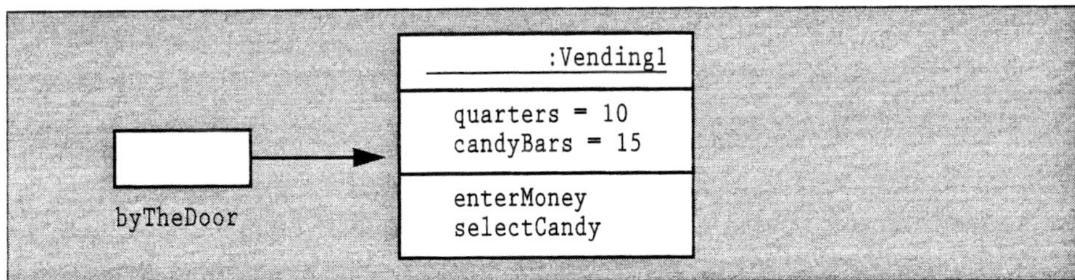

In Java, a declaration such as

```
Vending1 machineA;
```

declares a variable of type `Vending1` but `machineA` does not refer to any object. Java uses a special value, **null**, to indicate that `machineA` does not refer to an object. Figure 2.8 shows this situation.

Figure 2.8 A `null` reference

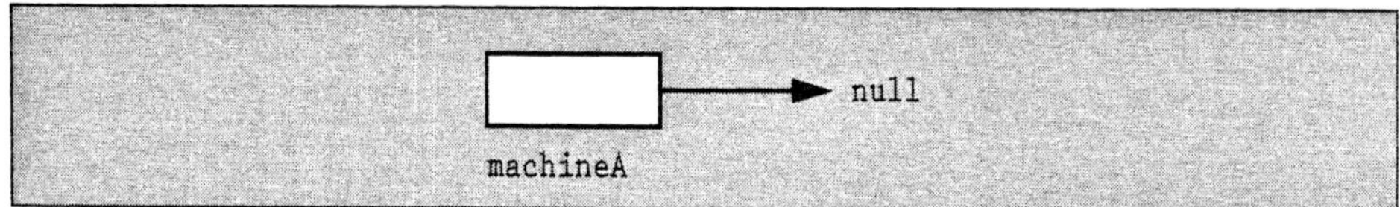

Invoking Behavior

When we enter money in a vending machine, we enter it into a particular machine. It changes the state of that machine and not of any others. We model the `enterMoney` method as an instance method. Each `Vending1` instance has an `enterMoney` method that changes the state of that instance. For the `byTheDoor` instance declared as

```
Vending1 byTheDoor = new Vending1(10, 15);
```

we invoke the `enterMoney` method using the form

```
byTheDoor.enterMoney(3);
```

assuming we deposit three quarters in this machine. Figure 2.9 shows the effect of the execution of this method, given the initial state of Figure 2.7

Figure 2.9 After executing `byTheDoor.enterMoney(3)`

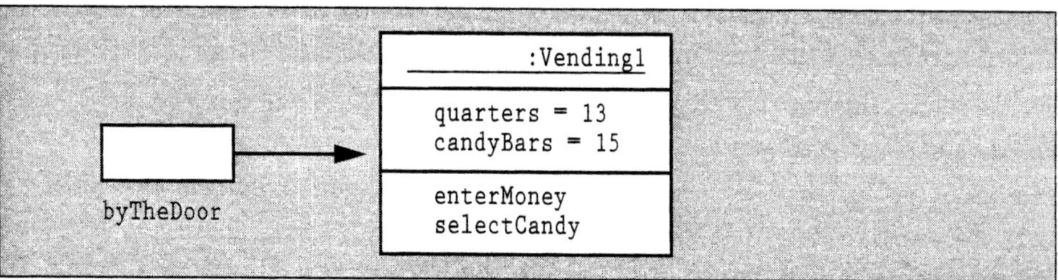

A dot separates the object on the left from the method on the right. The dot might remind us of a vending machine button. The `enterMoney` operation only makes sense when we invoke it on a specific machine in which we wish to enter money. It changes the state of that particular machine by adding the number of quarters entered to the previous amount of quarters.

Similarly the `selectCandy` method operates on a specific `Vending1` instance. It changes the state, reducing the number of candy bars by one, and returns a description of the item it dispensed. We call it using the syntax

```
byTheDoor.selectCandy()
```

and can assign the return value to a String using

```
String result = byTheDoor.selectCandy();
```

Figure 2.10 show how the state changes from that of Figure 2.9 after the execution of this method.

Figure 2.10 After executing `byTheDoor.selectCandy()`

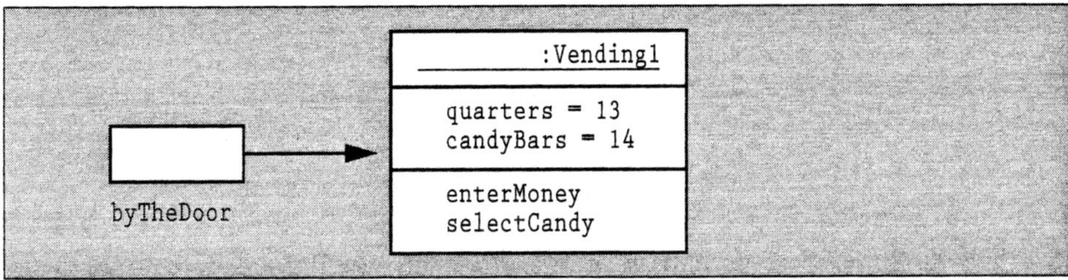

A Class for Testing

The purpose of the `Vending1` class is to provide a definition of `Vending1` instances. It contains instance variables to describe the state, instance methods to implement the behavior, and a constructor. We can also use a class to create objects and invoke their behavior.

Our `TestVending1` class will not have any instance variables, instance methods, or constructors, because we are not using it to create a type definition. It will have one class method, a special startup method named `main`. An instance method is part of an object. It may change the state of that object as the `enterMoney` and `selectCandy` methods change the state of the object to which `byTheDoor` refers.

A **class method** is shared by all instances. It uses the modifier `static` . We will use more interesting class methods later. Here we use the `main` method, which we always declare as

```
public static void main(String[] args) {
  // code goes here
}
```

The parameter is an array of `String` that we do not use now. We will discuss arrays and program arguments later. We use `void` as the return type, because `main` never returns a value.

The `TestVending1` class has the structure

```
public class TestVending1  {
  public static void main(String[] args) {
    // code goes here
  }
}
```

The Java interpreter calls the class method `main` to start executing a Java program. We put the test code inside the `main` method.

Local Variables

We declare local variables inside a method, in contrast to instance variables, which we declare outside of any method. We use local variables to refer to the objects we use or to hold values of primitive types. They only exist when the method is invoked, and can only be used inside the method in which they are declared.

In Example 2.2 we will declare three Vending1 instances

```
Vending1 choc1 = new Vending1(20, 10);
Vending1 peanut = new Vending1(15, 8);
Vending1 choc2 = new Vending1(20,10);
```

inside the `main` method. We will enter money in each and select candy. We will display the result of the candy selection in two different ways.

Output

First we will output to a console window, and then we will revise our example to output using message dialogs. The Java `System` class contains the standard output field, `out`. We refer to it as `System.out`. It has type `PrintStream`, which is another Java class that provides display services. `PrintStream` has `println` methods to display data in the console window. It positions output at the next line after executing, while the `print` methods remain on the same line. Thus

```
System.out.println("Have a nice day ");
System.out.println(12345);
```

displays

```
Have a nice day
12345
```

while

```
System.out.print("Have a nice day ");
System.out.print(12345);
```

displays

```
Have a nice day 12345
```

Using a Package

We have put the `Vending1` class in the `vend` package. In the `main` method of the `TestVending1` class we want to declare `Vending1` objects. We use the `import` statement to identify the package where the `Vending1` class file can be found. We use

```
import vend.Vending1;
```

which states that the `Vending1` class is found in the package named `vend`.

We also use the `System` class in Example 2.2, in `System.out.println` statements. The `System` class is part of the Java library, and is found in the `java.lang` package. However we do not need the import statement

```
import java.lang.System;
```

because Java automatically looks in the `java.lang` package to find classes it needs.

EXAMPLE 2.2 TestVending1.java

```
/* Creates Vending1 instances and invokes their
 * behavior.  Displays in a console window.
 */

import vend.Vending1;                                    // Note 1
public class TestVending1 {
  public static void main(String[] args) {
    Vending1 choc1 = new Vending1(20, 10);               // Note 2
    Vending1 peanut = new Vending1(15, 8);               // Note 3
    Vending1 choc2 = new Vending1(20,10);                // Note 4
    choc1.enterMoney(3);                                 // Note 5
    String result = choc1.selectCandy();                 // Note 6
    System.out.println("Dispensing " + result);          // Note 7
    peanut.enterMoney(3);
    result = peanut.selectCandy();
    System.out.println("Dispensing " + result);
    choc2.enterMoney(3);
    result = choc2.selectCandy();
    System.out.println("Dispensing " + result);
  }
}
```

Output

```
Dispensing Candy
Dispensing Candy
Dispensing Candy
```

Note 1: This `import` statement states that the `Vending1` class can be found in the `vend` package. In Java a package name corresponds to a directory name. Java needs to know where to find the `vend` directory. Below we show how to use the `classpath` to indicate the location of the `vend` directory.

Note 2: The local variable `choc1` can only be used inside the `main` method, where it is declared. We call it `choc1` to suggest that the candy bars it contains are made of chocolate, but `Vending1` instances do not include the type of candy as part of their state. We will design more complex vending machines later.

Note 3: We name this variable peanut to suggest that the candy is made of peanuts, but the `Vending1` state has no way to make this distinction.

Note 4: This vending machine has the same state and behavior as the one referred to by `chocl`. But it is a different machine. Its constructor allocates a location in memory for it separate from the location of the `chocl` machine.

Note 5: We always invoke instance methods on a specific object. Here we add three quarters to the `chocl` machine.

Note 6: `String result = chocl.selectCandy();`
The `selectCandy` method returns a description of the item dispensed. The description will be the same for each `Vending1` instance. We use a `String` variable to refer to the description, because the `selectCandy` method returns a `String`.

Note 7: `System.out.println("Dispensing " + result);`
We could have used `System.out.println(result);`but describing the result is more informative. The plus sign, +, functions as a concatenation operator when at least one of its arguments is a `String`. Concatenating two strings joins them together in a longer string. The output is thus

```
Dispensing Candy
```

Notice that we left a blank space after the first word. Otherwise the display would have been

```
DispensingCandy
```

TIP

Using an `import` statement is a convenience. We could eliminate an `import` statement by always using the fully qualified name for the class. For example if we had used

```
vend.Vending1 chocl = new vend.Vending1(20, 10);
```

instead of

```
Vending1 chocl = new Vending1(20, 10);
```

and similarly changes the other uses of `Vending1` to `vend.Vending1`, we would not have needed the `import` statement. Using fully qualified names makes the code more cumbersome to write and to read.

Classpath

The `classpath` lists the directories where user-defined classes may be found. If we only use classes in the Java library, we can ignore the `classpath`. However Example 2.2 uses the user-defined `Vending1` class in the `vend` package. We need to indicate the location of the `vend` directory. The easiest way to do that is make sure that the `vend` directory is contained in the current directory.* Java looks in the current directory by default, so it will find the `vend` directory automatically.†

* We will show other ways to indicate the classpath later.

For example, suppose we put the source code of Example 2.2, `TestVending1.java`, in the `d:\` directory. Placing `vend` as a subdirectory, `d:\vend`, will make it available to the `javac` compiler. We can then compile using the command

```
javac TestVending1.java
```

To run the tests in the `main` method of `TestVending1` we use

```
java TestVending1
```

A Message Dialog

Rather than displaying output in a console window, we can use a popup message dialog as shown in Figure 2.11.

Figure 2.11 A message dialog

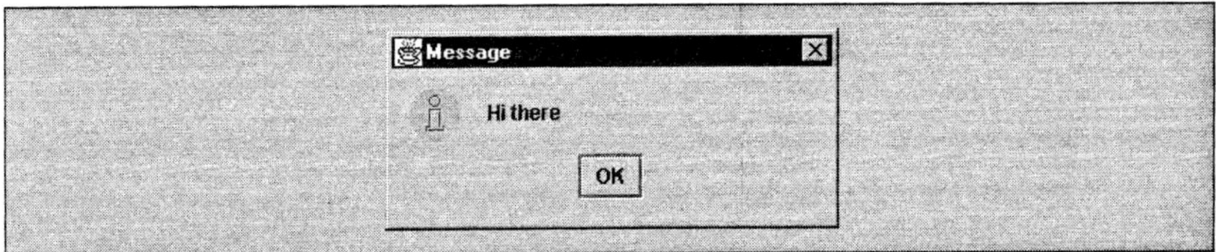

In addition to the message, the dialog shows an icon signifying that the message presents information. The user must press the *OK* button to close the dialog.

To obtain this dialog we invoke the `showMessageDialog` method of the `JOptionPane` class,

```
JOptionPane.showMessageDialog(null, "Hi there");
```

The first argument specifies the component containing the dialog. Passing `null` tells Java to use a default window frame to hold the dialog. The second argument represents the object to be displayed. We pass the `String` `"Hi there"` to display.

Because `showMessageDialog` is a class method, we call it prefixed by its class name, `JOptionPane`. The `JOptionPane` class is performing a class method. This contrasts with an invocation such as

```
byTheDoor.enterMoney(3);
```

where the instance `byTheDoor` is invoking its `enterMoney` method which changes its state.

The `javax.swing` package contains the `JOptionPane` class. We include the import statement

```
import javax.swing.JOptionPane;
```

† Integrated Development Environments provide options or preferences menus to set the `classpath`. We must always set these preferences. Placing the package directory as a subdirectory of the current directory will not be sufficient. See Appendix E for instructions in using an IDE.

to identify the package containing the `JOptionPane` class.

When we run Example 2.3 we get three dialog windows each of which looks like Figure 2.12.

Figure 2.12 The message dialog of Example 2.3

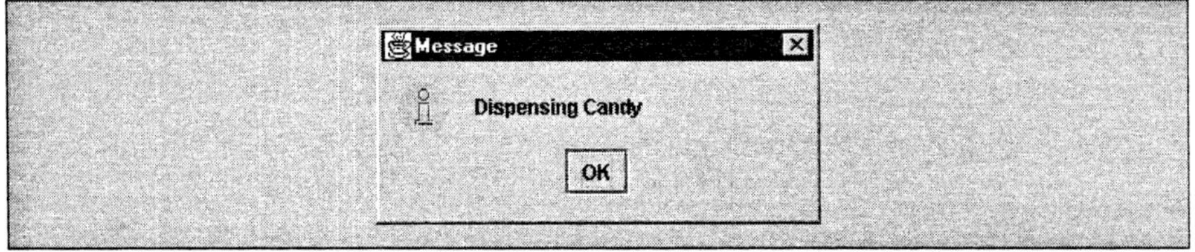

EXAMPLE 2.3 TestVending1Pop

```
/* Creates Vending1 instances and invokes their
 * behavior.  Displays in a dialog frame.
 */

import vend.Vending1;
import javax.swing.JOptionPane;

public class TestVending1Pop {
  public static void main(String[] args) {
    Vending1 choc1 = new Vending1(20, 10);
    Vending1 peanut = new Vending1(15, 8);
    Vending1 choc2 = new Vending1(20,10);
    choc1.enterMoney(3);
    String result = choc1.selectCandy();
    JOptionPane.showMessageDialog(null, "Dispensing " + result);
    peanut.enterMoney(3);
    result = peanut.selectCandy();
    JOptionPane.showMessageDialog(null, "Dispensing " + result);
    choc2.enterMoney(3);
    result = choc2.selectCandy();
    JOptionPane.showMessageDialog(null, "Dispensing " + result);
    System.exit(0);                                          // Note 1
    }
}
```

Note 1: The message dialog window becomes invisible after we click the *OK* button, but our program is still actively managing the dialog window. In order to terminate the program we use the `exit` method of the `System` class, which terminates the program. The argument `0` signifies normal termination, whereas a nonzero value would signify an abnormal termination due to some error.

A LITTLE EXTRA—USING A METHOD TO TEST

Examples 2.2 and 2.3 put all the `Vending1` test code inside the `main` method. The code repeated the steps of constructing a vending machine and calling the `enterMoney` and `selectCandy` methods three times, once for each vending machine. We can eliminate this repetition by creating a `test` method and calling that method three times. Example 2.4 shows this approach.

EXAMPLE 2.4 TestVending1Method.java

```
/* Create Vending1 instances and invokes their
 * behavior.  Displays in a console window.  Uses
 * a static test method.
 */

import vend.Vending1;
public class TestVending1Method {
  public static String test(Vending1 v) {                // Note 1
    v.enterMoney(3);
    return "Dispensing " + v.selectCandy();
  }
  public static void main(String[] args) {
    System.out.println(test(new Vending1(20, 10)));      // Note 2
    System.out.println(test(new Vending1(15,  8)));
    System.out.println(test(new Vending1(20, 10)));
  }
}
```

Output

```
Dispensing Candy
Dispensing Candy
Dispensing Candy
```

Note 1: Using the `static` modifier makes `test` a class method.

Note 2: In general, we prefix the class name when calling static methods to indicate the class containing that method. In this example we could have invoked the `test` method using

```
TestVending1Method.test(new Vending1(20, 10))
```

However because the `main` method is in the same class as the `test` method, we are able to omit the prefix.

THE BIG PICTURE

We use `new` to create an instance of a class with its own identity. The constructor may take arguments to initialize state variables. When invoking an instance method we are getting an object to provide a service, representing one of its behaviors. The `classpath` locates user-defined packages. Java calls the `main` method to start execution. It is a class method, not part of any object.

TEST YOUR UNDERSTANDING

5. a. Write a Java statement that creates a `Vending1` instance with 30 quarters and 20 candy bars. Assign it to a variable.

   b. Write a Java statement to invoke the `selectCandy` method of the object created in part a.

6. Which modifier does Java use to indicate that a method is a class method rather than an instance method?

7. Where are local variables declared?

8. Which package contains the class whose method we use to display a message dialog?

2.4 Arithmetic Expressions

In the process of solving problems, we perform operations on the data. Each type of data has suitable operations associated with it. Integer data in Java has the familiar arithmetic operations addition, subtraction, multiplication, division, and negation, and a remainder operation. We illustrate arithmetic expressions with example programs and use them to improve our vending machine simulation.

A **binary** operator, such as '+,' takes two operands, as in `3 + 4`, where the numbers `3` and `4` are the operands. Java supports these binary arithmetic operators:

```
+    addition
-    subtraction
*    multiplication
/    division
%    remainder
```

A **unary** operator takes one operand as in `-3`. Java supports these unary arithmetic operators:

```
-   negation
+   (no effect)
```

If the operands are integers then the result of an arithmetic operation will be an integer. Addition, subtraction, and multiplication behave as we expect from ordinary arithmetic. Some examples are:

Operation	Result
`32 + 273`	`305`
`63 - 19`	`44`
`42 * 12`	`504`

Integer division produces an integer result, truncating toward zero if necessary, meaning that it discards the fractional part, if any.

Operation	Result	
`12 / 3`	`4`	Comes out even.
`17 / 5`	`3`	Discards the 2/5.
`-17 / 5`	`-3`	Discards the –2/5.

The operation `x % y` gives the remainder when `x` is divided by `y`. The remainder operation obeys the rule

`(x/y)*y + x%y = x`

Operation	Result	(x/y)*y + x%y = x
`17 % 5`	`2`	`3*5 + 2 = 17`
`-17 % 5`	`-2`	`(-3)*5 + -2 = -17`

Examples of the unary operations are `-7`, which negates the seven, and `+3`. In summary, Figure 2.13 shows the Java arithmetic operations for integers.

Figure 2.13 Java arithmetic operations

Operation	Math notation	Java (constants)	Java (variables)
Addition	`a + b`	`3 + 4`	`score1 + score2`
Subtraction	`a - b`	`3 - 4`	`bats - gloves`
Multiplication	`ab`	`12 * 17`	`twelve * dozens`
Division	`a/b`	`7 / 3`	`total / quantity`
Remainder	`r in a=qb+r`	`43 % 5`	`cookies % people`
Negation	`-a`	`-6`	`-amount`

EXAMPLE 2.5 **BasicFive.java**

```
/* Tests the addition, sustraction, multiplication,
 * division, and remainder operators.
 */
```

```
public class BasicFive {
  public void test(int a, int b) {
    System.out.println("Numbers " + a + " and " + b);
    System.out.println("a + b = " + (a + b));              // Note 1
    System.out.println("a - b = " + (a - b));              // Note 2
    System.out.println("a * b = " + (a * b));
    System.out.println("a / b = " + (a / b));
    System.out.println("a % b = " + (a % b));
  }
  public static void main(String[] args) {
    BasicFive basic = new BasicFive();
    basic.test(17,6);                                      // Note 3
  }
}
```

Output

```
Numbers 17 and 6
a + b = 23
a - b = 11
a * b = 102
a / b = 2
a % b = 5
```

Note 1: The parentheses in `"a + b = " + (a + b)` are essential. The expression `"a + b = " + a + b` produces the output `a + b = 176` We leave it to the exercises to explain this result.

Note 2: The parentheses in `"a - b = " + (a - b)` are essential. The expression `"a - b = " + a - b` will not compile. We leave it to the exercises to explain this result.

Note 3: We hard code the data 17 and 6. Later in the chapter we shall see how to input values so we can rerun the code with different inputs.

TEST YOUR UNDERSTANDING

TRY IT YOURSELF 9. Change the test arguments in Example 2.5 to `12` and `5`. What output do you expect from this modified program? Compile and run it to see if your expectations are correct.

10. If `a=4`, `b=23`, `c=-5`, and `d=61` evaluate

a. `b/a` b. `b%a` c. `a%b` d. `b/c` e. `c*d` f. `d%b` g. `c/a` h. `c%a`

TRY IT YOURSELF 11. Modify Example 2.5 to remove the parentheses in the expression `"a + b = " + (a + b)`. Explain the output that results.

TRY IT YOURSELF 12. Modify Example 2.5 to remove the parentheses in the expression `"a - b = " + (a - b)`. Does the revised program compile and run? Explain.

Precedence of Arithmetic Operators

In Mathematics, we apply some common rules to decide how each operation gets its operands. For example, in the expression `3 + 4*5` we would multiply `4*5` giving `20`, and then add `3+20` to get the result of `23`. We say the multiplication has higher precedence than addition, meaning that it gets its operands first. In Figure 2.14 we show that `*` gets its operands first by drawing a box around the expression `4*5`.

Figure 2.14 Multiplication gets its operands first.

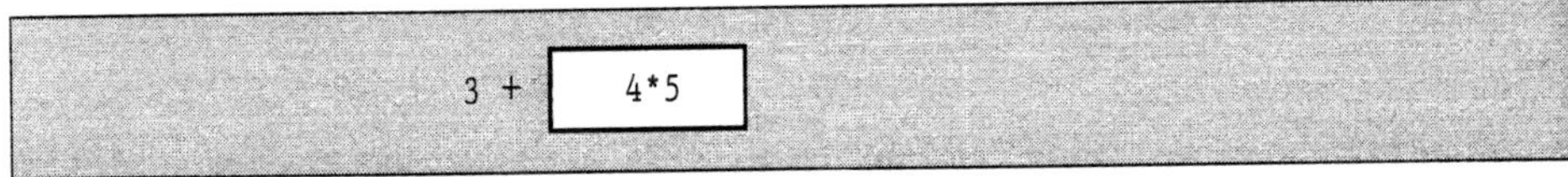

If we want to do the addition first, we would need to use parentheses, as in `(3+4)*5`, shown in Figure 2.15 We compute everything inside parentheses

Figure 2.15 Compute within parentheses first

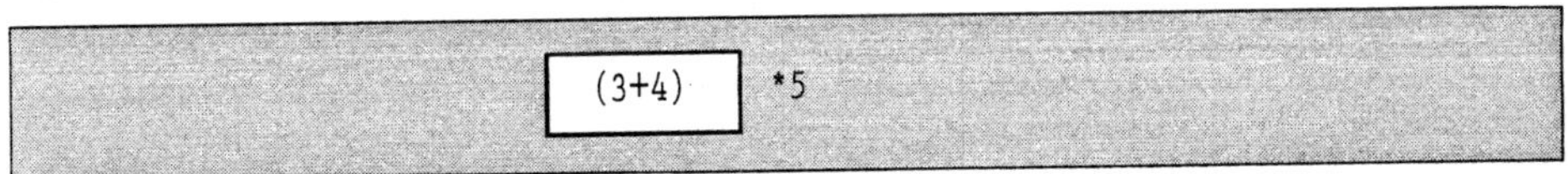

first, so we would add `3+4` giving `7`, and then multiply `7*5` giving `35`. By remembering the rules of precedence we can often avoid using parentheses. We could have written parentheses in the original expression, which would then be `3+(4*5)`, but these parentheses are not needed since we know that multiplication goes first.

Higher precedence

-, +	Unary Negation and Plus
*, /, %	Multiplication, Division, and Remainder
+, -	Binary Addition and Subtraction
=	Assignment

Lower Precedence

We evaluate `x-3/y` as `x-(3/y)` since '/' has higher precedence than '-.' We evaluate `-7+10` as `(-7)+10` or `3`, since negation has higher precedence than addition. In the case of arithmetic operators of equal precedence we evaluate from left to right. Thus we compute `3+x+7` as `(3+x)+7` and `10-7-5` as `(10-7)-5` which is `-2`.

EXAMPLE 2.6: Precedence.java

```
/* Illustrates precedence rules for arithmetic operators.  */

public class Precedence {
  public void noParen(int a, int b, int c) {              // Note 1
    System.out.println("a+7*b = " +(a+7*b));
```

```
    System.out.println("c/a + 4 = " + (c/a + 4));                    // Note 2
    System.out.println("c-a % b-a = " + (c-a % b-a));                // Note 3
    System.out.println();
  }
  public void sameParen(int a, int b, int c) {                       // Note 4
    System.out.println("a+(7*b) = " +(a+(7*b)));
    System.out.println("(c/a) + 4 = " + ((c/a) + 4));
    System.out.println("(c-(a%b))-a = " + ((c-(a%b))-a));
    System.out.println();
  }
  public void changeParen(int a, int b, int c) {                     // Note 5
    System.out.println("(a+7)*b = " +((a+7)*b));
    System.out.println("c/(a + 4) = " + (c/(a + 4)));
    System.out.println("(c-a) % (b-a) = " + ((c-a) % (b-a)));
    System.out.println();
  }
  public static void main(String[] args) {
    Precedence test = new Precedence();
    test.noParen(3,4,5);
    test.sameParen(3,4,5);
    test.changeParen(3,4,5);
  }
}
```

Output

```
a+7*b = 31
c/a + 4 = 5
c-a % b-a = -1

a+(7*b) = 31
(c/a) + 4 = 5
(c-(a%b))-a = -1

(a+7)*b = 40
c/(a + 4) = 0
(c-a) % (b-a) = 0
```

Note 1: We use the `noParen` method to compute the value of expressions without parentheses. The precedence order will determine which operation to perform first

Note 2: Recall that integer division gives an integer value so `5/3 = 1`.

Note 3: Recall that '`%`' is the remainder operator, so `3%4 = 3`.

Note 4: The `sameParen` method shows the expression fully parenthesized, but computed in the same order specified by the precedence. Thus the output of `noParen` and `sameParen` should be equal.

Note 5: The `changeParen` method computes the same expression, but now with parentheses placed to change the order of evaluation to be different than the order specified by precedence. Thus the value of `changeParen` may be different than `noParen`.

TEST YOUR UNDERSTANDING

TRY IT YOURSELF 13. Change the arguments in Example 2.6 to `a=7`, `b=3`, and `c=-2`. What output do you expect from this modified program? Compile and run it to see if your expectations are correct.

14. Evaluate the following Java expressions, where `x=2`, `y=3`, `z=-4`, and `w=5`.

    a. `x + w / 2`   b. `z * 4 - y`   c. `y + w % 2`   d. `x + y - z`
    e. `x * z / y`   f. `x + z * y / w`   g. `y * x - z / x`
    h. `w * x % y - 4`   i. `14 % w % y`

15. Insert parentheses in each expression in problem 14, following the Java operator precedence order. This will show what you would have to write if Java did not use precedence rules. For example, inserting parentheses in `x+w*z+3` gives `(x+(w*z))+3`, because '`*`' has the highest precedence, and Java evaluates the left '`+`' first.

Combining Assignment and Arithmetic*

Suppose we want to add `5` to a variable `x`. We could do that with the assignment statement

```
x = x + 5;
```

Java has an operator that combines the assignment and the addition, into one operator, `+=`. We can write the above statement more simply as

```
x += 5;
```

Java also has operators that combine assignment with the other arithmetic operators, `-=`, `*=`, `/=`, and `%=`. We must type these two-character operators without any space between the two symbols. Some examples:

Combined Form	Equivalent Form
`y -= 7;`	`y = y - 7;`
`a *= x;`	`a = a * x`
`x /= y;`	`x = x / y;`
`w %= z;`	`w = w % z;`
`b *= z + 3;`	`b = b*(z + 3);`

* While these operators provide no new functionality they do make it easier for the compiler to generate efficient code.

Note in the last example that we put parentheses around the entire right-hand side expression, `z + 3`, and multiplied that entire expression by the left-hand side variable, `b`.

EXAMPLE 2.7 AssignOps.java*

```
/*  Uses the operators which combine arithmetic and assignment */

public class AssignOps {
  public static void main(String [ ] args) {
    int  a = 2, b = 4, x = 3, y = 5, z = 6, w = 14;           // Note 1
    y -= 7;
    System.out.println("y = " + y);
    a *= x;
    System.out.println("a = " + a);
    x /= y;                                                   // Note 2
    System.out.println("x = " + x);
    w %= z;
    System.out.println("w = " + w);
    b *= z + 3;                                               // Note 3
    System.out.println("b = " + b);
  }
}
```

Output

```
y = -2
a = 6
x = -1
w = 2
b = 36
```

Note 1: We must initialize all variables since we use each before we compute a value for it.

Note 2: The program changed the value of `y`, so that the value of `y` used here is its current value `-2`, rather than its initial value, `5`.

Note 3: Recall that the equivalent expression is `b*(z+3)`, since the entire right-hand side expression is multiplied by the left-hand side variable, `b`.

* We put the code to illustrate assignment operators inside the `main` method. Another approach would be to put this code in a `test` instance method. In `main` we would create an `AssignOps` instance and invoke the `test` method. For this simple example we prefer not to create an object.

TEST YOUR UNDERSTANDING

TRY IT YOURSELF

16. Change the variable initializations in Example 2.7 to `a=7`, `b=2`, `x=12`, `y=4`, `z=-6`, and `w=8`. What output do you expect from this modified program? Compile and run it to see if your expectations are correct.

17. What value would Java assign each variable if, for each expression, `j=7`, `k=11`, and `n=-4`.

    a. `j += 31;` b. `k *= n;` c. `k -= n + 7;`
    d. `k %= j` e. `k /= n - 1`

Increment and Decrement Operators

Java has simple forms for the frequent operations of adding one to a variable (incrementing) or subtracting one from a variable (decrementing). To increment the variable `x` using the postfix form of the increment operator, we write `x++`. If `x` had a value of `5`, executing `x++` would give it a value of `6`.

There is significance to putting the plus signs after the variable (postfix). If you use this postfix increment in an expression, the computation uses the old value of the variable, and then increments it. So if `x` is `5`, evaluating the expression `3 + x++` will give `8`, and then the value of `x` changes to `6`. Figure 2.16 shows that evaluating `3 + x++` is like evaluating two expressions, first `3 + x`, and then `x++`.

Figure 2.16 Expression a) and equivalent expressions b)

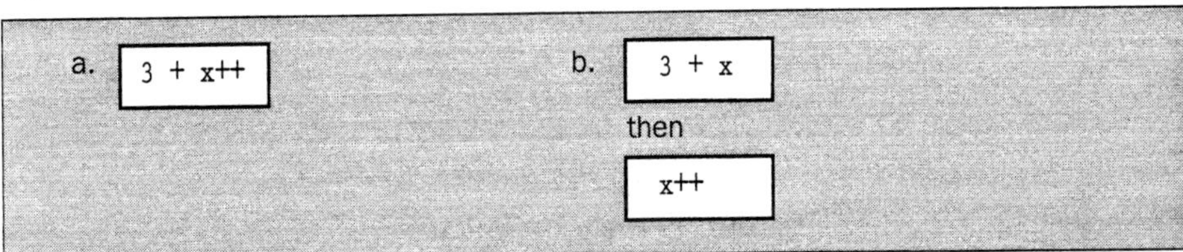

The prefix form of the increment operator, `++x`, also increments the variable by one, but it does it before the variable is used in an expression. If `x` had a value of `5`, evaluating the expression `3 + ++x` would increment `x` to `6` and then evaluate the expression giving a value of `9`. Figure 2.17 shows that evaluating `3 + ++x` is like evaluating two expressions, first `++x`, and then `3 + x`.

Java has two forms of the decrement operator. The postfix decrement, `x--`, uses the value of `x`, then decrements it, so that if `x` is `3`, then `2 + x--` evaluates to `5`, and `x` changes to `2`. The prefix decrement, `--x`, decrements `x` and then uses that new value of `x`, so that if `x` is `3` then `2 + --x` evaluates to `4`, since `x` was decremented to `2` before the expression was evaluated.

Figure 2.17 Expression a) and equivalent expressions b)

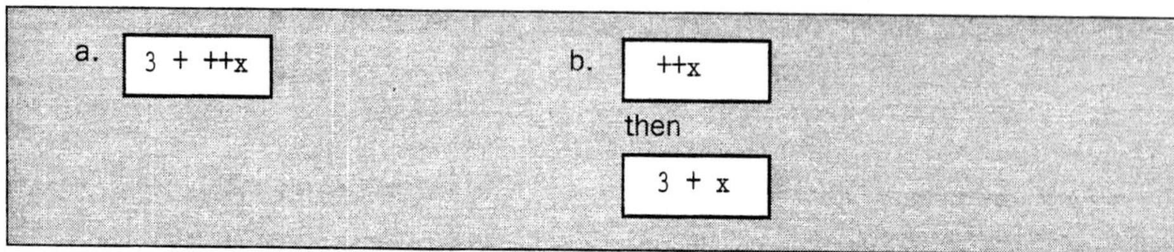

EXAMPLE 2.8 Increment.java

```
/*  Uses the prefix and postfix increment and decrement operators */

public class Increment {
  public static void main(String [ ] args) {
    int  x = 5, y = 5, a = 3, b = 3, j = 7, k = 7, result;
    j++;  ++k;                                                    // Note 1
    System.out.println(“j and k are " + j + “ and “ + k);
    j--;   --k;
    System.out.println(“j and k are " + j + “ and “ + k);
    result = 3 +  x++;
    System.out.println(“result and x are " + result + “ and “ + x);
    result = 3 + ++y;                                             // Note 2
    System.out.println(“result and y are " + result + “ and “ + y);
    result = 2 + a--;
    System.out.println(“result and a are " + result + “ and “ + a);
    result = 2 + --b;
    System.out.println(“result and b are " + result + “ and “ + b);
  }
}
```

Output

```
j and k are 8 and 8
j and k are 7 and 7
result and x are 8 and 6
result and y are 9 and 6
result and a are 5 and 2
result and b are 4 and 2
```

Note 1: We can put more than one statement on a single line as we have here for such short expressions. Usually the better style puts each statement on a separate line.

Note 2: Be sure to leave a space after the first plus sign, otherwise if you wrote `3 +++ y` Java would try to evaluate `3++ +y` which would give a compiler error, since you can only increment a variable, not a number like `3` which is constant.

TEST YOUR UNDERSTANDING

TRY IT YOURSELF

18. Initialize the variables in Example 2.8 to `x=7`, `y=6`, `a=5`, `b=-2`, `j=4`, and `k=3`. What output do you expect from this modified program? Compile and run it to see if your expectations are correct.
19. Evaluate each of the following Java expressions, where for each, `x=5`, `y=7`.

a. `x--`	b. `y++ + 6`	c. `y * --x`
d. `x++/3`	e. `++x/3`	f. `++y + --x`

Running a Test in a Package

Our `Vending1` class included no test code. The `TestVending1` class, which was not in the package `vend`, tested `Vending1` objects. Our `Vending2` class includes a `test` method and a `main` method to call it. Later we will improve it to be able to enter input interactively. Often a class includes a `main` method with some test code even though the class will be primarily used by applications outside its class and its package.

We use compound assignment and increment operators to simplify the expressions used in `Vending2` methods compared with those in `Vending1`. We add dimes and nickels to the coins we pass to the `enterMoney` method, and compute the total amount entered.

Because `Vending2` is in the `vend` package, its code must be in the `vend` directory. Suppose the source code, `Vending2.java`, is in the directory `d:\vend`. To compile Example 2.9 from a command prompt we go to that directory and execute

```
javac Vending2.java
```

When we execute a `main` method of a class inside a package we prefix the class name with the package name. In Example 2.9 this name is `vend.Vending2`.

Java needs to find the `vend` directory. One approach is to change the command prompt directory to the directory containing `vend`, `d:\`, say. We can then use the command

```
java vend.Vending2
```

This works because Java always looks in the current directory for package directories. It finds that `vend` is a subdirectory of the current directory. Figure 2.18 illustrate this approach.

EXAMPLE 2.9 Vending2.java

```
/* Uses compound assignment and the decrement operator.
 * Takes quarters, dimnes, and nickels.
 */
```

Figure 2.18 Running from the directory containing `vend`

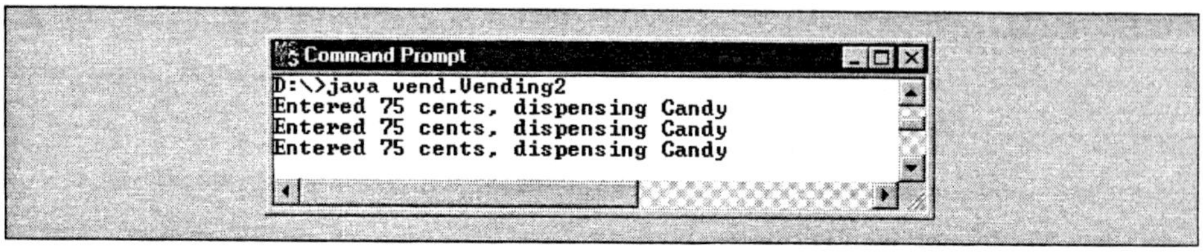

```
D:\>java vend.Vending2
Entered 75 cents, dispensing Candy
Entered 75 cents, dispensing Candy
Entered 75 cents, dispensing Candy
```

```
package vend;
public class Vending2 {
  private int quarters;
  private int dimes;
  private int nickels;
  private int candyBars;

  public Vending2(int q, int d, int n, int cStart) {
    quarters = q;
    dimes = d;
    nickels = n;
    candyBars = cStart;
  }
  public int enterMoney(int q, int d, int n) {
    quarters += q;                                              // Note 1
    dimes += d;
    nickels += n;
    return 25*q + 10*d + 5*n;                                   // Note 2
  }
  public String selectCandy() {
    candyBars--;                                                // Note 3
    return "Candy";
  }
  public String test(int q, int d, int n) {
    return "Entered " + this.enterMoney(q,d,n)
        + " cents, dispensing "  + this.selectCandy();          // Note 4
  }
  public static void main(String[] args) {
    Vending2 v = new Vending2(20,20,20,10);
         System.out.println(v.test(2,2,1));
    v = new Vending2(15,15,15, 8);
    System.out.println(v.test(2,2,1));
    v = new Vending2(20,10,10,10);
    System.out.println(v.test(2,2,1));
  }
}
```

Output

```
Entered 75 cents, dispensing Candy
Entered 75 cents, dispensing Candy
Entered 75 cents, dispensing Candy
```

Note 1: Using the += operator shortens the expression.

Note 2: We return the amount of money entered in cents.

Note 3: Using the -- operator shortens the expression.

Note 4: Our test uses fixed values for the quarters, dimes, and nickel entered. Later we will see how to input these values interactively. We use the optional syntax `this.enterMoney(2,2,1)` rather than the simpler `enterMoney(2,2,1)` to emphasize that every instance method is invoked from an object. Because the `test` method is also an instance method, it is understood that `enterMoney` is invoked from that same instance. Java uses `this` to refer to the current instance. In the `main` method we invoke the `test` method from a new `Vending2` instance, which is the same instance that invokes the `enterMoney` method. `enterMoney` changes the state of this instance, by adding to the quarters, dimes, and nickels.

THE BIG PICTURE

Arithmetic expressions use precedence rules that model those of mathematics. These allow fewer parentheses, making expressions easier to read and write. Like C and C++, Java can combine arithmetic and assignment operators and includes simple increment and decrement operators.

TEST YOUR UNDERSTANDING

20. Suppose the `Vending2` class is in the directory `c:\java\vend`. From which directory can we use the command `java vend.Vending2` to run the `Vending2` test program of Example 2.9?

TRY IT YOURSELF

21. Put the source code, `Vending2.java`, in the directory `c:\vend`. Change to the `c:\` directory, and compile using the command

```
javac vend\Vending2.java
```

What command could we use to run the program from `c:\`?

2.5 Parameters and Input

We have used methods in each of our examples. The `Vending2` class of Example 2.9 has an `enterMoney` instance method. We created a `Vending2` instance and executed `this.enterMoney(2,2,1)`. We explain the process of passing values to a method and how we can make our programs more flexible by inputting argument values interactively.

In this text we use the term `argument` to denote the actual value passed when we call a method, reserving the term `parameter` for the formal parameter which we use in the definition of the method.

We can think of arguments as the raw materials of the method that is like a machine that uses the raw materials to produce a product, the return value. We create a `Vending2` instance

```
Vending2 v = new Vending2(20,20,20,10);
```

and consider

```
v.enterMoney(2,2,1);
```

Figure 2.19 shows this view of the `enterMoney` method. We show the method as a black box because we can use it without having to look inside to see how it works.

Figure 2.19 The `enterMoney` "machine"

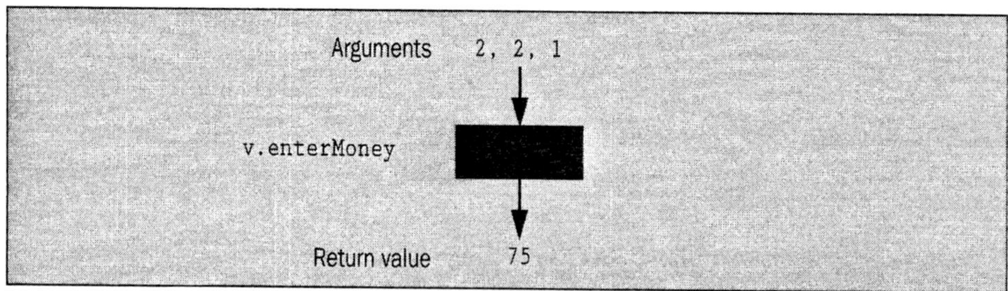

Figure 2.20 shows the changes to the state of the `Vending2` instance.

Figure 2.20 The state change from `enterMoney`

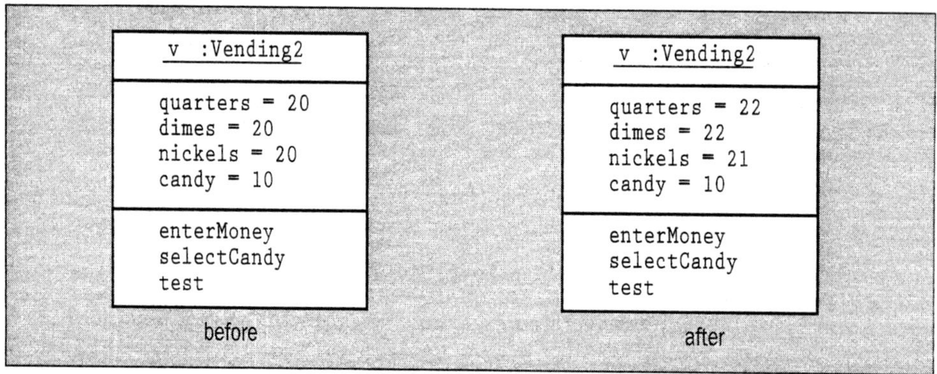

Passing by Value*

Java always passes arguments by value, meaning that the called method receives the value of the argument rather than its location.† Example 2.11 illustrates the effect of passing by value. We create a method that returns the cube of the argument passed to it. Passing `x`, which has a value of `12`, will cause the `cube` method to return `1728` which

* We discuss parameter passing further in Section 8.3 and compare values and references in Sections 5.1 and 8.2.

† Some language pass arguments by reference, passing a location rather than a value. Java, like C, always passes a value.

equals 12*12*12. We named the parameter to the cube method, aNumber. Inside the cube method we add 5 to the value of aNumber, but this has no effect on the argument x, defined in the main method, which remains 12.

We added a local variable, result, to the cube method. Local variables are declared inside a method and may only be used inside the method in which they are declared. The scope of a variable signifies the region of code in which it is visible. The scope of a local variable is the method in which it is declared.

EXAMPLE 2.10 PassByValue.java

```
/*  Illustrates pass by value
 */

public class PassByValue {
  public static int cube(int aNumber) {
    int result = aNumber*aNumber*aNumber;                      // Note 1
    aNumber += 5;                                              // Note 2
    return result;
  }
  public static void main(String [ ] args) {
    int x = 12, value;
    value = cube(x);
    System.out.println("The cube of " + x + " is " + value);   // Note 3
    System.out.println("The value of x is still " + x);        // Note 4
  }
}
```

Output

```
The cube of 12 is 1728
The value of x is still 12
```

Note 1: The variable result is local to the cube method and may only be used there.

Note 2: We add five to aNumber to show that this change affects only aNumber, and not the variable x which we pass to it from main.

Note 3: When we pass x to the cube method, Java copies its value, 12 , to the parameter aNumber, which functions as a local variable of the cube method.

Note 4: Changing aNumber has no effect on the value of the variable x, which remains 12.

Figure 2.21 illustrates the operations of Example 2.10. We see that local variables and parameters are only alive during the method call.* They do not exist before or after the call. We see that Java copies the value of the argument, so that the change to the

* A parameter acts as a local variable that is initialized by the calling argument.

parameter `aNumber` inside the `cube` method has no effect on the value of the argument `x` in the `main` method.

Figure 2.21 Memory usage

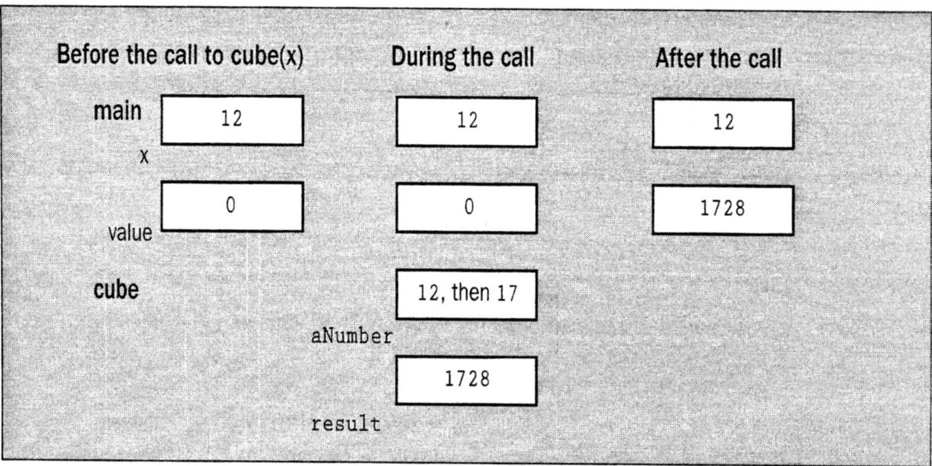

An Input Dialog

In our programs so far, we have assigned values to the variables we used. We could make our programs more flexible by allowing the user to input values from the keyboard. Java, to be robust and secure, does not make it easy to input values. The easiest approach uses the **Swing** input dialog.*

The `showInputDialog` method pops up a window, shown in Figure 2.22, containing a text field in which the user can enter a value.

Figure 2.22 An input dialog

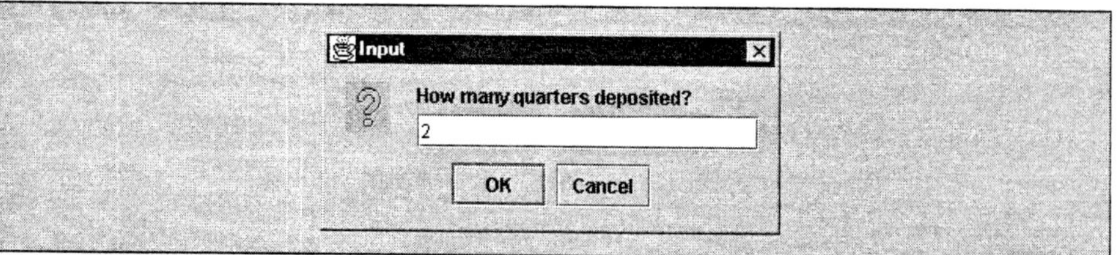

In Example 2.11, we call the `showInputDialog` method using

```
JOptionPane.showInputDialog
            ("How many quarters deposited? ")
```

The `showInputDialog` method has one parameter, which is the message that prompts the user what to input. In Java, every method is defined in a class. The `showInputDialog` method is a class method in the `JOptionPane` class, so we prefix the name of method with the class name. In Example 2.10 we were able to call the `cube` method without

* We introduce Swing components in Chapter 12.

prefixing it with its class name, because we called it inside the PassByValue class, in which it is declared. It would be correct, but redundant and unnecessary to call

```
PassByValue.cube(x)
```

instead of

```
cube(x)
```

in Example 2.10. However In Example 2.11, we must prefix the class name JOptionPane, because we call the showInputDialog method from the main method of a different class, TestVending2.

We have seen that Java organizes code into packages that correspond to directories in the computer's file system. A package can be either named or unnamed. The System class, which we have used in several examples, is in the java.lang package. Package names in Java correspond to directories, so the java.lang package can be found in a java\lang subdirectory in the Java distribution. Java automatically looks in the java.lang package when it runs our programs, but we need include import statements to indicate the locations of classes in other packages.

The JOptionPane class is in the javax.swing package, so we can indicate its location using the statement

```
import javax.swing.JOptionPane;
```

We could also use the statement

```
import javax.swing.*;
```

which will cause Java to look in the java\swing directory to find classes used in the program. The import statement does not include any code in our file. In this example, it tells the compiler to look in the directory javax\swing when looking for the JOptionPane class.

We use the UML notation for the package diagrams in Figure 2.23. The rectangle with a tab denotes a package. We show the package name in the tab and the classes of the package inside the larger rectangle. The TestVending2 class of Example 2.11 is in a default package consisting of all classes in the same directory in which it is contained. The dashed arrow shows a dependency in which the default package uses a class from the javax.swing package. We designate this dependency as <<imports>> showing that the default package imports javax.swing. Running Example 2.11 produces the three input dialogs of Figure 2.24, in which we enter the values of 2, 3, and 1.

The input dialog treats the value the user enters as a string, so that entering 2 in the first input dialog produces the string value "2" rather than the integer 2. We need the integer value 2 to decrement the number of quarters in the machine. The parseInt method of the Integer class will convert the string "2" to the corresponding integer 2. Because we call this method from the TestVending2 class we need to prefix it with its class name, as in

```
Integer.parseInt("2");
```

Figure 2.23 Package diagram

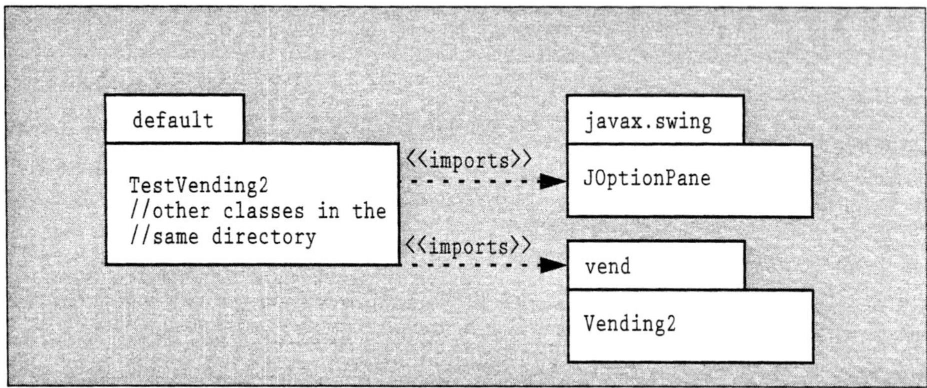

Figure 2.24 The input dialogs for Example 2.11

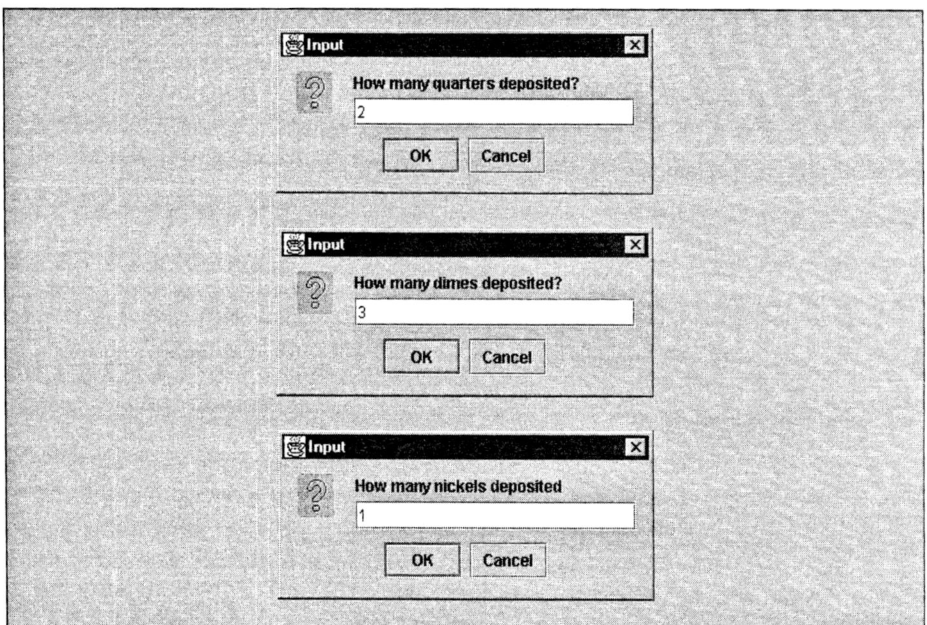

Because the `Integer` class is in the `java.lang` package, Java finds it automatically and we do not need an `import` statement.

Example 2.11 computes the total number of cents entered, which we could display in the console window using

```
System.out.println(v.test(q,d,n))
```

but we prefer to use the Swing message dialog. The command

```
JOptionPane.showMessageDialog(null, v.test(q,d,n))
```

produces the message dialog of Figure 2.25, which displays the sum of the three numbers we entered in the input dialogs. The first argument specifies a window in which to show the dialog. We pass `null`, which allows Java to create a default window.

Figure 2.25 The result for Example 2.11

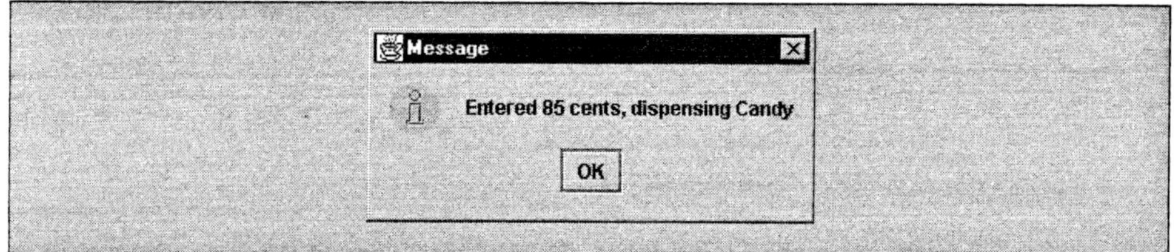

EXAMPLE 2.11 TestVending2.java

```
/* Creates a Vending2 instance and invokes its
 * behavior.  Displays in a console window. Uses
 * a dialog to input test values.
 */

import vend.Vending2;
import javax.swing.*;

public class TestVending2 {
  public static void main(String[] args) {
    String s = JOptionPane.showInputDialog
                     ("How many quarters deposited?");          // Note 1
    int q = Integer.parseInt(s);
    s = JOptionPane.showInputDialog
                     ("How many dimes deposited?");
    int d = Integer.parseInt(s);
    s = JOptionPane.showInputDialog
                     ("How many nickels deposited");
    int n = Integer.parseInt(s);
    Vending2 v = new Vending2(20,20,20,10);                     // Note 2
    JOptionPane.showMessageDialog(null,v.test(q,d,n));
    System.exit(0);
  }
}
```

Run

`Figure 2.24 shows the input and Figure 2.25 shows the output for Example 2.11.`

Note 1: After we cover exception handling, we will be better able to handle errors that would arise from improper input. For example, hitting the *`Cancel`* button will cause the input dialog to return null, which will cause the `parseInput` method to throw a `NumberFormatException`. The same exception will be thrown if the user enters text that cannot be converted to an integer, such as `47.1` or `hat`.

Note 2: We could have input the values to pass to the constructor from an input dialog. We leave this improvement for the exercises.

THE BIG PICTURE

A method contains code for an operation. We use parameters to pass values to a method, and may return a value from it. When we change the value of a parameter inside a method, it has no effect on the value of the variable passed from the caller. Local variables are declared inside a method, and can only be used there.

The Swing input dialog conveniently inputs values from the user. It allows us to rerun the program with different test values without changing the program itself or having to recompile it.

TEST YOUR UNDERSTANDING

22. Suppose that `x` has the value `9` in Example 2.10. What value will the local variable `aNumber` have when `cube` is called? What value will `aNumber` have just before `cube` returns? What value will `x` have after `cube` finishes executing? What value will `cube` return?

23. Consider the method declaration

```
int myAgeIs (int myAge) {
  return 39;
}
```

a. What is the name of this method?

b. What is the type of its return value?

c. What is the name of its formal argument?

d. What is the type of its formal argument?

e. Write a statement which calls the method, with the argument `55`.

TRY IT YOURSELF 24. Run Example 2.11, entering *hat* instead of a valid integer. Describe the result.

TRY IT YOURSELF 25. Rewrite Example 2.6 to enter the values for the test in input dialogs instead of hardcoding them in the program. Compile and run this modified program with different inputs. Calculate the outputs by hand and compare them with the program results.

2.6 Getting Started with Applets and Events

We introduce applets and events here in a friendly way, and begin a more detailed treatment later. Fortunately the browser or applet viewer manages the life cycle of an applet, so we can defer these details.

Objects

Objects have services that define their behavior. The list of services an object can perform is its interface to the programmer, who does not need to know how the object performs each service. For example a worker might provide a digging service, which in Java we might invoke as

```
worker.dig()
```

The notation we use starts with the name "`worker`" which refers to the object. We then give the name of the service, "`dig`," that we want the worker to perform. Writing "`workerdig`" would not be very clear, so we use a dot, `.`, as a separator.

A great feature of object-oriented programming is that the programmer does not have to know how the object performs the service. The worker could use a shovel, or a backhoe, or some other means.

In this section we use a `Graphics` object that knows how to draw text and shapes. It provides services such as `drawString` for drawing text or `drawRect` for drawing a rectangle. Programmers use these services without needing to know how they are implemented. The Java platform will give us a `Graphics` object designed to work on the machine we are using.

Graphics Mode

A `Graphics` object draws each pixel (picture element) in a window. Pixels are dots on the screen used to create graphic images. A screen may show 25 columns of 80 characters each, for a total of 2000 characters. At a resolution of 1024 by 768, the screen displays 786,432 pixels, while at a resolution of 640 by 480, the screen displays 307,200 pixels.

We use coordinates to denote each point of the window. Figure 2.26 shows that (0,0) is the upper-left corner of the window. The x-coordinates increase in value from left to right, while the y-coordinates increase from top to bottom. We illustrate with a window that is 400 pixels wide and 300 high. Since we start numbering with 0, the bottom left corner of this window has coordinates (399,299).

To display "`Hello World!`" in a graphics window, we will ask a `Graphics` object to perform its `drawString` behavior. We need to pass it the text we wish to display, and the `(x,y)` coordinates of the desired position for the lower-left corner of the text. If we use the name `g` to refer to our `Graphics` object, we can ask `g` to draw "`Hello World!`" at `(30,40)` using the command

```
g.drawString("Hello World!", 30,40);
```

Figure 2.26 Coordinates, in pixels, for 400 by 300 window

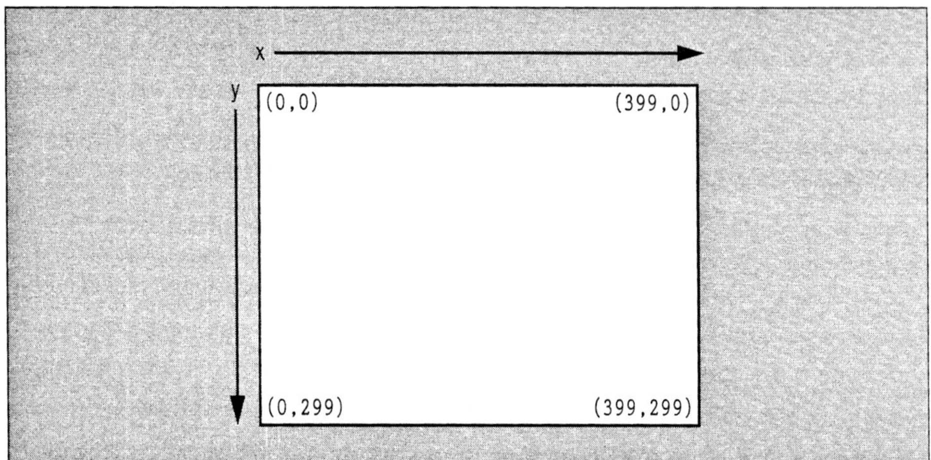

In Java each service is implemented by a method. The `Graphics` class that is part of the `java.awt` package contains a `drawString` method. The first argument to the `drawString` method is the text we wish to display. The second argument is the x-coordinate of the lower-left corner of the text, and the third argument is the y-coordinate.

Applets

An applet is a Java application that runs in a browser or an applet viewer. Java provides an `Applet` class that provides services including `init`, `start`, `stop`, and `destroy`, which the browser uses to manage applets. For simple applets, we let the browser use the default implementations of these services that the `Applet` class provides.

We saw how to run an applet in Section 1.3. Example 2.12 repeats Example 1.2 for convenience.

EXAMPLE 2.12 HelloApplet.java

```
/* Displays the message "Hello World!" in
 * a browser or appletviewer window.
 */

import java.awt.Graphics;                          // Note 1
import java.applet.Applet;                         // Note 2
public class HelloApplet extends Applet {          // Note 3
  public void paint(Graphics g) {                  // Note 4
    g.drawString("Hello World!",30,30);            // Note 5
  }
}
```

Note 1: We need a `Graphics` object to provide us the `drawString` service. The import statement tells the compiler that the `Graphics` class is located in the `java.awt` package, which is one of the standard Java libraries.

Note 2: The `java.applet` package in the Java library contains the `Applet` class. We need to inform the compiler where to find all classes we use except those in the `java.lang` package.

Note 3: Sometimes we cannot use a class directly because its services are not exactly what we need. We want to draw in the `Applet` window, and the `Applet` class has a `paint` service for that purpose. However, the `Applet` class has no idea what we want to draw, so it implements the `paint` method to do nothing. In order to draw, we must **extend** the `Applet` class and **override** the `paint` method to do our drawing. Extending a class illustrates the **inheritance** concept that we explore in detail later in the text. The syntax uses the keyword **extends.** `HelloApplet` extends Applet. The `HelloApplet` class is an `Applet`, so it inherits all of the `Applet` methods. It can use these methods unchanged or change them as needed. The code in the `HelloApplet` class specifies the changes we make to the `Applet` class.

Note 4: The only change `HelloApplet` makes to `Applet` is to override the `paint` method. Overriding a method means that we are implementing a new version of the behavior it represents. The `Applet paint` method does nothing. We override it to display "`Hello World!`" The argument to the `paint` method is a `Graphics` object `g` that provides services to draw text and shapes. Java passes a suitable `Graphics` object to the `paint` method, so the programmer does not need to create one.

Note 5: The three arguments to the `drawString` method are a message string and the `(x,y)` coordinates of the lower-left corner of the text. The applet uses a default font that we will learn how to change later.

An applet is part of a web page. We will study HTML tags later. For now we use the file `HelloApplet.html` which contains

```
<applet code="HelloApplet"  width="400" height="300">
</applet>
```

The `HelloApplet` files are located in the `D:\bookla\ch2` directory. Entering `D:\bookla\ch2\HelloApplet.html` in the browser's address field displays the applet as shown in Figure 2.27. Internet Explorer gives the applet a gray background.

We could also use the applet viewer that comes with the Java 2 SDK to view the applet, by entering the command

```
appletviewer HelloApplet.html
```

The applet viewer is a good way to test applets before deploying them on a web site for others to use.

Figure 2.27 Internet Explorer displaying HelloApplet

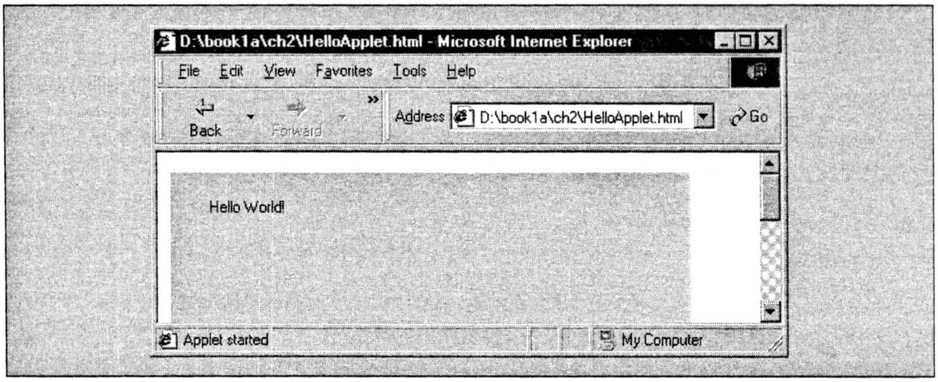

A LITTLE EXTRA

Observant readers may have noticed that we called the `showInputDialog` method by prefixing it with its class name `JOptionPane`, as for example

```
JOptionPane.showInputDialog("Enter the first number");
```

However we called the `drawString` method using a `Graphics` object `g`, as for example

```
g.drawString("Hello World!",30,40);
```

In Chapter 5, we will explore the difference between class methods such as `showInputDialog`, and instance methods such as `drawString`.

Events

In event-driven programming, the user generates an event that our program handles. We write event-handlers that wait until the user performs the appropriate action. The operating system responds to the user action, and passes the event to Java, which calls the event-handler to respond to it.

The `paint` method in `HelloApplet` is an event handler for `paint` events. The user of `HelloApplet` can generate `paint` events in several ways. For example,

- Enter the address of `HelloApplet.html` in the browser's address field.
- Restore the browser window after it has been minimized.
- Uncover the browser window from under other windows that were covering the applet.

These generate `paint` events because they require the applet to be redrawn. The `paint` method contains the code that specifies what to draw in the applet. Java calls the `paint` method whenever the user performs an action that requires the applet to be redrawn. `HelloApplet` remains active as long as the user remains browsing the page containing it.

Later we will investigate event handling in more detail, looking at paint events, and user interface events such as button presses.

THE BIG PICTURE

Objects provide services. For example, a `Graphics` object provides a `drawString` method to draw a string. An applet displays in a browser or applet viewer. The `paint` method handles paint events generated when a user-generated event requires it to be redrawn.

TEST YOUR UNDERSTANDING

TRY IT YOURSELF

26. We can avoid using import statements if we always refer to classes by their fully qualified names, for example `java.awt.Graphics` and `java.applet.Applet`. Rewrite Example 2.12 omitting the import statements. Compile and run the new version.
27. If a worker provides a `washCar` service, which is the object-oriented way to invoke it, `washCar(myCar, worker)`, or `worker.washCar(myCar)`?
28. Which method does Java call when the user uncovers an applet window?

SUMMARY

- We name our data and other items using identifiers which must start with a letter (including underscore, _, and dollar sign, `$`), followed by letters or digits or both, and can be of any length. Java is case-sensitive, distinguishing between identifiers `fruit` and `Fruit`, for example, which have the same letters, the first using a lower-case `f`, and the second using an upper-case `F`. Keywords, such as `int`, are reserved for special uses and cannot be used as identifiers. Java uses the Unicode character set which contains thousands of characters, including all the commonly used ASCII characters.
- A variable holds data that the program uses. Every Java variable has a type and a name that the programmer must declare. Java uses the keyword `int` for the integer data type. Declaring an `int` variable specifies its type as integer. Integer variables can hold values of up to 10 decimal digits. We can initialize a variable in its declaration that will give that variable an initial or starting value. We use the assignment statement to change a variable's value during the execution of the program.
- An object has state, behavior, and identity. A class defines a type of object. Instance variables define the state. Instance methods specify the behavior. Constructors create distinct objects with their own memory locations.
- A package holds Java classes. A directory of the same names contains the class files. The package statement appears first in a Java program.
- We invoke instance methods from an object instance using the dot to separate the instance from the method being invoked. A method contains the code for an operation. We use parameters to communicate with methods and to make them more flexible. A method can return a value, the result of the operation. We use the `return` statement to specify the result. We pass arguments to methods by

value, meaning that Java copies their value into local variables. Local variables exist only in the block in which they were created.

- To perform computations, Java provides the binary arithmetic operators +, -, *, / , and %, and the unary arithmetic operators + and -. Java uses precedence rules to evaluate arithmetic expressions without having to clutter them with too many parentheses. Multiplication, division, and remainder have higher precedence than addition and subtraction. Java has operators, -=, *=, /=, and %=, that combine assignment with the other arithmetic operators, and increment and decrement operators, ++ and --, which come in either prefix or postfix forms.
- We put the startup code in a `main` method, which is itself enclosed in braces in the definition of a class. We declare the `main` method with the `static` modifier. It is a class method, meaning that it is part of the class, not part of any object. The Java interpreter executes the code in our `main` method.
- We use the `showInputDialog` method of the `JOptionPane` class in the `javax.swing` package to input values. We call it by prefixing its class name. We pass a message describing the input to the user as the argument.
- The `import` statement helps the compiler to find the location of a class. It names a package that corresponds to a directory in the file system. For example,

  ```
  import java.awt.Graphics;
  ```

  indicates that the `Graphics` class can be found in the `java\awt` directory, and

  ```
  import javax.swing.*;
  ```

  adds the `javax\swing` directory to the search path for classes used in the program. In the Java 2 SDK the Java classes are in a compressed format which we would have to uncompress to see the location of these directories, but Java can find them.
- Objects perform services that define their behavior. Programmers can use a service without knowing how it is implemented. We used a Graphics object `g` to perform its `drawString` service. Java provides an object, `g`, appropriate for the system we are using. The three arguments to the `drawString` method specify the text to display, and the (x,y) coordinates of the lower-left corner of the text.
- Applets run in a browser or applet viewer. They extend the `Applet` class. The default `paint` method does nothing, but we can give it a new definition to specify what we would like to draw.
- The `paint` method handles paint events generated by the user by uncovering the applet, for example. The operating system informs Java that the user has uncovered its window and Java schedules a call to the `paint` method to redraw it. Much of event-driven programming consists in writing event handlers which wait for user generated events to occur.

Skill Builder Exercises

1. Find the mistakes in each of the following (and correct them if possible):

   a. `integer x;`

   b. `public void main (String [] args) { // code goes here }`

   c. `z + y = 17;`

   d. `public Class MyClass { // put code here }`

2. What will be the output when the following code fragment is run?

```
int x = 12, y = 14, z;
z = y / x +7;
x = z * z;
System.out.println(x);
```

3. Match each term on the left with its meaning on the right.

a. `main`	i. the type for integer variables
b. **return**	ii. the startup method
c. **void**	iii. a Java statement
d. **int**	iv. denotes the absence of a return value

Critical Thinking Exercises

4. Which of the following expressions, if any, have the same value for integers `x`, `y`, and `z`?

   a. `(x + y) * z`
   b. `x + y * z`
   c. `x + (y * z)`

5. Which of the following statements, if any, have the same result for integers `x` and `y`?

   a. `x += y;`
   b. `y += x;`
   c. `x = x + y;`

6. Fill in the blanks in the following:

   a. If `x++` evaluates to `3`, the value of `x` before the evaluation was _____, and its value after the evaluation will be ______.

   b. If `++x` evaluates to `3`, the value of `x` before the evaluation was _____, and its value after the evaluation will be ______.

7. Which of the following uses of the `multiplyBy4` method of Example 2.6 are incorrect? The variable `r` has type **int**.

a. `r = multiplyBy4(r);`
b. `r = multiplyBy4(12);`
c. `System.out.println(multiplyBy4(12));`
d. The above are all correct.

Debugging Exercise

8. The following program attempts to test the `Vending1` class of Example 2.1. Find and correct any errors.

```
import vend.Vending1;
public class Test {
  public static void main(String[] args) {
    Vending1 vending = Vending1(9,12);
    System.out.println(vending.enterMoney(3));
    System.out.println(vending.selectCandy());
  }
}
```

Program Modification Exercises

9. Add a default constructor to Example 2.1. Recall that a default constructor has no arguments. Have it initialize the state to default values of 10 quarters and 15 candy bars.
10. Modify Example 2.2 to use a message dialog for the output.
11. Modify Example 2.4 to use message dialogs for output.
12. Modify Example 2.5 to use message dialogs for output.
13. Modify Example 2.10 to use an input dialog to enter the value `x`.
14. Modify Example 2.5 to enter the arguments to the `test` method from an input dialog. Test with various inputs.
15. Modify Example 2.6 to enter the arguments to the methods from an input dialog. Test with various inputs.

Program Design Exercises

16. Write a program that displays a letter `T` like the one shown below

```
***********
     *
     *
     *
     *
```

17. Write a program that initializes three integer variables to `35`, `67`, and `452`, and outputs their sum and their product.

    a. Use only a `main` method to solve the problem.

    b. Develop an object-oriented solution with three instance variables, and `sum` and `product` instance methods.

18. Write a program that inputs three integers and outputs their sum and product.

    a. Use only a `main` method to solve the problem.

    b. Develop an object-oriented solution with three instance variables, and `sum` and `product` instance methods.

19. Write a **static** method with three integer parameters which returns the product of these parameters. Call this method from the `main` method and output the result.

20. Write a program to enter the height and width of a rectangle and output the area of the rectangle.

    a. Use only a `main` method to solve the problem.

    b. Develop an object-oriented solution with two instance variables, and an `area` instance method.

21. Write a `static` method with two integer parameters, the height and the width of a rectangle, which returns the perimeter of that rectangle. Call this method from the `main` method twice, each time with different arguments, and output the results.

22. Write a `static` method with one integer parameter and let it return the remainder of that integer when divided by seven. For example, `findRemainder(19)` should return 5. In the `main` method initialize two variables, `x` and `y`, with values `73` and `16`. Call the `findRemainder` method three times, with the arguments `x`, `y`, and `x+y`, each time displaying the result returned by `findRemainder`.

23. Write a program which reads an integer number of miles, converts it to an equivalent number of feet, and outputs the result. (There are 5280 feet in a mile.)

    a. Use only a `main` method to solve the problem.

    b. Develop an object-oriented solution with an instance variable, and a `convert` instance method.

24. Write a program to convert degrees Fahrenheit to degrees Celsius. Input an integer Fahrenheit temperature and convert to an integer Celsius temperature using the formula `Celsius=5(Fahrenheit-32)/9`. Output the result.

    a. Use only a `main` method to solve the problem.

    b. Develop an object-oriented solution with an instance variable, and an `fToC` instance method.

25. Write a method with one integer parameter, `x`, which returns the value of the polynomial `3x2 - 7x + 2`. Call this method twice from the `main` method each time reading in the value of `x`, and displaying the result.

    a. Solve using a `static` method.

    b. Solve using an instance method.

26. Write a method with one integer parameter, `x`, which returns the value of the polynomial `4x2 + 3x - 5`. Call this method twice from the `main` method each time reading in the value of `x`, and displaying the result.

    a. Solve using a `static` method.

    b. Solve using an instance method.

27. Write a program to convert an integer number of seconds to an equivalent number of hours, minutes, and seconds. For example, an input of 52,400 should give 14 hours, 33 minutes, and 20 seconds. (Dividing 52,400 by 3600 gives a quotient of 14 hours while the remainder is 2000 seconds. Dividing the remainder of 2000 by 60 gives a quotient of 33 minutes with a remainder of 20.)

    a. Use only a `main` method to solve the problem.

    b. Develop an object-oriented solution with an instance variable, and a `convert` instance method.

Applet Exercises

28. Write an applet that displays "`Have a nice day`" at position `(100,50)` in an applet of size 300 by 200.

29. Write an applet which displays "`Java is fun`" at position `(20,100)` in an applet of size 300 by 200.

30. Write an applet that displays your name and below that your birthday.

CHAPTER

3 Software Engineering with Control Structures

OUTLINE

Introduction

Our Java programs so far have been fairly simple. All we have learned to do so far is to execute one statement after another in order. We have not had any choices. If we lived life like that, then, no matter how we felt, we would get up, get dressed, and have breakfast. In reality, we make decisions among alternatives. If we are very sick we might stay in bed and not get dressed. (If we are real lucky, someone might bring us breakfast in bed.) We might not be hungry one morning so we would get up, get dressed, but skip breakfast. Here is a description of our morning, with decisions,

```
if (I feel ill)
  stay in bed;
else  {
  get up;
  get dressed;
  if (I feel hungry)
    eat breakfast;
}
```

In this "program," what I do depends upon whether "I feel ill" is true or false. We will see in this chapter how to write Java expressions that are either true or false, and how to write Java statements that allow us to choose among alternatives based on the truth or falsity of a test expression.

Making choices gives us more flexibility, but we need even more control. For example, if I am thirsty, I might drink a glass of water, but one glass of water might not be enough. What I really want to do is to keep drinking water as long as I am still thirsty. I need to be able to repeat an action. The kind of program I want is:

```
while (I feel thirsty)
  drink a glass of water;
```

We will see in this chapter how to write Java statements which allow us to repeat steps in our program.

We think of the Java interpreter as flowing from one statement to the next as it executes our program. The `if` and `while` statements will allow us to specify how Java should flow through our program as it executes its statements.

Controlling the flow of execution gives us flexibility as to which statements we execute, but we also need some choices about the type of data we use. So far we have declared variables only of type `int`, representing whole numbers. In this chapter we will introduce the type `double` to represent decimal numbers.

With the `if-else` and `while` statements, and the type `double`, we have the language support to create more complex programs*, but how do we use these tools to solve problems? In this chapter we introduce a process of careful design which we can use to develop problem solutions. We look at object-oriented design in more detail in Chapter 5.

Finally, in the last section we continue our introduction to applets, showing how to draw shapes.

Figure 3.1 shows our `AtmScreen` applet of Example 1.5 just after the user entered the PIN. The system prompts the user to select a transaction. Making selections is one of the themes of this chapter. We use the topics covered in the `AtmScreen` applet.

---

* For pedagogical purposes we introduce a basic set of control structures and the type double in this chapter, leaving the variations and additional features to Chapter 4, in preference to putting all selection structures in one chapter and loops in another with a third chapter for types.

Figure 3.1 The `AtmScreen` prompting for a selection

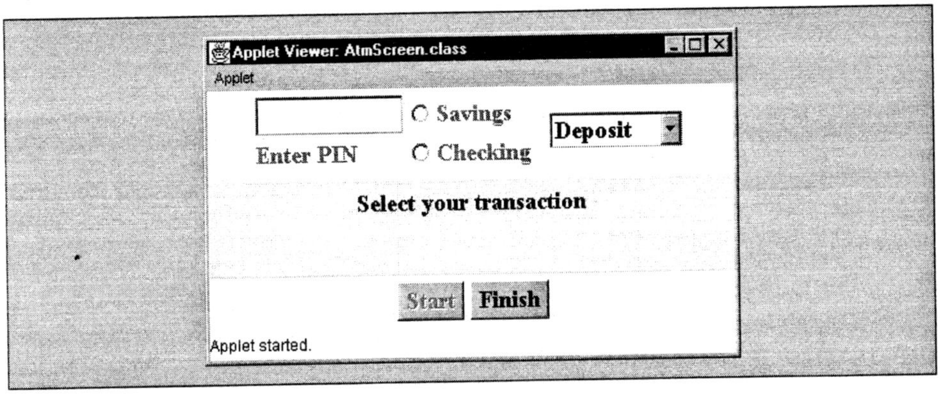

OBJECTIVES:

- Learn the basic sequence, selection, and repetition statements necessary for a general purpose programming language.
- Identify objects and their responsibilities to design solutions to problems.
- Introduce simple debugging techniques.
- Use the **double** type.
- Continue the study of applets and objects, drawing various shapes.

3.1 Relational Operators and Expressions

Arithmetic operators take numeric operands and give numeric results. For example, the value of `3+4` is an integer, `7`. By contrast an expression such as `3 < 4`, stating that `3` is less than `4`, gives the `boolean` value, `true`, and the expression `7 < 2` gives the `boolean` value, `false`. Type `boolean`, named for the British mathematician and logician, George Boole (1815-1864), provides two values, `true` and `false`, which we use to express the value of relational and logical expressions.

Java provides relational and equality operators, listed in Figure 3.2, which take two operands of a primitive type and produces a `boolean` result.

Figure 3.2 Java relational and equality operators.

Operator Symbol	Meaning	Example
<	less than	31 < 25 is false
<=	less than or equal to	464 <= 7213 is true
>	greater than	-98 > -12 is false
>=	greater than or equal to	9 >= 99 is false
==	equal to	9 == 12 + 12 is false
!=	not equal to	292 != 377 is true

TIP

The operators <=, >=, ==, and != are two-character operators which must be together, without any spaces between the two characters. The expression `3 <= 4` is fine, but `3 < = 4` will give an error. (The compiler thinks you want the '<' operator and cannot figure out why you did not give a correct right-hand operand.)

We can mix arithmetic operators and relational operators in the same expression, as in

```
643 < 350 + 450
```

which evaluates to true. We can omit parentheses because Java uses precedence rules, as we saw in Section 2.3. Arithmetic operators all have higher precedence than relational operators, so Java adds `350 + 450` giving `800`, and then determines that 643 is less than `800`. We could have written the expression using parentheses, as in

```
643 < (350 + 450)
```

but in this case we can omit the parentheses and let Java use the precedence rules to evaluate the expression.*

We can use variables in relational expressions, and can declare variables of type `boolean`. For example, if `x` is an integer variable, the expression

```
x < 3
```

is true if the value of `x` is less than three, and false otherwise. The expression

```
x == 3
```

evaluates to `true` if `x` equals three, and to `false` otherwise.

TIP

Be careful not to confuse the equality operator, ==, with the assignment operator, =. If `x` has the value `12`, then `x == 3` evaluates to false, but `x = 3` assigns the value `3` to `x`, changing it from `12`.

EXAMPLE 3.1 Relational.java

```
/*  Use relational expressions
 *  and boolean variables
 */

public class Relational {
  public static void main(String [] args) {
    int i = 3;
    boolean result;                                    // Note 1

    result = (32 > 87);                                // Note 2
```

* See Appendix C for the operator precedence table.

```
    System.out.println(" (32 > 87) is " + result);
    result = (-20  == -20);                              // Note 3
    System.out.println(" (-20 == -20) is " + result);
    result = -20 == -20;                                 // Note 4
    System.out.println(" -20 == -20 is " + result);
    result = -20 == -10 - 10;                            // Note 5
    System.out.println(" -20 == -10 - 10 is " + result);
    System.out.println(" 16 <= 54 is " + (16 <= 54));    // Note 6
    System.out.println(" i != 3 is " + (i != 3));        // Note 7
  }
}
```

Output

```
(32 > 87) is false
(-20 == -20) is true
-20 == -20 is true
-20 == -10 - 10 is true
16 <= 54 is true
i != 3 is false
```

Note 1: We can declare variables of type `boolean` which will have the values `true` or `false`.

Note 2: For clarity we use parentheses, but we could have omitted them, since the greater than operator, >, has higher precedence than the assignment operator, =. The value of the `boolean` variable `result` is `false`, a literal of the `boolean` type.

Note 3: We could omit the parentheses, since the equality operator, ==, has higher precedence than the assignment operator, =.

Note 4: We do not need parentheses, since == has higher precedence than =.

Note 5: `result = -20 == -10 - 10;`
This expression uses the equality operator, the subtraction operator and the negation operator. Again, we do not need parentheses.

Note 6: `System.out.println(" 16 <= 54 is " + (16 <= 54));`
We can use a relational expression in a `println` statement without assigning it to a variable. Java will evaluate the expression and display its value. Here we do need to enclose `16<=54` in parentheses. The '+' operator has higher precedence than '<=' so had we written

```
"16 <= 54 is " + 16 <= 54
```

Java would treat it as if we had written

```
("16 <= 54 is " + 16) <= 54
```

and we would get a compilation error because the left operand is a string while the right is an integer.

Note 7: `System.out.println(" i != 3 is " + (i != 3));`
Here we used a variable, `i`, in a relational expression, `i != 3`. Since `i` has the value `3`, the value of this expression is `false`.

THE BIG PICTURE

The relational operators `<=`, `>=`, `==`, and `!=` return `boolean` values. They are two-character operators and we must type them without any space between the two characters. They have lower precedence than the arithmetic operators, but higher precedence than assignment.

TEST YOUR UNDERSTANDING

1. Write a relational expression in Java for each of the following:

   a. 234 less than 52 b. 435 not equal to 87
   c. -12 equal to -12 d. 76 greater than or equal to 54

2. Evaluate the following relational expressions:

   a. `23 < 45` b. `49 >= 4 + 9`
   c. `95 != 100 - 5`

3. What is wrong with the expression `(3 < 4) < 5` in Java?
4. If `x` has the value `7`, and `y` is `12`, evaluate each of the following:

   a. `y == x + 5` b. `x >= y - 7`
   c. `2 * x < y` d. `y + 3 != x`

5. Explain the difference between `x = 5` and `x == 5`.
6. Explain why the expression `x > = 3` is not a correct Java expression to state that `x` is greater than or equal to `3`.

3.2 If and If-Else Statements*

We are now ready to make choices about which statements to execute.

Three Java statements permit us to make choices. We cover the `if` and `if-else` statements in this section. We cover the `switch` statement, which allows a choice among multiple alternatives, in the next chapter.

The If Statement

The `if` statement is essential because:

- it allows us to make choices

* We cover the basic form of the `if` and `if-else` statements in this section, leaving nested `if` statements and the `switch` statement until Chapter 4. In this way we can develop a basic set of control structures in this chapter, including both selection and repetition, and discuss problem-solving methods earlier.

- it allows us to solve more complex problems

The if statement has the pattern

```
if (condition)
  if_true_statement
```

as in the example:

```
if (x > 2)
  y = x + 17;
```

The condition is an expression, like `x > 2`, that evaluates to `true` or `false`. The `if_true_statement` is a Java statement such as `y = x + 17`. If the condition is true then execute the `if_true_statement`, but if the condition is `false` skip the `if_true_statement` and go on to the next line of the program. In this example, if `x` happened to have the value 5, we would assign `y` the value `22`, but if `x` had the value 1, we would skip the statement `y = x + 17`.

To illustrate the `if` statement we create a `Pay1` class to define objects whose state holds the hours worked and the hourly wage. It has an `overtime` method that indicates if there was overtime work, and a `pay` method that returns the pay for the hours, worked. This version has some limitations that we will remove in later versions.

We put the Pay1 class in the `pay` package. We use the command

```
javac Pay1.java
```

to compile it, and run the tests with the command

```
java pay.Pay1
```

issued from the directory containing the `pay` directory.

EXAMPLE 3.2 Pay1.java

```
/* Illustrates the if statement.
 */

package pay;
import javax.swing.*;

public class Pay1 {
  private int hours;
  private int wage = 11;                              // Note 1

  public Pay1(int h) {
    hours = h;
  }
  public boolean overtime() {                         // Note 2
    return hours > 40;
  }
  public int pay() {                                  // Note 3
    int amount = wage * hours;                        // Note 4
```

```
    if (hours > 40)
      amount += wage*(hours - 40);                         // Note 5
    return amount;
  }
  public static void main(String[] args) {
    String s = JOptionPane.showInputDialog("Hours worked?");
    Pay1 p = new Pay1(Integer.parseInt(s));
    JOptionPane.showMessageDialog(null, "Overtime -- " + p.overtime()
                          + ", Pay is " + p.pay() + " dollars.");
    System.exit(0);
  }
}
```

First Run

Input

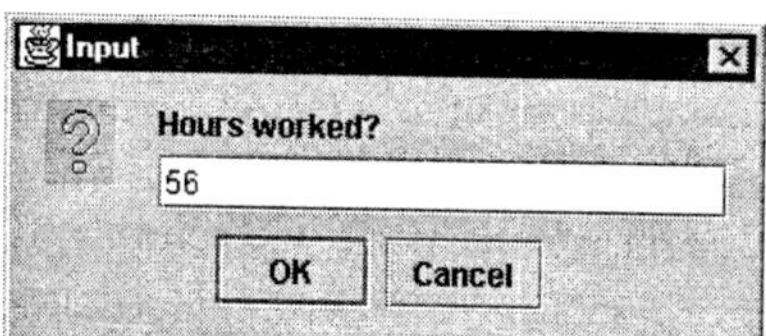

Output

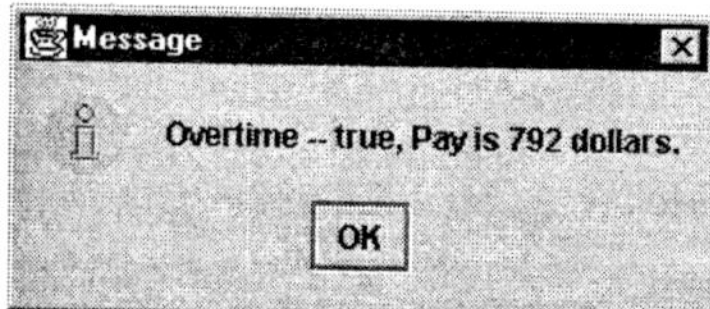

Second Run

Input

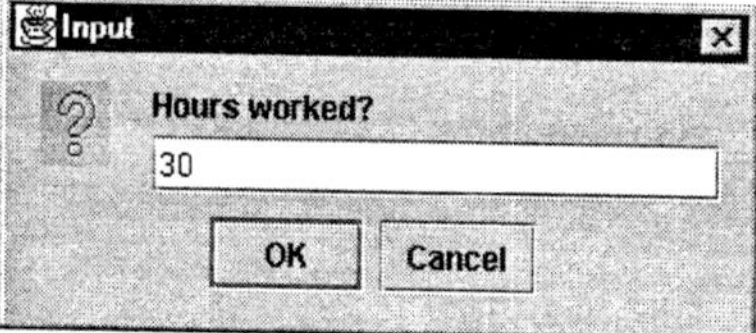

Output

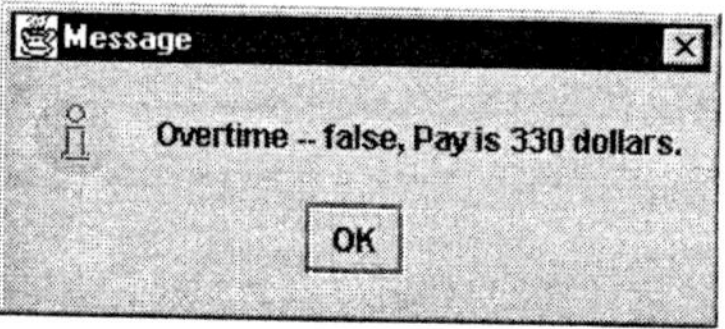

Note 1: We use a fixed wage of $11 per hour. We leave it to the exercises to modify the class to use different wages. After we introduce the type `double` we will allow wages in dollars and cents such as $11.50.

Note 2: The `overtime` method returns `true` if there was overtime work, and `false` otherwise.

Note 3: The `pay` method returns the amount of the pay in dollars. The wage is double the hourly rate for overtime.

Note 4: We initialize the amount with the normal hourly wage for each hour worked, and will add in any overtime pay earned.

Note 5: We add the normal wage for each overtime hours to the amount already computed. This result is double pay for overtime. We prefer the usual time and a half, but integer arithmetic may lead to errors. For example the expression `wage/2` will be `5` instead of `5.5` if `wage` is `11`. After we introduce the type `double` we will compute overtime pay at one and one half times the normal amount, rather than at twice.

Style

We could write a short `if` statement on one line, as in

```
if (x > 2)  y = x +17;
```

If we write the `if` statement on more than one line, then we should indent all lines after the first to show that these lines are part of the `if` statement, and to make it easier to read.

Do

```
if (myItem > 10)
    System.out.println("Greater than ten");
```

Don't

```
if (myItem > 10)
System.out.println("Greater than ten");
```

Control Flow

Control flow refers to the order in which Java (the controller) executes the statements in a program. For example, Java executes the three statements

```
int item1 = 25;
int item2 = 12;
item2 = item1+15;
```

one after the other. These three statements are in a sequence. We call this type of control flow, executing one statement after another in sequence, the **sequence** control structure. We can visualize the sequence structure in Figure 3.3 in which we write each statement inside a box, and use directed lines to show the flow of control from one statement to the next.

The `if` statement allows us to make a choice about the control flow. In Example 3.2, if the hours worked is greater than forty, we print a message about overtime, otherwise we skip this message. We use a diamond shape to represent a decision based on the truth or falsity of a condition. One arrow, called the true branch, shows what comes next if the condition is true. Another arrow, called the false branch, shows what comes next if the condition is `false`. Figure 3.4 shows the control flow for an `if` statement. When the condition is true, Java will execute an additional statement.

Figure 3.3 The `sequence` control flow

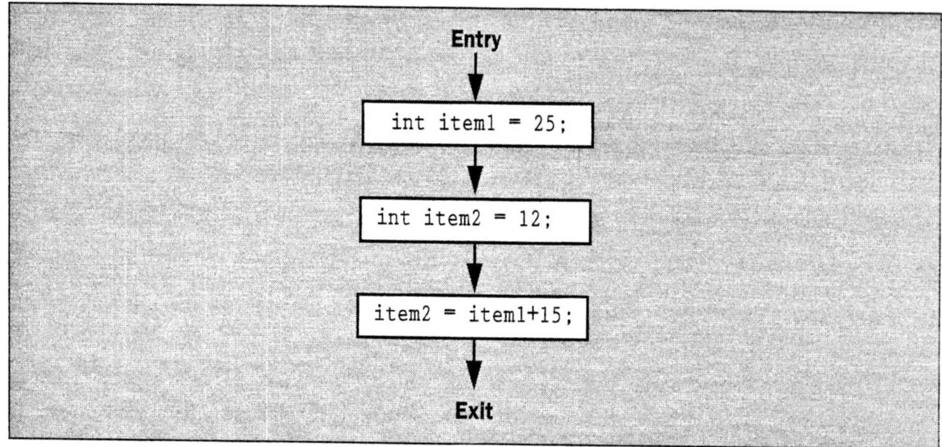

Figure 3.4 Control flow for the `if` statement

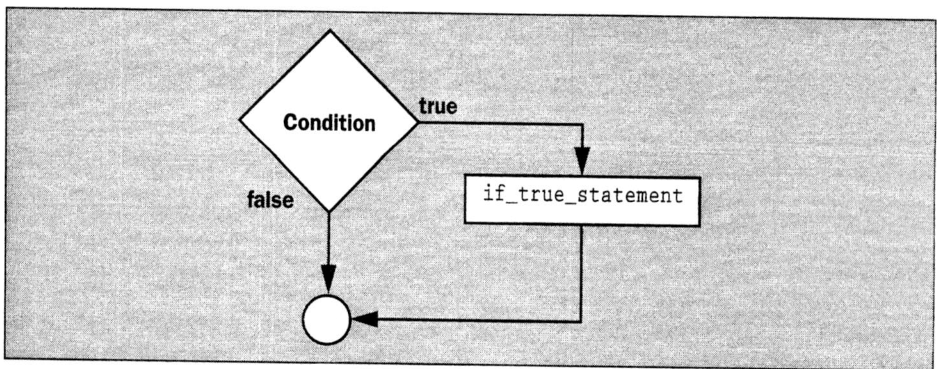

Figure 3.5 shows the control flow for the program of Example 3.2.

The If-Else Statement

The `if` statement allows us to choose to execute a statement or not to execute it depending on the value of a test expression. With the `if-else` statement we can choose between two alternatives, executing one when the test condition is true and the other when the test condition is false.

The `if-else` statement has the form

```
if (condition)
    if_true_statement
else
    if_false_statement
```

For example,

```
if (x <= 20)
    x += 5;
```

Figure 3.5 Control Flow for Example 3.2

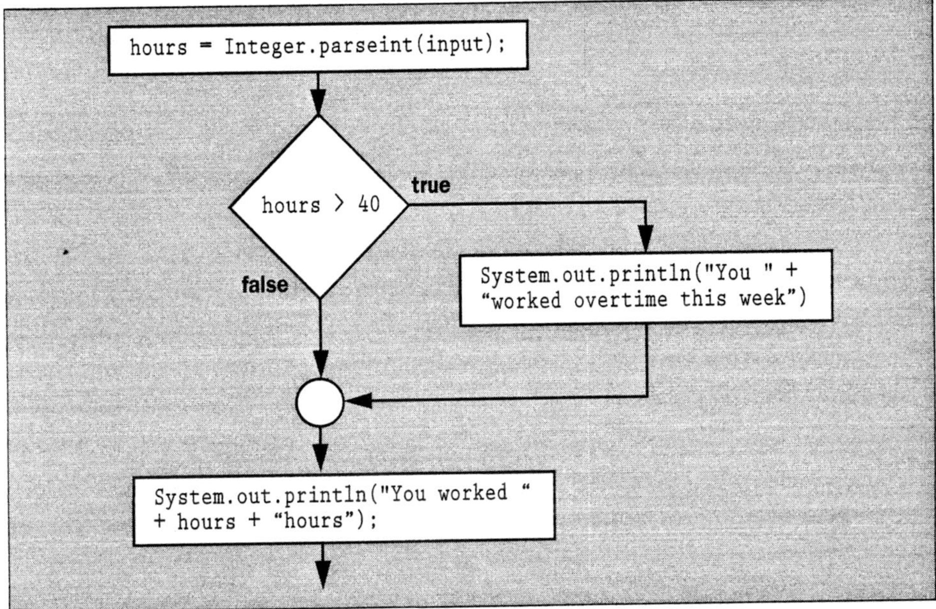


```
else
   x += 2;
```

If x is less than or equal to 20, then we add 5 to it, otherwise we add 2 to it. The if-else statement gives us a choice between two alternatives. We choose if_true_statement if the condition is true and if_false_statement if the condition is false.

Figure 3.6 shows the flow chart for the if-else statement.

Figure 3.6 Flow chart for the if-else statement

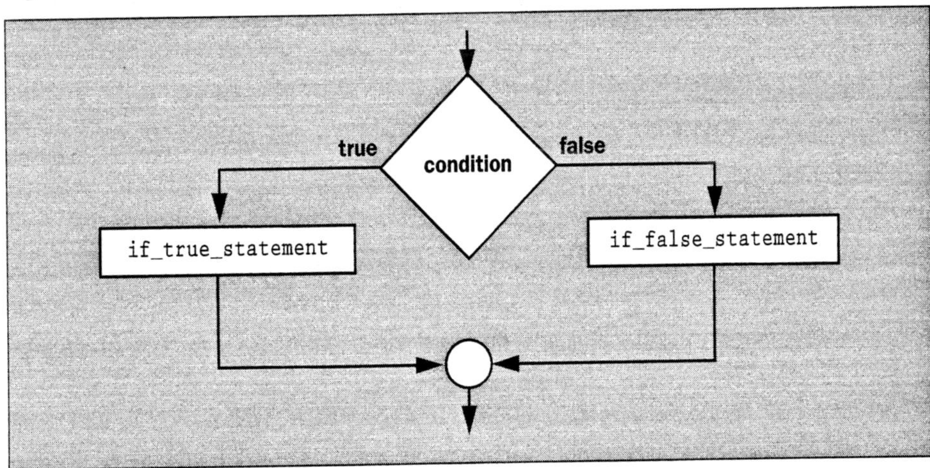

Blocks

We can group a sequence of statements inside braces to form a **block** as in

```
{
   x = 5;
   y = -8;
   z = x * y;
}
```

We can use a block as a statement in an `if` or an `if-else` statement, as in:

```
if (y > 5) {
  x = 5;
  y = -8;
  z = x * y;
}
```

By using a block we can perform more than one action if the test condition is `true`. In this example, if `y` is greater than `5`, we want to set `x`, `y`, and `z` to new values.

TIP

Do not forget to enclose the statements in braces that you want to execute if a condition is `true`. Just indenting them, as in

```
if (y > 5)
  x = 5;
  y = -8;
  z = x * y;
```

will not group the three statements together. We indent to make the program easier to read, but indenting does not affect the meaning of the program. Without the braces, Java will interpret the code as

```
if (y > 5)
  x = 5;
y = -8;
z = x * y;
```

If `y` is greater than five, then Java will set `x` to five. Whether or not `y` is greater than `5`, Java will always set `y` to `-8`, and `z` to `x*y`. This is quite a different result than we would get if we grouped the three statements in a block, and changed the values of `x`, `y`, and `z` only if the condition is true.

Style

Use a consistent style for blocks, so that it is easy to match the opening brace, `{`, with the closing brace, `}`. One choice is to put the left brace on the same line as the `if` or `else`, and to align the right brace with the `if` or `else`, as in

```
if (x < 10)  {
  y = 5;
  z = 8;
}
else  {
  y = 9;
  z = -2;
}
```

Using this style, we can match the keyword `if` or `else` with the closing brace, `}`, to keep our code neatly organized. Another choice is to align the left brace with the `if` or `else`, as in

```
if (x < 10)
{
  y = 5;
  z = 8;
}
else
{
  y = 9;
  z = -2;
}
```

Either of these styles allows us to add or delete lines within a block without having to change the braces. The latter style makes it easier to match opening with closing braces, but uses an extra line to separate the opening brace from the code. We could make the code more compact by putting the braces on the same line as the code, but the code would be harder to read and modify.

A LITTLE EXTRA—FLOW CHARTS FOR IF STATEMENTS WITH BLOCKS

Figure 3.4 shows the flow chart for the `if` statement. If the condition in the diamond is `true`, then the control flows to the statement in the box on the right. Remember that this statement can be a block, such as

```
{
  x = 2;
  y = 7;
}
```

which has the flow chart

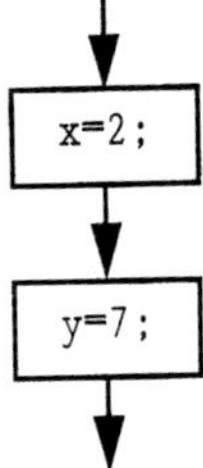

When the statement in the box is a block, we replace the box by the flow chart for that block. We find the flow chart for the `if` statement

```
if (z <= 10) {
   x = 2;
   y = 7;
}
```

in two steps. First, Figure 3.7 applies the pattern of Figure 3.4 to this example.

Figure 3.7 Flow chart for `if` statement with block, step 1

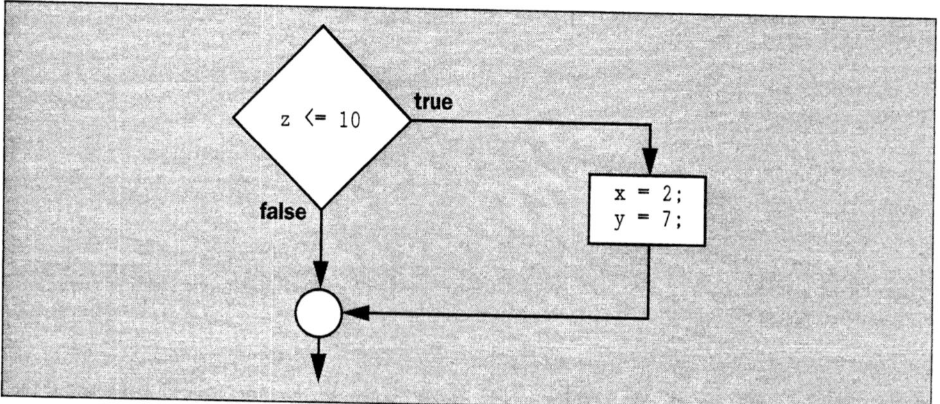

Second, in Figure 3.8 we replace the block statement by its flow chart.

Figure 3.8 Flow chart for `if` statement with block, step 2

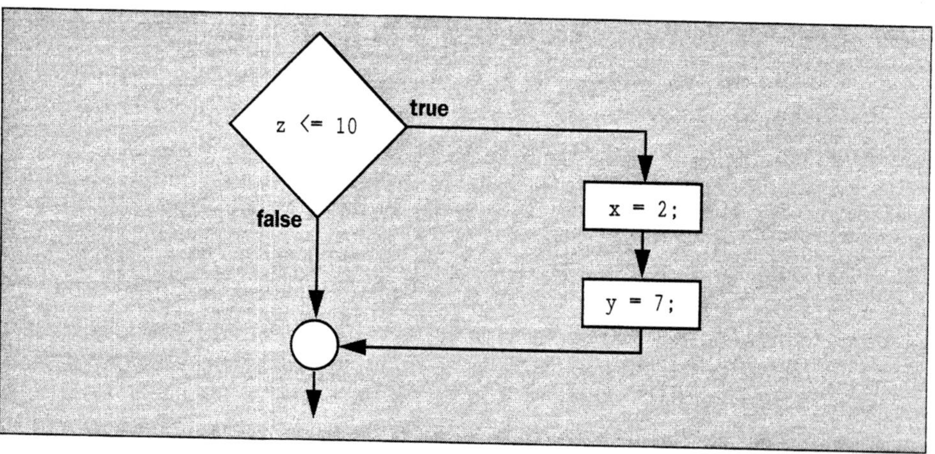

The `Vending3` class of Example 3.3 revises the `Vending2` class of Example 2.10 to use `if-else` statements where appropriate. The `makeChange` method can now determine the coins with which to make change.

EXAMPLE 3.3 Vending3.java

```
/* Uses if and if-else statements to determine
 * the coins needed to make change.
 */

package vend;
import javax.swing.*;

public class Vending3 {
  public static final int PRICE = 65;
  private int quarters;
  private int dimes;
  private int nickels;
  private int candyBars;
  private int deposited = 0;                                          // Note 1

  public Vending3(int q, int d, int n, int cStart) {
    quarters = q;
    dimes = d;
    nickels = n;
    candyBars = cStart;
  }
  public int enterMoney(int q, int d, int n) {
    quarters += q;
    dimes += d;
    nickels += n;
    deposited = 25*q + 10*d + 5*n;
    return deposited;
  }
  public String selectCandy() {
    if (deposited >= PRICE) {                                         // Note 2
      candyBars--;
      return "Dispensing Candy, " + makeChange(deposited - PRICE);
    }
    else
      return "Deposit " + (PRICE - deposited) + " cents.";
  }
  public String makeChange(int amount) {                              // Note 3
    String change = "Change: ";
    if (amount >= 25) {
       int q = amount/25;                                             // Note 4
       quarters -= q;                    // Fix needed                // Note 5
       change += q + " quarter";                                      // Note 6
       if (q==1)
         change += " ";
       else
         change += "s ";
       amount %= 25;                                                  // Note 7
    }
```

```
    if (amount >= 10) {                                       // Note 8
      int d = amount/10;
      dimes -= d;
      change += d + " dime";
      if (d==1)
        change += " ";
      else
        change += "s ";
      amount %= 10;
    }
    if (amount >= 5) {
      int n = amount/5;
      nickels -= n;
      change += n + " nickel";
      if (n==1)
        change += " ";
      else
        change += "s ";
      amount %= 5;
    }
    return change;
  }
  public String test(int q, int d, int n) {
    return "Entered " + this.enterMoney(q,d,n) + " cents, "
                                      + this.selectCandy();
  }
  public static void main(String[] args) {
    String s = JOptionPane.showInputDialog
                              ("How many quarters deposited?");
    int q = Integer.parseInt(s);
    s = JOptionPane.showInputDialog
                                ("How many dimes deposited?");
    int d = Integer.parseInt(s);
    s = JOptionPane.showInputDialog
                              ("How many nickels deposited");
    int n = Integer.parseInt(s);
    Vending3 v = new Vending3(20,20,20,10);
    JOptionPane.showMessageDialog(null,v.test(q,d,n));
    System.exit(0);
  }
}
```

Input—First Run

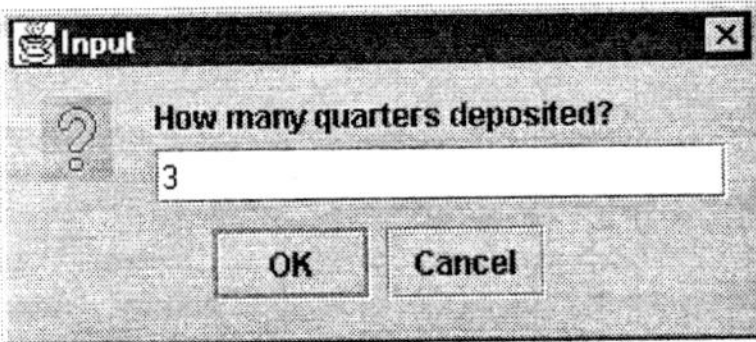

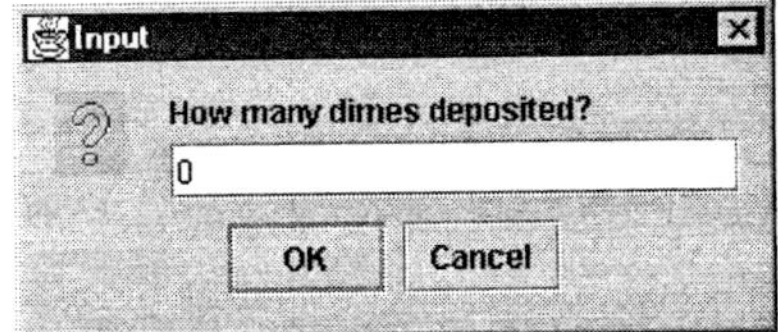

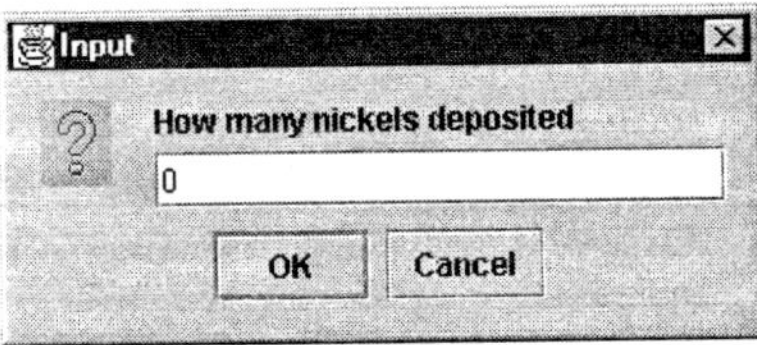

Output—First Run

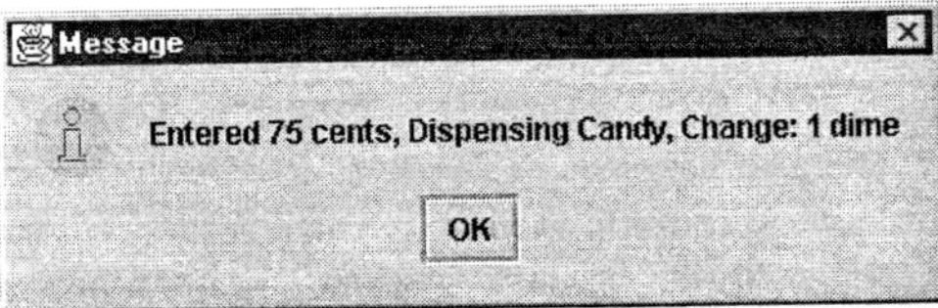

Input—Second Run

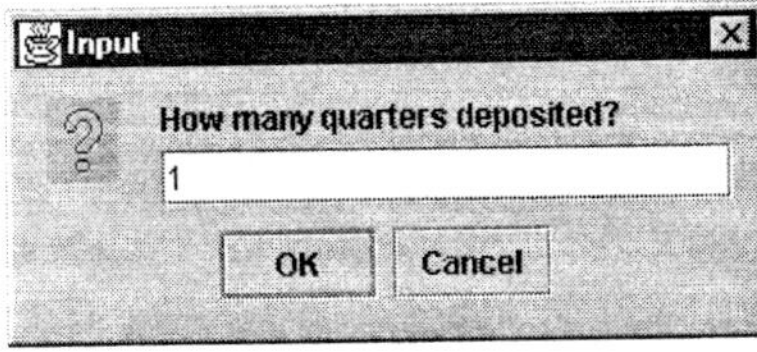

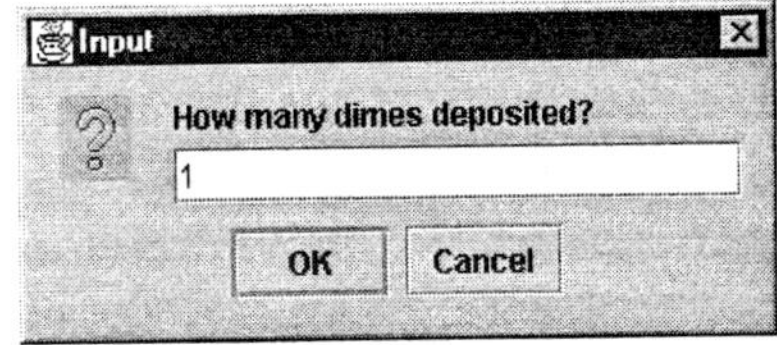

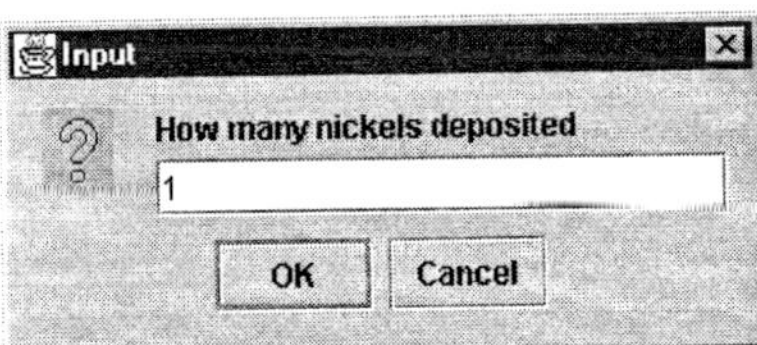

Output—Second Run

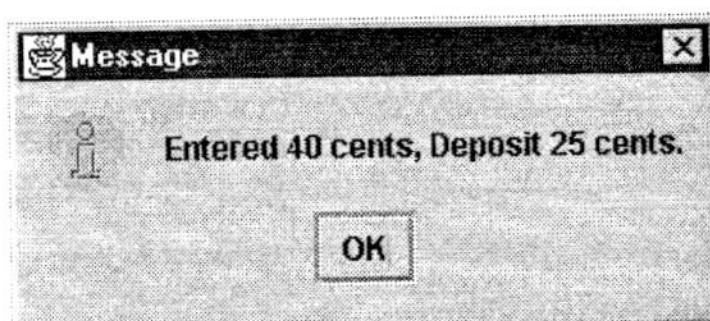

Note 1: We add another state variable to hold the amount of money deposited. We use it to make change.

Note 2: If the amount of money deposited is enough to pay for the candy we dispense the candy and make change. Otherwise we request the needed amount of money.

Note 3: The `makeChange` method receives the amount of change necessary and returns a string describing the coins used.

Note 4: We try making change with the largest coin first. q is the number of quarters needed.

Note 5: We remove the number of quarters used for change from the amount available. We need to check that enough quarters are available. This is an essential part of making change, but in the interests of simplicity we leave it for the exercises.

Note 6: `change += q + " quarter"`
We want the output to be `1 quarter`, but `2 quarters`. We start with the minimum, `quarter`, and add an `s` only if the number of quarters is not `1`.

Note 7: `amount %= 25;`
The remainder `amount%25` computes the amount remaining after making change with quarters. We need to make change from this amount using dimes and nickels.

Note 8: `if (amount >= 10) {`
We repeat the process we used for quarters for dimes, and then for nickels. The code is quite repetitious. We leave it to the exercises to make it into a method that we can call three times.

THE BIG PICTURE

The `if` statement allows us to make a choice to execute a statement or not. The `if-else` statement lets us choose between two alternatives. Each alternative may be a simple statement or a block, which uses braces to enclose Java code. Flow charts show the flow of control in diagram form.

TEST YOUR UNDERSTANDING

7. Correct the error in each of the following:

a. `if {x == 12} y += 7;`

b. `if (x=12) y += 7;`

c. `if (x == 12) then y += 7;`

8. Correct the error in each of the following:

a.
```
if (y > 5)
   z = 7;
   x = 5;
else
   w = 4;
```

b.
```
if  y > 5
   z = 3;
else
   x = y + 2;
```

c.
```
if (y > 5)
   z = 3;
else  (
   s = y + 7;
   z = s - 2;
);
```

9. How would you improve the style in each of the following?

a.
```
if (y <= 6)
z += 5;
```

b.
```
if (x != 0)
y+=5;
else
z = y + 9;
```

10. Draw the flow chart for each of the following `if` statements:

a.
```
if (x == 17)
   y += 6;
```

b.
```
if (s > 12)
   z = 52;
```

11. Draw the flow chart for each of the following `if-else` statements.

a.
```
if (z <= 10)
   y -= 11;
else
   y += 10;
```

b.
```
if (x == 0)
   z = 3*x;
else
   y = 4 + x;
```

A LITTLE EXTRA 12. Draw the flow chart for each of the following `if` statements with blocks.

a.
```
if (s > 4) {
   y = s - 30;
   z = 2;
}
```

b.
```
if (r != 0) {
   x = 4*r + 3;
   w = 3;
   y = x + w;
}
```

3.3 The Type Double*

In this section we introduce the type double for decimal values. In the next chapter, we will cover other numeric types.

Scientific Notation

In many applications, we need to use decimal numbers such as `2.54`, the number of centimeters in an inch. Small decimal numbers like `.00000003937`, the number of inches in a nanometer, are harder to read, but we can use a floating-point notation, `3.937E-8`. The number following the `E`, `-8` in this example, tells us that we need to move the decimal point eight places to the left to get the value `.00000003937`. We can write `5,880,000,000,000`, the number of miles in a light-year, more conveniently as

* We deferred type double to this chapter to allow Chapter 2 to introduce programming without presenting any more concepts than needed to get started writing programs.

5.88E12; the positive exponent, 12, in 5.88E12 informs us that we need to shift the decimal point twelve places to the right to get the number 5880000000000.0.

The number following the E, called the exponent, tells us how many places to shift the decimal point. To write very large or very small numbers in a way that is easier to read, we float the point to a more convenient location, to the right of the first non-zero digit, and adjust the exponent to keep the value of the number unchanged.

We often call this notation using exponents, as in 3.937E-8, scientific notation, because of its usefulness in expressing the varied sizes of numbers used in scientific calculations. Options in scientific notation are to use a lower-case e, as in 5.88e12, and to use a plus sign with a positive exponent, as in 5.88E+12. Of course, we can use both options, as in 5.88e+12.

We can express the same number in many ways using scientific notation. For example, each of the following expresses the value .00000003937

```
3.937E-8      393.7E-10     .03937E-6     .00000000003937E+3
```

The usual choice is to float the decimal point just to the right of the first non-zero digit, as in 3.937E-8.

For display purposes, we write numbers that are not too small or too large without exponents, as in 2.54 or 2755.323 or .01345. Very small or very large numbers are easier to read in scientific notation, as in 5.88E+12.

TEST YOUR UNDERSTANDING

13. Express the following without using exponents:

    a.345.22E-2 b. -2.98765e4
    c..000098765E+8 d. 435e-2

14. Express the following in scientific notation with the decimal point to the right of the first non-zero digit:

    a. 893.454 b. .000345722
    c. 98761234. d. .090909

15. Which of the following express the same value?

    a. .6789E+2 b. 6.789e-2
    c. 67.89 d. 678.9e-2
    e. 0.006789

Double Values

Now that we have seen how to write decimal numbers using scientific notation we can introduce the type double that Java provides for decimal numbers. Numbers of type double provide 16 decimal digits accurately. If you are using scientific notation, the exponents for double values can range from -324 to 308. A literal of type double may have a decimal point or an exponent or both, and it must have at least one digit. Some valid values of type double are:

```
22.7
4.123E-2
36e2
3.
0.54296
.1234
```

When you write a decimal literal such as `2.54`, Java treats it as a value of type `double`. We can declare variables of type `double`, as, for example

```
double length;
double height;
```

and we can initialize variables in the declaration, as, for example

```
double length = 173.24E5;
double height =  1.83;
```

We can use the arithmetic operators, +, -, *, and /, with `double` operands. For example,

Expression	Value
`6.2 + 5.93`	`12.13`
`72.34 - 2.97`	`69.37`
`32.3 * 654.18`	`21130.014`
`3.0 / 2.0`	`1.5`

TIP

When dividing numbers of type `double`, be sure to include the decimal points. If you write `3/2` then you will get integer division, which will truncate the value to `1`. Writing `3.0/2.0` gives the decimal value `1.5`.

Output

If we output values of type `double` using the `println` method, then Java will write the numbers in the most convenient form, using scientific notation for numbers greater than `10,000,000` or less than `-10,000,000`, and for numbers between `-.001` and `.001`.

EXAMPLE 3.4 DoubleOut.java

```
/* Creates double values to see
 * how Java displays them.
 */

public class DoubleOut {
    public static void main(String [] args) {
        double five3rds = 5.0/3.0;                              // Note 1
        System.out.println("double 5.0/3.0 = " + five3rds);     // Note 2
        double threeHalves = 3.0/2.0;
```

```
        System.out.println("double 3.0/2.0 = " + threeHalves);        // Note 3
        System.out.println
                ("big               " + 1234567898765.4);              // Note 4
        System.out.println("notSoBig    " + 12345.678987654);
        System.out.println("notSoSmall " + .0123456789);
        System.out.println
               ("small            " + .0000123456789);                 // Note 5
    }
}
```

Output

```
double 5.0/3.0   = 1.6666666666666667
double 3.0/2.0   = 1.5
big              1.2345678987654E12
notSoBig         12345.678987654
notSoSmall       0.0123456789
small            1.23456789E-5
```

Note 1: Java treats decimal literals, such as `5.0`, as type `double`.

Note 2: A `double` value is accurate to 16 decimal digits. The display includes a 17th digit that may be the result of rounding or truncation. Java converts the internal binary number to the closest decimal equivalent. If we divided 5.0/3.0 by hand we would keep getting sixes. The last digit is not significant.

Note 3: Java does not print zeroes at the end of a number. Every `double` value has 16 digits, but Java does not display the trailing zeroes.

Note 4: Java uses scientific notation for this value since it is greater than `10,000,000`.

Note 5: Java uses scientific notation for this value since it is between `-.001` and `.001`.

Input and Formatted Output

To input values of type `double` from the keyboard, we use the `JOptionPane.showInputDialog` method that we used for integer input. In Java 2, we can use the `Double.parseDouble` method to covert the input `String` to a `double` value.*

In Example 3.4, we have seen how Java displays decimal numbers. We would like to be able to specify the number of decimal digits in the displayed number. We can use the `NumberFormat` class from the `java.text` package to format decimal numbers.

The `getNumberInstance` method returns a `NumberFormat` object that we can use.

```
NumberFormat nf = NumberFormat.getNumberInstance();
```

---

* If our program needs to run on an earlier Java version, we convert a `String s` to a `double` using `new Double(s).doubleValue()` which is a little more cumbersome.

The `setMaximumFractionDigits` method will limit the output to at most that many digits. It will use less if the number requires less. The code

```
nf.setMaximumFractionDigits(1);
```

specifies one place after the decimal point. Once we configure the `NumberFormat` object in this way, the format method will output numbers with at most one decimal place. For example, if d = 345.678

```
nf.format(d)
```

will convert it to 345.7. The `format` method rounds numbers correctly when necessary.

The `NumberFormat` object will output numbers according the locale setting of the user's machine. In France, for example, the number we write in the United States as 3,456.78 is written 3 456,78. We do not use this feature in this text.

A `NumberFormat` object also helps when outputting currency values. For that purpose we use

```
NumberFormat cf = NumberFormat.getCurrencyInstance();
```

For example, if d= 345.678

```
cf.format(d);
```

will convert it to $345.68. It will also localize the conversion to reflect the currency of the user's locale. In France, the result would be 345,68 Frs.

The `Pay2` class of Example 3.5 modifies `Pay1` to use `double` values for the wages and hours.

EXAMPLE 3.5 Pay2.java

```
/* Uses type double for hours and wage.
 * Computes overtime at one and a half regular pay.
 */

package pay;
import javax.swing.*;
import java.text.*;

public class Pay2 {
  private double hours;
  private double wage = 11.50;

  public Pay2(double h) {
    hours = h;
  }
```

```
  public boolean overtime() {
    return hours > 40;
  }
  public double pay() {
    double regular = wage*hours;
    if (hours < 40)
       return regular;
    else
       return regular + (hours-40)*wage/2;                          // Note 1
  }
  public static void main(String[] args) {
    NumberFormat nf = NumberFormat.getCurrencyInstance();
    String s = JOptionPane.showInputDialog("Hours worked?");
    Pay2 p = new Pay2(Double.parseDouble(s));
    JOptionPane.showMessageDialog
              (null, "Overtime -- " + p.overtime()
                  + ", Pay is " + nf.format(p.pay()));              // Note 2
    System.exit(0);
  }
}
```

Input

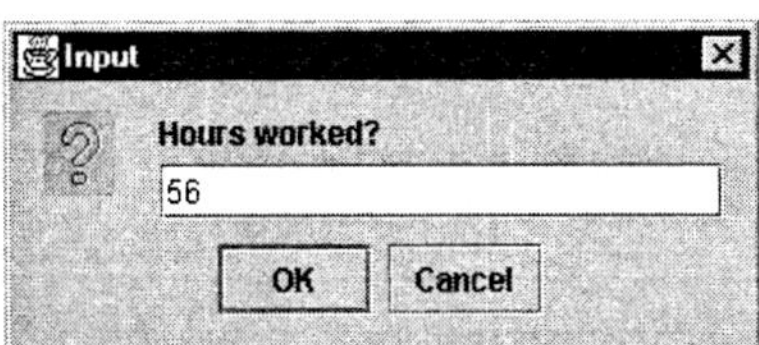

Output

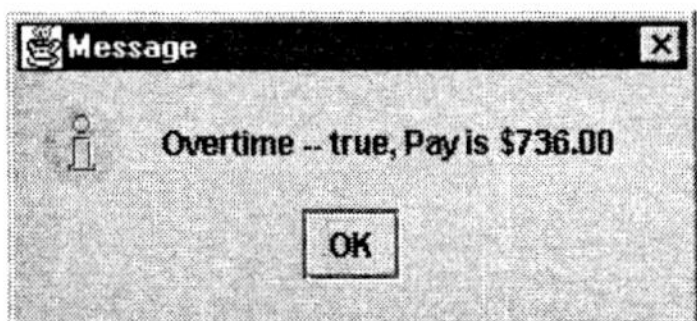

Note 1: We add half the wage for the overtime hours to the regular wage for all hours. For simplicity we use 2 instead of 2.0 and 40 instead of 40.0 in the `double` expressions. We take up mixed-type expressions next.

Note 2: The `NumberFormat` instance will format the amount in the currency of the locale set in the user's machine. In the US, that will be dollars and cents by default.

Mixed-Type Expressions

Usually a numeric expression uses all variables and literals of type `int`, or all of type `double`. For example, `2.54 + 3.61` is a `double` addition and `254 + 361` is an `int` addition. The addition operator `'+'` looks the same in both cases, but `int` addition is quite different from `double` addition, because, in the computer memory, `int` and `double` values are stored differently. For convenience, we use the same `'+'` symbol to represent these two different kinds of addition.

When we mix types in an expression, as in `2.54 + 361`, which type of addition does Java use, `int` or `double`? As they say, it is like adding apples and oranges. We cannot just add a `double` to an `int` because they are different types. We cannot convert real apples to real oranges, or oranges to apples, but in the numeric case, we have better luck. We cannot convert a `double` such as `2.54` to an `int` without losing information. Rounding it to `3` probably is not a good choice. But we can convert an `int` to a `double` without losing information, for example, by changing `361` to `361.0`.

Although we do not lose any information by converting `361` to `361.0`, it does require a change inside memory since `361` has an internal representation which is a lot different than that for `361.0`. Since we can always convert an `int` to a `double` without losing information, Java will do it for us automatically. If we write `2.54 + 361`, Java will convert `361` to `361.0`, and use type `double` addition to get the result `363.54`. Figure 3.9 illustrates this conversion process.

Figure 3.9 Conversion of a mixed-mode expression

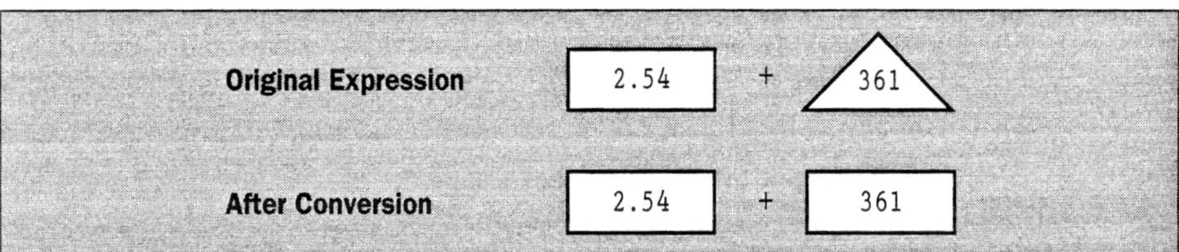

We used this automatic conversion in Example 3.5, where we used the expression

```
(hours-40)*wage/2
```

in which we wrote all the literals as integer values, `40` and `2`.

TIP

Java only converts from `int` to `double` in a mixed-mode expression, where one operand has type `int` and the other has type `double`. The expression

```
9/5*C + 32
```

looks fine, but it will not give the result we expect. The division `9/5` has both operands, `9` and `5`, integers, so Java uses integer division obtaining the integer quotient of `1`, not the value `1.8` that we want. Writing the expression as

```
9*C/5 + 32
```

where `C` has type `double`, works because `9*C` is a mixed-mode expression in which one operand, `9`, has type `int` and the other, `C`, has type `double`. The result, `9*C`, is a `double` value so `(9*C)/5` is a mixed-mode expression and Java will convert the `5` from `int` to `double`. Finally, `(9*C)/5` has type `double`, so Java will convert `32` from an `int` to a `double`, before doing the addition.

Java will also convert from `int` to `double` in an assignment statement. For example, in

```
double d = 4;
```

Java will assign the `double` value `4.0` to the variable `d`. However, Java will not automatically convert a `double` to an `int` in order to assign it to an integer variable, since a `double` value may be out of the range of values that an `int` variable can hold.

The general rule that Java follows for these implicit conversions of one primitive type to another is that any numeric value can be assigned to any numeric variable whose type supports a larger range of values.

A LITTLE EXTRA—TYPE CASTS

As we saw, Java will do an implicit conversion from `int` to `double` in a mixed-type expression. We could explicitly cast the type from `int` to `double` by putting the desired type, `double`, in parentheses to the left of the `int` literal or variable that we wish to convert. For example, in the expression

```
2.54 + (double)361
```

Java converts the value `361` to type `double` before adding it to `2.54`.

By using an explicit cast, we show that we really want Java to convert from one type to another. If we always use explicit type casts, then when checking our code, we would recognize an implicit mixed-type expression, such as `2.54 + 361`, as an error, say of omission of a decimal point in `361`. We might have meant to write `2.54 + 3.61`, and instead got a mixed-type expression. Since Java does not treat such a mixed-type expression as an error, we would have to inspect our results carefully to see that they are not correct.

TIP

Just because your program compiles and runs does not mean that the results are correct. Always check that your results are reasonable. Make a prediction before you run your program. If you expect the result to be positive, do not accept a negative value without further investigation. If you expect the result to be about `10`, do not accept a value of `17234` without more checking.

THE BIG PICTURE

Floating-point notation allows us to write large and small numbers conveniently. The type `double` provides 16-place accuracy. By default, Java will output very small and very large numbers in scientific notation. We use `NumberFormat` objects to specify the number of decimal places to display, or to display currency. Java lets us use some forms of mixed-type expressions.

TEST YOUR UNDERSTANDING

16. What will be the result of each division?

    a. `5.0 / 2.0`
    b. `5 / 2`
    c. `12 / 5`
    d. `12.0 / 5.0`

17. Suppose that the `double` variable, `x`, has the indicated value. Will `System.out.println(x)` display `x` in scientific notation? Show the result.

    a. `3456.789`
    b. `0000023456`
    c. `09876543`
    d. `1234567890.987`
    e. `-234567.765432`

18. Which of the following expressions will Java compute correctly if C and F have type `double`?

    a. `F = 9.0/5.0*C + 32.0`
    b. `F = 9*C/5 + 32`
    c. `F = 9/5*C + 32`

A LITTLE EXTRA

19. Rewrite each of the following to use explicit type casts:

    a. `72 + 37.5`
    b. `23.28 / 7`
    c. `double d = 874;`

3.4 Program Design with the While Loop*

The `if` and `if-else` statements give us the ability to make choices. In this section we will see how the `while` statement enables us to repeat steps.

Repetition

The `while` statement follows the pattern

```
while (condition)
  while_true_statement
```

with the flow chart shown in Figure 3.10.

* We cover the `while` loop here, deferring the `for` and `do-while` loops until Chapter 4. In this way we can develop a basic set of control structures in this chapter and discuss problem-solving methods earlier.

Figure 3.10 Flow chart for the `while` loop

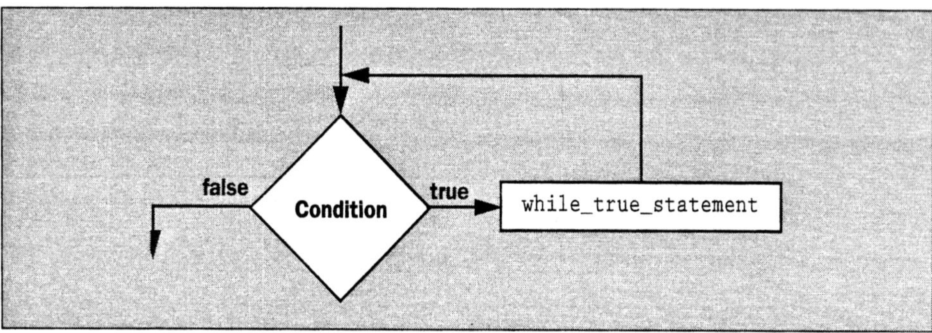

where the condition evaluates to `true` or `false`, and the `while_true_statement` can be any Java statement including a code block. If the condition is `true`, Java executes the `while_true_statement` and goes back to check the condition again. If the condition is still `true`, Java executes the `while_true_statement` and goes back to check the condition again, and so on. This process repeats until the condition is `false`.

For example, suppose that the variable `x` has the value `7` just before Java starts to execute the `while` statement

```
while (x < 10)
  x += 2;
```

Since `7 < 10` is true, Java executes the statement `x+= 2` which changes the value of `x` to `9`. Remember, this is a `while` statement, so Java again checks the condition, `x < 10`. Since `9 < 10` is still true Java again executes, `x += 2`, giving `x` the value `11`. Now checking the condition `x < 10`, Java finds that `11<10` is false so the execution of the `while` statement is finished.

The `while` statement is a type of `loop`, so called because execution keeps looping back to check the condition after every execution of the `true_statement`, which we call the **body** of the loop. The body of the loop could be a block, in which case Java executes every statement in the block while the condition is true. For example, if `x` had the value `5` before the loop, the `while` statement

```
while (x < 10) {
     System.out.println("x is now " + x);
     x += 2;
}
```

would output

```
x is now 5
x is now 7
x is now 9
```

The condition in a `while` statement may evaluate to `false` on the first entry to the loop, in which case Java never executes the body of the loop. For example, if `x` has the value 3 before executing the loop

```
while (x >= 5)
     x -= 4;
```

then the condition, `3 >= 5`, is `false`, and the loop body, `x -= 4`, is never executed.

Planning Programs using Pseudocode

With the `while` statement, we can solve more interesting problems. However, as problems get more complex, we need to carefully plan our solutions. Section 3.5 discusses problem-solving techniques in more detail.

In this section, we develop a program, Example 3.6, which uses a `while` loop to find and display the sum of test scores inputted by the user. Before coding, we need to plan our approach. The user will keep entering test scores which are nonnegative. To signal to the program that no more score are available the user can enter a negative number, which cannot be a valid score. We call this value a **sentinel**. The program checks each value that the user inputs. If it is the sentinel, it exits the while loop and outputs the total of all the scores. If it is not the sentinel, it adds the score to the total. We can use a `while` loop to code these repetitive steps. Informally, we could write the loop as

```
Read the next score;
while ( the score is not the sentinel) {
  Add the score to the total so far;
  Read the next score;
}
Output the total of all the scores.
```

We call this informal way of writing the program **pseudocode**. Pseudocode helps us to design the Java program. It is easier to understand than the very specific programming language statements, so we can correct logical errors before they get into the actual program.

We can use a flow chart in the same way as pseudocode to show the structure of a program as we develop the detailed solution. For small programs both techniques work well, but for larger programs it becomes cumbersome to manage the flow charts so that pseudocode is a better choice.

Continuing the problem solution, we create a `ScoreSum` class with responsibilities needed to solve this problem. In a later chapter we will introduce techniques and diagrams for object-oriented design. Here we begin with the simplest approach, identifying the behavior our object needs to supply. From the pseudocode, we identify the responsibilities of a `ScoreSum` instance as

```
Input a score from the user.
Add the score to the total.
```

```
Output the total.
```

The `ScoreSum` state will consist of the total of the scores that have been entered.

Pseudocode makes sense. We can execute it mentally with some test data as a further check. Suppose the scores are `56`, `84`, and `75`, and that the user follows them with the sentinel, `-1`. Let us number each line and trace, line by line, how the pseudocode would execute.

Pseudocode:

```
1   Read the next score;
2   while ( the score is not the sentinel) {
3       Add the score to the total so far;
4       Read the next score;
5   }
6   Output the total of all the scores.
```

Trace of the pseudocode:

Line	**NumberAction**
1	Read the next score: 56
2	56 is not the sentinel.
3	Add score to total : total is 56
4	Read the next score: 84
2	84 is not the sentinel.
3	Add score to total : total is 140
4	Read the next score: 75
2	75 is not the sentinel.
3	Add score to total : total is 215
4	Read the next score: -1
2	-1 is the sentinel.
6	Output the total of 215.

This trace looks correct. We should also check our pseudocode when the user has no scores to enter.

Line	**NumberAction**
1	Read the next score: -1
2	-1 is the sentinel.
6	Output the total of ???.

Here we get to line 6 without ever adding any scores to the total. The pseudocode always displays the total, whether or not the user entered any scores. We need to make sure that whenever we get to line six, we have a total to display. If the user has no scores to enter, we could display zero. To set this initial value for the total, we could add a line at the beginning of the pseudocode, say line 0,

0 Initialize the total to zero.

which sets the total to zero. Then, if we do not read any scores, we will still have a total to display. Actually, we implicitly use the initial value of total in line 3 after we read the very first score. Line 3 states `add the score to the total so far`, but before reading any scores the total does not have a value unless we give it an initial value in line 0.

If we want to be really picky, we might want to distinguish between the case when the total is zero because no scores were entered, and when it is zero because a bunch of zero scores were entered. More broadly, we might want to keep track of the number of scores entered. Should we do these things or not? In this example, the problem does not explicitly ask to keep track of the number of scores, and for simplicity, we will not add this feature now. The problem does not say what to do if no scores are available, but we assume that displaying zero is sensible and to be sure we check with the proposer of the problem who agrees.

We have taken a lot of trouble to design a solution to a simple problem. Because we have been careful, we should be able to convert the pseudocode to a Java program that solves the problem. We need to choose variables to hold the values we need. We could use any valid identifiers, not keywords, for our variable names. To make our program as readable as possible, we choose meaningful variable names. Let us use a variable, `total`, of type `int`, to hold the sum of the scores, and a variable, `score`, of type `int`, to hold each score

EXAMPLE 3.6 ScoreSum.java

```
/*  Uses a while loop to compute the sum of
 *  test scores. getScore returns an integer score
 *  input by the user. addScore adds a score to the total.
 *  getTotal returns the total.
 */

import javax.swing.*;

public class ScoreSum  {
  private int total = 0;            // sum of scores                 // Note 1

  public int getScore() {                                            // Note 2
    String input = JOptionPane.showInputDialog
                      ("Enter the score, -1 to quit");
    return Integer.parseInt(input);
  }
  public void addScore(int score) {
    total += score;
  }
  public int getTotal() {
    return total;
  }
```

```
  public static void main(String [] args) {
    ScoreSum scorer = new ScoreSum();
    int score = scorer.getScore();                          // Note 3
    while (score >= 0) {
      scorer.addScore(score);
      score = scorer.getScore();
    }
    JOptionPane.showMessageDialog
        (null, "The total is " + scorer.getTotal());
    System.exit(0);
  }
}
```

Input

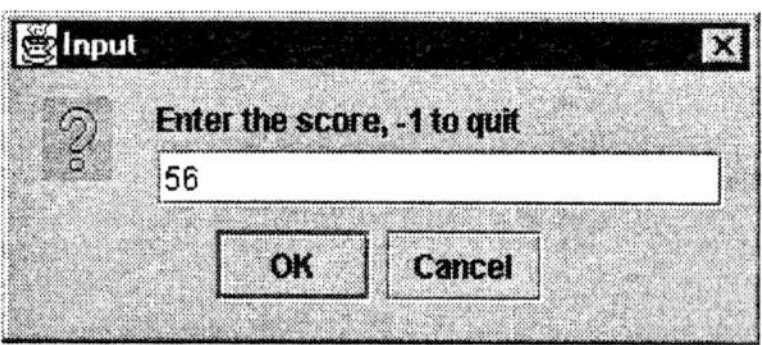

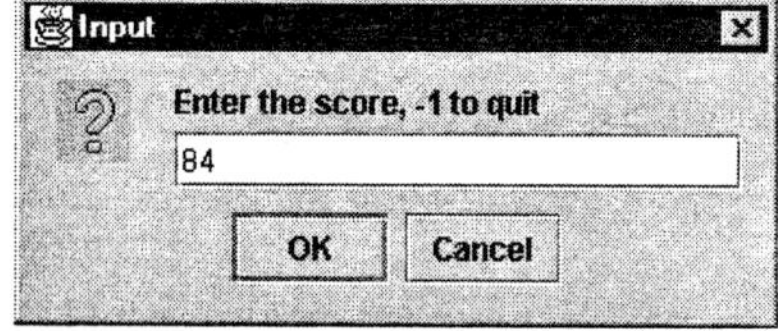

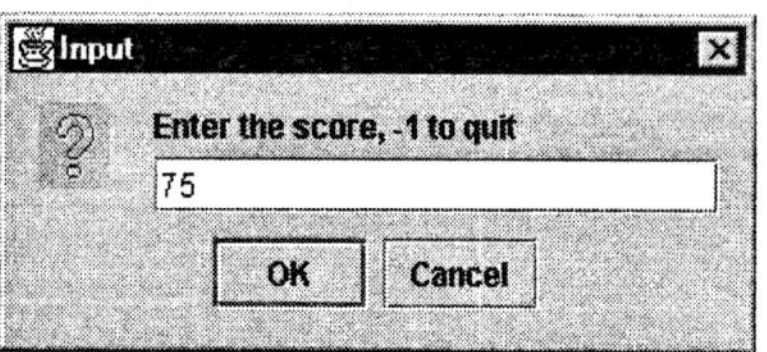

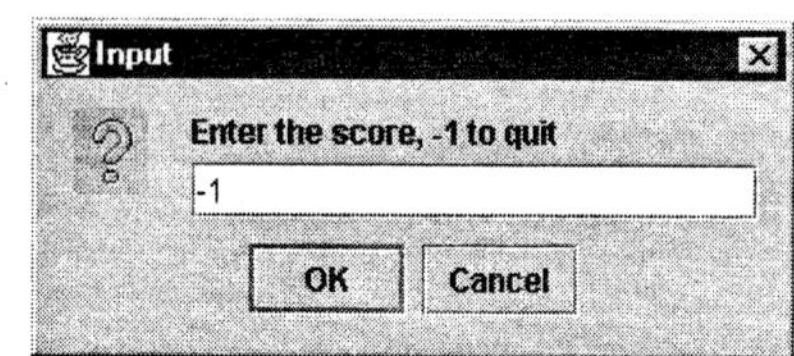

Output

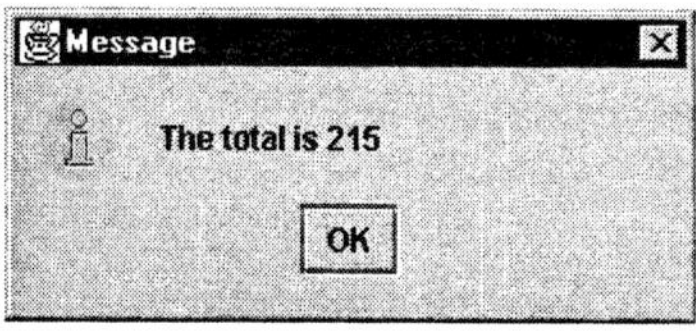

Note 1: We initialize total to 0 representing the sum of scores before the user has entered any scores. If the user enters the sentinel, -1, before entering any scores, the output will be 0.

Note 2: The `getScore` method returns the score entered by the user, who enters a negative value to terminate the input.

Note 3: The Java code closely follows the steps of the pseudocode.

Having completed this program nicely, we might ask about alternative solutions, in case another approach might allow us to improve our program. Instead of using a sentinel to signify the end of the input, the user might specify how many scores are available. Then we can have our loop condition check to see if all scores have been entered. If not, the body of the loop reads the next score and adds it to the total. The pseudocode for this approach is:

```
Read the quantity of scores to read;
while (number of scores read so far < quantity to read) {
  Read the next score;
  Add the score to the total so far
}
Display the total;
```

Each time around the loop we need to check the condition `number of scores read so far < quantity to read`. We know how many scores the user will enter. If we have not read that many, there are more scores; otherwise, we have read them all. But how many scores have we read? Let us keep track as we read. We could include another state variable, `count`, to hold the number of scores read so far. We initialize `count` to `0`, and each time we read a score, we increase `count` by 1. Here is the revised pseudocode.

Figure 3.11 Pseudocode for the sum of test scores problem

```
Read the quantity of scores;
while (count < quantity) {
     Read the next score;
     Add the score to the total so far;
     Increment the count of scores;
}
 Display the quantity and the total;
```

We leave the next steps in this solution process, which include tracing the execution of the pseudocode with sample data and converting it to a Java program, to the exercises. Note that to solve the problem using this approach, we had to know the quantity of test scores, so we added that to the output to make it more informative.

TIP

Think carefully when writing the condition (often called the test) for the `while` loop. Getting it correct can be tricky. In the above example we might easily have written `count <= quantity` which is incorrect, because when `count` equals `quantity`, then we have already read all the scores and should terminate the loop rather than ask for another score.

A LITTLE EXTRA

In Example 3.6, we assumed that the user would enter correct data. Entering a value such as `34.5` or "`hat`" will cause the program to abort. Later we will introduce exception handling which we can use to recover from such input errors. Even if the user enters a correct `int` value, that value could be `312017` or `-52`, neither of which is likely to be a test score. We could have prompted the user to enter a value from `0` to `100`, as in

```
Enter a score between 0 and 100
```

Even then a careless user could enter an invalid value.*

Style

Example 3.6 illustrates several important style rules for programs.

Do

Declare each variable on a separate line and use a comment to specify the use of that variable in the program.

Do

Use meaningful variable names that remind us of the purpose of that variable.

Do

Precede the program with a comment that describes the intent of the program, and the input and output. This comment is a good place to put the programmer's name and the date.

Do

Include comments to explain any parts of the code that might require help in understanding it. (In our examples, we use Notes at the end of the code for this purpose.)

Loop Termination

TIP

Beware of loops that never terminate. We use loops because we want repetition, but we must make sure that the repetition stops. Study the examples below and check each loop that you write to make sure that it will terminate.

Each time the loop condition is `true` Java executes the loop body. In order for the loop to terminate, something must change that causes the condition to fail. In the loop

```
while ( x < 10)
     x += 2;
```

we add 2 to `x` each time we execute the body. Eventually `x` will become greater than or equal to `10` so the condition `x < 10` will fail and the loop will terminate.

* In the next chapter we will see how to add error checking code to make our programs more robust.

If we were just to display the value of x, and not increase it, then the loop may never stop. For example, if x has the value 5 when Java executes the loop

```
while (x < 10)
    System.out.println("x is now " + x);
```

the result will be an unending sequence

```
x is now 5
x is now 5
x is now 5
...
```

and so on until someone aborts the program. (Holding the `Control` key down and pressing the `C` key will interrupt the program on Windows systems.)

The last example, repeatedly displaying `x is now 5`, made it easy to spot that something was very wrong. Sometimes an unending loop (often called an **infinite loop**) may have the opposite behavior, showing nothing at all to the user while it goes on computing. For example, if x has the value 5, the loop

```
while (x < 10)
  x -= 2;
```

keeps on subtracting 2 from x, never terminating. The value of x is 5, 3, 1, -1, -3, -5, -7,.. and so on. The condition, `x < 10`, is always true, so the loop keeps on executing, but displays nothing to the user. The programmer's first response is to blame the computer for being awfully slow, because nothing seems to be happening, but that eerie stillness could be a symptom of an infinite loop. If so, the user must interrupt, aborting the program.

Remember when writing a `while` statement, that the body of the loop must do something which will eventually cause the condition to be `false`.

Finding the Maximum

We close this section by solving another problem.

> Find the largest of the prices entered. The user will input a sequence of prices, and input a negative item as a sentinel to indicate that input has ended. The program will output the maximum of the prices.

To help us, we define a `Max` class with state the maximum so far and responsibilities

```
input a price
update the maximum
get the maximum
```

We repeatedly check that each new price is not the sentinel, and then update the maximum if that price is larger than the maximum so far. The pseudocode is

```
Input a price.
while (the price is not the sentinel) {
  Update the maximum.
  Input a price.
}
Output the maximum.
```

EXAMPLE 3.7 **Max.java**

```
/*  Finds the maximum of prices that the user enters.
 *  The user enters a negative value to indicate that
 *  no more data is available. The program displays the
 *  maximum value.
 */

import javax.swing.*;
import java.text.*;

public class Max {
  private double maxSoFar = 0;    // Max of prices entered              // Note 1
  public double getPrice() {
    String input = JOptionPane.showInputDialog
                         ("Enter a price, -1 to quit");
    return Double.parseDouble(input);
  }
  public void updateMax(double price) {                                 // Note 2
    if (price > maxSoFar)
       maxSoFar = price;
  }
  public double getMax() {
    return maxSoFar;
  }
  public static void main(String [] args) {
    Max max = new Max();
    double price = max.getPrice();                                      // Note 3
    while (price >= 0 ) {
      max.updateMax(price);
      price = max.getPrice();
    }
    NumberFormat nf = NumberFormat.getCurrencyInstance();
    JOptionPane.showMessageDialog
          (null, "The maximum is " + nf.format(max.getMax()));
    System.exit(0);
  }
}
```

Input

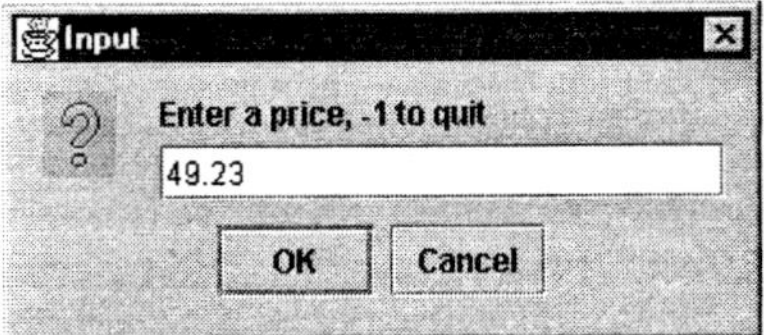

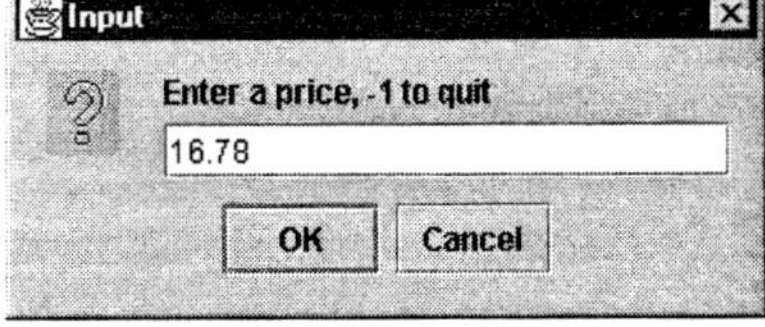

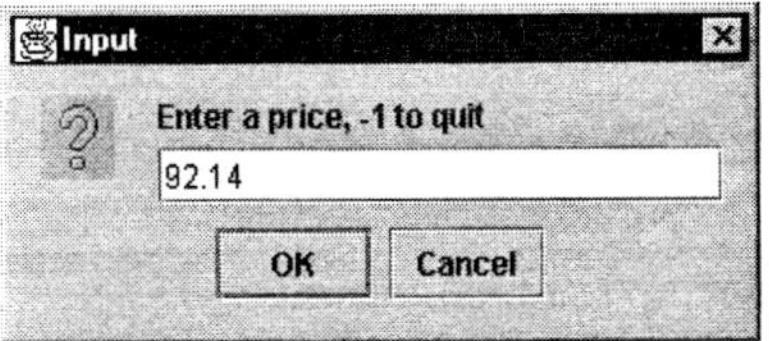

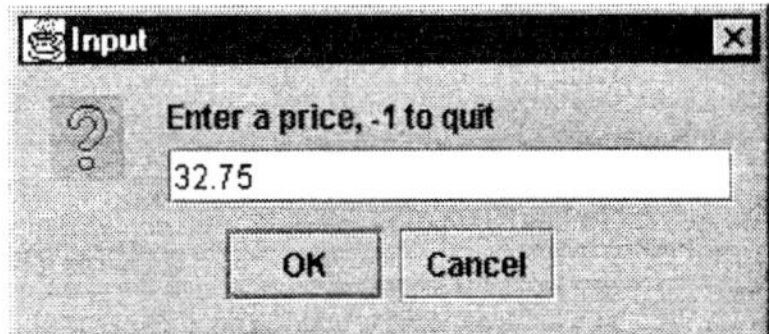

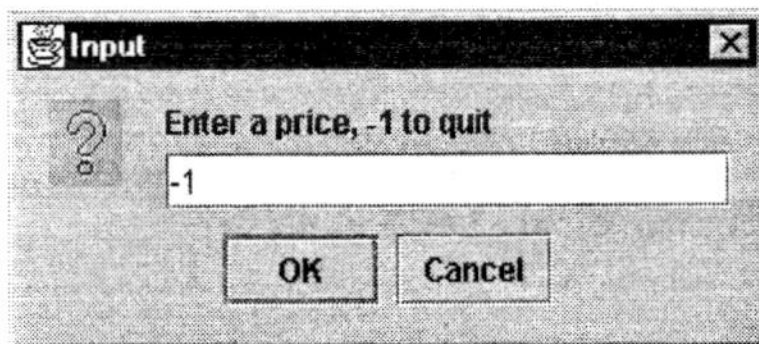

Output

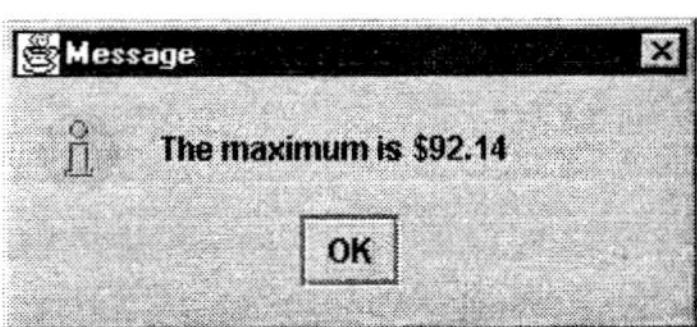

Note 1: We initialize `maxSoFar` to 0 because the prices are all nonnegative so the maximum must be at least 0.

Note 2: `updatePrice` changes `maxSoFar` if a larger price is passed to it.

Note 3: We get the first price before entering the loop because the while loop checks the price to see if it is the sentinel before trying to update the maximum. We could have simply initialized the price to zero with the declaration

```
double price = 0;
```

The update step would harmlessly check the zero value and go on to read the first price the user enters.

THE BIG PICTURE

The `while` statement enables us to repeat steps. We use pseudocode to plan problem solutions carefully. When writing `while` loops, we must make sure that the condition becomes false so that the loop terminates.

TEST YOUR UNDERSTANDING

20. How many times will the body of each of following `while` loops be executed if `x` has the value 5 at the start of the loop?

a.
```
while (x <= 10)
  x +=3;
```
b.
```
while (x == 2)
  x -= 7;
```
c.
```
while (x > 1)
  x--;
```

21. Find any errors in the following `while` loops:

a.
```
while (x != 9}
  x +=4;
```
b.
```
while (x)
  x *= 2;
```
c.
```
while (x =! 7)
  x++;
```

22. Trace the execution of the pseudocode in Figure 3.11 assuming test scores of:

a. `95, 46, 68,` and `79` b. `14, 87, 35, 76,` and `80`

23. Which of the following loops terminate? Assume that `x` has the value `12` at the start of the loop.

a.
```
while (x != 5)
  x++;
```
b.
```
while (x != 5)
  x--;
```
c.
```
while (x != 5)
  x = 5;
```

24. Draw the flow chart for each of the following `while` loops

a.
```
while(y < 7)
  y += 4;
```
b.
```
while(y > 5) {
  x = y + 10;
  y --;
}
```
c.
```
while (z != 0) {
  x = 4 * z;
  z++;
}
```

25. Develop a solution in pseudocode to the problem of looking up a number in the telephone directory.

26. Develop a solution in pseudocode to the problem of finding the minimum of a sequence of nonnegative numbers entered by the user, where the user enters a negative number to terminate the input.

27. Trace the execution of the pseudocode preceding Example 3.7, for finding the maximum of numbers input by the user, with the input data `49.23, 16.789, 92.145, 32.7,` and `-1`.

28. Develop a solution in pseudocode to the problem of finding the maximum of a sequence of nonnegative numbers entered by the user. In this solution, before reading the numbers, ask the user to enter how many numbers will be input.

29. Develop a solution in pseudocode to the problem of finding both the maximum and the minimum of a sequence of nonnegative numbers entered by the user. In this solution, before reading the numbers, ask the user to input how many numbers will be input.

30. Develop a solution in pseudocode to the problem of counting the number of negative numbers in a sequence of numbers that the user inputs. In this solution, before reading the numbers, ask the user to input how many numbers will be input. (Example: For input `32, 76, -12, 49, -11,` and `-3` the output should be that there are three negative numbers.)

3.5 Debugging

Following the careful problem solving methods described in the last section will help us to produce programs free from errors. Hasty coding, before developing a careful solution, is much more likely to lead to errors. In this section, we discuss some simple approaches to **debugging**, which is the finding and correcting any errors in the program.

We seek to correct errors in logic in a program that compiles but either aborts with an error message while running, or produces incorrect results. Those learning a new language or with little prior programming experience make many syntax errors, writing Java statements and expressions incorrectly, as part of the learning process. The compiler catches these syntax errors, and provides messages to help the programmer correct the syntax.

Our examples in this section compile but do not produce the desired results. We suggest some simple techniques for finding and correcting the observed errors. We take a simple problem to sum the squares of the integers from `1` to a high value entered by the user. Example 3.8 is an attempted solution.

EXAMPLE 3.8 Mistake1.java

```
/* Incorrect attempt to sum the squares of
 * numbers from 1 to a high value entered
 * by the user
 */

import javax.swing.*;

public class Mistake1 {
  public static void main(String [] args) {
    int sum = 0;
    int count = 1;
    String input = JOptionPane.showInputDialog
              ("Enter the number of squares to sum");
    int high = Integer.parseInt(input);
    while (count <= high)
      sum += count*count;
    System.out.println("The sum of the first " + high +
                             " squares is " +sum);
    System.exit(0);
  }
}
```

When we run Example 3.8, we find that there is no output. Nothing happens, and the program does not terminate. We must abort the program. Reading the code, we see that the `println` statement comes after the `while` loop. Since the `println` statement never gets executed, it seems like the `while` loop is not terminating. To see more clearly what is happening we add a `println` statement in the body of the loop.

EXAMPLE 3.9 Mistake2.java

```
/* Adds a println statement in the body of
 * the while loop of Example 3.8
 */

import javax.swing.*;

public class Mistake2 {
  public static void main(String [] args) {
    int sum = 0;
    int count = 1;
    String input = JOptionPane.showInputDialog
               ("Enter the number of squares to sum");
    int high = Integer.parseInt(input);
    while (count <= high) {                                    // Note 1
      sum += count*count;
      System.out.println("Sum is " + sum);
    }
    System.out.println("The sum of the first " + high +
                                  " squares is " +sum);
    System.exit(0);
  }
}
```

Run

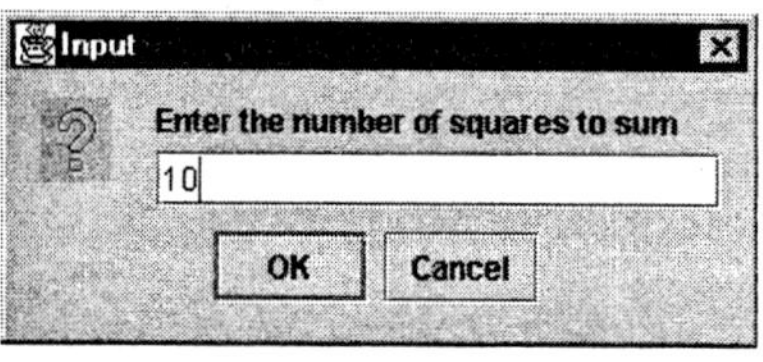


```
Sum is 1
Sum is 2
Sum is 3
.....(nonterminating)
```

Note 1: We make the `while` loop body a block, enclosing the two statements in braces. We did not need the braces in Example 3.8 since the `while` loop body was a single assignment statement.

The output of Example 3.9 continues until we abort the program. It is clear that the `while` loop does not terminate. Looking more closely at the code, we see that we forgot to increment the count after adding the next square to the sum.

EXAMPLE 3.10 Mistake3.java

```
/* Modifies Example 3.9 to increment the count.
 */

import javax.swing.*;

public class Mistake3 {
  public static void main(String [] args) {
    int sum = 0;
    int count = 1;
    String input = JOptionPane.showInputDialog
                 ("Enter the number of squares to sum");
    int high = Integer.parseInt(input);
    while (count <= high) {
       sum += count*count;
       count++;
    }
    System.out.println"The sum of the first "
                   + high + " squares is " +sum);
    System.exit(0);
  }
}
```

Run

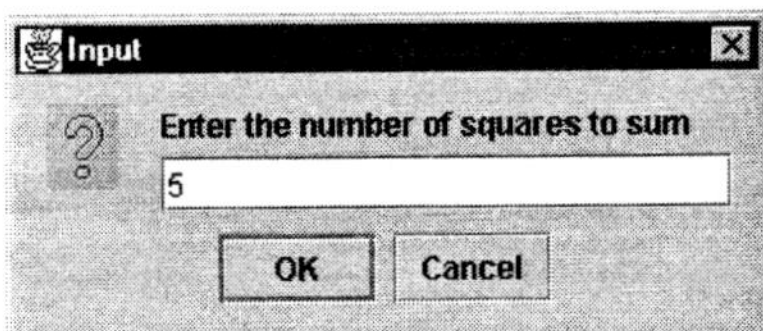


```
The sum of the first 5 squares is 55
```

The output looks correct. Checking it by hand, we see that the sum of the first five squares, `1 + 4 + 9 + 16 + 25`, is indeed `55`. It is tempting to conclude that our program is correct, but we should never make such a conclusion on the basis of one test case. Let us do some more testing, trying larger high values such as `100`, `1000`, and `10000`. The output of these tests is:

> Enter the number of squares to sum: 100
> The sum of the first 100 squares is 338350
>
> Enter the number of squares to sum: 1000
> The sum of the first 1000 squares is 333833500

Enter the number of squares to sum: 10000
The sum of the first 10000 squares is -1624114088

Surely something is wrong here. The sum of the first `10000` squares is certainly not negative. Remember that the `int` type can hold values up to 2,147,483,647. Trying to store values larger than `2,147,483,647` will give spurious results.

We leave it to the exercises to determine the largest number of squares we can sum correctly using the program of Example 3.10. The debugging techniques we illustrated in these examples are:

`Read the code carefully to determine where the error might be located.`

In Example 3.8 we could tell from reading the code that the error was in the while loop.

`Add println statements to get more information.`

The added `println` statement in Example 3.9 clearly demonstrated the error.

`Test thoroughly.`

Even though our first result was correct, more extensive testing of Example 3.10 found an error.

THE BIG PICTURE

We debug a program to find and correct errors. Simple techniques include reading the program carefully, adding println statements to display values, and testing the program thoroughly.

TEST YOUR UNDERSTANDING

TRY IT YOURSELF 31. Run Example 3.10 to find the largest value, `n`, such that Example 3.9 finds the sum of the first `n` squares correctly.

TRY IT YOURSELF 32. Modify Example 3.10 to inform the user of the largest acceptable input in the prompt, and to reject any input greater than that value.

3.6 Getting Started with Applets: Drawing Shapes

We introduce the methods of the `Graphics` class for drawing lines, rectangles, ovals, and arcs.

Graphics Drawing

The `Graphics` class contains a number of methods for drawing various shapes. We will draw lines, rectangles, ovals, rounded rectangles, and arcs. In each case, we will do our drawing in the `paint` method which Java calls when events affecting our window cause it to need repainting.

The `drawLine` method has four `int` parameters, the x- and y-coordinates of each endpoint of that line segment. For example

```
g.drawLine(70,80,130,230)
```

draws the line between (70,80) and (130,230).

Figure 3.12 Drawing a line

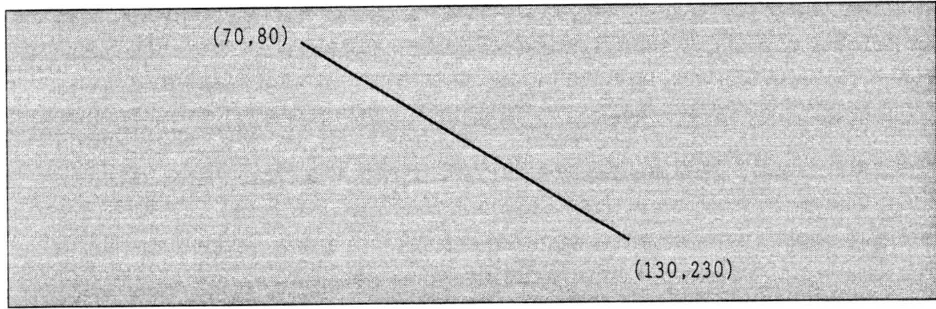

The `drawRect` method

```
g.drawRect(int x, int y, int w, int h)
```

draws the rectangle with upper-left corner `(x,y)`, width `w`, and height `h`. Figure 3.13 shows the rectangle produced by

```
g.drawRect(50,50,200,100)
```

Figure 3.13 Drawing a rectangle

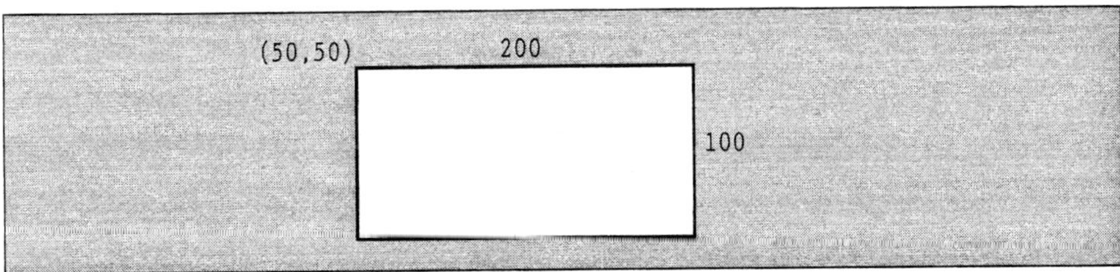

To draw an oval, we need to specify the rectangle that bounds the oval, just as we did in the `drawRect` method. Java draws an oval that just touches the center points of its bounding rectangle. The arguments specify the corner `(x,y)`, `width`, and `height` of the bounding rectangle. For example, Figure 3.14 shows the oval resulting from

```
g.drawOval(50,50,200,100)
```

Figure 3.14 An oval with its bounding rectangle

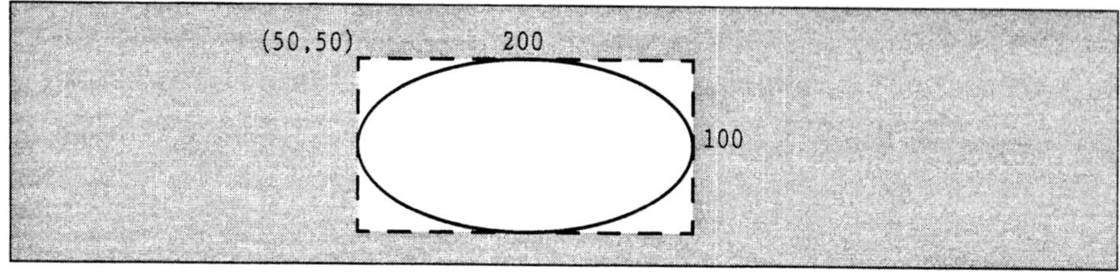

To draw a circle, we use a bounding rectangle that is a square.

An arc is a piece of an oval. The `drawArc` method has six parameters; the first four specify the bounding rectangle while the fifth gives the start angle for the arc and the sixth gives the angle swept out by the arc. Referring to the face of a clock, the zero-degree angle is at three o'clock, and angles increase counterclockwise with 360 degrees in the full circle, as Figure 3.15 shows.

Figure 3.15 Degree measure around a circle

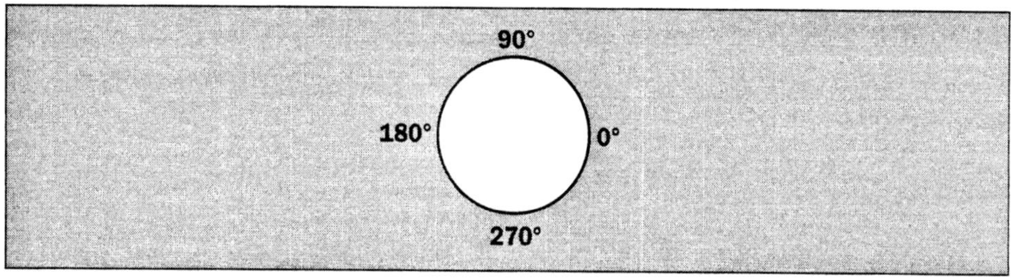

Figure 3.16 shows the part of the oval of Figure 3.14 that starts at 45° and sweeps out an arc of 90°, drawn by the method

Figure 3.16 An arc from the oval of Figure 3.14

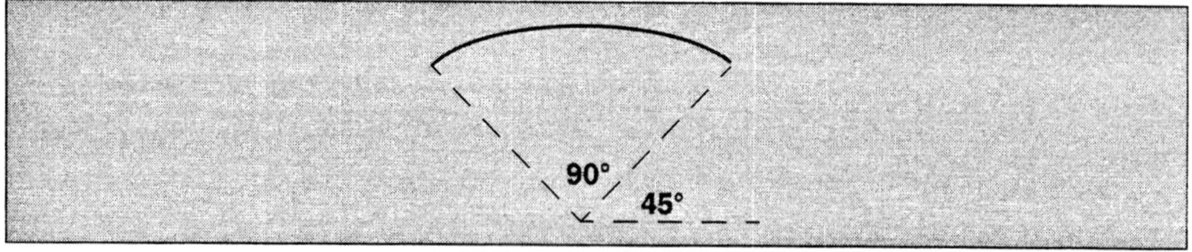


```
g.drawArc(50,50,200,100,45,90);
```

Positive angles sweep out an arc from the starting angle in the counterclockwise direction.

Java lets us draw a rounded rectangle, which is a rectangle with the corners rounded. For example,

```
g.drawRoundRect(50,50,200,100,30,30);
```

will draw a rounded rectangle of width 200 and height 100 with each corner replaced by an arc of an oval of diameter 30 in each direction. Figure 3.17 shows the basis for the drawing. The rectangle has upper-left corner `(50,50)`, width `200`, and height `100`. We placed an oval of width 30 and height 30 in each corner. To obtain the rounded rectangle, we follow the perimeter of the rectangle, but traverse a quarter of each oval rather than the corners. In this example, the rounded rectangle cuts off 15 pixels from each corner to do the rounding. The value 15 represents half the diameter of 30 in each direction.

Figure 3.17 The structure of a rounded rectangle

The drawRect, drawOval, drawArc, and drawRoundedRect methods draw the outlines of the shapes. To draw filled ovals, arcs, rectangles, or rounded rectangles, we use the `fillOval`, `fillArc`, `fillRect`, and `fillRoundRect` methods which have the same arguments as the corresponding `draw` methods shown above. The default color for drawing and filling is black, but we will add color later.

Example 3.11 demonstrates these `draw` and `fill` methods. The `paint` method of this applet draws various shapes when the Java system calls it in response to events requiring the applet to be painted.

Figure 3.18 shows the applet viewer running the applet of Example 3.11 using `DrawFill.html` given by

```
<applet code=DrawFill.class width=500 height=400>
</applet>
```

Figure 3.18 The `DrawFill` applet of Example 3.11

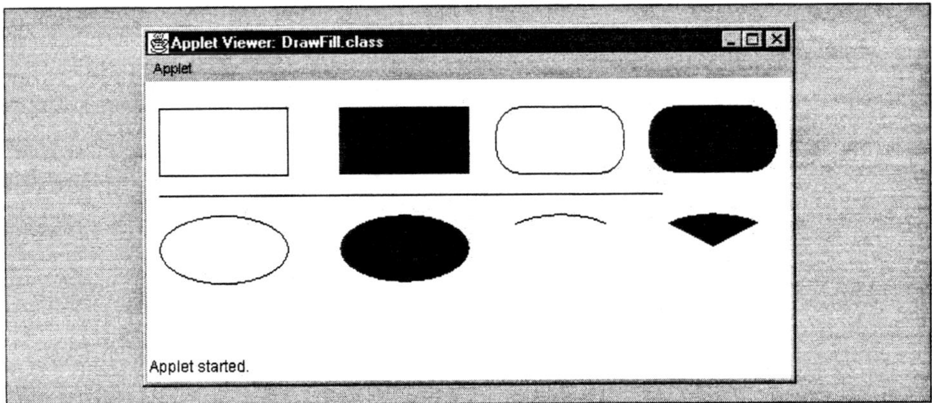

EXAMPLE 3.11 DrawFill.java

```
/* Uses Graphics draw and fill methods for various shapes.
 * The Java system calls the paint method when the applet
 * needs repainting.
 */

import java.awt.Graphics;
import java.applet.Applet;

public class DrawFill extends Applet {
  public void paint(Graphics g) {
    g.drawRect(10,20,100,50);                              // Note 1
    g.fillRect(150,20,100,50);
    g.drawRoundRect(270,20,100,50,40,40);                  // Note 2
    g.fillRoundRect(390,20,100,50,40,40);
    g.drawLine(10,85,400,85);                              // Note 3
    g.drawOval(10,100,100,50);                             // Note 4
    g.fillOval(150,100,100,50);
    g.drawArc(270,100,100,50,45,90);                       // Note 5
    g.fillArc(390,100,100,50,45,90);
  }
}
```

Note 1: The rectangle has upper left corner `(10,20)`, width `100`, and height `50`.

Note 2: Rounds the corner with an arc of a circle of diameter `40`.

Note 3: Draws the line from `(10,85)` to `(400,85)`.

Note 4: Draws the oval whose bounding rectangle has corner `(10,100)`, width `100` and height `50`.

Note 5: Draws the arc, starting from a 45 degree angle and sweeping out a 90 degree angle counterclockwise, which is part of the oval whose bounding rectangle has upper left corner `(270,100)`, width `100`, and height `50`.

TIP ☛

Test applets using the applet viewer rather than a browser. Browsers store your class file in a cache. When you make changes and recompile, they load your Java class from the cache, using the old file, not the changed version. Even pressing the Reload button does not help as that just reloads the HTML file. To load the new version of the Java class you have to clear the cache or exit the browser and start it again.

We are not developing web pages, so we can just use an applet viewer to test our applets. Even when we include an applet in a web page, we can still test it with the applet viewer, using the browser only when we have completed the applet development.

In Example 3.11 we passed numbers as arguments to the drawing methods, drawing the filled rounded rectangle, for example, starting from the point (390,20). We gave the applet a width of 500 in the HTML file, so there was space in the applet to draw this rectangle. Had we given the applet a width of 350, the filled rounded rectangle would not have appeared. Our program would be more flexible if we drew the figures relative to the size of the applet.

Drawing Relative to the Screen

We can get the size of the applet using the getSize. The getSize method returns an object of type Dimension, a class in the java.awt package, which has public data fields, width and height, that tell us the width and height of the applet.

Drawing relative to the size of the applet takes more effort to implement, but will work correctly when we change the applet's width and height in the HTML file. For example, to draw a rectangle whose width is one-third the width of the applet, whose height is one-third the height of the applet, and which appears at the upper-right of the applet, we could use the code of Figure 3.19.

Figure 3.19 Drawing a rectangle relative to the applet's size

```
Dimension d = getSize();
int w = d.width;
int h = d.height;
g.drawRect(2*w/3,0,w/3,h/3);
```

No matter what the size the applet has, the rectangle of Figure 3.19 has its corner at a point two-thirds of the width from the left. Its width and height are always one-third the width and height of the applet. To use the Dimension class, we must import java.awt.Dimension. We will leave the revision of Example 3.12 to draw figures relative to the size of the applet to the exercises. We will use this technique later when we draw text.

THE BIG PICTURE

Given a Graphics object for our platform, we draw lines, rectangles, rounded rectangles, ovals, and arcs and fill all but the lines. When drawing ovals and arcs, we specify the dimensions of their bounding rectangles. We can draw relative to the size of the applet so the figures will resize when the applet does.

TEST YOUR UNDERSTANDING

33. Write a statement to draw a horizontal line of length 12 whose left endpoint is (3,5).

34. Write a statement to draw a rectangle whose opposite corners are (10,10) and (100,200).

35. Write a statement to draw a square of side `50` whose upper left corner is `(30,60)`.
36. Write a statement to draw an oval which touches the left side of its bounding rectangle at `(100,100)` and the top of its bounding rectangle at `(200,50)`.
37. Write a statement to draw an arc of the oval of question 36, which starts at `90` degrees and sweeps out an angle of `120` degrees.
38. Write Java code to draw a rounded rectangle with lower-right corner `(200,150)`, width `130`, and height `80`. Round by cutting off `20` pixels on each side of each corner.

SUMMARY

- In this chapter we develop the tools to solve problems using Java. To make our programs more flexible, we need to make decisions based on the value of a test condition which can be either true or false. Java provides the `boolean` type which has values `true` and `false`. We write our test conditions as relational or equality expressions. The relational expressions use the operators `<`, `>`, `<=`, and `>=` and produce `boolean` values. The equality expressions use the operators `==` and `!=` and also produce `boolean` values. We can include arithmetic operators in our test conditions. Java will use precedence rules to help evaluate such expressions, with arithmetic expressions having higher precedence than relational expressions.
- Once we know how to write a test condition, we use the `if` and `if-else` statements to make choices based upon the result of a test condition. In the `if` statement, we execute the next statement if the condition is `true`, and skip it if the condition is `false`. The `if-else` statement gives us two alternative statements, one to execute if the test condition is `true`, and the other to execute if the test condition is `false`. Each of these statements can be a simple statement or a code block enclosed by braces. Flow charts give a visual representation of the control flow.
- The `if` and `if-else` statements give us choices in control flow. We discuss decimal numbers and the type `double` to add a choice of data in addition to the `int` type covered in Chapter 2. One can use scientific notation to express decimals, so that we can write `.000000645` as `6.45E-7`. The type `double` represents decimal numbers with 16-digit accuracy. We can declare variables of type `double`, and perform the usual arithmetic operations of `+`, `-`, `*`, and `/`.
- Java displays numbers of type `double` without using exponents for numbers between `.001` and `10,000,000` or between `-.001` and `-10,000,000`, and uses scientific notation otherwise, making very small or very large numbers easier to read.
- If an operator, say `+`, has one `int` operand and one `double` operand, then Java will convert the `int` operand to a `double`, and add the two doubles, producing a result of type `double`. Java will not automatically convert a `double` to an `int`, but we can use an explicit type cast should we need this conversion.

- To complete our set of basic control structures we have the `while` loop to handle repetition. While the test condition is `true`, Java repeats the body of the `while` loop, which can be either a simple Java statement or a block enclosed by braces.
- With the ability to do one statement after another in sequence, the `if` and `if-else` statements to make choices, and the `while` statement for repetition, we can solve complex problems. For clarity we use pseudocode, a program-like notation showing the three control structures of sequence, choice, and repetition, but expressing the refinements informally in English. The method of stepwise refinement allows us to use these three structures: sequence, choice, and repetition, to refine the given problem to show enough detail so that it can be easily coded in Java. In this stepwise refinement process, we can check that the pseudocode accurately solves the problem, and make necessary corrections before the details of the programming language obscure the meaning of the steps.
- To debug our programs, finding and correcting any errors, we read our code carefully, inserting `println` statements to get more information, and testing our code thoroughly with several test cases.
- The `Graphics` class has methods to draw lines, rectangles, ovals, arcs, rounded rectangles, 3-d rectangles, and polygons, and to fill any of them (except, of course, the line). We specify

  a `line` with the coordinates of its endpoints,

  a `rectangle` with its upper left corner, width, and height

  an `oval` with the arguments for its bounding rectangle

  an `arc` with the arguments for an oval, a start angle, and a sweep angle,

  a `rounded rectangle` with the arguments for a rectangle, and the width and height of the oval used to round each corner.

Skill Builder Exercises

1. What will the following program fragment output?

```
        int x=10, y=12, r, t;
if (y > x) {
   t = y;
   y = x;
   x = t;
}
while (y != 0) {
    r = x % y;
    x = y;
    y = r;
}
        System.out.println(x);
```

2. Select the output on the right produced from the statement on the left.

a.	`System.out.println(3.0/2);`	i.	`67.5`
b.	`System.out.println(30*45E-1/2);`	ii.	`1.5000000000000000`
c.	`System.out.println(3*.000045/2)`	iii.	`6.75E1`
		iv.	`6.75E-5`
		v.	`1.5`
		vi.	`.0000675`

3. Write Java statements which will

   a. print `x > y` if `x` is greater than `y` and print `y >= x` otherwise.

   b. loop while `x` is greater than `10`, each time decreasing `x` by `2`.

Critical Thinking Exercises

4. Which of the following correctly lists the sequence of statements that Java executes, given the code fragment?

```
1. int  x = 1, y = 4;
2. if (x >= 2)
3.     x = 7;
4.     y = 9;
5.     x = 8;
```

   a. 1, 2, 3, 4, 5
   b. 1, 2, 5
   c. 1, 2, 4, 5
   d. 1, 2, 3, 5
   e. none of the above

5. Removing which of the lines below will make the result a legal Java program fragment?

```
1. int  x = 7;
2. int  y;
3. if (x <= 10)
4.       x = 9;
5.       y = 3;
6. else
7.       x = 12;
```

   a. 5 and 6
   b. 5
   c. 2 and 5
   d. all of the above
   e. none of the above

6. How many times does the body of the `while` statement below get executed?

```
int x = 3;
while (x < 9)
  x += 2;
x++;
```

a. 6
b. 3
c. 4
d. 9
e. none of the above

7. The following program is supposed to output the sum of the integers one through ten. Choose the statement that best describes the result.

```
public class Sum  {
  public static void main(String [] args) {
    int x = 0;
    int total = 0;
    while ( x < 10) {
      total += x;
    }
    System.out.println("The sum of 1 through 10 is " + total);
  }
}
```

a. the output will be correct
b. the output will be correct, but an extra zero was added at first
c. there will be no output
d. the output will be too small

Debugging Exercise

8. The following program is supposed to find the total sales tax paid when making purchases in county A, in which the sales tax is 4%, and in county B, in which the sales tax is 5.5%. The user first inputs the prices, excluding sales tax, of all purchases in county A terminated by a negative value, then inputs the prices of all purchases in county B, excluding sales tax, terminated by a negative value. The program should output the total sales tax paid. Find and fix any errors in this program.

```
public class SalesTax {
  public static void main(String [] args) {
    double taxA = .05, taxB= .04;
    double priceA =Double.parseDouble
                  (JOptionPane.showInputDialog
                  ("Enter a purchase price in County A, -1 to quit"));
```

```
      double totalA = 0.0, totalB = 0.0;
      while (priceA >= 0) {
        totalA += priceA;
        priceA = Double.parseDouble(JOptionPane.showInputDialog
                 ("Enter a purchase price in County A, -1 to quit"));
      }
      while (priceB >= 0) {
        totalB += priceB;
        priceB = Double.parseDouble(JOptionPane.showInputDialog
                 ("Enter a purchase price in County B, -1 to quit"));
      }
      double tax = priceA*taxA + priceB*taxB;
      NumberFormat cf = NumberFormat.getCurrencyInstance();
      System.out.println("The total sales tax is " + cf.format(tax));
    }
  }
```

Program Modification Exercises

9. Modify Example 3.2 to input the wage in a dialog. Add a `Pay1` constructor that initializes both the hours and the wage.
10. Modify Example 3.3 to check that the coins are available before making change.
11. Modify the `makeChange` method of Example 3.3 to use methods to avoid the repetitious code for the different coins.
12. Modify Example 3.4 to output using message dialogs.

Program Design Exercises

13. Write a Java program that computes the weekly pay for an employee. Input the number of hours worked. The employee receives $7.50 per hour for the first forty hours and $11.25 per hour for each additional hour.

    a. Use only a `main` method to solve the problem.

    b. Develop an object-oriented solution with an instance variable, and a `getPay` instance method.

14. Write a Java program that checks a grade point average that the user inputs, and outputs `Congratulations, You made the honor roll` if the average is 3.5 and above, but outputs `Sorry, You are on probation` if the average is below 2.0.

    a. Use only a `main` method to solve the problem.

    b. Develop an object-oriented solution with an instance variable, and a `message` instance method.

15. Write a Java program that inputs the prices of a box of cereal and a quart of milk at store A and the prices of the same items at store B. The program should output the total cost of three boxes of cereal and two quarts of milk at whichever store has the lower cost. Either store is acceptable if the cost is the same at both.

    a. Use only a `main` method to solve the problem.

    b. Develop an object-oriented solution with class `Store` that has instance variables for the prices of milk and cereal, and instance methods `getMilkPrice` and `get-CerealPrice`.

16. Write a Java program to make change. Enter the cost of an item that is less than one dollar. Output the coins given as change, using quarters, dimes, nickels, and pennies. Use the fewest coins possible. For example, it the item cost 17 cents, the change would be three quarters, one nickel, and three pennies.

    a. Use only a `main` method to solve the problem.

    b. Develop an object-oriented solution with an instance variable, and a `makeChange` instance method.

17. Write a Java program to convert kilograms to pounds or ounces. There are .45359237 kilograms in one pound, and 16 ounces in one pound. If the weight is less than one pound, just report the number of ounces. Thus 3.4 kilograms converts to 7.4957 pounds, while .4 kilograms converts to 14.1096 ounces.

    a. Use only a `main` method to solve the problem.

    b. Develop an object-oriented solution with instance variables, and a `convert` instance method.

18. Write a Java program to convert meters to feet or inches. There are 39.37 inches in one meter and 12 inches in a foot. If the length is less than one foot, just report the number of inches. Show two digits after the decimal point. Thus 3.4 meters converts to11.15 feet, while .2 meter converts to 7.87 inches.

    a. Use only a `main` method to solve the problem.

    b. Develop an object-oriented solution with an instance variable, and a `convert` instance method.

19. Write a Java program to find the sum of the test scores input by the user. Use the pseudocode of Figure 3.11, in which the user inputs the number of test scores, and each score.

    a. Use only a `main` method to solve the problem.

    b. Develop an object-oriented solution with instance variables and methods.

20. Write a Java program to find the minimum of a sequence of nonnegative numbers entered by the user, where the user enters a negative number to terminate the input. (Use the pseudocode from Test Your Understanding, question 28.)

    a. Use only a `main` method to solve the problem.

    b. Develop an object-oriented solution with instance variables and methods.

21. Write a Java program to find the maximum of a sequence of nonnegative numbers entered by the user. In this solution, before reading the numbers, ask the user to input how many numbers will be input. (Use the pseudocode from Test Your Understanding, question 30.)

    a. Use only a `main` method to solve the problem.

    b. Develop an object-oriented solution with instance variables and methods.

22. Write a Java program to find both the maximum and the minimum of a sequence of nonnegative numbers entered by the user. In this solution, before reading the numbers, ask the user to input how many numbers will be input. (Use the pseudocode from Test Your Understanding, question 31.)

    a. Use only a `main` method to solve the problem.

    b. Develop an object-oriented solution with instance variables and methods.

23. Write a Java program to count the number of negative numbers in a sequence of numbers that the user inputs. In this solution, before reading the numbers, ask the user to input how many numbers will be input. For example: For input 32, 76, -12, 49, -11, and -3 the output should be that there are three negative numbers. (Use the pseudocode from Test Your Understanding, question 32.)

    a. Use only a `main` method to solve the problem.

    b. Develop an object-oriented solution with instance variables and methods.

24. Write a Java program to find the average of a sequence of nonnegative numbers entered by the user, where the user enters a negative number to terminate the input.

    a. Use only a `main` method to solve the problem.

    b. Develop an object-oriented solution with instance variables and methods.

25. Suppose you have an account that earns five percent interest that is credited to your account at the end of each year. Write a Java program to calculate the number of years it will take before the account balance is at least $2000, if the initial account balance is $1000.

    a. Use only a `main` method to solve the problem.

    b. Develop an object-oriented solution with instance variables and methods.

26. Generalize Exercise 21 by having the user enter the interest rate, the initial balance, and the final balance. Write a Java program to calculate the number of years it will take before the account balance reaches the specified final balance.

    a. Use only a `main` method to solve the problem.

    b. Develop an object-oriented solution with instance variables and methods.

27. Suppose an annual inflation rate of four percent. Because of inflation, an item that costs $1.00 today will cost $1.04 one year from now. (We assume, for simplicity, that the item we consider will rise in price exactly at the rate of inflation.) Write a Java program which inputs the cost of an item and outputs its cost three years from now.

    a. Use only a `main` method to solve the problem.

    b. Develop an object-oriented solution with instance variables and methods.

28. Generalize Exercise 23 by having the user input the annual inflation rate, the cost of the item, and the number of years. Write a Java program which outputs the cost of that item after the specified number of years.

    a. Use only a `main` method to solve the problem.

    b. Develop an object-oriented solution with instance variables and methods.

29. Suppose you borrow $1000 at 12% annual interest, and make monthly payments of $100. Write a Java program to calculate how many months it will take to pay off this loan. (Each month you pay interest on the remaining balance. The interest rate is 1% per month so the first month you pay $10 interest and $90 goes to reduce the balance to $910. The next month's interest is $9.10, and $90.90 is applied to reduce the balance, and so on. The last month's payment may be less than $100.)

    a. Use only a `main` method to solve the problem.

    b. Develop an object-oriented solution with an instance method.

30. Generalize Exercise 25 by having the user input the loan amount, the annual interest rate, and the monthly payment.

    a. Use only a `main` method to solve the problem.

    b. Develop an object-oriented solution with instance variable and methods.

Applet Exercises

31. Modify Example 3.12 to draw each figure relative to the size of the applet, so when the applet is resized, the figures will be resized proportionally.

32. Write an applet that draws a maze of your own design. You might sketch a maze on paper and work out the coordinates of the lines to draw.

33. Write an applet that draws a happy face of your own design.

34. Write a Java applet that displays a store's daily sales over the period of one week in a bar graph. It should look like the figure below.

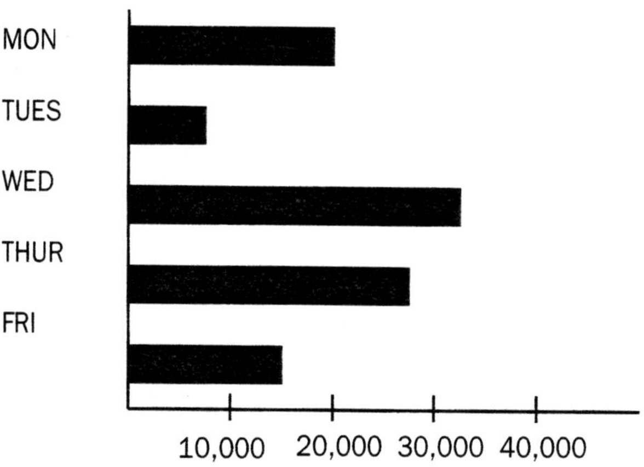

CHAPTER

4 More Control Structures and Types

OUTLINE

Introduction

In Chapters 2 and 3 we covered the essential concepts needed to start solving problems with Java. With the types `int` and `double`, the assignment, `if-else` and `while` statements, we can use Java to solve problems. But this is a bare bones set of tools. A good carpenter can do some fine construction with a few tools, but will be much more productive with a variety of tools to make the job easier. In this chapter we will add some tools to build Java programs more easily.*
Logical operators make it easier to use more complex tests such as

```
I am hungry and I am thirsty
```

* Chapter 3 contains a basic set of tools, while this chapter develops an enchanced set. An alternative organization would discuss all primitive types together, and all control structures together. The unifying theme of this chapter is enhancements to the basic constructs, in a software engineering context..

which is true if `I am hungry` and `I am thirsty` are both true.

The `if-else` statement lets us choose between two alternatives. Nested `if` statements and `switch` statements expand our choices to multiple alternatives. The `while` statement repeats while a condition is true. The `for` statement and the `do-while` statement make it easier to handle repetition.

We use the `int` and `double` types most frequently, but Java provides additional primitive types including `long`, `float`, and `character` which can sometimes be useful.

In addition to the statements and types in the Java language, Java libraries provide a wide range of methods to create user interfaces, connect across a network, and generally make Java a more powerful tool. In this chapter, we look at the collection of methods in the Math library which allow us to find powers, roots, maxima, minima, and evaluate natural logarithms and other functions.

Our problem-solving case study uses these topics to design a program to convert lengths between the English and Metric systems. We use this case study to introduce good software engineering techniques.

The `BigAtmScreen` applet in Figure 4.1 shows a delightfully large account balance. `BigAtmScreen` is a modification of the `AtmScreen` applet of Example 1.5, which uses the `BigDecimal` class from the Java library to allow larger numbers for our account balances (wishful thinking). Both applets use many of the concepts covered in this chapter including the `OR` operator, nested `if` and `switch` statements, and the `for` loop. Each defines several classes, but also makes use of predefined class types from the Java library.

Figure 4.1 The BigAtmScreen applet

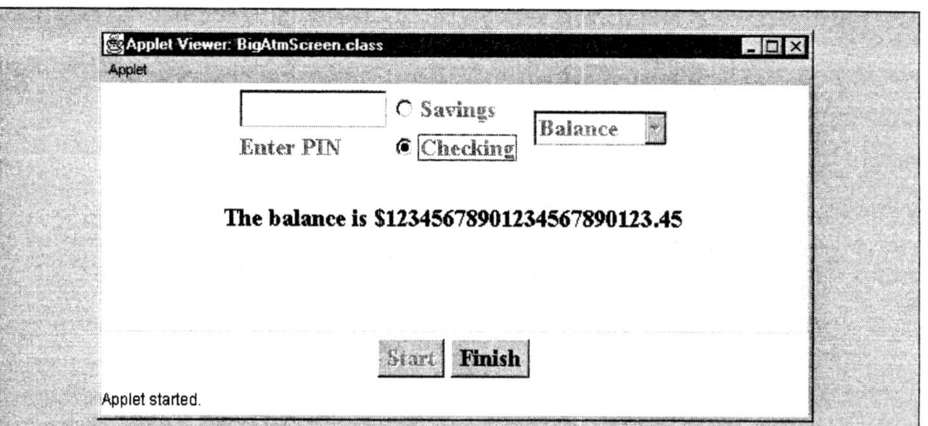

OBJECTIVES:

- Learn useful selection and repetition statements.
- Use additional primitive types and operators.
- Use the Math library.
- Build software using an iterative development cycle.

4.1 Conditional AND, Conditional OR, and Logical Complement

The Java conditional operators express the familiar `and`, and `or` operations, which we can use to write conditions such as

John's age is greater than 20 **and** John's age is less than 35.
John's height is greater than 78.5 **or** John's weight is greater than 300.

Figure 4.2 shows the Java symbols for the conditional operators.

Figure 4.2 Conditional Operators

Symbol	Meaning	Example
&&	conditional AND	(age > 20) && (age < 35)
||	conditional OR	(height > 78.5) || (weight > 300)

Note that the operands of the conditional operators have type `boolean`. The expression `age > 20` is either `true` or `false`, and so is `age < 35`.

TIP

The `&&` and `||` operators use two-character symbols which must be typed without any space between them. Using `& &` instead of `&&` would give an error.

Conditional AND

The `conditional AND` expression `(age > 20) && (age < 35)` will be `true` only when both of its operands are `true`, and `false` otherwise. If the variable `age` has the value `25`, then both operands are `true` and the whole `&&` expression is `true`, but if `age` has the value `17`, then the first operand, `age > 20` is `false`, and the whole `&&` expression is `false`. Note that when the first operand is `false`, as it is when `age` is `17`, we know that the `conditional AND` is `false` without even checking the value of the second operand. Figure 4.3 shows some sample evaluations of a `conditional AND` expression, illustrating how the value of an `&&` expression depends upon the values of its arguments.

Figure 4.3 Evaluating an example of a conditional AND expression

Age	age > 20	age < 35	age > 20 && age < 35
10	false	true	false
25	true	true	true
40	true	false	false

In general, Figure 4.4 shows how the value of a `conditional AND` expression, `A && B`, depends on the value of its operands, `A` and `B`.

Figure 4.4 Evaluating a `conditional AND` expression

A	B	A && B
True	true	true
True	false	false
False	(don't care)	false

Both `A` and `B` must be `true` in order for `A && B` to be `true`. If `A` is `false`, then Java knows that `A && B` is `false` without even evaluating `B`. Thus when `A` is `false`, Java does not bother to evaluate `B`, so we do not care what the value of `B` is. We say that Java short-circuits the evaluation by not evaluating the second argument when it already knows the value of the expression.*

Conditional OR

The `conditional OR` expression `(height > 78.5) || (weight > 300)` is `true` if either one of its operands is `true`, or if both are `true`. If `height` has the value `72` and weight has the value `310`, then the first operand is `false` and the second operand is `true`, so the `||` expression is `true`. Figure 4.5 shows some sample evaluations of a `conditional OR` expression, illustrating how the value of an `||` expression depends upon the values of its arguments.

Figure 4.5 Evaluating an example of a `conditional OR` expression

Height	weight	height > 78.5	weight > 300	(height>78.5) || (weight>300)
62	125	false	false	false
80	250	true	false	true
72	310	false	true	true
80	325	true	true	true

In general, Figure 4.6 shows how the value of a `conditional OR` expression, `A || B`, depends on the value of its operands, `A` and `B`.

Either `A` or `B`, or both, must be `true` in order for `A || B` to be `true`. If `A` is `true`, then Java knows that `A || B` is `true` without even evaluating `B`. Thus when `A` is true,

* This short-circuiting behavior is the reason why this operator is called the `conditional AND`, not simply `AND`. It evaluates the second argument on the condition that the first is true.

Figure 4.6 Evaluating a `conditional OR` expression

A	B	A || B
True	(don't care)	true
False	true	true
false	false	false

Java does not bother to evaluate `B`, so we do not care what the value of `B` is. As with the `conditional AND` operator, Java short-circuits the evaluation by not evaluating the second argument when it already knows the value of the expression.

Logical Complement

Java uses the symbol `!` for the `logical complement`, or `NOT`, operator, which has only one operand. The `logical complement` negates the value of its operand, as Figure 4.7 shows.

Figure 4.7 Evaluating a `logical complement` expression

A	!A
True	false
False	true

If the `boolean` variable, `on`, has the value `true`, then `!on` is `false`, but if `on` is `false`, then `!on` is true. Example 4.1 allows the user to enter different values of `height` and `weight` and displays the value of `conditional AND`, `conditional OR`, and `logical complement` expressions.

EXAMPLE 4.1 Measure.java

```
/*  Evaluates AND, OR, and NOT expressions
 *  involving height and weight measurements.
 */

import javax.swing.*;

public class Measure {
  public static void main(String [] args) {
    double height, weight;
    String input = JOptionPane.showInputDialog
                     ("Enter a height in inches");                 // Note 1
    height = Double.parseDouble(input);
    input = JOptionPane.showInputDialog
                      ("Enter a weight in pounds");
```

```
    weight = Double.parseDouble(input);
    System.out.print("height < 65 && weight < 130 is ");            // Note 2
    System.out.println((height < 65) && (weight  < 130));
    System.out.print("height < 65 || weight  < 130 is ");
    System.out.println((height < 65) || (weight  < 130));
    boolean heavy = (weight > 250);                                  // Note 3
    System.out.println("heavy is " + heavy);
    System.out.println("!heavy is " + !heavy);
  }
}
```

First Run

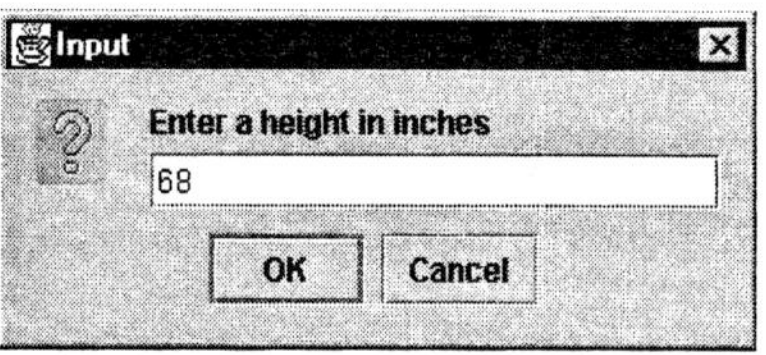

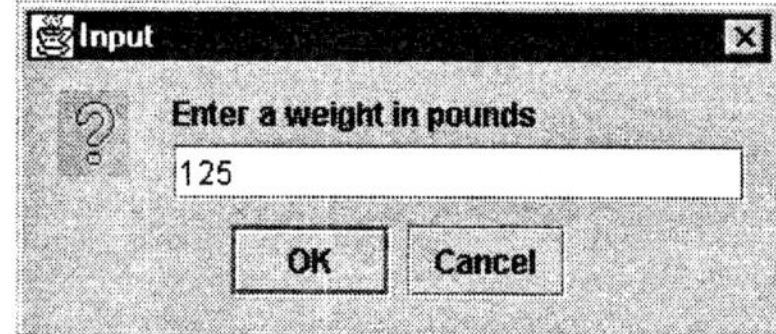


```
height < 65 && weight < 130 is false
height < 65 || weight < 130 is true
heavy is false
!heavy is true
```

Second Run

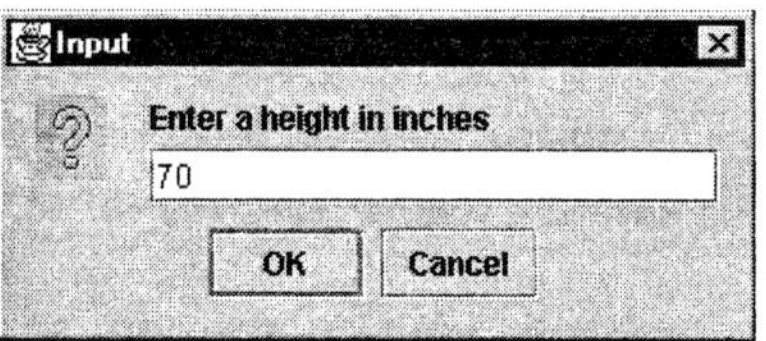

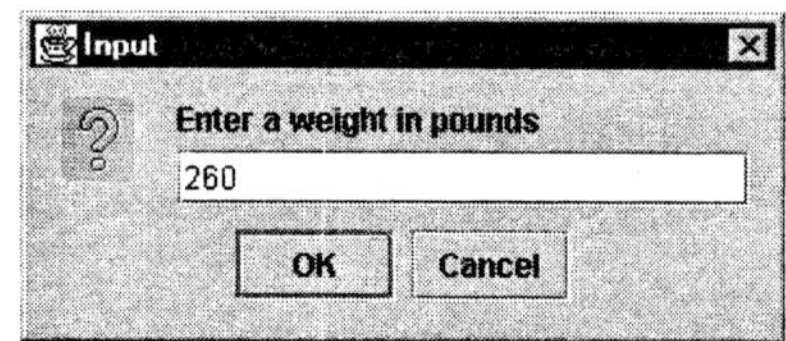


```
height < 65 && weight < 130 is false
height < 65 || weight < 130 is false
heavy is true
!heavy is false
```

Note 1: We can enter a decimal number such as 62.5 or an integer such as 68,which Java will convert to a `double`.

Note 2: This statement displays the description of the expression, while the next statement displays the value of the expression.

Note 3: The variable `heavy` holds the value of the condition, `weight > 250`. This is often how we use the `NOT` operator. We call these conditions **flags** meaning that they send a signal. In this example, the flag `heavy` signals that the weight is over 250.

Operator Precedence

The `conditional AND` and `conditional OR` operators have lower precedence than the relational and equality operators, as shown in Figure 4.8 where we show operators of equal precedence on the same line.

Figure 4.8 Operator precedence*

```
Highest
    NOT                 !
    multiplicative      * / %
    additive            + -
    relational          < > <= >=
    equality            == !=
    conditional AND     &&
    conditional OR      ||
    assignment          = += -= *= /= %=
Lowest
```

* See Appendix C for the complete operator precedence table.

Remember that Java follows precedence rules in evaluating expressions, with the higher precedence operators getting their arguments first. In the expression

```
(age > 20) && (age < 35),
```

we can omit the parentheses, writing it as

```
age > 20  && age < 35
```

The < and > operators have higher precedence than the `&&` operator, so Java will first evaluate `age > 20`. If `age > 20` is `false`, Java will short circuit the evaluation knowing that the result of the `&&` operation must be `false`. If `age > 20` is `true`, then Java will evaluate `age < 35` to determine the value of the `&&` expression.

Similarly, we can omit the parentheses in

```
height > 78.5) || (weight > 300)
```

writing it as

```
height > 78.5 || weight > 300
```

The operator > has higher precedence than `||` so Java will evaluate `height > 78.5` first. If `height > 78.5`, then the result of the `OR` operation, ||, will be `true`, and Java will short circuit the evaluation. If `height > 78.5` is `false`, then Java will evaluate `weight > 300` to determine the value of the `||` expression.

The logical complement operator has higher precedence than the arithmetic, relational, equality, and conditional operators. We must include parentheses in the expression

```
!(x < 10)
```

because we want Java to evaluate the relational expression `x < 10`, and then apply the `NOT` operator, `!`. If we write

```
!x < 10
```

then, because `!` has higher precedence than `<`, Java will try to evaluate `!x` which will give an error, since the variable `x` is an integer, and `NOT` operates on `boolean` values, not integers.

Style

Use parentheses, even when not necessary, if they help to make the steps in the evaluation of the expression clearer, but omit them if they add too much clutter, making the expression harder to read. In Example 4.1, we chose to include the parenthesis for clarity.

To show the use of the `conditional AND` in a program, we modify Example 3.6, which computes the sum of test scores, to add only those scores between zero and 100.

EXAMPLE 4.2 Zero100.java

```
/*  Computes the sum of test scores between
 *  zero and 100.  The program adds scores from 0 to 100
 *  to the total, and terminates, displaying the total,
 *  when a score outside that range is entered.
 */

import javax.swing.*;

public class Zero100  {
  private int total = 0;

  public boolean addValidScore() {                          // Note 1
    String input = JOptionPane.showInputDialog
                          ("Enter the score, -1 to quit");
    int score = Integer.parseInt(input);
    if (score >= 0 && score <= 100){                        // Note 2
      total += score;
      return true;
    }
    else
      return false;
  }
  public int getTotal() {
    return total;
  }
  public static void main(String [] args) {
    Zero100 test = new Zero100();
    while (test.addValidScore());                           // Note 3
```

```
    JOptionPane.showMessageDialog
                (null,"The total is " + test.getTotal());
    System.exit(0);
  }
}
```

Input

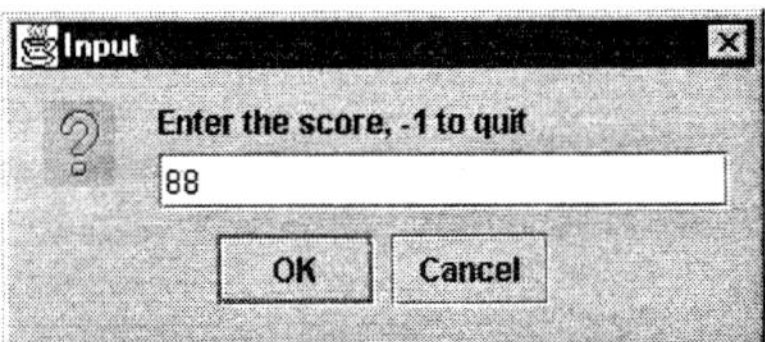

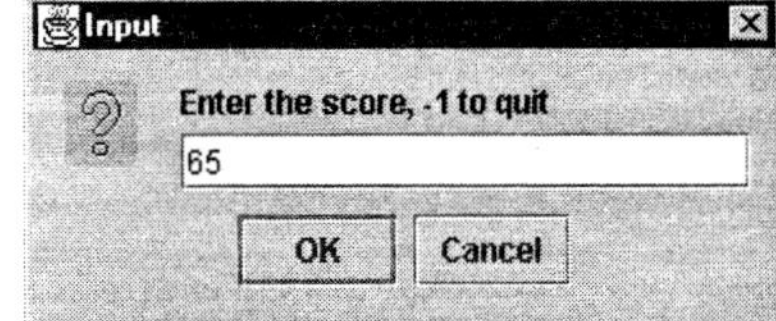

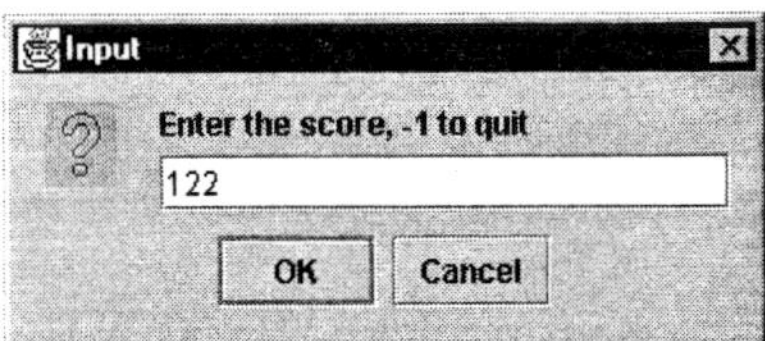

Output

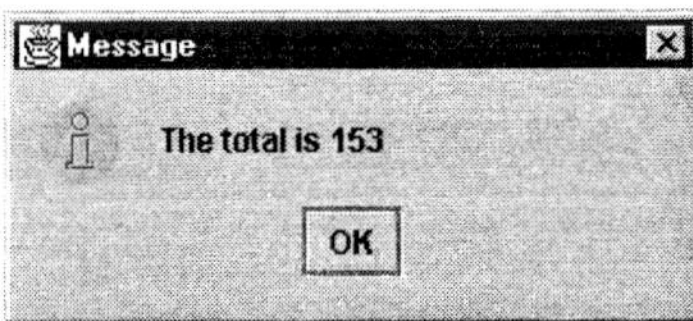

Note 1: The `addValidScore` method gets a score from the user. It returns `true` if that score is between 0 and 100 and `false` otherwise. It adds valid scores to the total.

Note 2: We check that the score is between zero and 100 before adding it to the total. We omit the parentheses in the `&&` expression, since, in addition to the necessary parentheses enclosing the if-test, they would add too much clutter.

Note 3: This `while` loop has an empty body. The `addValidScore` method that we use for the test also adds a valid score to the total. When the user enters a score less than 0 or greater than 100, the loop terminates.

TIP

Using an `OR` instead of an `AND` in Example 4.2 would not give the desired result . The expression `(score >= 0)||(score <= 100)` is true whenever either the score is greater than zero or less than 100, so that any score makes it true.

Combining AND with OR

We can use both the `&&` and `||` operators in the same expression,as in:

```
age > 50 && (height > 78.5 || height < 60)
```

where we need the parentheses since the AND operator has higher precedence than the OR operator. Without parentheses, as in:

```
age > 50 && height > 78.5 || height < 60
```

Java will evaluate the expression as if we had written it as:

```
(age > 50 && height > 78.5) || height < 60
```

which is not what we intended.

THE BIG PICTURE

The &&, ||, and ! operators allow us to use logical expressions in our programs. Conditional AND and OR short-circuit, only evaluating their second argument when necessary to determine the value of the expression.

TEST YOUR UNDERSTANDING

1. For each expression, find values for `x` and `y` that make it `true`.

   a. `(x == 2) && (y > 4)` b. `(x <= 5) || (y >= 5)`

   c. `x > 10 || y != 5` d. `x > 10  &&  y < x + 4`

2. For each expression in question 1, find values for `x` and `y` that make it `false`.
3. For each expression in question 1, find values for `x` that allow Java to short-circuit the evaluation and not evaluate the right-hand argument. What is the value of the conditional expression?
4. For each expression in question 1, find values for `x` that require Java to evaluate the right-hand argument.
5. For each expression, find a value for `x` that makes it `true`.

   a. `!(x == 5)` b. `! (x <= 10)c.!(x > 10 && x < 50)`

   d. `!(x == 5 || x > 8)`

6. For each expression in question 5, find a value for `x` that makes it `false`.
7. Omit any unnecessary parentheses from the following expressions.

   a. `((a > 1) || (c == 5))` b. `((x < (y+5)) && (y > 2))`

   c. `!((x >2)||(y != 8))`

4.2 Nested Ifs and the Switch Statement

With the `if-else` statement, we can choose between two alternatives. In this section we show two ways to choose between multiple alternatives, nested `if` statements and the `switch` statement.

Nested If Statements

Suppose we grade test scores 60–79 C, 80–89 B, and 90–100 A. Given a test score between 60 and 100, we can determine the grade by first checking if the score is between 60–79 or higher, using the `if-else` statement of Figure 4.9.

Figure 4.9 `If-else` statement to choose between two alternatives

```
if (score >= 60 && score < 80)
  System.out.println("Score " + score + " receives a C");
else
  System.out.println("Score " + score + " receives a B or an A");
```

This `if-else` statement only chooses between the two alternatives, grades C and B or better. To choose between the three alternatives, grades A, B, or C, we nest another `if-else` statement as the body of the else-part of our original `if-else` statement.

Figure 4.10 Nested `if-else` statement to choose among three alternatives

```
if (score >= 60 && score < 80)
  System.out.println("Score " + score + " receives a C");
else if (score >=80 && score < 90)
  System.out.println("Score " + score + " receives a B");
else
  System.out.println("Score " + score + "receives an A");
```

The code in Figure 4.10 has a problem. If we assume that score is always between 60 and 100 then the code does what we expect, but let's trace the code if the score has a value of 40. Then the first test, `score >=60 && score < 80`, fails, so we execute the `else-part` which is a nested `if-else` statement. Its condition, `score >= 80 && score < 90`, also fails, so we execute the `else-part` which indicates that a score of 40 receives an A grade, not what we expect.

We can improve the code of Figure 4.10, by nesting an `if` statement, in the last `else`, to check that score is really between 90 and 100, as shown in Figure 4.11.

Figure 4.11 Improved version of Figure 4.10

```
if (score >= 60 && score < 80)
  System.out.println("Score " + score + " receives a C");
else if (score >=80 && score < 90)
  System.out.println("Score " + score + " receives a B");
else if (score >= 90 && score <= 100)
  System.out.println("Score " + score + "receives an A");
```

We see that using nested `if-else` statements allow us, in this example, to choose among three alternatives:

scores between 60 and 79
scores between 80 and 89
scores between 90 and 100

Style

Figure 4.11 illustrates the style for nested `if-else` statements to choose from multiple alternatives. The general pattern is

```
if ( Is it the first alternative? ){
  First alternative code
}
else if ( Is it the second alternative? ) {
  Second alternative code
}
  ...
else if ( Is it the last alternative? ) {
  Last alternative code
}
```

We could add an optional last line to execute when none of the alternatives is true

```
else {
  Code when none of the above alternatives is true
}
```

Figure 4.12 shows the flow chart for the nested `if-else` statement with the optional `else` part at the end.

TIP

If you use code like Figure 4.10, having a final `else` with no nested `if`, then be sure that the code in the final `else` does handle everything else, that is, every case that does not come under one of the tested alternatives in the preceding `if` statements.

Pairing Else with If

Without an additional rule, we cannot always determine how to read nested `if` statements. For example, contrast Figure 4.13 with Figure 4.14. In Figure 4.13, we would like to pair `else` with the first `if`, but in Figure 4.14, we would like to pair the `else` with the second `if`. Unfortunately aligning the `else` under the first `if` in Figure 4.13 will not achieve the outcome we want. As we know, Java does not consider spacing significant, so both examples will produce the same result. Java uses the rule that pairs an `else` with the nearest `if`. Figure 4.14 is the correct version, and would be correct even if we type the `else` under the first `if`, as in Figure 4.13.

Figure 4.12 Flow chart for nested `if-else` statements

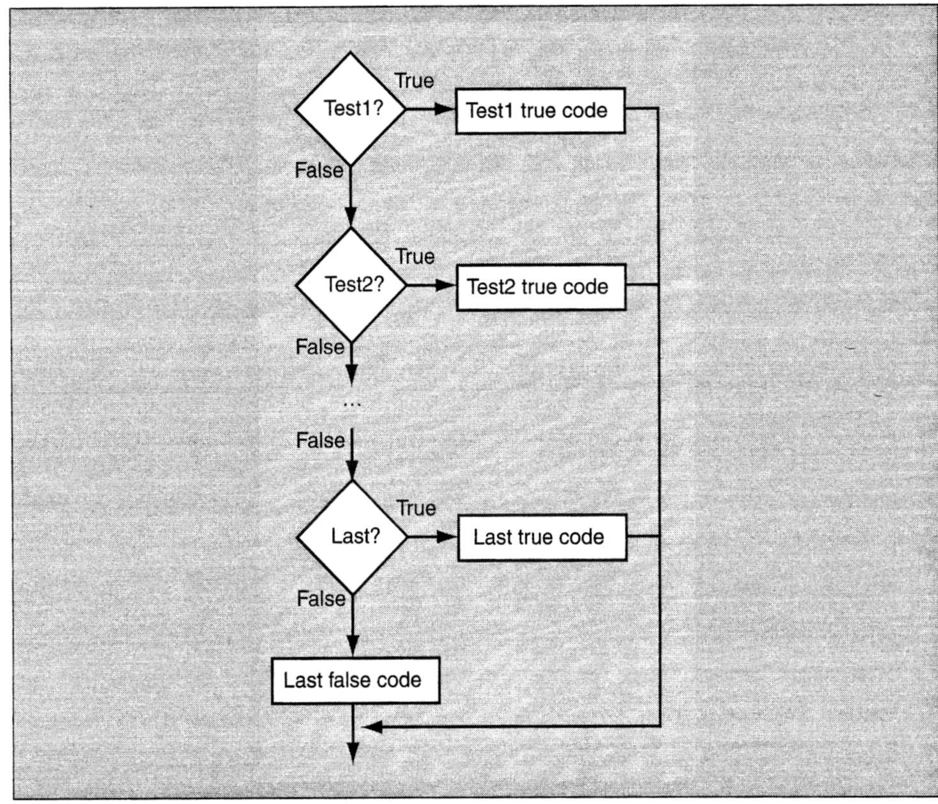

Figure 4.13 Incorrect attempt to pair an `else` with an `if`

```
if (score >= 60)
  if (score >= 80)
    System.out.println("You got a B or an A");
else
  System.out.println("You got a D or an F");  // Wrong pairing
```

Figure 4.14 Corrected pairing of `else` and `if`

```
if (score >= 60)
  if (score >= 80)
    System.out.println("You got a B or an A");
  else
    System.out.println("You got a C");    // Correct pairing
```

Both Figures 4.13 and 4.14 are `if` statements with nested `if-else` statements. What we tried to do in Figure 4.13, was to write an `if-else` statement whose `if-part` contained a nested `if` statement. To do that, we need to enclose the nested `if` statement in braces, as in Figure 4.15.

Figure 4.15 Figure 4.13 rewritten as an `if-else` with nested `if`

```
if (score >= 60) {
  if (score >= 80)
    System.out.println("You got a B or an A");
}
else
  System.out.println("You got a D or an F");  // Paired to first 'if'
```

TIP

Remember the Rule:

> Pair an `else` with the nearest preceding `if`

Trace each branch of nested `if` statements, checking carefully which values of the data will cause execution to flow to that branch.

Example 4.3 uses nested `if-else` statements to assign letter grades to test scores. The `Score` class keeps the last score entered. It has responsibilities to get a valid score (between 0 and 100) and to return a letter grade for that score.

EXAMPLE 4.3 Score.java

```
/*  Uses nested if-else statements
 *  to choose among alternatives
 *  to assign letter grades to test scores.
 */

import javax.swing.*;

public class Score {
  int score;

  public boolean getValidScore() {
    String input = JOptionPane.showInputDialog
                          ("Enter a score (0-100)");
    int temp = Integer.parseInt(input);
    if (temp >= 0 && temp <= 100){
      score = temp;
      return true;
    }
    else
      return false;
  }
  public String letterGrade() {
    String grade = "";
    if (score < 50)                                          // Note 1
      grade =  "F";
```

```
    else if (score >= 50 && score < 60)
      grade =  "D";
    else if (score >= 60 && score < 80)
      grade =  "C";
    else if (score >=80 && score < 90)
      grade =  "B";
    else if (score >= 90 && score <= 100)
      grade =  "A";
    return grade;
  }
  public static void main(String [] args) {
    Score s = new Score();
    String message = "Score is not valid";                    // Note 2
    if (s.getValidScore())
       message = "Grade: " + s.letterGrade();
    JOptionPane.showMessageDialog(null, message);
    System.exit(0);
  }
}
```

First Run

Input

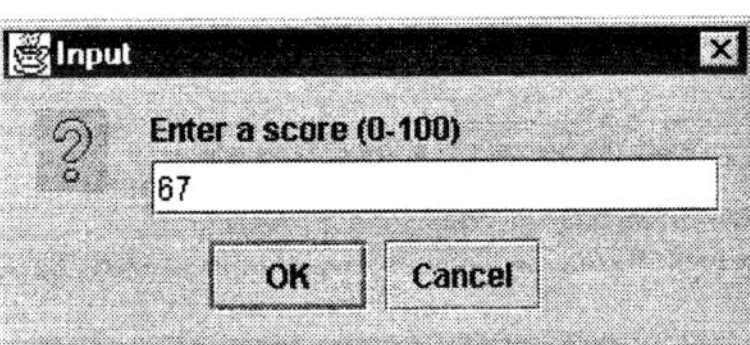

Output

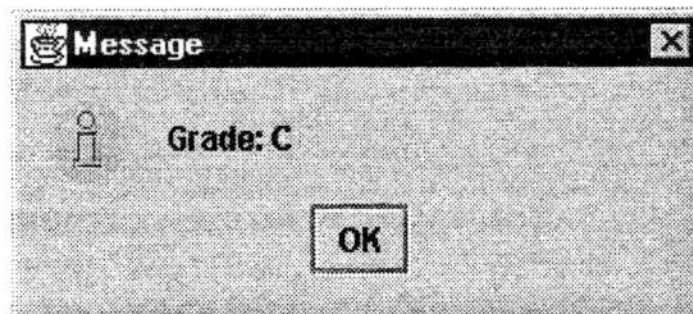

Second Run

Input

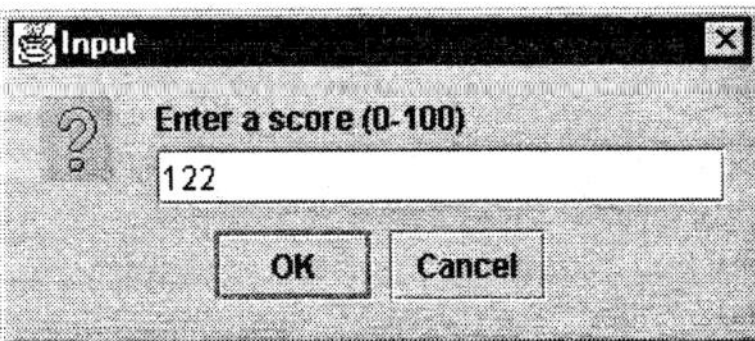

Output

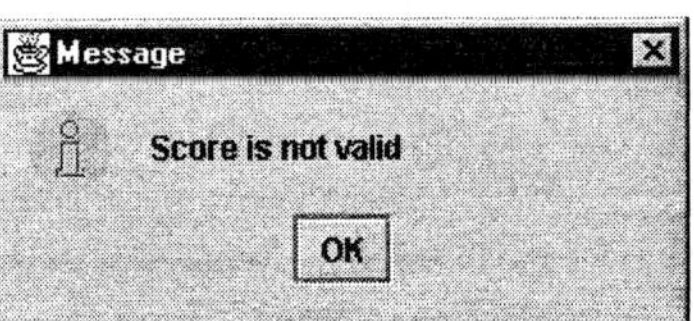

Note 1: We extend the `if-else` statement from Figure 4.11 to interpret all test score values. We choose among five alternatives. Because we have already checked that the score is valid we do not need a final `else` alternative to handle invalid scores.

Note 2: If the score is valid we will change this message to output the grade. This message displays when the user enters an invalid score.

TIP Be sure to test each alternative of nested `if-else` statements. For Example 4.3, we would need to test the A, B, D, and F alternatives.

The Switch Statement

Choosing among six alternatives is stretching the use of nested `if-else` statements. The efficiency of this construction declines as we add more alternatives. For example, to interpret a score of 98, Example 4.3 tests five conditions, the first four of which fail. The **switch** statement allows us to check a large number of alternatives more efficiently.

A `switch` statement chooses alternatives based upon the value of a variable. In this section we use an `int` variable in our `switch` statement. In Section 4.4 we introduce character variables which may also be used to indicate choices in a `switch` statement.

The `switch` statement has the form

```
switch (test_expression)  {
  case expression1:
                      statement1;
  case expression2:
                      statement2;
                .....
  default:
                      default_statement;
}
```

We can use a `switch` statement to replace the nested `if-else` statements of Example 4.3. Computing `score/10` will give a number from zero to ten since each score is between 0 and 100. For example `87/10` is `8`, and `35/10` is `3`. We can assign `score/10` to a variable `mark` as in:

```
int mark = score/10
```

and use `mark` in the switch statement of Figure 4.16 to determine the grade for that score.

In Figure 4.16, Java evaluates the variable `mark`, jumping directly to one of twelve cases depending upon the value of `mark`. We specify each case with a case label such as `case 5:` which is made up of the word `case` followed by the number `5`, followed by a colon. The label marks the place in the code to jump to when the switch variable value matches that case label. If `mark` is `5`, Java executes the code following the label, `case 5:`, which displays the grade of `D`; the **break** statement then causes a jump out of the `switch` statement, to the code following the closing brace, `}`.

If `mark` is `10`, then Java jumps to the code at the label, `case 10:`, which displays an `A` and breaks to the end of the `switch`. If `mark` is any integer other than 0 through 10, then Java jumps to the **default** case and displays an error message. The `default` case is

Figure 4.16 An example of a `switch` statement

```
switch(mark) {
  case 0:
  case 1:
  case 2:
  case 3:
  case 4:  System.out.println("F");
           break;
  case 5:  System.out.println("D");
           break;
  case 6:
  case 7:  System.out.println("C");
           break;
  case 8:  System.out.println("B");
           break;
  case 9:
  case 10: System.out.println("A");
           break;
  default: System.out.println("Incorrect score");
}
```

optional. Had we omitted the `default` case in Figure 4.13, then Java would simply do nothing if the variable `mark` had any value other than 0 through 10. Note that several labels can refer to the same code, as for example `case 6` and `case 7` which both label the statement that displays a `C`.

We usually want to include the `break` statement after each `case`; without it the code "falls through" to the code for the next case. Without the `break` statement to end case 7, when `mark` has the value `7`, Java would first display a `C`, and then continue on to the code for case 8, displaying a `B` before breaking to the end of the `switch`.

Example 4.4 illustrates a good use for `switch` statements which is to provide a menu to input choices from the user. We convert our programs from Examples 3.6 and 3.7 to methods to use as two of the menu choices. Since we did not use named packages for these classes, we need to copy `ScoreSum.class` and `Max.class` to the current directory to be part of the default package for Example 4.4

EXAMPLE 4.4 UserMenu.java

```
/*  Uses a switch statement to input a user's selection of
 *  an alternative. Uses code from Examples 3.6 and 3.7.
 */

import javax.swing.*;
import java.text.*;

public class UserMenu {
  public void sum() {                                    // Note 1
    ScoreSum scorer = new ScoreSum();
```

```
    int score = scorer.getScore();
    while (score >= 0) {
      scorer.addScore(score);
      score = scorer.getScore();
    }
    JOptionPane.showMessageDialog
            (null, "The total is " + scorer.getTotal());
  }
  public void max() {                                          // Note 2
    Max max = new Max();
    double price = max.getPrice();
    while (price >=0 ) {
      max.updateMax(price);
      price = max.getPrice();
    }
    NumberFormat nf = NumberFormat.getCurrencyInstance();
    JOptionPane.showMessageDialog
          (null, "The maximum is " + nf.format(max.getMax()));
  }
  public static void main(String [] args) {
    UserMenu menu = new UserMenu();
    String input = JOptionPane.showInputDialog
                 ("Choose: 1-Sum, 2-Max, 3-To Do, or 4-Quit");
    int choice = Integer.parseInt(input);
    while (choice != 4) {
      switch (choice) {                                        // Note 3
              case 1:
                  menu.sum();                                  // Note 4
                  break;                                       // Note 5
              case 2:
                  menu.max();
                  break;
              case 3:
                  JOptionPane.showMessageDialog
                            (null, "Fill in code here");       // Note 6
                  break;                                       // Note 7
      }                                                        // Note 8
      input = JOptionPane.showInputDialog
                 ("Choose: 1-Sum, 2-Max, 3 To Do, or 4-Quit");
      choice = Integer.parseInt(input);
    }
    System.exit(0);
  }
}
```

Run

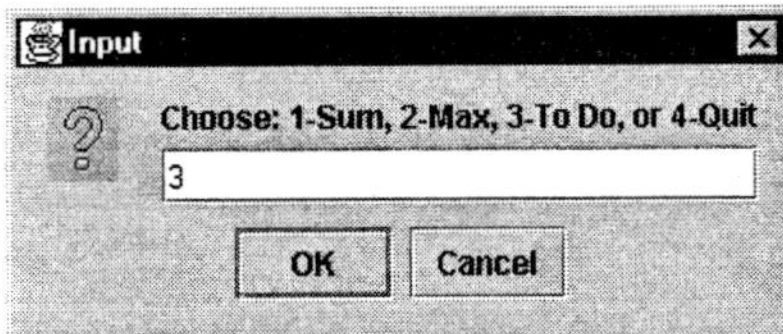

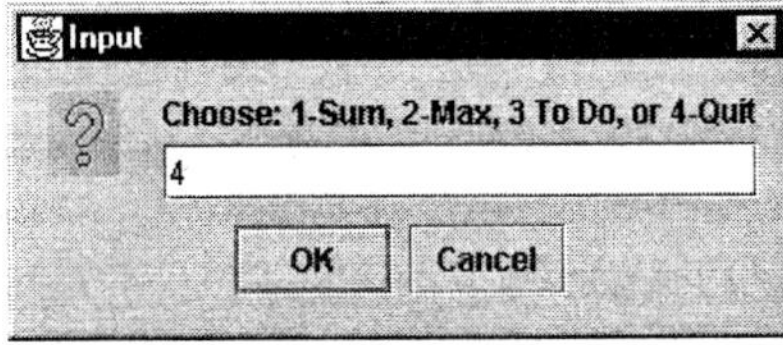

Note 1: This is the code from Example 3.6 to sum test scores entered by the user. We put it in a method, `sum`, to call if the user selects choice 1. We copy `ScoreSum.class` to the current directory to make it accessible in the default package.

Note 2: This is the code from Example 3.7 to find the maximum of the values input by the user. We put it in a method, `max`, to call if the user selects choice 2. We copy `Max.class` to the current directory to make it accessible in the default package.

Note 3: If `choice` has the value one, two, or three, then the `switch` jumps to the code for that case. For a choice of four, the `while` condition fails, and the program finishes without executing the `switch` statement. If `choice` has any other value, then the `switch` does nothing, and execution continues after the `switch` by reading the user's next choice.

Note 4: If `choice` has the value one, then we call the `sum` method to add test scores. We can execute any Java statements, including `if-else` and `while` statements as well as method calls, after a `case` label.

Note 5: This `break` statement causes execution to jump to the end of the `switch` statement, so that the next statement will be the call to print the menu.

Note 6: `JOptionPane.showMessageDialog (null, "Fill in code here");`
We have not really specified what to do if the user selects 3. We want to get the whole program working without adding any more code for additional choices. This illustrates a principle of program design, to solve the problem in stages, getting one stage right before going on to the next. We build a good framework, and can fill in the details later.

Note 7: `break;`
Even though we do not really need a `break` statement here since this is the end of the `switch`, we include it in case we add more alternatives later, and might forget to add the `break` statement here.

Note 8: We do not need a `default` case in this example. If the user enters any value but one, two, three, or four, then the `switch` does nothing, the menu prints again, and Java asks the user for another choice. This is just what we want to happen, so there is no need for a `default` case.

THE BIG PICTURE

Nested `if` statements work for a choice among a few alternatives. With the `switch` statement we can choose among many. `switch` statements can implement a menu of choices.

TEST YOUR UNDERSTANDING

8. A charity designates donors who give more than $1,000 as Benefactors, those who give $500-$999 as Patrons, and those who give $100-$499 as Supporters. Write a nested `if-else` statement that, given the amount of a contribution, outputs the correct designation for that contributor.

9. Write a nested `if-else` statement that includes the categories from question 8 and identifies donors of $1-99 as Contributors.

10. What value will the variable `x` have after executing

```
x = 6;
if (k < 10)
  if (k < 5)
    x = 7;
  else
    x = 8;
```

if `k` has the value

a. `9` b. `3` c. `11` d. `-2`

11. What value will the variable `x` have after executing

```
x = 6;
if (k < 10)
  if (k < 5)
    x = 7;
else
    x = 8;
```

if `k` has the value

a. 9 b. 3 c. 11 d. -2

12. What value will the variable `x` have after executing

```
x = 6;
if (k < 10)  {
  if (k < 5)
    x = 7;
}
else
    x = 8;
```

if `k` has the value

a. 9 b. 3 c. 11 d. -2

13. What value will the variable `x` have after executing

```
x = 5;
switch(k) {
  case 2:
  case 3:    x = 6;
             break;
  case 5:    x = 7;
             break;
  case 9:    x = 8;
             break;
  default:   x = 9;
}
```

if `k` has the value

a. 1 b. 3 c. 5 d. 6 e. 9 f. -5 g. 10

14. Answer question 13 for the code

```
x = 5;
switch(k) {
  case 2:
  case 3:    x = 6;
  case 5:    x = 7;
  case 9:    x = 8;
  default:   x = 9;
}
```

15. Answer question 13 for the code

```
x = 5;
switch(k) {
  case 2:
  case 3:      x = 6;
  case 6:      x = 7;
               break;
  case 9:      x = 8;
  default:     x = 9;
}
```

16. Answer question 13 for the code

```
x = 5;
switch(k) {
  case 2:
  case 3:    x = 6;
             break;
  case 5:    x = 7;
             break;
  case 9:    x = 8;
             break;
}
```

4.3 The For and Do-While Loops

In this section we introduce the **for** statement, which makes it easy to repeat a block of code a fixed number of times, and the **do-while** statement, which is like the `while` statement, with the difference that it tests the condition after executing a block of code, rather than before. These new statements help us to write programs requiring repetition.

The For Statement

We use a `for` statement when we know the number of repetitions. Technically we could use a `while` statement instead of a `for` statement in these cases, but it is much more convenient to say

```
Do this calculation 10 times.
```

than it is to write

```
Declare and initialize a count variable to zero.
while (count < 10) {
    doSomething;
    count ++;
}
```

The `for` statement performs the same steps but packages them more conveniently, following the pattern

```
for (initialize; test; update)
    for_statement
```

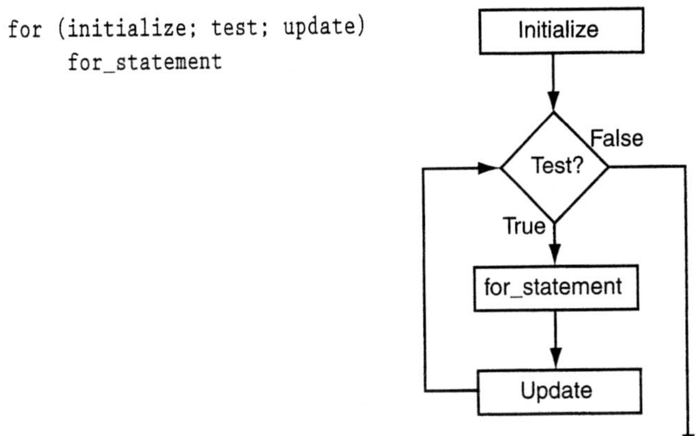

where the `for_statement` can be a simple statement or a block. The code in Figure 4.17 uses a `for` statement to add the numbers from one to four. The `initialize` part declares and initializes a variable, i, called the index or

Figure 4.17 A `for` statement for the sum 1+2+3+4

```
int sum = 0;
for (int i = 1; i <= 4; i++)
  sum += i;
```

counter, which will count the repetitions. The `test` expression, i <= 4, checks if we need more repetitions. Java will execute the statement, sum += i, of the for loop body, if the test condition is true, in this case if the count, i, is less than or equal to four. The loop terminates when the `test` condition becomes false, in this case, when i is greater than four. The `update` expression, i++ in this example, increments the count, i, by one. Java executes the `update` expression, after executing the for loop body. Figure 4.18 traces the execution of the `for` loop of Figure 4.17.

Figure 4.18 Trace of execution of the `for` loop of Figure 4.17

```
initialize      i = 1
test            1 <= 4 is true
execute body    sum += 1            (result:  sum = 0 + 1 = 1)
update          i++                 (result:  i = 2)
test            2 <= 4 is true
execute body    sum += 2            (result:  sum = 1 + 2 = 3)
update          i++                 (result:  i = 3)
test            3 <= 4 is true
execute body    sum += 3            (result:  sum = 3 + 3 = 6)
update          i++                 (result:  i = 4)
test            4 <= 4 is true
execute body    sum += 4            (result:  sum = 6 + 4 = 10)
update          i++                 (result:  i = 5)
test            5 <= 4 is false
```

The `update` expression can be more general than the increment in Figure 4.17. In Figure 4.19, we find the sum of the positive odd numbers less than 10.

Figure 4.19 A `for` statement for the sum 1+3+5+7+9

```
int sum = 0;
for (int i = 1; i < 10; i += 2)
  sum += i;
```

In each iteration, we add two to the index variable, `i`, which gets the values 1, 3, 5, 7, and 9, each of which is added to `sum`, whose final value is `25`.

Normally the index variable increases at each iteration, as in the code of Figures 4.17 and 4.19, but we can initialize the index to its highest value and decrement it at each iteration, as in Figure 4.20 which also computes the sum of the first four positive integers.

Figure 4.20 A `for` statement for the sum 4+3+2+1

```
int sum = 0;
for (int i = 4; i >= 1; i--)
  sum += i;
```

Now that we have seen how to write a `for` statement, we will use it in Example 4.5. We find how much our money will grow in a bank account if earning interest at a certain rate over a specified time period, assuming that interest is compounded yearly (At the end of the year the interest due for that year is added to the principal).

To develop a solution, let us start with a simple case, $1000 at 5% for three years. For each year, we have to find the interest earned and add it to the account balance, as the following table shows.

Year	Interest	New Balance
1	1000 * .05 = 50	1000 + 50 = 1050
2	1050 * .05 = 52.50	1050 + 52.50 = 1102.50
3	1102.50 * .05 = 55.13	1102.50 + 55.13 = 1157.63

From this example, we see that each year we find the interest and add it to the balance to get the new balance. We will put these two steps in the body of our `for` statement.

String Tokenizer

In Example 4.5 the user will input three items, the interest rate, the initial amount of money on deposit, and the number of years. Rather than using three input dialogs, we would like to have the user enter all three items in one dialog, separated by spaces, as for example

```
4.5  1000  10
```

The `StringTokenizer` class in the `java.util` package makes it easy to separate the line into the three individual items, called tokens. We pass the line we wish to tokenize to the constructor

```
StringTokenizer line = new StringTokenizer("4.5 1000 10");
```

and use the `nextToken` method to get the next token from the line. The first call to `line.nextToken()` will return `4.5`, the second will return `1000` and the third will return `10`.

The `Growth` class uses a constructor to initialize the rate, balance, and years. Its `futureBalance` method uses a `for` loop to compute the amount in the account at the end of the specified time period assuming interest is compounded annually at the specified rate.

EXAMPLE 4.5 **Growth.java**

```
/*
 * Input:  Rate, a double value giving the yearly percent interest rate
 *         Balance, a double value giving the amount deposited
 *         Years, an int value giving the time period for the deposit
 *
 * Output: Amount, the total amount in the account at the end of the
 *                time period.
 */

import javax.swing.*;
import java.util.*;
import java.text.*;

public class Growth {
  private double rate;             // yearly percent interest rate
  private double balance;          // amount on deposit
  private int years;               // time period of the deposit

  public Growth(double r, double b, int y) {
    rate = r;
    balance = b;
    years = y;
  }
  public double futureBalance() {
    double future = balance;
    double interest;
    for (int i = 1; i <= years; i++)  {                            // Note 1
      interest = future * rate/100;                                // Note 2
      future += interest;
    }
    return future;
  }
  public static void main(String [] args) {
    NumberFormat nf = NumberFormat.getCurrencyInstance();
    String input = JOptionPane.showInputDialog
```

```
                      ("Enter rate, balance, and years");
    StringTokenizer tokens = new StringTokenizer(input);
    Growth g = new Growth(Double.parseDouble(tokens.nextToken()),
    Double.parseDouble(tokens.nextToken()),
    Integer.parseInt(tokens.nextToken()));                    // Note 3
    JOptionPane.showMessageDialog(null,"The future balance will be "
                               + nf.format(g.futureBalance()));
    System.exit(0);
  }
}
```

Input

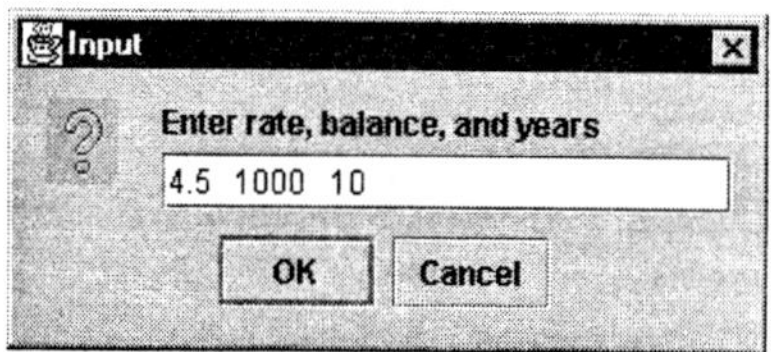

Output

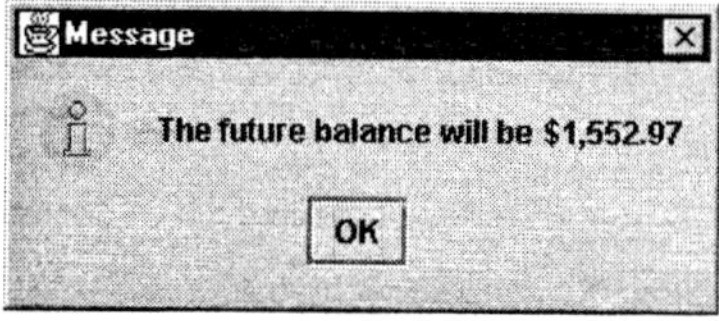

Note 1: The body of a `for` loop can be a block enclosed by curly braces, as it is here.

Note 2: Using two statements, one to calculate the interest, and one to calculate the balance, makes the steps clearer. We could have written the formula in one line as

```
balance *= (1 + rate/100);
```

The rate is input as a percent, which we divide by 100 to get the multiplier needed to compute the interest. Since rate has type `double`, Java will use floating point division to compute the quotient, converting 100 to a type `double` value.

Note 3: The `nextToken` method returns a `String`. In this example we need to convert the rate and balance to type `double`, and the years to an `int`.

A Little Extra

Declaring the index variable in the initialize part of the `for` statement, makes it visible only within the `for` loop. For example, the index variable, `i`, in Figure 4.20, can only be used within the `for` loop. Any reference to it outside of that loop would be an error.

We could declare the index variable prior to the loop, as in Figure 4.21, in which case we could use the variable, `i`, before or after the `for` loop.

Figure 4.21 Declaring an index variable before the `for` loop

```
int i;                          // declare loop index
int sum = 0;
for (i = 4; i >= 1; i--)  // initialize loop index
  sum += i;
...
i += 17;                        // use variable i
```

In most instances, we prefer to declare the index variable inside the `for` loop and use it only as an index inside the loop. Using a variable for more than one purpose can obscure the program.

The Do-While Statement

The `while` statement lets us repeat a block of code; it checks the condition before executing the loop body. In some problems, when we know we will execute the body at least once, it is more natural to check the condition after executing the body. The `do-while` statement, having the syntax shown in Figure 4.22, lets us do that. Java executes the statement, then checks the condition. If the

Figure 4.22 Syntax for the `do-while` statement

```
do
  statement
while (condition) ;
```

condition is true, Java executes the statement again, otherwise it proceeds to the next statement after the loop. The statement in the body of the `do` loop can be a simple statement, but most often it is a `block`, a group of statements enclosed in curly braces.

As a rule,

- use a `do-while` statement when the loop body will always be executed at least once.
- use a `while` statement when the loop body may (possibly) never be executed.

As an example, notice that Example 4.5 terminates after one input. Instead of rerunning the program from the operating system, suppose we add another loop to ask the user whether or not to rerun the example with different data, while we are still executing the program. Figure 4.23 shows the pseudocode for this enhancement.

Figure 4.23 Pseudocode for Example 4.5 enhancement

```
do {
  Compute balance as in Example 4.5
  Ask the user -- Repeat or Quit?
} while (User chooses to repeat);
```

EXAMPLE 4.6 DoGrowth.java

```
/*          Enhances Example 4.5 to ask if the user wants to
 *            repeat the calculation
 *
 * Input:   Rate, a double value giving the yearly percent interest rate
 *          Balance, a double value giving the amount deposited
 *          Years, an int value giving the time period for the deposit
 *          Repeat, 1 to repeat, 0 to quit
 *
 * Output:  Amount, the total amount in the account at the end of the
 *            time period.
 */

public class DoGrowth {
  public static void main(String [] args) {
    NumberFormat nf = NumberFormat.getCurrencyInstance();
    int repeat;
    do {
      String input = JOptionPane.showInputDialog
                  ("Enter rate, balance, and years");                // Note 1
      StringTokenizer tokens = new StringTokenizer(input);
      Growth g = new Growth(Double.parseDouble(tokens.nextToken()),
                            Double.parseDouble(tokens.nextToken()),
                             Integer.parseInt(tokens.nextToken()));
      JOptionPane.showMessageDialog(null,"The future balance will be "
                                     + nf.format(g.futureBalance()));
      input = JOptionPane.showInputDialog
                            ("Enter 1 to repeat, 0 to quit");        // Note 2
      repeat = Integer.parseInt(input);
    } while (repeat == 1);                                           // Note 3
    System.exit(0);
  }
}
```

Run

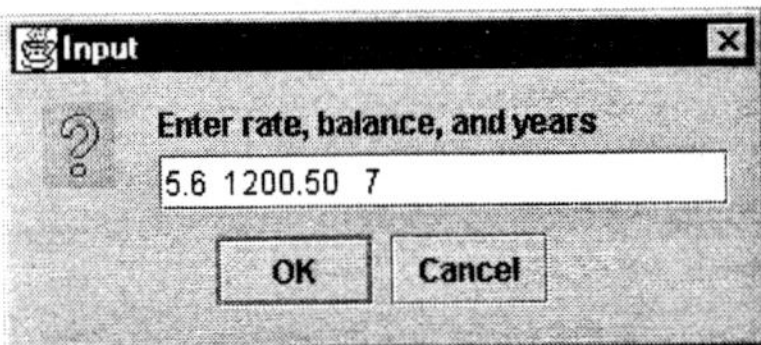

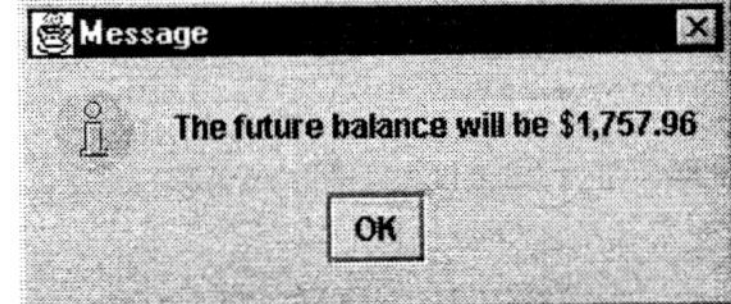

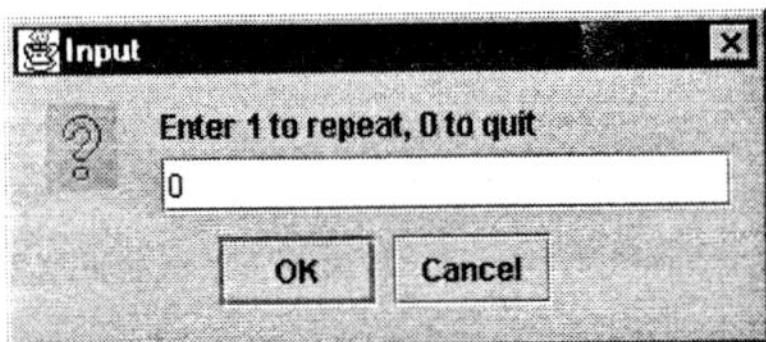

Note 1: The code starting here comes from Example 4.5. We assume that `Growth.class` is in the same directory because we did not use a named package.

Note 2: Having finished the code from Example 4.5, we ask the user whether or not to repeat the calculation.

Note 3: The `do-while` statement works very well here. We check the user's response after each execution of the calculation.

Style

In all loops, indent the body relative to the keywords.

Good

```
do {
  statements
} while (condition);
```

Bad

```
do {
statements
} while (condition);
```

THE BIG PICTURE

The `for` statement and the `do-while` statement provide useful options for repetition. The `for` statement is especially useful for a fixed number of repetitions, and the `do-while` works when we wish to test the condition after executing the loop body rather than before.

TEST YOUR UNDERSTANDING

17. Write a `for` statement which will display the numbers from one through ten.
18. Write a `for` statement which will display the numbers from seven through 12.
19. Write a `for` statement which will display the numbers from nine through three, in that order.
20. Write a `for` statement which will display the even numbers from four through twenty.
21. What value will the variable `sum` have after the execution of the following code?

```
int sum = 0;
for (int i = 0; i < 8; i++)
  sum += i;
```

22. What value will the variable `sum` have after the execution of the following code?

```
int sum = 100;
for (int i = 2; i < 6; i++)
  sum -= i;
```

23. What value will the variable `sum` have after the execution of the following code?

```
int sum = 100;
for (int i = 20; i > 16 ; i--)
  sum -= i;
```

24. What value will the variable `sum` have after the execution of the following code?

```
int sum = 0;
for (int i = 1; i <= 20 ; i += 3)
  sum -= i;
```

25. What value will the variable `sum` have after the execution of the following code?

```
int sum = 100;
for (int i = 20; i > 6 ; i -= 5)
  sum -= i;
```

26. Find the value of the variable `i` after the execution of the following code.

```
int i = 1;
int total = 0;
do {
  total += i;
  i++ ;
} while (total < 25);
```

27. Find the value of the variable `i` after the execution of the following code.

```
int i = 10;
int total =100;
do {
  total -= i;
  i += 5;
} while (total > 25);
```

28. Find the value of the variable `total` after the execution of the following code.

```
int i = 1;
int total = 10;
do {
  total += i;
  i++ ;
} while (i < 5);
```

29. Find the value of the variable `total` after the execution of the following code.

```
int i = 1;
int total = 100;
do {
  total -= i;
  i++ ;
} while (i <= 7);
```

30. Draw the flow diagram for the `do-while` statement.

4.4 Additional Primitive Types

So far we have used the `int` type for integers, the `double` type for decimal numbers, and the `boolean` type. In this section we introduce the **char** type for characters, the **long** type for long integers, and the **float** type, for decimal numbers, which uses less precision than the type `double`.

The Char Type

Java represents characters using single quotes, as in, for example, 'a,' 'A,' 'b,' 'B' for letters, '0,' '1' for numerals, '+,' '-' for operators, and '?,' ',' for punctuation. Internally, Java uses the Unicode® character set which has thousands of characters, including those needed for the world's major languages.* We will only need the ASCII (American Standard Code for Information Interchange) character set which has 128 characters. (See Appendix D for a table of the ASCII characters.) Each ASCII character has an equivalent Unicode character. Java converts from ASCII input to Unicode, and from Unicode to ASCII output; we will not need to use Unicode explicitly, since internationalizing Java is beyond the scope of this text.

We call the first thirty-two ASCII characters `control characters`; they are nonprinting, but control functions such as formatting, including `tab`, `newline`, and `return`. For example, the `enter` key and the `tab` key have no visible symbol, but they control the position of the next input. To represent these control characters, and other special characters, in our program we use the escape character, the backslash, '\.' When Java sees the backslash it escapes from its normal reading of printing characters and interprets the following character as a special character. Figure 4.24 shows some of these special characters.

---

* See http://unicode.org for more information about Unicode.

Figure 4.24 Escape sequences for special characterst

Special Character	Meaning
\n	newline, move to the start of the next line
\t	tab
\b	backspace
\r	return, move to the start of the current line
\"	double quote
\\	backslash

Double quote and backslash are printing characters, but they have special functions in Java. Normally we enclose strings within double quotes, as in `"The result is "`. Occasionally, we want to use a string that itself uses double quotes, as in

```
"Do you like the movie, \"Gone With The Wind\"? "
```

Using the backslash, in `\"`, tells Java that the double quote is part of the string and not the terminating double quote.

EXAMPLE 4.7 Special.java

```
/*  Shows the effect of the
 *  special characters.
 */

public class Special {
  public static void main(String [] args) {
    System.out.println("Use \n to go to the next line");          // Note 1
    System.out.println
          ("**************************\r back to start");          // Note 2
    System.out.println("1234\b\b5678");                           // Note 3
    System.out.println("***\t tab here");                         // Note 4
    System.out.println
            ("Do you like \"Gone With the Wind\"?");              // Note 5
    System.out.println("The directory is c:\\newstuff");          // Note 6
  }
}
```

Output

```
Use
 to go to the next line
 back to start************
125678
***      tab here
Do you like "Gone With the Wind"?
The directory is c:\newstuff
```

Note 1: The `newline`, `'\n'`, positions the next output at the start of the next line. The blank space after the `newline` shows up as the first character on the next line.

Note 2: The `return`, `'\r'`, positions the next output at the start of the current line.

Note 3: The `backspace`, `'\b'`, positions the next output one character to the left. The backspaces here position the next output to write over the preceding digits, 3 and 4.

Note 4: The `tab`, `'\t'`, positions the next input at the next tab position.

Note 5: Uses double quote inside the quoted string.

Note 6: `System.out.println("The directory is c:\\newstuff");`
We want to indicate that the directory is `c:\newstuff`. But Java treats the backslash as the escape character, so it would interpret the `'\n'` as a `newline` character. To use the backslash itself inside of a string we treat it as a special character `'\\'`.

We can declare variables of type `char`. Using `char` variables we could improve Example 4.6 to allow the user to input `Y` or `y` to repeat, and `N` or `n` to quit, instead of `1` or `0`. We leave this improvement as an exercise and will use this technique in Example 4.8.

The Long Type

The range of values for `int` variables is from `-2,147,483,648` to `2,147,483,647`. Java provides the type `long` which can represent integer values outside of this range. `long` values range from `-9,223,372,036,854,775,808` to `9,223,372,036,854,775,807`. By default, when we use a whole number such as `25` in a program, Java assumes it is an `int`. We can specify a `long` value by adding an `l` or `L` suffix, as in `25L`. We can declare variables of type `long`, but would only use `long` variables instead of `int` when we need values that the `int` type cannot handle. It takes more space to hold `long` values, and more time to process them.

To illustrate the use of the `long` type, we solve the problem suggested by a folk tale from India. In that story a young girl greatly helped a rich Rajah who was reluctant to offer her any reward. Coming from a poor village, the girl wanted to help her people, and seeing a chessboard nearby,

she asked the Rajah just to give her some grains of rice as her reward. She asked that on the first day the Rajah place one grain of rice on the first square of the chessboard, on the second day he place two grains on the second square, on the third day four grains on the third square, each day doubling the number of grains until all 64 squares were filled.

Example 4.8 attempts to find out the size of the reward placed on any one of these squares. We will see that even the `long` type is not quite able to handle all the values we need, but we could use the `BigInteger` type in the `java.math` package, which handles arbitrarily large integers.

The `Reward` class keeps the number of the square whose reward is sought. The `riceGrains` method returns the number of rice grains the Rajah must deposit on that square.

EXAMPLE 4.8 Reward.java

```
/* How many grains of rice does the Rajah place on
 * square n if the Rajah places one grain on
 * the first square of a chessboard, and
 * places double the amount of the previous
 * square on the next square, and so on. Allow
 * the user to repeat for different n.
 */

import javax.swing.*;

public class Reward {
  private int squarenum;

  public Reward(int days) {
    squarenum = days;
  }
  public long riceGrains() {
    long amount = 1;                                    // Note 1
```

```
    for (int i = 2; i <= squarenum; i++)
      amount += amount;                                         // Note 2
    return amount;
  }
  public static void main(String [] args) {
    long amount;
    char repeat;
    int squarenum;

    do {
      amount = 1;
      String input = JOptionPane.showInputDialog
                              ("Which square, 1-64?");
      Reward r = new Reward(Integer.parseInt(input));
      JOptionPane.showMessageDialog(null,"The reward is "
                                     + r.riceGrains());
      input = JOptionPane.showInputDialog
                     ("Enter 'Y' to repeat, 'N' to quit");
      repeat = input.charAt(0);                                 // Note 3
    } while (repeat == 'Y' || repeat == 'y');                   // Note 4
    System.exit(0);
  }
}
```

Run

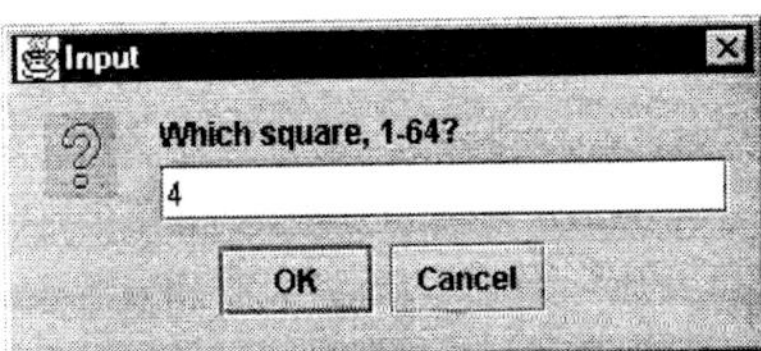

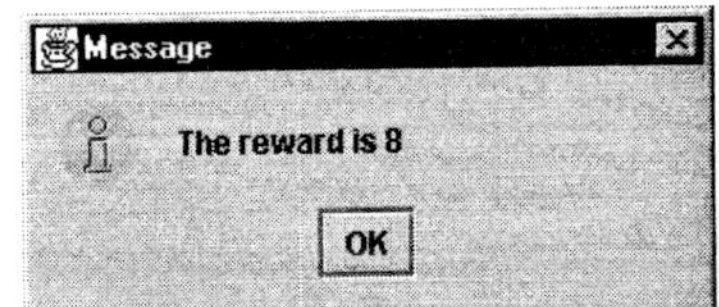

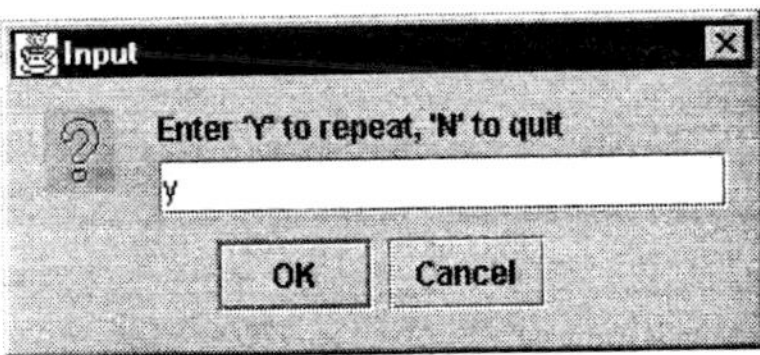

// Note 5

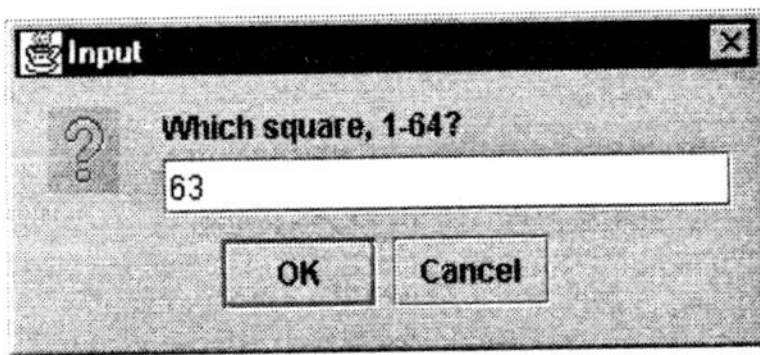

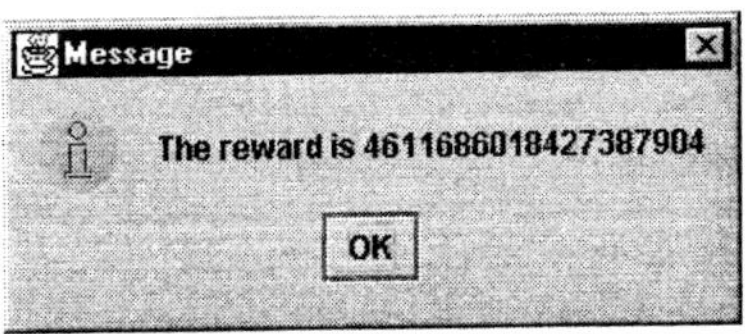

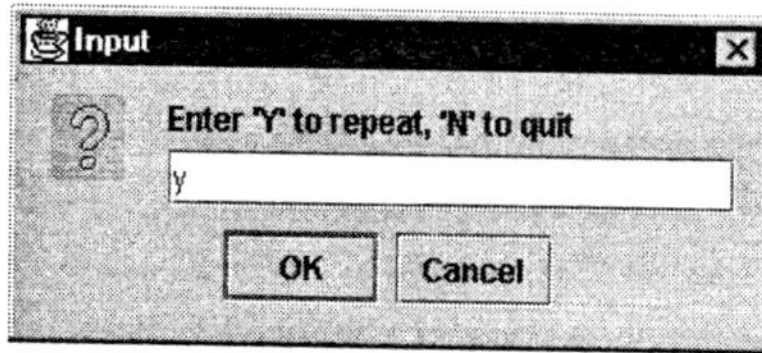

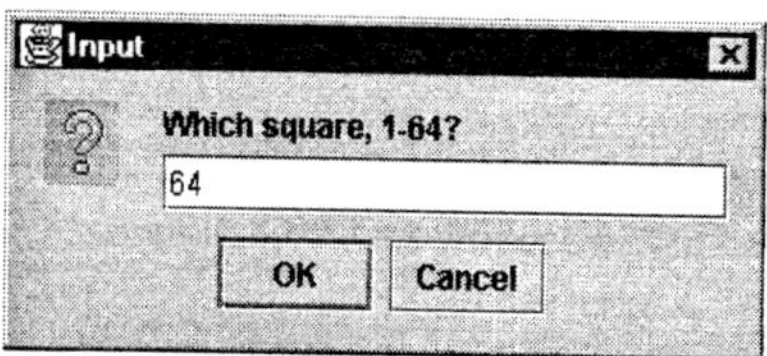

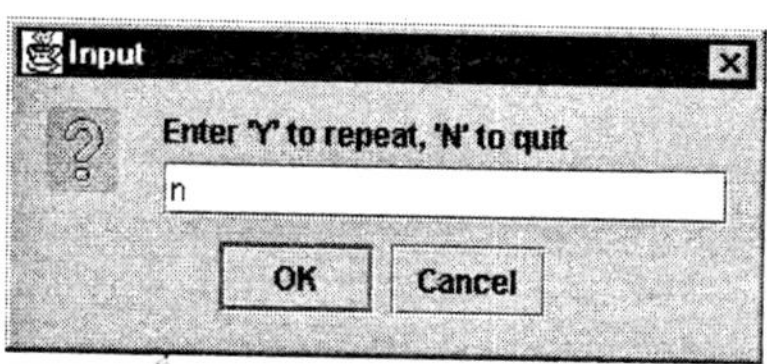

Note 1: We assign the `int` value, 1, to the `long` variable, `amount`. Java converts the `int` value to a `long` value. We could have specified a `long` value by writing `amount = 1L;`

Note 2: We could use the expression `2*amount` to double the amount, but the expression `amount+amount` is more efficient, since addition executes much faster than multiplication.

Note 3: The `charAt` method return the character at the specified position in the string. Specifying `0` gives the first character. Section 5.1 presents the methods of the String class.

Note 4: We only do the repeat if the character typed is `Y` or `y`. The prompt says to type an `N` or an `n` to quit, but actually any character other than `Y` or `y` will cause the program to quit. Following English usage, we might be tempted to say `while (repeat == 'Y' || 'y')`, but that is incorrect because each operand of an `OR` operator must have type `boolean`.

Note 5: It is always a good idea to try some small values that we can check by hand to see that our program is correct.

Note 6: Now we have passed the limit of `9,223,372,036,854,775,807` that a `long` variable can hold, so we get an erroneous negative value. Actually, we were very close here. Multiplying the previous value for square 63 by 2, we see that the correct answer is just one greater than the largest value that a `long` variable can hold.

TIP Always check your result for reasonableness. Just because the computer gives you some output, does not mean that it is correct.

Figure 4.25 shows the rapid growth of the reward graphically for the first few days.

Figure 4.25 Size of the reward given each day.

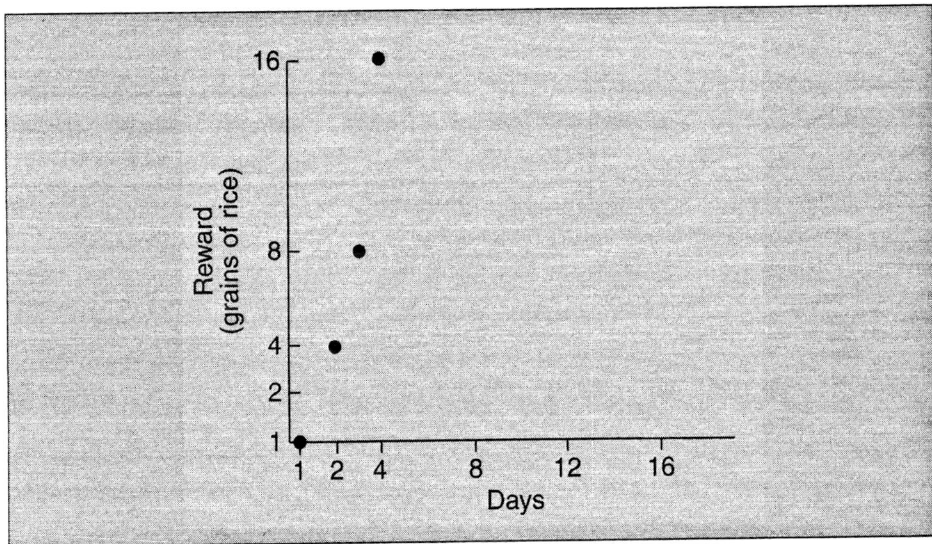

The Byte, Short, and Float Types

Java has the types **byte** and **short** for small integers that are used for specialized purposes; we do not use these types in this text. Java provides a **float** type for decimal numbers that uses less precision than the type `double`. In contrast to the integer types, where the smaller type `int` is the default and the bigger type `long` is less often used, for floating point types, the larger type `double` is the default, and `float` is less often used. In the modern world, we often deal with decimal numbers requiring a wide range of values and high precision, whether in scientific calculations or financial transactions, and need the values that type `double` provides.

`Float` values are accurate to seven digits and range from `1.4E-45` to `3.4028235E38`. To represent a `float` literal add an `F` or an `f`, as in `3.14f`. We can declare variables of type `float`, but must initialize them with `float` values. The declaration

```
float good = 4.25f;     // Valid
```

is fine, but the declaration

```
float bad = 4.25;       // Invalid
```

will cause an error, since the value `4.25` has type `double` by default. Java will not automatically convert from type `double` to type `float`, since, in general, a `double` value may be out of the range that a `float` variable accepts. We will use `float` variables when we want to output values of seven digits rather than the sixteen digits of the type `double`.

THE BIG PICTURE

With the16-bit `char` type, Java can handle the character sets of most of the world's languages. The 64-bit `long` type holds integers of up to 19 digits. The 8-bit `byte` and 16-bit `short` integer types have specialized uses. The 32-bit `float` type provides seven decimal places.

TEST YOUR UNDERSTANDING

31. Show the output from each of the following statements.

a.
```
System.out.println
    ("I like \n\nto write Java programs.");
```
b.
```
System.out.println
      ("Ali Baba said, \"Open, Sesame!\"");
```
c.
```
System.out.println("12345\r678");
```
d.
```
System.out.println("Find 3\\4 of 24");
```

32. Show the output from each of the following statements.

a.
```
System.out.println
      ("Descartes said, \"I think\ntherefore\nI am\"");
```
b.
```
System.out.println("set path=c:\\java\\bin");
```
c.
```
System.out.println("12345\b678");
```
d.
```
System.out.println("'i' before 'e' except after 'c'");
```

TRY IT YOURSELF

33. Change the declaration of the variable, `amount`, in Example 4.8 to have type `int`. Rerun the program and determine the largest square number for which the reward is computed correctly. How much is that reward?

34. Variables of type `long` can hold much larger values than variables of type `int`; would it be a good idea to declare all integer variables as type `long` and not use type `int`? Why or why not?

4.5 Using the Math Library

The Java language provides the basic arithmetic operations of addition, subtraction, multiplication, and division, but not exponentiation, max, min, and other mathematical functions. As we shall see, Java adds many resources as classes that we can use in our programs.

In this section, we introduce methods of the `Math` class to compute square root, absolute value, powers, max, min, random numbers, and other mathematical functions that we can use to solve problems in the remainder of the text. To use these methods, we prefix the method name with the class name, `Math`, as in `Math.sqrt(2.0)`, which computes the square root of 2.0.

TIP When calling class methods (methods which use the `static` modifier) from a method of the same class, as in Example 4.4, where we call `sum()` and `max()` from `main`, we do not need to use the class prefix. Optionally, we could use the class prefix, calling the method as `UserMenu.sum()`. When calling class methods from a method of a different class, as in Example 4.4, where we call `Integer.parseInt`, we must use the class prefix.

Powers and Roots

The power method, `pow`, takes two arguments of type `double` and returns a `double` value which is the result of raising the first argument to the exponent given by the second argument. Some examples:

```
Math.pow(2.0,3.0)  returns 8.0    (2.0^3.0)
Math.pow(3.0,2.0)  returns 9.0    (3.0^2.0)
```

The square root method, `sqrt`, takes a `double` argument and returns a `double` value, the square root of its argument. Some examples:

```
Math.sqrt(2.0)     returns 1.4142135623730951
Math.sqrt(16.0)    returns 4.0
```

Maximum, Minimum, and Absolute Value

Java provides `max`, `min`, and `abs` methods for each of the four numeric types, `int`, `long`, `float`, and `double`.

For each type, the `max` method returns the maximum of its two arguments of that type, and the `min` method returns the minimum of its two arguments. Some examples:

```
Math.max(3, 4)              returns   4
Math.max(17.32, 5.8567)     returns  17.32
Math.max(-9, -11)           returns  -9
Math.min(3, 4)              returns   3
Math.min(17.32, 5.8567)     returns   5.8567
Math.min(-9, -11)           returns -11
```

For each type, the `abs` method returns the absolute value of its argument, which, by definition, is

```
Math.abs(x)  =  x, if x >= 0
             = -x, if x < 0
```

Informally, the `abs` method removes the minus sign, if any. Some examples,

```
Math.abs(-10)    returns 10
Math.abs(12.34)  returns 12.34
```

Floor and Ceiling

Informally, just as the absolute value removes the minus sign, the `floor` removes the fractional part of its `double` argument, returning the largest `double` value that is not greater than the argument and is equal to a mathematical integer. Some examples:

```
Math.floor(25.194) returns 25.0
Math.floor(-134.28) returns  -135.0
```

The `ceiling` also removes the fractional part, but it returns the smallest `double` value that is not less than the argument and is equal to a mathematical integer. Some examples:

```
Math.ceil(25.194) returns 26.0
Math.ceil(-134.28) returns -134.0
```

Pi and e

In addition to methods, the `Math` class contains two important constants, `Math.PI`, the circumference of a circle of diameter one, and `Math.E`, the base for natural logarithms. We will use `Math.PI` in our calculations of areas and volumes.

EXAMPLE 4.9 Library.java

```
/* Uses methods from the Math class.
 */

import java.text.*;
public class Library {
  public static void main(String [] args)  {
    System.out.println("Two cubed is " + Math.pow(2.0,3.0));
    System.out.println("Three squared is " + Math.pow(3.0,2.0));
    System.out.println("The square root of two is " + Math.sqrt(2.0));
    System.out.println("The square root of 16 is " + Math.sqrt(16.0));
    System.out.println("The max of 2.56 and 7.91/3.1 is " +
                              Math.max(2.65,7.91/3.1));          // Note 1
    System.out.println("The min of -9 and -11 is " + Math.min(-9,-11));
    System.out.println("The absolute value of -32.47 is "
                                        + Math.abs(-32.47));
    System.out.println("The floor of 25.194 is " + Math.floor(25.194));
    System.out.println("The ceiling of 25.194 is " + Math.ceil(25.194));
    System.out.println("Pi is " + Math.PI);
    System.out.print("Pi, to six decimal places, is ");
    NumberFormat nf = NumberFormat.getNumberInstance();
    nf.setMaximumFractionDigits(6);
    System.out.println(nf.format(Math.PI));                        // Note 2
    System.out.println
            ("The base of natural logarithms, e, is " + Math.E);
  }
}
```

Output

```
Two cubed is 8.0
Three squared is 9.0
The square root of two is 1.4142135623730951
The square root of 16 is 4.0
The max of 2.56 and 7.91/3.1 is 2.65
The min of -9 and -11 is -11
The absolute value of -32.47 is 32.47
The floor of 25.194 is 25.0
The ceiling of 25.194 is 26.0
Pi is 3.141592653589793
Pi, to six decimal places, is 3.141593
The base of natural logarithms, e, is 2.718281828459045
```

Note 1: The argument can be an expression that evaluates to a `double`, as here for the second argument of `max`.

Note 2: We format the output to show only the first six decimal places of pi.

A LITTLE EXTRA ➪

The `Math` class has methods to compute the trigonometric functions, sine, cosine, and tangent. These methods each take a `double` argument representing an angle in radians, and produce a `double` result. Some examples:

```
Math.sin( Math.PI )  returns 0.0
Math.cos(Math.PI)    returns -1.0
Math.tan(Math.PI/4)  returns 1.0
```

The exponential function computes e^x, where `e` is the base of natural logarithms. The `exp` method of the `Math` class computes the exponential function. The `log` method computes the natural logarithm function, `log x`.

Some examples:

```
Math.exp(1.0)       returns 2.718281828459045
Math.exp(2.0)       returns 7.38905609893065
Math.log(Math.E)    returns 1.0
Math.log(10.0)      returns 2.302585092994046
```

Random Numbers

Sometimes we cannot predict the outcome of an event precisely, but can specify a probability that it will occur. For example, in tossing a fair coin, we cannot predict the outcome of any one toss. We can say that there is a 50% chance that it will be heads and a 50% chance that it will be tails, meaning that in a long series of coin tosses we expect about half of each outcome.

We do not usually use computers to toss coins, but we can use a computer generated sequence of numbers, which appear to be random, to simulate coin tossing, and many events such as the arrival of traffic at an intersection or customers at a bank.

The method, `Math.random()`, returns a double value between 0 and 1. Each time we call this method we get a different number between 0 and 1, and the numbers appear to be randomly scattered in that interval. Example 4.10 shows the result of calling `Math.random()` five times.

EXAMPLE 4.10 Coin.java

```
/* Gets five random numbers.
 */

public class Coin {
    public static void main(String [] args) {
        System.out.println(Math.random());
        System.out.println(Math.random());
        System.out.println(Math.random());
        System.out.println(Math.random());
        System.out.println(Math.random());
    }
}
```

Output—First Run

```
0.8725085781998776
0.9683048650459913
0.4434762410550146
0.651420385198781
0.4919912263574404
```

Output—Second Run

```
0.6282741848920075                        // Second run is different
0.9053726508413159
0.773087388472337
0.22610509763572595
0.07427409526097717
```

To simulate coin tossing, we need an event with two outcomes, each of which occurs in 50% of a long series of trials. Since the random numbers are evenly distributed in the interval from 0 to 1, about half the time a random number, `r`, will be in the lower half, satisfying `0<=r < .5`, and about half the time it will be in the upper half, satisfying `.5 <= r < 1.0`. Let us interpret an `r` in the lower half as an outcome of heads, and an `r` in the upper half as an outcome of tails. With this interpretation, the outcomes of the first run of Example 4.10 represent `tails`, `tails`, `heads`, `tails`, `heads`, and the outcomes of the second run represent `tails`, `tails`, `tails`, `heads`, `heads`. Figure 4.26 shows our interpretation of random numbers as heads and tails.

Figure 4.26 Using random numbers to represent heads and tails

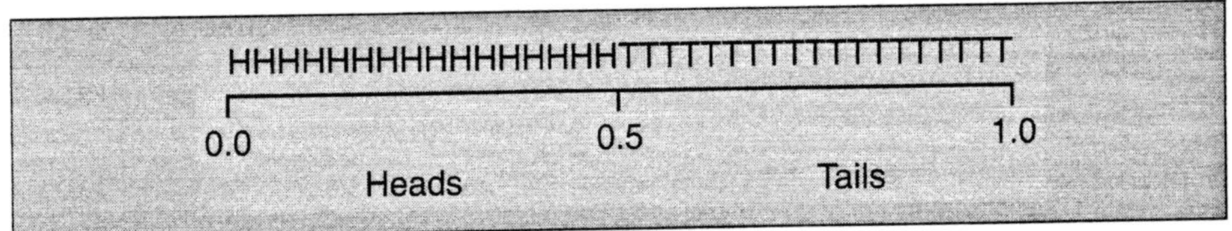

In Example 4.11, we play a game with the user who has to guess if the next simulated coin toss will be heads or tails. The `Toss` class represents a single toss of a coin. Its state holds the face showing as a character, `H` or `T`. The `Toss` class has two constructors. The default constructor uses a `flip` method to determine the face using a random number. We put the `Toss` class in the `coins` package.

EXAMPLE 4.11 Toss.java

```
/* Represents a toss of a fair coin.
 */

package coins;

public class Toss {
  private char face;

  public Toss(char f) {
    face = f;
  }
  public Toss() {                                             // Note 1
    flip();
  }
  public void flip() {
    if (Math.random() < .5)
      face = 'H';
    else
      face = 'T';
  }
  public char getFace() {
    return face;
  }
}
```

CoinToss.java

```
/*  The user guesses heads or tails and
 *  wins if the computer's toss matches
 *  that guess.
 */
```

```
import javax.swing.*;
import coins.*;

public class CoinToss {
  public static void main(String [] args)  {
    Toss computerToss;
    Toss yourToss;
    char repeat;
    String input, result;

    do {
      computerToss = new Toss();
      input = JOptionPane.showInputDialog
                ("Enter 'H' for heads, 'T' for tails");          // Note 2
      yourToss = new Toss(input.charAt(0));
      if (computerToss.getFace() == yourToss.getFace())
        result = "You win!";
      else
        result = "Computer wins";
      JOptionPane.showMessageDialog(null, result);
      input = JOptionPane.showInputDialog
                  ("Enter 'Y' to play again, 'N' to quit");
      repeat = input.charAt(0);
    } while (repeat == 'Y' || repeat == 'y');
    System.exit(0);
  }
}
```

Run

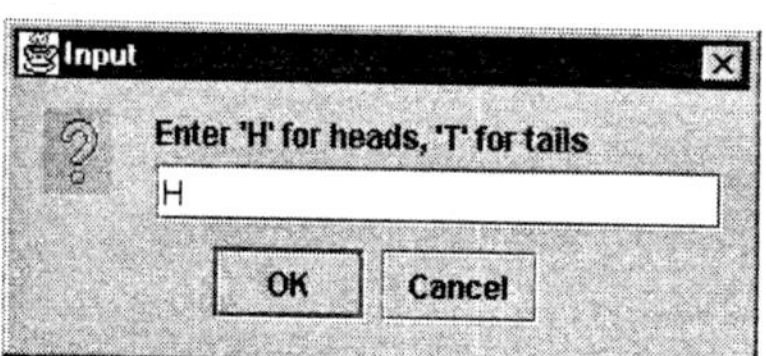

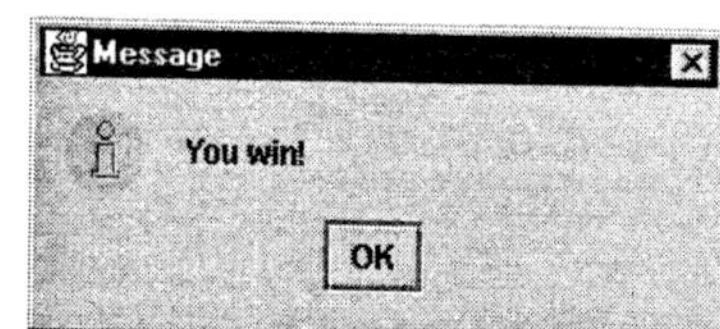

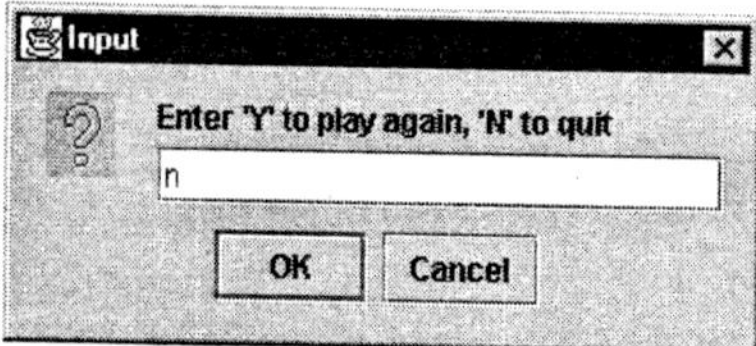

Note 1: Creates a `Toss` of a fair coin with a 50% chance of heads and a 50% chance of tails.

Note 2: The user must enter an upper case `H` or `T` to match our computer toss. See the tip below for an improvement.

TIP

Make your program user friendly. If the first input is incorrect, let the user try again, until it is correct. We could improve Example 4.11 by putting the user input of `H` or `T` in a `do-while` loop

```
do {
  input = JOptionPane.showInputDialog
         ("Enter 'H' for heads, 'T' for tails");
  }while(input.charAt(0) != 'H'
                   && input.charAt(0) != 'T');
```

that would force the user to input an uppercase `H` or `T`.

THE BIG PICTURE

The `Math` class contains the commonly used mathematical methods. The random method returns a decimal randomly distributed between 0 and 1. We can use random numbers to create simulations.

TEST YOUR UNDERSTANDING

35. Use methods from the `Math` class to compute each of the following.
    a. Seven to the fourth power.
    b. The square root of 43.
    c. The maximum of 476.22 and -608.90.
    d. The minimum of 58.43 and 6.32*8.87.
    e. The absolute value of -65.234.
    f. The floor of -43.99.
    g. The ceiling of -3.01.
36. Use methods from the `Math` class to compute each of the following.
    a. Four to the seventh power.
    b. The square root of 117.45.
    c. The maximum of 32.1*33.9 and 1000.2.
    d. The minimum of the square root of 32 and 5.613.
    e. The absolute value of 1089.9.
    f. The floor of 43.99.
    g. The ceiling of 3.01.
37. Using `Math.PI`, write a Java expression for the area of a circle or radius r.
38. Using `Math.PI`, write a Java expression for the circumference of a circle of radius `r`.

39. How would you use random numbers to simulate rolling of a fair six-sided die. Each face of the die has a number from one to six; each of these outcomes, one through six, is equally likely to occur.

4.6 Solving Problems with Java: An Iterative Development Cycle

In this section we develop the solution of a problem from original statement to Java code. Figure 4.27 shows the steps of the iterative process we use.

Figure 4.27 Iterative problem-solving process

```
Formulate the problem;
do {
  Develop pseudocode;
  Implement pseudocode in Java program;
  Test program;
} while (More subproblems to refine);
```

We use an iterative development cycle, designing part of the program, implementing that part, and testing it. The goal is to keep control of the design and implementation, so that we have confidence that we are producing a correct, well-designed solution to the problem.

In this case study, we use many concepts from this and earlier chapters including the `do-while` statement, the `switch` statement, nested `if` statements, a conditional expression, a `Math` library method, and type casting. We reuse designs from earlier examples and think about reuse for this design, since it is much more productive to build on earlier work than to start every project from scratch.

Defining the Problem

Let us develop a program to convert distances from the metric system to the English system or from the English system to the metric system. We start with some examples of uses of the system. A user may choose which conversion to do. If the user chooses to convert from the metric system, then an input might be `1222.32 meters` which our program will convert to an equivalent number of yards, feet, and inches. If the user chooses to convert from the English system, input might be `793 yards, 2 feet, 6 inches` which our program will convert to an equivalent number of meters. We use the conversion factors of .9144 meters in one yard and .0254 meters in one inch. Each yard has three feet, and each foot has 12 inches.

We should think about valid inputs and outputs. In converting to the English system, the number of feet should satisfy `0 <= feet < 3`, and the number of inches should satisfy `0 <= inches < 12`. Converting from the English system, we can accept as input any nonnegative values of yards, feet, and inches. For example, `10.3 yards, 4.5 feet, 17 inches` would be an acceptable, though unlikely, input.

Toward a Solution

The Iterative Process—Develop pseudocode, a Java program, and Test

Following the process of Figure 4.27, we repeat the three steps of developing pseudocode, implementing that pseudocode in a Java program, and testing the program, until we have completed the solution to the problem. In this example we use three iterations of the development steps to attain the solution.

Toward a Solution: First Iteration—Pseudocode, Program, Test

It is always a good idea to reuse techniques that have worked before. In solving this problem we can reuse the idea introduced in Example 4.4 of providing a menu for the user to choose the type of conversion. By using the `do-while` statement, instead of the `while` statement that we used in Example 4.4, we can avoid printing the menu from two different places in our program.

Figure 4.28 shows the pseudocode for the overall solution.

Figure 4.28 Top-level pseudocode

```
do {
  Display the menu;
  Get the user's choice;
  Execute the user's choice;
} while (user does not choose to quit);
```

The pseudocode of Figure 4.28 is actually a general pattern for a menu-driven application; we can reuse it in solving other problems. In refining the three subproblems, we follow a pattern for each refinement that we can apply to other problems that use menus. These three patterns are:

```
Display the menu using a dialog.
Convert the dialog response to get the user's choice.
Use a switch statement to execute the user's choice.
```

Figure 4.29 shows the refinements following these patterns. It shows the overall operation of the menu before getting into the details of the conversion operations. We can reuse this basic design for other menu-driven applications.

In Figure 4.29 we have a reusable design for a menu-driven application, with choices designed for our converting lengths application. To handle the details of the conversion we use two methods, `MetricToEnglish` and `EnglishToMetric`. Before trying to design these two methods, we can execute and test the design we have so far. Of course, we cannot do any conversion of lengths yet, but we can test the overall structure of the program. Since we have not designed the `MetricToEnglish` and `EnglishToMetric` methods yet, we will use stubs, methods that execute in a trivial way, just printing a message. Example 4.12 tests our high-level design, before our program gets too large for us to manage.

Figure 4.29 Pattern for a menu-driven application

```
do {
  System.out.println();
  System.out.println("Choose from the following list");
  System.out.println
           ("1.  Convert from meters to yds,ft,in");
  System.out.println
           ("2.  Convert from yds,ft,in to meters");
  System.out.println("3.  Quit");
  String input = JOptionPane.showInputDialog
           ("Enter your choice, 1, 2 or 3");
  int choice = Integer.parseInt(input);
  switch (choice) {
    case 1:
            MetricToEnglish();
            break;
    case 2:
            EnglishToMetric();
            break;
    case 3:  System.out.println("Bye, Have a nice day");
  }
} while (choice != 3);
```

TIP

Do not try to write the whole program and then test it. Even smaller programs provide many opportunities to introduce errors. Our defense against errors is to develop code in small pieces that we can test and debug. Use stubs to test before all methods have been coded.

EXAMPLE 4.12 ConvertMenu.java

```
/*  Tests the structure of the program
 *  to convert length using a menu to
 *  get the user's choice.  Uses stubs
 *  for the actual conversion methods.
 */

import javax.swing.*;
public class ConvertMenu {
  public void MetricToEnglish() {                          // Note 1
    JOptionPane.showMessageDialog
              (null, "Converting from meters to yds,ft,in");
  }
  public void EnglishToMetric() {                          // Note 2
    JOptionPane.showMessageDialog
              (null, "Converting from yds,ft,in to meters");
  }
```

```
  public static void main(String [] args) {
    ConvertMenu menu = new ConvertMenu();
    int choice;
    do {
       String input = JOptionPane.showInputDialog("Choose:\n"        // Note 3
                    + "1.  Convert from meters to yds,ft,in \n"
                    + "2.  Convert from yds,ft,in to meters \n"
                    + "3.  Quit");
       choice = Integer.parseInt(input);
       switch (choice) {                                             // Note 4
          case 1:
                   menu.MetricToEnglish();
                   break;
          case 2:
                   menu.EnglishToMetric();
                   break;
          case 3: JOptionPane.showMessageDialog
                               (null, "Bye, Have a nice day");
       }
    } while (choice != 3);
    System.exit(0);
  }
}
```

Run

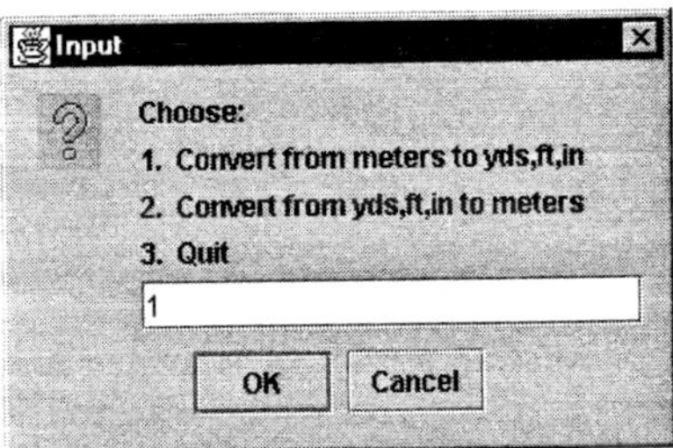

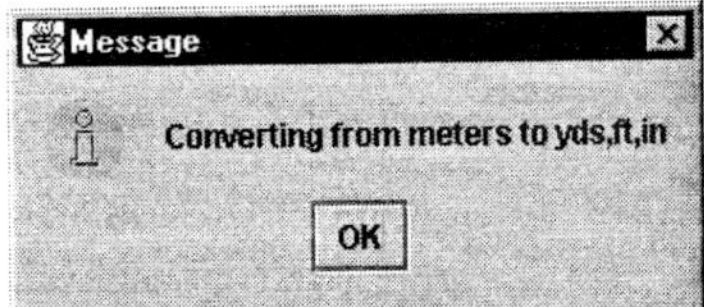

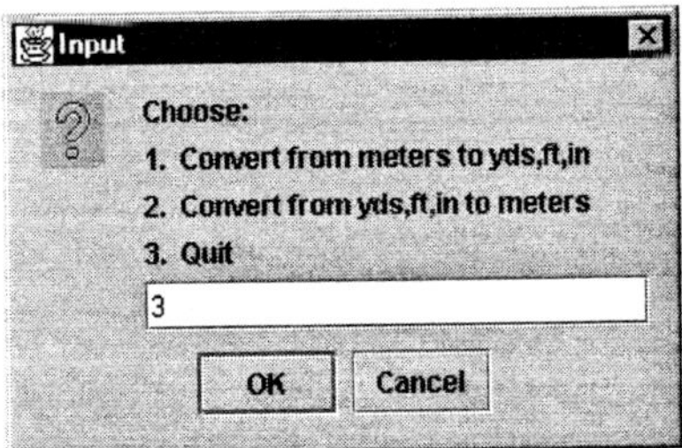

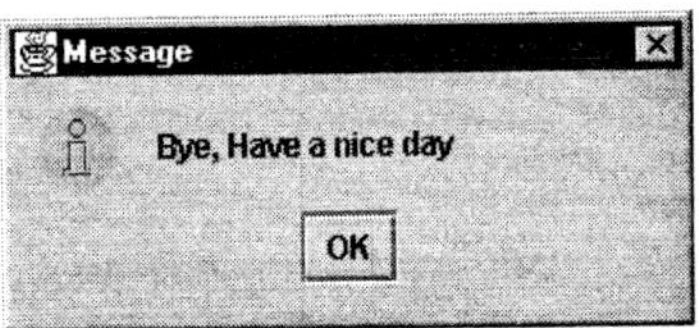

Note 1: This stub for the `MetricToEnglish` method just prints a message. We will implement this method later.

Note 2: This stub for the `EnglishToMetric` method just prints a message. We will implement this method later.

Note 3: We add the newline character, '`\n`,' to display each choice on a separate line.

Note 4: If the user chooses a number other than 1, 2 or 3, the `switch` statement does nothing, and because the choice is not three, the menu prints again giving the user another chance to enter a correct choice.

A LITTLE EXTRA The user of Example 4.12 will cause an error by pressing the *OK* or *Cancel* button before entering any input in the dialog. To recover from this error we could change the conversion to

```
if (input==null || input.equals(""))
  choice=3;
else
  choice = Integer.parseInt(input);
```

Toward a Solution: Second Iteration – Pseudocode, Program, Test

The output from Example 4.12 shows that the menu structure works fine, so we proceed to design the `MetricToEnglish` and `EnglishToMetric` methods. Let us try a hand example to review how to convert. The 100-meter dash is one of the highlights of the Olympic Games. We convert 100 meters to yards, feet, and inches. There are exactly .9144 meters in one yard. The calculations are

```
(100 meters) (1 yard / .9144 meters)   =  109.36133 yards
    giving 109 yards and an excess of .36133 yard
(.36133 yards) (3 feet / yard)  = 1.08399 feet
    giving 1 foot and an excess of .08399 foot
(.08399 foot) (12 inches / foot) = 1.00788 inches
```

which gives an output of 109 yards, 1 foot, 1.00788 inches.

We try another case close to the boundary, say a small value such as .05 meter. The calculations are

```
(.05 meter) (1 yard / .9144 meters) = .0546806 yard
    giving 0 yards and an excess of .0546806 yard
(.0546806 yard) (3 feet / yard) = .1640419 foot
    giving 0 feet and an excess of .1640419 foot
(.1640419 foot) (12 inches / foot) = 1.9685039 inches
```

which gives an output of 1.9685039 inches.

Looking at our calculations, we find that we may or may not have nonzero values for yards and feet. For the output, we have to distinguish between the singular forms, "inch," "foot," "yard," and the plural forms, "inches," "feet," and "yards." Figure 4.30 expresses the conversion process in pseudocode.

Figure 4.30 Pseudocode for the `MetricToEnglish` method

```
Input the number of meters, x, to convert;
Convert x meters to y yards;
Separate y into yInteger yards and yFraction yards;
Convert yFraction yards to f feet.
Separate f into fInteger feet and fFraction feet.
Convert fFraction feet to i inches.
Display the output.
```

On output, we want to be sure not to display zero of any unit, so we will check to see that each value is greater than zero before displaying it. Any value between zero and one should use the singular form of the unit name. Figure 4.31 shows this refinement.

Figure 4.31 Refinement: Display the output

```
if (yInteger > 0)
   if (yInteger  <= 1)  Display yInteger yard;
   else Display yInteger yards;
if (fInteger > 0)
   if (fInteger <= 1) Display fInteger foot;
   else Display fInteger feet;
if (i > 0)
   if (i <= 1) Display i inch;
   else Display i inches;
if (yInteger == 0 && fInteger == 0 && i == 0)
   Display 0 yards;
```

Example 4.13 adds the code for the `MetricToEnglish` method, based on the pseudocode of Figure 4.30 and 4.31, to Example 4.12. We just show the added part here, but the complete program is on the CD included with this book. We test the conversion from meters to yards, feet, and inches.

EXAMPLE 4.13 ConvertFromMetric.java

```
/*  Adds the implementation of
 *  the MetricToEnglish method to the
 *  code of Example 4.12.
 */

 public void MetricToEnglish() {
   double meters;            //  number of meters to convert
   double toYards;           //  meters converted to yards
   int yards;                //  integer part of toYards
   double excessYards;       //  fractional part of toYards
   double toFeet;            //  excessYards converted to feet
   int feet;                 //  integer part of toFeet
   double excessFeet;        //  fractional part of toFeet
```

```
      float toInches;            //  excessFeet converted to inches
      String output = "";        //  Concatenate output for message dialog

      String input = JOptionPane.showInputDialog
                          ("Enter the number of meters to convert");
      meters =  Double.parseDouble(input);
      toYards = meters / .9144;                                    // Note 1
      yards = (int)Math.floor(toYards);                            // Note 2
      excessYards = toYards - yards;                               // Note 3
      toFeet = 3 * excessYards;
      feet = (int)Math.floor(toFeet);
      excessFeet = toFeet - feet;
      toInches = (float)(12 * excessFeet);                         // Note 4
      if (meters <= 1)                                             // Note 5
        output += meters + " meter converts to";
      else
        output += meters+ " meters convert to";
      output += "\n   ";                                           // Note 6
      if (yards > 0)                                               // Note 7
        if (yards  <= 1)
          output += yards + " yard  ";
        else
          output += yards + " yards  ";
      if (feet > 0)
        if (feet <= 1)
           output += feet + " foot  ";
        else
           output += feet + " feet  ";
      if (toInches > 0)
        if (toInches <= 1)
          output += toInches + " inch";
        else
          output += toInches + " inches";
      if (yards == 0 && feet == 0 && toInches == 0)                // Note 8
        output += 0 + " yards";
      JOptionPane.showMessageDialog(null, output);
    }

        //  The rest of the program is the same as Example 4.12
}
```

Run

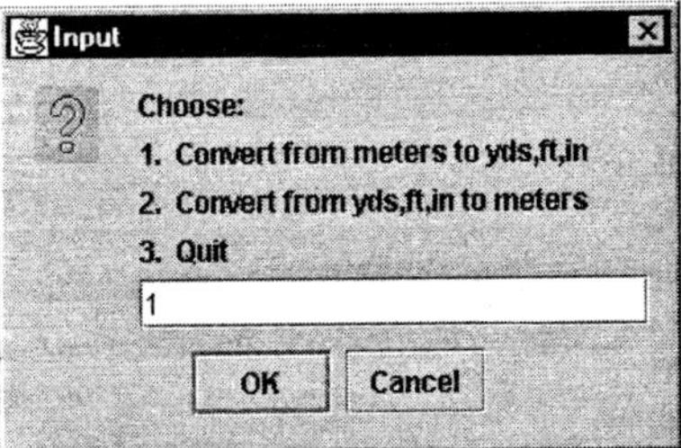
Input
Choose:
1. Convert from meters to yds,ft,in
2. Convert from yds,ft,in to meters
3. Quit
1
OK
Cancel

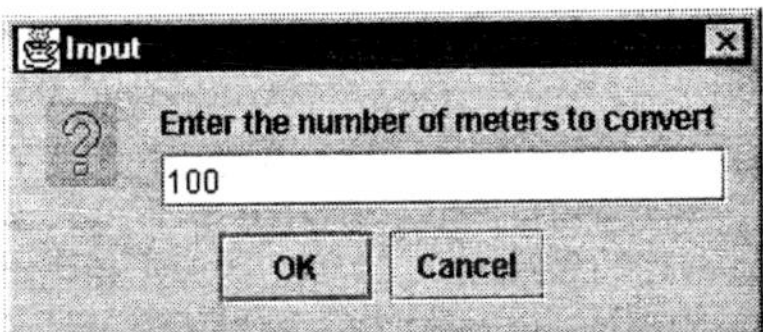
Input
Enter the number of meters to convert
100
OK
Cancel

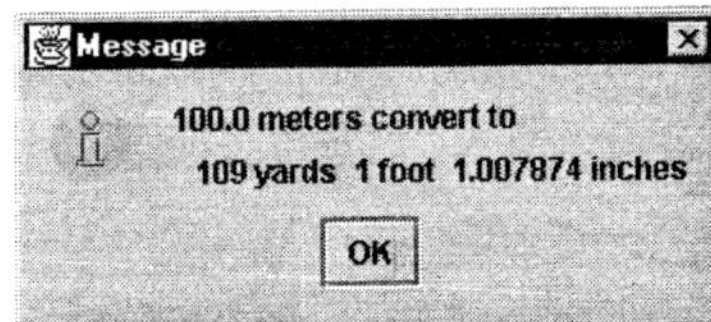
Message
100.0 meters convert to
109 yards 1 foot 1.007874 inches
OK

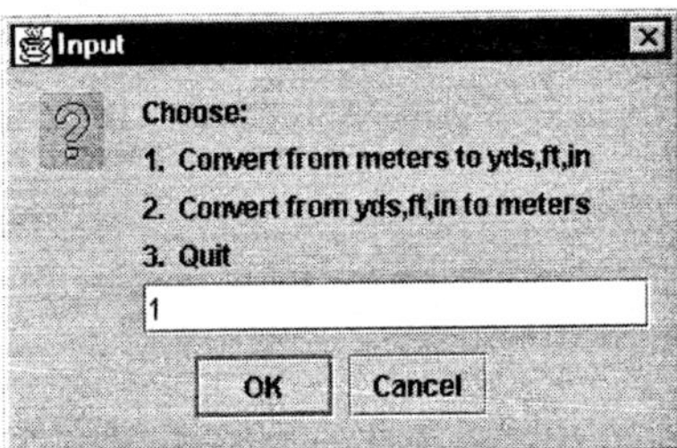
Input
Choose:
1. Convert from meters to yds,ft,in
2. Convert from yds,ft,in to meters
3. Quit
1
OK
Cancel

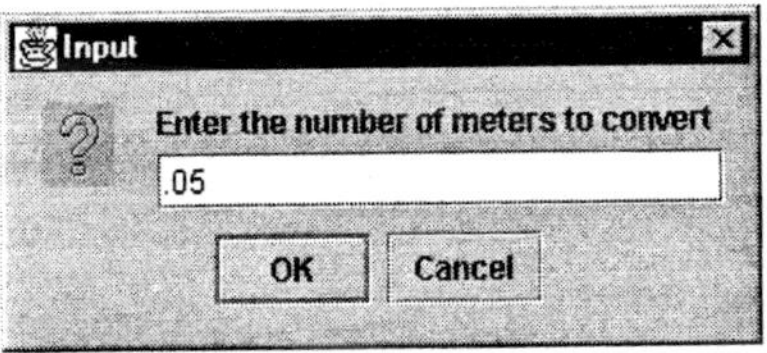
Input
Enter the number of meters to convert
.05
OK
Cancel

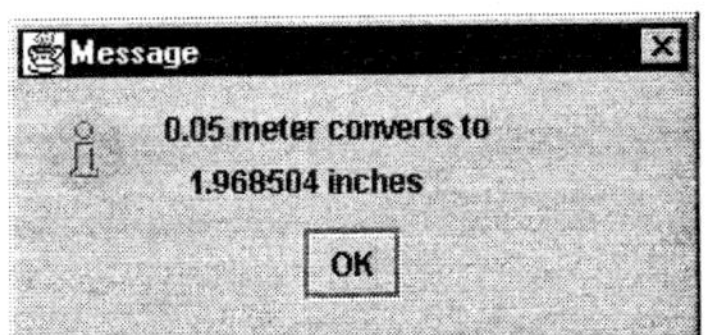
Message
0.05 meter converts to
1.968504 inches
OK

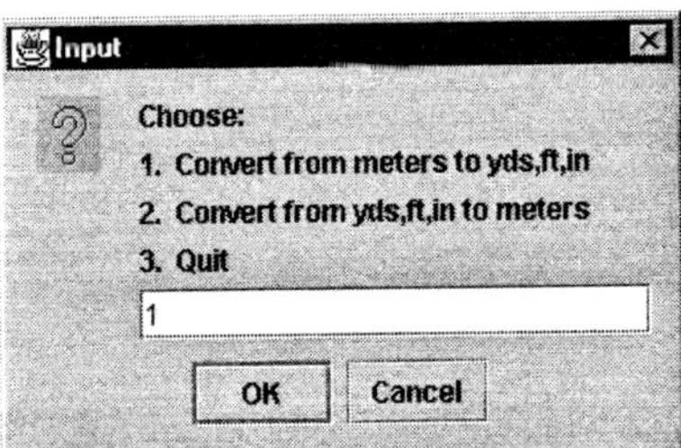
Input
Choose:
1. Convert from meters to yds,ft,in
2. Convert from yds,ft,in to meters
3. Quit
1
OK
Cancel

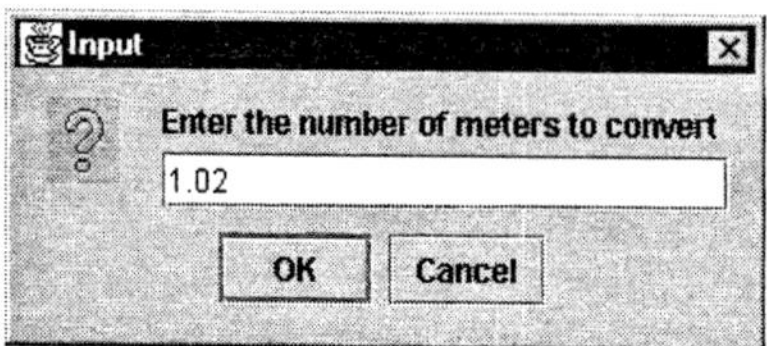

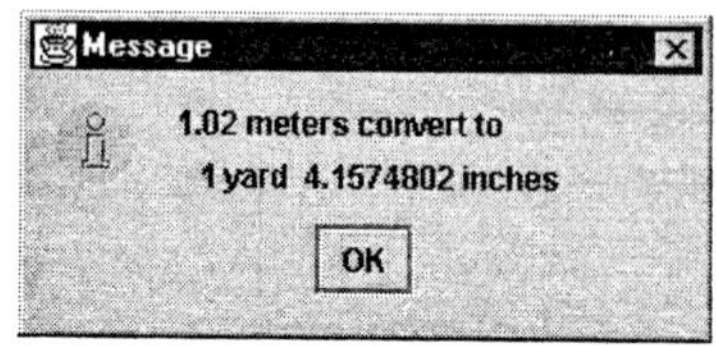

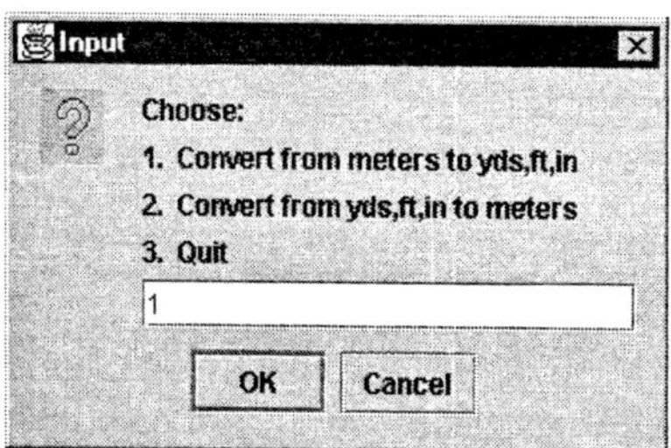

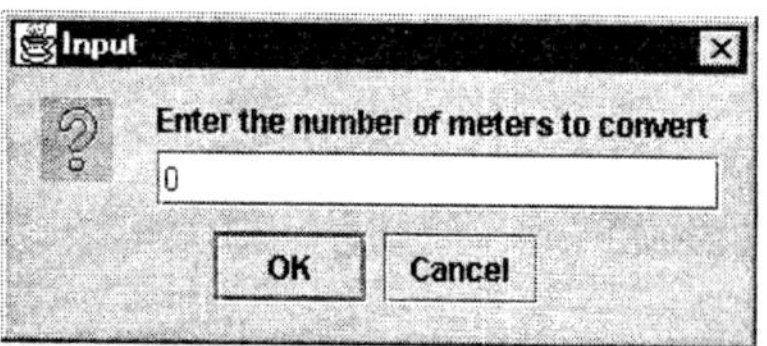

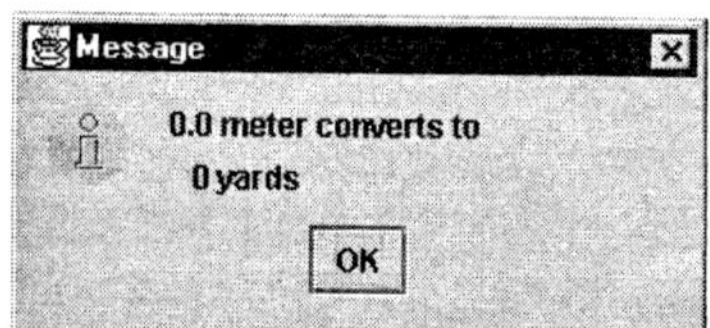

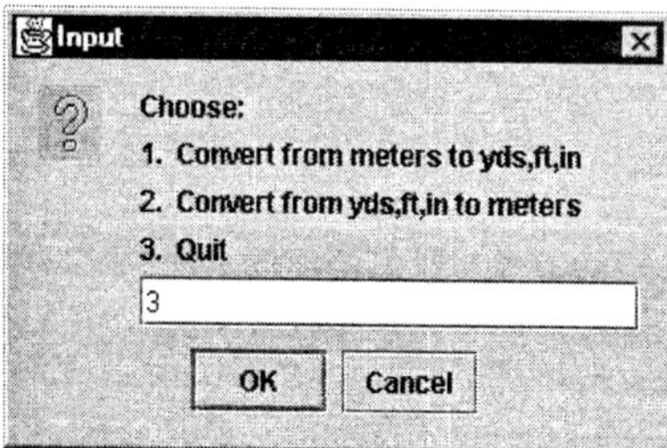

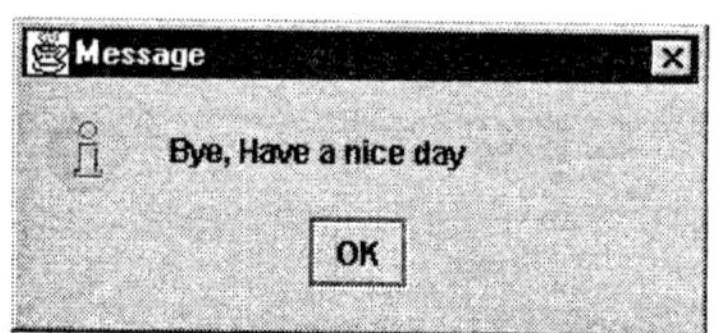

Note 1:

```
toYards = meters / .9144;
```

There are .9144 meters in one yard.

Note 2:

```
yards = (int)Math.floor(toYards);
```

The floor returns the integer part of `toYards` as a value of type `double`. We want to display it as an integer, so we cast it to an `int`, using the type cast, `(int)`.

Note 3:

```
excessYards = toYards - yards;
```

We get the fractional part of `toYards` by subtracting its integer part.

Note 4:

```
toInches = (float) (12 * excessFeet);
```

We will display the remaining inches as a decimal number. Using the type `double` would show 16 digits, so we cast the `double` value to a `float` which will display seven digits. We need the parentheses in `(12*excessFeet)`, since we want to convert the result to a `float` value, not the number `12`.

Note 5: `if (meters <= 1)`
If meters is less than or equal to one, we use the singular "meter," otherwise we use the plural "meters."

Note 6: `output += "\n   ";`
We go to the next line and indent a few spaces.

Note 7: `if (yards > 0)`
We only want to print nonzero values. Thus `.05` meters converts to `1.968504` inches, not to `0` yards `0` feet `1.968504` inches.

Note 8: `if (yards == 0 && feet == 0 && toInches == 0)`
This makes sure that we display the result when the input is zero.

Completing the Java Code: Third Iteration—Pseudocode, Program, Test

We have yet to design the `EnglishToMetric` method. Let us try an example to see how it should go. To convert 7 yards, 2 feet, 5 inches to meters we could convert to inches computing

```
(7 yards)*(36 inches / yard) + (2 feet)*(12 inches / foot) + 5 inches = 281
inches
```

and then convert to meters using the conversion factor of exactly .0254 meters per inch giving

```
(281 inches)*(.0254 meters / inch) = 7.1374 meters
```

Figure 4.32 shows the pseudocode for the `EnglishToMetric` method.

Figure 4.32 Pseudocode for the `EnglishToMetric` method

```
Input yards, feet, and inches to convert;
Convert to inches;
Convert inches to meters;
Output the result;
```

Example 4.14, the complete conversion program, adds the code for the `EnglishToMetric` method to Example 4.13. We only show the added part here, but the complete program is on the disk that comes with this book.

EXAMPLE 4.14 Convert.java

```
/*  Adds the implementation of
 *  the EnglishToMetric method to the
 *  code of Example 4.13
 */
```

```
import javax.swing.*;
import java.util.*;

public class Convert {
               // MetricToEnglish same as Example 4.13

  public void EnglishToMetric() {
    double yards, feet, inches;     //  amount to convert
    double total;                   //  input converted to inches
    float meters;                   //  converted amount

    String input = JOptionPane.showInputDialog
                           ("Enter yards, feet, and inches");
    StringTokenizer tokens = new StringTokenizer(input);
    yards = Double.parseDouble(tokens.nextToken());
    feet =  Double.parseDouble(tokens.nextToken());
    inches = Double.parseDouble(tokens.nextToken());
    total = 36*yards + 12*feet + inches;                        // Note 1
    meters = (float)(.0254*total);                              // Note 2
    if (meters <= 1)                                            // Note 3
       JOptionPane.showMessageDialog
            (null, "Your input converts to " + meters + " meter");
    else
       JOptionPane.showMessageDialog
            (null, "Your input converts to " + meters + " meters");
    }
          // The rest is the same as Example 4.13
}
```

Run

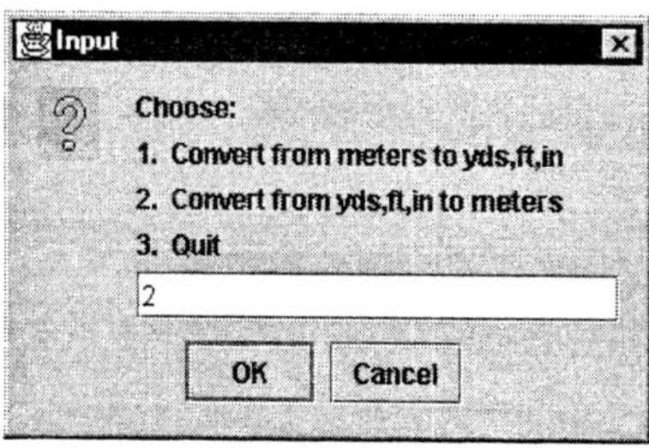

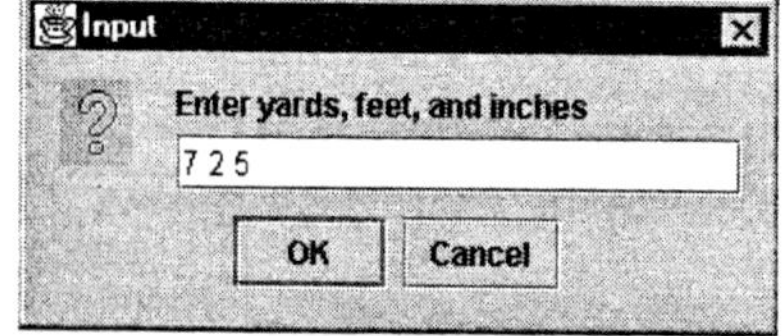

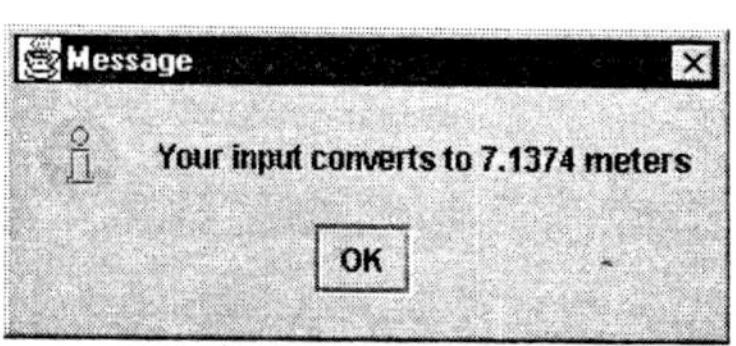

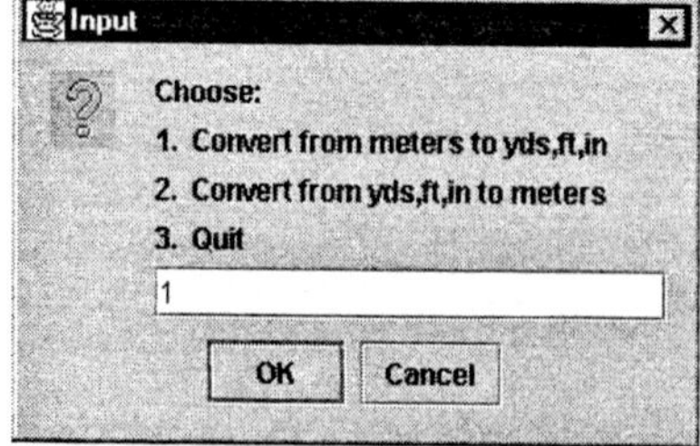

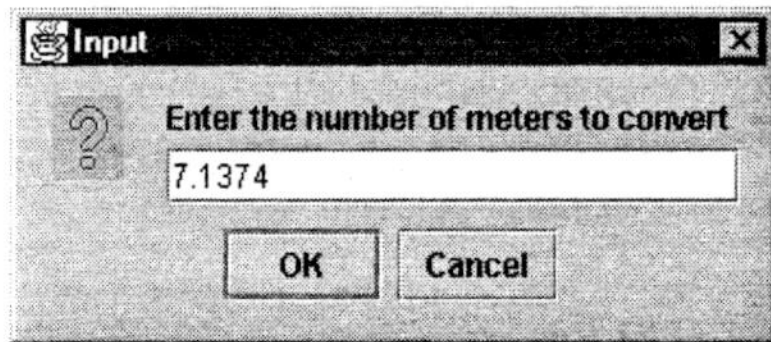

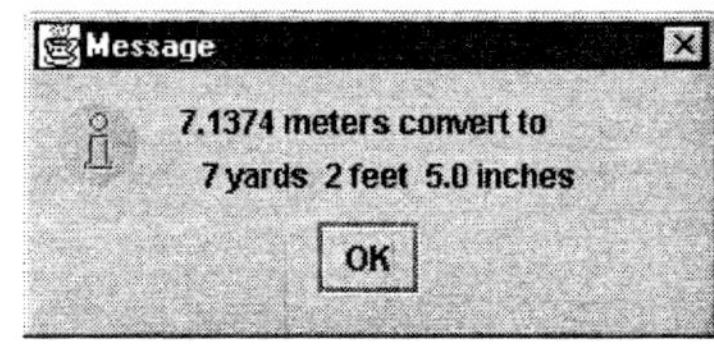

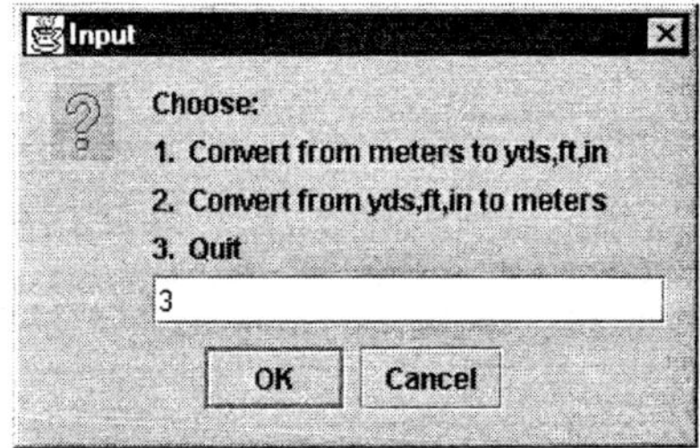

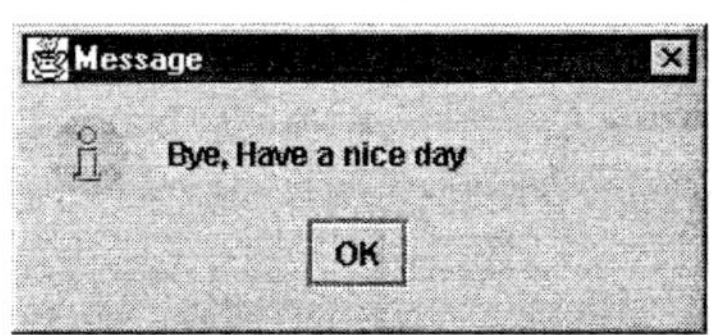

Note 1: This expression converts the yards, feet, and inches input to a total number of inches.

Note 2: Multiplying by .0254 converts inches to meters. The result has type `double` which we cast to type `float` so the output will have seven digits instead of 16.

Note 3: We use the singular "meter" if the value is between zero and one, and the plural "meters" otherwise. We do not display the user's input of yards, feet, and inches to avoid dealing with singular and plural. See the `MetricToEnglish` method which handles singular and plural unit names.

Testing the Java Code

This conversion problem allowed us to use our own program to provide a check on our results. In the first test, 7 yards 2 feet 5 inches converted to 7.1374 meters. In the second test, we converted 7.1374 meters, noting that it did in fact convert back to 7 yards 2 feet 5 inches. To save space we do not include any other tests, but leave such testing to the exercises.

TIP

Whenever possible do some tests where you know the expected result and can check if your program produces that result. Test each feature of your program, and include unusual input as well as typical cases. Test input errors to see how your program behaves when confronted with erroneous data.

We have been testing the program at each iteration. Rerunning the previous tests as we implement more features will allow us to check that the newly incorporated features have not affected the functioning of the previously tested code.

THE BIG PICTURE

Using the iterative method for software development lets us test the overall structure with stubs. We then develop one piece at a time, testing carefully at each iteration. We try to get once piece of the program correct before going on to the next.

TEST YOUR UNDERSTANDING

TRY IT YOURSELF 40. Test Example 4.14 thoroughly. For each test case determine whether or not the program is performing properly.

41. Modify the pseudocode of Figure 4.23 to provide pseudocode for a menu-driven program to convert between British currency of pounds and pence, in which one pound contains 100 pence, and US currency in dollars and cents. Do not compile or execute any code.

TRY IT YOURSELF 42. Add a section to the `EnglishToMetric` method in Example 4.14 to display the user's input before displaying the result of the conversion. Use the correct singular or plural form of the unit names. You may use the code in the `MetricToEnglish` method as a model.

TRY IT YOURSELF 43. Using stubs for the conversion functions, implement and test the high-level menu program for converting currencies between British pounds and pence and US dollars and cents. Use the pseudocode from question 41, and follow the model of Example 4.12 which implements the pseudocode of Figure 4.29.

SUMMARY

- This chapter covers Java operations, statements and types which facilitate the writing of good programs. The `conditional AND`, `conditional OR` and `NOT` operators take `boolean` operands and produce a `boolean` value. An `AND` expression is `true` only when both its operands are `true`, an `OR` expression is `true` when either or both of its operands is `true`, and a `NOT` expression is `true` when its operand is `false`. We use these operators to write more complex conditions, useful as tests in `if-else` and `while` statements.
- To choose among multiple alternatives we can use nested `if-else` statements. A final `else` without any following conditional test can be used to handle the case when all the previous conditions are false. Ambiguity can arise when nesting `if` and `if-else` statements. Java uses a rule that pairs each `else` with the preceding `if`, but programmers can override this rule by enclosing a nested `if` statement in curly braces.
- A `switch` statement is a better choice than nested `if-else` statements to handle more than a few alternatives. We mark each alternative in the code with a `case`

label. When Java executes a switch statement, it jumps to the code at the case label specified by the value of the switch variable, and continues executing code from that point on. break statements separate one alternative from the other. A break statement causes Java to jump to the end of the switch statement, bypassing the code associated with any cases that follow that break. The default label will handle any alternatives not covered by other case labels. We often use the switch statement to provide a menu of choices for the user.

- The for statement and the do-while statement make it easier to write programs requiring repetition. The for statement has four parts: initialize, test, update, and body. The initialize part initializes, and may declare, an index variable that identifies each repetition. The test condition evaluates to true or false; Java repeats the execution of the body, a simple statement or a block enclosed in curly braces, as long as the condition is true. After each repetition, Java evaluates the update expression, which often increments the value of the index variable. The flexible for statement allows a number of variations in its use. It is ideal when we have a fixed number of repetitions.
- The do-while statement is like the while statement, but it checks the test condition after executing the loop body instead of before; the loop body will be executed at least once. Java executes the body of a do-while statement, then terminates the loop if the test condition is false, but evaluates the body again if the test is true. The repetition will only terminate when the test condition becomes false. In writing a do-while statement, as well as in writing a for statement or a while statement, we must be very careful to make sure that the test condition eventually fails or the loop will never terminate.
- The switch, for, and do-while statements give the programmer options to design the program control flow. Java has data types, char, long, and float, which add choices for the program's data. The character type, char, internally uses Unicode to represent the many characters used in different locales. In this text we use the ASCII character set which includes lower and upper case letters, numerals, punctuation, various operators, and special characters some of which are non-printing control characters. Java uses single quotes to represent characters such as 'A.' The backslash. '\,' is an escape character, signaling to Java that the next character is a special character such as '\n,' the newline character. We can declare variables of type char, and input character data from the keyboard.
- The long type allows us to use integers of up to 19 digits, roughly twice as many as the 10 digit maximum for type int. The long type has the arithmetic operators +, -,*, /, and %; we represent literals of type long using the suffix L or l to distinguish these values from those of type int. For decimal numbers, the type float uses less precision, seven digits, than the type double, and also uses less space internally. Each float literal is suffixed with an F or an f to distinguish it from a value of type double.

- The `Math` class contains methods to compute a number of mathematical functions including powers, square roots, absolute value, maxima, minima, floor, and ceiling. There are methods for evaluating the natural logarithm, exponential, and trigonometric functions. A random number generator enables us to do simulations of events that occur with certain probabilities. In using any of the methods from the `Math` class we prefix the method name with the class name, `Math`, as for example in `Math.sqrt(2.0)` which computes the square root of two.
- We apply these statements, data types, operations and `Math` functions to solve problems, using an iterative process that repeats the steps of developing pseudocode, translating the pseudocode to a Java program, and testing that program, until all subproblems have been refined and the solution is complete. In the early stages of development, we use stubs for methods that will be designed later in the development process. By building our program in stages, we keep control of the design, clearly thinking through the steps that will lead to a correct, efficient, and maintainable solution.

Skill Builder Exercises

1. Rewrite the following `switch` statement using `if-else` statements.

```
switch(i) {
  case 1:
            j += 2;
            break;
  case 3:
            j -= 5;
            break;
  case7:
  case10:
            j *= 17;
            break;
  default:
            j = 0;
}
```

2. Rewrite the following `for` loop using a `while` loop.

```
for (int i = 0; i <= 20; i++)
  sum += i * i;
```

3. Rewrite the following fragment using a `do-while` loop instead of a `while` loop.

```
int sum = 0;
String input =
    JOptionPane.showInputDialog("Enter an integer");
int i = Integer.parseInt(input);
```

```
while (sum < 100) {
  sum += i;
  input =
    JOptionPane.showInputDialog("Enter an integer");
  i = Integer.parseInt(input);
}
```

Critical Thinking Exercises

4. Which of the following expressions is equivalent to

   `((x + 3) < (y - 10)) && ((!(x > 4)) == (y + (2 * x)))`

   where `x` and `y` are of type `int`?

   a. `x + 3 < y - 10 && !x > 4 == y + 2 * x`

   b. `(x + 3 < y - 10) && (!x > 4 == y + 2 * x)`

   c. `x + 3 < y - 10 && !(x > 4) == y + 2 * x`

   d. all of the above

   e. none of the above

5. Which of the following statements is equivalent to the `switch` statement

```
switch(x) {
  case 2: y = 3;
  case 5: y = 7;
          break;
  case 7:  y = 9;
}
```

   a.
```
if (x == 2)
    y = 3;
else if (x == 5)
    y = 7;
else if (x == 7)
    y = 9;
```

   b.
```
if (x == 2 || x == 5)
    y = 7;
else if (x == 7)
    y = 9;
```

   c.
```
if (x == 2)
    y = 7;
else if(x == 5)
    y = 7;
else  y = 9;
```

   d. none of the above

6. Which of the following `for` statements computes the same value for `sum` as `for (int x = 0; x < 15; x+=2) sum += x + 5;`?

   a. `for (int x = 5; x < 20; x+=2) sum += x;`

   b. `for (int x = 5; x < 20; sum += x-2) x += 2;`

   c. `for (int x = 0; x < 15; sum += x+3) x += 2;`

   d. all of the above

   e. none of the above

7. Which of the following do statements is equivalent to

```
y = x + 7;
x++;
while (x < 9) {
  y = x + 7;
  x++;
}
```

a.
```
y = x + 7;
x++;
do {
    y = x + 7;
    x++;
} while (x < 9);
```

b.
```
do {
    y = x + 7;
    x++;
} while (x < 9);
```

c.
```
do {
    y = x + 7;
    x++;
} while
    (x < = 9);
```

d. none of the above

Debugging Exercise

8. The program below attempts to calculate the total commission received by a salesperson who earns 7% on sales of product A which total less than $40,000 and 10% of the amount above $40,000. For example a sale of $50,000 would earn a commission of $3800. The salesperson receives a commission of 5% on sales of product B under $20,000, 6.5% on the amount of sales over $20,000 but under $50,000, and 7.5% on the amount over $50,000. Find and correct any errors in this program.

```
public class Commission {
  public static void main(String [] args) {
    String input = JOptionPane.showInputDialog
           ("Enter the amount of Product A sales");
    double salesOfA = Double.parseDouble(input);
    input = JOptionPane.showInputDialog
           ("Enter the amount of Product B sales");
    double salesOfB = Double.parseDouble(input);
    double amount = 0;
    if (salesOfA < 40000.00)
      amount += .07 * salesOfA;
    else
      amount = .1 * (salesOfA - 40000.0);
    if (salesOfB < 20000.00)
      amount += .05 * salesOfB;
    else if (salesOfB > 20000.00 || salesOfB < 50000.00)
      amount += 1000  + .065 * (salesOfB - 50000.00);
    else
      amount = .075 * (salesOfB - 50000.00);
    NumberFormat nf =
             NumberFormat.getCurrencyInstance();
    System.out.println("The commission is " +
             nf.format(amount));
```

```
        System.exit(0);
    }
}
```

Program Modification Exercises

PUTTING IT ALL TOGETHER 9. Do Exercise 9 of Chapter 3

Write a Java program which computes the weekly pay for an employee. Input the number of hours worked. The employee receives $7.50 per hour for the first forty hours and $11.25 per hour for each additional hour.with the added condition that the number of hours worked is between 0 and 80.

PUTTING IT ALL TOGETHER 10. Do Exercise 10 of Chapter 3

Write a Java program which checks a grade point average that the user inputs, and outputs "Congratulations, You made the honor roll" if the average is 3.5 and above, but outputs "Sorry, You are on probation" if the average is below 2.0.with the added condition that the grade point average is between 0.0 and 4.0.

11. Modify Example 4.6 to let the user type 'Y' or 'y' instead of 1 and 'N' or 'n' instead of 0 to indicate whether or not to repeat the calculation.

12. Modify Example 4.3 to use the `switch` statement of Figure 4.13 instead of nested `if-else` statements.

Program Design Exercises

13. Write a Java program that inputs the radius of a circle and outputs its area. Allow the user to repeat the calculation as often as desired. Use `Math.PI` for the value of pi. The area of a circle is pi times the square of the radius.
    a. Use only a `main` method to solve the problem.
    b. Develop an object-oriented solution with instance variables and methods.

14. Write a Java program that inputs the radius of a circle and outputs its circumference. Allow the user to repeat the calculation as often as desired. Use `Math.PI` for the value of pi. The circumference of a circle is pi times the diameter. The diameter of a circle is twice the radius.
    a. Use only a `main` method to solve the problem.
    b. Develop an object-oriented solution with instance variables and methods.

15. Write a Java program that inputs the radius of the base of a circular cylinder and its height and outputs its volume. Allow the user to repeat the calculation as often as desired. Use `Math.PI` for the value of pi. The volume of a cylinder is the height times the area of the base.
    a. Use only a `main` method to solve the problem.
    b. Develop an object-oriented solution with instance variables and methods.

16. The ancient Babylonians used a divide and average method for computing the square root of a positive number `x`. First estimate the square root by some value `r`; any positive estimate will do. Then compute the quotient, `x/r`. Averaging `r` and `x/r` gives a better estimate, so continue the process, dividing and averaging until the estimates agree to the desired number of places. For example, to compute the square root of two

estimate 1	divide 2/1 = 2	average (1+2)/2 = 1.5
estimate 1.5	divide 2/1.5 = 1.33	average (1.5+1.33)/2 = 1.415
estimate 1.415		

and so on. Write a Java program to compute the square root of a number input by the user. Use the divide and average method and stop after ten repetitions of the divide and average steps. Compare your result with the value produced by the `sqrt` method of the `Math` class.

    a. Use only a `main` method to solve the problem.

    b. Develop an object-oriented solution with instance variables and methods.

17. Write a Java program to compute square roots, as described in Exercise 16, but stop the repetitions when two successive estimates differ by less than `1.0E-6`. Also, output the number of repetitions of the divide and average process.

    a. Use only a `main` method to solve the problem.

    b. Develop an object-oriented solution with instance variables and methods.

18. The greatest common divisor (gcd) of two integers is the largest positive number that divides evenly into both numbers. For example, `gcd(6,9) = 3`, `gcd(4,14)=2`, and `gcd(5,8) = 1`. The Euclidean algorithm computes the gcd by a repetitive process. Find the remainder resulting from dividing the smaller number into the larger. Repeat this process with the smaller number and the remainder until the remainder is zero. The last non-zero remainder is the greatest common divisor. For example, to find the gcd of 54 and 16, the steps are

    54 % 16 = 6
    16 % 6 = 4
    6 % 4 = 2
    4 % 2 = 0

    so `gcd(54,16) = 2`. Write a Java program to compute the greatest common divisor of two integers.

    a. Use only a `main` method to solve the problem.

    b. Develop an object-oriented solution with instance variables and methods.

19. When we convert a fraction of the form `1/n`, where neither two nor five divide `n`, to a decimal, we find that the digits repeat a pattern over and over again. For example,

1/3 = .333333333333... repeat pattern 3
1/7 = .142857142857142857... repeat pattern 142657
1/37 = .027027027 .... repeat pattern 027

The number of digits in the pattern for `1/n`, called the period, is equal to the number of zeros in the smallest power of 10 that has a remainder of one when divided by `n`. For example, to find the number of digits on the pattern for `1/37`, we calculate

10 % 37 = 10
100 % 37 = 26
1000 % 37 = 1

Write a Java program to find the length of the repeating pattern for fractions 1/n, where neither two nor five divide `n`.

a. Use only a `main` method to solve the problem.

b. Develop an object-oriented solution with instance variables and methods.

20. Write a Java program that converts currencies between British currency of pounds and pence, in which one pound contains 100 pence, and US currency in dollars and cents. Assume an exchange rate of 1.6595 US dollars per British pound. Give the user a menu to choose the type of conversion. Allow the user to repeat as often as desired. (See Test Your Understanding questions 42 and 43.)

    a. Use only a `main` method to solve the problem.

    b. Develop an object-oriented solution with instance variables and methods.

21. Write a Java program to perform geometric calculations. Let the user choose whether to find the area of a circle (See Exercise 13), the circumference of a circle (See Exercise 14), or the volume of a cylinder (See Exercise 15). Allow the user to repeat as often as desired.

22. Suppose you are able to pay $400 per month to buy a car. Write a Java program to determine if you can afford to buy a car which costs $15,000 if the interest rate is 6% and you make payments for 48 months. (Hint: Each month, determine how much of the $400 payment will be used to pay interest, then deduct the remaining payment from the principal.)

    a. Use only a `main` method to solve the problem.

    b. Develop an object-oriented solution with instance variables and methods.

23. Generalize Exercise 22 to have the user input the size of the payment, the price of the car, the interest rate, and the number of monthly payments.

    a. Use only a `main` method to solve the problem.

    b. Develop an object-oriented solution with instance variables and methods.

24. The Sturdy company invests \$100,000 in a project that earns 10% compounded annually. Assuming that the interest is allowed to compound, what is the value of the investment after seven years? Use the formula

    $$V = P(1 + r/100)^N$$

    where `r` is the interest rate, `N` is the number of years, `P` is the initial investment, and `V` is the value after N years.

    a. Use only a `main` method to solve the problem.

    b. Develop an object-oriented solution with instance variables and methods.

25. The Sturdy company is evaluating an investment that will return \$400,000 at the end of five years. The company wants to earn an interest rate of 20% compounded annually. How much should they pay for this investment? Use the formula

    $$P = V / (1 + r/100)^N$$

    where `V` is the investment's value after `N` years and `r` is the interest rate.

    a. Use only a `main` method to solve the problem.

    b. Develop an object-oriented solution with instance variables and methods.

26. Use random numbers to simulate the toss of a fair coin. Letting the user input the number of tosses, report the percentage of outcomes that are heads. Allow the user to repeat the calculation as often as desired.

    a. Use only a `main` method to solve the problem.

    b. Develop an object-oriented solution with instance variables and methods.

27. Calculate pi by throwing darts. In the figure below, the area of the circle divided by the area of the square is equal to `pi / 4`. Throw darts randomly at the square, counting the total number of darts thrown, and the number of darts that land inside the circle. The ratio of the latter to the former is an estimate of `pi /4`. Multiplying that ratio by four, gives an estimate for pi. Use random numbers to simulate dart throwing. Get two random numbers, for the `x` and `y` coordinates. If $(x-0.5)^2 + (y-0.5)^2 < .25$, then the dart landed inside the circle. Let the user input the number of dart throws.

    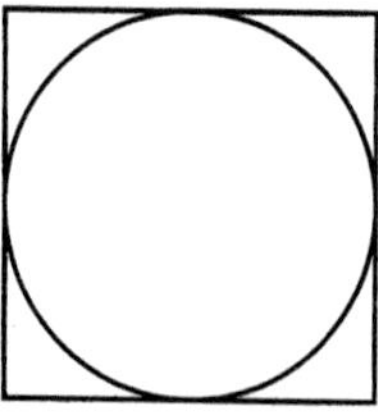

    a. Use only a `main` method to solve the problem.

    b. Develop an object-oriented solution with instance variables and methods.

28. Calculate pi using the series

    pi / 4 = 1 - 1/3 + 1/5 - 1/7 + 1/9 - ... and so on.

    Output the estimate of pi after computing 100, 1000, 10000, and 100000 terms of the series

    a. Use only a `main` method to solve the problem.

    b. Develop an object-oriented solution with instance variables and methods.

29. Compute e^x where

    $e^x = 1 + x/1! + x^2/2! + x^3/3! + \ldots\ldots \quad \ldots + x^n/n! + \ldots\ldots$

    and `n! = n(n-1)(n-2)...   ...1`, the product of the integers from one to `n` (We pronounce the expression `n!` as `n factorial`.) Let the user input the value of `x`, of type `double`, to use. Continue adding terms until the difference of successive terms is less than `1.0 E-6`. Compare your answer with the Java method `Math.exp(x)`. (Hint: Compute each term from the previous one. For example, the fourth term is `x/3` times the third term.)

    a. Use only a `main` method to solve the problem.

    b. Develop an object-oriented solution with instance variables and methods.

CHAPTER 5

Object-Oriented Design and Programming

OUTLINE

Introduction

In this chapter we introduce some basic concepts of object-oriented programming and design. We start by illustrating how to use `String` methods. Using two simple examples from section 1.7, a restaurant and an automated teller, we introduce object-oriented design with use cases and scenarios, which lets us identify the objects in the system. An object-oriented program shows that control and interactions are found in each object rather than in a master controller.

Looking at these design examples shows us the need for class definitions to define the state and responsibilities of our objects. Writing a simple `BankAccount` class illustrates the basic concepts of instance variables and methods, constructors, and overloading. We then complete the restaurant code to show a complete object-oriented program while introducing some UML diagrams. We conclude by discussing object composition, designing classes that include other classes as fields. In later chapters, we continue with object-oriented concepts, including inheritance, polymorphism, abstract classes, interfaces, and design with use cases and scenarios to complete the ATM example.

Objectives:

- Create and use objects.
- Learn selected `String` methods.
- Understand Java primitive type variables hold values, while object variables hold references.
- Understand the difference between a concept and its instances.
- Understand that a class defines a type of object.
- Write a class, including instance variables and methods, and constructors.
- Create UML sequence diagrams.
- Implement an object-oriented design.
- Use object composition.

5.1 Using Objects

We look at Java strings more carefully and contrast object variables, which hold references, with primitive type variables that hold values. Before getting to the Java details, we look at a string informally as we did the vending machine. Inside a `String` object is a sequence of characters, such as `"Java is fun"`. The state of a `String` object is private. Perhaps the letters of the string are wooden blocks numbered to indicate their position in the string, so block 'J' would have number 1, block 'a' would have number 2, and so on. Users of `String` objects do not need to know how the characters are represented.

Strings have many public operations to provide their services. We can ask the length of a string, or ask for the first position that contains the letter 'a.' The drawing of the `String` object, `"Java is fun"` in Figure 5.1 does not have a window to see inside, because strings do not show any of their state; it is all private. Strings provide many operations; we show only a few.

Figure 5.1 **A `String` object (for `"Java is fun"`)**

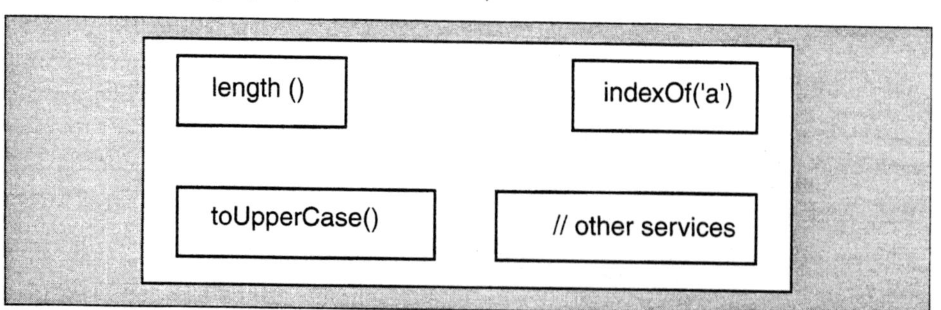

When we press the `length()` button in Figure 5.1 we get the result of 11 because `"Java is fun"` has 11 characters. The result of an operation depends on the state of the object. For this object the `indexOf('a')` operation returns 1. The first 'a' occurs as the second character, but for technical reasons we start the numbering with 0, so 'J' is at index 0, and 'a' is at index 1.

Strings in Java never change. The `String` object in Figure 5.1 will always represent `"Java is fun"`. When we execute the `toUpperCase()` operation, we do not change the object, but rather we get a new `String` object representing `"JAVA IS FUN"` shown in Figure 5.2.

Figure 5.2 A `String` object (for "`JAVA IS FUN`")

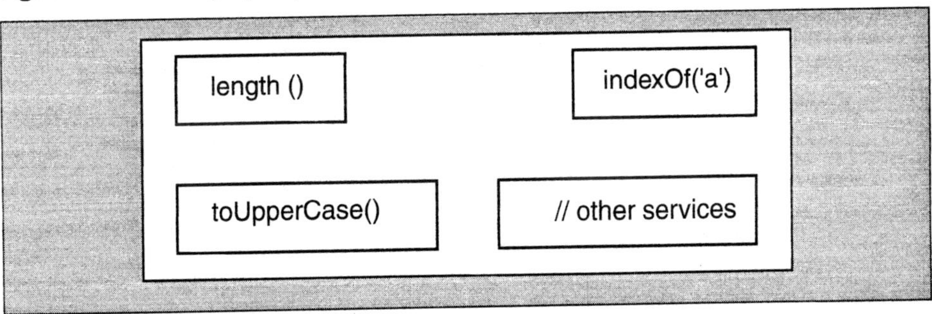

Because the state is hidden, Figure 5.2 looks just like Figure 5.1, but it operates differently. Executing the `indexOf('a')` operation will return –1, signifying the character 'a' does not appear in `"JAVA IS FUN"`. Java is case-sensitive; a lowercase 'a' differs from an uppercase 'A.'

Visualizing a `String` object as a vending machine really helps us to keep in mind the object concept: state, behavior, and identity. To use strings in Java programs, we need to learn the notation used to create a string, and to ask it to provide one of its services. The declaration

```
String s = "Java lets us use objects.";
```

creates and initializes a `String`, which we refer to as `s`, while the method

```
s.length();
```

will return the number of characters in `s`, 25 in this example.

Note the object-oriented flavor of the invocation `s.length()`. We ask the object referred to by `s` to determine its length. Finding its length is one of the behaviors a string can exhibit. The syntax we use can serve as a reminder. We might think of the dot in the expression `s.length()` as a vending machine button. Calling the `length` method is like pressing a vending machine button. The `length` method is part of the `String` object, and its result depends on the state of that object. Just as it would not make any sense to push a candy button not connected to the vending machine, trying to call `length()` instead of `s.length()` would not connect with any string and would be meaningless.

Figure 5.3 shows some of the many `String` methods:

Figure 5.3 Selected `String` methods

```
public char charAt(int index)                 character at the specified
                                              index
public int compareTo(String anotherString)    0 if equal to anotherString
                                              negative if less
                                              positive if greater
public boolean equals(Object anObject)        true for equal Strings
public int indexOf(char ch)                   index of first occurrence of ch
public int indexOf(char ch, int from)         index of first occurrence of ch
                                              starting at index from
public int indexOf(String str)                index of first occurrence of str
public int indexOf(String str, int from)      index of first occurrence of ch
                                              starting at index from
public int length()                           string length
public String substring                       new string with characters from
   (int beginIndex, int endIndex)             beginIndex to endIndex - 1
public String toLowerCase()                   returns a lowercase string
public String toUpperCase()                   returns an uppercase string
public String trim()                          removes leading and trailing
                                              whitespace
public static String valueOf(int i)           creates a string from an int
public static String valueOf(double d)        creates a string from a double
```

Figure 5.4 presents examples of the use of these methods on the string given by

```
String s = "Java lets us use objects. ";
```

Figure 5.4 Examples of `String` methods

Method	Return value	Description of return value
`s.charAt(6)`	'e'	The character at position 6 is an 'e.'
`s.compareTo("Toast")`	negative integer	The string referred to by s is alphabetically less than "Toast" so the return value is a negative integer.
`s.equals("Java is fun")`	false	The string referred to by s does not have the same characters as "Java is fun" .
`s.indexOf('e')`	6	The leftmost 'e' in the string occurs at index 6.

Figure 5.4 Examples of `String` methods (continued)

Method	Return value	Description of return value
`s.indexOf('e',8)`	15	The first occurrence of 'e,' starting from index 8, is at index 15.
`s.indexOf("us")`	10	The leftmost occurrence of "us" starts at index 10.
`s.indexOf("us",11)`	13	The first occurrence of "us", starting from index 11, begins at index 13.
`s.indexOf("us",15)`	–1	There is no occurrence of "us" starting at index 15.
`s.length()`	27	This string contains 27 characters.
`s.substring(13,24)`	A new String with characters "use objects"	The string "use objects" starts at index 13 and continues up to index 24.
`s.toLowerCase()`	A new String with characters "java lets us use objects. "	Returns a new string with all lowercase characters.
`s.toUpperCase()`	A new String with characters "JAVA LETS US USE OBJECTS. "	Returns a new string with all uppercase characters.
`s.trim()`	A new String with characters "Java lets us use objects."	Returns a new string with leading and trailing blanks removed.

Each method in these examples refers to a specific `String` object. We call these methods **instance methods**, because each refers to a specific instance of a string. Just as selection buttons are part of a specific instance of a vending machine, instance methods are part of a specific instance of an object. In the expression `s.length()`, the length request goes to the string referred to by `s`, not to some other string. Not all the methods of Figure 5.3 are instance methods. We leave consideration of the `valueOf` methods to a later section.

To illustrate the use of objects, Example 5.1 replaces every occurrence of the word "fish," in a string entered by the user, with the word "fowl." Example 5.1 demonstrates the use of `String` objects, but is not an object-oriented program in which objects cooperate to perform a task. We will see an object-oriented program in the next section.

EXAMPLE 5.1 Replace.java

```
/* Replaces every occurrence of "fish" with "fowl"
 */

import javax.swing.*;
public class Replace {
  public static void main(String[] args) {
    String s = JOptionPane.showInputDialog
           ("Enter a String which includes \"fish\" ");
    int length = s.length();
    int position = s.indexOf("fish");                     // Note 1
    while (position != -1) {
      s = s.substring(0,position) + "fowl"
          + s.substring(position+4, length);              // Note 2
      position = s.indexOf("fish", position + 4);         // Note 3
    }
    JOptionPane.showMesageDialog
          (null,"The new string is: " +s);
    System.exit(0);
  }
}
```

First Run

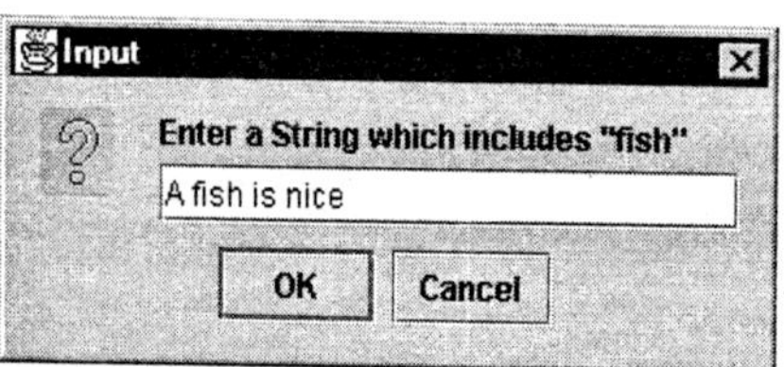

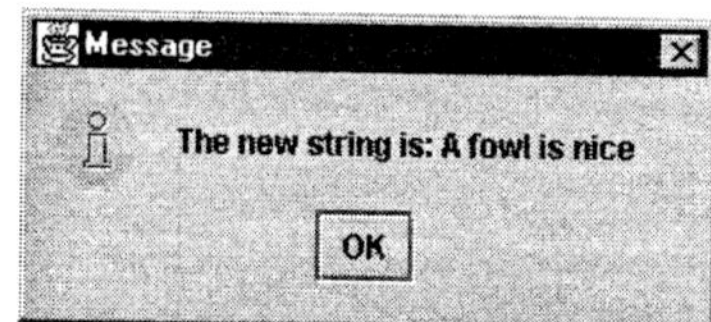

Second Run

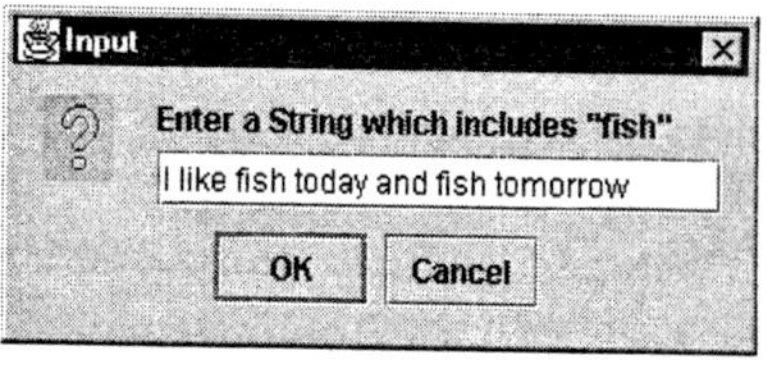

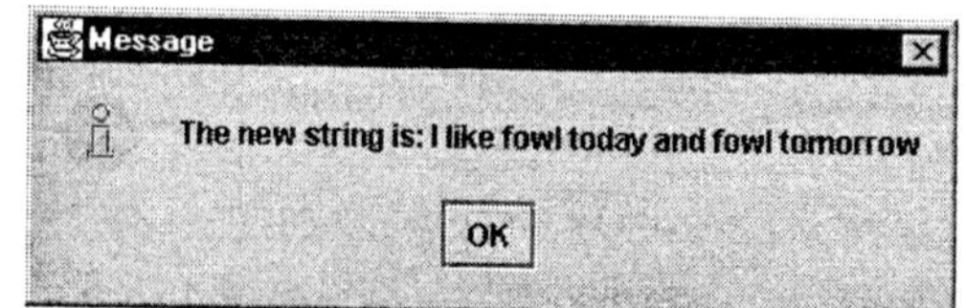

Note 1: We initialize position with the index of the first occurrence of "fish," or -1 if it does not occur in s.

Note 2: When we find "fish" in the string s, we create a new string with that occurrence of "fish" replaced by "fowl." We have already used the string concatenation operator, +, in `println` statements.

Note 3: We continue the search from the character after "fowl."

THE BIG PICTURE

An object has state, behavior, and identity. We picture a vending machine in a given configuration which provides services and has an identity distinct from other vending machines. A `String` object hides its state, but provides many methods to access its services.

We ask an object to perform an operation using one of its instance methods. Such an instance method refers to that object. Thus `s.length()` returns the length of a specific `String` object referred to by s. Just as a selection button is part of a vending machine, an instance method is part of an object.

Values vs. References

Java uses variables for objects such as strings differently than variables for basic data types such as integers. Let us review how we created variables to hold integers. The statement

```
int x = 4;
```

declares a variable, `x`, of type integer, and initializes it with the value of 4. Inside the computer, the variable `x` has a storage location and the computer places the value `4` into that location. Here the variable holds the value `4`. A real world analogy might involve me asking at the dinner table to please pass the salt, and my wife graciously handing me the salt shaker. My wife can easily move the small salt shaker to my hand. My hand is like the variable `x`, and the salt is like the value `4`.

By contrast, suppose I would like to stand next to the Grand Canyon. Even if I had a hundred helpers, they could not pass me the Grand Canyon. If I want to stand next to the Grand Canyon, I have to go there. In fact my wife might pass me a map showing how to get to there. When I hold that map in my hand I am holding a reference to the Grand Canyon, telling me where it is.

In Java, an object is like the Grand Canyon. An object may be large, so we do not want to pass it around. We put it in one place and tell users where it is. A variable for an object holds a reference to that object, telling where to find it in the computer's memory. If we declare

```
String myString= "We want a big car";
```

then the variable `myString` contains a reference to a `String` object, rather than the object itself. We leave the object in one place, and variables in our program refer to it.

When we declare and initialize an integer variable,

```
int x = 4;
```

we get a single entity that holds an integer value (see Figure 5.5a). When we declare and initialize a `String` variable,

```
String myString = "We want a big car";
```

Figure 5.5b shows we get two entities, an object representing `"We want a big car"` and a variable, `myString`, that refers to that `String` object. We show the reference as an arrow pointing to the object. The reference has a name, `myString`, while the string itself remains nameless.

Figure 5.5 Value vs. reference

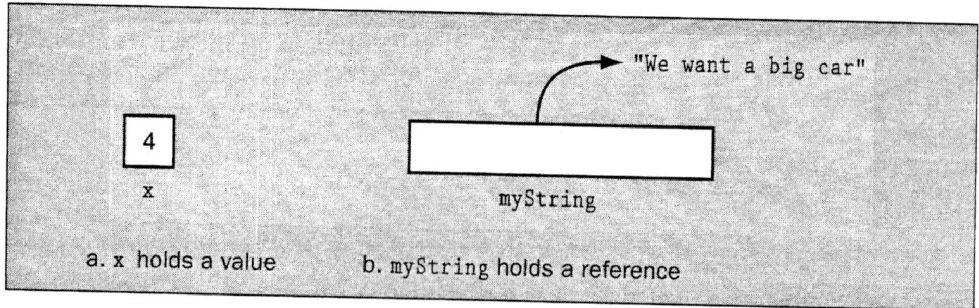

A big difference between **int** variables which hold values, and string variables which hold references occurs as a result of assignment. The assignment operation copies the contents of one variable to another. For primitive types such as **int**, assignment copies the integer value from one variable to another, as shown in Figure 5.6. The effect of the assignment statement `y = x;` is to copy the value 4, stored in `x`, to `y`, overwriting the previous value of 5 that `y` had.

Figure 5.6 Assignment of an integer

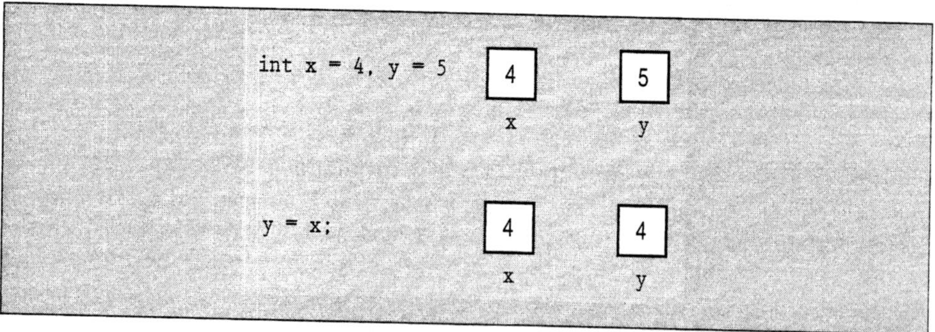

For object types such as `String`, assignment still copies the contents of one variable to another. A string variable holds a reference, so assignment copies that reference as Figure 5.7 shows. After the assignment, the variable `t` has the same reference as `s`. Both refer to "soup." The string "fish" has no references to it and is termed **garbage**. Java will automatically reclaim the memory used for "fish" with a process known as a **garbage collection.**

Figure 5.7 Assignment of a string

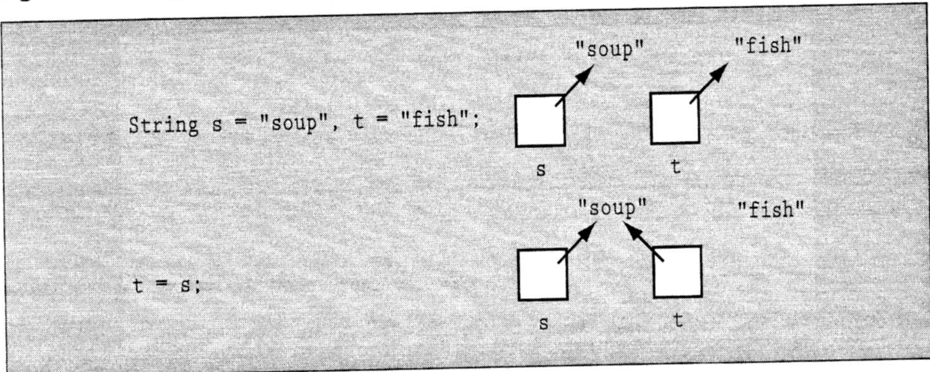

Comparing Figures 5.6 and 5.7, we see that, after the assignment, `x` and `y` each have their own copy of the value 4, but that `s` and `t` refer to the same string "soup." Figure 5.7 uses strings, but the same sharing would result from the assignment of any type of object, whereas no sharing results from assignment of primitive types.

We access objects through references to them. For example, to find the number of characters in "We want a big car" we invoke

```
myString.length()
```

accessing the string using the `myString` variable.

If we declare a string without initializing it, as in

```
String s;
```

then we have a variable, `s`, which does not refer to any string yet, as shown in Figure 5.8. Java uses `null` to represent the value of a reference before we create an object for it to refer to, so `s` is `null` until we give it a reference to a string.

Figure 5.8 An object declaration without object creation

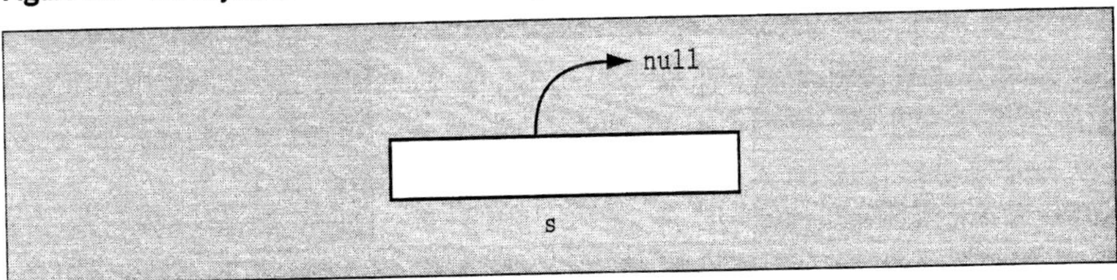

Comparing Strings

Often we need to check two strings for equality, meaning both strings have the same characters at each position. For example, for the strings `s1`, `s2` and `s3` given by

```
String s = "a houseboat";
String s1 = "house";
String s2 = s.substring(2,7);
String s3 = "horse";
```

```
String s4 = s1;
```

we would like `s1` and `s2` to be equal, because each has the same characters, but expect `s1` to be unequal to `s3`, because these strings differ at index 2. Of course, `s1` and `s4` are equal, because they refer to the same string.

The equality operator, ==, which we have used many times to test the equality of primitive values, can mislead us when applied to strings. This operator compares the contents of each variable, returning true if both are the same. Figure 5.9 illustrates the problem.

Figure 5.9 `s1 == s4` **but** `s1 != s2`

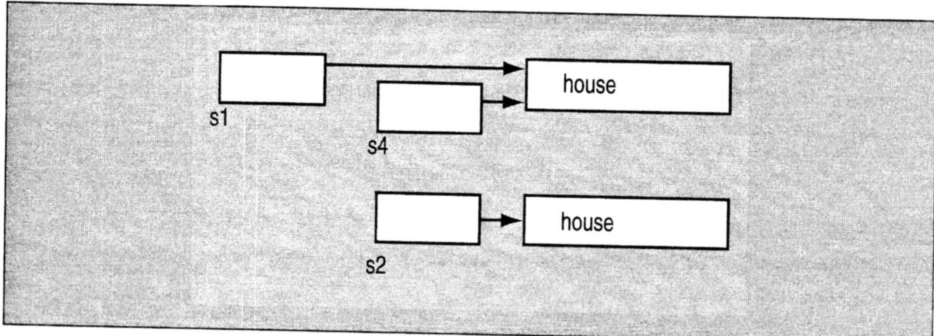

Object variables hold references to objects. The equality operator, ==, compares the contents of these variables, comparing the references, not the objects to which they refer. Both `s1` and `s4` refer to the same object, so `s1 == s4` evaluates to **true**. The expression `s1 == s2` will be false as these references are not equal; they refer to different objects. While these objects are not identical they are equal because they each contain the same sequence of characters. We need a replacement for the equality operator which compares the objects themselves, not the references to them.

The `equals` method solves our problem. It returns true if both strings have the same sequence of characters. Thus `s1.equals(s4)` and `s1.equals(s2)` will both return **true**. Figure 5.3 shows the argument to the `equals` method is of type `Object`. We will discuss the `Object` type in Section 9.1 and will see a `String` is a type of `Object` so we can use `String` arguments such as `s4` and `s2`, as we did above.

In applications such as alphabetizing we need to determine whether one string is greater than another. Java provides a `compareTo` method which, comparing strings lexicographically, returns a negative number if the string is less than the string argument, returns zero if both strings are equal, and returns a positive number if the string is greater than the string argument. For our strings `s1`, `s2`, and `s3` above,

```
s1.compareTo(s2) returns zero
s1.compareTo(s3) returns a positive number
s3.compareTo(s1) returns a negative number
```

THE BIG PICTURE

Variables declared with primitive types such as **int** hold values of those types. We can compare values using the == operator.

`String` variables, and those with other object types, are references to objects which are themselves nameless. To compare `String` values we use the `equals` method.

TEST YOUR UNDERSTANDING

1. Given the `String` object

```
String s = "The three did feed the deer";
```

find

a. `s.length()` b. `s.charAt(5)` c. `s.indexOf('e')`
d. `s.indexOf("did")` e. `s.substring(4,9)` f. `s.toUpperCase()`

2. Given the `String` objects

```
String s = "a good time";
String s1 = "time";
String s2 = s.substring(7,11);
String s3 = s2;
```

find

a. `s1 == s2` b. `s1 == s3` c. `s2 == s3`
d. `s1.equals(s2)` e. `s1.equals(s3);`

3. Given the `String` objects

```
String s1 = "Happy days";
String s2 = "Hello world";
String s3 = "77 Sunset Strip";
```

determine whether the value returned by each of the following calls to the `compareTo` method returns zero, a negative value, or a positive value.

a. `s1.compareTo(s2);` b. `s2.compareTo(s3)` c. `s1.compareTo("Happy days");`

5.2 Developing Java Classes

Our scenarios from Section 1.7 showed objects invoking each other's services. One of the responsibilities of a bank account is to provide a deposit operation which the teller can invoke. Each bank account has a state given by the value of its balance. The `BankAccount` class defines the state and behavior of bank account objects. In this section we develop and test the `BankAccount` class, leaving the full development of the ATM system, which uses inheritance and other object-oriented concepts until Section 9.5. In the next section we implement the classes for the `QuickFood` application introduced in Section 1.7.

The Structure of the `BankAccount` Class

Our analysis in Section 1.7 used a `BankAccount` object in the scenarios for the ATM system. In discussing classification, we saw that, in Java, a class defines the state and behavior of its object instances. To use `BankAccount` objects we need to specify them in a `BankAccount` class. The `BankAccount` class we will develop in this section will have a structure shown in Figure 5.10.

Figure 5.10 The `BankAccount` class

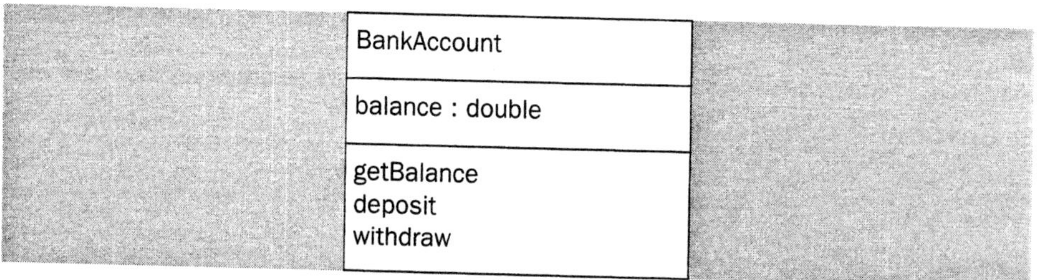

This `BankAccount` class specifies the account `balance` to represent the state of each account, and `deposit`, `withdraw`, and `getBalance` as an account's behavior. The UML notation allows us to specify the type of the state variables; here `balance` is of type **double**. For simplicity we do not show the arguments to the methods or their return types.

The overall structure of the `BankAccount` class in Java is

```
public class BankAccount {
  // put code to specify BankAccount objects here
}
```

A class is like a dictionary entry. The dictionary entry for *chair* defines what it means to be a chair. The `BankAccount` class defines what it means to be a bank account object. Each bank account has state, behavior, and identity. In Java, we use instance variables to hold the state of an object, and instance methods to implement the services needed to meet its responsibilities, which is what we call its behavior. We also have constructors to create bank accounts each with its own memory location distinct from other objects. Thinking of the `BankAccount` class as a definition of bank account objects, it will have the structure:

```
public class BankAccount {

  // instance variables go here    (for state)
  // constructors go here          (for identity)
  // instance methods go here      (for behavior)

}
```

We now discuss each of the three parts of the `BankAccount` class: instance variables, instance methods, and constructors.

Instance Variables

An **instance variable**, also called a **field**, is a variable declared inside the class but outside of any method. The name, *instance variable* reminds us these variables will be part of object instances. Analogously, the `Chair` concept includes mention of legs, but the concept does not have legs, only actual chairs do.

Our programs have used variables, but we have always declared these variables inside the `main` method. We call these variables **local variables** because they are declared inside one method, and cannot be used outside that method.

In Java, we declare instance variables to hold the state of an object. For a bank account we might declare

```
double balance;
```

to hold an account balance. The declaration (incomplete) for the bank account class shows how we declare the account balance outside of any method.

```
public class BankAccount {
  private double balance;

  // fill in the rest of the declaration here
}
```

In contrast to local variables, instance variables are available to all services of an object. Making a deposit to a bank account will increase its balance while making a withdrawal will reduce it.

Note the use of the modifier `private`. Using `private` signifies we want to keep the account balance data hidden within the object, accessible only by the services the object provides. The object appears as a black box to a user of its services. The user of an account can only inspect its balance by calling the object's `getBalance` method, and can only change its balance by making a deposit or a withdrawal.

Instance Methods

To specify an object's behavior we declare methods inside the class, such as a `deposit` method in the `BankAccount` class.

```
public class BankAccount {
  private double balance;

  public void deposit(double amount) {
    balance += amount;
  }

  // fill in the rest of the declaration here
}
```

The `deposit` method adds the amount passed in as a parameter to the balance. We call it an instance method because it is part of a specific bank account instance. Each bank account will have its own `balance` and its own `deposit` method. To put it simply, when I make a deposit into my account I want the money to increase my balance, not yours.

Our `BankAccount` class defines the concept of a bank account. Analyzing the ATM system with use cases and scenarios shows us each bank account should provide services to get its balance and to make a withdrawal, in addition to the deposit service. Thus we must add `getBalance` and `withdraw` operations to the `BankAccount` class.

The code for `getBalance()` simply returns the balance

```
public double getBalance() {
  return balance;
}
```

The `withdraw` method uses an `if-else` statement to check whether the account balance is large enough to make the withdrawal, printing an error message otherwise.

```
public void withdraw(double amount) {
  if (balance >= amount)       // check for sufficient funds
    balance -= amount;
  else
    System.out.println("Insufficient funds");
}
```

With the addition of the `getBalance` and `withdraw` methods the `BankAccount` class now has the structure

```
public class BankAccount {
    private double balance;

    public void deposit(double amount) {
      balance += amount;
  }
    public double getBalance() {
      return balance;
  }
    public void withdraw(double amount) {
      if (balance >= amount)
        balance -= amount;
      else
        System.out.println("Insufficient funds");
  }

    // fill in the rest of the declaration here
}
```

Constructors

Our `BankAccount` class now defines the concept we identified in the analysis of the ATM system. It provides an instance variable, `balance`, for the state, and `getBalance`, `deposit`, and `withdraw` methods for the services. However, we do need to add code to enable us to create and initialize `BankAccount` objects. These special methods, called **constructors**, always have the same name as the class, and never have a return value.

Every bank account has a `balance`. We can use the constructor to initialize the balance of a new account. The `BankAccount` constructor

```
public BankAccount () {
  balance = 0.0;
}
```

initializes the balance of a new `BankAccount` object to zero. We call a constructor with no arguments a **default constructor.**

We would also like a constructor to create a bank account with a specified initial balance. Using method overloading, which we discuss later in this section, we can use the constructor

```
public BankAccount(double initialAmount) {
  balance = initialAmount;
}
```

to create a bank account with a balance initialized to `initialAmount`.

Figure 5.11 shows the class diagram for the `BankAccount` class as we developed it in this section.

Figure 5.11 The revised `BankAccount` class

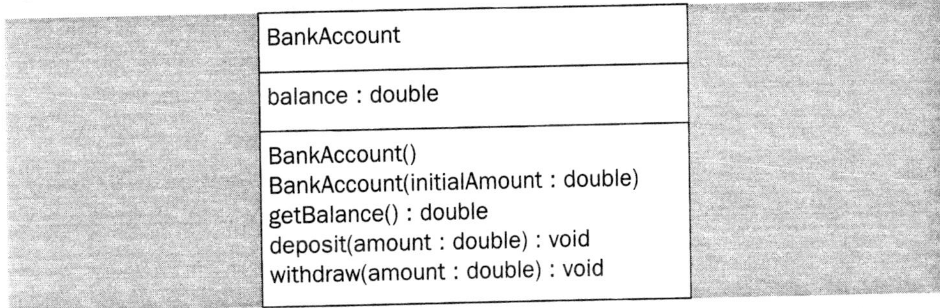

We usually do not show this amount of detail in our class diagrams. The UML notation uses a different style than Java for specifying method parameters and return values. Whenever possible we omit parameters and return values from class diagrams to avoid confusion.

Example 5.2 shows the Java code for our `BankAccount` class. This class has no `main` method. We can compile it, but not execute it. Remember the `BankAccount` class defines `BankAccount` objects. We need to learn how to create and use `BankAccount` objects.

EXAMPLE 5.2 BankAccount.java

```
/* Declares a BankAccount class with an account balance,
 * two constructors, and getBalance, deposit, and
 * withdraw operations.
 */

public class BankAccount {
```

```
  private double balance;                                // Note 1

  public BankAccount() {                                 // Note 2
    balance = 0;
  }
  public BankAccount(double initialAmount) {             // Note 3
    balance = initialAmount;
  }
  public double getBalance() {                           // Note 4
    return balance;
  }
  public void deposit(double amount) {                   // Note 5
    balance += amount;
  }
  public void withdraw(double amount) {
    if (balance >= amount)
      balance -= amount;
    else
      System.out.println("Insufficient funds");
  }
}
```

Note 1: We declare the variable `balance` outside of any method. Each object has its own `balance` variable which stores the balance for that specific account. We declare `balance` private so only `BankAccount` operations can use it.

Note 2: `BankAccount()` is a constructor. A constructor has no return value, not even **void**. It has the same name as the class, in this case, `BankAccount`. We need a `BankAccount` constructor to initialize the balance because `balance` is a private field, and can only be changed by `BankAccount` operations. A constructor is a special operation which we use when we create a new object as in the expression `new BankAccount()`.

Note 3: This constructor overloads the name `BankAccount`, but it has a parameter giving the initial balance for the new account, so Java can tell the difference between it and the `BankAccount` constructor with no parameters. We discuss overloading later in this section.

Note 4: We include the `getBalance` method to tell us the account balance. Because `balance` is a private variable, we can only access it by using a method which is a member of the `BankAccount` class. The `getBalance` method has no parameters but returns a double value which is the balance.

Note 5: The `deposit` method refers to a specific `BankAccount` object. It adds the specified amount to the balance of that specific bank account. Depositing to my account will increase my account balance, while depositing to your account will increase yours.

Style

Our `BankAccount` class declares the data first, then the constructors, and finally the other methods. Even though we cannot directly use the private data, we like to place it in an easy to spot location at the top of the class definition. Many programmers prefer a different style, which places the private data after the methods, which are usually public. The public methods provide the interface the programmer will use directly, and some feel that for this reason they should be at the top. For your programs choose one of these styles and use it consistently.

Using BankAccount Objects

Now that we have defined the `BankAccount` class, we can create `BankAccount` objects and invoke their services.

Creating Objects

For creating objects Java provides an operator, appropriately enough called **new**. We can declare a new bank account with the expression

```
new BankAccount();
```

which creates the bank account object, reserving space in memory, and calling the default `BankAccount` constructor to initialize it. This expression creates a new bank account, but does not tell anyone where it is. Figure 5.12 shows there are no references to this new account, and it has no name.

Figure 5.12 Result of new `BankAccount()`

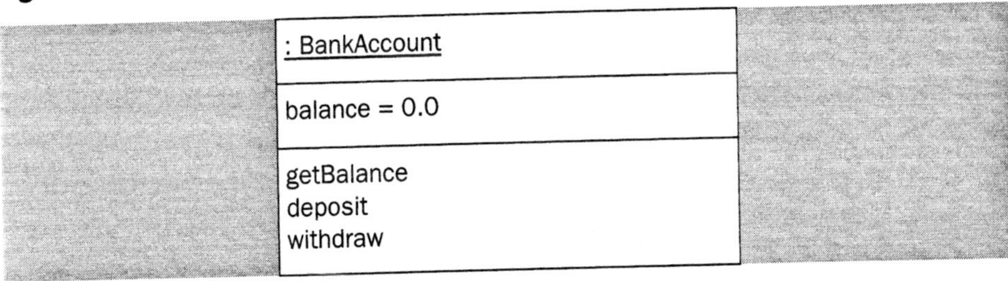

To use a `BankAccount` object we must declare a variable to refer to it, as in the statement

```
BankAccount myAccount = new BankAccount();
```

which declares the variable `myAccount` to have type `BankAccount` and to refer to a specific new `BankAccount` created with the `new` operator. The `new` operator allocates space in memory for a `BankAccount` object, calls the default constructor, and returns a reference to the object which the assignment operator stores in the variable `myAccount`. The `myAccount` variable has a reference to the newly created `BankAccount`, so it knows where to find that account in the computer's memory. We say the account is an **instance** of the `BankAccount` class. Figure 5.13 shows the variable `myAccount` referring to a newly created `BankAccount` instance.

Figure 5.13 `myAccount` **refers to a new** `BankAccount`

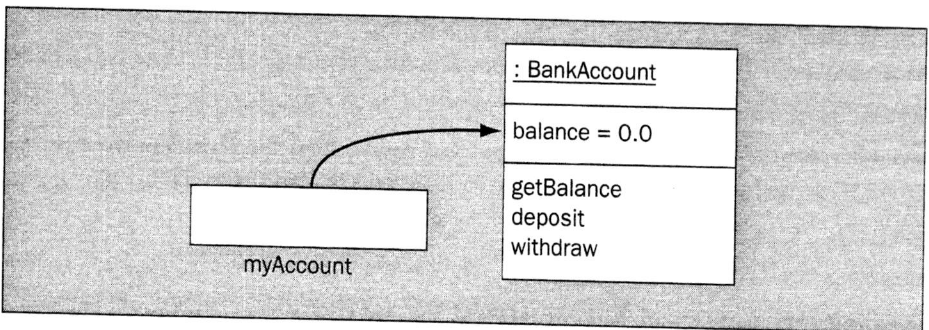

TIP

We always use the `new` operator to create an object. For `String` objects, we used a special form, for example

```
String fruit = "apple";
```

which is equivalent to

```
String fruit = new String("apple");
```

Declaring a `BankAccount` variable without creating a `BankAccount` object for it to refer to, as in

```
BankAccount anAccount;
```

would cause `anAccount`, shown in Figure 5.14, to have the value **null**.

Figure 5.14 An object declaration without object creation

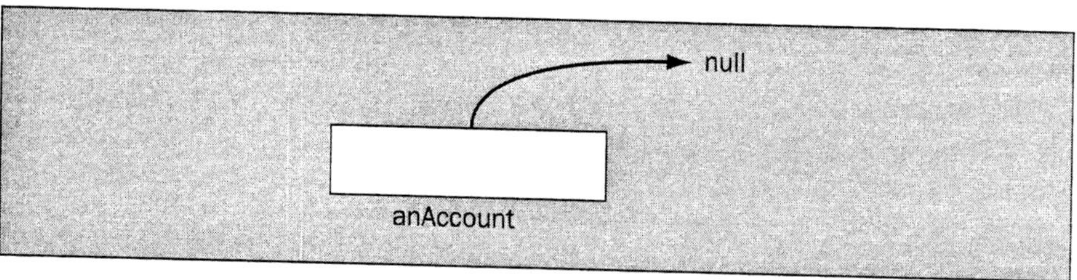

Making an Object Behave

Once we have created a new `BankAccount` object we need to get it to perform its operations. Java uses a syntax that looks like we are commanding an object to perform a service. Informally, we might command `myAccount` to deposit $100 with

```
myAccount deposit $100
```

In Java, the code for `myAccount` to make a deposit is

```
myAccount.deposit(100.00);
```

The bank account object referred to by `myAccount` deposits 100 dollars. The `deposit` method adds the amount of the deposit to the `balance` field of the object referred to by `myAccount`. The code for this instance method is

```
public void deposit(double amount) {
  balance += amount;
}
```

Note we do not refer to the object explicitly in the code. We understand the `balance` field is the account balance of the specific `BankAccount` object that is getting the deposit, which in the statement `myAccount.deposit(100.00)` is the object referred to by `myAccount`.

A LITTLE EXTRA—THE this REFERENCE

Java uses `this` to refer to the current object whose method we are invoking. We could write the `deposit` method as

```
  public void deposit(double amount) {
    this.balance += amount;
}
```

which shows explicitly that we are adding the amount to the balance of `this`, referring to the current object, the account to which we are depositing.

When we invoke `myAccount.deposit(100.00)`, the variable `this` refers to the current object, the `BankAccount` object referred to by `myAccount`. When we invoke `yourAccount.deposit(100.00)`, the variable `this` refers to the `BankAccount` object referred to by `yourAccount`. English usage is similar. When I say "My book is on the table" the word *my* refers to my book, but when you say "My book is on the table" the word *my* refers to your book. When we use `this` inside the `deposit` method it refers to the account into which the deposit is being made.

The use of `this` is optional. We introduce it here to emphasize that instance variables and methods are always invoked by an object, even if that object is not explicitly mentioned.

As with the `deposit` method, each `BankAccount` object has its own `getBalance` method which we invoke using the dot notation as in

```
double money = myAccount.getBalance();
```

If the object referred to by `myAccount` has a balance of $24.50, the variable `money` will have the value 24.5.

Calling the `withdraw` method, as in

```
myAccount.withdraw(20.00);
```

will cause $20.00 to be deducted from the balance of the object referred to by `myAccount` if that balance is greater than or equal to $20.00, and will print a message otherwise.

Now that we have seen how to create a bank account and invoke its services, in Example 5.3 we create two accounts and use their services. Inside `main` we create a `BankAccount` object, as in:

```
BankAccount myAccount = new BankAccount(25.00);
```

and get its balance using the `getBalance` method, as in:

```
myAccount.getBalance();
```

which will return the $25.00 balance with which we initialized the account. In this example, we use the `BankAccount` class of Example 5.2.

EXAMPLE 5.3 TestBankAccount.java

```
/* Creates and uses some BankAccount objects.
 */

import java.text.*;
public class TestBankAccount {                                    // Note 1
  public static void main (String [ ] args) {
    NumberFormat nf = NumberFormat.getCurrencyInstance();
    BankAccount myAccount = new BankAccount(25.00);
    System.out.println("My balance = "
          + nf.format(myAccount.getBalance()));
    myAccount.deposit(700.00);                                    // Note 2
    System.out.println("My balance = "
          + nf.format(myAccount.getBalance()));
    myAccount.withdraw(300.00);
    System.out.println("My balance = "
          + nf.format(myAccount.getBalance()));
    myAccount.withdraw(450.00);
    System.out.println("My balance = "
          + nf.format(myAccount.getBalance()));                   // Note 3
    BankAccount yourAccount = new BankAccount();
    yourAccount.deposit(1234.56);
    System.out.println("Your balance = "
          + nf.format(yourAccount.getBalance
  }
}
```

Output

```
My balance = $25.00
My balance = $725.00
My balance = $425.00
Insufficient funds
My balance = $425.00
Your balance = $1,234.56
```

Note 1: The BankAccount class defines a type of BankAccount object. The TestBankAccount class is a procedural program which we use to try out the BankAccount type. We could have included the main method in the BankAccount class itself, but it helps to differentiate between a class such as BankAccount, used to define a type, and a class such as TestBankAccount which contains a main method to test the type. Including a main method in a class such as BankAccount is the usual way to provide testing, but such mixing of functions in a class can be confusing when first creating class definitions.

Note 2: The variable myAccount invokes its deposit operation. Each object has certain operations that express its behavior. A BankAccount can deposit, and here myAccount deposits 700 dollars by adding that amount to its balance. We can think of deposit(700.00) as a message sent to myAccount asking it to handle this request according to its deposit method. The instance method deposit always refers to a specific BankAccount object.

Note 3: The balance remains the same because the previous withdrawal request was rejected for insufficient funds.

Style

The objects referred to by myAccount and yourAccount are instances of the class BankAccount. Note the common style which uses capital letters to start class names and lowercase letters to start object names and method names.

Method Overloading

We use **method overloading** to define more than one method with the same name. Such overloaded methods must have differences in their arguments lists. For example, the String class contains overloaded methods. Two methods have the same name, indexOf, but one has a char parameter while the other has a parameter of type String. Their signatures are:

```
public int indexOf(char c);
public int indexOf(String s);
```

Programmers find it less cumbersome to use overloaded methods. For example if the indexOf method were not overloaded, we would have to use something like indexOfChar and indexOfString as the names for these two methods. Method overloading helps when we have methods which are similar except that they operate with different arguments.

When we use an overloaded method in a program, Java can determine which method to call by looking at the type of argument we pass to it. For example, in

```
String food = "potato";
int a= food.indexOf('a');
int to = food.indexOf("to");
```

Java will call the `indexOf(char c)` method to find the index of the first 'a' in "potato," because the argument 'a' passed in the call `indexOf('a')` has type `char`. However, Java will call `indexOf(String s)` to find the index of the first occurrence of "to," because the argument "to" has type `String`.

Another common use of method overloading is for constructors. We often overload constructors to provide different way of creating objects. The `BankAccount` class of Example 5.2 has two constructors, one with no parameters and one with a single parameter specifying an initial balance. In Example 5.3, we used the constructor with no arguments to create `yourAccount` and the constructor with one argument to create `myAccount`.

When two methods have the same name, Java uses the argument types to determine which method to call. Thus Java will not let us define two methods with the same name and the same types of parameters; it could not determine which one to call when we invoke the method in our program.

Class Variables and Methods

Our `BankAccount` class of Example 5.2 has only instance variables, instance methods, and constructors. It defines a new type of object, a `BankAccount`. When we use `BankAccount` methods in Example 5.3, we first create a bank account using a constructor.

```
BankAccount myAccount = new BankAcccount(25.00);
```

Only then can we perform transactions such as

```
myAccount.deposit(700.00);
```

It would not make sense to invoke `deposit(700.00)` without prefixing it with the object name `myAccount`. The `deposit` method deposits into a specific account and can only be called as an operation of an account.

A class may also include **class variables** and **class methods**, which are associated with the class, rather than with a particular instance of the class. They are declared using the `static` modifier. The word *static* may remind us that class variables and methods stay with the class. The `main` method is always static, a class method, because Java calls it to start the program when there are no objects of ours.

To illustrate class variables and methods, we modify the `BankAccount` class of Example 5.2 to count the total number of `deposit`, `withdraw`, and `getBalance` transactions successfully completed by all bank accounts created in a test program. We change the class name to `Acct` to avoid confusion with the unmodified `BankAccount` class. The `Acct` class has a class variable, `transactions`,

```
public static int transactions = 0;
```

which keeps count of the number of transactions. The `Acct` class has only one copy of the `transactions` class variable, whereas each `Acct` object has its own copy of the `balance` instance variable. Thus, if `myAcct` makes a deposit and `yourAccount` performs a withdrawal, the total number of transactions will increase by two. We modify the `deposit`, `withdraw`, and `getBalance` methods to increment the transactions variable.

We include a class method

```
public static int getTransactionCount() {
  return transactions;
}
```

that returns the total number of successful transactions by all `Acct` objects.

EXAMPLE 5.4 Acct.java

```
/* Modifies the BankAccount class to include a class variable
 * to store the total number of successful deposit, withdraw, and
 * getBalance operations by any Acct object.
 */

public class Acct {
  private double balance;
  private static int transactions = 0;                    // Note 1

  public Acct() {
    balance = 0;
  }
  public Acct(double initialAmount) {
    balance = initialAmount;
  }
  public void deposit(double amount) {
    balance += amount;
    transactions++;
  }
  public void withdraw(double amount) {
    if (balance >= amount) {
      balance -= amount;
      transactions++;                                     // Note 2
    }
    else
      System.out.println("Insufficient funds");
  }
  public double getBalance() {
    transactions++;
    return balance;
  }
  public static int getTransactionCount() {               // Note 3
    return transactions;
  }
}
```

Note 1: The `static` modifier signifies that `transactions` is a class variable. We initialize it to 0 because a test program starts with no transactions completed initially.

Note 2: We only increase the count of transactions when the withdrawal is successful.

Note 3: The `static` modifier signifies that `getTransactionCount` is a class method.

Example 5.5 tests the `Acct` class. We create `myAcct` and execute the `deposit`, `getBalance`, and `withdraw` methods. Because the last withdraw is unsuccessful, we get a transaction count of 3. Creating `yourAcct` and executing the `deposit` and `getBalance` methods, we find that the transaction count becomes 5. The `transactions` class variable is part of the class and is incremented by all instances. Of course each object only reads or writes its own `balance` instance variable. Figure 5.15 illustrates this difference between class and instance variables.

Figure 5.15 The difference between class and instance variables

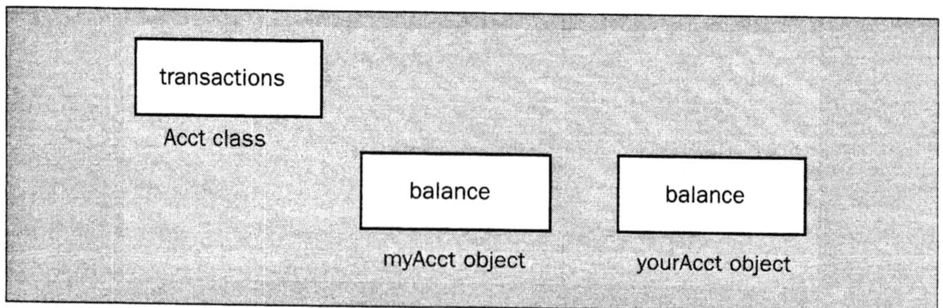

When calling the `getTransactionCount` method, we prefix the class name, as in

```
Acct.getTransactions
```

reminding us that `getTransactionCount` is a class method, not part of any instance of the `Acct` class.

EXAMPLE 5.5 TestAcct.java

```
/* Creates some Acct objects and illustrates the use of
 * class variables and methods.
 */

public class TestAcct {
  public static void main (String [ ] args) {
    NumberFormat nf = NumberFormat.getCurrencyInstance();
    Acct myAcct = new Acct(25.00);
    myAcct.deposit(700.00);
    myAcct.withdraw(300.00);
    myAcct.withdraw(450.00);
    System.out.println("My balance after completing transactions is "
        + nf.format(myAcct.getBalance()));
    System.out.println
        ("The number of transactions is " + Acct.getTransactionCount());
```

```
        Acct yourAcct = new Acct();
        yourAcct.deposit(1234.56);
        System.out.println("Your balance after completing transactions is "
            + nf.format(yourAcct.getBalance()));
        System.out.println
            ("The number of transactions is " + Acct.getTransactionCount());
    }
}
```

Output

```
Insufficient funds
My balance after completing transactions is $425.00
The number of transactions is 3
Your balance after completing transactions is $1,234.56
The number of transactions is 5
```

TIP

In `main` we cannot write

```
deposit(100.00);
```

because `deposit` is a method of a specific `Acct` object, and `main` is a class method. We must write

```
myAcct.deposit(700.00);
```

where `myAcct` refers to an `Acct` object.

THE BIG PICTURE

The `BankAccount` class implements a programmer-defined type. It contains constructors, with the same name as the class, which initialize the private instance variable, `balance`, when a `BankAccount` object is created. The instance methods `getBalance`, `deposit`, and `withdraw` allow a `BankAccount` object to fulfill its responsibilities. Because Java supports method overloading we were able to include two constructors with the same name.

A user creates a `BankAccount` object with the `new` operator, and invokes its behavior with a message sending style,

```
myAccount.deposit(50.00);
```

Class variables and methods, declared with the `static` modifier, are part of the class but not part of any instance.

TEST YOUR UNDERSTANDING

4. Write the declaration for an integer account number instance variable in the `BankAccount` class. Restrict access to the account number to methods of the `BankAccount` class.

5. Where do we declare an instance variable of a class? Give an example of an instance variable in Example 5.2.

6. Rewrite the declaration

   ```
   BankAccount theAccount;
   ```

   so `theAccount` will refer to a newly created `BankAccount`.

7. What value does the variable `theAccount` have after the following declaration?

   ```
   BankAccount theAccount;
   ```

8. Given a `BankAccount`, `myAccount`, write Java statements to
   a. deposit $35.50
   b. get the current balance
   c. deposit $999

9. Which method does the `new` operator call in the following expression:

   ```
   new BankAccount();
   ```

TRY IT YOURSELF

10. In Example 5.4, add a line

    ```
    deposit(439.86);
    ```

    to the `main` method of the `TestBankAccount` class which tries to use the `deposit` instance method without referring to a specific `BankAccount` object. Try to compile this modified program and see what error you get.

TRY IT YOURSELF

11. Replace the first `myAccount.getBalance()` method call in the `TestBankAccount` class with a field access

    ```
    myAcccount.balance.
    ```

    This will create errors because the `balance` field is `private` and not accessible outside the `BankAccount` class. What errors do you get when you try to compile this modified version of Example 5.3?

12. We can overload methods other than constructors. Write another `withdraw` method, with no parameters, which will withdraw $40 if that amount is available. This method provides a quick withdrawal where the user does not have to specify any amount.

13. Suppose we want to add a third constructor to Example 5.2 which would take no parameters, but would set the initial balance to $25.00. We could code it as

    ```
    public BankAccount () {
      balance = 25.00;
    }
    ```

    Could we add this constructor to Example 5.2 or will Java not allow it? Explain.

TRY IT YOURSELF 14. Add the `withdraw` method written in question 14 to Example 5.3. Modify Example 5.4 to test the new `withdraw` method.

5.3 The QuickFood Example

The `BankAccount` class we wrote in the last section defines the state and services for bank account objects. The `QuickFood` example of Section 1.7 uses `Customer`, `Waiter`, and `Cook` objects. We need to write the `Customer`, `Waiter`, and `Cook` classes which define the state and services for these objects. We introduce the UML class and sequence diagrams to illustrate the design.

Class Diagrams

We use the UML **class diagram** to show the associations between classes. An association represents a relationship between instances of the associated classes. For example, a customer places an order with a waiter, while a waiter asks the cook to make a burger (see Figure 5.16).

Figure 5.16 A class diagram

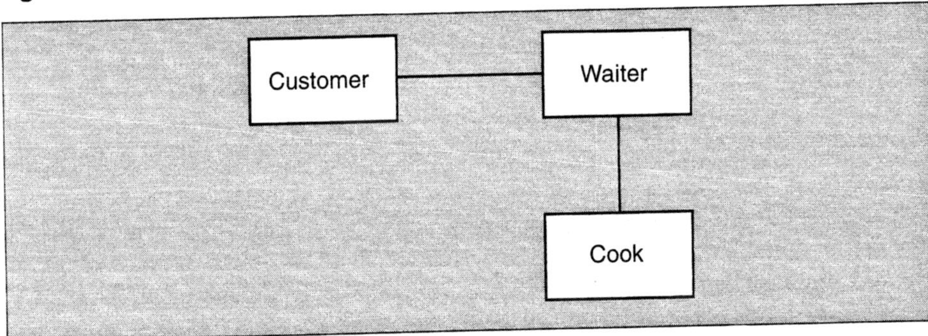

Sequence Diagrams

We can visualize the scenario of Figure 1.15, repeated here

```
The customer orders a burger, soda, and fries from the waiter.
The waiter asks the cook to make a burger.
The waiter serves the soda to the customer.
The waiter asks the cook to make the fries.
The cook gives the waiter the burger to serve.
The cook gives the waiter the fries to serve.
The waiter asks the customer to pay.
```

in a **sequence diagram**, another part of the UML, that shows object interactions arranged in time sequence. Each object appears at the top (see Figure 5.17), with a dashed line descending, called its **lifeline**. We represent each message from one object to another using a horizontal arrow.

Figure 5.17 A sequence diagram for a food order

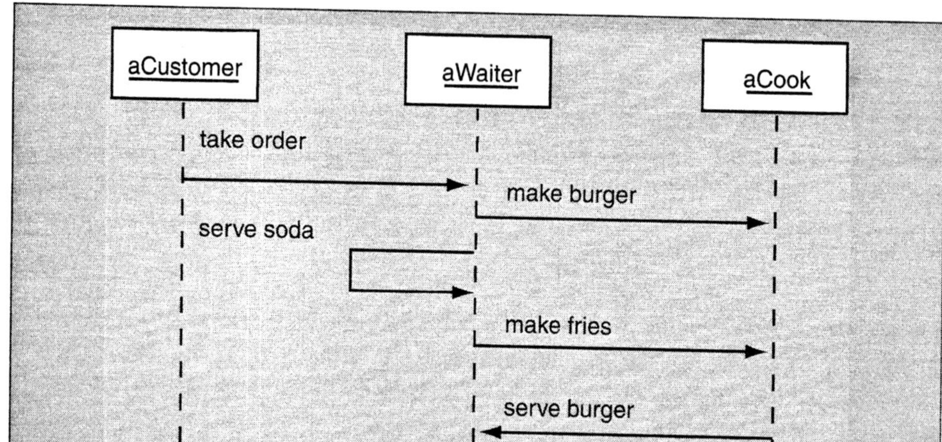

For ease of implementation of this introductory example, we change the model to serve each item as it is ordered. Figure 5.18 shows the new sequence diagram.

Figure 5.18 A revised sequence diagram for a food order

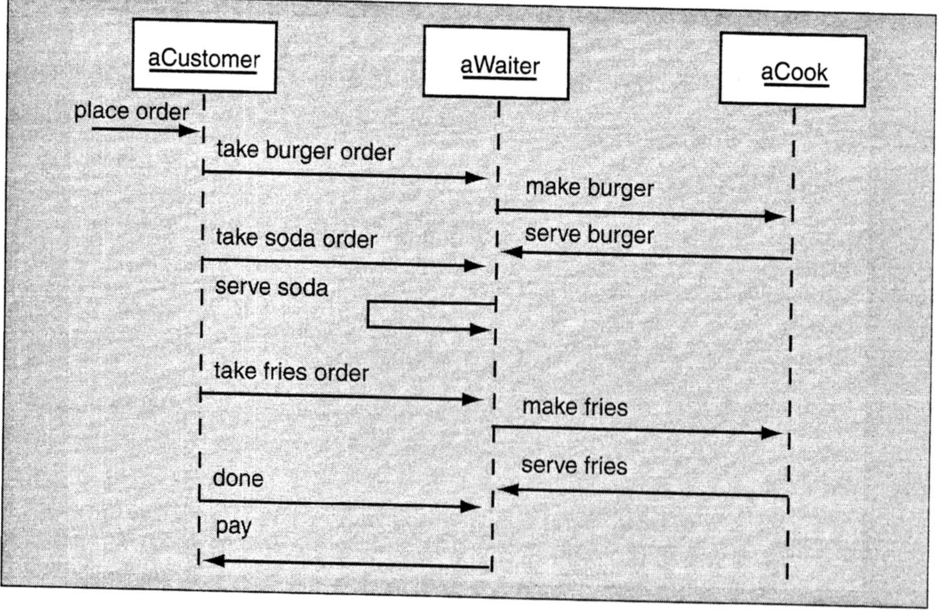

Our code for the `Customer`, `Waiter`, and `Cook` classes includes the state and responsibilities identified in the scenario. For simplicity the `placeOrder` method just orders a burger, fries, and a soda. A more detailed implementation would provide a user interface for the customer to make selections. The `pay` method reduces the customer's money by the amount of the bill.

In implementing associations, we include a reference in one object to the object to which it is associated. The `Customer` constructor saves a reference to a `Waiter`.

```
public Customer(Waiter w) {
  waiter = w;
}
```

In taking an order, the waiter adds the price to the customer's bill and asks the cook to prepare the burger or fries, or serves the soda. The cook makes the burger or fries and asks the waiter to serve it. Example 5.6 shows the complete code for the simple fast food simulation.

EXAMPLE 5.6 QuickFood.java

```
/* Adds the Customer, Waiter, and Cook classes
 * to define the objects used in Example 5.2.
 */

import java.text.*;

class Customer {                                              // Note 1
  private double money = 30.00;
  private Waiter waiter;

  public Customer(Waiter w) {
    waiter = w;
  }
  public void placeOrder() {
    waiter.takeOrder("Burger",this);
    waiter.takeOrder("Soda",this);
    waiter.takeOrder("Fries",this);
    waiter.takeOrder("Done",this);                            // Note 2
  }
  public double pay(double amount) {
    NumberFormat nf = NumberFormat.getCurrencyInstance();
    money -= amount;
    System.out.println("Customer pays " + nf.format(amount));
    return amount;
  }
}
```

```
class Waiter {
  private double cash = 200.00;
  private Cook cook;
  private Customer customer;
  private double bill = 0;

  public Waiter(Cook c) {                                            // Note 3
    cook = c;
  }
  public void takeOrder(String item, Customer c) {
    customer = c;
    if (item.toUpperCase().equals("BURGER")){                       // Note 4
      System.out.println("Waiter places BURGER order");
      bill += 1.99;
      cook.makeBurger(this);
    }
    else if (item.toUpperCase().equals("FRIES")){
      System.out.println("Waiter places FRIES order");
      bill += 1.19;
      cook.makeFries(this);
    }
    else if (item.toUpperCase().equals("SODA")){
      serveFood("SODA");                                             // Note 5
      bill += .99;
    }
    else if (item.toUpperCase().equals("DONE"))
      cash += customer.pay(bill);;
    }
  public void serveFood(String item) {
    System.out.println("Waiter serves " + item.toUpperCase());
  }
}
class Cook {
  private int burgers = 10;
  private int fries = 10;

  public void makeBurger(Waiter waiter) {                            // Note 6
    if (burgers > 0) {
      System.out.println("Cook making BURGER");
      waiter.serveFood("Burger");
      burgers--;
    }
    else
      System.out.println("Sorry -- No more BURGERS");
  }
  public void makeFries(Waiter waiter) {
    if (fries > 0) {
      System.out.println("Cook making FRIES");
      waiter.serveFood("Fries");
      fries--;
    }
```

```
    else
      System.out.println("Sorry -- No more FRIES");
    }
  }
public class QuickFood {
  public static void main(String[] args) {
    Cook joe = new Cook();                                    // Note 7
    Waiter suzy = new Waiter(joe);
    Customer fred = new Customer(suzy);
    fred.placeOrder();
  }
}
```

Output

```
Waiter places BURGER order
Cook making BURGER
Waiter serves BURGER
Waiter serves SODA
Waiter places FRIES order
Cook making FRIES
Waiter serves FRIES
Customer pays $4.17
```

Note 1: We have omitted the public modifier on the `Customer`, `Waiter`, and `Cook` classes, because at most one public class may appear in any file, and for simplicity we wanted to include all the classes in the same file. Generally, classes define types that can be used in many applications, and should be declared using the **public** modifier and placed in separate files. We discuss the use of access modifiers in Section 9.4.

Note 2: The customer passes `"Done"` to signal the order is complete.

Note 3: Reflecting the association between a waiter and a cook, we pass a reference to a cook when we construct a waiter.

Note 4: Converting the item to upper case allows the comparison to be case insensitive, so `"burger"`, when converted, would be equal to `"BURGER"`.

Note 5: The waiter calls its own `serveFood` method, so the object is implicit. We could have used `this.serveFood("SODA")` to make the object explicit.

Note 6: `public void makeBurger(Waiter waiter) {`
We do not need an explicit constructor for the `Cook` class because the waiter passes a reference to itself to the cook when it calls the `makeBurger` method.

Note 7: `Cook joe = new Cook();`
We did not include a constructor in `Cook` class. Even though `Cook` has an association with `Waiter`, a cook does not initiate contact with a waiter, but

only responds to requests. The cook receives a reference to a waiter as an argument to its `makeFries` and `makeBurger` methods.

THE BIG PICTURE

A large part of an object-oriented program involves writing the classes which define the state and responsibilities of its object instances. In meeting its responsibilities an object uses the services of other objects.

The UML class diagram shows the associations between classes, while the sequence diagram shown the sequence of interactions between objects, from the earliest at the top to the latest at the bottom.

TEST YOUR UNDERSTANDING

15. Redraw the sequence diagram of Figure 5.18 so the waiter asks the customer to take each item as it becomes available.

5.4 Object Composition

Our `BankAccount` class has an instance variable `balance` of type **double**. **Composition**, a powerful object-oriented design concept, builds objects that have references to other objects as data fields. Our Java objects can be composed of other objects, just as a computer, for example, is composed of a CPU, a keyboard, a monitor, a disk drive, and so on. Composition models the HAS-A relationship in which one object contains another. An automobile has tires and an engine, for example.

We shall build `Name` and `Address` objects that have fields defined as `Strings`, and `Person` objects that each have a field defined as a `Name` and another defined as an `Address`. Composition, along with inheritance, which we cover in Chapter 9, is one of the two ways of defining new classes using those previously defined. Composition models the whole-part relationship; the whole object is composed of its parts.

We define a class `Person` we can use in applications when we need data associated with a specific individual. We need many data items for each person, including first name, last name, street address, city, and so on. We choose to organize this data into coherent `Name` and `Address` classes rather than as an unorganized group of individual fields. Organizing our data will make our class easier to read. We can use the `Name` and `Address` classes in other applications.

Figure 5.19 lists the fields for our `Name`, `Address`, and `Person` classes.
Each class in Figure 5.19 contains data fields that are objects. The `Name` class has two `String` objects and a `char`. Each `Address` has four `String` objects. The zip code, `zip`, uses digits, but because we do not do arithmetic on zip codes, we have no need to store it as an integer. Our `Person` class uses a `String`, a `Name` and an `Address`. As we did with the zip code, we treat the `id`, usually the social security number, as a `String`.

Figure 5.19 Fields for the `Name`, `Address`, and `Person` classes

```
Name
  private String first
  private char initial
  private String last
  public Name(String f, String l)
  public Name(String f, char i, String l)
  public String toString()

Address
  private String street
  private String city
  private String state
  private String zip
  public Address(String st, String cy, String se, String zp)
  public String toString()

Person
  private String id
  private Name name
  private Address address
  public Person(String i, Name n, Address a)
  public String getId()
  public String toString()
```

Figure 5.20 illustrates composition. A `Person` contains references to a `String`, a `Name`, and an `Address`. A `Name` contains two `String` references and a character, while an `Address` contains four `String` references. We are especially interested in the fields, so we omit the operations from the class diagrams.

Figure 5.20 Composition: The `Person`, `Name`, and `Address` classes

Person	Name	Address
id : String name : Name address : Address	first : String initial : char last : String	id : String name : Name address : Address zip : String

Each of the three classes has a constructor to initialize its fields (the `Name` class has two), and each has a `toString` method to provide a string representation for display purposes. Java provides a `toString` method for its library classes whose objects we need to display. The `println` method calls this `toString` method when asked to display an object, as in:

```
System.out.println(aPerson);
```

which calls `aPerson.toString()` to get the string representation for the object `aPerson` of type `Person`.

TIP

Define a `toString` method for each class whose objects you need to display. Then you will be able to display your objects using the `println` statement. When your object is a component of another object, its string representation will be part of the string representation of the containing object.

Style

Do group fields into classes such as `Name` and `Address` that give meaning to the fields, help to organize your data, and can be reused in other applications.

Don't build a class with a long list of unorganized fields.

None of the fields listed in Figure 5.19 are static. The `Name`, `Address`, and `Person` classes define the data and operations that will be part of each object of these types. Each object is an instance of its class type. For example the object given by

```
Name composer = new Name("Wolfgang", 'A', "Mozart");
```

shown in Figure 5.21, is an instance of the `Name` class, just as the `String` objects `s1`, `s2`, `s3`, and `s4`, defined on page 213, are instances of the `String` class.

Figure 5.21 An instance of `Name`

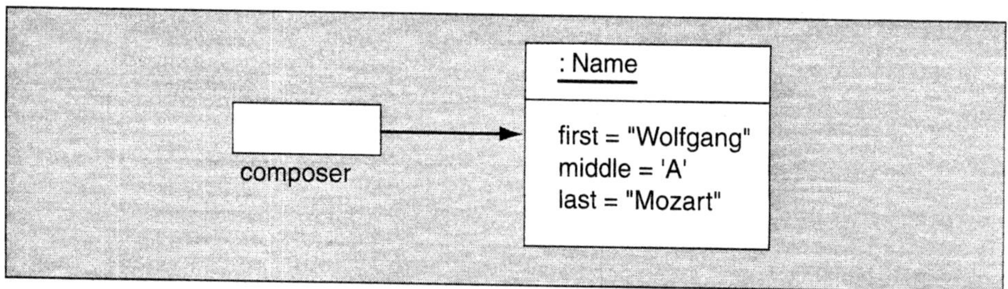

The `composer` object has private data, its `first`, `initial`, and `last` fields, and a method, `toString`, which returns its string representation. When we create an object instance of some type, we say we are **instantiating** an object of that type.

In contrast to the classes of many of our earlier examples, our classes in this chapter contain non-static fields which are instance variables meant to be part of each object instance.

Example 5.7 creates our `Name`, `Address`, and `Person` classes, which we will use in applications later in this chapter. To allow us to use each class in future applications, we make each public in its own file. The `TestPerson` class contains a `main` method to test the `Person`, `Name`, and `Address` classes, also illustrating some of the `String` methods of Section 5.1.

EXAMPLE 5.7 Name.java

```
/* Groups fields for a name.
 * Uses toString to display.
 */

public class Name {
  private String first = "";
  private char initial = '\u0000';                          // Note 1
  private String last = "";

  public Name(String f, String l) {
    first = f; last = l;
  }
  public Name(String f, char i, String l) {
    this(f,l);                                              // Note 2
    initial = i;
  }
  public String toString() {
    if (initial == '\u0000')                                // Note 3
      return first + " " + last;
    else
      return first + " " + initial + " " + last;            // Note 4
  }
}
```

Address.java

```
/* Groups fields for an address.
 * Uses toString to display.
 */

public class Address {
  private String street;
  private String city;
  private String state;
  private String zip;
  public Address(String st, String cy, String se, String zp) {
    street = st; city = cy; state = se; zip = zp;
  }
  public String toString() {
    return street + "\n" + city + ", " + state + " " + zip;  // Note 5
  }
}
```

Person.java

```
/* Groups fields for a person.
 * Uses toString to display.
 */
```

```
public class Person {
  private String id;
  private Name name;
  private Address address;
  public Person(String i, Name n, Address a) {
    id = i; name = n; address = a;
  }
  public String getId() {                                   // Note 6
    return id;
  }
  public String toString() {
    return name + "\n" + address;                           // Note 7
  }
}
```

TestPerson.java

```
/* Tests the Person, Name, and Address classes, and uses String
 * methods.
 */

import javax.swing.*;
public class TestPerson {
  public static void main (String [] args) {
    Name aName = new Name("Henry", "Johnson");
    Address anAddress =
      new Address("1512 Harbor Blvd.", "Long Beach",
                  "CA", "99919");
    String anId = JOptionPane.showInputDialog
                  ("Enter an id string");
    Person aPerson = new Person(anId,aName,anAddress);
    System.out.println("Our person is ");
    System.out.println(aPerson);
    System.out.println(" with id " + aPerson.getId());
    System.out.println("\n And now some tests of string methods");
    String address = anAddress.toString();
    int i = address.indexOf("Harbor");                      // Note 8
    System.out.println("The index of Harbor in address is " + i);
    String z1 = String.valueOf(99919);                      // Note 9
    int l = address.length();                               // Note 10
    System.out.println("The length of address is " + l);
    String z2 = address.substring(l-5,l);                   // Note 11
boolean same = z2.equals(z1);                      // Note 12
    System.out.println("These two zip codes are the same? " + same);
    int less = z1.compareTo("Harbor");                      // Note 13
    System.out.println("Compare returns the negative number " + less);
    String hat = " hat ";
    System.out.println(hat+"rack");
    System.out.println(hat.trim()+"rack");                  // Note 14
}
}
```

Run

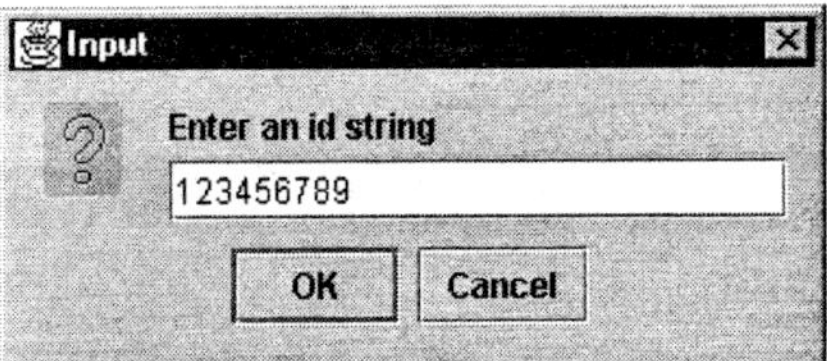


```
Our person is
Henry Johnson
1512 Harbor Blvd.
Long Beach, CA 99919
 with id 123456789

 And now some tests using string methods
The index of Harbor in address is 5
The length of address is 38
These two zip codes are the same? true
Compare returns the negative number -15
   hat rack
hatrack
```

Note 1: Java automatically initializes data fields with default values if none are supplied by the user. However, it is good practice to initialize them. We initialize the middle initial with the default value for the type character which is the character with numerical code zero. We can write this character as either `'\u0000'`, where the `'u'` stands for Unicode, or `'\000'`.

Note 2: One constructor can call another constructor in the same class by using the name `this` which refers to the current object. Here we call the other `Name` constructor, passing it a name and an address, and then initialize the middle initial.

Note 3: We do not display the middle initial when it has the default value of `'\u0000'`, the character code with value zero.

Note 4: The concatenation operator '+' converts any primitive type, such as `char`, to a String representation.

Note 5: We add the string `"\n"` to include a `newline` in the string, so the street will appear on a separate line from the city, state, and zip code.

Note 6: `public String getId() {`
We do not want to output the id every time we display the person's name and address. We can use this method to get the id when we need it.

Note 7: `return name + "\n" + address;`
The one string argument, `"\n"`, tells Java the `'+'` is the string concatenation operator rather than an arithmetic addition. The string concatenation operator uses the `toString` methods we defined for `Name` and `Address` to get

the string representations for the name and address fields, without having to write `name.toString()` or `address.toString()`.

Note 8: `int i = address.indexOf("Harbor");`
The `indexOf` method returns the position of the first occurrence of its argument in the string, or `-1` if the argument is not found. Here `"Harbor"` occurs starting at position five.

Note 9: `String z1 = String.valueOf(99919);`
The static method `valueOf` makes a string from its argument. Java overloads `valueOf` to make strings from several primitive types.

Note 10: `int l = address.length();`
The `length()` method returns the length of the String.

Note 11: `String z2 = address.substring(l-5,l);`
The `substring` method returns a string made from a range of characters of the given `String` object. Here we make a string from the last five characters, those at position `l-5` up to position `l`, which is just the zip code of the address.

Note 12: `boolean same = z2.equals(z1);`
The two strings, `z1` and `z2`, are different objects but have the same characters, the zip code, so they are equal.

Note 13: `int less = z1.compareTo("Harbor");`
Digits come before letters in the ASCII and Unicode character orderings so a string of digits will be less than a string of letters. The `compareTo` method will return a negative number.

Note 14: `System.out.println(hat.trim()+"rack");`
The `trim` method removes the leading and trailing blanks from `hat`.

THE BIG PICTURE

Composition models the HAS-A relationship between objects in which one object contains another. We represent the contained object as an instance variable in the containing object.

TEST YOUR UNDERSTANDING

16. Declare and initialize a `Name` object using your own name.
17. Declare and initialize an `Address` object using your own address. List the four objects of which this `Address` is composed.
18. Declare and initialize a `Person` object using data of your choice. List the three objects of which this `Person` is composed.

SUMMARY

- An object has state, behavior, and identity. In analogy with a vending machine, the services an object provides are like the buttons of the machine. Users access an object via its services, which express the behavior of that object and meet its responsibilities. Using classes from the Java library, we can create objects and use the operations Java provides for them. Strings are a special class of great importance; Java provides a large library of `String` methods. A few, such as `valueOf`, are class methods which we invoke as if we were sending a message to the class, for example `String.valueOf(1234)`. Most, including `charAt`, `compareTo`, `equals`, `indexOf`, `length`, `substring`, `toUpperCase`, and `toLowerCase`, are instance methods which we invoke as if sending a message to a particular object, for example `myName.length()`, where `myName` is the string given by `String myName = "Art"`. The concatenation operator, +, not only concatenates strings, but converts primitive types to a string representation, and uses the `toString` method to get the string representation for objects. We can initialize a string using a string literal such as `"house"`.
- Java implements primitive types such as integers and class types such as bank accounts differently. Primitive types have small fixed sizes, so Java variables hold their values. An integer variable stores the values of an integer. By contrast, objects may be quite large and have varying sizes, so it is easier for an object variable to store a reference to an object rather than trying to hold it directly.
- Procedural programming focuses mainly on the function performed by the program and only incidentally on the data. The function performed is the aspect most likely to change, so a more stable and maintainable system results from object-oriented programming which focuses on the objects that comprise the system. These objects have data representing their states and operations representing their behavior. The operations give each object an active role in the system. Objects communicate with each other by invoking operations that allow an object to meet its responsibilities. We can use scenarios for typical uses of the system to find the relevant objects and identify their responsibilities.
- In Java, we use a class to define a type of object. Each object has state, data which we represent using instance variables which are non-static variables declared inside the class but outside of any method. Our `BankAccount` class defines an instance variable, `balance`, to hold the account balance. By contrast, local variables are declared inside methods and available only inside the method in which they are declared.
- We add methods to our class to implement the behavior of its type of objects. In our `BankAccount` class we add instance methods to deposit an amount, to withdraw an amount, and to get the account balance. These methods are not static, signifying they will be operations of each `BankAccount` object, representing that object's behaviors. Static methods such as the `getTransactionCount` method of Example 5.4 are sometimes called class methods because they are class tools, not associated with any object.

- We access objects using methods which are operations representing their behavior. Java uses the period to separate the name of the object from the operation it is invoking. This notation emphasizes that an object such as `myAccount` is performing one of its operations such as `deposit`. Usually, we make the object's data fields private, requiring that users of our objects access fields only via the object's operations.
- A special kind of method, called a constructor, helps the user to construct an object. Constructors have the same name as the class and no return value. We define a `BankAccount` constructor which creates a `BankAccount` object with an initial balance of zero. We create objects with the `new` operator which allocates space for the object, calls the object's constructor, and returns a reference to the object. Java uses a **null** reference to represent an uncreated object.
- Java supports method overloading, where two methods have the same name but different parameters. One important use of overloading is to provide multiple constructors for objects of a given class. We add another constructor to our `BankAccount` class to create a `BankAccount` with a specified initial balance.
- We use composition, a powerful design tool, for building objects composed of other objects. Example 5.8 builds a `Name` and an `Address` from strings, and a `Person` class from a name and an address.

Skill Builder Exercises

1. Match the concept name on the left with its function on the right.

   a. instance variablei. stores a value within a method

b. local variable	ii. represents a behavior of an object
c. class method	iii. represents an attribute of an object
d. instance method	iv. used by the class as a whole

2. Fill in the blanks in the following:

   A variable of a primitive type holds a __________, while a variable of a class type holds a __________.

3. What will be the output from the following

```
String s = "hat";
String t = s + " rack";
System.out.println(s.substring(0,1) + t.substring(5,8));
```

Critical Thinking Exercises

4. Declaring a bank account as

```
BankAccount acct;
```

and making a deposit using

```
acct.deposit(500.00);
```

will have the following result:

a. The compiler will generate an error message.
b. The account `acct` will have a balance of $500.00.
c. The account `acct` will have its previous balance increased by $500.
d. none of the above.

5. A constructor

a. must have the same name as the class it is declared within.
b. is used to create objects.
c. may be overloaded.
d. b and c above
e. all of the above

6. Which of the following are never part of a class definition?

a. instance variables
b. static methods
c. instance methods
d. constructors
e. none of the above

7. Suppose `acct1` refers to a `BankAccount` with a balance of $300, while `acct2` refers to a `BankAccount` with a balance of $200. After the assignment

```
acct1 = acct2;
```

which of the following is true?

a. Withdrawing $100 from `acct1` will leave its balance at $200.
b. Withdrawing $100 from `acct2` and then withdrawing $100 from `acct1` will leave the balance of `acct1` at $100.
c. Withdrawing $100 from `acct1` and then withdrawing $100 from `acct2` will leave the balance of `acct1` at $0.00.
d. none of the above
e. all of the above

Debugging Exercise

8. The following `isEqual` method, for the `Name` class of Example 5.7, attempts to check two names for equality. They should be equal if they have the same first name, middle initial, and last name. Find and correct any errors.

```
public boolean isEqual(Name name) {
  boolean result = false;
  if (first == name.first &&
      initial == name.initial &&
      last == name.last)
    result = true;
  return result;
}
```

Program Modification Exercises

9. Add a `compareTo` method to the `Name` class of Example 5.7. The `compareTo` method should return a negative integer when the object is less than the argument, zero when equal, and a positive number when greater. Compare last names first. If the last names are equal, compare first names. If the first names are equal, compare the middle initial.

10. Revise the `BankAccount` class of Example 5.2 to overload the `withdraw` method. Include a `withdraw` method with no parameters, which will withdraw $40 if available, and display a message otherwise. Add tests of this new method to the `main` method.

11. Modify Example 5.6 to add a `pickUpOrder` method to the `Customer` class, and let the waiter invoke this method when each item is ready.

12. Modify Example 5.2 to include an account holder of type `Person` in the `BankAccount` class.

Program Design Exercises

13. Write a Java program which illustrates the use of each of the `String` methods in Figure 5.4.

14. Write a class for soccer game scoring. Provide a constructor which starts each team with a score of zero. Include instance variables to keep the score for both teams. Include a method to add one to the score of the first team and a method to add one to the score of the second team. Include a method which displays the

score of both teams, and the `main` method to test, creating two different soccer games. Score points so the first game is 3–2 and the second game is 0–1. Display the scores of each game.

15. Write a class which uses the soccer game class of Exercise 14. In the `main` method create some games, score points, and display the results.

16. Write a class for a warehouse which hold radios, televisions, and computers. Provide a constructor which starts a warehouse with no items. Include instance variables to store the quantity of each item in the warehouse. Include methods to add to the stock of each item, and a method to display the contents of the warehouse. Test in a `main` method, creating two warehouses. Add items to each and display the final contents of each warehouse.

17. Write a class to use the warehouse class of Exercise 16. In the `main` method create some warehouses, add some items to each and display the contents of each warehouse.

18. Write a class to keep track of the movement of a cat. Include three instance variables to hold the `x`, `y`, and `z` positions of the cat. Include a method for the cat to walk to another position. This method has two parameters specifying the change in `x` and the change in `y`. If the cat is at `(3,4,5)` and we ask it to `walk(1,4)` then it will be at `(4,8,5)`. (Walking is a horizontal action here.) Include a method for the cat to jump to another position. This method has one parameter specifying the change in the cat's vertical position. If the cat is at `(3,4,5)` and we ask it to `jump(5)` it will be at `(3,4,10)`. Include a method to display a cat's position. Test in a `main` method, creating a few cats and have them `walk` and `jump`. Display their final positions.

19. Write a class to use the cat tracking class of Exercise 18. In the `main` method, create some cats, make them `walk` and `jump`, and display their final positions.

20. For the `Warehouse` class of Exercise 16 overload the `Warehouse` constructor by adding another constructor to create a warehouse with specified initial quantities of radios, televisions, and computers. Revise the `main` method to include tests of this new constructor.

21. For the `Warehouse` class of Exercise 16, add methods to remove a specified quantity of each item. If the quantity specified is greater than the amount of that item in the warehouse then no items are removed. Add tests of the `remove` methods to the `main` method.

22. Write a coffee vending machine class. Include fields giving the number of cups of coffee available, the cost of one cup of coffee, and the total amount of money inserted by the user. This machine requires exact change. Include one constructor which stocks the machine with a quantity and price of coffee specified as

parameters, and another with no parameters which stocks the machine with 10 cups of coffee at fifty cents each. Include the following methods:

```
menu()      // displays the quantity and price of coffee
insert(int quarters, int dimes, int nickels) // inserts the given amount
select()    // dispenses a cup of coffee if user has inserted enough
            // money and coffee is available, otherwise displays a message.
refund()    // returns the money inserted
```

Write a `main` method to create some vending machines and test their operation.

23. Create a `Fraction` class to provide a data type for rational numbers. Each `Fraction` will have an integer numerator and denominator. Include a constructor with two integer arguments to initialize the numerator and denominator. Include methods to add, multiply, subtract, and divide, each having a `Fraction` argument and returning a `Fraction` result. Use the `main` method to test the `Fraction` class.

CHAPTER

6 Event-Driven Programming

OUTLINE

Introduction

In this chapter we discuss event-driven programming. Event-driven programs will respond to external events generated by the user or the operating system.

Figure 6.1 shows the `AtmScreen` applet of Example 1.5 after the user, John Venn in this case, has entered his name, entered a PIN, and chosen to withdraw from his savings account. The `AtmScreen` prompts Mr. Venn to specify the amount of the withdrawal, and waits for an event. In this simple example, Mr. Venn has two choices: either enter an amount or press the *`Finish`* button. The `AtmScreen` passively waits for one of these events to occur.

Figure 6.1 shows the graphical style. Notice that we drew the text in a bigger font than that used for character output, and centered the prompt "Specify the amount" horizontally in the window. Running the applet will show the yellow canvas on which we drew the prompt.

Figure 6.1 The `AtmScreen`: specify the amount

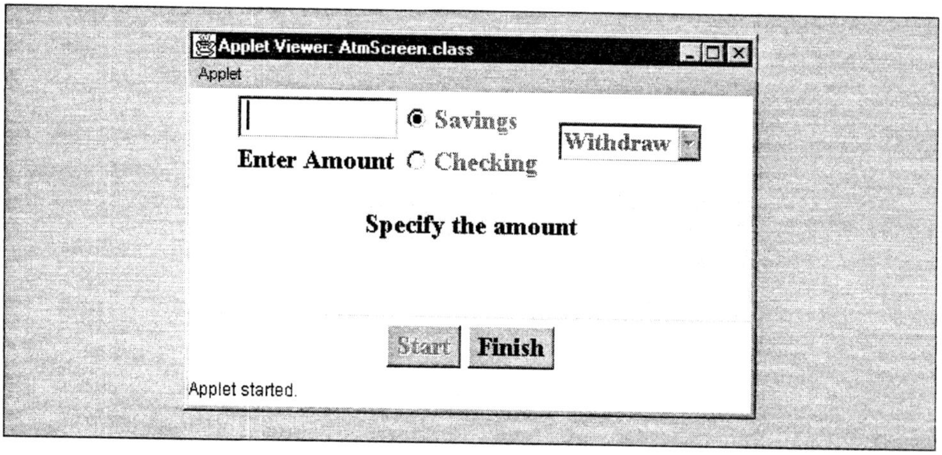

In this text we introduce event-driven programming in three chapters graded according to complexity. In this chapter, continuing our previous introduction to applets, we deal only with events which cause the screen to be drawn or redrawn. These events are coordinated by the operating system and our program only has to specify what to draw. In Chapter 7 we cover high-level events associated with a component of a user interface such as a button. The button deals with the mouse directly and just tells us when the user presses it. In Chapter 10 we discuss the low-level mouse, key, and window events.

The `AtmScreen` shown in Figure 6.1 is an applet. It shows, at a simple level, how a bank might serve customers using the Internet. A customer could use a browser to connect to the bank's web site and download a Java applet to perform banking transactions.

With applets we enter the world of distributed computing, rapidly growing in importance, in which computers at different locations coordinate their efforts. We start with an introduction to the World Wide Web.*

Objectives:

- Learn the uses of protocols.
- Learn basic HTML tags.
- Write and test applets.
- Understand the idea of event-handling code.
- Respond to paint events.
- Take a first look at inheritance.
- Know AWT classes needed for drawing.
- Draw in color.

---

* For a thought provoking article on the significance of interaction in computing see "Why Interaction is More Powerful than Algorithms," Peter Wegner, *Communications of the ACM,* May 1997, pp. 80–91.

6.1 The World Wide Web and Applets

The Internet includes many applications of which the most used is email. The rapidly growing **World Wide Web (WWW)** allows computers all over the world to explore the enormous web of links from one site to another for educational, commercial, and recreational purposes. We will explain a little about how the World Wide Web works, and then show how Java applets enhance its capabilities.

Protocols

Diplomats and heads-of-state follow protocol, special rules of etiquette governing their formal interactions. Each knows what is expected in a particular situation. Similarly computers have rules of interaction, called protocols, specifying how they interact. To send email, a computer uses **SMTP** (Simple Mail Transfer Protocol). To receive email, a computer uses **POP3** (Post Office Protocol-version 3). Computers can transfer files using **FTP** (File Transfer Protocol). The `java.net` package that we introduce in Chapter 15 makes it easy to use these protocols from a Java program.

For web programs, we most often use **HTTP** (Hypertext Transfer Protocol). Hypertext, text augmented with links to other files, images, and other resources, makes the Web a web of links connecting one document to another document on the same computer or on one perhaps halfway around the world. As Java programmers, we are not required to know the details of HTTP.

Clients and Servers

A salesperson serves a customer who is sometimes called a client. Computers follow this analogy. A client can ask a server for service. The server may be a program that will give a client its email if both client and server send each other messages using POP3. The server may be ready to serve hypertext files to a client, both using HTTP to communicate. We call the client getting hypertext files a browser, while the server sending hypertext files is called a web server. Popular browsers include Communicator from Netscape and Internet Explorer from Microsoft.

The URL

We use a **URL** (Uniform Resource Locator) to specify an Internet resource. For example, the URL

```
http://java.sun.com/applets/index.html
```

specifies the page on Sun Microsystems' web site that provides applets. The URL has three parts,

`http`	specifies the protocol, in this case HTTP.
`java.sun.com`	specifies the domain name of the server. (a unique address for that computer)
`applets/index.html`	the path to the resource

If we enter this URL in the location field of a browser, then the browser will connect to Sun's computer, and using HTTP, ask the web server for the `index.html` file in the specified path. Sometimes we do have a reference, like this one, to a specific file that we request; more often we go to a home page and click on links from that home page to find the information we want. For example, Sun's Java home page has the URL

```
http://java.sun.com/
```

Clicking on the word Applets on that page gets the page given by the first URL above. When the URL does not include a path to the resource, then the server returns a file with a default file name, usually `index.html`.

HTML

Notice that the page providing applets has the `.html` extension. We use HTML (Hypertext Markup Language) to create the hypertext files found on the Web. This markup language adds tags to specify the formatting of the text. For example the tag `<br>` causes a break to a new line. The browser interprets these tags, formatting the page for the client. Using tags allows browsers of different capabilities to interpret the tags differently. For example, the tag `<em>`, requesting emphasis for the text that follows, might cause one browser to display the text in italics, but another browser, without the capability to use italics, might underline that text for emphasis.

The World Wide Web must adapt itself to many computers with differing capabilities. By using **HTML tags**, web documents can be displayed by a variety of browsers including those on terminals without graphics capabilities.

We will soon see how to include Java applets in web pages. Although HTML is not hard to learn to use, we do not really need to design web pages to learn how to use Java applets. Nevertheless, a brief introduction to HTML here will remove some of the mystery from the Web, and provide a foundation for further study for those who may wish to integrate Java into web applications.

To get the flavor of HTML we list a few tags in Figure 6.2 and use them to write a rudimentary web page. Tags are not case sensitive; the tag `<BR>` is the same as `<br>`.

We can insert an empty tag like `<br>` anywhere to cause a line break. Non-empty tags like `<em>` have a closing form using the forward slash that marks the end of the text covered by that tag. Thus

```
<em> Java is fun. </em>
```

would emphasize the text, *Java is fun*. The six levels of header tags specify the importance of the header, with `h1` being the most important, and `h6` the least. Browsers will try to make the more important headers larger and more impressive. An unordered list includes, between its starting and ending tags, various list elements with tags `<li>`.

Some tags use attributes embedded in the tag to provide information needed to interpret that tag. The **anchor tag** uses the `href` attribute to specify the URL of a hypertext link. For example to link to Sun's Java home page we can use the anchor

```
<a href = "http://java.sun.com/"> Sun's home page. </a>
```

Figure 6.2 Some HTML tags

` `	Break to the next line.
`<p>`	New paragraph (after a blank line).
`<em> ... </em>`	Emphasize the text.
`<strong>...</strong>`	Strongly emphasize the text.
`<title>... </title>`	Title, displayed separately from text.
`<h1>... </h1>`	Top-level header.
`<h3>... </h3>`	Third-level header, (lowest is sixth).
`<ul> ... </ul>`	An unordered list.
`<li>`	Element of a list.
`<a>... </a>`	An anchor, a hypertext link.
`<img>`	An image.
`<applet>...</applet>`	A Java applet.

The `href` attribute gives the URL for Sun's Java home page. The text, *Sun's home page* will usually appear underlined and in blue, indicating that a mouse click will cause the browser to request, using HTTP, the Sun server to serve up its home page HTML file, which the browser then interprets, displaying Sun's Java home page.

The client must be connected to the Internet to link to other computers. Anchors can also link to files on the same machine using a relative URL. For example, to link to a file `funStuff.html` in the same directory, we could use the anchor

```
<a href = "funStuff.html"> some fun stuff </a>
```

Use the `<img>` tag to display an image, with an `src` attribute which gives the URL of the source of the picture. For example to display a picture of the author of the text, found in the same directory as the web page itself, use

```
<img src="gittleman.gif">
```

A browser that cannot display graphics will fill the space with text such as `[IMAGE]`.

The **applet tag** will, in Java enabled browsers, cause the Java interpreter to execute a Java applet. The `code` attribute specifies the class file for the applet, while the `width` and `height` attributes give the size of the applet in **pixels**. For example,

```
<applet code="Sort.class" width="300" height="200">
If you see this, your browser is not Java enabled.
</applet>
```

will cause Java enabled browsers to execute the `Sort` applet of Example 1.3 and other browsers to display the message between the `<applet>` and `</applet>` tags.

The World Wide Web really is worldwide. In our browser we access web pages developed on a variety of machines running various operating systems. Java byte-code is platform-independent, so the server and client can use different hardware and software, but the client can still execute the applet developed on the server. This platform independence makes Java an ideal language for network applications, including the WWW.

Example 6.1 shows an HTML file for a very simple web page, displayed in Figure 6.3, which uses some of the tags from Figure 6.2.

Figure 6.3 Displaying `WebPage.html` in a browser

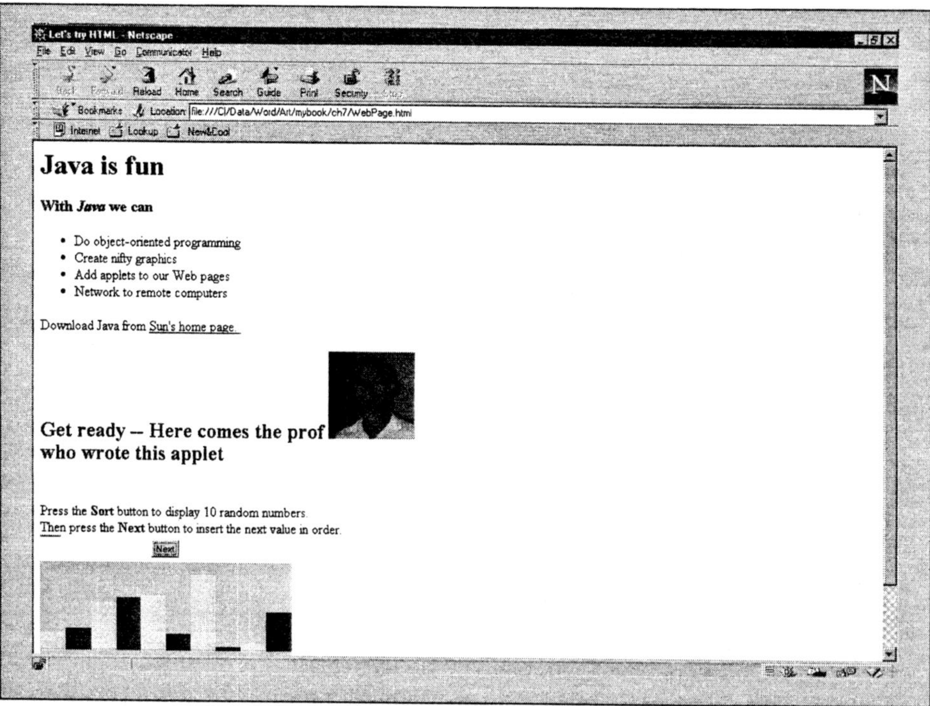

EXAMPLE 6.1 WebPage.html

```
<!-- Illustrates some html tags in                              // Note 1
  -- a simple web page.
  -->
<title> Let's try HTML </title>                                 // Note 2
<h1> Java is fun </h1>                                          // Note 3
<p>
<h3> With <em>Java</em> we can </h3>                            // Note 4
<ul> <li> Do object-oriented programming                        // Note 5
        <li> Create nifty graphics
        <li> Add applets to our web pages
        <li> Network to remote computers
    </ul><p>
    Download Java from
  <a href = "http://java.sun.com/"> Sun's Java home page. </a>  // Note 6
    <br>
    <h2> Get ready -- Here comes the prof
    <img src=gittleman.gif><br>                                 // Note 7
    who wrote this applet </h2><br>
```

```
Press the <strong> Sort </strong> button to display 10 random numbers.<br>
Then press the <strong> Next </strong> button to insert the next value in
order.<br>
<applet code=Sort.class width=300 height=200>                    // Note 8
   If you see this, your browser is not Java enabled.
</applet>
```

Note 1: Comments in HTML documents start with `<!--` and end with `-->`

Note 2: The title displays at the top of the frame, not in the document itself. Web search engines use the title in their searches.

Note 3: The text between the `h1` tags has the largest size.

Note 4: The `em` tag causes the text to be displayed in italics.

Note 5: Each item of an unordered list is preceded by a bullet.

Note 6:

```
<a href = "http://java.sun.com/">
Sun's home page. </a>
```

The URL of the anchor does not show up; the blue text is underlined.

Note 7:

```
<img src=gittleman.gif><br>
```

The image is a `.gif` file, a graphics format.

Note 8:

```
<applet code=Sort.class width=300 height=200>
```

`Sort.class` was compiled from the `Sort.java` program containing the Java code for the applet of Example 1.3 that displays 10 random numbers in a bar chart when the user presses the Sort button and inserts the next bar in order with respect to its predecessors when the user presses the Next button. In this chapter we will learn how to write applets; we will study the code for a more complex version of this applet in Section 8.6.

Use a browser to see this page. In Netscape Communicator, click on `File`, click on `Open Page`, and click on `Choose File` to locate the `WebPage.html` file. In Microsoft Internet Explorer , click on `File`, click on `Open`, and click on `Browse` to locate `WebPage.html`.* The URL is a file URL, using the `file` protocol. The domain name of the server is just the local host, which can be omitted, so the URL looks like

```
file:///path/WebPage.html
```

where `path` is the path on the local machine to the `WebPage.html` file.

We created a very simple web page in Example 6.1, but to illustrate Java applets we could have made it a lot simpler, leaving out everything but the applet tags, as in the following code for the HTML file `Sort.html`.

```
<applet code="Sort.class" width="300" height="200">
</applet>
```

* Browsers may not be configured with the latest versions of Java. The Java Plugin (See Appendix E) can be used to provide the latest Java version.

Loading `Sort.html` in a Java enabled browser will cause the `Sort` applet to execute; the page will just contain the bar chart and the button we use to sort the bars. To test applets without using a browser, development environments provide an applet viewer that executes only the applets in an HTML file, and ignores everything else.* Using an applet viewer, both Example 6.1 and `Sort.html` would produce the same result.

THE BIG PICTURE

Using a browser, we can connect to sites anywhere in the World Wide Web. Web pages, written using HTML, the Hypertext Markup Language, may include applets, which are Java programs that the browser downloads and executes on our machine. A browser displays the full web page, while an applet viewer just tests any applets on the page, ignoring other HTML tags.

TEST YOUR UNDERSTANDING

1. Which protocol does the browser use to download web pages?
2. Given the URL

   `http://developer.javasoft.com/developer/readAboutJava/jpg/ball.html`

   a. What is the protocol?
   b. What is the domain name of the server?
   c. What is the path to the resource?
3. What language do we use to write Web pages?
4. What are the three required attributes in the `<applet>` HTML tag? What does each specify?
5. For what purpose is an HTML anchor tag used?
6. Which header tag, `h2` or `h5`, will most likely cause a more prominent display of the text to which it applies?

6.2 Paint Events

Redrawing a window gives a gentle introduction to event-driven programming. The operating system manages its windows, notifying Java when a Java window needs refreshing. In our program we write the code to execute when our applet window needs to be redrawn. However, we do not call this code, but rather we wait for an event such as a user resizing the window to cause Java to call our `paint` method.

* The JDK provides the applet viewer which we use from the console window, as for example,

```
appletviewer WebPage.html
```

See Appendix E for instructions on creating applets with other development environments.

Responding to Paint Events

Example 6.1 showed an applet executed from a web page, but we will not see until Section 8.7 how the code for that `Sort` applet works. Let us look at the simple applet in Example 6.2 to illustrate event-driven programming.

EXAMPLE 6.2 HelloCount.java

```
/* Displays the message "Hello World!" in
 * a browser or applet viewer window.
 */
import java.applet.Applet;
import java.awt.Graphics;
public class HelloCount extends Applet {
  private int count = 1; // counts paint calls

  public void paint(Graphics g) {
    g.drawString("Hello " + count++,30,30);                    // Note 1
  }
}
```

Note 1: We increment `count` each time we call `paint` so we can see how events that the user creates cause calls to the `paint` method to redraw the applet.

We will discuss the code further after we see how `HelloCount` works. Notice that the `HelloCount` class has no `main` method. We always run applets using a browser or applet viewer that initializes and starts them. We implement the `paint` method, but we do not call it. The Java system calls our `paint` method when our applet needs to be redrawn. It needs to draw the window when the applet starts running, and again in response to external events such as a user minimizing the window, resizing it, or just changing to another web page and then returning back to this one. Figure 6.4 shows the applet when we first start it.

Figure 6.4 `HelloCount` **just starting**

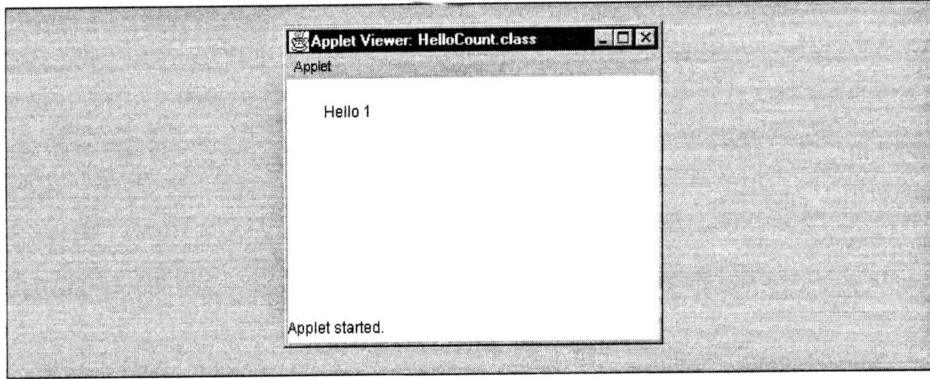

The `paint` method increments the `count` variable by one every time Java calls it so we can see how the user's actions cause Java to call `paint`. Figure 6.5 shows the applet window after the user resizes it with the mouse, making it smaller. The `count` goes up to 2, showing that Java called the `paint` method to redraw the applet when the user resized it.

Figure 6.5 `HelloCount` **after the user resizes it**

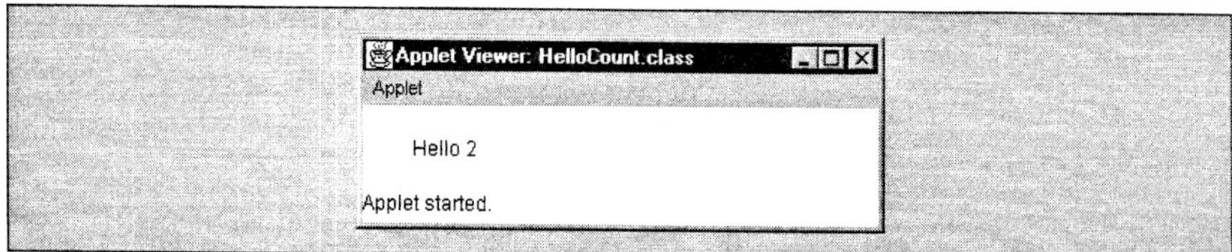

Covering the applet with another window and then uncovering it will cause Java to call our `paint` method to redraw the applet. Figure 6.6 shows the applet partially covered, while Figure 6.7 shows it uncovered again, now showing a count of three indicating another call to `paint`.

Paint events are simpler than those we study later because the operating system coordinates these events, keeping all its windows properly painted, not just our Java programs. All our Java program has to do is to implement the `paint` method.

Figure 6.6 `HelloCount` **partially covered**

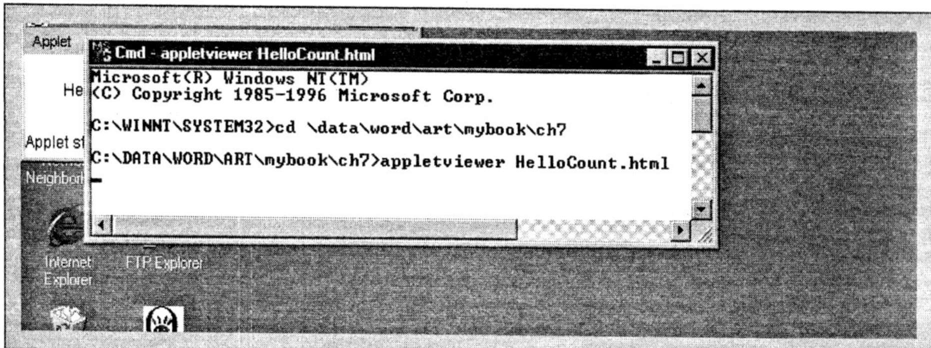

Figure 6.7 `HelloCount` **uncovered again**

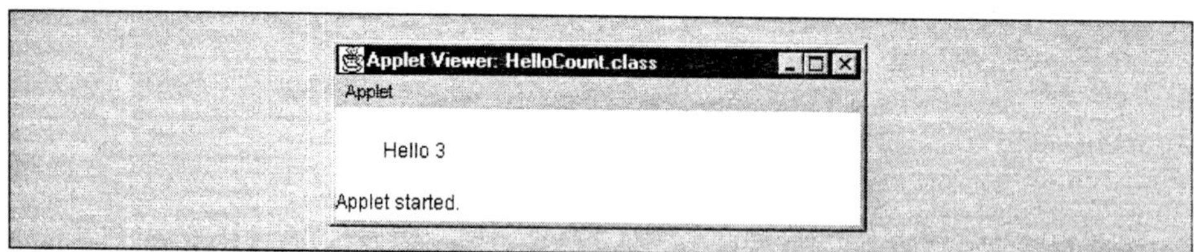

Our code in an event-driven program such as `HelloCount.java` implements the `paint` method, which is a type of event handler. It contains the code to draw the applet window when an event causes the window to need to be drawn again. Although this example is an applet, we will see in Section 10.2 that we can create standalone event-driven programs. Now that we have seen how `HelloCount` works, responding to paint events, we will look at more detail at some other aspects of that code.

An applet looks much like any other Java program. The `HelloCount` class can have data fields and methods just like other Java classes. In this example, `HelloCount` implements just one method, `paint`, which overrides the `paint` method it inherits from the `Container` class.

The `paint` method has a formal parameter `g` of type `Graphics`, a class of the AWT. Java has a reason to call the AWT abstract. The same Java code runs on vastly different systems. Windows, UNIX, and Macintosh systems each have their own windowing libraries. A Java program that used graphics would be very difficult to write if it had to refer specifically to each of the many windowing libraries. The `Graphics` package provides an abstract interface to these windowing libraries. When we run a Java program that uses graphics, the local system provides an implementation of the `Graphics` class that uses the windowing library available on that system. As Java programmers, we just use the methods of the `Graphics` class for all systems, and let each system give us an implementation that works on that system.

Running the `HelloCount` applet of Example 6.2 displays the string Hello n starting at position (30,30) which is near the upper-left corner of the screen. Here n is the number of times Java has called the `paint` method. To run the `HelloCount` applet, we compile that code, and write an HTML file,

```
<applet code="HelloApplet.class" width="300" height="200">
</applet>
```

which we load in the browser or applet viewer.

THE BIG PICTURE

We write code in an event-driven program that is called by the system when an event occurs. Our `paint` method indicates how to redraw the window when the user resizes it or uncovers it from behind another window. The Abstract Windowing Toolkit (AWT) includes the `Graphics` class whose methods let us draw shapes and text in a platform-independent manner.

TEST YOUR UNDERSTANDING

TRY IT YOURSELF

7. Run Example 6.2 and generate `paint` events by repeatedly minimizing and restoring the window in which the applet is displayed.
8. Explain how the `Graphics` class helps provide platform independence for Java.
9. We use coordinates to represent each pixel in a window or panel. What is the position of the origin `(0,0)`?
10. Give some examples of events that would cause the `paint` method of the `Hello-Count` applet of Example 6.2 to be called.

6.3 Drawing Text

In this section, we will draw text in graphics mode where we can choose different fonts, sizes, and styles for our text.

Fonts

The `Font` class in the `java.awt` package lets us create fonts of different types, with various sizes, and a choice of four styles. Java distinguishes between logical and physical font names. The logical font name describes a font style that can be implemented by different physical fonts on different systems. Java logical font names are:

`Serif`	The letters have hooks at the ends of the strokes.
`SansSerif`	The letters do not have hooks.
`Monospaced`	Each character has the same width.
`Dialog`	Used in dialog boxes.
`DialogInput`	Used for dialog input.

These logical font names are mapped to actual fonts available on the user's machine. For example Windows systems use the `Times New Roman` font for `Serif`, the `Arial` font for `SansSerif` and `Dialog`, and the `Courier` font for `Monospaced` and `DialogInput`.

Physical font names correspond to fonts installed on the user's machine. Java 2 recommends using physical font names. We mentioned `Times New Roman`, `Arial`, and `Courier`, three commonly available fonts. The Java 2 distribution includes fonts from the Lucinda family, such as `Lucinda Sans Regular`.

Java provides four styles, `Font.PLAIN`, `Font.ITALIC`, `Font.BOLD`, and `Font.ITALIC + Font.BOLD`, which are constants of the `Font` class. We measure the character size in points; one inch is equal to 72 points.

The `Font` constructor takes three arguments: the name, style, and size.

```
Font serifBold24 = new Font("Serif",Font.BOLD,24);
```

Notice that the three arguments are all constants. We really only need to construct the font `serifBold24` once, but if we put the call to the constructor in the `paint` method, we will construct the same font again each time Java calls our `paint` method.

Constructing this font should be part of the applet's initialization, done only once when the applet is first loaded.

Initializing an Applet

The `Applet` class has just the method we need. The browser calls the applet's `init` method, which has the form

```
public void init() {
  // do initialization here
}
```

once when it loads the applet. The default implementation of `init` in the `Applet` class does nothing, so we override it to provide any needed initialization for our applet, such as the creation of a font.

TIP Use the `init` method to compute values that will not change during the life of the applet. Do not compute something that might change, such as the applet's width, in the `init` method, because `init` is called only once when the applet is loaded.

We can specify the font for the applet in the `init` method using the `setFont` method, as in

```
setFont(serifBold24);
```

which would cause all the strings in the applet to appear in the font `serifBold24`. If we want to change the font in the `paint` method, then we can use the `setFont` method of the `Graphics` class:

```
g.setFont(serifBold24);
```

We will draw all our text at positions defined in terms of the dimensions of the applet, so if the size of our applet changes, then our text will still be displayed at the same relative positions. We can use the `getSize` method to return a `Dimension` object, which gives us the height, h, and width, w, of our applet.

Suppose we want to center a string in the applet, horizontally. If we know the number of pixels, n, that a string will use when displayed in a given font, we can easily center it horizontally. If the applet's width is w, then w-n gives the number of pixels on both sides of the string. Dividing w-n in half gives the number of pixels on each side of the string needed to make it centered, as shown in Figure 6.8.

Figure 6.8 Centering a string

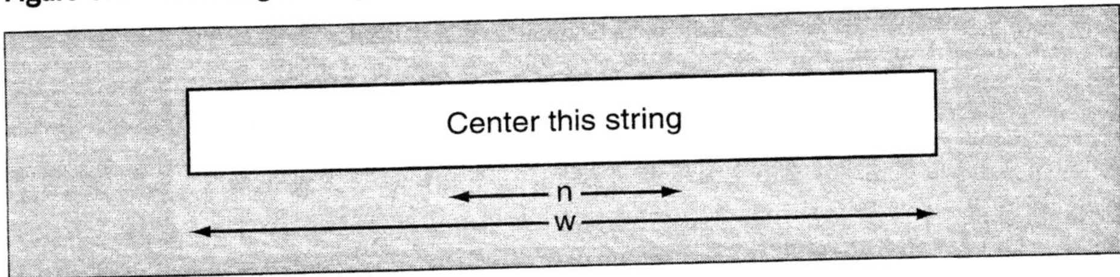

Font Metrics

To find the width of a string drawn in our applet using a certain font, we can get the `FontMetrics` object that will give us information about the font. We get a `FontMetrics` object using the `getFontMetrics` method, as in:

```
FontMetrics metrics = getFontMetrics(serifBold24);
```

which gives us the `metrics` object for the `serifBold24` font as it will appear in this applet. To get the width of a string, we use the `stringWidth` method:

```
n = metrics.stringWidth("Center this string");
```

We can get the `metrics` object and find the width of a string in the `init` method because these values do not change, even if the applet changes size. However, we need to find the height and width of the applet in the `paint` method. Java calls our `paint` method whenever events require our applet to be redrawn. Many of these events, including maximizing, minimizing, and other resizing operations, change the size of our applet, so we need to compute the applet's size in the `paint` method, which will be called in response to such changes in its size.

In Example 6.3 we will draw five lines of text, each one using a different font name. We illustrate the four font styles and choose different point sizes for the fonts. For the text of each line, we draw the font name given by the `getName` method, as in:

```
serifBold24.getName()
```

which will return the string `Serif`.

We will center the first line horizontally, and start each of the other four lines one-fourth of the way in from the left. Vertically, we will position the five lines so they always divide the applet into six equal parts. We put as much of the computation as possible in the `init` method that is called just once, rather than in `paint`, which is called whenever the applet needs to be redrawn.

Figure 6.9 shows the `Text` applet of Example 6.3 running in the applet viewer.

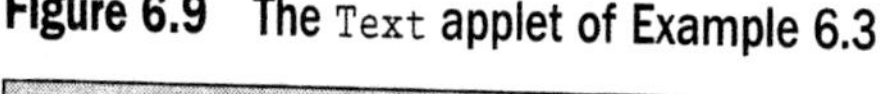

Figure 6.9 The `Text` applet of Example 6.3

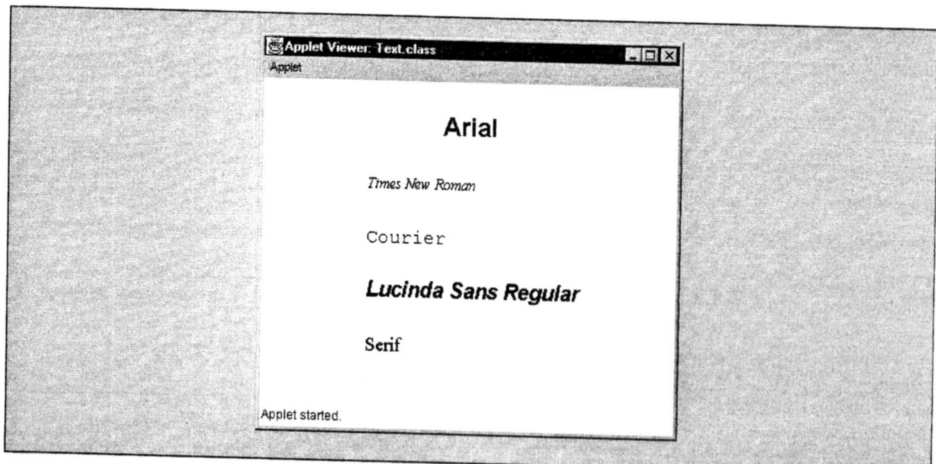

EXAMPLE 6.3 **Text.java**

```
/* Draws the different fonts, trying all the
 * styles, and using various point sizes. Draws
 * all text relative to the applet's size. Uses
 * the init method to compute quantities that
 * do not change.
 */
                                                            // Note 1
import java.awt.*;
import java.applet.Applet;
public class Text extends Applet {
                                                            // Note 2
     private Font arialBold24;
     private Font timesItalic14;
     private Font courierPlain18;
     private Font lucindaBI20;
     private Font serifPlain18;
     private String arial;          // The string we want to center
     private int arialStart;        // The distance in for the centered string
     private int arialWide;         // The width of the centered string.
     public void init() {
                                                            // Note 3
       arialBold24 = new Font("Arial",Font.BOLD,24);
       timesItalic14 = new Font("Times New Roman",Font.ITALIC,14);
       courierPlain18 = new Font("Courier",Font.PLAIN,18);
       lucindaBI20 = new Font
               ("Lucinda Sans Regular",Font.BOLD+Font.ITALIC,20);
       serifPlain18 = new Font("Serif",Font.PLAIN,18);
                                                            // Note 4
       setFont(arialBold24);
                                                            // Note 5
       FontMetrics metrics = getFontMetrics(arialBold24);
                                                            // Note 6
       arial = arialBold24.getName();
                                                            // Note 7
       arialWide = metrics.stringWidth(arial);
     }
     public void paint(Graphics g) {
                                                            // Note 8
       Dimension d = getSize();
       int w = d.width;             // The width of the applet
       int h = d.height;            // The height of the applet
                                                            // Note 9
       arialStart = (w-arialWide)/2;
                                                            // Note 10
       int otherStart = w/4;
                                                            // Note 11
       g.drawString(arial,arialStart,h/6);
                                                            // Note 12
       g.setFont(timesItalic14);
                                                            // Note 13
       g.drawString(timesItalic14.getName(),otherStart,2*h/6);
       g.setFont(courierPlain18);
       g.drawString(courierPlain18.getName(),otherStart,3*h/6);
       g.setFont(lucindaBI20);
       g.drawString(lucindaBI20.getName(),otherStart,4*h/6);
       g.setFont(serifPlain18);
       g.drawString(serifPlain18.getName(),otherStart,5*h/6);
     }
}
```

Note 1: Because we have to use `Graphics`, `Font`, and `FontMetrics` from `java.awt`, it is easier just to use the `*` which stands for any class in the `java.awt` package, rather than to import each class individually.

Note 2: We will create this font in the `init` method, but we declare it here because we need to use it in both the `init` and the `paint` methods.

Note 3: The three arguments to the `Font` constructor are the font name, the style, and the point size. Note that styles are constants of the `Font` class.

Note 4: Using the `setFont` method from the `Component` class sets the font for the applet. Setting the font here does not help us in this example, because we are going to change the font several times in the `paint` method, but if our applet used one font, then this would be the best way to set it.

Note 5: We get the font metrics for the `arialBold24` font as it will appear in this applet. The `FontMetrics` class has many methods to provide data about the font; we use just one in this example. Each font has its own `FontMetrics` object; we illustrate just this one.

Note 6:
```
arial = arialBold24.getName();
```
The `getName` method returns the name of the font, which in this case is Arial.

Note 7:
```
arialWide = metrics.stringWidth(arial);
```
The `stringWidth` method of the `FontMetrics` class returns the width in pixels of its string argument as drawn in this font.

Note 8:
```
Dimension d = getSize();
```
The `getSize` method returns the size of the applet as a `Dimension` object which we can use to get the height and width of the applet. We get the applet's size in `paint` which is called when the size changes; we need to find the new size before drawing the strings again.

Note 9:
```
arialStart = (w-arialWide)/2;
```
We divide the whitespace into two equal parts so the first string will be centered as in Figure 6.8.

Note 10:
```
int otherStart = w/4;
```
The other four strings will start at a distance `w/4` from the left of the applet, where `w` is the applet's width.

Note 11:
```
g.drawString(arial,arialStart,h/6);
```
We draw the first string with the x-coordinate computed so as to center the string horizontally and the y-coordinate at `h/6` which will always be one-sixth of the way down from the top, no matter what height, `h`, the applet has.

Note 12:
```
g.setFont(timesItalic14);
```
Inside the `paint` method, we use the `setFont` method of the `Graphics` class to change the font.

Note 13: `g.drawString(timesItalic14.getName(),otherStart,2*h/6);`
We draw each of the other strings starting at a horizontal position one-fourth of the way across from the left. We position the strings vertically using the applet's height to divide it into six equally spaced parts each separated by one of our strings.

THE BIG PICTURE

Using the graphics mode we can draw text in different fonts, with italics, boldface, and in different sizes. Using a `FontMetrics` object, we can find properties of a particular font, which we can use to position text.

We override the `init` method of the `Applet` class to include code that needs to be executed only once when the applet is initialized.

TEST YOUR UNDERSTANDING

11. Declare and initialize a monospaced, italic, 30-point font.
12. Declare and initialize a 12-point sansserif font that is both bold and italic.
13. Write a statement to draw a string `s` of width 50 centered horizontally in an applet whose width is 400 and height is 200.
14. Write a statement to draw a string `s` of width 100 centered both horizontally and vertically in an applet of width 300 and height 200. The font height is `20`.

6.4 Using Color

Using Java, we can easily draw in any of over 16,000,000 colors. Using colors we can illustrate 3D rectangles.

Creating Colors

The `Color` class, found in the `java.awt` package, defines the color name constants

```
Color.black         Color.magenta
Color.blue          Color.orange
Color.cyan          Color.pink
Color.darkGray      Color.red
Color.gray          Color.white
Color.green         Color.yellow
Color.lightGray
```

We can construct other colors using their red, green, and blue components. One `Color` constructor uses values between 0 and 255 for each component. Thus

```
Color itsRed = new Color(255,0,0);
```

constructs a color, `itsRed`, that is equal to the `Color.red`, while

```
Color itsGreen = new Color(0,255,0);
```

constructs another `Color.green`.

We can find the components of a color by using the `getRed`, `getGreen`, and `getBlue` methods. For example, the methods

```
Color.pink.getRed();
Color.pink.getGreen();
Color.pink.getBlue();
```

will return the values 255, 175, and 175 for the red, green, and blue components of `Color.pink`.

Another way to specify colors uses float values between 0.0 and 1.0. Using the constructor which takes three arguments of type float,

`new Color(1.0f, 0.0f, 0.0f)`	would be red,
`new Color(0.0f, 1.0f, 0.0f)`	would be green, and
`new Color(1.0f, 175f/255, 175f/255)`	would be pink.

To initialize the applet's background and foreground colors we can use the `setBackground` and `setForeground` methods inherited from the `Component` class:

```
setBackground(Color.yellow);
setForeground(new Color(100,150,200));
```

Inside the `paint` method we can change the drawing color using the `setColor` method of the `Graphics` class:

```
g.setColor(Color.blue);
```

If we need to get any of these colors, perhaps to save them to use later, we can use the `getBackground`, `getForeground`, and `g.getColor` methods.

Example 6.4 makes a 10 by 10 grid with each cell colored with a color chosen at random. Figure 6.10 shows a black and white version of this applet. Run it to get the effect of the color.

EXAMPLE 6.4 ColorChips.java

```
/* Draw each of 100 cells with randomly
 * chosen colors.
 */
import java.awt.*;
import java.applet.Applet;
public class ColorChips extends Applet {
  public void paint(Graphics g) {
    int h = getSize().height;
    int w = getSize().width;
```

Figure 6.10 The applet of Example 6.4

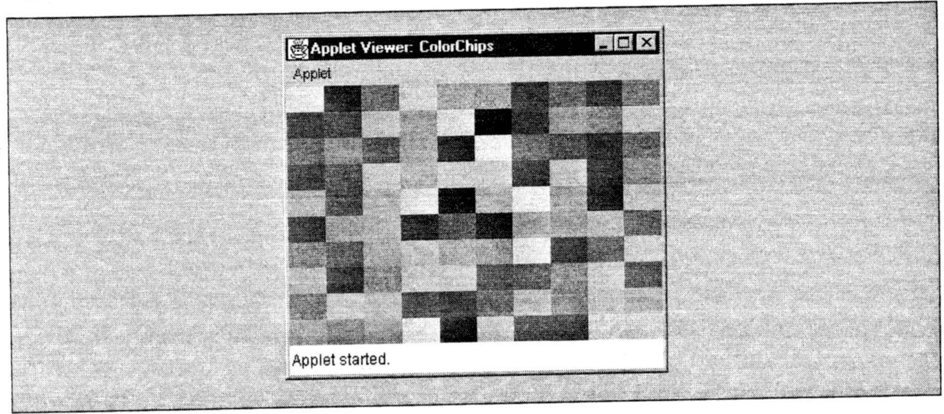


```
    for (int i = 0; i < 10; i++)                        // Note 1
     for (int j = 0; j < 10; j++) {
      float red = (float)Math.random();                  // Note 2
      float green = (float)Math.random();
      float blue = (float)Math.random();
      Color color = new Color(red,green,blue);
      g.setColor(color);
      g.fillRect(i*w/10,j*h/10,w/10,h/10);               // Note 3
     }
  }
}
```

Note 1: We use one for loop to divide the width of the applet into 10 parts and another to divide its length into 10 parts.

Note 2: The `random` method return a double value, so we cast it to the float needed in the `Color` constructor.

Note 3: Each cell is a rectangle of width `w/10` and height `h/10`.

3D Rectangles

The **Graphics** class has two drawing methods, `draw3DRect` and `fill3DRect`, that we did not mention in Section 3.7 because we need to set a different color than the default black to see these effects, which brighten and darken the drawing color to provide a very thin shading to give a slight three-dimensional effect. These methods have a fifth parameter of type boolean which we set to true to show the rectangle raised and to false to show it recessed. Thus the statement

```
g.fill3DRect(150,20,100,50,true);
```

draws a raised, filled rectangle with upper-left corner `(150,20)`, width `100`, and height `50`.

The `Color` class has methods, `brighter` and `darker`, which modify the color, so

```
Color.orange.brighter()
```

will brighten `Color.orange`. We can call the method twice to achieve a greater effect, as in

```
Color.orange.darker().darker()
```

which darkens the darkened `Color.orange.darker()`. Figure 6.11 shows the applet of Example 6.5 which displays these effects.

Figure 6.11 The applet of Example 6.5

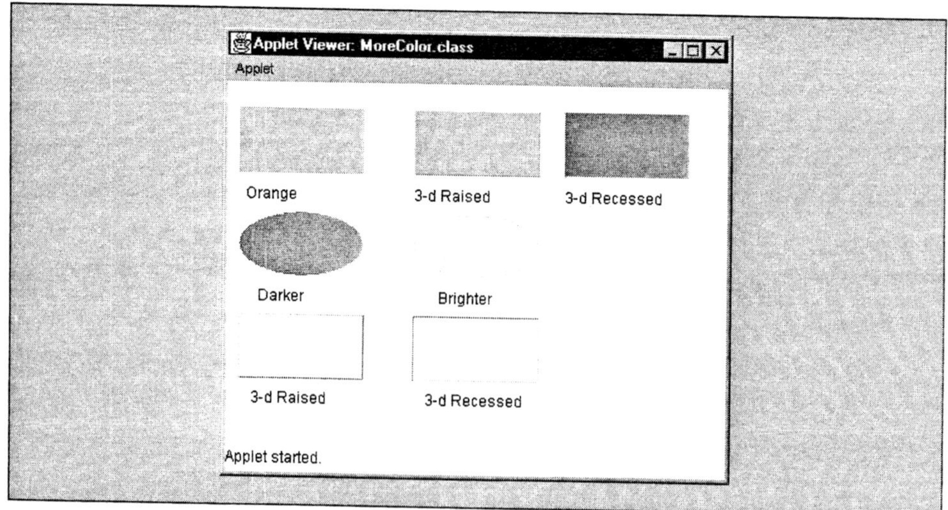

EXAMPLE 6.5 MoreColor.java

```
/* Demonstrates drawing and filling 3D
 * rectangles, and brightening and darkening
 * colors.
 */

import java.awt.*;
import java.applet.Applet;

public class MoreColor extends Applet {
  public void paint(Graphics g) {
     g.setColor(Color.orange);
     g.fillRect(10,20,100,50);
     g.fill3DRect(150,20,100,50,true);                    // Note 1
     g.fill3DRect(270,20,100,50,false);
     g.setColor(Color.orange.darker());
     g.fillOval(10,100,100,50);
     g.setColor(Color.orange.brighter());
     g.fillOval(150,100,100,50);
     g.setColor(Color.orange);
     g.draw3DRect(10,180,100,50,true);
     g.draw3DRect(150,180,100,50,false);                  // Note 2
```

```
        g.setColor(Color.black);                                // Note 3
        g.drawString("Orange",15,90);                           // Note 4
        g.drawString("3-d Raised",150,90);
        g.drawString("3-d Recessed",270,90);
        g.drawString("Darker",25,170);
        g.drawString("Brighter",170,170);
        g.drawString("3-d Raised",20,250);
        g.drawString("3-d Recessed",160,250);
    }
}
```

Note 1: The argument true specifies a raised rectangle.

Note 2: The argument false specifies a recessed rectangle.

Note 3: We want the text in black. We do not have to draw the text right after the figure it describes, which would have forced us to keep changing colors between black and orange. We can set the color to black after drawing all the figures, and then draw all the text.

Note 4: To draw the text we use the default font name, style, and point size.

THE BIG PICTURE

The `Color` class has 13 predefined colors. We can define others using red, green, and blue values, either integers from 0 to 255, or floats from 0.0f to 1.0f. We can set the foreground and background colors for any component and set the drawing color used by a `Graphics` object.

TEST YOUR UNDERSTANDING

15. Construct a color which is the same as `Color.blue`, using the constructor that takes three integer arguments.
16. Construct a color which is the same as `Color.blue`, using the constructor that takes three float arguments.
17. Find the red, green, and blue components for `Color.black`.
18. Find the red, green, and blue components for `Color.white`.

6.5 Interfaces

Before continuing with event-driven programming, we need to introduce interfaces, which the Java event model uses heavily.

Declaring an Interface

An interface specifies behavior but omits any implementation. The interface specifies a type for objects, and can be implemented in various ways by Java classes.

For example, a `Drivable` interface might specify operations used in driving a vehicle (See Figure 6.12).

Figure 6.12 The `Drivable` interface

```
public interface Drivable {
  public static final int LEFT = 0;
  public static final int RIGHT = 1;
  public void start();
  public void stop();
  public void accelerate();
  public void decelerate();
  public void turn(int direction);
}
```

The `Drivable` interface contains two constants, `LEFT` and `RIGHT`, that we use as arguments to the `turn` method, and five methods. The interface states what a `Drivable` object can do, but not how. We cannot implement any methods in an interface, nor can we include variables.

Interfaces limit the dependencies between various parts of a program, making programs easier to maintain, which is a very important consideration when developing large software systems that will be used for many years.

A nice interface promotes portability. A program written using interface methods will work with any implementation of that interface.

Before we get to a Java example, consider driving an automobile. We do not have to learn a new set of skills to drive each of the many makes and models of automobiles. We usually start a car using a key, accelerate using the gas pedal, decelerate using the brake, and turn using the steering wheel. The implementation of these methods can be quite different, with a great impact on comfort and performance, but as drivers we do not need to delve into these implementation details.

In Java we can use interface methods without knowing the details of any implementation of that interface. The `goForward` method of Figure 6.13 will work for any `Drivable` object. It starts, accelerates to pick up speed, and decelerates to slow down.

Figure 6.13 Using `Drivable`

```
public static void goForward(Drivable d) {
  d.start();
  d.accelerate();
  d.decelerate();
}
```

We can pass any object that implements the `Drivable` interface to the `goForward` method. The developer of the `goForward` method does not need to know about implementations of the interface.

Implementing an Interface

We can define various classes, which implement `Drivable` in their own way. A class that implements an interface must implement each method of that interface. It may implement more than one interface, and add instance variable and additional methods. We use the `implements` keyword when defining a class that implements an interface. For example,

```
public class SportsCar implements Drivable {
  // implement Drivable methods here
}
```

In Example 6.6, we define two implementations of `Drivable`: `SportsCar` and `Van`. For simplicity they just display messages that describe what each method does.

EXAMPLE 6.6 SportsCar.java, Van.java, TestDrivable.java

SportsCar.java

```
/* Implements the Drivable interface to drive
 * like a sports car.
 */
public class SportsCar implements Drivable {                    // Note 1
  public void start() {
    System.out.println("Starting like a sports car");
  }
  public void stop() {
    System.out.println("Stopping like a sports car");
  }
  public void accelerate() {
    System.out.println("Accelerating quickly");
  }
  public void decelerate() {
    System.out.println("Decelerating rapidly");
  }
  public void turn(int direction) {
    System.out.println("Turning like a sports car");
  }
}
```

Van.java

```
/* Implements the Drivable interface to drive
 * like a van.
 */
public class Van implements Drivable {
  public void start() {
    System.out.println("Starting like a van");
  }
  public void stop() {
    System.out.println("Stopping like a van");
  }
```

```
  public void accelerate() {
    System.out.println("Accelerating cautiously");
  }
  public void decelerate() {
    System.out.println("Decelerating gradually");
  }
  public void turn(int direction) {
    System.out.println("Turning like a van");
  }
}
```

TestDrivable.java

```
/* Uses the Drivable interface.
 */

public class TestDrivable {
  public static void goForward(Drivable d) {
    d.start();
    d.accelerate();
    d.decelerate();
  }
  public static void main(String[] args) {
    Van mini = new Van();                          // Note 2
    SportsCar hot = new SportsCar();
    goForward(mini);                               // Note 3
    System.out.println();
    goForward(hot);
  }
}
```

Output

```
Starting like a van
Accelerating cautiously
Decelerating gradually

Starting like a sports car
Accelerating quickly
Decelerating rapidly
```

Note 1: `SportsCar` must implement all five methods of the `Drivable` interface. It may add instance variables and methods. For example, a `SportsCar` might have a `race` method for fast driving that other implementations of `Drivable` would not support.

Note 2: Neither the Van nor the SportsCar classes define constructors explicitly, because there are no instance variables to initialize. Java will automatically create a default constructor in this case.

Note 3: We can pass any object that implements the `Drivable` interface to the `goForward` method. In this example we pass two types of motor vehicle, but we could pass a `Tricycle` object, if it implemented `Drivable`.

THE BIG PICTURE

An interface declares methods but provides no implementation. Programmers using an interface do not need to know the details of any of its implementations. A class implements an interface by implementing each of its methods. An interface may also declare constants.

TEST YOUR UNDERSTANDING

19. Write an `aroundBlock` method with a `Drivable` parameter. The method should enable the `Drivable` object to traverse a rectangular city block.
20. Describe some other classes that might implement the `Drivable` interface.

6.6 Event Listeners

An event signifies an occurrence. Users create events when they press buttons, enter text in a field, change the size of the window, or select from a list, for example. Our program must respond to these user-generated events to accomplish the desired results. We show how the Java event model works to connect events with the event-handlers in our program.

To get the flavor of the Java event model, we use a familiar situation. A promoter schedules concerts. Many people would like to buy tickets to these concerts. The promoter is the event generator, like the user who presses a button or enters text. The prospective buyers wish to respond to announcements from the promoter. These buyers are like the pieces of our program that respond to button presses and text entries.

To have a successful concert, the promoter must let the prospective buyers know that a concert has been scheduled. This promoter uses a callback system. Buyers sign up with the promoter, indicating they want to be notified when a new concert is scheduled. The promoter keeps a list of all those who signed up and notifies each of them about the new event. Each person receiving the notification decides whether or not to buy tickets.

The Java event model uses an interface to enable the event generator to notify event handlers. In our illustration, we use a `TicketListener` interface, which every ticket buyer must implement. It contains one method, `concertComing`, which has a `TicketEvent` argument describing the event.

```
public interface TicketListener {
  void concertComing(TicketEvent event);
}
```

The `concertComing` method contains the prospective buyer's response to the new concert event. Each buyer can implement it differently, but the promoter knows that each buyer does implement it. For example, a student may only buy tickets if the price is low. A scalper only buys tickets to popular events.

The `TicketEvent` argument has information about the concert to enable buyers to decide what to do. For simplicity, `TicketEvent` only contains a style field, which specifies the type of concert, rock, country, classical, or jazz. Ticket buyers make their decisions based on that style.

To use the Java event model, in this example our program

- Defines an interface that declares the method that an event handler will use to respond to an event. These interfaces often end with the suffix `Listener`, because objects that implement them are listening for events to happen. The `TicketListener` interface declares the `concertComing` method.
- Defines classes that implement the interface. In this example, we define the `Student` and `Scalper` classes. These classes implement the `concertComing` method to specify how they will respond to a `TicketEvent`.
- Defines an event source that generates events. In this example, we define a `Promoter` that creates a `TicketEvent`.

The scenario of Figure 6.14 shows how the student, scalper, and promoter objects interact in generating and handling events.

Figure 6.14 Student, scalper, and promoter interactions

The student registers with the promoter as a `TicketListener`.
The scalper registers with the promoter as a `TicketListener`.
The promoter creates a `TicketEvent`.
The promoter passes the `TicketEvent` to the student's `concertComing` method.
The student's `concertComing` method decides whether to buy tickets.
The promoter passes the `TicketEvent` to the scalper's `concertComing` method.
The scalper's `concertComing` method decides whether to buy tickets.

We must inform the promoter that the student and the scalper want to listen for ticket events. The `Promoter` class has a method

```
addTicketListener(TicketListener listener)
```

that saves its `TicketListener` argument. The student and the scalper both implement `TicketListener`. We pass each to the `addTicketListener` method of the promoter. Until we study arrays, we configure the promoter to save at most two listeners.

EXAMPLE 6.7 **TicketEvent.java, TicketListener.java, Student.java, Scalper.java, Promoter.java, TicketTest.java**

TicketEvent.java

```
/* Describes a concert. Includes the style,
 * but not the artist, day, time, location, or price.
 */
public class TicketEvent {
  public static final int ROCK = 0;
  public static final int COUNTRY = 1;
  public static final int CLASSICAL = 3;
  public static final int JAZZ = 4;
  private int style;

  public TicketEvent (int kind) {
    style = kind;
  }
  public int getStyle() {
    return style;
  }
}
```

TicketListener.java

```
/* Handles a TicketEvent.
 */
public interface TicketListener {
  void concertComing(TicketEvent event);
}
```

Student.java

```
/* The concertComing method responds to ticket events.
 * A student may also study.
 */
public class Student implements TicketListener {
  public void study() {
    System.out.println("Working hard to get better grades.");
  }
  public void concertComing(TicketEvent event) {
    if (event.getStyle() == TicketEvent.ROCK)
      System.out.println("Student buys rock concert tickets");
    if (event.getStyle() == TicketEvent.JAZZ)
      System.out.println("Student buys jazz concert tickets");
  }
}
```

Scalper.java

```
/* The concertComing methods responds to ticket events.
 * A scalper may drive a fancy car.
 */
```

```
public class Scalper implements TicketListener {
  public void driveFancyCar() {
    System.out.println("Driving my fancy car");
  }
  public void concertComing(TicketEvent event) {
    if (event.getStyle() == TicketEvent.ROCK)
      System.out.println("Scalper buys lots of rock concert tickets");
  }
}
```

Promoter.java

```
/* The promoter add ticket listeners, who wish to be called
 * back when a new concert is scheduled. The createConcert method
 * creates a concert event and send it to all ticket listeners.
 */
public class Promoter {
  private TicketListener customer1;
  private TicketListener customer2;

  public void addTicketListener(TicketListener buyer) {
    if (customer1 == null)
      customer1 = buyer;
    else if (customer2 == null)
      customer2 = buyer;
    else
      System.out.println("Cannot accept any more customers now.");
    }
  public void createConcert(int style) {
    TicketEvent event = new TicketEvent(style);
      if (customer1 != null) customer1.concertComing(event);
      if (customer2 != null) customer2.concertComing(event);
  }
}
```

TicketTest.java

```
/* Tests Student, Scalper, Promoter, and
 * TicketEvent.
 */
public class TicketTest {
  public static void main(String[] args) {
    TicketListener student = new Student();
    TicketListener scalper = new Scalper();
    Promoter promoter = new Promoter();
    promoter.addTicketListener(student);
    promoter.addTicketListener(scalper);
    promoter.createConcert(TicketEvent.ROCK);
    promoter.createConcert(TicketEvent.CLASSICAL);
    promoter.createConcert(TicketEvent.JAZZ);
  }
}
```

Output

```
Student buys rock concert tickets
Scalper buys lots of rock concert tickets
Student buys jazz concert tickets
```

THE BIG PICTURE

The Java event model allows the source of an event to communicate its occurrence to various listeners who will take appropriate action. In the concert example, a `Promoter` generates a `TicketEvent`. We use the `addTicketListener` method to register a `Student` and a `Scalper` with the `Promoter`. Both `Student` and `Scalper` implement the `TicketListener` interface. When scheduling a new concert, the `Promoter` calls the `concertComing` method of all registered ticket listeners. The `concertComing` method handles the `TicketEvent` by implementing the desired action such as purchasing tickets.

TEST YOUR UNDERSTANDING

21. In the `createConcert` method, the `Promoter` calls the `concertComing` method for each customer. How do we know that each customer has a `concertComing` method?
22. Suppose the `Promoter` knows that `customer1` in the `concertComing` method is a `Student`. Can the `Promoter` call `customer1.study`? Why or why not?

6.7 A First Look at Inheritance and the AWT

In the next chapter, we use the Abstract Windowing Toolkit (AWT) to create user interfaces. The AWT contains many classes related by inheritance, which we introduce briefly, leaving a thorough study to Chapter 9.

The Component Class

The `Component` class defines objects that have a graphical representation and can interact with users, such as buttons, checkboxes, and lists. It abstracts behavior common to all components, so that each does not have to duplicate the code. For example, we would like to be able to set the size of a button, or a list, or any other component. Java could have added a `setSize` method to the `Button` class, the `List` class, the `Checkbox` class, and so on, but it uses a better approach by adding the `setSize` method to a `Component` class from which `Button`, `List`, and `Checkbox` inherit.

Using inheritance, the code for the `setSize` method appears once in the `Component` class, rather than being duplicated many times in `Button`, `List`, `Checkbox`, and the other types of components. Many other methods, including `setBackground`, which sets the background color, and `setName`, which allows us to specify a name, are common to all components. Java includes these methods in the `Component` class.

Introducing Inheritance

Inheritance models the IS-A relationship. For example, a dog is a mammal and an automobile is a vehicle. When we characterize a dog, we do not have to state that it has hair, because all mammals have hair. We can assume the properties that a dog has in common with other mammals and just add those that are special to dogs.

Similarly, in Java, rather than developing each class independently, we can let one class inherit from another. For example, the `Button`, `List`, and `Checkbox` classes each inherit from `Component`. Each `Button` is a `Component` and may use any methods of the `Component` class in addition to its own. To set the size of a button, we call the `setSize` method and to set its background color, we call `setBackgound`. Both these methods are defined in the `Component` class. In this example `Component` is the `superclass` and `Button` is the `subclass`.

The Container Class

Java distinguishes between those components that can contain other components and those that cannot. Buttons, checkboxes, and lists cannot contain other components, but windows and panels can. Figure 6.15 shows an applet that contains a button, a checkbox, a list, and a panel. The panel has a blue background to make it easier to see. We placed a button inside the panel to show that it can hold other components.

Figure 6.15 Components in an applet.

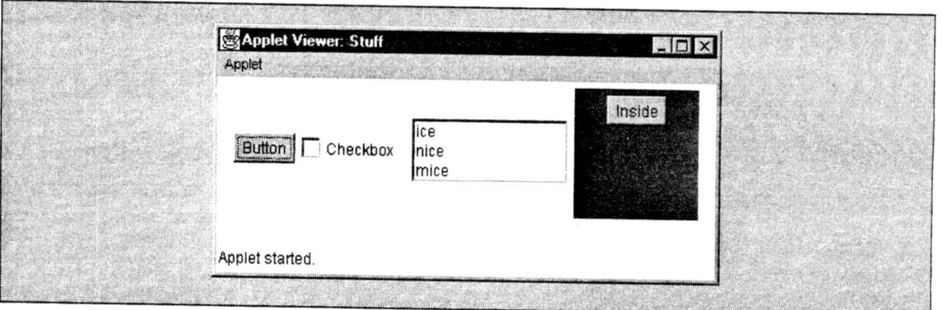

Java abstracts behavior common to those components that can hold other components into a `Container` class. `Container` has an `add` method to add a component to it. Defining the `add` method in the `Container` class is a much better approach than it would be to require each of the `Panel`, `Window`, and other similar classes to implement their own `add` methods.

As Figure 6.15 illustrates, a `Panel` is a `Container` that is itself part of another `Container`. By contrast a `Window` stands alone. We will use `Window` objects later in the text. An `Applet` is a type of `Panel`. It is contained in the browser's window. Because an `Applet` is a `Panel`, we can add components to it. In addition, the `Applet` class provides methods that the browser uses to execute it.

So far we illustrated inheritance using AWT classes. Our user-defined classes often inherit from AWT classes. The line

```
public class HelloCount extends Applet
```

from Example 6.2 declares that the class `HelloCount` inherits from the class `Applet`. `HelloCount` is a subclass of `Applet`. We redefined the `paint` method in the `HelloCount` class in order to define what we wanted to draw on our applet. This redefining of an inherited method is called overriding, and we will discuss it further in Chapter 9.

The purpose of this brief section has been to introduce inheritance as it is used in the AWT to prepare for the building of user interfaces in the next chapter.

THE BIG PICTURE

Inheritance models the IS-A relationship. A `Button` is a `Component`. It inherits the `Component` methods. `List`, `TextField`, and other classes also inherit `Component` methods. The `Component` class abstracts behavior common to all `Components`. A `Container` is a `Component` that can hold other components. A `Panel` and a `Window` are types of containers.

TEST YOUR UNDERSTANDING

23. In Example 6.3, the `Text` applet invokes the `getName` method. Use the Java documentation to find out which superclass of `Text` contains the `getName` method that `Text` inherits.
24. Is `Container` a superclass or a subclass of `Component`?
25. What class does every applet extend? In what package is that class found?
26. Arrange the following classes in order, from left to right, so that each class, except the rightmost, extends the class on its right.

    `Component, Applet, Container, Object, Panel`

27. Which classes from the `java.awt` package did we mention is this section?

SUMMARY

- Web pages may include Java applets, which we download and execute. Our computer communicates with a Web server using HTTP, one of several networking protocols. HTML uses tags to markup text, images, and applets for display in a browser. We can write web pages using just a few tags, but web page design is beyond the scope of this Java text. The `<applet>` tag allows Java enabled browsers to run Java applets. This tag requires us to specify code, width, and height attributes of the applet.
- The AWT (Abstract Windowing Toolkit) has many classes for graphical user interface (GUI) design. The `Applet` class is part of the `java.applet` package, but it inherits from `Panel`, a container that is itself part of another container such as a browser window. The `Panel` class inherits from `Container` which inherits from `Component`, a class representing the various components of a user interface, some of which we will study in Chapter 7.

- Applets do use some of the methods they inherit from the `Component` class, including the `paint` method, which has a `Graphics` object, `g`, as its parameter. The `Graphics` class provides abstract methods for drawing, so we can write a Java applet or application that runs on any platform without knowing the specific windowing library used on that system. We write our Java programs using the abstract methods of the `Graphics` class, and the system gives us a graphics object which implements these methods on that system.
- In the `paint` method we include statements describing what text and shapes we want to draw, but our program does not call the `paint` method. The Java system calls our `paint` method when events cause our applet to need repainting. For example, if the user resizes the applet, making it larger or smaller, or transfers back to the applet from another web page, then the applet needs to be redrawn. The operating system handles the events from the user, passing them to Java which calls our `paint` method to redraw our applet. In this chapter our programs only respond to paint events, but in the next two chapters we will learn to respond to mouse, key, button, checkbox, and other user-interface generated events.
- The `drawString` method of the `Graphics` class has three parameters, the string to draw, and the x and y position at which to draw it. We can construct a font, specifying a font name, style, and point size. Java uses several generic font names to allow implementation of diverse character sets. The style can be plain, bold, italic, or bold and italic.
- The `Applet` class has an `init` method which the browser calls when it first loads the applet. The default `init` method does nothing, but we can override it to initialize our applet, for example, creating a font. It is best to put code that needs to be executed only once in the `init` method rather than in `paint` which will cause that code to be executed every time Java calls the `paint` method.
- The `Color` class provides 13 predefined colors and allows us to construct other colors specifying their red, green, and blue components either as integers from 0 to 255 or as float values from 0.0 to 1.0. We can set the foreground and background colors for the whole applet and set drawing colors using a `Graphics` object, usually in the `paint` method. The `Color` class has methods to brighten and darken a color.
- An interface specifies behavior without implementing it. A user of an interface does not need to know how it is implemented. The user may invoke any methods of the interface. Each object that implements the interface will have an implementation of that interfaces methods.
- The Java event model uses interfaces. Event handlers implement an interface and register with the source of the event. When the event occurs, the source calls an interface method that the event handlers have implemented. In that method the handler implements the response to the event that occurred.

Skill Builder Exercises

1. Match the protocol names on the left with their functions on the right.

a. POP3	i. send email
b. FTP	ii. not a protocol
c. SMTP	iii. web file server
d. HTTP	iv. receive email
e. HTML	v. transfer files

2. Describe what the following applet will display.

```
import java.awt.*;
import java.applet.Applet;

public class Skill extends Applet {
  public void paint(Graphics g) {
    Dimension d = getSize();
    int w = d.width;
    int h = d.height;
    g.drawRect(w/4,h/4,w/2,h/2);
  }
}
```

3. A student was unsuccessful in trying to run the `DrawFill` applet using the following HTML file. Identify and correct the problem.

```
<applet code=DrawFill.class, width=500, height=320>
  </applet>
```

Critical Thinking Exercises

4. (40,40)

Which of the following will draw the arc shown above with center at (40,40) and radius 40?

a. `g.drawArc(0,0,40,40,0,90);`
b. `g.drawArc(40,40,0,0,0,90);`
c. `g.drawArc(0,0,80,80,90,90);`
d. `g.drawArc(0,0,80,80,90,180);`
e. `g.drawArc(40,40,0,0,90,90);`

5. Which of the following colors is most like the color given by

   `new Color(51,85,85)?`

   a. `new Color(.20f,.33f,.33f)`
   b. `Color.pink`
   c. `new Color(.51f,.85f,.85f)`
   d. `new Color(53,87,87)`

6. In an applet shown in a 500 x 300 area, where is the point (50,150) relative to the point (50,50)?

   a. 100 pixels above it
   b. 100 pixels to the right of it
   c. 100 pixels below it
   d. 100 pixels to the left of it

7. Which of the following HTML tags does not require an end tag?

   a. `<h1>`
   b. `<ul>`
   c. `<em>`
   d. `<li>`
   e. `<title>`

Debugging Exercise

8. The following applet attempts to center a string horizontally. Find and fix any errors in it.

```
import java.awt.*;
import java.applet.Applet;
public class Center extends Applet {
  Font f;
  String s;
  int x, w;
  public void init() {
    f = new Font("Monospaced",Font.PLAIN,18);
    setFont(f);
    FontMetrics metrics = getFontMetrics(f);
    s = f.getName();
    w = metrics.stringWidth(s);
  }
  public void paint(Graphics g) {
    Dimension d = getSize();
    int x = w-d.height;
    g.drawString(s,x,50);
  }
}
```

Program Modification Exercises

9. Modify Example 6.3 so that each line of text is centered horizontally.
10. Modify the applet of Example 6.5 to draw the shapes relative to the size of the applet.

Program Design Exercises

11. Write a method, `getPointSize`, which has formal parameters, a string, a font, an applet width, and an applet height, and which returns the largest point size such that drawing the string in that point size just fits within the applet. Write an applet which draws the string using that point size.
12. Write an HTML file that provides links to each of the Java example programs of this chapter. Test it using a browser.
13. Write an applet that centers your name both vertically and horizontally. (The `getHeight` method of the `FontMetrics` class gives the height of a font.)
14. The Tomato Soup Company wants a new logo on their web site. Write an applet containing a design for the logo which includes a nice red tomato with a green stem. Include the name of the company in the applet.
15. Write an applet which draws a happy face of your design. Use colors as desired.
16. Draw the happy face of Exercise 15 so it resizes when the applet changes size.
17. Write an applet that draws a clock (the old-fashioned kind with an hour hand, a minute hand, and numerals for each hour.)
18. Write an applet that draws a maze of your own design.
19. Write an applet which draws a pentagon inscribed in a circle. Connect the diagonals of the pentagon forming a star (which will contain a smaller pentagon in its center). Use the `sine` and `cosine` methods from the `Math` class with arguments `0`, `2pi/5`, `4pi/5`, `6pi/5`, and `8pi/5` to get the coordinates of the points as `(r*cos x, r*sin x)` where `r` is the radius of the circle, and `x` is one of the five angles listed.
20. Write an applet to draw a chessboard which has 64 squares alternating in color.

CHAPTER

7 User Interfaces

OUTLINE

Introduction

Graphical user interface components such as buttons and text fields let the user communicate directly with our program. We introduce graphical user interfaces (or GUI's as they are often called) with our `AtmScreen` of Figure 7.1 which shows the applet of Example 1.5 just after the user has finished a transaction. The applet is still active, waiting for the next user to press the Start button to begin another transaction. The user has finished a transaction; in this chapter we finish presenting the topics needed to understand the `AtmScreen` code.

The `AtmScreen` presents a graphical interface to the user, with

- a text field to enter the user's name and PIN, and the amount of the transaction,
- two checkboxes for selecting the type of account,
- a choice box, which will pop up with three choices for the type of transaction: deposit, withdraw, or balance,
- a canvas to display prompts and transaction results, and

Figure 7.1 The `AtmScreen` ready to start another transaction

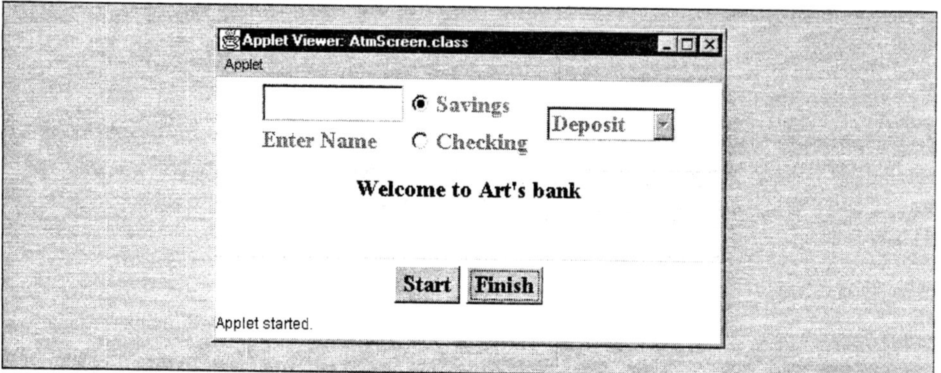

- two buttons for the user to start and finish a transaction.

When the user presses the `Start` button, that event causes the applet to take some actions:

- Enable the text field to permit the entry of the user name
- Enable the `Enter Name` label, making it dark instead of gray
- Direct key presses to the text field
- Disable the `Start` button

The `Start` button is the source of this event, while the applet is the event handler. The text field, checkboxes, and choice box also generate events which the applet handles. The events a user might generate using the `AtmScreen` interface of Figure 7.1 are:

Event source	User behavior	Event generated
text field	Enter text and press Enter key	action event
checkbox	Select a checkbox	item event
choice box	Select an item	item event
button	Press the button	action event

We previously stated that when the user presses the `Start` button, the applet takes four actions, but how does the applet know that the user pressed the button? The Java event model uses interfaces to support callbacks* to communicate from the event source to the event handler. The applet registers with the button, requesting to be notified when the user presses it. When such an event occurs the button calls the applet which can take the desired actions.

TIP

Event-handling for redrawing the screen is simpler than for user interface events. Redrawing the screen involves windows from the environment outside our Java

* See Section 6.6 where we used interfaces to support callbacks by the Promoter to interested listeners for newly scheduled concerts.

window. For example, the user can obscure our Java applet with a window from a different program which will cause our applet to need to be redrawn when the user removes the obstruction. The window manager part of the operating system coordinates this painting of its windows, so all we have to do is to handle the event generated by writing a `paint` method with the code needed to draw our Java component.* In contrast, the `Start` button is part of our Java program and we have full responsibility for communicating the occurrence of a button press from the source button to the event handler wishing to take appropriate action.

An even more basic question about the user interface of Figure 7.1 is how do we position the components? Looking at Figure 7.2 shows us what happens to this interface when the user resizes the applet.

Figure 7.2 The `AtmScreen` resized

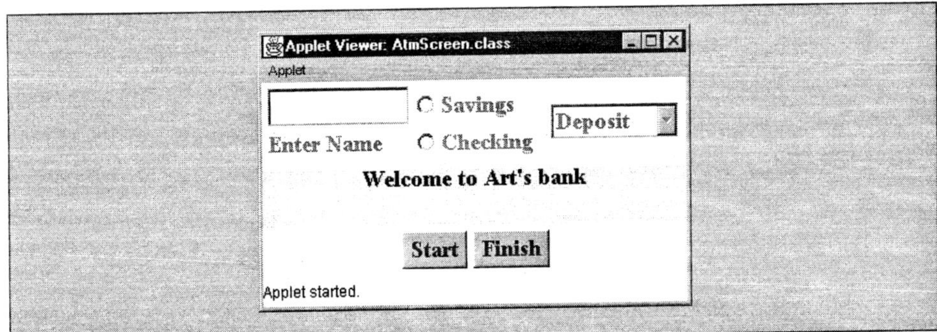

We see the canvas is thinner while the text field, choice box, and buttons remain the same size. The buttons are still centered so the `Start` button is closer to the left edge of the applet than it was in Figure 7.1. The programmer could not easily anticipate in advance all the possible resizings and changes to the layout needed in each case. Java uses layout managers, objects that know how to layout components to figure out the new layout when necessary.

We have a lot to cover in this chapter, first introducing the various user interface components, next showing how the Java 1.1 event model allows button, text field, checkbox, and choice box event sources to communicate with event handlers, and then exploring layout managers. Along the way we introduce panels, labels, number formatting, wrapper classes, and inner classes.

We show the displays from our examples and the code, but running these highly interactive programs will give the best sense of how they work.

OBJECTIVES:

- Know important `Component` subclasses
- Understand the purpose of layout managers.

* We considered this simpler case of event-driven programming in Chapter 6

- Use flow, border, grid, and gridbag layouts.
- Draw on a canvas.
- Understand the Java event model.
- Use buttons, text fields, and labels.
- Use inner classes.
- Use checkboxes and choice boxes.

7.1 Using a Layout

After presenting the user interface components that we will study, we demonstrate the role of a layout manager in displaying components in a container. We illustrate to the use of a canvas component for drawing.

The Component Hierarchy

The `Component` class is the parent class for the graphical objects on the screen that provide the interface to the user. Figure 7.3 shows the subclasses of `Component` that we will treat in this text.

Figure 7.3 Some subclasses of `Component`

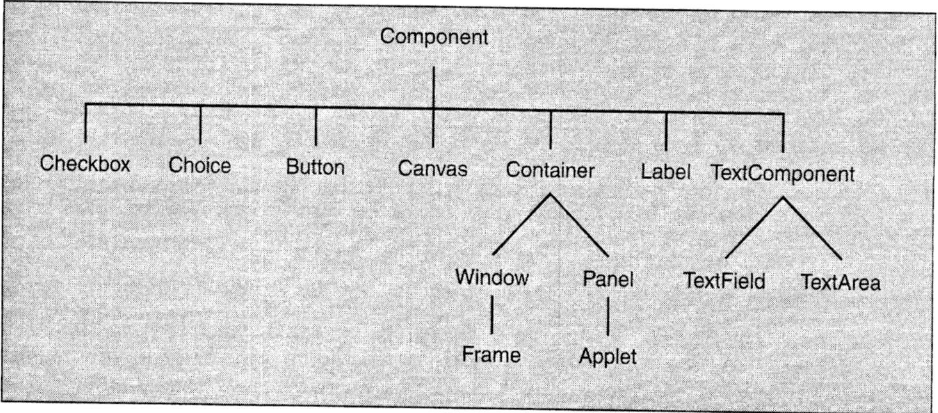

`Checkbox`, `Choice`, `Button`, `Label`, `TextField`, and `TextArea` objects provide the actual graphical components with which the user interacts. The `Container` class is the parent of components that contain other components. The `Window` and `Frame` containers are used by standalone applications.* The **panel** defines containers that are part of another container, which might be a panel, or a frame, or a browser window. Our applets inherit from the `Applet` class. We see from Figure 7.3 that an applet is a container, and we will soon learn how to add components to it.

* We cover standalone graphics application in Section 10.2

Adding Buttons to a Container

Java places components in a container, which can adjust the positions of the components, as needed when a component or the container itself is resized. For example, Figure 7.4 shows a container with five buttons arranged in a row. When the user resizes the container, there may only be room for three buttons in one row, so Java will put the other two buttons in a second row below the first as shown in Figure 7.5.

Figure 7.4 Five buttons in a row

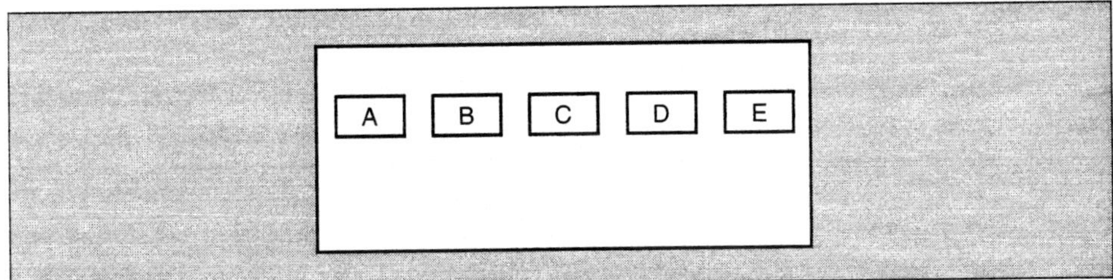

Figure 7.5 The five buttons after resizing Figure 7.4

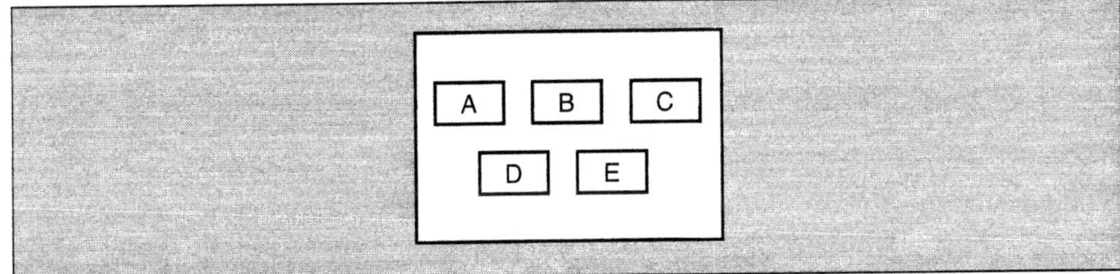

Of course, the button positions can only adjust if they are not specified with fixed numbers. For example if the rightmost button in Figure 7.4 was fixed at position (400,20), there would be no place for it in the 300 × 200 container of Figure 7.5. The position (400,20) would be too far to the right. For this reason, Java does not assign fixed positions to components, but uses a **layout manager** to arrange the components in the container.

Every time a container is resized, the layout manager repositions its components. A layout manager does not always succeed. If a user constricts the container of Figure 7.5 to have size 20 × 200, then none of the buttons will fit in such a thin container. But in most cases the layout manager can reposition the components to fit within the newly dimensioned container.

Flow Layout

Java has five layout managers, each useful in certain situations, and allows us to create custom layout managers if desired. The **flow layout** is the default layout manager for applets. The flow layout manager arranges components in a left-to-right flow until no more fit in a row, and centers any remaining components in the last row.

We can add components to an applet in its `init` method. For example, we can declare a button

```
Button button = new Button("Press me");
```

and add it to an applet using the `add` method of the `Container` class

```
add(button);
```

The flow layout manager will add the button in the next available space according to its flow layout method.

In Example 7.1 we try adding five buttons to an applet. By changing the size of the applet in the HTML file, we can see how the layout manager adjusts the placement of the buttons. Of course the buttons do not have any effect yet; we will learn how to respond to button presses in the next section.

Figure 7.6 Layout of five buttons in different size containers

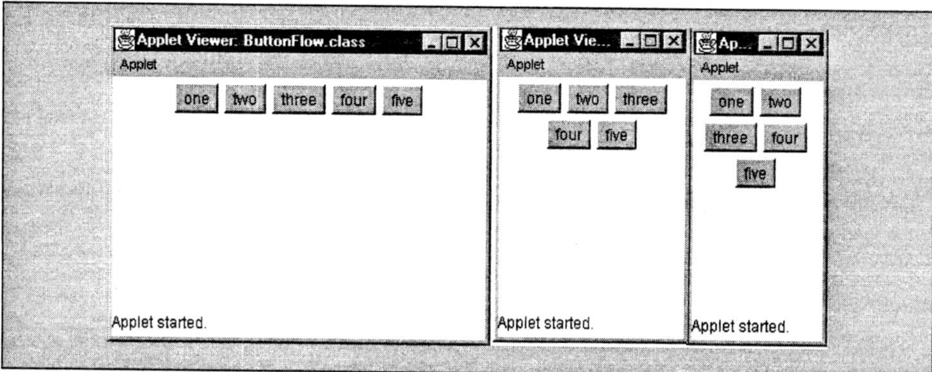

Figure 7.6 shows the layout using the `ButtonFlow` code from Example 7.1 with each of the following three HTML files:

- <applet code = ButtonFlow.class width=300 height=200> </applet>
- <applet code = ButtonFlow.class width=150 height=200> </applet>
- <applet code = ButtonFlow.class width=100 height=200> </applet>

EXAMPLE 7.1 ButtonFlow.java

```
/* Adds five buttons to an applet.
 * Tries different sizes for the applet
 * to see how the flow layout manager
 * adjusts the placement of the buttons.
 */

import java.awt.*;
import java.applet.Applet;

public class ButtonFlow extends Applet {
  public void init() {                                    // Note 1
    add(new Button("one"));                               // Note 2
```

```
    add(new Button("two"));
    add(new Button("three"));
    add(new Button("four"));
    add(new Button("five"));
  }
}
```

Note 1: We do not even override the `paint` method in this example, because we do not draw anything. We just want to show how the flow layout manager arranges the buttons.

Note 2: We add buttons without specifying precisely where to position them. The flow layout manager handles the positioning of these components.

Drawing on a Canvas

So far we have not added any components to our applets, and did all our drawing in the applet itself by overriding its `paint` method. As we add components, such as buttons, to make a user interface, we want to be careful where we draw so we are not trying to draw on top of these components.

Java provides the `Canvas` class, a component on which we can draw text and shapes. Figure 7.7 shows the applet of Example 7.2 in which we use two buttons and a canvas on which to draw so as not to interfere with the buttons.

Figure 7.7 The applet of Example 7.2

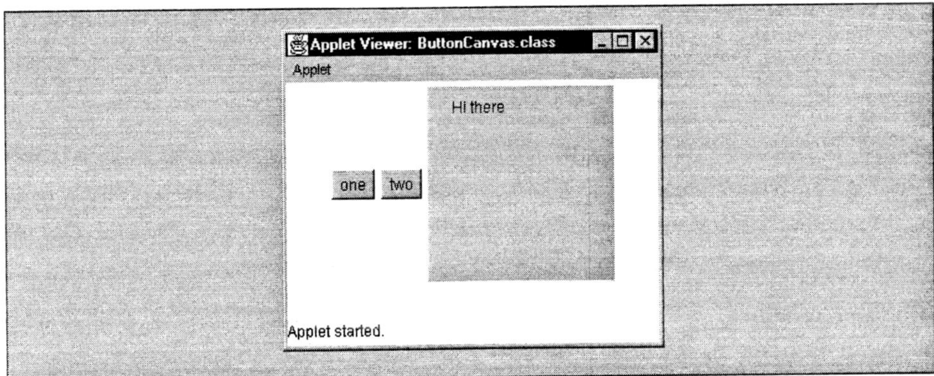

To use a canvas to do our drawing, we must define a subclass in which we override the `paint` method, as in

```
class DrawOn extends Canvas {
  public void paint(Graphics g) {
    g.drawString("Hi there",20,20);
  }
}
```

We create a new canvas and add it to our applet, setting its background color to pink to make it visible:

```
DrawOn canvas = new DrawOn();
add(canvas);
canvas.setBackground(Color.pink);
```

Java creates each component with a preferred size. The flow layout manager uses these preferred sizes for each component when it lays out the applet. Java made 0 x 0 the preferred size for a canvas, so we must set the size of the canvas, as in

```
canvas.setSize(150,150);
```

EXAMPLE 7.2 ButtonCanvas.java

```
/* Adds two buttons and a canvas to an applet.
 * Sets size of canvas, which by default is 0x0.
 * Sets background to pink to see the canvas.
 * Overrides paint to draw on the canvas.
 */

import java.awt.*;
import java.applet.Applet;

public class ButtonCanvas extends Applet {
  public void init() {
    add(new Button("one"));
    add(new Button("two"));
    DrawOn canvas = new DrawOn();
    add(canvas);
    canvas.setBackground(Color.pink);                    // Note 1
    canvas.setSize(150,150);                             // Note 2
  }
}
class DrawOn extends Canvas {
  public void paint(Graphics g) {
    g.drawString("Hi there",20,20);                      // Note 3
  }
}
```

Note 1: White is the default background color for both the canvas and the applet. Leaving the canvas white would blend it in with the applet. Even though our drawing would appear, we would not see the borders of our canvas. Setting the background to pink makes the canvas stand out.

Note 2: If we do not set its size, the canvas will have the default 0×0 size, so we will not see any of our drawing, which will always be too large to fit.

Note 3: We are drawing on the canvas component, so the coordinates are relative to the canvas. We position the string 20 pixels in each direction from the upper-left corner of the canvas, not the applet.

A LITTLE EXTRA—GETTING THE PREFERRED SIZE

The flow layout manager finds the preferred size of a component by calling its `getPreferredSize` method. We can override this method for our subclass of `Canvas` to give our canvas a preferred size of our choosing, rather than the 0×0 default. Overriding this method, as in

```
public Dimension getPreferredSize() {
  return new Dimension(150,150);
}
```

would remove the need for the applet to set the size of the canvas.

THE BIG PICTURE

We add components to make a user interface. Layout managers place components in relation to the dimensions of the window. When the user resizes the window, the layout manager rearranges the components. The flow layout manager adds components one after another until it fills a row. We draw on a canvas to separate our drawing from other user interface components such as buttons.

TEST YOUR UNDERSTANDING

1. Describe the way the flow layout manager positions components in an applet.
2. Which of the classes shown in Figure 7.3 can be instantiated to create components we can add to an applet, and are abstract without instances? (The JDK documentation will show which classes are abstract.)

TRY IT YOURSELF

3. Remove the `setSize` statement from Example 7.2, rerun that example, and explain the result.

7.2 Button and TextField

In Examples 7.1 and 7.2 we added buttons to an applet, but pressing these buttons had no effect. In this section we learn how to respond to button presses. We introduce the `TextField`, a component for entering text, in this section as both text fields and buttons generate action events.

The Java Event Model* and Action Events

Our applets have provided a `paint` method to be called when events such as resizing caused our applet to need to be redrawn. The applet did not have to ask to be redrawn; a windowing operating system keeps its windows properly drawn as part of

* Starting with version 1.1, Java introduced a new event model. We do not use the older 1.0 event model in this text.

its normal functioning. The operating system listens for events that require a window to be redrawn, passing these events to the Java event handler which calls the appropriate method to actually do the redrawing.

To make buttons work, Java follows a similar approach. The user pressing the button generates an event, called an **action event** because it will cause some action. The action event object, of type `ActionEvent`, contains information describing the event. The button keeps a list of any objects (listeners) that want to be notified when the button is pressed. When the user presses a button, the button notifies each object that is listening, passing it the action event that describes the button press. The listeners implement the actions they wish to take as a result of the button press.

This process of registering to listen for button presses is like a student and a scalper registering with the promoter to be notified when a new concert is scheduled.* The student and the scalper implement the `TicketListener` interface to provide the `concertComing` method to handle changes in the interest rate. The promoter calls the `concertComing` method whenever a new concert is scheduled.

The `TicketListener` interface allows the student and the scalper to register with the promoter and be notified about new concerts. For button presses and other action events, Java provides the `ActionListener` interface which has one method

```
public void actionPerformed(ActionEvent event);
```

To be notified about a button press, an object registers as an action listener with the button, and implements the `actionPerformed` method to define what it will do when the button notifies it that an action event representing the button press has occurred.

Making Buttons Work

The button keeps a list of listeners, and when the user presses the button, passes an action event as the argument to the `actionPerfomed` method of each object that registered as an action listener.

To illustrate this process, Example 7.3 will add two buttons to an applet. A *`Print`* button will display a message, and a *`Clear`* button will erase the message. We let the applet listen for button presses, and implement the `actionPerformed` method to display a message when the user presses the *`Print`* button, and to erase the message when the *`Clear`* button is pressed. One scenario might proceed as follows:

- The applet registers with the *`Print`* button as an action listener.
- The user presses the *`Print`* button.
- The *`Print`* button sends an action event as an argument to the applet's `actionPerformed` method.
- The applet's `actionPerformed` method displays a message `Hi there`.

To be an action listener, the applet must declare that it implements the `ActionListener` interface, using the keyword `implements`, as in:

* See Section 6.6 for an introduction to event handling in Java.

```
public class ButtonPress extends Applet
  implements ActionListener
```

To register with the button, the applet calls the button's `addActionListener` method, passing itself as the listener, as in

```
print.addActionListener(this);
```

where `print` refers to the *Print* button. The `this` argument is the applet itself which waits for notification about button presses.

To handle button presses, when it is notified that one occurred, the applet implements the `actionPerformed` method. We use two buttons in this example, so the applet, in the `actionPerformed` method, calls `event.getSource()` which will return the object that generated the event, either the *Print* button or the *Clear* button.

Using Labels

To display a message, we use a `Label` component. We generally use a label object to label a text field or other component, but it serves here to illustrate the action of a button to change the text of a label. Figure 7.8 shows the applet initially, and just after the *Print* button was pressed. The button just pressed has a border around it. Run this applet to see how it responds to button presses.

Figure 7.8 The applet of Example 7.3

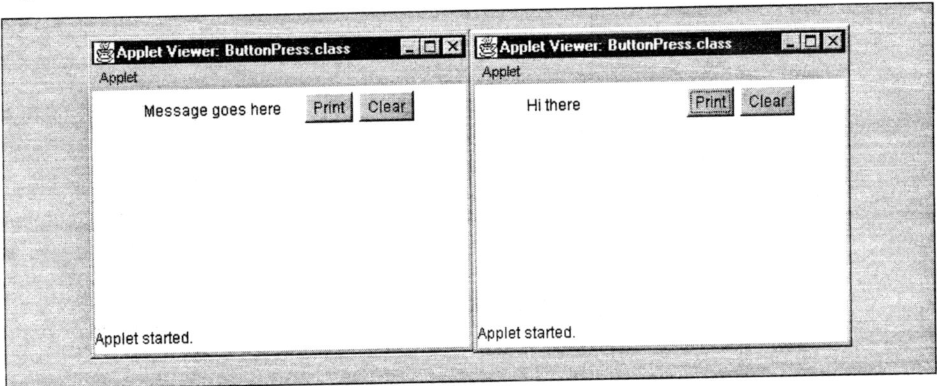

EXAMPLE 7.3 ButtonPress.java

```
/* A Print button prints a message.
 * A Clear button erases the message.
 * We use a Label component to hold
 * the message.
 */

import java.awt.*;                                    // Note 1
import java.awt.event.*;
import java.applet.Applet;
```

```
public class ButtonPress extends Applet
                implements ActionListener {                    // Note 2
  private Button print = new Button("Print");
  private Button clear = new Button("Clear");
  private Label message = new Label("Message goes here");      // Note 3

  public void init() {
    add(message);
    add(print);
    add(clear);
    print.addActionListener(this);                             // Note 4
    clear.addActionListener(this);
  }
  public void actionPerformed(ActionEvent event) {             // Note 5
    Object source = event.getSource();                         // Note 6
    if (source == print)
      message.setText("Hi there");                             // Note 7
    else if (source == clear)
      message.setText("");                                     // Note 8
  }
}
```

Note 1: We must import the `java.awt.event` package to use the event classes such as `ActionEvent`.

Note 2: The applet declares it will implement the `ActionListener` interface, meaning it must implement the `actionPerformed` method to receive action events from components with which it registers.

Note 3: Java allocates space for the label based on the size of the initial message. Using the default constructor, `Label()`, may not allow enough space for the text we use later.

Note 4: The applet registers with the *`Print`* button as an action listener, passing itself (`this`) as an argument to the `addActionListener` method, so the button will know who needs to be notified when the user presses this button.

Note 5: When the user presses either button, the button calls the `actionPerformed` method, passing it an action event that describes the button press.

Note 6: `Object source = event.getSource();`
The applet registered itself with two buttons and will be notified if either is pressed. The `getSource` method returns the object that generated the action event, so the applet can determine if it was the *`Print`* button or the *`Clear`* button.

Note 7: `if (source == print) message.setText("Hi there");`
If the user pressed the *`Print`* button, then the applet sets the text of the label to *Hi there*.

Note 8: `else if (source == clear) message.setText("");`
If the user pressed the *Clear* button, then the applet sets the text of the label to the empty string.

We want to revise Example 7.3 to use a canvas and do the drawing in the `paint` method of that canvas, as we did in Example 7.2. The canvas will do the drawing, so the canvas should register with the button to listen for button presses. When the user presses a button, the canvas will find out which button the user pressed and save the button's label, so when Java calls the `paint` method it will know whether to display a message or to erase the message.

Remember that the `paint` method is also event-driven, activated by users who resize the applet or return to it after browsing another page. Rather than waiting for one of these events to happen, the canvas asks Java to schedule a call to the `paint` method by calling `repaint()`. A scenario for this process is

- The canvas registers with the *Print* button as an action listener.
- The user presses the *Print* button.
- The *Print* button sends an action event as an argument to the canvas' `actionPerformed` method.
- The canvas' `actionPerformed` method saves the label of the button which the user pressed.
- The canvas' `actionPerformed` method calls the `repaint` method, which asks Java to schedule a call the `paint` method to redraw the canvas.
- Java calls the `paint` method of the canvas.
- The canvas' `paint` method uses the button's label to determine that the *Print* button was pressed, and displays the message.

TIP

For simplicity, we left out one important step involved when the applet calls `repaint()`. Java actually calls the `update` method which the applet inherits from `Component`. The `update` method first clears the component and then calls the `paint` method. Because the `update` method clears the component by default, we do not have to write code to clear it.

In Example 7.3, the listener used the `getSource` method to find the object that generated the action event. In Example 7.4 the listener, our canvas, uses the `getActionCommand` method to determine the name of the action that caused the event. By default, Java uses the button's label to name the action, so `getActionCommand` will return the label of the button that was pressed.

Figure 7.9 shows the applet just after the user pressed the *Print* button.

Figure 7.9 The applet of Example 7.4

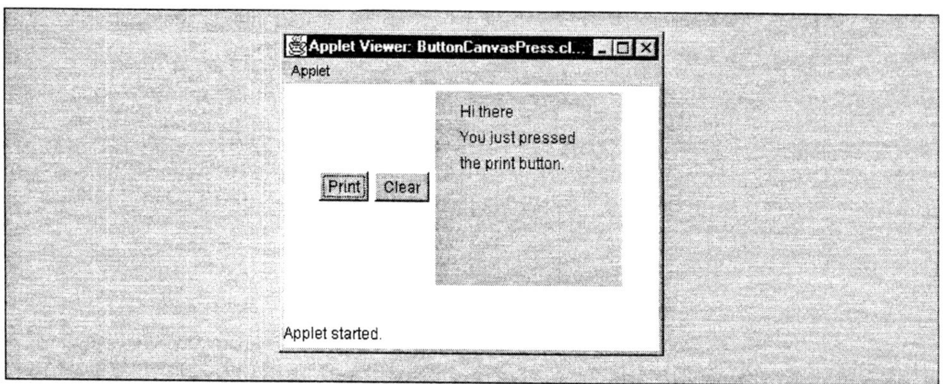

EXAMPLE 7.4 ButtonCanvasPress.java

```
/* Adds two buttons and a canvas to an applet.
 * The canvas registers with each button to
 * listen for button presses. Its actionPerfomed
 * method saves the button label, and asks Java
 * to redraw the canvas (calling update which calls
 * paint). Paint displays a message if Print was
 * pressed but clears the canvas if Clear was pressed.
 */

import java.awt.*;
import java.awt.event.*;
import java.applet.Applet;

public class ButtonCanvasPress extends Applet {
  private Button print = new Button("Print");
  private Button clear = new Button("Clear");
  private Draw canvas = new Draw();

  public void init() {
    add(print);
    add(clear);
    print.addActionListener(canvas);                    // Note 1
    clear.addActionListener(canvas);
    add(canvas);
    canvas.setBackground(Color.pink);
    canvas.setSize(150,150);
  }
}
  class Draw extends Canvas implements ActionListener {  // Note 2
      String command = "";                               // Note 3

  public void actionPerformed(ActionEvent event) {
      command = event.getActionCommand();                // Note 4
```

```
      repaint();                                         // Note 5
  }
  public void paint(Graphics g) {
    if (command.equals("Print")){                        // Note 6
      g.drawString("Hi there",20,20);
      g.drawString("You just pressed",20,40);
      g.drawString("the print button.",20,60);
    }
  }
}
```

Note 1: The canvas registers with the buttons to listen for button presses.

Note 2: The `Draw` class declares that it implements the `ActionListener` interface, which requires it implement the `actionPerformed` method to specify what it will do when notified about a button press.

Note 3: We need to initialize the command string, because the `paint` method needs to refer to it when the applet is initialized which is before it gets the label of the button which the user pressed.

Note 4: The `getActionCommand` method returns the name of the command for the action that generated the event. By default, the name of the action command for a button is its label.

Note 5: Java calls the `paint` method in response to events. When we want to refresh the screen to show the changes we made, we call `repaint()` to ask Java to schedule such a call to `paint` (via `update` which clears the canvas before calling `paint`). The call to `update` will clear the canvas, so the `paint` method does not need to supply any code for the case when the user presses the *Clear* button.

Note 6: `if (command.equals("Print")){`
For strings, we want to check the equality of the characters even if they are in different objects, so we use the `equals` method rather than the equality operator, `==`, which checks the equality of references.

Number Formatting

In Example 7.4 we displayed text, but in Example 7.5 we will need to display decimal numbers or currency values in a graphical user interface.

The `java.text` package has a `NumberFormat` class* which allows us to output decimal and currency values using the default format for the user's locale. Decimal output in the US will use the dot, ., for the decimal point, and currency output in the US will appear as dollars and cents with a dollar sign preceding the amount.

To format decimal numbers, we use the `getInstance` method to get an instance of a `NumberFormat` class, and use the `setMaximumFractionDigits` method to specify the number of places to the right of the decimal point. For example, the code

---

* We used the `NumberFormat` class to format decimal output in Section 3.3.

```
NumberFormat n = NumberFormat.getInstance();
n.setMaximumFractionDigits(3);
System.out.println(n.format(Math.PI));
```

will output the value 3.142.

To format a currency value, we use the `getCurrencyInstance` method, as in:

```
NumberFormat nf = NumberFormat.getCurrencyInstance();
```

to get a `NumberFormat` object `nf` and then use that object to display **double** values in a currency format, using the `format` method, as in:

```
g.drawString(nf.format(cost), 20, 30);
```

which would display `$2.10` if the variable `cost` had the value `2.1`.

Wrapper Classes

In graphics mode, we would like to enter data in a text field. If those entries represent numerical values we need to convert them from the strings that the user inputs. We use wrapper classes to do these conversions. Java provides **wrapper classes:** `Integer`, `Double`, `Byte`, `Float`, `Long`, `Short`, `Boolean`, and `Character`, corresponding to each primitive type.

An object of type `Integer` contains a data field of type **int**. The code

```
Integer wrapsFive = new Integer(5);
```

creates an object, `wrapsFive`, which contains an **int** field with value 5.

We can use the `intValue()` method to retrieve the **int** value of `5` which is wrapped inside the `wrapsFive` object.

To convert a string such as "345" to the integer 345, we can use

```
int converted = new Integer("345").intValue();
```

which creates a new `Integer` and uses the `intValue` method to retrieve the **int** value it contains. We could also use the static `parseInt` method, as in

```
int alsoConverted = Integer.parseInt("345");
```

to do the conversion.

Similarly the class `Double` wraps a **double** value inside an object of type `Double`, and the `doubleValue()` method retrieves it, as in:

```
Double wrapsPI = new Double(Math.PI);
double itsPI = wrapsPI.doubleValue();
```

To convert from a string to a **double** value, we use the `doubleValue` method, as, for example,

```
double converted = new Double("345.67").doubleValue();
```

The Java 2 Platform introduced the `parseDouble` method, which is somewhat simpler.

```
double alsoConverted = Double.parseDouble("345.67");
```

Entering Data in Text Fields

A button enables a user to indicate an action, but does not allow the user to input any data. A text field provides a line for the user to input data. When the user presses the *Enter* key on the keyboard, after entering data in a text field, Java sends an action event to all listeners who registered with that text field. Another way to use a text field is to get its contents when the user presses a button.

We can specify the number of columns for the text field in the constructor, as in

```
TextField text = new TextField(5);
```

which gives us a text field five columns wide. We use the `getText` method to retrieve the text that the user enters in the text field. This text is always of type `String` even if it is meant to represent a number such as 100 or 52.7.

In Example 7.5 we add a text field for the user to input **double** values. If the user presses the *Enter* key or the *Enter Price* button, we add the value in the text field to the sum of the numbers entered so far. After we get the string entered by the user we set the text in the text field to the empty string using the `setText` method, as in:

```
text.setText("");
```

so that the user does not have to erase the old value before entering the next.

If the user presses the *Average* button, we output, in a label, the average of the numbers entered. Figure 7.10 shows the applet of Example 7.5 just after the user pressed the average button.

Figure 7.10 The applet of Example 7.5

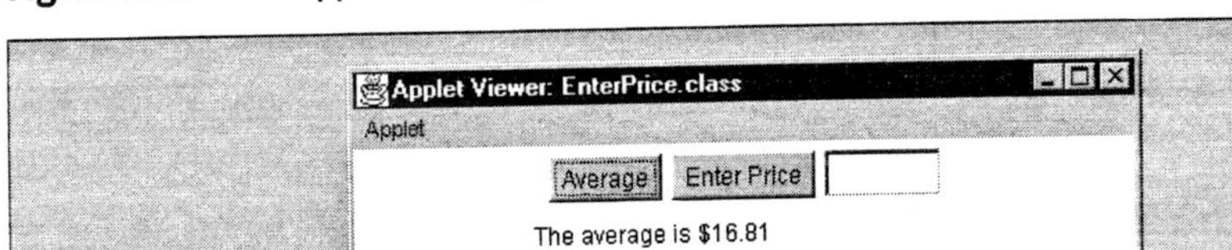

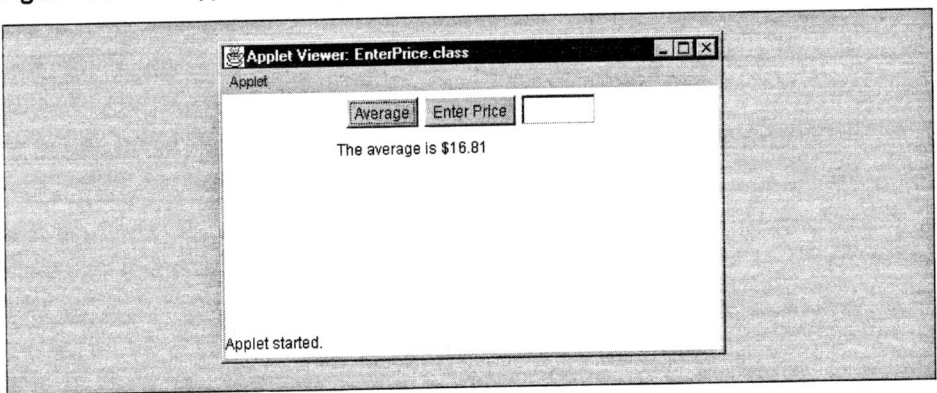

Because the text in a text field is of type `String` we need to convert it to a **double** which we do using a wrapper class, `Double`. The expression

```
new Double(text.getText()).doubleValue()
```

converts the string, `text.getText()`, that the user entered in the text field to a value of type **double**.

The applet registers itself as a listener with the text field, so the applet will be notified when the user hits the *Enter* key. The applet is also listening for button presses, and will be notified when the user presses the *Enter Price* button, another way to signify the entry of a number in the text field. The *Average* button will notify the applet when the user presses it requesting the average, which the applet will display in a label.

EXAMPLE 7.5 EnterPrice.java

```
/* Converts the price the user enters in the text field to a
 * double and adds it to the sum when the user hits the
 * Enter key or presses the Enter button. Displays the
 * average in a label when the user presses the Average button.
 */

import java.awt.*;
import java.awt.event.*;
import java.applet.Applet;
import java.text.NumberFormat;

public class EnterPrice extends Applet
                  implements ActionListener {
  private Button average = new Button("Average");
  private Button enter = new Button("Enter Price");
  private TextField text = new TextField(5);                    // Note 1
  private Label answer = new Label("Enter prices -- the average goes here");
  private double sum = 0.0;
  private int count = 0;
  private NumberFormat nf;

  public void init() {
    add(average);
    add(enter);
    add(text);                                                   // Note 2
    add(answer);
    average.addActionListener(this);
    enter.addActionListener(this);
    text.addActionListener(this);                                // Note 3
    nf = NumberFormat.getCurrencyInstance();
  }
  public void actionPerformed(ActionEvent event) {
    Object source = event.getSource();
    if (source == text || source == enter){                      // Note 4
      sum += new Double(text.getText()).doubleValue();           // Note 5
```

```
      count++;
      text.setText("");                                     // Note 6
    }
    else if (source == average) {
      answer.setText("The average is "+ nf.format(sum/count));    // Note 7
    }
  }
}
```

Note 1: The text field shows five columns, but the user can enter more digits that will not all show.

Note 2: We add the text field component to the applet.

Note 3: The applet registers as a listener to be notified whenever the user hits the *Enter* key.

Note 4: Hitting the *Enter* key and pressing the *Enter Price* button generates action events. We could have used one or the other but wanted to show both approaches are possible.

Note 5: We use the `getText` method to get the string from the text field. The expression `new Double(text.getText()).doubleValue()` converts the string to a **double** which we then add to the sum.

Note 6: `text.setText("");`
Clears the text field of its previous contents.

Note 7: `answer.setText("The average is "+ nf.format(sum/count));`
When the user presses the *Average* button, we use the `format` method to display the average as a string with a currency format in dollars and cents.

THE BIG PICTURE

In the Java event model, listeners, who want to handle an event, register with the event source. When the event occurs, the source notifies the registered listeners. Buttons and text fields both generate action events. An action listener registers with a button, and when the user presses that button it notifies listeners by calling their `actionPerformed` methods, which each action listener must have implemented to make the button work as desired.

The `NumberFormat` class helps us format decimal numbers and currency values, using any locale specific variants. Wrapper classes include primitive types in objects. We use them here to convert strings to numbers.

TEST YOUR UNDERSTANDING

4. Write a scenario showing the interactions in the applet of Example 7.3, for the case when the user presses the *Clear* button after pressing the *Print* button.

5. Write a scenario showing the interactions in the applet of Example 7.4, for the case when the user presses the `Clear` button after pressing the `Print` button.

6. Write a scenario showing the interactions in the applet of Example 7.5, for the case when the user enters two values, hitting the `Enter` key after entering each, and then presses the `Average` button.

7.3 Checkbox and Choice

Checkboxes and **choice boxes** allow us to make selections. They generate an **item event** when the user makes a selection, but we can also use them with a button to signify that the user has finished making selections. We show both approaches in this section. First we introduce inner classes which we illustrate in our checkbox and choice box examples.

Inner Classes

An **inner class** can be defined as a member of another class or within a block of code. It has access to the fields of the outer class, which simplifies code, and keeps its name nested within the outer class, avoiding conflict with the same name used elsewhere. We often use inner classes for event handlers. Inner classes add some complexity to Java; we only introduce them here, omitting some of the details we do not use.

The following code fragments illustrate the differences.

```
class A {
  String s = "potato";
}
class B extends Canvas {
  A other;
  public B(A a) {
    other = a;
  }
  public void paint(Graphics g) {
    g.drawString(other.s, 20, 20);
  }
}
```

```
class C {
  String s = "tomato";
  class D extends Canvas {
      public void paint(Graphics g) {
      g.drawString(s, 20, 20);
    }
  }
}
```

In the fragment on the left we need to pass an object of class A to class B to draw its instance variable `s`. Compiling a program with this structure will produce the class files `A.class` and `B.class`, so the class named `B` may be confused with other classes of the same name.

In the fragment on the right, the inner class `D`, declared as a member of `C`, has access to the instance variable, `s`, of `C`. Compiling a program with this structure will produce the class files `C.class` and `C$D.class`, so the class named `D` only appears prefixed by `C$` and will not be confused with another class named `D`.

We use inner classes in the following examples and in other examples throughout the text.

Checkbox and Choice with a Button

Checkboxes and choice boxes allow us to make selections, rather than initiate actions. Figure 7.11 shows two checkboxes, for selecting bold or italic fonts. The user can select none, either, or both styles.

Figure 7.11 Checkboxes with both selected

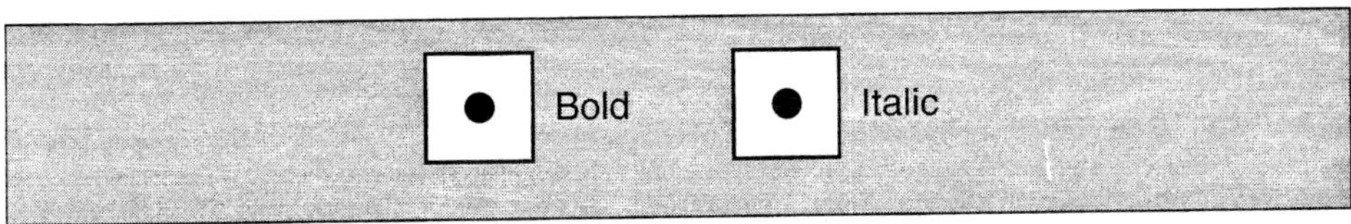

Figure 7.12 shows two checkboxes, for selecting large or small size. We put these in a **checkbox group** so exactly one is selected. Checkboxes in a checkbox group are often called radio buttons, referring to the use of buttons on older radios used to select stations.

Figure 7.12 Checkboxes in a checkbox group

We can construct a checkbox in several ways, by passing a string to label the checkbox

```
Checkbox bold = new Checkbox("Bold");
```

or by passing a string and a **boolean** value indicating whether that item is selected initially

```
Checkbox italics = new Checkbox("Italics", true);
```

or we can pass a string, a **boolean**, and a `CheckboxGroup` object

```
Checkbox large = new Checkbox("Large",false,size);
```

where `size` is a checkbox group and is declared as:

```
CheckboxGroup size = new CheckboxGroup();
```

The declaration for `large` puts it in the checkbox group `size`. Each checkbox has a `getState` method which returns **true** if that checkbox is selected, and **false** otherwise.

A choice box shows one item, but allows the user to pop up other choices. Figure 7.13 shows a choice box containing the items `Red`, `Green`, and `Blue` to allow the user to choose a color. The item `Red` shows, but clicking on the button at the right will cause all three choices to pop up.

Figure 7.13 A choice box

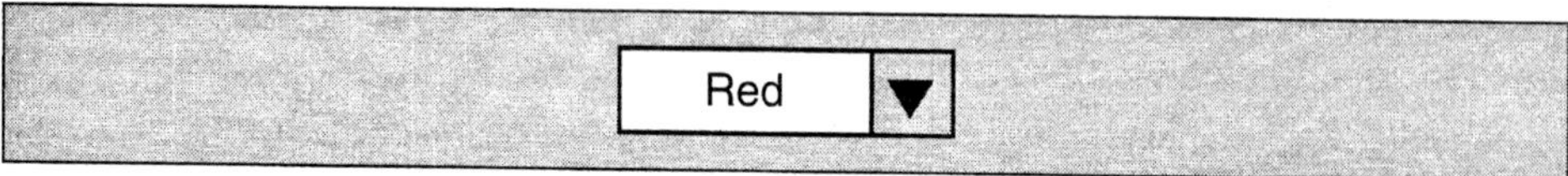

The choice box has a simple constructor

```
Choice color = new Choice();
```

We use the `add` method to add each choice item to the choice box:

```
color.add("Red");
```

We can get the selected item using `getSelectedItem()` or get the index of the selected item using the `getSelectedIndex` method. We can initialize a choice box by selecting an item using its index

```
color.select(0);
```

or using its label

```
color.select("Red");
```

We can use checkboxes and choice boxes in two ways. In the first approach we add a button to the applet, and when the user presses the button signifying the selections have been made, we find those selections, taking whatever action is appropriate. In this approach the selections only take effect when the user presses a button. The only event the program responds to is the user's button press.

In the second approach, the program responds to each selection as it is made. Both the checkbox and the choice box generate an item event when the user makes a selection, and send that item event, which describes the item selected, to all objects that registered as item listeners with that checkbox or choice box.

To illustrate these two ways of using checkboxes and choice boxes we program the same example using both approaches. In each program we include a choice box to select one of three colors, red, green, or blue, and two checkboxes, one to select a square and the other to select a circle. We put the checkboxes in a checkbox group so that we must select exactly one shape, a square or a circle, but not both.

In Example 7.6, illustrating the first approach, we add a *`Draw`* button. When the user presses the *`Draw`* button, we draw the selected shape in the selected color. The canvas, an instance of the `DrawOn` class, listens for button presses.

We declare the `DrawOn` class inside the applet class, as an inner class. Inner classes have access to the fields of the classes in which they are defined, so the `DrawOn` class will have access to the fields of the applet.

Figure 7.14 shows the applet initially, displaying a red circle, and then, after the user presses the draw button, displaying the green square that the user selected.

Figure 7.14 The applet of Example 7.6

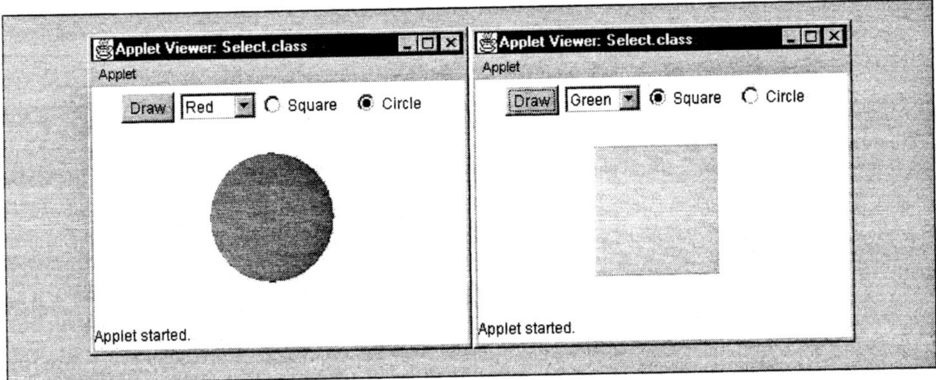

EXAMPLE 7.6 Select.java

```
/* Uses a choice box to choose a color, and
 * two checkboxes to choose a shape. Uses a Draw button
 * to request drawing the selected shape in the
 * selected color. Declares the DrawOn class as an
 * inner class, inside the class Select.
 */

import java.awt.*;
import java.awt.event.*;
import java.applet.Applet;

public class Select extends Applet {
  private Button draw = new Button("Draw");
  private DrawOn canvas = new DrawOn();
  private Choice color = new Choice();
  private CheckboxGroup shapes = new CheckboxGroup();
  private Checkbox square =
          new Checkbox("Square",false,shapes);                    // Note 1
  private Checkbox circle = new Checkbox("Circle",true,shapes);

  public void init() {                                            // Note 2
    add(draw);
    add(color);
    add(square);
    add(circle);
    add(canvas);
    color.add("Red");
    color.add("Green");
    color.add("Blue");
    color.select(0);                                              // Note 3
    canvas.setSize(150,150);
    draw.addActionListener(canvas);                               // Note 4
  }
```

```
  class DrawOn extends Canvas implements ActionListener {          // Note 5
    public void actionPerformed(ActionEvent event) {               // Note 6
      repaint();                                                   // Note 7
    }
    public void paint(Graphics g) {
      Color c;
      if(color.getSelectedItem().equals("Red"))                    // Note 8
        c = Color.red;
      else if(color.getSelectedItem().equals("Green"))
        c = Color.green;
      else
        c = Color.blue;
      g.setColor(c);
      if (circle.getState())                                       // Note 9
        g.fillOval(20,20,100,100);
      else
        g.fillRect(20,20,100,100);
    }
  }
}
```

Note 1: The argument false specifies that checkbox `square` will not be selected initially. The third argument, `shapes`, names the checkbox group to which this checkbox belongs. We must select exactly one checkbox of a group.

Note 2: We add five components to the applet.

Note 3: We select the first color, `Color.red`, as the initial drawing color, used when the applet starts running, before the user has a chance to select a color.

Note 4: The canvas registers with the button to listen for button presses, which indicate the user has selected a color and a shape and wants us to draw it. The choice box and the checkboxes generate item events, but in this program no one registers to listen to them. In Example 7.7, we listen for item events rather than the action events created by button presses.

Note 5: We declare `DrawOn` as an inner class, meaning it is defined inside the class `Select` of our applet. As an inner class it can access the fields of the `Select` class. The `DrawOn` class declares that it implements the `ActionListener` interface, which means it must implement the `actionPerformed` method.

Note 6: `public void actionPerformed(ActionEvent event) {`
This is the method that the source of an action event, such as a button, calls to notify a listener when an action event occurs.

Note 7: `repaint();`
When the user presses the *Draw* button, the button will call the canvas' `actionPerformed` method. The canvas wants to be redrawn to implement the user's selections, so it calls its `repaint` method which requests Java to schedule a call to its `paint` method to redraw the canvas.

Note 8: `if(color.getSelectedItem().equals("Red"))`
The `getSelectedItem` method gives the user's choice of a color. We cannot use the choice items directly because they are strings such as `Green`, not colors such as `Color.green`. Because `DrawOn` is an inner class it can access the `color` field of the `Select` class containing it.

Note 9: `if (circle.getState()) g.fillOval(20,20,100,100);`
The `getState` method returns **true** if the user selected that checkbox. If the user selected circle, then we draw a circle, otherwise the user must have selected square, so we draw a square. Because `DrawOn` is an inner class it can access the circle data field of the `Select` class.

Checkbox and Choice Item Events

To illustrate the second approach, we respond to the item events generated by the checkboxes and the choice box. When the user selects a color we immediately redraw the current shape in that color. When the user selects a shape, we immediately draw that shape in the current color. The canvas, an instance of the `DrawOn` class, listens for checkbox or choice box selections.

In the second approach the `DrawOn` class listens for item events rather than action events. A class that wants to listen to item events must implement the `ItemListener` interface, which requires the class to implement the `itemStateChanged` method.

In our example, the `DrawOn` class will implement the `ItemListener` interface. The canvas will register as an item listener to listen for item events generated by the choice box when the user chooses a color, or generated by a checkbox when the user selects a square or a circle. When the user selects the color green, for example, the choice box calls the `itemStateChanged` method of all registered listeners, passing an `ItemEvent` object describing the selection to each listener. The `itemStateChanged` method calls the `repaint` method to ask Java to redraw the selected shape in green. A scenario for a choice box selection is:

- The canvas registers with the choice box as an item listener.
- The user chooses the color green.
- The choice box sends an item event describing this selection to the canvas' `itemStateChanged` method.
- The canvas' `itemStateChanged` method asks Java to schedule a call to the `paint` method to redraw the canvas.
- Java calls the canvas' `paint` method (via `update`).
- The `paint` method draws the currently selected shape in the selected color.

Choice boxes and checkboxes generate item events when the user selects an item or when the user deselects an item. We only want to draw the shape in the color that the user selects, and do not care about the shapes or colors that were deselected. An item event has a method, `getStateChange`, which returns either `ItemEvent.SELECTED` or `ItemEvent.DESELECTED`. We can use this method to allow us to handle only item events that return `ItemEvent.SELECTED`, ignoring the deselection events.

TIP

In our example, when the user selects an item, the previous item is automatically deselected, but in cases where the checkboxes are not in a checkbox group, it is possible to select an item without a corresponding deselection of the previous item. It is also possible to deselect an item without selecting another one.

An item event has a `getItem` method that returns an `Object` which represents the selected item. If a choice box selection generated the item event, then the `getItem` method returns the string selected. If a checkbox generated the item event, then the `getItem` method returns the label of that checkbox. For example if the event `evt` represents the selection of green in a choice box, then

```
(String)evt.getItem()
```

returns the string `Green`. Java declares the return type of `getItem` to be `Object`, so we need to explicitly cast the return value to a `String`. The `getSource` method returns the object that generated the event.

Example 7.7 uses much of the same code as Example 7.6, but because the canvas is an item listener rather than an action listener, the selections take effect immediately, not when the user presses a button as in Example 7.7. Figure 7.15 shows the `SelectItem` applet after the user selects the square shape.

Figure 7.15 The applet of Example 7.7

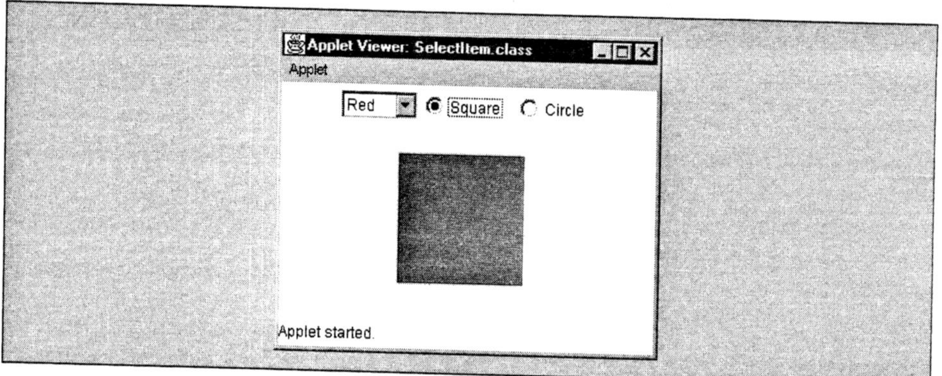

EXAMPLE 7.7 SelectItem.java

```
/* Revises Example 7.6 to listen for item
 * events rather than action events.
 */
```

```
import java.awt.*;
import java.awt.event.*;
import java.applet.Applet;

public class SelectItem extends Applet {
  private DrawOn canvas = new DrawOn();
  private Choice color = new Choice();
  private CheckboxGroup shapes = new CheckboxGroup();
  private Checkbox square = new Checkbox("Square",false,shapes);
  private Checkbox circle = new Checkbox("Circle",true,shapes);

 public void init() {
   add(color);
   add(square);
   add(circle);
   add(canvas);
   color.add("Red");
   color.add("Green");
   color.add("Blue");
   color.select(0);
   canvas.setSize(150,150);                              // Note 1
   color.addItemListener(canvas);
   square.addItemListener(canvas);
   circle.addItemListener(canvas);
 }

 class DrawOn extends Canvas implements ItemListener {   // Note 2
   public void itemStateChanged(ItemEvent event) {        // Note 3
     if (event.getStateChange() == ItemEvent.SELECTED)    // Note 4
       repaint();
   }
     public void paint(Graphics g) {
       Color c;
       if(color.getSelectedItem().equals("Red"))
         c = Color.red;
       else if(color.getSelectedItem().equals("Green"))
         c = Color.green;
       else
         c = Color.blue;
       g.setColor(c);
       if (circle.getState())
         g.fillOval(20,20,100,100);
       else
         g.fillRect(20,20,100,100);
     }
   }
 }
```

Note 1: We register the canvas to listen for item events generated by the choice box and the two checkboxes.

Note 2: We make the `DrawOn` class an inner class, as in Example 7.6. The `DrawOn` class declares that it implements the `ItemListener` interface which requires that it implement the `itemStateChanged` method to handle item events.

Note 3: An item event source, such as a choice box, calls the `itemStateChanged` method of all registered listeners, passing them an item event object containing information about that event.

Note 4: The `getStateChange` method tells us whether the item event was a selection or a deselection. We ignore deselection events, just repainting according to the user's selection.

THE BIG PICTURE

When using checkboxes and choice boxes we can respond to the item events generated when the user makes a selection, which will cause the selection to take effect immediately, or we can have the selection take effect when the user presses a button.

Inner classes, nested within another class, often simplify code, allowing access the outer class fields.

TEST YOUR UNDERSTANDING

7. Write a scenario showing the interactions in the applet of Example 7.6, for the case when the user selects a green square and presses the *`Draw`* button.
8. Write a scenario showing the interactions in the applet of Example 7.7, for the case when the user selects a square.

TRY IT YOURSELF

9. Modify Example 7.6 to add four additional colors. Rerun the applet to try out the new colors.

7.4 Border and Grid Layouts

Thus far in Chapter 7 we have used only the flow layout, which is the default for applets. Java provides other layouts to give some other options when designing a user interface. In this section we look at the border layout and the grid layout. We also show how to use panels to group components nested inside another container, an approach that often enables us to achieve a better design.

The Border Layout

The **border layout** divides the container into five regions, `North`, `South`, `East`, `West`, and `Center`, as shown in Figure 7.16.

Figure 7.16 The border layout

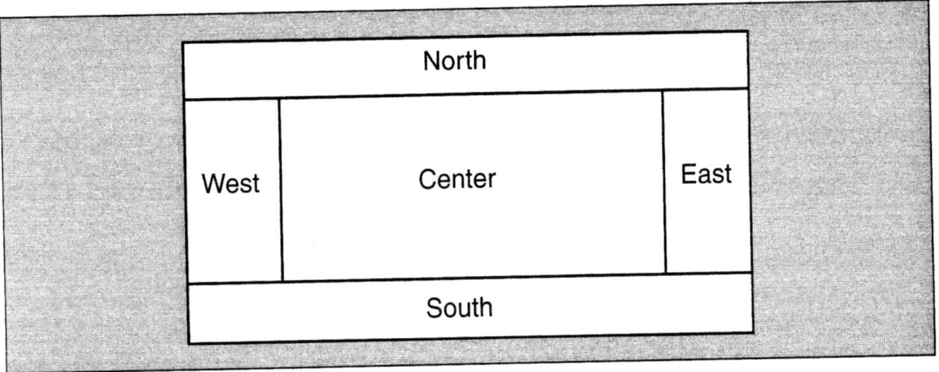

To use a border layout for an applet, we need to explicitly call the `setLayout` method to override the default

```
setLayout(new BorderLayout());
```

To add a component, we specify the region along with the component, as in

```
add(draw,"North");
```

where `draw` is a component such as a button.

Each component has a preferred size, and the flow layout respects that size, but the border layout does not. For example, the preferred size of a button just covers the text of its label, as, for example, in Figure 7.14 which shows a *Draw* button. The flow layout, used in Example 7.6, displays the *Draw* button in its preferred size. If we add this button to the `North` or `South` regions of a border layout, the border layout manager will stretch it horizontally until it fills the entire region. Adding the *Draw* button to the `East` or `West` regions, will cause the border layout to stretch it vertically, and adding it to the `Center` will cause it to be stretched in both directions.

To see these effects we revise Example 7.6 to use a border layout. Figure 7.17 shows the unsatisfactory result.

Figure 7.17 The applet of Example 7.8

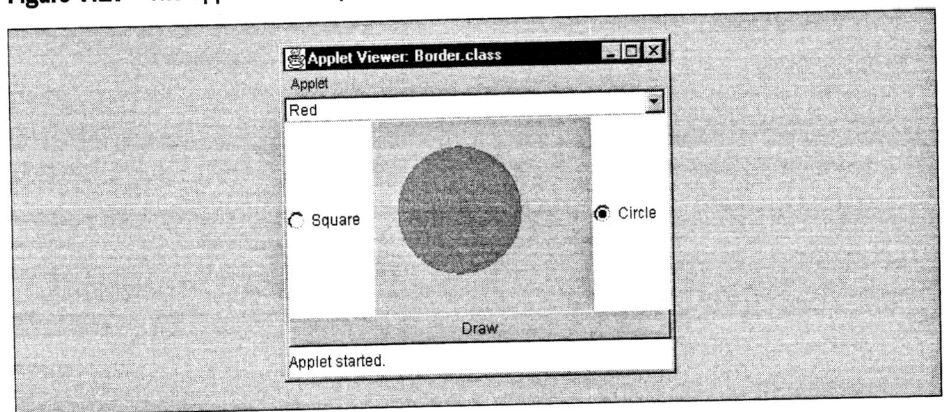

The border layout stretched the choice box in the `North` and the button in the `South` horizontally, and stretched the canvas in both directions to fill the `Center` region. While this is not what we want for the button, it improves the canvas. Remember that the default preferred size of the canvas is 0 by 0, so using the flow layout we had to set the size of the canvas. Because the border layout stretches the component in the center we do not need to set the size of the canvas.

Example 7.8 shows the code for the `init` method (which is the only part that differs) of this border layout revision of Example 7.6. We will show in Example 7.9, how to use a panel to make a better border layout for this example.

EXAMPLE 7.8 Border.java

```
/* Revises Example 7.6 to use a
 * border layout.
 */

public class Border extends Applet{
  // the rest is the same as Example 7.6
  public void init() {
    setLayout(new BorderLayout());                          // Note 1
    add(draw,"South");                                      // Note 2
    add(color,"North");                                     // Note 3
    add(square,"West");
    add(circle,"East");
    add(canvas,"Center");                                   // Note 4
    color.add("Red");
    color.add("Green");
    color.add("Blue");
    color.select(0);
    canvas.setBackground(Color.pink);                       // Note 5
    draw.addActionListener(canvas);
  }
}
```

Note 1: To use any layout for an applet (or any panel) except the flow layout, we need to set it explicitly, in this case passing a new `BorderLayout` object to the `setLayout` method.

Note 2: Directly adding a button to a border layout stretches it so it no longer looks like a normal button.

Note 3: Directly adding a choice box to a border layout stretches it, making it too wide, in this example.

Note 4: Adding a canvas to a border layout stretches it to fill the region, which means we no longer have to set its size.

Note 5: Setting the canvas color to pink allows us to see its extent.

Panels

To use the border layout more effectively, we can put the button, the choice box, and the two checkboxes into a panel, and then add that panel to the `North` region. The panel, which uses a flow layout by default, shows these components in their preferred sizes, if possible. We put the canvas in the `Center` region which will take up the rest of the applet's space because we do not put anything in the `East`, `West`, or `South` regions.

To use a panel, we first create it,

```
Panel p = new Panel();
```

then add components to it, as in

```
p.add(draw);
```

which adds the *Draw* button. Finally we use the statement

```
add(p,"North");
```

to add the panel `p` to the `North` region. Figure 7.18 shows the improved layout given by the applet of Example 7.9.

Figure 7.18 The applet of Example 7.9

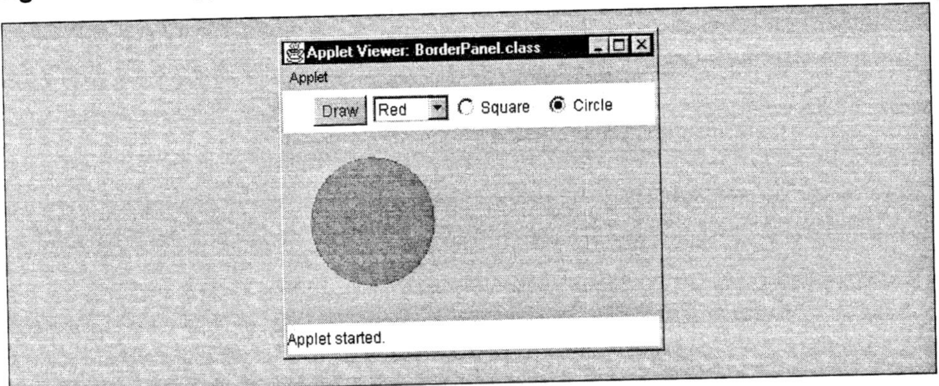

EXAMPLE 7.9 BorderPanel.java

```
/* Revises Example 7.8 to put the button,
 * the choice box, and the two checkboxes into
 * a panel. Adds the panel to the North region,
 * and the canvas in the Center.
 */

public class BorderPanel extends Applet {
   // the rest is the same as Example 7.8

   public void init() {
     setLayout(new BorderLayout());                    // Note 1
     Panel bar = new Panel();                          // Note 2
     bar.add(draw);
```

```
        bar.add(color);
        bar.add(square);
        bar.add(circle);
        add(bar,"North");                                  // Note 3
        add(canvas,"Center");                              // Note 4
      ...
    }
}
```

Note 1: We create a new panel which is a container that is itself contained in a container, in this case the applet.

Note 2: The panel uses the flow layout; adding the button, the choice box, and the two checkboxes to the panel keeps these components at their preferred sizes.

Note 3: We add the panel to the `North` region.

Note 4: We add the canvas to the `Center` region, which takes up the remaining space, as none of the other regions contain any components.

The Grid Layout

The grid layout divides the container into a rectangular grid. Figure 7.19 shows a 2 x 3 grid layout.

Figure 7.19 A 2×3 grid layout

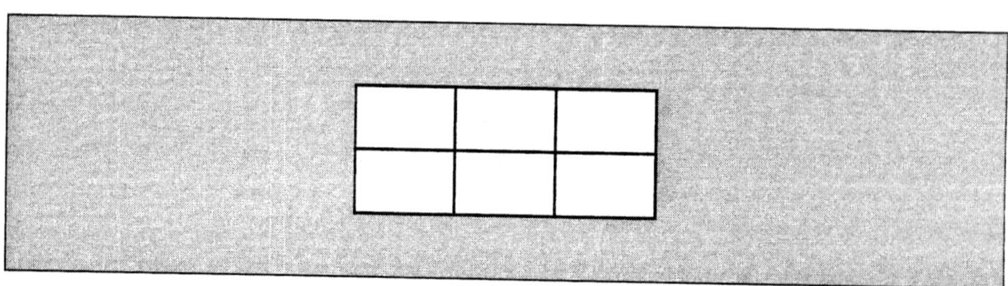

The grid layout stretches a component to fill the grid cell to which it has been added. This might be useful for a calculator applet in which each grid cell contains a button. To keep a component at its preferred size, we could add it to a panel, and then add the panel to a grid cell.

We can specify a 2×3 grid layout using the statement

```
setLayout(new GridLayout(2,3));
```

and can add a button using the statement

```
add(draw);
```

which adds the *`Draw`* button. Example 7.10 creates a 2 x 3 grid layout and adds a button to each of the six cells. We do not make the buttons do anything other than illustrate the appearance of the grid layout.

Figure 7.20 shows the applet of Example 7.10 in which the each button fills its grid cell.

Figure 7.20 The applet of Example 7.10

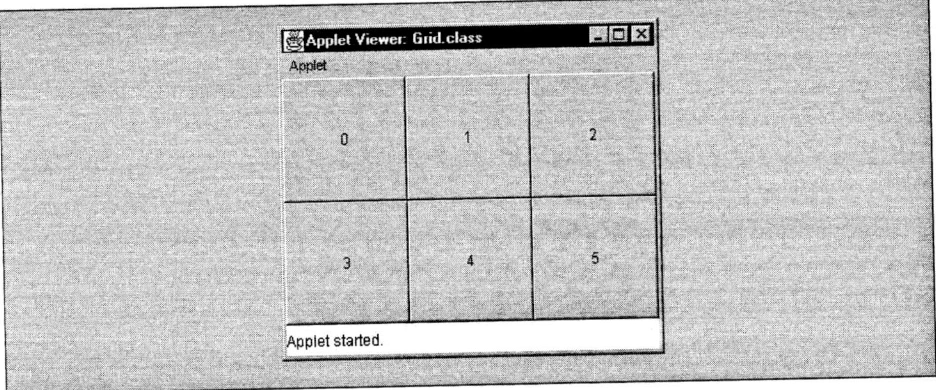

EXAMPLE 7.10 Grid.java

```
/* Adds six buttons to illustrate the use
 * of the grid layout. The buttons do not
 * do anything
 */

import java.awt.*;
import java.applet.Applet;

public class Grid extends Applet {
  public void init() {
    setLayout(new GridLayout(2,3));
    for (int i=0; i<6; i++)
      add(new Button(String.valueOf(i)));                 // Note 1
  }
}
```

Note 1: We convert the index `i` to a string to use as the label for the button. Note that the grid layout manager adds the buttons across the row first, and when the first row is full, goes to the second row.

THE BIG PICTURE

The border layout provides five regions to add components. It does not respect the preferred sizes of its components, but we can nest components in a panel, which uses the flow layout, and then add the panel to one of the border layout regions. Using a panel allows us to arrange components within one of the regions of the grid layout, which also does not respect preferred sizes. The grid layout divides the window into an $m \times n$ grid of rows and columns.

TEST YOUR UNDERSTANDING

10. For each region of a border layout, specify the dimensions of a component, `width` or `height`, or both, that the border layout ignores when laying out the component in that region.
11. Compare the flow layout with the grid layout with respect to how they use the preferred sizes of their components.

TRY IT YOURSELF

12. Modify Example 7.10 to display the buttons at their preferred size, rather than expanded to fill the grid cell, while still using the grid layout?

7.5 List and TextArea

We introduce the useful `List` and `TextArea` components. Our example uses a `StringBuffer` to build a string.

List

The `List` displays items, using scrollbars if necessary. We can create a `List` which allows either a single selection or multiple selections. For example

```
new List(5);
```

will construct a `List` that shows five items and which allows the user to select one item at a time. The constructor

```
new List(4,true);
```

creates a `List` that shows four items and allow the user to make multiple selections. The `add` method will add a `String` item to a `List`.

Clicking once on an item in a `List` to select it generates an `ItemEvent`. Clicking twice on an item or hitting the *Enter* key when an item is selected generates an `ActionEvent`. We may respond to these events in a `List` that allows only single selections. We prefer to use a `Button` to work with a `List` that allows multiple selections.

TextArea

A `TextArea` displays text in a rectangular region. Java provides several `TextArea` constructors. For example,

```
new TextArea(8,40);
```

constructs a `TextArea` with 8 rows of 40 columns each. It includes both vertical and horizontal scrollbars. The constructor

```
new TextArea("Until we meet again.",8,40);
```

creates a `TextArea` that contains initial text.

The `setText` method will update the text in a `TextArea`. By default the user can edit the text, but we can change the default by using

```
setEditable(false);
```

The `append` method will add text at the end of the current text.

Figure 7.21 shows the applet of Example 7.11, which contains a `List` of animals, a `List` of things, a `TextArea` and a *`Choose Animals`* Button. We may select multiple animals but can only select one thing.

Figure 7.21 The applet of Example 7.11

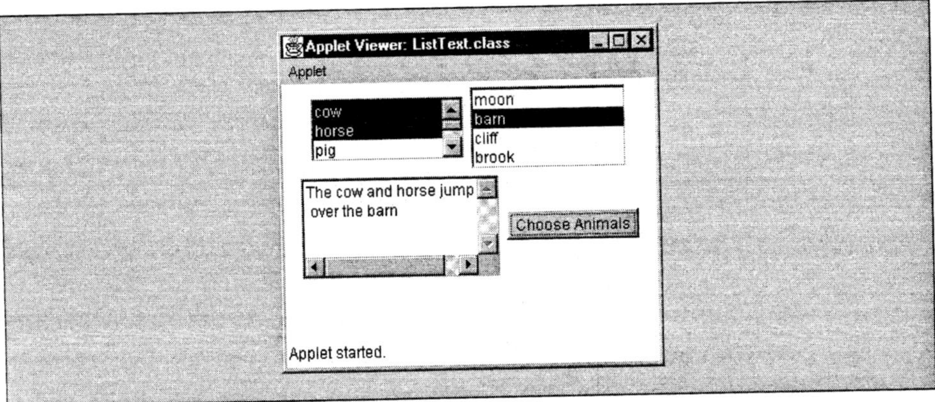

When the user presses the *`Choose Animals`* button, the message in the text area states that the chosen animals jumped over the selected thing. When the user single clicks a thing, a message echoes the user's selection. When the user double clicks on a thing, the message states that the chosen animals jumped over that thing.

StringBuffer

A Java `String` is immutable. It cannot be changed. The concatenation operator causes new temporary strings to be created. Creating a simple message,

```
String message = "The cow jumped over the moon";
```

presents no problem, but suppose the animal names and the thing they jump over are stored in variables. For example, suppose we have two variables, `animal1` and `animal2`, that hold the names of animals, and a variable, `thing`, that holds the name of a thing. To construct a similar `String` we could use the statements

```
String message = "The ";
message += animal1;
message += " and ";
message += animal2;
message += " jumped over the ";
message += thing;
```

Each concatenation would create a temporary `String` and change the message variable to refer to it. Figure 7.22 shows how the first step would work.

Figure 7.22 Concatenating strings

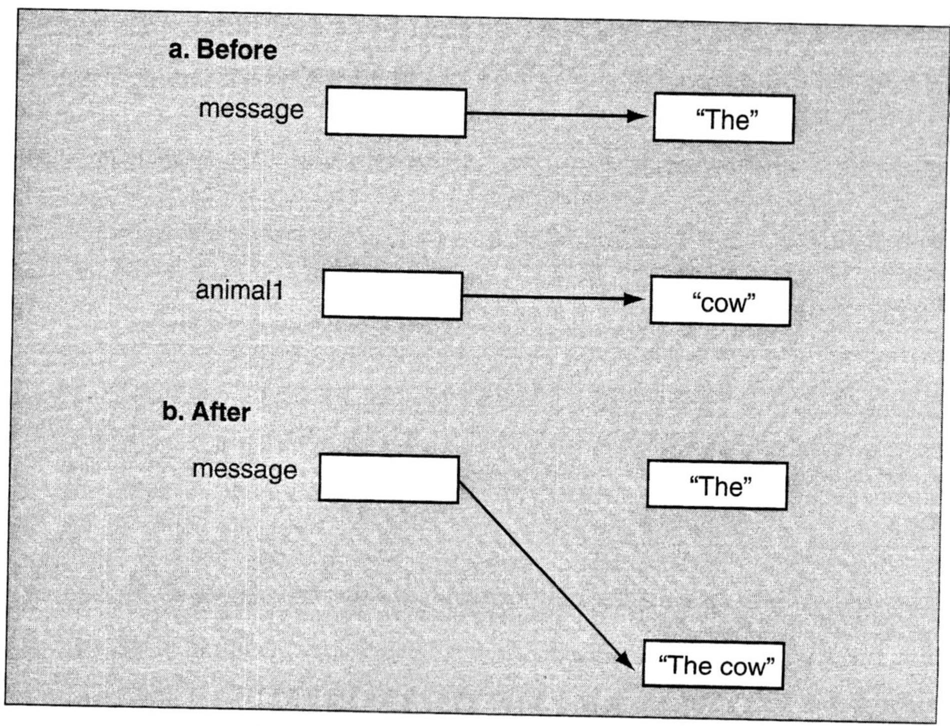

By contrast, we can change a `StringBuffer`. The `append` method adds a string to the existing `StringBuffer` and does not need to create a new object. Using a `StringBuffer` we could create the message with the code

```
StringBuffer mess = "The ";
mess.append(animal1);
mess.append(" and ");
mess.append(animal2);
mess.append(" jumped over the ");
mess.append(thing);
String message = mess.toString();
```

We use a `StringBuffer` in Example 7.11, where we need to make choices concerning the punctuation of the message.

EXAMPLE 7.11 ListText.java

```
/* Illustrates the List and TextArea components.
 */

import java.awt.*;
import java.awt.event.*;
import java.applet.Applet;
```

```
public class ListText extends Applet
               implements ActionListener, ItemListener {
  private List animals = new List(3,true);                    // Note 1
  private List things = new List(4);
  private TextArea text = new TextArea(4,20);                 // Note 2
  private Button choose = new Button("Choose Animals");

  public void init() {
    animals.add("cow");
    animals.add("horse");
    animals.add("pig");
    animals.add("elephant");
    animals.add("flea");
    add(animals);
    things.add("moon");
    things.add("barn");
    things.add("cliff");
    things.add("brook");
    things.select(0);
    add(things);
    add(text);
    add(choose);
    choose.addActionListener(this);
    things.addActionListener(this);                           // Note 3
    things.addItemListener(this);
  }
  public String buildString(String[] animals, String thing) {
    StringBuffer message = new StringBuffer(50);
    message.append("The ");
    int length = animals.length;
    switch(length) {
      case 0: message.append("??");                           // Note 4
        break;
      case 1: message.append(animals[0]);                     // Note 5
        break;
      case 2: message.append(animals[0]);
        message.append(" and ");                              // Note 6
        message.append(animals[1]);
        break;
      default:
        for(int i = 0; i < length-1; i++){
          message.append(animals[i]);
          message.append(", ");                               // Note 7
        }
          message.append("and ");
          message.append(animals[length-1]);
    }
    message.append(" jumped\n over the ");
    message.append(thing);
    return message.toString();
  }
```

```
    public void actionPerformed(ActionEvent event) {
      Object source = event.getSource();
      if (source==choose || source==things)                     // Note 8
        text.setText( buildString
          (animals.getSelectedItems(), things.getSelectedItem()));    // Note 9
    }
    public void itemStateChanged(ItemEvent e) {
      Object source = e.getSource();
      if (source==things)
            text.setText("You selected " + things.getSelectedItem());  // Note 10
    }
}
```

Note 1: The user will be able to select more than one animal from this list.

Note 2: This `TextArea` of 4 rows and 20 columns will be empty initially.

Note 3: We listen for action and item events from the `List` of things. The user may only select one item.

Note 4: We append question marks if the user has not selected any animals.

Note 5: When the user selects one animal we do not need any commas.

Note 6: `message.append(" and ");`
When the user selects two animals we use an "and" but no commas.

Note 7: `message.append(", ");`
When the user chooses more than two animals, we need a comma after each except the last.

Note 8: `if (source==choose || source==things)`
When the user presses the button or double clicks on an item from the `thing List`, we display a message in the `TextArea`.

Note 9: `(animals.getSelectedItems(), things.getSelectedItem()));`
The `getSelectedItems` method returns the multiple selections of animals. The `getSelectedItem` method returns the single selection of a thing.

Note 10: `text.setText("You selected " + things.getSelectedItem());`
When the user single clicks on a thing, we echo the selection in the `TextArea`.

THE BIG PICTURE

The `List` and `TextArea` add to our repertoire of user interface components. We cannot change a `String`, but can change a `StringBuffer`. Using a `StringBuffer` avoids needless `String` creation in certain situations.

TEST YOUR UNDERSTANDING

13. What is the main difference between a `String` and a `StringBuffer`?
14. What does the second argument in the `List` constructor signify?
15. What is the main difference between a `TextArea` and a `TextField`?

7.6 Gridbag Layout

The gridbag layout provides a grid of variable-sized cells, giving more flexibility than the flow, border, or grid layouts, but is more complex and difficult to learn. The best way to understand its features is through experimentation with simple examples. Figure 7.23 shows a form designed using a gridbag layout whose code appears as Example 7.27.

Figure 7.23 A form with a gridbag layout

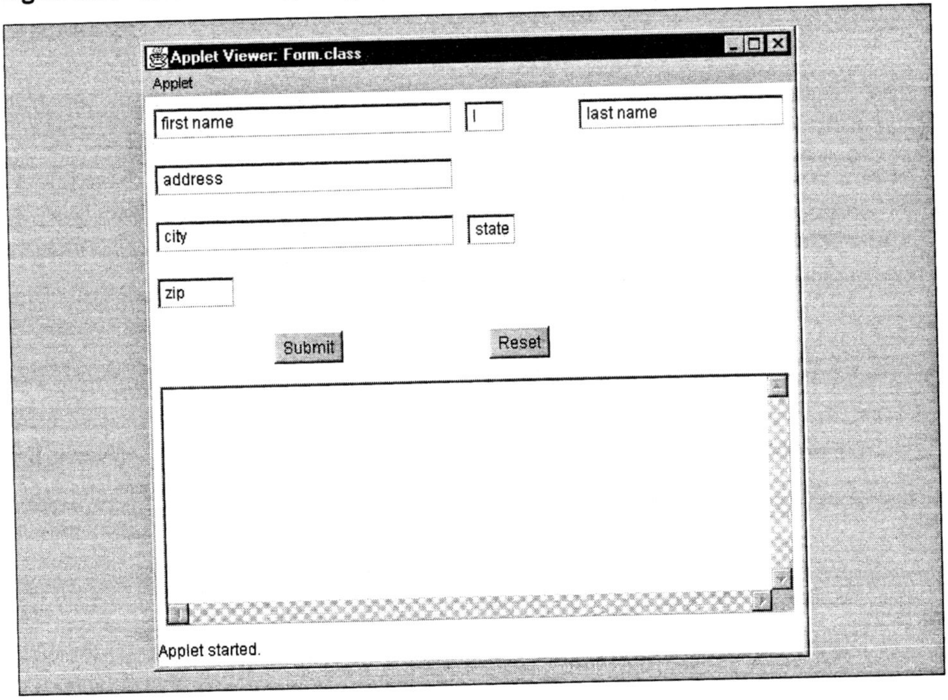

Default GridBag Constraints

A `GridBagConstraints` object holds the values which customize the location and appearance of each component. Setting the values of these constraint variables determines how the layout manager will display a component. The `GridBagConstraints` variables, with their default values and uses, are:

Variable	Default value	Use
`gridx, gridy`	RELATIVE	Upper-left corner of display area
`gridwidth`	1	Number of cells used for width
`gridheight`	1	Number of cells used for height
`fill`	NONE	Resizing behavior
`ipadx, ipady`	0	Internal padding
`insets`	new Insets(0,0,0,0)	External padding
`anchor`	CENTER	Placement
`weightx`	0.0	Distribute row space
`weighty`	0.0	Distribute column space

As we experiment, we will come to understand the meaning of these default values.

The applet of Example 7.12, shown in Figure 7.24, adds two buttons to an applet using all default settings for the `GridBagConstraints`. We do not activate the buttons; our purpose is to discuss the layout.

Figure 7.24 Using the `GridBagConstraints` defaults in Example 7.12

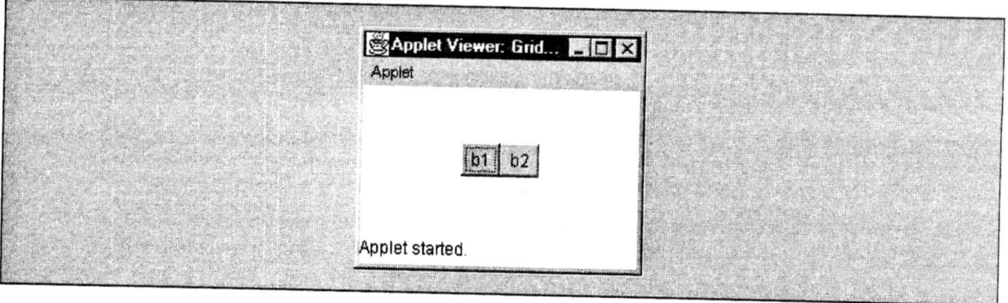

`gridx` and `gridy` each start out at 0, indicating column 0 and row 0. The default of `GridBagConstraints.RELATIVE` positions the component just to the right of the previous component (or below if placing it in a column). Thus `b2` is just to the right of `b1`. Because `gridwidth` and `gridheight` are 1, they each use one row and one column. Because `weightx` and `weighty` are each 0.0, the extra space in the applet is outside the layout of the two components, which are clustered in the center. The `fill` constraint has no effect as there is no extra space to fill.

EXAMPLE 7.12 GridBag1.java

```
/* Uses default settings for GridBagConstraints.
 */

import java.awt.*;
import java.applet.*;
public class GridBag1 extends Applet {
    private Button b1 = new Button("b1");
    private Button b2 = new Button("b2");
    public void init() {
    GridBagLayout gbl = new GridBagLayout();
    setLayout(gbl);
    GridBagConstraints c = new GridBagConstraints();        // Note 1
    gbl.setConstraints(b1, c);                              // Note 2
    add(b1);
    gbl.setConstraints(b2, c);
    add(b2);
  }
}
```

Note 1: We only need one `GridBagConstraints` object, `c`, which we can reuse for each component. In this example, we do not change any values of its variables, using the default settings.

Note 2: Before adding a component to the applet, we call the `setConstraints` method to associate the current constraint settings with the component to be added.

Setting Weight and Fill

The weight and the fill determine how a component uses the available space. `weightx` and `weighty` distribute the space and `fill` specifies how a component uses it.

In Example 7.13, we set `weightx` to .7 for button `b1` and `weightx` to .3 for `b2`. We see, in Figure 7.25, that `b1` is centered in the left 70 percent of the applet while `b2` is centered in the right 30 percent. Had we left the default `fill` of `NONE`, the buttons would have remained their normal size as in Figure 7.24. By giving `b1` `VERTICAL` fill, it expands to fill its space vertically. Button `b2`, with `HORIZONTAL` fill, expands horizontally. Had we chosen `BOTH` for `fill` the button would have expanded to fill its entire area. Had we left `weightx` and `weighty` at the default of 0.0, no additional area would have been allocated to each component and the setting `fill` would have no effect. Had we left `weighty` at 0.0, specifying `VERTICAL` fill would have no effect.

EXAMPLE 7.13 GridBag2.java

```
/* Sets weightx, weighty, and fill.
 */
```

Figure 7.25 Using `weightx`, `weighty`, and `fill` in Example 7.13

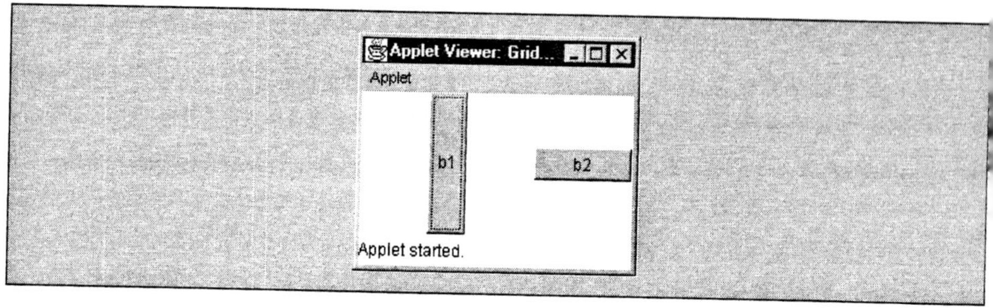


```
import java.awt.*;
import java.applet.*;
public class GridBag2 extends Applet {
  private Button b1 = new Button("b1");
  private Button b2 = new Button("b2");
  public void init() {
    GridBagLayout gbl = new GridBagLayout();
    setLayout(gbl);
    GridBagConstraints c = new GridBagConstraints();
    c.weightx = .7;                                        // Note 1
    c.fill = GridBagConstraints.VERTICAL;
    gbl.setConstraints(b1, c);
    add(b1);
    c.weightx = .3;
    c.weighty = 1.0;                                       // Note 2
    c.fill = GridBagConstraints.HORIZONTAL;
    gbl.setConstraints(b2, c);
    add(b2);
  }
}
```

Note 1: The `weightx` setting applies to the whole column of components. In this case we have only `b1` in the first column, but with more components the layout manager takes `weightx` for the column to be the maximum of `weightx` for each component.

Note 2: The `weighty` setting applies to the whole row of components. The layout manager takes `weighty` for the row to be the maximum of `weighty` for each component. Thus `b1` expands vertically even though its `weighty` setting is 0.0, because the `weighty` setting for the entire row is 1.0.

Anchoring and Internal Padding

Example 7.14 illustrates anchoring and internal padding. We use the anchor field to position a component that is smaller than its display area. Its possible values are `CENTER`, `NORTH`, `NORTHEAST`, `EAST`, `SOUTHEAST`, `SOUTH`, `SOUTHWEST`, `WEST`, and `NORTHWEST`.

Internal padding adds to the dimensions of the component. Setting ipadx to 25 causes the buttons in Figure 7.26 to have 25 pixels of internal padding on both the left and the right. Similarly, setting ipady to 25 causes the buttons to have 25 pixels of top and bottom padding. We anchor b1 to the WEST of its area and b2 to the NORTH. In this example, we return to the default NONE for fill.

Figure 7.26 Anchoring and internal padding in Example 7.14

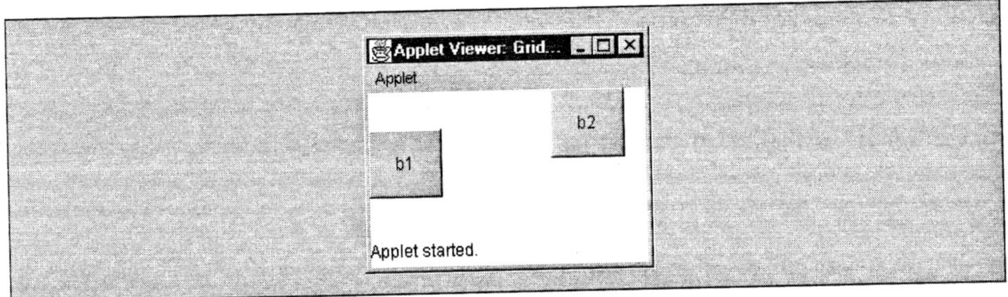

EXAMPLE 7.14 GridBag3.java

```
/*Illustrates anchoring and internal padding
 */

import java.awt.*;
import java.applet.*;
public class GridBag3 extends Applet {
  private Button b1 = new Button("b1");
  private Button b2 = new Button("b2");
  public void init() {
    GridBagLayout gbl = new GridBagLayout();
    setLayout(gbl);
    GridBagConstraints c = new GridBagConstraints();
    c.weightx = .7;
    c.anchor = GridBagConstraints.WEST;
    c.ipadx = 25;
    c.ipady = 25;
    gbl.setConstraints(b1, c);
    add(b1);
    c.weightx = .3;
    c.weighty = 1.0;
    c.anchor = GridBagConstraints.NORTH;
    gbl.setConstraints(b2, c);
    add(b2);
  }
}
```

Insets

The insets determine the external padding around a component. In Example 1.25, we set `fill` to `BOTH` so the buttons expand to fill their display areas. However, we set the external padding for `b2` to provide a border of 10 pixels around it. The type of the `insets` variable is `Insets`, a class used to specify the four values for the border in each direction., top, left, bottom, and right.

Figure 7.27 `Insets` **and** `fill.BOTH` **in Example 7.15**

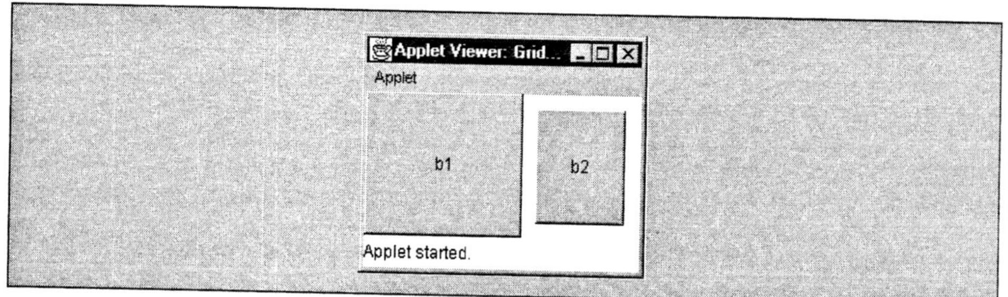

EXAMPLE 7.15 GridBag4.java

```
/* Illustrates Insets and fill BOTH
 */

import java.awt.*;
import java.applet.*;
public class GridBag4 extends Applet {
  private Button b1 = new Button("b1");
  private Button b2 = new Button("b2");
  public void init() {
    GridBagLayout gbl = new GridBagLayout();
    setLayout(gbl);
    GridBagConstraints c = new GridBagConstraints();
    c.weightx = .7;
    c.fill = GridBagConstraints.BOTH;
    gbl.setConstraints(b1, c);
    add(b1);
    c.weightx = .3;
    c.weighty = 1.0;
    c.insets = new Insets(10,10,10,10);
    gbl.setConstraints(b2, c);
    add(b2);
  }
}
```

Positioning Constraints

By setting gridx and gridy we can locate a component at a specific row and column, while setting gridwidth and gridheight defines the number of cells for a component. The constant GridBagConstraints.REMAINDER specifies the remaining space in the row or column, while GridBagConstraints.RELATIVE indicates a position next to the preceding component.

In Example 7.16, shown in Figure 7.28, we use six buttons to illustrate the use of positioning constraints.

Figure 7.28 The applet of Example 7.16

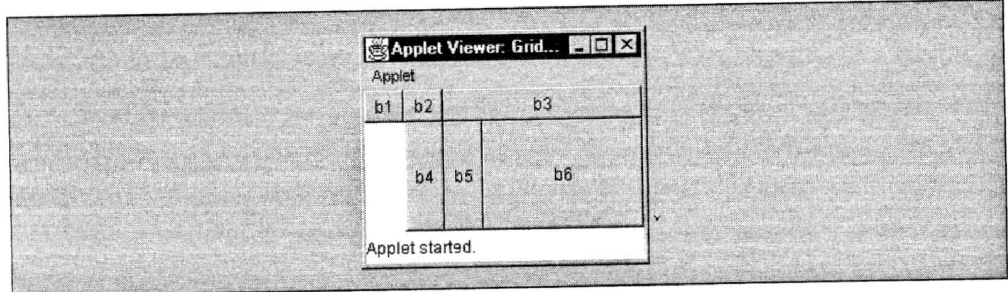

EXAMPLE 7.16 GridBag5.java

```
/* Illustrates positioning constraints
 */

import java.awt.*;
import java.applet.*;
public class GridBag5 extends Applet {
  private void makebutton(String name,                        // Note 1
      GridBagLayout gridbag, GridBagConstraints c) {
    Button button = new Button(name);
    gridbag.setConstraints(button, c);
    add(button);
  }
  public void init() {
    GridBagLayout gbl = new GridBagLayout();
    setLayout(gbl);
    GridBagConstraints c = new GridBagConstraints();
    c.fill=GridBagConstraints.BOTH;
    makebutton("b1",gbl,c);
    makebutton("b2",gbl,c);
    c.gridwidth = GridBagConstraints.REMAINDER;               // Note 2
    makebutton("b3",gbl,c);
    c.gridwidth = 1;                                          // Note 3
    c.gridx = 1;                                              // Note 4
```

```
        makebutton("b4",gbl,c);
        c.gridx = GridBagConstraints.RELATIVE;          // Note 5
        makebutton("b5",gbl,c);
        c.weightx = 1.0;                                 // Note 6
        c.weighty = 1.0;
        makebutton("b6",gbl,c);
    }
}
```

Note 1: Because we are using six buttons, we use a method to create each button, set its constraints, and add it to the applet.

Note 2: Using `REMAINDER` for `gridwidth` specifies that it is the last component in its row.

Note 3: We set `gridwidth` back to its default value of 1. Had we not done that, buttons `b5` and `b6` would appear under `b4`, each filling an entire row.

Note 4: Setting `gridx` to 1 positions `b4` in the second column, because a value of 0 represents the first column.

Note 5: Returning to the default `RELATIVE` for `gridx` keeps `b5` and `b6` in the same row as `b4`; otherwise they would each be positioned with `gridx` equal to 1, underneath `b4`.

Note 6: `c.weightx = 1.0;`
The other buttons in the second row, `b4` and `b5`, have `weightx` equal to 0.0, so `b6`, with `weightx` equal to 1.0, gets all the extra space. Because `b3` occupies the remainder of the first row, it gets stretched along with `b6`.

The Form Applet

Finally, Example 7.17 contains the code for the `Form` applet shown in Figure 7.23. Typically, the user would be filling out the form to buy a product or register for access to a restricted site. The information would go to a web site server which would return a response. In this example, since we do not really submit the data anywhere, we just display the information the user enters in a text area.

A text area provides a rectangular area in which to display information. We can specify initial text and the number of rows and columns of the display using the constructor

```
public TextArea(String initialText, int rows, int cols);
```

or use the default constructor

```
public TextArea();
```

to get a blank text area with a default size. The text area comes with scroll bars to see the text that is not visible.

We want this form to look good when the applet is resized, so we keep the `fill HORIZONTAL` for all text fields except those with a small fixed size, which along with the buttons have `fill NONE`. The text area for messages expands in both directions.

EXAMPLE 7.17 Form.java

```
/* Illustrates creating a form with a GridBagLayout.
 */

import java.awt.*;
import java.applet.*;
public class Form extends Applet implements ActionListener {
  private TextField first = new TextField("first name",12);
  private TextField middle = new TextField("I",1);
  private TextField last = new TextField("last name",15);
  private TextField address = new TextField("address",25);
  private TextField city = new TextField("city",20);
  private TextField state = new TextField("state",2);
  private TextField zip = new TextField("zip",5);
  private Button submit = new Button("Submit");
  private Button reset = new Button("Reset");
  private TextArea message = new TextArea();

  public void init() {
    GridBagLayout gbl = new GridBagLayout();
    setLayout(gbl);
    GridBagConstraints c = new GridBagConstraints();
    c.anchor = GridBagConstraints.WEST;
    c.weightx=1.0;
    c.weighty=1.0;
    c.fill=GridBagConstraints.HORIZONTAL;
    c.insets = new Insets(5,5,5,5);
    gbl.setConstraints(first,c);            add(first);
    c.fill=GridBagConstraints.NONE;
    gbl.setConstraints(middle,c);           add(middle);
    c.fill=GridBagConstraints.HORIZONTAL;
    gbl.setConstraints(last,c);             add(last);
    c.gridy=1;
    gbl.setConstraints(address,c);          add(address);
    c.gridy=2;
    gbl.setConstraints(city,c);             add(city);
    c.fill=GridBagConstraints.NONE;
    gbl.setConstraints(state,c);            add(state);
    c.gridy=3;
    gbl.setConstraints(zip,c);              add(zip);
    c.gridy=4;
    c.anchor = GridBagConstraints.CENTER;
    gbl.setConstraints(submit,c);           add(submit);
    gbl.setConstraints(reset,c);            add(reset);
    c.gridy=5;
    c.gridwidth=3;
    c.fill=GridBagConstraints.BOTH;
    gbl.setConstraints(message,c);          add(message);
    submit.addActionListener(this);
    reset.addActionListener(this);
  }
```

```
public void actionPerformed(ActionEvent event) {
  Object source = event.getSource();
  if (source == submit){
    String initial = middle.getText();
      if (initial != null)
        initial += ". ";
      message.setText(first.getText() + ' ' + initial + last.getText());
      message.append('\n' + address.getText());
      message.append('\n' + city.getText() + ", " + state.getText());
      message.append(' ' + zip.getText());
    }
    else if (source == reset) {
      message.setText("");
      first.setText("");
      middle.setText("");
      last.setText("");
      address.setText("");
      city.setText("");
      state.setText("");
      zip.setText("");
    }
  }
}
```

THE BIG PICTURE

The gridbag layout gives us the most flexibility in arranging components. The various gridbag constraints allow us to specify the starting position of a component, the number of rows and columns it takes, internal padding, anchoring, external padding, the direction(s) in which it will fill up its allocated cell, and its weighting relative to other components which determines how much screen space it gets relative to them. The gridbag layout manager uses the largest weight in a row or column to determine how to allocate space to that row or column. The fill for a component determines how it will appear within its allocated space. Experimenting, as we did in Examples 1.22–1.27, helps to understand the effect of the different constraints.

TEST YOUR UNDERSTANDING

TRY IT YOURSELF 16. Modify Example 7.13 so `b1` has a `weighty` of `1.0` and `b2` has a `weighty` of 0.0. Explain the result.

TRY IT YOURSELF 17. Modify Example 7.16 to omit the line `c.gridwidth = 1.` Explain the result.

TRY IT YOURSELF 18. Modify Example 7.16 to omit the line `c.gridx = GridBagConstraints.RELATIVE;` Explain the result.

TRY IT YOURSELF 19. Modify Example 7.16to omit the line `c.gridwidth = GridBagConstraints.REMAINDER;` Explain the result.

SUMMARY

- In this chapter we created graphical user interfaces. The `Component` class of the AWT is the superclass of the various components we can add to containers such as applets to make a user interface. The `Container` class describes components that are themselves containers. We use the `Panel` and its `Applet` subclass inside another window such as a browser, while we can use the window and its `Frame` subclass in standalone applications.*
- The Java event model allows objects that want to be notified about an event to register with the event source as a listener. The listener promises to implement an interface consisting of a method (or methods) to handle the event(s). The event source will call this method for each registered listener when the event occurs.
- Both buttons and text fields generate action events. An object that wants to be notified of these events implements the `ActionListener` interface, requiring that it implement the `actionPerformed` method stating how it wants to handle an action event. The object registers with the button or text field requesting to be notified when the user presses the button or when the user hits the `Enter` key after entering a string in the text field. When one of these events occurs, the event source, button or text field, calls the object's `actionPerformed` method, passing it an action event describing the button press or text entry event.
- We use the `Canvas` class to get an object to draw on, so we do not overwrite other components by drawing directly in the container. We use the `Label` class to label text fields, and can use it for a simple text display. Neither the canvas nor the label generates any events.
- Both checkboxes and choice boxes generate item events when the user makes a selection. An object that wants to be notified of these events implements the `ItemListener` interface, requiring that it implement the `itemStateChanged` method stating how it wants to handle an item event. The object registers with the checkbox or choice box requesting to be notified when the user makes a choice or checks a box. When one of these events occurs, the event source, the checkbox or the choice box, calls the object's `itemStateChanged` method, passing it an `ItemEvent` describing that selection.
- Java uses layout managers to position components in a container. The layout manager adjusts the positions of the components when necessary as a consequence of resizing a component or the whole container. The default for an applet or a panel is the flow layout, which adds components from left to right until no more will fit in a row, centering any remaining components in the last row. The flow layout uses the preferred sizes of its components in laying them out.
- The border layout uses five regions, `North`, `South`, `East`, `West`, and `Center`. We add a component to a border layout specifying the region in which to place it. It stretches components horizontally in the `North` and `South`, vertically in the `East` and `West`,

* We cover standalone graphics applications in Section 10.2.

and in both directions in the `Center`. The grid layout uses a grid of m rows and n columns, adding components from left to right across each row before moving to the next lower row. The grid layout expands each component to fill its grid cell. We can use panels to nest components, to give us more flexibility in designing user interfaces.

- A `List` displays item. It generates an `ItemEvent` when a user selects an item, and an `ActionEvent` when a user double clicks on an item. A `List` may or may not allow multiple selections. A `TextArea` presents a rectangular text display. A `String` cannot change, but we can append characters to a `StringBuffer`.
- The gridbag layout flexibly positions components by appropriately setting the `gridx`, `gridy`, `gridwidth`, `gridheight`, `fill`, `ipadx`, `ipady`, `insets`, `anchor`, `weightx`, and `weighty` constraint variables.

Skill Builder Exercises

1. Fill in the blanks below to show the correct listener type for the indicated object.

   a. button.add ________ Listener where `button` is a button.

   b. choice.add ________ Listener where `choice` is a choice box.

   c. check.add ________ Listener where `check` is a checkbox.

   d. text.add ________ Listener where `text` is a text field.

2. Match a layout type on the left with a description on the right of how it uses the preferred size of its components.

a. Grid layout	i. always respects the preferred sizes
b. Flow layout	ii. never respects the preferred sizes
c. Border layout	iii. partially respects preferred sizes

3. Fill in the blanks in the following:

   To be notified about a button press, an object must be instantiated from a class that ________ the __________ interface which means that it implements the ____________ method. To be notified about a checkbox selection, an object must be instantiated from a class that __________ the __________ interface which means that it implements the ______________ method.

Critical Thinking Exercises

4. Suppose we add a button, a text field, a choice box, and a checkbox to an applet using the default flow layout. Choose the best description below of how these components will be positioned in the applet.

   a. Centered in a row across the top of the applet

b. The number of rows used depends upon the size of the applet

c. In the top row if the applet is wide enough, and in two rows otherwise

d. At the positions where we add them

e. None of the above

5. For an `ItemEvent e`, the method call `e.getItem()` returns

   a. the object that was the source of the event.

   b. the object that is listening for the event.

   c. the object that represents the item selected.

   d. none of the above.

6. For checkboxes in a `CheckboxGroup`

   a. at most one may be selected.

   b. exactly one must be selected.

   c. more than one may be selected.

   d. more than one may be selected only if we set a flag in each checkbox to **true** when we construct it.

7. The border layout uses five regions in which to arrange components. To use more than five components we can

   a. add more than one component directly into each region.

   b. add more than one component directly to the Center region, but not to the others.

   c. add some components into a component that is a type of container and then add the container to one of the regions.

   d. none of the above.

Debugging Exercise

8. The following applet attempts to draw the figure selected in a checkbox, with the name of the shape displayed inside it, when the user presses the Draw button. Find and fix any errors.

```
import java.awt.*;
import java.awt.event.*;
import java.applet.Applet;
public class NameIt extends Applet {
  Button draw = new Button("Draw");
  DrawOn canvas = new DrawOn();
  CheckboxGroup shapes = new CheckboxGroup();
  Checkbox square = new Checkbox("Square",false,shapes);
  Checkbox circle = new Checkbox("Circle",true,shapes);
```

```
    public void init() {
      add(draw);
      add(square);
      add(circle);
      add(canvas);
      draw.addActionListener(canvas);
    }
    class DrawOn extends Canvas implements ActionListener {
    public void actionPerformed(ActionEvent event) {
      repaint();
    }
    public void paint(Graphics g) {
      if (circle.getState()){
        g.fillOval(20,20,100,100);
        g.drawString("Circle",40,40);
      }
      else {
        g.fillRect(20,20,100,100);
        g.drawString("Square",40,40);
      }
    }
  }
}
```

Program Modification Exercises

9. Modify Example 3.11 to draw on a `Canvas` object rather than drawing directly on the applet.

10. Modify Example 6.3 to draw on a `Canvas` object rather than drawing directly on the applet.

11. Modify Example 6.4 to draw on a `Canvas` object rather than drawing directly on the applet.

A LITTLE EXTRA 12. Modify Example 7.2 to override the `getPreferredSize` method to set the size of the canvas, rather than calling the `setSize` method.

13. Modify Example 7.6 to use a `List` instead of a `Choice` box.

PUTTING IT ALL TOGETHER 14. a. Example 6.3 displayed text in various fonts. Develop a GUI to allow the user to select a font from a choice box, to select a style from checkboxes, and to enter a point size in a text field. Display a message, using the selected font, in a canvas.

b. Check that the message will fit on one line. If it does not fit in the point size that the user requested, reduce the point size so it does fit.

c. Allow the user to select a color, and display the text in that color.

PUTTING IT ALL TOGETHER 15. a. Example 3.11 displayed various shapes. Develop a GUI to allow the user to select a shape from a choice box. Use checkboxes for the user to select whether to draw the shape filled or unfilled. If the user selects a line, then disable the checkboxes. Display the selected shape in a canvas.

b. Allow the user to select a color, and display the shapes in that color.

16. Modify Example 7.11 to allow multiple selections in the `things List`.

PUTTING IT ALL TOGETHER 17. Modify Exercise 30 of Chapter 3 to add a text field for the user to input the sales values for each day.

18. Modify Example 7.8 to center the figure in the canvas.

19. Modify Example 7.9 to center the figure in the canvas.

Program Design Exercises

20. a. Develop a GUI for a four-function (+,-,*,/) calculator. Use a text field for the display and a grid of buttons for the input. Just provide the interface. Do not try to implement the calculator functions.

    b. Implement the calculator functions, +,-,*, and /.

21. Write a program that lets the user input, in a text field, the number of fair coins to toss. Using random numbers to simulate the toss of a coin, repeat this experiment 100 times, and display a bar chart showing the distribution of the outcomes for each possible number of heads obtained. For example, tossing six coins 100 times might give no heads twice, one head 10 times, two heads 20 times, three heads 30 times, four heads 24 times, five heads 13 times, and six heads once.

22. a. A market sells eggs at $1.90 per dozen, milk at $1.47 per quart, and bread and $2.12 per loaf. Use a choice box to allow the user to select an item, and a text field for the user to input the quantity desired. Include an `Order` button for the user to order the specified quantity of the selected item. When the user selects an item, the price should appear in a label. When the user presses the `Order` button, a description and the total cost of the order should appear in a canvas. Design the applet using a layout of your choice.

    b. Allow the user to order more than one type of food. Each time the user presses the `Order` button, describe the purchase. Add a `Total` button and when the user presses this button display the total prices of all items ordered.

23. Every brokerage firm has its own formulas for calculating commissions when stocks are purchased or sold. Many of these formulas are based on the number of round lots (groups of 100) purchased and the number of stocks in any odd lot (less than 100) purchased as well as the price of the stock. To keep things simple, our company will only charge according to the number of stocks purchases as follows:

    $30 per round lot

    $.50 per stock in any odd lot

Thus, for example, if the purchaser buys 110 shares of stock, he or she is charged $35 in commissions. Include three text fields for the user to enter the name of a stock, the quantity desired, and the cost of one share. Include a *Buy* button and when the user presses this button display the total cost of that stock, including the commission. Design the applet using a layout of your choice.

24. Write a Java applet that prints the message listing the capital of a country using the interface shown in Figure 7.23 where the style can be bold or italic, and the size, large or small, refers to the point size of the font.

Figure 7.29 User Interface for Exercise 24

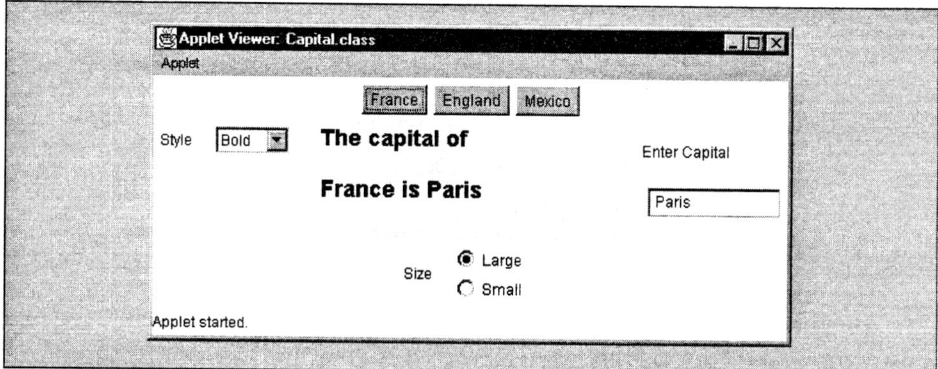

25. Using a gridbag layout, design a form for a program to send email. Include such items as text fields to enter the sender's name, the addresses of the recipient(s), a text area to enter the message, and a checkbox to indicate whether to save the message. Rather than actually sending email, save the message to a file if the checkbox is checked, and display it on standard output otherwise.

CHAPTER

8 Arrays

OUTLINE

Introduction

Each variable whose type is one of the primitive types holds a single value. Using an integer variable `score` to hold a single test score, we can write a program to add a list of test scores. Once we add a score to the total we no longer need that value and could read the next test score saving it in the same variable, `score`.

Suppose, however, that we want to arrange the scores from highest to lowest, displaying an ordered list of all scores. To sort the scores, we need to have them all available so that we can compare one score with another. Using variables of type **int** would hardly be feasible. For 50 scores we would need variables `score1`, `score2`, `score3`, and so on up to `score50`. We might manage the burdensome task of typing 50 variable declarations, but suppose we had 500 scores, or 5000. Fortunately, the **array** concept solves this problem. An array provides a collection of values.

Figure 8.1 shows the `AtmScreen` applet of Example 1.5 when the `user` tries to deposit to a non-existent checking account. To find that the `account` does not exist,

Figure 8.1 The **AtmScreen** applet: No such account

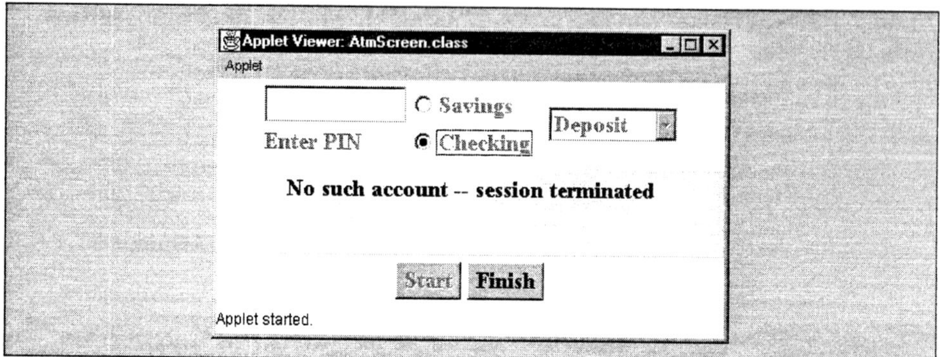

the `bank` searched an array of its accounts. Arrays are a useful data structure in many applications.

Our examples show how to use an array to handle large sets of data. We search an array for a given value, and reverse its elements. As we learn more about arrays we revisit and revise our reversing program to explicitly allocate space for an array and to use methods which have array arguments and which return array values. Our discussion of array references in Section 8.2 is independent of the discussion in Section 5.1 of object references where we introduce related ideas.

Arrays of arrays extend the array concept to multidimensional sets of data. We illustrate with an example of a class of students each of whom has a set of test scores. Our program, using an array of arrays, computes average scores.

Our case study takes up the important problem of sorting, arranging data in order. We introduce insertion sort, developing a complete sorting program. As an extra topic, we show how to add timing statements to determine the efficiency of this sorting algorithm. We then do some exploratory programming to develop a graphical user interface for insertion sorting. With a GUI we will be able to see each step of the sorting as it happens.

OBJECTIVES:

- Know how to create and use Java arrays.
- Understand that array variables hold references.
- Understand memory allocation for arrays, and arrays of objects.
- Copy arrays and pass array arguments.
- Use arrays of arrays.
- Implement insertion sort using an array to hold the data.
- Estimate efficiency using timing statements.
- Design a GUI for insertion sorting.

8.1 Using Arrays

As we noted in the introduction, it is not feasible to have 500 variables, score1, score2, ..., score500, to hold 500 test scores. The Java array lets us use one variable to refer to a collection of elements. We declare and initialize an array of type **int** that holds three integer elements as follows:

```
int[] score = {74, 38, 92};
```

Adding the square brackets to a type name, as in **int [ ]**, indicates an array type, in this case, a collection of **int** values. Java uses the values listed inside the curly braces to initialize the components of the array, which are called elements.

We use an integer index to access an array element. Array indices always start with zero, so we denote the three elements of the score array as score[0], score[1], and score[2]. The declaration above for score initialized score[0] to 74, score[1] to 38, and score[2] to 92. Figure 8.2 shows the score array.

Figure 8.2 The **score** array

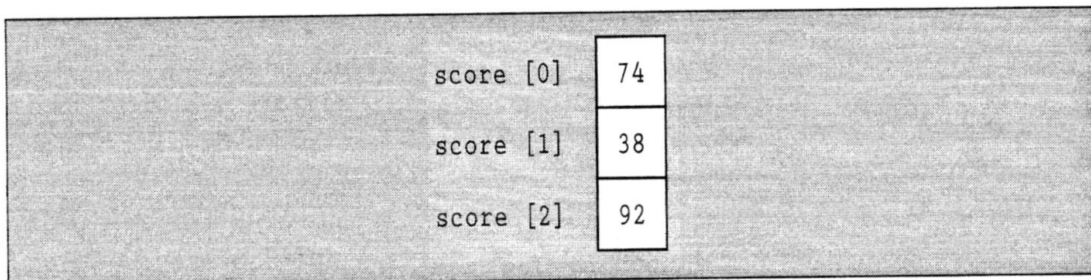

The score array conveniently groups three integer elements which we can use in expressions as we would any other variables. For example,

```
x = score[1] + score[2];
```

adds the values of score[1] and score[2], storing the result in the variable x, and

```
score[0] = 87;
```

assigns the value 87 to score[0].

Comparing Figures 8.3 and 8.4 will demonstrate the advantage of using an array. Each program fragment searches for a score of 90 among the three scores.

Figure 8.3 Searching using **int** variables

```
if (score1 == 90)
  System.out.println("It's score1");
else if (score2 == 90)
  System.out.println("It's score2");
else if (score3 == 90)
  System.out.println("It's score3");
```

Figure 8.4 Searching using an array

```
for (int i = 0; i < 3; i++)
  if (score[i] == 90)
    System.out.println("It's at index " + i);
```

Suppose we have 500 scores instead of three. To use integer variables we would need to add hundreds of lines to Figure 8.3, but to use an array, we need only change the test condition in Figure 8.4 to `i < 500` and the same three line program will perform the search. We could revise Figure 8.4 so that it will work no matter what the size of the array. Each array keeps its length in a field that we can access. The field `score.length` holds the length of the score array, three in this example. Figure 8.5 shows how to rewrite the code of Figure 8.4 to use the array length, so that the code will work whatever the length of the array.

Figure 8.5 Search any size `score` array

```
for (int i = 0; i < score.length; i++)
  if (score[i] == 90)
    System.out.println("It's at index " + i);
```

We can declare arrays of any type. For example we declare an array of **char**, `vowel`, to hold the five vowels,

```
char[] vowel = {'a','e','i','o','u'};
```

Java initializes the `vowel` array so that `vowel[0] = 'a'`, `vowel[1] = 'e'`, and so on. The **double** array

```
double[] prices = {31.22,44.50,7.98,3.99,77.88,103.99};
```

has six elements, each of type **double**.

Example 8.1 searches an array for the first occurrence of a value inputted by the user. If we find our value in the array, we use the **break** to jump out of the **for** loop; there is no need to check any more values once we have found the first occurrence.

Figure 8.6 The applet of Example 8.1

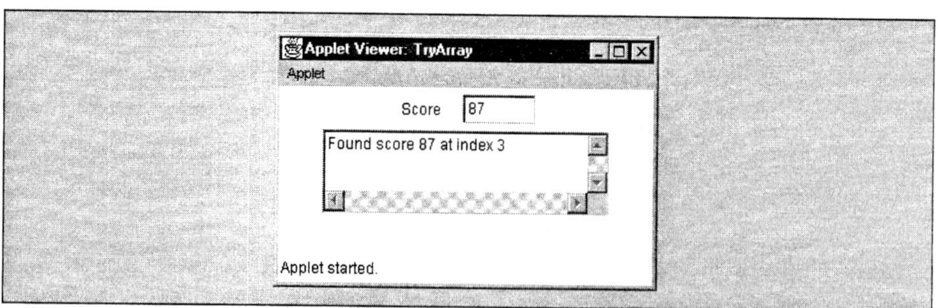

EXAMPLE 8.1 TryArray.java

```
/* Searches an array for the first occurrence of a value
 * input by the user.
 */

import java.applet.Applet;
import java.awt.*;
import java.awt.event.*;

public class TryArray extends Applet implements ActionListener{
  int [] score = {56, 91, 22, 87, 49, 89, 65};                    // Note 1
  private TextField text = new TextField(5);
  private Label label = new Label("Score");
  private TextArea result = new TextArea(3,30);

  public void init() {
    add(label);
    add(text);
    add(result);
    text.addActionListener(this);
    result.setText("Score not found yet");
  }
  public void actionPerformed(ActionEvent e) {
    int testValue = Integer.parseInt(text.getText());
    result.setText("Score not found");                            // Note 2
    for (int i=0; i < score.length; i++)                          // Note 3
      if (testValue == score[i]) {                                // Note 4
        result.setText("Found score "+ testValue +" at index "+i);
      break;                                                      // Note 5
    }
  }
}
```

Note 1: `Score` will have elements `score[0] = 56, ..., score[6] = 65.`

Note 2: We initially indicate that the test value is not found, and change the message if we find it.

Note 3: `Score.length` is seven. We use < in the test, rather than <=, because the highest index is six.

Note 4: We compare the item for which we are searching, `testValue`, to the current array element, `score[i]`.

Note 5: The **break** statement causes a jump out of the loop; once we have found the first occurrence of the value, we do not need to search any longer.

Style

We have written our array declarations so far with the square brackets after the type name, but before the variable name, as in

```
int[] score = {20,50,80};
```

In this form of the array declaration, the type designation, **int [ ]**, for an array of integers, is separated from the variable name, `score`.

Another correct form for an array declaration places the brackets after the variable name, as in

```
int score[] = {20,50,80};
```

This form of the array declaration is like that used in C and C++. We will use the former style exclusively in this text.

Changing an Array

In Example 8.1, we use an array, searching for a value inputted by the user. We can also change individual array elements. For the score array of Example 8.1, if we executed the assignment `score[3] = 74`, then the array would be changed to

```
{56, 91, 22, 74, 49, 89, 65}
```

Let us write a program to reverse an array. Our program should change the score array of Example 8.1 to `{65, 89,49, 87, 22, 91, 56}` **L** and **R** to denote the left and right indices of the values that we will swap, starting with `L=0` and `R=score.length-1`. After we swap two values we increment **L** and decrement **R**, repeating these steps until `L >= R`. Figure 8.7 shows the steps for the score array of Example 8.1

Figure 8.7 Reversing the array of Example 8.1

```
{56, 91, 22, 87, 49, 89, 65}          swap 56 and 65
  L                       R

{65, 91, 22, 87, 49, 89, 56}          swap 91 and 89
      L               R

{65, 89, 22, 87, 49, 91, 56}          swap 22 and 49
          L       R

{65, 89, 49, 87, 22, 91, 56}          reverse completed
              L
              R
```

Figure 8.8 shows the pseudocode describing this algorithm to reverse an array.

Each step of the reversing process swaps two elements. We have to be very careful in doing a swap not to write over the data before we copy it. For example, if `x = 3` and `y = 4`, then the code,

```
x = y;
```

Figure 8.8 Pseudocode to reverse an array

```
Initialize the array;
Initialize L to the smallest index;
Initialize R to the largest index;
while (L < R) {
  Swap the array elements at positions L and R;
  Increment L;
  Decrement R;
}
Output the reversed array;
```

```
y = x;
```

which looks like it swaps `x` and `y`, causes both `x` and `y` to have the value four. The first assignment, `x = y`, erases the value of `x` that we need in the next assignment to assign to `y`. Consequently the second assignment, `y = x`, assigns the new value of `x`, 4, instead of its old value, 3. To swap correctly, we need to save the value of `x` before we copy the value of `y` into it. The correct code is

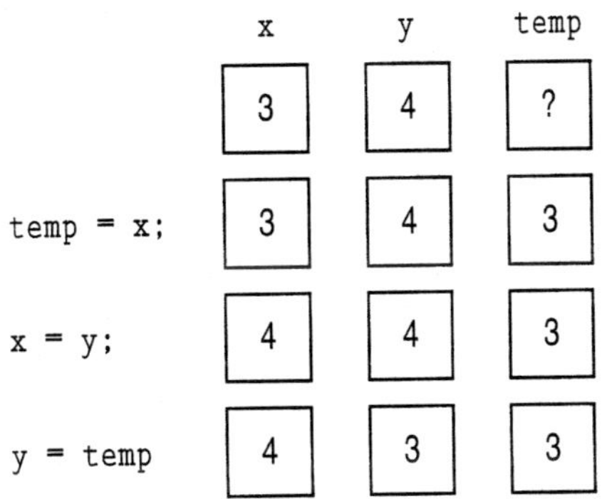

	x	y	temp
	3	4	?
`temp = x;`	3	4	3
`x = y;`	4	4	3
`y = temp`	4	3	3

which saves the value of `x` in the variable `temp`, copies `y` to `x`, and then copies `temp` to `y`.

To output an array, we output the left brace, then each element, one at a time, then the right brace. We want to separate the values by commas, so before each element except the first we need to output a comma.

Before writing a program to reverse an array, we should check that our algorithm works for arrays with an even number of elements, and for boundary cases. The array `{21,31,41,51,61,71}` has six elements. Applying our algorithm (steps omitted) will cause the while loop to terminate when we reach the position

```
{71,61,51,41,31,21}
        R  L
```

where **R** is less than **L**. For an array of one element, such as `{56}`, the algorithm will terminate without entering the `while` loop, since initially `L` starts out equal to `R` and the test condition fails. Example 8.2 reverses an array.

EXAMPLE 8.2 ReverseArray.java

```
/*  Reverses an array.  Tested with
 *  an array initialized in the program.
 */

public class ReverseArray {
  public static void main(String [] args)  {
    int [] score = {56, 91, 22, 87, 49, 89, 65};
    int temp;                          // used to store a value during a swap
    int left = 0;                      //  index of the left element to swap
    int right = score.length -1;       //  index of the right element to swap

    while (left < right) {                                         // Note 1
      temp         = score[left];                                  // Note 2
      score[left]  = score[right];
      score[right] = temp;
      right--;
      left++;
    }
    System.out.print("{");                                         // Note 3
    for (int i=0; i<score.length; i++) {
      if (i!=0) System.out.print(",");                             // Note 4
      System.out.print(score[i]);
    }
    System.out.println("}");
  }
}
```

Output

```
{65,89,49,87,22,91,56}
```

Note 1: `left` starts out at zero, and `right` starts out at the highest index, `score.length-1`. As long as `left < right`, there are two array elements to swap. For arrays of even length, the condition will fail with `right < left`. For arrays of odd length, it will fail with `right = left`.

Note 2: The `temp` variable saves the value `score[left]`, so that we can change `score[left]` to have the value `score[right]`, and then assign `temp` to `score[right]`, completing the swap.

Note 3: We display the array using a `for` loop to display each element; the `print` statement keeps the output on the same line.

Note 4: Before every element except the first, we output a comma to separate the next element from the preceding one.

A LITTLE EXTRA—COMBINING INCREMENT WITH ASSIGNMENT

For clarity, we adjusted the variables `left` and `right` after doing the swap, but we could have made these adjustments in the assignments themselves. The **while** loop of Example 8.2 would then read

```
while (left < right) {
  temp              = score[left];
  score[left++]     = score[right];
  score[right--]    = temp;
}
```

One defect of Example 8.2 is that we hard-coded the score array (initializing it with specific values in the code itself), rather than inputting it from the keyboard. In order to test other arrays, we would have to change the initialization of the score array in the program and recompile. To improve this example to let the user input array values, we need to learn more about arrays in the next section.

THE BIG PICTURE

An array is a sequence of elements. In Java, we may declare an array variable as `int[ ] x` or `int x[ ]`, which creates an array variable `x` to refer to an array. The variable `x` has the value `null` until we refer it to an array. We can initialize an array with a sequence of values. We refer to an array element using its index. Array indices start at 0.

TEST YOUR UNDERSTANDING

1. Declare and initialize an array with values 37, 44, 68, and –12. Replace the second element with 55.
2. Declare and initialize an array with values –4.3, 6.8, 32.12, –11.4, and 16.88. Copy the element in the fourth location into the first.
3. Declare and initialize an array with values 's,' 'y,' 't,' 'c,' 'v,' and 'w.'
4. Write a `for` loop to find the sum of the elements of the array of question 1.
5. Show the steps of the algorithm to reverse the elements of the array `{21,31,41,51,61,71}`, as we did in Figure 8.7 for the seven-element array.

8.2 Reference versus Value Again

Data, like many things, comes in different sizes. Many people have a cat that runs around their house, and which they even pick up and hold from time to time. If the cat is sitting on your lap, and your sister wants to hold it, you can pass it to her. Some people have horses, but they do not give them free rein in the house, nor do they hold them on their laps. Horses are too big. Both you and your sister know where to find the horses, in the stable.

Values of primitive types, like 10, 'e,' or 3.14, have fixed small sizes. Variables hold values of primitive types and assignment copies the value from one variable to another, as Figure 8.9 shows.

Figure 8.9 Primitive types hold values

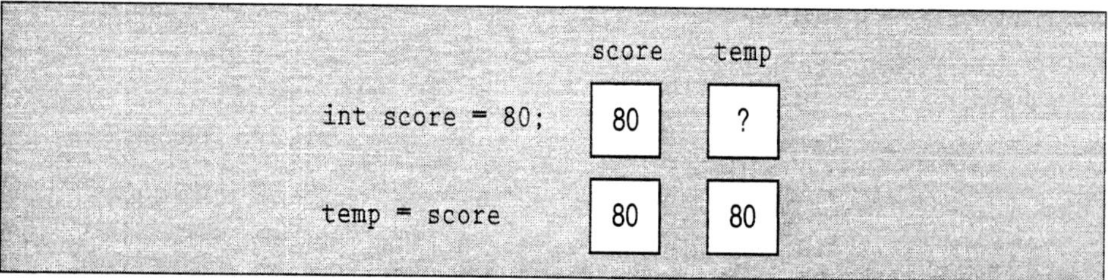

Values of array types, like {10,20,30,40,50,60,70}, can often be quite large. Variables do not hold array values, but hold references to them. A **reference** is a memory address, it tells where to find the item, in this case an array. We indicate a reference by an arrow pointing to the location of the array. Figure 8.10 shows the memory usage for the array given by

```
int[] score = {26,73,92};
```

Figure 8.10 Memory usage for score

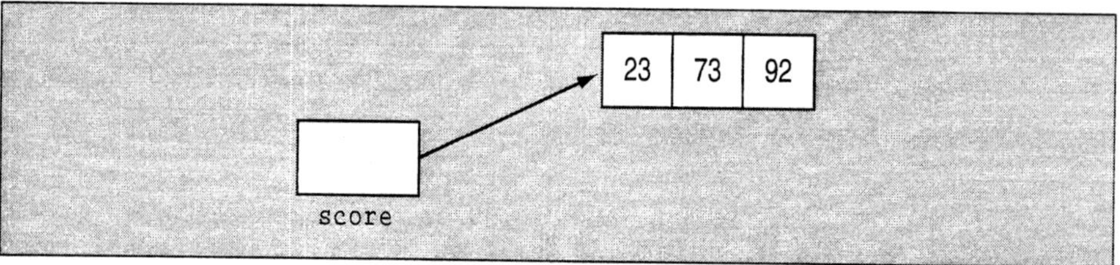

The variable `score` holds a reference to the array of three **int** elements.

Assigning one array to another copies the reference, not the array value. For example, Figure 8.11a diagrams the memory Java uses for an array variable `x` initialized to refer to an array of five integers, and an uninitialized array variable `y`. Figure 8.11b show the memory usage after we assign `x` to `y`.

We see that the assignment copies the reference from the variable `x` into the variable `y`. After the assignment, both variables refer to the same array. Copying a reference is more efficient that copying the whole array, which can be quite large. It takes time to copy the array values, and space to hold them.

Since the variables `x` and `y` in Figure 8.11b refer to the same array, any changes made using `x` will affect `y`, and vice versa. For example, if we execute

```
y[2] = -38;
System.out.println(x[2]);
```

Figure 8.11 Memory usage for an array assignment

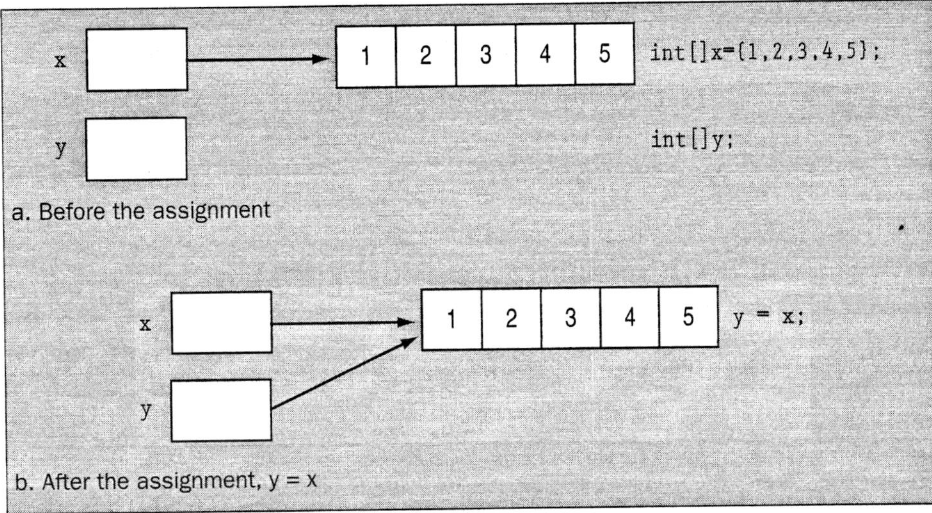

we will see that `x[2]` has the value `-38`; `x` and `y` refer to the same array so their elements must be the same. Figure 8.12 shows the effect of the assignment to `y[2]`.

Figure 8.12 Memory usage after the assignment `y[2] = -38`

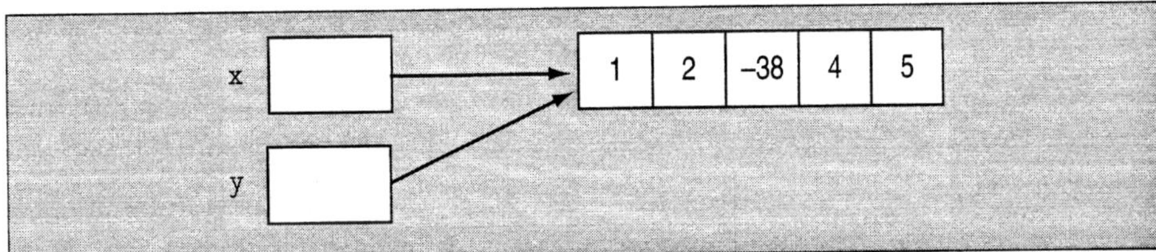

Creating an Array

So far we have created each array by initializing it using an array **initializer**, which is a list of values enclosed in curly braces. Figure 8.10 shows that the array variable refers to the collection of array elements specified in the array initializer `{26,73,92}`. If we just declare an array, but do not initialize it, as in

```
int [] anArray;
```

then the memory looks like Figure 8.13, where an array variable exists but has no values to which to refer.

Figure 8.13 Memory usage for `anArray`

anArray

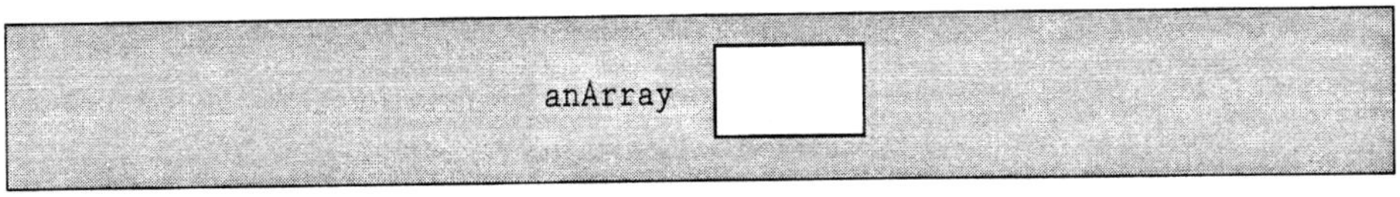

Java has an operator, `new`, to allocate space for the array elements. We can use the expression

```
new int[3]
```

to allocate an array with space for three elements. Figure 8.14 shows the memory after execution of the statement `anArray = new int[3];`

Figure 8.14 Memory allocation using the operator `new`

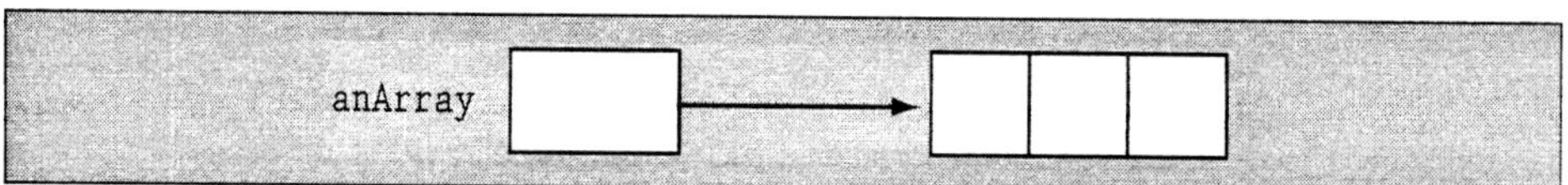

Having allocated the memory for the array elements, we can assign values to them, as in

```
anArray[0] = 17;
anArray[1] =  3 + x;
anArray[2] = Integer.parseInt(JOptionPane.showInputDialog("Enter an integer"));
```

The first of these statements assigns a constant value, the second assigns the value of an expression, while the third assigns a value input by the user. Figure 8.15 diagrams the memory, if the variable `x` has the value `7`, and the user inputs `22`.

Figure 8.15 Figure 8.15 Memory configuration for anArray

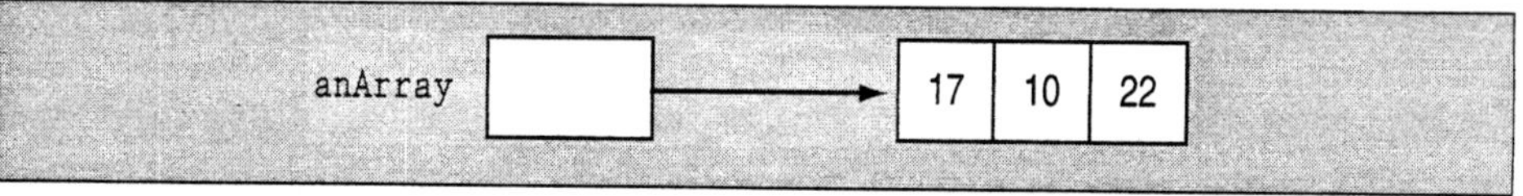

We declared `anArray` to have three elements. By using a variable, `size`, in the declaration instead of the constant, `3`, as in:

```
int[] myArray = new int[size];
```

we can declare an array `myArray` whose size depends upon the value of the variable `size`. By allowing the user to input the value of `size` before making the declaration, as in:

```
string input = JOptionPane.showInputDialog ("Enter the size of the array");
int size = Integer.parseInt(input);
int[]  myArray = new int[size];
```

we can create the `myArray` at runtime to have the desired size.

To summarize, an array variable holds a reference to a collection of elements. If we declare an array without initializing it, we create an array variable but no space for array elements (Figure 8.13). We create the space for the array elements either by initializing the array with a list of elements, or using the operator **new**. Initializing the array with a list of elements causes Java to allocate the memory for the array elements and initialize the memory with the specified values (Figure 8.10). Using the operator

new allocates the memory for the array elements (Figure 8.14); we can then assign values to the elements (Figure 8.15).

To illustrate the use of the operator **new**, Example 8.3 revises Example 8.2 to allow the user to enter the array elements from the keyboard. The user first enters the size of the array; we then create an array of that size.

Figure 8.16 The applet of Example 8.3

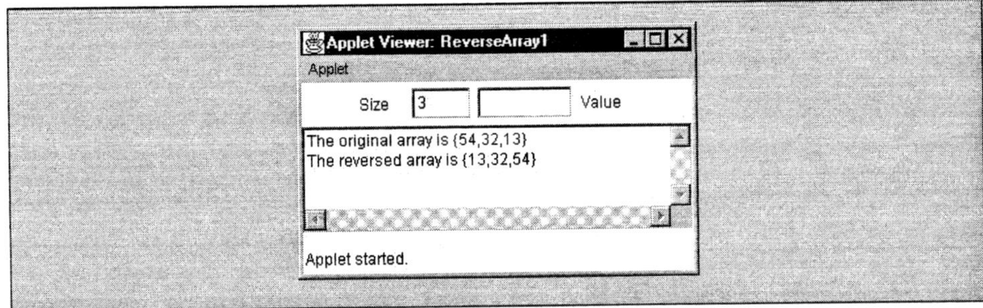

EXAMPLE 8.3 ReverseArray1.java

```
/*  Reverses an array.  The user inputs the
 *  size of the array and enters its components.
 */

import java.applet.Applet;
import java.awt.*;
import java.awt.event.*;

public class ReverseArray1 extends Applet implements ActionListener {
  private int[] score;
  private TextField size = new TextField(3);                    // Note 1
  private Label sizeLabel = new Label("Size");
  private TextField value = new TextField(7);
  private Label valueLabel = new Label("Value");
  private int index = 0;
  private TextArea result = new TextArea(4,40);

  public void init() {
    add(sizeLabel);
    add(size);
    add(value);
    add(valueLabel);
    add(result);
    size.addActionListener(this);
    value.addActionListener(this);
  }
  public void actionPerformed(ActionEvent e) {
    Object source = e.getSource();
    int count = Integer.parseInt(size.getText());
```

```
    if (source==size)
      score = new int[count];                                          // Note 2
    else if (source==value) {
      int num = Integer.parseInt(value.getText());
      if(index==0)
        result.append("The original array is {");
      if (index!=0)
        result.append(",");
      result.append(String.valueOf(num));                              // Note 3
      score[index++] = num;
      value.setText("");                                               // Note 4
      if (index == count){
        result.append("}\n");
        value.setEnabled(false);                                       // Note 5
        int temp;                         // used to store a value during a swap
        int left = 0;                     // index of the left element to swap
        int right  = score.length -1;     // index of the right element to swap
        while (left < right) {
          temp          = score[left];
          score[left]   = score[right];
          score[right]  = temp;
          right--;
          left++;
        }
        result.append("The reversed array is {");
        for (int i=0; i<score.length; i++) {
          if (i!=0) result.append(",");
          result.append(String.valueOf(score[i]));
        }
        result.append("}");
      }
    }
  }
}
```

Note 1: The user enters the size of the array, so that we can run the program with arrays of different sizes.

Note 2: The operator `new` allocates memory for an array of **int** type. Note that we can specify the number of components as the value of the `count` variable, which we input from the user. This gives much more flexibility than if we had specified a constant number of components as in the expression `new int[10]`.

Note 3: Each time the user enters a value, we display it as part of the original array.

Note 4: We clear the field to make it easier to enter the next value.

Note 5: We disable the text field to prevent the user from entering additional values, because the array is now full.

The assignment in Figure 8.11b copies the reference in the variable x, resulting in two variables, x and y, referring to the same array. If we want to copy the array elements, not the reference, then we need to use the new operator to allocate space for a second array, as in

```
int[] y = new int[x.length];
```

and write a loop to copy each element from the old array to the new array, as in

```
for (int i=0; i<y.length; i++)
y[i] = x[i];
```

We can also use the arraycopy method to copy an array. The statement

```
System.arraycopy(x, 0, y, 0, y.length);
```

will copy the entire array x to the array y. The five arguments to the arraycopy method are the source array, the starting index in the source, the target array, the starting index in the target, and the number of elements to copy.

Figure 8.17 shows the result of copying the array x to the array y.

Figure 8.17 Copying array elements

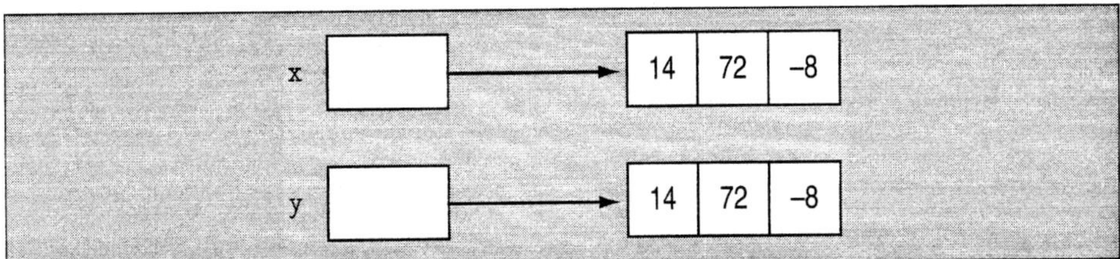

With the arrays in Figure 8.17, if we change the x array, say by the assignment x[1] = 11, then the y array will not change, since y refers to a different array than x. Example 8.4 demonstrates the difference between copying a reference and copying the array itself.

EXAMPLE 8.4 ArrayCopy.java

```
/*  Illustrates the difference between array
 *  assignment, which copies a reference to an array,
 *  and making a copy of one array in a new array.
 */

public class ArrayCopy  {
  public static void main(String [] args) {
    int [] x = {4,5,6};
    int [] z = x;                                          // Note 1
    int [] y = new int[x.length];                          // Note 2
    for (int i=0; i<y.length; i++)                         // Note 3
      y[i] = x[i];
```

```
        x[1] = 7;                                                   // Note 4
        System.out.println ("The x array is now {"                  // Note 5
            + x[0]+ "," + x[1]+ "," + x[2] + "}");
        System.out.println ("The y array, after changing x, is {"   // Note 6
            + y[0] + "," + y[1]+ "," + y[2] + "}");
        System.out.println ("The z array, after changing x, is {"   // Note 7
            + z[0]+ "," + z[1]+ "," + z[2] + "}");
    }
}
```

Output

```
The x array is now {4,7,6}
The y array, after changing x, is {4,5,6}
The z array, after changing x, is {4,7,6}
```

Note 1: Assigning x to z copies the reference in x, so that z refers to the same array as x does.

Note 2: We allocate space for a new array with the same number of elements as the x array.

Note 3: The for loop copies the elements from the x array to the y array.

Note 4: This assignment changes the x array to see how it affects the y and z arrays.

Note 5: This code displays the changed x array. For brevity we write a simple println statement for the three array values. Better code would use a for loop like those in Examples 8.2 and 8.3. Since we have to display three arrays, we opted for the less general, but briefer form. In the next section we will see how to use array arguments so that we can write a method to display an array.

Note 6: Since the array variable y refers to a true copy of the x array, changing x has no effect on the y array; it retains its original values.

Note 7: Since the array variable z refers to the same array the x does, changing the x array also changes the z array.

THE BIG PICTURE

The new operator allocates storage for array elements. Array variables, like object variables, are references. Assignment copies one reference to another and both variables refer to the same array. To make a copy of an array, we need to allocate storage for the new array and copy the elements. We can use the arraycopy statement to copy one array to another.

TEST YOUR UNDERSTANDING

6. Diagram the memory usage for each of the following

   a. `int[] intArray;` b. `char[] charArray = {'a','b','c'};`

   c. `double[] doubleArray = new double[6];`

7. Diagram the memory usage for each of the following

   a. `int[] intArray = {2,-4,5,9,-1};`

   b. `char[] charArray = new char[8];`

   c. `double[] doubleArray;`

8. Diagram the memory usage resulting from the execution of

```
int[] a = {36, -2, 44, 55};
int[] b = a;
```

9. Write Java code to make a copy of the array `a` of question 8.

10. Diagram the memory configuration resulting from the variables and arrays of question 9.

8.3 Passing Array Arguments and Returning Arrays

In this section, we will learn to write methods that have array parameters and that return array values. In Example 8.5, we improve Example 8.4, which uses three ugly `println` statements to output three arrays, by writing a method which displays an array that we pass in as an argument.

In Example 8.6, we reverse an array using three methods, the `display` method, a `readIntArray` method that returns an array input by the user, and a `reverse` method to reverse the array that was inputted. We allow the user to run the program again to reverse additional arrays.

We name three pieces of the code, placing each piece inside a method of the chosen name. In effect, we are creating three new operations, `readIntArray`, `display`, and `reverse`. The `main` method of Example 8.6 will call these three operations to perform the tasks of reading, displaying, and reversing an array. This makes our program much easier to understand, since the human mind finds it much easier to grasp a few large steps, than to follow dozens of small details.

TIP Group major operations into methods, using the method names to invoke the operations. Organizing your program, naming operations, makes it much easier to understand, write correctly, and change when needed.

Passing an Array Argument: The `display` Method

To write a method to display an array, we can take the code that we used to display an array in Example 8.2, and copy it to the body of the `display` method. Figure 8.18 shows the `display` method, which has a formal parameter, `anArray`, of type **int**[ ], an array of integers.

Figure 8.18 The `display` method

```
public static void display(int [] anArray) {
  System.out.print("{");
  for (int i=0; i<anArray.length; i++) {
    if (i!=0) System.out.print(",");
    System.out.print(anArray[i]);
  }
  System.out.println("}");
}
```

To call the `display` method we pass it an array argument, as in the code fragment

```
int[] score = {40, 50, 60};
display(score);
```

which displays the array `{40, 50, 60}` on the screen.

The actual argument, `score`, refers to the array `{40,50,60}`. When we call the method `display(score)`, Java copies `score` to the formal parameter `anArray`; Figure 8.19 displays the memory configuration.

Figure 8.19 Passing the `score` reference to the `anArray` parameter

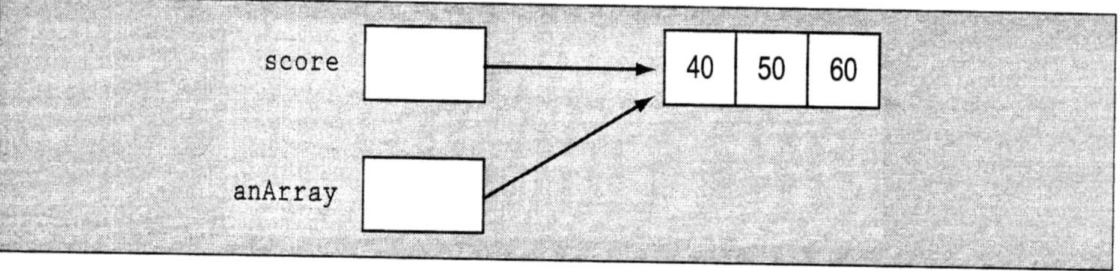

The code inside the `display` method uses the reference given by the `anArray` variable to display each of the elements of the array. We can use the `display` method again with a different argument. In Example 8.4 we displayed three arrays. In Example 8.5 we revise Example 8.4 to use the `display` method to display the arrays. We only have to write the code once, in the `display` method, but call it three times. Each time we call the `display` method, the parameter, `anArray`, refers to the array that we pass in as the argument.

EXAMPLE 8.5 DisplayArray.java

```
/*  Revises Example 8.4 to use a display
 *  method to output an array.
 */

public class DisplayArray  {
  public static void display(int [] anArray) {              // Note 1
    System.out.print("{");
    for (int i=0; i<anArray.length; i++) {
      if (i!=0) System.out.print(",");
      System.out.print(anArray[i]);
    }
    System.out.println("}");
}

public static void main(String [] args) {
  int [] x = {4,5,6,7,8,9,10,11};                              // Note 2
  int [] z = x;
  int [] y = new int[x.length];
  for (int i=0; i<y.length; i++)
    y[i] = x[i];
  x[1] = 7;
  System.out.print("The x array is now ");
  display(x);                                                  // Note 3
  System.out.print("The y array, after changing x, is ");
  display(y);                                                  // Note 4
  System.out.print("The z array, after changing x, is ");
  display(z);                                                  // Note 5
  }
}
```

Output

```
The x array is now {4,7,6,7,8,9,10,11}
The y array, after changing x, is {4,5,6,7,8,9,10,11}
The z array, after changing x, is {4,7,6,7,8,9,10,11}
```

Note 1: The `display` method outputs the values of the array argument passed to it.

Note 2: The `x` array has seven elements and would be more tedious to display using a loop like that of Example 8.4.

Note 3: We pass the `display` method the array that we wish to display. This is the first of three calls to the `display` method. In this call the formal parameter, `anArray`, refers to the array to which `x` refers.

Note 4: In this call the formal parameter, `anArray`, refers to the array to which `y` refers.

Note 5: In this call the formal parameter, `anArray`, refers to the array to which `z` refers.

Returning an Array: The `readIntArray` Method

The `display` method of Example 8.5 has an array parameter, but does not return any value. However, methods can return array values. The `readIntArray` method will not have any parameters but it will have a return value which will be the array that the user inputs. Inside the `readIntArray` method, we first ask the user to input the size of the array, then use the operator `new` to allocate memory for an array of that size. Finally, we ask the user to input each element of the array, and use the `return` statement to return that array to the caller of the method. Figure 8.20 contains the code for the `readIntArray` method.

Figure 8.20 The `readIntArray` method

```
public static int[] readIntArray() {
  String input = JOptionPane.showInputDialog("Enter the array size");
  int size = Integer.parseInt(input);
  int [] anArray = new int[size];
  for (int i=0; i<size; i++){
    input = JOptionPane.showInputDialog("Enter anArray["+i+"] ");
    anArray[i] = Integer.parseInt(input);
  }
  return anArray;
}
```

In the `readIntArray` method, we specify the return type as `int[ ]`, an array of integers. We use the `return` statement to return the array, `anArray`, that we get from the user. To use the `readIntArray` method, we can declare an array in our program and initialize that array with the value returned by the `readIntArray` method, as in

```
int[] score = readIntArray();
```

where the variable `score` will refer to the array returned by the `readIntArray` method.

TIP

When calling a method, such as `display`, that does not return a value, we use it like a statement, as in

```
display(score);
```

When calling a method , such as `readIntArray`, that returns a value, we use it like an expression, assigning the return value to a variable, as in

```
int[] score = readIntArray();
```

Changing an Array: The `reverse` Method

The algorithm to reverse an array, whose steps are shown in Figure 8.4, changes the original array. We can write a method to reverse an array that similarly changes the array argument passed to it. The body of the reverse method in Figure 8.21 comes from Example 8.2.

Figure 8.21 The **reverse** method

```
public static void reverse(int[] anArray) {
  int temp;                              // used to store a value during a swap
  int left = 0;                          // index of the left element to swap
  int right = anArray.length -1;         // index of the right element to swap
  while (left < right) {
    temp             = anArray[left];
    anArray[left]    = anArray[right];
    anArray[right]   = temp;
    right--;
    left++;
  }
}
```

When we call the reverse method, we pass it an array to reverse, as in

```
int[] score = {40,50,60};
reverse(score);
```

which will output the array {60,50,40}. Java passes the reference to the argument score to the formal parameter anArray so that when we begin executing the code for the reverse method in Figure 8.21, both the argument score and the formal parameter anArray refer to the same array as shown in Figure 8.19. The code in the reverse method shown in Figure 8.21 changes the array to that shown in Figure 8.22.

Figure 8.22 Reversing the **score** array.

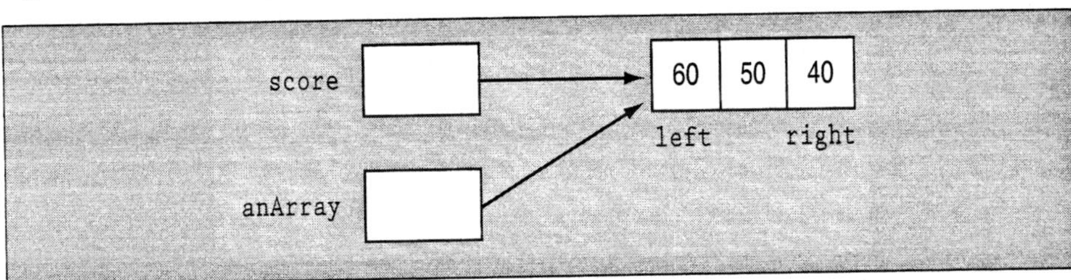

The steps in the body of the reverse method make the changes in that array needed to reverse it. Inside the reverse method we refer to the array using the anArray reference. When the reverse method completes its execution, Java destroys the local variables anArray, left, and right, but the variable score refers to the reversed array and we can pass it to the display method, as in:

```
display(score);
```

which outputs the array {60,50,40} to which score now refers.

An Example: Using Methods to Name Operations

Having developed the `display`, `readIntArray`, and `reverse` methods, we can use them to reverse an array. We allow the user to repeat, reversing additional arrays during the same run of the program.

EXAMPLE 8.6 RepeatReverse.java

```
/*  Reverses an array.  The user inputs the
 *  size of the array and enters its components.
 *  Uses readIntArray, reverse, and display
 *  methods.  Allows user to repeat with
 *  additional arrays.
 */

import javax.swing.*;
public class RepeatReverse {
  public static int[] readIntArray() {                                   // Note 1
    String input = JOptionPane.showInputDialog("Enter the array size");
    int size = Integer.parseInt(input);
    int [] anArray = new int[size];
    for (int i=0; i<size; i++) {
      input = JOptionPane.showInputDialog("Enter anArray["+i+"] ");
      anArray[i] = Integer.parseInt(input);
    }
    return anArray;                                                      // Note 2
  }
  public static void reverse(int [] anArray) {                           // Note 3
    int temp;                          // used to store a value during a swap
    int left = 0;                      // index of the left element to swap
    int right = anArray.length -1;     // index of the right element to swap
    while (left < right) {
      temp           = anArray[left];
      anArray[left]  = anArray[right];
      anArray[right] = temp;
      right--;
      left++;
    }
  }
  public static void display(int [] anArray) {
    System.out.print("{");
    for (int i=0; i<anArray.length; i++) {
      if (i!=0) System.out.print(",");
      System.out.print(anArray[i]);
    }
    System.out.println("}");
  }
  public static void main(String [] args)  {
```

```
    char repeat;           // 'Y' to repeat, 'N' to quit
    int [] theArray;       // the array to reverse
    do {
      theArray = readIntArray();                              // Note 4
      System.out.print("The input array is ");
      display(theArray);                                      // Note 5
      reverse(theArray);                                      // Note 6
      System.out.print("The reversed array is ");
      display(theArray);                                      // Note 7
      String input = JOptionPane.showInputDialog
                       ("Enter 'Y' to repeat, 'N' to quit");
      repeat = input.charAt(0);
    } while (repeat == 'Y' || repeat == 'y');
    System.exit(0);
  }
}
```

Run

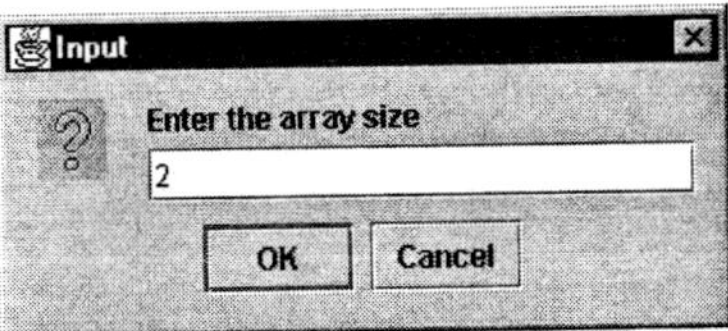

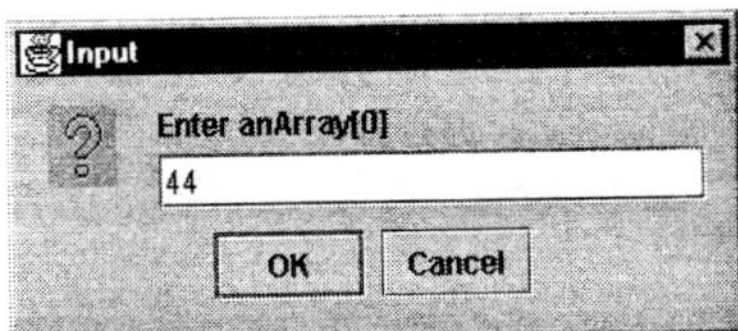

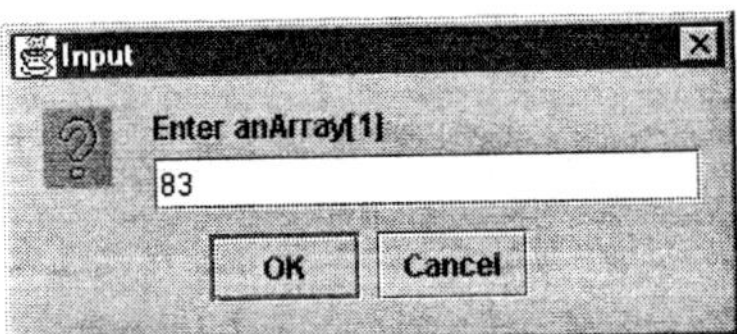

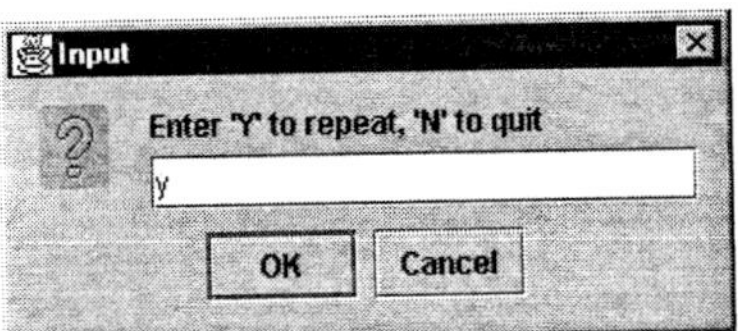


```
The input array is {44,83}
The reversed array is {83,44}
```

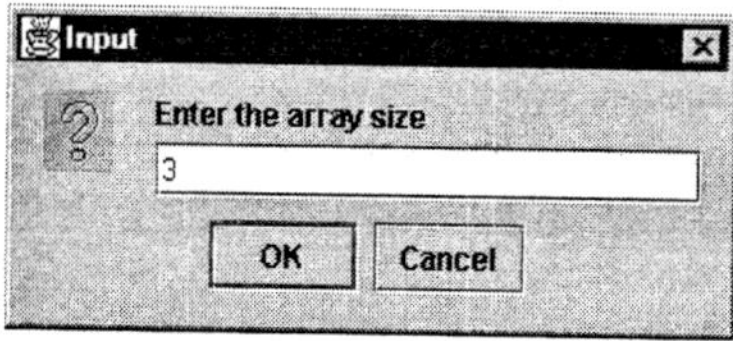

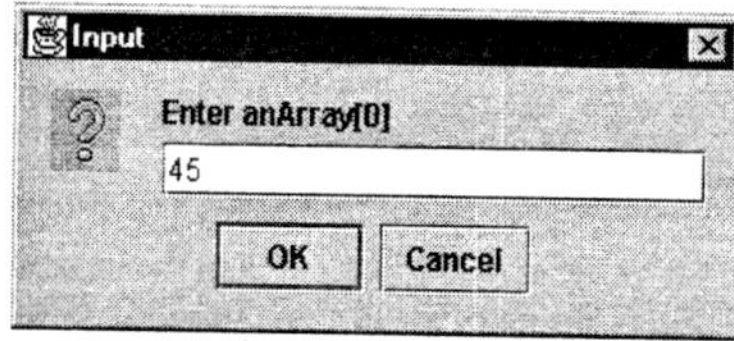

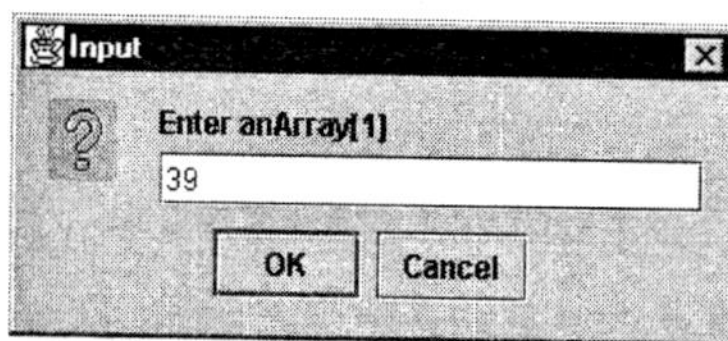

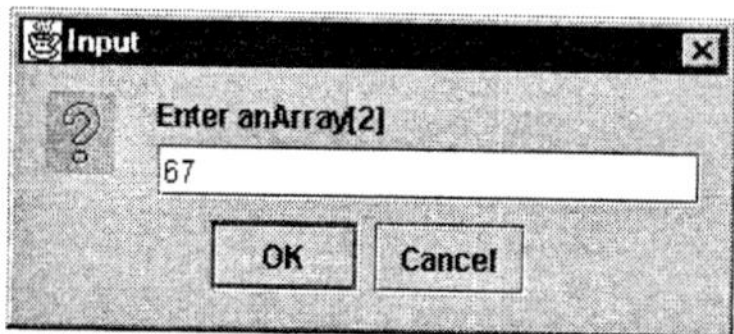

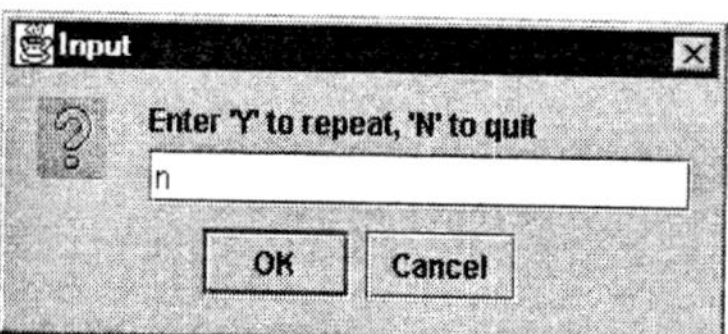


```
The input array is {45,39,67}
The reversed array is {67,39,45}
```

Note 1: The `readIntArray` method returns an `int[ ]` value, an array of integers.

Note 2: Any method that returns a value needs to have a `return` statement. Here the `return` statement returns the variable `anArray` whose type is an array of integers.

Note 3: The `reverse` method has as its formal parameter the array of integers, `anArray`, to reverse. There is no return value since this method changes the array passed to it rather than creating a new array to return. We leave as an exercise the revision of this method to return a new array.

Note 4: We assign the array returned from the `readIntArray` method to the `theArray` variable.

Note 5: We pass `theArray` to the `display` method to echo what the user input.

Note 6: We pass `theArray` to the `reverse` method to reverse it.

Note 7: Now the variable `theArray` refers to the reversed array, which we display.

A LITTLE EXTRA—COMPARING `int[ ]` AND `int` ARGUMENTS

When we pass an array to a method, we pass a reference, so that as in Figure 8.19, we get two references to the same array, one from the actual argument passed in, and one from the formal parameter. We do not copy the array, so that when we use the formal parameter to change the array inside the method, as in the code

```
anArray[left] = anArray[right];
```

from the `reverse` method of Example 8.6, the change affects the `score` array that we pass as the argument when we call the `reverse` method.

By contrast, when we pass a primitive type to a method, the formal parameter is a copy of the actual argument and changing it has no effect on the actual argument. To illustrate this, consider the `assign4` method given by

```
public static void assign4(int someNumber) {
  someNumber = 4;
}
```

which we might call with the code

```
int x = 27;
assign4(x);
```

When we pass the variable `x` to `assign4`, Java copies its value, 27, to the formal parameter `someNumber`; Figure 8.23 shows the result.

Figure 8.23 Memory configuration after passing `x` to `assign4`

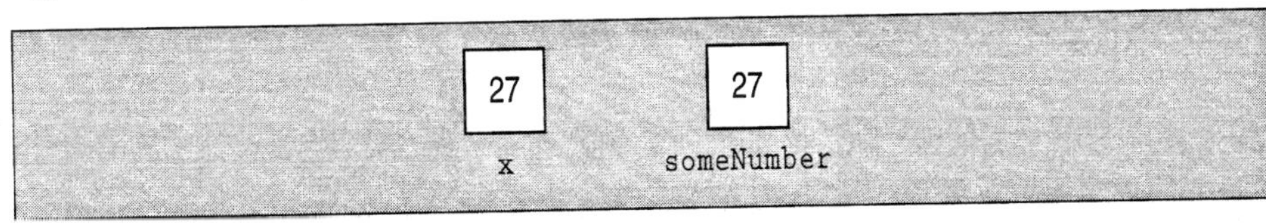

When Java executes the `assign4` method, the formal parameter changes its value to 4, but the actual argument `x` is unchanged, as Figure 8.24 shows.

Figure 8.24 Effect of the `assign4` method

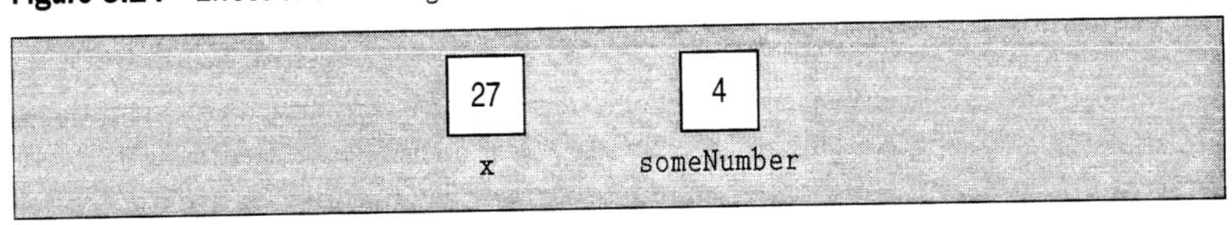

THE BIG PICTURE

We can pass array arguments to and return array values from methods. The formal array parameter, used in the body of the method, refers to the array passed from the calling program, whereas for primitive types, changes to the formal parameter do not affect the value passed from the caller.

TEST YOUR UNDERSTANDING

11. Write a statement to call the `display` method of Figure 8.18 to display the array `myArray = {52, 63, 74, 85};`
12. Write a statement which assigns the array returned by the `readIntArray` method of Figure 8.20 to the variable `myArray`.
13. Write a statement which uses the `reverse` method of Figure 8.21 to reverse the array `myarray = {52, 63, 74, 85}`.
14. The `display` method of Figure 8.18 uses a formal parameter, `anArray`, to refer to the array. Suppose we call the `display` method with the argument `myArray = {52, 63, 74, 85}`. Diagram the memory configuration, showing both `anArray` and `myArray`.

8.4 An Example: Simulating Rolls of the Dice

Before continuing with arrays of arrays, we present another example to gain further practice using arrays. In our `Dice` class we use random numbers to simulate the tossing of two dice. Assuming that each die has an equal chance of landing so that any one of its six faces, numbered 1 through 6, will be showing, we tabulate the frequency of each of the sums, 2 through 12, of the numbers showing on each die.

We write a method, `roll`, that simulates the roll of two dice, returning the sum of the numbers showing on each face. The `Random` class of the `java.util` package contains a `nextInt` method that returns an integer that appears to be randomly chosen. For example,

```
random.nextInt(6)
```

returns either 0, 1, 2, 3, 4, or 5., where `random` is a `Random` instance. Adding one gives an integer from 1 through 6, and each of these should occur with equal frequency since the random numbers are distributed evenly. Thus the formula

```
random.nextInt(6) + 1
```

simulates the effect of tossing a die. We toss two and return the sum.

The method `tossResults` tabulates the frequencies of each outcome, 2 through 12, in an array named `result`, so that `result[i]` is the number of times that the sum on the two dice was `i`. We use the array elements `result[2]` through `result[12]`, leaving `result[0]` and `result[1]` unused. We simply store the outcome of the `roll` method in the `result` array by incrementing the value in the array. For example if the outcome is 6, we execute `result[6]++`.

Example 8.7 shows the code for this dice simulation. To find the expected frequencies, make a 6x6 grid with row labels 1-6, and column labels 1-6, and enter the sum of the row and column labels in the grid as shown in Figure 8.25

Figure 8.25 Outcomes when tossing two dice

	1	2	3	4	5	6
1	2	3	4	5	6	7
2	3	4	5	6	7	8
3	4	5	6	7	8	9
4	5	6	7	8	9	10
5	6	7	8	9	10	11
6	7	8	9	10	11	12

Tabulating the 36 outcomes from Figure 8.25 gives

Sum	2	3	4	5	6	7	8	9	10	11	12
Frequency	1	2	3	4	5	6	5	4	3	2	1

showing, for example, that 6 of the 36 outcomes are 7 while 3 are 10. If the number of rolls is a simple multiple of 36, such as 36, 360, 3600, and so on, we can easily see how closely the simulation matches the prediction. For example, for 360 tosses we expect, on average, to get a distribution like

Sum	2	3	4	5	6	7	8	9	10	11	12
Frequency	10	20	30	40	50	60	50	40	30	20	10

EXAMPLE 8.7 Dice.java

```
/* Simulates the rolling of two dice.
 * The user inputs the number of tosses.
 * Uses arrays to tabulate the results.
 */

import javax.swing.*;
import java.util.Random;
public class Dice {
  private Random random = new Random();
```

```
  public static int roll() {
    int die1 = random.nextInt(6) + 1;                          // Note 1
    int die2 = random.nextInt(6) + 1;
    return die1 + die2;
  }
  public static int[] tossResults(int number) {
    int[] result = {0,0,0,0,0,0,0,0,0,0,0,0,0};                // Note 2
    for (int i=0; i<number; i++)
      result[roll()]++;                                        // Note 3
    return result;
  }
  public static void main(String[] args) {
    int[] diceThrows;            // Elements 2-12 store frequencies
    int numberOfRolls;           // Number of rolls of the dice
    String input = JOptionPane.showInputDialog
        ("Enter the number of rolls of the dice");
    numberOfRolls = Integer.parseInt(input);
    diceThrows = tossResults(numberOfRolls);
    System.out.println("Sum\tFrequency");
    for (int i=2; i<=12; i++)
      System.out.println(i + "\t" +diceThrows[i]);
    }
    System.exit(0);
}
```

Run

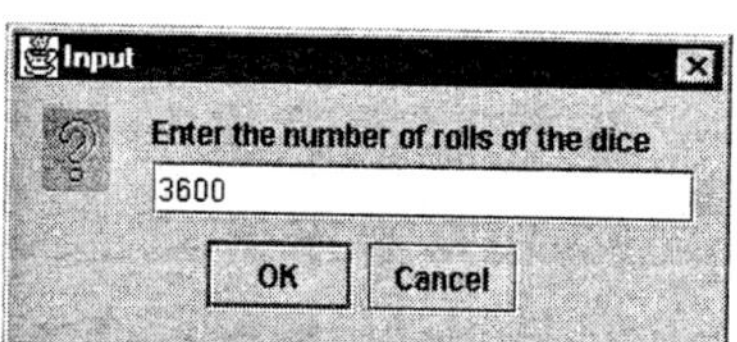


```
Sum     Frequency
2         101
3         209
4         307
5         402
6         498
7         590
8         481
9         403
10        308
11        213
12         88
```

Note 1: This formula produces values 1 through 6 with equal expected frequency, as we explained in the text above.

Note 2: We initialize the array with 13 components, all zero, but only use the last 11, with `result[i]` holding the number of times the sum on the two dice was `i`.

Note 3: The call to `roll()` returns a value from 2 through 12. We increment the number stored in the array element `result[roll()]` to indicate the occurrence of the value returned by `roll`. For example, if `roll()` returns five, we increment `result[5]`.

THE BIG PICTURE

Arrays have many uses. The `Random` class has methods to generate random values to use in simulations.

TEST YOUR UNDERSTANDING

15. Write a Java expression which generates a random integer greater than or equal to 50 but less than 500.
16. If in Example 8.7 we were to roll three dice instead of two how many elements would we need in the roll array? Which elements would be unused?

8.5 Arrays of Arrays

Arrays let us access a collection of data. An array `score` might have ten elements, or 100, which we access using an array index, as in `score[9]`. An instructor might have an array of scores for each student in the class. For example,

```
student1 has scores {52, 76, 65}
student2 has scores {98, 87, 93}
student3 has scores {43, 77, 62}
student4 has scores {72, 73, 74}
```

and so on for the thirty students (or is it 300?) in the class.

We do not want to declare 30 or 300 variables. We have the same problem that we faced with one set of scores, where we had to declare variables `score1`, `score2`, `score3`, and so on, until we learned to declare an array variable score of type **int**[ ]. The type **int**[ ] has two parts, the type of each element, **int**, followed by the square brackets, `[]`, to indicate an array.

What we need here is an array with one element for each student, where the type of each element is **int**[ ], an array of integers. This array will hold the student's test scores. Again we write the type declaration in two parts, the type of each element, **int**[ ], followed by the square brackets, `[]`, to indicate an array of an array of integers. For a class of thirty students with three scores each, we would declare

```
int[][] s =  new int[30][3];
```

We initialize the array, as we did for arrays of integers, by giving a list of elements. Here each element of the array is itself an array of integers. To shorten the example, we declare an array of four students with three scores each,

```
int[][] student =
        {{52,76,65},{98,87,93},{43,77,62},{72,73,74}};
```

Each element of the student array is itself an array of integers. In fact,

```
student[0] is {52, 76, 65}
student[1] is {98, 87, 93}
student[2] is {43, 77, 62}
student[3] is {72, 73, 74}
```

Figure 8.26 shows the student array of array of scores for each student.

Figure 8.26 The `student` array

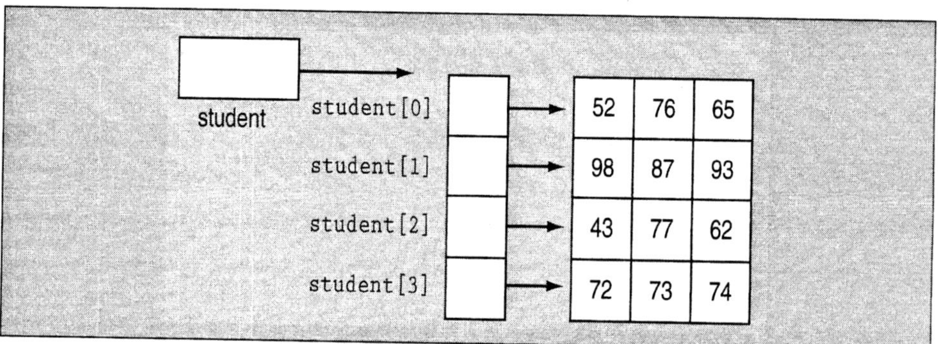

We can get individual scores by referring to components of these arrays, as in

```
student[1][0] is 98
student[2][2] is 62
```

The length of the student array, given by `student.length`, is four. Each element of the student array is itself an array. The length of element `i`, `student[i]`, is given by `student[i].length`, which in this example is three.

Example 8.8 computes the average score for each student. To compute the average we use nested **for** statements. The outer loop uses an index `i` to refer to student `i`. The inner loop uses an index `j` to refer to the grades of student `i`.

EXAMPLE 8.8 StudentScore.java

```
/* Uses an array of arrays.  Computes the average
 * score of each student.
 */

import java.text.*;
public class StudentScore {
```

```
  public static void main(String [] args) {
    int [] [] student = {{52, 76, 65},{98, 87, 93},{43, 77, 62},{72, 73, 74}};
                                                                    // Note 1
    double sum;                                                     // Note 2
    for (int i=0; i<student.length; i++) {                          // Note 3
      sum = 0;                                                      // Note 4
      for (int j=0; j<student[i].length; j++)                       // Note 5
        sum += student[i][j];
      System.out.print("The average score for student " + i + " is ");
      NumberFormat nf = NumberFormat.getNumberInstance();
      nf.setMaximumFractionDigits(1);
      System.out.println(nf.format(sum/student[i].length));         // Note 6
    }
  }
}
```

Output

```
The average score for student 0 is 64.3
The average score for student 1 is 92.7
The average score for student 2 is 60.7
The average score for student 3 is 73.0
```

Note 1: We declare `sum`, representing the sum of the scores for each student, as type **double** so that when we compute the average it will be of type **double**.

Note 2: The index `i` runs through the students. The field `student.length` gives the length of the array of score arrays, which is four in this example.

Note 3: We must initialize `sum` for each student, so this statement must occur inside the outer loop. Forgetting to initialize `sum` here would cause the second student's scores to be added to the those of the first, giving an incorrect result.

Note 4: This loop runs through the array of scores for student `i`. The length of this array is `student[i].length`.

Note 5: We add score `j` of student `i` to the sum of scores for student `i`.

Note 6: We output the average, which is the sum of the scores divided by the number of scores. Here the number of scores is the length of the array of scores for student `i`.

A LITTLE EXTRA—ELEMENTS OF DIFFERENT SIZES

In Example 8.8, each student had three scores, but the code will work properly if these arrays are not all the same size. For example,

```
int[ ][ ] student = { {56,76}, {83}, {34,78, 67} };
```

To allocate space without initializing the array we could use

```
int[ ][ ] student = new int[4][3];
```

for the case where each student has three scores, and

```
int[ ][ ] student = new int[3][ ];
student[0] = new int[2];
student[1] = new int[1];
student[2] = new int[3];
```

when the first student has two scores, the second one, and the third three.

THE BIG PICTURE

An array of arrays is an array whose elements are also arrays. These element arrays do not have to be the same size. When declaring a variable for an array of arrays, we can either initialize it to refer to a specific array of arrays, or we can use the new operator. Declaring `int [ ][ ] x = new int [4][3]` will create an array x whose four elements are each arrays of three elements. Declaring `int [ ] [ ] y = new int [4][ ]` will create an array y whose four elements may have different sizes. Executing `y[0] = new int [5]` will give the first element of the y array five elements.

TEST YOUR UNDERSTANDING

17. Declare and initialize an array of arrays of scores for two students. The first student has scores 55, 66, 87, and 76, while the second's scores are: 86, 92, 88, and 95.
18. Declare and initialize an array of arrays of batting averages for five baseball players for each of the last three years. Batting averages are typically computed to three decimal places and range from .150 to .400.
19. Given `char[][] letter ={{'a','b','c'}, {'x','y','z','w'}}`, find

    a. `letter[0][1]` b. `letter[1][0]`

    c. `letter[1][3]` d. `letter[0][2]`

8.6 Solving Problems with Java: Insertion Sort

In this section we develop a program to sort an array, arranging its elements in order, using insertion sort. Sorting has many uses; various algorithms have been developed to solve this important problem. Insertion sort is useful for smaller data sets, while other methods such as quicksort or merge sort work much more efficiently for larger sets of data.

Defining the Problem

To understand how insertion sort works, we start with an example. Given the values

```
54 23 78 42 26 12 41 64
```

the sorted array should be

12 23 26 41 42 54 64 78.

Insertion sort takes each element from the second element to the last element and inserts it in its proper place with respect to the preceding elements. Starting with the second element, which we underline

54 <u>23</u> 78 42 26 12 41 64

we see that 23 < 54, so we move 54 to the right one position in the array, and insert 23 in the beginning of the array giving

23 54 78 42 26 12 41 64

Next we insert 78.

23 54 <u>78</u> 42 26 12 41 64

Since 78 > 23, we compare 78 to 54. Since 78 > 54, we know that 78 is greater than all its predecessors, so we leave it where it is in position three, and the array is unchanged. At this point we have the first three elements in order.

Next we insert the fourth element, 42.

23 54 78 <u>42</u> 26 12 41 64

Since 42 > 23 and 42 < 54, we move both 78 and 54 to the right by one position and insert 42 in the second position giving

23 42 54 78 26 12 41 64

Figure 8.27 shows the array at this point, with its first four elements in order. In the next section we will use Java to draw such a diagram.

Figure 8.27 Partially sorted array

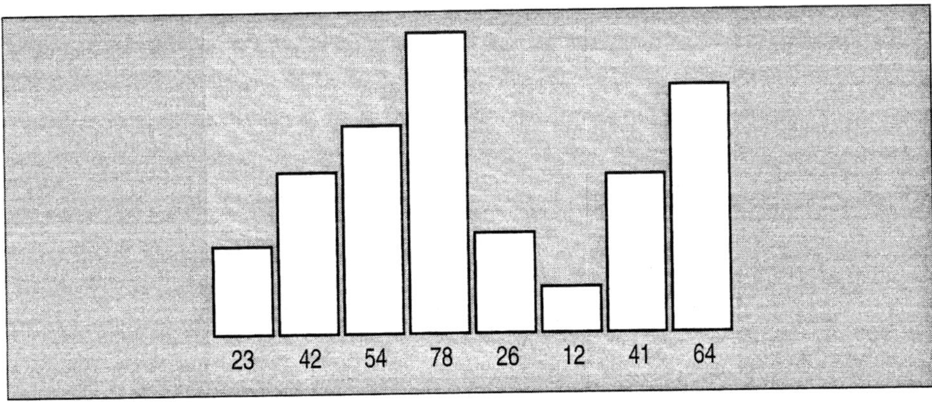

The fifth element, 26, is greater than 23 and less than 42, so we move the elements 42, 54, and 78 to the right and insert 26 in the second position giving

23 26 42 54 78 12 41 64

Since 12 is smaller than 23, we move the first five elements to the right, and insert 12 at the start of the array, giving

```
12  23  26  42  54  78  41  64
```

The seventh element, 41, is greater than the first three elements, but less than 42, so we move 42, 54, and 78 to the right and insert 41 as the fourth element of the array, giving

```
12  23  26  41  42  54  78  64
```

Finally, the last element, 64, is greater than all elements but 78, so we move 78 to the right, and insert 64 as the seventh element and the array is fully sorted.

Toward a Solution: Developing the Pseudocode

Figure 8.28 expresses the overall solution in pseudocode.

Figure 8.28 Insertion Sort: Top-level pseudocode

```
Get the data to sort;
Display the data to sort;
Insert each item in the correct
  position in its predecessors;
Display the sorted data;
```

To get the data, we can allow the user to input data, or we can generate random numbers to test without requiring user input. Figure 8.29 shows this refinement.

Figure 8.29 Refinement: Get the data to sort

```
Ask if the user wants to enter data;
if (yes) Get data from the user;
else Generate random data;
```

In previous examples, we have used three ways to get data from the user. Since the data could be positive or negative we do not really have a convenient sentinel value that we can distinguish from a valid data value, so we will rule out the use of a sentinel. We could ask the user each time if there is more data to input, which does not require the user to know the size of the data set, but does require an extra response to input the next item. The last alternative, which we choose, is to have the user input the size of the data, as shown in the refinement in Figure 8.30, where we use **loop** to represent a loop that we will implement using one of the Java repetition statements.

Figure 8.30 Refinement: Get data from the user

```
Input the size of the data;
loop
  Get the next item;
```

To generate random data, we first ask the user to input the size of the data and then use a loop to generate the required number of random values. Having got this far we see that no matter how we get the data, we will ask the user to input the size of the data. Rather than coding this request twice, we can get the data size before deciding whether to input from the user or generate random numbers. Figure 8.31 shows this revision of the refinement in Figure 8.29, including the refinements for the subproblems.

Figure 8.31 Revised Refinement: Get the data to sort

```
Input the size of the data;
Ask if the user wants to enter the data;
if (yes)
  loop
    Get the next item;
else
  loop
    Generate the next random item;
```

To sort the data we insert one element at a time, starting with the second element, in the correct position in its predecessors. Figure 8.32 shows this loop.

Figure 8.32 Refinement: Insert items

```
loop, from second item to last
  Insert item i in the correct position
    in its predecessors;
```

From our example, we see that to insert the item at index `i` we first find its correct position, say `j`, then move the elements at positions `j` through `i-1` to the right by one position. Lastly we insert the item in the correct position. Figure 8.33 shows this refinement

Figure 8.33 Refinement: Insert item i

```
Find the correct position, say j, for item i;
Move elements at j to i-1 one position to the right;
Insert item i at position j.
```

To find the correct position for item `i`, we start at the leftmost element of the array, with `j` initialized to zero, and while item `i` is greater than item `j`, we increment `j`. In our example above, when we insert item 6, which is 41, we do the following steps

```
41 > 12 so increment j to 1
41 > 23 so increment j to 2
41 > 26 so increment j to 3
41 < 42 so stop, finding that index 3 is the correct position
```

Figure 8.34 shows the refinement for finding the correct position.

Figure 8.34 Refinement: Finding the correct position for item i

```
j = 0;
while (item i > item j) j++;
```

We have to be careful to move the items starting at the right, so that we do not overwrite any items before they are moved, and to save item i before writing over it. In our example above, since we found that index 3 is the correct position for 41, we need to move items 3 to 5 to the right; the steps are:

```
save the 41 that we want to insert
move 78 to the right, storing it as the item at index 6
move 54 to the right, storing it as the item at index 5
move 42 to the right, storing it as the item at index 4
```

Figure 8.35 shows the for loop we need to move the elements at indices from j to i-1 to the right by one position

Figure 8.35 Refinement: Move elements j to i-1 to the right

```
Save item i;
for (int k=i; k>j; k--)
  item[k] = item[k-1];
```

To insert item i at position j we use the simple assignment

```
item[j] = item[i];
```

To display the data we can use the `display` method we wrote in Example 8.5. We leave that refinement until we write the Java code. We will also postpone the decision as to which random numbers to use until we write the code. We have refined all but the simplest subproblems and can put the complete pseudocode together in Figure 8.36.

Figure 8.36 Pseudocode for insertion sort

```
Input the size of the data;
Ask if the user wants to enter the data;
if (yes)
  loop
    Get the next item;
else
  loop
    Generate the next random item;
```

(Continues)

Figure 8.36 Pseudocode for insertion sort (continued)

```
Display the data to sort;
loop, from second item to last {
j = 0;
  while (item i > item j) j++;
  Save item i;
  for (int k=i; k>j; k--)
    item[k] = item[k-1];
  item[j] = item[i];
}
Display the sorted data;
```

Toward a Solution: Alternatives

Having completed the pseudocode for the insertion sort, we might think about other possible solutions. One alternative would allow us to combine the steps of finding the correct position and moving the elements to the right. For this alternative, when we insert element `i` we start checking at element `i-1` instead of at element 0. We leave the development of this alternative solution to the exercises.

Completing the Java Code

The pseudocode in Figure 8.36 gives us a good basis for writing the Java program.

EXAMPLE 8.9 InsertionSort.java

```
/* Sorts an array of data using the
 * insertion sort algorithm.  Uses
 * data from the user or random data.
 */

import javax.swing.*;
import java.util.*;

public class InsertionSort {
  public static void main(String [] args)  {
    String input = JOptionPane.showInputDialog
                    ("Enter the number of data items");
    int size = Integer.parseInt(input);
    int[] item = new int[size];       // allocate array to hold data
    input = JOptionPane.showInputDialog
              ("Enter 'Y' to enter data, 'N' for random data");
    char enter = input.charAt(0);
    if (enter=='Y' || enter=='y')
      for (int i=0; i<size; i++) {
        input = JOptionPane.showInputDialog("Enter item[" + i + "]");
        item[i] = Integer.parseInt(input);
```

```
      }
      else{
        Random random = new Random();
        for (int i=0; i<size; i++)
        item[i] = random.nextInt(100);                    // Note 1
    }
    System.out.print("The data to sort is ");
    DisplayArray.display(item);                           // Note 2
    for (int i=1; i<size; i++) {
      int current = item[i];                              // Note 3
      int j = 0;
      while (current > item[j]) j++;                      // Note 4
      for (int k=i; k>j; k--)
        item[k] = item[k-1];
      item[j] = current;
    }
    System.out.print("The sorted data is ");
    DisplayArray.display(item);
    System.exit(0);
  }
}
```

First Run

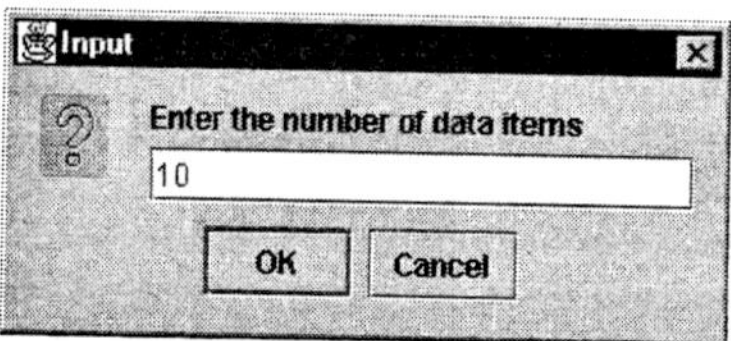

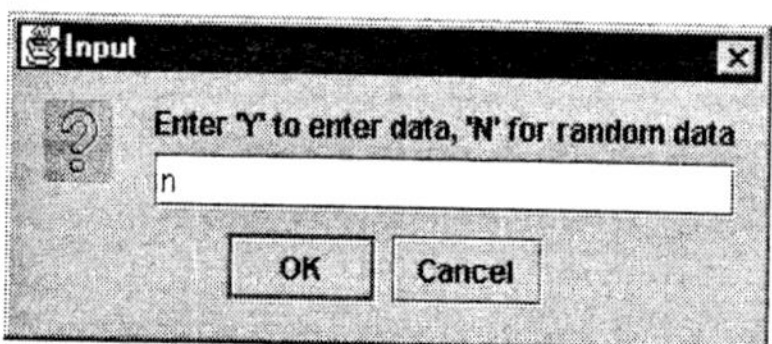


```
The data to sort is {51,70,41,62,95,89,63,78,80,5}
The sorted data is {5,41,51,62,63,70,78,80,89,95}
```

Second Run

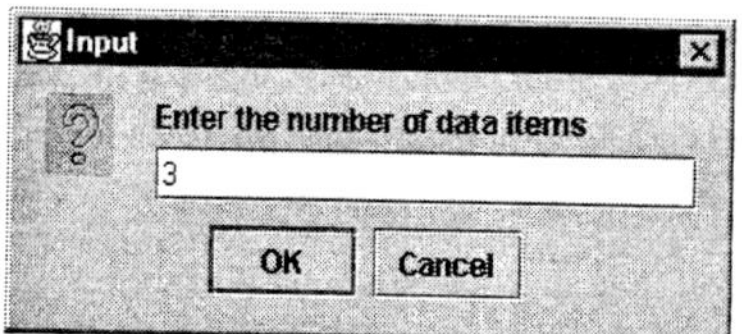

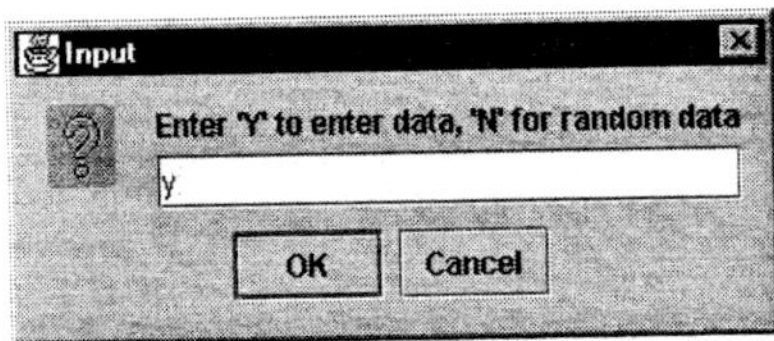

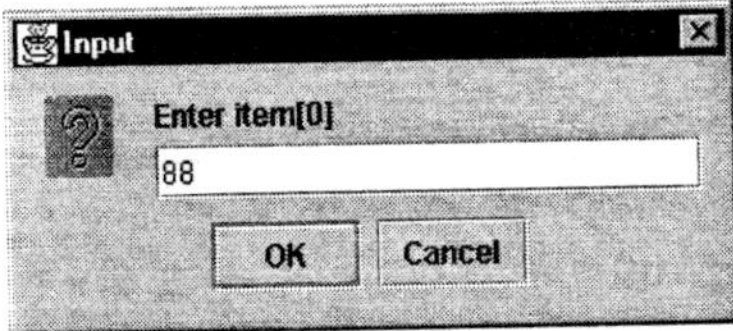

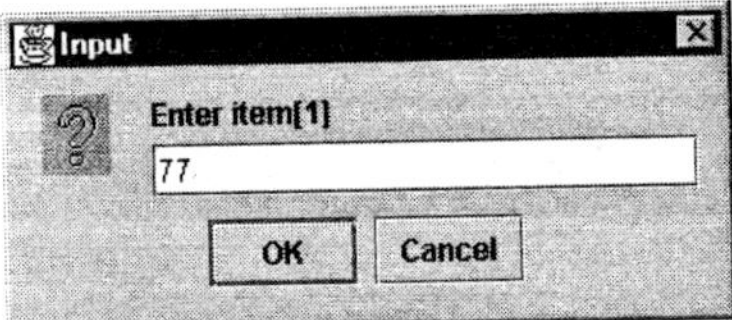

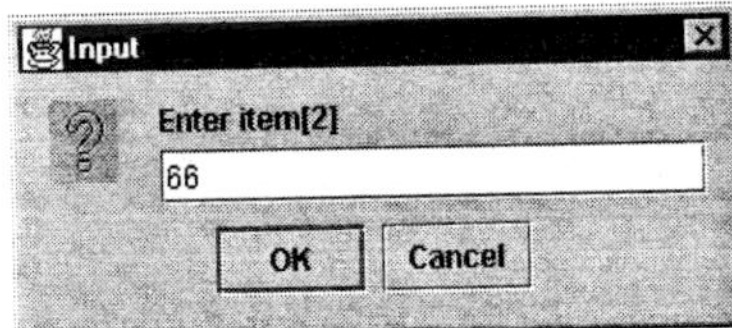


```
The data to sort is {88,77,66}
The sorted data is {66,77,88}
```

Note 1: To make the display shorter, we restrict our random numbers to the range 0 to 99.

Note 2: We could have included a display method in the `InsertionSort` class, but all we need is a generic method to display any array, and we already have such a display method in the `DisplayArray` class. We can call a `public` method from a class in the same package without using an `import` statement. All the code from Chapter 8 is in the same directory, which means all these classes are in the default package which is the current directory.

Note 3: We store the element at index `i` before we write over it. This store occurs in the pseudocode just before the inner for loop when we are about to write over item `i`. Since we refer to item `i` earlier in the code, in the `while` statement, we decided to store it earlier, before the `while` statement. This has the small advantage that, in the `while` statement, we can use the value of the variable `current` which is a little easier to look up than the array element, `item[i]`. It is like the difference between looking up a number in your personal address book or the big phone book. Either way you look up a value, but one way is a little easier. For beginning programmers, we rank clarity and ease of understanding higher than efficiency concerns, but good programmers need to be aware of performance. See the `A Little Extra` section which follows for a more important discussion of efficiency.

Note 4: Such a short loop body fits easily on the same line. It might make it stand out more to put it on its own line.

Testing the Code

We tested `InsertionSort` with two cases, one using random numbers and one with user supplied data. The user supplied the data in reverse order which is a special case worthy of testing. Realistically we should provide many more tests, but because of space limitations we defer that to the exercises.

A LITTLE EXTRA—GROWTH RATES

Polishing your code to improve efficiency is important since getting results fast is always a selling point in commercial projects. However, the best performance increases will come from using the best algorithm for the task. Data structures and algorithm analysis courses show how to analyze algorithms for efficiency, and present good algorithms for important computing tasks. As an introduction to this area, we will investigate the efficiency of the `InsertionSort` algorithm of Example 8.9.

The `System` class has a method, `currentTimeMillis()`, which returns a **long** value containing the current time in milliseconds from a starting point of January 1, 1970. We call this method, just before the loop to do the insertion sort, to get the start time, and just after to get the stop time. Computing `stoptime-starttime` tells us the time spent doing the insertion sort.

Example 8.10 revises Example 8.9 to add these timing statements.* We omit the output of the array since we want to run the program for very large arrays. For the same reason, we use only random number input, omitting the choice to let the user input the data.

The most interesting statistic about an algorithm is its growth rate. We want to know not just how much time insertion sort will take for a single array, but how does that time grow as the size of the array grows. In our test, sorting an array of size 1000 takes 210 milliseconds, while sorting an array of size 10000 takes 20149 milliseconds. If we repeat with the same size arrays, we will get similar results. The size of the data increased 10-fold from 1000 to 10000, while the time increased about 100-fold from 210 to 20149 milliseconds.

We say that the time needed by insertion sort has a rate of growth that varies as the square of the size of the data. Based on this growth rate, we would predict that running this program with an array of size 2000 should take about 800 milliseconds.

* In running this example we disabled the JIT (Just-In-Time compiler) which compiles the byte code during runtime to improve performance. The results will be similar with the JIT enabled, but we need to use larger data sizes, because the processing is so fast. To disable the JIT in Java 2, use the command `java -Djava.compiler=NONE InsertionSortTiming`.

Try it and see how good our prediction is. Figure 8.37 shows the number of steps plotted as a function of the size of the data.

Figure 8.37 Figure 8.37 Rate of growth of insertion sort

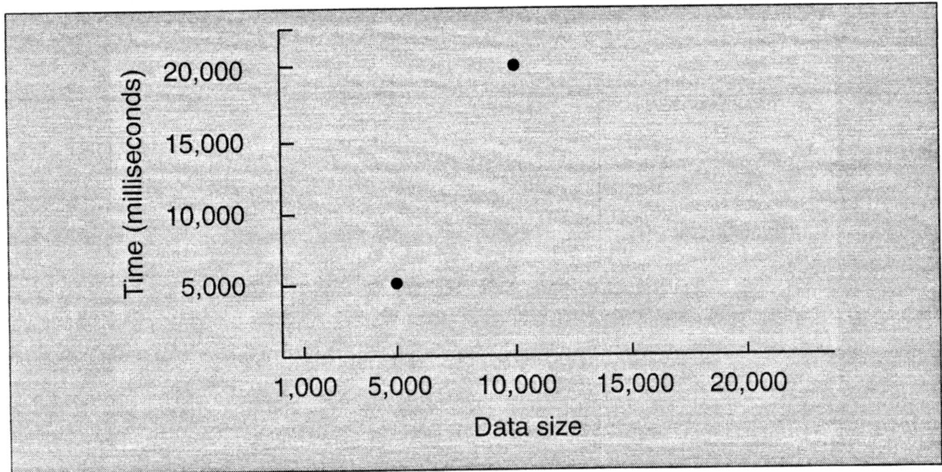

EXAMPLE 8.10 InsertionSortTiming.java

```
/* Sorts random numbers using the insertion sort algorithm.  Uses
 * random data. Outputs the milliseconds taken to sort.  Use this
 * program to estimate the efficiency of insertion sort.
 */

import javax.swing.*;
import java.util.*;

public class InsertionSortTiming {
  public static void main(String [] args)  {
    String input = JOptionPane.showInputDialog
                        ("Enter the number of data items");
    int size = Integer.parseInt(input);
    int[] item = new int[size];      // allocate array to hold data
    Random random = new Random();
    for (int i=0; i<size; i++)
      item[i] = random.nextInt(100);
    long starttime = System.currentTimeMillis();                // Note 1
    for (int i=1; i<size; i++) {
      int current = item[i];
      int j = 0;
      while (current > item[j]) j++;
```

```
      for (int k=i; k>j; k--)
        item[k] = item[k-1];
      item[j] = current;
    }
    long stoptime = System.currentTimeMillis();                    // Note 2
    System.out.println("The time used in milliseconds is "
                  + (stoptime-starttime));
    System.exit(0);
  }
}
```

First Run

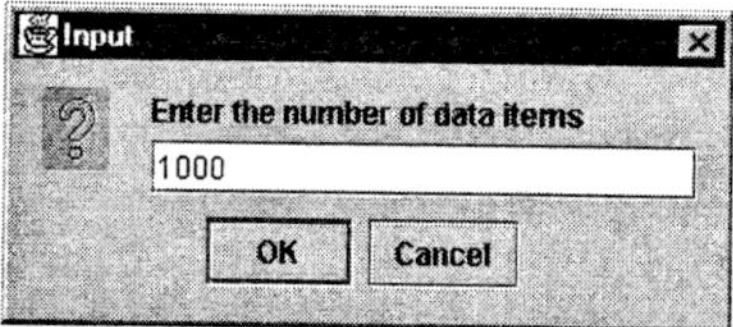


```
The time used in milliseconds is 210
```

Second Run

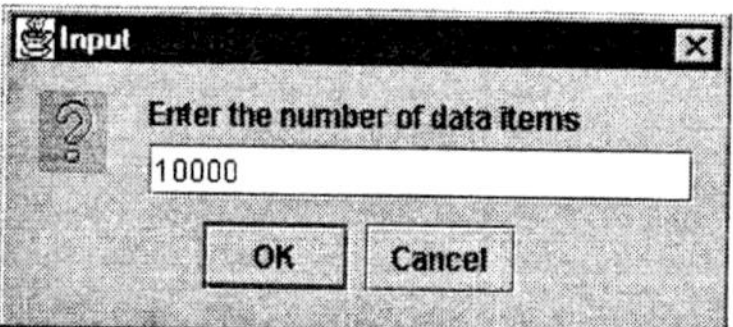


```
The time used in milliseconds is 20149
```

Note 1: We save the time just before the loop to do the sorting.

Note 2: We save the time just after the sorting loop, so that subtracting the start time from the stop time will give the time used by the sort.

> **THE BIG PICTURE**
>
> Carefully developed pseudocode makes it much easier to code correctly in Java. Insertion sort is one of many algorithms that use data stored in arrays. By adding timing statements we can estimate the efficiency of the code. For insertion sort, we find that the time used grows proportionally to the square of the size of the data.

TEST YOUR UNDERSTANDING

20. Show the stages of insertion sort by starting with the array 52, 38, 6, 97, 3, 41, 67, 44, 15 and showing that array after each insertion of an element in the correct position in its predecessors.

21. Change the insertion sort algorithm by providing a different refinement for the `insert item i` subproblem of Figure 8.32. In this solution, compare item `i` to item `i-1`, exchanging the two if item `i` is less than item `i-1`. Repeat this process of moving the original item `i` to the left until either that item is greater than or equal to its predecessor or there are no more predecessors.

TRY IT YOURSELF

22. Test Example 8.9 carefully with a range of test data.

23. Using the data of question 20, show each change in that array following the revised insertion sort algorithm of question 21.

TRY IT YOURSELF

24. (A LITTLE EXTRA) Add timing statements before and after the call to the `reverse` method in Example 8.6. Try test cases to estimate the rate of growth of time to reverse an array as the size of the array increases. If the size of the array doubles, by what factor does the time increase? Modify Example 8.6 to use random numbers to generate data to reverse.

8.7 A GUI for Insertion Sorting

With user interface components, we can enhance our console applications, make them more user friendly and interactive.

Defining the Problem

In this section we develop a graphical user interface to sort by insertion. In Example 8.9, we sorted data inputted by the user in a console window, displaying the sorted array in the same way, with no graphics. Here we provide a user-friendly interface that lets us see the insertion sort proceed graphically, step by step.

Designing a Solution: The Exploratory Process

Sometimes problems come to us fully formulated, with our job being to develop a good solution. Other times we have a general goal, but have not yet settled on the specific requirements. For example, we have the goal of providing a GUI for insertion sort, but have not decided on a specific design. A good approach in this situation is to do a little exploratory programming, trying out some ideas on a small scale to determine what might work nicely.

We will want to display the data in a bar chart, so let us start the exploratory process by trying to display data in a chart. We can use a text field to enter the data and a canvas to display it.

Our applet can register with the text field to be notified when the user hits the `Enter` key, after entering the next value. The applet implements the `actionPerformed` method, (which the text field will call when the user hits the `Enter` key), to get the data from the text field, and ask the canvas to repaint, displaying the data entered so far in a bar chart. Our program will be event-driven, getting the data and displaying when the user hits the `Enter` key.

Designing a Solution: Making a Chart

We need to figure out how to draw the chart. We might have very large or very small values, positive or negative values. The best approach is to simplify as much as possible, adding refinements later when we master the simpler cases. For now, let us use a 100x100 canvas, and integer data between 0 and 99, which will eliminate the problem of figuring out the vertical scale; we represent a value of 59 with a bar of height 59 pixels. To find the width of each bar, we divide the width of the canvas, 100, by the size of the data, dividing the canvas into equal parts for each bar.

To use the `fillRect` method to draw our bars, we need the upper-left corner for each bar and its height and width. Figure 8.38 shows the canvas with a few bars (unfilled).

Figure 8.38 Part of a bar chart

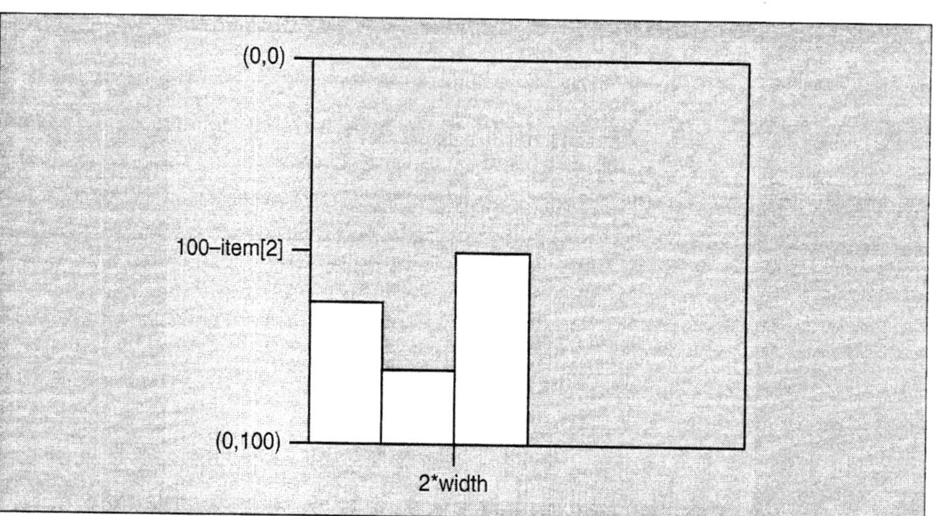

Because the coordinate origin is in the upper-left corner of the canvas, the upper-left corner of the bar representing the array element `item[i]` is `(i*width,100-item[i])` where `width` is the common width of each bar, given by `100/count`, and `count` is the number of elements entered thus far.

In the `paint` method, we draw a bar chart showing the values entered so far. Figure 8.39 shows the chart after the user entered the values 53, 22, and 75. Example 8.11 gives the code for this exploration.

Figure 8.39 The applet of Example 8.11

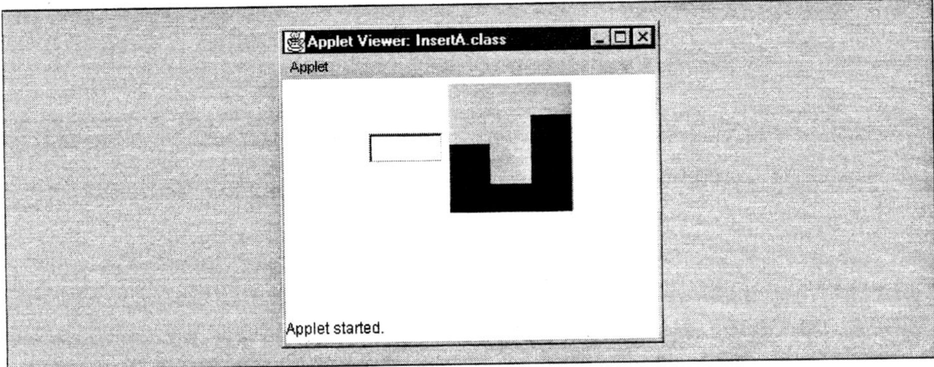

EXAMPLE 8.11 InsertA.java

```
/* Uses a text field to enter data and a canvas
 * to display the chart.  This is an exploratory
 * program to develop a GUI for insertion sort.
 */

import java.awt.*;
import java.awt.event.*;
import java.applet.Applet;

public class InsertA extends Applet implements ActionListener{
  public static int ITEM_SIZE = 10;
  public static int CHART_SIZE = 100;
  private TextField number = new TextField(5);
  private DrawOn canvas = new DrawOn();
  private int [] item = new int[ITEM_SIZE];                    // Note 1
  private int count = 0;     // number of item entered

  public void init() {
    add(number);
    canvas.setSize(CHART_SIZE,CHART_SIZE);
    canvas.setBackground(Color.pink);
    add(canvas);
    number.addActionListener(this);
  }
  public void actionPerformed(ActionEvent event) {
    item[count++] = new Integer(number.getText()).intValue();  // Note 2
    number.setText("");
    canvas.repaint();                                          // Note 3
  }
  class DrawOn extends Canvas {
    public void paint(Graphics g) {
    if (count > 0){                                            // Note 4
      int width = CHART_SIZE/count;                            // Note 5
      for (int i=0; i<count; i++)
```

```
            g.fillRect(i*width, CHART_SIZE-item[i],width,item[i]);       // Note 6
          }
        }
      }
    }
```

Note 1: We use an array of size 10, for simplicity, but later will allow different sizes of data.

Note 2: The only action listener is the applet who registers with the text field which generates an action event when the user hits the `Enter` key after entering a value. Here the applet gets the value from the text field, converts it to an integer using the expression

```
new Integer(number.getText()).intValue()
```

saves it in the next position in the array, and increments the count of the items entered so far.

Note 3: Because the user just entered another value, the applet asks the canvas to repaint the chart including this new value.

Note 4: When the applet starts, Java will call this `paint` method to draw the canvas once before the user has a chance to enter any values. While the count is still zero, we do not want to draw a chart.

Note 5: To get the width of each bar, we divide the width of the canvas, CHART_SIZE, by the number of data items, `size`.

Note 6: `g.fillRect(i*width,CHART_SIZE-item[i],width,item[i]);`
Figure 8.38 shows the canvas' coordinates and a few bars. We can see from this figure how to get the coordinates of the upper-left corner of each bar. The data value itself gives the height of the bar, because we do not need to scale the data.

Designing a Solution: Sorting

We can improve the chart later, but at least Example 8.11 shows that we are on the right track. For our next step, let us try to sort the data. Each time the user enters another value, we can insert it in the order of its predecessors. To do this we can just copy the code from Example 8.9 into an `insertNext` method to which we pass the array of data and the number of elements so far. The array holds ten elements but if the user just entered the third element, for example, the `insertNext` method should insert that value in the correct position with respect to its two predecessors, ignoring the array values beyond the third.

Figure 8.40 shows the chart just after the user entered the values 53, 22, and 75; as we can see, the values are sorted. Example 8.12 shows the additions to Example 8.11 needed to do the sorting.

Figure 8.40 The applet of Example 8.12

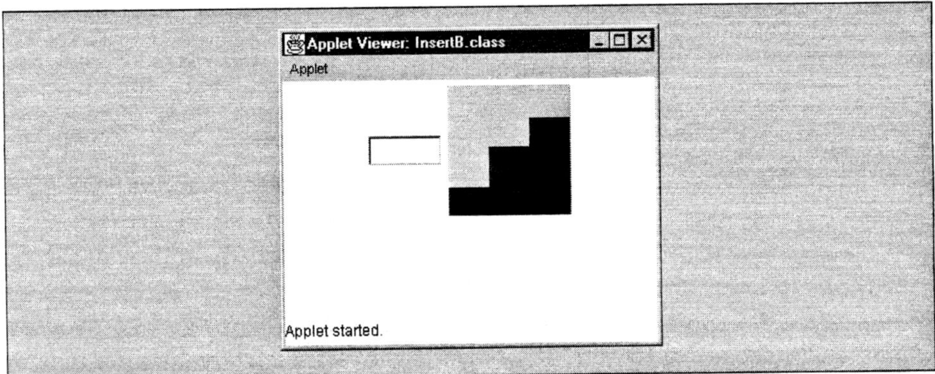

EXAMPLE 8.12 InsertB.java

```
/* Add an insertNext method to insert
 * each value in order as soon as the
 * user enters it
 */

  public class InsertB extends Applet implements ActionListener {
// The rest is the same as Example 8.11

public void actionPerformed(ActionEvent event) {
    item[count] = new Integer(number.getText()).intValue();
    insertNext(item,count++);                                    // Note 1
    canvas.repaint();
  }
  public void insertNext(int [] data, int size) {                // Note 2
    int current = data[size];
    int j = 0;
    while (current > data[j]) j++;
    for (int k=size; k>j; k--)
      data[k] = data[k-1];
    data[j] = current;
  }
}
```

Note 1: The applet inserts the next value in the correct position as soon as the user enters it in the text field and hits the *Enter* key to generate the action event.

Note 2: We copied the code for inserting the next element from Example 8.9.

We are making progress, but the chart does not look very nice with each bar the same color. We can greatly improve the appearance of the chart by drawing adjacent bars in different colors. To do this we add a simple statement

```
if (i%2==0) g.setColor(Color.green);
else g.setColor(Color.blue);
```

to the `paint` method to set the color to green if the index is even and to blue otherwise. We will see this improvement in our next example.

Designing a Solution: The User Interface

Now that we are comfortable with the sorting and drawing, we can think about the user interface. We will keep the text field for the user to enter data values, and add another text field for the user to specify the size of the array.

As in Example 8.9, it is nice to be able to select random input generated by the computer, or manual input from the user in the text field. We add two checkboxes in a checkbox group to make these selections. The user must select a method of input and specify the amount of input, so we add a button for the user to indicate the desired selections have been made.

Although we started our exploration using the default flow layout, the idea of putting a row of components in the `North` region of a border layout and the canvas with the chart in the `Center` appeals to us. We could create a panel and add four components to it, which are:

- A panel containing checkboxes for random or manual input, which uses a 2x1 grid layout so one checkbox will appear above the other.
- A panel containing a text field to input the size of the data and a label for the text field, which uses a 2x1 grid layout so that the label will appear above the text field.
- A button for the user to start the sorting (used when random input is selected).
- A panel containing a text field for the user to enter data and a label for the text field, which uses a 2x1 grid layout so the label will appear above the text field (used when the user enters data manually).

Let us see how the GUI looks before we try to make it work. In Example 8.13 we add the new components using the border layout, but do not respond to any events other than the text entry of Example 8.12. Figure 8.41 shows our new GUI.

EXAMPLE 8.13 InsertC.java

```
/* Adds components to the North region
 * of a border layout, and a canvas in
 * the Center.  Handles the same event as
 * Example 8.12, but no other events.
 */

public class InsertC extends Applet implements ActionListener {
  public static int ITEM_SIZE = 10;
  public static int CHART_SIZE = 100;
  private TextField number = new TextField(5);
```

Figure 8.41 The applet of Example 8.13

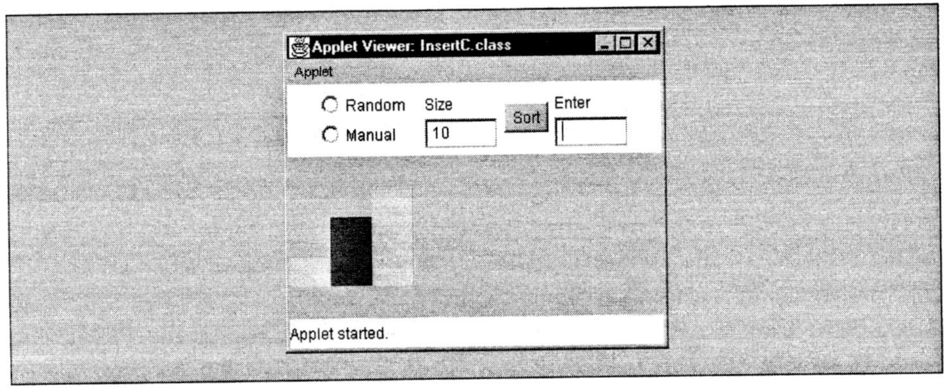


```
private DrawOn canvas = new DrawOn();
private int [] item = new int[10];
private int count = 0;
private CheckboxGroup acquire = new CheckboxGroup();
private Checkbox random = new Checkbox("Random",false,acquire);
private Checkbox manual = new Checkbox("Manual",false,acquire);
private Label size = new Label("Size");
private TextField getSize = new TextField("10",5);
private Button sort = new Button("Sort");
private Label enter = new Label("Enter");

public void init() {
  setLayout(new BorderLayout());
  Panel p = new Panel();                                    // Note 1
  Panel p1 = new Panel();                                   // Note 2
  p1.setLayout(new GridLayout(2,1));
  p1.add(random);
  p1.add(manual);
  p.add(p1);
  Panel p2 = new Panel();
  p2.setLayout(new GridLayout(2,1));
  p2.add(size);
  p2.add(getSize);
  p.add(p2);
  p.add(sort);
  Panel p4 = new Panel();
  p4.setLayout(new GridLayout(2,1));
  p4.add(enter);
  p4.add(number);
  p.add(p4);
  add(p,"North");
  canvas.setBackground(Color.pink);
  add(canvas, "Center");
  number.addActionListener(this);
}
```

```
// The rest is the same as Example 8.12
}
```

Note 1: `Panel p` is the panel we will add to the `North` region. We will add four components to it using its default flow layout.

Note 2: `Panel p1` is the first of the four components that we add to `p`.

Completing the Java Code: Making the User Interface Work

Our attempt at a GUI, shown in Figure 8.41, looks reasonable enough to attempt to continue the implementation. Before getting into the details of the implementation we need to look at a few techniques that we will need.

We can disable a component `c` using the statement

```
c.setEnabled(false);
```

and enable it with

```
c.setEnabled(true);
```

We should disable components when they should not be used. For example, when the user selects random data, we should disable the text field that allows the user to input data manually. Until we are ready to handle repeated sorting with different data, we should disable most of the components after we complete the first sort.

In addition to getting data from a text field, or reading the label of a button, we can also set these strings to desired values. We can clear the text field after each data entry, so that the user will not have to delete the previous value to enter a new one. After the user presses the *`Sort`* button to start the sorting, we can change that button's label to *`Next`* so the user can command that we insert the next value.

Returning to our GUI, we will start with both the *`Sort`* button and the data entry text field disabled. If the user selects random input we enable the *`Sort`* button, while if the user selects manual input we enable the data entry field. No matter what type of input the user selects, we disable both checkboxes after the first selection because we will not yet handle repeated sorting, or changes in the input method. We handle the item events generated by the checkboxes in the `itemStateChanged` method.

When the user enters the first number, the applet, registered with that text field as an action listener, will be notified, and will allocate an array whose size it gets from the other text field in which the user specified the array size. We initialize this field with a default size of 10. We only accept a data entry until the user has entered the specified number of elements. After processing the latest entry we set the text field to the empty string to make it easier for the user to enter the next element.

The applet also listens for button presses. On the first press, when the button has its original label, *`Sort`*, the applet gets the desired size of the data, creates the array, and fills it with random numbers from 0 to 99. The applet then asks the canvas to display the data, and changes the button's label to *`Next`* so the user can start inserting the items one by one.

Each time the user presses the *Next* button, the applet inserts the next element in order with respect to its predecessors and asks the canvas to display the data. Thus we see the sorting process step-by-step. The applet disables the button when all the elements have been inserted and the data is completely sorted.

In Figure 8.41 the canvas fills the whole center region, but the chart, using bar widths based on the 100 × 100 canvas size used in the flow layout, is over on the far left side of the canvas. To use the whole canvas, we get the size of the applet and compute the width of each bar as `(applet width)/count`, where `count` gives the number of data elements.

Figure 8.42 shows the sorting partially completed. Example 8.14 shows the changes from Example 8.13 needed to make the applet respond to the events generated by the user.

Figure 8.42 The applet of Example 8.14

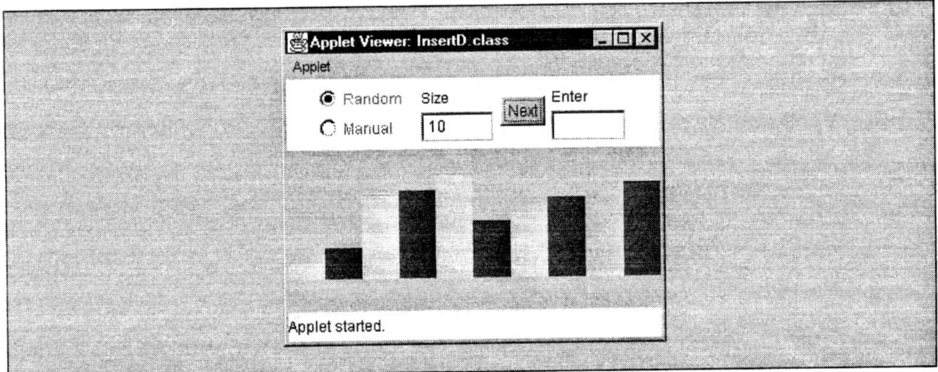

EXAMPLE 8.14 InsertD.java

```
/* Provides a user interface for insertion sorting.
 * The user can choose random data or input values
 * manually.  The user specifies the size of the data.
 * As the user inserts each item, the chart is redisplayed.
 */

public class InsertD extends Applet
               implements ActionListener, ItemListener {
  // The rest is the same as Example 8.13

int nextCount = 1;    // next random number to insert
int itemSize = 0;     // size of the data to sort
Dimension d;          // size of the applet

public void init() {
  ...
```

```
    d = getSize();
    number.setEnabled(false);                                   // Note 1
    sort.setEnabled(false);
    sort.addActionListener(this);                               // Note 2
    random.addItemListener(this);                               // Note 3
    manual.addItemListener(this);
  }
  public void itemStateChanged(ItemEvent event) {               // Note 4
    String label = (String)event.getItem();
    if (label.equals("Random"))
      sort.setEnabled(true);                                    // Note 5
    else if (label.equals("Manual"))
      number.setEnabled(true);                                  // Note 6
    random.setEnabled(false);                                   // Note 7
    manual.setEnabled(false);
  }
  public void actionPerformed(ActionEvent event) {
    Object source = event.getSource();
    String name = event.getActionCommand();
    if (source == number) {
      if (count == 0) {                                         // Note 8
        itemSize = new Integer(getSize.getText()).intValue();
        item = new int[itemSize];
      }
      if (count < itemSize) {
        item[count] = new Integer(number.getText()).intValue();
        insertNext(item,count++);
        canvas.repaint();
        number.setText("");                                     // Note 9
      }
      if (count == itemSize)  number.setEnabled(false);        // Note 10
    }
    else if (name.equals("Sort")) {
      itemSize = new Integer(getSize.getText()).intValue();
      item = new int[itemSize];
      count = itemSize;
      for (int i=0; i<itemSize; i++)
        item[i] = (int)(100*Math.random());
      canvas.repaint();
      if (count == 1)                                           // Note 11
        sort.setEnabled(false);
      else
        sort.setLabel("Next");                                  // Note 12
    }
    else if (name.equals("Next")) {
      insertNext(item,nextCount++);                             // Note 13
      canvas.repaint();
```

```
    if (nextCount == count) sort.setEnabled(false);                 // Note 14
    }
  }

  // Also change width in paint to d.width/size.
}
```

Note 1: Until the user selects either the random or the manual data entry, we disable both the *Sort* button and the data entry text field.

Note 2: The applet registers to listen for button presses.

Note 3: The applet registers to listen for checkbox selections.

Note 4: The checkbox calls this method when the user makes a selection.

Note 5: When the user selects random input, we enable the *Sort* button.

Note 6: `if (label.equals("Manual"))number.setEnabled(true);`
When the user selects manual input, we enable the data entry text field.

Note 7: `random.setEnabled(false); manual.setEnabled(false);`
We disable both checkboxes, so that the user cannot change the selection before the sorting is finished, and cannot repeat with new data.

Note 8: `if (count == 0) {`
When the user enters the first data element, we get the size of the data and allocate an array to hold the values.

Note 9: `number.setText("");`
We erase the current entry in the text field to make it easier for the user to enter the next value.

Note 10: `if (count == itemSize) number.setEnabled(false);`
When the user has entered all the values, we disable the text field.

Note 11: `if (count == 1)`
When count is 1 we have nothing more to do so we disable the *Sort* button. We really do not expect the user to choose to sort only one item, but our program should be correct if that unlikely event does occur.

Note 12: `sort.setLabel("Next");`
We change the button's label to *Next* to allow the user to insert each random number in the correct position in its predecessors.

Note 13: `insertNext(item,nextCount++);`
When the user presses the *Next* button, we insert the next item in order and display all the values, so the user can see the sorting step by step.

Note 14: `if (nextCount == count) sort.setEnabled(false);`
We disable the button when the sorting is complete.

Testing the Code

By developing our program in stages, we are also able to test it in stages. We tested the making of the chart in `InsertA`, the sorting in `InsertB`, and the look of the user interface in `InsertC`. Finally we test the implementation of the user interface in `InsertD`.

We should carefully test the two main use cases of this system, sorting with random input and sorting manually. When we select random input we check that the *Sort* button becomes enabled and the text field remains disabled. First we check the sorting using the default size of 10 and then check with size 1. With size 10, pressing the *Sort* button does display the chart properly and change the button label to *Next*. Pressing the *Next* button the first time inserts the second element in the correct place with respect to the first element. Pressing the *Next* button nine times results in a completely sorted array, at which time the *Next* button becomes disabled. Using size 1 causes the *Sort* button to be immediately disabled after we press it, which is what we want because there is no need to do anything further to sort one element.

When we select manual input of 10 items, we see that the *Sort* button is disabled and the *Enter* text field is enabled so we can enter the data to sort. Entering each value causes it to be placed in the correct order with respect to the data previously entered. After entering 10 items, the *Enter* text field becomes disabled.

In industrial strength systems much effort is spent in validating the input to ensure the program does not crash if the user enters incorrect data.*

> **THE BIG PICTURE**
>
> The development of a GUI for insertion sorting illustrates the exploratory development process. First we make the chart, then we add the sorting algorithm. Next we design the user interface, and finally we make the user interface work. At each stage we have a complete program we can test.

SUMMARY

- Arrays allow us to refer to large collections of elements conveniently. An array variable refers to the array; we use an index to refer to a specific element such as `myArray[2]`.
- To indicate an array type we add the square brackets, `[]`, to the element type. Thus **int**[ ] denotes the type of an array whose elements have type **int**, and **int**[ ][ ] denotes the type of an array whose elements have type **int**[ ].
- The statement `int[] myArray = {4,5,6};` declares an array variable, allocates space for three elements, and initializes the three elements to have values four, five, and six. Array indices start at zero, so that `myArray[0]` has the value four.
- Array variables refer to an array of elements. The statement `int[] myArray;` declares an array variable, but does not allocate space for elements to which it can

* We will cover the Java exception handling facility, which helps us check for and recover from errors, in Section 11.2.

refer. The statement `int[] myArray = new int[3];` uses the operator `new` to allocate space for an array of three integers to which the variable `myArray` refers. We still need to initialize this array with desired values.

- We can pass array arguments to methods and return array values from methods. A formal parameter of an array type has a copy of the reference to an array passed as the actual argument to the method, so that inside the method we can change the actual array argument passed from the caller, as we did in the `reverse` method of Example 8.6.
- An array of arrays is a collection of elements which are themselves arrays. Our test score example uses an array of arrays of test scores, where each array of test scores contains the scores for a single student. We can initialize an array of arrays with a literal, as in `int[][] x = {{2,3}, {4,5}};` and refer to elements using two indices, as in `x[1][0]` which has the value 4 in this example.
- Many applications involve sorting. The insertion sort arranges the elements of an array in order, by inserting each element in the correct position in its predecessors. It is useful for small arrays, but gives way to more efficient methods for larger arrays. We can add timing statements to determine the time taken by an algorithm as a function of the size of the data; we call this the growth rate of the algorithm. For insertion sort, we found that the time increased as the square of the size of the data.
- We can use exploratory programming to develop an interface step by step. At each stage we have a working program that provides some of the functionality we want, and can focus all our attention on the next enhancement. We used this technique to provide an interface for insertion sorting which lets us see each step of the sorting process.
- Arrays, which allow us to group data, are a part of almost every major programming language.

Skill Builder Exercises

1. Given the array

```
static int[] nums = {45,23,67,12,11,88,3,77};
```

what value does `split(0,7)` return, and how does the `nums` array change given the following Java code?

```
static void interchange (int a, int b){
  int temp = nums[a];
  nums[a] = nums[b];
  nums[b] = temp;
}
static int split (int first, int last) {
  int x, splitPoint;
```

```
    x = nums[first];
    splitPoint = first;
    for (int i = first;i <= last; i++)
      if (nums[i] < x) {
        splitPoint++;
        interchange (splitPoint,i);
    }
    interchange(first,splitPoint);
    return splitPoint;
  }
```

2. Find the array that results from the execution of `f(3,4,21)` where the code for the method `f` is:

```
public static int[] [] f(int n, int m, int value) {
  int[] [] x = new int[n] [m];
    for (int i=0; i < x.length; i++)
      for (int j=0; j < x[i].length; j++)
        x[i] [j] = value;
  return x;
}
```

3. Find the array that results from the execution of `g(5,34)` where the code for the method `g` is:

```
public static int[] [] g(int n, int value) {
  int[] [] x = new int[n] [];
  for (int i=0; i < x.length; i++) {
    x[i] = new int[i+1];
    for (int j=0; j < x[i].length; j++)
      x[i] [j] = value;
  }
  return x;
}
```

Critical Thinking Exercises

4. For each statement below, choose one of the following which best describes it

   i. declares an array only

   ii. declares an array, and allocates space for array elements

   iii. declares an array, allocates space for and initializes its elements with values supplied by the user

   iv. is incorrectly formed

   a. `int[] x;`

   b. `int y = {32, 41};`

   c. `int[] z = new int[5];`

   d. `int[] w = {5, 6};`

5. Consider the code

```
int[] x = {5,6,7,8,9};
int[] y = x;
y[2] = 3;
```

Which of the following is correct?

a. `x[2]` has the value `7`.

b. `x[2]` has the value `6`.

c. `x[2]` has the value `3`.

d. `y[3]` has the value `7`.

6. Choose one of the following which best describes the result of the statement

```
int[] myArray = display(score);
```

where `display` is the method of Example 8.5.

a. The array `myArray` will refer to the same array as `score` does.

b. The array `myArray` will refer to a different array than `score` does.

c. This statement is incorrectly formed.

d. None of the above

7. The statement

```
import java.util.Random;
```

as used in Example 8.7, tells the Java compiler that the code for

a. the file `Random.class` must be in the same directory as the file `Dice.class`.

b. the file `Random.class` must be in a directory named `java\util` which is a subdirectory of a directory in the classpath.

c. the file `Dice.class` must be in a directory named `java\util\Random`.

d. None of the above.

Debugging Exercise

8. A word is a palindrome if it reads the same backwards and forwards. For example, `dad` and `otto` are palindromes while `hat` and `boat` are not. The following program attempts to find if a word is a palindrome. The user enters the number of characters in the word, and then enters each character, using only lower-case characters. Find and correct any errors in this program.

```
public class Pal {
  public static void main(String [] args) {
    int size = Io.readInt("How many characters?");
    char [] a = new char[size];
```

```
      for (int i=0; i<a.length; i++)
      a[i] = Io.readChar("Enter next character");
      System.out.print("The word ");
      for (int i=0; i<a.length; i++)
        System.out.print(a[i]);
      for (int i=1; i<a.length/2; i++)
        if (a[i] != a[a.length-i]) {
          System.out.println(" is not a palindrome");
          System.exit(0);
        }
        System.out.println(" is a palindrome");
    }
  }
```

Program Modification Exercises

9. Modify the program to reverse an array in Example 8.3 to allow the user to repeat the code, reversing additional arrays during the same run of the program. Do not use any methods.
10. Modify Example 8.6 so that the `reverse` method returns a new array rather than changing the array argument passed to it. Display the original array after reversing it, to show that the original array has not changed.
11. Modify Example 8.8 to use a method to return the average score for each student.
12. Modify Example 8.8 to compute the class average for each test, rather than the average of the test scores for each student.
13. a. Modify the insertion sort program of Example 8.9 to use the insertion method described in the pseudocode of Test Your Understanding question 21.

    A LITTLE EXTRA b. Add timing statements to the code of to estimate the growth rate for the insertion algorithm (See Example 8.10).
14. Modify the insertion sort algorithm of Example 8.9 to sort an array of `String` objects. Use the `compareTo` method to replace the less than operator, <, used for integers.
15. Modify the array search program of Example 8.1 to search an array of `String` objects. Use the `equals` method to replace the equality operator, ==, used for integers.
16. Modify Example 8.3 to reverse an array of `String` objects.
17. Modify Example 8.6, which uses methods, to reverse an array of `String` objects.
18. Modify Example 8.14, the GUI for insertion sort, to indicate the number below each bar in the chart.

Program Design Exercises

19. a. Generate an array of 20 random integers from zero to nine. Search for the first occurrence, if any, of the number seven, and report its position in the array.

    b. Repeat the computation of part a 1000 times and for each position in the array, report the number of times that the first occurrence of a seven in the array is at that position.

20. Generate an array of 10,000 random numbers from zero to four. Report the percentage of each of the numbers, zero, one, two, three, and four in the array.

21. The standard deviation is a measure of the spread of the data with respect to the mean (average). Data with a small standard deviation will be clustered close to the mean and data with a larger standard deviation will be more spread out. To compute the standard deviation, find the mean, find the difference of each item from the mean, square those differences, find the average of those squares, and, finally, find the square root of that average which is the standard deviation. For example, given the data 10, 20, and 30,

mean	(10+20+30)/3 = 20
differences	(10-20) = -10 (20-20) = 0 (30-20) = 10
squares of differences	100, 0, 100
average of the squares	(100+0+100)/3 = 66.7
square root of the average	8.2

    Write a Java program to compute the mean and standard deviation of the elements in an array with elements of type **double**.

22. A company has five stores. Input the weekly sales for each store. Find the store with the maximum sales, the one with the minimum sales, and find the average weekly sales for the five stores.

23. A company has three regions, with five stores in the first region, three in the second, and two in the third. Input the weekly sales for each store. Find the average weekly sales for each region, and for the whole company.

24. A company has five stores. Input the weekly sales for each store. Determine which stores have sales in the top half of the sales range. In order to find the range of sales, first find the maximum and minimum sales. The range is the maximum minus the minimum.

25. a. Write a program to partition an array. Read in `n` values to an array, and a test value `x`. Rearrange the array, so that the elements up to and including index `p` are less than or equal to `x` and the elements from `p+1` to `n` are greater than `x`. Elements may be repeated. The test value, `x`, may be larger than all values or smaller than all values or in between somewhere. You may only visit each element once, and may not copy it to another array. For example, given

```
28 26 25 11 16 12 24 29 6 10
```

with test 17 the result might be

```
10 6 12 11 16 25 24 29 26 28
```

with partition index 4.

An outline of an algorithm is:

Start with markers at each end. Move markers towards each other until you find a wrongly placed pair. Allow for `x` being outside the range of array values.

While the two markers have not crossed over

> exchange the wrongly placed pair and move both markers inward by one.
>
> move the left marker to the right while elements are less than or equal to `x`.
>
> move the right marker to the left while elements are greater than `x`.

b. Add timing statements to the code of part a to estimate the growth rate of the array partitioning algorithm (See Example 8.10).

26. a. Write a Java program to perform a selection sort of an array of integers. In a selection sort, we find the smallest element of the array and interchange it with the first element. We repeat this process, finding the smallest element of the remaining elements and exchanging it with the first of the remaining elements. At each repetition the number of elements remaining decreases by one, until the whole array is sorted.

A LITTLE EXTRA

b. Add timing statements to the code of part a to estimate the growth rate of the selection sort algorithm (See Example 8.10).

27. Write a `Matrix` class to operate with `N×N` matrices. For example, we represent a 3×3 matrix as

```
{{2.3,4.1,-1.7}, {12.4,15.0,1.2},{2.0,3.0,4.0}}.
```

Provide the addition, subtraction, and scalar multiplication operations. Adding or subtracting two matrices `x` and `y` produces a matrix with each element the sum or difference of the corresponding elements of `x` and `y`. In formulas,

`z[i][j] = x[i][j] + y[i][j]` for the sum
`z[i][j] = x[i][j] - y[i][j]` for the difference

The scalar multiplication of a matrix `x` by a number `n` produces a matrix with each element the product of `n` times `x[i][j]`. For example 2.0 times the matrix above produces the matrix

```
{{4.6,8.2,-3.4},{24.8,30.0,2.4},{4.0,6.0,8.0}}.
```

Include a constructor with parameters to specify the dimension `n` of the matrix, and the array of arrays for its initial value. Use the `main` method to test, applying `Matrix` operations to several `Matrix` objects.

CHAPTER

9 Inheritance

OUTLINE

Introduction

Java is an object-oriented programming language. Object-oriented programming is especially useful in managing the complexity of very large software systems. It focuses on the objects, which are the most stable aspect of these systems. Designing with objects is natural for us and allows us to reuse designs in new contexts, making software less expensive to produce and easier to maintain. To get these benefits we need to use the full range of object-oriented techniques.

In this chapter, we focus on inheritance and include discussions of polymorphism and abstract classes, leading to a case study illustrating the flavor of the object-oriented programming paradigm using the object-oriented design techniques of use cases and scenarios. This case study develops the `AtmScreen` applet shown in Figure 9.1 prompting the user to select an account type. These account types, Savings and Checking use inheritance to extend the basic `Account` type.

Figure 9.1 The `AtmScreen` applet: select an account type

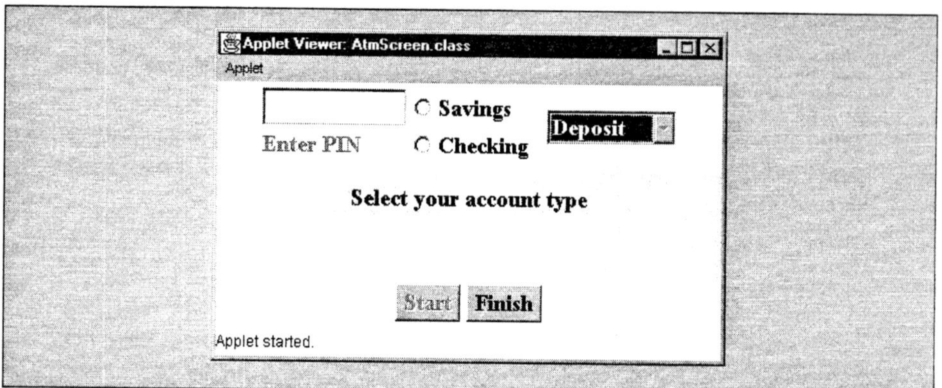

OBJECTIVES:

- Use inheritance to relate classes.
- Use polymorphism to improve design.
- Use abstract classes to achieve implementation independence.
- Understand the use of modifiers in specifying access.
- Develop an object-oriented design from use cases and scenarios.

9.1 Subclasses

Inheritance lets us do in Java what we do when classifying natural objects, which is to group common properties and behavior into a higher-level superclass. We can talk about objects generally on a higher level or more specifically with lower-level details.

Classification Revisited

Classification organizes knowledge. We divide living things into plant and animal categories. Among animals we differentiate reptiles from mammals, and among mammals we can tell cats from bats. Finally, we recognize individual cats, Tabby and Tom.

Using these categories we can refer to the `Animal` class for behavior, such as movement, that Tabby and Tom share just by being animals. The `Mammal` class stores the common property of having hair, and all `Cat` instances are carnivorous. Finally some properties differ from cat to cat. We have thin cats and fat cats, feisty cats and fraidy cats.

Classification reflects the IS-A relationship in that every `Mammal` is an `Animal`, and every `Cat` is a `Mammal`.

Class Hierarchies

Java lets us organize our classes into a hierarchy in which a class can have several **subclasses**, each of these subclasses can itself have subclasses, and so on. For example, our

BankAccount class could specify the state and behavior common to all bank accounts. A SavingsAccount subclass of BankAccount will define accounts that earn interest. SavingsAccount might have a TimedAccount subclass to define accounts in which we deposit funds for a fixed period of time. A CheckingAccount subclass of BankAccount will define accounts with check writing privileges. Figure 9.2 shows this

Figure 9.2 The account hierarchy

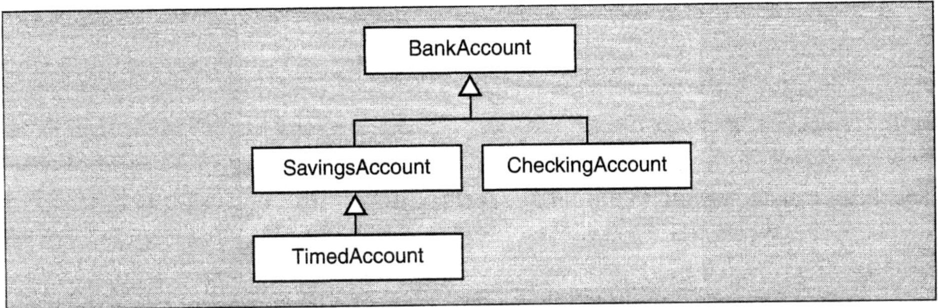

hierarchy of account classes.

Constructing a Subclass

To create a subclass, we **extend** a class, inheriting all the attributes and behavior of that class. A declaration for a SavingsAccount subclass would have the pattern

```
public class SavingsAccount extends BankAccount {
  .....
}
```

where the keyword **extends** tells us that SavingsAccount is a subclass of the BankAccount class. Here SavingsAccount is a subclass of BankAccount, and BankAccount is the **superclass** of SavingsAccount.

Example 9.1 creates a SimpleSavings1 class that simply extends BankAccount and does nothing more. We normally would not make such a simple extension that adds or changes nothing in BankAccount. We do it to illustrate that the subclass SimpleSavings1 inherits the state and behavior from its superclass BankAccount.

EXAMPLE 9.1 SimpleSavings1.java

```
/* Illustrates the simplest inheritance.
 */

public class SimpleSavings1 extends BankAccount {                // Note 1
}
```

Note 1: The `SimpleSavings1` inherits from the `BankAccount` class. Since the `BankAccount` class is in an unnamed package, it needs to be in the directory containing this example.

Example 9.2 tests the `SimpleSavings1` class. We see that we can declare a `SimpleSavings1` object which has an initial balance `$0.00`. `SimpleSavings1` inherits the `getBalance`, `deposit`, and `withdraw` methods from its `BankAccount` superclass.

EXAMPLE 9.2 UseSimpleSavings1.java

```
/* Tests the SimpleSavings1 class.
 */

public class UseSimpleSavings1 {
  public static void main(String[] args) {
    SimpleSavings1 ss1Acct = new SimpleSavings1();                // Note 1
    System.out.println("Initial balance is " + ss1Acct.getBalance());
    ss1Acct.deposit(400.00);                                      // Note 2
    ss1Acct.withdraw(50.00);
    System.out.println("Current balance is " + ss1Acct.getBalance());
  }
}
```

Output

```
Initial balance is 0.0
Current balance is 350.0
```

Note 1: The `SimpleSavings1` class of Example 9.1 does not contain any constructor. When a class has no constructors, Java will create a default constructor for it. Because `SimpleSavings1` is a subclass of `BankAccount`, its constructor will call a superclass constructor to initialize instance variables of its superclass, `BankAccount`. Because the default `SimpleSavings1` constructor has no arguments, it will call the default `BankAccount` constructor, which also has no arguments. The `BankAccount` default constructor initializes its balance variable to `$0.00`.

Note 2: A `SimpleSavings1` object inherits the behavior of its `BankAccount` superclass. It inherits the `deposit`, `withdraw`, and `getBalance` methods.

We cannot create a `SimpleSavings1` object with an initial balance different from `$0.00`. To do that, we need to add a constructor and pass the initial balance to it.

Subclasses do not inherit the constructors of their superclasses. Even though `SimpleSavings1` does not inherit the `BankAccount` constructors, it is a `BankAccount` and, as part of its construction, must use one of the `BankAccount` constructors to initialize the `balance` field it inherits. A subclass constructor calls a constructor for its superclass by calling the `super` method in the first statement, passing it any arguments that the superclass constructor needs.

We create another class, `SimpleSavings2`, to add the constructor. The code for the `SimpleSavings2` constructor is

```
public SimpleSavings2(double amount) {
  super(amount);
}
```

Java uses the keyword **super** to represent the superclass. The call

```
super(amount);
```

indicates a call to a superclass constructor for the `BankAccount` superclass of `SimpleSavings2`. Because we pass one argument of type **double**, the `BankAccount` superclass must have a constructor with one argument of type **double**.

EXAMPLE 9.3 SimpleSavings2.java

```
/* Creates a constuctor for the subclass which calls the
 * superclass constructor.
 */

public class SimpleSavings2 extends BankAccount {            // Note 1
  public SimpleSavings2(double amount) {                     // Note 2
    super(amount);
  }
}
```

Note 1: It would not work to extend `SimpleSavings1`. We leave it as an exercise to explain why not.

Note 2: Whenever a class has at least one constructor, Java will not create any others. By including only this constructor with one parameter, we have made it impossible to use a default constructor (with no arguments) for `SimpleSavings2`.

Example 9.4 tests the `SimpleSavings2` class. We create a `SimpleSavings2` object with an initial balance of $500.00.

EXAMPLE 9.4 UseSimpleSavings2.java

```
/* Tests the SimpleSavings2 class.
 */

public class UseSimpleSavings2 {
  public static void main(String[] args) {
    SimpleSavings2 ss2Acct = new SimpleSavings2(500.00);      // Note 1
```

```
      System.out.println("Initial balance is " + ss2Acct.getBalance());
      ss2Acct.deposit(400.00);
      ss2Acct.withdraw(50.00);
      System.out.println("Current balance is " + ss2Acct.getBalance());
  //  ss2Acct = new SimpleSavings2();                              // Note 2
    }
}
```

Output

```
Initial balance is 500.0
Current balance is 850.0
```

Note 1: The `SimpleSavings2` constructor passes the argument, `500.00`, to the `BankAccount` superclass constructor to initialize the account balance.

Note 2: We commented out this line because `SavingsAccount2` has no default constructor, and Java will not create one as it did for `SavingsAccount1`.

Adding State and Behavior to a Subclass

A subclass inherits the state and behavior of its superclass. The SavingsAccount class inherits the data fields and methods of the `BankAccount` class. Every `SavingsAccount` is a `BankAccount`. Our `BankAccount` class of Example 5.3 has an instance variable, `balance`, to hold the balance, and instance methods, `getBalance`, `deposit`, and `withdraw`. The `SavingsAccount` class extends `BankAccount`, so it will inherit the `balance` field, and the `getBalance`, `deposit`, and `withdraw` methods. The `SavingsAccount` class is a subclass of the `BankAccount` class, and the `BankAccount` class is a superclass of `SavingsAcccount`.

`SavingsAccount` can add additional state and behavior, which would only apply to the subclass. The `SavingsAccount` class needs an `interestRate` field to store the interest rate for an account, and a `postInterest` method to compute the interest and add it to the account balance. Example 9.5 shows these additions.

EXAMPLE 9.5 SavingsAccount.java

```
/* Defines a SavingsAccount subclass of BankAccount.
 */

public class SavingsAccount extends BankAccount {
  private double interestRate;                                      // Note 1

  public SavingsAccount(double amount, double rate) {               // Note 2
    super(amount);                                                  // Note 3
    interestRate = rate;                                            // Note 4
  }
  public void postInterest() {
    double balance = getBalance();
```

```
    double interest = interestRate/100*balance;                    // Note 5
    deposit(interest);                                             // Note 6
  }
}
```

Note 1: We add the `interestRate` field, where we intend the user to enter 5.0 for an interest rate of 5%.

Note 2: The `SavingsAccount` constructor has two parameters, the first to pass the initial account balance, and the second to pass the interest rate. We leave for the exercises the addition of additional constructors, such as a default constructor, or a constructor that passes an interest rate but not an initial balance.

Note 3: We pass the initial account balance to the superclass, `BankAccount`, constructor. This call to `super` must be the first line in the constructor.It would not work to try to initialize the balance field directly using

```
balance = amount;
```

`balance` is a private field and not directly accessible in the subclass. Even if it were permitted it would be less efficient. If we do not call a constructor Java will call a default constructor and initialize `balance` to `0.0`. We would then change it to `amount`, doing a second step when only one call to the correct superclass constructor is necessary.

Note 4: After calling the superclass constructor to initialize the superclass variables, we initialize `interestRate` directly.

Note 5: To convert a percent to a decimal, we divide by 100.

Note 6: `deposit(interest);`
We cannot add the interest to the private `balance` field directly, so we call the `deposit` method to deposit the interest to the savings account.

Example 9.6 tests the `SavingsAccount` class. The `NumberFormat` class helps to display the account balance nicely. We use the methods, `deposit`, `withdraw`, and `getBalance`, that `SavingsAccount` inherits from `BankAccount` as well as the `postInterest` method that it adds. If we create a `BankAccount`, we cannot call the `postInterest` method.

EXAMPLE 9.6 UseSavingsAccount.java

```
/* Tests the SavingsAccount class.
 */

import java.text.*;

public class UseSavingsAccount {
  public static void main(String [] args) {
    NumberFormat nf = NumberFormat.getCurrencyInstance();          // Note 1
```

```
      SavingsAccount s =  new SavingsAccount(500.00, 4.5);
      s.deposit(135.22);
      s.postInterest();
      s.withdraw(50);
      System.out.print("The balance of SavingsAccount s is "
                                   + nf.format(s.getBalance()));
   }
}
```

Output

```
The balance of SavingsAccount s is $613.80
```

Note 1: The `getCurrencyInstance` method returns a `NumberFormat` object configured for the user's locale. A user in France might see the amount in francs, while one in Mexico would see pesos.

Overriding Behavior

Objects exhibit their unique behavior. Each type of account can handle a withdraw request, for example, in its own way. A subclass automatically inherits the public methods of its superclass, but it may choose to **override** some of them to implement its own specific behavior.

The `SavingsAccount` class accepted the behavior it inherited. The `deposit`, `withdraw`, and `getBalance` methods work in the same way for the `SavingsAccount` subclass as they do for its `BankAccount` superclass. However, a class does not have to accept the implementations that it inherits.

We define a `CheckingAccount` class that charges a service charge for each check cashed unless the account balance is above a specified minimum balance, in which case check cashing incurs no charge. A `CheckingAccount` inherits the balance instance variable from `BankAccount`, and we add two additional instance variables,

`charge` The service charge if the balance is below the minimum

`minBalance` The minimum balance necessary to waive the check cashing charge.

The `CheckingAccount` class will inherit the `getBalance` and `deposit` methods from `BankAccount`, but will override the `withdraw` method to call a `processCheck` method because this type of checking account only permits withdrawals by check. A `CheckingAccount` is a kind of `BankAccount`, but it handles withdrawals in its own way. Figure 9.3 contains the code for the `CheckingAccount withdraw` method which overrides the `BankAccount withdraw` method.

The `CheckingAccount` class adds the `processCheck` method. It determines if the account contains the minimum balance necessary for free checks. If so it withdraws the amount of the check. If not, it withdraws the amount of the check plus the service charge. To remove the funds from the account `processCheck` uses the `withdraw` method of the `BankAccount` class. But there are two different `withdraw` methods. We

Figure 9.3 `Withdraw` method overrides `BankAccount` withdraw

```
public void withdraw(double amount) {
  processCheck(amount);
}
```

need to distinguish the superclass `BankAccount withdraw` method from the subclass `CheckingAccount withdraw` method.

When implementing `CheckingAccount` methods, calling

```
withdraw(40.00)
```

refers to `CheckingAccount withdraw`, while

```
super.withdraw(40.00)
```

refers to the superclass method, `BankAccount withdraw`.

TIP

Do not confuse overriding with overloading. An overloaded method has the **same** name as the original method, but **different** parameters. It provides an **additional** method for a class. For example, the `BankAccount` class of Example 5.3 has overloaded constructors, one with no parameters and the other with a single parameter of type **double**. A user of the `BankAccount` class may call either constructor,

```
new BankAccount()
```

or

```
new BankAccount(500.00)
```

An overridden method has the **same** name as the original method, and the **same** parameters. The new implementation of the method in the subclass **replaces** the old implementation of that method in the superclass. For example, the `CheckingAccount withdraw` method overrides the `withdraw` method of the `BankAccount` class. Each has one parameter of type **double.** We could overload the `withdraw` method by declaring a `CheckingAccount withdraw` method of the form

```
public void withdraw(int amount)
```

where the parameter has type **int**. The `CheckingAccount` class would then have two `withdraw` methods, one inherited from `BankAccount`, and one added with an **int** parameter. If you intend to override a method, make sure to use the same parameters that are used in the method you are overriding.

Figure 9.4 shows the inheritance relationship between the `BankAccount` class and its `SavingsAccount` and `CheckingAccount` subclasses. The UML uses the unfilled arrow to denote the inheritance relationship. The subclasses inherit from their parent superclass.

In Example 9.7, we illustrate inheritance with the code for subclass `CheckingAccount` of the `BankAccount` class.

Figure 9.4 Inheritance

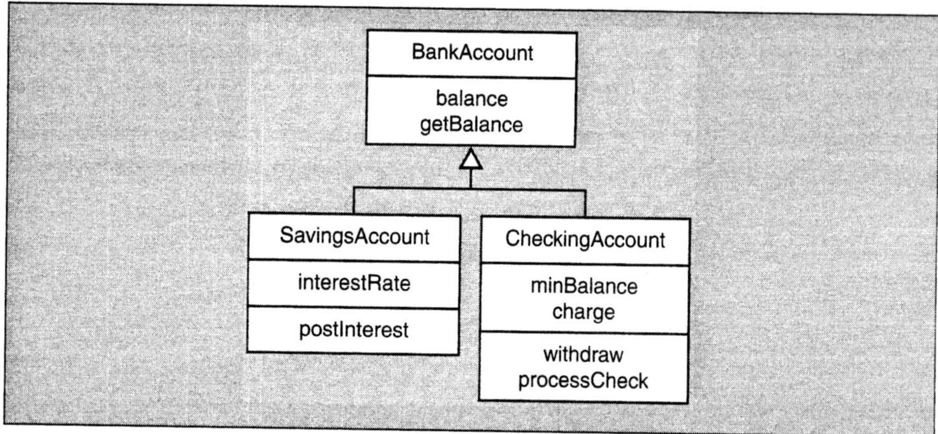

EXAMPLE 9.7 CheckingAccount.java

```
/* Defines CheckingAccount subclass of BankAccount.
 */

public class CheckingAccount extends BankAccount {
  private double minBalance; // Balance needed to avoid charge
  private double charge;     // Per check charge

  public CheckingAccount(double minAmount, double charge) {     // Note 1
    super();                                                     // Note 2
    minBalance = minAmount;
    this.charge = charge;
  }
  public void processCheck(double amount)  {
    if (getBalance() >= minBalance)
      super.withdraw(amount);                                    // Note 3
    else
      super.withdraw(amount + charge);                           // Note 4
  }
  public void withdraw(double amount) {                          // Note 5
    processCheck(amount);
  }
}
```

Note 1: We only define one `CheckingAccount` constructor. The arguments are the minimum balance needed for free checking, and the charge per check if the balance is below the minimum. We do not pass an initial balance to the `CheckingAccount` constructor, but do pass it to the constructor for the

SavingsAccount class to see the contrast. Each CheckingAccount object will start with an initial balance of $0.00.

Note 2: Because we do not specify an initial balance, we call the default constructor (the one with no arguments which sets the balance to zero) for the BankAccount superclass. If we omit this line, Java will add it anyway, because a subclass constructor must always call some superclass constructor to correctly initialize the part of the object inherited from the superclass.

Note 3: To call the BankAccount withdraw method, we use the prefix super. Because the balance is above the minimum needed for free checks, we withdraw the amount requested. We do not have to check if the amount requested is available, since the withdraw method performs that check.

Note 4: The balance is below the minimum so we withdraw the amount requested plus the service charge for the check.

Note 5: We override the BankAccount withdraw method to permit withdrawal only by check.

Example 9.8 tests the CheckingAccount class.

EXAMPLE 9.8 UseCheckingAccount.java

```
/* Tests the CheckingAccount class.
 */

import java.text.*;

public class UseCheckingAccount {
  public static void main(String [] args) {
    NumberFormat nf = NumberFormat.getCurrencyInstance();
    CheckingAccount c = new CheckingAccount(2500.00, .50);           // Note 1
    c.deposit(1000.00);                                               // Note 2
    c.processCheck(200.00);                                           // Note 3
    c.withdraw(100.00);                                               // Note 4
    System.out.println("The balance of CheckingAccount c is "
                          + nf.format(c.getBalance()));
  }
}
```

Output

```
The balance of CheckingAccount c is $699.00
```

Note 1: The minimum balance for free checking is $2500 and the service charge per check if the balance is below $2500 is $.50.

Note 2: Because the initial account balance is zero, we first make a deposit.

Note 3: Because the balance is below $2500, we will withdraw $200.50 to cover the amount requested and the service charge.

Note 4: Because the balance is below $2500, we will withdraw $100.50 to cover the amount requested and the service charge.

The Object Class

The `Object` class, in the `java.lang` package, is a superclass of every Java class. A class, such as `Person` from Example 5.8, that does not explicitly extend any class, implicitly extends `Object`. Java treats the `Person` class as if we had declared it as

```
public class Person extends Object {// same as Example 5.8}
```

Our `SavingsAccount` class from Example 9.5 explicitly extends `BankAccount`, while `BankAccount` implicitly extends `Object`. The Java library classes all directly or indirectly extend `Object`.

The `Object` class provides a default implementation of the `toString` method that returns an empty string. Because every class inherits from `Object`, every class can invoke its `toString` method. For example, a `BankAccount` object, `myAccount`, is also an `Object`, so we can invoke the `toString` method, explicitly as in

```
System.out.println( myAccount.toString());
```

or implicitly, as in

```
System.out.println(myAccount);
```

either of which will display an empty string. Any class that wants to have a string representation should override the `toString` method as we did in Example 5.8 for the `Name`, `Address`, and `Person` classes. Figure 9.5 shows the `BankAccount` class inheriting the `toString` method from `Object`, while the `Person` class overrides it.

TEST YOUR UNDERSTANDING

1. Each class, except `Object`, extends another class either implicitly or explicitly. For each of the following classes, which class does it extend?

   a. `SavingsAccount` b. `String` c. `BankAccount` d. `Address` e. `CheckingAccount`

2. Declare and initialize a `SavingsAccount`, `s`, with an initial balance of $50.00 and an interest rate of 3.5 percent.

3. Declare and initialize a `CheckingAccount`, `c`, which requires a minimum balance of $1500 to avoid the $.35 service charge per check.

4. Describe the output from each of the following, where `s` is the `SavingsAccount` defined in question 2, and

Figure 9.5 Inheriting from `Object`

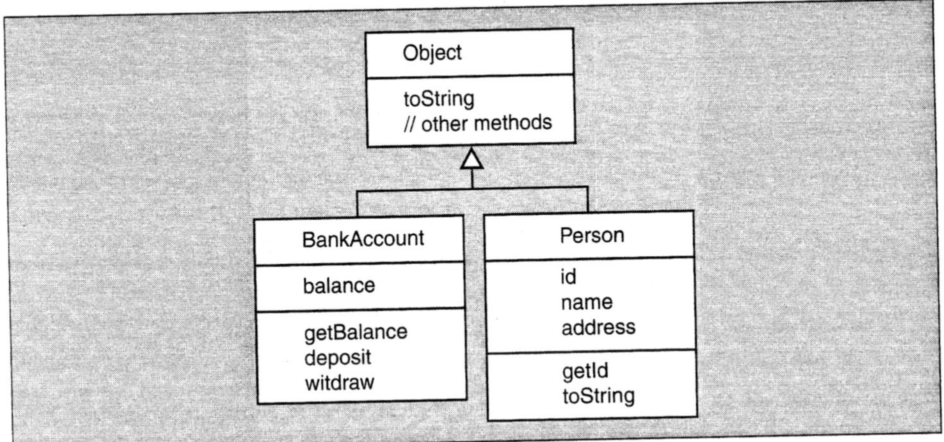

THE BIG PICTURE

The superclass contains data and operations common to all subclasses. Rather than duplicating these fields in each subclass, we let the subclasses inherit them from the superclass. A subclass can override inherited methods and/or add additional methods and data fields.

Inheritance supports the IS-A relationship in which a subclass object is also a type of superclass object.

```
Name president = new Name("Abraham", "Lincoln");
String s3 = "horse";
```

a. `System.out.println(s);` b. `System.out.println(s3);`

c. `System.out.println(president);`

5. Suppose we add a `withdraw` method to the `SavingsAccount` class, using the pattern

```
public void withdraw(double amount, boolean receipt)
      { ... },
```

which would perform the withdrawal giving a receipt if the **boolean** variable `receipt` is **true**. Would we be overriding the `withdraw` method of the `BankAccount` superclass, or overloading it? Explain.

9.2 Polymorphism

With **polymorphism** we get the benefit of letting each type of object define its own behavior. Our programs ask objects to do something, but each does that operation in its own way. Our programs are easier to create and maintain because we leave to the objects the details of how to perform their operations.

Polymorphic Operations

When we say "that animal is eating," it could mean that a lion is tearing flesh from its kill or that a giraffe is munching tree leaves. Each subclass of `Animal` has its own way of eating. The eating operation is **polymorphic**, meaning that it has many structures. A lion implements it in one way, while a giraffe does something quite different, but they both eat.

Most of us do not talk to the animals, but if we did, we could command `animal1 eat, animal2 eat,...` and so on. Each animal knows how to eat, and will do so in its own way. We do not even have to know what kind of animals we are talking to, or how they eat. Our command is like a program that will execute correctly, even if other animals come along later that we had not known about. We say `animal902 eat`, and it eats because it knows how to eat.

Our command program would not be nearly as flexible if we had to know the type of each animal. We could start commanding `lion eat, giraffe eat`, but this program only works for a lion followed by a giraffe, and does not allow for some other type of animal. Our earlier command was more flexible because we used the superclass type, `Animal`, in our command, rather than the subclass types, `Lion` and `Giraffe`.

Compile-time and Run-time Types

Our common usage shows that we talk of animals in general, but, of course, each animal is really a specific type such as a lion or a giraffe. In Java we distinguish between the compile-time type of an object variable and its run-time type.

- `Compile-time type` The variable's declared type.
- `Run-time type` The type of the object to which the variable currently refers.

The run-time type may be the same as the compile-time type or it may be any subclass of it. For example, if we declare

```
Animal herman;
```

`herman` has the compile-time type `Animal`. After the code

```
herman = new Lion();
```

`herman` has the run-time type `Lion`, because the variable `herman` refers to a `Lion`.

Inheritance allows us to assign a subclass object to a superclass variable. It works because a subclass object is also a superclass object. A `Lion` is an `Animal`. Later on in code, we might include the lines

```
Animal zelda;
zelda  = new Giraffe();
```

zelda has the compile-time type Animal, and the run-time type Giraffe, which is also an Animal.

The power of polymorphism comes when we write code that is very general and easy to maintain. Figure 9.6 shows a feed method that will feed any type of animals.

Figure 9.6 Illustrating polymorphism

```
public void feed(Animal[] theZoo) {
  for (int i= 0; i < theZoo.length; i++)
    theZoo[i].eat();
}
```

We can use the feed method to feed lions or giraffes or any kind of animal. For example, we feed herman and zelda using the code

```
Animal[] two = {herman, zelda};
feed(two);
```

When Java executes the feed method it uses the run-time type of each array element to determine which method to call. If theZoo[i] refers to a Lion, it calls the Lion eat method, but if it refers to a Giraffe it calls the Giraffe eat. As programmers, we do not have to distinguish one animal from another. We let each object eat in its own way.

We must remember however that any method we expect to work for each subclass must occur in the common superclass.

TIP ☛

Suppose we try another command,

```
theZoo[i].brushTeeth();
```

If theZoo[i] refers to our brother, this command might be diligently executed, but if theZoo[i] refers to a lion, that lion might show us his teeth, but he would not be brushing them. Not every animal brushes its teeth. To use specialized methods we must declare the object to have the subclass type containing those methods. For example to use an attack method that a Lion has but not a Giraffe, we use the code

```
Lion salina = new Lion();
salina.attack();
```

The attack method does not apply to all animals.

Example 9.9 illustrates polymorphism with the simplified Animal hierarchy for clarity. We provide a first version of an Animal class, which we will revise when we discuss abstract classes.

EXAMPLE 9.9 Animal.java, Lion.java, Giraffe.java, UseAnimals.java

Animal.java

```
/* A first version of the Animal class.
 */

public class Animal {
    public void eat() {                                      // Note 1
    }
}
```

Lion.java

```
/* Lions eat and attack.  The Lion class overrides the Animal
 * eat method, and adds an attack method.
 */

public class Lion extends Animal {
    public void eat() {                                      // Note 2
        System.out.println("Eating like a lion");
    }
    public void attack() {                                   // Note 3
        System.out.println("Attacking like a lion");
    }
}
```

Giraffe.java

```
/* Giraffes eat and look around.  The Giraffe class overrides
 * Animal eat and adds a lookAround method.
 */

public class Giraffe extends Animal {
    public void eat() {
        System.out.println("Eating like a giraffe");
    }
    public void lookAround() {
        System.out.println("Looking around like a giraffe");
    }
}
```

UseAnimals.java

```
/* Uses Animal objects polymorphically.
 */

public class UseAnimals {
    public static void feed(Animal[] theZoo) {
        for (int i= 0; i < theZoo.length; i++)
            theZoo[i].eat();
    }
    public static void main(String[] args) {
```

```
        Animal herman = new Lion();
        Animal zelda = new Giraffe();
        Animal[] two = {herman, zelda};
        feed(two);                                    // Note 4
        Lion leo = new Lion();
        leo.attack();                                 // Note 5
    }
}
```

Output

```
Eating like a lion
Eating like a giraffe
Attacking like a lion
```

Note 1: We implement the `eat` method to do nothing, because `Animal` is a general category with no method of eating that applies to it.

Note 2: `Lion` overrides the `eat` method of `Animal` to eat like a lion. We omit more realistic descriptions of lions eating.

Note 3: We add the specialized `attack` method to the `Lion` class. Because it does not occur in the `Animal` class we cannot invoke it for an object declared as an `Animal`.

Note 4: The `feed` method is very general. It runs through its array argument, invoking the `eat` method for each `Animal`. At run time Java determines what each array element refers to and calls the correct `eat` method. Because `herman` refers to a `Lion`, Java will call the `Lion eat` method, rather than `Animal eat`. For `zelda`, Java will call `Giraffe eat`. Because Java determines which method to call while the program is running, we call this process **dynamic binding**.

Note 5: Because we declared `leo` to have type `Lion`, we can call the specialized `attack` method. We cannot call the `attack` method for `herman`, because we declared `herman` to have type `Animal`. The compile-time type determines which method we can invoke for an object.

To appreciate the advantages of polymorphism, we show that the same feed method works even if we add a new type of `Animal`. We add a `Duck` class and create a new `Animal` array including a duck. Our test program shows that the feed method needs no changes to work correctly.

EXAMPLE 9.10 Duck.java, UseNewAnimal.java

Duck.java

```
/* A Duck eats.  The eat method overrides Animal eat.
 */
```

```
public class Duck extends Animal {
  public void eat() {
    System.out.println("Eating like a duck");
  }
}
```

UseNewAnimal.java

```
/* Shows that the feed method works unchanged
 * when ducks are included.
 */

public class UseNewAnimal {
  public static void feed(Animal[] theZoo) {
    for (int i= 0; i < theZoo.length; i++)
      theZoo[i].eat();                                    // Note 1
}
  public static void main(String[] args) {
    Animal herman = new Lion();
    Animal zelda = new Giraffe();
    Animal don = new Duck();
    Animal[] three = {herman, zelda, don};
    feed(three);
  }
}
```

Output

```
Eating like a lion
Eating like a giraffe
Eating like a duck
```

Note 1: Java will check at run time to determine what type of `Animal` each array element references. It will call the correct eat method. The programmer of the `feed` method does not have to know how each `Animal` eats. Each subclass of `Animal` implements the eat method in the manner appropriate for it.

The BankAccount Hierarchy

Now that we have illustrated polymorphism using `Animal` and its subclasses, we return to the `BankAccount` hierarchy. We cannot make our bank accounts eat, but we can make withdrawals. To use polymorphism, we refer to all our accounts using the superclass type `BankAccount`. After all, every `SavingsAccount` or `CheckingAccount` is a `BankAccount`, just as every lion or giraffe is an animal.

Suppose we have several `BankAccount` objects, `b1`, `b2`, and `b3`. We can command them to withdraw $50 each with the statements

```
b1.withdraw(50.00);  b2.withdraw(50.00);
b3.withdraw(50.00);
```

We do not have to know what kind of bank accounts `b1`, `b2`, and `b3` are, because every bank account knows how to withdraw, just as every animal knows how to eat. This is the beauty of object-oriented programming—each object implements its own behavior.

If bank account `b1` happens to be a checking account, it will deduct a service charge if the balance is below the minimum for free checking; we just ask it to withdraw, and trust `b1` to know how to process a `withdraw` request. Our little program is quite flexible. We can apply it at some future time when we have written a `TimedAccount` subclass of `BankAccount` which overrides the `withdraw` method to prohibit withdrawals. If `b2` happens to refer to a `TimedAccount` then Java will execute the `withdraw` method defined in the `TimedAccount` class.

The `withdraw` operation has many structures, depending upon which subclass of `BankAccount` is processing the withdrawal. As we saw with animals, to get the flexibility of polymorphism, we need to refer to objects by their superclass type. We start by creating two BankAccount objects (see Figure 9.7)

Figure 9.7 Two BankAccount objects

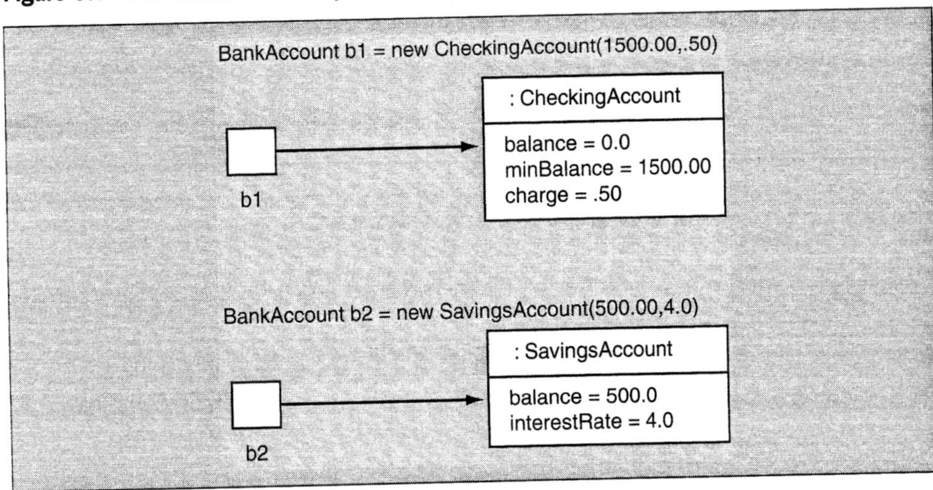

We declare `b1` with type `BankAccount`, but actually assign it a value of type `CheckingAccount` which is a subtype of `BankAccount`. Similarly, we declare `b2` with type `BankAccount`, but assign it a `SavingsAccount`. If we make a deposit and withdrawals

```
b1.deposit(400.00);
b1.withdraw(50.00);
b2.withdraw(50.00);
```

`b1` will process the `withdraw` using `CheckingAccount withdraw`, deducting a service charge, while `b2` will process the `withdraw` using `SavingsAccount withdraw` (inherited from `BankAccount`), not deducting a service charge.

If we now change `b2` to refer to the `CheckingAccount` to which `b1` refers, and then do a withdrawal, as in

```
b2 = b1;
b2.withdraw(50.00);
```

the account b2 will now process the withdrawal using `CheckingAccount withdraw`, and will deduct a service charge, because as shown in Figure 9.8, b2 refers to a checking account.

Figure 9.8 Variable b2 refers to a checking account

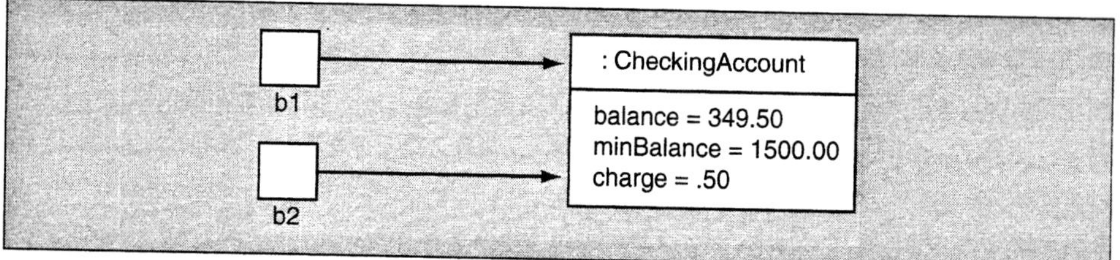

As the program is running, Java determines to which type object the variable `b2` refers, and invokes the `withdraw` method for that type.

EXAMPLE 9.11 Withdraw.java

```
/*  Uses the withdraw operation of  BankAccount and its
 *  subclasses to illustrate polymorphism.
 */

import java.text.*;

public class Withdraw {
  public static void main(String [] args) {
    NumberFormat nf = NumberFormat.getCurrencyInstance();
    BankAccount b1 = new CheckingAccount(1500.00,.50);         // Note 1
    BankAccount b2 = new SavingsAccount(500.00, 4.0);
    b1.deposit(400.00);
    b1.withdraw(50.00);                                        // Note 2
    System.out.println
      ("The balance of the BankAccount to which b1 refers is "
          + nf.format(b1.getBalance()));
    b2.withdraw(50.00);                                        // Note 3
    System.out.println
      ("The balance of the BankAccount to which b2 refers is "
        + nf.format(b2.getBalance()));
    b2 = b1;                                                   // Note 4
    b2.withdraw(50.00);                                        // Note 5
    System.out.println
    ("The balance of the BankAccount to which b2 refers is "   // Note 6
      + nf.format(b2.getBalance()));
  }
}
```

Output

```
The balance of the BankAccount to which b1 refers is $349.50
The balance of the BankAccount to which b2 refers is $450.00
The balance of the BankAccount to which b2 refers is $299.00
```

Note 1: The key to using polymorphism is to declare objects of a general superclass type but assign instances of various subclasses. We do that here, declaring `b1` to have type `BankAccount`, but assigning it an object of type `CheckingAccount`.

Note 2: Because `b1` refers to a `CheckingAccount`, the `withdraw` deducts a service charge.

Note 3: Because `b2` currently refers to a `SavingsAccount`, the `withdraw` does not deduct a service charge.

Note 4: We change `b2` to refer to a `CheckingAccount`.

Note 5: Because `b2` now refers to a `CheckingAccount`, the `withdraw` deducts a service charge.

Note 6: `"The balance of the BankAccount to which b2 refers is"`
The variable `b2` refers to some bank account object, either a `SavingsAccount` or a `CheckingAccount`. This example shows that we can change this reference during the course of the program among various subclasses of `BankAccount` which is the declared type of `b2`.

We illustrated polymorphism with animals eating and withdrawals from bank accounts. Every bank account can process a withdrawal and every animal can eat. Just as we cannot expect every animal to brush its teeth, we cannot expect every bank account to process a check. Only a `CheckingAccount` has a `processCheck` method. If we declare `b` as a `BankAccount`, we can only call methods of the `BankAccount` class, even though `b` might actually refer to a `CheckingAccount` at some point in the code. For example, given the code

```
BankAccount b;
 ...
b = new CheckingAccount(750.00, .75);
 ...
b.processCheck(50.00);        // rejected
```

Java will reject the `processCheck` statement. We declared `b` to have type `BankAccount`, which cannot always process a check. At runtime `b` might actually refer to a `CheckingAccount` which can process a check, but then again it might refer to a `SavingsAccount` which cannot. The Java compiler stops us from making a fatal runtime error, allowing only a method, like `deposit` or `withdraw`, that every account can execute.

If we want to use methods that apply only to a certain type of account, then we should declare our objects to be of that type. For example, declaring b to be a `CheckingAccount` will allow us to execute `b.processCheck`.

THE BIG PICTURE

Polymorphism is one of the key benefits of object-oriented programming. A statement such as `animal.eat()` will apply to objects of any subclass of animal, such as lions and giraffes, and will apply to those objects yet to be defined, such as ducks. Such code needs less modification because it is independent of the details of how each type of animal eats, which are left to the subclasses to implement.

TEST YOUR UNDERSTANDING

6. If we declare `b` as in

```
BankAccount b = new CheckingAccount(1500.00,.50);
```

which of the following will generate a compiler error?

a. `b.deposit(100.00);` b. `b.processCheck(25.25);`

c. `b.postInterest();` d. `b.getBalance();`

e. `b.withdraw(75.00);`

7. If we declare `b` as in

```
CheckingAccount b = new CheckingAccount(1500.00,.50);
```

which of the method calls of question 6 will generate a compiler error?

9.3 Abstract Classes

`Abstract classes` let us talk about operations in general without creating instances. They may defer implementation details to concrete subclasses. For example, nothing is just an `Animal`. Every animal is a member of some subclass such as `Lion` or `Giraffe`. The class `Animal` has no instances, in contrast to the class `Lion`, which has various, perhaps ferocious, instances.

Declaring an Abstract Class

Java uses the modifier `abstract` to denote that a class cannot have any instances. Figure 9.9 revises the `Animal` class to be abstract. The only change we make to the `Animal` class in Example 9.9 is to add the `abstract` modifier in the class declaration.

Figure 9.9 Making the `Animal` class abstract

```
public abstract class Animal {
  public void eat() {
  }
}
```

By making `Animal` abstract, we prohibit the creation of `Animal` objects. The code

```
Animal error = new Animal();      // incorrect
```

will not compile. Remember that `Animal` is a general concept. We never want just an `Animal`, but rather we would like one of its subclasses such as `Lion` or `Giraffe`.

TIP We can still declare an object whose compile-time type is an abstract class.

The declaration

```
Animal anAnimal;
```

is legal. Until `anAnimal` refers to an object it has the value **null**. We can assign any concrete subclass of `Animal` to `anAnimal`. For example,

```
anAnimal = new Giraffe();
```

is legal.

Polymorphism and Abstract Classes

Polymorphism does not require abstract classes but often works together with them. We use an abstract class to specify the behavior common to a number of concrete classes, just as the `Animal` class specifies that every `Animal` can eat. Programs that use the operations of the abstract class will work for objects of any subclass of that class. We saw in Example 9.10 that the `feed` method continued to work with `Duck` objects that were not even created when `feed` was first used in Example 9.9 with `Lion` and `Giraffe` objects.

In retrospect, now that we have `SavingsAccount` and `CheckingAccount` classes, our `BankAccount` class might be better defined to have no instances. We never want an object that is just a `BankAccount`; every account is either a `CheckingAccount` or a `SavingsAccount`. Declaring `BankAccount` using the pattern

```
public abstract class BankAccount { // same as before }
```

will cause the Java compiler to reject any attempts to instantiate `BankAccount` objects, as for example,

```
BankAccount b = new BankAccount(1000.00);  // rejected now
```

By using the `abstract` modifier we can make `BankAccount` an abstract class. Nevertheless, `BankAccount` implements the `deposit`, `withdraw`, and `getBalance` methods, which its subclasses inherit. The `BankAccount` class implements all its methods. An abstract class can implement only some of its methods and leave others to be implemented by subclasses as we will see when we develop the `Shape` class next.

A Shape Class

`Shape` is an abstract concept. Nothing is just a `Shape`, but `Shape` has subclasses such as `Line` and `Circle` that have instances. We define an abstract `Shape` class to allow programmers to work with shapes in general and get the advantages of polymorphism. We include in `Shape` the state and behavior that apply to all subclasses of `Shape` such as `Line` and `Circle`.

We will create every `Shape` with a center point, which determines where it is located. The center point will have a specific interpretation for each subclass of `Shape`. Java provides a `Point` class in the `java.awt` package that we can use for the center.

We want to be able to draw and move every concrete shape, so we add `draw` and `move` methods to the `Shape` class. To provide a `String` representation for every `Shape` we override the `Object toString` method.

A `Shape` has no particular form, so we make the `draw` operation abstract, to be implemented only in subclasses of `Shape`. Java allows us to do this by using the `abstract` modifier, as in

```
public abstract void draw();
```

which declares, but does not implement, the `draw` method.

Declaring an abstract method is a good choice when we have no useful implementation in the superclass, and only want to implement it in subclasses. We could have declared the `eat` method in the `Animal` class abstract,

```
public abstract void eat();
```

rather than implementing it with an empty body

```
public void eat() {  }
```

The difference is:

- Abstract method — Concrete subclasses **must** override to provide an implementation.
- Empty body — Concrete subclasses **may** override to provide an implementation, **or** may inherit the empty body implementation.

TIP

Any class that has an abstract method must be declared abstract using the `abstract` modifier.

Even though `Shape` is abstract, we can implement the `move` method. When we move any `Shape` we must move its center. We pass two arguments to the `move` method, the distances to move in the x- and y-directions. Every `Shape` moves by moving its `center` by the specified distances in each direction. We can make use of the `translate` method of the `Point` class which does just what we need.

We use a Point constructor

```
public Point(int x, int y);
```

that creates a `Point`, given its `x` and `y` coordinates. The method

```
public void translate(int x, int y);
```

translates a `Point` by the specified `x` and `y` values. Translating a point `p` at `(3,4)` by 2 in the x-direction and 5 in the y-direction, as in:

```
Point p = new Point(3,4);
p.translate(2,5);
```

would move the point `p` to `(5,9)`.

We implement the `toString` method to display the center point of the `Shape`, using the `toString` method of the `Point` class.

Figure 9.10 shows the diagram for the abstract `Shape` class. Using the UML notation, we italicize the class name and the abstract `draw` method, and also designate `Shape` as abstract, using `{abstract}`.

Figure 9.10 The abstract **`Shape`** class

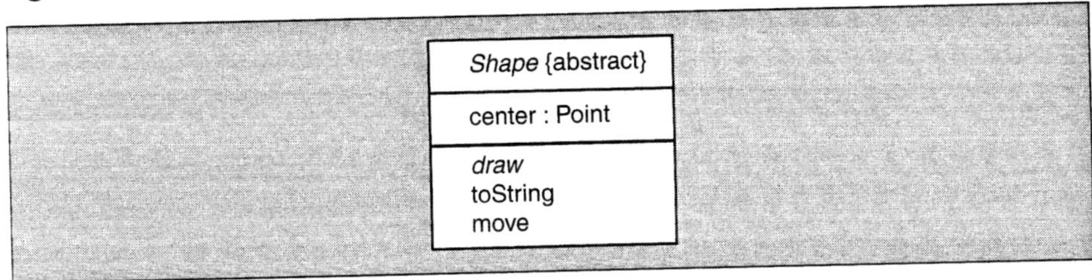

EXAMPLE 9.12 Shape.java

```
/* An abstract Shape class specifies state and behavior
 * common to all Shapes.
 */

import java.awt.*;

public abstract class Shape {                          // Note 1
  Point center;                                        // Note 2
  public Shape() {                                     // Note 3
    center =  new Point(0,0);
  }
  public Shape(Point p) {
    center = p;
  }
  public abstract void draw(Graphics g);               // Note 4
  public String toString() {
    return "Shape with center " + center;              // Note 5
  }
  public void move(int xamount, int yamount) {
    center.translate(xamount,yamount);                 // Note 6
  }}
```

Note 1: The `abstract` modifier indicates that `Shape` will have no instances.

Note 2: We omit the `public` modifier to make the center `Point` visible to other classes in the package. We discuss modifiers and access in Section 9.4. We could have used the `private` modifier and provided a public method, `getCenter`, to access the center point.

Note 3: The default constructor sets `center` to the origin, (0,0).

Note 4: We declare the `draw` method as abstract. Any class with an abstract method is an abstract class with no instances. Any subclass that we want to instantiate must implement the `draw` method. We pass a `Graphics` argument to use the drawing methods it provides.

Note 5: Java invokes the `center.toString` method to get the string representation for the center.

Note 6: `center.translate(xamount,yamount);`
The translate method of the `Point` class moves the `center` point by the specified `x` and `y` values.

Because `Shape` is abstract, we cannot instantiate any `Shape` objects, but we can write a method which uses a `Shape` array. Figure 9.11 shows a `moveDraw` method that takes a `Shape` array, the amounts to move in the x- and y-directions, and a `Graphics` object. It moves and draws each `Shape` in the array. The `moveDraw` method will work for any subclasses of `Shape` that we choose to put into an array.

Figure 9.11 Moving and drawing shapes

```
public void moveDraw
  (Shape[] theShapes,  int xAmount,  int yAmount, Graphics g) {
  for (int I = 0; I < theShapes.length; I++)  {
    theShapes[I].move(xAmount,yAmount);
    theShapes[I].draw(g);
  }
}
```

Line and Circle

The `Line` class extends `Shape`, adding an instance variable, `end`, of type `Point` to represent the other end of the line (the center point of the parent shape represents one end of the line). Because `Line` is a `Shape` it inherits the `Shape draw`, `move`, and `toString` methods, however it overrides all three of them.

`Line` must override the abstract `Shape draw`. It uses the `Graphics` object to draw the line from the `center` point to the `end` point.

`Line` overrides the `Shape move` method by extending its function. To move a `Line` we must move both the `center` and the `end` points. The `Shape move` method already moves the `center` point, so `Line move` first calls `Shape move` to move the `center`, and then move the `end` point. This illustrates a common form of overriding in which the subclass extends the behavior of the superclass.

The `Line` class overrides the `toString` method to describe the line between the `center` and `end` points. It lets each point use its `toString` method to display itself. This illustrates a common technique of building on what was already done. When writing toString methods, we use the toString methods of the components parts of the object.

The Circle class extends Shape, adding an instance variable, radius, of type **int** to represent the radius. (The center point of the parent shape represents the center of the circle.)

The Circle class inherits the Shape draw, move, and toString methods. It must override Shape draw. Circle draw displays a circle with the given center and radius. Circle implements its own toString method, using the toString method of its center point in the process.

The Circle class has no need to override the inherited move method, which moves the center point by the specified amounts in the x- and y-directions.

Example 9.13 contains the Line and Circle classes, and a UseShapes test program. We add a main method to the Shape class to test our classes. We create two shapes, assigning a line to the first and a circle to the second. Because the Shape class declares draw and move methods, the Java compiler lets each of our shapes invoke them. Java, at runtime, finds the right version of each method. If we move a shape that is a line, then Java executes the move defined in the Line class. If we move a shape that is a circle, then Java, realizing that circles inherit the move operation from the Shape class, calls the move method defined in the Shape class. Figure 9.12 shows the UseShapes applet.

Figure 9.12 The UseShapes applet

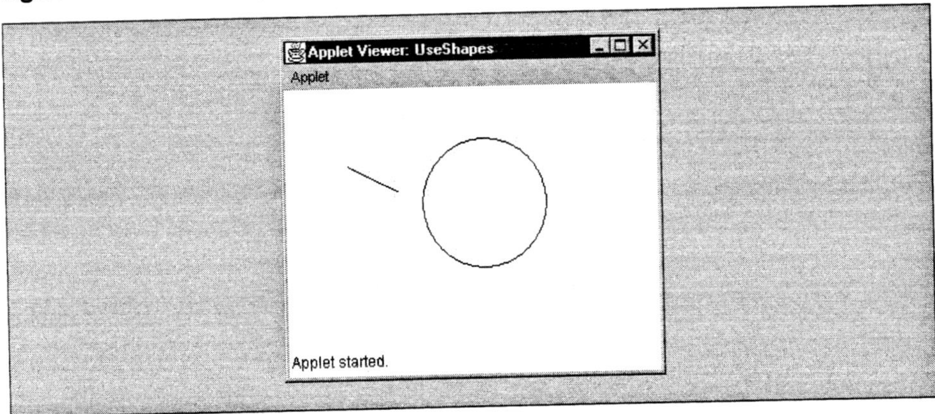

EXAMPLE 9.13 Line.java, Circle.java, UseShapes.java

Line.java

```
/*  Extends the Shape class.
 */

import java.awt.*;
public class Line extends Shape {
  Point end;
```

```
    public Line(int x1, int y1, int x2, int y2) {                // Note 1
      super(new Point(x1,y1));                                   // Note 2
      end = new Point(x2,y2);
    }
    public void draw(Graphics g) {
      g.drawLine(center.x,center.y,end.x,end.y);                 // Note 3
    }
    public String toString() {
      return  "Line from "+center + " to " + end;                // Note 4
    }
    public void move(int xamount, int yamount) {
      super.move(xamount,yamount);
      end.translate(xamount,yamount);
    }
}
```

Circle.java

```
/* Extends the Shape class.
 */

import java.awt.*;

  public class Circle extends Shape {
    int radius;

  public Circle(Point p, int r) {
    super(p);
    radius = r;
  }
  public void draw(Graphics g) {
    g.drawOval
      (center.x-radius, center.y-radius, 2*radius, 2*radius);    // Note 5
  }
  public String toString() {
    return "Circle at "+center+" with radius "+radius;
  }
}
```

UseShapes.java

```
/* Moves and draws an array of Shapes polymorphically.
 */

import java.applet.Applet;
import java.awt.*;

public class UseShapes extends Applet{
  Shape[] s = new Shape[2];                                      // Note 6

  public void moveDraw
      (Shape[] theShapes, int xAmount, int yAmount, Graphics g) {
      for (int i= 0; i < theShapes.length; i++)  {
```

```
      theShapes[i].move(xAmount, yAmount);
      theShapes[i].draw(g);
    }
  }
  public void init() {
    s[0] = new Line(20,50,60,70);                          // Note 7
    s[1] = new Circle( new Point(130,80) ,50);
  }
    public void paint(Graphics g) {
      moveDraw(s, 30, 10, g);                              // Note 8
  }
}
```

Note 1: We pass the `x`- and `y`-coordinates of the two endpoints of the line. Alternatively, we could have defined the constructor to accept two `Point` arguments.

Note 2: When constructing a subclass, we often call the superclass constructor to construct the superclass part of the object. Here we call the `Shape` constructor to initialize the `center` point. It would be a mistake to omit this call, because Java will call the default `Shape` constructor, which initializes the `center` to `(0,0)`instead of `(x1,y1)`. Because the `Shape` constructor requires a `Point` argument, we create a `Point` from `x1` and `y1`.

Note 3: The `drawLine` method requires the x- and y-coordinates of the two points that determine the line. The `Point` class has public instance variables `x` and `y`, which we use to get the coordinates of the `center` and `end` points.

Note 4: When an object, such as `center`, appears as an argument of a `String` concatenation, Java automatically calls its `toString` method to obtain its String representation.

Note 5: The point `(center.x-radius, center.y-radius)` gives the upper-left corner of the square surrounding the circle we want to draw. The side of the bounding square is `2*radius`.

Note 6: `Shape[] s = new Shape[2];`
We create array of two references, which Java initializes to **null**. We declare the references to the abstract `Shape` class, but the objects we create for these references will have types that are concrete subclasses of `Shape`, such as `Line` or `Circle`.

Note 7: `Shape s[0] =new Line(20,50,60,70);`
The line has coordinates (2,5) and (6,7).

Note 8: `moveDraw(s, 30, 10, g);`
Java determines at runtime that `s[0]` refers to a `Line` and calls the correct version of `move` from the `Line` class. Because `s[0]` refers to a `Line`, Java calls the `draw` method from the `Line` class, which is no longer abstract. Because `s[1]` refers to a `Circle`, Java uses the `move` method inherited from `Shape`. Because `s[1]` refers to a `Circle`, Java calls the `draw` method defined in `Circle`.

THE BIG PICTURE

By declaring a reference, s, as an abstract `Shape`, we can ask it to draw or move,

```
s.draw(g);    s.move(30,40);
```

leaving the details of how a concrete shape such as a line moves or draws itself to the details of the implementation of the subclass. The same operations will apply to any subclass of Shape, even those, such as Rectangle, Polygon, or Ellipse, which we have not yet defined.

Our program will depend on the abstract class, which is less likely to change than are the details of the concrete subclasses that extend it.

TEST YOUR UNDERSTANDING

TRY IT YOURSELF

8. What will be the result if in the `Shape` class of Example 9.12 we declare it without the `abstract` modifier, declaring it as

   `public class Shape { // same as Example 9.12 };?`

   Revise Example 9.12 to omit the modifier at that position. Does the compiler allow this change?

9. Will the `Shape` class of Example 9.12 still be abstract if we revise that example to implement the `draw` method in the `Shape` class to return the string representation of a `Shape`? Explain.

10. Where does the point p, where p = newPoint(3,4), move to as a result of p.translate(-1,6)?

9.4 Modifiers and Access

In a library, we may use reference books such as encyclopedias but not take them home, whereas we are encouraged to borrow non-reference books to read at home. Rare books may be restricted to scholars with special credentials.

Just as access to library books varies, so can access to Java classes, data fields, and methods vary. Java uses the **modifiers** public, private, and protected to specify the type of access. Before we consider modifiers and access we need to take a second look at packages, as package access is one of the topics we will discuss.

A Second Look at Packages*

Java groups related code into packages. Figure 9.13 shows some of the Java packages that we use in this text.

We can put our own code in a package and would certainly do so whenever our code is to be used by others or is part of a larger system. To put code in a named package, we use a `package` statement as the first statement in the file. For example, to

* Section 2.5 contains a first look at packages.

Figure 9.13 Some of the Java packages used in this text

Package Name	Description
java.applet	applets
java.awt	abstract windowing toolkit
java.awt.event	event handling in the AWT
java.io	input and output
java.lang	classes central to Java
java.text	formatting and internationalization
java.util	utility classes

use the `Name`, `Address`, and `Person` classes from Example 5.8 in other applications we put them in a package `personData` by adding the statement

```
package personData;
```

as the first line in each of these programs and placing the files `Name.class`, `Address.class`, and `Person.class` in a directory named `personData`.

All files that are part of a package must be in a directory with the same name as that of the package. Because the `Person` class is in the package `personData`, the file `Person.class` must be in a directory named `personData`, the same name as the package. Java has to find the classes that we use, and it uses the directory structure on the host machine to locate these classes.

If we want to use the classes from the package `personData` in a program, we have to tell Java which package they are in. We can do this in two ways. One way is to use the fully qualified name of the class, as in

```
personData.Name aName =
          new personData.Name("Henry", "Johnson");
personData.Address anAddress = new personData.Address
           ("1512 5th St.","Long Beach","CA", "99919");
personData.Person aPerson =
       new personData.Person("123456789",aName,anAddress);
```

where we prefix each name with the package name, `personData.` which tells Java to look in the directory `personData` to find the `Name`, `Address`, and `Person` classes. Using this approach will result in many longer method names.

The other way is to use an `import` statement at the beginning of our program, as in

```
import personData.*;
```

which tells Java to look in the personData directory for classes referenced in the program. Using the star, *, makes available all the classes in the personData package. We could have used an import statement for each class, as in:

```
import personData.Name;
import personData.Address;
import personData.Person;
```

Using the import statement, we can omit the package prefixes, as in:

```
Name aName = new Name("Henry", "Johnson");
Address anAddress =
  new Address("1512 5th St.","Long Beach","CA", "99919");
Person aPerson = new Person("123456789",aName,anAddress);
```

Classpath

The import statement adds a directory name that Java should search to find class files. But Java must be able to find that directory. Java knows how to find directories in the Java core packages. For example, using

```
import java.awt.*;
```

makes available the classes in the java\awt subdirectory of the library classes, whose location Java knows.

However, the statement

```
import personData.*;
```

refers to a user-defined personData directory that Java knows nothing about. The **classpath** environment variable contains a list of user-defined directories that contains classes used in the program being compiled and run. We compile a program named Test.java that contain this import statement using the command*

```
javac -classpath .;c:\booklr Test.java
```

and run it with

```
java -classpath .;c:\booklr Test
```

We separate each directory in the classpath with a semicolon. The dot, ., represents the current directory, which we should always include in the classpath so Java can find our program. c:\booklr is the directory that contains the personData directory.

Now that we have seen how to put classes in a package, we return to the topic of modifiers and access.

Class (and Interface) Visibility

(Replace 'class' everywhere in this section by 'class or interface'; the visibility rules are the same for both.)

We can declare a class using the public modifier, as in

* Each IDE has its own way of setting the classpath. See Appendix E for some examples.

```
public class SendRateChange { ... }
```

or without any modifier, as in

```
class Investor { ... }
```

We can access a `public` class from other packages, but we can only access a class that lacks the `public` modifier from the package it is defined in. We say that a class declared without the `public` modifier has package visibility, meaning that it is visible only in its own package.

Our small examples are self-contained; each would perform the same with or without the `public` modifier for classes. The significance of the `public` modifier only shows up if we want to use a class outside of its package. For example, our `Name` class is public in the package `personData`. Leaving off the `public` modifier would make the `Name` class visible only within the package `personData`, defeating its purpose of providing methods to use in classes outside of the `personData` package.

Java library classes, such as the `String` class from the `java.lang` package, are public. If they were not, we could not have used them. We can put at most one public class on any file. Each Java library public class is in a separate file, which has the same name as that class.

Data Field and Method Visibility

We can declare data fields and methods using at most one of the modifiers `public`, `private`, or `protected` to specify the type of access we want for that data field or method. Figure 9.14 lists these modifiers with the least restrictive at the top and the most restrictive at the bottom.

Figure 9.14 Access modifiers for data fields and methods

`public`	Accessible anywhere the class name is accessible.
`protected`	Accessible in the package that contains the class in which the data field or method is declared, and in any subclass of that class.
`(no modifier)`	Accessible in the package that contains the class in which the data field or method is declared.
`private`	Accessible only in the class in which the data field or method is declared.

Access to Data Fields

In our examples, we usually make data fields private to hide the data, allowing users to access it only by means of the public methods of the class.

When we define a class that we expect to be a superclass of various subclasses, we have to decide how we would like these subclasses to have access to data of this superclass. Had we declared the center `Point` as private in the `Shape` class of Example 9.12, then the `toString` methods of subclasses `Line` and `Circle` would not have had access to the `center` variable.

In Example 9.12, we declared the center `Point` without using any access specifier, meaning that the `center` variable is accessible in the package containing the `Shape` class, which in this example is the current directory. Another choice would be to declare `center` with private access, and include a method, `getCenter`, as in,

```
public Point getCenter() {
  return center;
}
```

which would allow all users of shapes to get the value of `center`. The `toString` method of the `Circle` class could use `getCenter` to find the center point, as in

```
public String toString() {
  return "Circle at " + getCenter() + " with radius " + dradius;
}
```

Comparing these two choices, using no modifier lets any class in the same package as `Shape` use the `center` variable directly. Typically the classes in a package have a common purpose; the package developer makes the compiled classes in the package available for use. Only the package developer would be using the data directly and could make desired changes without affecting users of the package.

Making the data private ensures that no other class can use the data directly. The developer can change the data without affecting any users as long as the public methods remain the same. This approach requires a method such as `getCenter()` if users need to read the data, and another method such as `setCenter()` if users need to change the data.

The other two modifiers, `public` and `protected`, have drawbacks when applied to data fields. Any user of the class can modify public data. We would like our classes to provide a carefully chosen interface using public operations, following the model of primitive types which we access using operations such as + and *, never using the representation of the primitive data.

Using the `protected` modifier makes a data field accessible in the current package, and in any subclass of the class in which the field is declared. Because a class has no way to know which classes may have extended it, it has no way to communicate a change in its data representation to subclasses who have access to protected data fields. For example, had we declared the center point as

```
protected Point center;
```

and then later change the representation to use x- and y-coordinates instead of a `Point`, all subclasses of `Shape` would have to be revised.

TIP

Avoiding public or protected data fields, will allow you to change the representation of the data without affecting users of your class. Provide methods if users need to access the data.

Access to Methods

Most often we make methods `public`. An object's methods provide its behavior for others to use. Our public `draw`, `move`, and `toString` methods allow users to perform these operations on any shape. Class developers might use a `private` method to help implement the `public` methods.

TIP

Make any methods private that are not intended for users of the class. Such a method might use an algorithm to help implement the public methods. You can change a private method later to use a better algorithm, knowing that no users of the class will be affected.

Protected methods also have their uses. For example, if we declare the `center` instance variable of the `Shape` class of Example 9.12 using the `private` modifier, we could declare `getCenter` and `setCenter` methods using the protected modifier, as in

```
protected Point getCenter() {
  return center;
}
protected void setCenter(Point p) {
  center = p;
}
```

which would limit access to these methods to the package containing `Shape` and to subclasses of `Shape`.

Example 9.14 illustrates the use of the access modifiers for classes, data fields, and methods. We put classes `A`, `B`, and `C` in a package named `visibility`, which means that they must be in a directory with the same name. Class `D` extends `A` but is not in the same package as `A`, while class `E` is another unrelated class. Inside `A`, we declare data fields and methods with each of the four kinds of access, and show in which classes these data fields and methods will be visible. We demonstrate the difference in visibility between the public class `A` and the non-public class `B`.

The UML notation allows us to indicate the access (visibility) of each field in a class diagram. Figure 9.15, for class `A` of Example 9.14, shows these symbols, which are useful when we wish to specify more details.

Figure 9.15 Indicating access in a class diagram

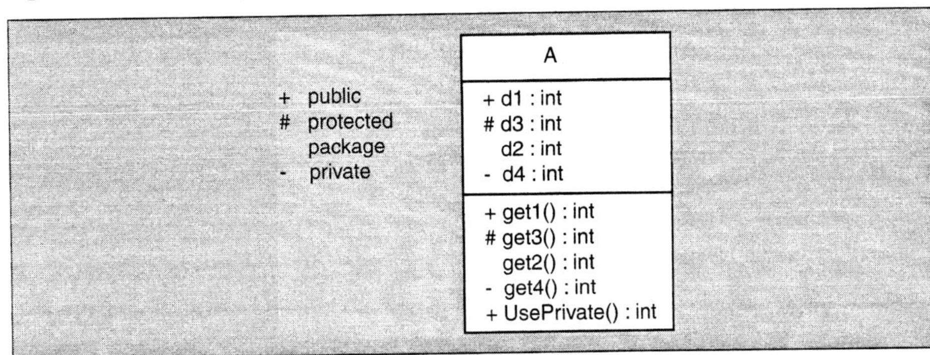

When we do not put our class in a named package by using a package statement at the beginning of the program, that class is in a default package consisting of all Java classes in the current directory. Figure 9.16 diagrams the two packages in Example 9.14, the package visibility and the default package. We do not show the class `B` in the diagram because access to it is limited to the classes in the visibility package.

Figure 9.16 The packages of Example 9.14

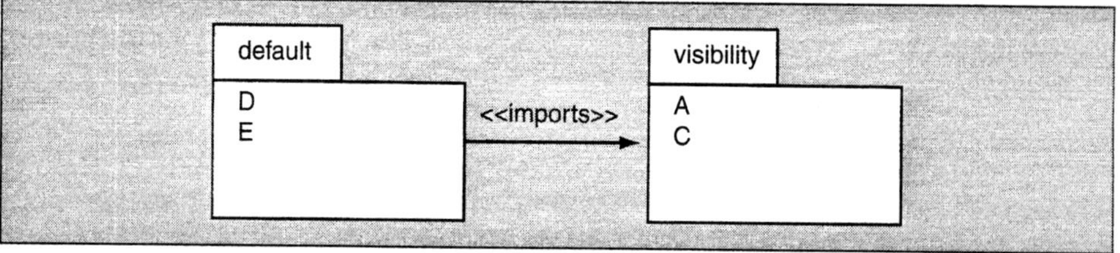

EXAMPLE 9.14 A.java, C.Java, and D.java

A.java

```
/* Public class A declares data fields and methods
 * with each of the four access modifiers
 * (including none) to illustrate their use.
 * Class B, not public, will be visible only in the
 * package visibility in which it is declared.
 */

package visibility;                                    // Note 1

public class A {                                       // Note 2
  public int d1=1;                                     // Note 3
  int d2=2;
  protected int d3=3;
  private int d4=4;

  public int get1() {
    return d1;
  }
  int get2() {
    return d2;
  }
  protected int get3() {
    return d3;
  }
  private int get4() {
    return d4;
  }
  public int usePrivate(){                             // Note 4
    return d4 + get4();
  }
}
```

```
class B {                                              // Note 5
  public int d5=5;
}
```

C.java

```
/*  Class C in the same package as A and B
 *  can use A, B and all data fields and methods
 *  except the private d4 and getd4().
 */

package visibility;

public class C {                                       // Note 6
  public static void main(String [] args) {
    A a = new A();
    B b = new B();
    int i, j;
    i = a.d1 + a.d2 + a.d3 + b.d5 + a.usePrivate();
    j = a.get1() + a.get2() + a.get3();
    System.out.println("i is " + i + " and j is " + j);
  }
}
```

D.java

```
/* Class D extends A but is not in the same package.
 * D cannot use d2, get2(), or the class B which are
 * visible only in the package in which they are declared.
 * D can use d3 and getd3(), but only from an object of
 * type D, not from an object of type A.  Class E can
 * only use public data and methods.
 */

import visibility.*;                                   // Note 7

public class D extends A {                             // Note 8
  public static void main(String [] args) {
    A a = new A();
    D d = new D();
    int i,j;
    i = a.d1 + d.d3 + a.usePrivate();                  // Note 9
    j = a.get1() + d.get3();
    System.out.println("i is " + i + " and j is " + j);
  }
}

class E {                                              // Note 10
  public static void main(String [] args) {
    A a = new A();
    D d = new D();
    int i,j;
```

```
    i = a.d1 + d.usePrivate();                                  // Note 11
    j = d.get1();
    System.out.println("i is " + i + " and j is " + j);
  }
}
```

Output—C

```
i is 19 and j is 6
```

Output—D

```
i is 12 and j is 4
```

Output—E

```
i is 9 and j is 1
```

Note 1: We put classes `A`, `B`, and `C` in a package to illustrate the effect of access modifiers.

Note 2: The public class `A` will be visible everywhere.

Note 3: We declare four variables and four methods using each of the three modifiers and no modifier. We will see which we can access in classes `C`, `D`, and `E`.

Note 4: We can directly access the private `d4` and `get4` only in `A`, but we can access a public method that uses them anywhere.

Note 5: Declared with no modifier, the class `B` is visible only in its package, `visibility`. The public `d5` is visible anywhere `B` is.

Note 6: `public class C {`
Class `C`, in the same package as `A` and `B`, can use both `A` and `B`, and all but the private `d4` and `get4`.

Note 7: `import visibility.*;`
This `import` statement tells Java to look in the `visibility` package for any classes it cannot otherwise find. The star `*` matches every class. We could have used two `import` statements to name the classes explicitly, as in:

```
import visibility.A;
import visibility.C;
```

Note 8: `public class D extends A {`
Class `D` extends `A`, but is not in the same package as `A`. `D` cannot use `B` or its data, or `d2` and `get2` all of which are visible only in the package in which they are declared.

Note 9: `i = a.d1 + d.d3 + a.usePrivate();`
A subclass object `d`, of type `D`, can use the protected `d3` and `get3`, but an object `a`, of type `A`, cannot access `d3` and `get3`.

Note 10: `class E {`
The class `E`, which is not in the same package as `A`, and not a subclass of `A`, can only access the public data fields and methods of `A`.

Note 11: `i = a.d1 + d.usePrivate();`
Either `a`, of type `A`, or `d`, of the subtype `D` of `A`, can access the public fields of `A`.

The steps to compile and run programs with named packages depend upon the development environment used.*

THE BIG PICTURE

Groups of related classes belong in a named package with each public class on a separate file, contained in a directory with the same name as the package. Java looks in the classpath to find the directory. Classes declared without using the public modifier may only be used inside the package.

Instance variables and methods can have four levels of access. Usually data is private; the default is access within the same package. Methods representing the behavior of the object are public, but the other access modes have their uses.

TEST YOUR UNDERSTANDING

11. What must be the first statement in a file whose contents we wish to include in a package named `stuff`?
12. Suppose you wish to use a class, `GoodStuff`, from the package `stuff`, in your program. Write the `import` statement that would allow Java to find the `GoodStuff` class.
13. Suppose you want to call the `static` method `doStuff()` from the class `GoodStuff` in the package `stuff`. How could you do it without using an `import` statement?
14. What must be the directory name which contains all files that are part of the package `stuff`?

---

* Using the JDK, execute the following commands from the directory which contains the `visibility` directory (on other than Windows systems replace the backslash with a forward slash)

```
javac visibility\A.java
javac visibility\C.java
javac D.java
java visibility.C
java D
java E
```

15. Example 9.12 uses the `Point` class from the `java.awt` package. Without looking at the source, can you tell whether or not `Point` is declared using the `public` modifier? Why or why not?
16. In Example 9.14, what is the difference in accessibility to `d2`, declared with no modifier, and accessibility to `d3`, which is protected?
17. In Example 9.14, what is the difference in accessibility to `get2()`, which is declared with no modifier, and accessibility to `get4()`, which is private?
18. Explain why the field `d5`, declared public in Example 9.14, is not visible in either class `D` or `E`.

9.5 Object-Oriented Design with Use Cases and Scenarios

In object-oriented programming, we solve our problem by identifying objects, each having certain responsibilities, and let these objects use each other's services. Each object's methods provide that object's services, which allow it to meet its responsibilities.

To identify the objects we analyze the system using use cases and scenarios. Each **use case** describes one function that the system should provide. For each use case, we develop several **scenarios**, which are step by step listings of the interactions among the user and other parts of the system to provide the function described by that use case. Usually for each use case there will be a primary scenario, which represents the interactions for a successful use, and several secondary scenarios representing the various errors that might occur.

Defining the Problem

For our example case study we will develop a simple automatic teller application. A user of the system should be able to choose an account, either savings or checking, and make deposits to, withdrawals from, or get the balance of that account. For simplicity, we assume that each user has at most one account of each type. (Figure 1.11 shows the initial screen for the `AtmScreen` applet.)

Object-Oriented Design—Developing Scenarios

For the automatic teller system our use cases consist of the deposit, withdrawal, and get balance transactions that the user can perform. To discover the objects we need, we can look at scenarios which represent each use case, first looking at scenarios where everything goes well, and then looking at some processing failures. Figure 9.17 describes a scenario for a successful deposit.

The scenario in Figure 9.17 involves four objects, `user`, `teller`, `bank`, and `account`. The user is an actor who interacts with the system via a user interface, which we model as an `AtmScreen`. We write an event-driven program that responds to user-generated events. For every successful scenario there are usually several scenarios where something goes wrong. Figure 9.18 shows one of them, when no account exists of the type specified by the user.

Figure 9.17 A scenario for a successful deposit

```
The user asks the teller to accept an ATM card.
The teller asks the user to enter a PIN.
The user asks the teller to accept a PIN.
The teller asks the user to select a transaction type.
The user asks the teller to accept a deposit.
The teller asks the user to select an account type.
The user asks the teller to accept a savings account type.
The teller asks the bank to find the account of the chosen
     type for the user with the specified PIN.
The bank gives the teller a reference to the account.
The teller asks the user to specify an amount.
The user asks the teller to accept an amount.
The teller asks the account to deposit the specified amount.
The teller asks the user to select another transaction, ...
```

Figure 9.18 A scenario when the specified account does not exist

```
The user asks the teller to accept an ATM card.
The teller asks the user to enter a PIN.
The user asks the teller to accept a PIN.
The teller asks the user to select a transaction type.
The user asks the teller to accept a get balance transaction.
The teller asks the user to select an account type.
The user asks the teller to accept a checking account type.
The teller asks the bank to find the account of the chosen
     type for the user with the specified PIN.
The bank gives the teller a null account.
The teller asks the user to select another transaction, ...
```

We leave to the exercises the writing of other scenarios to explore possible uses (and misuses) of the automatic teller system.

Object-Oriented Design—Assigning Responsibilities

Using scenarios gives us an idea of the responsibilities for each object. Figure 9.19 shows these responsibilities.

Figure 9.19 Objects and their responsibilities

Object	Responsibilities
AtmScreen	Enter a PIN Select a transaction type Select an account type Specify an amount
Bank	Find a specified account
Account	Deposit Withdraw Get balance

Figure 9.19 Objects and their responsibilities (continued)

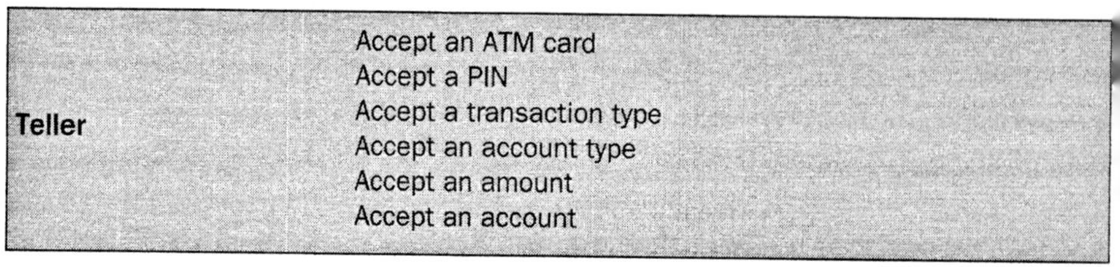

Teller	Accept an ATM card Accept a PIN Accept a transaction type Accept an account type Accept an amount Accept an account

Figure 9.20 shows the relationships between classes we have identified. Each line represents an association between the two classes it connects. These associations are evident from the scenarios in which one class makes a request of another.

Figure 9.20 Class relationships

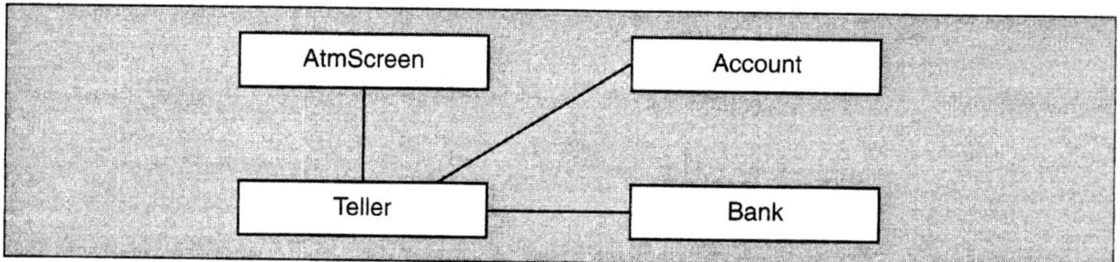

Object-Oriented Design—Defining the Classes

We can define our classes and create methods to handle each of these responsibilities. The `AtmScreen` has methods to present the appropriate screen to the user to meet each of its responsibilities, entering a PIN, selecting a transaction type, selecting an account type, and specifying an amount. The `Teller` methods accept information from the user and the bank, and use the information to initiate the next step of the transaction. When the teller accepts the account from the bank, it can ask the account to execute a `getBalance` transaction, but needs to wait for the user to enter the amount to deposit or withdraw before asking the account to execute one of these transactions. When a transaction is complete, the teller asks the user to select another transaction, until the user cancels the session.

The `Account` class revises the `BankAccount` class of Example 5.3 by making `Account` abstract and adding a `Person` data field for the account holder. The `Savings` class revises class `SavingsAccount` of Example 9.5 to inherit from `Account` and accept a `Person` in its constructor. The `Checking` class revises class `CheckingAccount` of Example 9.7 to inherit from `Account` and accept a `Person` in its constructor.

Large systems use databases to hold account data. Here we simply create three accounts in the `Bank` class. When asked to find an account, the bank checks each account to see if the account id matches the PIN specified by the user and if its type matches the type specified by the user.

We purposely avoid complicating the system. Obviously a real ATM system would be orders of magnitude more complex. We omit any security considerations for entering PINs and greatly simplify the interactions with the bank. Normally the user would have an id such as a social security number and a separate PIN for a bank account. We use only one identification number, which we store as the `id` field in the `Person` class. Each account has a `holder` field of type `Person`, which allows the bank to compare the PIN entered by the user to the id of the account holder.

Completing the Java Code

The event-driven, object-oriented programming style really becomes evident when we look at the `init` method, which just creates the user interface. The applet waits for user actions, which cause objects to interact in fulfilling their responsibilities.

For the user interface, we place the input components in the north region of a border layout. A text field allows the user to enter a name, a PIN, and an amount. Checkboxes let the user choose the type of account, and a choice box presents the types of transaction. *Start* and *Finish* buttons appear in the south region, while a canvas displays the results in the center.

Figure 9.21 shows the applet after a user has made a deposit.

Figure 9.21 **Figure 9.21 The applet of Example 9.15**

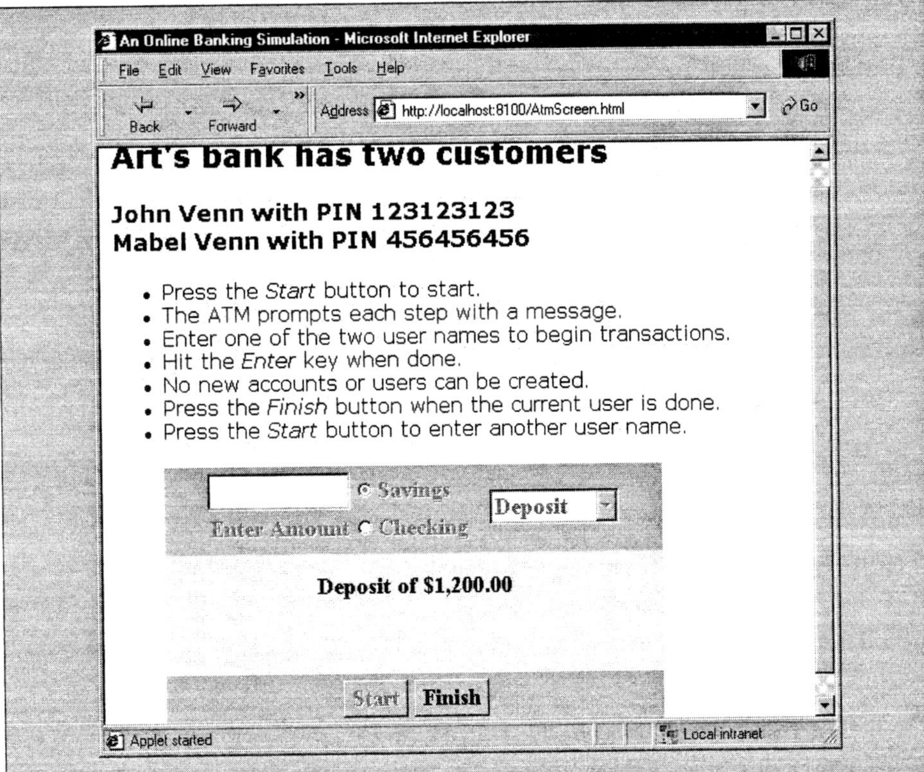

We find modeling with objects natural, because it mirrors our world of objects, even though objects in our programs can also model abstractions not based upon real-world analogies. The process of developing scenarios modifies the stepwise refinement process to apply to interacting objects. Traditional stepwise refinement is essential in implementing those methods of a class which use more complex algorithms.

EXAMPLE 9.15 AtmScreen.java

```
/* Illustrates event-driven object-oriented
 * programming
 /

import personData.*;
import java.applet.Applet;
import java.awt.*;
import java.awt.event.*;
import java.text.NumberFormat;

public class AtmScreen extends Applet
                    implements ActionListener, ItemListener {
  private Button start = new Button("Start");
  private Button finish = new Button("Finish");
  private TextField dataEntry = new TextField(10);
  private CheckboxGroup group = new CheckboxGroup();
  private Checkbox savings = new Checkbox("Savings",false,group);
  private Checkbox checking = new Checkbox("Checking",false,group);
  private Choice transaction = new Choice();
  private String message = "Welcome to Art's Bank";
  private MyCanvas canvas = new MyCanvas();
  private Label textLabel = new Label("Enter Name");
  private Bank bank = new Bank();
  private Person[] person = Database.personData();
  private Teller teller;
  private Font font = new Font("Serif",Font.BOLD,18);
  private FontMetrics metrics = getFontMetrics(font);

  public void init() {
    setLayout(new BorderLayout());
    setFont(font);
    Panel text = new Panel();
    text.setLayout(new GridLayout(2,1));
    text.add(dataEntry);
    text.add(textLabel);
    Panel north = new Panel();
    north.add(text);
    Panel checkboxes = new Panel();
    checkboxes.setLayout(new GridLayout(2,1));
    checkboxes.add(savings);
    checkboxes.add(checking);
    north.add(checkboxes);
    transaction.add("Deposit");
    transaction.add("Withdraw");
    transaction.add("Balance");
```

```
    north.add(transaction);
    add(north,"North");
    Panel south = new Panel();
    south.add(start);
    south.add(finish);
    add(south,"South");
    canvas.setBackground(Color.yellow);
    add(canvas,"Center");
    dataEntry.addActionListener(this);
    savings.addItemListener(this);
    checking.addItemListener(this);
    transaction.addItemListener(this);
    start.addActionListener(this);
    finish.addActionListener(this);
    clear();
}
public void actionPerformed(ActionEvent e) {                    // Note 1
  Object source = e.getSource();
  if (source==dataEntry){
    String s = textLabel.getText();
    if (s.equals("Enter Name")){                                // Note 2
        String name = dataEntry.getText();
        if (name.equals("John Venn"))
          teller.acceptCard(person[0]);
        else if (name.equals("Mabel Venn"))
          teller.acceptCard(person[1]);
        else {
          message = "Enter John Venn or Mabel Venn";
          dataEntry.setText("");
          canvas.repaint();
        }
      }
      else if (s.equals("Enter PIN"))
        teller.acceptPIN(dataEntry.getText());
      else if (s.equals("Enter Amount"))
        teller.acceptAmount
            (new Double(dataEntry.getText()).doubleValue());
   }
   else if (source == finish)clear();
   else if (source == start){
     dataEntry.setEnabled(true);
     dataEntry.requestFocus();                                  // Note 3
     textLabel.setEnabled(true);
     start.setEnabled(false);
   }
  }
  public void itemStateChanged(ItemEvent e) {                   // Note 4
    Object item = e.getItemSelectable();
    if (item == transaction)
      teller.acceptTransaction(transaction.getSelectedIndex());
```

```
    else if (item == savings)
      teller.acceptType(Bank.SAVINGS);
    else if (item == checking)
      teller.acceptType(Bank.CHECKING);
  }
  public void enterPIN() {
    dataEntry.setText("");
    textLabel.setText("Enter PIN");
    message = "Enter your PIN number";
    canvas.repaint();
  }
  public void selectTransaction() {
    dataEntry.setText("");
    dataEntry.setEnabled(false);                          // Note 5
    textLabel.setEnabled(false);
    transaction.setEnabled(true);
    message = "Select your transaction";
    canvas.repaint();
  }
  public void selectType() {
    savings.setEnabled(true);
    checking.setEnabled(true);
    transaction.setEnabled(false);
    message = "Select your account type";
    canvas.repaint();
  }
  public void specifyAmount() {
    dataEntry.setEnabled(true);
    dataEntry.requestFocus();
    textLabel.setEnabled(true);
    textLabel.setText("Enter Amount");
    savings.setEnabled(false);
    checking.setEnabled(false);
    message = "Specify the amount";
    canvas.repaint();
  }
  public void display(String s) {
    dataEntry.setText("");
    textLabel.setEnabled(false);
    dataEntry.setEnabled(false);
    checking.setEnabled(false);
    savings.setEnabled(false);
    message = s;
    canvas.repaint();
  }
  public void clear() {                                   // Note 6
    start.setEnabled(true);
    savings.setEnabled(false);
    checking.setEnabled(false);
```

```
    transaction.setEnabled(false);
    textLabel.setText("Enter Name");
    textLabel.setEnabled(false);
    dataEntry.setText("");
    dataEntry.setEnabled(false);
    message = "Welcome to Art's bank";
    canvas.repaint();
    teller = new Teller(bank,this);
  }
  class MyCanvas extends Canvas {
    public void paint(Graphics g) {
      int w = metrics.stringWidth(message);                          // Note 7
      g.drawString(message, (getSize().width-w)/2, getSize().height/3);
    }
  }
}

class Teller {
  public static final int DEPOSIT = 0;                               // Note 8
  public static final int WITHDRAW = 1;
  public static final int BALANCE = 2;
  private String id;
  private int transType;
  private intacctType;
  private Person user;
  private Bank bank;
  private Account account;
  private AtmScreen screen;
  private NumberFormat nf = NumberFormat.getCurrencyInstance();

  public Teller(Bank b, AtmScreen s) {
    bank = b;                                                        // Note 9
    screen = s;
  }
  public void acceptCard(Person p) {
    user = p;                                                        // Note 10
    screen.enterPIN();                                               // Note 11
  }
  public void acceptPIN(String s) {
    id = s;
    screen.selectTransaction();
  }
  public void acceptTransaction(int trans) {
    transType = trans;
    screen.selectType();
  }
  public void acceptType(int type) {
    acctType = type;
    bank.find(id,acctType,this);
  }
```

```
  public void acceptAccount(Account a) {
    account = a;
    if (account != null)                                              // Note 12
      if (transType == BALANCE){
        screen.display("The balance is "
           + nf.format(account.getBalance()));
      }
      else {
         if (transType == DEPOSIT || transType == WITHDRAW){
          screen.specifyAmount();
         }
      }
    else
      screen.display("No such account -- session terminated");
  }
  public void acceptAmount(double amount) {
    switch(transType) {
      case DEPOSIT :
        account.deposit(amount);
        screen.display("Deposit of " + nf.format(amount));
        break;
      case WITHDRAW:
        double taken = account.withdraw(amount);
        if (taken >= 0)
          screen.display("Withdrawal of " + nf.format(taken));
        else
          screen.display("Insufficient funds");
        break;
    }
  }
}

class Database {
  public static Person[] personData() {
    Name n1 = new Name("John","Venn");
    Address a1 = new Address( "123 Main St.", "Tyler","WY", "45654");
    Person p1 = new Person("123123123",n1,a1);
    Name n2 = new Name("Mabel","Venn");
    Person p2 = new Person("456456456",n2,a1);
    Person[] p = {p1,p2};
    return p;
  }
  public static Account [] accountData() {
    Person[] p = personData();
    Account p1Savings = new Savings(1500.00,p[0],4.0);               // Note 13
    Account p1Checking = new Checking(p[0],2500.00,.50);
    Account p2Savings = new Savings(1000.00,p[1],3.5);
    Account[] a = {p1Savings,p1Checking,p2Savings};
    return a;
  }
```

```
}
class Bank {
  public static final int SAVINGS = 1;
  public static final int CHECKING = 2;
  private Account [] accounts = Database.accountData();
  public void find(String id, int acctType, Teller teller) {          // Note 14
    for (int i=0; i<accounts.length; i++) {
      Account acct = accounts[i];
      if (acct.getId().equals(id))
        switch(acctType) {
      case SAVINGS:
        if (acct instanceof Savings){
          teller.acceptAccount(acct);
          return;
        }
      case CHECKING:
        if (acct instanceof Checking){
          teller.acceptAccount(acct);
          return;
        }
      }
     }
     teller.acceptAccount(null);                                      // Note 15
   }
 }
 abstract class Account {
   private double balance;
   private Person holder;
   public Account(Person p)    {
     this(0,p);
   }
   public Account(double initialAmount, Person p) {
     balance = initialAmount;
     holder = p;
   }
   public String getId() {
     return holder.getId();
   }
   public void deposit(double amount) {
     balance += amount;
   }
   public double withdraw(double amount) {
     if (balance >= amount){
        balance -= amount;
        return amount;
     }
     else
        return -1.0;
   }
   public double getBalance() {
```

```
      return balance;
    }
  }
  class Checking extends Account {
    private double minBalance;
    private double charge;
    public Checking(Person p,double minAmount, double charge) {
      super(p);
      minBalance = minAmount;
      this.charge = charge;
    }
    public double processCheck(double amount){
      if (getBalance() >= minBalance)
        return super.withdraw(amount);
      else
        return super.withdraw(amount + charge);
    }
    public double withdraw(double amount) {
      return processCheck(amount);
    }
  }
  class Savings extends Account{
    private double interestRate;
    public Savings(double amount, Person p, double rate) {
      super(amount,p);
      interestRate = rate;
    }
    public void postInterest(){
      double balance = getBalance();
      double interest = interestRate/100*balance;
      deposit(balance + interest);
    }
  }
```

Note 1: `public void actionPerformed(ActionEvent e)`
We respond here to the text field entries and the button presses.

Note 2: `if (s.equals("Enter Name")){`
We use the text field to enter the name, the PIN, and the amount, so we check the label to determine which of these the user entered.

Note 3: `dataEntry.requestFocus();`
Text entry does not have a natural association with any component. Requesting the focus for the text field directs text entry to it.

Note 4: `public void itemStateChanged(ItemEvent e)`
We respond here to the checkbox and choice selections.

Note 5: `dataEntry.setEnabled(false);`
When we want the user to choose the transaction type, we disable the text

field, which is not needed, to avoid confusion. We disable unnecessary components whenever possible.

Note 6: `public void clear() {`
We reset the user interface initially, and when the user finishes a transaction.

Note 7: `int w = metrics.stringWidth(message);`
We get the width of each message so we can center it in the canvas.

Note 8: `public static final int DEPOSIT = 0;`
Named constants make the program easier to maintain and modify. We use the C-C++ style, naming constants with uppercase identifiers. The `final` modifier indicates that the variable cannot change so that it becomes a constant.

Note 9: `bank = b;`
The teller saves the reference to the bank so that it can find accounts.

Note 10: `user = u;`
The teller saves the reference to the user, to continue communication during the execution of the transactions for that user.

Note 11: `screen.enterPIN();`
After getting the user's name, the teller asks the screen to set up the interface for the user to enter the PIN.

Note 12: `if (account != null)`
The bank sends a **null** account to the teller if it cannot find an account of the specified type for that user.

Note 13: `Account p1Savings = new Savings(1500.00,p1,4.0);`
We create three accounts to test our program.

Note 14: `public void find (String id, int acctType, Teller teller)`
The `find` method checks that the requested account exists.

Note 15: `teller.acceptAccount(null);`
If none of the accounts match the id and account type specified by the user, the bank sends the value **null** back to the teller.

Testing the Code

We test the code with the scenarios of Figures 9.17 and 9.18, leaving other tests for the exercises. The first user, John Venn, makes a deposit of $1200 to a savings account. This transaction succeeds (Figure 9.21), because this user has a savings account. The second user, Mabel Venn, attempts to get the balance of a checking account, but this transaction fails (Figure 9.22) because this user does not have a checking account.

Figure 9.22 Another scenario for the applet of Example 9.15

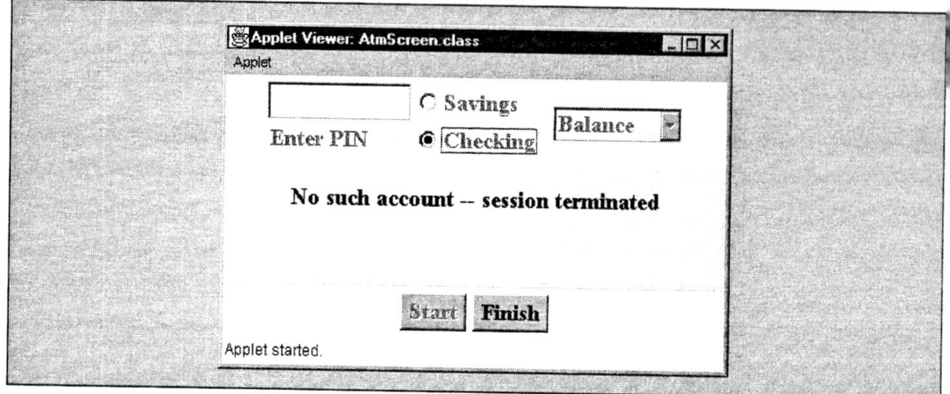

The use cases and scenarios express the intended functionality of the system, so testing based on these scenarios will help ensure that our system correctly provides the required behavior.

THE BIG PICTURE

Use cases and scenarios help us to identify the objects and their responsibilities. A class implementing an object type includes methods to enable objects of that type to meet their responsibilities. Rather than following a recipe, as in a procedural program, the `init` method merely creates a user interface. User-generated events cause objects to interact with one another.

TEST YOUR UNDERSTANDING

19. Write a scenario for a successful withdrawal of $100 from a checking account.
20. Write a scenario for a user who chooses to cancel rather than input a transaction type.
21. Write a scenario for a user who cancels a deposit while specifying the account type.
22. Write a scenario for a successful `getBalance` transaction from a savingaccount.

TRY IT YOURSELF

23. Run Example 9.15 testing the scenarios of questions 19–22.

SUMMARY

- Inheritance, often contrasted with composition, is another way to relate objects. A class that extends another class, said to be a subclass of the class it extends, can add data fields and methods to those of its parent class; it can also override methods, tailoring their implementations to express its own behavior. In our bank account example, a savings account adds an interest rate field, and a method to post the interest. A checking account overrides the `withdraw` method of its bank account superclass to deduct a service charge if the balance is below the minimum needed for free checking. Every class, directly or indirectly, extends the `Object` class which provides a default implementation for the `toString` method that returns an empty string.

- Polymorphism, the many forms that operations can have, distinguishes object-oriented programming from other paradigms. A superclass variable can refer to objects of any of its subclasses. A bank account variable might refer to a savings account or it might refer to a checking account; its withdraw behavior will be different in each case. As programmers, we just ask the object to execute its withdraw behavior. Our programs can have broad applicability, leaving each object to implement the specifics of its behavior. We use the same name, `withdraw`, but the result depends on the type of object whose `withdraw` method we invoke.
- Often the superclasses we use polymorphically are abstract, not having any instances. In Example 9.12 the abstract `Shape` class implements its `move` method, but not its `draw` method. Subclasses `Line` and `Circle` must override `draw`, but may either override or inherit the `move` method from `Shape`. When we draw or move shapes, each instance will draw or move itself behaving according to its subclass type.
- Java uses modifiers to specify the type of access for classes, interfaces, data fields, and methods. We can declare a class or interface public, making it visible everywhere, or without any modifier, restricting its visibility to the package it is declared in. We can declare data fields and methods with the `private`, `protected`, or `public` modifiers or without any modifier. Using the `private` modifier restricts access to the methods of the class in which the data field or method is declared. This is the most restrictive modifier. Using no modifier restricts access to the package containing the data field or method. We can use the `package` statement to put our code in a package.
- Using the `protected` modifier restricts access to the containing package or to any subclasses of the containing class. Finally, the `public` modifier makes the data field or method visible anywhere its containing class is visible. Generally speaking, we declare data fields `private` or with no modifier. Methods are most often `public`, but the other access types can be useful.
- Our case study demonstrates the object-oriented programming methodology. Thinking in objects fits in with our normal experiences. To develop a system, we look at the uses of that system, giving scenarios for each use which step through the interactions needed to accomplish that use. We construct normal scenarios describing successful outcomes, and scenarios for the many cases when something goes wrong. From these scenarios we identify the objects of the system and their responsibilities. We implement methods to allow objects to satisfy these responsibilities. The system runs by creating objects and letting them interact serving each other with their methods that execute their responsibilities. Our automatic teller application is quite simple, but illustrates this approach nicely.

Skill Builder Exercises

1. Fill in the blanks in the following:

   A class can extend one __________ but may implement more than one __________. An __________ class has no instances, but it can implement some of its __________. Redefining an operation in a subclass is called __________. The behavior expressed by that operation depends on the __________ of the object that invokes it.

2. Fill in the modifier needed to provide the desired access for the following declarations in a public class C which is defined in a package P.

   a. __________ int a; access only in the package P

   b. __________ double d; access in P and in subclasses of C

   c. __________ String s; access everywhere C is accessible

   d. __________ char c; access only within C

3. What will be the output from the following program?

```
class H {
  int a;
  public H() {
    a = 0;
  }
  public H(int i) {
       a = i;
  }
  public void display() {
    System.out.println(a);
  }
}
class K extends H {
  public K(int i) {
    a = i*i;
  }
}
public class HK {
  public static void main(String[] args) {
    H first = new H(4);
    H second  = new K(5);
    first.display();
    first = second;
    first.display();
  }
}
```

Critical Thinking Exercises

4. Using the `Name` class of Example 5.8 and the `SavingsAccount` class of Example 9.5, given

```
Name name = new Name("Ben","Franklin");
SavingsAccount savings = new SavingsAccount(500.00,4.0);
String s = "The account of " + name + " is " + savings;
```

choose the correct value of the string s.

a. `"The account of Ben Franklin is $500 at 4% interest"`

b. `"The account of Ben Franklin is "`

c. `"The account of Franklin, Ben is $500 at 4% interest"`

d. None of the above.

5. A subclass can override a method of its superclass or overload it. Choose the correct description from the following:

a. Overriding replaces the method of the superclass, while overloading adds another method with the same name.

b. Overloading replaces the method of the superclass, while overriding adds another method with the same name.

c. Both overriding and overloading replace the method of the superclass.

d. None of the above.

6. Which of the following best describes the relation between an abstract class and an interface?

a. An interface is another name for an abstract class.

b. An abstract class must be totally abstract, but an interface may be partially implemented.

c. Every abstract class implements an interface.

d. None of the above.

7. Given

```
BankAccount b = new SavingsAccount(500.00,4.0);
```

referring to the classes of Examples 5.3 and 9.5, choose which of the following is correct.

a. The statement `b.postInterest()` is not valid.

b. Later in the program, the variable `b` may refer to a `CheckingAccount` object.

c. The statement `b.withdraw(100.00)` will invoke the `withdraw` method from the `BankAccount` class.

d. All of the above.

Debugging Exercise

8. The following class, `Check`, might be useful for validating account inquiries by telephone. It attempts to check the four digits submitted by the inquirer against the last four digits of the account id. It uses the `Account` class of Example 9.15, and the `Name` and `Address` classes of Example 5.8. Find and fix any errors in the code below.

```
public class Check {
  Account account;
  public Check(Account a){
    account = a;
  }
  public boolean checkId(String id){
    String s = account.getId();
    int length = s.length();
    boolean result = false;
    if (s.substring(length-4,length)==id)
      result = true;
    return result;
  }
  public static void main (String[] args) {
    Name name = new Name("Java", 'A', "Student");
    Address address =
      new Address("76 Applet Way","Web City","FL","44444");
    Person person = new Person("123456789",name,address);
    Account a = new Savings(1500.00,person,4.0);
    Check c = new Check(a);
    System.out.println(c.checkId("6789"));
  }
}
```

Program Modification Exercises

9. Modify Example 5.3 to add a `readAccount` method to the `BankAccount` class which will return a `BankAccount` constructed from data input from the keyboard. Override `readAccount` in `SavingsAccount` to return an account which refers to a `SavingsAccount` that you construct, again initializing it with data from the keyboard. Similarly implement `readAccount` in the `CheckingAccount` class.

10. Create a `TimedAccount` subclass of the `SavingsAccount` class of Example 9.5, which has an instance variable, `fundsAvailable`, to indicate that part of the balance is available for withdrawal. Override the `withdraw` method to check that the amount requested does not exceed the funds available for withdrawal. Override the `deposit` method to permit, at most, three deposits during the life of the account. Use an instance variable to hold the number of deposits made.

11. Create a `Rectangle` subclass of the `Shape class` of Example 9.12. Let the center point of the shape represent the upper-left corner, and add another point which represents the lower-right corner of the rectangle.

12. Modify the `Line`, `Circle`, and `Shape` classes of Examples 9.12 and 9.13 to make all data fields private and add public methods, such as `getCenter`, to access those fields.

Program Design Exercises

13. Implement a set of classes for dining out which will demonstrate polymorphism. An abstract `Restaurant` class will have abstract methods such as `getMenu`, `getBill`, `orderFood`, `payBill`, and so on. Implement an `eatOut` method by calling the abstract methods in the order they would occur in a typical restaurant scenario. Implement `FastFood`, `CoffeeShop`, and `Fancy` subclasses of `Restaurant`, which each implement all the abstract methods using stubs to print messages describing what would happen in that type of restaurant. For example the `orderFood` method in the `FastFood` class might describe talking to a machine from a car window in a drive through line, while the `orderFood` method in the `Fancy` class might call a method to order wine to go with the meal.

    To demonstrate the polymorphism, declare several restaurant objects, which refer to the various subclasses. Calling the `eatOut` method for each restaurant will show that each behaves in its own way, appropriate to that type of restaurant. A subclass may override the `eatOut` method if the order of method calls defined in the `eatOut` method in the `Restaurant` class is not appropriate for that subclass.

14. Implement a set of classes for accommodations which will demonstrate polymorphism. An abstract `Accommodation` class will have abstract methods such as `reserve`, `checkIn`, `tipStaff`, `payBill`, and so on. Implement a `sleepOut` method by calling the abstract methods in the order they would occur in a typical accommodation scenario. Implement `LuxuryHotel`, `Motel`, and `Campground` subclasses of `Accommodation`, which each implement all the abstract methods using stubs to print messages describing what would happen in that type of accommodation. For example the `checkIn` method in the `Campground` class might describe pitching a tent, while the `checkIn` method in the `LuxuryHotel` class might call a method to have the luggage carried to the room.

    To demonstrate the polymorphism, declare several accommodation objects, which refer to the various subclasses. Calling the `sleepOut` method for each accommodation will show that each behaves in its own way, appropriate to that type of accommodation. A subclass may override the `sleepOut` method if the order of method calls defined in the `sleepOut` method in the `Accommodation` class is not appropriate for that subclass.

15. Identify use cases and develop scenarios for a car rental system in which users may reserve a car in advance, cancel a reservation, and pick up or return a car. The company has different types of cars, such as compact cars and luxury cars. Make a list of the responsibilities of each object you identify from the scenarios. Implement the rental system using an object-oriented approach, developing methods to implement an object's responsibilities, and letting the objects interact. There is no "right" answer for this exercise. Good solutions will differ in many respects from one another.

16. a. Create an interface, Bendable, with one method, bend. Create two classes, Spoon, and Arm, which implement Bendable. Spoon will also have an `eat` method, and Arm will also have a `raise` method. Each of these methods prints a message indicating its function. Write another class with a `main` method, declaring two objects of type Bendable, one a spoon and another an arm.

    b. Put the Bendable interface, and the Arm and Spoon classes in a named package. The test class will not be in that package. Put it in a directory which does not contain the package. Show how you configure your system to provide the test class access to the package.

17. Create a `Picture` subclass of the `Shape` class of Example 9.12. A picture contains an array of shapes, which may themselves be pictures, or any other shapes. Implement the `draw`, `move`, and `toString` methods for pictures. Implement an `add` method which will add shapes to the picture. The center of a shape will be the center of the picture. When drawing a picture, draw its shapes relative to the center of the picture. For example, if a picture has center (100,100) and contains a circle with center (20,30) and radius 10, then draw that circle at center (120,130) with radius 10.

18. Create an applet to display a circle and a line and allow the user to choose which figures to move. Add text fields to allow the user to input the amounts to move in the x and y directions, and a button for the user to request the move. Move the selected figure, when the user presses the button.

CHAPTER

10 Window, Mouse, and Key Events

OUTLINE

Introduction

Thus far we have not needed to handle window events. Our graphics programs have been applets run by the browser or applet viewer, which opens and closes the windows for us. To create standalone graphics applications we will need to handle window events, and can then use the same graphics techniques and user interface components that we used in our applet examples. We will show the steps needed to convert an applet to a standalone application or to convert a standalone application to an applet.

When we use the mouse to press buttons, and to select checkbox and choice items, we do not handle the mouse events directly. The button responds to a mouse click, generating an action event describing the button press. The checkbox and choice box respond to the mouse click by generating an item event. We refer to these action and item events as high-level or semantic events because they incorporate the meaning of the mouse click as a button press or item selection.

In this chapter we learn to handle mouse events directly, and in the process introduce the concept of an adapter class, a useful tool for implementing interfaces containing multiple methods. By responding directly to low-level mouse events, we will be able to use the mouse to drag shapes, change colors, and play games. Figure 10.1 shows a simple screen for playing tick tack toe with the computer. We leave the implementation of this and a Nim game for the exercises.

Figure 10.1 Tick tack toe

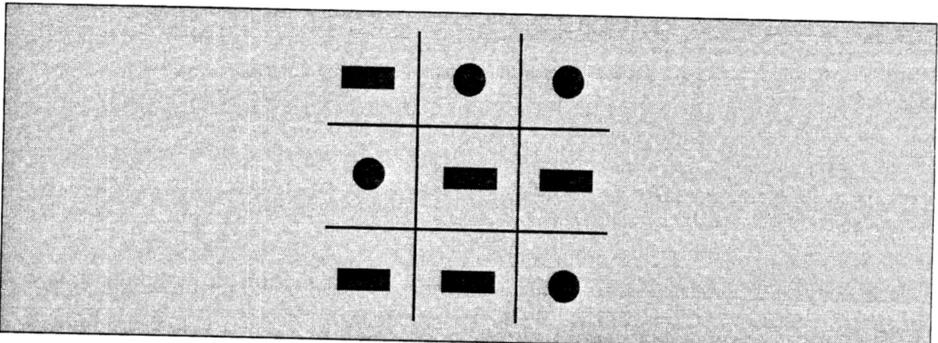

When we use the keyboard to enter text in a text field, we do not handle the key events directly. When we hit the `Enter` key, the text field generates an action event describing the text entry. In this chapter we learn to handle key events. We will use keys to rotate shapes in solving the tangram puzzle.

OBJECTIVES:

- Handle window events.
- Use adapter classes.
- Convert applets to standalone applications.
- Write standalone applications.
- Convert standalone applications to applets.
- Handle mouse events.
- Handle key events.
- Use the mouse and the keyboard to solve tangram puzzles.

10.1 Closing Windows

Thus far in our GUI examples we have not had to close any windows. Our applets are panels, which are not standalone windows. Applets are displayed by a browser or applet viewer which is responsible for closing the window containing the applet. Preparing to create standalone GUI applications, we present the `WindowEvent` class and

WindowListener interface that allow us to respond to window events in a **top-level window.**

Frames

Recall from our introduction to components that the Frame class is a container we can use as a standalone window. Frames are top-level windows, not nested inside other containers. We, not the browser or applet viewer, are responsible for creating frames and closing them when we are done using them. In this section we popup a top-level window from an applet, while in the next we will see how to write standalone applications using frames.

To create a frame, we pass a title to the Frame constructor

```
Frame f = new Frame("MyFrame");
```

The title will appear in the frame that comprises the window's border. To specify the size of the frame, we use the setSize method

```
f.setSize(150,150);
```

To make the frame visible we can call

```
f.setVisible(true);
```

while calling

```
f.setVisible(false);
```

will hide the frame. The show method will make a frame visible and if the frame is already visible it will bring it to the top.

Window Events and WindowListener

In the Java event model, a source object generates the event and a handler object handles it. Pressing a button generates a high-level action event. An event handler implementing the ActionListener interface has only to implement the actionPerformed method. Low-level window events have a more complex interface.

To listen for window events, an object must be registered as a window listener, using the addWindowListener method. It must implement the seven methods of the WindowListener interface, which are:

windowActivated	The window gets the focus.
windowDeactivated	The window loses the focus.
windowOpened	The window is opened.
windowClosed	The window is closed.
windowClosing	The user asks to close the window.
windowIconified	The window is minimized as an icon.
windowDeiconified	The window is restored from an icon.

In Example 10.1 we create a frame in an applet, letting the applet implement the window listener interface. It ignores all events except `WINDOW_CLOSING`, generated when the user clicks on the `X` in the upper-right corner of the frame, or chooses *Close* from the menu in the upper-left corner of the frame. The purpose of this example is to construct our first standalone frame.

Running Example 10.1 involves two windows; the first contains the applet while the second is the frame. Figure 10.2 shows the two windows. We handle the window event that the user generates to close the `MyFrame` window, but the applet viewer handles the event the user generates to close the applet.

Figure 10.2 The frame and the applet

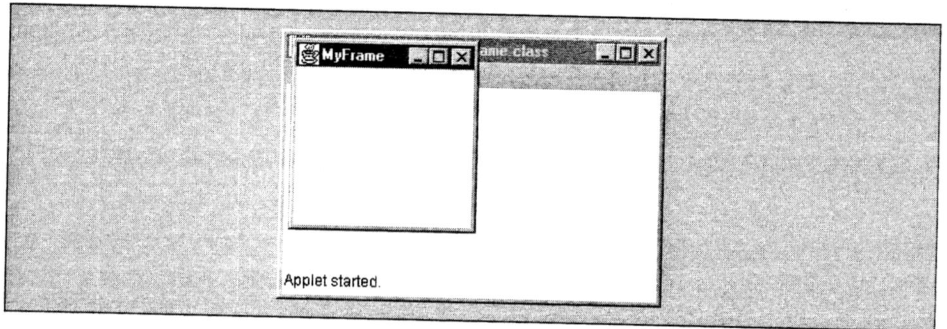

In Example 10.1, six of the seven window handling methods have empty bodies. The `windowClosing` method hides the window, and calls the `dispose` method to free up the system resources used for that window.

EXAMPLE 10.1 AppletFrame.java

```
/*  Shows the use of a Frame as a top-level
 *  window.  Each window event causes the
 *  applet to display a message in the console.
 */

import java.awt.*;
import java.awt.event.*;
import java.applet.Applet;

public class AppletFrame extends Applet
            implements WindowListener {                    // Note 1
  private Frame f;

  public void init() {
    f = new Frame("MyFrame");                               // Note 2
    f.setSize(150,150);
    f.show();
    f.addWindowListener(this);                              // Note 3
  }
```

```
public void windowActivated(WindowEvent evt) {                    // Note 4
}
public void windowDeactivated(WindowEvent evt) {
}
public void windowClosed(WindowEvent event) {
}
public void windowDeiconified(WindowEvent event) {
}
public void windowIconified(WindowEvent event) {
}
public void windowOpened(WindowEvent event) {
}
public void windowClosing(WindowEvent event) {
  f.setVisible(false);
  f.dispose();                                                    // Note 5
}
}
```

Note 1: The applet implements the `WindowListener` interface, which requires that it implement the seven window event-handling methods. We will see in Example 10.2 how to use the `WindowAdapter` class when we do not want to handle all seven window events.

Note 2: We have to create the frame, set its size, and show it. In this example we did not use the frame, but in the next we will show we can create a subclass of `Frame` on which we can draw and to which we can add components.

Note 3: The applet registers itself with the frame as a listener of window events.

Note 4: Each of the seven window event-handling methods displays a message in the console, so we can see when that event occurs.

Note 5: When the user asks to close the window, we hide it to remove the display and then dispose of it, freeing up the system resources that were used for it.

Adapter Classes

An **adapter class** connects the source of an event with its target, implementing the methods of a listener interface. In Example 10.1 the applet implemented all seven methods of the `WindowListener` interface, six of them with empty bodies because we are not interested in those events. We could have used a separate class to implement the window listener interface, registering it as a window listener rather than the applet. Using such an adapter class would separate the event-handling code from the application code.

To simplify the handling of low-level events, Java provides adapter classes with default implementations of each method of the appropriate interface. The `WindowAdapter` class implements each of the seven methods of the `WindowListener` interface with empty bodies. We can define a subclass of `WindowAdapter` to override just those methods that handle the events we are interested in.

For example, if we just want to handle the window closing event, as was the case in Example 10.1, we can define a class `WindowClose` which extends the `WindowAdapter` class and just overrides the `windowClosing` method. Example 10.2 revises Example 10.1 to make this change.

TIP

For easier handling of window events we use the `WindowAdapter` class from the AWT, but this technique is generally applicable. Whenever we define an interface, say

```
public interface Chores {
  public void washCar(Car aBigCar);
  public void feedDog(Dog iggy);
  public void makeCoffee(Coffee brew);
}
```

we should define an adapter class which implements the interface with empty bodies

```
  public abstract class ChoresAdapter
              implements Chores {
  public void washCar(Car aBigCar) {  }
  public void feedDog(Dog iggy) {  }
  public void makeCoffee(Coffee brew) {  }
}
```

Classes that implements the Chores interface can override those methods of the ChoresAdapter class which handle events of interest to it. For example, a class that just wants to feed the dog could override `ChoresAdapter` to provide an implementation for the `feedDog` method, inheriting the do nothing implementations for the `washCar` and `makeCoffee` methods.

```
  public class DogFeeder extends ChoresAdapter {
    public void feedDog(Dog iggy) {
      // routine to feed the dog goes here
  }
}
```

WindowAdapter

In Example 10.1 we implemented all seven window event-handling methods of the `WindowListener` interface. In many window applications we may only wish to respond to the user's request to close the window. Implementing the window listener interface directly in this situation requires us to provide empty bodies for the six methods that handle the six events to which we do not want to respond. In Example 10.2, we define a subclass of `WindowAdapter` to override the `windowClosing` method.

In Example 10.2 we define a subclass of `Frame` and add a text field to it, showing that we can add components to standalone windows just as we have added them to applets and panels. When the user enters text in the text field we display it in our frame using a larger point size and a bold style. We define a subclass of `WindowAdapter` that overrides the `windowClosing` method to allow the user to close the frame, but accepts the default implementations of the other six window event-handling methods inherited from the `WindowAdapter` class. Figure 10.3 shows the applet and the frame just after the user entered "hi there" in the text field.

Figure 10.3 The applet of Example 10.2

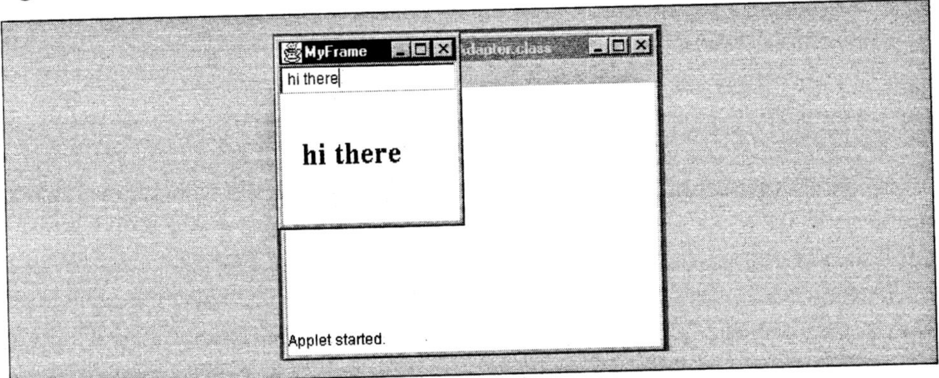

Panels and applets, which inherit from `Panel`, use the flow layout as the default, but frames use the border layout as the default. In Example 10.2, we add the text field to our subclass of `Frame` in the North region.

EXAMPLE 10.2 FrameAdapter.java

```
/*  Defines a subclass of WindowAdapter, overriding
 *  the windowClosing method but inheriting the default
 *  implementations of the other six window handling
 *  methods. Defines a subclass of Frame, adding a text
 *  field, and displaying the string the user enters.
 */

import java.awt.*;
import java.awt.event.*;
import java.applet.Applet;
public class FrameAdapter extends Applet {
  private MyFrame f;

  public void init() {                                    // Note 1
    f = new MyFrame("MyFrame");
    f.setSize(150,150);
    f.show();                                             // Note 2
    f.addWindowListener(new CloseWindow());
  }
                                                          // Note 3
  class CloseWindow extends WindowAdapter {
    public void windowClosing(WindowEvent event) {
      f.setVisible(false);
      f.dispose();
    }
  }
}
```

```
class MyFrame extends Frame
              implements ActionListener{
  Font font = new Font("Serif",Font.BOLD,24);
  TextField text = new TextField(10);

  public MyFrame(String title) {                               // Note 4
    super(title);                                              // Note 5
    add(text,"North");                                         // Note 6
    text.addActionListener(this);
  }
  public void actionPerformed(ActionEvent event) {             // Note 7
    repaint();
  }
  public void paint(Graphics g) {
    g.setFont(font);
    g.drawString(text.getText(),20,100);
  }
}
```

Note 1: We need to define a subclass, `MyFrame`, of `Frame`, to override the `paint` method, and to add components to it.

Note 2: We create an instance of the inner `CloseWindow` class to handle the window events generated by our frame.

Note 3: We define the `CloseWindow` subclass of `WindowAdapter` which has default implementations of all seven window handling methods of the `WindowListener` interface. We only override the `windowClosing` method.

Note 4: Top-level frames add components in their constructors, in contrast to applets which add components in the `init` method called by the browser or applet viewer before starting the applet.

Note 5: We pass the title to the constructor of the `Frame` superclass.

Note 6: `add(text,"North");`
Frames use the border layout by default.

Note 7: `public void actionPerformed(ActionEvent event)`
`{ repaint();}`
When the user presses the *`Enter`* key after entering text in the text field, we repaint the frame drawing the text entered in a larger font.

THE BIG PICTURE

When using a top-level window such as a `Frame`, we need to close it ourselves. The `WindowEvent` class represents seven window events. A class that handles these events can either implement the seven methods of the `WindowListener` interface or extend `WindowAdapter`, overriding the methods that handle the events of interest. To close a window, we need only override the `windowClosing` method.

TEST YOUR UNDERSTANDING

Y IT YOURSELF

1. Omit the `windowIconified` method from Example 10.1. Compile the modified program and see what happens.

Y IT YOURSELF

2. a. Omit the statement `f.show()` from Example 10.2. Run the modified program and see what happens.

   b. Change the statement `f.show()` in Example 10.2 to f.setVisible(true). Run the modified program and see what happens.

0.2 Applets <-- --> Standalone Applications

Having learned how to create frames and close them in the last section we can now write standalone applications with graphical user interfaces. We will find we can use the text and shapes we drew in applets, and the components we added to applets in standalone applications. In fact, a graphical standalone application is not very much different from a graphical applet. We can easily convert an applet to a standalone application and vice versa.

Applets to Applications

To illustrate, we convert the applet, `ButtonPress`, of Example 7.3 to the standalone application `ButtonPressFrame`, which will have a `main` method that we call using the Java interpreter. Because we are writing event-driven programs, the `main` method is very simple; it just creates our subclass of `Frame`, sets its size, and shows it. When the user presses one of the buttons, our program responds. Pressing the *Print* button causes the string `"hi there"` to be displayed, while pressing the *Clear* button causes it to be erased. We define the `windowClosing` method so clicking the button in the upper-right corner of the frame causes the program to terminate.

Figure 10.4 shows our top-level window for Example 10.3, which looks like the right window of Figure 7.8 except that this top-level window, titled `MyFrame`, is the one we created, whereas the applet viewer created the window of Figure 7.8.

Figure 10.4 The frame of Example 10.3

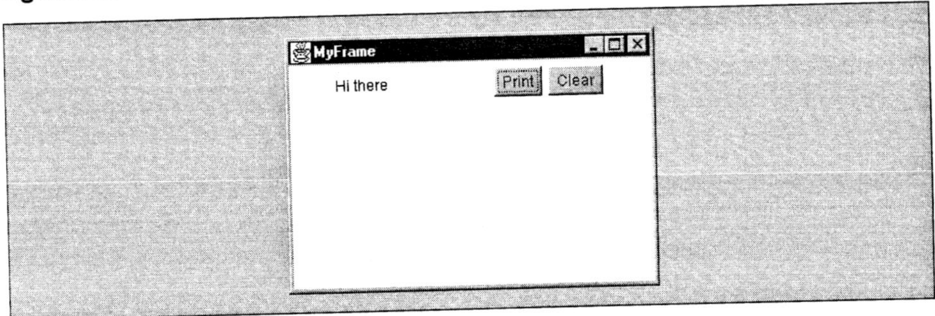

The changes from Example 7.3 to Example 10.3 in the order they appear are:

- Omit "`import java.applet.Applet`" because we are not using an applet.
- Extend `Frame`, rather than `Applet`, because we want a top-level window.
- Use a constructor rather than the `init` method of the applet.
- Add a string argument to the constructor to pass the title to the `Frame`. (Applets, appearing inside other windows, do not have titles.)
- Set the layout to flow layout to preserve the default layout of the applet.
- Add a window listener. (We have to close our top-level window, whereas the applet viewer or browser closed the applet.)
- Add a `main` method to create our subclass of `Frame`, set its size, and show it. (The applet viewer or browser did that for applets.)
- Add a `CloseWindow` subclass of `WindowAdapter` to handle window events.

Otherwise the code in Example 10.3 is the same as the code in Example 7.3.

EXAMPLE 10.3 **ButtonPressFrame.java**

```
/* Converts Example 7.3, ButtonPress.java
 * from an applet to a standalone application.
 */

import java.awt.*;
import java.awt.event.*;

public class ButtonPressFrame extends Frame                      // Note 1
                  implements ActionListener {
  private Button print = new Button("Print");
  private Button clear = new Button("Clear");
  private Label message = new Label("Message goes here");

  public ButtonPressFrame(String title) {                        // Note 2
    super(title);
    setLayout(new FlowLayout());                                 // Note 3
    add(message);
    add(print);
    add(clear);
    print.addActionListener(this);
    clear.addActionListener(this);
    addWindowListener(new CloseWindow());                        // Note 4
  }
  public void actionPerformed(ActionEvent event) {
    Object source = event.getSource();
    if (source == print)
      message.setText("Hi there");
    else if (source == clear)
      message.setText("");
  }
```

```
  public static void main(String [ ] args) {                    // Note 5
   ButtonPressFrame f = new ButtonPressFrame("MyFrame");
   f.setSize(300,200);
   f.show();
  }

 class CloseWindow extends WindowAdapter {                      // Note 6
   public void windowClosing(WindowEvent event) {
     System.exit(0);                                            // Note 7
   }
  }
}
```

Note 1: To make a top-level window to which we can add components, we extend the `Frame` class.

Note 2: We put the code in the applet's `init` method in our frame's constructor. In addition we pass a title to the constructor of the superclass, `Frame`.

Note 3: The applet had a flow layout by default. To keep that same flow layout we need to set it explicitly because frames have a default border layout.

Note 4: We have to handle the window closing that the applet viewer or the browser handled for the applet.

Note 5: The `main` method creates our frame, sets its size, and shows it. User events such as button presses and window closing drive our program after the `main` method has set up the frame.

Note 6: `class CloseWindow extends WindowAdapter {`
The inner class `CloseWindow` overrides the `windowClosing` method of the `WindowAdapter` class so the user can close the window.

Note 7: `windowClosing(WindowEvent event) {`
When the user closes the window we terminate the program, returning control to the operating system.

Console Application to GUI Application

We can convert a standalone application to an applet even more easily than we converted the applet of Example 7.3 to the standalone application of Example 10.3. However we have not yet written any standalone GUI programs that we can convert to applets, so we first convert Example 4.5, `Growth.java`, to a GUI application, Example 10.4, `GrowthFrame.java`.

In Example 4.5 we input the interest rate, the beginning account balance, and the term of the account, then output the amount of the balance at the end of the term. We make a GUI similar to that of Example 8.13 in which we put the user interface components in the `North` region and drew on a canvas in the center. In the `Growth` program we input three values. To input three values graphically we can use three text fields, with each text field having a label.

Six components, the three labels and the three text fields would be too wide to fit in one row side by side, so we put each text field and its label into a panel with a 2x1 grid layout, so the text field will appear below its label. We add the three panels to a containing panel, which we add to the `North` region. We do not want to compute the resulting balance until the user has entered the desired values in all three text fields. Rather than handling the action events generated by the text fields, we add a button in the `South` region that the user can press when all the data has been entered.

Figure 10.5 shows the standalone graphical application of Example 10.4.

Figure 10.5 The standalone application of Example 10.4

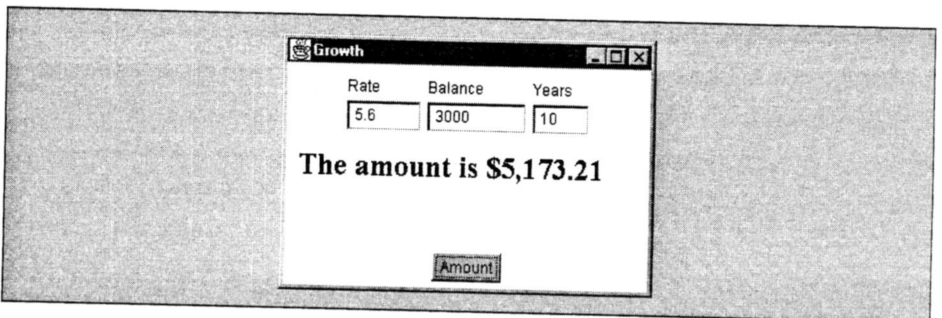

When the user presses the button, we use the `getText` method to get the text from each of the three text fields. The text in a text field has type `String`, so we need to convert the entries to type **double** for the interest rate and the balance, and to type **int** for the years. As in Section 7.2, we use the expression

```
double rate =  new Double(getRate.getText()).doubleValue();
```

to convert the rate to a **double**. To convert the years from `String` to **int** we use the analogous expression

```
int years = new Integer(getYears.getText()).intValue();
```

In Example 10.4, the user can change one or more values and press the button again to calculate the amount that will result if the specified balance earns interest at the specified rate for the specified number of years. In addition to notes, we annotate the code with change items, which identify the simple changes needed to convert this standalone application to an applet.

EXAMPLE 10.4 GrowthFrame.java

```
/* Revises Example 4.5, Growth.java, to make it a graphical
 * rather than a console program.
 */

import java.awt.*;
import java.awt.event.*;
```

```
import java.text.NumberFormat;                          // Change 1
                                                        // Change 2
public class GrowthFrame extends Frame
         implements ActionListener {
  private TextField getRate = new TextField(5);
  private TextField getBalance = new TextField(8);
  private TextField getYears = new TextField(3);
  private Label rate = new Label("Rate");
  private Label balance = new Label("Balance");
  private Label years = new Label("Years");
  private MyCanvas canvas = new MyCanvas();
  private Button button = new Button("Amount");
  private String amount = "Press button";                       // Note 1
  private NumberFormat nf;

  public GrowthFrame(String title) {                    // Change 3
     super(title);                                      // Change 4
     Panel p1 = new Panel();
     p1.setLayout(new GridLayout(2,1));
     p1.add(rate);
     p1.add(getRate);

     Panel p2 = new Panel();
     p2.setLayout(new GridLayout(2,1));
     p2.add(balance);
     p2.add(getBalance);

     Panel p3 = new Panel();
     p3.setLayout(new GridLayout(2,1));
     p3.add(years);
     p3.add(getYears);

     Panel p = new Panel();
     p.add(p1);
     p.add(p2);
     p.add(p3);

     Panel p4 = new Panel();
     p4.add(button);
     add(p,"North");
     add(canvas,"Center");
     add(p4,"South");
     addWindowListener(new CloseWindow());              // Change 5
     button.addActionListener(this);                            // Note 2
     nf = NumberFormat.getCurrencyInstance();
  }
```

```
  public String computeGrowth() {                                // Note 3
    double rate = new Double(getRate.getText()).doubleValue();
    double balance = new Double(getBalance.getText()).doubleValue();
    int years = new Integer(getYears.getText()).intValue();
    for (int i = 1; i <= years; i++)
      balance += balance * rate / 100;
    return nf.format(balance);                                   // Note 4
  }

  public void actionPerformed(ActionEvent event) {               // Note 5
    amount = "The amount is " + computeGrowth();
    canvas.repaint();
  }

  public static void main(String [ ] args) {                     // Change 6
    GrowthFrame f = new GrowthFrame("Growth");
    f.setSize(300,200);
    f.show();
  }

  class CloseWindow extends WindowAdapter {                      // Change 7
    public void windowClosing(WindowEvent event) {
      System.exit(0);
    }
  }

  class MyCanvas extends Canvas {
    public MyCanvas() {
      Font f = new Font("Serif",Font.BOLD,24);
      setFont(f);
    }
    public void paint(Graphics g) {
      g.drawString(amount,10,30);
    }
  }
}
```

Note 1: The applet will display the string "Press button" when it starts running.

Note 2 We only listen for action events generated by button presses, not text fields. The user presses the button after entering the desired values in each of the three text fields.

Note 3: The `computeGrowth` method gets the text from the text fields, converting the rate and balance to type **double** and the years to type **int**, and then computing the amount of the balance at the end of the term.

Note 4: We format balance as currency.

Note 5: When the user presses the button, we call the `computeGrowth` method to do the computation, and ask to repaint the canvas which will draw a string showing the resulting amount.

andalone Application to Applet

We can easily convert the standalone application of Example 10.4 to an applet, mostly by omitting lines. We show the necessary changes, referring to the change items annotating Example 10.4.

Change 1: Add the line `import java.applet.Applet` here.

Change 2: Replace with `public class GrowthApplet extends Applet`

Change 3: Replace with `public void init() {`

Change 4: Replace with `setLayout(new BorderLayout());` to preserve the border layout which is the default for the frame of the standalone application.

Change 5: Omit this line, as the browser or applet viewer handles the windows.

Change 6: Omit the `main` method, because an applet is called from a browser or applet viewer.

Change 7: Omit the `CloseWindow` class because we do not need to handle window events.

Because there are so few changes to Example 10.4 needed to convert it to an applet we do not print the full code here, but provide the `GrowthApplet.java` file on the disk that accompanies this text. Running the applet gives a user interface that looks just like Figure 10.5.

THE BIG PICTURE

We started graphical user interfaces using applets, but the same drawing and user interface components can be used in standalone applications. A standalone application extends `Frame` rather than `Applet`, uses a constructor rather than an `init` method, and must close the window itself. It is easy to convert a standalone application to an applet or an applet to a standalone application.

TEST YOUR UNDERSTANDING

TRY IT YOURSELF 3. Modify Example 10.3 to omit adding a window listener and the `CloseWindow` class. Run the modified program to see what happens. (To abort the program, hold the `Control` key and hit the `C` key in the console window.)

TRY IT YOURSELF 4. Another way to convert a numerical string s to a double d uses the `valueOf` method, as in

```
d = Double.valueOf(s).doubleValue();
```

Modify Example 10.4 to use this method to convert the rate and balance strings entered in the text fields to type **double**. Run the modified example to see that it still works properly.

10.3 Using the Mouse

Our three examples illustrate three aspects of using the mouse. The first concerns the mouse in a fixed location, while the second concerns a moving mouse. Finally, for mouse events, we utilize the general technique of providing a trivial implementation of an interface that we can override to implement those methods in which we are interested.

Mouse Events

In the Java event model, a source object generates the event and a handler object handles it. With the mouse, the user can generate seven types of **low-level events** in a component source:

`MOUSE_PRESSED`	user pressed the mouse in a component
`MOUSE_RELEASED`	user released the mouse in a component
`MOUSE_CLICKED`	user clicked the mouse in a component
`MOUSE_ENTERED`	the mouse entered a component
`MOUSE_EXITED`	the mouse exited a component
`MOUSE_MOVED`	the mouse moved (no button down) in a component
`MOUSE_DRAGGED`	the mouse moved (button down) in a component

These are seven types of `MouseEvent`, which is a class in the `java.awt.event` package. The `MOUSE_CLICKED` type refers to a mouse click which consists of a mouse press followed by a mouse release, with no intervening mouse drag.

MouseListener and MouseMotionListener

Java uses two types of listener interfaces to handle mouse events. An object that wants to be notified of any of the first five mouse events, mouse pressed, released, clicked, entered, or exited, needs to register, using the `addMouseListener` method, as a `MouseListener` with the component that is the event source. It must implement each of the five methods of the `MouseListener` interface:

```
public void mousePressed(MouseEvent e);
public void mouseReleased(MouseEvent e);
public void mouseClicked(MouseEvent e);
public void mouseEntered(MouseEvent e);
public void mouseExited(MouseEvent e);
```

An object that wants to be notified of any of the last two mouse events, mouse moved or dragged, needs to register as a `MouseMotionListener` using the `addMouseMotionListener` method. It registers with the component that is the event source and must implement each of the two methods of the `MouseMotionListener` interface:

```
public void mouseMoved(MouseEvent e);
public void mouseDragged(MouseEvent e);
```

We can choose which mouse events we want to handle in our applications. If we only care about the mouse click, then we can ignore the mouse pressed, mouse released, mouse entered, and mouse exited events. To ignore a low-level mouse event we implement its handler method with an empty body. For example, implementing the `mousePressed` method as

```
public void mousePressed(MouseEvent e) { }
```

with an empty body will ensure nothing will happen in response to a mouse pressed event.

As an example, let us suppose when we press the mouse inside a polygon that we want to change its color to red. A scenario describing the interactions of the objects is:

```
The applet registers as a mouse listener with the polygon.
The user presses the mouse inside the polygon.
The applet (the component in which the user pressed the mouse) passes a mouse
  event describing the mouse press to the applet's mousePressed method.
The applet's mousePressed method changes the foreground color to red and asks
  Java to redraw it.
Java calls the applet's paint method which fills the polygon in red.
```

To illustrate the handling of mouse events, our first example program of this chapter will fill a triangle in red if the user presses the mouse inside it, and fill it in blue if the user releases the mouse inside it. If the user presses the mouse inside the triangle, but then drags the mouse outside of it, the triangle will remain red, as it only turns blue if the user releases the mouse inside it. Nothing happens if the user presses the mouse outside the triangle first, but if the user then drags the mouse inside the polygon and releases it, the polygon will turn blue. We also draw the strings "Got the mouse" when the mouse enters the applet, and "Lost the mouse" when the mouse leaves the applet.

Figure 10.6 shows the applet after the user pressed the mouse inside the triangle and released it outside, moving the mouse outside the applet. In color, the string and triangle are red.

Figure 10.6 The applet of Example 10.5

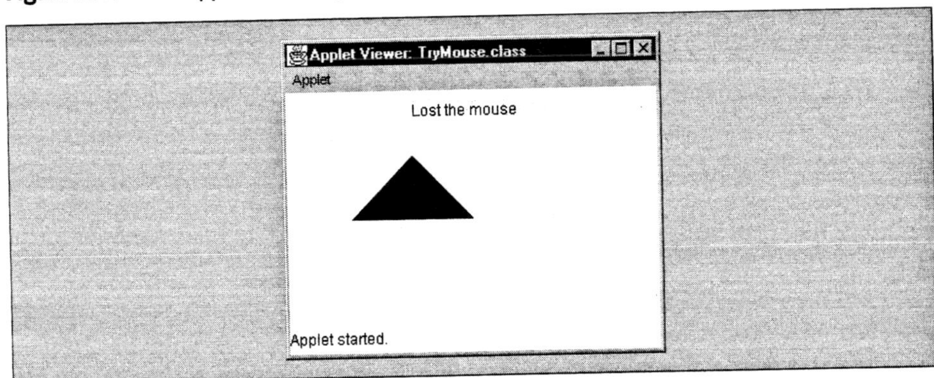

To implement these effects, the applet defines the mouse event-handling methods to change the settings and repaint so that the `paint` method can draw using the new settings. The `mousePressed` method sets the foreground color to red, while the `mouseReleased` method sets it to blue. The `mouseEntered` method sets the display string to "Got the mouse," while the `mouseExited` method sets that string to "Lost the mouse." In this example, we implement the `mouseClicked` method with an empty body, meaning we do not care about that type of event.

We can get the position of any mouse event using the `getX` and `getY` methods, as in

```
int x = event.getX();
```

where `event` is one of the seven types of mouse events. We can use the `contains` method of the `Polygon` class to see if the user pressed the mouse inside a polygon, as in

```
boolean inside = p.contains(event.getX(),event.getY());
```

where `p` is a polygon, and `event` is a mouse event describing a mouse press.

EXAMPLE 10.5 TryMouse.java

```
/* Fills a red triangle when the user presses the mouse
 * inside it.  Fills the triangle in blue when the user
 * releases the mouse inside it.  Draws "Got the mouse"
 * when the mouse enters the applet, and draws "Lost
 * the mouse" when the mouse exits the applet.  Provides
 * an empty body for mouseClicked.
 */

import java.awt.*;
import java.awt.event.*;
import java.applet.Applet;

public class TryMouse extends Applet
          implements MouseListener {                    // Note 1
  private int [ ] x = {50,100,150};
  private int [ ] y = {100,50,100};
  private Polygon p = new Polygon(x,y,3);               // Note 2
  private String mouse = "";                            // Note 3

  public void init() {
   addMouseListener(this);                              // Note 4
  }
  public void paint(Graphics g) {
   g.drawString(mouse,20,20);
   g.fillPolygon(p);
  }
  public void mousePressed(MouseEvent event) {
   if (p.contains(event.getX(), event.getY()))  {      // Note 5
     setForeground(Color.red);
     repaint();
```

```
    }
  }
  public void mouseReleased(MouseEvent event) {
    if (p.contains(event.getX(), event.getY()))  {
      setForeground(Color.blue);
      repaint();
    }
  }
  public void mouseClicked(MouseEvent event) {  }              // Note 6
  public void mouseEntered(MouseEvent event) {
    mouse = "Got the mouse";                                   // Note 7
    repaint();
  }
  public void mouseExited(MouseEvent event) {
    mouse = "Lost the mouse";
    repaint();
  }
}
```

Note 1: A class that implements the `MouseListener` interface must implement the five methods `mousePressed`, `mouseReleased`, `mouseClicked`, `mouseEntered`, and `mouseExited` to handle each of these events.

Note 2: We construct a triangle from arrays of its x- and y-coordinates.

Note 3: The `mouseEntered` and `mouseExited` methods will set this string. We initialize it to the empty string so the string will not be `null` when the applet is initialized.

Note 4: The applet registers to listen to its own mouse events. We could have created another class to listen to these events. With this approach, we use `addActionListener(new MouseHandler())` adding the `MouseHandler` class given by

```
class MouseHandler implements MouseMotionListener {
  /* Code for mousePressed, mouseReleased, mouseClicked,
   * mouseEntered, and mouseExited goes here.
}
```

In a small illustrative example we find it simpler to let the applet handle events itself, but in general, code quality improves when we separate GUI event handling from the code needed for other processing.

Note 5: The `getX()` and `getY()` methods return the position at which the user pressed the mouse. If that position is contained inside the polygon, then we set the foreground color to red, so the triangle will be redrawn in red.

Note 6: `public void mouseClicked(MouseEvent event) {  }`
A mouse listener must implement all five mouse event handling methods. We do not care about the mouse clicked event, so we just provide an empty body for the `mouseClicked` method.

Note 7: `mouse = "Got the mouse";`

When the mouse enters the applet, we set the display string to "Got the mouse" and then repaint so that the `paint` method will draw this string.

Moving the Mouse

Java separates the mouse moved and mouse dragged events from the other mouse events. Mouse motion events occur in great numbers and users not interested in them should not have to be bothered by them. As noted above, the `MouseMotionListener` interface has two methods, `mouseMoved` and `mouseDragged`, that need to be implemented by mouse motion listeners interested in these events. A mouse moved event occurs when the user moves the mouse with no buttons pressed, while a mouse dragged event occurs when the user moves the mouse while pressing a button.

A sample scenario in which the user drags a polygon to a new position is:

```
The applet registers as a mouse listener.
The applet registers as a mouse motion listener.
The user presses the mouse inside a polygon.
The applet sends a mouse event describing the mouse press to the applet's
  mousePressed method.
The applet's mousePressed method saves the position of the mouse.
The user drags the mouse to a new position.
The applet sends a mouse event describing the mouse drag to the applet's
  mouseDragged method.
The applet's mouseDragged method translates the polygon to the new mouse
  position, saves that position in case the user drags the polygon again, and
  asks Java to redraw the applet.
Java calls the applet's paint method to redraw the applet with the polygon
  in its new position.
```

Example 10.6 enables the user to drag a triangle with the mouse. Figure 10.7 shows the triangle when the applet has just started, and then after the user dragged it to the lower-left.

Figure 10.7 The applet of Example 10.6

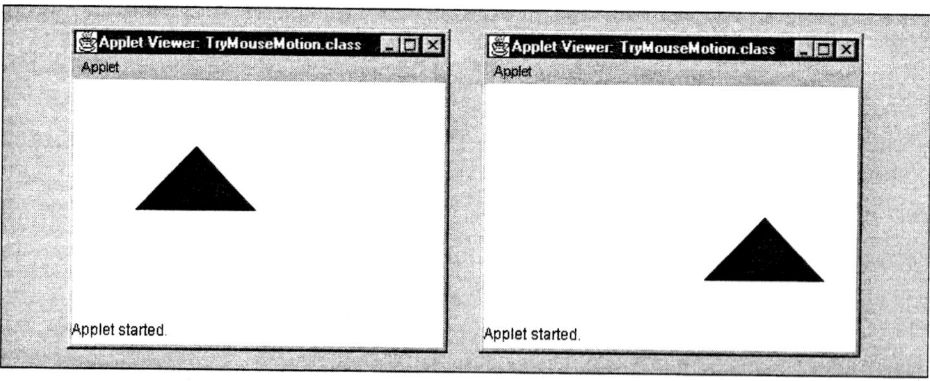

This applet implements both the `MouseListener` and the `MouseMotionListener` interfaces. When the user presses the mouse inside the polygon, the `mousePressed` method saves the x- and y-coordinates of the mouse press for use if the user drags the mouse to a new position.

When the user does drag the mouse to a new position, the `mouseDragged` method translates the polygon by the amount `(x-oldx,y-oldy)` where `(x,y)` is the new location of the mouse, and `(oldx,oldy)` is its previous location. The `mouseDragged` method then updates the `oldx` and `oldy` values to the current position, `(x,y)`, in case the user continues to drag the mouse.

EXAMPLE 10.6 TryMouseMotion.java

```
/*  Drags a triangle to a new location
 *  using the position of the mouse to
 *  determine how to move the polygon.
 */

import java.awt.*;
import java.awt.event.*;
import java.applet.Applet;

public class TryMouseMotion extends Applet
        implements MouseListener, MouseMotionListener {            // Note 1
  private int [ ] x = {50,100,150};
  private int [ ] y = {100,50,100};
  private Polygon p = new Polygon(x,y,3);
  private int oldx;                          // saves previous polygon position
  private int oldy;

  public void init() {
     addMouseListener(this);
     addMouseMotionListener(this);                                  // Note 2
  }
  public void paint(Graphics g) {
     g.fillPolygon(p);
  }
  public void mousePressed(MouseEvent event) {
     int x = event.getX();
     int y = event.getY();
     if (p.contains(x,y)){                                          // Note 3
      oldx = x;
      oldy = y;
    }
  }
  public void mouseReleased(MouseEvent event) {  }
  public void mouseClicked(MouseEvent event) {  }
```

```
    public void mouseEntered(MouseEvent event) {  }
    public void mouseExited(MouseEvent event) {  }
    public void mouseMoved(MouseEvent event) { }
    public void mouseDragged(MouseEvent event) {
      int x = event.getX();
      int y = event.getY();
      if (p.contains(x,y)){
        p.translate(x - oldx, y - oldy);                          // Note 4
        oldx = x;
        oldy = y;
        repaint();
      }
    }
  }
```

Note 1: The applet implements the `MouseListener` interface to respond to mouse pressed events and the `MouseMotionListener` interface to respond to mouse dragged events. We could have used another class to implement these listener interfaces.

Note 2: The applet registers with itself to listen for mouse events. The applet will the listener who responds to these events.

Note 3: When the user presses the mouse, we check to see if the mouse is inside the triangle, and if so we save the mouse position to use if the user drags the mouse to a new position.

Note 4: When the user drags the mouse to a new position, we translate the polygon to that position.

MouseAdapter

The `MouseAdapter` class implements each of the five methods of the `MouseListener` interface with empty bodies. If we want to handle the mouse pressed event, and do not want to handle mouse released, mouse clicked, mouse entered, and mouse exited, as was the case in Example 10.6, we can define a class `MousePressListener` which extends the `MouseAdapter` class and just overrides the `mousePressed` method. Example 10.7 revises Exam,ple 10.6 to make that change.

EXAMPLE 10.7 TryMouseAdapter.java

```
/*  Revises TryMouseMotion.java using
 *  an inner class to extend MouseAdapter,
 *  overriding the mousePressed method.
 */

import java.awt.*;
import java.awt.event.*;
import java.applet.Applet;
```

```
public class TryMouseAdapter extends Applet
  implements MouseMotionListener {                              // Note 1
  private int [ ] x = {50,100,150};
  private int [ ] y = {100,50,100};
  private Polygon p = new Polygon(x,y,3);
  private int oldx; // Saves previous polygon position
  private int oldy;
  public void init() {
     addMouseListener(new MousePressListener());                // Note 2
     addMouseMotionListener(this);
  }
  public void paint(Graphics g) {
     g.fillPolygon(p);
  }
  public void mouseMoved(MouseEvent event) { }
  public void mouseDragged(MouseEvent event) {
     int x = event.getX();
     int y = event.getY();
     if (p.contains(x,y)){
      p.translate(x - oldx, y - oldy);
      oldx = x;
      oldy = y;
      repaint();
     }
  }

  class MousePressListener extends MouseAdapter {               // Note 3
    public void mousePressed(MouseEvent event) {
      int x = event.getX();
      int y = event.getY();
      if (p.contains(x,y)){
        oldx = x;
        oldy = y;
      }
    }
  }
}
```

Note 1: The applet implements the `MouseMotionListener` interface, but uses a `MousePressListener` class, which extends the `MouseAdapter` class, to handle mouse events. We could have defined another class, extending the `MouseMotionAdapter` class, to handle mouse motion events, instead of having the applet implement the mouse motion listener interface, but we will leave that to the exercises.

Note 2: We create a new `MousePressListener` class to listen for mouse press events. `MousePressListener` extends `MouseAdapter` so it only has to implement the methods for the events it wants to handle.

Note 3: `MousePressListener` is an inner class, defined inside the applet. It implements the `mousePressed` method to handle mouse pressed events. The `MouseAdapter` class provides default implementations of all five mouse listeners methods; we only have to override the handlers for the events in which we are interested.

THE BIG PICTURE

Unlike the `ActionEvent` and `ItemEvent` classes that represent higher-level events, `MouseEvent` deals with basic mouse operations. In contrast to the `ActionListener` interface which needs only one method, the `MouseListener` interface has five methods and the `MouseMotionListener` interface has two. The `MouseAdapter` and `MouseMotionAdapter` classes provide trivial implementations of these interfaces, in which the methods do nothing. A class can either implement all five methods of the `MouseListener` interface or extend `MouseAdapter` and override only those methods needed to handle the mouse events of interest.The choice is similar for events involving mouse motion.

TEST YOUR UNDERSTANDING

5. Write a scenario showing the interactions of the objects in Example 10.5 if the user presses the mouse outside the triangle and releases the mouse inside it.

TRY IT YOURSELF

6. Add `print` statements to the `mousePressed`, `mouseReleased`, and `mouseClicked` methods in Example 10.5 to see in what order the mouse pressed, released, and clicked events are generated when the user clicks the mouse. In addition, try to press the mouse, drag it, and release it so a mouse clicked event is not generated.

TRY IT YOURSELF

7. Add a `print` statement to the `mouseDragged` method of Example 10.7 to see how frequently mouse dragged events are generated. The statement should print the value of a counter which `mouseDragged` increments each time it handles an event.

10.4 Using the Keyboard

When using the keyboard we have to distinguish between the physical keys pressed and the characters they might represent. For example, we use two keys to represent uppercase letters. With the `KeyEvent` class and the `KeyListener` interface Java lets us respond to user generated keyboard events.

Focus

We press the mouse at a specific point, in a specific component. An applet may contain several panels and other components. When we press the mouse, the component in which the mouse was pressed receives the mouse event. By contrast, pressing a key has no association with any specific component in the user interface. Java sends key events to the currently selected component, which is said to have the **focus**. A component that wants to receive key events must execute the `requestFocus` method to get the focus.

ey Events

Java defines three key events, `KEY_PRESSED`, `KEY_RELEASED`, and `KEY_TYPED`. Java generates the key pressed or key released events for each physical key that is pressed or released, and generates the key typed event when a Unicode character is typed. The `KEY_TYPED` event allows Java to give meaning to sequences of key presses used to represent a single Unicode character. We press two keys, the *Shift* key and a letter key, to represent an uppercase letter. This facility is very useful in adapting keyboards to input characters from diverse languages.

To represent the physical keys, Java uses key codes, (named integer constants), starting with the letters `VK_` (for virtual key). Some of these key codes are listed below:

Key Code	Physical Key
VK_A, ... , VK_Z	The keys A to Z
VK_0, ... , VK_9	The keys 0 to 9
VK_SHIFT	The shift key
VK_CONTROL	The control key
VK_DOWN, VK_UP	The down and up arrow keys
VK_RIGHT, VK_LEFT	The right and left arrow keys

Pressing the *G* key will generate a key pressed event and a key released event; it will also generate a key typed event which will indicate a `G` if the user pressed the *Shift* key while pressing the *G* key , or indicate a g otherwise. The key events that occur when the user types the uppercase letter `G` are:

Event	Description
KEY_PRESSED	Press the VK_SHIFT key
KEY_PRESSED	Press the VK_G key
KEY_TYPED	G was typed
KEY_RELEASED	Release the VK_G key
KEY_RELEASED	Release the VK_SHIFT key

KeyListener

An object that wishes to respond to key events must register as a key listener, using the `addKeyListener` method, with the source of these key events. The `KeyListener` interface has three methods,

```
public void keyPressed(KeyEvent e);
public void keyReleased(KeyEvent e);
public void keyTyped(KeyEvent e);
```

that a class wanting to listen to key events must implement. The source of a key event passes a `KeyEvent` object to the appropriate method. For example, pressing the *G* key will cause the component that has the focus to pass a `KeyEvent` object to the `key-Pressed` method of any objects registered as key listeners with that component.

To see how we handle key events, consider a simple applet which displays the letter a user types, moving it to the left when the user presses the `<-` key, and moving it to the right when the use presses the `->` key. If we move the letter using the arrow key alone, we change the position of the letter by two pixels, but if we hold down the *`Ctrl`* key while we move the letter using an arrow key, then we change the position of the letter by ten pixels. To implement this, the `keyPressed` method changes the increment to ten pixels when the user presses the *`Ctrl`* key, and the `keyReleased` method changes the increment back to two pixels when the user releases the *`Ctrl`* key.

Figure 10.8 shows, on the left, the applet of Example 10.8 initially displaying an `A`, and, on the right, displaying a `G` that the user typed and moved to the right of the applet.

Figure 10.8 The applet of Example 10.8

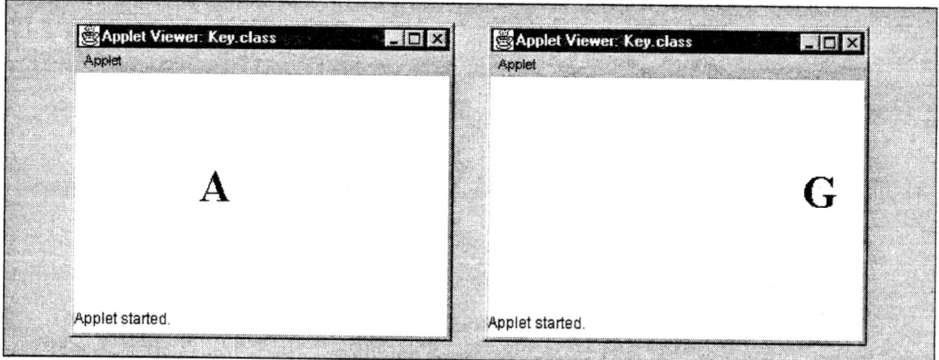

To find the physical key that was pressed or released we can use the `getKeyCode` method, as in:

```
event.getKeyCode();
```

where `event` describes the key event that occurred. The `getKeyCode` method returns a value of type **int** which gives the virtual key code for the key that was pressed or released. For example, it returns `VK_G` when the user presses or releases the *`G`* key, and `VK_LEFT` when the user presses or releases the left arrow key.

To find the character that was typed we can use the `getKeyChar` method, as in:

```
event.getKeyChar();
```

where `event` describes the key event that occurred. The `getKeyChar` method returns a value of type **char** which gives the character that was typed. For example, it will return `g` if the user types the *`G`* key alone, but will return `G` if the user presses and releases the *`G`* key while pressing the *`Shift`* key.

EXAMPLE 10.8 Key.java

```
/* Displays a key pressed by the user.  Moves the
 * character to the right if the user presses the ->
 * key and to the left if the user presses the <-
 * key.  Moves ten pixels if the user holds down the
 * Ctrl key and two pixels otherwise.
 */

import java.awt.*;
import java.awt.event.*;
import java.applet.Applet;

public class Key extends Applet
                 implements KeyListener {                            // Note 1
  public static int SLOW = 2;   // pixel change using arrow keys
  public static int FAST = 10;  // pixel change using arrow and Ctrl keys
  private int x = 100,y = 100;  // position of the character displayed
  private char theKey = 'A';
  private Font f = new Font("Serif",Font.BOLD,36);
  private int deltaX = SLOW;
  public void init() {
    setFont(f);
    addKeyListener(this);                                            // Note 2
    requestFocus();                                                  // Note 3
  }
  public void paint(Graphics g) {
      g.drawString(String.valueOf(theKey),x,y);                      // Note 4
  }
  public void keyPressed(KeyEvent event){
     int code = event.getKeyCode();                                  // Note 5
     if (code == KeyEvent.VK_CONTROL) {                              // Note 6
          deltaX = FAST;
     }
     else if (code == KeyEvent.VK_RIGHT){                            // Note 7
          x += deltaX;
          repaint();
     }
     else if (code == KeyEvent.VK_LEFT) {
         x -= deltaX;
         repaint();
     }
  }
  public void keyReleased(KeyEvent event) {
    if (event.getKeyCode() == KeyEvent.VK_CONTROL)
        deltaX = SLOW;                                               // Note 8
  }
```

```
  public void keyTyped(KeyEvent event) {
    theKey = event.getKeyChar();                              // Note 9
    repaint();
  }
}
```

Note 1: To handle key events a class can implement the `KeyListener` interface which consists of the methods `keyPressed`, `keyReleased`, and `keyTyped`.

Note 2: The applet registers with itself as a key listener, meaning it wants to be notified when key events occur. We could have defined another class to handle the key events.

Note 3: The applet must request the focus to receive key events. Unlike clicking the mouse, pressing a key does not associate that key press with any specific location in the applet. Any component in the applet could request the focus, but in this simple example, there are no components other than the applet itself.

Note 4: We convert the character that the user pressed (or A initially) to a string to display at the current (x,y) position.

Note 5: The `getKeyCode` method returns the number of the actual key that the user pressed. For example, pressing the *`G`* key would return `VK_G` from `getKeyCode`, and pressing the *`Ctrl`* key would return `VK_CONTROL`.

Note 6: `if (code == KeyEvent.VK_CONTROL) {`
When the user presses the *`Ctrl`* key, we set the increment to 10 pixels, so that if the user presses a left or right arrow key the letter will move by ten pixels as long as the user does not release the *`Ctrl`* key.

Note 7: `else if (code == KeyEvent.VK_RIGHT){`
If the user presses the -> key, we add the increment to the current value of x and ask that the applet be repainted. When Java calls the `paint` method the character will be drawn `deltaX` pixels to the right of its current position.

Note 8: `deltaX = SLOW;`
If the user releases the *`Ctrl`* key, we set the increment back to two pixels, so that if the user presses a left or right arrow key the letter will move by two pixels as long as the user does not press the *`Ctrl`* key.

Note 9: `theKey = event.getKeyChar();`
If the user types a Unicode character then the applet will generate a `keyTyped` event and the `getKeyChar` method will return the character typed (not the key pressed). If the user presses the *`G`* key without pressing the Shift key, then `getKeyChar` will return `g`.

Just as there is a `MouseAdapter` class which provides implementations of the five methods of the `MouseListener` interface, there is a `KeyAdapter` class that provides implementations, with empty bodies, of the three methods of the `KeyListener` interface. We did not use the `KeyAdapter` class in Example 10.8.

THE BIG PICTURE

A component that wishes to receive key events can use the `requestFocus` method to get the focus. To handle key events, a class either implements each of the three methods of the `KeyListener` interface or extends `KeyAdapter`, overriding those methods of interest. Two of the key events, `KEY_PRESSED` and `KEY_RELEASED`, represent physical key presses, while the third, `KEY_TYPED` represents a Unicode character typed. The `getKeyCode` method returns the physical key code, while the `getKeyChar` method returns the character typed.

TEST YOUR UNDERSTANDING

8. List the key events that occur if the user presses the *G* key without holding down the *Shift* key.

TRY IT YOURSELF 9. Add `print` statements to the `keyPressed`, `keyReleased`, and `keyTyped` methods of Example 10.8 to see in what order these events are generated when the user presses the *R* key. Try this with and without holding down the *Shift* key.

TRY IT YOURSELF 10. Remove the `requestFocus()` from the `init` method of Example 10.8 and note what happens when you run the modified program.

10.5 Solving Problems with Java: Drawing the Tangram Puzzle

The traditional tangram puzzle uses seven plastic or wooden pieces that fit nicely into a square shape, but which can be moved to create other figures. In this section we begin to computerize the tangram puzzle.

Defining the Problem

In this section we begin to experiment with the ancient Chinese tangram puzzle, in which a square is cut into five triangles, a square, and a parallelogram. The object of the puzzle is to reassemble the pieces into various fanciful shapes. Figure 10.9 shows the seven pieces in the square, and Figure 10.10 shows a cat into which they can be arranged.

In this section we build the puzzle pieces, and in the next we move the pieces around. To start, we create polygons to represent each of the pieces, draw the original square, and translate the pieces to a new location. Doing these things will not only prepare us to solve the puzzle, but will give us an opportunity to review arrays from Chapter 8.

Figure 10.9 The Seven Tangram Pieces

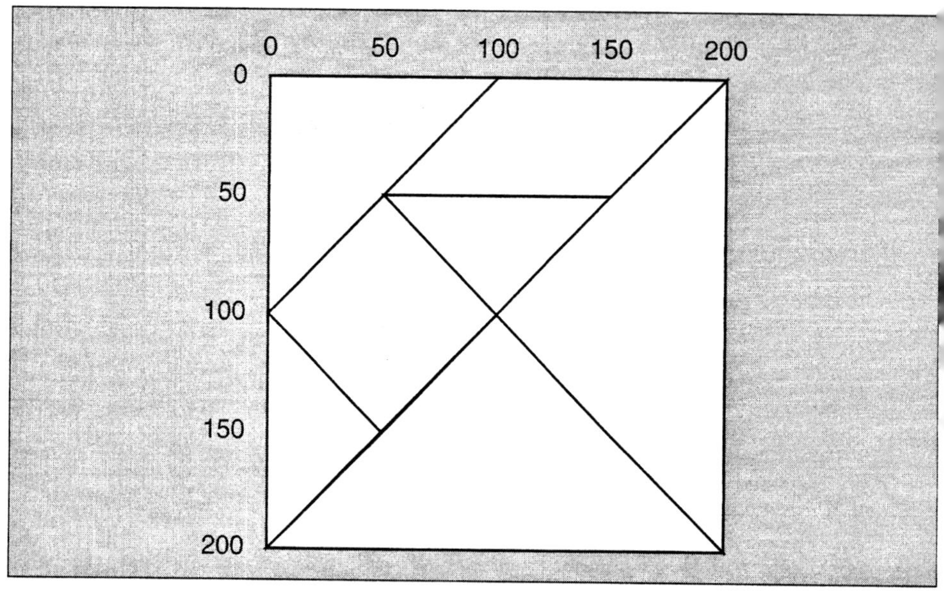

Figure 10.10 The Cat

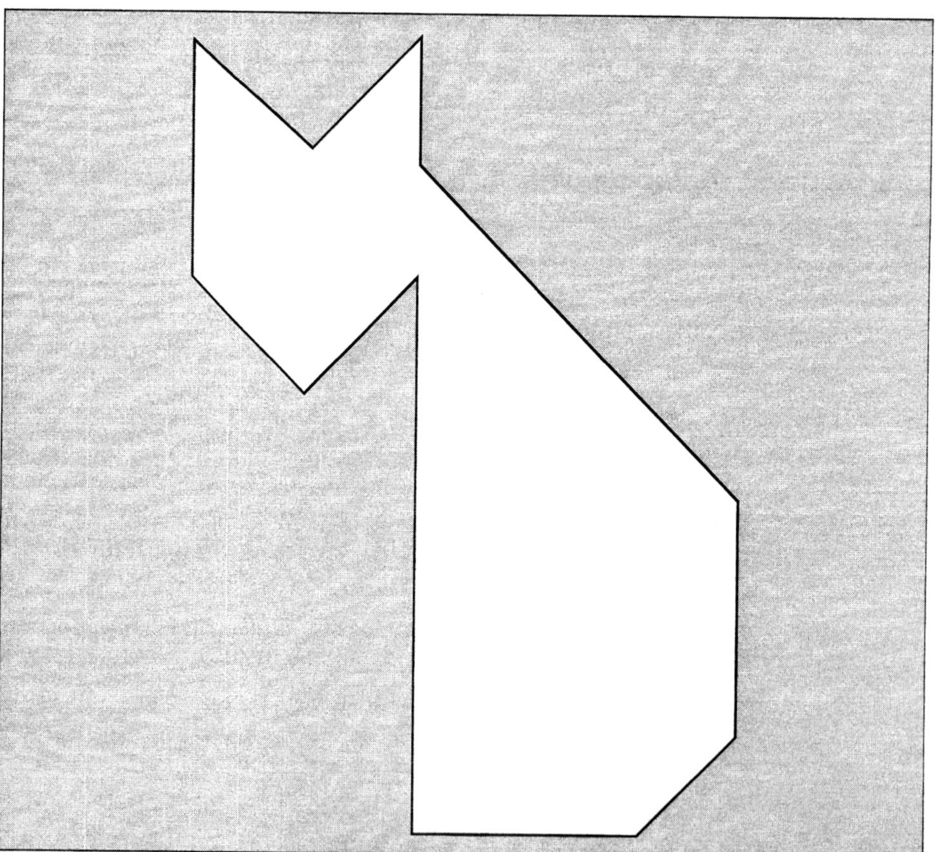

esigning a Solution: Starting with One Polygon

To begin to build our tangram solver, we first work with a single polygon, constructing, translating, and drawing it to prepare ourselves to manipulate the puzzle with its seven polygons.

The `Polygon` class in the `java.awt` package has the constructor

```
Polygon(int[] x, int[] y, int n)
```

where `x` and `y` are arrays of x- and y-coordinates and `n` is the number of vertices. Once we construct a polygon `p`, we draw it using

```
g.drawPolygon(p);
```

where `g` is a `Graphics` object.

The `Polygon` class has some methods that help us solve this puzzle problem. For example, if `p` is a polygon, then

```
p.contains(x,y)
```

tells us if the point `(x,y)` is inside `p`. We will use the `translate` method of the `Polygon` class, as in:

```
p.translate(x,y)
```

which will add `x` to the x-coordinate of every point in `p`, and add `y` to the y-coordinate of every point in `p`.

Before we try to construct all seven polygons, let us get started by working with the triangle in the upper-left corner of Figure 10.9. From that figure we learn the coordinates of its three corners are (0,0), (100,0), and (0,100). To construct this triangle in Java we need the arrays of the x- and y-coordinates for these points, which are:

```
int[] x = {0,100,0};  // x-coordinates
int[] y = {0,0,100};   // y-coordinates
```

The number of points to connect to form the triangle is 3. We use the `Polygon` constructor to construct this triangle:

```
Polygon triangle = new Polygon(x,y,3);
```

If we translate this triangle 100 pixels across to the right and 50 pixels down, as in:

```
triangle.translate(100,50);
```

we will move the triangle to the position shown in Figure 10.11

To draw the triangle we use the `drawPolygon` method, as in:

```
g.drawPolygon(triangle);
```

which will display the triangle in its original position if we call it before we translate the triangle, and in its new position if we call it after we translate the triangle.

Translating the triangle moves it to its new location. If we want to show the original position of the triangle and its new position in the same figure, we need

Figure 10.11 The translated triangle

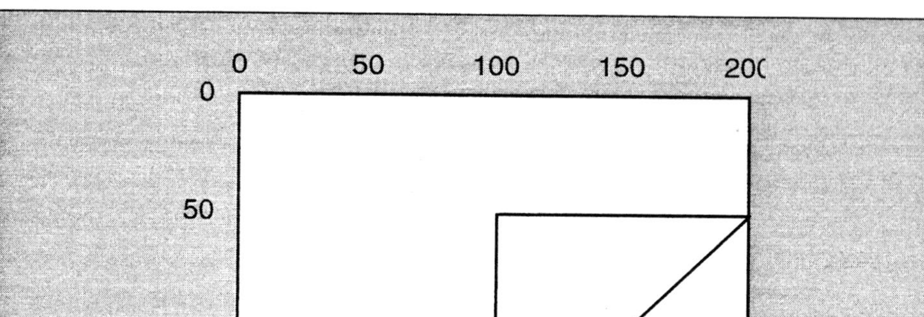

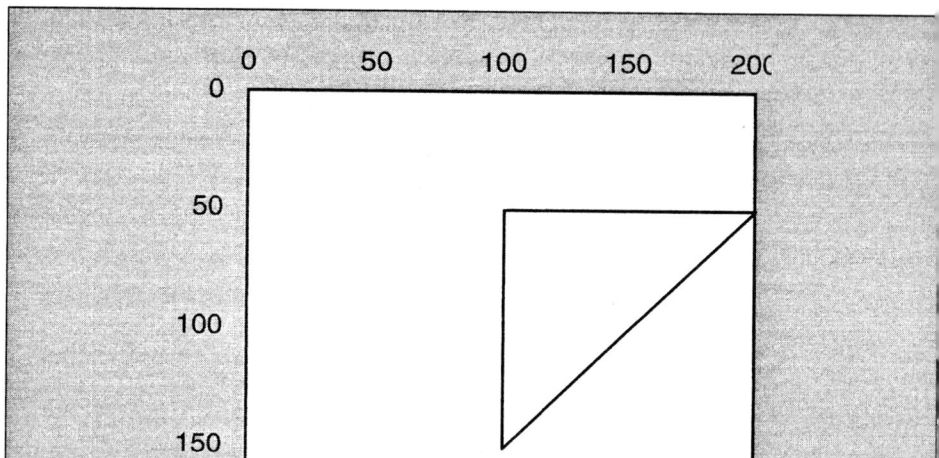

to construct two triangles, one that remains in its original position, and one that we translate to the new position. The following code will construct and display both triangles:

```
Polygon stay = new Polygon(x,y,3);
Polygon go = new Polygon(x,y,3);
go.translate(100,50);
g.drawPolygon(stay);
g.drawPolygon(go);
```

Having constructed one polygon, translated it, and drawn it, we can begin to solve the tangram puzzle containing seven polygons.

Designing a Solution: Solving a Simpler Problem

Before tackling the tangram puzzle, we solve the simpler problem of drawing the puzzle in its original configuration, moving all seven polygons to the right, and drawing them with different colors in the translated position.

In Figure 10.11, we made a 200 x 200 square. Using the numerical values shown, we can get the array of points for each polygon. For example, the big triangle at the bottom of the square connects the three points (0,200), (100,100), and (200,200). The array, `xpoints`, of x-coordinates, that we need is `{0,100,200}`, while the array, `ypoints`, of y-coordinates, is `{200,100,200}`.

Because we have seven polygons to construct, we have to create 14 arrays and call seven constructors. To save our fingers from this excessive amount of typing, we use an array of arrays* and write a loop to create the seven polygons. From Figure 10.11

* See Section 8.5, Arrays of Arrays

we can get the coordinates of all the points and define the arrays for each polygon, as we did above for the big triangle at the bottom.

We put the seven arrays of x-coordinates into an array, `x`,

```
int[][] x =
  {{0,100,200},{100,200,200},{0,100,0},{0,50,0},
  {50,150,100},{0,50,100,50},{100,200,150,50}};
```

and the seven arrays of y-coordinates into an array, `y`,

```
int[][] y =
  {{200,100,200},{100,0,200},{0,0,100},{100,150,200},
  {50,50,100},{100,50,100,150},{0,0,50,50}};
```

The order of the polygons in the arrays is as follows:

Array index	Polygon
0	big triangle at bottom
1	big triangle at right
2	medium triangle at upper left
3	small triangle at lower left
4	small triangle in center
5	square
6	parallelogram

To construct the seven polygons, we use the loop

```
for (int i=0; i<x.length; i++)
  polygons[i] = new Polygon(x[i],y[i],x[i].length);
```

where `x[i]`, the ith element of the `x` array is itself an array of the x-coordinates for the ith polygon, `y[i]` is the array of the y-coordinates for the ith polygon, and `x[i].length` is the number of points in the ith polygon.

To draw these polygons we could use a loop

```
for (int i=0; i<x.length; i++)
  g.drawPolygon(polygons[i]);
```

in the `paint` method, but we would like to be more flexible, choosing a drawing color, and choosing whether or not to fill the polygon, so we write a `showPolygon` method. We pass a polygon, a color, a graphics object, and a **boolean** flag, indicating whether or not to fill the polygon, to the `showPolygon` method. The pseudocode for `showPolygon` is:

```
Save the current drawing color;
Set the color to the desired color;
if (fill flag is true)
   Fill the polygon;
else
   Draw the polygon;
Restore the saved drawing color.
```

For our initial tangram display, we would like to draw the polygons in their original configuration, as shown in Figure 10.11, on the left of the applet, and show them filled with different colors on the right of the applet. The `translate` operation moves the polygon to a new position. If we just translate the polygons on the left, then we will get polygons on the right, but nothing on the left.

We need two sets of polygons, one to draw on the left, and one to show, filled and colored, on the right. We have all the coordinates for the polygons in the `x` and `y` arrays, so we can create another array of seven polygons, and translate each to the right.

Completing the Java Code

Example 10.9 will draw the original configuration on the left and the colored, filled configuration on the right. We use an array to specify the colors for the filled polygons. Figure 10.12 shows this `Tangram` applet.

Figure 10.12 The applet of Example 10.9

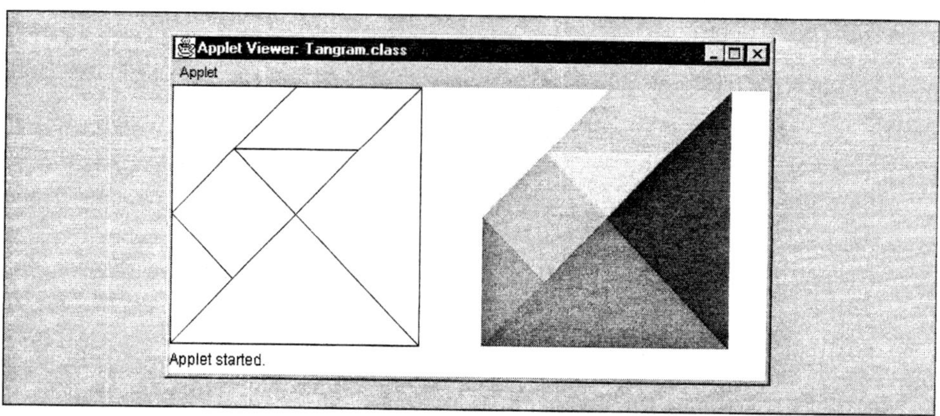

EXAMPLE 10.9 Tangram.java

```
/*  Draws the seven polygons of the
 *  tangram puzzle on the left, and, filled
 *  and colored, on the right.
 */

import java.awt.*;
import java.applet.Applet;

public class Tangram extends Applet {
  private int [][] x = {{0,100,200},{100,200,200},{0,100,0},{0,50,0},
                        {50,150,100},{0,50,100,50},{100,200,150,50}};
  private int [][] y = {{200,100,200},{100,0,200},{0,0,100},{100,150,200},
                        {50,50,100},{100,50,100,150},{0,0,50,50}};
  private Color [] colors = {Color.red,Color.blue,Color.yellow,
```

```
                 Color.magenta,Color.cyan,Color.pink,Color.orange};
private Polygon [] polygons = new Polygon[7];
private Polygon [] translates = new Polygon[7];

  public void init() {
    for (int i=0; i<x.length; i++) {
      polygons[i] = new Polygon(x[i],y[i],x[i].length);
      translates[i]= new Polygon(x[i],y[i],x[i].length);           // Note 1
      translates[i].translate(250,0);                               // Note 2
    }
  }
  public void showPolygon
        (Polygon p, Color c, Graphics g, boolean fill) {
    Color oldColor = g.getColor();                                  // Note 3
    g.setColor(c);
    if (fill)
      g.fillPolygon(p);
    else
      g.drawPolygon(p);
    g.setColor(oldColor);                                           // Note 4
  }
  public void paint(Graphics g) {
    for (int i=0; i<polygons.length; i++) {
      showPolygon(polygons[i],Color.black,g,false);                 // Note 5
      showPolygon(translates[i],colors[i],g,true);                  // Note 6
    }
  }
}
```

Note 1: We construct a second array of polygons having the same points as the first.

Note 2: Each polygon moves 250 pixels to the right.

Note 3: We save the current drawing color, so we can restore it later.

Note 4: After drawing the polygon in the desired color, we restore the previous drawing color.

Note 5: We set the `fill` argument to **false** to draw the polygons unfilled.

Note 6: `showPolygon(translates[i],colors[i],g,true);`
We choose a color from the color array, and set the `fill` argument to **true** to fill the polygon with the chosen color.

Testing the Code

We cannot test the tangram solver until we complete the code for it in the next section, where we use the mouse and the keyboard to drag and rotate the polygons to solve tangram puzzles.

THE BIG PICTURE

By constructing polygons and passing them to the `drawPolygon` method, we can use polygon methods such as `translate` to move polygons to new locations. Had we drawn the polygons directly from the arrays of the x- and y-coordinates of their vertices, we would not have had access to the `translate` method.

10.6 Solving Problems with Java: Tangrams with the Mouse and Keys

We return to the tangram puzzle we set up in Example 10.9. To solve tangram puzzles on the computer we need to drag polygons to new locations and rotate them. We use the mouse to drag polygons and key presses to rotate them.

Defining the Problem

In this section we will use the mouse to translate a polygon, use the *B* key (for back) to rotate a polygon counterclockwise, and use the *F* key (for forward) to rotate the polygon clockwise. With these translation and rotation operations we can move the puzzle pieces to form other designs. We leave to the exercises the implementation of an operation to reflect the parallelogram, in effect flipping it over, to allow the user to form even more shapes.

The ability to rotate a polygon is an important piece of the solution.

Designing a Solution: Solving a Subproblem—Rotating a Polygon

To **rotate** a polygon we **translate** the polygon to center it at the origin. We then rotate each of the vertices `(x,y)` of the polygon by an angle `z` using the formulas

```
x =  (cos z)x - (sin z)y
y =  (sin z)x + (cos z)y
```

where `sin z` represents the sine of the angle `z` and `cos z` represents its cosine. Using a positive angle will cause the polygon to rotate clockwise, while using a negative angle will cause it to rotate counterclockwise. Finally we translate the rotated polygon back to its original position.

While the formulas define the correct values mathematically for the rotated points, they cause a problem for our implementation. The `cosine` and `sine` methods return **double** values so the x and y values of the exact rotated point will have **double** values. For example the triangle we use has points (50,100), (100,50), and (150,100). Translating the triangle to be centered about the origin changes its coordinates to (-50,25), (0,-25), and (50,25). Rotating counterclockwise by .05 radians (just less than three degrees) changes these points to (-48.68, 27.46), (-1.24, -24.96), and (51.18,22.46) which do not have integer values for the coordinates. We must either truncate or round to get integer pixel values that we can plot.

If we truncate the rotated points to (-48,27), (-1,-24), and (51,22), then the triangle gets slightly smaller, and as we repeat a few dozen times to rotate by a larger angle, the triangle will get smaller and smaller, eventually disappearing. We can round, rather than truncating, which keeps the triangle about the same size, but after dozens of repetitions, its shape will be a bit distorted. In the above example rounding would give the points (-49,27), (-1,-25), and (51,22).

We need to be able to rotate by a small angle to form our polygons into various shapes, but only rotating by a small angle will sometimes take too many rotations, and the roundoff error will cause the polygons to become distorted. We need to rotate by a larger angle until we get close to the final angle, and then rotate by a smaller angle to fit the polygon into the new shape. By using a larger angle first, we will reduce the number of rotations, and thus reduce the distortion to an acceptable level.

In Example 10.10, pressing the uppercase `B` or `F` will rotate the polygon by pi/6 radians (30 degrees) while pressing the lowercase `b` or `f` will rotate the polygon by pi/60 radians (3 degrees). We use the 30-degree rotation to get close to the desired total rotation angle, and the 3-degree rotation to finish. By not using too many rotations, we will not cause too much distortion.

Figure 10.13 shows the triangle when the applet starts, and then after the user has rotated it counterclockwise a few times.

Figure 10.13 The applet of Example 10.10

We initialize a point `(rotx, roty)` to the center of the triangle; this will be the point which will move to the origin when we translate the triangle before rotating it about the origin and translating it back. A polygon object has an `npoints` field which gives the number of points in a polygon, and `xpoints` and `ypoints` fields which are arrays that give the x- and y-coordinates of the polygon's points.

EXAMPLE 10.10 Rotate.java

```
/* Displays a triangle which the user can
 * rotate counterclockwise by pressing the
 * B key, and clockwise by pressing the F key.
 */

import java.awt.*;
import java.awt.event.*;
```

```
import java.applet.Applet;

public class Rotate extends Applet
           implements KeyListener {

  private int [] xcoord = {50,100,150};
  private int [] ycoord = {100,50,100};
  private Polygon p = new Polygon(xcoord,ycoord,3);
  public static final double PCOS = Math.cos(Math.PI/60);             // Note 1
  public static final double NCOS = Math.cos(-Math.PI/60);
  public static final double PSIN = Math.sin(.Math.PI/60);
  public static final double NSIN = Math.sin(-.Math.PI/60);
  public static final double BIGPCOS = Math.cos(Math.PI/6);
  public static final double BIGNCOS = Math.cos(-Math.PI/6);
  public static final double BIGPSIN = Math.sin(Math.PI/6);
  public static final double BIGNSIN = Math.sin(-Math.PI/6);
  private int rotx = 100; // x-coordinate of the center
  private int roty = 75; // y-coordinate of the center

  public void init() {
    addKeyListener(this);
    requestFocus();                                                   // Note 2
  }
  public void paint(Graphics g) {
    g.fillPolygon(p);
  }
  public void keyTyped(KeyEvent event) {
    char key = event.getKeyChar();
    double C;
    double S;
    switch(key) {                                                     // Note 3
      case 'b' : C = NCOS; S = NSIN; break;
      case 'f' : C = PCOS; S = PSIN; break;
      case 'B' : C = BIGNCOS; S = BIGNSIN; break;
      case 'F' : C = BIGPCOS; S = BIGPSIN; break;
      default  : return;
    }
    p.translate(-rotx,-roty);                                         // Note 4
    for (int i=0; i<p.npoints; i++) {                                 // Note 5
      int x = p.xpoints[i];
      int y = p.ypoints[i];
      p.xpoints[i] = (int)Math.round(x*C - y*S);                      // Note 6
      p.ypoints[i] = (int)Math.round(x*S + y*C);
    }
    p.translate(rotx,roty);                                           // Note 7
    repaint();
  }
  public void keyReleased(KeyEvent event) { }
  public void keyPressed(KeyEvent event) { }
}
```

Note 1: It is generally more efficient to compute the sine and cosine values once rather than each time we press a key to rotate the triangle. We rotate by an angle of `Math.PI/60` radians which is three degrees. (There are pi radians in 180 degrees.)

Note 2: To receive key events a component must request the focus.

Note 3: If the user types `b` we use the negative angle, `-Math.PI/60`, while if the user types `f` we use the positive angle, `Math.PI/60`. Typing `F` causes a rotation by `Math.PI/6`, while typing `B` causes a rotation by `-Math.PI/6`. If the user presses any other key we return immediately. By choosing the angle here we can use the same rotation formula for both forward and backward rotations.

Note 4: We translate the triangle so its center `(rotx,roty)` moves to the origin.

Note 5: This loop rotates each point of the polygon by the given angle.

Note 6: `p.xpoints[i] = (int)Math.round(x*C - y*S);`
The sine and cosine values have type **double**, so the rotation formulas compute **double** values. We use integer-valued pixels so we need to cast the result to an **int**. If we did not round first we would keep underestimating the size of the rotated vector, so the triangle would gradually get smaller. (See Test Your Understanding question 12.) Rounding sometimes rounds up, overestimating the pixel values of the rotated point, and sometimes rounds down, underestimating the pixel values. On the average these estimations balance and the triangle stays the same size, but may be slightly distorted.

Note 7: `p.translate(rotx,roty);`
We translate the rotated triangle back to its original position.

Completing the Java Code

We combine the setup of the polygons forming the square from Example 10.9, the dragging a polygon with the mouse from Example 10.7, and the rotating a polygon from Example 10.10 to write a program to transform the polygons into other shapes.

As in Example 10.7, we store the current location of the polygon when the user presses the mouse in it, but here we have to loop through the seven polygons to find in which one, if any, the user pressed the mouse.

If the user releases the mouse inside one of the polygons, we save the point where the user releases the mouse as the new center (approximately) of the polygon in case the user decides to rotate that polygon. We also save the index of that polygon which tells us which polygon to rotate if the user types `b`, `B`, `f`, or `F`. Usually the user will rotate the polygon just after dragging it, but the user can rotate another polygon by clicking the mouse in it, which will generate a mouse released event.

EXAMPLE 10.11 TangramSolver.java

```
/*  Start with the seven polygons forming
 *  a square. Drag them with the mouse, and rotate
 *  them with the F and B keys to form other shapes.
 */

import java.awt.*;
import java.awt.event.*;
import java.applet.Applet;

public class TangramSolver extends Applet
      implements MouseMotionListener, KeyListener {
public static final double PCOS = Math.cos(Math.PI/60);
public static final double NCOS = Math.cos(-Math.PI/60);
public static final double PSIN = Math.sin(Math.PI/60);
public static final double NSIN = Math.sin(-Math.PI/60);
public static final double BIGPCOS = Math.cos(Math.PI/6);
public static final double BIGNCOS = Math.cos(-Math.PI/6);
public static final double BIGPSIN = Math.sin(Math.PI/6);
public static final double BIGNSIN = Math.sin(-Math.PI/6);
int [ ][ ] x = {{0,100,200},{100,200,200},{0,100,0},{0,50,0},
                {50,150,100},{0,50,100,50},{100,200,150,50}};
int [ ][ ] y = {{200,100,200},{100,0,200},{0,0,100},{100,150,200},
                {50,50,100},{100,50,100,150},{0,0,50,50}};
Color [ ] colors = {Color.red,Color.blue,Color.yellow,Color.magenta,
              Color.cyan,Color.pink,Color.orange};
Polygon [ ] polygons = new Polygon[7];
int [ ] oldx = new int[7]; // Saves previous polygon position
int [ ] oldy = new int[7];
int rotate;                // Index of polygon to rotate
int rotx;                  // x-coordinate of a point inside
int roty;                  // y-coordinate of a point inside

public void init() {
  for (int i = 0; i < x.length; i++) {
    polygons[i] = new Polygon(x[i], y[i], x[i].length);
  }
  addMouseListener(new MousePressListener());
  addMouseMotionListener(this);
  addKeyListener(this);
  requestFocus();
}
public void mouseMoved(MouseEvent event) { }
public void mouseDragged(MouseEvent event) {
  int x = event.getX();
  int y = event.getY();
  for (int i = 0; i < 7; i++){
    if (polygons[i].contains(x,y)){                          // Note 1
      polygons[i].translate(x - oldx[i], y - oldy[i]);
```

```
      oldx[i] = x;
      oldy[i] = y;
      repaint();
      break;                                          // Note 2
    }
  }
}

class MousePressListener extends MouseAdapter {
  public void mousePressed(MouseEvent event) {
    int x = event.getX();
    int y = event.getY();
    for (int i = 0; i < 7; i++)
      if (polygons[i].contains(x,y)){                // Note 3
      oldx[i] = x;
      oldy[i] = y;
      break;
    }
  }
  public void mouseReleased(MouseEvent event) {
  int x = event.getX();
  int y = event.getY();
  for (int i = 0; i < 7; i++)
    if (polygons[i].contains(x,y)){                  // Note 4
      rotate = i;
      rotx = x;
      roty = y;
      break;
    }
  }
}

public void showPolygon                              // Note 5
      (Polygon p, Color c, Graphics g, boolean fill) {
  Color oldColor = g.getColor();
  g.setColor(c);
  if (fill)
   g.fillPolygon(p);
  else
   g.drawPolygon(p);
  g.setColor(oldColor);
}
public void paint(Graphics g) {
  for (int i = 0; i < polygons.length; i++)
    showPolygon(polygons[i], colors[i], g, true);
}
public void keyTyped(KeyEvent event) {
  char key = event.getKeyChar();
  double C = PCOS;
  double S = NCOS;
```

```
      switch(key) {
        case 'b' : C = NCOS; S = NSIN; break;
        case 'f' :  C = PCOS; S = PSIN; break;
        case 'B' : C = BIGNCOS; S = BIGNSIN; break;
        case 'F' : C = BIGPCOS; S = BIGPSIN; break;
        default  : return;
      }
      polygons[rotate].translate(-rotx,-roty);                  // Note 6
      for (int j = 0; j < polygons[rotate].npoints; j++) {
        int x = polygons[rotate].xpoints[j];
        int y = polygons[rotate].ypoints[j];
        polygons[rotate].xpoints[j] = (int)Math.round(x*C - y*S);
        polygons[rotate].ypoints[j] = (int)Math.round(x*S + y*C);
      }
      polygons[rotate].translate(rotx,roty);
      repaint();
      }
    public void keyReleased(KeyEvent event) { }
    public void keyPressed(KeyEvent event) { }
}
```

Note 1: We perform the same translation steps as in Example 10.7, but first we check to see which polygon the mouse is dragging. The point (x,y) is the point to which the user dragged the mouse. It does not take much motion to generate a drag event (See Test Your Understanding question 7) so (x,y) will still be inside the same polygon in which the user pressed the mouse to start dragging it.

Note 2: Once we find the polygon, we break out of the loop as there is no need to check any of the other polygons.

Note 3: Again as in Example 10.7, we save the position at which the user presses the mouse, if that position is contained in one of the seven polygons.

Note 4: When the user releases the mouse inside a polygon, we save the index of that polygon and the coordinates of that mouse release. We will rotate this polygon if the user types `b`, `f`, `B`, or `F`.

Note 5: We include this method from Example 10.9 which allows us to draw the polygons with different colors, and to choose whether or not to fill them. We might prefer to draw the polygons unfilled to reduce the flicker that comes from repainting the polygons on a white background. (See Test Your Understanding question 11.)

Note 6: `polygons[rotate].translate(-rotx,-roty);`
We rotate as in Example 10.11, using the saved index, `rotate`, and the position inside polygon i, `(rotx,roty)`, that we saved when the user released the mouse.

Testing the Code

Figure 10.14 shows the polygons dragged and rotated into the shape of a cat. Test Your Understanding questions 14 and 15 provide other tests of the tangram solver.

Figure 10.14 The applet of Example 10.11

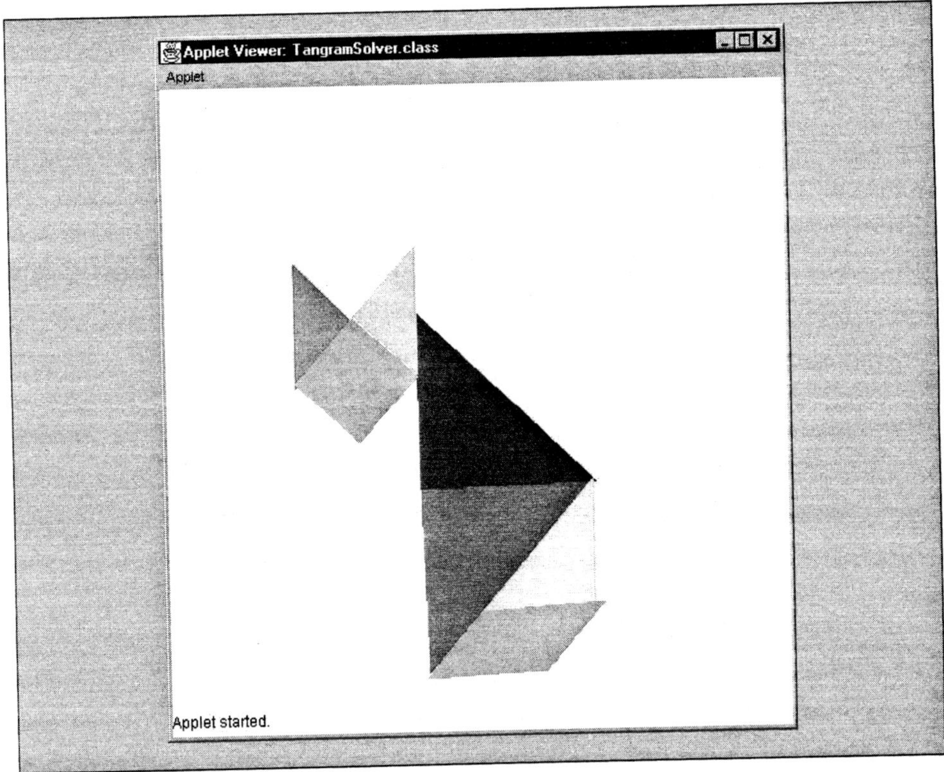

THE BIG PICTURE

We use the mouse to drag polygons and the keyboard to rotate them. Rotating distorts the polygon slightly due to the limitations of a fixed number of pixels. By using both small and large rotations we can minimize this distortion, dragging and rotating polygons to solve tangram puzzles.

TEST YOUR UNDERSTANDING

TRY IT YOURSELF

11. Modify Example 10.11 by changing the last argument in the call to `showPolygons` in the `paint` method from true to false, so that we draw the polygons without filling them. Also change the second argument to `Color.black`. Run the modified program to see that these changes greatly reduce the amount of flicker.

TRY IT YOURSELF

12. Modify Example 10.10 to remove the two calls to `Math.round` from the `keyTyped` method computing the rotated point as

```
polygons[rotate].xpoints[j] = (int)(x*C - y*S);
polygons[rotate].ypoints[j] = (int)(x*S + y*C);
```

Rotate the triangle many times and see what happens.

TRY IT YOURSELF 13. In Example 10.11, in the `mouseReleased` method, save the coordinates (x,y) in rotx and roty before checking if (x,y) is inside a polygon. Run the modified program to see what happens. Test rotations carefully.

TRY IT YOURSELF 14. Run the tangram solver of Example 10.11 to transform the seven polygons into the boat shown in Figure 10.15.

Figure 10.15 Form the seven polygons into this boat

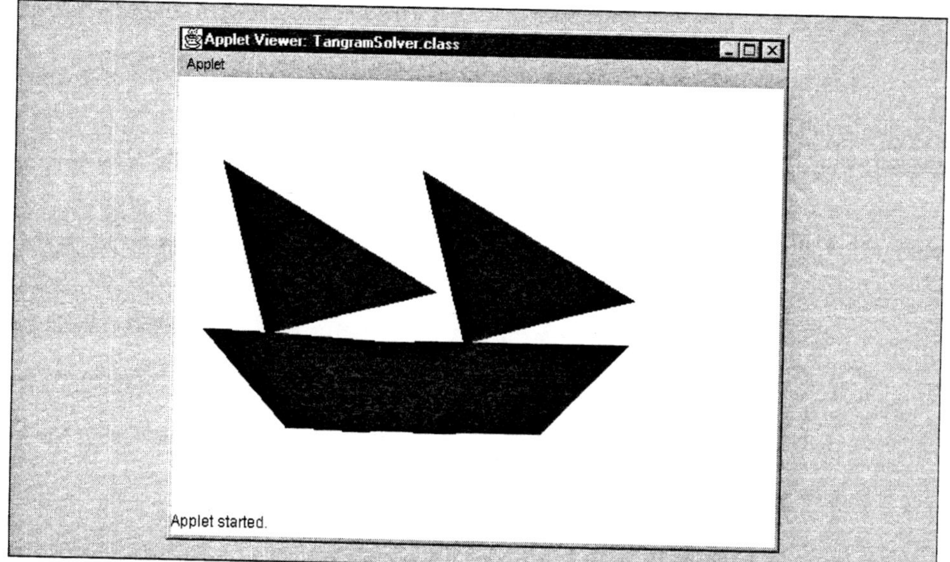

TRY IT YOURSELF 15. Run the tangram solver of Example 10.11 to transform the seven polygons into the duck shown in Figure 10.16.

SUMMARY

- The `ActionListener` and `ItemListener` interfaces each have only one method, but the interfaces for the low-level mouse, key, and window events of this chapter each have several methods. The `MouseListener` interface has the `mousePressed`, `mouseReleased`, `mouseClicked`, `mouseEntered`, and `mouseExited` methods. A class that implements the `MouseListener` interface must implement each of these methods, but may use an empty body for those methods which handle events in which it is not interested. Another approach to handling mouse events is to extend the `MouseAdapter` class which provides default implementations for the five events. By extending the `MouseAdapter` class, we only have to implement the methods for those events we wish to handle.
- The `MouseMotionListener` interface specifies two methods, `mouseDragged` and `mouseMoved`. A class can implement this interface or extend the `MouseMotionAdapter`

Figure 10.16 Form the seven polygons into this duck

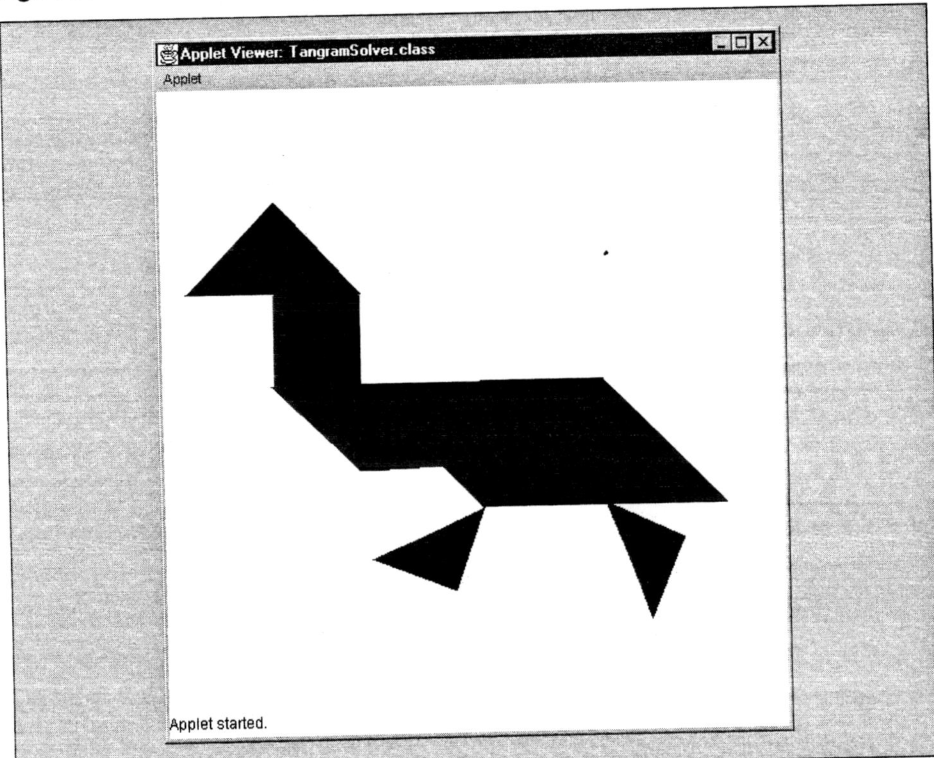

class. Java generates the mouse moved event when the user moves the mouse without holding down a button, while the mouse dragged event represents the user moving the mouse with a button held down. A mouse click occurs when the user presses and releases the mouse without dragging it in between.

- An implementor of the `KeyListener` interface defines the `keyPressed`, `keyReleased`, and `keyTyped` methods. We refer to physical keys using integer codes such as `VK_A` or `VK_SHIFT`. Pressing the `F` key will generate a `keyPressed` event; the `keyCode` method will return `VK_F` for this event. If the user also holds down the Shift key, then the `keyTyped` method would return the `F` character, but if the user does not hold down the *`Shift`* key, then the `keyTyped` event would return the character f. A class that wants to handle key events can implement the three methods of the `keyListener` interface or subclass the `KeyAdapter` class, overriding only those methods for events that it wants to handle.
- Frames are essential to making standalone applications. A frame is a standalone window, not a panel in the applet viewer or the browser. If we use frames, we are responsible for showing them, defining their size, and closing them properly. The `WindowListener` interface has seven methods, `windowActivated`, `windowDeactivated`, `windowIconified`, `windowDeiconified`, `windowOpened`, `windowClosed`, and `windowClosing`. If we just want

to close the window, we can extend the `WindowAdapter` class, overriding only the `windowClosing` method.

- Once we know how to close a frame, we can write standalone graphical applications. Applets and applications use the same graphical components, but a standalone application has to make its window visible and handle window events. We easily converted an applet to an application. After converting a standalone program to have a graphical user interface, we then converted this standalone graphical program to an applet.
- In the final sections we used the mouse to drag and keystrokes to rotate the polygons of the tangram puzzle into various shapes.

Skill Builder Exercises

1. The following, showing the key events generated when the user types an uppercase T, does not list these events in they order in which they occur. Rearrange the list to reflect the order in which they are generated.

   `KEY_TYPED, KEY_PRESSED, KEY_RELEASED, KEY_PRESSED, KEY_RELEASED`

2. Fill in the blanks in the code below to create an applet that draws a red circle of radius 25 centered where the user clicks the mouse.

```
import java.awt.________;
import java.awt.________ ;
import java.applet.________;
public class MouseClickRed __________ {
  int x = 25, y = 25;
  public ______________() {
    setForeground(___________);
    addMouseListener(new ______________);
  }
  public void paint(Graphics g) {
    g.fillOval(x - 25,y - 25,___ ,___ );
  }
  class MouseHandler extends MouseAdapter {
    public void __________ (___________) {
      x = ______________;
      y = ______________;
      ______________
    }
  }
}
```

3. Fill in the blanks in the code below to create a standalone application that draws a red circle of radius 25 centered where the user clicks the mouse.

```
import java.__________;
import java.__________;
public class MouseClickRedAlone ______ F____ {
```

```
int x = 25,.y = 25;
public ______________() {
  setForeground(_________);
  add_____Listener(new ________());
  add_______Listener(new ________());
}
public void paint(Graphics g) {
  g.fillOval(x - 25,y - 25,___,___);
}
class MouseHandler extends MouseAdapter {
public void ____________(__________) {
    x = _______________ ;
    y = _______________ ;
    ___________________;
  }
}
class WindowClose extends WindowAdapter {
  public void __________(___________) {
    _______________;
  }
}
public _____ void main(_________) {
  __________ m = new ______________();
  m.______________;
  m.______________;
}
}
```

Critical Thinking Exercises

4. The `MouseAdapter` class
   a. implements the five methods of the `MouseListener` interface.
   b. allows the user to override any of the `MouseListener` or `MouseMotionListener` methods.
   c. can be used by applets, but not by standalone applications.
   d. none of the above.
   e. all of the above.
5. Invoking `event.getKeyCode()`, where event is a `KeyEvent` will return
   a. the character that the user typed, even if it required pressing two keys, for example typing an uppercase `G`.
   b. an integer representing the character typed, so a lowercase `g` will be distinguished from an uppercase `G`.
   c. an integer representing the physical key generating the event.
   d. none of the above.

6. Which of the following are steps we need to perform when converting an applet to a standalone application? More than one choice may be correct.

   a. Remove "extends Applet"

   b. Add a call to the `addWindowListener` method

   c. Add a `main` method

   d. All of the above

7. To handle a window closing event, a class could

   a. implement the `WindowListener` interface, overriding the `windowClosing` method.

   b. extend the `WindowAdapter` class, overriding the `windowClosing` method.

   c. directly implement the `windowClosing` method, without implementing the `WindowListener` interface or extending the `WindowAdapter` class.

   d. none of the above.

   e. all of the above.

Debugging Exercise

8. The following standalone application attempts to increase the radius of a circle by three pixels when the user presses the B key and decrease it by three pixels when the user presses the S key. Find and correct any errors.

```
import java.awt.*;
import java.awt.event.*;
public class CircleSize extends Frame{
   int width = 50, height = 50;
   int x = 140, y = 90;
   public CircleSize()  {
     addKeyListener(this);
     addWindowListener(this);
   }
   public void paint(Graphics g) {
     g.drawOval(x,y,width,height);
   }
   public void keyPressed(KeyEvent e) {
     int i = e.getKeyCode();
     if (i == KeyEvent.VK_B) {width += 6; height += 6; x -= 3; y -= 3;}
     else if (i == KeyEvent.VK_S) {width -= 6; height -= 6; x += 3; y += 3;}
     repaint();
   }
   public void keyTyped(KeyEvent e) {}
     public static void main(String[] args) {
       CircleSize cs = new CircleSize();
     cs.setSize(300,200);
     cs.show();
   }
```

```
class WindowHandler extends WindowAdapter {
  public void widowClosing(WindowEvent e) {
    System.exit(0);
  }
 }
}
```

Program Modification Exercises

9. Modify Example 10.7 to define a subclass of `MouseMotionAdapter` to handle mouse motion events rather than having the applet implement the `MouseMotionListener` interface.
10. Modify Example 10.7 so the user cannot drag the triangle out of the visible region of the applet.
11. Modify Example 10.8 to move the character using the up and down arrow keys in addition to moving it with the left and right arrow keys.
12. Modify Example 10.8 to ensure that the character stays within the visible region of the applet.
13. Modify Example 10.2 to draw on a canvas, rather than directly in the frame itself.
14. In Example 10.4 we create three panels, each time setting the layout to the grid layout, and adding a label and a text field. Modify Example 10.4, writing a method to create and initialize these panels, and then calling this method three times when building the user interface.

PUTTING IT ALL TOGETHER 15. Convert the applet of Example 6.4 to a standalone application.

PUTTING IT ALL TOGETHER 16. Convert the insertion sort applet of Example 8.14 to a standalone application.

17. Convert the tangram solver of Example 10.11 to a standalone program.
18. Modify the tangram solver of Example 10.11 so the parallelogram flips over when the user presses the `R` key. Figure 10.17 shows the positions of the parallelogram before and after the flip.

Figure 10.17 The parallelogram positions

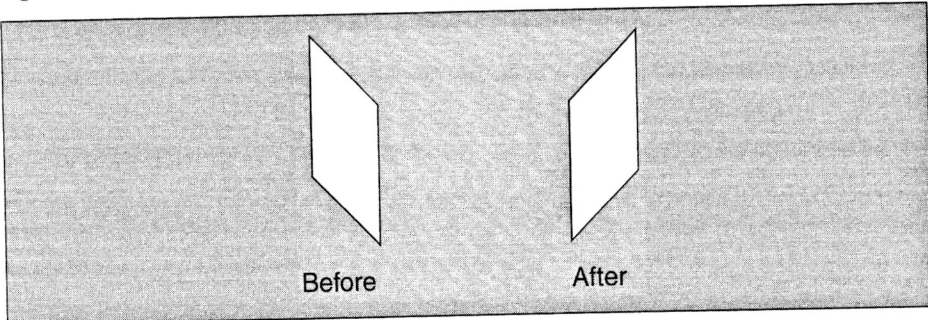

Program Design Exercises

19. Write an applet that displays a red oval which turns green when the user moves the mouse over it and turns back to red when the user moves the mouse outside of the oval.

20. Write an applet that causes a blue rectangle to appear where the user clicks the mouse, and to disappear when the user double-clicks the mouse inside of it. (Use the `getClickCount()` method of the `MouseEvent` class to get the click count. A double-click is two mouse clicks in quick succession.)

21. Write an applet that prints the user's name wherever the user clicks the mouse.

22. Write an applet that displays a circle that changes its color to red when the user presses the *R* key, to yellow when the user presses the *Y* key, to blue when the user presses the *B* key, and to green when the user presses the *G* key.

23. Write an applet that displays a string, changing it to bold if the user presses the *B* key, to italics if the user presses the *I* key, to all uppercase if the user presses the *Shift* key, and to all lowercase if the user presses the *Ctrl* key.

PUTTING IT ALL TOGETHER

24. Design a graphical user interface for the `QuickFood` application of Example 5.7. Let the user order by clicking the mouse on icons for a burger, fries, and a drink. Write this program as a standalone application.

25. Write a Java applet to play the game of Nim with the computer. To play Nim, start with a certain number of tokens. Each player takes from one up to a maximum number of tokens at each turn, and the player taking the last token loses. Provide a GUI to input the total number of tokens, and the maximum number each player can take at each move. Randomly choose whether the user or the computer moves first. At startup, display all the tokens. Let the user select a token with a mouse click which should cause that token to be erased. When finished selecting tokens, the user should press the *N* key. The computer should print a message stating how many tokens it chooses, and these tokens should be erased. When the game is over, display a message announcing the winner. Use colors to enhance the display.

26. Write a Java applet to play a game of Tick Tack Toe with the computer. You may use the interface of Figure 10.1. Let the player move by clicking the mouse in an available square.

    a. For an easier version, let the computer make its move in any available square.

    b. For a more challenging program, have the computer find its best move.

27. Develop a simplified Blackjack game. Create a deck of 51 cards, 17 each of threes, sevens, and tens. Deal two cards face down to the player and two cards to the computer, one face up and one face down. Allow the user to turn over the player's cards by clicking on them. The user will hit the *H* key to get another card and the *S* key to stop drawing cards. The player loses if his total is greater than 21. If not, the dealer draws cards until the dealer's total is greater than 16. The dealer loses if her total is over 21. Otherwise the one with the greater score wins.

CHAPTER

11 Exception Handling and Input/Output

OUTLINE

Introduction

In this chapter we input and output in Java. Before we can use data files in Java, we must explore exceptions, which signal data errors. Exception handling enables us to manage serious errors that might occur such as trying to read from a file that does not exist. It is essential for implementing input and output operations and networking where errors beyond the control of the programmer may easily occur.

After we discuss exception handling, we shall show how to read from and write to external files. Files persist after our program is finished, keeping data for later use. Business applications, and many others, are heavily dependent on good access to external data. Because handling data carefully is important, it is not easy to do it well. We left it until this chapter when we have developed sufficient background to tackle these concepts. We first work with text and then consider binary data.

Inside our programs we have passed data as arguments to individual methods but not to the `main` method called at the start of execution or to applets. We start this chapter by showing how to use program arguments to pass data to the `main` method of a standalone application, so we can use this technique in the rest of the chapter. We also show how to use a tag in the HTML file to pass data to an applet.

OBJECTIVES:

- Handle exceptions.
- Read and write text files using reader and writer classes.
- Input and output binary files.
- Read and write objects to and from files.
- Pass arguments to the `main` method of a standalone application
- Pass arguments to an applet.

11.1 Program Arguments and Applet Parameters

In Sections 2.4 and 8.3 we showed how to pass arguments to methods of a class other than the `main` method. In this section we show how to pass arguments to the `main` method and how to pass parameters to an applet.

Program Arguments

In all our standalone application examples we have diligently declared the `main` method as

```
public static void main(String [] args)
```

but have yet to use the `String` array, `args`, that we specify as its parameter.

When we call a method, we pass it its arguments. For example, we can pass the values 4.5, 1000.0, and 7 to the `amount` method of Example 4.5, as in `amount(4.5, 1000, 7)`. However, we do not call the `main` method, the Java interpreter does. The technique for passing arguments to the `main` method depends on which environment we are using. **Program arguments**, passed to the `main` method, are often called command-line arguments because they are placed just after the program name when a **command line** is used to run the program.

In Example 11.1, we adapt the temperature conversion program of Example 3.5 to use program arguments to input the temperatures to convert. Using the Java 2 Platform Standard Edition from Sun, we enter a hot temperature and a cold temperature on the command line*

```
java PassArguments  56.0  -19.33
```

The method to pass the arguments in to the `main` method depends on which environment we are using, but inside the program we use the arguments in the same way, referring to the strings passed as program arguments using the `String` variable, `args`. When executing the program, Java sets `args[0]` to the hot temperature, 56.0, and `args[1]` to the cold temperature, –19.33, passing these values to the `main`

* See Appendix E to see how to pass program arguments using other environments.

method. We can run our program again passing different program arguments, such as 49.7 and -12.44. When passed these arguments, our program will output the Fahrenheit values of the two Celsius tempertatures.

If the user does not pass two program arguments we display a message and abort the program. To abort a Java program we can use the statement

```
System.exit(1);
```

which exits, returning the value of its argument to the operating system. By convention, a non-zero value indicates an error caused the program to terminate.

Each program argument is passed as a string. The arguments in our example specify **double** values. Inside the program we need to convert the strings `args[0]` and `args[1]` to type **double**.

EXAMPLE 11.1 PassArguments.java

```
/* Converts degrees Celsius to degrees Fahrenheit.
 * Uses program arguments to input values to convert.
 * Uses a NumberFormat object to output the results.
 */


import java.text.*;

public class PassArguments {
  public static void main(String [ ] args) {
    double  hotC, coldC;
    double  hotF, coldF;
    if (args.length != 2) {                                    // Note 1
       System.out.println
           ("Enter a hot and a cold temerature as program arguments.");
       System.exit(1);
    }
    NumberFormat nf = NumberFormat.getNumberInstance();
    nf.setMaximumFractionDigits(1);
    hotC = Double.parseDouble(args[0]);                        // Note 2
    hotF = 9.0*hotC/5.0 + 32.0;
    System.out.println("The Fahrenheit temperature is: "
                         + nf.format(hotF));
    coldC = Double.parseDouble(args[1]);
    coldF = 9.0*coldC/5.0 + 32.0;
    System.out.println("The Fahrenheit temperature is: "
                         + nf.format(coldF));

  }
}
```

Output (Using `java PassArguments 56.0 -19.33`)

```
The Fahrenheit temperature is: 132.8
The Fahrenheit temperature is: -2.8
```

Note 1: We check that the user entered two arguments. If not, we print a message indicating the arguments the user needs to specify, and exit the program by calling `System.exit` with an argument of 1, indicating that an error occurred.

Note 2: The program arguments are strings. Since they represent temperatures we use the `parseDouble` method, available starting with the Java 2 Platform, to convert them to **double** values.

Applet Parameters

An applet does not have a `main` method; a browser or an applet viewer loads an applet when it encounters the `applet` tag in an HTML file. **Applet parameters** allow us to pass information to an applet. To pass parameters to an applet, we use the `param` tag in the HTML file. For example, we can use a `param` tag to specify the name of the font in which we will draw strings. The `param` tag has an attribute, `name`, which gives the name of the parameter, and an attribute, `value`, which gives the desired value of the parameter with that name.

The `param` tag

```
<param name=fontName value="Serif">
```

describes a parameter named `fontName` whose value is `Serif`. In our code for the applet, we can obtain the value of any parameters using the `getParameter` method, as in:

```
String fontName = getParameter("fontName");
```

The argument to the `getParameter` method is the parameter name found in the `name` attribute of a `param` tag in the HTML file. In this example, the `getParameter` method finds the `param` tag with the `name` attribute and returns the string specified in the `value` attribute. For the above `param` tag, the `getParameter` method would return the string, "Serif."

The `getParameter` method always returns a string. For example, we could use the `param` tag

```
<param name=size value=36>
```

to specify the point size to use for the font. In our applet, calling the `getParameter` method to get the size, as in:

```
getParameter("size");
```

will return "36" as a string which we must convert to an **int** value, as in:

```
int size = Integer.parseInt(getParameter("size"));
```

The param tag occurs in the HTML file between the <applet> and the </applet> tags, as in:

```
<applet code = PassToApplet.class   width = 200   height = 200>
<param  name = fontName   value = "SansSerif">
</applet>
```

We can include several param tags to specify the names and values for several parameters.

Example 11.2 gets the fontName and size parameters from the HTML file, creating a bold font with the specified font name and point size.

EXAMPLE 11.2 PassToApplet.java

```
/* Uses parameters set in the HTML file to
 * specify the font name and size.
 */

import java.awt.*;
import java.applet.Applet;

public class PassToApplet extends Applet {
  private Font font;
  private int size;
  private String fontName;

  public void init() {
    fontName = getParameter("fontName");
    if (fontName == null) fontName = "Serif";                // Note 1
    String temp = getParameter("size");
    if (temp != null)                                        // Note 2
      size = Integer.parseInt(temp);
    else
      size = 12;
    font = new Font(fontName, Font.BOLD, size);              // Note 3
    setFont(font);
  }
  public void paint(Graphics g) {
    g.drawString("Uses applet parameters", 20, 70);
  }
}
```

Note 1: If the HTML file has no param tag with a name attribute of fontName, the getParameter method will return null, in which case we set the fontName to the default value of Serif.

Note 2: If the HTML file has no param tag with a name attribute of size, the getParameter method will return null, which will cause the parseInt method to throw a number format exception. In the next section we will learn how to handle this exception. For now, we assign `size` a default value of 12 when it has not been specified in the HTML file.

Note 3: We construct the font using the `fontName` and `size` parameters obtained from the HTML file. We could also have input the style as a parameter to the applet. We leave this modification for the exercises.

Figure 11.1 shows an HTML file with two `param` tags for the font name and the point size. Figure 11.2 shows the applet of Example 11.2 run using the HTML file of Figure 11.1.

Figure 11.1 The file `PassToAppletA.html`

```
<applet code = PassToApplet.class width=400 height=200>
<param name=fontName value="Serif">
<param name=size value=36>
</applet>
```

Figure 11.2 Example 11.2 run using `PassToAppletA.html`

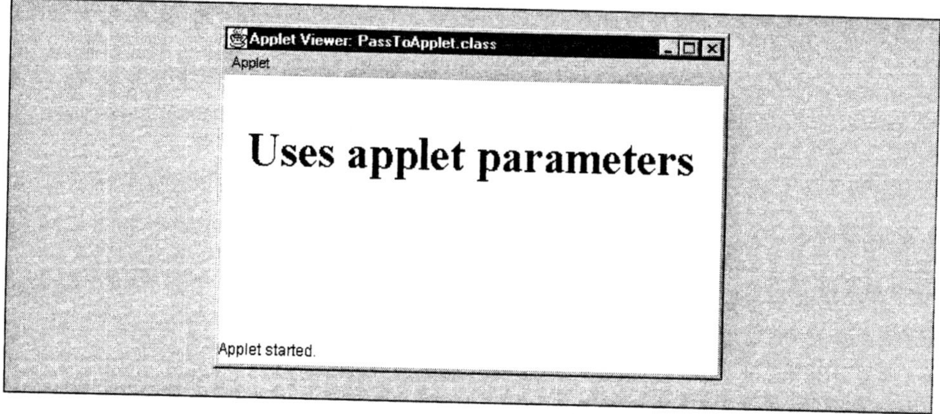

Figure 11.3 shows another HTML file, with different values for the `fontName` and `size` parameters. Figure 11.4 shows the applet of Example 11.2 run using the HTML file of Figure 11.3.

Figure 11.3 The file `PassToAppletB.html`

```
<applet code = PassToApplet.class width=200 height=200>
<param name=fontName value="SansSerif">
<param name=size value=14>
</applet>
```

Figure 11.4 The applet viewer processing `PassToAppletB.html`

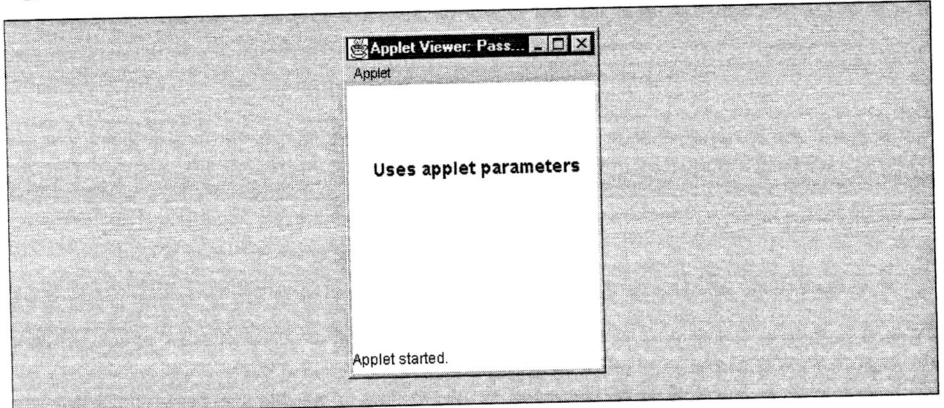

THE BIG PICTURE

Program arguments allow us to pass data to the `main` method of a standalone program. Applet parameters, placed in the HTML file, let us pass data to an applet.

TEST YOUR UNDERSTANDING

1. The **parseDouble** method used in Example 11.1 is not available in earlier Java versions. What could we use instead to do the conversion from `String` to **double** that would work in all Java versions?

TRY IT YOURSELF

2. Revise the HTML file of Figure 11.1 to omit both `param` tags. Run the applet of Example 11.2 using this revised file and explain what happens.

11.2 Exception Handling

We do not want our programs to crash or to produce erroneous results. When inputting a test score we can check that the value entered was between 0 and 100. We can easily include this check on the value of the score in our program, but sometimes we have no control over circumstances that might affect our program. For example, if our program tries to read from a file that does not exist, it may abort. Someone else may have deleted that file without our knowledge, or the disk drive may have failed.

Java provides an exception handling facility to allow the programmer to insert code to handle such unexpected errors and allow the program to recover and continue executing, or to terminate gracefully, whichever is appropriate. An **exception** signals that a condition such as an error has occurred. We **throw** an exception as a signal, and **catch** it to handle it and take appropriate action. We will not cover all of the features of exception handling in this text, but will show how to handle exceptions that Java generates.

Exception Classes

In Java, exceptions are instances of a class derived from `Throwable`. Figure 11.5 shows the exception classes that we discuss in this chapter (the ... indicates a class that we do not use is omitted from the display.)

Figure 11.5 Classes of Exceptions

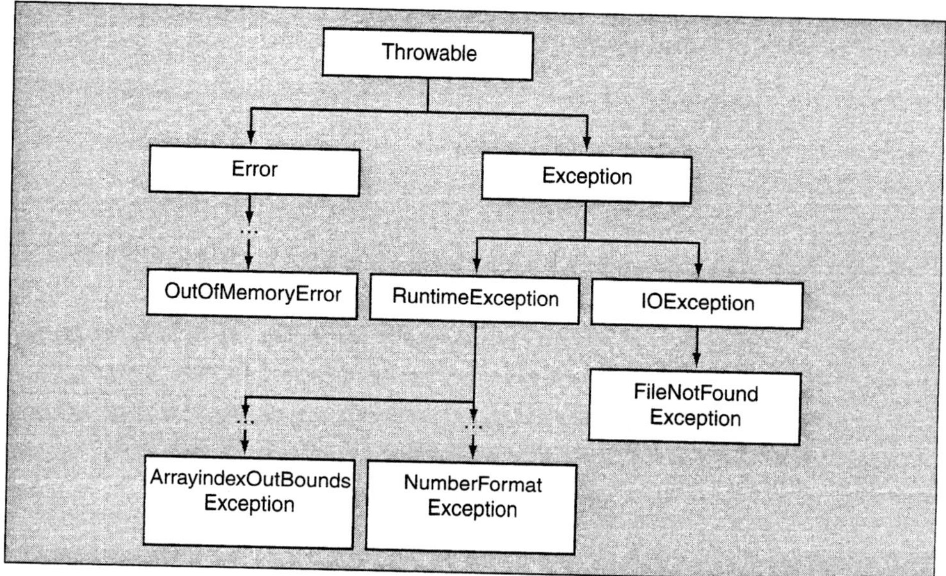

In this section we consider array index out of bounds and number format exceptions, leaving the IO exceptions to the next section. Java allows us to handle array index out of bounds and number format exceptions, but does not require us to handle them. Java requires that we handle IO errors, usually beyond our control, which would otherwise cause our program to abort.

The Array Index Out of Bounds Exception

The array

```
int[] a = {4,5,6};
```

has three elements which we can access using the indices `0`, `1`, and `2`. If we try to use an index other than these three, as for example in the expression `i=a[3]`, Java will throw an array index out of bounds exception. Each exception is an instance of a class. We can write our own classes to define new types of exceptions, which we do in Section 13.3, but in this text we mostly use the Java exception classes shown in Figure 11.5.

Throwing an exception interrupts the program, transferring control to a user-defined catch clause, if any, which specifies how to handle the exception, or aborting if no catch clause is found. Example 11.3 shows the latter case when no catch clause is found. Java **aborts** execution with a message when it reaches the statement that uses an index that is out of bounds, and will not return to execute the rest of the program.

EXAMPLE 11.3 Abort.java

```
/* Shows that Java aborts when it encounters
 * an out of bounds array index.
 */

public class Abort{
    public static void main(String [] args) {
      int [ ] anArray = {5,6,7};                                // Note 1
      int badIndex = 5;
      int causesError;

      causesError = anArray[badIndex];                          // Note 2
      System.out.println("This statement never gets executed.");  // Note 3
    }
}
```

Output

```
java.lang.ArrayIndexOutofBoundsException: 5
  at Abort.main(Abort.java:10)
```

Note 1: Only 0, 1, and 2 are valid indices for `anArray`.

Note 2: Java throws an array index out of bounds exception when it encounters this use of the bad index 5; it prints a message naming the type of exception, and showing the bad value. Java outputs the class, method name, and line number causing the exception.* Because the program does not handle this exception, Java aborts the program.

Note 3: Java aborted the program before reaching this line, thus it never gets executed.

We can easily fix Example 11.3 so it does not abort. Example 11.4 asks the user to input an index, but confirms that the index is between zero and two so that the program does not abort. If the index is out of bounds, then we display an error message.

EXAMPLE 11.4 ValidateInput.java

```
/* Validates the index that the user inputs
 * so the program does not abort.
 */
```

* To see the line numbers in the stack trace we disabled the JIT (Just-In-Time compiler) which compiles the byte code during runtime to improve performance. To disable the JIT in java 2, use the command `java -Djava.compiler=NONE InsertionSortTiming`. Some JDK version 1.1 compilers omit the second line of the error message in this example.

```
public class ValidateInput{
  public static void main(String [] args) {
    int [ ] anArray = {5,6,7};
    int index = Integer.parseInt(args[0]);
    int value;
    if (index >= 0 && index <= 2) {                          // Note 1
      value = anArray[index];
      System.out.println("Execution does not get here if index is bad");
    }
    else
      System.out.println("Stick with 0, 1, or 2");
  }
}
```

Output (Using `java ValidateInput 1`)

```
Execution does not get here if index is bad
```

Output (Using `java ValidateInput 34`)

```
Stick with 0, 1, or 2
```

Note 1: We validate the user's input, accepting indices in the correct range, and displaying an error message otherwise.

TIP If there is a good way to validate the input, do so yourself. Much code in many applications is devoted to validating the data. Unsophisticated users may be unsure of the proper way to enter data, and even professionals make occasional errors.

Java does not require the programmer to handle the array index out of bounds exception, but it allows the programmer to do so. To handle an exception, we put the code that could cause that exception to occur in a `try` block followed by a `catch` clause to handle the exception, as in:

```
try {
  // some code that might generate an out of bounds exception
} catch(ArrayIndexOutOfBoundsException e) {
  // some code to execute when that exception occurs
}
```

where `ArrayIndexOutOfBoundsException` is the type of exception we are trying to catch. Java passes an instance, `e`, of this exception, which contains information about the array index out of bounds exception that occurred, to the `catch` clause.

If an exception occurs in the `try` block then Java looks for a `catch` clause that handles that exception. If it finds such a `catch` clause, it jumps immediately to execute that code, never returning to any code in the `try` block after the code which caused the exception. If Java does not find such a catch clause, it will abort the program with an error message, as happened in Example 11.3.

In Example 11.5 we put our use of the array index into a `try` block, and when Java throws the array index out of bounds exception, we catch it and display an error message. Our program does not abort, and execution continues after the `catch` clause. With a little more effort, we could use a loop to give the user another chance to input a correct value after making an error. We leave this enhancement to the exercises.

EXAMPLE 11.5 TryException.java

```
/* Puts the array code in a try block and
 * catches the array index out of bounds exception
 * if it occurs.
 */

public class TryException{
  public static void main(String [] args) {
    int value;
    try {
      int [ ] anArray = {5,6,7};
      int index = Integer.parseInt(args[0]);
      value = anArray[index];                                    // Note 1
        System.out.println("Execution does not get here if index is bad");
      }catch (ArrayIndexOutOfBoundsException e) {               // Note 2
        System.out.println("Stick with 0, 1, or 2");
      }
      System.out.println("This is the end of the program");    // Note 3
  }
}
```

Output (Using `java TryException 2`)

```
Execution does not get here if index is bad
This is the end of the program
```

Output (Using `java TryException 89`)

```
Stick with 0, 1, or 2
This is the end of the program
```

Note 1: Java will throw an array index out of bounds exception if index < 0 or if index >2.

Note 2: After throwing an array index out of bounds exception, Java jumps here to the handler, skipping any code remaining in the try block.

Note 3: After executing the code in the `catch` clause, Java continues executing here. Handling the array index out of bounds exception allows the program to continue executing whether or not Java throws an array index out of bounds exception.

If there is no catch clause for an exception immediately following the try block, then, when that exception occurs, Java looks for the catch clause in the caller of the method in which the try block is contained. In Example 11.6, we use an out of bounds array index in the getAndSetValue method, but do not include a catch clause in that method. When Java encounters the invalid index during execution it throws an array index out of bounds exception and looks for a catch clause which handles that exception. Not finding one in getAndSetValue, Java looks in the caller of the getAndSetValue method, the main method, which does have a clause that catches the exception. Java jumps to the catch clause in the main method in which we call e.printStackTrace(), where e is the array index out of bounds exception which Java passes to the catch clause.

We will implement a Stack class in Section 13.3. For now, think of a stack in the sense we use it in English as a stack of books or a stack of dishes. An important use of stacks is in implementing method calls in programming languages. We stack up arguments passed to the method and local variables. When starting to execute the main method, Java puts the data that main needs onto the stack. When the main method calls the getAndSetValue method, Java pushes the data that getAndSetValue needs onto the top of the previous data on the stack. In Example 11.6, we have only two methods, but in larger examples we could have half a dozen or more methods using the stack, many of them from the Java library packages.

The data for the method that Java is currently executing is on the top of the stack. When Java throws an array index out of bounds exception it passes an object of that exception type to the catch clause for that exception. This object contains a list of all the methods whose data is on the stack when the exception occurred. To see this list, we call the printStackTrace() method, which outputs

```
java.lang.ArrayIndexOutOfBoundsException: 98
  at TryExceptionTrace.getAndSetValue(TryExceptionTrace.java:11)
  at TryExceptionTrace.main(TryExceptionTrace.java:16)
```

The first line names the exception that occurred and displays the invalid value, 98. The next two lines are the stack entries. TryExceptionTrace is the class name for Example 11.6. The data for getAndSetValue is on the top of the stack and the exception occurred at line 11 of the program. Thus by printing the **stack trace** we can find the line at which the exception occurred. The second stack entry says that the bottom of the stack contains the data for the main method, and that the main method called the getAndSetValue method at line 16 of the program.

By reading the stack trace, we can follow the sequence of method calls that culminated in the throwing of the exception. After executing the code in the catch clause, Java continues execution with the code following the catch clause. Had we omitted the catch clause, Java would have aborted the program with an error message, as in Example 11.3. Handling the exception allows us to recover from the error and continue executing the remainder of the program.

EXAMPLE 11.6 TryExceptionTrace.java

```
/* Shows the use of the printStackTrace method
 * to obtain the sequence of method calls that
 * culminated in the throwing of the array index
 * out of bounds exception.
 */

public class TryExceptionTrace{
  public static int getAndSetValue(String value) {
    int [ ] anArray = {5,6,7};
    int index = Integer.parseInt(value);
    return anArray[index];                                    // Note 1
  }
  public static void main(String [ ] args) {
    int value;
    try {
      value = getAndSetValue(args[0]);                        // Note 2
      System.out.println("Execution does not get here if the index is bad");
    }catch (ArrayIndexOutOfBoundsException e) {
       e.printStackTrace();
    }
    System.out.println("This is the end of the program");
  }
}
```

Output (Using `java TryExceptionTrace 98`

```
java.lang.ArrayIndexOutOfBoundsException: 98
  at TryExceptionTrace.getAndSetValue(TryExceptionTrace.java:11)
  at TryExceptionTrace.main(TryExceptionTrace.java:16)
This is the end of the program
```

Note 1: This is line 11 which causes the exception.*

Note 2: This is line 16, where the main method calls the `getAndSetValue` method that produces the exception.

The Number Format Exception

Java allows us to construct an `Integer` object from a string, as in:

```
Integer i = new Integer("375");
```

If we provide a string that is not a valid integer constant, as in:

```
Integer j = new Integer("3.75");
```

* Some JDK 1.1 compilers report this exception on line 10 because Java checks that the index is between 0 and 2 before executing line 11.

then Java will throw a number format exception. If we do not handle the exception in a catch clause, Java will abort the program with an error message.

Example 11.7 shows both valid and invalid attempts to construct `Integer` and `Double` objects from strings. As in Example 11.6, we call the `printStackTrace` method to determine the exception and where it occurred. In this example the stack of method calls shows three entries, the bottom from our `main` method and the top two from the `Integer` class of the Java library. Java uses `<init>` to denote a constructor.

EXAMPLE 11.7 StringToNumber.java

```
/* Illustrates wrapper classes used to convert
 * a string to an int or a double, and the number format
 * exception when the string has an invalid format.
 */

public class StringToNumber {
  public static void main(String [] args) {
    try {
      int i = new Integer("435").intValue();              // Note 1
      System.out.println("i = " + i);
      int j = new Integer("45.2").intValue();             // Note 2
      System.out.println("j = " + j);
    }catch(NumberFormatException e) {
      e.printStackTrace();                                // Note 3
    }
    double d = new Double("3.14").doubleValue();// Note 4
    System.out.println("d = " + d);
  }
}
```

Output

```
i = 435
java.lang.NumberFormatException: 45.2
    at java.lang.Integer.parseInt(Integer.java:238)
    at java.lang.Integer.<init>(Integer.java:342)
    at StringToNumber.main(StringToNumber.java:11)
d = 3.14
```

Note 1: We construct an `Integer` object from the string "435" which represents an integer literal. The `intValue` method returns a value, 435, of type **int**.

Note 2: Passing the string "45.2" to the `Integer` constructor causes Java to throw a number format exception, as 45.2 is not a valid integer literal.

Note 3: The stack trace shows two methods from the `Integer` class. The bottom line of the trace shows that line 11 of our program caused Java to throw the exception.

Note 4: After handling the exception, we wrap a valid **double** value as a `Double`.

Style

Even though the catch clause in Example 11.7 has just one statement, `e.printStackTrace()`, we still need to enclose it in curly braces. If a try block contains just one statement, that statement needs to be enclosed in curly braces.

THE BIG PICTURE

Enclosing code that can throw an exception in a `try` block allows us to handle that exception in a `catch` clause. When Java throws an exception it will jump to a `catch` clause for that exception in the same method if there is one, and continue searching for a `catch` clause in the calling method, if there is not one. Printing the stack trace shows the methods that were in progress when the exception occurred.

TEST YOUR UNDERSTANDING

TRY IT YOURSELF 3. Run Examples 11.5 and 11.6, entering a negative value for the index to see that Java throws an exception in this case.

TRY IT YOURSELF 4. Revise Example 11.7 to remove the `try` statement and the `catch` clause for the `NumberFormatException`. Rerun the revised code and note what happens and what code gets executed.

TRY IT YOURSELF 5. Write a small test program to create an array with elements of type `Object`. Show that you can include `Integer` and `Double` objects in the array. What happens if you try to include an **int** value?

6. Which of the following will cause Java to throw a `NumberFormatException`?

   a. `Integer i = new Integer("-7200");`

   b. `Double d = new Double("PI");`

   c. `String s = new String("PI");`

   d. `String s = new String("64000");`

   e. `Double d = new Double(".123");`

11.3 Text File Input and Output

So far we have done our character mode input from the keyboard, and our character mode output to the screen. In this section we will see how to read from and write to external files.

Reading from a File

The `FileReader` class allows us to read from an external file stored on a disk. We pass the name of the file to the constructor, as in:

```
FileReader input = new FileReader("myFile.data");
```

Many errors can occur during the input and output process. For example if the file `myFile.data` does not exist, (it may have been accidentally deleted, or never created), then Java will throw a `FileNotFoundException`. In our file IO programs in this section we catch `IOException` which is a superclass of all the IO exceptions so we will be notified if any IO exception occurs such as an unexpected end of file or a file not found.

We have no way of knowing that a file is missing from the disk, so we cannot validate the file name the same way we validated the array index in Example 11.4. If Java raises an IO exception and we do not handle it, the program will abort. To prevent this, Java requires that we handle the IO exception, and will not compile a call to any method that can generate an IO exception unless it is in a try block that handles that exception.

Example 11.8 shows an attempt to construct a `FileReader`. It compiles because the constructor is in a `try` block with a `catch` clause which catches the IO exception. This program generates a `FileNotFoundException` at runtime because there is no external file named `zxcvb.data`. We print the stack trace and let the program terminate. We leave it to the exercises to improve the program by allowing the user to enter another file name if the current name causes an exception.

EXAMPLE 11.8 IoError.java

```
/* Throws an IO exception because the
 * file zxcvb.data does not exist.
 */

import java.io.*;                                          // Note 1
  public class IoError {
    public static void main(String [] args) {
    try {
       FileReader f = new FileReader("zxcvb.data");       // Note 2
    }catch(IOException e) {
      e.printStackTrace();                                 // Note 3
    }
  }
}
```

Output

```
java.io.FileNotFoundException: zxcvb.data
    at java.io.FileInputStream.<init>(FileInputStream.java:64)
    at java.io.FileReader.<init>(FileReader.java:43)
    at IoError.main(IoError.java:9)
```

Note 1: We tell the compiler to look for the classes used for input or output, such as `FileReader`, in the package `java.io`.

Note 2: This line will not compile unless it is included in a `try` block with a `catch` clause for the IO exception. (See the A Little Extra section for an amendment to this rule.) If the file does not exist at runtime, Java will throw a file not found exception. The file, `zxcvb.data`, named in this example does not exist.

Note 3: The stack shows three methods, `main` from our `IoError` class, the `FileReader` constructor, and the constructor from the `FileInputStream` class in the Java library that the `FileReader` class uses.

A LITTLE EXTRA—CHECKED EXCEPTIONS AND THE THROWS CLAUSE

Java divides exceptions into two categories:

unchecked	subclasses of `Error` or `RuntimeException`
checked	subclasses of `Exception` (but not of `RuntimeException`)

As we have seen, we have a choice whether or not to handle an **unchecked exception** such as `ArrayIndexOutOfBoundsException` or `NumberFormatException`. If a method does not want to handle a **checked exception** it can use a `throws` clause to declare that it may pass along that exception to its caller. For example, in

```
public FileReader createFile(String s) throws IOException {
  return new FileReader(s);
}
```

the `createFile` method does not put the `FileReader` in a `try` block, and does not catch the `IOException`; it declares that it may throw the `IOException` to whomever calls it. The `main` method could call the `createFile` method, putting that call in a `try` block and adding a `catch` clause for the `IOException` that `createFile` may throw because it does not catch the error caused when the file `zxcvb.data` is not found.

The code for `main` would look like Example 11.8, except that `FileReader("zxcvb.data")` would change to `createFile("zxcvb.data")`. A method might use the `throws` clause when it does not know what to do when the exception occurs. The caller of the method might have more information to help handle the error appropriately.

Reading Lines and Fields

Java provides classes for both binary and text input and output. Binary IO uses the internal representations of the data without converting them to the character representations using digits and letters that humans can more easily read. Such binary IO can be very useful for transferring data from one file to another. We will concentrate on text IO in this section and binary IO in the next.

Disk storage units have mechanical parts so we access external data much more slowly than that residing in the computer's memory. Reading one character at a time from a disk would be very inefficient. A better plan is to read a whole block of data from the disk, say 1024 characters, storing these characters in an area of the computer memory called a **buffer**. We then read the characters, when we need them, from the buffer. Because the buffer is in memory rather than on the disk, we can access the data much faster. When we have read all the characters in the buffer, we again read another block of data from the disk.

The process works in reverse for output. We write each character into a buffer, and when the buffer is full we write the entire buffer to the external disk. Java provides a `BufferedReader` class to allow us to read blocks of data into a buffer. We pass a `FileReader` to the `BufferedReader` constructor

```
BufferedReader f = new BufferedReader
                   (new FileReader("messages.data"));
```

To read from the buffer, we use the `readLine` method, which reads a line of text returning it as a string.

Example 11.9 reads the strings from the `messages.data` file, which we created by typing some lines of our choosing using a simple text editor (that is, not using a fancy editor with hidden formatting characters). The **while** loop terminates when the `readLine` method returns **null**, indicating it is at the end of the file. After reading the strings we close the file, releasing any resources used back to the operating system.

EXAMPLE 11.9 FileReadStrings.java

```
/* Reads strings from a file created in
 * a text editor.
 */
import java.io.*;
  public class FileReadStrings {
    public static void main(String [ ] args) {
      String line;
      try {
        BufferedReader f = new BufferedReader
                (new FileReader("messages.data"));                // Note 1
        while((line = f.readLine()) != null)                      // Note 2
        System.out.println(line);
        f.close();                                                // Note 3
      }catch(IOException e) {
        e.printStackTrace();
    }
  }
}
```

Output

```
Java is fun.
The three did feed the deer.
An apple a day keeps the doctor away.
```

Note 1: We pass the name of the external file, `messages.data`, to the `FileReader` constructor, and pass the `FileReader` that we construct to the `BufferedReader` constructor, so that we can read blocks of data into a buffer rather than reading one character at a time from the external file.

Note 2: We read a line from the file, assigning it to the variable `line`. We terminate the loop when `line` is `null` which indicates we are at the end of the file.

Note 3: We close the file to release the resources it used back to the operating system.

A LITTLE EXTRA—THE FINALLY CLAUSE

Java provides a `finally` clause to cleanup after it completes the execution of the code in the `try` clause, either normally or by throwing an exception. We could use the `finally` clause in Example 11.9 to close the file `f`. The `close()` method at the end of the `try` clause in Example 11.9 will not be invoked if the `readLine` method throws an exception. Putting the statement `f.close()` in the `finally` clause will make sure that it gets executed whether or not an exception occurs. The revised code fragment using the `finally` clause is:

```
BufferedReader f = null;
try {
  f = new BufferedReader(new FileReader("messages.data"));
  while((line = f.readLine()) != null)
    System.out.println(line);
}catch(IOException e) {
  e.printStackTrace();
}finally {
  try{
    f.close();
  }catch(IOException e) {
    e.printStackTrace();
  }
}
```

Because the `close()` method can generate an `IOException`, we put it in a `try` block.

In Example 11.9 we read one string from each line. Typically, data files contain records with several fields on each line. We will separate fields by a delimiter which we can choose. For example, if we use the vertical bar to separate the fields, we can write the name, product number, color, and price of an item as

```
shirt|12345|blue|15.99
```

We can use the `StringTokenizer` class to read several fields from a single line. Each field on the line is called a **token**. We first read the line using the `readLine` method. Suppose we read the line of data above for the shirt storing it in a variable named `line`, and then pass `line` to the `StringTokenizer` constructor, as in:

```
StringTokenizer strings = new StringTokenizer(line,'|');
```

where the second argument to the constructor specifies the vertical bar, |, as the delimiter, dividing the line into separate string tokens. We use the `nextToken()` method to get each token. Calling `strings.nextToken()` will return the string, shirt, the characters up to the vertical bar delimiter. Calling `nextToken()` three more times will return the strings 12345, blue, and 15.99, in that order.

In Example 11.10 we will enter the four fields, street, city, state, and zip, of the `Address` class of Example 5.8 on a single line separating them with the vertical bar, as in:

```
77 Sunset Strip|Hollywood|CA|90048
```

To read the next string we use the `nextToken` method, as in:

```
strings.nextToken();
```

which for the above line will return `77 Sunset Strip` the first time it is called, `Hollywood` the second time, and so on. We use the `countTokens` method to check that the line has exactly four strings, skipping it if it does not.

EXAMPLE 11.10 FileReadAddresses.java

```
/* Reads the four fields of an Address, separated by vertical bars,
 * from a single line. Uses a StringTokenizer to get each string.
 */

import java.io.*;
import personData.*;
import java.util.StringTokenizer;                              // Note 1
public class FileReadAddresses {
  public static void main(String [ ] args) {
    String line;
    String street, city, state, zip;
    StringTokenizer strings;
    Address address;

    try {
      BufferedReader f = new BufferedReader(new
                            FileReader("addresses.data"));
      while ((line = f.readLine()) != null){
        strings = new StringTokenizer(line,"|");
        if (strings.countTokens() == 4) {
          street = strings.nextToken();
          city = strings.nextToken();
          state = strings.nextToken();
          zip = strings.nextToken();
```

```
          address = new Address(street,city,state,zip);              // Note 2
          System.out.println(address);                               // Note 3
          System.out.println();
        }
      }
      f.close();
    }catch(IOException e) {
      e.printStackTrace();
    }
  }
}
```

Output

```
77 Sunset Strip
Hollywood, CA 90048

222 Bridge Road
Grand Palabra, ND 58585
```

Note 1: We tell the Java compiler to find the `StringTokenizer` class in the `java.util` package.

Note 2: We create an `Address` object as defined in Example 5.8.

Note 3: The `println` method uses the `toString` method of the `Address` class to print the `address` object on the screen. Notice that the `address` object rearranges the fields input from the file to look like an address on two lines.

In Example 11.10 we read lines containing four strings. Often our lines may contain other types of data such as **int** or **double**. For example we might have a line with three fields, an item which is a string, an **int** quantity and a price of type **double,** as in:

```
Milk  3  2.10
```

where for variety we separate the fields using blank spaces. Using the blank spaces to delimit the fields prevents us from including an item such as ice cream which has an internal blank.

When we read each token, using the `StringTokenizer` object, we get values of type `String`. We use the wrapper classes introduced in section 7.2 to convert the string representing the quantity to an **int**, and the string representing the price to a **double**. Java allows us not to handle the number format exception that would be generated if, for example, our file had a value of 3.5 in the field for the quantity. In that case our program would abort, so it is better to include a catch clause to handle the number format exception. We leave this improvement for the exercises.

Writing to a File

Java makes it easy to write values of different types to an external file. We first create a `FileWriter`, passing it the name of the external file on which we want to write our data, and then pass the `FileWriter` object to a `PrintWriter` constructor, as in:

```
PrintWriter p = new PrintWriter
            (new FileWriter("totalCost.data"), true);
```

The second argument, **true**, to the `PrintWriter` constructor indicates that we want Java to flush the buffer whenever it executes a `println` statement, instead of waiting until the buffer fills up before writing its contents to the file. Using `p.print` and `p.println` statements we will write to the external file `totalCost.data` overwriting its previous contents.

TIP

To append to the end of `totalCost.data` instead of overwriting its contents use the constructor

```
new FileWriter("totalCost.data", true);
```

where the second argument is an `append` flag set to **true** to append to the file and **false** to overwrite it.

We can format the output using the `NumberFormat` class.

EXAMPLE 11.11 Prices.java

```
/* Reads records from a file, each containing an item, a
 * quantity, and a price.  Computes the total cost of each item,
 * uses NumberFormat objects to write a double to a file, and
 * to write in a currency format to the screen.
 */

import java.io.*;
import java.text.*;
import java.util.StringTokenizer;
public class Prices {
   public static void main(String [ ] args) {
    String line;
    String item;
    int quantity;
    double price;
    double cost;
    StringTokenizer strings;
    NumberFormat decimal = NumberFormat.getInstance();
    decimal.setMaximumFractionDigits(2);
    NumberFormat currency = NumberFormat.getCurrencyInstance();
    try {
     BufferedReader f =
        new BufferedReader(new FileReader("prices.data"));
     PrintWriter p = new PrintWriter(new FileWriter("totalCost.data"),true);
     while ((line = f.readLine()) != null){
       strings = new StringTokenizer(line);                       // Note 1
       if (strings.countTokens() == 3) {
        item = strings.nextToken();
```

```
            quantity = new Integer(strings.nextToken()).intValue();   // Note 2
            price = new Double(strings.nextToken()).doubleValue();    // Note 3
            cost = price*quantity;
            System.out.println("Total cost of "+ item + " is " +
                               currency.format(cost));
            p.print(item + " ");
            p.println(decimal.format(cost));
          }
        }
        f.close();
        p.close();
      }catch(IOException e) {
        e.printStackTrace();
      }
    }
}
```

Output

```
Total cost of Milk is $6.30
Total cost of Coffee is $6.78
Total cost of Bread is $5.67

The file totalCost.data

Milk 6.30
Coffee 6.78
Bread 5.67
```

Note 1: We use the `StringTokenizer` constructor with one argument, the string whose parts we wish to read. We use the default delimiters, space, tab, and newline, often called **whitespace** characters, so that we do not need to specify the delimiters in the second argument.

Note 2: The `nextToken` method returns a string which we have to convert to an `int` for the quantity field.

Note 3: The `nextToken` method returns a string which we have to convert to a `double` for the price field.

Reading an Integer

We develop a `readInt` method that makes it easy for a user to enter an integer from the keyboard. It handles errors, such as poorly formatted values, gracefully.

Example 11.12 shows the `readInt` method, which accepts a `String` argument to prompt the user about the input. We add a trailing colon to the prompt to indicate that the input should follow it. We use a `print`, rather than a `println`, statement to print the prompt, so the user can input the integer on the same line as the prompt.

The `print` statement adds the prompt to the buffer but does not automatically output the buffer to the screen. To quickly output the prompt immediately, we use the `flush` method to flush the buffer. A `System.out.println` statement would flush the buffer, but we do not want to go to the next line.

When reading from a file, as in Example 11.11, we pass the file name to a `FileReader` constructor, and then pass a new `FileReader` object to a `BufferedReader` constructor. For input from the keyboard we pass the standard input stream, `System.in`, to an `InputStreamReader` constructor, which converts the bytes to characters, and then pass a new `InputStreamReader` to a `BufferedReader` constructor to buffer the input.

We expect the user to enter a string representing a valid integer literal which we convert to a value of type **int** using the static `parseInt` method of the `Integer` class. We could have done the conversion, as we did in Example 11.11, by constructing an `Integer` object from the input string, and using the `intValue` method to get the **int** value wrapped inside it. The conversion code using that approach would be

```
i = new Integer(s).intValue();
```

We handle exceptions inside a `while` loop so that if an error occurs we can recover and continue with the program. We initialize the integer variable `i` to zero. If an IO exception occurs, we exit the loop and return `i`, which will have the default value of zero. If the user inputs a string that does not represent an **int**, such as 34.5 or `cat`, then Java will throw a number format exception which we catch inside the loop, printing a message so, hopefully, the user will enter a correct value at the next iteration of the loop.

EXAMPLE 11.12 EnterInt.java

```
/* Create a readInt method to input
 * an integer from the console.
 */

import java.io.*;
public class EnterInt {
  public static int readInt(String prompt) {
    boolean done = false;
    String s;
    int i = 0;
    while (!done) {
      System.out.print(prompt+ ":  ");
      System.out.flush();
      try {
        BufferedReader in = new BufferedReader
                              (new InputStreamReader(System.in));
```

```
        s = in.readLine();
        i = Integer.parseInt(s);
        done = true;
      }catch (IOException e){                                    // Note 1
        done = true;
      }catch (NumberFormatException e1){                         // Note 2
        System.out.println("Error -- input an integer -- Try again");
      }
    }
    return i;
  }
  public static void main(String [ ] args) {
    System.out.println(readInt("Enter an integer"));
  }
}
```

Output—First Run

```
Enter an integer:  57
57

Output -- Second Run

Enter an integer:  cat
Error -- input an integer -- Try again
Enter an integer:  54
54
```

Note 1: If an IO error occurs, we exit the loop and return the default value of zero.

Note 2: We can catch more than one type of exception that might be thrown in a try block. Here we have two catch clauses, one for an IO exception, and another for a number format exception.

THE BIG PICTURE

Code that might throw an `IOException` must be enclosed in a `try` block with a `catch` clause to handle that exception, or in a method that declares that it may throw an `IOException` to its caller.

The `FileReader` lets us read characters from a file. To gain efficiency by buffering, we pass it to a `BufferedReader` which has a `readLine` method we use to read from the file. We can use a `StringTokenizer` to retrieve fields from a line. Similarly a `FileWriter` lets us write characters to a file. The `PrintWriter`, automatically buff-ered, lets us use the familiar `print` and `println` methods.

TEST YOUR UNDERSTANDING

TRY IT YOURSELF 7. Create a `prices.data` file, in which each row has a string naming an item, an integer representing the quantity desired of that item, and a **double** representing the unit price for that item, which contains data in an invalid format, such as a value of 3.5 for the quantity. Run Example 11.11, explaining the result.

TRY IT YOURSELF 8. Write your own `messages.data` file with one string on each line, and run the code of Example 11.9, checking that the program does list the strings from your file.

TRY IT YOURSELF 9. Change the file `prices.data`, used in Example 11.11, to include ice cream as an item. Run the program and explain what happens.

11.4 Binary and Object Input and Output

We use binary input and output for data in 8-bit byte form rather than the character form needed for 16-bit Unicode characters. Such binary data can be stored in files, but it is not meant to be read by humans.

When reading and writing objects, we must be very careful in dealing with shared objects. Fortunately the Java object serialization facilities handle these details automatically, allowing us to easily store and retrieve objects.

The File Class

The `File` class has several methods, which return properties of the file. Example 11.13 uses some of these methods, whose names nicely signify their functions.

EXAMPLE 11.13 FileProperties.java

```
/* Creates a file and returns some
 * of its properties.
 */

public class FileProperties {
  public static void main(String [ ] args) {
    File f = new File(args[0]);
    System.out.println("Name: "+f.getName());
    System.out.println("Path: "+f.getPath());
    System.out.println("Can write: "+f.canWrite());
    System.out.println("Is directory: "+f.isDirectory());
    System.out.println("Length: "+f.length());
    System.out.println("Parent directory: "+f.getParent());
  }
}
```

Output (Using java `FileProperties FileProperties.java`)

```
Name: FileProperties.java
Path: FileProperties.java
Can write: true
Is directory: false
Length: 638
Parent directory: d:\booklr\gittleman\ch11
```

Reading and Writing Bytes

The abstract `InputStream` class contains three read methods. The method

```
public native int read( ) throws IOException;
```

where the modifier **native** indicates that Java implements this method in a platform-dependent manner, reads a single byte. The **int** return type guarantees that the return value will be positive. The **byte** type represents values from –128 to 127. Character codes use unsigned values better represented using the **int** type where a single byte will have a value between 0 and 255.

The method

```
public int read(byte[ ] b) throws IOException;
```

reads into a byte array. It may not fill the array if not enough input bytes are available. The three-argument version of `read`,

```
public int read(byte[] b, int off, int len)
                          throws IOException;
```

reads into an array of bytes, with the second argument specifying the starting offset in the file, and the third giving the number of bytes to read. The last two `read` methods return the number of bytes read, or –1 if at the end of the file.

Because files represent external resources there is always a possibility of hardware failure or corruption or deletion by other users, so Java requires that we catch the `IOException` that would be thrown when such an error occurs. Omitting the `try-catch` code in Example 11.14 will cause a compiler error.

In Example 11.14, we read and display bytes from standard input by default, but can read from a file by entering its name on the command line. Java declares the standard input stream, `System.in`, usually the keyboard, as an `InputStream`. The `FileInputStream` class lets us read from a file.

EXAMPLE 11.14 ReadBytes.java

```
/* Reads and displays bytes until end-of-file. Reads from the keyboard
 * or from a file name entered as a program argument.
 */

import java.io.*;
```

```
public class ReadBytes {
  public static void main(String[] args) {
    InputStream input;
    try {
       if (args.length == 1)
        input = new FileInputStream(args[0]);
       else
        input = System.in;
       int i;
       while((i = input.read()) != -1)
         System.out.print(i + " ");
       input.close();
    }catch(IOException e) {
       e.printStackTrace();
    }
  }
}
```

Output (from `java ReadBytes`)

```
a big car
97 32 98 105 103 32 99 97 114 13 10 ^Z                          // Note 1
```

Output (from `java ReadBytes test.data` where `test.data` contains `á big car`)

```
225 32 98 105 103 32 99 97 114                                  // Note 2
```

Note 1: The program outputs the ASCII values for the characters. The last two values, `13` and `10`, represent carriage return and newline generated in Windows by pressing the *Enter* key. Java buffers the standard input so that the user can backspace and make changes. Hitting the *Enter* key signals that the user is satisfied with the input. To signal the end of the input, the user enters `Control Z` on a separate line of input.

Note 2: We added an accented character, `á`, to show a value, `225`, that would be negative if the return type was **`byte`**. In Notepad, entering Alt 0225 produces the character á. The Unicode value for á is 225.

We can make reading from a file much more efficient by buffering the input. Buffering involves reading a block, say 2048 bytes, from the disk to an internal memory buffer. The next reads will take bytes from the buffer rather than having to make inefficient disk accesses. When the buffer is empty, the next read will grab another block to fill it. We could have buffered the file input in Example 11.14 using the constructor

```
new BufferedInputStream(new FileInputStream(args[0]))
```

Example 11.15 uses a `read` statement to read a file, and copies it to a new location with the `write` method of `FileOutputStream`. We can copy either text files or binary files this way. The `FileOutputStream` class has three versions of the `write` method: write one byte, write an array of bytes, or write a given length of an array of bytes from a starting offset in the file.

We close the file in a `finally` clause, which is an extra exception handling option to ensure proper clean up. Java executes the `finally` clause whether or not an exception was thrown.

EXAMPLE 11.15 FileCopy.java

```
/* Copies a file using read and write statements.
 * Pass source and target file names as program arguments.
 */

import java.io.*;
public class FileCopy {
  public static void main(String [] args) {
    FileInputStream input = null;
    FileOutputStream output = null;
    try {
      File f = new File(args[0]);
      input = new FileInputStream(f);                  // Note 1
      int length = (int)f.length();                    // Note 2
      byte [] data = new byte[length];                 // Note 3
      input.read(data);                                // Note 4
      output = new FileOutputStream(args[1]);          // Note 5
      output.write(data);
    }catch (IOException e) {
      e.printStackTrace();
    }finally {
      try {
        input.close();                                 // Note 6
        output.close();
      }catch(IOException ex) {
        ex.printStackTrace();
      }
    }
  }
}
```

Output

The command `java FileCopy FileCopy.java NewFileCopy.java` copies `FileCopy.java` to `NewFileCopy.java`

Note 1: We create a `File` object, `f`, and pass it rather than the file name, because we need a `File` object to get the file's length. We leave the buffering of the input as an exercise.

Note 2: The `length` method returns a value of type **`long`**, which we must cast to an **`int`** because the **`new`** operator creates an array with size given by a value of type **`int`**.

Note 3: We create an array large enough to hold the entire file.

Note 4: We created the data array to have the size of the file, so we use the `read` method that fills the entire array. This is equivalent to `read(data,0,length)`.

Note 5: We do not need a `File` object for the output file, so we just pass the file name directly to the constructor.

Note 6: We close each file to release any operating system resources used. Closing them in the `finally` clause means that Java will close the files whether or not an exception occurs. The `close` statements may throw an exception and need to be in a `try-catch` block.

For greater efficiency, we could have buffered the output using the constructor.

```
new BufferedOutputStream(new FileOutputStream(target))
```

We leave the buffering of the output as an exercise.

Reading and Writing Primitive Types

The `DataOutputStream` class has methods for writing each of the primitive types in binary form, including `writeBoolean`, `writeChar`, `writeDouble`, `writeFloat`, `writeInt`, and `writeLong`, while `DataInputStream` has methods for reading these types including `readBoolean`, `readChar`, `readDouble`, `readFloat`, `readInt`, and `readLong`.

To create a `DataOutputStream`, we first create a `FileOutputStream`

```
new FileOutputStream(args[0])
```

where `args[0]` is the name of the file to which we write. We pass this `FileOutputStream` to a `BufferedOutputStream`

```
new BufferedOutputStream(new FileOutputStream(args[0]))
```

so that each `write` statement does not force an expensive write to external storage, but rather writes to a buffer which, when filled, is written to the disk. Finally, we construct the `DataOutputStream` from the `BufferedOutputStream`

```
new DataOutputStream(new BufferedOutputStream(
                     new FileOutputStream(args[0])))
```

In Example 11.16, we use the `writeDouble` method to write the integers 0 through 9 and the decimals from 0.0 through 9.0 to a file. The binary format, used internally, is not suitable for human reading. We use the `readDouble` method to read from the newly created file, displaying the values on the screen using the `System.out.print` method to verify the file was written correctly.

XAMPLE 11.16 Binary.java

```
/* Illustrates the DataOutputStream and DataInputStream
 * classes for primitive type IO using int and double.
 */

import java.io.*;

public class Binary {
  public static void main(String [] args) {
    try {
      DataOutputStream output = new DataOutputStream
                              (new BufferedOutputStream
                              (new FileOutputStream(args[0])));
      for (int i = 0; i < 10; i++) output.writeInt(i);
      for (double d=0.0; d < 10.0; d++) output.writeDouble(d);        // Note 1
      output.close();
      DataInputStream input = new DataInputStream
                              (new BufferedInputStream
                              (new FileInputStream(args[0])));
      for (int i=0; i<10; i++)
        System.out.print(input.readInt() + " ");
      for (int i=0; i<10; i++)
        System.out.print(input.readDouble() + " ");
      input.close();
    }catch (IOException e) {
       e.printStackTrace();
    }
  }
}
```

Output (from `java Binary primitive.data`)

```
0 1 2 3 4 5 6 7 8 9 0.0 1.0 2.0 3.0 4.0 5.0 6.0 7.0 8.0 9.0
```

Note 1: Although for loops usually use integer indices, using a **double** index suits this example well. We illustrate the `DataOutputStream` and `DataInputStream` classes using types **double** and **int**, leaving the use of other primitive types for the exercises.

Example 11.16 writes the **int** and **double** values in binary form, using four bytes for each **int** and eight for each **double**. Running Example 11.14 to inspect this representation, using the command

```
java ReadBytes primitive.data
```

produces

```
0 0 0 0  0 0 0 1  0 0 0 2  0 0 0 3  0 0 0 4  0 0 0 5
0 0 0 6  0 0 0 7  0 0 0 8  0 0 0 9
```

```
0 0 0 0 0 0 0 0   63 240 0 0 0 0 0 0 64 0 0 0 0 0 0 0
64 8 0 0 0 0 0 0  64 16 0 0 0 0 0 0  64 20 0 0 0 0 0 0
64 24 0 0 0 0 0 0 64 28 0 0 0 0 0 0  64 32 0 0 0 0 0 0
64 34 0 0 0 0 0 0
```

The first ten entries show the four-byte integer values, while the second ten show eight-byte doubles. The **double** format is not obvious, and not meant for human reading. It separates each number into a fraction part and an exponent, and includes a sign bit.

Random Access Files

We access `FileInputStream`, `FileOutputStream`, `DataInputStream`, and `DataOutputStream` objects sequentially. We read one item after another, going forward in the file, but cannot go back to data before the current file position. Similarly, when writing data, we cannot return to an earlier position in the file. By contrast, the **random access file**, which we can use for both reading and writing, allows us to read or write at any position in the file.

A random access file implements the methods to write primitive types that a `DataOutputStream` does, and provides the same methods to read primitive types as found in a `DataInputStream`. The `seek` method locates a position in the file. Calling `seek(20)` sets the position at the twentieth byte in the file, at which position we can either read or write. After completing a read or write operation, we can use `seek(4)` to move the position to the location further back in the file at byte 4.

When creating a random access file, we use the second argument in its constructor to specify the access mode, "r" for read-only or "rw" for read-write access. For example,

```
new RandomAccessFile("random.dat", "rw");
```

creates a random access file with read and write capabilities on the file `random.dat`. The system will create `random.dat` if it does not exist.

EXAMPLE 11.17 RandomAccess.java

```
/* Seek forward and back, and writes and reads
 * in a random access file.
 */

import java.io.*;
public class RandomAccess {
  public static void main(String [ ] args) {
    try {
       RandomAccessFile raf = new RandomAccessFile("random.dat", "rw");
       for (int i = 0; i < 10; i++)
        raf.writeInt(i);
       raf.seek(20);                                              // Note 1
       int number = raf.readInt();
```

```
      System.out.println("The number starting at byte 20 is " + number);
      raf.seek(4);                                              // Note 2
      number = raf.readInt();
      System.out.println("The number starting at byte 4 is " + number);
      raf.close();
    }catch (IOException e) {
      e.printStackTrace();
    }
  }
}
```

Output

```
The number starting at byte 20 is 5
The number starting at byte 4 is 1
```

Note 1: Each integer is 32 bits or 4 bytes, so the position at byte 20 will bypass the first five integers, 0, 1, 2, 3, and 4, in the file. (The bytes are numbered 0, 1, .., 19.) Reading at byte 20 should result in reading the integer 5.

Note 2: Going back to byte 4 will position the file after the first integer, 0, so reading an integer at this position should return the value 1.

Reading and Writing Objects

Anyone who has tried to write objects to external storage in C++ or even to understand various C++ implementations of object persistence will appreciate how nicely Java has set up **object persistence**, the ability to write objects to and read them from external files. Each class whose objects we wish to store must implement the `Serializable` interface, which has no methods. Implementing `Serializable` shows we intend to write objects of that class to disk. For security reasons, Java did not make the capability for persistence the default, but requires programmers to explicitly permit persistence by implementing the `Serializable` interface.

Java, transparently to the programmer, writes type information to the file, so reading an object will automatically recover its type. Shared objects could cause problems. References are memory addresses which would be meaningless when we reload the objects. Saving a copy of a shared object each time we refer to it, would cause problems trying to maintain several copies of the formerly shared object. Java solves these problems by automatically numbering objects and using these numbers to refer to shared objects which need to be saved only once. This process of coding objects so they can be written to external storage and recovered properly is called **object serialization.**

Example 11.18 illustrates the saving and restoring of objects. An `Account`, `general`, and a `SavingsAccount`, `savings`, share an account holder, `fred`, of type `Person`. We use simplified versions of these classes to create these objects.

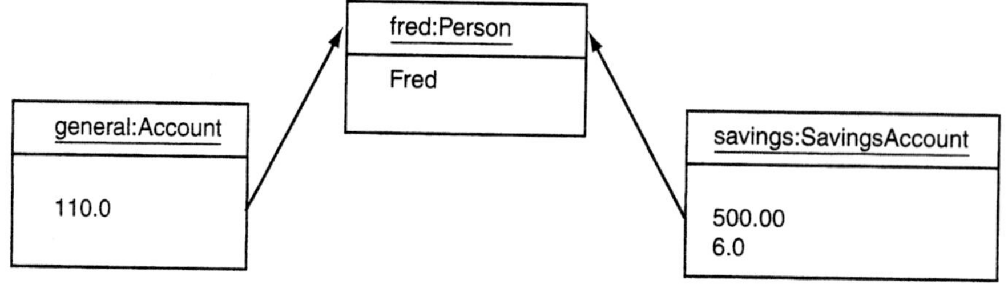

To show that Java handles types correctly, we declare both accounts as `Account` and create an `ObjectOutputStream`, calling `writeObject` to serialize these objects to a file. The classes, `Account`, `BankAccount`, and `Person` all implement `Serializable`.

`ObjectInputStream` provides the `readObject` method to read our objects, which we cast to their compile-time type, `Account`, checking that Java restored the types correctly. The `aGeneral` object should be just a plain `Account`, not an instance of the subclass `SavingsAccount`, while the `aSavings` object should be a `SavingsAccount`. We also check that both the `aGeneral` and the `aSavings` accounts have the identical account holder, `fred`, which shows that Java restored the shared object correctly. Using object serialization, Java saves all the type information and does the object numbering automatically.

EXAMPLE 11.18 ObjectIO.java

```
/* Illustrates object persistence.
 */

import java.io.*;
public class ObjectIO {
  public static void main(String [] args) {
    try {
      Person fred = new Person("Fred");
      Account general = new Account(fred, 110.0);
      Account savings = new SavingsAccount(fred, 500.0, 6.0);       // Note 1
      ObjectOutputStream oos = new ObjectOutputStream(
                  new FileOutputStream("Objects.dat"));
      oos.writeObject(general);                                     // Note 2
      oos.writeObject(savings);
      oos.close();
      ObjectInputStream ois = new ObjectInputStream(
                  new FileInputStream("Objects.dat"));
      Account aGeneral = (Account)ois.readObject();
      Account aSavings = (Account)ois.readObject();                 // Note 3
      if (aGeneral instanceof SavingsAccount)
        System.out.println("aGeneral account is a SavingsAccount");
      else if (aGeneral instanceof Account)
        System.out.println("aGeneral account is an Account");       // Note 4
      if (aSavings instanceof SavingsAccount)
        System.out.println("aSavings account is a SavingsAccount");
```

```
      else if (aSavings instanceof Account)
        System.out.println("aSavings account is an Account");       // Note 5
      if (aGeneral.holder == aSavings.holder)                       // Note 6
        System.out.println("The account holder, fred, is shared");
      else
        System.out.println("The account holder, fred, has been duplicated");
      ois.close();
    }catch (IOException ioe) {
      ioe.printStackTrace();
    }catch (ClassNotFoundException cnfe) {                           // Note 7
      cnfe.printStackTrace();
    }
  }
}
class Person implements Serializable {                               // Note 8
  String name;
  Person (String name) { this.name = name; }
}
class Account implements Serializable {
  Person holder;
  double balance;
  Account(Person p, double amount) {
    holder = p;
    balance = amount;
  }
}
class SavingsAccount extends Account implements Serializable {
  double rate;
  SavingsAccount(Person p, double amount, double r) {
    super(p,amount);
    rate = r;
  }
}
```

Output

```
aGeneral account is an Account
aSavings account is a SavingsAccount
The account holder, fred, is shared
```

Note 1: We declare `savings` to have type `Account`, but assign it an instance of the `SavingsAccount` subclass to check that `writeObject` saves the object's actual type correctly.

Note 2: Besides the `writeObject` method, `ObjectOutputStream` provides the primitive type output methods such as `writeDouble` and `writeInt`. The object written, `general`, is of type `Account` which implements the `Serializable` interface.

Note 3: The second object written had type `SavingsAccount`. Reading it should create an object of type `SavingsAccount`. The `readObject` method returns type `Object`, so we cast the return value to type `Account` and assign it to an `Account` reference, but will check later that its original `SavingsAccount` type has been preserved.

Note 4: The object `aGeneral` was read from the first object written, `general`, so it should be an `Account` object.

Note 5: The object `aSavings` was read from the second object written, `savings`, so it should be a `SavingsAccount`.

Note 6: `if (aGeneral.holder == aSavings.holder)`
We check that these references are equal, meaning they point to the identical object. This shows using the object serialization facility, we preserve the structure of the objects. Objects shared before writing are still shared after being read again. In our example both accounts have the identical account holder, `fred`.

Note 7: `}catch (ClassNotFoundException cnfe) {`
The `readObject` method may throw a `ClassNotFoundException`.

Note 8: `class Person implements Serializable {`
The `Person`, `Account`, and `SavingsAccount` classes are simplified versions of these classes which we use to illustrate object serialization. Each implements the `Serializable` interface, as it must in order to be serializable.

THE BIG PICTURE

The `File` class allows us to get file properties. To read binary files we can use one of the three `read` methods of a `FileInputStream`. To read primitive types we construct a `DataInputStream` from the basic `FileInputStream`, and use the `readInt` and other similar methods. To read objects we construct an `ObjectInputStream` and use the `readObject` method. Such objects must implement the `Serializable` interface. Analogous classes and methods exist for writing. A random access file, used for both input and output, allows us to seek specific locations without having to process the file sequentially.

Test Your Understanding

TRY IT YOURSELF 10. Modify Example 11.15 to add buffering using the `BufferedInputStream` and `BufferedOutputStream` classes.

TRY IT YOURSELF 11. Modify Example 11.15 to close the files in a finally clause so that the files will be closed even if an exception is thrown.

TRY IT YOURSELF 12. Modify Example 11.16 to use the `readLong` and `writeLong` methods instead of `readDouble` and `writeDouble`.

TRY IT YOURSELF

13. Modify Example 11.17 to write the same values using type **double** instead of **int**. Seek the position of 5.0, and then the position of 1.0.

SUMMARY

- We can use program arguments to pass data to the `main` method of a standalone application. If the formal parameter to the `main` method is `String[] args`, then `args[0]` will represent the first program argument, `args[1]` the second, and so on. These values are strings which we may need to convert to type **int** or **double**.
- To pass parameters to an applet, we use the `param` tag in the HTML file. The `name` attribute in that tag specifies the name of the parameter, while the `value` attribute specifies its value. In the applet's code, we use the `getParameter` method, with the `name` attribute as its argument, to get the value of the parameter. The value is of type `String`, which we may need to convert to an **int** or a **double**.
- Java provides an exception handling facility with a hierarchy of predefined exception classes. Some of the methods in the Java library packages throw exceptions when error conditions occur. Java will throw an array index out of bounds exception when a user tries to find an array element having an index outside the bounds specified in the creation of the array. The program aborts when an unhandled exception occurs.
- To handle an exception, we put the code that can throw that exception in a `try` block followed by a `catch` clause for that exception. Java passes an object representing that exception to the `catch` clause. Inside the `catch` block, we can put the code we want to execute after an exception has occurred. Java jumps from the line where the exception occurred to the `catch` clause, and continues execution from there, never returning to the code that caused the exception.
- If there is no `catch` clause in the method where the exception occurs, Java will look for one in the caller of that method, and so on to its caller, finally aborting the program if no `catch` clause is found. Inside the `catch` block, we can call the `printStackTrace` method to show which exception occurred and to see the sequence of method calls that led to the exception.
- To prevent the program from aborting, we can sometimes validate our data; for example, we can check that array indices are valid or that objects are non-null before we try to access their fields. For these types of exceptions Java gives us the option to handle them or not. By contrast, Java requires that we handle IO exceptions from which we could not otherwise recover and continue with the program.
- Java has classes for binary IO, in which data is kept in an internal format not easily readable, and for text IO where we convert internal values to text output, and text input to binary internal values. We can read from an external text file by passing the file name to the `FileReader` constructor. For efficiency we pass the file reader to a buffered reader so we can minimize the number of accesses to the external disk, and do most of our reading from a buffer in memory. The `readLine` method reads a

line from the file, returning `null` when at the end of the file. We must handle the `IOException` that the constructors and methods might generate. The `close` method releases resources back to the operating system.

- We use the `StringTokenizer` class to read more than one field from a single line. The default `StringTokenizer` constructor assumes that whitespace separates the strings, but an optional second argument allows us to specify other delimiters, such as the vertical bar. The `nextToken` method returns the next item on the line as a string, which we convert to an **int** for integer data, and to a **double** for decimal values.
- To write to a text file, we pass the file name to a `FileWriter` constructor. Passing the file writer to a `PrintWriter` constructor will allow us to use the familiar `print` and `println` methods to output values of any of the primitive types, or string representations of objects using the `toString` method.
- The `File` class has methods to obtain the properties of a file. We use the `read` method of the `FileInputStream` class to read bytes from a file and the write method of the `FileOutputStream` class to write bytes to it. The methods of the `DataInputStream` and `DataOutputStream` classes allow the input and output of primitive types in binary format. We can seek a specific position in a `RandomAccessFile`. The `writeObject` and `readObject` methods use object serialization to store and retrieve objects.

Skill Builder Exercises

1. For each code fragment in the left column choose the exception from the right column that it might throw.

a. `r.readLine()`	i. `ArrayIndexOutOfBoundsException`
b. `a[index]`	ii. `NumberFormatException`
c. `new Integer(s)`	iii. `IOException`
d. `new FileReader("abc.data")`	

2. Fill in the blanks in the code to create a reader to read text from a file `text.data` buffering it for efficiency.

```
BufferedReader buffer
  = new __________ (new __________ (________));
```

3. Fill in the blanks in the code to create a writer to write text to a file `text.out` using `print` and `println` methods.

```
PrintWriter writer
  = new __________ (new ____________ (________));
```

Critical Thinking Exercises

4. If we use the tag

   `<param name=font  value=Monospaced>`

   to pass the font to an applet, which of the following expressions can be used in the applet to retrieve the font name?

   a. `getName(font);`

   b. `getParameter(font);`

   c. `getParameter(name);`

   d. `getParameter("font");`

   e. none of the above

5. If we include the statement

   ```
   FileReader reader = new FileReader("test.dat");
   ```

   in our program without putting it in a try block with a catch clause for the `IOException` (and without declaring that the method containing this line can throw an `IOException`)

   a. the compiler will report an error.

   b. the program will compile, but will abort when running if there is no file named `test.dat` on the user's machine.

   c. the program will always run, using a default file if `test.dat` is not available.

   d. none of the above.

6. If we include the statement

   ```
   Integer i = new Integer("3.14");
   ```

   in our program without putting it in a `try` block with a `catch` clause for the `NumberFormatException` (and without declaring that the method containing this line can throw a `NumberFormatException`)

   a. the compiler will report an error.

   b. the program will compile, but will abort when it reaches this statement.

   c. the program will always run, truncating the value 3.14 to 3.

   d. none of the above.

7. Given the statement

   ```
   StringTokenizer s =
       new StringTokenizer("123|abc|456","|");
   ```

   which statement below will cause the **int** variable `i` to have the value `123`?

a. `int i = s.nextToken();`

b. `int i = Integer.parseInt(s.nextToken());`

c. `int i = Integer.parseInt(s);`

d. `int i = nextToken(s);`

e. none of the above.

Debugging Exercise

8. The following program attempts to read a fixed number of lines from a file, and display them on the screen. The file name if the first program argument and the number of lines is the second. Find and correct any errors in this program.

```
import java.io.*;
public class ReadFile {
   public static void main(String [] args) {
     String line;
     int totalLines;   // number of lines to read from the file
     int count = 0;       // number of lines read so far
     totalLines = Integer.parseInt(args[2]);
     BufferedReader f = new BufferedReader(new FileReader(args[1]));
     while((line=f.readLine()) != -1 && count++ < totalLines)
      System.out.println(line);
    f.close;
  }
}
```

Program Modification Exercises

9. Modify Example 11.5 to give the user another chance to enter a correct value after Java throws an exception.

PUTTING IT ALL TOGETHER 10. Modify Example 8.8, `StudentScore`, to read the test scores from a file. The first line will contain the number of students. Put each student's scores on a separate line, with each score separated by a blank. Prompt the user to enter the file name.

11. Modify Example 11.2, `PassToApplet`, to input the font style using a `param` tag in the HTML file.

12. Modify Example 11.11, `Prices`, to catch the number format exceptions that might be generated. Test with a file that includes some values that will cause the exception to be thrown.

13. Modify Example 11.9 to allow the user to enter another file name if an exception is thrown.

PUTTING IT ALL TOGETHER 14. Modify Example 8.14, to input the two colors of the bars as applet parameters.

Program Design Exercises

15. Write an applet which draws a rectangle. Use applet parameters to specify the position and size of the rectangle.
16. Write a Java standalone application that presents data read from a file in a bar chart. Enter the file name as a program argument.
17. Write a Java program that searches a file for a string. Pass the string and the file name as program arguments.
18. Write a Java program that reads a text file, removing any extra spaces between words, and writes the output to a file. Enter the file names to read from and write to as program arguments.
19. Write a Java program to update an inventory file. Each line of the inventory file will have a product number, a product name, and a quantity separated by vertical bars. The items in the inventory file will be ordered by product number. The transaction file will contain a product number and a change amount which may be positive, for an increase, or negative, for a decrease. Assume the transaction file is also ordered by product number. Use the transaction file to update the inventory file, writing a new inventory file with the updated quantities. Assume there is at most one transaction for each item in the inventory, and that no new items occur in the transaction file.
20. Write a Java program which provides a GUI to copy Java programs to the screen or to another file. List the Java programs in a choice box. Use checkboxes in a checkbox group to indicate whether to copy the file to the console window or to another file. Use a text box to enter the name of the file receiving the copy.
21. Write an applet which draws a circle and a rectangle. Use applet parameters to specify the color of the circle and the color of the rectangle.

CHAPTER

12 Swing Components

OUTLINE

Introduction

The Abstract Windowing Toolkit (`AWT`) uses native methods to create heavyweight components that use the platform's windowing system. This gives components a different look and feel on each platform, rather than appearing uniformly on all platforms. The peer classes that Java uses to access the native code require extra resources. The AWT has a limited set of components for user interface design; professional designers need a more powerful system.

Swing is such a more powerful set of user interface components, implemented in Java so the components have the same look and feel across platforms. The user can change the look and feel among several choices. With a separate download one can use Swing with the JDK 1.1. It is included in the Java™ 2 platform along with other parts of the Java Foundation Classes such as a greatly enhanced 2D API, accessibility support, printing, cut-and-paste, clipboard, and drag-and-drop capabilities.

The `SwingSet` demo, found in `\JAVA_HOME\demo\jfc\SwingSet\`, where `JAVA_HOME` is the directory in which the `JDK` is installed, shows all the components in a very impressive way. In the Java™ 2 release, the Swing classes are in packages starting with the `javax` prefix, meaning they are not part of the core Java packages but are a standard extension. The Swing classes appeared in other packages in earlier Java versions.

OBJECTIVES:

- Convert AWT applets and applications to Swing.
- Make look and feel choices.
- Use buttons with images and borders.
- Take advantage of double buffering.
- Use lists, checkboxes, radio buttons, and combo boxes.
- Use menus and dialogs.
- Use tabs and tables.

12.1 Starting to Swing

We explore the Swing hierarchy of classes, show how to convert AWT applets and applications to Swing, and learn to specify the desired look and feel from among the three choices Java currently provides.

The Swing Classes

Many of the Swing classes have the J prefix. The `JComponent` class is a subclass of the AWT `Container` class. It is lightweight, having no native code peer. Figure 12.1 shows some of the Swing classes we will use.

Figure 12.1 Some Swing subclasses of `JComponent`

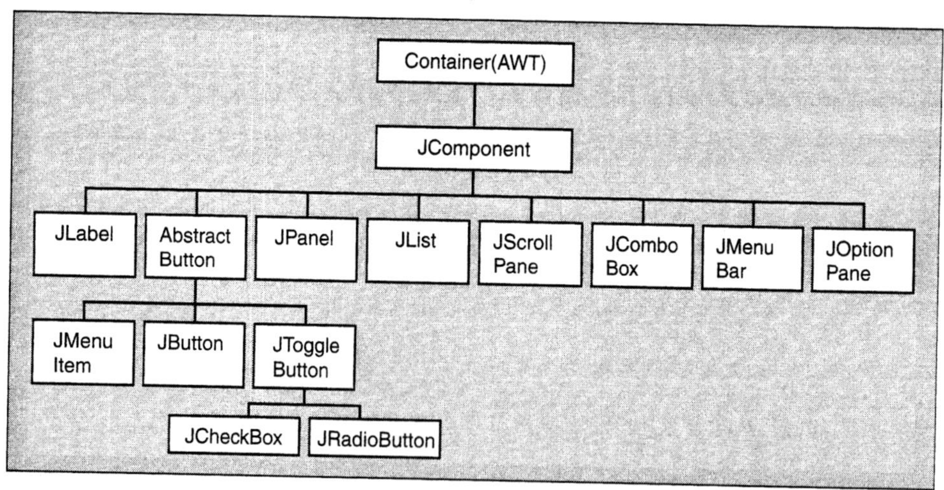

Converting an AWT Applet to Swing

Before Swing, applet writers used the AWT classes. We begin by converting an AWT applet to use Swing. Figure 12.2 shows the applet of Figure 12.3 that we will convert from AWT to Swing.

Figure 12.2 The applet of Figure 12.3

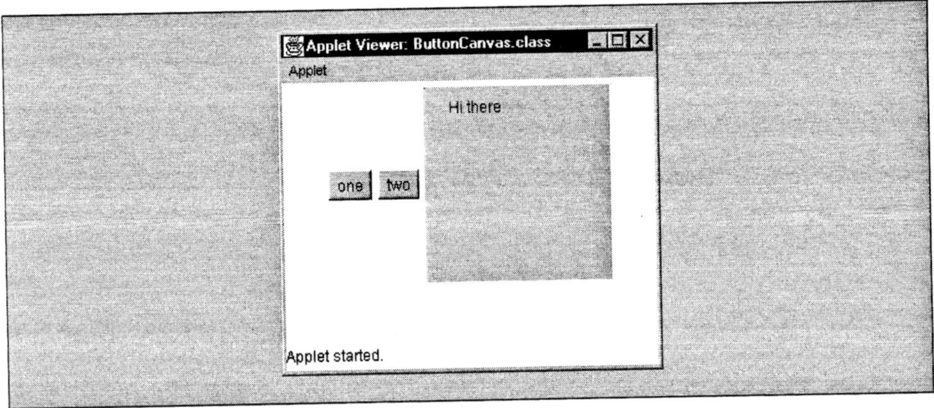

Figure 12.3 An AWT applet

```
import java.awt.*;
import java.applet.Applet;

public class ButtonCanvas extends Applet {
    public void init() {
      add(new Button("one"));
      add(new Button("two"));
      DrawOn canvas = new DrawOn();
      add(canvas);
      canvas.setBackground(Color.pink);
      canvas.setSize(150,150);
    }
    class DrawOn extends Canvas {
      public void paint(Graphics g) {
        g.drawString("Hi there",20,20);
      }
    }
}
```

To write an applet in Swing, we extend the `JApplet` class, which is a subclass of `Applet`. We never add components directly to the outermost window, but rather call the `getContentPane` method to get a `Container` in which to add them.

Swing has no need for a `Canvas` class. We can subclass the `JComponent` or `JPanel` classes instead. Lightweight components can be transparent, taking on the color of their containing window in areas on which we do not draw. Extending `JComponent` always gives us transparency, but we can get a `JPanel` to paint its background, by calling its `paintComponent` method. For drawing in Swing, we use the `paintComponent` method rather than the `paint` method. To set the size we use the `setPreferredSize` method rather than the `setSize` method. Making these changes gives the applet of Example 12.1 shown in Figure 12.4. The Metal look and feel is the default in Swing. Later we will see how to change to another look and feel.

Figure 12.4 The Swing version of the applet

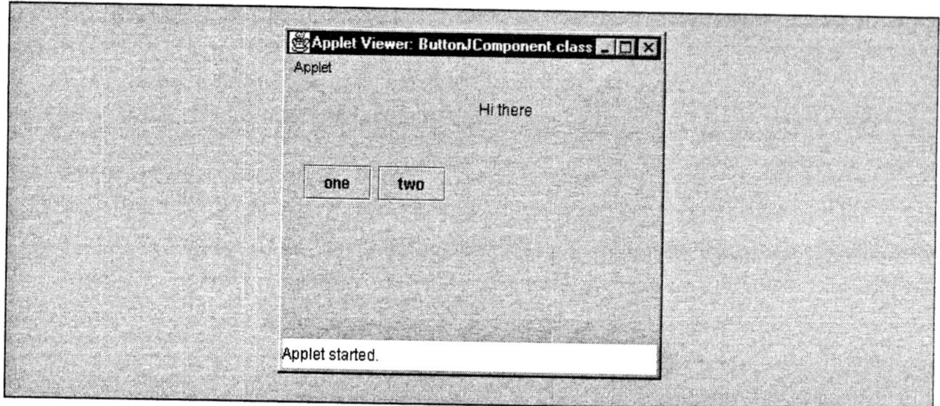

Example 12.1 overrides `JComponent` to draw on, so the drawing component is transparent and the background of the containing content pane shows through. It uses the Swing `JButton` class that we will discuss further in the next section.

EXAMPLE 12.1 ButtonJComponent.java

```
/* Converts the AWT applet of Figure 12.3 to Swing
 */

import javax.swing.*;                                              // Note 1
import java.awt.*;                                                 // Note 2

public class ButtonJComponent extends JApplet {
  public void init() {
    Container c = getContentPane();
    c.setLayout(new FlowLayout());
    c.add(new JButton("one"));
    c.add(new JButton("two"));
    DrawOnJComponent canvas = new DrawOnJComponent();
//      canvas.setBackground(Color.pink);                          // Note 3
    canvas.setPreferredSize(new Dimension(150,150));               // Note 4
    c.add(canvas);
    }
    class DrawOnJComponent extends JComponent {                    // Note 5
      public void paintComponent(Graphics g) {
//        super.paintComponent(g);                                 // Note 6
        g.setColor(Color.black);
        g.drawString("Hi there",20,20);
      }
    }
  }
}
```

Note 1: The `javax.swing` package in Java 2 contains the basic Swing classes. Earlier releases used different package names.

Note 2: Even though it uses Swing components, this example also uses `Container`, `FlowLayout`, `Color`, `Dimension`, and `Graphics` classes from the AWT.

Note 3: We commented this line out because it would have no effect. A `JComponent` has no background.

Note 4: The `setPreferredSize` method takes an argument of type `Dimension`, rather than the `width` and `height` arguments used in `setSize`.

Note 5: We have no need for a `Canvas` class in Swing. We subclass `JComponent` here to draw on. In the next example we use a `JPanel`, which can have a background.

Note 6: `//  super.paintComponent(g);`
The purpose of this line is to fill in the background. Because a `JComponent` has no background it has no effect and we comment it out. We will see it used with `JPanel` in the next example.

Figure 12.5 Using a `JPanel` to draw on

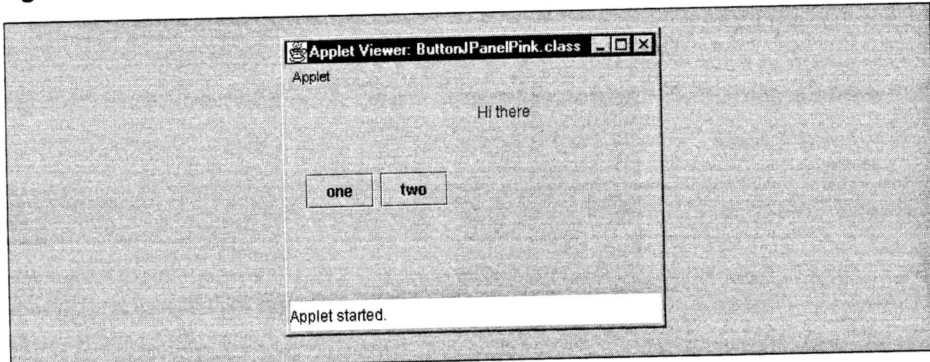

If we use a `JPanel` to draw on instead of a `JComponent`, we can fill in the background and make it pink, as in Figure 12.5. To do that we remove the two comments placed in the Example 12.1 code.

EXAMPLE 12.2 ButtonJPanelPink.java

```
/* Converts Example 12.1 to draw on a JPanel instead of
 * JComponent and to fill in its background in pink.
 */

import javax.swing.*;
import java.awt.*;

public class ButtonJPanelPink extends JApplet {
    public void init() {
```

```
        Container c = getContentPane();
        c.setLayout(new FlowLayout());
        c.add(new JButton("one"));
        c.add(new JButton("two"));
        DrawOnJPanelPink canvas = new DrawOnJPanelPink();
        canvas.setBackground(Color.pink);
        canvas.setPreferredSize(new Dimension(150,150));
        c.add(canvas);
    }
    class DrawOnJPanelPink extends JPanel {
        public void paintComponent(Graphics g) {
            super.paintComponent(g);                              // Note 1
            g.setColor(Color.black);
            g.drawString("Hi there",20,20);
        }
    }
}
```

Note 1: Causes the `JPanel` to fill in its background. If we omit this line, the `JPanel` will be transparent and the applet will look like Figure 12.4.

Text Components and Labels

The `JTextField` class extends `JTextComponent` as does `JTextArea`, which we use in later examples. We use the constructors

```
public JTextField(int columns)
public JTextArea(int rows, int columns)
```

and others are available. As with the corresponding AWT components, text fields hold a single line of text, while text areas can contain a number of rows. To access text we use the method

```
public String getText()
```

while to replace it we use

```
public void setText(String s)
```

We label a text component with a `JLabel` using the constructor

```
public JLabel(String label)
```

but we could also use

```
public JLabel(Icon icon)
```

which uses an icon for a label. We discuss the `Icon` interface in the next section. The `setText` and `setIcon` methods let us make changes to a label.

A Swing Application with Look and Feel Demo

A look and feel defines a consistent style for all components. Because the AWT uses the native windowing platform found on the host machine, AWT interfaces have the look and feel of the host windows. With Swing components we can choose the look and feel. The Metal look and feel is the default for Java, but we can also choose the Windows look and feel which will make our interfaces appear like those on Windows platforms, or the Motif look and feel which will cause them to look like Unix X-Windows applications.

Example 12.3 is a standalone application rather than an applet. A Swing application extends `JFrame` rather than `Frame`. As with a Swing applet, we enter components in the content pane rather than the frame itself, extend `JComponent` to draw rather than `Canvas`, and use `paintComponent` rather than `paint`.

To illustrate we convert, to Swing, Example 10.4 in which the user enters an interest rate, an initial balance, and a number of years in text fields, and presses a button to see the final balance if the interest is compounded annually.

We use the `UIManager.getInstalledLookAndFeels` method to show the choices for a look and feel, and the `UIManager.setLookAndFeel` method to dynamically install our choice. Figure 12.6 shows the Metal look and feel, while Figure 12.7 shows the one for Motif.

Figure 12.6 The Metal look and feel

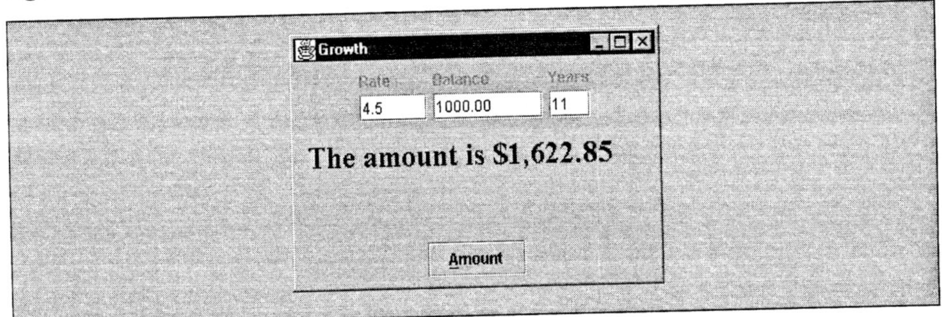

Figure 12.7 The Motif look and feel

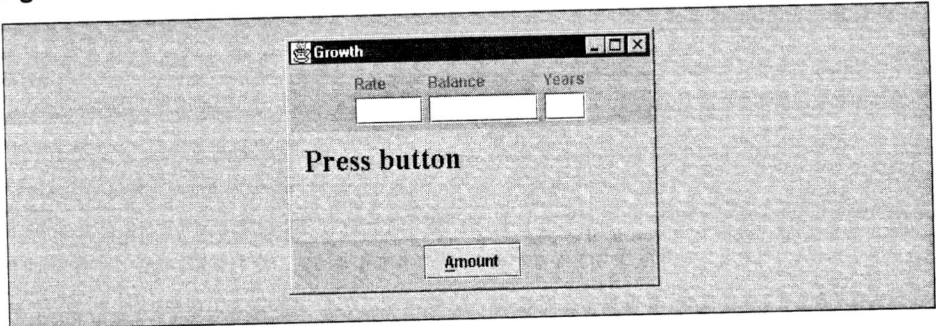

EXAMPLE 12.3 GrowthFrameSwing.java

```
/* Illustrate look and feel using a standalone application.
 */
```

```
import javax.swing.*;
import java.awt.*;
import java.awt.event.*;
import java.text.NumberFormat;
import java.util.Enumeration;

public class GrowthFrameSwing extends JFrame
                              implements ActionListener {
   private JTextField getRate = new JTextField(5);
   private JTextField getBalance = new JTextField(8);
   private JTextField getYears = new JTextField(3);
   private JLabel rate = new JLabel("Rate");
   private JLabel balance = new JLabel("Balance");
   private JLabel years = new JLabel("Years");
   private MyCanvas canvas = new MyCanvas();
   private JButton button = new JButton("Amount");
   private String amount = "Press button";
   private NumberFormat nf;

   public GrowthFrameSwing(String title, String[] args) {
     super(title);
     UIManager.LookAndFeelInfo[] info =
                 UIManager.getInstalledLookAndFeels();          // Note 1
     for(int i=0; i<info.length; i++)
        System.out.println(info[i]);
     try {
        UIManager.setLookAndFeel
              (info[Integer.parseInt(args[0])].getClassName()); // Note 2
     }catch(Exception e) {
          e.printStackTrace();
     }
     Container pane = getContentPane();
     JPanel p1 = new JPanel();
     p1.setLayout(new GridLayout(2,1));
     p1.add(rate);
     p1.add(getRate);
     JPanel p2 = new JPanel();
     p2.setLayout(new GridLayout(2,1));
     p2.add(balance);
     p2.add(getBalance);
     JPanel p3 = new JPanel();
     p3.setLayout(new GridLayout(2,1));
     p3.add(years);
     p3.add(getYears);
     JPanel p = new JPanel();
     p.add(p1);
     p.add(p2);
     p.add(p3);
     JPanel p4 = new JPanel();
     p4.add(button);
     pane.add(p,"North");
```

```
    pane.add(canvas,"Center");
    pane.add(p4,"South");
    addWindowListener(new CloseWindow());
    button.addActionListener(this);
    nf = NumberFormat.getCurrencyInstance();                    // Note 3
  }
  public String computeGrowth() {
    double rate = new Double(getRate.getText()).doubleValue();
    double balance = new Double(getBalance.getText()).doubleValue();
    int years = new Integer(getYears.getText()).intValue();
    for (int i = 1; i <= years; i++)
        balance += balance * rate/100;
    return nf.format(balance);
  }
  public void actionPerformed(ActionEvent event) {
    amount = "The amount is " + computeGrowth();
    canvas.repaint();
  }
  public static void main(String [] args) {
    GrowthFrameSwing f = new GrowthFrameSwing("Growth",args);
    f.setSize(300,200);
    f.show();
  }
  class CloseWindow extends WindowAdapter {
    public void windowClosing(WindowEvent event) {
        System.exit(0);
    }
  }
  class MyCanvas extends JComponent {
    public MyCanvas() {
      Font f = new Font("Serif",Font.BOLD,24);
      setFont(f);
    }
    public void paintComponent(Graphics g) {
      g.drawString(amount,10,30);
  }
 }
}
```

Output (`java GrowthFrameSwing 0` produces Figure 12.6)
(`java GrowthFrameSwing 1` produces Figure 12.7)

```
javax.swing.UIManager$LookAndFeelInfo
      [Metal  javax.swing.plaf.metal.MetalLookAndFeel]
javax.swing.UIManager$LookAndFeelInfo
      [CDE/Motif com.sun.java.swing.plaf.motif.MotifLookAndFeel]
javax.swing.UIManager$LookAndFeelInfo
      [Windows com.sun.java.swing.plaf.windows.WindowsLookAndFeel]
```

Note 1: The `UIManager` class keeps track of the current look and feel. The `LookAndFeelInfo` class is an inner class of `UIManager`. The `getInstalledLookandFeels` method returns a `LookAndFeelInfo` array. Each `LookAndFeelInfo` object displays two fields, the look and feel name and the name of the Java class that implements the look and feel.

Note 2: The `getClassName` method of the `LookAndFeelInfo` class returns the class name of a class that implements this look and feel. The `setLookAndFeel` method uses this class name to set the look and feel. The integer `0` will generate the Metal look and feel because it is first in the look and feel array returned by the `getInstalledLookAndFeels` method. Similarly, index `1` generates Motif, and `2` generates the Windows look and feel.

Note 3: We use the `getCurrencyInstance()` method of the `NumberFormat` class to output the resulting amount formatted in the local currency, dollars and cents in the United States.

THE BIG PICTURE

Swing provides many user interface components, greatly improving the limited selection in the AWT. We can easily convert AWT applets and applications to use Swing classes, and create transparent components. Look and feel classes let our windows conform to a desired style.

TEST YOUR UNDERSTANDING

TRY IT YOURSELF 1. Uncomment the commented lines in Example 12.1 and rerun it. What can you say about the result?

TRY IT YOURSELF 2. Comment the lines in Example 12.2 that are commented in Example 12.1 and rerun it. What can you say about the result?

TRY IT YOURSELF 3. Figures 12.6 and 12.7 show Example 12.3 with the Metal and Motif look and feels. Run Example 12.3 with the Windows look and feel.

12.2 Images and Buttons

Using Swing we can add an image to a button or label, change the image when the mouse rolls over it or presses it, add a tool tip, and specify a keyboard mnemonic. We start by looking at how Swing handles images so we can add images to our buttons.

Images

The `Icon` interface, for a small fixed-sized picture often used to decorate components, has three methods

```
int getIconHeight()
int getIconWidth()
void paintIcon(Component c, Graphics g, int x, int y)
```

The `paintIcon` method draws the icon at the location (x,y) and may use its `Component` argument to get properties such as the background color.

The `ImageIcon` class implements the `Icon` interface to paint icons from images. Image loading can be a slow process. Java has a `MediaTracker` class that helps track the progress of the loading. An `ImageIcon` automatically uses a media tracker to wait for the images to load, so the programmer does not need to provide a media tracker explicitly. Two `ImageIcon` constructors are:

```
public ImageIcon(String filename)
public ImageIcon(URL location)
```

For example, for a local image file we can use

```
ImageIcon("images/gittleman.gif")
```

for the image `gittleman.gif` which is in the `images` subdirectory of the directory containing the `.class` and `.html` files. We use the forward slash separator on all systems because Java creates a URL to find the image. For a remote image we can use

```
ImageIcon(new URL("http://www.cecs.csulb.edu/~artg/gittleman.gif"))
```

Rather than using an `ImageIcon`, we can implement the `Icon` interface to get an icon that we can add to a button or a label. The `paintIcon` method specifies how to draw the icon. In Example 12.4 we create the `RoundIcon` class which implements the `Icon` interface to provide a round icon which we add to two buttons. We leave it to the exercises to add an image icon to a button.

Buttons

From Figure 12.1, we see that the `JButton` class is a subclass of `AbstractButton`, along with `JMenuItem`, and `JToggleButton`, which itself has the `JRadioButton` and `JCheckbox` subclasses. We work with `JButton` in this section, leaving the other button types until later in the chapter.

We can add images to any of the button types. To add an image to a `JButton` we use the constructor

```
public JButton(String text, Icon icon)
```

We could also construct a button with only a text label or only an icon. The `setPressedIcon` method allows us to specify a different icon that appears when the user presses the button. The `setRolloverIcon` method sets an icon that appears when the user rolls the mouse over the button.

The `JButton` class has a `setMnemonic` method to allow users to push a button from the keyboard by holding down the *Alt* key while pressing the key passed as the argument to the method. Thus

```
print.setMnemonic('p')
```

enables `Alt + p` to activate the print button. The `setToolTipText` method displays the tip passed as its argument (and the mnemonic, if any) when the user holds the mouse over the button for a few seconds.

Figure 12.8 The `ButtonIcon` applet

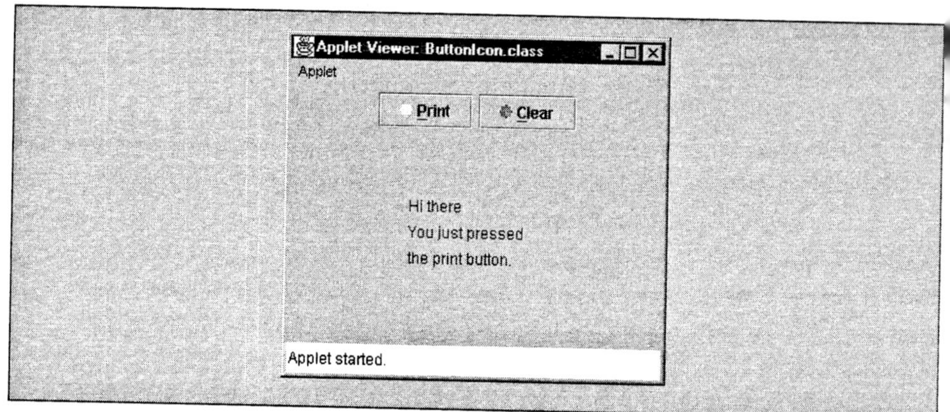

EXAMPLE 12.4 ButtonIcon.java

```
/* Illustrates JButton with mnemonics, images, and rollover images.
 */

import java.awt.*;
import java.awt.event.*;
import javax.swing.*;

public class ButtonIcon extends JApplet {
    private JButton print = new JButton("Print",
                            new RoundIcon(Color.yellow));          // Note 1
    private JButton clear = new JButton("Clear",new RoundIcon(Color.red));
    private DrawOn canvas = new DrawOn();

    public void init() {
      Container c = getContentPane();
      c.setLayout(new FlowLayout());
      RoundIcon brightGreen = new RoundIcon(Color.green.brighter().brighter());
      RoundIcon white = new RoundIcon(Color.white);
      print.setPressedIcon(brightGreen);                           // Note 2
      print.setRolloverIcon(white);                                // Note 3
      print.setMnemonic('p');                                      // Note 4
      print.setToolTipText("Print a message");                     // Note 5
      clear.setPressedIcon(brightGreen);
      clear.setRolloverIcon(white);
      clear.setMnemonic('c');
      clear.setToolTipText("Erase the message");
      print.addActionListener(canvas);
      clear.addActionListener(canvas);
      c.add(print);
      c.add(clear);
      c.add(canvas);
      canvas.setPreferredSize(new Dimension(150,150));
```

```
      print.requestFocus();                                     // Note 6
    }
    class DrawOn extends JComponent implements ActionListener {
      String command = "";

      public void actionPerformed(ActionEvent event) {
        command = event.getActionCommand();
        repaint();
      }
      public void paintComponent(Graphics g) {
        if (command.equals("Print")){
          g.drawString("Hi there",20,60);
          g.drawString("You just pressed",20,80);
          g.drawString("the print button.",20,100);
        }
      }
    }
    class RoundIcon implements Icon {                           // Note 7
      public static final int SIZE = 10;
      Color color;
      public RoundIcon(Color c) {
        color = c;
      }
      public int getIconWidth() {
        return SIZE;
      }
      public int getIconHeight() {
        return SIZE;
      }
      public void paintIcon(Component c, Graphics g, int x, int y) {
        Color oldColor = g.getColor();
        g.setColor(color);
        g.fillOval(x,y,SIZE,SIZE);
        g.setColor(oldColor);
      }
    }
}
```

Note 1: The second argument in this `JButton` constructor allows us to specify an image to place on the button.

Note 2: We make the button image bright green when the user presses the button. We could also have used a different image.

Note 3: We make the button image white when the mouse rolls over the button.

Note 4: Keyboard users can press `Alt+p` to press this button.

Note 5: When the mouse is over the button a tool tip pops up, explaining the effect of the button and giving the keyboard shortcut. The argument gives the text the tool tip displays.

Note 6: We request the focus for the `Print` button, so the user can use the keyboard mnemonic to press it.

Note 7: Implementing the `Icon` interface allows us to implement our own image to place on a button.

Automatic Double Buffering

Double buffering uses an offscreen image to do drawing, and then copies the offscreen image to the screen. This avoids the flicker that often occurs when moving figures directly on the screen. The flicker results from clearing the screen between the drawing of successive frames. Using Swing automatically enables double buffering. The `TryMouseAdapter` applet of Example 10.7 flickers using the AWT, but does not when using Swing classes.

EXAMPLE 12.5 TryMouseNoFlicker.java

```
/* Revises TryMouseAdapter to use Swing components, which
 * automatically enables double buffering to avoid flicker.
 */

import java.awt.*;
import java.awt.event.*;
import javax.swing.*;

public class TryMouseNoFlicker extends JApplet
                    implements MouseMotionListener {
  private int [] x = {50,100,150};
  private int [] y = {100,50,100};
  private Polygon p = new Polygon(x,y,3);
  private int oldx;
  private int oldy;
  private DrawOn canvas = new DrawOn();

  public void init() {
    addMouseListener(new MousePressListener());
    addMouseMotionListener(this);
    getContentPane().add(canvas);
  }
  public class DrawOn extends JPanel {                          // Note 1
    public void paintComponent(Graphics g) {
      super.paintComponent(g);
      g.fillPolygon(p);
    }
  }
```

```
    public void mouseMoved(MouseEvent event) { }
    public void mouseDragged(MouseEvent event) {
      int x = event.getX();
      int y = event.getY();
      if (p.contains(x,y)){
        p.translate(x-oldx,y-oldy);
        oldx=x;
        oldy=y;
        repaint();
      }
    }

  class MousePressListener extends MouseAdapter {
    public void mousePressed(MouseEvent event) {
      int x = event.getX();
      int y = event.getY();
      if (p.contains(x,y)){
        oldx = x;
        oldy = y;
      }
    }
  }
}
```

Note 1: We draw on a `JPanel` to get the benefit of double buffering in Swing. Running both this applet and Example 10.7 will show the difference.

THE BIG PICTURE

The Swing image icon makes it easy to add an image to a button or a label. We can draw our own icon to add to these components. Buttons may have a different image when pressed as well as a rollover image. We may press the button from the keyboard and and a tool tip to remind users of its function.

Swing provides automatic double buffering to avoid flicker.

TEST YOUR UNDERSTANDING

TRY IT YOURSELF 4. Remove the `requestFocus` call from Example 12.4. What happens when you rerun the modified example?

TRY IT YOURSELF 5. Modify Example 12.4 to add an `ImageIcon` to the button instead of the `RoundIcon`.

TRY IT YOURSELF 6. Modify Example 12.4 to draw an `ImageIcon` instead of displaying a message when the user presses the *`Print`* button.

12.3 Lists and Toggle Buttons

We discuss some useful Swing controls including `JList`, `JScrollPane`, `JCheckbox`, `JRadioButton`, and `JComboBox`. `JRadioButton` and `JCheckbox`, each a subclass of `JToggleButton`, have many similarities, as do `JList` and `JComboBox` which both hold lists of items.

Lists

Using an AWT `List` we have to add each element separately, but we can create a `JList` from an array using the constructor

```
public JList(Object[] listData)
```

Selecting an item from a `JList` generates a `javax.swing.event.ListSelectionEvent`. To handle such an event, we implement the `ListSelectionListener` interface, which has one method

```
public void valueChanged(ListSelectionEvent e)
```

and use the `addListSelectionListener` method to register with the `JList`.

We use the method

```
void setSelectionMode(int selectionMode)
```

to specify whether multiple selections are permitted. The `selectionMode` argument has three possible values

`ListSelectionModel.MULTIPLE_INTERVAL_SELECTION`
Select one or more contiguous ranges of indices at a time.

`ListSelectionModel.SINGLE_INTERVAL_SELECTION`
Select one contiguous range of indices at a time.

`ListSelectionModel.SINGLE_SELECTION`
Select one list index at a time.

The `JList` class uses an internal field that implements the `ListSelectionModel` interface to keep track of the list properties.

Scroll Panes

The `JScrollPane` class lets us add scroll bars to any component that implements the `Scrollable` interface, including `JList` and `JTextComponent` which is a superclass of `JTextField` and `JTextArea`. We use the constructor

```
public JScrollPane(Component view)
```

which passes the component which gets the scroll bars as an argument. We add the scroll pane to a container. In Example 12.6, we create a scroll pane from a list, giving the list vertical and horizontal scrollbars.

heckboxes

In the AWT, the `Checkbox` class allowed the selection of multiple checkboxes, but adding checkboxes to a checkbox group would restrict the user to select exactly one of the group, making them behave like radio buttons. In Swing the `JToggleButton` class has two subclasses:

`JCheckBox`	usually allows multiple selections
`JRadioButton`	usually requires one and only one button to be selected (as in the old-time radios).

The seven `JCheckBox` constructors allow us to specify some or all of the three arguments:

a String to identify the checkbox
an icon to add
whether the checkbox is selected initially

They are:

```
public JCheckBox()
public JCheckBox(Icon icon)
public JCheckBox(Icon icon, boolean selected)
public JCheckBox(String text)
public JCheckBox(String text, boolean selected)
public JCheckBox(String text, Icon icon)
public JCheckBox(String text, Icon icon, boolean selected)
```

In constructors without the boolean argument, the checkbox is initially unselected. These checkboxes generate an item event when their state changes. The `ItemEvent` class has a `getStateChange` method which returns `SELECTED` or `DESELECTED`. The `getItem` method returns an object which represents the item selected or deselected.

Example 12.6 uses `JList`, `JScrollPane`, and `JCheckbox` to produce the applet of Figure 12.9.

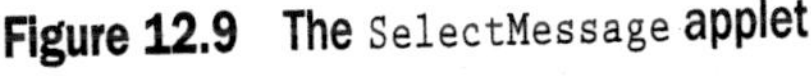

Figure 12.9 **The** `SelectMessage` **applet**

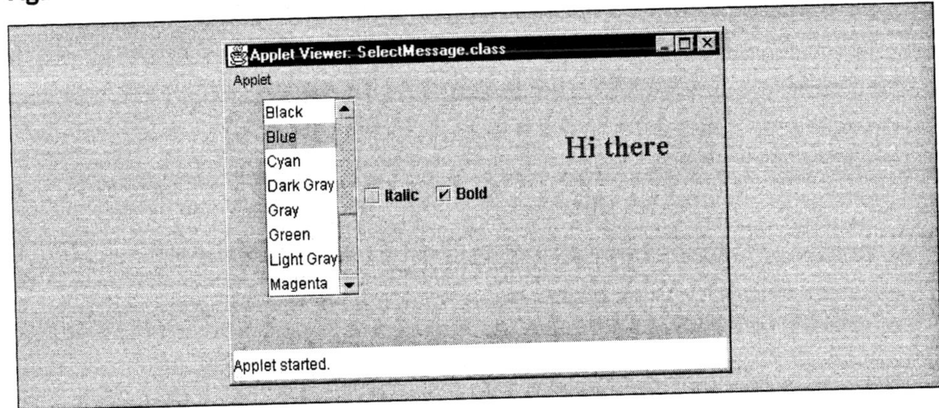

EXAMPLE 12.6 SelectMessage.java

```
/* Illustrates the use of JList, JScrollPane, and
 * JCheckbox components.
 */

import java.awt.*;
import java.awt.event.*;
import javax.swing.*;
import javax.swing.event.*;                                    // Note 1

public class SelectMessage extends JApplet {
    private DrawOn canvas = new DrawOn();
    private String [] colorName = {"Black","Blue","Cyan","Dark Gray","Gray",
       "Green","Light Gray","Magenta","Orange","Pink","Red","White","Yellow"};
    private JList names = new JList(colorName);                 // Note 2
    private JScrollPane color = new JScrollPane(names);         // Note 3
    private JCheckBox italic = new JCheckBox("Italic");         // Note 4
    private JCheckBox bold = new JCheckBox("Bold");
    private Color [] theColor =
              {Color.black,Color.blue,Color.cyan,Color.darkGray,
       Color.gray,Color.green,Color.lightGray,Color.magenta,Color.orange,
       Color.pink,Color.red,Color.white,Color.yellow};
    private String message = "Hi there";

    public void init() {
      Container c = getContentPane();
      c.setLayout(new FlowLayout());
      c.add(color);
      c.add(italic);
      c.add(bold);
      c.add(canvas);
      names.setSelectionMode(ListSelectionModel.SINGLE_SELECTION);
      names.setSelectedIndex(0);                                // Note 5
      names.addListSelectionListener(canvas);                   // Note 6
      canvas.setPreferredSize(new Dimension(150,150));
      italic.addItemListener(canvas);
      bold.addItemListener(canvas);
    }
    class DrawOn extends JPanel implements
                           ItemListener, ListSelectionListener {
       int style = Font.PLAIN;
       public void itemStateChanged(ItemEvent event) {
         Object source = event.getItem();
         int change = event.getStateChange();
         if (source == italic)
            if (change == ItemEvent.SELECTED)                   // Note 7
             style += Font.ITALIC;
            else
             style -= Font.ITALIC;
```

```
        if (source == bold)
          if (change == ItemEvent.SELECTED)
            style += Font.BOLD;
          else
            style -= Font.BOLD;
        repaint();
      }
      public void valueChanged(ListSelectionEvent e) {           // Note 8
        if (e.getValueIsAdjusting() == false)                    // Note 9
            repaint();
      }
      public void paintComponent(Graphics g) {
        super.paintComponent(g);
        g.setFont(new Font("Serif",style,24));
        g.setColor(theColor[names.getSelectedIndex()]);
        g.drawString(message, 50,50);
      }
    }
}
```

Note 1: The `javax.swing.event` package contains event classes such as `ListSelectionEvent` and `ListSelectionListener`.

Note 2: This `JList` constructor enters the strings from its array argument into the list.

Note 3: We pass the component to a `JScrollPane` to add scrollbars to it.

Note 4: We use the constructor that leaves the checkbox initially unchecked. To check it initially we could use the constructor

```
JCheckbox("Italic", true)
```

Note 5: The `setSelectedIndex` initializes a `JList`, giving the index of the item initially selected.

Note 6: `names.addListSelectionListener(canvas);`
A `ListSelectionListener` must implement the `valueChanged` method to respond to a `ListSelectionEvent`, which characterizes a change in the current selection.

Note 7: `if (change == ItemEvent.SELECTED)`
We can select italic and/or bold styles. When we check the box, we select that style, and when we uncheck we deselect the style. When we select a style, we add its value to those selected, and when we deselect an item, we subtract its value.

Note 8: `public void valueChanged(ListSelectionEvent e)`
We implement the `valueChanged` method to handle a `ListSelectionEvent`.

Note 9: `if (e.getValueIsAdjusting() == false)`
Several changes occur when we make a selection. The previously selected item becomes deselected and the new item is selected. With multiple selections more changes occur. The `getValueIsAdjusting` method returns false only for the final event, at which point we repaint using the new selections.

Radio Buttons

A `JRadioButton`'s constructors are similar to those for `JCheckBox`.

```
public JRadioButton()
public JRadioButton(Icon icon)
public JRadioButton(Icon icon, boolean selected)
public JRadioButton(String text)
public JRadioButton(String text, boolean selected)
public JRadioButton(String text, Icon icon)
public JRadioButton(String text, Icon icon, boolean selected)
```

To insure the radio button property that exactly one button is selected, we add the radio buttons to a `ButtonGroup`. The user can select only one from the group. Radio buttons generate item events when selected or deselected.

Combo Boxes

The `JComboBox` is the Swing version of the AWT `Choice`. It is similar to a `JList` but displays only one item with the others displayed in a drop-down menu. We can construct it to hold an array or a vector of items using

```
public JComboBox(Object[] items)
public JComboBox(Vector items)
```

A combo box generates an item event when selected or deselected. The `getSelectedIndex` method returns the index of the selected item.

Figure 12.10 The SelectItem applet

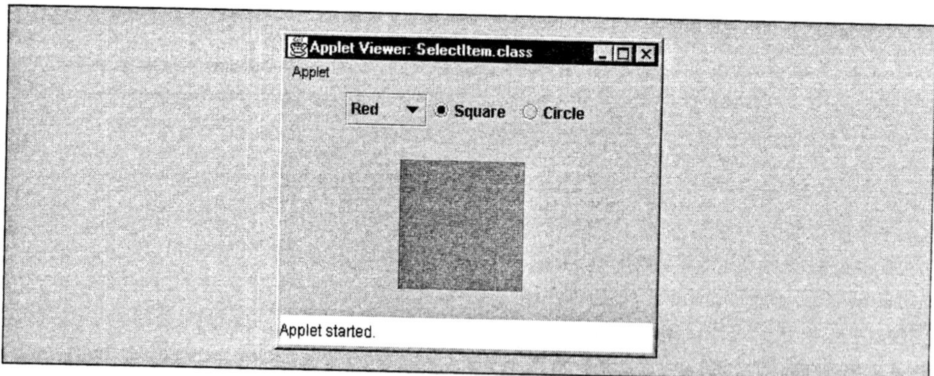

XAMPLE 12.7 SelectItem.java

```
/* Illustrates JRadioButton and JComboBox.
 */

import java.awt.*;
import java.awt.event.*;
import javax.swing.*;

public class SelectItem extends JApplet {
    private DrawOn canvas = new DrawOn();
    private ButtonGroup group = new ButtonGroup();
    private JRadioButton square = new JRadioButton("Square");
    private JRadioButton circle = new JRadioButton("Circle", true);  // Note 1
    private Color [] theColor = {Color.red,Color.green,Color.blue};
    private String [] colorName = {"Red","Green","Blue"};
    private JComboBox color = new JComboBox(colorName);               // Note 2

    public void init() {
      Container c = getContentPane();
      c.setLayout(new FlowLayout());
      c.add(color);                                                   // Note 3
      group.add(square);
      group.add(circle);
      c.add(square);
      c.add(circle);
      c.add(canvas);
      canvas.setPreferredSize(new Dimension(150,150));
      color.addItemListener(canvas);
      square.addItemListener(canvas);
      circle.addItemListener(canvas);
    }
    class DrawOn extends JPanel implements ItemListener {
      boolean isCircle = true;
      public void itemStateChanged(ItemEvent event) {                 // Note 4
          Object source = event.getItem();
          if (source == circle)
             isCircle = true;
          else if (source == square)
             isCircle = false;
          repaint();
      }
      public void paintComponent(Graphics g) {
          super.paintComponent(g);
          g.setColor(theColor[color.getSelectedIndex()]);             // Note 5
          if (isCircle)
            g.fillOval(20,20,100,100);
```

```
          else
            g.fillRect(20,20,100,100);
      }
    }
}
```

Note 1: Setting the second argument to true makes this button selected initially.

Note 2: We construct the combo box to contain the color names in the array argument.

Note 3: We add the square and circle radio buttons to a `ButtonGroup` to require that the user choose only one at a time.

Note 4: The radio buttons and the combo box generate item events when their states change. When we select the radio button for a shape we set a flag and repaint so that shape will appear in the applet. When we select a color we just repaint, using the shape last selected.

Note 5: We use the `theColor` array of colors to convert the string selected in the combo box to a `Color`.

THE BIG PICTURE

Swing has a number of user interface components. We can create a `JList` from an array. Adding a `JList` to a `JScrollPane` will provide the list with scrollbars. Selecting a list item generates a list selection event. Both `JCheckbox` and `JRadioButton` extend `JToggleButton`. Each has seven constructors which let us choose to add a string, or an icon, or to initially select it. They generate an item event when the user makes a selection. We add radio buttons to a button group to require that exactly one radio button of the group is selected. A `JComboBox` may have multiple items, but only one is displayed. It also generates an item event to indicate a selection.

TEST YOUR UNDERSTANDING

TRY IT YOURSELF 7. Omit the `setSelectionMode` statement from Example 12.6. Rerun the example and describe what happens.

TRY IT YOURSELF 8. In Example 12.6, modify the constructor so that the *`Italic`* checkbox is selected initially. Rerun the example to see if the text is initially displayed in italics.

TRY IT YOURSELF 9. Modify Example 12.7 to remove the button group. Rerun the example and describe what happens.

12.4 Menus and Dialogs

The AWT had some classes for menus and dialogs, but Swing greatly extends Java's capabilities for these component types.

Menus

When using a menu, we create a `JMenuBar` and use the `setJMenuBar` method to install it in a `JFrame`. We create a `JMenu` for each menu, using the `add` method to place it on the `JMenuBar`, and create a `JMenuItem` for each item, adding it to its `JMenu`. We call the `addActionListener` method to provide a listener to respond to menu selections. In Example 12.8, we use menus to illustrate the various Swing dialog classes.

Dialogs

The `JOptionPane` class provides four types of dialogs, three of which, `Confirm`, `Option`, and `Input`, we illustrate in the *Feedback* menu shown as one of the menus in the menu bar of Figure 12.11. Each of these three provides feedback.

Figure 12.11 The *`Feedback`* menu of `MenuDialog`

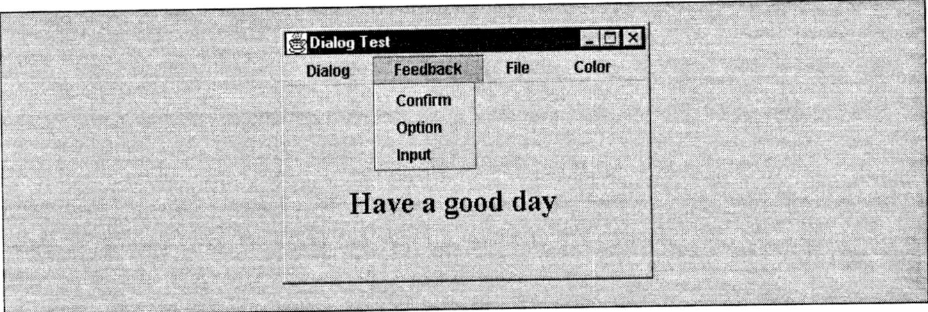

Pressing *`Confirm`* pops up the window of Figure 12.12, in which the user can choose `Yes`, `No`, or `Cancel`. The `showConfirmDialog` method returns the user's response to the program, which in Example 12.8 responds with a message dialog saying `"Great!"`

Figure 12.12 A `Confirm` Dialog

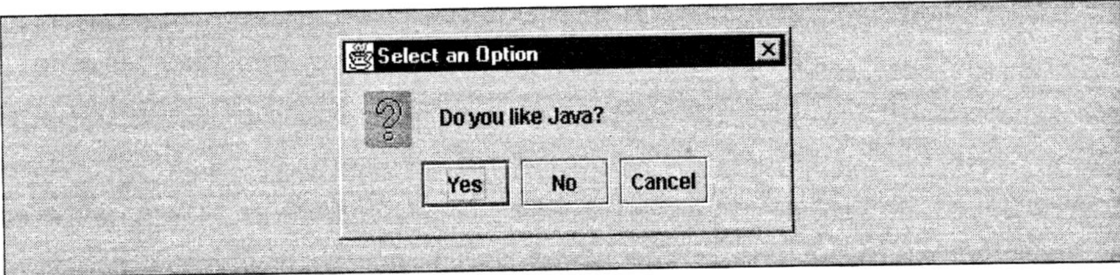

We can configure the `Option` dialog in many ways using the various parameters. Figure 12.13 shows the configuration in Example 12.8. Choosing `Quite well` causes the program to display a congratulatory message.

Figure 12.13 An `Option` dialog

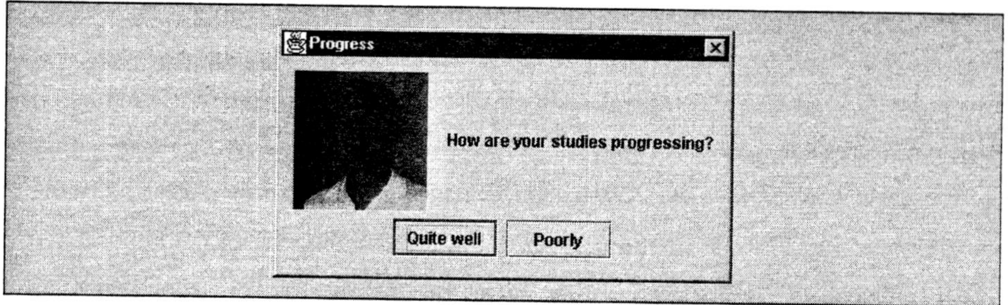

Pressing the *`Input`* menu item pops up an input dialog with a text field for user input and `OK` and `Cancel` buttons. In Example 12.8, we respond with a message echoing the user's input.

The `Message` dialog is the fourth type of dialog box provided by `JOptionPane`. The *`Dialog`* menu of Figure 12.14 shows the generic `Message` dialog, and then the five message dialog types, each of which includes a distinctive image and a message we have supplied as an argument. For example, Figure 12.15 shows the `Error` message, in which we specify both the title and the display message.

Figure 12.14 The *`Dialog`* menu

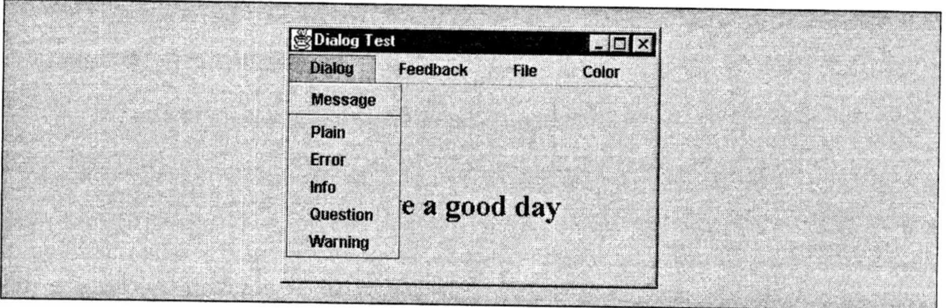

Figure 12.15 The `Error Message` dialog

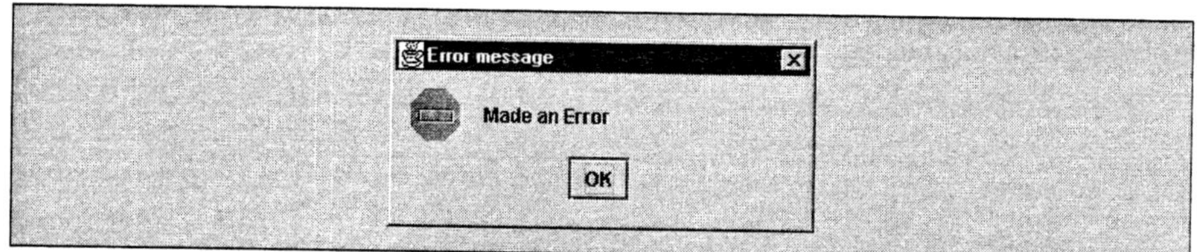

The *`File`* menu in Example 12.8 has only one menu item, `Open`. When we press it a dialog pops up that lets us choose a file. We display the chosen file in a `JTextArea` of a new `JFrame`. The *`Color`* menu has one entry, `Choose`, which when pressed pops up the color dialog of Figure 12.16. We repaint the text in the chosen color.

Figure 12.16 A color dialog

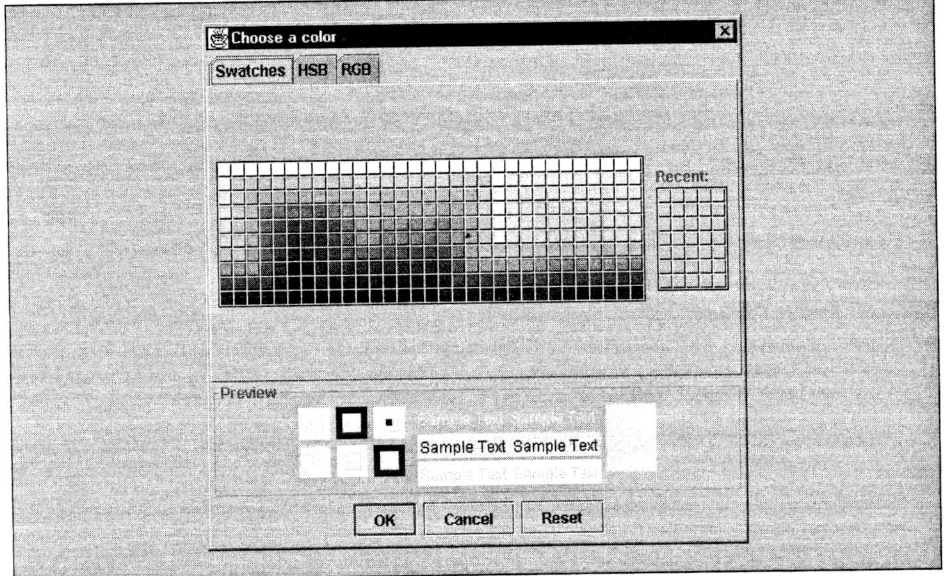

EXAMPLE 12.8 MenuDialog.java

```
/* Illustrate some Swing menu and dialog features.
 */

import javax.swing.*;
import java.awt.*;
import java.awt.event.*;
import java.io.*;

public class MenuDialog extends JFrame
                    implements ActionListener {
    JMenuItem message = new JMenuItem("Message");
    JMenuItem plain = new JMenuItem("Plain");
    JMenuItem error = new JMenuItem("Error");
    JMenuItem info = new JMenuItem("Info");
    JMenuItem question = new JMenuItem("Question");
    JMenuItem warning = new JMenuItem("Warning");
    JMenuItem confirm = new JMenuItem("Confirm");
    JMenuItem option = new JMenuItem("Option");
    JMenuItem input = new JMenuItem("Input");
    JMenuItem open = new JMenuItem("Open");
    JMenuItem choose = new JMenuItem("Choose");
    Color color = Color.black;
    DrawOn canvas = new DrawOn();
```

```
  public MenuDialog(String title) {
    super(title);
    Container c = getContentPane();
    c.add(canvas);
    JMenuBar bar = new JMenuBar();
    setJMenuBar(bar);

    JMenu dialogMenu = new JMenu("Dialog");
    bar.add(dialogMenu);
    dialogMenu.add(message);
    dialogMenu.addSeparator();
    dialogMenu.add(plain);
    dialogMenu.add(error);
    dialogMenu.add(info);
    dialogMenu.add(question);
    dialogMenu.add(warning);
    message.addActionListener(this);
    plain.addActionListener(this);
    error.addActionListener(this);
    info.addActionListener(this);
    question.addActionListener(this);
    warning.addActionListener(this);

    JMenu feedbackMenu = new JMenu("Feedback");
    bar.add(feedbackMenu);
    feedbackMenu.add(confirm);
    feedbackMenu.add(option);
    feedbackMenu.add(input);
    confirm.addActionListener(this);
    option.addActionListener(this);
    input.addActionListener(this);

    JMenu fileMenu = new JMenu("File");
    bar.add(fileMenu);
    fileMenu.add(open);
    open.addActionListener(this);

    JMenu colorMenu = new JMenu("Color");
    bar.add(colorMenu);
    colorMenu.add(choose);
    choose.addActionListener(this);

    addWindowListener(new CloseWindow());
  }
  public void actionPerformed(ActionEvent event) {
    Object source = event.getSource();
    if (source == message)
       JOptionPane.showMessageDialog
                (this,"Your message goes here");                // Note 1
```

```
else if (source == plain)
   JOptionPane.showMessageDialog(this,"Very Plain",
        "Plain message", JOptionPane.PLAIN_MESSAGE);         // Note 2

else if (source == error)
   JOptionPane.showMessageDialog(this,"Made an Error",
                      "Error message", JOptionPane.ERROR_MESSAGE);

else if (source == info)
   JOptionPane.showMessageDialog(this, "Information",
             "Some Info", JOptionPane.INFORMATION_MESSAGE);

else if (source == question)
   JOptionPane.showMessageDialog(this, "?????????",
                      "?????", JOptionPane.QUESTION_MESSAGE);

else if (source == warning)
    JOptionPane.showMessageDialog(this, "This is a warning",
                      "Uh-oh!!", JOptionPane.WARNING_MESSAGE);

else if (source == confirm) {
    int answer =
         JOptionPane.showConfirmDialog(this,"Do you like Java?");
    if (answer == JOptionPane.YES_OPTION)
         JOptionPane.showMessageDialog(this,"Great!");
}

else if (source == option){
    int answer = JOptionPane.showOptionDialog(this,
       "How are your studies progressing?", "Progress",
       JOptionPane.DEFAULT_OPTION,
       JOptionPane.QUESTION_MESSAGE,
        new ImageIcon("images/gittleman.gif"),
        new String[] {"Quite well","Poorly"}, "Quite well");   // Note 3
    if (answer == 0)                                            // Note 4
        JOptionPane.showMessageDialog(this,"Great!");
}

else if (source == input){
    String name = JOptionPane.showInputDialog
                 (this,"Please enter your name");
    JOptionPane.showMessageDialog(this,"Hi " + name);
}

else if (source == open) {
   JFileChooser jfc = new JFileChooser();                       // Note 5
   int answer = jfc.showOpenDialog(this);
   if (answer == JFileChooser.APPROVE_OPTION) {                 // Note 6
       File file = jfc.getSelectedFile();
       JFrame f = new JFrame(file.getName());
```

```
                Container c = f.getContentPane();
                JTextArea text = new JTextArea(10,50);
                JScrollPane scroll = new JScrollPane(text);            // Note 7
                c.add(scroll);
                int length = (int)file.length();
                char[] buffer = new char[length];
                try {
                 BufferedReader br = new BufferedReader(new FileReader(file));
                 br.read(buffer);                                      // Note 8
                 text.setText(new String(buffer));                     // Note 9
                 f.pack();
                 f.setLocation(300,200);                               // Note 10
                 f.setVisible(true);
                }catch(IOException e) {
                   e.printStackTrace();
                }
            }
        }
        else if (source == choose){
           color = JColorChooser.showDialog(this,"Choose a color",Color.yellow);
        }
        repaint();
      }
      class DrawOn extends JPanel {
         public void paintComponent(Graphics g) {
           super.paintComponent(g);
           Color oldColor = g.getColor();
           g.setColor(color);
           g.setFont(new Font("Serif",Font.BOLD,24));
           g.drawString("Have a good day",50,100);
           g.setColor(oldColor);
         }
      }
      public static void main(String [] args) {
        MenuDialog f = new MenuDialog ("Dialog Test");
        f.setSize(300,200);
        f.setVisible(true);
      }
      class CloseWindow extends WindowAdapter {
        public void windowClosing(WindowEvent event) {
            System.exit(0);
        }
      }
}
```

Note 1: The two arguments of the generic `Message` dialog, obtained using the `showMessageDialog` method, are the component containing the dialog and the message.

Note 2: The additional two arguments for the special `Message` dialogs are the title and the message type.

Note 3: The eight arguments of the `showOptionDialog` method are:

parent Component

message

title

option type

```
DEFAULT_OPTION
YES_NO_OPTION
YES_NO_CANCEL_OPTION
OK_CANCEL_OPTION
```

message type

```
ERROR_MESSAGE
INFORMATION_MESSAGE
WARNING_MESSAGE
QUESTION_MESSAGE
PLAIN_MESSAGE
```

icon

options

initial option

Note 4: The answer `0` represents the first option string, "`Quite well.`"

Note 5: The `JFileChooser` class lets the user choose a file to open or save, using the `showOpenDialog` or `showSaveDialog` methods.

Note 6: `if (answer == JFileChooser.APPROVE_OPTION)`
The `APPROVE_OPTION` value represents a positive response such as clicking the `OPEN` button, while the `CANCEL_OPTION` represents a negative response such as clicking the `CANCEL` button.

Note 7: `JScrollPane scroll = new JScrollPane(text);`
As we did with the `JList` in Example 12.6, we add the `JTextArea` to a `JScrollPane`.

Note 8: `br.read(buffer);`
We read the entire file that we have selected.

Note 9: `text.setText(new String(buffer));`
We convert the character array to a string and enter it in the text area.

Note 10: `f.setLocation(300,200);`
Rather than accepting the default location of `(0,0)`, we position the frame at `(300,200)` so as not to cover the dialog.

THE BIG PICTURE

To use menus we create a menu bar, set it in a frame, and add menus with their menu items. Each menu choice generates an action event when the user presses it. `JOptionPane` provides `confirm`, `option`, `input`, and `message` dialogs. Types of `message` dialogs include `plain`, `error`, `information`, `question`, and `warning`. A file dialog lets the user choose a file, while a `color` dialog lets the user choose a color.

TEST YOUR UNDERSTANDING

TRY IT YOURSELF 10. Modify Example 12.8 to show a message dialog when the user presses the *No* button in the `Confirm` dialog.

TRY IT YOURSELF 11. Modify the option dialog of Example 12.8 to use `YES_NO_OPTION` for the option type, and null for the last three arguments. Describe how the resulting option dialog works.

TRY IT YOURSELF 12. Modify the option dialog of Example 12.8 to display a message when the user presses the *Poorly* button.

12.5 Tabs and Tables

Tabbed components allow the user to select from multiple screens to provide more options without crowding a single screen. Swing tables can be configured to display data with great flexibility. We just introduce the basic table in this section.

Tabbed Panes

We construct a tabbed pane with the constructor

```
JTabbedPane()
```

which places the tabs on top. Using the constructor

```
JTabbedPane(int tabPlacement)
```

places the tabs at `SwingConstants.TOP`, `SwingConstants.BOTTOM` , `SwingConstants.LEFT`, or `SwingConstants.RIGHT`.

We use one of the methods

```
void addTab(String title, Component component)
void addTab(String title, Icon icon, Component component)
void addTab(String title, Icon icon, Component component, String tip)
```

to add a component as one of the tabs. The added components have indices `0`, `1`, `2`, . . ., determined in the order they were added. The `setSelectedIndex` method chooses the tab to display.

In Example 12.9 we illustrate a tabbed pane with two tabs, one for the `SelectItem` screen of Example 12.7 and one for the `SelectMessage` screen of Example 12.6.

Figure 12.17 The tabbed pane of Example 12.9

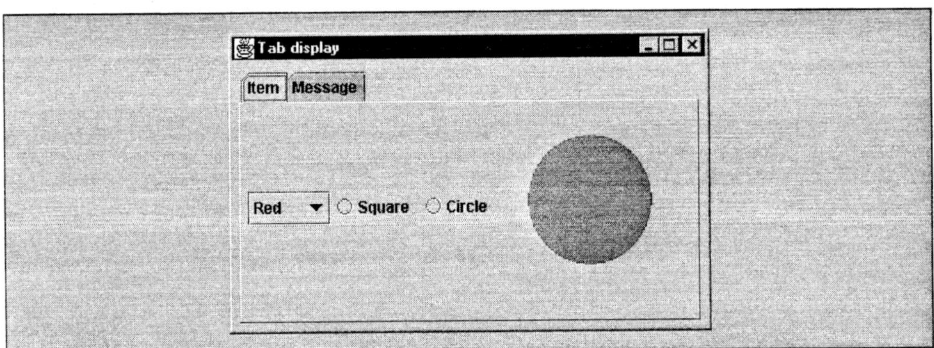

EXAMPLE 12.9 Tabs.java

```
/* Illustrates a tabbed pane.
 */

import javax.swing.*;
import javax.swing.event.*;
import java.awt.*;
import java.awt.event.*;

public class Tabs extends JFrame {

    public Tabs(String title) {
      super(title);
      JTabbedPane tabPane = new JTabbedPane();
      Container c = getContentPane();
      c.add(tabPane,"Center");
      SelectItem item = new SelectItem();
      tabPane.addTab("Item",item);
      SelectMessage message = new SelectMessage();
      tabPane.addTab("Message",message);
      tabPane.setSelectedIndex(0);
      addWindowListener(new CloseWindow());
    }
    public static void main(String [] args) {
      Tabs t = new Tabs("Tab display");
      t.pack();                                                    // Note 1
      t.show();
    }
    class CloseWindow extends WindowAdapter {
       public void windowClosing(WindowEvent event) {
         System.exit(0);
       }
    }
    class SelectItem extends JPanel {
       // same as SelectItem.java
```

```
    }
    class SelectMessage extends JPanel {
      // same as SelectMessage.java
    }
}
```

Note 1: The `pack` method arranges the components in the minimum space necessary.

Tables

Swing provides a powerful table component `JTable` and a package, `javax.swing.table`, of utilities to help configure tables. A `TableModel` interface separates the data from views, so that we can display several different views of the same table, showing different columns or rearranging columns, for example. A `TableColumnModel` interface separates the column configuration from the data itself so that we can change columns without affecting the data model. A `JTableHeader` class manages table headers.

The methods of the `TableModel` interface are:

`void addTableModelListener(TableModelListener l)`
Adds listener notified of changes to the data model.

`Class getColumnClass(int columnIndex)`
Returns the lowest common denominator Class in the column.

```
int getColumnCount()
String getColumnName(int columnIndex)
int getRowCount()
Object getValueAt(int rowIndex, int columnIndex)
boolean isCellEditable(int rowIndex, int columnIndex)
void removeTableModelListener(TableModelListener l)
void setValueAt(Object aValue, int rowIndex, int columnIndex)
```

For simple tables, we do not need to use all of these capabilities. The `AbstractTableModel` class implements the `TableModel` interface, but the `getRowCount`, `getColumnCount`, and `getValueAt` methods are abstract. To use the `AbstractTableModel` class, we subclass it, implementing these three methods and optionally overriding others. In Example 12.10 we choose to also implement the `getColumnName` method to provide headings for each column. Otherwise Swing will create single-letter labels for each column.

Table entries must be objects, so we need to wrap primitive types in wrapper classes. The easiest way to provide data is to hardcode it into the program as an `Object[][]` array, and return these array values in the `getValueAt` method. We use a `String[]` array to specify the column names which we return in the `getColumnName` method.

When we have created an instance of our subclass of `AbstractTableModel`, we pass it to the `JTable` constructor

```
JTable(TableModel dataModel)
```

Figure 12.18 The table of Example 12.10

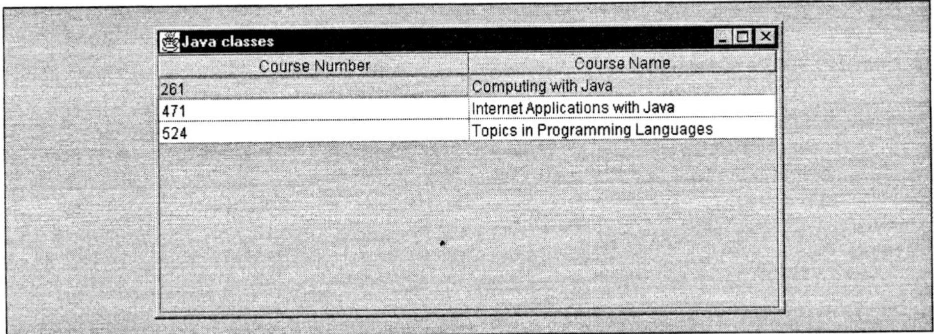

EXAMPLE 12.10 Table.java

```
/* Illustrates a JTable.
 */

import javax.swing.*;
import javax.swing.table.*;
import java.awt.*;
import java.awt.event.*;

public class Table extends JFrame {
    public Table(String title) {
      super(title);
      Container c = getContentPane();
      JTable table = new JTable(new QuickModel());                  // Note 1
      JScrollPane scrollpane = new JScrollPane(table);              // Note 2
      scrollpane.setPreferredSize(new Dimension(500,200));          // Note 3
      c.add(scrollpane);
      addWindowListener(new CloseWindow());
    }
    public static void main(String [] args) {
      Table t = new Table("Java classes");
      t.pack();
      t.show();
    }
    class QuickModel extends AbstractTableModel {
      Object[][] courses = { {"261", "Computing with Java"},
                   {"471", "Internet Applications with Java"},
                   {"524", "Topics in Programming Languages"} };
      String[] headings = { "Course Number", "Course Name" };

      public int getRowCount() {
        return courses.length;
      }
      public int getColumnCount() {
        return courses[0].length;
      }
```

```
      public Object getValueAt(int row, int col) {              // Note 4
        return courses[row][col];
      }
      public String getColumnName(int i) {                      // Note 5
        return headings[i];
      }
    }
    class CloseWindow extends WindowAdapter {
      public void windowClosing(WindowEvent event) {
        System.exit(0);
      }
    }
}
```

Note 1: `QuickModel` is our subclass of `AbstractTableModel`.

Note 2: We add our table to a scroll pane because in general it will not all fit in the display window.

Note 3: Setting the preferred size reduces the amount of wasted space when the layout manager displays the table.

Note 4: The `getValueAt` method uses the `courses` array to specify the data in the table.

Note 5: The `getColumnName` method uses the `headings` array to specify the column headings.

The `SwingSet` provides much more than we are able to explore.

THE BIG PICTURE

Tabbed panes and tables help us to create professional looking user interfaces. Each tab provides a user interface for a facet of the application. Tables present data nicely in rows and columns without the need for the programmer to determine spacing. A table model separates the data from the views displayed.

TEST YOUR UNDERSTANDING

TRY IT YOURSELF 13. Modify Example 12.9 to make the *`Message`* tab appear on top initially.

TRY IT YOURSELF 14. Modify Example 12.10 to omit the `headings` array and the `getColumnName` method. Describe the changes to the table.

TRY IT YOURSELF 15. Modify Example 12.10 to add another row to the table. Make up your own course number and name.

SUMMARY

- Swing components allow us to develop professional looking user interfaces for applications and applets. Using Swing, we do not add components directly to the top level window or applet, but rather to a content pane container. For drawing we subclass `JComponent` or `JPanel` rather than the AWT Canvas class. Subclasses of

`JComponent` always produce transparent components whose background shows through. When drawing on a `JPanel` we can use the `JPanel paintComponent` method to make it opaque.

- Because Swing uses lightweight components each component does not have a corresponding native object that uses the local windowing system. This reduces overhead and allows us to use different look and feels for our components. Swing provides a Metal look and feel, developed for Java, and Windows and Motif look and feels for Windows and Unix systems.
- Swing components have much more functionality than their AWT counterparts. We can easily add images, keyboard shortcuts, and tool tips to buttons, for example. Different images could appear when the user presses the button or when the user rolls the mouse over it.
- We can implement the `Icon` interface, for a small image to decorate components, to draw an icon, or we can use the `ImageIcon` to load a graphic image. The `ImageIcon` class uses a media tracker internally to fully load an image. The `getImage` method returns an `Image` object from an `ImageIcon`. Swing automatically uses double buffering to avoid flicker in animations.
- We construct a `JList` from an array of objects. Selecting a list item generates a list selection event which is handled by implementing the `valueChanged` method of the `ListSelectionListener` interface. A list may or may not allow multiple selections. Passing a list to the `JScrollPane` constructor will cause scrollbars to be added to view lists that do not fit in the available space.
- Check boxes and radio buttons may be labeled by text and/or icons and may or may not be selected initially. Typically, we put radio buttons in a button group so that exactly one will be selected. Check boxes and radio buttons generate item events. The `getItem` method returns an object that represents the item selected. The `getStateChange` method returns the type of item event, selection or deselection.
- We construct a combo box from an array of objects or a vector. A combo box differs from a list in that only one item shows and the other pop up. Selecting an item generates an item event. The `getSelectedIndex` method returns the index of the item selected.
- To use menus, we set a menu bar in a frame, adding menu items to menus which we add to the menu bar. Pressing a menu item generates an action event.
- Swing provides various dialogs to communicate with users. The `JOptionPane` class has methods to create `message`, `confirm`, `input`, and `option` dialogs. The `message` dialog can send a `plain`, `error`, `information`, `question`, or `warning` message. The constructor we used displays a default icon for each message type. Another constructor allow us to add our own icon. The confirm dialog allows the user to answer a question with choices like *Yes*, *No*, and *Cancel*. The input dialog prompts the user for input. The option dialog uses a constructor with eight arguments to allow us to customize the dialog messages, response buttons, and icon.

A file dialog lets the user select a file, and a color dialog lets the user select a drawing color.

- Tabbed panes let us include more components than can fit on one screen. Tables display data in an attractive manner managing the details of its specific placement. A model separates the data from various presentations of it.

We do not have space to discuss all the many features of these and other Swing components.

Skill Builder Exercises

1. Fill in the blanks with the correct class names.

   The ________________ class creates a menu bar. The ________________ class creates a menu, and the ____________________ class creates an entry in a menu.

2. Fill in the blanks with the correct method names.

   We use the ____________________________ to register an event handler for an event generated by a `JList`. The event handler implements the ________________________ method.

3. To create a table model by overriding the `AbstractTableModel` class, which methods must be implemented?

Critical Thinking Exercises

4. Which best describes the use of a look and feel?

   a. The look and feel depends on the user's machine.

   b. A Java program can use a Windows look and feel on a Unix machine.

   c. The look and feel has to be specified when the program is compiled.

   d. All of the above

   e. None of the above.

5. Which of the following can a `JButton` have?

   a. A rollover image.

   b. A mnemonic.

   c. A tool tip.

   d. All of the above.

6. Which of the following is true about `JRadioButton`.

   a. It might be added to a `ButtonGroup`.

   b. It is an abstract class.

c. It must be added to a `ButtonGroup`.

d. It replaces the `Checkbox` class form the AWT.

e. None of the above.

7. Which of the following is not a type of `JOptionPane` dialog?

a. message

b. input

c. confirm

d. option

e. None of the above

Debugging Exercise

8. The following applet attempts to display the message in the text field whenever the user presses the *Print* button. Find and correct any errors.

```
import java.awt.*;
import java.awt.event.*;
import javax.swing.*;

public class ButtonField extends JApplet {
  private JButton print = new JButton("Print");
  private JTextField text = new JTextField(12);
  private DrawOn canvas;

  public void init() {
    canvas = new DrawOn();
    print.addActionListener(canvas);
    add(print);
    add(text);
    add(canvas);
  }
  class DrawOn extends JComponent implements ActionListener {
    String message = "";

    public void actionPerformed(ActionEvent event) {
      Object object = event.getSource();
      if (object == print) {
      message = text.getText();
      repaint();
      }
    }
    public void paintComponent(Graphics g) {
      g.drawString(message,20,100);
    }
  }
}
```

Program Modification Exercises

9. Modify Examples 12.1 and 12.2 to draw a happy face instead of printing a message. Rerun the examples and compare how they look.
10. Modify Example 12.6 to be able to change the look and feel. Run it with each of the three look and feel types and compare the results.
11. Modify Example 12.6 to use a combo box instead of a list for the color names.
12. Modify Example 12.7 to use a `JList` instead of a `JComboBox` for the colors.
13. a. Convert Example 12.7 to a standalone application.

    b. Use menus for the colors and shapes instead of a combo box and radio buttons.
14. Modify Example 12.8 to draw an icon to display in the option dialog, rather than the image of the author.
15. Modify Example 12.9 to add a third tab for the `GrowthFrameSwing` component of Example 12.3.
16. Modify Example 12.10 to use `Integer` data for the course number rather than `String`.

PUTTING IT ALL TOGETHER 17. Modify Example 8.14 to use Swing components for the sorting interface.

PUTTING IT ALL TOGETHER 18. Modify Example 9.15 to use Swing components for the ATM screen interface.

Program Design Exercises

PUTTING IT ALL TOGETHER 19. Write a Java program to enter an order in a Swing `JTextField`. Connect to a servlet which returns a message describing the order. Display the message in a `JTextArea`.

20. Write a Swing interface with menu items for an integrated development environment. Just implement the menu items to display a message, because we are not developing a programming environment tool, just the user interface.
21. Display sales figures for four items in each of five stores using a `JTable`.
22. Display sales figures for four items in each of five stores using a `JTable`. Add a menu with items for adding, inserting, and deleting a row. Add a row at the end of the table. Insert a row after the currently selected row. Use an input dialog to prompt for values. Before deleting the currently selected row, use a dialog to ask the user to confirm the deletion.
23. Use a button with an image of a square to trigger the drawing of a square, and a button with an image of a circle to draw a circle. Add a tip for each button and a mnemonic to allow it to be used from the keyboard. Include a `Color` menu item which pops up a color dialog to let the user choose the drawing color.
24. Use a `JTabbedPane` , providing one tab to input user data such as the name and address, and another to input information about a pizza order. Just echo the data submitted.

CHAPTER

13 Data Structures

OUTLINE

Introduction

Recursion is another approach to repetition. In recursion, instead of spelling out each step of the repetition the way loops do, we do one step and call the recursive method again to complete the remaining steps. We illustrate recursion with two important data processing applications, searching and sorting.

Data structures allow us to organize data for efficient processing. In this chapter we introduce several of the most important data structures, linked lists, queues, stacks, vectors, and hash tables.. In contrast to an array which stores its elements together, a linked list uses a link to refer to the location of its next item, making it easier to add and remove elements but harder to search for them. Choosing the right data structure is an engineering decision based on the requirements of the problem being solved.

Programmers familiar with C or C++ might be familiar with the use of pointers to create linked lists. Java does not need explicit pointers. Each object variable contains a reference to an object, so we can easily create linked lists in Java. Our linked list class includes operations to insert and remove items from a list, and other useful operations.

The stack in computer science is like a stack of books; putting data on a stack has the last in, first out (LIFO) property that the last item placed on it is the first removed. We implement our stack using an array, but could make a more flexible stack using a linked list to hold its elements. The model for a queue is a line of customers. The head of the line gets served first. New customers go to the end of the line.

A vector keeps elements together, but in a more flexible way than an array. A hash table provides quick access to individual elements, but not to a range of elements. In the next chapter we study the collection classes that Java added starting with the Java 2 Platform.

OBJECTIVES:

- Use recursive methods.
- Be familiar with binary search and merge sort algorithms.
- Implement the linked list, stack, and queue data structures.
- Experiment with vector and hash table operations.

13.1 Recursion: Searching and Sorting

Iteration and recursion allow us to repeat steps in a program. The `while`, `for`, and `do-while` loops use iteration to repeat steps where continuing the repetitions is based on the value of a test condition. Using iteration, our program shows the detailed mechanics of the repetition process. By contrast **recursion** deals with repetition at a higher level, letting Java manage the details hidden in calls to recursive methods. Some problems are much easier and more natural to solve using recursion, but in some situations using recursion can be
inefficient. With experience, which comes with further study, one can judge when a recursive solution is appropriate.

An old proverb says that the journey of a thousand miles begins with the first step. This proverb captures the essence of recursion. Take one step and you start toward your goal. To achieve the goal you just have to repeat the process beginning at your new position, one step along the road. We can express this proverb in a Java method, `travel`:

```
public void travel(int start, int finish) {
  if (start < finish) {
    takeOneStep(start);
    travel(start + 1,finish);
  }
}
```

The `travel` method is **recursive**; it recurs inside of itself. One reason recursion is an important concept is that recursive methods are easy to read. The code is like a specification of the travel process. The `travel` code says that to complete the trip from start to finish, if you are not already at the finish, then take one step and travel from that point to the finish, a method that certainly works.

Another reason for the importance of recursion is that recursive methods are usually short because we do not need to specify each detailed step of the solution. We call the method recursively, as in:

```
travel(start+1,finish);
```

letting the `travel` method fill in one more step every time it recurs. Another old proverb says that one picture is worth a thousand words, which we modernize to: One program is worth a thousand words. (The number 1000 seems to have some significance in proverbs.) Our one program is Example 13.1.

EXAMPLE 13.1 Journey.java

```
/* Use a recursive method, travel, to journey from start
 * to finish, printing messages to show its progress.
 */

public class Journey {
  private static String indent = "";                          // Note 1
  public static void takeOneStep(int step) {
    System.out.println(indent + "Taking step " + step);
  }
  public static void travel(int start, int finish) {
    String oldIndent = indent; // save indent to restore it later
    System.out.println
      (indent + "Starting travel from " + start + " to " + finish);  // Note 2
    if (start < finish) {
      takeOneStep(start);
      indent += " ";                                          // Note 3
      travel(start + 1,finish);                               // Note 4
      indent = oldIndent;                                     // Note 5
    }
    System.out.println
      (indent + "Finishing travel from " + start + " to " + finish); // Note 6
  }
  public static void main(String [ ] args) {
    int start = Integer.parseInt(args[0]);                    // Note 7
    int finish = Integer.parseInt(args[1]);
    travel(start, finish);
  }
}
```

Output from java `Journey 1 4`

```
Starting travel from 1 to 4
Taking step 1
  Starting travel from 2 to 4
```

```
      Taking step 2
        Starting travel from 3 to 4
        Taking step 3
          Starting travel from 4 to 4
          Finishing travel from 4 to 4
        Finishing travel from 3 to 4
      Finishing travel from 2 to 4
    Finishing travel from 1 to 4
```

Note 1: We use a static field to keep the string which specifies the amount to indent the message. Each time we call the `travel` method we increase the indent by three spaces, and each time we return we restore the previous indent three spaces to the left.

Note 2: We print the message using the current indent.

Note 3: We increase the indent before calling the `travel` method recursively.

Note 4: This recursive call starts executing the `travel` method with new arguments. This new activation of the `travel` method starts before the previous call to `travel` has returned.

Note 5: We restore the previous indent when we finish executing the `travel` method.

Note 6:
```
System.out.println(indent + "Finishing travel
                 from " + start + " to " + finish);
```
We display a message to show when this call to `travel` completes.

Note 7:
```
int start = Integer.parseInt(args[0]);
```
We use program arguments to specify the start and finish values.

We see from the output that `travel(1,4)` takes the first step and calls `travel(2,4)` to complete the trip. `travel(2,4)` takes the second step and calls `travel(3,4)` to complete the trip. `travel(3,4)` takes the third step and calls `travel(4,4)` to complete the trip. `travel(4,4)` concludes that the trip is complete and terminates. `travel(3,4)` terminates, `travel(2,4)` terminates, and finally `travel(1,4)` terminates.

A recursive method needs an alternative that does not involve making another recursive call, or it will never terminate. The `travel` method terminates if start >= finish. At each call to `travel`, we increase start by one, getting closer to the finish, so eventually the program will terminate.

Before tackling the interesting binary search and merge sort problems we use recursion to sum an array of prices. Like the `travel` method, our recursive `sum` method adds the sum of the remaining elements of the array to the start element. We find the sum of 12.23 + 3.68 + 34.99 + 8.87 + 63.99 by adding 12.23 to the sum of 3.68 + 34.99 + 8.87 + 63.99 which we find by adding 3.68 to the sum of 34.99 + 8.87 + 63.99 and so on.

EXAMPLE 13.2 SumPrices.java

```
/* The recursive sum method sums the elements
 * from start to end of the array passed to it.
 */

public class SumPrices {
  public static double sum(double[ ] p, int start, int end) {
    if (start < end)
      return p[start] + sum(p,start+1,end);                  // Note 1
    else
      return 0;                                              // Note 2
  }
  public static void main(String[ ] args) {
    double[ ] prices = {12.23, 3.68, 34.99, 8.87, 63.99};
    System.out.println("The sum is $" + sum(prices,0,prices.length));
  }
}
```

Output

```
The sum is $123.76
```

Note 1: This is the recursive call where we add the start element of the array to the remaining elements.

Note 2: When start reaches end we have added all the elements and no longer need to make a recursive call. We return a zero as the sum of the remaining (none) elements.

Binary Search

A simple way to search for a value in an array compares the value with each element of the array until we find the element or reach the end of the array. In the worst case, when the element sought is not an element of the array, we must check each element.

If we keep the elements in the array in order from smallest to largest, then we can find an element using binary search, a much more efficient algorithm. We can program binary search as a recursive method or using a loop. In this section we will write a recursive method to perform a binary search.

The idea behind binary search is quite simple. Compare the element sought, called the key, with the middle element in the array. If the key equals the middle element, then we have found it and we are done.

If the key is smaller than the middle element, we know we need only search the left half of the array; because the array is ordered, a key smaller than the middle element can only be found in the left half of the array. In this case we call the binary search method recursively to search the array elements to the left of the middle.

If the key is greater than the middle element, then we need only search the right half of the array. In this case we call the binary search method recursively to search the array elements to the right of the middle.

In the journey of a thousand miles we take the first step, and then travel the rest of the way. In binary search we compare our key to the middle element of the array, and if it is not the value for which we are searching we search either the left half or the right half of the array for the key.

Figure 13.1 shows a trace of a binary search for 78 in an array, data, where `data = {2,5,7,12,23,34,56,78,99,123,234,345,567}`, whose leftmost element has index 0, and whose rightmost element has index 12.

Figure 13.1 Trace of a binary search for 78 in the data array

```
binarySearch(data,78,0,12)
                                middle = (0 + 12)/2  = 6
                                78 >  data[6]         // data[6]==56
                                // search index 7 to index 12.
binarySearch(data,78,7,12)      middle = (7 + 12)/2 = 9
                                78 < data[9]          //data[9]==123
                                // search from index 7 to index 8.
binarySearch(data,78,7,8)       middle = (7 + 8)/2 = 7
                                78 == data[7]         // data[7]==78
                                // return the index 7 to the caller.
```

Example 13.3 shows the code for binary search. The user inputs the array elements as program arguments to the `main` method, entering the elements in order from smallest to largest. The program prompts the user for the key to search.

EXAMPLE 13.3 BinarySearch.java

```
/* Inputs integers in order from smallest to largest on the
 * command line.Uses a recursive method to implement binary
 * search.
 */

import java.io.*;

public class BinarySearch {
public static int binarySearch(int [ ] data, int key, int left, int right) {
    if (left <= right) {                                              // Note 1
      int middle = (left + right)/2;
      if (key == data[middle])
        return middle;
      else if (key < data[middle])
        return binarySearch(data,key,left,middle - 1);                // Note 2
      else                                                            // Note 3
        return binarySearch(data,key,middle + 1,right);
```

```
    }
    return -1;
}
public static void main(String [] args) {
    int key;                                  // the search key
    int index;                                // the index returned
    int [] data = new int[args.length];
    for (int i=0; i < data.length; i++)
      data[i] = Integer.parseInt(args[i]);                    // Note 4
    try {
      BufferedReader input =
        new BufferedReader(new InputStreamReader(System.in));
      System.out.print("Enter the search key: ");
      System.out.flush();
      key = Integer.parseInt(input.readLine());
    } catch(Exception e) {
        key = 10;
    }
    index = binarySearch(data,key,0,data.length-1);
    if (index == -1)
      System.out.println("Key " + key + " not found");
    else
      System.out.println("Key " + key + " found at index " + index);
  }
}
```

Output (using program arguments 2 5 7 12 23 34 56 78 99 123 234 345 567)

```
Enter the search key: 78
Key 78 found at index 7
```

Output (using program arguments 2 5 7 12 23 34 56 78 99 123 234 345 567)

```
Enter the search key: 8
Key 8 not found
```

Note 1: We do not use a `while` loop here, because the recursive call will start the rest of the search. We just determine one of three conditions: either we found the key, or it can only be found in the left half of the data, or it can only be found in the right half of the data. In the first case, we return the index at which we found the key. In the second and third cases, we return the result of the recursive call to the binary search method on the appropriate half of the array.

Note 2: We know that `data[middle]` is greater than the key, so we only need to search the array up to and including the element at index `middle-1`.

Note 3: In this third case, the only possibility remaining is that

```
key > data[middle]
```

so we call the binary search method to search the array from position `middle+1` to `right`.

Note 4: We convert the program arguments to **int** values, storing them in the data array that we will search.

We can also program binary search using a `while` loop, without recursion. We leave this approach for the exercises.

Merge Sort

We introduced the insertion sorting method in Section 8.6, and developed a GUI for it in Section 8.7. The **merge sort** algorithm, easily programmed recursively, is much more efficient than insertion sort especially for larger sets of data.

Merge sort uses the merge operation to sort the data. The merge operation takes two sorted arrays, merging them into a larger sorted array containing all the elements of the original two arrays. For example, the arrays `{2,4,6,8}` and `{1,3,5,7}` merge into the array `{1,2,3,4,5,6,7,8}`. Figure 8.7 traces a merge operation. At each step, we compare the initial elements of the first and second array, adding the smallest of these two elements to the merged array. When we have added all the elements of one array to the merged array, we simply copy the remaining elements in the other array to the merged array.

Figure 13.2 Merging two sorted arrays

First Array	Second Array	Merged Array
{2,5,7,8}	{3,4,9,10}	{2}
{5,7,8}	{3,4,9,10}	{2,3}
{5,7,8}	{4,9,10}	{2,3,4}
{5,7,8}	{9,10}	{2,3,4,5}
{7,8}	{9,10}	{2,3,4,5,7}
{8}	{9,10}	{2,3,4,5,7,8}
{}	{9,10}	{2,3,4,5,7,8,9,10}

To make an analogy illustrating merge sort, we could say that a journey of a thousand miles ends with a single step. Given an array, such as `{8,5,2,7,10,9,3,4}`, to sort we first sort each half, `{8,5,2,7}` and `{10,9,3,4}`, obtaining the two sorted arrays `{2,5,7,8}` and `{3,4,9,10}`, and then, as the final step, merge the two sorted halves into the final sorted array as shown in Figure 13.2.

We can write the merge sort program very simply, just as described in the last paragraph. The details of sorting the two arrays `{8,5,2,7}` and `{10,9,3,4}` are hidden in further recursive calls. To sort {8,5,2,7} we first sort each half, {8,5} and {2,7}, giving the two arrays {5,8} and {2,7}, and then merge these two sorted arrays into {2,5,7,8}. To sort {8,5} we first sort each half, {8} and {5} -- the recursion stops here because single-element arrays are already sorted -- and then merge these two sorted arrays into the array {5,8}. We have not traced all the steps involved in the merge sort. Tracing shows how the merge sort works, but we do not need these details to write the program.

EXAMPLE 13.4 MergeSort.java

```
/* Implements the recursive merge sort
 * algorithm to sort an array that the user
 * inputs as program arguments.
 */

public class MergeSort {
  public static void mergeSort (int [ ] data, int left, int right) {
    if (left < right) {
      int middle = (left + right)/2;
      mergeSort(data,left,middle);                // sort the left half
      mergeSort(data,middle + 1,right);           // sort the right half
      merge(data,left,middle,middle + 1,right);  // merge the left and right
    }
  }
  public static void merge(int[ ] data, int l1, int r1, int l2, int r2) {
    int oldPosition = l1;// save position to copy sorted array
    int size = r2 - l1 + 1;
    int [ ] temp = new int[size];
    int i = 0;
    while (l1 <= r1 && l2 <= r2) {                                   // Note 1
      if (data[l1] <= data[l2])
        temp[i++] = data[l1++];
      else
        temp[i++] = data[l2++];
    }
    if (l1 > r1)                                                     // Note 2
      for (int j = l2; j <= r2; j++)
        temp[i++] = data[l2++];
    else
      for (int j = l1; j <= r1; j++)
        temp[i++] = data[l1++];
      System.arraycopy(temp,0,data,oldPosition,size);                // Note 3
    }
    public static void display(int [ ] anArray) {                    // Note 4
      System.out.print("{");
      for (int i = 0; i < anArray.length; i++) {
        if (i != 0) System.out.print(",");
        System.out.print(anArray[i]);
      }
```

```
    System.out.println("}");
  }
  public static void main (String [ ] args) {
    int [ ] data = new int[args.length];
    for (int i = 0; i < data.length; i++)
      data[i] = Integer.parseInt(args[i]);
    mergeSort(data,0,data.length - 1);
    display(data);
  }
}
```

Output (using program arguments 8 5 2 7 10 9 3 4 6 11 77 1)

```
{1,2,3,4,5,6,7,8,9,10,11,77}
```

Note 1: As long as both arrays that we are merging are not empty, we copy the smallest element of both arrays into a temporary array, and increment the index, either l1 or l2, to the array containing the smallest element.

Note 2: If the first array empties first we copy the remaining elements of the second array into the temporary array, otherwise we copy the remaining elements of the first array.

Note 3: We want to copy the merged elements in the temporary array back to the original array that we are sorting. We use the `arraycopy` method of the `java.lang.System` class, which takes as its arguments

```
source array
starting index in the source array at which to start copying
destination array
starting index in the destination array for the copied elements
number of elements to copy
```

Note 4: We use the `display` method of Example 8.5.

THE BIG PICTURE

Iteration, used in `for` and `while` loops, manages each step of a repetition explicitly. Recursion takes a higher level approach to repetition, doing one step, which reduces the problem to a smaller size, and then asking to repeat that process. The system, behind the scenes, attends to the details. Binary search and merge sort, two important algorithms, illustrate recursion

TEST YOUR UNDERSTANDING

1. Trace all the steps of the merge sort method on the array `{8,5,2,7,10,9,3,4}`.
2. As we did in Figure 13.1, trace the steps in the binary search for `8` in the array `{2,5,7,12,23,34,56,78,99,123,234,345,567}`.

TRY IT YOURSELF 3. Run the merge sort of Example 13.4 to sort the array `{34,23,67,87,2,45,98,12,16,78,32}`.

13.2 Linked Lists

Data structures, ways of organizing data, are an important computer science topic because they are an important tool for programmers to develop efficient solutions to a variety of problems. Having a repertoire of data structures and the knowledge of their characteristics needed to use them effectively is essential. In this and the next section we introduce two of the most important data structures, the linked list and the stack, to add to the array that we have already introduced.

The very efficient binary search method of Example 13.3 uses an ordered array to hold the data to be searched. We can search array data efficiently, but inserting or deleting elements from an ordered array is not very efficient. For example, to insert 17 in the array `{1,3,5,9,12,15,19,23,34,36,45}`, we would have to move the elements greater than 17 one position to the right, assuming space is available in the array. If the array is full, then we have to allocate a new array and copy the whole array into the larger array.

The **linked list** data structure makes it easy to add or remove elements which is why it is so important, but searching for an item may be less efficient than the best array searches. In a linked list, we keep each data item in a node which also contains a reference to the next node in the list. Figure 13.3 shows a linked list containing integer data.

Figure 13.3 A linked list

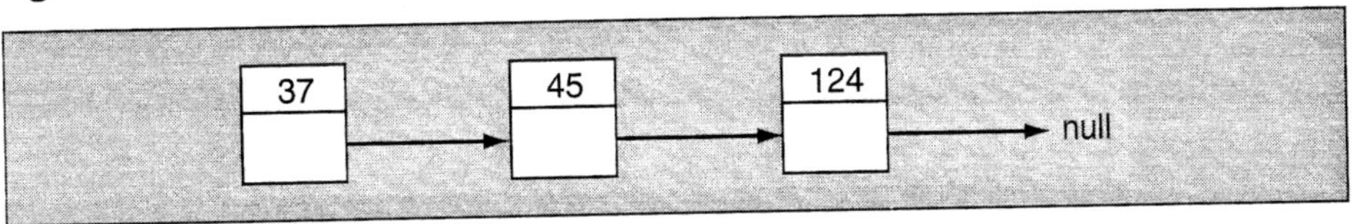

We show the reference in each node as an arrow pointing to the next node. In contrast to arrays, which store their elements contiguously, linked lists allocate each individual node as needed. No matter the size of the list, adding an element to it only requires us to change two references, which is why lists are especially useful when we have to perform many additions and deletions. For example to add 40 to the list of Figure 13.3, we need to allocate a new node, enter 40 in its data field, enter a reference to the node containing 45, and change the node containing 37 to refer to this new node. Figure 13.4 shows these changes.

We can implement a linked list in a variety of ways. We choose to use an inner class, `Node`, for the individual nodes of the list. The private field, `head`, refers to the head node, which is the front of the list. The private field, `current`, refers to the current element; we can advance to the next element of a list, so at any given time we may be inspecting any of the list elements. We need the field, `previous`, which refers

Figure 13.4 Adding 40 to the linked list of Figure 10.8

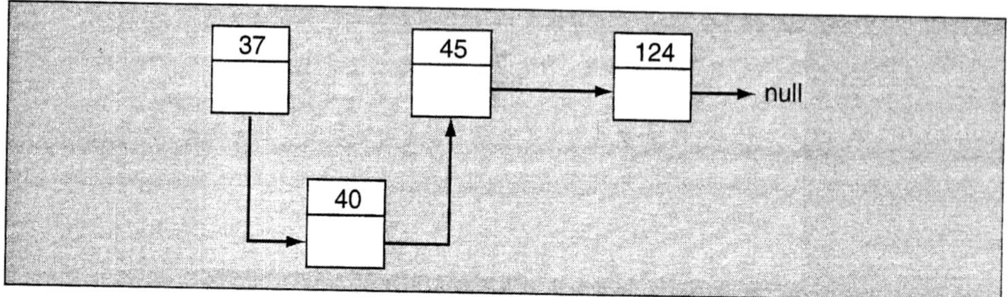

to the list element just before the current element, when we remove the current element.

Figure 13.5 shows the list operations we include in our `LinkedList` data type.

Figure 13.5 The operations of the `LinkedList` class

`public LinkedList()`
Constructs an empty linked list, with the head, previous, and current nodes null.

`public boolean isEmpty()`
Returns **true** if the list is empty and **false** otherwise.

`public void insert(Object o)`
Creates a node containing the object o, inserting it before the current element.

`public void remove()`
Removes the current element.

`public Object getData()`
Gets the data field from the current element. Returns **null** if the current element is null.

`public boolean atEnd()`
Returns **true** if the current element is **null**, false otherwise.

`public void advance()`
If current is not null, advances the previous and current references.

`public void reset()`
Resets the current reference to refer to the head of the list.

`public void display()`
Prints each element of the list on a separate line.

Example 13.5 shows the code for the `LinkedList` class. The `main` method tests the class. We can use `LinkedList` objects in other classes.

EXAMPLE 13.5 LinkedList.java

```
/* Implements the LinkedList data structure.
 */

public class LinkedList {

  class Node {
    Object data;
    Node next;

    public Node(Object o, Node n){
      data = o;
      next = n;
    }
  }

  private Node head;
  private Node previous;
  private Node current;

  public LinkedList() {
    head = null;
    previous = null;
    current = null;
  }
  public boolean isEmpty() {
    if (head == null)
      return true;
    else
      return false;
  }
  public void insert(Object o) {                                  // Note 1
    Node n = new Node(o,current);                                 // Note 2
    if (previous == null)
      head = n;
    else
    previous.next = n;                                            // Note 3
    current = n;
      }
  public void remove() {
    if (head != null){                                            // Note 4
    if (previous == null)
      head = head.next;
    else
      previous.next = current.next;                               // Note 5
    current = current.next;
    }
  }
```

```
    public Object getData(){
      if (current != null)
        return current.data;
      return null;
    }
    public boolean atEnd() {
      return current == null;
    }
    public void advance(){
      if (!atEnd()){
        previous = current;
        current = current.next;
      }
    }
    public void reset() {
      previous = null;
      current = head;
    }
    public void display() {
      reset();                                                          // Note 6
      if (head != null)
        do {
          System.out.println("" + getData());
          advance();
        }while (!atEnd());
    }
    public static void main(String [ ] args) {
      LinkedList list = new LinkedList();
      System.out.println("It is " + list.isEmpty() + " that this list in empty");
      list.insert("Happy days");
      list.insert("Pie in the sky");
      list.insert("Trouble in River City");
      System.out.println("The original list is:");
      list.display();
      list.reset();                                                     // Note 7
      list.advance();
      System.out.println("The current list element is " + list.getData());
      list.remove();
      System.out.println("The list, after removing the current element, is:");
      list.display();
    }
}
```

Output

```
It is true that this list is empty
The original list is:
  Trouble in River City
  Pie in the sky
  Happy days
The current list element is Pie in the sky
```

```
The list, after removing the current element, is:
  Trouble in River City
  Happy days
```

Note 1: We insert the new node before the current element, passing the current element to the next field of the new node.

Note 2: If we are inserting a node before the head node, we make head refer to the new node, otherwise we set the next field of the previous node to refer to the new node.

Note 3: The node being inserted becomes the current node.

Note 4: If we remove the head node, then we update the head reference, otherwise we change the next field of the previous node to refer to the node following the current node. This change unlinks the current node from the list.

Note 5: The node following the current node becomes the new current node, when we remove the current node.

Note 6: `reset();`
We reset to the beginning of the list to display the entire list.

Note 7: `list.reset();`
After displaying the list, the current node is `null`, at the end of the list. We need to reset to the beginning of the list to process the list further.

A LITTLE EXTRA—RUNNING OUT OF MEMORY

Whenever we use the `new` operator, as we do in creating nodes in a linked list, we are allocating memory. Java uses garbage collection to reclaim memory no longer in use by our program, but programs that use a lot of memory may cause memory to run out. If not enough memory is available, Java throws an `OutOfMemoryError` exception. As our examples have been relatively small we have not been concerned with running out of memory, and have not caught this exception which Java designates as unchecked to give us this option.

THE BIG PICTURE

In contrast to an array, a linked list does not keep its data in neighboring locations, but rather each node has a field which refers to its successor. This structure makes it easier to add and delete elements because we do not have to move as many items as we would in an array. However we can use an index to directly access an array element, but must traverse the list to reach a list element.

TEST YOUR UNDERSTANDING

4. Using the `insert` method for a `LinkedList`, is the element inserted before or after the current element?

TRY IT YOURSELF

5. Devise a thorough series of tests for the `LinkedList` class of Example 13.5. Run these tests and note the results.

13.3 Stacks and Queues

Stack and queues carefully control access to the data. A stack allow insertion and deletion only at one end of the sequence of values. A queue deletes from the front and adds to the back.

Stacks

The stack is one of the most useful data structures. We have already seen it in Section 11.1 in the listing by the `printStackTrace` method of the stack of method calls in progress when an exception occurs.

Often technical terms mirror familiar terms that provide good analogies to the technical concepts. **Stack** is such a term. A stack of data is similar to a stack of books or a stack of dishes. We add a book to the top of the stack, and remove a book from the top. Sometimes we call the stack a LIFO stack, where **LIFO** stands for last in, first out. The last dish we stacked is the first that we remove, because it is on the top of the stack.

Of course computer people have to introduce some jargon, so we call the add operation **push** and the remove operation **pop**. In addition to the `push` and `pop` operations, we want an operation, `isEmpty`, to tell us if the stack is empty, an operation, `isFull`, to tell us if the stack is full, and an operation, `top`, to tell us what is on top of the stack without removing it.

Users of stacks just need to know the stack operations to work with stacks. As implementers of the `Stack` class, we can hide the representation of the stack by using private data fields. Let us use the elements of an array to hold the stack data, which for this example will be integers such as 15, 7, or 12. Stacks of books or dishes grow vertically, but we draw our arrays horizontally, so our stack will grow from left to right. Figure 13.6 shows a stack with space for six integers, which currently contains three integers.

Figure 13.6 A stack growing from left to right

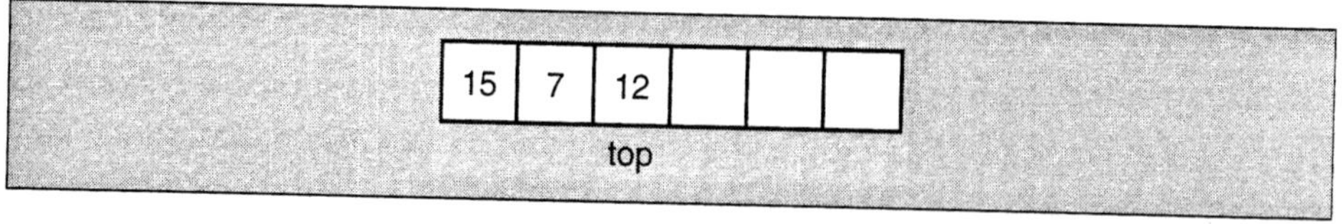

A field, `top`, tells us the index of the top element on the stack. In Figure 13.6, `top` has the value two. The `top` method returns the element on the top of the stack without changing or removing it. Figure 13.7 shows an empty stack, in which case we assign top a value of `-1` to indicate that nothing is on the stack yet.

Figure 13.7 An empty stack

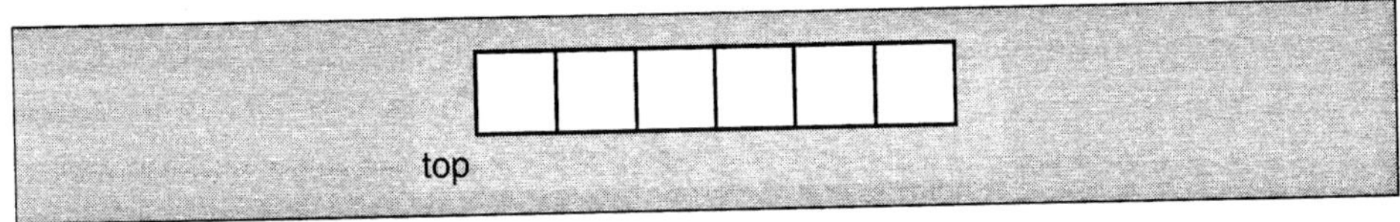

When the stack is full, as in Figure 13.8, then top has the value `size-1`, where the `size` field gives the number of elements allocated for the array.

Figure 13.8 A full stack

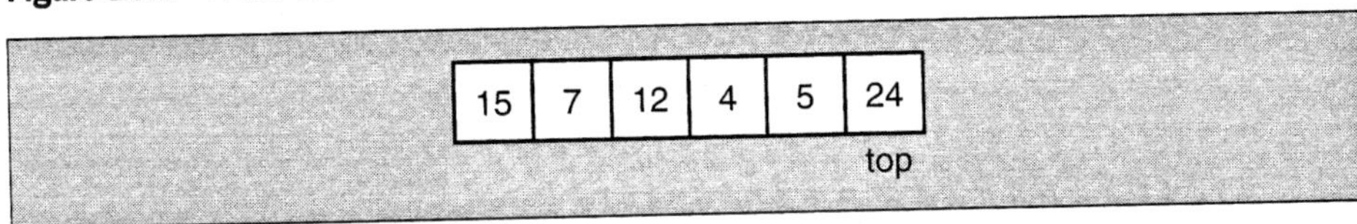

Using our array, we implement the push operation with the pseudocode:

```
if (stack full)
   throw an exception;
else {
   Increment top;
   Add item to the array at index top;
}
```

Figure 13.9 shows the result of pushing 4 onto the stack of Figure 13.6.

Figure 13.9 Pushing 4 onto the stack of Figure 13.6

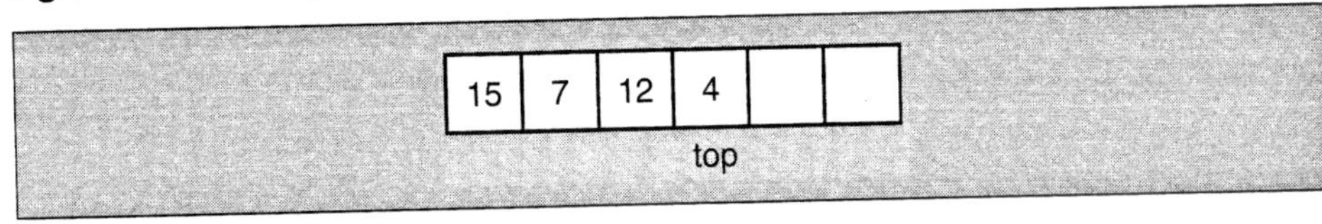

The `pop` method returns and removes the element on the top of the stack, which presents a problem when the stack is empty, in which case we throw an exception. The pseudocode for the pop operation is:

```
if (stack empty) {
   throw an exception;
}
Return the top of the stack
   and decrement top;
```

Figure 13.10 shows the stack resulting from popping the stack of Figure 13.9. The integer 4 is still at index three of the array, but top is now two, so we ignore it.

Figure 13.10 Popping the stack of Figure 13.9

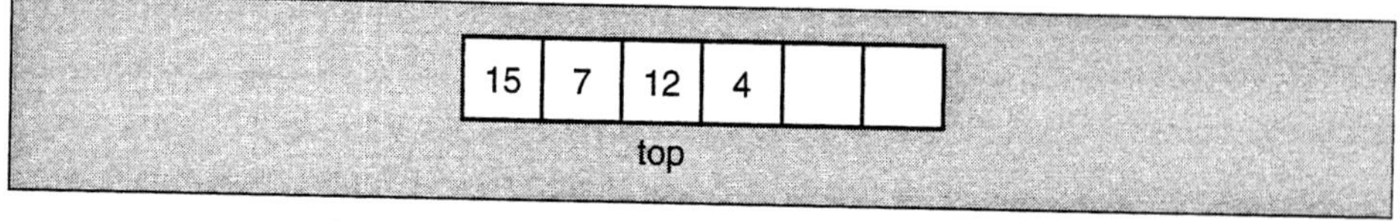

When the `push` method encounters a full stack, it can throw a standard `RuntimeException`, passing it a message describing the nature of the error. Similarly the `pop` method can throw a `RuntimeException` when it tries to remove an element or return the top from an empty stack. We can also define our own exception classes with names specific to the error identified. For example, to handle a stack empty error, we can define a `StackEmptyException` class, which has a constructor with a string parameter which we pass to the superclass which saves it. When Java throws a `StackEmptyException` the `printStackTrace` method will display this error message, and a stack trace.

Example 13.6 shows the code for the stack data type implemented using an array for the stack data, a size field giving the number of elements allocated, and a top field which holds the index of the top element of the stack. We provide two constructors, one that allocates an array with a default size of 10, and one that allocates an array with a size passed in as an argument. Note that using an array to hold the stack values limits the size of the stack to the number of elements allocated for that array. We leave to the exercises the use of a linked list to create a stack which would remove this limitation.

EXAMPLE 13.6 Stack.java

```
/* Implements the stack data type using
 * an array and fields top and size.
 */

public class Stack {
  private int [] data;         // holds the stack data
  private int size;            // holds the size allocated
  private int top = -1;        // holds the index of the top          // Note 1
                               // element, or -1 if none
  public Stack() {                                                    // Note 2
    size = 10;
    data = new int[size];
  }
  public Stack(int size) {
    this.size = size;                                                 // Note 3
    data = new int[size];
  }
  public boolean isEmpty() {                                          // Note 4
    return top == -1;
  }
```

```
public boolean isFull() {                                           // Note 5
  return top == size - 1;
}

public void push(int i) {
  if (isFull())
    throw new RuntimeException("Stack full -- cannot push");        // Note 6
  else
    data[++top] = i;                                                // Note 7
}
public int pop() {
  if (isEmpty())
    throw new StackEmptyException("Stack empty-- cannot pop");
  else
    return data[top--];                                             // Note 8
}
public int top() {
  if (isEmpty())
    throw new StackEmptyException("Stack empty-- top undefined");
  else
    return data[top];
}
public static void main(String [ ] args) {
  try {
    Stack stack1 = new Stack();
    Stack stack2 = new Stack(3);
    stack2.push(4);
    stack2.push(5);
    System.out.println("The top is now " + stack2.top());
    stack2.push(6);
    System.out.println("Popping stack 2 returns " + stack2.pop());
    System.out.println("Stack 1 has size " + stack1.size);
    System.out.println("Stack 1 empty? " + stack1.isEmpty());
    stack1.pop();
    System.out.println("Throws exception before we get here");
  } catch(Exception e) {
    e.printStackTrace();
  }
}
class StackEmptyException extends RuntimeException {
  public StackEmptyException(String message) {
    super(message);
  }
}
}
```

Output

```
The top is now 5
Popping stack 2 returns 6
Stack 1 has size 10
Stack 1 empty? true
Stack$StackEmptyException: Stack empty -- cannot pop
  at Stack.pop(Stack.java:35)
  at Stack.main(Stack.java:57)
```

Note 1: We always construct empty stacks to start, so, no matter which constructor we use, the correct initial value of `top` is `-1`.

Note 2: This constructor initializes the stack with a default size of 10.

Note 3: This constructor initializes the stack with the size passed in as an argument. The formal parameter has the same name as the field, so we refer to the field as `this.size`, where the variable `this` refers to the current object. We do not often need to refer to the current object explicitly, but here is an example where we need to use the variable `this`.

Note 4: `top` holds the index of the top element on the stack. When the stack is empty, `top` has the value `-1`.

Note 5: When the stack is full, `top` holds the index, `size-1`, of the last element in the array.

Note 6: `throw new RuntimeException ("Stack full -- cannot push");`
When the array is full we cannot add any more elements. Trying to add more would cause Java to throw an array index out of bounds exception and abort. We can detect this condition and throw an exception ourselves to allow users of a stack to catch the exception and to continue processing. We could have written our own exception class but for simplicity chose to throw a runtime exception which is unchecked so that stack users can ignore it if they wish. The message we pass to the exception object we create will be displayed by the `printStackTrace` method used in the catch clause.

Note 7: `data[++top] = i;`
The expression `++top` increments top to point to the next free space in the array, and returns the new value to use as the array index. This is equivalent to the code

```
top++;
data[top] = i;
```

Note 8: `return data[top--];`
When the stack is not empty, we return the integer, `data[top]`, at index top and decrement top. We do not have to remove the value from the array. The index top tells us where the top of the stack is; we ignore any array elements with index higher than top.

A LITTLE EXTRA—USING A STACK

Stacks have many uses, including the evaluation of expressions. To evaluate an expression, we write it in **postfix** form, sometimes called reverse Polish notation, in which the operands occur first followed by the operator. The expression 5 + 6 has the postfix form 5 6 +, while the expression (7 + 8)*(4 + 5) has the postfix form 7 8 + 4 5 + *. Remember the postfix form follows the pattern

```
left operand   right operand   operator
```

We will not cover methods for converting an infix expression to its postfix form. It helps to add parentheses and then follow the pattern. For example, given the expression 3 + 4 * 5, multiplication has higher precedence, so we add parentheses to give 3 + (4*5). Following the pattern, the postfix is

```
3    4 5 *     +
```

or 3 4 5 * +.

Once we have a postfix expression, we can easily evaluate it using a stack. Let us assume, for simplicity, that all operands are single digits 0 to 9, and that the operators are the binary arithmetic operators, +, -, *, and /. The algorithm for evaluating a postfix expression is:

```
do {
  Read the next character;
  if (next character is a digit)
    Convert the digit to an integer
      and push the integer on the stack;
  else if (next character is an operator) {
    Pop two operands from stack;
    Perform the operation;
    Push the result onto the stack;
    }
} while (more characters);
Display the top of the stack;
```

Figure 13.11 applies this algorithm to the expression `7 8 + 4 5 + *`.

Figure 13.11 Evaluating the expression `7 8 + 4 5 + *`

Read '7'	
Push the integer 7	7
Read '8'	
Push the integer 8	7 8
Read '+'	
Pop 8 and pop 7	empty
Add, getting 15	
Push 15	15
Read '4'	
Push the integer 4	15 4
Read '5'	
Push the integer 5	15 4 5
Read '+'	
Pop 5 and pop 4	15
Add, getting 9	
Push 9	15 9
Read '*'	
Pop 9 and pop 15	empty
Multiply, giving	135
Push 135	135
Pop 135 and display it.	

TIP

When evaluating subtraction we take the top entry on the stack and subtract it from the next to the top entry. For example, when evaluating `7 5 -` we follow the steps:

push 7, push 5, pop 5 and 7, subtract 7-5, push 2

When evaluating division we take the top entry on the stack and divide it into the next to the top entry. For example, when evaluating 14 3 / we follow the steps:

push 14, push 3, pop 3 and 14, divide 14/3, push 4

We can input the postfix expression one character at a time. To convert from a character c, where the value of c is a digit such as 9, to an integer, use the method `Character.digit(c,10)` where the number 10 refers to base 10. We leave the writing of a program to evaluate a postfix expression using a stack to the exercises.

Queues

A **queue** is like a waiting line in that the first element added is the first removed. We term this a FIFO queue, where **FIFO** stands for First In First Out. front and back fields keep track of the positions of the first and last elements in the queue. Figure 13.12 shows a queue containing three elements. It holds five.

Figure 13.12 A queue containing three elements

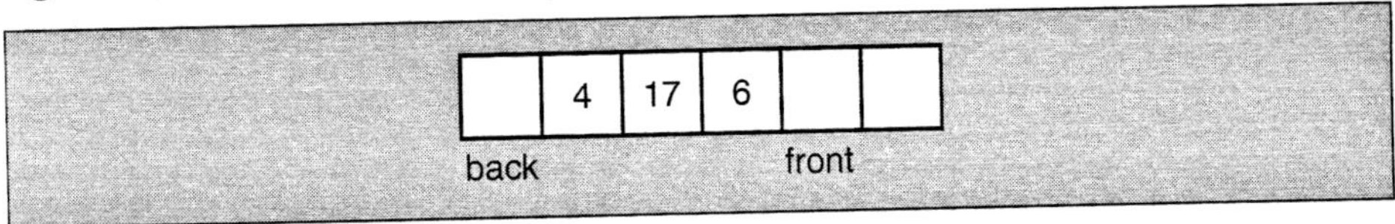

The `front` field holds the index of the position before the first element, and the `back` field holds the index of the position after the last element. We add an element at the `back` position and then increment `back` so that it still marks the position after the last element. Before removing an element, we increment `front`, and then remove the element at the `front` position. After the removal, `front` will still be the position before the first element.

We start entering queue elements at index 0 of the array, but as we use the queue, removing elements from the front and adding elements to the back we might reach the end of the array while free space remains at the front where elements were removed. To make full use of the array we create a circular queue, where we treat the array as if it were arranged in a circle. In that configuration, position `0` would follow position `size-1`, as Figure 13.13 shows.

Figure 13.13 A circular queue

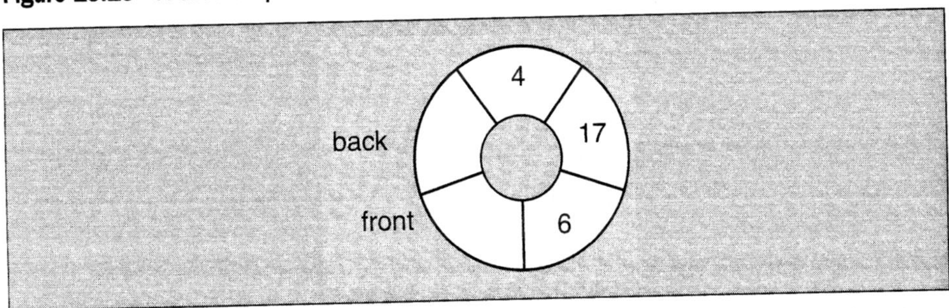

When entering elements we cannot simply increment the back index using back++. If the array holding the data has size 5, the valid array indices are 0, 1, 2, 3, and 4. If `back` is 4, then `back++` would be 5 which is invalid. We use the expression

```
back++ % size
```

which evaluates to `5%5` which equals `0`. Using this expression causes the index 0 to follow the index 4, so the array, in effect, wraps around in a circle. We use similar expressions for all the index calculations. Example 13.7 contains the code for this circular queue.

EXAMPLE 13.7 Queue.java

```
/* Implements the queue data type using
 * an array, and fields front, back, and size.
 */
```

```
public class Queue {
  private int [] data;          // stack data
  private int size;             // size allocated
  private int front = -1;       // index of the front, -1 if empty
  private int back = 0;         // index of the first free spot.
  private int count = 0;        // number of elements in the queue

  public Queue() {
    size = 10;
    data = new int[size];
  }
  public Queue(int size) {
    this.size = size;
    data = new int[size];
  }
  public boolean isEmpty() {
    return count == 0;                                         // Note 1
  }
  public boolean isFull() {
    return count == size;                                      // Note 2
  }
  public void add(int i){
    if (isFull())
      throw new RuntimeException("Queue full -- cannot add");
    else {
      count ++;
      data[back++ % size] = i;
    }
  }
  public int remove(){
    if (isEmpty())
      throw new RuntimeException("Queue empty -- cannot remove");
    else {
      count --;
      return data[++front % size];
    }
  }
  public int head(){
    if (isEmpty())
      throw new RuntimeException("Queue empty -- head undefined");
    else
    return data[(front+1) % size];
  }
  public static void main(String [] args) {
    try {
      Queue q1 = new Queue();
      Queue q2 = new Queue(3);
      q2.add(4);
      q2.add(5);
```

```
      System.out.println("The front is now " + q2.head());
      q2.add(6);
      System.out.println("Removing from q2 returns " + q2.remove());
      System.out.println("Queue 1 has size " + q1.size);
      System.out.println("Queue 1 empty? " + q1.isEmpty());
      q1.remove();
      System.out.println("Throws exception before we get here");
    }catch(Exception e) {
      e.printStackTrace();
    }
  }
}
```

Output

```
The front is now 4
Removing from q2 returns 4
Queue 1 has size 10
Queue 1 empty? true
java.lang.RuntimeException: Queue empty -- cannot remove
 at Queue.remove(Queue.java:36)
 at Queue.main(Queue.java:60)
```

Note 1: We use a `count` field to keep track of the number of elements in the queue. The queue is empty when `count` is 0.

Note 2: When the queue is full, `count` equals `size`, the capacity of the array.

THE BG PICTURE

A stack allows us to add and remove data at the top. Because we implemented a stack using an array, we throw an exception if the user tries to pop an empty stack or push onto a full stack. We illustrated by throwing a standard `RuntimeException` and creating our own `StackEmptyException` class. Stacks have many uses; one is evaluating postfix expressions. A queue allows us to add at the front and remove from the back

TEST YOUR UNDERSTANDING

6. Show the stack of Figure 13.6 after performing the operations `pop()`, `pop()`, and `push(19)`, in that order.

7. Show the stack of Figure 13.6 after performing the operation `push(pop())`. What can you conclude about the relationship between the push and pop operations?

A LITTLE EXTRA

8. Use a stack to evaluate the following postfix expressions:

   a. 2 3 4 * + 6 2 - +   b. 9 9 + 9 9 * -

   c. 6 3 / 4 9 8 + - +

TRY IT YOURSELF

9. Run additional tests of the stack operations for the `Stack` class of Example 13.6.
10. Will a test front == back determine when the queue of Example 13.7 is full? Explain.

13.4 Vectors and Enumerations

A **vector** is like an array, but it can grow in size. The cost of this flexibility is a decrease in performance compared to arrays. Vectors are useful in multithreaded applications as they are designed for safe access from concurrent threads.*

The `Vector` class, in the `java.util` package, has three constructors. We can specify the initial size of the vector and the amount to increase its size when it becomes full. Using the default

```
new Vector();
```

will give us a vector of capacity 10 which doubles in size when more space is needed. The constructor

```
new Vector(20);
```

creates a vector with the capacity to hold 20 elements, which doubles in size when necessary. Finally,

```
new Vector(15,5);
```

starts out with a capacity of 15 which increases by 5 when necessary.

To add an element to the end of a vector, we use the `addElement` method which has a parameter of type `Object`. Because every class is, directly or indirectly, a subclass of `Object`, we can add any object to a vector. The code

```
Vector v = new Vector();
String s = "Happy days";
v.addElement(s);
```

creates a vector and a string and adds the string to the vector. We can only add objects to a vector. To add primitive types we must use the wrapper classes discussed in Section 6.2.

Using the `addElement` method, as in

```
v.addElement("A big car");
v.addElement("Less is more");
```

adds the strings at the end of the vector

---

* Threads allow different parts of the program to proceed in parallel, sharing the processor. We introduce threads in Chapter 15.

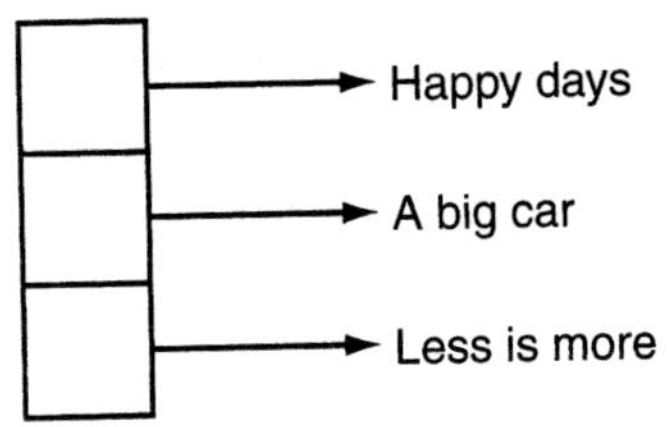

We could use the `insertElementAt` method to insert an item at a given index in the vector, but that is less efficient than adding at the end. For example,

```
v.insertElementAt("Candy and cake",1);
```

changes `v` to

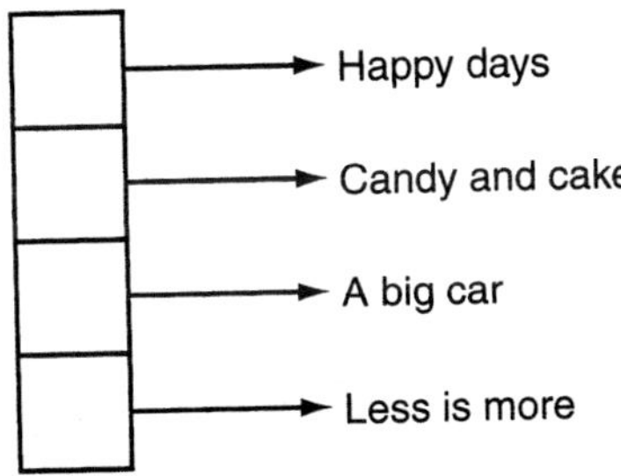

requiring the moving of two elements. In a large vector, insertion might require moving a large number of elements.

The `elementAt` method lets us get the element at a given index. For example,

```
String atTwo = (String)v.elementAt(2);
```

assigns `"A big car"` to `atTwo`. Because `elementAt` returns a value of type `Object`, we must cast it to a string to assign it to a string variable. The vector `v` contains only string elements so we know casting to a string will not cause an error.

The `Vector` class provides several methods to locate elements in a vector. The `contains` method returns true if its argument is an element of the vector and false otherwise. Thus

```
v.contains("A big car");
```

returns true, while

```
v.contains("Sweet dreams");
```

returns false. If we need the exact location of an element, the `indexOf` method returns the index of its first occurrence in the vector, or -1 if it does not occur. For example,

```
v.indexOf("A big car");
```

would return 2, while

```
v.indexOf("Sweet dreams");
```

returns -1. The call

```
v.indexOf("Happy days",1);
```

returns −1, because there is no occurrence, in `v`, of `"Happy days"` starting at index 1.

The `capacity` method returns the number of elements allocated for the vector, while the `size` method returns the number of its elements. Thus

```
v.capacity();
```

returns 10, while

```
v.size();
```

returns 4.

Either

```
v.removeElement("Candy and cake");
```

or

```
v.removeElementAt(1);
```

would remove the element at index `1` from `v`.

The `elements` method returns an enumeration which allows us to get all the elements of a vector. The `Enumeration` interface is a general facility for retrieving the elements of a container. It has two methods, `nextElement`, which returns the `nextElement` in an arbitrary order, and `hasMoreElements` which returns true if there are more elements not yet returned. We can use the method

```
public void listAll(Enumeration e) {
  while(e.hasMoreElements())
    System.out.println(e.nextElement());
}
```

to list the elements of any enumeration. This `listAll` method applies to any container that has an enumeration, completely separating the details of the container type, `Vector`, `Stack`, `List`, or other container, from the listing process. We could list the elements of `v` with

```
Enumeration e = v.elements();
listAll(e);
```

To illustrate `Vector` objects, we create a vector of the first 1000 Fibonacci numbers. The Fibonacci sequence starts with its first two elements, $f_1 = f_2 = 1$, and the remaining computed by

$$f_{i+1} = f_i + f_{i-1}$$

so the first 10 Fibonacci numbers are 1, 1, 2, 3, 5, 8, 13, 21, 34, and 55. The Fibonacci numbers have useful applications in numerical analysis and occur in nature, but here we use them solely to illustrate vectors.

We use the `BigInteger` class, in the `java.math` package, to handle large Fibonacci numbers. We create big integers from strings as for example,

```
BigInteger twentyDigits =
      new BigInteger("12345678909876543210");
```

and add them using the add method, as in

```
BigInteger stillTwentyDigits =
      twentyDigits.add(twentyDigits);
```

EXAMPLE 13.8 Fibonacci.java

```
/* Uses the Fibonacci sequence to
 * illustrate vectors.
 */

import java.util.*;
import java.math.BigInteger;

public class Fibonacci {
  public static void main(String[] args) {
      Vector fib = new Vector(1000);
      BigInteger previous = new BigInteger("1");
      BigInteger current = previous;
      fib.addElement(previous);
      fib.addElement(current);
      BigInteger temp;
      for(int i=2; i<fib.capacity(); i++) {                         // Note 1
        temp = current;
        current = previous.add(current);
        previous = temp;
        fib.addElement(current);
      }
      System.out.println
           ("The fifth Fibonacci number is " + fib.elementAt(4));    // Note 2
      System.out.println("The one-thousandth Fibonacci number is "
                    + fib.elementAt(999));
      Vector prime = new Vector();
      for (int i = 0; i < 100; i++) {
        BigInteger aFib = (BigInteger)fib.elementAt(i);
        if (aFib.isProbablePrime(10))                               // Note 3
          prime.addElement(aFib);
     }
     System.out.println
       ("The probable primes in the first 100 Fibonacci numbers are:");
     Enumeration e = prime.elements();                               // Note 4
     while(e.hasMoreElements())
       System.out.println("\t" + e.nextElement());
     System.out.println("Vector prime's capacity is " + prime.capacity());
```

```
                                                                    // Note 5
    System.out.println("Vector prime's size is " + prime.size());
    System.out.println("The ninth probable prime is the "
               + (fib.indexOf(new BigInteger("514229")) + 1)       // Note 6
               + "th Fibonacci number");
    int count = 0;
    BigInteger random100;
    do {
      random100 = new BigInteger
            (String.valueOf((int)(100*Math.random()) + 1));         // Note 7
      count++;
    }while (!fib.contains(random100));                              // Note 8
    System.out.println("It took " + count
         + " tries to find a Fibonacci number randomly");
  }
}
```

Output

```
The fifth Fibonacci number is 5
The one-thousandth Fibonacci number is
  43466557686937456435688527675040625802564660517371780402481 7
  29089536555417949051890403879840079255169295922593080322634 7
  75209689623239873322471161642996440906533187938298969649928 5
  16003704476137795166849228875
The probable primes in the first 100 Fibonacci numbers are:
  2
  3
  5
  13
  89
  233
  1597
  28657
  514229
  433494437
  2971215073
  99194853094755497
Vector prime's capacity is 20
Vector prime's size is 12
The ninth probable prime is the 29th Fibonacci number
It took 12 tries to find a Fibonacci number randomly
```

Note 1: We fill `fib` to its capacity of 1000. We use two variables, `previous` and `current` to represent the last two Fibonacci numbers computed. Each time through the loop we save the current number, add it to the previous number to get the updated `current`, and then copy the saved old `current` to get the new `previous`.

Note 2: It is always a good practice to check a computation with a known value,which we do here, checking that the fifth Fibonacci number is 5.

Note 3: We create a new vector containing those of the first 100 Fibonacci numbers that are probably prime. Determining whether a number is prime (has no divisors other than itself and 1) can be time consuming for large numbers. The `BigInteger` class has a method, `isProbablyPrime`, that determines with a certain probability that a number is prime. Making the probability higher, makes the computationlonger. This method uses the probability `1 - (1/2)`^{n} where `n` is its argument. We pass the argument `10`, so it uses the probability `1 - 1/1024`, which means there is greater than a `99.9%` chance that the number is prime.

Note 4: Because we are using the `Vector` class, from the `java.util` package, we can use the `elements` method to get an enumeration. When creating our own container such as the `Linked List` of Section 13.2, we can implement an enumeration by implementing the `hasMoreElements` and `nextElement` methods.

Note 5: There turned out to be 12 probable primes in the first 100 Fibonaaci numbers, so the vector, `prime`, automatically grew to capacity 20 from its initial capacity of 10.

Note 6: We check which Fibonacci number happens to be the ninth probable prime.

Note 7: We get a random number between 1 and 100 and then convert it to a string, using the `valueOf` method, so we can construct a `BigInteger` from that random number.

Note 8: We keep computing random numbers from 1 to 100 as long as they are not Fibonacci numbers. Because there are 11 Fibonacci numbers between 1 and 100, we expect about `100/11 = 9.09` trials, on the average, until we find a Fibonacci number.

THE BIG PICTURE

A vector grows automatically to accommodate more data. We add values of type `Object`, or any of its subtypes, to a vector. An enumeration, with `hasMoreElements` and `nextElement` methods, lets us iterate through the elements of a vector.

TEST YOUR UNDERSTANDING

11. Declare a vector which initially can hold 25 elements, and grows by seven when it becomes full.
12. Explain the difference between the `capacity` and the `size` methods for the `Vector` class.

13.5 Hash Tables

A hash table takes a totally different approach to storing data. A **hash table** maps keys to values. We use a hash function to compute an integer from the data that will tell us where to add or search for that item. Suppose we want to create a symbol table of identifiers in a program. Each identifier is the name of a variable or other entity. We associated various properties with a variable such as its type and memory location. For simplicity, in Figure 13.14 we associate only a type with each variable.

Figure 13.14 Identifiers and their types

```
sum           int
average       double
count         int
number        int
name          String
address       String
repeat        char
line          String
background    Color
g             Graphics
print         Button
text          TextField
```

The idea of hashing is that we compute an integer from the key, and use that integer as an array index to enter the identifier and its associated data. For example, suppose that the hash function computes 10 when given the identifier `sum`. Then we enter `sum` at index 10 in the array. When we need to look up the data for `sum`, we compute the hash value, 10, and find `sum` in position 10 without searching any other elements.

In this ideal case, hashing is very fast, because with only a simple computation and no search, we can find the data. In practice collisions occur because hash functions produce duplicate values. If the hash value for `count` is also 10, then we cannot put `count` in position 10 because `sum` is already there. Various collision resolution algorithms find another location for `count`. When we look up `count` we first expect it to be in location 10, but not finding it there we have to continue the search, which becomes less efficient.

A good hash function distributes the hash values with few duplicates. Ideally the 12 entries in Figure 13.14 would have 12 different hash values, so there would be no conflicts. The worst hash function gives the 12 identifiers a single value such as 10. A typical hash function uses the features of the data it is hashing. A hash function might add the values of each character and shift bits to increase randomness.

A class whose objects might be hashed should implement the `hashCode` method, which returns an integer value. The hash values might be rather large numbers and we may have a relatively small table. For example to store the 12 identifiers of Figure 13.13 we could use a table of size 23. This allows some extra space to reduce the chance of collisions. If the hash value is larger than 22, we find its remainder when divided by 23 to get its table index. For example, if `repeat` has a hash value of 12345, we compute `12345 % 23` which gives 17 as the table index.

Figure 13.14 contains `String` data, and fortunately the `String` class has a `hashCode` method. Example 13.9 computes the hash values for each identifier and the table indices based on a table size of 23.

EXAMPLE 13.9 HashValues.java

```
/* Computes the hash values of 12 identifiers, and
 * the index of each in a table of size 23.
 */

public class HashValues {
  public static void main(String[] args) {
    String[] identifiers =
      {"sum","average","count","number","name","address","repeat",
      "line","background","g","print","text"};
    String spaces = "                    ";                       // Note 1
    for (int i = 0; i < identifiers.length; i++)
      String id = identifiers[i];
      int hash = id.hashCode();
      int code = hash % 23;
      if (code < 0) code += 23;                                   // Note 2
        System.out.println(id + spaces.substring(0,20-id.length())  // Note 3
          + hash + spaces.substring(0,20-String.valueOf(hash).length())
          + code);
    }
  }
}
```

Output

```
sum                 114251              10
average             -631448035          14
count               94851343            10
number              -1034364087         9
name                3373707             21
address             -1147692044         21
repeat              -934531685          14
line                3321844             0
background          -1332194002         15
g                   103                 11
print               106934957           22
text                3556653             2
```

Note 1: We use a string of blank to space the three fields of the output nicely.

Note 2: If the hash code is negative, we add 23 to give it a positive value. For example,

`-60 = -(2)23 + -14` giving a hash code of -14

or

`-60 = -(3)23 + 9` giving a hash code of 9

Note 3: To make the hash codes display in column 20, we add enough spaces after the identifier. We concatenation a substring of the `spaces` `String`. The length of this substring is just enough to position the next character of the output in position 20.

We use the `put` method

```
Object put(Object key, Object value)
```

to enter data in a hash table, and the `get` method

```
Object get(Object key)
```

to retrieve it. The `keys` method returns an `Enumeration` of all the keys in the table. Example 13.10 puts all the values from Figure 13.13 into a hash table.

EXAMPLE 13.10 HashPut.java

```
/* Enters 12 identifiers in a hash table.
 */

import java.util.*;

public class HashPut {
  public static void main(String[] args) {
    String[] identifiers =
      {"sum","average","count","number","name","address","repeat",
      "line","background","g","print","text"};
    String[] types = {"int","double","int","int","String","String",
      "char","String","Color","Graphics","Button","TextField"};
    Hashtable table = new Hashtable(23);                       // Note 1
    for(int i = 0; i < identifiers.length; i++)
      table.put(identifiers[i], types[i]);                     // Note 2
    System.out.println("The type of background is " +
                  table.get("background"));                    // Note 3
    System.out.println("The keys are:");
    Enumeration e = table.keys();
    while (e.hasMoreElements()){                               // Note 4
      System.out.print(e.nextElement());
      System.out.print(' ');
    }
  }
}
```

Output

```
The type of background is Color
The keys are:
print background name repeat average number g count sum address text line
```

Note 1: We choose a table size to be a prime number. By choosing it to be about double the size of the data we reduce the number of collisions expected. The ratio of the number of keys in the table to the size of the table is called the **load.** In order not to degrade performance, we like to keep the load under .75.

Note 2: We put each identifier into the table and associate its type with it.

Note 3: The `get` method returns the object associated with the key.

Note 4: When we use an `Enumeration` to list the keys in the has table, we see they do not appear in alphabetical order. A hash table is not a suitable data structure when we need to find a range of elements such as all keys beginning with the letter `'m'`.

THE BIG PICTURE

A hash table maps keys to values. A hash function computes an integer index used to enter the key and its associated value into the table. Different keys may have the same has value, which causes a collision, which degrades performance. Keeping the load factor below .75 helps avoid collisions. A class implements the `hashCode` method to provide a hash value for its instances.

TEST YOUR UNDERSTANDING

TRY IT YOURSELF 13. Change the keys in Example 13.9 and rerun. Is the number of collisions about the same?

TRY IT YOURSELF 14. Change the table size to 67 in Example 13.9 and rerun it. How many collisions are there?

SUMMARY

- Recursion deals with repetition by describing a process whose structure recurs within itself. In binary search, we compare the key with the middle element. If equal, we have found it; if the key is greater than the middle element we have only to search the upper portion of this sorted array. Calling binary search recursively, we compare our key to the middle of the upper portion, either returning, if we found it, or starting yet another binary search of the upper or lower half (of the upper half of the original array). While the trace of a recursive algorithm can get complicated, the program is usually very simple.

- Merge sort is a very efficient sorting method which has a very nice recursive implementation. We call merge sort recursively to sort the left and right halves of the array, and then merge the resulting sorted arrays into the final result.
- The linked list data structure makes it easy to add and remove elements but loses some of the advantages of arrays for searches, and takes extra space to hold the node references. Each node of a linked list contains a data field and a reference to another node. When we add an item to the list, or remove an item from a list, we just have to change two references. If the `Stack` class used a linked list to store its data, rather than an array, it would be able to grow in size without being restricted to the size of its internal array.
- The useful Stack type has operations `push`, `pop`, `top`, `isEmpty`, and `isFull`. `push` adds an item to the top of the stack. `pop` removes the item on the top of the stack, while `top` inspects the top item without removing it. `isEmpty` and `isFull` tell us whether the stack is empty or full. We operate on stacks using just these operations and constructors. The representation of the stack, which is hidden from the user, uses an array to hold the data, a size field to hold the size of the array, and a top field which gives the index of the top element of the stack, or holds -1 if the stack is empty.
- A queue has operations `add`, `remove`, `head`, `isEmpty`, and `isFull`. `add` enters an item at the back of the queue. `remove` takes it away from the front. `head` returns the front element without removing it. We implement the queue using an array, in a way that makes it appear circular, with index `0` following index `size-1` if necessary.
- A vector is like an array, but it can grow in size. The `addElement` method adds an element, of type `Object` or a subtype, to the end of a vector, causing the vector to grow in size to accommodate it, if necessary. We get an element using the `elementAt` method. Other methods help us find an element in a vector. The `elements` method returns an `Enumeration` object with which we can list the elements of an array using the `hasMoreElements` and `nextElement` methods. Enumerations are useful for listing object from many types of containers.
- A hash table uses a integer computed from the key to find the index at which to enter the key and its value in the table. It can be extremely efficient.

Skill Builder Exercises

1. What is the output if 7 is passed as a program argument to the following program?

```
public class Fun {
  public static int f(int n) {
    if (n==1 | n==2) return 1;
    else return f(n-1) + f(n-2);
  }
```

```
  public static void main(String[] args) {
    System.out.println(f(Integer.parseInt(args[0])));
  }
}
```

2. What is the output if 2, 3, and 5 are passed as a program arguments to the following program?

```
public class Ack {
  public static int a(int x, int y, int z) {
    if (x == 0) return y + z;
    if (z == 0) {
      if(x == 1) return 0;
      if(x == 2) return 1;
      if(x > 2) return y;
    }
    if(x>0 && z>0)
      return a(x-1, y, a(x,y,z-1));
    return -1;
  }
  public static void main(String[] args) {
    System.out.println(a(Integer.parseInt(args[0]),
      Integer.parseInt(args[1]),
      Integer.parseInt(args[2])
    ));
  }
}
```

3. Match the `Vector` method name on the left with its description on the right.

a. capacity	i. returns an enumeration
b. size	ii. returns the allocated size
c. elements	iii. returns an array element
d. elementAt	iv. returns the current size

Critical Thinking Exercises

4. A difference between a stack and a queue is?

   a. We can add to and remove from a stack, but can only add to a queue.

   b. The last one in is the first one out for a queue, but is the last one out for a stack.

   c. The first one in for a queue is the first one out, but is the last one out for a stack.

   d. We can add to and remove form a queue, but can only add to a stack.

5. Which of the following is true about a hash table?
   a. Decreasing the load improves performance.
   b. Increasing the load improves performance.
   c. Hash tables keep data in alphabetical order.
   d. Hash values are almost always strings.
   e. None of the above.
6. Which of the following is not a linked list operation?
   a. Insert an element.
   b. Check if the list is empty.
   c. Remove an element.
   d. None of the above.
7. In the merge sort algorithm, we
   a. sort the left part of the data before the right.
   b. merge the two sorted parts of the data.
   c. may use recursion.
   d. all of the above.

Debugging Exercise

8. The following program attempts to compute the product of the first n integers where n is passed as a program argument. For example, passing a program argument of 4 should generate a result of 24 because 4*3*2*1 = 24. Find and correct any errors in this program.

```
public class Factorial {
  public static int product(int n) {
    return n*product(n - 1);
  }
  public static void main(String[ ] args) {
    System.out.println(product(Integer.parseInt(args[0])));
  }
}
```

Program Modification Exercises

9. Modify Example 13.6 to define an `Object` stack rather than an integer stack.
10. Modify Example 13.7 to define an `Object` queue rather than an integer queue.

11. Modify the `Stack` class of Example 13.6 to use the `LinkedList` of Example 13.5, rather than an array, to hold the stack elements.
12. Modify Example 13.6 to create a graphical interface for the user to perform stack operations. Include *Push* and *Pop* buttons and text field to enter data. After each operation draw the current stack.
13. Modify Example 13.3, `BinarySearch`, to use Swing dialogs to input the data and display the result of the search.
14. Modify the merge sort program of Example 13.4 to input the numbers to be sorted from a file, rather than as program arguments. Pass the file name as a program argument.
15. Modify the merge sort program of Example 13.4 to sort `String` objects. Input the strings from a file, rather than as program arguments, and write the sorted strings to a file. Pass the file name as a program argument.
16. Modify Example 13.6 by writing an exception class `StackFullException` and throwing this exception instead of `RuntimeException`.
17. Modify Example 13.5 to include an inner class which implements the `Enumeration` interface. Add an `elements` methods to the `LinkedList` class which returns an `Enumeration` for the list. In the `main` method, use the `nextElement` and `hasMoreElements` methods of the `Enumeration` interface to display the elements of a list.

Program Design Exercises

18. Create a user interface to manipulate and display a linked list. Include buttons to insert and remove a string entered in a text field, and a button to reset the list to its head. Display the list using rectangles for the nodes.
19. Write a Java program that searches a file for a string. Pass the string and the file name as program arguments.
20. Write a Java program that uses a stack to reverse an array.
21. Write a Java program, which does not use recursion, to perform a binary search of an array input from a file.
22. Write a Java program to search for an item in a linked list. Use the `LinkedList` class of Example 13.5. Use a recursive method to do the search.
23. Write a Java program to check if a string is a palindrome (reads the same backward and forward, as, for example, "toot"). Use a recursive method to do the checking.
24. (Towers of Hanoi)
    Suppose we have n disks on a peg, each of different sizes, stacked in order of size, with the largest on the bottom, and two other pegs, as shown in Figure 13.15.

Figure 13.15 The Towers of Hanoi puzzle

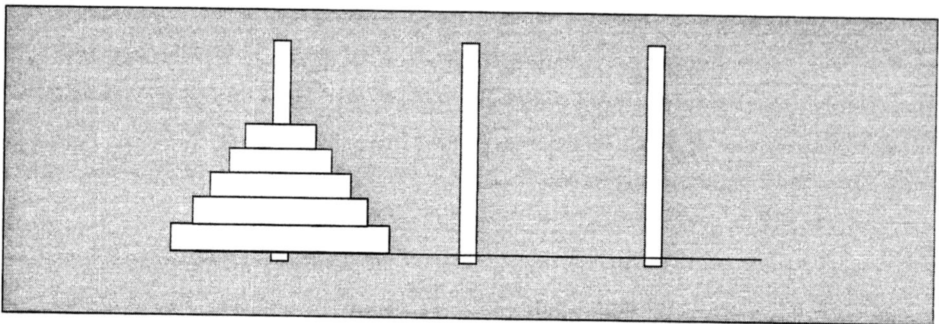

What is the sequence of moves needed to transfer the rings to the second peg, in the same configuration, in order from largest to the smallest, with the largest at the bottom, if we can move only one disk at a time, and we cannot place a larger disk on top of a smaller disk? We may use the last peg to store disks, but the same rules apply. Use a recursive method to provide the solution. To move n disks from peg 1 to peg 2, move n-1 disks to peg 3, move the bottom disk to peg 2, then move n-1 disks from peg 3 to peg 2. For this problem, print out the sequence of moves, as for example, "Move disk from peg 1 to peg 2," and so on.

A LITTLE EXTRA

25. In Section 13.3, we showed how to use a stack to evaluate a postfix expression. Write a program to allow the user to input a postfix expression, of the form described in Section 13.3, in a text field. Add a button for the user to ask the program to process the next character. Make a graphical display which shows the stack as it grows and shrinks, and display the result of the evaluation.

26. Draw the Towers of Hanoi configuration in Figure 13.15. Allow the user to drag the disks to new locations to solve the puzzle. Include a text field for the user to enter the number of disks.

27. Write a Java program that uses a recursive method to reverse an array.

CHAPTER

14 Collections

OUTLINE

Introduction

Programmers often use collections of data such as lists and sets. The Java 2 release includes a `Collection` hierarchy in the `java.util` package, which allows us to use these data structures without having to code them ourselves.

After introducing the overall hierarchy, we look at sets, lists, and maps in detail. Comparing elements of a collection lets us arrange a collection in order. Algorithms implement standard computations so users do not have to implement these basic operations.

OBJECTIVES:

- Know the hierarchy of `Collection` classes.
- Use the methods of the `Collection` interface.
- Use sets, lists, and maps.
- Compare collection elements to enable sorting.
- Use collection algorithms.

14.1 The Collection Interfaces and Classes

Java interfaces provide the framework for the various data structures included in the collection utilities. Figure 14.1 shows that these interfaces occur in two groups.

Figure 14.1 The `Collection` interfaces

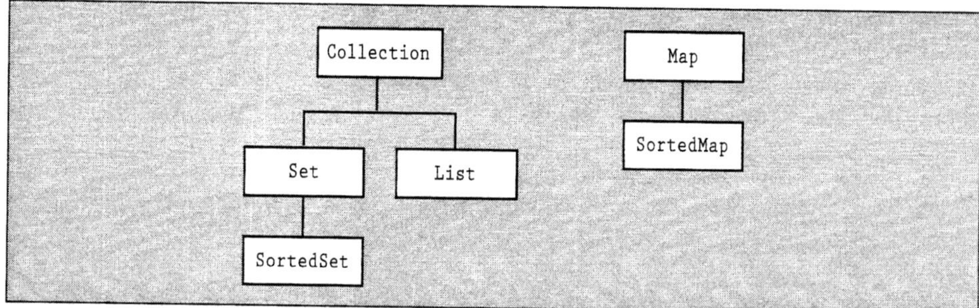

The `Collection` interface represents a group of objects, known as its elements. It abstracts the behavior common to both sets and lists. The `Set` interface supports unordered elements; we can determine if an element is in a set but there is no order relation between one element and another in the set. By contrast, the `List` interface supports a sequence in which elements are ordered from first to last. The `SortedSet` interface represents a set whose elements can be retrieved in sorted order.

The `Map` interface represents (key, value) pairs, such as a dictionary in which we look up a word (the key) and obtain its definition (the value). Typically a map does not keep its elements in order, but the `SortedMap` interface allows us to retrieve map elements in order of their keys. For example, a dictionary is actually a sorted map.

All of these interfaces specify operations in two main groups:

- Accessors that get information, but do not change the collection.
- Mutators that change the collection.

The Collection Interface

The `Collection` interface specifies the operations common to sets and lists. It contains the following operations:

Accessors:

```
boolean contains(Object o)
boolean containsAll(Collection c)
boolean equals(Object o)
int hashCode()
boolean isEmpty()
Iterator iterator()
int size()
Object[] toArray()
Object[] toArray(Object[] a)
```

Mutators:

```
void clear()
boolean add(Object o)
boolean addAll(Collection c)
boolean remove(Object o)
boolean removeAll(Collection c)
boolean retainAll(Collection c)
```

Interfaces formally just specify the name, parameters, and return value for each method. Informally the documentation states conditions that implementers of the interface are expected to observe. For example, in getting the size of a collection, if it contains more than `Integer.MAX_VALUE` elements, the size method returns `Integer.MAX_VALUE`.

Sets

The `Set` interface has the same methods as the `Collection` interface, but in a few instances the conditions on the methods are more stringent. For example, a `Set` cannot contain duplicates so the `add` method must refuse to add a duplicate. In general, this requirement does not apply to the `add` method for a `Collection`. We will look at each method of the `Set` interface when we present Examples 14.1 and 14.2.

In order to give some examples we need to introduce some implementations of these interfaces.

Interface	Class implementing that interface
Set	HashSet
SortedSet	TreeSet
List	ArrayList, LinkedList
Map	HashMap
SortedMap	TreeMap

The `HashSet` class uses hashing techniques which we will discuss later to implement the `Set` interface. We use a `HashSet` to store the words of the Gettysburg address, keeping count of the duplicates which will be eliminated, and listing the resulting unique words. We will extend this example to illustrate other `Set` methods.

EXAMPLE 14.1 WordsSet.java

```
/* Adds the words of the Gettysburg address to a set, counting
 * the number of duplicates and listing the unique words.
 */

import java.util.*;
import java.io.*;

public class WordsSet {
  public static void main(String[ ] args) {
    try {
```

```
      File f = new File(args[0]);
      BufferedReader in = new BufferedReader(new FileReader(f));
      Set set = new HashSet();                                  // Note 1
      String line;
      int duplicates = 0;
      while((line = in.readLine()) != null) {
         StringTokenizer tokens =
                    new StringTokenizer(line,"-,. \n\r\t");
                                                                // Note 2
         while(tokens.hasMoreTokens()) {
           String tok = tokens.nextToken().toLowerCase();       // Note 3
           if (!set.add(tok))                                   // Note 4
             duplicates++;
         }
      }
      System.out.println
         (args[0] + " has " + set.size() + " distinct words.");
      System.out.println("There are " + duplicates + " duplicate words.");
      System.out.println("The distinct words are:");
      System.out.println(set);                                  // Note 5
    }catch(IOException e) {
      e.printStackTrace();
    }
  }
}
```

Output (from `java WordsSet gettysburg.txt`**)**

```
gettysburg.txt has 138 distinct words.
There are 129 duplicate words.
The distinct words are:
[live, great, men, add, fitting, under, struggled, did, might, resolve, our, inc
reased, proper, these, remaining, living, government, sense, earth, never, say,
power, do, dead, should, consecrate, created, they, will, full, nobly, devotion,
 who, birth, new, forth, battlefield, last, war, task, testing, vain, remember,
world, we, portion, advanced, hallow, seven, it, dedicated, is, note, any, in, b
y, consecrated, continent, shall, the, or, fourscore, on, and, a, honored, ago,
take, which, be, of, forget, field, us, here, endure, what, freedom, final, civi
l, years, highly, poor, their, for, as, but, this, brave, perish, died, gave, be
fore, detract, proposition, now, resting, not, to, nor, fathers, far, conceived,
 come, engaged, all, nation, whether, unfinished, above, dedicate, equal, those,
 thus, brought, rather, long, fought, ground, people, measure, that, larger, cau
se, little, lives, so, are, work, have, cannot, altogether, liberty, god, from,
place, can, met]
```

Note 1: We declare our collection as a `Set`, using only the methods of the `Set` interface. Java provides a `HashSet` implementation of the `Set` interface. We use the default constructor, but will discuss other constructors later in this section.

Note 2: We do not want to include punctuation as parts of the words, so we include these characters in the `StringTokenizer` constructor to signal the end of words.

Note 3: Words such as `"The"` and `"the"` would both appear in the set unless we first convert each word to lower case.

Note 4: The `add` method returns false if the set already contains the element passed as its argument.

Note 5: The `HashSet` class inherits the `toString` method from the `AbstractCollection` class which provides a skeletal implementation of the `Collection` interface.

Iterators

Many of the methods of the `Collection` interface have names which clearly describe their behavior. For example, `isEmpty()` returns true if the collection has no elements and false otherwise. The `iterator` method requires some explanation. It returns an `Iterator` object which is very much like an `Enumeration`, allowing us to iterate through the elements of the `Collection`. An `Iterator` differs from an `Enumeration` in two ways. First we can remove elements from a `Collection` while iterating through it, and second the method names are shorter.

Iterator methods	Enumeration methods
`hasNext`	`hasMoreElements`
`next`	`nextElement`
`remove`	

If we just want to list the elements of a `Set` we can use the `toString` method implicitly in a print statement, as for example,

```
System.out.println("The set is " + set);
```

where `set` is a `Set`. But if we need to process each element then we use a loop such as

```
Iterator i = set.iterator();
while (i.hasNext()) {
  // do processing here
  i.next();
}
```

In Example 14.2 we use an iterator to remove all words of less than eight letters from the Gettyburg set and illustrate other methods of the `Set` interface.

EXAMPLE 14.2 SetMethods.java

```
/* Illustrates the methods of the Set interface.
 */

import java.util.*;
import java.io.*;

public class SetMethods {
  public static void main(String[ ] args) {
    try {
      File f = new File(args[0]);
      BufferedReader in = new BufferedReader(new FileReader(f));
      Set set = new HashSet();
      String line;
      while((line = in.readLine()) != null) {
        StringTokenizer tokens = new StringTokenizer(line,"-,. \n\r\t");
        while(tokens.hasMoreTokens()) {
          String tok = tokens.nextToken().toLowerCase();
          set.add(tok);
        }
      }
      System.out.println("Contains \"fourscore\"? " + set.contains("fourscore"));
      System.out.println
          ("Contains \"computer\"? " + set.contains("computer"));     // Note 1
      Collection start = new HashSet();                                // Note 2
      start.add("fourscore");
      start.add("and");
      start.add("seven");
      start.add("years");
      System.out.println("Contains \"fourscore, and, seven, years\" ? "
                      + set.containsAll(start));                       // Note 3
      Set newStart = new HashSet();
      newStart.addAll(start);                                          // Note 4
      System.out.println("newStart equals start? " + newStart.equals(start));
      newStart.add("computer");                                        // Note 5
      System.out.println
         ("newStart with \"computer\" equals start? " + newStart.equals(start));
      System.out.println("The newStart set is now " + newStart);
      newStart.retainAll(set);                                         // Note 6
      System.out.println
        ("newStart equals start after retainsAll? " + newStart.equals(start));
      Object[] startArray = start.toArray();                           // Note 7
      System.out.print ("The start array is now: " );
      for (int i = 0; i < startArray.length; i++)
         System.out.print(startArray[i] + " ");
      System.out.println();
```

```
      start.add(new Integer(5));                              // Note 8
      start.add(new Double(Math.PI));
      startArray = start.toArray();
      System.out.print("The start array is now: ");
      for (int i = 0; i < startArray.length; i++)
        System.out.print(startArray[i] + " ");
      System.out.println();
      System.out.println("Removing pi worked? "
                 + start.remove(new Double(Math.PI)));        // Note 9
      System.out.println("The start set is now " + start);
      System.out.println("Removing newStart elements from start worked? "
             + start.removeAll(newStart));                    // Note 10
      System.out.println("The start set is now " + start);
      Iterator setIterator =  set.iterator();                 // Note 11
      while(setIterator.hasNext()) {
        String next = (String)setIterator.next();
        if (next.length() < 8)
          setIterator.remove();                               // Note 12
      }
      System.out.println("The long words in " + args[0] + " are " + set);
    }catch(IOException e) {
        e.printStackTrace();
    }
  }
}
```

Output (using the command `java SetMethods gettysburg.txt`)

```
Contains "fourscore"? true
Contains "computer"? false
Contains "fourscore, and, seven, years" ? true
newStart equals start? true
newStart with "computer" equals start? false
The newStart set is now [and, seven, fourscore, years, computer]
newStart equals start after retainsAll? true
The start array is now: and seven fourscore years
The start array is now: 3.141592653589793 and seven fourscore years 5
Removing pi worked? true
The start set is now [and, seven, fourscore, years, 5]
Removing newStart elements from start worked? true
The start set is now [5]
The long words of gettysburg.txt are: [struggled, increased, remaining,
   government, consecrate, devotion, battlefield, remember, advanced,
   dedicated, consecrated, continent, fourscore, proposition, conceived,
   unfinished, dedicate, altogether]
```

Note 1: The `contains` method returns true if its argument is in the set and false otherwise.

Note 2: We create a new `Collection`, adding the first four words of the Gettysburg address to it.

Note 3: The `containsAll` method return true if each member of its `Collection` argument is contained in the `Set` and false otherwise.

Note 4: The `addAll` method adds each member of its `Collection` argument to the `Set`, returning true if the set is changed and false otherwise. A false value will be returned if the argument is empty so there are no elements to add or if all the elements are duplicates. Because we are adding just the elements of `start` to an empty `newStart`, the sets `start` and `newStart` will be equal.

Note 5: Adding another element to `newStart` will make `start` and `newStart` unequal.

Note 6: `newStart.retainAll(set);`
The `newStart` set will retain only those elements contained in `set`.

Note 7: `Object[] startArray = start.toArray();`
The `toArray` method places the elements of the `start` set into an array, `startArray`. This is useful when using older API's that expect array input.

Note 8: `start.add(new Integer(5));`
Sets contain objects, so we need to wrap the integer `5` in an `Integer` object in order to add it to the `start` set.

Note 9: `start.remove(new Double(Math.PI))`
The `remove` method removes its argument from the `start` set, returning true if `start` is changed, and false otherwise, as for example, when the argument is not in the set.

Note 10: `start.removeAll(newStart)`
The `removeAll` method removes all the elements of `newStart` that are members of `start`.

Note 11: `Iterator setIterator =  set.iterator();`
The `iterator` method returns an `Iterator` object that we use to iterate through each element of the set. When we find an element `String` with less than eight characters, we remove it from the set. When we exit the loop, `setIterator` has traversed all set elements. Had we wanted to process the set elements once more, we could have called the `iterator` method again.

Note 12: `setIterator.remove();`
The `remove` method removes the last element returned by the `next` method. It will throw an `IllegalStateException` if the `next` method has not been called or if the `remove` method has already been called after the last call to `next`.

THE BIG PICTURE

A group of interfaces specify the methods for `Collection` classes. The `Collection` interface has subinterfaces for `Sets`, which are unordered, and `Lists`, which are ordered by position. The `Map` interface describes a collection of keys and the value to which each key is mapped. The `SortedSet` and `SortedMap` interfaces describe collections which keep elements in sorted order. Java provides classes that implement these interfaces. Each collection type has a number of accessor methods to inspect element values and mutator methods to change them.

TEST YOUR UNDERSTANDING

1. The `Collection` and `Set` interfaces have the same methods. What is the difference between them?
2. Why does the `Collection` interface need an `equals` method, because Java has the == operator?
3. Can you add a primitive type such as an **int** to a `Collection`? Why or why not?

TRY IT YOURSELF

4. How does the output of Example 14.1 change if we do not change a word to lower-case before adding it to the set?

TRY IT YOURSELF

5. How does the output of Example 14.1 change if we use the default argument for the string tokenizer separator instead of passing the separators explicitly in the second argument?

TRY IT YOURSELF

6. Run Example 14.2 taking input from a file of your choosing and describe the results.

14.2 Lists

In contrast to a set, the elements of a list have an order. A list has a first element, a second, and so on until its last element. A list is a sequence of elements. The `List` interface extends the `Collection` interface. The methods it adds are:

Accessors:

```
Object get(int index)
int indexOf(Object o)
int lastIndexOf(Object o)
ListIterator listIterator()
ListIterator listIterator(int index)
List subList(int fromIndex, int toIndex)
```

Mutators:

```
void add(int index, Object element)
boolean addAll(int index, Collection c)
Object remove(int index)
Object set(int index, Object element)
```

The new `List` operations refer to the index to locate a specific position in a list. For example, if `myList` is an object of type `List`,

```
myList.add(3, "Have a good day");
```

would add the string "Have a good day" at position `3` in `myList`. Because a list starts at position `0`, this would be the fourth element in the list. Any elements that were at positions `3` and above would be shifted one position higher.

The `ListIterator` interface extends the `Iterator` interface with the additional methods

```
void add(Object o)
boolean hasPrevious()
int nextIndex()
Object previous()
int previousIndex()
void set(Object o)
```

With a `ListIterator` we can traverse the list both forward and backward. We will discuss these methods further when we use them in example programs.

Implementations

Java provides the `ArrayList` and `LinkedList` implementations of the `List` interface. Most often the `ArrayList` is more efficient. Our examples will compare the efficiency of each and then we will discuss the differences. Example 14.3 uses the `ArrayList` implementation while Example 14.4 executes the same methods using the `LinkedList` implementation. We repeat each method 10,000 times to do enough computation to obtain a timing estimate.

EXAMPLE 14.3 ArrayListTiming.java

```
/* Checks time needed for list operations
 * using an ArrayList implementation.
 */

import java.util.*;

public class ArrayListTiming {
  public static void main(String[] args) {
  List arrayImp = new ArrayList();
  Date today = new Date();
  long time1, time2;
  time1 = System.currentTimeMillis();                          // Note 1
  for(int i = 0; i < 10000; i++)
     arrayImp.add(today);                                      // Note 2
  time2 = System.currentTimeMillis();
  System.out.println("Time for 10000 adds: " + (time2 - time1));
  time1 = System.currentTimeMillis();
```

```
    for(int i = 0; i < 10000; i++)
      arrayImp.add(50, today);                              // Note 3
    time2 = System.currentTimeMillis();
    System.out.println
         ("Time for 10000 adds at position 50: " + (time2 - time1));
    time1 = System.currentTimeMillis();
    for(int i = 0; i < 10000; i++)
      arrayImp.get(5000);                                   // Note 4
    time2 = System.currentTimeMillis();
    System.out.println("Time for 10000 gets at position 5000: "
         + (time2 - time1));
  }
}
```

Output

```
Time for 10000 adds: 110
Time for 10000 adds at position 50: 3275
Time for 10000 gets at position 5000: 10
```

Note 1: The `currentTimeMillis` method returns the number of milliseconds since January 1, 1970. We only use the difference between two times in our examples.

Note 2: Because we are adding at the end of the array, we do not have to move any elements.

Note 3: Adding at position 50 in this array requires us to move at least 9950 elements one position to the right to make room for the added element.

Note 4: Using the index we can retrieve the element at position 5000 without accessing any other array elements.

The results show that adding elements to the end of an array is efficient. As Figure 14.2 shows we do not need to move any elements to add at the end.

Figure 14.2 Adding an element at the end of a `ArrayList`

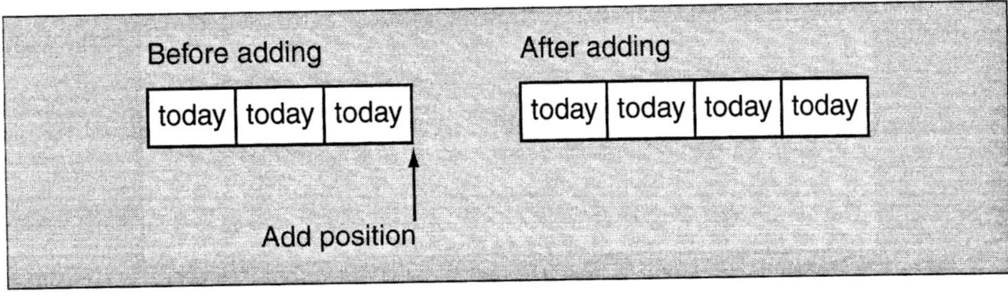

By contrast, adding an element at position 50 to an array that is at least of size 10000 requires moving all the elements one position to the right, as shown in Figure 14.3.

Figure 14.3 Add an element at position 50 in an `ArrayList`

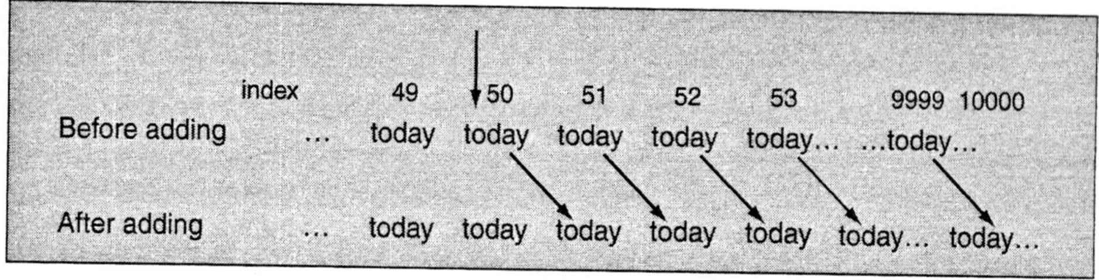

The timing result shows that we can get an element at position 5000 very efficiently using an array because we can retrieve it using the index without accessing any other array elements. Arrays use contiguous storage for their elements, so a simple computation finds the location of a particular element. The results using a linked list implementation will be quite different.

EXAMPLE 14.4 LinkedListTiming.java

```
/* Checks time needed for list operations
 * using a LinkedList implementation.
 */

import java.util.*;

public class LinkedListTiming {
  public static void main(String[] args) {
  List linkImp = new LinkedList();
  Date today = new Date();
  long time1, time2;
  time1 = System.currentTimeMillis();
  for(int i = 0; i < 10000; i++)
     linkImp.add(today);                                    // Note 1
  time2 = System.currentTimeMillis();
  System.out.println("Time for 10000 adds: " + (time2 - time1));
  time1 = System.currentTimeMillis();
  for(int i = 0; i < 10000; i++)
     linkImp.add(5000, today);                              // Note 2
  time2 = System.currentTimeMillis();
  System.out.println("Time for 10000 adds at position 5000: " + (time2 - time1));
  time1 = System.currentTimeMillis();
  for(int i = 0; i < 10000; i++)
     linkImp.get(5000);                                     // Note 3
  time2 = System.currentTimeMillis();
  System.out.println("Time for 10000 gets at position 5000: " + (time2 - time1));
  }
}
```

Output

```
Time for 10000 adds: 180
Time for 10000 adds at position 5000: 2423
Time for 10000 gets at position 5000: 2447
```

Note 1: Adding at the end of a list can be efficient if the implementation keeps a reference to the end of the list. In that case adding an element does not require traversing other list elements.

Note 2: To add an element at position 5000, we must traverse the first 5000 list elements to get to position 5000.

Note 3: To get the element at position 5000, we must traverse the first 5000 list elements to get to position 5000.

The timing results show adding at the end of a list is efficient, but adding or retrieving an item at a specified position is expensive. As Figure 14.4 shows, to get to a position in a linked list, we must start at the head of the list at position 0 and follow the links until we reach element 5000. Linked lists do not use contiguous storage, so the only way to access an element is to follow the links from the head of the list.

Figure 14.4 Finding element 5000 in a linked list

index 0 1 2 3 4 5000
today → today → today → today → today... → ...today →
head

These timing results confirm our understanding of how an array works. We see the `get` and `set` operations will be efficient for an `ArrayList` implementation of a `List`. In this respect the `ArrayList` implementation makes the `List` an improvement over the `Vector` class which has survived in the `Collection` class modified from earlier implementations to implement the `List` interface.

Adding and removing elements from linked lists can be efficient if we are positioned at the element we wish to add or remove, so we do not have the overhead of traversing the links to find the element. Adding and deleting while using a `ListIterator` to traverse a list should be efficient because we are making changes at the current cursor position.

EXAMPLE 14.5 LinkedListIterator.java

```
/* Illustrates List and ListIterator methods.
 */
```

```
import java.util.*;
import java.awt.Point;

public class LinkedListIterator {
  public static void main(String[] args) {
    List linkImp = new LinkedList();
    Date today = new Date();
    long time1, time2;
    for(int i = 0; i < 10000; i++)
      linkImp.add(today);
    ListIterator iterator = linkImp.listIterator(50);           // Note 1
    System.out.println("Previous index is " + iterator.previousIndex());
                                                                 // Note 2
    time1 = System.currentTimeMillis();
    for(int i = 0; i < 10000; i++)
      iterator.add(today);
                                                                 // Note 3
    time2 = System.currentTimeMillis();
    System.out.println("Time for 10000 adds at position 50: " + (time2 - time1))
    int previousIndex = iterator.previousIndex();
    System.out.println("Previous index is " + previousIndex);
    System.out.println("Previous item is: " + iterator.previous());
    Point point = new Point(5,7);
    iterator.set(point);
                                                                 // Note 4
    System.out.println("The item at the previous index is now: "
                 + linkImp.get(previousIndex));                  // Note 5
    System.out.println("Next index is " + iterator.nextIndex()); // Note 6
    List threeItems = linkImp.subList(10048,10051);             // Note 7
    System.out.println("The sublist in reverse is:");
    for (ListIterator i = threeItems.listIterator(threeItems.size());
          i.hasPrevious();)
                                                                 // Note 8
      System.out.println("\t" + i.previous());
    threeItems.set(0, new Point(3,4));
                                                                 // Note 9
    System.out.println("Changing threeItems(0) changes linkImp(10048) to:");
    System.out.println("\t" + linkImp.get(10048));
  }
}
```

Output

```
Previous index is 49
Time for 10000 adds at position 50: 100
Previous index is 10049
Previous item is: Mon Aug 23 12:51:04 PDT 1999
The item at the previous index is now: java.awt.Point[x=5,y=7]
Next index is 10049
The sublist in reverse is:
    Mon Aug 23 12:51:04 PDT 1999
    java.awt.Point[x=5,y=7]
    Mon Aug 23 12:51:04 PDT 1999
Changing threeItems(0) changes linkImp(10048) to:
    java.awt.Point[x=3,y=4]
```

Note 1: Calling `listIterator(50)` returns a list iterator starting at element 50. Using the default `listIterator()` will return a list iterator which starts at the beginning of the list.

Note 2: The `previousIndex` method returns the index of the element that would be returned by a call to `previous`, or -1 if the iterator is positioned at the beginning of the list.

Note 3: Using a list iterator to add is efficient, because it adds at the current position. In Example 14.4, using `add(5000, today)` was not efficient because it required a traversal of the first 5000 elements of the list to find the position at which to add.

Note 4: The `set` method changes the list element returned by the last call to `next` or `previous`. In this case that would be the previous item at index 10049. Java throws an `IllegalStateException` if neither `next` nor `previous` have been called, or `remove` or `add` (from the `ListIterator` interface) have been called after the last call to `next` or `previous`.

Note 5: Using this `List` method to find the item at index `previousIndex` is less efficient than using the `previous` method of the `ListIterator` class, again because it requires starting at the beginning of the list and traversing element by element to reach the element at index 10049.

Note 6:
```
System.out.println ("Next index is " + iterator.nextIndex());
```
We displayed the index of the previous element, which was 10049. Calling `previous` moved the iterator one position to the left so the previous index is 10048 and the next index is 10049.

Note 7:
```
List threeItems = linkImp.subList(10048,10051);
```
The `subList` method creates a view of a portion of the list. Making changes to this list will change the list of which it is a view. The `threeItems` list contains the three items starting at index `10048` and going up to but not including the element at index `10051`.

Note 8:
```
for(ListIterator i = threeItems.listIterator(threeItems.size());
i.hasPrevious(); )
```
We can process the elements of a list in reverse order by starting a list iterator at the index one greater than the index of the last element in the list. At each iteration of the loop we process the element returned by `previous`, continuing until `hasPrevious` returns false. Because we call `previous` in the body of the loop to process the previous element we do not need any code in the `for` loop to decrement the index.

Note 9:
```
threeItems.set(0, new Point(3,4));
```
Changing element 0 of this view will change element 10048 in the list, `linkImp`, backing this view.

THE BIG PICTURE

The two List implementations, `ArrayList` and `LinkedList`, differ in their performance. In an `ArrayList` finding an element at a fixed position is very efficient while inserting an element there is inefficient. Using a `LinkedList` finding an element at a fixed position is inefficient, but using a list iterator to insert at the current position is efficient.

TEST YOUR UNDERSTANDING

7. The `List` `add` and `set` methods have two arguments, while the `ListIterator` methods have one. Explain the difference.
8. What is the maximum size of the `linkImp` list of Example 14.4?

TRY IT YOURSELF

9. How much time does it take to get the element at position 9000 in Example 14.4? To get the element at position 1000?
10. Describe the contents of the `linkImp` list of Example 14.5 just before execution completes.

14.3 Maps

A **map** associates a **value** with a **key**. Each key occurs at most once in a map. A key in the map has one value. For example, Figure 14.5 shows the lengths of some of the world's major rivers. The key is the name of the river, while the value is its length.

Figure 14.5 Rivers of the world and their lengths (in miles)

```
Amazon            4000    Indus          1800
Chang (Yangtze)   3964    Mekong         2600
Colorado          1450    Mississippi    2340
Columbia          1243    Missouri       2315
Congo             2718    Niger          2590
Danube            1776    Nile           4160
Euphrates         1700    Rio Grande     1900
Ganges            1560    Volga          2290
Huang (Yellow)    3395
```

The methods of the `Map` interface are:

```
void clear()
boolean containsKey(Object key).
boolean containsValue(Object value)
Set entrySet()
boolean equals(Object o)
```

```
Object get(Object key)
int hashCode()
boolean isEmpty()
Set keySet()
Object put(Object key, Object value)
void putAll(Map t)
Object remove(Object key)
int size()
Collection values()
```

Implementations

The `Map` interface has two implementations, `HashMap` and `TreeMap`. A hash map is more efficient at accessing a single key, but does not easily permit a listing in alphabetical order, whereas a tree map does keep elements in alphabetical order.

A hash map uses a hash function to map each key to a location. In our example we have 17 rivers. We create a hash map with 37 spaces to reduce the chance of collisions. There are thousands of possible river names. A hash function associates a position in a hash table with a name. For example, a simple hash function might add up the ASCII values of the characters in the name and divide by the table size to get the remainder, which gives the table position. For Nile that calculation would be

```
N=78, i=105, l=108, e=101
78+105+108+101 = 392
392 = 10*37 + 22
```

So Nile would go in position 22 in the table.

Because Java implements the hashing function, we do not need to know the details, but it helps to see the basic concept to understand the efficiency of the operation. To enter Nile in the table or to search for it requires just a computation of the hash function without traversing other elements in the table except to resolve collisions which arise when another element also hashes to the same value of 22.

The reason an alphabetical listing is difficult is that adjacent elements alphabetically may have totally different hash values. For example to hash Rio Grande

```
R=82, i=105, o=111, blank=32, G=71, r=114, a=97, n=110, d=100, e=101
82+105+111+32+71+114+97+110+100+101 = 923
923 = 24*37+35
```

So Rio Grande would go in position 35 if this hash function were used.

A tree uses two dimensions to arrange data so as to include many data elements without requiring extensive search to find an element. A tree is a compromise between an array and a list which is not as good as either at their best, but not as bad as either at their worst. To get good performance we must keep the tree balanced, making it spread out as much as possible rather than branch unnecessarily deep. For example, the tree of Figure 14.6a is unbalanced, while that of Figure 14.6b is balanced.

Figure 14.6 Examples of trees

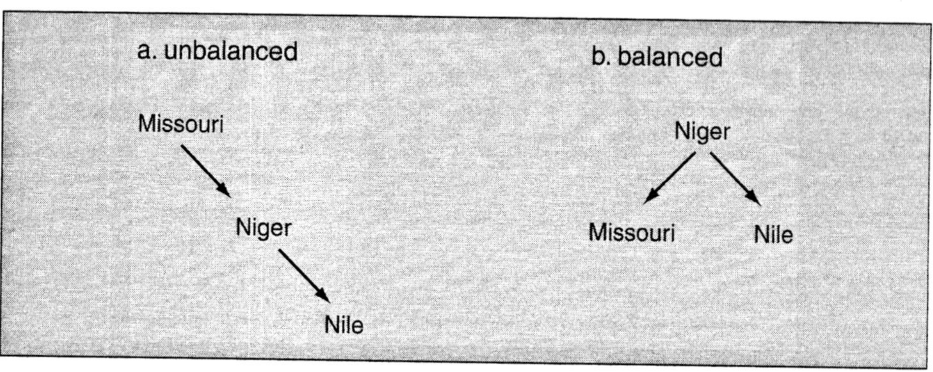

The tree map implementation uses a red-black tree which keeps itself balanced so the worst-case search time is of the order of `ln n` where n is the size of the data in the tree. We will look at efficiency further in Example 14.7. First Example 14.6 illustrates how to use a map.

EXAMPLE 14.6 RiverMap.java

```
/* Illustrates Map methods
 */

import java.util.*;

public class RiverMap {
  public static void main(String[] args) {
    Map rivers = new HashMap(37);                                   // Note 1
    int[] lengths = {4000,3964,1450,1243,2718,1776,1700,1560,3395,
                 1800,2600,2340,2315,2590,4160,1900,2290};
    String[] names = {"Amazon", "Chang", "Colorado", "Columbia", "Congo",
                    "Danube", "Euphrates", "Ganges", "Huang", "Indus",
                    "Mekong", "Mississippi", "Missouri", "Niger", "Nile",
                    "Rio Grande", "Volga"};
    for (int i = 0; i < names.length; i++)
      rivers.put(names[i], new Integer(lengths[i]));                // Note 2
    System.out.println("The size of the rivers map is: " + rivers.size());
                                                                    // Note 3
    System.out.println("Rivers map contains key 'Congo': "
            +  rivers.containsKey("Congo"));                        // Note 4
    System.out.println("Rivers map contains value 3500: "
            + rivers.containsValue(new Integer(3500)));             // Note 5
    System.out.println();
    System.out.print(rivers.keySet());                              // Note 6
    System.out.println();
    System.out.println();
    System.out.println(rivers);                                     // Note 7
    Map riversTree = new TreeMap();
```

```
    riversTree.putAll(rivers);                                  // Note 8
    System.out.println();
    System.out.println(riversTree);                             // Note 9
    System.out.println();
    for (Iterator i = rivers.entrySet().iterator(); i.hasNext(); ) { // Note 10
      Map.Entry item = (Map.Entry)i.next();
      int size = ((Integer)item.getValue()).intValue();         // Note 11
      if (size >= 3000)
        System.out.println("\t" + item.getKey() + '\t' + size);
    }
    long starttime = System.currentTimeMillis();
    for (int i = 0; i < 100000; i++)
       rivers.get("Columbia");                                  // Note 12
    long stoptime = System.currentTimeMillis();
    System.out.println("Time for 100000 gets in a hash map is "
                    + (stoptime-starttime));
    starttime = System.currentTimeMillis();
    for (int i = 0; i < 100000; i++)
      riversTree.get("Columbia");
    stoptime = System.currentTimeMillis();
    System.out.println("Time for 100000 gets in a tree map is "
                    +  (stoptime-starttime));
  }
}
```

Output

```
The size of the rivers map is: 17
Rivers map contains key 'Congo': true
Rivers map contains value 3500: false

Mekong Ganges Colorado Euphrates Amazon Mississippi Rio Grande Volga Missouri
Indus Huang Congo Danube Niger Nile Columbia Chang

{Mekong=2600, Ganges=1560, Colorado=1450, Euphrates=1700, Amazon=4000, Missis-
sippi=2340, Rio Grande=1900, Volga=2290, Missouri=2315, Indus=1800, Huang=3395,
Congo=2718, Danube=1776, Niger=2590, Nile=4160, Columbia=1243, Chang=3964}

{Amazon=4000, Chang=3964, Colorado=1450, Columbia=1243, Congo=2718,
Danube=1776, Euphrates=1700, Ganges=1560, Huang=3395, Indus=1800, Mekong=2600,
Mississippi=2340, Missouri=2315, Niger=2590, Nile=4160, Rio Grande=1900,
Volga=2290}

    Amazon  4000
    Huang   3395
    Nile4160
    Chang   3964
Time for 100000 gets in a hash map is 110
Time for 100000 gets in a tree map is 671
```

Note 1: We choose a table size of 37 because it is the nearest prime to twice the size of the data. We want the data to be spread as uniformly as possible in the table to minimize the chance of collisions and a prime table size helps spread the values to each possible location using the common hash functions.

Note 2: The `put` method enters a key and its associated value in the map. Both the key and value are of type `Object`. In this example the river name key is a string which inherits from `Object`, but the river length is an integer that we need to wrap inside an Integer object so it will inherit from `Object`.

Note 3: The `size` method returns the number of elements in the map. Each element is a `(key, value)` pair.

Note 4: The `containsKey` method returns true if the key is contained in the map and false otherwise.

Note 5: The `containsValue` method returns true if the value is associated with some key in the map and false otherwise.

Note 6: `System.out.println(rivers.keySet());`
The `keySet` method returns a `Set` of all the keys in the map. Note that the elements do not appear in alphabetical order, but rather in the order they were hashed into the map.

Note 7: `System.out.println(rivers);`
The `Map` implementations inherit the `toString` method in `AbstractMap` so we can list the entire map with a simple `println`. Note that the elements do not appear in alphabetical order, but rather in the order they were hashed into the map.

Note 8: `riversTree.putAll(rivers);`
The `putAll` method lets us put all the elements of one map into another.

Note 9: `System.out.println(riversTree);`
The `treeMap` elements appear in alphabetical order because they were added to the tree in such a way as to preserve that order.

Note 10: `for (Iterator i = rivers.entrySet().iterator(); i.hasNext(); )`
The `entrySet` method returns a set of elements of type `Entry`, an inner interface of `Map`. The `Entry` interface has three methods:

```
Object getKey();
Object getValue();
Object setValue(Object value);
```

We use this set to iterate through the map, processing each entry in turn. The loop needs no update expression because the `next` method is executed in the loop body to update to the next element.

Note 11: `int size = ((Integer)item.getValue()).intValue();`
In the body of the loop, we get the value from each entry and list all rivers whose length is greater than or equal to 3000 miles.

Note 12: `for (int i = 0; i < 100000; i++) rivers.get("Columbia");`
Executing a `get` in a hash map is more efficient than in a tree map. We will explore this difference further in the next example.

We compare the hash map with the tree map implementation in the next example. We compare searches of maps with different sizes. The search time for a hash map depends on the load factor which is the ratio of the number of items in the table to the table capacity. In our example, the load factor is always .5 because our hash map is constructed with capacity twice the number of elements we add.

As we add more nodes to a tree map, the tree gets deeper, but slowly. The maximum number of comparisons occurs when we search for an item not in the tree. In a balanced tree, the growth in the search time varies as the logarithm of the data size. In running Example 14.7 we use data sets of size 100, 1000, 10,000, and 100,000. Figure 14.7 shows the natural logarithms of these numbers, the ratios compared to the logarithm of 100 as a base, the observed time and the predicted time.

Figure 14.7 Predictions based on `ln n` efficiency

Size	Natural logarithm	Ratio	Observed time	Predicted time
100	4.6	1.0	1953	1953
1000	6.9	1.5	2814	2929
10000	9.2	2.0	3685	3906
100000	11.5	2.5	4777	4882

EXAMPLE 14.7 CompareMaps.java

```
/* Compares the efficiency of the hash map
 * implementation with the tree map.
 */

import java.util.*;

public class CompareMaps {                                          // Note 1
  public static final int MAX  = 500000;                            // Note 2
  public static final Integer TEST = new Integer(100000);

  public static String time(Map map, Integer test) {                // Note 3
    Object value = null;
    long starttime = System.currentTimeMillis();
    for (int i = 0; i < MAX; i++) {
      value = map.get(test);
    }
    long stoptime = System.currentTimeMillis();
```

```
    return (value + " took " + (stoptime - starttime));
  }
  public static void main(String[] args) {
    int SIZE = Integer.parseInt(args[0]);                    // Note 4
    Map hash = new HashMap(2*SIZE);                          // Note 5
    Map tree = new TreeMap();
    Random random = new Random();                            // Note 6
    for (int j = 0; j < SIZE; j++) {                         // Note 7
      Integer i = new Integer(random.nextInt(5000000));      // Note 8
      hash.put(i, i);                                        // Note 9
      tree.put(i,i);
    }
    System.out.println("Hash for " + time(hash, TEST));
    System.out.println("Tree for " + time(tree, TEST));
  }
}
```

Output

```
C:\book3\collections>java CompareMaps 100
Hash for null took 200
Tree for null took 1953

C:\book3\collections>java CompareMaps 1000
Hash for null took 241
Tree for null took 2814

C:\book3\collections>java CompareMaps 10000
Hash for null took 210
Tree for null took 3685

C:\book3\collections>java CompareMaps 100000
Hash for null took 210
Tree for null took 4777
```

Note 1: `MAX` is the number of times we repeat the `get` operation when we estimate the time it takes. One or a few calls would be too quick to time.

Note 2: We define the key for which we will search as a constant before the search loop so computing the test value does not affect the search time.

Note 3: The `time` method returns a string stating the time taken for `MAX` searches in the map passed as the first argument for the key passed as the second argument.

Note 4: We pass the number of items in the table as a program argument.

Note 5: Creating the hash map with a load factor of .5 (fraction of the table that will be filled) gives it good performance. High load factors can degrade the performance.

Note 6: `Random random = new Random();`
Java 2 added the `Random` class in the `java.util` package.

Note 7: `for (int j = 0; j < SIZE; j++)`
We create both the hash map and the tree map with a `SIZE` which we vary as a program argument. Increasing the number of elements in the hash map will not affect performance as long as the load factor remains the same. Increasing the number of elements in the tree map causes the worst case number of comparisons to increase by one as we double the number of items in the tree. As a balanced tree gets one level deeper the number of items it can hold doubles. This gives the logarithmic performance shown in Figure 14.7.

Note 8: `Integer i = new Integer(random.nextInt(5000000));`
The `nextInt` method returns a random number between 0 and 4,999,999. Because we put at most 100,000 numbers in the map, it is unlikely that the test value of 100,000 will be found in the map and we will be estimating the worst case behavior when we have search until we determine that the sought for element is not present.

Note 9: Because we are just comparing the hash map and tree map implementations, we do not use the value associated with the key, and put the key itself as an arbitrary value.

THE BIG PICTURE

A `Map` associates a value with each key. We can get the value associated with a key. The `HashMap` implementation is very efficient but does not keep the keys in sorted order. It uses a hash function computed from the key to find a location in the map. Performance does not depend on the size of the data, but will degrade if the load factor increases because more conflicts will occur with multiple keys hashing to the same location. The search time using the `TreeMap` implementation increases proportional to `ln n` where `n` is the size of the map. It is useful if getting the data in sorted order is important.

TEST YOUR UNDERSTANDING

11. Modify Example 14.7 to make the size of the map five greater than the size of the data. How do the performance figures change?
12. We see from Figure 14.7 that squaring the size from 100 to 10000 doubles the logarithm. Using this rule what is the predicted search time in a `TreeMap` of size 40000 compared to one of size 200? Run Example 14.7 to check your prediction.
13. What advantage would a tree map have over a hash map if used for a spell checker?

14.4 Comparisons and Ordering

Thus far in this chapter we have been adding strings to our collections. Part of the Java library, the `String` class is well behaved in that comparison between strings work as expected. In this section we learn to make our user classes implement the necessary comparison operations properly, so we can add them to collections and arrange them in order.

Inheriting From Object

Class `Object` provides default implementations of the methods

```
public boolean equals(Object o);
public int hashCode();
public String toString();
```

so every class inherits these methods. However `Object` implements these methods based on a reference to an object, and not based on the state of the object itself. Subclasses normally must override these methods for them to work properly, as the `String` class does. To see why such overriding is necessary we use the `Name` class of Figure 14.8, with the instances of Figure 14.9.

Figure 14.8 A `Name` class

```
/* Groups fields for a name.
 * Uses toString to display.
 */

package personData;

public class Name {
  String first;
  char initial;
  String last;

  public Name(String f, String l) {
    first = f;
    last = l;
  }
  public Name(String f, char i, String l) {
    this(f,l);
    initial = i;
  }
  public String toString() {
    if (initial == '\u0000')
      return first + " " + last;
    else
      return first + " " + initial + " " + last;
  }
}
```

Figure 14.9 Two **Name** instances

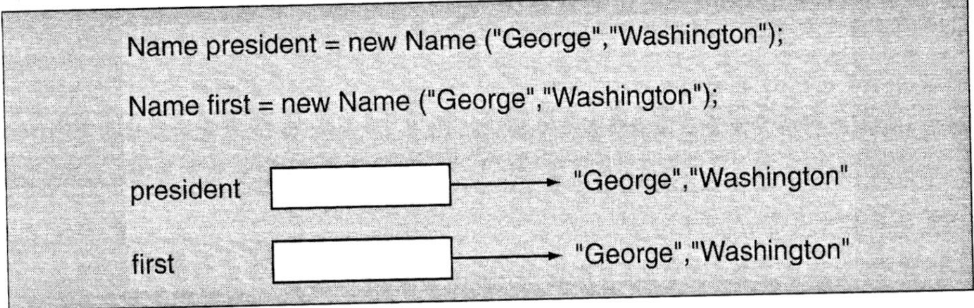

Example 14.8 shows what happens when a class uses the default implementations that it inherits from `Object`.

EXAMPLE 14.8 BadCompare.java

```
/* Shows that the Name class does not behave properly
 * using inherited equals and hashCode methods.
 */

import personData.Name;
import java.util.*;

public class BadCompare {
  public static void main(String[] args) {
    Name president = new Name ("George", "Washington");
    Name first = new Name ("George", "Washington");              // Note 1
    System.out.println("Should be equal, but equals returns: "
                + first.equals(president));                      // Note 2
    System.out.print("The hash codes for first and president are: ");
    if (president.hashCode() == first.hashCode())
      System.out.println("equal");
    else
      System.out.println("not equal");                           // Note 3
    Set s = new HashSet();
    s.add(president);
    System.out.println("Should contain George Washington, but "
          + "contains returns: " + s.contains(first));           // Note 4
    Map m = new HashMap();
    m.put(president, "first");
    System.out.println("Should get 'first', but get returns: "
                                + m.get(first));                 // Note 5
    System.out.println("toString overridden so first is: " + first); // Note 6
  }
}
```

Output

```
Should be equal, but equals returns: false
The hash codes for first and president are: not equal
Should contain George Washington, but contains returns: false
Should get 'first', but get returns: null
toString overridden so first is: George Washington
```

Note 1: Figure 14.9 shows that `first` and `president` refer to different objects.

Note 2: The `equals` method inherited from `Object` checks the equality of references. The two references, `president` and `first`, are not equal even though the names they point to are.

Note 3: The `hashCode` method inherited from `Object` computes a hash value based on the reference, so the two references, `president` and `first`, have different hash codes. Any implementation that uses these hash values to find locations for objects will put `first` and `president` in two different locations.

Note 4: The `HashSet` implementation uses the `hashCode` method to check whether an object is contained in a set. After adding `president` the set will contain the name of the first president, but the `contains` method returns false because the `hashCode` method inherited from `Object` looks for the object referred to by `first` in a different location from the one containing the object referred to by `president`.

Note 5: The `HashMap` implementation uses the `hashCode` method to store and retrieve items from the map. Because `president` and `first` have different hash codes they will be stored in different locations. Calling `m.get(first)` will only look in the location found using the hash code of `first` and thus will not find the name placed using the `president` reference.

Note 6: `System.out.println ("toString overridden so first is: " + first);`
Because the `Name` class overrides the `toString` method, we do obtain the desired result. Had `Name` not overriden `toString`, the inherited implementation from object would have been used which displays an empty string.

Overriding Object Methods

To make the `Name` class function properly we must override the `equals` and `hashCode` methods. Example 14.9 shows the rewritten class, where we rename the `Name` class as `NewName` to avoid confusion with the incomplete version in Figure 14.8.

EXAMPLE 14.9 NewName.java

```
/* Groups fields for a name. Overrides equals, hashCode
 * and toString.
 */
```

```
package personData;

public class NewName extends Name {

  public NewName(String f, String l) {
    super(f,l);
  }
  public NewName(String f, char i, String l) {
    super(f,i,l);
  }
  public boolean equals(Object object) {                    // Note 1
    if (!(object instanceof NewName))
      return false;                                          // Note 2
    NewName name = (NewName)object;
    return first.equals(name.first) && initial == name.initial
          && last.equals(name.last);                         // Note 3
  }
  public int hashCode() {                                    // Note 4
    return first.hashCode() + (int)initial + last.hashCode();
  }
}
```

Note 1: The `equals` method overrides the method inherited from `Object` which of course has a parameter of type `Object`. The actual argument we pass to the `equals` method can be any subclass of `Object`. Because we are checking equality of `NewName` objects, we use the `instanceof` operator to rule out any object which is not of that type.

Note 2: If execution gets here we know that the object is an instance of `NewName` so we perform this cast to be able to refer to the `first`, `initial`, and `last` fields.

Note 3: The two objects are equal if they have the same first and last names and middle initial. Because the first and last names are strings, we can use the `equals` method of the `String` class to do these checks.

Note 4: To compute a hash code for a name we add the hash codes of the first and last names and the ASCII value of the middle initial. The first and last names are strings which implement the `hashCode` method properly. We could have constructed a more complex hash function, for example by shifting the hash code for the first name right by several bits before adding the middle initial and last name hash code. Such a tweaking of the function might make the distribution of hash values more uniform thus reducing the number of collisions and improving the efficiency of the hashing.

Example 14.10 shows that using the `NewName` class the problems encountered in Example 14.8 using the `Name` class are corrected.

EXAMPLE 14.10 GoodCompare.java

```
/* Shows that the NewName class behaves properly
 * using overridden equals and hashCode methods.
 */

import personData.NewName;
import java.util.*;

public class GoodCompare {
  public static void main(String[] args) {
    NewName president = new NewName ("George", "Washington");
    NewName first = new NewName ("George", "Washington");
    System.out.println("Should be equal, and equals returns: "
                  +  first.equals(president));
    System.out.print("The hash codes for first and president are: ");
    if (president.hashCode() == first.hashCode())
      System.out.println("equal");
    else
      System.out.println("not equal");
    Set s = new HashSet();
    s.add(president);
    System.out.println("Should contain George Washington, "
                 + "and contains returns: " + s.contains(first));
    Map m = new HashMap();
    m.put(president, "first");
    System.out.println("Should get 'first', and get returns: " + m.get(first));
    System.out.println("toString overridden so first is: " + first);
  }
}
```

Output

```
Should be equal, and equals returns: true
The hash codes for first and president are: equal
Should contain George Washington, and contains returns: true
Should get 'first', and get returns: first
toString overridden so first is: George Washington
```

The `Comparable` Interface

Classes implement the `Comparable` interface to allow objects to be ordered. The wrapper classes such as `Integer` and `Double` implement it, as do the `String`, `BigInteger`, and `Date` classes. The `Comparable` interface has one method,

```
public int compareTo(Object object);
```

which returns a negative integer if the result is less, zero if equal, and a positive integer if greater.

The TreeSet and TreeMap implementations require that their elements implement the Comparable interface, because they use the compareTo method to arrange them in order. In Examples 14.6 and 14.7 we successfully added strings to a TreeMap. In Example 14.8 trying to add a Name to a TreeSet would have caused a ClassCastException to be thrown because Name does not implement the Comparable interface. Algorithms such as sort, which we will consider later, naturally require that elements to be sorted implement the Comparable interface.

Names do have a natural alphabetical ordering. In Example 14.11 we revise the NewName class to implement the Comparable interface.

EXAMPLE 14.11 NewOrderedName.java

```
/* Groups fields for a name. Overrides NewName and
 * implements the Comparable interface.
 */

package personData;

public class NewOrderedName extends NewName implements Comparable {
  public NewOrderedName(String f, String l) {
    super(f,l);
  }
  public NewOrderedName(String f, char i, String l) {
    super(f,i,l);
  }
  public int compareTo(Object object) {                         // Note 1
    NewOrderedName name = (NewOrderedName)object;
    int lastResult = last.compareTo(name.last);
    if (lastResult != 0)                                        // Note 2
      return lastResult;
    else {
      int firstResult = first.compareTo(name.first);
      if (firstResult != 0)
        return firstResult;
      else                                                      // Note 3
        return (int)initial - (int)name.initial;
    }
  }                                                             // Note 4
  public static void main(String[] args) {
    NewOrderedName jAdams = new NewOrderedName("John", "Adams");
    NewOrderedName jqAdams =
                  new NewOrderedName("John", 'Q', "Adams");
    NewOrderedName hAdams = new NewOrderedName("Henry", "Adams");
    System.out.println("jAdams vs. jqAdams " + jAdams.compareTo(jqAdams));
    System.out.println("jAdams vs. hAdams " + jAdams.compareTo(hAdams));
    System.out.println("hAdams vs. hAdams " + hAdams.compareTo(hAdams));
  }
}
```

Output

```
jAdams vs. jqAdams -81
jAdams vs. hAdams 2
hAdams vs. hAdams 0
```

Note 1: The conditions specified in the `Comparable` interface require the `compareTo` method to throw a `ClassCastException` if the object argument cannot be compared to a `NewOrderedName`. If this cast fails Java will throw such an exception.

Note 2: We first check last names using the `compareTo` method for strings and return if the last names are unequal.

Note 3: If the first and last names are equal, we return the different of the ASCII values of the middle initials.

Note 4: It is a good idea to include some tests of the class methods in the `main` method.

Sorted Sets and Maps

The `SortedSet` and `SortedMap` interfaces keep the elements in order. Each adds additional operations to make use of the ordering of their elements. Additional method in the `SortedSet` interface include:

```
Object first()
SortedSet headSet(Object toElement)
Object last()
SortedSet subSet(Object fromElement, Object toElement)
SortedSet tailSet(Object fromElement)
```

Additional methods in the `SortedMap` interface include:

```
Object firstKey()
SortedMap headMap(Object toKey)
Object lastKey()
SortedMap subMap(Object fromKey, Object toKey)
SortedMap tailMap(Object fromKey)
```

EXAMPLE 14.12 Ordering.java

```
/* Illustrates the SortedSet interface
 */

import java.util.*;
import personData.*;
```

```
public class Ordering {
  public static void main(String[] args) {
    SortedSet set = new TreeSet();                                    // Note 1
    NewOrderedName jackson, madison;
    set.add(new NewOrderedName("George", "Washington"));
    set.add(new NewOrderedName("John", "Adams"));
    set.add(new NewOrderedName("Thomas", "Jefferson"));
    set.add(madison = new NewOrderedName("James", "Madison"));
    set.add(new NewOrderedName("James", "Monroe"));
    set.add(new NewOrderedName("John", 'Q', "Adams"));
    set.add(jackson = new NewOrderedName("Andrew", "Jackson"));
    set.add(new NewOrderedName("Martin", "Van Buren"));
    set.add(new NewOrderedName("William", 'H', "Harrison"));
    set.add(new NewOrderedName("James", 'K', "Polk"));
    System.out.println("The first element is: " + set.first());       // Note 2
    System.out.println("The last element is: " + set.last());         // Note 3
    System.out.println("The J's are: " + set.subSet(jackson, madison));
                                                                      // Note 4
    System.out.println("A-I are: " + set.headSet(jackson));           // Note 5
    System.out.println("M-Z are: " + set.tailSet(madison));           // Note 6
  }
}
```

Output

```
The first element is: John Adams
The last element is: George Washington
The J's are: [Andrew Jackson, Thomas Jefferson]
A-I are: [John Adams, John Q Adams, William H Harrison]
M-Z are: [James Madison, James Monroe, James K Polk, Martin Van Buren,
        George Washington]
```

Note 1: `TreeSet` implements the `SortedSet` interface while `HashSet` does not.

Note 2: The `first` method returns the first element according to the natural ordering implemented by the `compareTo` method.

Note 3: The `last` method returns the last element according to the natural ordering implemented by the `compareTo` method.

Note 4: The `subSet` method returns the sorted set starting with the first argument and continuing up to but not including the second argument.

Note 5: The `headSet` method returns elements in the sorted set starting with the first element and continuing up to but not including the argument.

Note 6: `System.out.println ("M-Z are: " + set.tailSet(madison));`
The `tailSet` method returns elements in the sorted set starting with the argument and continuing to the end of the set.

THE BIG PICTUIRE

To add our own object types to containers we need to override the `equals`, `hashCode`, and `toString` method inherited from `Object`. To be able to sort our own object types, we need to make them implement the `Comparable` interface and implement the `compareTo` method. We can add types that implement `Comparable` to sorted sets and sorted maps, which keep them in order.

TEST YOUR UNDERSTANDING

TRY IT YOURSELF 14. What happens if you change the implementation of the set `s` in Example 14.10 from a `HashSet` to a `TreeSet`? Explain.

TRY IT YOURSELF 15. What happens in Example 14.11 if you try to compare `jAdams` to the `String` "John Adams"? Explain.

TRY IT YOURSELF 16. What happens in Example 14.12 if you change the declaration of set to have type `Set` instead of `SortedSet`? Explain.

14.5 Algorithms

The `Collections` class in the `java.util` package contains static methods including algorithms which operate on certain `Collection` objects. These algorithms include:

```
static int binarySearch(List list, Object key)
static void copy(List dest, List src)
static void fill(List list, Object o)
static Object max(Collection coll)
static Object min(Collection coll)
static List nCopies(int n, Object o)
static void reverse(List list)
static void shuffle(List list)
static void sort(List list)
```

EXAMPLE 14.13 Algorithms.java

```
/* Illustrates algorithms in the Collections class.
 */

import java.util.*;

public class Algorithms {
  public static void main(String[] args) {
    String[] words =
{"sat","tat","hat","fat","vat","cat","rat","bat","mat","oat","pat"};
    List list = new ArrayList();
    for (int i = 0; i < words.length; i++)
      list.add(words[i]);
```

```
    Collections.reverse(list);                                    // Note 1
    System.out.println("Reverse of list is: " + list);
    System.out.println("Max is: " + Collections.max(list));       // Note 2
    System.out.println("Min is: " + Collections.min(list));
    Collections.sort(list);                                       // Note 3
    System.out.println("Sorted list is: " + list);
    System.out.println
          ("Index of rat is: " + Collections.binarySearch(list, "rat"));
                                                                  // Note 4
    System.out.println("Searching for potato returns: "
          + Collections.binarySearch(list, "potato"));            // Note 5
    Collections.shuffle(list);                                    // Note 6
    System.out.println("Shuffled list is: " + list);
    Collections.copy(list,list.subList(5,8));                     // Note 7
    System.out.println("List changed at indices 0-2 is:\n\t " + list);
    Collections.fill(list.subList(0,3),"fill");                   // Note 8
    System.out.println("List filled at indices 0-2 is:\n\t " + list);
    System.out.println
         ("List with 5 fives is: " + Collections.nCopies(5,"five")); // Note 9
  }
}
```

Output

```
Reverse of list is: [pat, oat, mat, bat, rat, cat, vat, fat, hat, tat, sat]
Max is: vat
Min is: bat
Sorted list is: [bat, cat, fat, hat, mat, oat, pat, rat, sat, tat, vat]
Index of rat is: 7
Searching for potato returns: -8
Shuffled list is: [cat, tat, mat, fat, vat, sat, pat, oat, rat, hat, bat]
List changed at indices 0-2 is:
     [sat, pat, oat, fat, vat, sat, pat, oat, rat, hat, bat]
List filled at indices 0-2 is:
     [fill, fill, fill, fat, vat, sat, pat, oat, rat, hat, bat]
List with 5 fives is: [five, five, five, five, five]
```

Note 1: The algorithms are static methods of the `Collections` class. The `reverse` method reverses the order of the elements in its list argument.

Note 2: The `max` method applies to any `Collection` whose elements implement the `Comparable` interface. Elements must be mutually comparable. For example a collection could not contain both strings and dates.

Note 3: The `sort` method arranges the elements of a list from smallest to largest. The elements must implement the `Comparable` interface and be mutually comparable.

Note 4: Uses the binary search algorithm to find an element in a list whose elements must be sorted. It will perform much better for a random access implementation such as an `ArrayList`.

Note 5: The search for "potato" returns -8 which equals -7 -1, where 7 is the position at which to insert "potato" in the list (just before "rat").

Note 6: `Collections.shuffle(list);`
Permutes the elements of the list randomly.

Note 7: `Collections.copy(list,list.subList(5,8));`
Copies the source list to the destination list which must be at least as long as the source. In this example, we copy elements at indices `5`, `6` and `7` to indices `0`, `1`, and `2`.

Note 8: `Collections.fill(list.subList(0,3),"fill");`
Fills the list with the specified object. In this example we fill the first three positions of the list with the word "fill."

Note 9: `("List with 5 fives is: " + Collections.nCopies(5,"five"));`
The `nCopies` method returns a list, in this example, with `5` copies of the word "five."

THE BIG PICTURE

A `Collections` class has static methods to implement useful algorithms. These include binary search, sort, reverse, shuffle, max, and min.

TEST YOUR UNDERSTANDING

17. Explain why most `Collections` methods take a `List` as the first argument instead of a `Collection`.

TRY IT YOURSELF

18. What happens in Example 14.13 if you add the line

```
list.add(new Date());
```

just after the loop which adds the words?

SUMMARY

- The `Collection` interface abstracts behavior common to both lists and sets. In a `Set`, elements are unordered, while in a list the elements have an order from first to last. A `Set` cannot contain duplicates. Trying to add an element already in the set will leave the set unchanged. A `Map` interface represents `(key, value)` pairs and allows us to look up the value associated with a key. Each interface includes accessor operations that inspect elements and mutator operations that modify them.
- The `Collection iterator` method allows us to process the elements of a collection, and remove elements while iterating, if desired. The `hasNext` method returns true when the iterator has not completed traversing the collection, and in that case, the `next` method returns the next element.
- The `List` interface adds methods which refer to the specific position of an element. A list iterator can traverse a list both forward and backward. The `ArrayList` implementation generally is more efficient than the `LinkedList` implementation, but is

inefficient when adding at the interior of a list because the elements to the right need to moved to make space. Adding at an interior position is efficient using a `LinkedListIterator` since the iterator is already positioned at the insertion position.

- A `Map` associates a value with a key. We use the `put` method to store a key and value pair, and the `get` method to retrieve the value associated with a key. The `HashMap` implementation is more efficient than the `TreeMap`, but does not keep the elements in sorted order.
- By default the `equals` method compares references and the `hashCode` method computes the hash value of references. Objects that we wish to add to collections must override these methods to check equality of objects, and to compute a hash value based on the object data. A class must implement the `Comparable` interface, providing a `compareTo` method, to allow its objects to be sorted, or placed in a sorted collection which keeps its elements in sorted order.
- The `Collections` class includes `binarySearch`, `copy`, `fill`, `max`, `min`, `reverse`, `s huffle`, `sort`, and `nCopies` methods which perform common operations.

Skill Builder Exercises

1. For each interface fill in the blank with the name of a class that implements it.

   a. `Set` ________________

   b. `SortedSet` ________________

   c. `List` ________________

   d. `Map` ________________

   e. `SortedMap` ________________

2. A class whose objects may be entered as keys in a hash table should override the __________ and the __________ methods.

3. A class whose object may be entered in an ordered data structure, should implement the __________ interface which has a __________ method.

Critical Thinking Exercises

4. Which of the following is most correct regarding `Iterator` and `Enumeration`?

   a. An `Iterator` can remove elements from the `Collection`, but an `Enumeration` cannot.

   b. The `Enumeration` interface has more methods than the `Iterator`

   c. An `Enumeration` only applies to a `Vector`, while an `Iteration` applies to any `Collection`.

   d. `Enumeration` methods have shorter names than `Iterator` methods.

5. Which of the following is not a method of the `Collections` class.
   a. shuffle
   b nCopy
   c. fill
   d. reverse
   e. none of the above.
6. Which of the following is not true about a `Map` whose keys have type `Integer`?
   a. It may be implemented by a tree structure.
   b. It may be implemented using hashing.
   c. We can get a `Set` of all the keys.
   d. W e can get a `Collection` of all its values.
   e. None of the above.
7. The `currentTimeMillis` methods returns
   a. the number of milliseconds since January 1, 1970.
   b. the number of milliseconds since the start of the program.
   c. the number of milliseconds since the start of the current method.
   d. the number of milliseconds since midnight.

Debugging Exercise

8. The following program attempts to find all the words starting with the letter 's'. Find and correct any errors.

```
public class LetterS {
  public static void main(String[] args) {
    Set s = new HashSet();
    s.add("apple");
    s.add("pickle");
    s.add("soup");
    s.add("spaghetti");
    s.add("tomato");
    System.out.println(s.subSet("saaaa","taaaa"));
  }
}
```

Program Modification Exercises

9. Modify Example 14.1 to use a sorted set so that the words will display in alphabetical order.
10. Modify Example 14.3 to also compare times for removing an element.
11. Modify Example 14.4 to also compare times for removing an element.
12. Modify Examples 14.3 and 14.4 to compare the time needed using an iterator to traverse the list.
13. Modify Example 14.6 to display any river names that start with a letter entered by the user.

Program Design Exercises

14. Make a `Map` containing the distinct words of the Gettysburg address as the keys and their frequency of occurrence as the values.
15. Create a list containing 1000 random numbers between 0 and 1,000,000 and sort it. Use binary search to find the index at which 500,000 occurs in the list or the index at which it should be inserted if it does not occur. Repeat for linear search that checks the elements successively beginning at the head of the list.
16. Create a deck of `Card` objects. Each card has a suit and a value. The suits are `Clubs`, `Diamonds`, `Hearts`, and `Spades`. The values, which can be characters, are `2, 3, 4, 5, 6, 7, 8, 9, 10, J, Q, K, A`. Shuffle the deck and deal 4 hands of 13 cards each. Use suitable collection methods wherever possible.
17. Keep the words macabre, `macaco, macadam, macadamia, macaque, macaroni, macaronic, macaroon, macaw,` and `maccaboy` in a list. When the user enters a word alphabetically greater than "mac," but less than "macd," and not in the list, show the nearest four words to it and let the user choose a replacement.

CHAPTER

15 Multimedia

OUTLINE

Introduction

To go on with Java we need to exploit its powerful capabilities for multimedia and networking. We introduce threads, which allow two or more pieces of a program to execute in their own threads of control, appearing to work simultaneously. Animation provides a good illustration of thread use. Running an animation in one thread allows the program to continue other processing. We can animate graphics that we draw on the screen or images that we can download from remote sites. In Java, we can play sound clips, and we add these to our animations. We introduce the Java Media Framework to display video.

OBJECTIVES:

- Add threads to Java programs.
- Use threads in animation.
- Use images and sound.
- Use the Java Media Framework to play video and audio clips.
- Introduce concurrent programming.

15.1 Introduction to Threads

The term **thread** is short for `thread of control`. Someone who can read a book and watch television at the same time is processing two threads. For a while she concentrates on the book, perhaps during a commercial, but then devotes her attention to a segment of the TV program. Since the TV program does not require her undivided attention, she reads a few more lines every now and then. Each thread gets some of her attention. Perhaps she can concentrate on both threads simultaneously, like musicians who are able to follow the different parts of the harmony.

If we have only one thread of control, then we have to wait whenever that thread gets delayed. For example, suppose our thread is downloading a picture from the Internet. It may have to wait while the system transfers all the pixels of the picture from some remote site. If our program can create a second thread to wait for the input from the remote site, it can go with other processing while the new thread is waiting. When some new data comes in from the remote site, the new thread can receive it while the first thread waits for a while. The two threads share the processor. Figure 15.1 illustrates this sharing.

Figure 15.1 Two threads sharing the processor

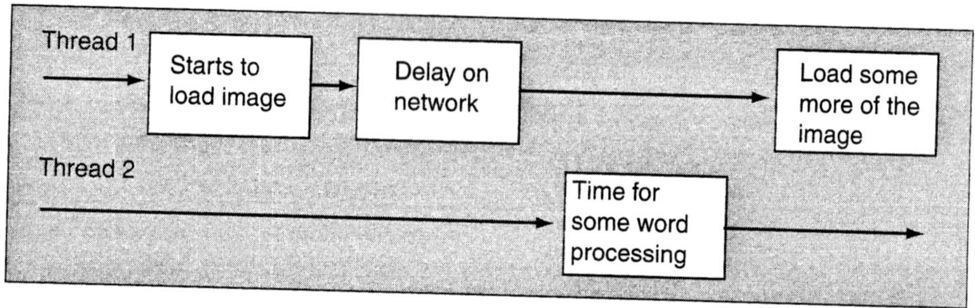

The Thread Class

Java allows us to use threads in our program. Our program can define two or more threads; the processor will divide its attention among the active threads. Each thread that we define executes a `run` method when it gets the processor. We can define a thread by extending the `Thread` class, overriding the `run` method to specify what our thread will do when it has control, as in:

```
public class MyThread extends Thread {
  ...
  public void run () {
    // put code here for thread to run
    // when it gets control
  }
}
```

To make thread, we can create a new thread and call its `start` method, as in:

```
MyThread t = new MyThread();
t.start();
```

This will make the thread ready, and when it gets scheduled, it will execute its `run` method. When another thread gets a turn, the thread, `t`, will stop executing the code in its `run` method, but will start again from where it left off, when it gets another turn.

Optionally, we can name our thread, passing the name to the constructor which it in turn passes it to the `Thread` superclass constructor, as in:

```
public MyThread(String name) {
  super(name);
  ...
}
```

The `Thread` class has a static method, `sleep(int milliseconds)`, which will cause its caller to sleep (be blocked from using the processor) for the specified number of milliseconds. While one thread sleeps, another will get a turn. We call the `sleep` method in a try block, as in:

```
try {
  Thread.sleep(1000);
}catch(InterruptedException e) { return;}
```

where we have to catch the `InterruptedException` which would occur if another thread interrupted this one. We will not consider interruption or other more advanced thread concepts in this text.

In Example 15.1 we create two threads, `Bonnie` and `Clyde`, and let them write their names five times, sleeping after each writing. Processors are so fast that a thread could do a large amount of output while it has its turn. We sleep here to slow the thread down to human scale, so that we only have to read a few lines of output. The `main` method runs in a thread, different from the two we create, so we will actually have three threads sharing the processor, writing their names when they get their turns.

EXAMPLE 15.1 NameThread.java

```
/* Creates two threads which write their names and
 * sleep.  The main thread also writes its name
 * and sleeps.
 */

import java.io.*;

public class NameThread extends Thread {
  int time;  // time in milliseconds to sleep

  public NameThread(String n, int t) {
    super(n);
    time=t;
  }
```

```
  public void run() {
    for (int i=1;i<=5;i++) {                                   // Note 1
      System.out.println(getName() + " " + i);                 // Note 2
    try {
      Thread.sleep(time);
    } catch (InterruptedException e) {return;}
  }
}

  public static void main(String argv[]) {                     // Note 3
      NameThread bonnie = new NameThread("Bonnie",1000);
      bonnie.start();
      NameThread clyde =  new NameThread("Clyde",700);
      clyde.start();
      for (int i=1;i<=5;i++) {                                 // Note 4
        System.out.println(Thread.currentThread().getName() + " " + i);
      try {
        Thread.sleep(1100);
      } catch (InterruptedException e) {return;}
    }
  }
}
```

Output

```
main 1
Bonnie 1
Clyde 1
Clyde 2
Bonnie 2
main 2
Clyde 3
Bonnie 3
Clyde 4
main 3
Clyde 5
Bonnie 4
main 4
Bonnie 5
main 5
```

Note 1: Each thread will print its name five times and sleep after each time, returning where it left off when it gets the processor again. We can see in the output that after `Bonnie` prints her name the first time, `Clyde` gets a turn and manages to print his name twice before `Bonnie` returns printing her name the second time. `Main` started first because it had the processor first, at the start of the program.

Note 2: The `getName` method of the `Thread` class returns the thread's name.

Note 3: We put the `main` method in the `NameThread` class for simplicity; we could have created another class, say `TryNameThread`, with a `main` method to create the threads.

Note 4: The `main` method also writes its name five times. Since we did not create this thread in our program we get it using the static `currentThread` method of the `Thread` class.

Figure 15.2 helps us to understand the order in which the three threads execute in Example 15.1. Each thread spends most of its time sleeping; printing its name takes a mere fraction of the time it sleeps. By graphing the sleep times in Figure 15.2 we can get a good idea of when each thread will be ready to run.

Figure 15.2 Threads of Example 15.1 sleeping and waking up

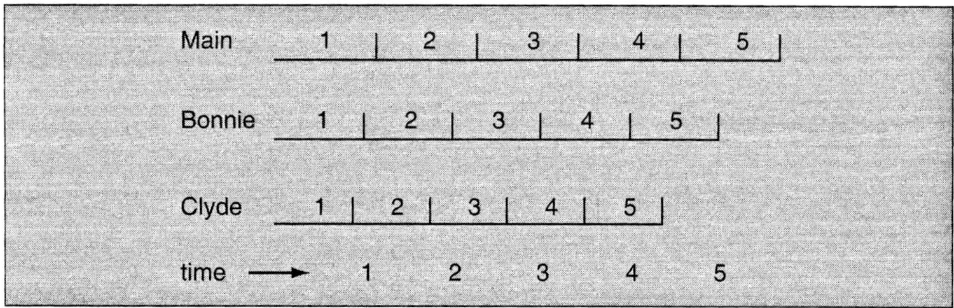

`Main` prints its name first and then sleeps for 1.1 seconds. `Bonnie` starts next, printing her name and sleeping for 1 second. `Clyde` prints his name and sleeps for .7 second. When he wakes up the other two threads are still sleeping so he prints his name again (#2). Since `Bonnie` woke up before `main`, she prints her name (#2) first, followed by `main` (#2). (Picking the thread that becomes ready first is a choice made by the thread scheduler.) When `main` finishes both `Bonnie` and `Clyde` are awake, but `Clyde` woke up first and executes first (#3). We leave it to the reader to continue following the diagram in Figure 15.2 to explain the results of Example 15.1.

The Runnable Interface

In Example 15.1 we extended the `Thread` class, creating a `NameThread` subclass which overrode the run method to provide the code for a `NameThread` object to execute in its thread of control. The `Runnable` interface provides an alternate method to use threads. In this approach we use an interface to perform a callback as we have been doing with the various listener interfaces used in event handling.

The `Runnable` interface contains just the one `run` method.

```
public interface Runnable  {
  public void run();
}
```

A concrete class that implements the `Runnable` interface must implement the `run` method. An object of this class must pass itself to a thread so that when that thread gets the processor it will execute the object's `run` method.

In Example 15.2 we rewrite Example 15.1, creating a class that implements the `Runnable` interface rather than extending `Thread`.

EXAMPLE 15.2 NameUsingThread.java

```
/* Revises Example 15.1 to implement the Runnable
 * interface rather than extending Thread.
 */

import java.io.*;

public class NameUsingThread implements Runnable {
  private int time;
  private Thread thread;      // the thread to execute the run method

  public NameUsingThread(String n, int t) {
    time=t;
    thread = new Thread(this,n);                              // Note 1
    thread.start();
  }
  public void run() {                                         // Note 2
    for (int i=1;i<=5;i++) {
      System.out.println(thread.getName() + " " + i);
      try {
        Thread.sleep(time);
      } catch (InterruptedException e) {return;}
    }
  }

  public static void main(String argv[]) {
    NameUsingThread bonnie = new NameUsingThread("Bonnie",1000);
    NameUsingThread clyde =  new NameUsingThread("Clyde",700);
    for (int i=1;i<=5;i++) {
      System.out.println(Thread.currentThread().getName() + " " + i);
      try {
        Thread.sleep(1100);
      } catch (InterruptedException e) {return;}
    }
  }
}
```

Output is the same as that from Example 15.1.

Note 1: We create a new thread, passing it the current object of type `NameUsingThread`, which implements the `run` method that the thread will run when it gets the processor, and the name of the thread. The next line starts the thread, making it ready to run when it gets its turn.

Note 2: The `NameUsingThread` class implements the `run` method which the thread will call when it gets the processor.

Either Example 15.1 or 15.2 works fine; there is no reason to prefer one approach over the other. When a class already extends a class, it cannot extend the `Thread` class, so in that case only the approach of Example 15.2, implementing the `Runnable` interface, would work.

THE BIG PICTURE

Threads allow two or more processes to proceed as if each had it own processor. A scheduler arranges for them to share processing time. One approach creates a thread by extending the `Thread` class. The other implements the `Runnable` interface. In either case, the `run` method contains the code that the thread executes when it gets its turn. The `start` method includes the thread in the group of those ready to run.

TEST YOUR UNDERSTANDING

TRY IT YOURSELF 1. In Example 15.1, change the sleep amounts for threads `Bonnie`, and `Clyde` to `300` and `200` milliseconds respectively. How does the output change when you rerun the example?

TRY IT YOURSELF 2. In Example 15.2, change the sleep times for the `main` thread to `200` milliseconds. How does the output change when you rerun the example?

TRY IT YOURSELF 3. What do you predict the output would be if you omit all the `sleep` statements from Example 15.1? Rerun the program with these changes, and see if your supposition is correct.

15.2 Animation

Animation provides an interesting application for threads. We will use a thread to show a ball moving across the screen. This thread computes the new position of the ball, asks the system to repaint the screen, showing the ball in the new position, and sleeps for a fraction of a second, so we can see the ball moving at human speed.

We start by exploring some possibilities for adding animation. Suppose we want to write an applet to move a ball across the screen. We can add a button, and whenever the user presses the button we can change the position of the ball, asking the system to repaint the screen. Figure 15.3 shows the `actionPerformed` method that handles the button press.

Each time we press the button, the browser or applet viewer executes the code of Figure 15.3. The call to `repaint` asks Java to paint the screen which, since `x` and `y` have increased, will show the ball in its new position. When the browser releases control, the system paints the screen. We can press the button several times, each time moving the ball further.

Figure 15.3 Figure 15.3 Handling a button press to move a ball

```
public void actionPerformed(ActionEvent event) {
  x+=9;
  y+=9;
  repaint();
}
```

Suppose we try to have the user initiate several moves with one button press; Figure 15.4 shows the `actionPerformed` method with a loop to repeat the move.

Figure 15.4 An attempt to move the ball 10 times with one button press

```
public void actionPerformed(ActionEvent event) {
  for (int i=0; i<10; i++) {
    x+=9;
    y+=9;
    repaint();
  }
}
```

When the user presses the button, the browser or applet viewer executes the `actionPerformed` method. Every time around the loop, it requests the system to paint the ball in its new position, but it does not release control until the loop is finished. Java combines all these `repaint` requests that it could not get to while the browser was executing the `actionPerformed` method, and just draws the ball in its final position

Example 15.3 shows the complete code using the `actionPerformed` method of Figure 15.3, which moves the ball once with each button press. We leave it as an exercise to modify this example to use the `actionPerformed` method of Figure 15.4 and see what happens (or does not happen).

Figure 15.5 shows the ball, which the user can move by pressing the button.

Figure 15.5 The applet of Example 15.3

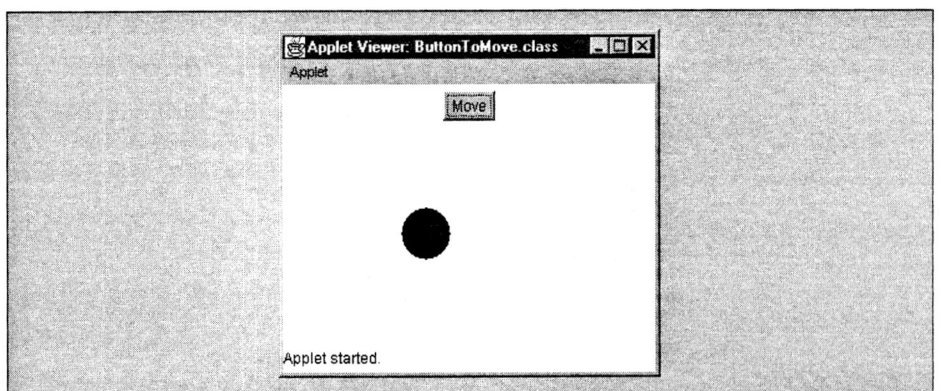

EXAMPLE 15.3 ButtonToMove.java

```
/* Moves a ball when the user presses a
 * button. Modifying the actionPerformed method
 * to put the code in a loop will cause the applet
 * to display only the ball's final position.
 */

import java.awt.*;
import java.applet.Applet;
import java.awt.event.*;

public class ButtonToMove extends Applet
            implements ActionListener {
  private int x = 50, y = 50;
  private Button move;

  public void init() {
    move = new Button("Move");
    add(move);
    move.addActionListener(this);
  }
  public void actionPerformed(ActionEvent event) {
    x+=9;
    y+=9;
    repaint();
  }
  public void paint(Graphics g) {
    g.fillOval(x,y,40,40);
  }
}
```

An applet needs its own thread of control to do animation. By using a separate thread, other system functions can proceed in parallel, sharing the processor, so that the animation will not monopolize the system's resources. As in Example 15.2, the applet implements the Runnable interface providing the run method shown in Figure 15.6 which the new thread it creates will execute when it gets its turn.
Our thread changes the position of the ball, calls the `repaint` method to show the ball in its new location, and sleeps for 300 milliseconds to do the animation on a human scale and allow the system to paint the screen. When a thread sleeps, other threads that are waiting to run, if any, get their turn to use the processor.

When the user presses the button, the applet creates an instance of `Thread`, passing itself as an argument, as in :

```
Thread t = new Thread(this);
```

so the thread will know whose run method to execute. To set up the thread and make it ready to run, the applet calls the thread's `start` method, as in:

Figure 15.6 The run method of a thread for an animation

```
public void run() {
 for(int i=0; i<10; i++) {
   x+=9;
   y+=9;
   repaint();
   try {
     Thread.sleep(300);
   }catch(InterruptedException e) {
     e.printStackTrace();
   }
  }
}
```

```
t.start();
```

As soon as it gets its turn, the thread will start executing the applet's `run` method, terminating when it has finished; while executing it takes turns with the system which paints the ball in the new position. Example 15.4 moves the ball ten times when the user presses the button. Each time the user presses the button, we return the ball to its start position and repeat the ten moves. Try it out; a static figure will not show how it works.

EXAMPLE 15.4 MoveBall.java

```
/* Uses a thread to move a ball ten times
 * when the user presses a button.
 */

import java.awt.*;
import java.applet.Applet;
import java.awt.event.*;
  public class MoveBall extends Applet
              implements ActionListener, Runnable {
  private int x = 50, y = 50;
  private Button move;

  public void init() {
    move = new Button("Move");
    add(move);
    move.addActionListener(this);
  }
  public void actionPerformed(ActionEvent event) {
    x = 50; y= 50;
    Thread t = new Thread(this);
    t.start();
  }
```

```
    public void paint(Graphics g) {
      g.fillOval(x,y,40,40);
    }
    public void run() {
        // See Figure 15.6
      }
    }
  }
```

Since the animation occurs in a thread and does not interfere with other processing, we can modify Example 15.4 to keep it going indefinitely, as long as the user remains viewing the page containing the applet. If the user moves to another web page, we want to terminate the thread; if the user returns to the page containing this applet, we start a new thread. The browser or applet viewer calls the `start` and `stop` methods of the `Applet` class to start the applet when we reenter the web page it is on, and to stop it when we leave that page. We override the `start` method to create a new thread and start it when the user initially views the page containing our applet, or returns to it. We override the applet's `stop` method to set a **boolean** flag when we leave the web page containing the applet. The `run` method periodically checks this flag, terminating when it becomes true.

TIP

The thread class has methods `suspend`, `resume`, and `stop` which were used to control a thread when the user leaves a web page or returns to it. In the Java 2 Platform these methods are **deprecated**, meaning that they are still available so that old programs will still run, but should not be used in new code.*

To move the ball continuously, we use a nonterminating loop in the `run` method, moving the ball ten times down and to the right, followed by ten moves up and to the left. While the ball moves, notice that we can edit text in another window, or run another program. As we will see in Section 15.4, we can perform other tasks in the same applet, such as whistling a tune, while the animation is continuing. The animation shares the processor rather than monopolizing it. In Example 15.5 the applet uses a thread to move the ball back and forth until the user aborts it.

* Using the JDK, the Java compiler will give a warning if a program uses any deprecated methods. To find out which methods caused the warning, compile the program using the deprecation option, as in:

```
javac -deprecation progname.java
```

Look up the deprecated methods in the JDK documentation to find suggested alternatives. For example, this documentation explains the reasons why suspend, resume, and stop were deprecated and suggests the approach of setting a flag that we use in Example 15.5.

EXAMPLE 15.5 AnimateBall.java

```
/* Animates a ball, moving it until the applet
 * quits.  Uses a thread to allow the system to
 * continue other processing.
 */

import java.awt.*;
import java.applet.Applet;

public class AnimateBall extends Applet implements Runnable {
  private int x, y;
  private boolean done;

  public void start() {
    x = 50; y = 50;                                            // Note 1
    done = false;
    Thread t = new Thread(this);
    t.start();
  }
  public void stop() {                                         // Note 2
    done = true;
  }
  public void paint(Graphics g) {
    g.fillOval(x,y,40,40);
  }
  public void run() {
    int dx=9, dy=9;
    while (true) {                                             // Note 3
      for(int i=0; i<10; i++) {
      if (done) return;                                        // Note 4
        x+=dx;
        y+=dy;
        repaint();
        try {
          Thread.sleep(300);
        }catch(InterruptedException e) {
          e.printStackTrace();
        }
      }
      dx = -dx; dy = -dy;                                      // Note 5
    }
  }
}
```

Note 1: The browser or applet viewer calls the applet's `start` method when the user enters or returns to the web page containing the applet. We start the ball at (50,50) and set the `done` flag, which the thread checks while running, to false.

Note 2: When the user leaves the web page containing the applet, the browser or applet viewer calls the applet's `stop` method, which we override to set the `done` flag to true. The thread checks this flag; it will terminate when the flag is true. When the user leaves the page containing the applet, we want the thread to finish and release the resources it uses.

Note 3: Often threads run in a nonterminating loop. Since they share the processor with other threads, they can keep running until the user terminates the applet. By contrast, a nonterminating loop in a program without threads would monopolize the processor, not allowing the program to perform other tasks.

Note 4: The thread checks the `done` flag at every iteration of the loop. When true, it returns, terminating itself.

Note 5: To get the applet to move back and forth, we change the direction of the increment after every ten moves.

TIP

The browser or applet viewer may call the `start` method of the applet many times, whenever the user returns to the web page containing the applet. We call the `start` method of a thread only once to make it ready to run. We may call the applet's `stop` method many times, whenever the user leaves the web page containing it.

We used a thread to animate a ball; we can use the same technique to do fancier animations, for example, to draw a sequence of figures that would change the appearance of each frame of the animation. To make a modest start in this direction, we animate a circular face with circles for eyes, a line for a nose, and an arc for a mouth. We use three different frames, and continually draw one after the other, sleeping for 300 milliseconds between each repainting with the next frame. Example 15.6 performs this animation. Figure 15.7 shows two of the three different faces we use in the animation.

Figure 15.7 Two faces from the applet of Example 15.6

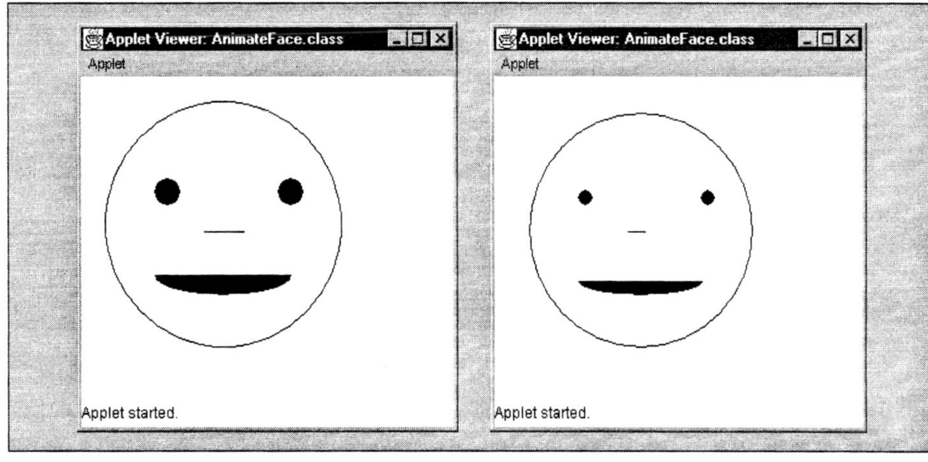

EXAMPLE 15.6 AnimateFace.java

```
/* Animates a face, drawing it in three different sizes
 * with an interval of 300 milliseconds between each
 * repainting.
 */

import java.awt.*;
import java.applet.Applet;

public class AnimateFace extends Applet implements Runnable {
  private int x, y, width, height;                    // circle for face
  private int leftEyeX, leftEyeY, lwidth, lheight;    // circle for left eye
  private int rightEyeX, rightEyeY, rwidth, rheight;  // circle for right eye
  private int leftNoseX, leftNoseY, rightNoseX, rightNoseY;  // line for nose
  private int mouthX, mouthY, mouthWidth, mouthHeight;       // arc for mouth
  private boolean done;

  public void start() {
    x=10;y=10;width=200;height=200;
    leftEyeX=50;leftEyeY=70;lwidth=30;lheight=30;
    rightEyeX=150;rightEyeY=70;rwidth=30;rheight=30;
    leftNoseX=90;leftNoseY=120;rightNoseX=140;rightNoseY=120;
    mouthX=50;mouthY=130;mouthWidth=120;mouthHeight=40;
    done = false;
    Thread t = new Thread(this);
    t.start();
  }
  public void stop() {
    done = true;
  }
  public void paint(Graphics g) {
    g.drawOval(x,y,width,height);
    g.fillOval(leftEyeX,leftEyeY,lwidth,lheight);
    g.fillOval(rightEyeX,rightEyeY,rwidth,rheight);
    g.drawLine(leftNoseX,leftNoseY,rightNoseX,rightNoseY);
    g.fillArc(mouthX,mouthY,mouthWidth,mouthHeight,180,180);
  }
  public void run() {
    int dx=9, dy=9;
    while (true) {
      for (int i=0;i<3;i++) {
        if (done) return;
        x+=dx; y+=dy; width-=dx; height-=dy;                    // Note 1
        leftEyeX+=dx; leftEyeY+=dy;lwidth-=dx;lheight-=dy;
        rightEyeX+=dx;rightEyeY+=dy;rwidth-=dx;rheight-=dy;
        leftNoseX+=dx;rightNoseX-=dx;
        mouthX+=dx;mouthY+=dy;mouthWidth-=dx;mouthHeight-=dy;
        repaint();
        try {
```

```
          Thread.sleep(300);
        }catch(InterruptedException e) {
          e.printStackTrace();
        }
      }
      dx = -dx; dy = -dy;
    }
  }
}
```

Note 1: We add a small amount to the position of each of the components of the face to move it slightly to the right three times, returning it to its original position in the next three moves. We decrease the size of the face, and its eyes, nose, an mouth as we move it to the right, increasing it to the original size as we move back to the original position.

TIP

See the author's textbook web page

`http://www.cecs.csulb.edu/~artg/cwj/`

which contains a colored version of the AnimateFace applet. It is convenient to test applets using an applet viewer, but when finished, we can deploy them on our websites. The site

`http://www.cecs.csulb.edu/~artg/projects.html/`

has various entertaining student projects.

THE BIG PICTURE

We change each frame of the animation in the run method. The thread displays the new drawing, sleeps and repeats this process over and over again. We terminate the thread when we stop the applet and create a new thread every time we start the applet.

TEST YOUR UNDERSTANDING

TRY IT YOURSELF 4. Change the `actionPerformed` method of Example 15.3 to the one of Figure 15.4. Run the code and observe the result. Does it draw the ball 10 times?

TRY IT YOURSELF 5. Start the animation of Example 15.5 and leave it running. Can you edit another program while the animation is running? Can you open another console window and run another Java program while the animation is running?

TRY IT YOURSELF 6. In Example 15.6, try different values for the sleep time and decide which you think makes the animation look best. How might we make it easier to try the applet with these different sleep times?

15.3 Images

An applet or an application can download an image from a remote site. Any component can create an image on which we can draw. Using the Swing `ImageIcon` class is a particularly convenient way to load an image. Once we have the `ImageIcon` we use its `getImage` method to get an `Image` object. We can create an `ImageIcon` from a URL specifying the location of an image, or a `String` specifying a local image file name.

We used URLs in Section 6.1 to specify resources available on computers at remote sites. We entered the URL (Uniform Resource Locator) in the browser and the browser connected to the remote site, displaying the resource for us in its window. In this section we use a URL to specify the location of an image. We can specify the complete URL, creating a URL object, as in:

```
URL url = new URL
    ("http://www.engr.csulb.edu/~artg/gittleman.gif");
```

and create the image using

```
Image pic = new ImageIcon(url).getImage();
```

We can create an image from the `gittleman.gif` file using

```
Image pic = new ImageIcon("gittleman.gif").getImage();
```

When Java has loaded the image we can draw it using the `drawImage` method of the `Graphics` class, as in:

```
g.drawImage(pic,10,10,null);
```

where the first argument is the image, and the next two arguments are the `(x,y)` coordinates of the position to display the image. The last argument is an `ImageObserver` which we could use to track the loading of the image. Because the ImageIcon class takes care to load the image completely, we do not use this argument, passing in `null`.

The four-argument version of the `drawImage` method draws the image in its normal size. A six-argument version of `drawImage` lets us scale the image, as in:

```
g.drawImage(pic,10,10,100,100,this);
```

which scales the image, drawing it in a `100x100` region.

We can use the `getWidth` and `getHeight` methods to get the width of an image, as in:

```
imageWidth = pic.getWidth(null);
imageHeight = pic.getHeight(null);
```

where the `null` argument indicates that we do not use an image observer since we call these methods after the image has been fully loaded.

Our first program to animate images follows the format of our animation programs of Section 15.2. In those examples we used a loop in the `run` method to change the location and/or the dimensions of the shapes to be drawn, to repaint, and to sleep. In Example 15.7 we load an image of the author from his home page (or from the current directory, for those not connected to the Internet). In the run method, we change the desired size of the image, repaint, and sleep for 300 milliseconds. The image expands, filling up more of the screen, and then contracts, repeating this behavior over and over again. It does flicker; we will eliminate the flicker in the Example 15.8.

Figure 15.8 shows the distorted image of the author, which occurs as part of the animation of Examples 15.7.

Figure 15.8 A step in the animation of Example 15.7

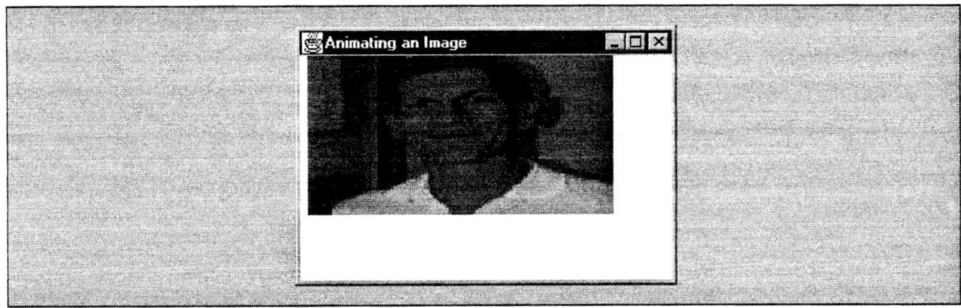

EXAMPLE 15.7 AnimateImage.java

```
/* Animates an image, loading it from a URL.  Uses a
 * thread to allow the system to continue other processing.
 */

import java.awt.*;
import java.awt.event.*;
import java.applet.Applet;
import java.net.URL;                                           // Note 1
import javax.swing.*;

public class AnimateImage extends Frame implements Runnable {
  private boolean done;        // should the thread stop?
  private Image pic;           // the image
  private int imageWidth, imageHeight;

  public AnimateImage(String title) {
    super(title);
    try{
      URL url = new URL
          ("http://www.cecs.csulb.edu/~artg/gittleman.gif");     // Note 2
      pic = new ImageIcon(url).getImage();
    } catch(Exception e) {
      pic = new ImageIcon("gittleman.gif").getImage();          // Note 3
    }
    imageWidth = pic.getWidth(null);
    imageHeight = pic.getHeight(null);
```

```
    Thread t = new Thread(this);
    t.start();
    addWindowListener(new CloseWindow());
  }
  public static void main(String[] args) {
    AnimateImage frame = new AnimateImage("Animating an Image");
    frame.setSize(300,200);
    frame.setVisible(true);
  }
  public void paint(Graphics g) {
    g.drawImage(pic,10,10,imageWidth,imageHeight,null);
  }
  public void run() {
    int dx=20, dy=5;
    while (true) {
      for(int i=0; i<10; i++) {
      if (done) return;
      imageWidth += dx;                                        // Note 4
      imageHeight += dy;
      repaint();
      try {
        Thread.sleep(300);
       }catch(InterruptedException e) {
          e.printStackTrace();
        }
      }
      dx = -dx; dy = -dy;
    }
  }
  public class CloseWindow extends WindowAdapter {
    public void windowClosing(WindowEvent e) {
      done = true;
      System.exit(0);
    }
  }
}
```

Note 1: We need to tell the compiler where to find the `URL` class.

Note 2: The image `gittleman.gif` will be loaded from the author's home page. If not connected to the Internet, change the `ImageIcon` constructor to the one used in the `catch` clause to load the image from a local file.

Note 3: The URL constructor throws the checked `MalformedURLException`. We catch any `Exception` and load the image from a local file.

Note 4: At each iteration of the loop we change the size of our scaled image. We loop ten times increasing the size of the display, alternating with ten iterations decreasing the size back to its original value.

Double Buffering

Running Example 15.7 animates the image in different sizes, but the animation flickers a lot, making it somewhat unpleasant to view. The flickering occurs because of the way the system repaints the image. Our call to the `repaint` method does not directly cause a call to the `paint` method, but rather causes a call to the `update` method which first clears the screen and then calls the `paint` method. Each time we repaint, we see a blank screen followed by the image. This alternation of blank screen and image appears as a distracting flicker.

To eliminate the flicker, we do our drawing, whether of graphical shapes, text, or images, on an offscreen buffer. Only when the drawing is done do we copy it to the visible screen. We use the `createImage` method to get an offscreen image on which to draw, passing it the size of our frame for its size, as in:

```
Image buffer =
   createImage(getSize().width,getSize().height);
```

Having created the offscreen image, we need to get a graphics context to use to draw on it. We get the `Graphics` object using the `getGraphics` method, as in:

```
bufferGraphics = buffer.getGraphics();
```

We do all our drawing in the buffer, only at the end copying the completed buffer to the screen. First we clear the buffer of the previous image. We then draw the scaled image, and a rectangular frame around it, to show that we can draw shapes as well as images in the offscreen buffer. The code is:

```
bufferGraphics.clearRect(0,0,getSize().width,getSize().height);
bufferGraphics.drawRect(8,8,imageWidth+3,imageHeight+3);
bufferGraphics.drawImage(pic,10,10,imageWidth,imageHeight,null);
g.drawImage(buffer,10,10,null);
```

The last change we need to make is to override the update method to just call `paint`, not clearing the screen every time. We do the clearing in the offscreen buffer, where it does not cause flicker. Example 15.8 revises Example 15.7 to eliminate flickering. We need to run Examples 15.7 and 15.8 to see the difference.

EXAMPLE 15.8 AnimateImageNoFlicker.java

```
/* Modifies AnimateImage.java to use double buffering
 * to eliminate flicker.
 */

import java.awt.*;
import java.awt.event.*;
import java.applet.Applet;
import java.net.URL;
import javax.swing.*;

public class AnimateImageNoFlicker extends Frame
```

```
          implements Runnable {
private boolean done;
private Image pic;
private int imageWidth, imageHeight;
private Image buffer;
private Graphics bufferGraphics;

public AnimateImageNoFlicker(String title) {
  super(title);
  try{
    URL url = new URL
      ("http://www.cecs.csulb.edu/~artg/gittleman.gif");
    pic = new ImageIcon(url).getImage();
  }catch(Exception e) {
    pic = new ImageIcon("gittleman.gif").getImage();
  }
  imageWidth = pic.getWidth(null);
  imageHeight = pic.getHeight(null);
  Thread t = new Thread(this);
  t.start();
  addWindowListener(new CloseWindow());
}
public static void main(String[] args) {
  AnimateImageNoFlicker frame =
          new AnimateImageNoFlicker("No Flicker");
  frame.setSize(300,200);
  frame.setVisible(true);
}
public void update(Graphics g) {                                    // Note 1
  paint(g);
}
public void paint(Graphics g) {
  buffer = createImage(getSize().width,getSize().height);
  bufferGraphics = buffer.getGraphics();
  bufferGraphics.clearRect(0,0,getSize().width,getSize().height);  // Note 2
  bufferGraphics.drawRect(8,8,imageWidth+3,imageHeight+3);         // Note 3
  bufferGraphics.drawImage(pic,10,10,imageWidth,imageHeight,null);
  g.drawImage(buffer,10,10,null);                                   // Note 4
}
public void run() {
  int dx=20, dy=5;
  while (true) {
    for(int i=0; i<10; i++) {
      if (done) return;
      imageWidth += dx;
      imageHeight += dy;
      repaint();
      try {
        Thread.sleep(300);
      }catch(InterruptedException e) {
        e.printStackTrace();
```

```
            }
          }
          dx = -dx; dy = -dy;
        }
      }
      public class CloseWindow extends WindowAdapter {
        public void windowClosing(WindowEvent e) {
          done = true;
          System.exit(0);
        }
      }
    }
```

Note 1: We override the `update` method to paint without clearing the screen first.

Note 2: We clear the offscreen buffer, which does not cause flicker. We clear a rectangle which has the size of the image. All the drawing on the offscreen image uses the `bufferGraphics` object that provides the graphics context for this image.

Note 3: To show that we can draw shapes on an offscreen image, as well as images, we draw a rectangle to frame the picture, making it a few pixels larger than the image.

Note 4: Having completed our drawing in the offscreen buffer, we copy it to the screen using the graphics context, `g`, for the frame.

Using Swing

If we draw on Swing components we can take advantage of the fact that Swing automatically implements double buffering. Example 15.9 executes the same animation in a Swing applet. Running it will show no flicker.

EXAMPLE 15.9 AnimateImageSwing.java

```
/* Illustrate the automatic double buffering of Swing.
 */

import java.awt.*;
import java.net.URL;
import javax.swing.*;

public class AnimateImageSwing extends JApplet implements Runnable {
  private boolean done;
  private Image pic = new ImageIcon("gittleman.gif").getImage();
  private int imageWidth = pic.getWidth(null);
  private int imageHeight = pic.getHeight(null);

  public void init() {
    Container c = getContentPane();
```

```
      DrawOn canvas = new DrawOn();
      c.add(canvas);
    }
    public void start() {
      done = false;
      Thread t = new Thread(this);
      t.start();
    }
    public void stop() {
      done = true;
    }
    public void destroy() {
      done = true;
    }
    class DrawOn extends JComponent {
      public void paintComponent(Graphics g) {
        super.paintComponent(g);
        g.drawImage(pic,10,10,imageWidth,imageHeight,null);
      }
    }
    public void run() {
      int dx=20, dy=5;
      while (true) {
        for(int i=0; i<10; i++) {
          if (done) return;
          imageWidth += dx;
          imageHeight += dy;
          repaint();
          try {
            Thread.sleep(300);
          }catch(InterruptedException e) {
            e.printStackTrace();
          }
        }
        dx = -dx; dy = -dy;
      }
    }
  }
```

TEST YOUR UNDERSTANDING

TRY IT YOURSELF 7. Modify Example 15.7 to use the image from the local machine.

TRY IT YOURSELF 8. Vary the sleep time in Example 15.7, running the example each time to see how the change in the sleep time affects the amount of flicker.

TRY IT YOURSELF 9. What happens in Example 15.8 when you omit the call to `clearRect` in the `paint` method?

15.4 Sound

Java lets us play sound clips in our applets. Java versions 1.0 and 1.1 support the AU format for audio files, while the Java 2 Platform adds support for MIDI (type 0 and type 1), RMF, WAVE, and AIFF files. Playing audio requires a machine with a sound card.

We can play an audio clip using the `play` method of the applet class, either with an absolute URL

```
public void play(URL url);
```

or a relative URL

```
public void play(URL url, String name);
```

The URL argument specifies a base location, and the String argument gives the path of the file relative to that base. We use

```
new URL(getDocumentBase(),"whistle.au");
```

to locate the `whistle` file, which is in the same directory as the HTML file, `PlayBall.html`. The `getDocumentBase` method returns the URL of that HTML file. We use

```
new URL(getCodeBase(),"boom.au");
```

to locate the `boom` file, which is in the same directory as the class file, `PlayBall.class`. The `getCodeBase` method returns the URL of the applet's class file. Very often the class file and the HTML file are in the same directory.

The `java.applet` package contains the `AudioClip` interface with methods `play`, `loop`, and `stop`. The `play` method plays an audio clip; the `loop` method plays an audio clip repeatedly until the `stop` method is invoked. The `Applet` class has methods

```
public AudioClip getAudioClip(URL url);
```

and

```
public AudioClip getAudioClip(URL url, String name);
```

enabling us to get an audio clip.

In Example 15.10 we add sounds to the `AnimateBall` applet of Example 15.5. Each time the ball moves we play a spoken word "boom." While the ball moves, we use another thread to loop a whistling rendition of the first few bars of a familiar tune. When the applet stops, we stop the animation and the whistling (mercifully).

We can use a browser or applet viewer to open the URL

```
http://www.cecs.csulb.edu/~artg/PlayBall.html
```

If not connected to the Internet, we can test the applet on our own machine.

EXAMPLE 15.10 PlayBall.java

```
/* Add sounds to the AnimateBall applet
 * of Example 15.5.
 */

import java.awt.*;
import java.applet.*;                                          // Note 1
  import java.net.*;

  public class PlayBall extends Applet
                    implements Runnable {
    private int x, y;
    private boolean done;
    private URL boomURL;
    AudioClip whistle;

  public void init() {
    try {
      URL url1 = new URL(getDocumentBase(),"whistle.au");      // Note 2
      boomURL = new URL(getCodeBase(),"boom.au");              // Note 3
      whistle = getAudioClip(url1);                            // Note 4
     }catch (MalformedURLException e) {
        e.printStackTrace();
     }
  }
   public void start() {                                       // Note 5
     x = 50; y = 50;
     done = false;
     Thread t = new Thread(this);
     t.start();
     Sound sound = new Sound(whistle);
     sound.start();
   }
   public void stop() {
     done = true;
     whistle.stop();                                           // Note 6
   }
   public void paint(Graphics g) {
     g.fillOval(x,y,40,40);
   }
   public void run() {
     int dx=9, dy=9;
     while (true) {
      for(int i=0; i<10; i++) {
        if (done) return;
        x+=dx;
        y+=dy;
        play(boomURL);                                         // Note 7
        repaint();
```

```
        try {
          Thread.sleep(1000);                                  // Note 8
        }catch(InterruptedException e) {
          e.printStackTrace();
        }
      }
      dx = -dx; dy = -dy;
    }
  }
  class Sound extends Thread {                                 // Note 9
    AudioClip clip;
    public Sound(AudioClip a) {
      clip = a;
    }
    public void run() {
      clip.loop();                                             // Note 10
    }
  }
}
```

Note 1: We import `java.applet.*` because we use both the `Applet` class and the `AudioClip` interface from the `java.applet` package.

Note 2: The `whistle.au` file is in the same directory as the document containing the applet, `PlayBall.html`. All versions of Java play the AU format used in this example (the 8000 Hz frequency can be played in all Java versions).

Note 3: The `boom.au` file is in the same directory as the applet code file, `PlayBall.class`.

Note 4: We use an audio clip because we want to loop this sound. The applet itself only includes a play method.

Note 5: When the applet starts we start the threads to do the animation and play the whistling.

Note 6: `whistle.stop();`
The `stop` method of the `AudioClip` class stops the looping of that clip.

Note 7: `play(boomURL);`
We use the `play` method of the applet to speak the word `boom` every time we move the ball.

Note 8: `Thread.sleep(1000);`
The thread sleeps for a full second, longer than in Example 15.5, in order to give the sound time to play.

Note 9: `class Sound extends Thread {`
We use a thread for the looping sound because we want it to continue concurrently with the animation and the other sound.

Note 10: `clip.loop();`
The `loop` method repeats the clip until the `stop` method is called.

TEST YOUR UNDERSTANDING

TRY IT YOURSELF 10. Run Example 15.10 with `PlayBall.html` in a different directory from the one containing `PlayBall.java`. In which of these directories should you place `whistle.au`? Which for `boom.au`?

TRY IT YOURSELF 11. What happens if you omit the call to `whistle.stop` from Example 15.10?

TRY IT YOURSELF 12. Modify Example 15.10 to loop the boom sound in the `Sound` thread rather than play it in thread `t`.

15.5 The Java Media Framework

The Java Media Framework (JMF) allows Java applications and applets to display and capture multimedia data. It supports many media content types including MPEG, QuickTime, AVI, WAV, AU, and MIDI. Various compression methods produce files in these formats. A codec performs media compression and decompression. Each codec has certain formats that it can handle. The Java Media Framework documentation lists the supported formats.

The Java 2 Platform Standard Edition does not include JMF, which may be downloaded from `http://java.sun.com/products/java-media/jmf`. JMF can also be used with Java 1.1. The installation program automatically adjusts the classpath. We introduce JMF, but do not begin to exploit its capabilities.

The JMF classes are a standard extension to core Java. The `javax.media` package contains the basic JMF classes. The JMF distribution comes with a media player, a Java program that plays media files. Our example will create a media player in an applet. A media player processes the data, rendering the sound or images. Timekeeping facilities allow synchronization of several players.

A media player can be in one of several states. For our simple example, we need to know when the player becomes realized so it can provide visual components and controls. The player generates controller events and sends them to controller listeners. We listen for a `RealizeCompleteEvent` subtype of `ControllerEvent` in order to know when to add the visual or control panel components, if they exist. We listen for an `EndOfMediaEvent` subtype to restart the clip when it ends.

The NASA site

`http://www-istp.gsfc.nasa.gov/istp/outreach/movies.html`

has links to interesting clips of astronomical phenomena which we use as illustrations. The site

`http://www.wavsounds.com`

has thousands of sound clips.

Figure 15.9 shows the applet of Example 15.11, which has a text field to enter the URL of a media clip, and a choice box with two preset video and two audio choices. When the user makes a selection a new window pops up to view or hear the clip.

Figure 15.9 The applet of Example 15.11

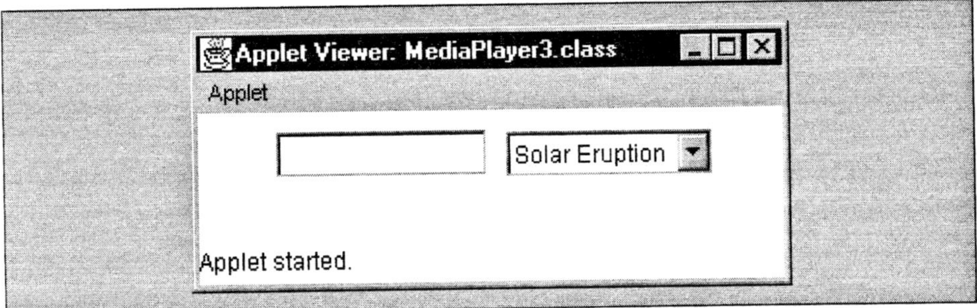

Figure 15.10 shows the media player started in response to the user's request to view a solar eruption.

Figure 15.10 Viewing a solar eruption (Example 15.11)

EXAMPLE 15.11 MediaPlayer3.java

```
/* Creates a media player to play
 * video and sound clips.
 */

import javax.media.*;
import java.awt.*;
import java.awt.event.*;
import java.net.URL;
import java.applet.Applet;
```

```
public class MediaPlayer3 extends Applet {
  Choice mediaChoice = new Choice();
  TextField mediaText = new TextField(12);
  static int position = 100;
  String[] clip = {
    "http://windows.engin.umich.edu/sun/movies/promerupt495.mpg",
    "/whistle.au",
    "/elephnt3.wav",
    "http://solar.physics.montana.edu/YPOP/Movies/sun_diver.mpg"
  };
  String[] titles = {"Solar Eruption", "Whistle", "Elephant",
                     "Solar Activity"};

  public void init() {
    Panel p = new Panel();
    p.add(mediaText);
    add(p);
    for(int i = 0; i < 4; i++)
      mediaChoice.add(titles[i]);
    add(mediaChoice);
    mediaText.addActionListener(new ActionListener() {          // Note 1
    public void actionPerformed(ActionEvent e) {
      new PlayerFrame(mediaText.getText());
    }
  });
  mediaChoice.addItemListener(new ItemListener() {              // Note 2
    public void itemStateChanged(ItemEvent e) {
      new PlayerFrame(clip[mediaChoice.getSelectedIndex()]);
    }
  });
}
class PlayerFrame extends Frame implements ControllerListener{  // Note 3
  Player player = null;
  public PlayerFrame(String s) {
    super(s);
    URL url;
    try {
      if (s.substring(0,4).equals("http"))
      url = new URL(s);
      else url = new URL (getCodeBase(),s);
      player = Manager.createPlayer(url);                       // Note 4
      player.addControllerListener(this);
      player.start();                                           // Note 5
    }catch (Exception e) {
      e.printStackTrace();
    }
  }
  public void controllerUpdate(ControllerEvent e) {             // Note 6
    Component c;
    if (e instanceof RealizeCompleteEvent) {                    // Note 7
      setSize(300,200);
```

```
      setLocation(position,0); // Note 8
      position += 100;
      setVisible(true);
      if ((c = player.getVisualComponent()) != null) // Note 9
        add(c,"Center");
      if ((c = player.getControlPanelComponent()) != null) // Note 10
        add(c,"South");
          validate();                                          // Note 11
          addWindowListener(new WindowAdapter() {
            public void windowClosing(WindowEvent e) {         // Note 12
              player.stop();
              player.deallocate();
              dispose();
            }
        });
      }
      else if (e instanceof EndOfMediaEvent) {                 // Note 13
        player.setMediaTime(new Time(0));
        player.start();
      }
    }
  }
}
```

Note 1: When the user enters a URL in the text field, we start a media player to play it.

Note 2: When the user selects a URL from the choice box, we start a media player to play it.

Note 3: The `PlayerFrame` creates a media player and implements the controller listener interface to handle controller events the player generates.

Note 4: Java provides the `Manager` class for obtaining system dependent resources such as media players.

Note 5: The `start` method starts the player as soon as possible.

Note 6: `public void controllerUpdate(ControllerEvent e)`
This is the only method of the controller listener interface. It handles controller events generated by the media player.

Note 7: `if (e instanceof RealizeCompleteEvent)`
When a player reaches the realized state, it knows the resources it needs. We can show the window and add the necessary components.

Note 8: `setLocation(position,0);`
We may have several players active at the same time. We create each at a separate position so it is at least partially visible to the user.

Note 9: `if ((c = player.getVisualComponent()) != null)`
If there is a visual component, we get it and add it in the center region.

Note 10: `if ((c = player.getControlPanelComponent()) != null)`
If there is a control panel component, we get it and add it to the south region.

Note 11: `validate();`
When adding components, we need to have the layout manager redo the layout.

Note 12: `public void windowClosing(WindowEvent e)`
When the user closes the window, we stop the clock, release resources the player is using, and free the window resources.

Note 13: `else if (e instanceof EndOfMediaEvent)`
When the clip finishes, we reset the clock and start the player again to repeat the clip.

THE BIG PICTURE

The Java Media Framework, a separate download, provides classes to play and capture multimedia data. Media players created in Java applets and applications handle many types of media files. They generate controller events that describe the state of the player.

TEST YOUR UNDERSTANDING

TRY IT YOURSELF 13. Modify Example 15.11 to omit the call to the `validate` method. Describe the result.

TRY IT YOURSELF 14. Find a multimedia file and enter its URL in the text field of Example 15.11.

15.6 Concurrent Programming

Having seen threads running independently in the last section, we take up the interesting and difficult problem of threads which share data and need to cooperate with each other to operate correctly.

An Example without Synchronization

To illustrate the problem, suppose that two threads are depositing to an account, and that a deposit involves two steps:

1. computing the new balance
2. recording the change in a log

We assume each thread computes the balance separately, but shares the log to enter the result.

A thread runs for a certain time period, and then another thread gets its turn. If each thread completes both steps when it has its turn, the balance and the log will be consistent, but perhaps thread1 loses its turn after completing step 1.

Figure 15.11 A problem with threads

```
thread1                  thread2
balance = $100
                         balance = $200
                         enter $200 in log
enter $100 in log
```

The execution sequence of Figure 15.11 shows that after thread1 computes a balance of $100 it loses its turn to thread2 which computes a balance of $200 and records the new balance in the log. When thread1 gets its turn again it finishes where it left off, entering $100 in the log, which is now incorrect.

To create a simple program to illustrate this phenomenon, we use a buffer that contains an integer, `number`, which two threads share. The `increment` method adds 1 to `number` and reports its new value, while the `decrement` method subtracts 1 and reports the new value. When the threads operate correctly, successive reports will display values that differ by one. For example, starting with `number` at 5, two increments give

```
thread1 increments to 6
thread1 reports 6
                         thread2 increments to 7
                         thread2 reports 7
```

while an increment followed by a decrement results in

```
thread1 increments to 6
thread1 reports 6
                         thread2 decrements to 5
                         thread2 reports 5
```

Only when the threads operate incorrectly do we get the same value on successive reports. For example, again starting at 5,

```
thread1 increments to 6
                         thread2 decrements to 5
                         thread2 reports 5
thread1 reports 5
```

Example 15.12 shows this behavior, but not very often. The `increment` and `decrement` methods are so short they are rarely interrupted before completion. For larger methods, this error would occur more often.

EXAMPLE 15.12 TallyWrong.java

```
/* Two threads occasionally err in reporting
 * values because they get interrupted before
 * finishing to execute a method.
 */
```

```
public class TallyWrong {
  class Buffer {
    int number = 0; // the number to increase or decrease
    int previous = 0;
    int total = 0; // total number of operations performed
    int errors = 0; // number of errors

  public void increment() {
    number++;
    report(number);
  }
  public void decrement() {
    number--;
    report(number);
  }
  public void report(int n) {
    total++;
    if (n == previous)                                            // Note 1
      System.out.println(++errors + "\t" + total );
    previous = n;
   }
  }
  class Plus extends Thread {
    Buffer buf;
    Plus(Buffer b) {
      buf = b;
   }
   public void run() {
    while (true)                                                  // Note 2
      buf.increment();
   }
  }
  class Minus extends Thread {
    Buffer buf;
    Minus(Buffer b) {
      buf = b;
    }
    public void run() {
    while (true)
      buf.decrement();
    }
  }
  public static void main(String[ ] argv) {
    TallyWrong tw = new TallyWrong();
    Buffer b = tw.new Buffer();                                   // Note 3
    Plus p = tw.new Plus(b);
    Minus m = tw.new Minus(b);
    p.start();
    m.start();
  }
}
```

Output

```
1     456250
2     4649634
3     7245105
4     12916833
5     14452346
6     23241347
7     24257947
8     29420248
9     30436644
10    36110307
```

Note 1: When the current and previous values of `number` agree, an error has occurred, and we output the number of errors and the total number of operations performed. We illustrated the error when a thread loses its turn after changing `number` but before reporting. It could also lose its turn while executing the `report` method. The point is that errors can occur due to the interleaving of execution of various threads.

Note 2: This thread keeps incrementing `number` in an unending loop. We need to abort execution manually.

Note 3: We used inner classes to make the class names local to the`TallyWrong` class. To access these classes we use an instance of `TallyWrong`.

Synchronization

To correct the problem exhibited by Example 1.18, we need to enable the `increment` and `decrement` methods to execute completely once they have begun. Java provides the **synchronized** keyword to enforce this behavior. We declare the `increment` method as

```
public synchronized void increment() {
number++;
report(number);
}
```

For example, when thread1 calls this method of the `buf` object,

```
buf.increment();
```

if no other thread is executing any method of `buf`, thread1 gets a **lock** for the object. Therefore no other thread can use `buf` until thread1 has finished executing the `increment` method. If another thread is executing a method of `buf`, then thread1 must wait until that operation completes. If several threads are waiting to get a lock on an object, the thread scheduler determines who will get it when it becomes available.

Figure 15.12 thread1 locks `buf` while thread2 waits

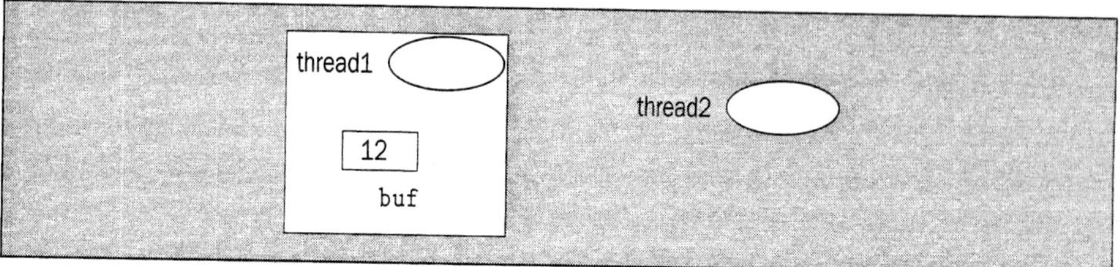

We only need make the `increment` and `decrement` methods in Example 15.12 synchronized to ensure that they work correctly when accessed by multiple threads. With synchronized methods, behavior like that shown in Figure 15.11 cannot occur because once a thread starts executing a synchronized method it is allowed to finish.

EXAMPLE 1.19 TallyRight.java

```
/* Uses synchronized methods to correct the
 * error in Example 5.12.
 */

public class TallyRight {

  // The rest of the code is the same as Example 15.12.

  public synchronized void increment() {
    number++;
    report(number);
  }
  public synchronized void decrement() {
    number--;
    report(number);
  }
}
```

Output

There is none, because no errors occur.

A LITTLE EXTRA

Synchronizing methods exacts a performance penalty. If only a portion of the code of a large method is critical, we can improve performance by only synchronizing that portion of the code. Schematically,

```
public returnType someMethod(someParameters) {
  // some code not synchronized

  synchronized(this) {
    // synchronize the critical code here
  }
```

```
  // more non-synchronized code
}
```

When a thread calls this method it will only lock the object while executing the synchronized block.

Communication

Synchronization allows threads to complete portions of code without interruption. Sometimes threads also need to communicate with one another to signal the occurrence of a condition that may affect their ability to proceed. For our example, we look at the classic **producer-consumer problem**, in which both producer threads and consumer threads access a data buffer. Producers add data to the buffer, while consumers remove it.

Assuming a fixed-size buffer, a producer cannot add more than the buffer can hold, while a consumer cannot retrieve data from an empty buffer. Each Java object has `wait` and `notify` methods which are useful in this situation.

When a producer has a lock on the buffer, and cannot add data because the buffer is full, it executes the `wait` method causing it to release the lock and wait to be notified the state of the buffer has changed. When a consumer removes an item from a full buffer, it executes the `notify` method to notify a waiting thread that the buffer is no longer full.

Similarly, when a consumer has a lock on the buffer, and cannot remove data because the buffer is empty, it executes the `wait` method causing it to release the lock and wait to be notified that the state of the buffer has changed. When a producer puts an item into an empty buffer, it executes the `notify` method to notify a waiting thread that the buffer is no longer empty.

Example 15.14 solves this producer-consumer problem. We input sleep times for each thread to see how the behavior varies depending on which thread has more time. We use one producer and one consumer thread.

EXAMPLE 15.14 PutGet.java

```
/* Uses wait and notify to enable
 * producer and consumer threads to
 * cooperate in using a buffer.
 */

public class PutGet {
  public static final int size = 3;
  class Buffer {
    int[ ] buffer = new int [size];         // the data
    int putpos = 0;                         // next position to put a value
    int getpos = 0;                         // next position to get a value
    int number = 0;                         // number of items in the buffer
```

```
  public synchronized void put(int value)
                          throws InterruptedException {       // Note 1
    if (number == size) {
      System.out.println("Cannot put -- Buffer full");
      wait();                                                 // Note 2
    }
    number++;
    buffer[putpos] = value;
    System.out.println("Put "+value);
    putpos = (putpos + 1) % size;                             // Note 3
    if (number == 1) notify();                                // Note 4
  }
  public synchronized int get() throws InterruptedException {
    if (number == 0) {
      System.out.println("Cannot get -- Buffer empty");
      wait();
    }
    number--;
    int n = buffer[getpos];
    System.out.println("Get "+n);
    getpos = (getpos + 1) % size;
    if (number == size - 1) notify();                         // Note 5
    return n;
  }
}
class Producer extends Thread {
  Buffer buf;
  int time;
  Producer(Buffer b, int t) {
    buf = b;
    time = t;
  }
  public void run() {
    for(int i = 1; i <= 10; i++)                              // Note 6
      try {
        buf.put(i);
        sleep(time);                                          // Note 7
      }catch (InterruptedException e){
        e.printStackTrace();
      }
    }
  }
class Consumer extends Thread {
  Buffer buf;
  int time;
  Consumer(Buffer b, int t) {
    buf = b;
    time = t;
  }
  public void run() {
    for (int i = 1; i <= 10;i++)
```

```
        try {
          buf.get();
          sleep(time);
      }catch (InterruptedException e) {
        e.printStackTrace();
      }
    }
  }
  public static void main(String[ ] args) {
    PutGet pg = new PutGet();
    Buffer b = pg.new Buffer();
    Producer p = pg.new Producer(b,Integer.parseInt(args[0]));
    Consumer c = pg.new Consumer(b,Integer.parseInt(args[1]));
    p.start();
    c.start();
  }
}
```

Output – from java PutGet 300 500

```
Put 1
Get 1
Put 2
Get 2
Put 3
Put 4
Get 3
Put 5
Put 6
Get 4
Put 7
Get 5
Put 8
Cannot put -- Buffer full
Get 6
Put 9
Cannot put -- Buffer full
Get 7
Put 10
Get 8
Get 9
Get 10
```

Note 1: The `wait` method may throw an `InterruptedException`, which we declare here to pass it on to the caller of the `put` method who will handle it.

Note 2: The `wait` method is a member of the `Object` class, so any object, such as a buffer in this example, may invoke it. `wait` must be invoked in a synchronized method so the thread invoking it has a lock on the object.

Note 3: We use a circular buffer. Visualizing the array as a circle shows that after filling position 2, we move to position 0 again. This formula computes indices in this way: 0, 1, 2, 0, 1, 2, ... and so on.

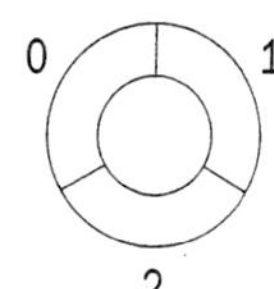

Note 4: After putting an item into an empty buffer, we call `notify`. The scheduler will notify one thread, making it ready to run. In our example, we have at most one thread waiting, so if it is waiting it will be notified that the buffer is non-empty. When more than one thread may be waiting, calling `notifyAll` will wake them all up.

Note 5: By removing an item from a full buffer, the consumer has just made it possible for a waiting producer to add an item. Calling `notify` will wake up a waiting producer.

Note 6: `for(int i = 1; i <= 10; i++)`
We let the producer produce 10 numbers, and the consumer consume these 10. We could have run these threads in an unending loop, and aborted the program manually.

Note 7: `sleep(time);`
Typically there will be some extended computation to produce the value to put in the buffer. For simplicity we sleep to simulate some computational time.

Deadlock

When threads wait for locks to be freed that cannot be freed we have **deadlock**. We can easily modify Example 15.14 to produce deadlock. If we change the condition for the producer to put only when the buffer is empty and the consumer to get only when the buffer is full we reach a deadlocked state almost immediately. The buffer starts out empty so the producer can put one item into it, but no more until the consumer removes that item, making the buffer empty again. The consumer cannot remove the one item in the buffer until the producer adds two more items to fill the buffer. Both the producer and consumer are stuck, each waiting an action by the other that can never occur.

Good programming is the only prevention for deadlock. In more complicated situations it can be very difficult to determine if deadlock can occur.

EXAMPLE 15.15 Deadlock.java

```
/* Modifies Example 15.14 to illustrate deadlock.
 */

public class Deadlock {

  // the rest of the code is the same as Example 15.14

  public synchronized void put(int value) throws InterruptedException {
    if (number != 0) {
      System.out.println("Cannot put -- Buffer not empty");
      wait();
  }
  ......
  }
  public synchronized int get() throws InterruptedException {
  if (number != size) {
    System.out.println("Cannot get -- Buffer not full");
      wait();
    }
  ......
  }
}
```

Output

```
Put 1
Cannot get -- Buffer not full
Cannot put -- Buffer not empty
```

(At this point the program hangs up because neither the producer nor the consumer can proceed.)

THE BIG PICTURE

Concurrent programming coordinates multiple threads. When threads share data we can synchronize access so that a thread using the data will be able to complete its operation before another thread gets access to that data. A thread gets a lock on the object which contains the data until it finishes the synchronized method or block.

Threads can wait on a condition, to be notified by other threads when changes occur that may make the condition satisfied. Deadlock occurs when threads wait for locks that can never be freed and no thread can proceed.

TEST YOUR UNDERSTANDING

TRY IT YOURSELF 15. Vary the sleep times when running Example 1.20, and determine how that affects the results.

TRY IT YOURSELF 16. Modify Example 1.20 to start two producers and two consumers, and explain the resulting behavior.

SUMMARY

- Java allows several threads of control to proceed simultaneously, sharing the processor. Each thread executes the code in a `run` method when it gets the processor. We can extend the `Thread` class to override the default `run` method, or another class can declare that it implements the `Runnable` interface. Such a class must implement the `run` method and pass itself to a thread that will execute its `run` method.
- Calling the `start` method of a thread makes it ready to run; when it gets the processor it will execute either its `run` method, if it is an extension of the `Thread` class, or the `run` method that a `Runnable` object passes to it otherwise. An applet often starts a thread in its `start` method, which is called by the browser or applet viewer whenever the user returns to the web page containing the applet. The best way to stop the thread is to set a flag and have the thread check the flag periodically during the execution of its `run` method. If the flag becomes **true** then the thread returns from the `run` method, terminating itself.
- A `Thread` can sleep for a specified number of milliseconds. A call to the static `sleep` method occurs in a `try` block with a `catch` clause to handle the `InterruptedException` that might be generated. We can construct a thread with a name which we can get later with the `getName` method. To get a thread that we did not create ourselves, such as the thread that runs the `main` method, we can use the static `currentThread` method of the `Thread` class.
- Animations run in threads, sharing the processor with the `main` method or the browser or applet viewer. We can run an animation in a nonterminating loop since other activities can proceed in other threads concurrently. In a simple example we display the same figure at different positions, allowing the thread to sleep for a fraction of a second between repaints of the screen. To make the animation more interesting, we change the figure before repainting it.
- We can use images and sounds in our Java programs. One approach uses the `getImage` method to obtain an image from a Swing `ImageIcon` constructed from a URL. We can specify either an absolute URL or a relative URL; using `getDocumentBase()`, we specify the path relative to the location of the document containing the applet, while using `getCodeBase()`, we specify the path relative to the location of the applet's code.
- The `drawImage` method has several versions. We use the simplest, with four arguments: the image, the `(x,y)` coordinates of the position at which to draw the image, and an `ImageObserver` which we do not use since we wait for the image to

load fully. This version of `drawImage` draws the image in its normal size. We also use the six-argument version of `drawImage` which includes two arguments representing the scaled size we prefer for the image.

- The images we animate will flicker a lot because the `repaint` method calls the `update` method, which clears the screen before calling the `paint` method to repaint the screen. The alternation of clear background and image causes the flicker. We can eliminate the flicker by the technique of double buffering. We create an offscreen image whose size is that of the applet. We override `update` to paint only, and not to clear the screen first. In the `paint` method we do all the drawing of graphics and images on the offscreen buffer. As the last step of `paint`, we draw the offscreen buffer on the screen. We can clear the offscreen image between repaints; we do not see this background, so this does not cause flicker. Swing components automatically implement double buffering.
- Java versions 1.0 and 1.1 support the AU audio format, while versions 1.2 and higher support additional formats, including Windows WAVE files. The applet class has a play method which can play a sound file specified by a URL. The applet can also get an audio clip. The `AudioClip` interface has methods to play a sound, to loop it, playing in until the `stop` method is invoked to terminate it. We can add additional threads to play sounds in the background while an animation is in progress. We can also add sounds to the thread in which the animation is running.
- Java has a `java.net` package that makes connecting to other computers easy. An applet can use the `getAppletContext` method to get the browser that called it to use the `showDocument` method to display a document specified by a URL. A standalone program can use the `getInputStream` method to read a resource specified by a URL. Such a resource may be an `HTML` file or another file type such as a Java program.
- We could use the `java.net` package to connect to one of the standard servers such as a `POP3` server from which we can get our email. We can write our own server using the accept method of the `ServerSocket` class to wait for a connection by a client. The client creates a socket specifying the address of the machine hosting the server, and the port number the server is using. The client and the server use input and output streams to communicate with one another. Further explorations of networking in Java are beyond the scope of this text.
- When threads share data we must be careful to ensure correct access. Using the keyword **synchronized** locks an object either for the duration of a method or block of code. The thread holding the lock may complete the method or block of code without interruption.
- The `wait` and `notify` methods help threads communicate. The `wait` method signals a condition is not satisfied, so the thread executing it must wait. The `notify` method wakes up one thread, signaling a condition has been satisfied. Concurrent programming requires great care to avoid problems such as deadlock where threads are unable to proceed, halting the system.

- The Java Media Framework allows Java applications and applets to display and capture multimedia data. It supports many media content types including MPEG, QuickTime, AVI, WAV, AU, and MIDI. The documentation indicates which compression formats it supports for each of these types. Using JMF, we can create a media player from within a Java program. The player generates controller events to inform a controller listener of its progress. The listener can add visual and control components to the interface and restart the clip when it finishes.

Skill Builder Exercises

1. For each method on the left, choose a property on the right that applies to it.

a. `start()` for a `Thread`	i. should not be used
b. `start()` for an `Applet`	ii. may be executed many times
c. `stop()` for a `Thread`	iii. executed once only
d. `stop()` for an `Applet`	

2. For each method on the left, choose the exception on the right that it might throw.

a. `Thread.sleep(100)`	i. none
b. `new URL("pic.gif")`	ii. `InterruptedException`
c. `url.openStream()`	iii. `MalformedURLException`
d. `clip.loop()`	iv. `IOException`

3. Match each method on the left with the class on the right of which it is a member.

a. `showDocument`	i. `Socket`
b. `loop`	ii. `AppletContext`
c. `getOutputStream`	iii. `Thread`
d. `sleep`	iv. `AudioClip`

Critical Thinking Exercises

4. To run itself in a separate thread an applet can
   a. extend the `Thread` class.
   b. implement the `Runnable` interface.
   c. either `a` or `b`.
   d. none of the above.

5. Adding the line

   `sleep(150.5)`

   to a Java program would cause an error because

   a. the argument must be an integer.

   b. the prefix `Thread.` should be used.

   c. exception handling has not been provided.

   d. none of the above.

   e. all of the above.

6. We can read from a `URL` object using the

   a. `openStream()` method.

   b. `getInputStream()` method.

   c. `openReader()` method.

   d. none of the above.

   e. all of the above.

7. We can read from a Socket object using the

   a. `openStream()` method.

   b. `getInputStream()` method.

   c. `openReader()` method.

   d. none of the above.

   e. all of the above.

Debugging Exercise

8. The following applet attempts to draw a rectangle in colors chosen at random, changing the color every two seconds. Find and correct any errors.

```
public class ColoredBoxes extends Applet {
  Color c;
  boolean done;
  public void start() {
    done = false;
    Thread t = new Thread(this);
    t.start();
  }
  public void stop() {
    done = true;
  }
  public void paint(Graphics g) {
    g.drawRect(100,100,30,30);
  }
```

```
    public void run(){
      while(! done) {
        c = new Color((int)(255*Math.random()),
                (int)(255*Math.random()), (int)(255*Math.random()));
        setForeground(c);
        Thread.sleep(200);
      }
    }
  }
```

Program Modification Exercises

9. Modify Example 15.6 to specify the sleep time as an applet parameter in the HTML file.
10. Modify Example 15.7 to specify the sleep time as an applet parameter in the HTML file.
11. Modify Example 15.5 to use double buffering to remove the flicker.
12. Modify Example 15.6 to use double buffering to remove the flicker.
13. Modify Example 15.5 to draw the ball in a color of your choice, other than black.
14. Modify Example 15.5 to draw the ball in a different color for each of the ten iterations of the loop.
15. Modify Example 15.6 to draw the eyes in one color and the mouth in another, both different from black.
16. Modify Example 15.5 so that instead of arbitrarily moving the ball ten times in each direction, we use the size of the applet, the size of the ball, and the size of the increment to determine how many times we can move the ball before it goes off the screen.
17. Modify Examples 15.13 and 15.14 to pass the port number as a program argument.
18. Modify Example 15.13 to put the `accept` statement and the code following it into a nonterminating loop, so that the server can accept another client as soon as the current client finishes.
19. Modify Example 15.13 so that the server can handle several clients simultaneously. After the server accepts a connection from the client, the server should create a separate thread to handle the communication with that client and loop back to the `accept` statement waiting for another client to connect.

Program Design Exercises

20. Write a Java applet which uses two threads, one to animate a ball, and one to animate a face. Make sure that the ball and the face do not collide.

PUTTING IT ALL TOGETHER 21. Example 8.14 provides a user interface for insertion sorting. In that example, the user inserts one element at a time, pressing a button to perform the next insertion. Write a Java program that will display the bar chart as the sorting progresses, without requiring the user to press a button to insert each item. Use a thread and let the sorting proceed, sleeping between each insertion to make it easier to view.

22. Write a Java program that displays a digital clock that shows the correct time. To get the current time, use the `getInstance()` method of the `Calendar` class, in the `java.util` package, to get a `Calendar` object, `c`. Then use the `Calendar` get method to get the hours, minutes, and seconds, as in:

```
int hour = c.get(Calendar.HOUR);
int minute = c.get(Calendar.MINUTE);
int second = c.get(Clandar.SECOND);
```

Use a thread to allow the clock to keep the correct time.

23. a. Write a Java program that moves a ball around the screen randomly. If you have access to sound, make a sound at each move. If the user clicks the mouse on the ball, increment a score showing in the corner of the screen. If the user reaches a score of 5, make the ball move faster so that it is more difficult to catch. If you are including sound, do so in a separate thread so that it does not slow the ball down. If the user reaches a score of 10 make the ball smaller.

    b. In part a, use an image of your choice instead of a ball.

24. Write an applet which provides a choice box naming several web sites. When the user makes a choice, have the browser show the document that the user has chosen.

25. Write a mail client which will connect to a POP3 server (find the address of your server) and retrieve the first message. Specify the server address, user name, and password as program arguments. The protocol of Figure 15.9 may be helpful.

26. Write a multithreaded server which will pass whatever message line it receives from a client to all the other clients that are connected. Write a client program to connect to this server, which sends its lines and receives the lines sent by the other clients.

PUTTING IT ALL TOGETHER 27. (Towers of Hanoi)
Suppose we have n disks on a peg, each of different sizes, stacked in order of size, with the largest on the bottom, and two other pegs, as shown in Figure 15.11.

Figure 15.13 The Towers of Hanoi puzzle

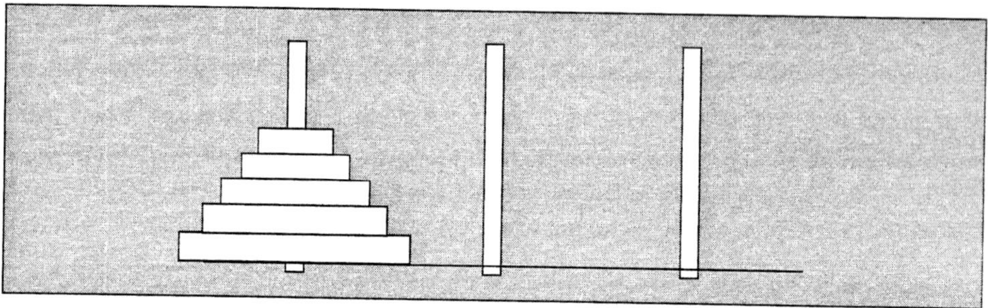

What is the sequence of moves needed to transfer the rings to the second peg, in the same configuration, in order from largest to the smallest, with the largest at the bottom, if we can move only one disk at a time, and we cannot place a larger disk on top of a smaller disk? We may use the last peg to store disks, but the same rules apply. Use a recursive method to provide the solution. To move n disks from peg 1 to peg 2, move n-1 disks to peg 3, move the bottom disk to peg 2, then move n-1 disks from peg 3 to peg 2. Use a thread to animate the solution, using various colors for the disks.

28. Create a Java application that displays the word "SUN" in larger and larger letters and then uses a media player to play the clip of solar activity from

    `http://solar.physics.montana.edu/YPOP/Movies/sun_diver.mpg`

    or another clip chosen from

    `http://www-istp.gsfc.nasa.gov/istp/outreach/movies.html/`

CHAPTER

16 Networking

OUTLINE

Introduction

Java makes it easy to connect to other computers, using classes from the `java.net` package. We first write client programs that connect to a server, which is a program that performs a task useful to its clients, and then write our own servers. A web server provides files such as web pages, Java applets, and images.

To write client programs, we first use Java classes that enable us to hide the details of the interaction between client and server. We then try classes that let us customize the connection, and present classes that give us full control of the communication, but require us then to know the details of the request and response commands.

The simplest clients connect to a server using a `URL` object, or for more flexibility, a `URLConnection` object. The `URLConnection` talks to a server using a specific protocol. We introduce HTTP, the Hypertext Transfer Protocol used to connect to a web server. Understanding HTTP allows us to customize a connection using `URLConnection` methods, and to write our own simple web client and web server using `Socket` and `ServerSocket` objects. This will enable us to develop and use our own protocols for clients and servers to communicate.

On a higher level, Remote Method Invocation (RMI) allows us to invoke objects on remote machines, introducing powerful distributed computing using Java.

OBJECTIVES:

- Use a URL to connect to a remote site from an applet or an application.
- Introduce HTTP to understand how web clients and servers communicate.
- Use `URLConnection` to customize a connection.
- Use `Socket` and `ServerSocket` objects to have full control over the communication.
- Write a very simple browser and a very simple web server.
- Use threads to enable a server to handle multiple clients.
- Introduce distributed computing using RMI.

16.1 Using a URL to Connect

Computers use **protocols** to communicate. A **client** sends requests using the commands provided by the protocol in the order specified in the protocol, and the **server** responds similarly. The `URL` class encapsulates several popular protocols, handling their details thereby making it easier for Java programmers to make network **connections** to display a page, retrieve a file, or get mail, for example.

We will describe a URL, then show how to use an applet to display a resource downloaded from a remote site. Finally we use a standalone application to make a connection using a URL.

The Uniform Resource Locator (URL)

A **URL** has four parts: the protocol name, the host address, the port, and the path to the resource file. The **port** number specifies a specific communication link between computers. For example, the full URL for Sun's Java home page is

```
http://java.sun.com:80/index.html
```

where HTTP is the protocol, `java.sun.com` is the host address, `80` is the port, and `index.html` is the path to the resource. Because `80` is the default port for the HTTP service, and `index.html` is the default file name, we can write the same URL more concisely as

```
http://java.sun.com/
```

Using the URL for Sun's Java home page, our Java client connects our machine to the web server on Sun's host machine. This server program must understand HTTP, which we will introduce in the next section. Using a URL and a `URLConnection` to write our client programs, we let Java handle the details of the messages specified by the HTTP protocol to communicate with a **web server**.

Connecting from an Applet

We can use the `URL` class in a Java applet to have the browser get and display a resource for us. We pass a string specifying a URL to the `URL` constructor, as in:

```
URL url = new URL("http://java.sun.com/");
```

for Sun's Java home page, or

```
URL myURL = new URL("http://www.cecs.csulb.edu/~artg/");
```

for the author's home page.

Each applet has a `getAppletContext()` method which returns an object that implements the `AppletContext` interface. The **applet context** is the **browser** or applet viewer that started the applet. Each object that implements the `AppletContext` interface has a `showDocument` method which will display the document specified by the `URL` object, if it is able to do so. We can use the applet context to display the resource using the `showDocument` method, as in:

```
getAppletContext().showDocument(url);
```

TIP

If the applet context is a browser, then the `showDocument` method will cause the browser to display the page requested in the `URL`. However, if the applet context is an applet viewer, then the `showDocument` method will only display the applets contained in the document, and not the rest of the page, as the applet viewer just runs applets and does not interpret HTML.

Example 16.1 shows how an applet can get the browser to display a document. We input the URL as a parameter in the HTML file to make it easier to change. The HTML file we use to run the applet of Example 16.1 is:

```
<applet code = ShowURL.class width=300 height=400>
<param name = url value = http://www.cecs.csulb.edu/~artg/>
</applet>
```

Naturally, when requesting a resource from a remote site, we must be connected to the Internet.

EXAMPLE 16.1 **ShowURL.java**

```
/* Running this applet in a browser will cause
 * the browser to display the resource specified
 * in the URL parameter in the HTML file used to run
 * the applet. The applet viewer cannot
 * show a document.
 */

import java.net.*;
import java.applet.Applet;

public class ShowURL extends Applet {
  public void init() {                                    // Note 1
    try {
      URL url = new URL(getParameter("url"));
      getAppletContext().showDocument(url);
```

```
      }catch(MalformedURLException e) {
        e.printStackTrace();
      }
    }
  }
```

Note 1: Java will throw a `MalformedURLException` if the argument to the constructor does not have the correct form for a URL.

Figure 16.1 Example 16.1 displaying a web site

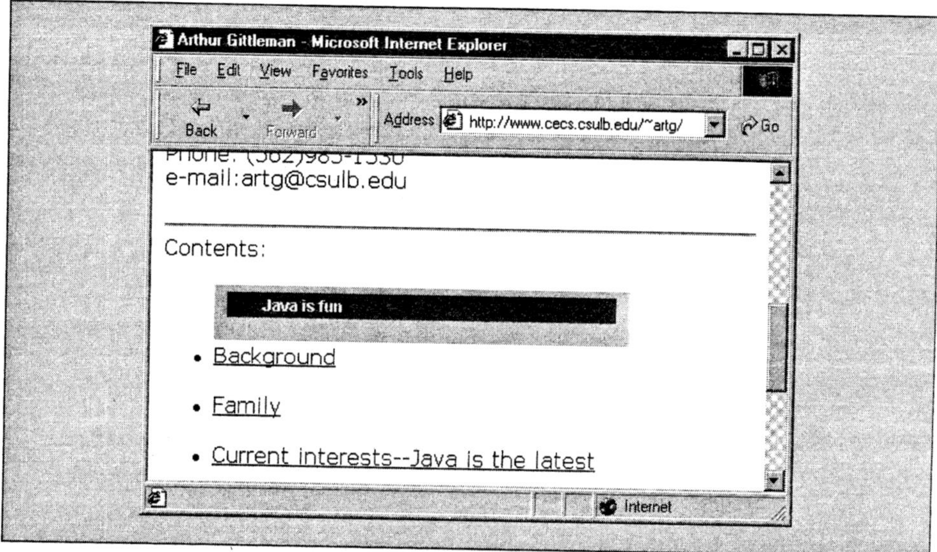

Connecting from a Standalone Application

We can use a `URL` object in a standalone program, reading characters from the resource specified by the URL. The `URL` class has a method, `openStream`, which opens a connection to the server, and allows us to read its responses to our client's request. The `openStream` method returns an `InputStream` that we pass to an `InputStreamReader` to convert the bytes to characters, and then pass the `InputStreamReader` to a `BufferedReader` to buffer the input so we can read one line at a time.

```
BufferedReader input = new BufferedReader
                 (new InputStreamReader(url.openStream()));
```

Example 16.2 reads one line at a time from the URL specified on the command line, writing each line to the screen. Our Java program is not a browser, so when we read HTML files we get output with the embedded HTML tags. Passing the program argument

```
http://java.sun.com/
```

will list the HTML file for Sun's Java home page.* Most files that we access on web servers are HTML files, but we can get other types of files too. Passing the program argument

```
http://www.cecs.csulb.edu/~artg/TryURL.java/
```

will connect to the web server at the California State University Long Beach, Engineering and Computer Science department, retrieving the source code file, `TryURL.java`. We could read a file from the local machine passing a file URL as a program argument, as in:

```
file:///java/TryURL.java/
```

where the file `TryURL.java` is in the directory `c:\java` on a Windows system.† Leaving the host name empty defaults to **localhost**, which is the user's machine rather than a remote host. Including localhost, as in,

```
file://localhost/java/TryURL.java/
```

gives the same URL.

TIP

Use forward slashes in writing URLs, even on Windows machines for which the default separator is the backslash.

EXAMPLE 16.2 TryURL.java

```
/* Displays the resource specified by the URL
 * entered on the command line.
 */

import java.net.*;
import java.io.*;

public class TryURL {
  public static void main(String[] args) {
    BufferedReader input;
    try {
      URL url = new URL(args[0]);
      input = new BufferedReader
        (new InputStreamReader(url.openStream()));
      String s;
      while ((s = input.readLine()) != null)
        System.out.println(s);

      input.close();
```

---

* Using the JDK we enter the URL on the command line,
`java TryURL http://java.sun.com/.`

† On Windows systems, we could include the drive letter, as for example
`file:///c:/java/TryURL.java/`

```
    }catch(Exception e) {                                   // Note 1
      e.printStackTrace();
    }
  }
}
```

Output

(The output will display the contents of any file we pass as the program argument. Passing

`http://www.cecs.csulb.edu/~artg/TryURL.java/`

will display the code for this example.)

Note 1: The `URL` constructor may throw a `MalformedURLException`, and the `readLine` method may throw an `IOException`. We could write a catch clause for each, but we are not taking the trouble to do anything special for these exceptions so we just catch the superclass `Exception` which is the parent of both of these exceptions. If Java throws either a `MalformedURLException` or an `IOException`, control will jump here to print the stack trace and the message indicating which exception occurred.

THE BIG PICTURE

Network clients and servers communicate using protocols. The `URL` class hides the details of some popular protocols, letting us make connections more easily. An applet can ask its context, the browser, to show a document. A standalone client uses streams to send data to the servers and receive its response. A URL consists of a protocol, a server address, a port, and a path to the resource.

TEST YOUR UNDERSTANDING

TRY IT YOURSELF 1. Try using an applet viewer, rather than a browser, to run Example 16.1. What is the result?

TRY IT YOURSELF 2. Use Example 16.2 to display the file `TryURL.java`. Use a file URL to get the program from the local disk. For example, using Windows, if the file is in the directory `c:\java`, use the URL `file:///c:/java/TryURL.java`

TRY IT YOURSELF 3. Use Example 16.2 to connect to the author's home page, `http://www.cecs.csulb.edu/~artg/`. Explain the result.

16.2 Protocols with a URLConnection

The `URLConnection` class makes a connection using a URL, but it adds methods for us to customize the connection and get its properties. It still hides the details of the protocol, while giving the programmer more control.

The Hypertext Transfer Protocol (HTTP)*

We used the **HTTP** protocol for our URL in Example 16.1, and suggested the HTTP or file protocols for the URL in Example 16.2. Java supports other protocols, including FTP (File Transfer Protocol) and `mailto`, when connecting using a URL, but here we concentrate on HTTP. Each protocol allows a formal exchange of messages using well-specified formats. Before going further with networking we describe HTTP, which we will use when customizing a `URLConnection`, and when writing our own HTTP client and server.

An HTTP client sends a **request** to the server in which the first line has the form

```
Method used     Identifier for the resource     Protocol version
```

The following lines of the request are various **request headers** which provide information about the capabilities of the client. After the request headers comes the data (if any) to be sent to the server. Figure 16.2, obtained using the HeaderServer program of Example 16.7, shows the request sent by the Java client of Example 16.2 when we pass it the argument

```
http://www.cecs.csulb.edu/~artg/TryURL.java
```

Figure 16.2 The HTTP client request from Example 16.2

```
GET /~artg/TryURL.java HTTP/1.0
User-Agent: Java1.3.0
Host: www.cecs.csulb.edu:80
Accept: text/html, image/gif, image/jpeg, *; q=.2, */*; q=.2
Connection: keep-alive
```

In the first line of Figure 16.2, `GET` is the method used; we are asking the server to get us a file. The path to that file is the second part of that first line, while the protocol, HTTP/1.0, is the third.

The next four lines of Figure 16.2 are request headers of the form

```
name: value
```

* See `http://www.w3.org/` for the complete HTTP specification.

They are:

Field	Description
User-Agent	Indicates that Java 1.3.0 is running our client.
Host	Identifies the server.
Accept	Specifies the types of files that the client is prepared to accept. Each type has a preference associated with it given by the value of q (for "quality"). This value ranges from a low of 0 to the default of 1. The three types* text/html, image/gif, and image/jpeg have the highest preference (the default of q=1 is not shown). If the server cannot send these types, then the client will accept any type, denoted by *, or any subtype of any type, denoted by */*. These latter generic types have preferences of q=.2.
Connection	Specifies the type of connection. Here keep-alive expresses the client's wish to keep the connection alive for multiple requests.

* The type names are MIME (Multipurpose Internet Mail Extensions) types.

Our Java client has sent a request followed by four request headers selected from various header types available. We will see in the next section how to determine the client's request, and will see that different clients such as Netscape and Internet Explorer send different request headers to the server.

An HTTP server responds to a request with a **status line** followed by various **response headers**. The status line has the form

```
HTTP Version     Status Code     Reason
```

We will use Example 16.3 to find the server's response to a request. Figure 16.3 shows the server's response to the client request of Figure 16.2.

Figure 16.3 The HTTP server response

```
Status line:
  HTTP/1.0 200 Document follows
Response headers:
  Date: Mon, 07 Dec 1998 21:12:05 GMT
  Server: NCSA/1.4.2
  Content-type: text/plain
  Last-modified: Wed, 11 Feb 1998 19:19:01 GMT
  Content-length: 439
```

The server sends a status line showing the HTTP version, 1.0 in this example, a code, 200, and the reason for the code, `Document follows`.

The response headers are:

Field	Description
Date	Gives the day and Greenwich Mean Time.
Server	Names the web server used.
Content-type	Describes the content. (Here `text/plain` for a Java program.
Content-length	Number of bytes in the file.

As we shall see in Example 16.3, other servers use different response headers.

A LITTLE EXTRA ➪

Status codes have five types, distinguished by their first digit. Some are:

Success	200	OK
Redirection	301	Moved Permanently
Client Error	400	Bad Request
	404	Not Found
	406	Not Acceptable

Using a URLConnection

Using a URL we can download a file. For more flexibility, we can use a `URLConnection` to set some capabilities of a connection, including the client request header fields, and to retrieve the server response status and headers.

We implicitly used a `URLConnection` in Example 16.2 because the URL `openStream` method is supplied by Java as a convenient shorthand for

```
openConnection().getInputStream()
```

where `openConnection` is a `URL` method that returns a `URLConnection` whose `getInputStream` method returns an `InputStream` to the caller. By using `URLConnection` explicitly, we can use the other `URLConnection` methods.

To get the names of the response header fields that the server sends, we use the `getHeaderFieldKey` method, and to get the field value we use `getHeaderField`. The first field returned is the status line.

EXAMPLE 16.3 GetResponses.java

```
/* Uses a URLConnection to find the response status
 * and headers sent by the server.
 */

import java.net.*;
import java.io.*;


public class GetResponses {
  public static void main(String[] args) {
    try {
      URL url = new URL(args[0]);
      URLConnection c = url.openConnection();                    // Note 1
      System.out.println("Status line: ");
      System.out.println('\t' + c.getHeaderField(0));            // Note 2
      System.out.println("Response headers:");
      String value = "";
      int n = 1;
      while (true){                                              // Note 3
        value = c.getHeaderField(n);
        if (value == null) break;
        System.out.println('\t' + c.getHeaderFieldKey(n++) + ": " + value);
      }
    }catch(Exception e) {
      e.printStackTrace();
    }
  }
}
```

Output – Connecting to http://www.cecs.csulb.edu/~artg/TryURL.java

See Figure 16.3

Output – Connecting to http://java.sun.com/

```
Status line:
  HTTP/1.1 200 OK
Response headers:
  Date: Mon, 07 Dec 1998 21:14:55 GMT
  Server: Apache/1.3.3 (Unix)
  Connection: close
  Content-Type: text/html
```

Output – Connecting to http://ibm.com/

```
Status line:
  HTTP/1.0 200 IBM-Planetwide Document OK
Response headers:
  MIME-Version: 1.0
  Server: Domino-Go-Webserver/4.6
  Title: IBM Corporation
  Date: Mon, 07 Dec 1998 21:17:45 GMT
  Last-modified: Mon, 07 Dec 1998 21:17:45 GMT
  Connection: keep-alive
  Expires: Tue, 08 Dec 1998 01:17:45 GMT
  Window-target: _top
  Vary: User-agent
  Reply-to: webmaste@us.ibm.com
  Content-type: text/html
  Content-Language: en-us
  Content-Length: 9919
```

Note 1: In contrast to Examples 16.1 and 16.2, we explicitly open a `URLConnection`. With its various methods we can customize a connection as we shall see in Example 16.4.

Note 2: We use the `getHeaderField` method that takes an integer argument which is the number of the header in the order sent by the server. Given the argument `0`, `getHeaderField` returns the status line sent by the server.

Note 3: The loop continues indefinitely until `getHeaderField` returns a **null** value, which it does when there is no header with number `n`.

In the output from the second run of Example 16.3 we see that the Sun server sends a `Connection: close` response header meaning that it closes the connection after each response. It sends `Content-type: text/html` because we have requested its Java home page which is an HTML file.

The IBM server, in the third run, includes an `Expires` response with an expiration date. This is to aid the client in using a **cache** to store the response. If we connect again to IBM's home page, we can save the time and effort of downloading that HTML file again by using the file that we saved in the cache the last time we browsed IBM's site. However when reading the cache, the client should connect with IBM's web server again if the date is later than the expiration date. By including an `Expires` response header, the server advises the client when it might be necessary to download a fresh copy of the file.

The `Vary` response header states the file the server returns may vary based on the fields indicated, in this case `User-agent`. IBM might have versions customized for particular browsers which do not always display HTML files in the same way.

The `Content-Language` header describes the language for the intended audience for the response, using first a language abbreviation such as "en" for English, and then a country code such as us for United States, to represent a dialect of the language.

A LITTLE EXTRA

The language abbreviations are registered with the International Standards Organization (ISO-639). Some abbreviations are:

Chinese	zh
French	fr
German	de
Greek	el
Spanish	sp

The country codes follow ISO-3166. Some country codes are:

Canada	CA
China	CN
Germany	DE
Great Britain	GB
Greece	GR
Spain	ES
Switzerland	CH
Taiwan	TW

In Example 16.3, we used the generic `getHeaderField` method to list all the response headers sent by the server. We can also get response headers using their names, as in

```
getHeaderField("Content-length")
```

The `URLConnection` class has separate methods for the most common header requests, so we could also get the content length using

```
getContentLength()
```

which returns -1 if the server does not send a Content-length response.

We can use the `setRequestProperty` method to customize the request headers sent by the client. For example,

```
setRequestProperty("Accept", "text/plain");
```

would indicate a client preference for a plain text file. The server should send a 406 (not acceptable) status code if it cannot supply an entity of that type for the request, but it is not required to do so.

Example 16.4 modifies Example 16.2 to use a `URLConnection` explicitly, using some of the `URL` methods to customize the connection and get information about the response.

TIP

When requesting a large file, the response will scroll out of the command window. In many operating systems we can redirect the output to a file. For example, the command

```
java TryURLConnect http://java.sun.com/ text/html
```

causes the output of the response to scroll out of the window, but

```
java TryURLConnect http://java.sun.com/ text/html >out
```

writes the output to a file named `out` which we can read using a text editor. In Windows, we can use the `MSDOS, Properties` menu to increase the height of the command window.

EXAMPLE 16.4 TryURLConnect.java

```
/* Displays the resource specified by the URL passed as the
 * first program argument, with the MIME types acceptable for
 * the response passed as the second program argument.
 * Uses URLConnection methods.
 */
import java.net.*;
import java.io.*;
import java.util.*;

public class TryURLConnect {
  public static void main(String[] args) {
    BufferedReader input;
    try {
      URL url = new URL(args[0]);
      URLConnection c = url.openConnection();
      c.setRequestProperty("Accept", args[1]);                   // Note 1
      input = new BufferedReader
          (new InputStreamReader(c.getInputStream()));
      String s;
      while ((s = input.readLine()) != null)
        System.out.println(s);
      input.close();
      System.out.println();
      System.out.println("Content type: " + c.getContentType());
      System.out.println("Content length: " + c.getContentLength()); // Note 2
      System.out.println("Length using getHeaderField: "
                    + c.getHeaderField("Content-length"));       // Note 3
    }catch(Exception e) {
      e.printStackTrace();
    }
  }
}
```

Output – arguments http://www.cecs.csulb.edu/~artg/TryURL.java text/plain
(The file of Example 16, not shown)

```
Content type: text/plain
Content length: 439
Length using getHeaderField: 439
```

Output—arguments http://www.cecs.csulb.edu/~artg/ShowURL.java text/plain
(The file of Example 1, not shown)

```
Content type: text/plain
Content length: 305
Length using getHeaderField: 305
```

Output—arguments http://java.sun.com/ text/html
(Sun's HTML file for its Java home page, not shown)

```
Content type: text/html
Content length: -1
Length using getHeaderField: null
```

Output—arguments http://ibm.com/ text/html
(IBM's HTML file for its home page, not shown)

```
Content type: text/html
Content length: 9924
Length using getHeaderField: 9924
```

Note 1: Passing `text/plain` as a program argument will change the client's default `Accept` request header to request `text/plain`. We could use the `setRequestProperty` method to set any of the client's request headers.

Note 2: In Example 16.3 we listed the response headers actually sent by the server. Here when we ask for the content length, the server may not have sent it, in which case the method returns -1.

Note 3: This version of the `getHeaderField` returns a response header for the field name passed as its argument. Its return value has type `String` so if the server has not sent any header for that field, it returns **null**.

THE BIG PICTURE

Using HTTP to communicate with a web server, the client sends a request followed by various request headers giving information about the client. The server responds with a status line and various response headers describing the server and the response. The `URLConnection` class still hides the details of the protocol, but allows us to customize the request and inquire about the response.

TEST YOUR UNDERSTANDING

4. For the `Accept` request header given by

   `Accept: text/plain; q=0.5, text/html, application/zip; q=0.8, image/gif`

   which two file types are most preferred, which is next, and which is least preferred.

TRY IT YOURSELF 5. Rewrite Example 16.2 to explicitly use `URLConnection` rather than implicitly using it via the `openStream` method.

TRY IT YOURSELF 6. Use Example 16.3 to connect to five different web sites, in addition to those tried in the text.

TRY IT YOURSELF 7. In Example 16.4 use the `getHeaderField` method to get the content type instead of `getContentType`.

16.3 Clients and Servers Using Sockets

The `URL` and `URLConnection` classes hide the details of a few common protocols, most importantly HTTP, so we can easily write programs to connect to a web server, for example. With the `Socket` and `ServerSocket` classes, we can write clients and servers using existing protocols, and develop our own protocols for communicating between client and server. After introducing ports, through which we connect, we use our own protocol, writing both a server and a client to illustrate the use of **sockets**. Finally, we use the HTTP protocol to write a server which echoes the requests sent by the client.

Server Ports

Each server listens on a numbered port. The system servers use port numbers below 1024; we can use higher numbered ports for our servers. The familiar services use standard port numbers. For example web servers usually use port 80, **SMTP** servers (Simple Mail Transfer Protocol) for sending mail use port 25, and **POP3** servers (Post Office Protocol-version3) for receiving mail use port 110.

We could use Java to write a client to connect to a system server. For example we could get our email by writing a client for a POP3 server. In writing such a client we would have to follow the Post Office Protocol-version 3 which specifies the form of the communication between the client and the server. Figure 16.4 shows sample interaction between a client and a POP3 server.

Figure 16.4 Interacting with the POP3 server

```
Server:   +OK POP3 server ready,      // server responds welcome
Client:   USER username               // client sends user's name
Server:   +OK                         // server responds OK
Client:   PASS password               // client sends the password
Server:   +OK 23 messages 3040 octets // server sends message info
Client:   RETR 23                     // asks for message 23
Server:   text of message 23, ending
          with a '.' alone on a line
Client:   QUIT
```

A Client-Server Example

If we write our own server we can use our own protocol for communicating with a client. We write a very simple server which reverses the text that the client sends it. Figure 16.5 shows the client window and the server window.

Figure 16.5 `ReverseClient` **and** `ReverseServer`

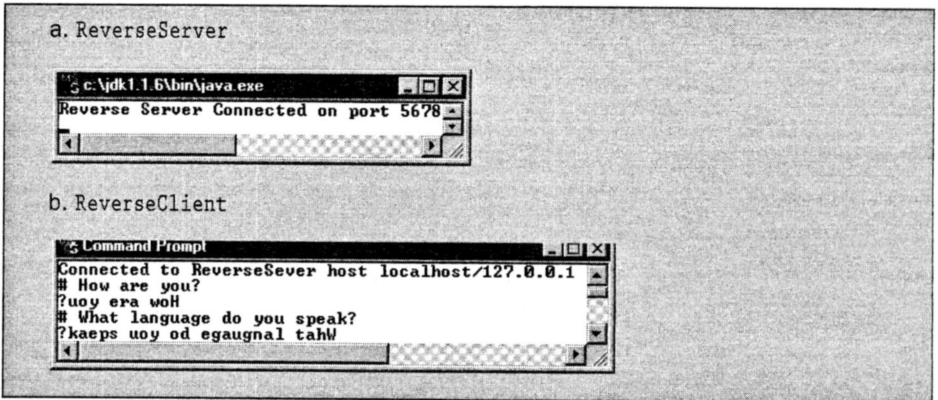

Java provides a `Socket` class for the client to connect to a server on a specific port, and a `ServerSocket` class for the server to listen for clients who wish to make a connection. Once the client connects with the server, they use the reader and writer classes to send and receive data to and from one another. Example 16.5 shows the code for a server that reverses whatever the client sends it.

We choose an arbitrary port number, 5678, on which our server will listen. The `accept` method waits for a client to make a connection. When a client connects, the `accept` method returns a client socket and our server prints a message announcing the connection. The client socket has a `getInputStream` method which the server uses to create a `BufferedReader` to read from the client. The server uses the client's `getOuput-Stream` method to create a `PrintWriter` to write to the client. The server reads one line at a time from the client, reversing it and sending it back.

EXAMPLE 16.5 ReverseServer.java

```
/* Listens on port 5678. When a client connects, the server
 * reverses whatever the client sends, and sends it back.
 */

import java.net.*;
import java.io.*;


public class ReverseServer {
  public static void main(String [] args) {
    String s;    // the string to reverse
```

```
    int size;   // the length of the string
    char[] c;   // the reversed characters
    try {
      ServerSocket server = new ServerSocket(5678);            // Note 1
      Socket client = server.accept();                         // Note 2
      BufferedReader input = new BufferedReader
            (new InputStreamReader(client.getInputStream()));
      PrintWriter output = new PrintWriter
            (client.getOutputStream(),true);                   // Note 3
      while ((s = input.readLine()) != null){
        size = s.length();
        c = new char[size];                                    // Note 4
        for (int i = 0; i < size; i++)
          c[i] = s.charAt(size - 1 - i);                       // Note 5
        output.println(c);                                     // Note 6
      }
      input.close();
      output.close();
      client.close();
    }catch(Exception e) {
      e.printStackTrace();
    }
  }
}
```

Note 1: We create a server to listen for connections on port 5678.

Note 2: The `accept` statement blocks any further progress in the program until a client connects; it then returns the client socket.

Note 3: We set the second argument to the `PrintWriter` constructor to **true** so `println` statements will flush the output, rather than waiting until the buffer fills up.

Note 4: We cannot change a `String` object, so we create an array of characters to hold the reverse of the line the client inputs. We could also have used a `StringBuffer` object which is like a `String` but allows changes.

Note 5: We use the `charAt` method to get the character which is `i` positions from the right end of the string and copy it into element `i` of the `char` array.

Note 6: `output.println(c);`
The array `c` contains the reversed characters of the string sent by the client. We send these reversed characters back to the client.

We can run the server on the same machine as the client or on a different machine.* The server does not terminate until we abort it, so we should run it in the back-

* When running a server on the same machine as the client in Windows, the machine does not need to be connected to the Internet, but the TCP/IP protocol should be installed. (Click on the *Start* button, *Settings*, *Control Panel*, *Network* icons, then *Protocol* tab to check the installed protocols.)

ground in its own thread, and we can do other things while it is waiting for clients to connect.* Figure 16.5 shows the client and server running on the same machine. The client connects using the address of the host which we pass as a program argument. The name localhost denotes the local machine so the client connects to the server on the same machine with the command

```
java ReverseClient localhost
```

Using two machines, we would have started the server on one machine and let the client connect to it using the server's name or its **IP address**†. We usually refer to machines by their names, as for example, `www.cecs.csulb.edu`, but underlying each name is a four byte IP (Internet Protocol) address, as for example 134.139.67.68. (The local machine, named localhost, has the IP address 127.0.0.1.) In connecting in a small lab, whose computers are linked to the Internet, we may just use these basic IP addresses. If we start ReverseServer on machine 134.139.67.68, we would connect to the server from another machine using the command

```
java ReverseClient 134.139.67.68.
```

The client creates a socket using the port, 5678, on which the server is listening. The client uses the `getInetAddress` method of the socket to display the address of the host to which it is connected. As in the server of Example 16.5, the client and the server use readers and writers to communicate with each other. The client uses the `getInputStream` method of the socket to create a `BufferedReader` to read from the server, and uses the `getOutputStream` method of the socket to create a `PrintWriter` to write to the server. The client also creates a `BufferedReader` to get the input from the user.

The client enters a loop printing a prompt, getting a line from the user, sending it to the server, getting the reversed line from the server, and displaying it on the screen, exiting when the user signals the end of input (Control + Z in Windows). Example 16.6 shows the client program which connects to a server that reverses its input.

EXAMPLE 16.6 ReverseClient.java

```
/* Connects to a server which reverses whatever
 * the user inputs. Specifies the host of the
 * server on the command line.
 */

import java.net.*;
import java.io.*;
```

* Using the JDK, in Windows systems, use the start command to run the server in the background: `start java ReverseServer`. On Unix systems, run in the background using the command `java ReverseServer &`. If using an integrated development environment, use separate projects for the server and client, running the server first.

† The IP address is actually associated with a network interface card.

```
public class ReverseClient {
  public static void main(String[] args) {
    String s; // the string to reverse
    if (args.length != 1){                                   // Note 1
      System.out.println("Pass the server's address");
      System.exit(1);
    }


    try {
      Socket server = new Socket(args[0],5678);              // Note 2
      System.out.println("Connected to ReverseServer host "
                          + server.getInetAddress());

      BufferedReader fromServer = new BufferedReader
               (new InputStreamReader(server.getInputStream()));
      PrintWriter toServer = new PrintWriter
               (server.getOutputStream(),true);
      BufferedReader input = new BufferedReader(
               new InputStreamReader(System.in));
      while (true) {
        System.out.print("# ");
        System.out.flush();
        if ((s=input.readLine()) == null)
          break;
        toServer.println(s);
        System.out.println(fromServer.readLine());
      }
      fromServer.close();
      toServer.close();
      input.close();
      server.close();
    }catch(Exception e) {
      e.printStackTrace();
    }
  }
}
```

Note 1: We check that the user passed the address of the server's host machine as a program argument. If not, we abort the program with a message indicating the omission.

Note 2: The client creates a socket connection to the server on port 5678, the port on which the server is listening.

A Request Header Server

While `ReverseServer` (Example 16.5) works fine when connected to by `ReverseClient` (Example 16.6), we will see it does not respond properly to an HTTP client such as our `TryURL` program of Example 16.2. `ReverseServer` does not respond properly to

`TryURL` because it does not follow HTTP. We modify it, producing a server, `HeaderServer`, that echoes the lines sent by the client.

We used `ReverseClient` to connect to `ReverseServer`, but we can use other clients to connect to `ReverseServer`. Using our `TryURL` client using the command

```
java TryURL http://localhost:5678/~artg/TryURL.java
```

gives the result shown in Figure 16.6.

Figure 16.6 Connecting to ReverseServer using `TryURL`

```
Command Prompt - java TryURL http://localhost:5678/~artg/TryURL.java
H avaj.LRUyrT/gtra~/ TEG
6.1.1avaJ :tnegA-resU
8765:tsohlacol :tsoH
2.=q ;*/* ,2.=q ;* ,gepj/egami ,fig/egami ,lmth/txet :tpeccA
evila-peek :noitcennoC
```

We wrote the `TryURL` program to connect to a server and request it to send us a file. `TryURL` does not send any user data to the server; it only sends its request headers. `ReverseServer` reverses those headers and sends them back to the client which displays them as if they were the sought after file. Thus Figure 16.6 looks almost like Figure 16.2, except in reverse, of course, because `ReverseServer` dutifully reverses everything sent to it before sending it back.

One difference is minor. Line 3 (reversed so that we can read it) shows the host as localhost:5678 because we connected to our `ReverseServer` on the local machine rather than to a web server at a remote site. The important difference is in the first line which is shortened in Figure 16.6 to

```
H avaj.LRUyrT/gtra~/ TEG
```

which reversed is `GET /~artg/TryURL.java H`.

The explanation for this mysterious shortening is that the client, `TryURL`, is using HTTP, and expects the server to follow that protocol. A web server should send the status line, any response headers, and then a blank line to signal the beginning of file to the client. The browser, or other web client, such as `TryURL`, uses the response headers internally but does not display them. It waits for the blank line, using the header information it received to appropriately display what follows the blank line.

`ReverseServer`, not using HTTP, does not send a blank line. This confuses `TryURL` which discards the first seven characters of the first line of data sent by `ReverseServer`. The first line that `TryURL` sent was the request, and we see in the result that the first seven characters, 0.1/PTT, of the reversed request line are missing from Figure 16.6.

By modifying `ReverseServer`, we can make a very simple server to show us the request and headers that an HTTP client sends. We send a status line

```
HTTP/1.0 200 OK
```

and the single response header

```
Content-type: text/plain
```

then send a blank line before sending any data to the client. We no longer want to reverse what the client sends, so we can remove the code from `ReverseServer` that does the reversing. Rather than trying to satisfy the client's request, our server will return to the client whatever it sent. An HTTP client sends a request and perhaps some request headers, so this is what the server will return.

Figure 16.7 A Netscape client connected to `HeaderServer`*

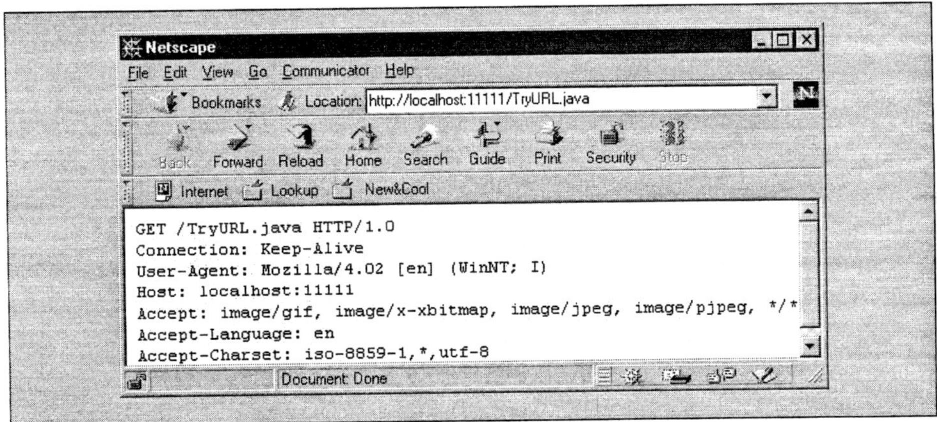

* Use the command `start java HeaderServer 11111`, where `11111` is the port number, to start header server running in the background in Windows. This server will terminate after one client connects.

Because the server indicates that every file has type `text/plain`, Internet Explorer, when connecting to `HeaderServer`, pops up a Notepad editor window, shown in Figure 16.8, to display the text.

Figure 16.8 An Internet Explorer client connected to `HeaderServer`

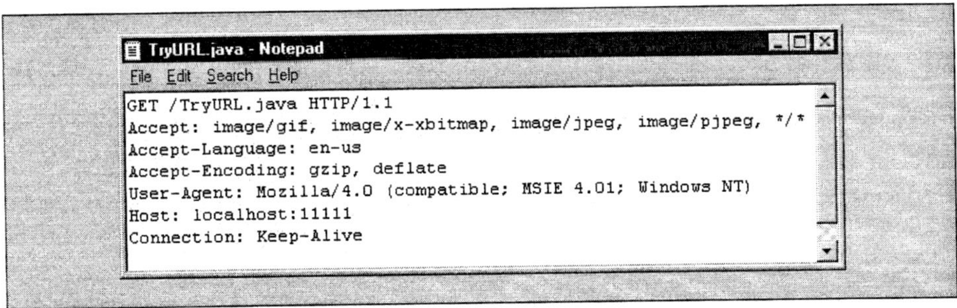

We see that each client has its own variants of the request headers that it sends to the server.

EXAMPLE 16.7 HeaderServer.java

```
/* When an HTTP client connects, the server sends
 * the client's request and its request headers back to it.
 */

import java.net.*;
import java.io.*;


public class HeaderServer {
  public static void main(String[] args) {
    String s;
    try {
      ServerSocket server = new ServerSocket(Integer.parseInt(args[0]));
      Socket client = server.accept();
      System.out.println("Header Server Connected on port " + args[0]);
      BufferedReader fromClient = new BufferedReader
          (new InputStreamReader(client.getInputStream()));
      PrintWriter toClient = new PrintWriter
          (client.getOutputStream(), true);
      toClient.println("HTTP/1.0 200 OK");                           // Note 1
      toClient.println("Content-type: text/plain");                  // Note 2
      toClient.println();
      while (!(s = fromClient.readLine()) .equals("")){              // Note 3
        toClient.println(s);
      }
      fromClient.close();
      toClient.close();
      client.close();
    }catch(Exception e) {
      e.printStackTrace();
    }
  }
}
```

Output from `java TryURL http://localhost:11111/TryURL.java.`
(See also Figures 7 and 8)

```
GET /TryURL.java HTTP/1.0
User-Agent: Java1.3.0
Host: localhost:11111
Accept: text/html, image/gif, image/jpeg, *; q=.2, */*; q=.2
Connection: keep-alive
```

Note 1: A web server must send a status line to the client which reflects the status of the request. For simplicity, we always send the code 200 meaning OK even though we make no attempt to serve the file requested. We leave improvements to the server to the exercises. Were we to omit sending the status line, HTTP clients would drop some characters from the response.

Note 2: If we do not send this header to the client, then both Netscape and Internet Explorer run all the headers together in a long line rather than displaying each header on a separate line as we see in Figures 16.7 and 16.8. This shows that HTTP clients use the response headers sent by the server to display the requested resource.

Note 3: We check for the empty string instead of **null**. The `ReverseClient` user sends an end-of-file which terminates `ReverseServer`. `TryURL` sends a request and then request headers terminated by an empty line, but not an end-of-file.

THE BIG PICTURE

Using a `Socket` to connect gives the most flexibility, but both client and server must follow the appropriate protocol. When writing our own server, we can define the protocol by which client and server communicate. The server creates a `ServerSocket` and uses an `accept` statement to wait for a client to connect.

TEST YOUR UNDERSTANDING

TRY IT YOURSELF 8. Start the `ReverseServer` of Example 16.5. Connect to it with a client. After sending some strings for the server to reverse, send an end-of-file to the server. What happens to the client and the server programs? In the Exercises we will suggest modifications to the `ReverseServer` to change this behavior.

TRY IT YOURSELF 9. Revise Example 16.7 to omit sending the status line to the client. What error occurs in the result?

TRY IT YOURSELF 10. Revise Example 16.7 to omit the `Content-type` response header. How does the output change when using either Netscape or Internet Explorer as the client?

16.4 Browsers and Web Servers

A browser is an HTTP client, which may use other protocols, while a web server is an HTTP server. In this section we write a very simple browser and a very simple web server, leaving to the exercises many improvements to make them more functional. We conclude with a threaded web server, which can handle multiple clients connected simultaneously.

A Very Simple Browser

An HTTP client sends a request to the server followed by request headers and a blank line. It then reads the status line, response headers, and the requested file from the server. A browser typically can handle several types of files, the most important being HTML files which define web pages. The browser has to interpret the HTML tags to guide it in displaying the page. With so many file types to handle, and such intricate processing necessary for web pages, a useful browser is not a small or simple undertaking. Our very simple browser just handles plain text files.

Figure 16.9 shows `VerySimpleBrowser` connecting to the author's web site to download a file using the command

```
java VerySimpleBrowser www.cecs.csulb.edu 80 /~artg/TryURL.java
```

where 80 is the standard HTTP port on which the server is running. An alternative approach would pass a URL, as in the command

```
java VerySimpleBrowser http://www.cecs.csulb.edu/~artg/TryURL.java
```

and use the URL methods `getFile`, `getHost`, and `getProtocol`, which each return a `String`, and `getPort`, which returns an **int**, to break the URL into the parts needed in Example 16.8.

Figure 16.9 `VerySimpleBrowser` **downloads a file**

```
Command Prompt
D:\book3\gittleman\ch2>java VerySimpleBrowser www.cecs.csulb.edu 80 /~artg/TryUR
L.java
Connected to host www.cecs.csulb.edu/134.139.4.17
import java.net.*;
import java.io.*;

public class TryURL {
  public static void main(String [] args) {
    BufferedReader input;
    try {
      URL url = new URL(args[0]);
      input = new BufferedReader(new InputStreamReader(url.openStream()));
      String s;
      while ((s=input.readLine())!= null)
        System.out.println(s);
    }catch(Exception e) {
        e.printStackTrace();
    }
  }
>
```

`VerySimpleBrowser` always sends a `GET` request, and a `Host` request header. It ignores the status line and response headers sent by the server, rather than trying to use them to get information that would help it to display the requested resource.

EXAMPLE 16.8 VerySimpleBrowser

```
/* Connects to a web server to download a text file.
 * Exercises suggest extensions to handle other file types.
 */

import java.net.*;
import java.io.*;

public class VerySimpleBrowser {
  public static void main(String[] args) {
    String s;
    if (args.length != 3){
```

```
      System.out.println("Usage: java VerySimpleBrowser host port file");
      System.exit(1);
    }
    try {
      int port = Integer.parseInt(args[1]);                          // Note 1
      Socket server = new Socket(args[0],port);
      System.out.println("Connected to host "
          + server.getInetAddress());
      BufferedReader fromServer = new BufferedReader
          (new InputStreamReader(server.getInputStream()));
      PrintWriter toServer = new PrintWriter
          (server.getOutputStream(),true);
      toServer.println("GET " + args[2] + " HTTP/1.0");             // Note 2
      toServer.println("Host: " + args[0]+ ':' + args[1]);
      toServer.println();
      while (!(s = fromServer.readLine()).equals(""));               // Note 3
      while ((s = fromServer.readLine()) != null)                    // Note 4
        System.out.println(s);
      fromServer.close();
      toServer.close();
      server.close();
    }catch(Exception e) {
      e.printStackTrace();
    }
  }
}
```

Note 1: The standard HTTP port is 80, but some servers use 8080. We run our simple web server on port 11111. The user should pass the server port number as the second program argument.

Note 2: We use the path to the resource, `/~artg/TryURL.java` in Figure 2.9, sending the host address and port in a separate `Host` header. Alternatively, we could have sent the `GET` command
`GET www.cecs.csulb.edu:80/~artg/TryURL.java HTTP/1.0`

Note 3: We read and ignore the status line and headers sent by the server, looking for the blank line that signals the end of the headers and the start of the file we requested. We leave it to the exercises to improve the browser to make use of this information.

Note 4: This loop reads the file we requested from the server, displaying it in the command window. Extending this very simple browser to display HTML would use graphics extensively.

A Very Simple Web Server

An HTTP server reads the request from the client, any headers, and in some cases additional data. It sends a status line followed by headers and the requested resource, if any. Web servers often transmit data from the client to other programs for processing before returning results to the client. Our very simple web server only responds to `GET` requests, and only serves text files. We leave it to the exercises to add features to make this server more functional.

To start `VerySimpleWebServer`, we use the command

```
start java VerySimpleWebServer 11111
```

which, on Windows systems, starts the server in a new window. Figure 16.10 shows Netscape connecting to `VerySimpleWebServer` to download a file. We could also have used `VerySimpleBrowser` as the client.

Figure 16.10 A Netscape client connecting to `VerySimpleWebServer`

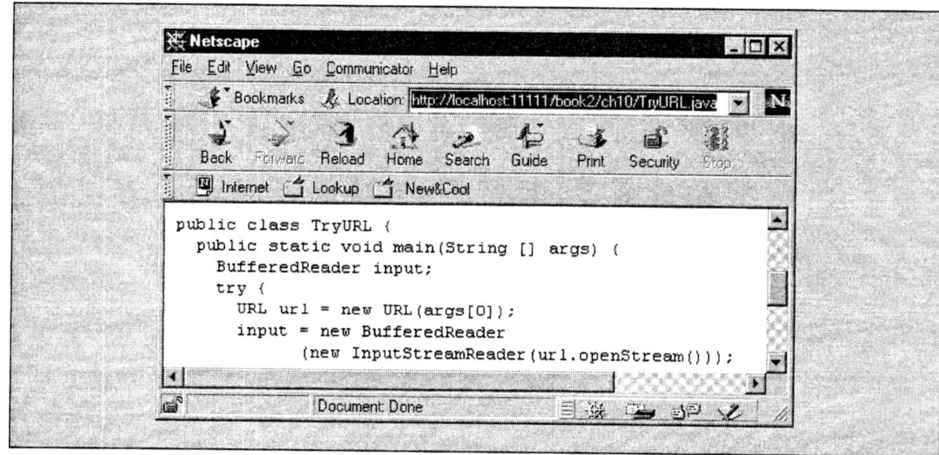

EXAMPLE 16.9 VerySimpleWebServer.java

```
/* Serves a text file to an HTTP client submitting a GET
 * request. Exercises suggest extensions to make the
 * server more functional.
 */

import java.net.*;
import java.io.*;
import java.util.StringTokenizer;

public class VerySimpleWebServer {
  public static void main(String[] args) {
    String s;
    try {
      ServerSocket server = new ServerSocket(Integer.parseInt(args[0]));
      Socket client = server.accept();
        System.out.println
            ("VerySimpleWebServer Connected on port " + args[0]);
        BufferedReader fromClient = new BufferedReader
            (new InputStreamReader(client.getInputStream()));
```

```
        PrintWriter toClient = new PrintWriter
            (client.getOutputStream(), true);
        s = fromClient.readLine();                              // Note 1
        StringTokenizer tokens = new StringTokenizer(s);        // Note 2
        if (!(tokens.nextToken()).equals("GET")) {              // Note 3
          toClient.println("HTTP/1.0 501 Not Implemented");
          toClient.println();
        }
        else {
          String filename = tokens.nextToken();                 // Note 4
          while (!(s = fromClient.readLine()) .equals(""));     // Note 5

          BufferedReader file =
              new BufferedReader(new FileReader(filename));     // Note 6
          toClient.println("HTTP/1.0 200 OK");                  // Note 7
          toClient.println("Content-type: text/plain");
          toClient.println();
          while ((s = file.readLine()) != null)                 // Note 8
            toClient.println(s);
          file.close();
        }
        fromClient.close();
        toClient.close();
        client.close();
      }catch(Exception e) {
        e.printStackTrace();
      }
    }
}
```

Note 1: We read the first line from the client to find the method and the identifier for the resource.

Note 2: Blanks separate each item of the request. We use a `StringTokenizer` to get the method and identifier parts of the request.

Note 3: If the request method is anything other than `GET`, the server sends a status line with a code of 501 to indicate the method is not implemented.

Note 4: The file name comes after `GET`, separated by a blank, in the request from the client. We save it here before we read the next line from the client which will overwrite the string `s`.

Note 5: We read and ignore any request headers sent by the client, looking for the blank line that separates the request and headers from any data the client might send.

Note 6: `BufferedReader file = new BufferedReader(new FileReader(filename));` If file cannot be found or another error occurs, the exception thrown will cause control to jump to the catch clause and the server to terminate.

We leave to the exercises the improvement of the server to handle the error and send an error message to the client

Note 7: `toClient.println("HTTP/1.0 200 OK");`
Having created the file to send, the server sends a status line with code 200 meaning OK, and follows with one header describing the content type to help the client to display it.

Note 8: `while ((s = file.readLine()) != null)`
This loop sends the file to the client.

A Threaded Web Server

Our `VerySimpleWebServer` has the very unusual behavior for a server in that it serves one request and terminates. We can easily modify Example 16.9 to put the server code in a loop. After it responds to one request, it can respond to another, and keep serving clients one at a time. Each client has to wait until the server finishes with the preceding client before being served.

Web servers may get requests from many clients at many dispersed locations. Using threads would allow the server to serve many clients simultaneously. The server interacts with one client while others are preparing their requests or displaying responses. It divides its attention among all connected clients so that they share the server. Large web sites may have a number of servers sharing the load of serving many, many clients.

Our `ThreadedWebServer` runs in an unending loop. Each time a client connects, the server creates a thread to handle its processing with that client. The client thread creates the files needed to communicate with the server in its constructor and starts itself running. Its `run` method contains the code from Example 16.9 in which the server responds to the client.

A good test for a threaded server would check how it handles simultaneous requests. We can make a step in that direction by starting two `VerySimpleBrowser` clients, each requesting a large file so the server will give each request some of its attention. We will see both browser windows scrolling the text of the file. The server will alternate, sending some of the first file to the first browser, then some of the second file to the second browser, then returning to the first, and so on until it has satisfied both requests.

We start `ThreadedWebServer` using the command

```
start java ThreadedWebServer 11111
```

on Windows systems, and

```
java ThreadedWebServer 11111 &
```

on Unix systems. Once the server is running, we start the two clients. Figure 16.11 shows both clients receiving the text of this chapter from a `ThreadedWebServer`.

Figure 16.11 Two browsers receiving text from `ThreadedWebServer`

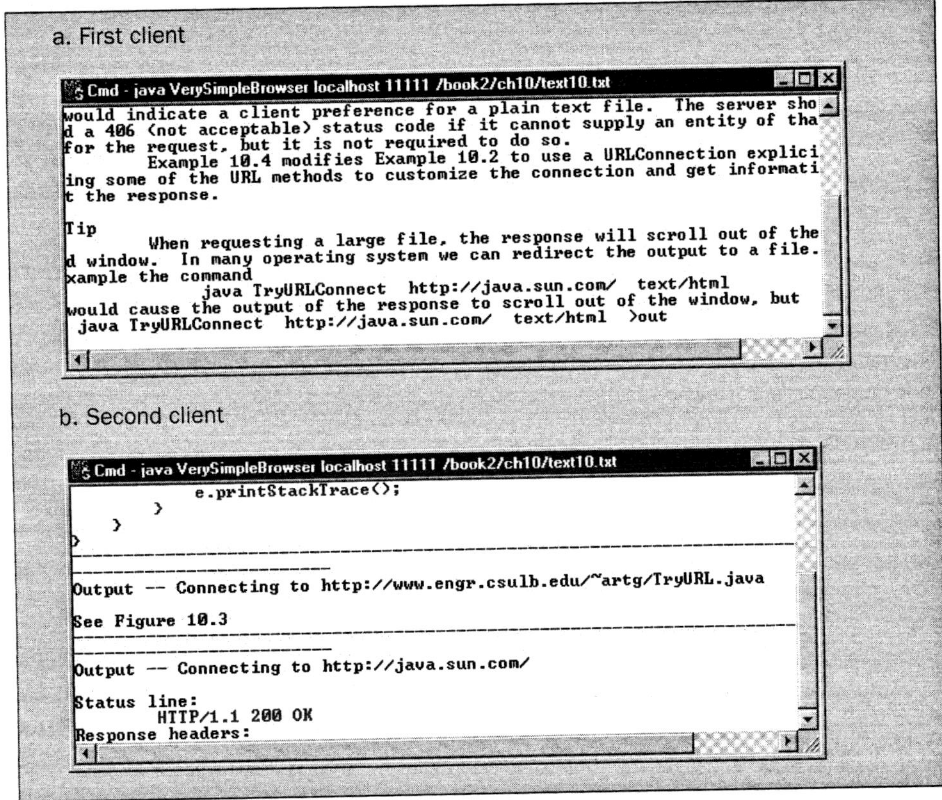

EXAMPLE 16.10 ThreadedWebServer.java

```
/* When an HTTP client connects, the server creates a thread
 * to respond to the client's request, so that multiple clients
 * can be connected simultaneously.
 */

import java.net.*;
import java.io.*;
import java.util.StringTokenizer;

public class ThreadedWebServer {
  public static void main(String [] args) {
    try {
      ServerSocket server = new ServerSocket(Integer.parseInt(args[0]));
      ThreadedWebServer web = new ThreadedWebServer();            // Note 1
      while(true) {                                                // Note 2
        Socket client = server.accept();
        web.new ClientThread(client);                              // Note 3
        System.out.println("ThreadedWebServer Connected to "
                      + client.getInetAddress());
      }
```

```
      }catch(Exception e) {
        e.printStackTrace();
      }
    }
    class ClientThread extends Thread {
      Socket client;
      BufferedReader fromClient;
      PrintWriter toClient;
      public ClientThread(Socket c) {
        try {
          client = c;
          fromClient = new BufferedReader
              (new InputStreamReader(client.getInputStream()));
          toClient = new PrintWriter
              (client.getOutputStream(), true);
          start();                                              // Note 4
        }catch(Exception e) {
          e.printStackTrace();
        }
      }
      public void run() {                                       // Note 5
        try {
          String s;
          s = fromClient.readLine();
          StringTokenizer tokens = new StringTokenizer(s);
          if (!(tokens.nextToken()).equals("GET")) {
            toClient.println("HTTP/1.0 501 Not Implemented");
            toClient.println();
          }
          else {
            String filename = tokens.nextToken();
              while (!(s = fromClient.readLine()) .equals(""));
              BufferedReader file =
                  new BufferedReader(new FileReader(filename));
              toClient.println("HTTP/1.0 200 OK");
              toClient.println("Content-type: text/plain");
              toClient.println();
              while ((s=file.readLine()) != null)
                toClient.println(s);
              file.close();
            }
            fromClient.close();
            client.close();
            toClient.close();
          }catch(Exception e) {
            e.printStackTrace();
          }
        }
      }
  }
```

Note 1: We need an instance of `ThreadedWebServer` to create the client thread to run each client. `ClientThread` is an inner class and must be created using a reference to its containing class, `ThreadedWebServer`.

Note 2: The server runs in an unending loop, until aborted, continuing to serve clients as they connect.

Note 3: By making `ClientThread` an inner class, we avoid conflicts in the global namespace. `ClientThread` has the full name `ThreadedWebServer$Client`, so the name `ClientThread` may be used in other contexts without conflict. Because `ClientThread` is an inner class of `ThreadedWebServer`, we create a `ClientThread` instance using the instance, `web`, of `ThreadedWebServer`. We leave the alternative, defining `Client` outside of `ThreadedWebServer`, as an exercise.

Note 4: This makes this thread runnable, so when it gets scheduled, Java will execute its `run` method.

Note 5: The `run` method contains the code from Example 16.9 by which the server and client communicate. If several threads are active, then the server will be communicating with several clients who are all connected simultaneously.

THE BIG PICTURE

Browsers and web servers use HTTP to communicate. Our `ThreadedWebServer` spawns a new thread to handle a connection from a client, so many clients may be connected to this server simultaneously. Rather than terminating after a client connects, `ThreadedWebServer` remains in a loop waiting for the next client.

TEST YOUR UNDERSTANDING

TRY IT YOURSELF 11. Modify Example 16.8 to use the `HEAD` method which just sends headers and does not ask for a resource in response. Connect with the very simple web server of Example 16.9. What happens?

TRY IT YOURSELF 12. Put the server of Example 16.9 into a loop so instead of terminating after each connection, it waits for another client to connect. Make the loop unending, so the server will have to be aborted to terminate it.

TRY IT YOURSELF 13. Test the threaded web server of Example 16.10 by connecting to it from two simple web browser clients at close to the same time. Find long text files to request so both clients will be connected to the server at the same time while downloading the requested files. Describe what you observe.

16.5 Remote Method Invocation (RMI)

Remote Method Invocation (**RMI**) takes networking to a higher level, providing distributed computing for Java programs. In distributed computing a program can be composed of parts located on more than one computer. So far we have used input and output streams to communicate between a client and server. These streams transfer data from one machine to another. Using RMI we can distribute our objects on various machines, invoking methods of objects located on remote sites.

Distributed Computing: The RMI Solution

We use a very simple example, a fortune server, to show how RMI works without introducing the extra complications of an involved example. The fortune server may be running on one machine. Clients, from remote sites, can request a fortune. In making these requests, clients will invoke a method of an object on the server. A **distributed computing** system must provide the following capabilities:

1. Clients must know what services the fortune server provides.
   RMI Solution: A `Fortune` interface lists the methods available to remote clients.
2. Clients must find a `Fortune` object on the server.
   RMI Solution: The fortune server registers an object with a special server, called the **rmiregistry**, so that clients can look it up by name.
3. Clients must be able to pass arguments to, and invoke a method of the `Fortune` object located on the server.
   RMI Solution: A special compiler, called **rmic**, creates a `stub` class for use on the client, and a `skeleton` class for use on the server. The stub takes the request from the client, passes the arguments to the skeleton which invokes the `Fortune` method and sends the return value back to the stub which passes it to the client.

Figure 16.12 shows how RMI operates.

Figure 16.12 The parts of RMI illustrated

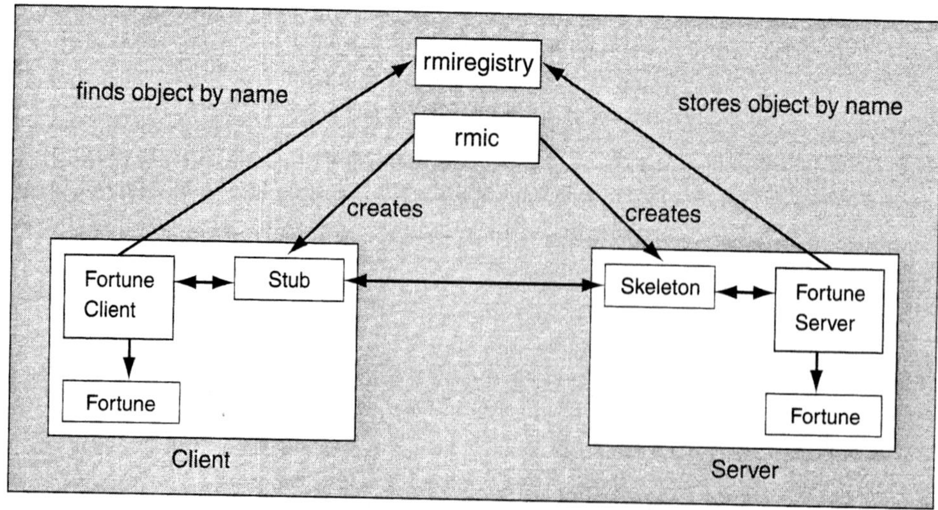

For our example which provides a fortune server that will enable clients to request fortunes (the fortune cookie kind, not the billionaire kind), we need to write the following programs:

`Fortune`	The interface that shows the client what remote methods it can invoke, the `getFortune` method in this example.
`FortuneServer`	The implementation of the `Fortune` interface to provide the remote object which is served to clients who wish to use its method to get a fortune.
`FortuneClient`	A client that gets a reference to a `Fortune` object and invokes its `getFortune` method remotely.

We run this example on one machine but use two directories, one for the client and one for the server, to simulate the use of a remote site. To compile and run our example we follow these steps:

In the server directory

1. Compile `Fortune.java` and `FortuneServer.java`.
2. Create the `stub` and `skeleton` classes using the command* `rmic FortuneServer`
3. Copy `FortuneServer_Stub.class` to the client directory.
4. Start the registry server using the command `start rmiregistry` on Windows systems, or `rmiregistry &` on Unix systems.
5. Start FortuneServer using the command† `start java FortuneServer localhost` on Windows systems, or `java FortuneServer localhost &` on Unix systems.

In the client directory

6. Compile `Fortune.java` and `FortuneClient.java`.
7. Run FortuneClient using the command† `java FortuneClient localhost`

TIP To run using two machines, follow the above steps, changing localhost, in steps 5 and 6, to the address of the server.

---

* If this command generates an error, it may be necessary to set the classpath.

† When using the Java™ 2 Platform, due to changes in the security model, we need to specify a security policy on the command line, so the command would be
`start java -Djava.security.policy=d:\policy FortuneServer localhost`
where `d:\policy` is the file containing the security policy. For testing RMI, the policy file grant { `permission java.security.AllPermission;` }; will work.

Figure 16.13 An RMI example

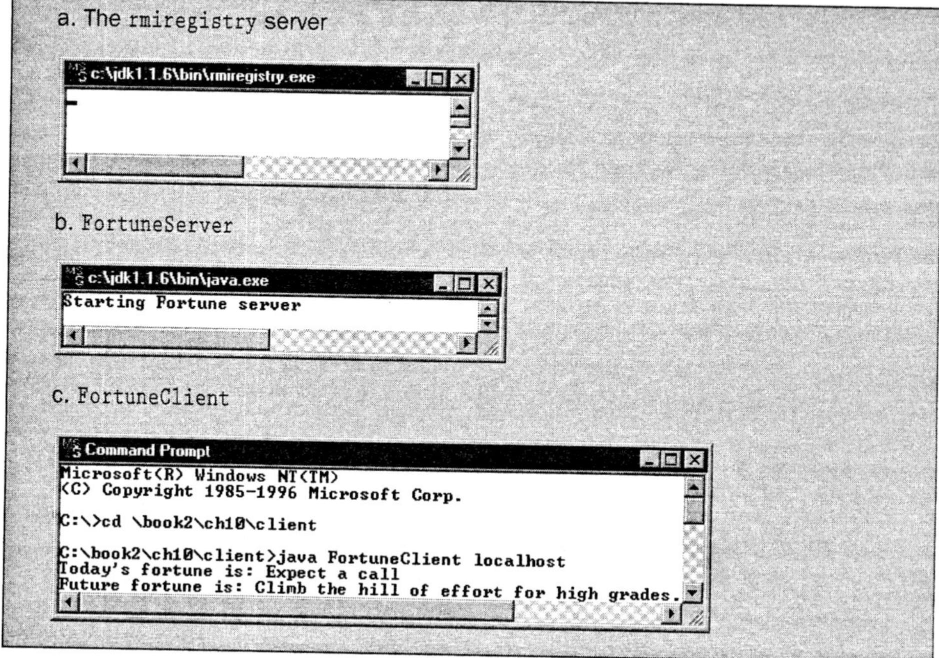

The Interface

Let us build each part of this example RMI application. The `Fortune` interface specifies the `getFortune` method. We ensure that objects that implement the `Fortune` interface can be used remotely by making `Fortune` extend the `Remote` interface. Because any network communication may fail, every method used remotely must declare that it may throw a `RemoteException`.

EXAMPLE 16.11 Fortune.java

```
/* The server implements this interface and clients call
 * its method remotely. Clients get a fortune from the server.
 */


import java.rmi.*;                                                    // Note 1
public interface Fortune extends Remote {
  public static final String NOW = "Now";                             // Note 2
  public static final String LATER = "Later";
  public String getFortune(String when) throws RemoteException;       // Note 3
}
```

Note 1: The `java.rmi` package contains the basic classes and interfaces needed for RMI, such as `Remote` and `RemoteException` in this example.

Note 2: In addition to methods, we can declare constants in an interface. We declare two `String` constants here to show clients the choices they have for arguments to the `getFortune` method. They can either request a fortune for NOW or for LATER.

Note 3: Using RMI, Java passes arguments and return values across the network using object serialization. Objects passed must have a type, such as `String`, that implements the `Serializable` interface.

The Server

On the server, the `FortuneServer` class implements the `Fortune` interface. Figure 16.12 shows the client uses the `Fortune` interface, and only sees that part of the `FortuneServer` object declared in the interface. The client only sees the `getFortune` method, and cannot access any other methods of the `FortuneServer` object. The `getFortune` method, which returns a message of good fortune to the client, must declare that it throws `RemoteException` because it will be called from a remote site. By contrast, the `find` method, used only within the `FortuneServer` class and declared as private, does not throw `RemoteException`.

We declare the `getFortune` method as synchronized because many clients may try to access the server simultaneously. Although our example is so simple it is really not necessary to synchronize access, in many cases we want a client to have exclusive access to the server object so any changes made will be completed before another client gets access.

The `java.rmi.server` package contains the classes needed for implementing servers of objects accessed remotely using RMI. Our `FortuneServer` class directly extends `UnicastRemoteObject`, a remote object sent to one destination at each request.

In the `main` method, we set up a server for a `FortuneServer` object, so remote clients can call its `getFortune` method to get a fortune. When using RMI, we may need to load class files from a remote site and need a security manager to ensure the safety of such operations. Java provides the `RMISecurityManager` class for this purpose, which we install using the `setSecurityManager` method of the `System` class.

The server and the client use the URL syntax with the RMI protocol to refer to remote objects. The server gives the object a name and places it, using that name, in the registry server, using the form

```
rmi://host:port/name
```

which the client also uses to locate that object. The `Naming` class handles interactions with the registry. Here the server uses the `rebind` method which registers the object with the rmiregistry server, replacing an earlier object of that name if any in the registry. In our example, the server binds a `FortuneServer` object in the registry under the name *Seer*.

EXAMPLE 16.12 FortuneServer.java

```
/* Implements the Fortune interface. Establishes a server
 * for remote clients to use a FortuneServer object.
 */

import java.rmi.*;
import java.rmi.server.UnicastRemoteObject;
import java.util.Vector;

public class FortuneServer extends UnicastRemoteObject
                              implements Fortune {
  public static final int SIZE = 3;
  private Vector now = new Vector(SIZE); // Fortunes for NOW
  private Vector later = new Vector(SIZE); // Fortunes for LATER
  public FortuneServer() throws RemoteException {
    now.addElement("A friend is near");
    now.addElement("Expect a call");
    now.addElement("Someone misses you");
    later.addElement("Wealth awaits -- if you desire it.");
    later.addElement("Climb the hill of effort for high grades.");
    later.addElement("The door to success is open to you.");
  }
  private Vector find(String when) {                          // Note 1
    if (when.equals(Fortune.NOW))
      return now;
    else return later;
  }
  public synchronized String getFortune(String when)
                                throws RemoteException {
    int number = (int)(SIZE*Math.random());                   // Note 2
    Vector fortunes = find(when);
    return (String)fortunes.elementAt(number);                // Note 3
  }
  public static void main(String[] args) {
    System.setSecurityManager(new RMISecurityManager());
    try {
      Fortune fortune = new FortuneServer();
      String url = "rmi://" + args[0] + "/Seer";              // Note 4
      Naming.rebind(url,fortune);                             // Note 5
      System.out.println("Starting Fortune server");
    }catch(Exception e) {
      e.printStackTrace();
    }
  }
}
```

Note 1: We only use the `find` method within `FortuneServer` to select a vector of fortunes based on the argument passed by the client. Just in case the client passes something other than NOW or LATER, we do not put a condition in the **else** clause and return LATER if the client passes anything but NOW.

Note 2: We get a random number between 0 and SIZE-1 to choose one of the fortunes to return to the client.

Note 3: Because `elementAt` returns type `Object`, we must cast the return value to type `String`. We know the elements of the vector have type `String` because we created them that way.

Note 4: We use the name `Seer` for the `fortune` object. The client uses the same name when looking up a reference to this object on the rmiregistry server. We pass the host and port as a program argument so that we can run our server on different machines without having to recompile the program. By default the rmiregistry server runs on port 1099; if we do not wish to change the port, we may omit it from the URL, just passing the host name as the program argument. Note that although we use the URL syntax, we do not declare a `URL` object, but rather a string.

Note 5: We associate the `fortune` object with the `Seer` URL when binding to the registry, so client can find it.

The Client

`FortuneClient` is the last program we need to complete our RMI example. It sets `RMISecurityManager`, just as the server does, and looks up a reference to the `Seer` object in the `rmiregistry` server. When the client calls the `getFortune` method of this remote object, it receives a fortune as the return value. From the client's point of view there is no difference between calling a method of a remote object and a method of a local object. RMI handles the details of the remote method call, using the `stub` and `skeleton` classes to pass arguments to the server and return values to the client.

EXAMPLE 16.13 FortuneClient.java

```
/* Looks up a Fortune object in the registry.
 * Invokes its getFortune method remotely to
 * get a fortune for now and for later.
 */

import java.rmi.*;

public class FortuneClient {
  public static void main(String[] args) {
    System.setSecurityManager(new RMISecurityManager());
    try {
      String url = "rmi://" + args[0] + "/Seer";                    // Note 1
      Fortune fortuneTeller = (Fortune)Naming.lookup(url);          // Note 2
      String fortune = fortuneTeller.getFortune(Fortune.NOW);       // Note 3
      System.out.println("Today's fortune is: " + fortune);
      fortune = fortuneTeller.getFortune(Fortune.LATER);
```

```
      System.out.println("Future fortune is: " + fortune);
    }catch(Exception e) {
      e.printStackTrace();
    }
  }
}
```

Note 1: We pass the host name of the server as a program argument, omitting the port number, because we have no need to change the default port of 1099 used by the `rmiregistry` server.

Note 2: The `lookup` method returns a reference, obtained from the `rmiregistry` server, to an object of type `Remote`, meaning it implements the `Remote` interface. We need to cast this reference to type `Fortune` to invoke the `getFortune` method.

Note 3: This remote method invocation looks like a method call of a local method, but the `fortuneTeller` object is actually on the server, which may be at a remote site. The `FortuneServer_Stub` sends the argument to `FortuneServer_Skel` on the host which invokes the `getFortune` method of the `fortuneTeller` object on the host. `FortuneServer_Skel` gets the return value from the `getFortune` method and sends it to the `FortuneServer_Stub` back on the client which returns it to the caller here to display. Fortunately, `RMI` handles all these details of communication using object serialization to transfer values.

THE BIG PICTURE

RMI lets us distribute our program across the network. We can bind an object in the `rmiregistry` server, so an object on another machine can look it up, and invoke its methods. The rmic compiler creates the `skeleton` and `stub` needed to call remote methods. Remote objects use interfaces to declare their remote methods.

TEST YOUR UNDERSTANDING

14. In Example 16.12 which classes from the `java.rmi` package are we using?

TRY IT YOURSELF

15. Run the RMI example of this section using port `3000` for the `rmiregistry` server. Start the registry with the command `start rmiregistry 3000`. Change the `localhost` program argument to `localhost:3000`.

SUMMARY

- Java makes it easy to connect to other computers. The `URL` class encapsulates some of the common communication protocols, such as HTTP (Hypertext Transfer Protocol) and FTP (File Transfer Protocol). Its four parts are the protocol name, the host name, port, and path to the resource. In an applet, we can use the `showDocument` method of the applet context to display a resource specified by a URL. The `openStream` method allows us to download the object referred to by a URL.
- The Hypertext Transfer Protocol specifies the messages by which browsers and web servers communicate. A browser or other web client sends a request, then some request headers, and a blank line to the server. The server sends a status line, followed by response headers, a blank line, and the requested resource. The examples show web clients and servers vary in the headers they choose to send.
- The `URLConnection` class has methods which allow us to set properties of the connection to customize it, or to get information about the connection. The `getHeaderField` method lets us determine the response headers sent by the server. The `setRequestProperty` method allows us to set request headers to send to the server. Special methods such as `getContentLength` return the value of specific headers.
- Sockets allow us to communicate using standard protocols, or to devise protocols of our own for use with clients and servers. A `ServerSocket` accepts connections on a numbered port. Standard services have default ports such as 80 for web servers, 25 for sending mail, and 110 for receiving it. Once we make a connection, we use input and output streams to send data back and forth between the client and the server. The `ReverseClient` example sends strings to the `ReverseServer` which sends them reversed back to the client. Modifying the `ReverseServer` produces `HeaderServer`, which just sends back to a web client the headers that it sent.
- To display a web page, a browser must interpret all the HTML tags embedded in that page. Our `VerySimpleBrowser` uses HTTP to communicate with web servers. It is a bare outline of a browser, following HTTP but ignoring the response headers and only displaying plain text, not HTML or images. Similarly our `VerySimpleWebServer` ignores any headers the client sends, and puts no effort into accurately sending response headers. Nevertheless our browser can connect and download files from various web servers and our web server can respond to plain text request from browsers. The exercises suggest many improvements. Our `ThreadedWebServer` permits several clients to be connected at the same time, each served in its own thread.
- Remote Method Invocation (RMI) takes networking to a higher level in which a client can invoke methods of a remote object on the server. The `rmiregistry` server allows the client to find a reference to a remote object. The `rmic` compiler creates the `stub` and `skeleton` files used to pass arguments and return values across the network. An interface, implemented on the server, specifies the remote methods available to the client.

Program Modification Exercises

1. Modify Example 16.3 to use a `String` argument to `getHeaderField` instead of an **int**. User `getHeaderFieldKey` to find the names of the headers.
2. Example 16.4 uses two program arguments. Add a check that the user passed two arguments and if not, print a message showing the proper usage and exit the program.
3. Modify Example 16.8 to pass a URL such as `http://www.cecs.csulb.edu/TryURL.java` rather than passing the host, port, and resource path program arguments. The `URL` methods `getHost`, `getPort`, `getHost`, and `getProtocol` will be helpful.
4. Modify Example 16.9 to send a status line with code 404 and reason Not Found when the file requested is not available on the server.
5. Modify Example 16.9 so when the server has responded to one client it can accept a request from another.
6. Modify Example 16.10 to avoid using any inner classes.
7. Modify Example 16.9 to send a Content-length header giving the length of the file in bytes.
8. Modify Examples 16.5 and 16.6 to pass the port number as a program argument.
9. Modify Example 16.5 to put the `accept` statement and the code following it into a nonterminating loop, so the server can accept another client as soon as the current client finishes.
10. Modify Example 16.5 so the server can handle several clients simultaneously. After the server accepts a connection from the client, the server should create a separate thread to handle the communication with that client and loop back to the `accept` statement waiting for another client to connect.
11. Modify Example 16.13 to ask if the user wants another fortune. When testing, let two clients stay connected at the same time.
12. Modify Examples 16.11, 16.12, and 16.13 to allow the client to request a lucky number. The server will return a number from 1 to 10 at random.

Program Design Exercises

13. Write an applet which lists URLs in a choice box. When the user selects a URL, use the `showDocument` method to display the page to which it refers.
14. Write a multithreaded server which will pass whatever message line it receives from a client to all the other clients that are connected. Write a client program to connect to this server, which sends its lines and receives the lines sent by the other clients.

15. Write a mail client which will connect to a POP3 server (find the address of your server) and retrieve the first message. Specify the server address, user name, and password as program arguments. The protocol of Figure 16.4 may be helpful.
16. Write a browser that displays a plain text file in a text area, rather than in the command window as `VerySimpleBrowser` does.
17. Write a piece of a browser which will display HTML files. This piece will only display text within header tags, `<h1>` ... `<h6>`. Use the largest point size for text between `<h1>` and `</h1>` tags, and the smallest for text between `<h6>` and `</h6>` tags.
18. Add to the browser of Exercise 16.17 the capability to handle `<em>` and `<strong>` tags.
19. Write a new version of `ReverseClient` in which the user enters the text to be reversed in a text field.
20. Use RMI to allow clients to connect to a broker to get the price of a stock, or to buy and sell some stock. Use just three stocks, StockA, StockB, and StockC, each with a price that varies randomly within a range. Assume two accounts numbered 1111 and 2222.

    a. For simplicity, do not maintain account information, so no records are kept about buy and sell orders.

    b. Add account information, so each account keeps a record of how many of each stock it contains.
21. Improve the very simple browser of Example 16.8. The browser should properly interpret HTML tags `<h1>`, ..., `<h6>`, `<em>`, `<strong>`, `<ul>`, `<li>`, `<br>`, `<p>`, `<a>`, and `<img>`.
22. Improve the very simple web server of Example 16.9. Use the status codes 200, 301, 400, 404, 406, and 501 appropriately. Send `Date`, `Last-modified`, `Content-type`, and `Content-length` response headers.
23. Implement a chess game in which the server relays moves from one player to the other. Two clients play against one another, with each showing the board and the moves as they are made. Players will use the mouse to drag a piece to its new position. (Alternatively, substitute another game for chess. For example, checkers would be simpler.)
24. Make a user interface for the mail-reading client of Exercise 16.15. The screen will show the message headers and allow the user to choose which message to read. For additional information on the POP3 protocol, search the Internet for RFC 1939 which contains its specification.
25. Implement an SMTP client to send email. Provide a user interface to compose and send the message. Testing requires access to an SMTP server. An example session is:

```
Server:   220 charlotte.cecs.csulb.edu ESMTP Sendmail 8.8.4/8.8.4;
              Thu, 11 Feb 1999 15:31:27 -0800 (PST)
Client:   HELO gordian.com                                // sent from

Server:   250 charlotte.cecs.csulb.edu Hello ppool3.gordian.com
              [207.211.232.196], pleased to meet you
Client:   MAIL FROM:artg@csulb.edu                        // email address
Server:   250 <artg@csulb.edu>... Sender ok
Client:   RCPT TO:artg@csulb.edu                          // recipient
Server:   250 artg@csulb.edu... Recipient ok
Client:   DATA                                            // signals message
Server:   354 Enter mail, end with "." on a line by itself
Client:   Subject: test                                   // message
          To: artgcsulb.edu
          This is
          a test.
          .                                               // signals end
Server:   250 PAA27651 Message accepted for delivery
Client:   QUIT
Server:   221 Closing connection.
```

Headers have the form `Name:Value` and are separated from the message body by an empty line.

CHAPTER

17 Java Database Connectivity (JDBC)

OUTLINE

Introduction

For small applications, we can use files to store data, but as the amount of data that we need to save gets larger the services of a database system become invaluable. A database system allows us to model the information we need while it handles the details of inserting, removing, and retrieving data from individual files in response to our requests.

Of course each database vendor provides its own procedures for performing database operations. The Java Database Connectivity (JDBC) programming interface hides the details of different databases; our programs can work with many different databases on many different platforms. JDBC can be used as part of large scale enterprise applications. In this chapter we cover the JDBC concepts using a small example which allows many extensions, some of which we pursue in the exercises.

The example programs illustrate JDBC concepts using console applications so as not to obscure them with the details involved in building a GUI. In the last section our extended case study develops a graphical user interface to a database.

OBJECTIVES

- Introduce relational database tables.
- Introduce SQL (Structured Query Language).
- Register a database as an ODBC data source.
- Connect to a database from Java, using JDBC.
- Build a database using JDBC and SQL.
- Use Java to query a database.
- Use metadata to obtain the properties of a database or a result set.
- Introduce selected aggregate functions.
- Use prepared statements for efficiency.
- Process database transactions.
- Provide a GUI for the user to query a database.

17.1 Database Tables and SQL Queries

Database design is best left to other texts and courses. We introduce a few database concepts here to provide an example with which to illustrate the Java Database Connectivity techniques for working with databases using Java. Relational databases provide an implementation-independent way for users to view data. The Structured Query Language (SQL) lets us create, update, and query a database using standard commands that hide the details of any particular vendor's **database system**.

Relational Database Tables

When designing a **database** we need to identify the entities in our system. For example, a company might use a database to keep track of its sales and associated information. In our example company, an order has one customer who can order several items. A salesperson may take several orders from the same customer, but each order is taken by exactly one salesperson.

Using a **relational database**, we keep our data in **tables**. In our example, we might have a `Customer` table with fields for the customer id, name, address, and balance due as shown in Figure 17.1.

Figure 17.1 The `Customer` table

CustomerID	CustomerName	Address	BalanceDue
1234	Fred Flynn	22 First St.	1667.00
5678	Darnell Davis	33 Second St.	130.95
4321	Marla Martinez	44 Third St.	0
8765	Carla Kahn	55 Fourth St.	0

Each row of the table represents the information needed for one customer. We assign each customer a unique customer ID number. Customer names are not unique; moreover they may change. `CustomerID` is a **key** that identifies the data in the row. Knowing the `CustomerID` we can retrieve the other information about that customer.

TIP

Do not embed spaces in field names. Use `CustomerID` rather than `Customer ID`.

Figures 17.2 and 17.3 show the `Salesperson` and `Item` tables which we define in a similar manner. A more realistic example would have additional fields, but our purpose here is only to illustrate JDBC.

Figure 17.2 The `Salesperson` table

SalespersonID	SalespersonName	Address
12	Peter Patterson	66 Fifth St.
98	Donna Dubarian	77 Sixth St.

Figure 17.3 The `Item` table

ItemNumber	Description	Quantity
222222	radio	32
333333	television	14
444444	computer	9

The `SalespersonID` serves as the key for the `Salesperson` table, while we use the `ItemNumber` to identify an item in the Item table. We have to be more careful in designing the `Orders` table, as an order can have multiple items. We use a second table, the `OrderItem` table, to list the items in each order. Figure 17.4 shows the `Orders` table with the fields `OrderNumber`, `CustomerID`, `SalespersonID`, and `OrderDate`. The `OrderNumber` is the key. `CustomerID` and `SalespersonID` are **foreign keys** that allow us to avoid redundancy by referring to data in other tables. For example, including the `CustomerID` lets us find the customer's name and address from the `Customer` table rather than repeating it in the `Orders` table.

Figure 17.4 The `Orders` table

OrderNumber	CustomerID	SalespersonID	OrderDate
1	1234	12	4/3/99
2	5678	12	3/22/99
3	8765	98	2/19/99
4	1234	12	4/5/99
5	8765	98	2/28/99

TIP

When choosing field names, avoid names like `Number`, `Value`, `Order`, `Name`, or `Date` that might conflict with reserved names in the database system.

The `OrderItem` table uses a **compound key** consisting of both the `OrderNumber` and the `ItemNumber` to identify a specific item that is part of an order. Figure 17.5 shows that each pair (`OrderNumber, ItemNumber`) occurs only once, identifying a row containing the data for a specific item in a particular order. For example, the first row shows that for order number one, and item 222222, four units were ordered at a price of $27 each.

Figure 17.5

OrderNumber	ItemNumber	Quantity	UnitPrice
1	222222	4	27.00
1	333333	2	210.50
1	444444	1	569.00
2	333333	2	230.95
3	222222	3	27.00
3	333333	1	230.95
4	444444	1	569.00
5	222222	2	27.00
5	444444	1	725.00

Now that we have defined our `Sales` database, we want to see how to get information from it, and how to make changes as needed.

Structured Query Language (SQL)

The Structured Query Language (SQL) is a standard language with which to get information from or make changes to a database. We can execute SQL statements from within Java. The SQL statements we shall use are `CREATE`, `SELECT`, `INSERT`, `DELETE`, and `UPDATE`. We illustrate these statements using the `Sales` database defined above. The names for the data types may depend on the actual database system used. Our examples work with Microsoft Access.

We could use the `CREATE` statement

```
CREATE TABLE Customer (CustomerID CHAR(4), CustomerName
  VARCHAR(25), Address VARCHAR(25), BalanceDue CURRENCY)
```

to create the `Customer` table, the statement

```
CREATE TABLE Orders (OrderNumber VARCHAR(4), CustomerID
    CHAR(4), SalespersonID CHAR(2), OrderDate DATE)
```

to create the `Orders` table, and the statement

```
CREATE TABLE OrderItem (OrderNumber VARCHAR(4), ItemNumber
    CHAR(6), Quantity INTEGER, UnitPrice CURRENCY)
```

to create the `OrderItem` table. We use character fields for `CustomerID`, `OrderNumber`, `SalespersonID`, and `ItemNumber`, even though they use numerical characters, because we have no need to do arithmetic using these values. By contrast, we use the type `INTEGER` for the `Quantity` field because we may wish to compute with it.

Standard SQL uses various types which are not all supported in every database system. Figure 17.6 shows the SQL types we use in this text.

Figure 17.6 SQL types

Type	Standard SQL	Description
CHAR(N)	Yes	Fixed size string of length N
VARCHAR(N)	Yes	Variable size string up to length N
INTEGER	Yes	32-bit integer
DATE	Yes	year, month, and day
CURRENCY	No	dollars and cents

The type `DECIMAL(M,N)`, where `M` is the maximum number of digits and `N` is the maximum number of digits after the decimal point, is standard SQL, but is not supported in Access.

To insert the first row in the `Customer` table, we could use the `INSERT` statement

```
INSERT INTO Customer VALUES (1234,'Fred Flynn','22 First St.',1667.00)
```

TIP Use the single quote, ', to enclose strings within an SQL statement.

The statement

```
INSERT INTO Orders VALUES (1,1234,12,'Apr 3, 1999')
```

inserts the first row into the `Order` table. We write dates in the form

```
Month Day, Year
```

to avoid confusion among date formats used in various locales and to indicate the century explicitly. The database system translates this form to its internal representation, and can present dates in various formats in its tables.

The `DELETE` statement

```
DELETE FROM OrderItem WHERE OrderNumber = '1'
```

will delete the first three rows of the `OrderItem` table in Figure 17.5. These rows contain the data for the three items comprising the order with an `OrderNumber` of 1.

TIP

Use the single equality sign, =, in the equality test, OrderNumber = 1, instead of the Java equality symbol, ==.

To delete just the televisions from that order and leave the order for radios and a computer, we could use the statement

```
DELETE FROM OrderItem
WHERE OrderNumber = '1' AND ItemNumber = '333333'
```

To update an existing row we use the `UPDATE` statement. For example, to reduce the number of radios in order number 1 to 3, we can use the statement

```
UPDATE OrderItem SET Quantity = 3
WHERE OrderNumber = '1' AND ItemNumber = '222222'
```

When we change an order we will also want to change the balance due in the `Customer` table, which we can do using

```
UPDATE Customer SET BalanceDue = 1640.00
WHERE CustomerID = '1234'
```

TIP

Because the `OrderItem` table uses a compound key `(OrderNumber, ItemNumber)` to identify a row, we needed to specify values for both in the `WHERE` clause. In updating the `Customer` table we only needed to specify the value of the single `CustomerID` key to identify a row.

The `CREATE` statement creates a table, and the `INSERT`, `DELETE`, and `UPDATE` statements make changes in a table. In many applications, we retrieve information from the database more frequently than we create a table or make changes to a table. To retrieve information we use the `SELECT` statement.

The simplest **query** we can make is to retrieve the entire table. For example, the statement

```
SELECT * FROM Customer
```

retrieves the entire `Customer` table. We use the star symbol, `*`, which matches every row. To retrieve the names and addresses of the customers we use the statement

```
SELECT CustomerName, Address FROM Customer
```

If we do not want data from the entire table, we can use a `WHERE` clause to specify a condition that the data of interest satisfy. For example, to retrieve all orders for radios we could use the statement

```
SELECT * FROM OrderItems
WHERE ItemNumber = '222222'
```

The power of database systems becomes evident when we use SQL to get information combined from several tables. For example, suppose we would like to know the names of all customers who placed orders on March 22, 1999. We can find that information using the statement

```
SELECT CustomerName FROM Customer, Orders
WHERE Customer.CustomerID = Orders.CustomerID
AND OrderDate = {d '1999-03-22'}
```

where `{d '1999-03-22'}` is an escape sequence.

Date formats vary among database systems. To make programs general Java uses a generic string format yyyy-mm-dd with a four-digit year, a two-digit month, and a two digit day. The curly braces, {}, enclose the escape sequence which tells the driver to translate it to the specific form used by the database system. The keyword, `d`, signifies that a date follows. The date format for the Access database we are using is #3/22/99#, which we could have used, but the escape sequence makes the code more general.

TIP When a field such as `Address` occurs in more than one table, prefix the field name with the table name, as in `Customer.Address`, to state precisely which `Address` field you desire. Similarly, use the prefixes `Customer` and `Orders` to refer to the `CustomerID` fields in each of these tables.

In finding the names of customers who placed orders on March 22, 1999, the database joins two tables. Customer names occur in the `Customer` table, while we find order dates in the `Orders` table, so we list both the `Customer` and the `Orders` tables in the `FROM` part of the query. We want to find which orders each customer placed. `CustomerID`, the primary key of the `Customer` table, is also a foreign key of the `Orders` table. For each `CustomerID` in the `Customer` table we only want to inspect the rows of the `Orders` table which have the same `CustomerID`, so we include the condition

```
Customer.CustomerID = Orders.CustomerID
```

in our query.

The first row of the `Customer` table has a `CustomerID` of `1234`. The first and fourth rows of the `Orders` table have the same `CustomerID` of `1234` but neither of the `OrderDate` fields equals `3/22/99`. The second row of the `Customer` table has `CustomerID 5678` as does the second row of the `Orders` table and the `OrderDate` is `3/22/99` so the system adds 'Darnell Davis' to the result set of customers placing orders on March 22, 1999. Continuing the search turns up no further matches. A three-line SQL statement can cause many steps to occur in the process of retrieving the requested information. The database handles all the details. We will use other interesting examples of `SELECT` statements when we develop our Java programs later in this chapter.

Figure 17.7 shows the general pattern for the `SQL` statements we have introduced so far.

Figure 17.7 Some patterns for SQL statements

```
CREATE TABLE tablename
(fieldname1 TYPE1, fieldname2 TYPE2, ... , fieldnameN TYPEn)

INSERT INTO tablename
VALUES (field1value,field2value, ..., fieldNvalue)

DELETE FROM tablename
WHERE fieldname1 = value1 ... AND fieldnameN = valueN

UPDATE tablename SET fieldnameToSet = newValue
WHERE fieldname1ToCheck = value1ToCheck

SELECT fieldname1, ..., fieldnameN FROM table1, ..., tableM
WHERE condition1 ... AND conditionN
```

THE BIG PICTURE

In a relational database, we keep our data in tables, making sure not to enter information redundantly. Using SQL, we can write statements to create a table, insert, delete, and update elements, and query the database. Generally SQL is standardized so queries do not reflect implementation details of specific database systems.

TEST YOUR UNDERSTANDING

1. Why is it a good idea to use `SalespersonID` as the key in the `Salesperson` table, rather than the salesperson's name?
2. Write an SQL statement to create the `Salesperson` table with the fields shown in Figure 17.2.
3. Write SQL statements to insert the data shown in Figure 17.2 into the Salesperson table.
4. Write an SQL statement to add a new salesman, Paul Sanchez, who lives at 88 Seventh St., and has an ID of 54, to the `Salesperson` table of Figure 17.2.
5. Write an SQL statement to delete Carla Kahn's order of a computer from the `Sales` database.
6. Write an SQL statement to find the names of all salespersons in the `Sales` database.
7. Write an SQL statement to find the order numbers of all orders taken by Peter Patterson.

17.2 Connecting to a Database

After an overview contrasting two-tiered with three-tiered architectures for software systems, we show how to connect to a database using the Java Database Connectivity programming interface.

Database and Application Servers

In building large systems, a **database server** may reside on one machine to which various clients connect when they need to access the stored data.

Figure 17.8 Client-server database access

In a three-tiered design, business logic resides in a middle machine, sometimes called an **application server**, which acts as a server to various application clients. These clients provide user interfaces to the business applications on the middle machine which is itself a client of the database server.

Figure 17.9 A three-tiered system architecture

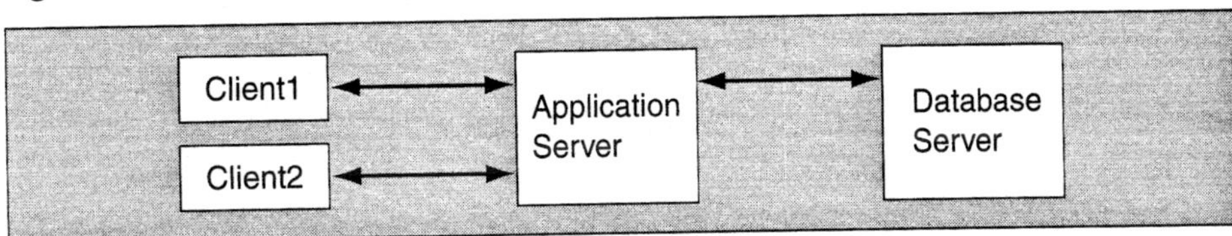

For example, a business may have an accounting department that runs a payroll client providing a user interface to the payroll application on the middle machine which itself is a client of the database server. The marketing department might have several client programs running in their sales offices enabling salespersons to get necessary information. Rather than configuring each salesperson's machine to process all the details of the application, the company just allows the sales staff to interact with the sales application on the middle machine. This sales program gets data from the database server as needed.

Java Database Connectivity (**JDBC**) allows us to write Java programs that will work no matter which database system we use. We can work entirely on one machine or use a two-tier, three-tier, or even more complex architecture for our system. What we need for any database system we wish to use is a JDBC driver. The driver provides a uniform interface to our Java programs. Many database vendors provide JDBC drivers for use with their products.

A JDBC Driver

A **driver** translates JDBC statements to the specific commands of a particular database system. Several different categories of drivers exist, but in this text we use the JDBC to ODBC bridge to allow JDBC to work with Microsoft Access which has an existing **ODBC** driver (for an earlier technology, Open Database Connectivity, that is still used). To connect to our database using Java, we need only specify our JDBC driver and the URL for the database

Creating an ODBC Data Source

Before using Java we need to register our database as an ODBC data source. The Microsoft Open Database Connectivity (ODBC) interface, introduced prior to the development of Java, provides an interface to many databases. Sun makes a JDBC to ODBC bridge available, so if a database has an ODBC driver, we can access it using the JDBC to ODBC bridge as our JDBC driver.

In this chapter, our examples will use Microsoft Access databases on Windows. Only the driver name and the data source URL need to be changed to use another database system.

The first step is to register the database we will be creating as an ODBC data source. The steps we use are:

1. Click on the My Computer icon and the Control Panel icon to open the Control Panel.
2. Click on the ODBC icon in the Control Panel, which pops up the ODBC Data Source Administrator window shown in Figure 17.10.

Figure 17.10 ODBC Data Source Administrator

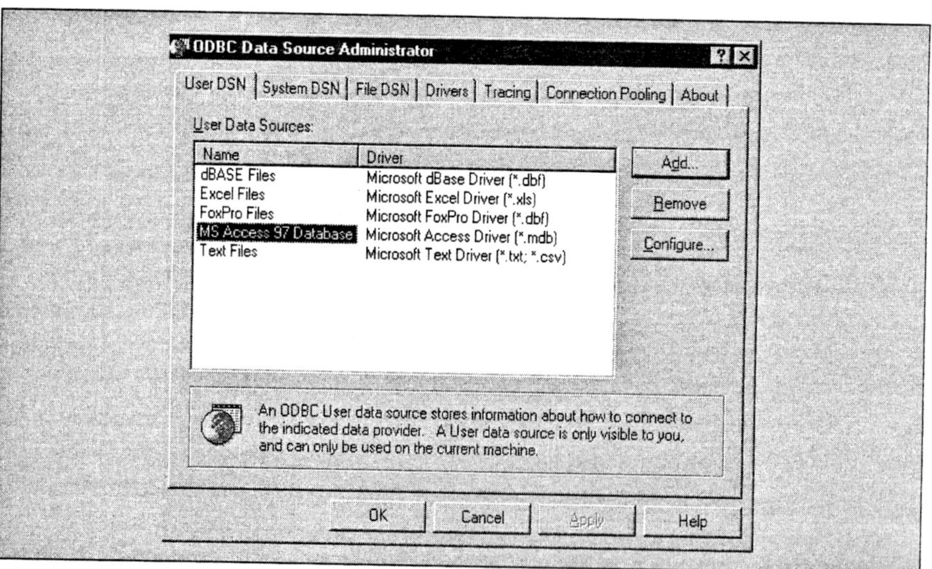

3. Select MS Access Database.
4. Click Add, which pops up the Create New Data Source window shown in Figure 17.11.

Figure 17.11 Create New Data Source

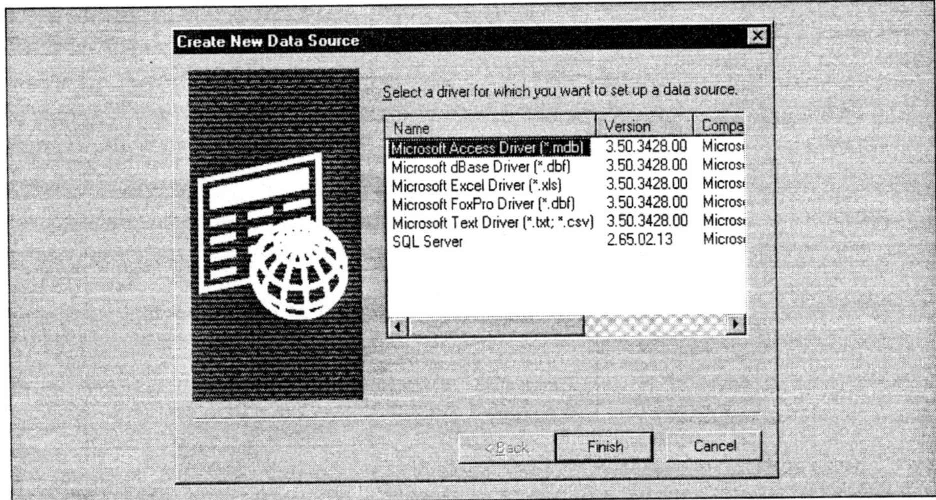

5. Select Microsoft Access Driver and click Finish, which pops up the ODBC Microsoft Access Setup window shown in Figure 17.12.

Figure 17.12 ODBC Microsoft Access Setup

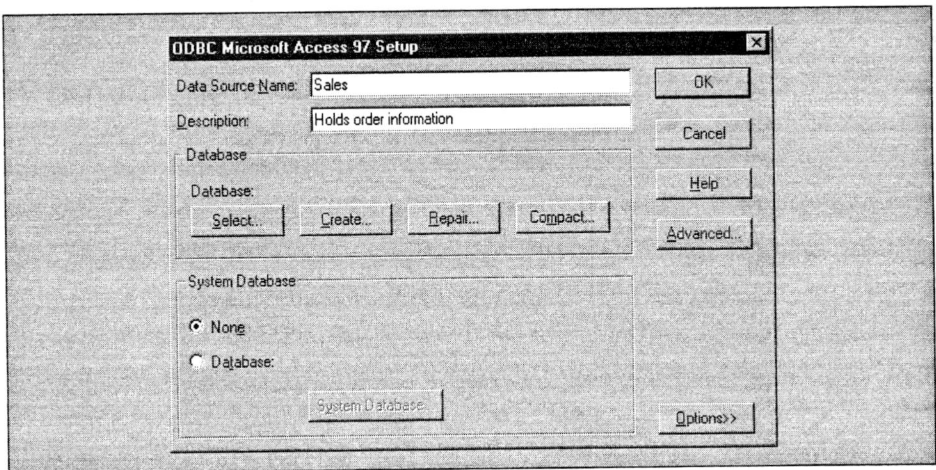

6. Fill in the Data Source Name. We use this name to refer to this database in our Java programs. We use the name `Sales` for our example.
7. Fill in a short description, such as "Holds order information" in the Description field.

8. Click `Create`, as we are creating a new database.

Figure 17.13 New Database

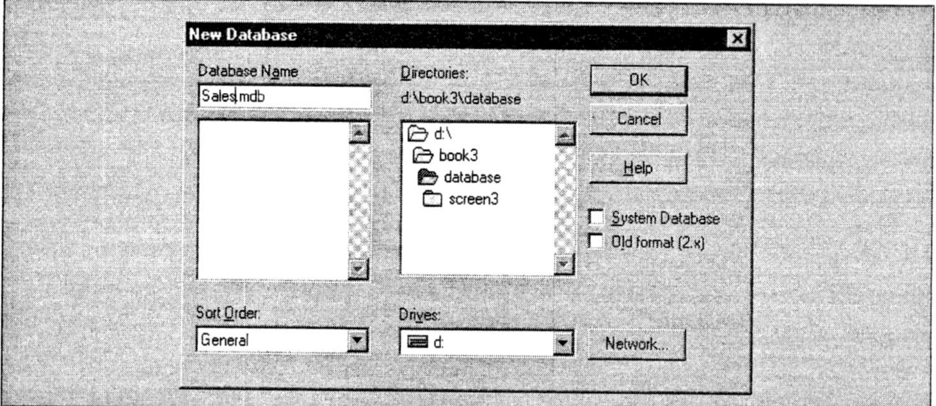

9. In the New Database window, shown in Figure 17.13, navigate to the directory in which to place the new database, give it a name, such as `Sales.mdb`, and click OK.
10. If all went well, a message that the database was successfully created will appear.

TIP

On a Windows system without Microsoft Access, much of what we do in this chapter can be done with ordinary text files. The steps for using text files are:

1. Click on the My Computer icon and the Control Panel icon to open the Control Panel.
2. Click on the ODBC icon in the Control Panel, which pops up the ODBC Data Source Administrator window.
3. Click on Text Files.
4. Click Add, which pops up the Create New Data Source window.
5. Select Microsoft Text Driver and click Finish, which pops up the ODBC Text Setup window.
6. Fill in the Data Source Name. We use this name to refer to this database in our Java programs. We use the name Sales for our example.
7. Fill in a short description, such as "Record sales orders" in the Description field.
8. Deselect the UseCurrentDirectory box, click Select Directory, navigate to the desired directory for the files, and click OK in all the open windows.

Connecting from Java

We want our `Sales` database to contain the five tables with the data shown in Figures 17.1–17.5. We could create these tables and populate them within Access, but prefer to show how to do this using Java.

Every Java program that uses JDBC to access a database must load the driver that it will use and connect to the desired database. To load the driver we create a new driver object. Sun provides the JDBC classes in the `java.sql` package and the JdbcOdbcDriver in the `sun.jdbc.odbc` package. The core Java packages all start with the java prefix. Sun includes the `JdbcOdbcDriver` with the JDK but it is not one of the core Java classes. Sun also includes the helper file, `JdbcOdbc.dll`, with the JDK.

The statement

```
new JdbcOdbcDriver();
```

will load a new driver object, calling its constructor. The drawback of using the **new** operator to load `JdbcOdbcDriver` is that if we want to use a different driver, we have to modify the program. Java has the ability to load classes while the program is running so that we could pass a class name in as a program argument and let Java load whichever driver we decide to use. We use the `forName` method of the class `Class` in the `java.lang` package

```
Class.forName("JdbcOdbcDriver");
```

to load `JdbcOdbcDriver`. To make the loading dynamic we could use

```
Class.forName(args[0]);
```

which would load the class whose name we pass as the first program argument.

TIP Each class loaded into the JVM has a Class object associated with it. This object has various methods that give information about the structure of the class. We do not use any of these methods, but use only the static `forName` method which loads the class whose full name is passed as the argument.

Once we load the driver, it registers with the `DriverManager` that keeps a vector of drivers to use when making a connection to a database. We connect to a database using the static `getConnection` method of the `DriverManager` class that returns a connection representing our session with the database.

We use a URL to locate the database to which we wish to connect. We could use a database server which would require a remote connection in which case the URL would include the Internet address of the server. The URL has the form

```
jdbc:<subprotocol>:<subname>
```

where the **subprotocol** is the name of the driver or a database connectivity mechanism such as **odbc** which is what we will use. The **subname** identifies the database. For the case of ODBC drivers we just need the name of the database that we registered with the ODBC Data Source Administrator, which is `Sales` for our example. Thus the URL we will use is

```
jdbc:odbc:Sales
```

The developer of the JDBC driver defines the URL needed.

Example 17.1 will just connect to the Sales database. The code we use will occur at the beginning of all of our examples in this chapter.

EXAMPLE 17.1 Connect.java

```
/* Connects to a Microsoft Access database
 * using the JDBC-ODBC bridge
 */

import java.sql.*;                                                    // Note 1
import java.io.*;
import sun.jdbc.odbc.*;                                               // Note 2

class Connect {
  public static void main (String args[]) {
    try{
      new JdbcOdbcDriver();                                           // Note 3
      String url = "jdbc:odbc:Sales";                                 // Note 4
      String user = "";                                               // Note 5
      String password = "";
      Connection con =
      DriverManager.getConnection(url, user, password);               // Note 6
      System.out.println("Made the connection to the Sales database");
    }catch (Exception e) {e.printStackTrace();}                       // Note 7
  }
}
```

Output

Made the connection to the Sales database

Note 1: The `java.sql` package contains the JDBC classes.

Note 2: The `sun.jdbc.odbc` package contains the JdbcOdbcDriver we use to access our ODBC data source, a Microsoft Access database.

Note 3: We create a new `JdbcOdbcDriver` which registers itself with the `DriverManager` which stores a vector of all the registered drivers. The driver hides the details of the specific database. We use JDBC generic methods which the driver translates to the specific procedures provided by the database vendor. By changing the driver, the same program can work with data on a different database system. We do not need to assign the driver to a variable, because we will not refer to it again explicitly.

Note 4: The supplier of the driver defines the URL needed. If we change the driver then we also need to change the URL. Making these changes will allow our program to work with another database system. Our programs would be more flexible, if rather than hard coding the driver and URL we pass them as program arguments. We leave this modification to the exercises.

Note 5: For the Access database we are using we do not need a user name or a password. For other databases we may need to log in to the server. For generality we left the user and password fields in the program and set them both to empty strings.

Note 6:
```
Connection con =
DriverManager.getConnection(url, user, password);
```
This static method looks through the vector of registered drivers to find a driver that can connect to this database, and throws an exception if one is not found. If it finds a suitable driver, it attempts to make the connection. In this example, we could have used the method
```
DriverManager.getConnection(url);
```
which omits the user and password arguments.

Note 7:
```
catch (Exception e) {e.printStackTrace();}
```
We catch all exceptions here. We could have used the `SQLException` class to catch exceptions relating to SQL.

Building the Database

Once we have a connection to the database we can execute SQL statements to create and **populate** our database. The `createStatement` method returns a `Statement` object that we use to send SQL statements to the database.

Some SQL statements, such as those used to create tables and insert values in a table, change the database but do not return any values to the program. To execute SQL `CREATE` and `INSERT` statements we use the `executeUpdate` method. The argument to `executeUpdate` is a `String`, which will be sent to the database. The string argument should represent an SQL statement in a form understandable by the database system. If not, Java will throw an exception. As an example,

```
stmt.executeUpdate
("INSERT INTO Item VALUES ('555555','CD player',10)");
```

would insert a fourth row into the `Item` table.

Example 17.2 uses Java to create and populate the `Sales` database. We create the five tables shown in Figures 17.1–17.5, using a `CREATE` statement to create each table, and `INSERT` statements to add the rows. Figure 17.14 shows the resulting Access `Sales` database and Figure 17.15 shows the `Customer` table that results from executing Example 17.2.

TIP ☛ After running this program, the database contains the five tables. Therefore running the program again will cause an error, unless the tables are first deleted from the database.

Figure 17.14 The Access `Sales` database created by Example 17.2

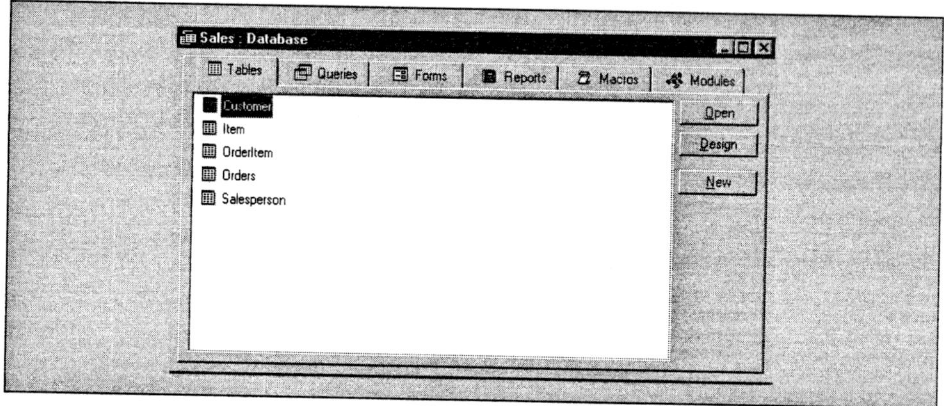

Figure 17.15 The `Customer` table created by Example 17.2

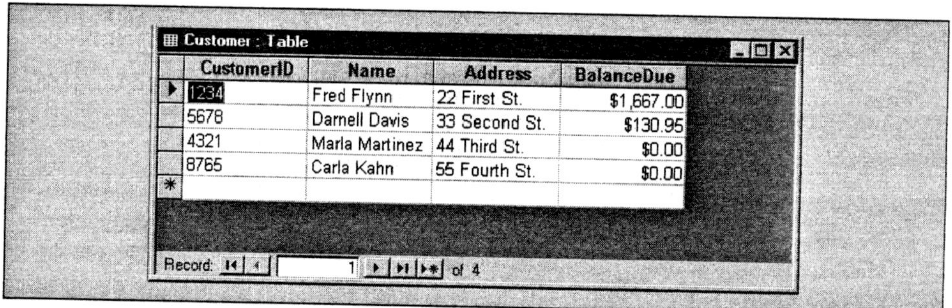
Customer : Table

CustomerID	Name	Address	BalanceDue
1234	Fred Flynn	22 First St.	$1,667.00
5678	Darnell Davis	33 Second St.	$130.95
4321	Marla Martinez	44 Third St.	$0.00
8765	Carla Kahn	55 Fourth St.	$0.00

Record: 1 of 4

EXAMPLE 17.2 Create.java

```
/* Creates and populates the Sales database.
 */

import java.sql.*;
import java.io.*;
import sun.jdbc.odbc.*;

public class Create {
  public static void main (String args[]) {
    try{
      new JdbcOdbcDriver();
      String url = "jdbc:odbc:Sales";
      String user = "";
      String password = "";
      Connection con = DriverManager.getConnection(url, user, password);
      Statement stmt = con.createStatement();

      stmt.executeUpdate ("CREATE TABLE Customer (CustomerID "
          + "VARCHAR(4), CustomerName VARCHAR(25), Address "
          + "VARCHAR(25), BalanceDue CURRENCY)");                // Note 1
```

```
stmt.executeUpdate ("INSERT INTO Customer "
    + " VALUES (1234,'Fred Flynn','22 First St.',1667.00)");    // Note 2
stmt.executeUpdate ("INSERT INTO Customer "
    + " VALUES (5678,'Darnell Davis','33 Second St.',130.95)");
stmt.executeUpdate ("INSERT INTO Customer"
    + " VALUES (4321,'Marla Martinez','44 Third St.',0)");
stmt.executeUpdate ("INSERT INTO Customer "
    + " VALUES (8765,'Carla Kahn','55 Fourth St.', 0)");

stmt.executeUpdate("CREATE TABLE Salesperson (SalespersonID "
    + " VARCHAR(2), SalespersonName VARCHAR(25), "
    + " Address VARCHAR(25))");
stmt.executeUpdate ("INSERT INTO Salesperson "
    + " VALUES (12,'Peter Patterson','66 Fifth St.')");
stmt.executeUpdate ("INSERT INTO Salesperson "
    + " VALUES (98,'Donna Dubarian','77 Sixth St.')");

stmt.executeUpdate("CREATE TABLE Item (ItemNumber VARCHAR(6),"
    + "Description VARCHAR(20), Quantity INTEGER)");
stmt.executeUpdate("INSERT INTO Item VALUES (222222,'radio',32)");
stmt.executeUpdate("INSERT INTO Item VALUES (333333,'television',14)");
stmt.executeUpdate("INSERT INTO Item VALUES (444444,'computer',9)");

stmt.executeUpdate("CREATE TABLE Orders (OrderNumber VARCHAR(4),"
    + " CustomerID VARCHAR(4), SalespersonID VARCHAR(2),"
    + " OrderDate DATE)");
stmt.executeUpdate
    ("INSERT INTO Orders VALUES (1,1234,12,'Apr 3, 1999')");
stmt.executeUpdate
    ("INSERT INTO Orders VALUES (2,5678,12,'Mar 22, 1999')");
stmt.executeUpdate
    ("INSERT INTO Orders VALUES (3,8765,98,'Feb 19, 1999')");
stmt.executeUpdate
    ("INSERT INTO Orders VALUES (4,1234,12,'Apr 5, 1999')");
stmt.executeUpdate
    ("INSERT INTO Orders VALUES (5,8765,98,'Feb 28, 1999')");

stmt.executeUpdate("CREATE TABLE OrderItem (OrderNumber CHAR(4),"
    + " ItemNumber CHAR(6), Quantity INTEGER, UnitPrice CURRENCY)");
stmt.executeUpdate("INSERT INTO OrderItem "                      // Note 3
    + " VALUES (1,222222,4,27.00)");
stmt.executeUpdate("INSERT INTO OrderItem "
    + " VALUES (1,333333,2,210.50)");
stmt.executeUpdate("INSERT INTO OrderItem "
    + " VALUES (1,444444,1,569.00)");
stmt.executeUpdate("INSERT INTO OrderItem "
    + " VALUES (2,333333,2,230.95)");
stmt.executeUpdate("INSERT INTO OrderItem "
    + " VALUES (3,222222,3,27.00)");
stmt.executeUpdate("INSERT INTO OrderItem "
    + " VALUES (3,333333,1,230.95)");
```

```
      stmt.executeUpdate("INSERT INTO OrderItem "
          + " VALUES (4,444444,1,569.00)");
      stmt.executeUpdate("INSERT INTO OrderItem "
          + " VALUES (5,222222,2,27.00)");
      stmt.executeUpdate("INSERT INTO "
          + " OrderItem VALUES (5,444444,1,725.00)");

      stmt.close();                                        // Note 4
    }catch (Exception e) {e.printStackTrace();}
  }
}
```

Note 1: Just as with any string, we need to split the SQL statement over multiple lines using the concatenation operator so that each string constant fits on one line.

Note 2: When splitting the SQL statement over multiple lines we must be sure to add spaces to separate identifiers. Without the spaces either after `Customer` or before `VALUES`, then the juxtaposition of `CustomerVALUES` would cause an error.

Note 3: Using nine statements to insert the nine rows into the `OrderItem` table is cumbersome, and would be more so if the table were larger. A better method is to read the data to enter from a file. We leave this improvement to the exercises.

Note 4: The `Statement` object, `stmt`, is closed automatically by the garbage collector and its resources freed, but it is good programming practice to close it explicitly.

THE BIG PICTURE

JDBC uses a driver to translate its platform-independent interface to work in a specific database system. We use the JDBC to ODBC bridge to connect to Access or a text file which have ODBC drivers. A URL, specific to the database system, locates the database. Once connected to the database, we can create tables and insert data into them from a Java program. Optionally we could have created the tables outside of Java.

TEST YOUR UNDERSTANDING

TRY IT YOURSELF 8. Register a new `Sales` database as an ODBC data source.

TRY IT YOURSELF 9. Modify Example 17.1 to input the JDBC driver and the database URL as program arguments.

TRY IT YOURSELF 10. Modify Example 17.2, as described in Note 2, to omit the spaces after `Customer` and before `VALUES`. What is the effect of this change?

17.3 Retrieving Information

Now that we have created the Sales database, we can use JDBC to extract information from it. When executing an SQL statement that returns results, we use the executeQuery method which returns a ResultSet containing the rows of data that satisfy the query. Executing

```
ResultSet rs = stmt.executeQuery
  ("SELECT CustomerName, Address FROM Customer");
```

returns the rows containing the names and address of all entries in the Customer table.

Viewing Query Results

To view the results, the ResultSet has getXXX methods where XXX is the Java type corresponding to the SQL type of the data field we are retrieving. Because CustomerName and Address both have the VARCHAR SQL type, we use the getString method to retrieve these fields. We can retrieve fields by name or by field number. The loop

```
while(rs.next())
  System.out.println(rs.getString(1) + '\t' + rs.getString("Address"))
```

will list the rows of names and addresses from the Customer table. We retrieve the CustomerName field using its column number 1 and the Address field using its name. The next() method returns **true** when another row is available and **false** otherwise. Figure 17.16 shows the Java methods corresponding to the SQL types we use.

Figure 17.16 Java methods for SQL types

Java method	SQL type
getInt	INTEGER
getString	VARCHAR
getBigDecimal	CURRENCY
getDate	DATE

SELECT Statement Options

The SELECT statement has additional options. The ORDER clause allows us to display the results sorted with respect to one or more columns. The query

```
SELECT CustomerName, Address FROM Customer ORDER BY CustomerName
```

returns the result set by name in alphabetical order. We could use

```
SELECT CustomerName, Address FROM Customer ORDER BY 1
```

to achieve the same result using the column number in the ORDER clause.

Sometimes a query may return duplicate rows. For example, in selecting customers who ordered computers we would get the result

```
Fred Flynn
Fred Flynn
Carla Kahn
```

because Fred Flynn bought computers in orders 1 and 4. We can remove duplicates by using the `SELECT DISTINCT` variant of the `SELECT` statement.

This query

```
SELECT DISTINCT CustomerName
FROM Customer, Item, Orders, OrderItem
WHERE Customer.CustomerID = Orders.CustomerID
AND Orders.OrderNumber = OrderItem.OrderNumber
AND OrderItem.ItemNumber = Item.ItemNumber
AND Description = 'computer'
```

joins rows from four tables to produce the result.

The `UPDATE` and `DELETE` statements change the database, but do not return results, so we use the `executeUpdate` method to execute them.

EXAMPLE 17.3 ExtractInfo.java

```
/* Demonstrates the use of SQL queries from
 * a Java program.
 */

import java.sql.*;
import java.io.*;
import sun.jdbc.odbc.*;
import java.text.*;

public class ExtractInfo {
  public static void main (String args[]) {
    try{
      new JdbcOdbcDriver();
      String url = "jdbc:odbc:Sales";
      String user = "";
      String password = "";
      Connection con = DriverManager.getConnection(url, user, password);
      Statement stmt = con.createStatement();

      String query = "SELECT CustomerName, Address FROM Customer "
          + "ORDER BY CustomerName";
      ResultSet rs = stmt.executeQuery(query);                    // Note 1
      System.out.println(" Names and Addresses of Customers");
      System.out.println("Name\t\tAddress");                      // Note 2
      while (rs.next())
      System.out.println
               (rs.getString("CustomerName") + '\t' + rs.getString(2));

      query = "SELECT * FROM OrderItem "
          + "WHERE ItemNumber = '222222'";
      rs = stmt.executeQuery(query);
      System.out.println();
      System.out.println(" Order items for radios");
      NumberFormat cf = NumberFormat.getCurrencyInstance():
```

```
System.out.println("OrderNumber\tQuantity\tUnitPrice");
while (rs.next())
  System.out.println(rs.getString(1) + "\t\t" + rs.getInt(3)
        + "\t\t" + cf.format(rs.getBigDecimal(4)));          // Note 3

query = "SELECT CustomerName FROM Customer, Orders "
+ "WHERE Customer.CustomerID = Orders.CustomerID "
+ "AND OrderDate = {d '1999-03-22'}";
rs = stmt.executeQuery(query);
System.out.println();
System.out.println(" Customer placing orders on Mar 22, 1999");
while(rs.next())
  System.out.println(rs.getString("CustomerName"));

query = "SELECT DISTINCT CustomerName "
    + "FROM Customer, Item, Orders, OrderItem "
    + "WHERE Customer.CustomerID = Orders.CustomerID "
    + "AND Orders.OrderNumber = OrderItem.OrderNumber "
    + "AND OrderItem.ItemNumber = Item.ItemNumber "
    + "AND Description = 'computer'";
rs = stmt.executeQuery(query);
System.out.println();
System.out.println(" Customers ordering computers");
while(rs.next())
  System.out.println(rs.getString(1));                       // Note 4

query = "SELECT OrderNumber FROM Orders "
    + "WHERE OrderDate "
    + "BETWEEN {d '1999-04-01'} AND {d '1999-04-30'}";
rs = stmt.executeQuery(query);
System.out.println();
System.out.println(" Order numbers of orders from 4/1/99 to 4/30/99");
while(rs.next())
  System.out.println(rs.getString("OrderNumber"));

String sql;
sql = "INSERT INTO Item VALUES (555555,'CD player',10)";       // Note 5
stmt.executeUpdate(sql);
sql = "UPDATE Item SET Quantity = 12 "
    + "WHERE Description = 'CD player'";
stmt.executeUpdate(sql);                                       // Note 6
System.out.println();
System.out.println(" Added and updated a new item");

System.out.println("Description");
query = "SELECT Description FROM Item";
rs = stmt.executeQuery(query);
while(rs.next())
  System.out.println(rs.getString(1));

sql = "DELETE FROM Item WHERE Description = 'CD player'";
stmt.executeUpdate(sql);
```

```
      query = "SELECT Description FROM Item";
      rs = stmt.executeQuery(query);
      System.out.println();
      System.out.println(" Deleted the new item");
      System.out.println("Description");
      while(rs.next())
        System.out.println(rs.getString(1));

      stmt.close();
    }catch (Exception e) {e.printStackTrace();}
  }
}
```

Output

```
Names and Addresses of Customers
Name            Address
Carla Kahn      55 Fourth St.
Darnell Davis   33 Second St.
Fred Flynn      22 First St.
Marla Martinez  44 Third St.

Order items for radios
OrderNumber   Quantity   UnitPrice
1             4          $27.00
3             3          $27.00
5             2          $27.00

  Customer placing orders on Mar 22, 1999
Darnell Davis

Customers ordering computers
Carla Kahn
Fred Flynn

  Order numbers of orders from 4/1/99 to 4/30/99
1
4

  Added and updated a new item
Description
radio
television
computer
CD player

  Deleted the new item
Description
radio
television
computer
```

Note 1: The SQL `SELECT` statement returns the selected rows in a `ResultSet`. We use the `executeQuery` method to execute `SELECT` statements.

Note 2: We embed tab characters, `\t`, in the string to space the data horizontally.

Note 3: We omitted field 2, `ItemNumber`, from the display because we selected all results to have `ItemNumber` = 222222. We could insert a single tab character using single quotes, `'\t'`, but inserting two characters requires the double-quoted string, `"\t\t"`. We use the `getInt` method because field 3, `Quantity`, has SQL type `INTEGER`. The argument, 4, to `getBigDecimal` is the field number. This `UnitPrice` field has type `Currency` in the database.

Note 4: We used the field number, 1, but could have used the field name, `CustomerName`, as the argument to `getString`. We will see in the next section how to get the number of fields and their names from the database if we do not know them.

Note 5: We add a new row to illustrate the `UPDATE` and `DELETE` statements which change the database. We update the new row, and then delete it, leaving the database unchanged when we exit the program. This is nice while learning JDBC because we can try various `SELECT` statements running the same program repeatedly without changing the data.

Note 6: `stmt.executeUpdate(sql);`
Because the `UPDATE` and `DELETE` statements do not return values, we use the `executeUpdate` method to execute them.

THE BIG PICTURE

When querying the database, a result set contains the selected rows. We use methods such as `getString` to display a value from a row of the result set. The SQL types have corresponding Java methods, so the Java `getInt` method retrieves `INTEGER` values, for example. We can write our SQL queries to order the results or to eliminate duplicate rows. A query may have to join several tables on common fields to obtain the desired information.

TEST YOUR UNDERSTANDING

11. Write an SQL statement to find names of salespersons and the customers that have placed orders with them. Be sure to eliminate duplicates.

TRY IT YOURSELF 12. Modify Example 17.3 to use only field names in the `getString`, `getInt`, and `getBigDecimal` methods.

TRY IT YOURSELF 13. Modify Example 17.3 to use only field numbers in the `getString`, `getInt`, and `getBigDecimal` methods.

TRY IT YOURSELF 14. Modify Example 17.3 to list `CustomerID` in addition to `CustomerName` and `Address`. Arrange the output rows so that the `CustomerID` numbers appear in numerical order.

15. Write a `SELECT` statement to find the names and addresses of customers who placed orders with Peter Patterson. Be sure to eliminate duplicates.

17.4 Metadata and Aggregate Functions

Java, with JDBC, allows us to get information about the database (**metadata**) with which we are working, and about any result sets we obtain. We can use SQL functions to compute with the data.

Database Metadata

The `DatabaseMetaData` methods return information about the database to which we are connected. To use these methods we first execute

```
DatabaseMetaData dbMetaData = con.getMetaData();
```

where `con` is the connection to the database. We can ask what level of SQL the database system supports by using the three methods

```
dbMetaData.supportsANSI92EntryLevelSQL();
dbMetaData.supportsANSI92IntermediateSQL();
dbMetaData.supportsANSI92FullSQL();
```

where ANSI (pronounced an´-see) stands for the American National Standards Institute. Java requires that JDBC drivers support ANSI92 entry level SQL so the first method must always return **true**. The Microsoft Access version 7.0 that we use supports ANSI89 but does not support ANSI92 intermediate or full SQL.

The method

```
dbMetaData.getIdentifierQuoteString();
```

returns the character used to delimit strings; in our database that is the single quote, `'`. Executing

```
ResultSet rs = dbMetaData.getTypeInfo();
```

gives us the type names used in the database itself, which may be different from the standard SQL types, or Java types. For example Microsoft Access uses the `CURRENCY` type and internally uses `TEXT` for the SQL `VARCHAR` type. We can list the type names from the result set using the loop

```
while(rs.next())
  System.out.println(rs.getString("TYPE_NAME"));
```

The very handy `getTables` method lets us obtain the names of the tables in our database. For example,

```
dbMetaData.getTables(null,null,"%",tables);
```

will return the names of the five tables in the `Sales` database. The first two arguments represent the catalog and schema facilities. Our application is not so elaborate, and here we pass **null** for these arguments.

The third argument to `getTables` is a string representing a search pattern for the tables we are seeking. In a large database with many tables, we might search for all tables starting with "Payroll" by using the string "Payroll%" where the % character matches zero or more characters. Because we want all tables, we use the string "%" which matches any string. To match a single character we could use the string "_", so "Payroll_" would match strings such as Payroll1, Payroll2, and so on.

The fourth argument to `getTables` uses an array of strings to specify the types of table for which to search. In addition to the tables that we created, there are various system tables in the database in which we are not interested. To limit our search we declare the fourth argument as

```
String[] tables = {"TABLE"};
```

which restricts the search to user-defined data tables.

We can also use database metadata to find the column names and types for each table. The method call

```
ResultSet rs = dbMetaData.getColumns(null,null,"Customer","%");
```

returns information about each column of the `Customer` table. As with the `getTables` methods we pass **null** arguments for the catalog and schema which we do not use. The third argument is a pattern for the tables to search; we pass the name `Customer` to get its columns. The fourth argument allows a string pattern to select the columns. We pass "%" to retrieve all columns. The details of interest about each column are its name and type which we access using

```
rs.getString("COLUMN_NAME");
```

and

```
rs.getString("TYPE_NAME");
```

Result Set Metadata

JDBC allows us to get information about each result set. We use

```
ResultSetMetaData rsMetaData = rs.getMetaData();
```

to get the `rsMetaData` object, and then use the methods

```
rsMetaData.getColumnCount();
```

to return the number of columns in the result set,

```
rsMetaData.getColumnLabel(i);
```

to return the name of column `i`, and

```
rsMetaData.getColumnTypeName(i);
```

to return its type.

Using the `getColumns` method, we suggested just listing the `COLUMN_NAME` and `TYPE_NAME` fields of the result set returned. In Example 17.4 we use result set metadata to list all the fields of the result set describing each column of the database. Perhaps not surprisingly, we found these result set fields differ from those described in the documentation included with the JDK, using versions 1.1.6 and 1.3.0.

The `colNamesTypes` method in Example 17.4 uses the `getColumnLabel` and `getColumnTypeName` methods to return the names and types of each of the columns of its result set argument. We can use it with any result set. For example, using it with the result set returned by

```
stmt.executeQuery("SELECT * FROM Item");
```

would list the all columns, with their types, from the Item table, because using the star, `*`, in the `SELECT` clause returns all the columns of the table.

Aggregate Functions

Aggregate functions compute values from the table data, using all the rows to produce the result. For example, the query

```
SELECT SUM(BalanceDue),
       AVG(BalanceDue),
       MAX(BalanceDue)
FROM Customer
```

returns the sum, average, and maximum of all the balances due in the customer table. These functions operate on the `BalanceDue` column for all rows in the `Customer` table. Using a `WHERE` clause, as in

```
SELECT COUNT(*), MIN(Quantity) FROM OrderItem
WHERE ItemNumber = '222222'
```

will limit the computation to the rows of the `OrderItem` table which correspond to orders for radios. The function `COUNT(*)` will return the total number of rows satisfying this condition. `MIN(Quantity)` returns the minimum quantity of radios ordered in one of the three rows of the `OrderItem` table which represent orders for radios (item number 222222).

EXAMPLE 17.4 DatabaseInfo.java

```
/* Illustrate DatabaseMetaData, ResultSetMetaData
 * and SQL aggregate functions.
 */

import java.sql.*;
import java.io.*;

class DatabaseInfo {
  public static void main (String args[]) {
    try{
      ResultSet rs;
      Class.forName("sun.jdbc.odbc.JdbcOdbcDriver");                // Note 1
      String url = "jdbc:odbc:Sales";
      Connection con = DriverManager.getConnection(url);             // Note 2

      DatabaseMetaData dbMetaData = con.getMetaData();
```

```
System.out.println("Supports entry level SQL: " +
       dbMetaData.supportsANSI92EntryLevelSQL());
System.out.println("Supports intermediate SQL: " +
       dbMetaData.supportsANSI92IntermediateSQL());
System.out.println("Supports full SQL: " +
       dbMetaData.supportsANSI92FullSQL());
System.out.println("Supports stored procedures: "+
       dbMetaData.supportsStoredProcedures());
System.out.println("Quote string: " +
       dbMetaData.getIdentifierQuoteString());
System.out.println("Types used in the database:");
System.out.print('\t');

rs = dbMetaData.getTypeInfo();
while (rs.next())
  System.out.print(rs.getString("TYPE_NAME") + " ");               // Note 3
System.out.println();

String[] tables ={"TABLE"};
rs = dbMetaData.getTables(null,null,"%",tables);
System.out.println("Tables in the Sales database:");
System.out.print('\t');
while(rs.next())
  System.out.print(rs.getString("TABLE_NAME") + " ");              // Note 4
System.out.println();

rs = dbMetaData.getColumns(null,null,"Customer","%");
System.out.println("Columns in the Customer table");
while(rs.next())
  System.out.println('\t'+rs.getString("COLUMN_NAME")+"             // Note 5
      "+rs.getString("TYPE_NAME"));
displayStrings("Fields describing each column",colNamesTypes(rs)); // Note 6
String query;
query = "SELECT * FROM Item";
Statement stmt = con.createStatement();
rs = stmt.executeQuery(query);
displayStrings("Item Columns",colNamesTypes(rs));                  // Note 7

query = "SELECT SUM(BalanceDue),AVG(BalanceDue), "
      + "MAX(BalanceDue) FROM Customer";
rs = stmt.executeQuery(query);
displayStrings("Function columns",colNamesTypes(rs));              // Note 8
System.out.println("Sum, average, and maximum balance due");
NumberFormat cf = NumberFormat.getCurrencyInstance();
while(rs.next())
  System.out.println(cf.format(rs.getBigDecimal(1))
    +" " + cf.format(rs.getBigDecimal(2))
    +" " + cf.format)rs.getBigDecimal(3)));
query = "SELECT COUNT(*), MIN(Quantity) FROM OrderItem "
      + "WHERE ItemNumber = '222222' ";
rs = stmt.executeQuery(query);
```

```
      while(rs.next()){
        System.out.println("Number of radio order items: " + rs.getInt(1));
        System.out.println("Minimum quantity of radios ordered in any order item: "
              + rs.getInt(2));
      }

      stmt.close();
    }catch (Exception e) {e.printStackTrace();}
  }
  public static String[] colNamesTypes(ResultSet rs) throws SQLException {
    ResultSetMetaData rsMetaData = rs.getMetaData();
    int cols = rsMetaData.getColumnCount();
    String[] s = new String[cols];                                    // Note 9
    String label, tab;
    for (int i =1; i <= cols; i++) {
      label = rsMetaData.getColumnLabel(i);
      if (label.length() < 8) tab = "\t\t"; else tab = "\t";          // Note 10
      s[i - 1] = '\t' + label + tab + rsMetaData.getColumnTypeName(i);   // Note 11
    }
    return s;
  }
  public static void displayStrings(String description, String[]s) { // Note 12
    System.out.println(description);
    for(int i = 0; i < s.length; i++)
    System.out.println(s[i]);
  }
}
```

Output

```
Supports entry level SQL: true
Supports intermediate SQL: false
Supports full SQL: false
Supports stored procedures: true
Quote string: `
Types used in the database:
      BIT BYTE LONGBINARY VARBINARY BINARY LONGTEXT CHAR
CURRENCY LONG COUNTER SHORT SINGLE DOUBLE DATETIME TEXT
Tables in the Sales database:
    Customer Item OrderItem Orders Salesperson
Columns in the Customer table
    CustomerID TEXT
    CustomerName TEXT
    Address TEXT
    BalanceDue CURRENCY
Fields describing each column
    TABLE_QUALIFIER TEXT
```

```
    TABLE_OWNER     TEXT
    TABLE_NAME      TEXT
    COLUMN_NAME     TEXT
    DATA_TYPE       SHORT
  TYPE_NAME     TEXT
  PRECISION     LONG
  LENGTH        LONG
  SCALE         SHORT
  RADIX         SHORT
  NULLABLE      SHORT
  REMARKS       TEXT
  ORDINAL       LONG
Item Columns
  ItemNumber    TEXT
  Description   TEXT
  Quantity      LONG
Function columns
  Expr1000      CURRENCY
  Expr1001      CURRENCY
  Expr1002      CURRENCY
Sum, average, and maximum balance due
$1797.95 $449.49 $1667.00
Number of radio order items: 3
Minimum quantity of radios ordered in any order item: 2
```

Note 1: To show how it works, we use the `forName` method to load the JDBC driver. The advantage of this approach is we could easily modify this program to pass the driver name as a program argument. We have no need to do that here but it might be useful in writing a general application designed to work with different databases.

Note 2: We use the form of the `getConnection` method that does not require a user name or a password because these are not needed for the Microsoft Access database system we are using.

Note 3: According to the JDK documentation, the `getTypeInfo` method returns 18 columns of information for each type provided by the database system. We only list one, `TYPE_NAME`, leaving as an exercise the use of the `colNamesTypes` to list the names and types of all columns of this result set to see if they correspond to the 18 listed in the documentation.

Note 4: According to the JDK documentation, the `getTables` method returns five columns of information for each table in the database. We list only `TABLE_NAME`. It is column 3 so we could have used `getString(3)` to retrieve it, but using the column name is much more helpful.

Note 5: According to the JDK documentation, the `getColumns` method returns 18 fields to describe each column. (However, see Note 6.) We list `COLUMN_NAME` and `COLUMN_TYPE`.

Note 6: `displayStrings ("Fields describing each column",colNamesTypes(rs));`
Using the `colNamesTypes` method to list the names and types of the columns in the result set returned by the `getColumns` method we see that the result set actually contains 13 columns, some of which are named differently than the columns listed in the JDK documentation.

Note 7: `displayStrings("Item Columns",colNamesTypes(rs));`
This shows that we can use the `colNamesTypes` method to display the names and types of the columns of any result set, in this case the one which selects all columns from the `Item` table.

Note 8: `displayStrings("Function columns",colNamesTypes(rs));`
The result set gives the values of the `SUM`, `AVG`, and `MAX` functions. These are not columns of the `Customer` tables, but rather they are values computed from the `BalanceDue` column. We use the `colNamesTypes` method to list the names and types of the columns in the result set. Because these columns have no names Java creates the names Expr1000, Expr1001, and Expr1003 for them. They have internal database types of `CURRENCY` which does not correspond to a SQL type. The Java `getBigDecimal` method will return the value of each function.

Note 9: `String[] s = new String[cols];`
We use a string array to hold the name and type of each column in the result set argument to this method.

Note 10: To keep the type column aligned we use two tab characters as a separator when the column name is less than eight characters in length, but one tab character otherwise.

Note 11:
```
s[i-1] = '\t' + label + tab +
rsMetaData.getColumnTypeName(i);
```
Column numbers start at 1, while array indices start at 0, so we store column `i` in array component `i-1`.

Note 12: The `displayStrings` method displays a description and a list of the elements of its `String` array argument.

THE BIG PICTURE

Database metadata tells us properties of the database such as the names of its tables, and the names and types of the columns in a table. Result set metadata lets us find properties of a result set. We can find the number of columns in the result set and the label and type of each column. We can use result set metadata on a result set from a database metadata method or on a result set from an SQL query. Aggregate functions compute values from the rows of a table.

TEST YOUR UNDERSTANDING

TRY IT YOURSELF 16. Modify Example 17.4 to pass **null** as the fourth argument to the `getTables` method, instead of the `tables` array. This will list all tables in the database, including the system tables.

TRY IT YOURSELF 17. Modify Example 17.4 to change the third argument to the `getTables` method to find the tables in the `Sales` database which start with `Order`.

TRY IT YOURSELF 18. Modify Example 17.4 to use the `colNamesTypes` method to list all the fields of the result set returned by the `getTypeInfo` method. Compare these fields to those listed in the JDK documentation, if available.

TRY IT YOURSELF 19. Modify Example 17.4 to use the `colNamesTypes` method to list all the fields of the result set returned by the `getTables` method. Compare these fields to those listed in the JDK documentation, if available.

17.5 Prepared Statements and Transactions*

A prepared statement lets us translate a statement to low-level database commands once, and execute it many times, thus avoiding the inefficient repetition of the translation process.

When making changes to a database we must be very careful that we complete all steps of the transaction. It would not do to withdraw funds from one account, but not have it deposited in another. **Transaction processing** allows us to explicitly control when changes become final, so that we only **commit** changes when all those desired have completed correctly.

Using Prepared Statements

Often we may wish to execute a query repeatedly using different conditions each time. The query

```
SELECT * FROM OrderItem
WHERE ItemNumber = '222222'
```

selects all order items with number 222222. To execute this query for each item, we could use a loop such as

```
String[] numbers = {"222222","333333","444444"}
ResultSet rs;
for (int i = 0; i < numbers.length; i++) {
  rs = stmt.executeQuery("SELECT * FROM OrderItem "
              + "WHERE ItemNumber = '" + numbers[i] + '\'');
  // process results
}
```

* The ODBC text driver does not handle prepared statements or transactions.

We have only three products in our database, but we might have had many more. For each product, the database system must process the SQL query analyzing how to find the requested data from the database in the most efficient way possible. Our query is quite simple, but it could have been much more complex. Each time we call `executeQuery`, we have to process the query, spending the time over and over again to find the best way to find the results that satisfy it.

The prepared statement allows the database system to process an SQL query once, determining the best way to get the results. We can then use this prepared statement over and over again with different data but without the overhead of translating it again.

We use the question mark, ?, to denote the arguments to query that we wish to change from one execution to the next. To make a prepared statement from our previous query, we write it as

```
String query = "SELECT * FROM OrderItem "
  + "WHERE ItemNumber = ?";
```

where the question mark stands for the item number that we will pass in. Next we create a prepared statement using

```
PreparedStatement pStmt = con.prepareStatement(query);
```

where `con` is the connection to the database.

To pass arguments to a query we use `setXXX` methods where `XXX` stands for the type of the argument. In our example, `ItemNumber` has type `VARCHAR` which corresponds to the string type in Java, so we use the `setString` method, as in

```
pStmt.setString(1,"222222");
```

where we enclose the item number in double quotes because we are inside Java and not writing an SQL statement for this database system. The first argument to `setString` is the number of the argument to which we want to pass the value specified. We number the arguments in the order they appear in the query, with the first argument having number 1. The statement

```
rs = pStmt.executeQuery();
```

executes the prepared query with the argument 222222.

TIP The `executeQuery` method takes no arguments when used with a prepared statement because we have already passed the query to the `prepareStatement` method.

We process the result set as we did with simple statements. The code

```
System.out.println("OrderNumber\tQuantity\tUnitPrice");
while (rs.next())
  System.out.println(rs.getString(1) + "\t\t" + rs.getInt(3)
    + "\t\t" + cf.format(rs.getBigDecimal(4)));
```

extracted from Example 17.3 will return the other columns of all rows in the `OrderItem` table having the specified item number.

After closing the result set with

```
rs.close();
```

we could pass another argument to the query and execute the query again as in

```
pStmt.setString(1,"333333");
rs = pStmt.executeQuery();
```

which would find the rows of the `OrderItem` table whose item number is 333333, representing a television order.

To pass multiple arguments we use additional question marks in the query. In the query

```
query = "SELECT OrderNumber FROM Orders "
      + "WHERE OrderDate BETWEEN ? AND ?";
```

the arguments represent the starting and ending dates of orders. After creating the prepared statement, we pass the arguments using the `setDate` method as in

```
pStmt.setDate(1, Date.valueOf("1999-04-01"));
```

which replaces the first question mark with April 1, 1999, and

```
pStmt.setDate(2, Date.valueOf("1999-04-30"));
```

which replaces the second question mark with April 30, 1999. The `Date` class, in the `java.sql` package, extends `java.util.Date`. The `valueOf` method translates a string representing the date to a `Date` that can be used in the database system.

In preparing a statement to which we pass an argument that is a currency amount, we use the `setBigDecimal` method to pass the currency value. For example, the query

```
SELECT CustomerName FROM Customer
WHERE BalanceDue > ?
```

has an argument for the `BalanceDue` value. To pass such a value to the prepared statement created from this query, we use

```
pStmt.setBigDecimal(1, new java.math.BigDecimal(0.0));
```

The `BigDecimal`, created from the double `0.0`, will represent the amount $0.00, so our query will return the names of all customers with a non-zero balance.

Transaction Processing

Often when using a database we need to execute several statements to perform the desired transaction. For example, if a customer places a new order we will update the `Order` table with another order, the `OrderItem` table with the items ordered, and the `Customer` table with a new `BalanceDue`. We would be unhappy if an error occurred after some, but not all of these changes were made. Java allows us to manage transactions so we only commit the changes to the database when they complete without error.

The JDBC default is to commit the change as soon as we execute the update. The statement

```
con.setAutoCommit(false);
```

changes from the default behavior to require that we explicitly commit changes using

```
con.commit();
```

If we have already executed some updates and decide we do not want to commit them, we can roll back to the point when we executed the last commit, undoing these changes using

```
con.rollback();
```

For example, if we have removed the auto commit default, after executing the queries

```
INSERT INTO Item VALUES (555555,'CD player',10)
```

and

```
UPDATE Item SET Quantity = 12
WHERE Description = 'CD player'
```

we can either commit them, making the changes permanent, using the `commit` method, or undo them using the `rollback` method.

EXAMPLE 17.5 Prepare.java

```
/* Illustrates prepared statements
 * and transaction processing.
 */

import java.sql.*;
import java.io.*;

class Prepare {
  public static void main (String args[]) {
    try {
      ResultSet rs;
      Class.forName("sun.jdbc.odbc.JdbcOdbcDriver");
      String url = "jdbc:odbc:Sales";
      Connection con = DriverManager.getConnection(url);
      con.setAutoCommit(false);                              // Note 1

      String query;
      query = "SELECT Quantity FROM Item "
            + "WHERE Description = ?";                       // Note 2
      PreparedStatement pStmt = con.prepareStatement(query);
      pStmt.setString(1, "radio");
      rs = pStmt.executeQuery();
```

```
System.out.println(" Using a prepared statement to find quantity of radios");
while(rs.next())
  System.out.println(rs.getInt("Quantity"));
rs.close();                                                       // Note 3

pStmt.setString(1, "computer");
rs = pStmt.executeQuery();
System.out.println
      (" Using a prepared statement to find quantity of computers");
while(rs.next())
  System.out.println(rs.getInt("Quantity"));
rs.close();

query = "SELECT OrderNumber FROM Orders "
      + "WHERE OrderDate BETWEEN ? AND ?";
pStmt =con.prepareStatement(query);
pStmt.setDate(1, Date.valueOf("1999-04-01"));                     // Note 4
pStmt.setDate(2, Date.valueOf("1999-04-30"));
rs = pStmt.executeQuery();
System.out.println(" Using a prepared statement to find orders in April");
while(rs.next())
  System.out.println(rs.getInt("OrderNumber"));
rs.close();

query = "SELECT CustomerName FROM Customer "
    + "WHERE BalanceDue > ?";
pStmt = con.prepareStatement(query);
pStmt.setBigDecimal(1, new java.math.BigDecimal(0.0));
rs = pStmt.executeQuery();
System.out.println(" Using a prepared statement to find customers "
    + "with non-zero balance");
while(rs.next())
  System.out.println(rs.getString("CustomerName"));
pStmt.close();                                                    // Note 5

Statement stmt = con.createStatement();
String sql;
sql = "INSERT INTO Item VALUES (555555,'CD player',10)";
stmt.executeUpdate(sql);

sql = "UPDATE Item SET Quantity = 12 "
    + "WHERE Description = 'CD player'";
stmt.executeUpdate(sql);
System.out.println();
System.out.println
       (" Before commit or rollback -- table changed, but can rollback");
System.out.println("Description");
query = "SELECT Description FROM Item";
rs = stmt.executeQuery(query);
while(rs.next())
  System.out.println(rs.getString(1));                            // Note 6
```

```
        con.rollback();                                              // Note 7
        System.out.println();
        System.out.println(" Rolled back insert and update -- table unchanged");
        System.out.println("Description");
        query = "SELECT Description FROM Item";
        rs = stmt.executeQuery(query);
        while(rs.next())
          System.out.println(rs.getString(1));

        sql = "INSERT INTO Item VALUES (555555,'CD player',10)";     // Note 8
        stmt.executeUpdate(sql);
        sql = "UPDATE Item SET Quantity = 12 "
            + "WHERE Description = 'CD player'";
        stmt.executeUpdate(sql);
        con.commit();                                                // Note 9
        System.out.println();
        System.out.println(" Committed insert and update -- table changed");
        System.out.println("Description");
        query = "SELECT Description FROM Item";
        rs = stmt.executeQuery(query);
        while(rs.next())
          System.out.println(rs.getString(1));

        sql = "DELETE FROM Item WHERE Description = 'CD player'";    // Note 10
        stmt.executeUpdate(sql);
        con.commit();                                                // Note 11
        query = "SELECT Description FROM Item";
        rs = stmt.executeQuery(query);
        System.out.println();
        System.out.println(" Deleted the new item");
        System.out.println("Description");
        while(rs.next())
          System.out.println(rs.getString(1));

        stmt.close();
      }catch (Exception e) {e.printStackTrace();}
    }
  }
```

Output

```
Using a prepared statement to find quantity of radios
32
  Using a prepared statement to find quantity of computers
9
  Using a prepared statement to find orders in April
1
4
  Using a prepared statement to find customers with non-zero balance
Fred Flynn
```

```
Darnell Davis

  Before commit or rollback -- table changed, but can rollback
Description
radio
television
computer
CD player

 .Rolled back insert and update -- table unchanged
Description
radio
television
computer

  Committed insert and update -- table changed
Description
radio
television
computer
CD player

  Deleted the new item
Description
radio
television
computer
```

Note 1: With auto commit off, we must execute the `commit` statement in order to make our updates permanent.

Note 2: The question mark indicates where we can substitute one of the descriptions, `radio`, `television`, or `computer`.

Note 3: With simple statements we do not need to close the result set after each query. The `stmt.close` method also closes the result set when we are done with the statement, `stmt`. For prepared statements we need to close the result set after each query.

Note 4: The `Date` class, in the `java.sql` package, extends `java.util.Date`.

Note 5: Closing the prepared statement, `pStmt`, automatically closes the last result set too.

Note 6: `while(rs.next()) System.out.println(rs.getString(1));`
Outputting the descriptions of the items in the database shows that the database system has entered the item `CD player` (with the updated quantity of `12` not shown). We have not yet executed the `commit` statement so we still have a chance to rollback this change.

Note 7: `con.rollback();`
After we rollback the updates we find only the original three items in the `Item` table.

Note 8: `sql = "INSERT INTO Item VALUES (555555,'CD player',10)";`
Now we make the same updates, this time actually committing them to the database.

Note 9: `con.commit();`
This will commit the previous updates to the database and prevent further rollbacks of them. Only updates executed after this can be rolled back.

Note 10: `sql = "DELETE FROM Item WHERE Description = 'CD player'";`
We delete the new row from the database, to leave it as we found it in this pedagogical example.

Note 11: `con.commit();`
We must commit the DELETE transaction for it to take effect.

THE BIG PICTURE

A prepared statement lets us translate a query once and substitute values for its parameters to execute it repeatedly. By deciding explicitly when to commit changes to the database, we reserve the option to rollback some changes if the entire transaction cannot be completed.

TEST YOUR UNDERSTANDING

20. Write a `SELECT` statement to return the names of customers who ordered an item given by its description in the Item table, which we pass in as an argument, so we can create a prepared statement from the query.

TRY IT YOURSELF 21. Modify Example 17.5 to omit the first `rs.close()` statement. Does any error result? If so, which?

TRY IT YOURSELF 22. Modify Example 17.5 to find the order numbers of orders placed in March. Use the same prepared statement.

TRY IT YOURSELF 23. Modify Example 17.5 to omit the last `commit` statement. Run the modified program and check the database afterward to see that the new row has not been deleted; it must be deleted manually.

17.6 A GUI for Database Queries

Our case study builds a graphical user interface for querying our `Sales` database. This example illustrates the JDBC techniques covered in this chapter, adding the user interface concepts studied earlier. Even as presented here it is large for an introductory example. It would need many extensions and much polishing to make it a really useful application. Some of these extensions are left to the exercises.

The `SearchSales` program allows the user to create a `SELECT` query, and executes it, displaying the resulting rows. We use the gridbag layout to arrange the components. Figure 17.17 shows the initial screen.

Figure 17.17 The `SearchSales` initial screen

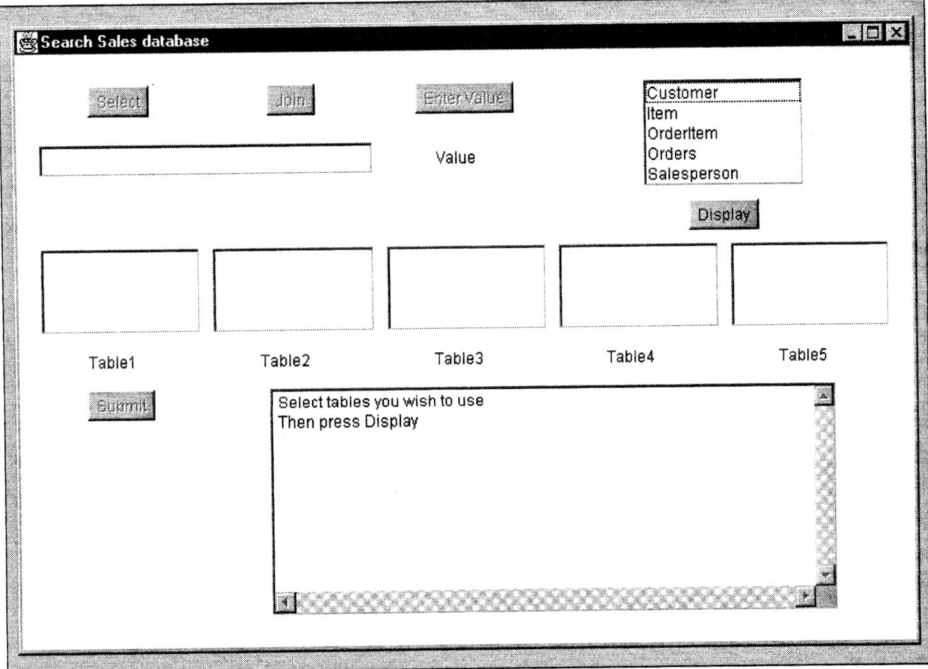

The `List` (we cover the `List` component below) at the upper-right shows the five tables of the `Sales` database. The user selects the tables to search. The names of these tables will appear after `FROM` in the query. The text area at the bottom gives instructions to the user, and displays the final results of the search. We disable all buttons, except `Display`, until we are ready to use them.

Figures 17.18–17.22 show the steps in the creation and execution of the query

```
SELECT CustomerName FROM Customer, Orders
WHERE Customer.CustomerID = Orders.CustomerID
AND OrderDate = {d '1999-03-22'}
```

Figure 17.18 shows the screen after the user has selected the `Customer` and `Orders` tables, and pressed the `Display` button. We have disabled the `Display` button because the user has already chosen the tables. The column names for the `Customer` table appear in the leftmost `List`, while those for the `Orders` table appear in the fourth `List`. The labels underneath now show the table names. Thus far our query is

```
SELECT ... FROM Customer, Order.
```

The user now selects the columns to be part of the result set, in this example choosing `CustomerName` and pressing the `Select` button. The partially constructed query is now

Figure 17.18 Screen to choose columns for the result

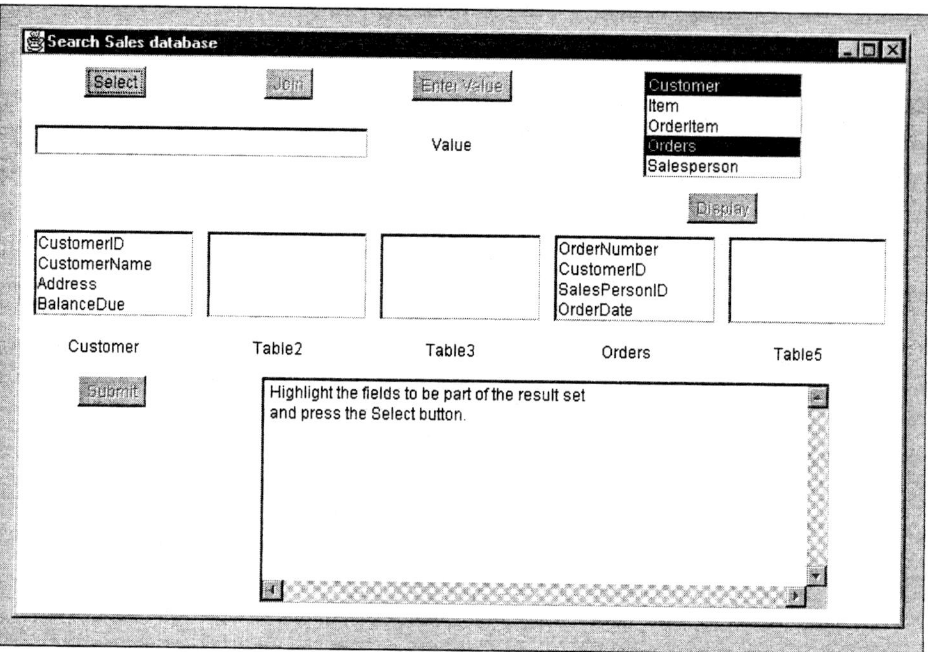


```
SELECT CustomerName FROM Customer, Order
```

Figure 17.19 shows the next screen in which we disabled the Select button, because we only select the fields of the result once. We deselect all fields so that the user will not have to deselect the fields before going on to the next step. At this point we enable the *Join*, *Enter Value*, and *Submit* buttons. The user would be ready to execute queries without conditions, such as

```
SELECT CustomerName FROM Customer,
```

so we enable the `Submit` button. The `Join` and `Enter Value` buttons allow us to add conditions that restrict the scope of the query.

In our example query we join the `Customer` and the `Orders` tables, requiring the condition

```
Customer.CustomerID = Orders.CustomerID.
```

We impose this condition to join the information from the two tables properly, and also impose the condition

```
OrderDate = {d '1999-03-22'}
```

to select orders placed on March 22, 1999.

Figure 17.20 indicates the user has selected the `CustomerID` field in the `Customer` table and the `CustomerID` field in the `Orders` table.

Figure 17.19 After pressing the `Select` button

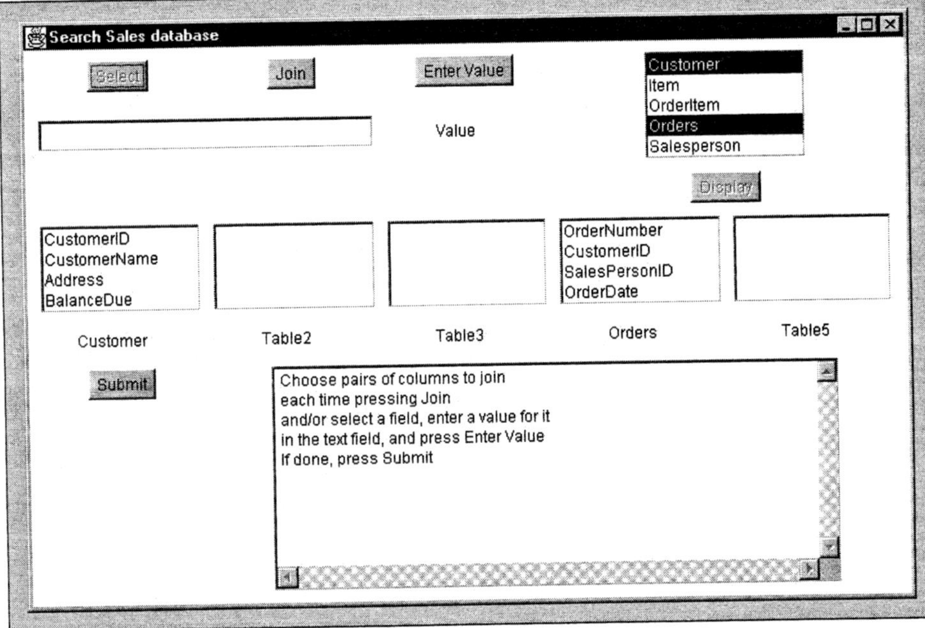

Figure 17.20 Adding a `Join` condition

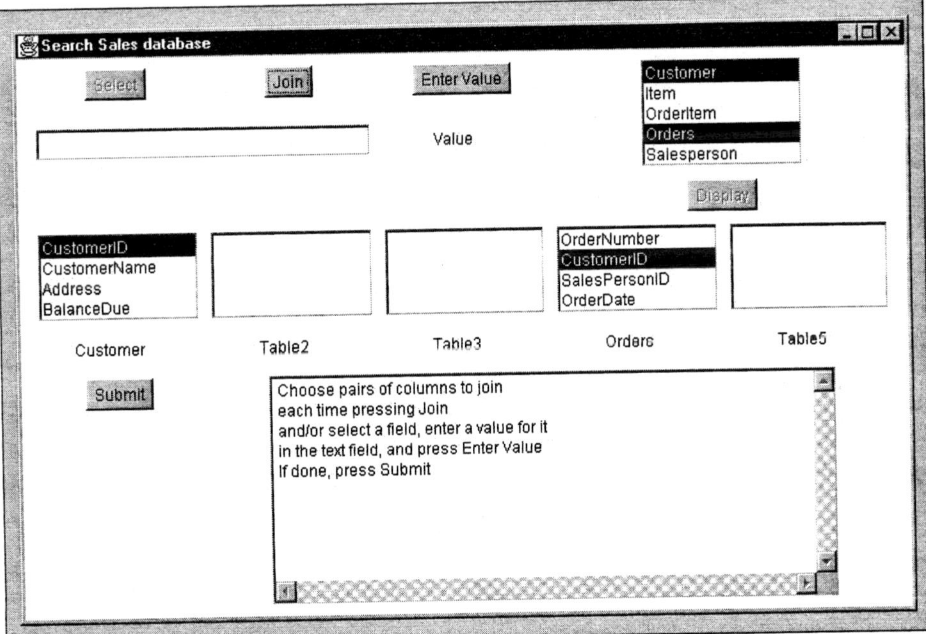

After pressing the `Join` button the partially completed query will be

```
SELECT CustomerName FROM Customer, Order
WHERE Customer.CustomerID = Orders.CustomerID
```

The next screen, Figure 17.21 has the same options as in Figure 17.20, because we can add conditions or submit the completed query. We choose the `OrderDate` column from the `Orders` table and enter the value `{d '1999-03-22}` in the text field. Pressing the `Enter Value` button will add to our query the condition that the order date be March 22, 1999. We only use the equality relation in our conditions leaving the extension to less than and greater than to the exercises.

Figure 17.21 Entering the `OrderDate` condition

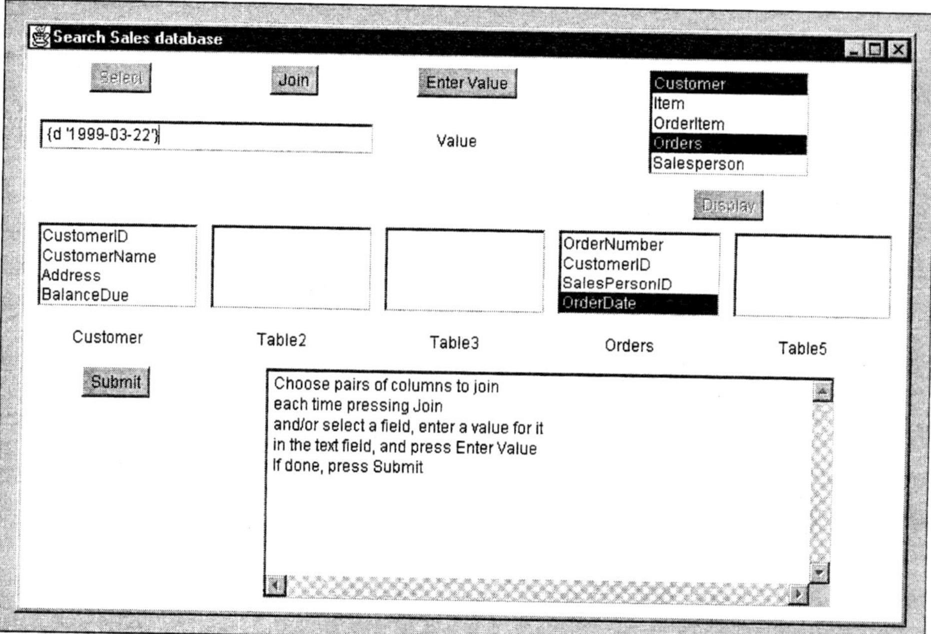

We could add more conditions, but this completes our query, so we press the `Submit` button. Figure 17.22, shows the resulting list (of only one customer, Darnell Davis) displayed in the text area. We disable all buttons, leaving for the exercises the option to continue executing additional queries.

The `List` Component

The `List` component we use in Example 17.6 differs from a choice box in that we can specify how many entries to display and select multiple entries.

The constructor

```
List(5,true)
```

specifies a box that will show five entries, providing a scroll bar if the list contains more than five items. A second argument of **true** permits multiple selections.

Figure 17.22 The query result

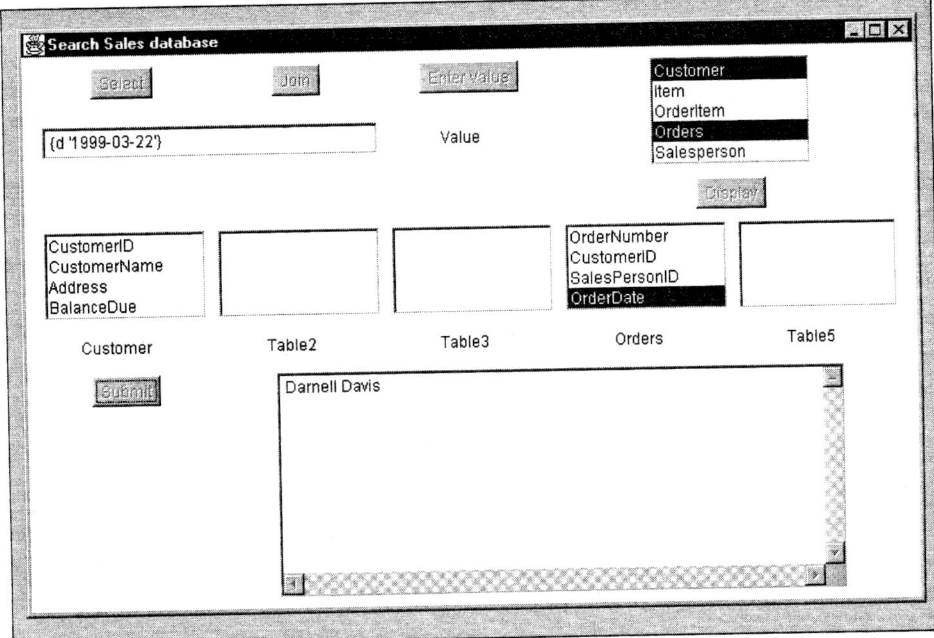

We add items to a `List` using the `add` method, as in

```
tables.add("Customer");
```

Single-clicking the mouse on a list item generates an `ItemEvent`, while double-clicking on an item generates an `ActionEvent`. We do not handle these events in this example, because we prefer to wait until the user selects all the desired items and presses the appropriate button to ask us to process the selections.

EXAMPLE 17.6 SearchSales.java

```
/* Provides a GUI to execute an SQL query
 * on the Sales database.
 * /

import java.awt.*;
import java.awt.event.*;
import java.sql.*;
import java.net.*;

public class SearchSales extends Frame implements ActionListener{
  public static final int SIZE = 5;
  List tables = new List(SIZE,true);        // tables in Sales database
  List[] columns = new List[SIZE];          // columns in each table
  Label[] colLabel = new Label[SIZE];       // label for each table's col list
  Label value = new Label("Value");
  TextField fieldValue = new TextField(12);  // enter a value in a condition
```

```
  Button submit = new Button("Submit");       // submit the query
  Button join = new Button("Join");           // choose common columns in a
                                                 condition
  Button enter = new Button("Enter Value");   // enter the value for the
                                                 condition
  Button select = new Button("Select");       // choose the columns for result
                                                 set
  Button display = new Button("Display");     // display the selected tables'
                                                 columns
  TextArea result = new TextArea();           // display prompts and final
                                                 result

  Connection con;
  Statement stmt;
  DatabaseMetaData dbMetaData;
  String[] tableName = new String[SIZE];      // names of the selected Sales
                                                 tables
  int[] indices = null;                       // indices of Sales tables
                                                 selected
  String resultCols = "";                     // result set columns, after
                                                 SELECT
  boolean firstJoin = true;                   // first time for join
  String joinClauses = "";                    // clauses to be joined, after
                                                 WHERE or AND
  String condition = "";                      // condition clauses, after WHERE
                                                 or AND
  String fromTables = "";                     // tables used, for FROM part of
                                                 query
  String query = "SELECT ";                   // the query to be executed
  int count = 0;                              // number of cols in result set

  public SearchSales(String title) {
    setTitle(title);
    for(int i = 0; i < SIZE; i++)                                  // Note 1
      columns[i] = new List(4,true);
    for(int i = 0; i < SIZE; i++)                                  // Note 2
      colLabel[i] = new Label("Table" + (i+1));
    GridBagLayout gbl = new GridBagLayout();
    setLayout(gbl);
    GridBagConstraints c = new GridBagConstraints();
    c.insets = new Insets(5,5,5,5);                                // Note 3
    gbl.setConstraints(select,c); add(select);
    gbl.setConstraints(join,c); add(join);
    gbl.setConstraints(enter,c); add(enter);

    c.gridwidth = GridBagConstraints.REMAINDER;                    // Note 4
    c.gridheight = 2;
    gbl.setConstraints(tables,c);add(tables);

    c.gridx = 0;
    c.gridy = 1;
```

```
c.gridwidth = 2;
c.gridheight = 1;
c.fill = GridBagConstraints.HORIZONTAL;                              // Note 5
gbl.setConstraints(fieldValue,c); add(fieldValue);

c.fill = GridBagConstraints.NONE;
c.gridwidth = 1;
c.gridx = 2;
gbl.setConstraints(value,c);              add(value);

c.gridx = 3;
c.gridy = 2;
c.gridwidth = GridBagConstraints.REMAINDER;
gbl.setConstraints(display,c);            add(display);

c.gridy = 3;
c.gridwidth = 1;
c.gridheight = 2;
for(int i = 0; i < SIZE; i++) {                                      // Note 6
  c.gridx = i;
  gbl.setConstraints(columns[i],c);
  add(columns[i]);
}

c.gridheight = 1;
c.gridy = 5;
for(int i=0; i<SIZE; i++) {
  c.gridx = i;
  gbl.setConstraints(colLabel[i],c);
  add(colLabel[i]);
}
c.gridx = 0;
c.gridy = 6;
gbl.setConstraints(submit,c);             add(submit);

c.gridx = 1;
c.gridheight = 2;
c.gridwidth = GridBagConstraints.REMAINDER;
gbl.setConstraints(result,c);             add(result);

addWindowListener(new WindowClose());
display.addActionListener(this);
select.addActionListener(this);
select.setEnabled(false);
join.addActionListener(this);
join.setEnabled(false);
submit.addActionListener(this);
submit.setEnabled(false);
enter.addActionListener(this);
enter.setEnabled(false);
```

```
    try {
      Class.forName("sun.jdbc.odbc.JdbcOdbcDriver");
      String url = "jdbc:odbc:Sales";
      con = DriverManager.getConnection(url);
      stmt = con.createStatement();
      result.setText("Select tables you wish to use\nThen press Display");
      dbMetaData = con.getMetaData();
      String[] tableTypes ={"TABLE"};
      ResultSet rs = dbMetaData.getTables(null,null,"%",tableTypes);
      int i = 0;
      while(rs.next())
        tables.add(tableName[i++] = rs.getString("TABLE_NAME"));      // Note 7
    }catch (Exception e) {e.printStackTrace();}
  }

  public void actionPerformed(ActionEvent event) {
    Object source = event.getSource();
    if (source == display) {
      indices = tables.getSelectedIndexes();                          // Note 8
      for(int i = 0; i < indices.length; i++){
        colLabel[indices[i]].setText(tableName[indices[i]]);          // Note 9
        colLabel[indices[i]].invalidate();                            // Note 10
        fromTables += tableName[indices[i]] +',';                     // Note 11
      }

      fromTables = fromTables.substring(0,fromTables.length() - 1);  // Note 12
      display.setEnabled(false);
      result.setText("Highlight the fields to be part of the result set\n"
      + "and press the Select button.");

      for(int i = 0; i < indices.length; i++) {
        try {
          ResultSet rs =
            dbMetaData.getColumns(null,null,tableName[indices[i]],"%");
                                                                      // Note 13
          while(rs.next())
            columns[indices[i]].add(rs.getString("COLUMN_NAME"));     // Note 14
        }catch(SQLException e) {e.printStackTrace();}
      }
      select.setEnabled(true);
      validate();                                                     // Note 15
    }

    else if (source == select) {
      for(int i = 0; i < indices.length; i++)
        count += columns[indices[i]].getSelectedIndexes().length;     // Note 16
      resultCols = build("",',');                                     // Note 17
      resultCols = resultCols.substring(0,resultCols.length() - 1);
      result.setText("Choose pairs of columns to join\n"
              + "each time pressing Join\n"
              + "and/or select a field, enter a value for it\n"
```

```
            + "in the text field, and press Enter Value\n"
            + "If done, press Submit");
  join.setEnabled(true);
  enter.setEnabled(true);
  select.setEnabled(false);
  deselectAll(columns,indices);                               // Note 18
  query += resultCols + " FROM " + fromTables;                // Note 19
  submit.setEnabled(true);
}

else if (source == join) {
  String keyword = "";                                        // Note 20
  if (firstJoin) {
    keyword = " WHERE ";
    firstJoin = false;
  }

  else
    keyword = " AND ";
  joinClauses = build(keyword,'=');
  joinClauses = joinClauses.substring(0,joinClauses.length()-1);
  deselectAll(columns,indices);
  query += joinClauses;
}

  else if (source == enter){
  String keyword = "";
  if (firstJoin) {
    keyword = " WHERE ";
    firstJoin = false;
  }

  else
    keyword = " AND ";
  condition = build(keyword,'=');
  condition += fieldValue.getText();
  query += condition;
 }

  else if (source == submit) {
    try {
      ResultSet rs = stmt.executeQuery(query);
      result.setText("");
      while(rs.next()) {
        String s = "";
        for(int i = 1; i <= count; i++)
        s += rs.getString(i) + ' ';                            // Note 21
      s += '\n';
      result.append(s);
    }
  }catch(Exception e) {
```

```
      e.printStackTrace();
    }
    submit.setEnabled(false);
    join.setEnabled(false);
    enter.setEnabled(false);
    }
  }

  public String build(String start, char c ) {                    // Note 22
    String s = start;
    String[] colNames;
    for(int i = 0; i < indices.length; i++) {
      colNames = columns[indices[i]].getSelectedItems();
      for (int j = 0; j < colNames.length; j++) {
        s += tableName[indices[i]]+ '.' + colNames[j] + c;
      }
    }
    return s;
  }

  public void deselectAll(List[] columns, int[] indices) {        // Note 23
    for(int i = 0; i < indices.length; i++)
      for(int j = 0; j < columns[indices[i]].getItemCount(); j++)
        columns[indices[i]].deselect(j);
  }

  public static void main(String[] args) {
    SearchSales search = new SearchSales("Search Sales database");
    Toolkit toolkit = Toolkit.getDefaultToolkit();                // Note 24
    Dimension d = toolkit.getScreenSize();                        // Note 25
    search.setSize(d.width,d.height - 30);
    search.setLocation(0,30);                                     // Note 26
    search.setVisible(true);
  }

  public class WindowClose extends WindowAdapter {
    public void windowClosing(WindowEvent e) {
      System.exit(0);
    }
  }
}
```

Note 1: We create a `List` box to hold the columns in each of the five tables in the `Sales` database.

Note 2: We create the `Label` objects to which the `Label` array, `colLabel`, refers. The constructor for `colLabel` initialized these references to **null**.

Note 3: Except for setting the insets to provide a border of five pixels around each component, we use the default values for the gridbag constraints.

Note 4: Setting the `gridwidth` to `GridBagContraints.REMAINDER` lets the list of tables use the remainder of the row. Because the `List` has a default width of 1, it is centered in the remaining two columns.

Note 5: We want the text field to fill two columns, so we set the `gridwidth` to 2 and the `fill` to `GridBagConstraints.HORIZONTAL` so it will expand horizontally to fill the two-column space available.

Note 6: `for(int i = 0; i < SIZE; i++) {`
This loop adds the five `List` boxes, one for each table of the `Sales` database.

Note 7: `tables.add(tableName[i++]=rs.getString("TABLE_NAME"));`
This statement concisely achieves several objectives. It gets the next table name from the result set, assigns it to the `tableName` array for use later, increments the index `i`, and finally adds the table name to the tables list.

Note 8: `indices = tables.getSelectedIndexes();`
We constructed the tables list to allow the user to select multiple items. The `getSelectedIndexes` method returns the array of index numbers corresponding to selected items.

Note 9: `colLabel[indices[i]].setText(tableName[indices[i]]);`
Initially, we labeled the five tables, `Table1,...,` `Table5`. We change the labels underneath the selected tables to their actual table names. We could have labeled all five tables correctly, but chose this to differentiate those tables the user selected from the unselected ones.

Note 10: `colLabel[indices[i]].invalidate();`
Because the new label may have a different length, we later invoke the `validate` method to get the layout manager to redo the layout. Each changed label calls `invalidate` here so the layout manager will know that it needs to be laid out with its new size.

Note 11: `fromTables += tableName[indices[i]] +',';`
We save the names of the selected tables in a string, separated by commas, to use after `FROM` when we construct the SQL `SELECT` query.

Note 12: `fromTables = fromTables.substring(0,fromTables.length()-1);`
This removes the last comma.

Note 13:
```
ResultSet rs = dbMetaData.getColumns
  (null,null,tableName[indices[i]],"%");
```
For each table the user selected, we get the names of its columns.

Note 14: `columns[indices[i]].add(rs.getString("COLUMN_NAME"));`
We add each column name to the `List` box representing the selected table.

Note 15: `validate();`
The gridbag layout manager will redo the layout, so components whose size has changed will be laid out properly.

Note 16: `count += columns[indices[i]].getSelectedIndexes().length;`
We save the total number of columns in the result set for the query, obtaining it by adding up the number of columns selected in each `List` box. After executing the query, we use `count` to list the results.

Note 17: `resultCols = build("",',');`
The `build` method combines the selected item into a string, using the second argument as the separator. The first argument is the initial value of the string.

Note 18: `deselectAll(columns,indices);`
The `deselectAll` method deselects each of the selected items so the user does not have to manually deselect the previous choices before making selections at the next step toward building the query.

Note 19: `query += resultCols + " FROM " + fromTables;`
We continue to build the query we wish to execute, adding the pieces we have constructed so far.

Note 20: `if (firstJoin) {`
The first condition, if any, in the query follows `WHERE`, while the remaining conditions follow `AND`. We use the **boolean** variable `firstJoin` to specify whether or not this is the first condition.

Note 21: `s += rs.getString(i) + ' ';`
For simplicity, we have not dealt with the types of each table column. Knowing the column type would allow us to use a more specific method than `getString`. For example, knowing the column has type `INTEGER` would allow us to use the `getInt` method, but the `getString` method will also work for every type, although sometimes the formatting will not be as nice.

Note 22: `public String build(String start, char c ) {`
The `build` method combines the selected `List` items into a string. The `start` argument is the initial value of the string, while the argument `c` is the character used to separate the selected items.

Note 23: `public void deselectAll (List[] columns, int[] indices) {`
For simplicity, this method deselects every column, even those the user had not selected. The arguments are the array of `List` boxes, one for each table, and the array of indices specifying which tables the user selected.

Note 24: `Toolkit toolkit = Toolkit.getDefaultToolkit();`
The `Toolkit` class allows us to access some properties of the host platform.

Note 25: `Dimension d = toolkit.getScreenSize();`
We get the screen size of the user's machine so we can size the frame to fill the screen. Setting the size using a fixed number of pixels, such as 500 by 300, as we have done in previous examples, will cause the frame to appear smaller on a higher resolution screen, and may make the frame too large for a low resolution screen.

Note 26: `search.setLocation(0,30);`
The `setLocation` method allows us to position the frame; otherwise we get the default of (0,0) for its upper-left corner.

THE BIG PICTURE

A graphical user interface lets the user compose a query. At each stage the user presses a button which causes some actions to occur and instructions to appear in the text area. The user first selects the tables to be used, then the fields to be displayed. The user may add conditions by joining tables or requiring a field have a specific value. After pressing the `Submit` button, the user sees the results in the text area.

TEST YOUR UNDERSTANDING

TRY IT YOURSELF 24. Run Example 17.6 to execute the query which returns the customer names who placed orders on March 22, 1999, but this time add the condition that the `OrderDate` is March 22, 1999 before the join condition that `Customer.CustomerID = Orders.CustomerID`. This shows we can enter conditions in any order.

TRY IT YOURSELF 25. Modify Example 17.6 to remove the call to the `validate` method. Run the modified program and describe any changes from the original version.

TRY IT YOURSELF 26. Modify Example 17.6 to omit setting `gridwidth` to `REMAINDER` for the tables list. Run the modified program and describe any changes from the original version.

TRY IT YOURSELF 27. Modify Example 17.6 to omit setting the `fill` for the `fieldValue` text field to `HORIZONTAL`. Run the modified program and describe any changes from the original version.

SUMMARY

- Java Database Connectivity (JDBC), in the `java.sql` package, allows us to create database tables, insert, update, and delete data, and query a database from a Java program. Relational databases store data in tables, and each table has a key that uniquely identifies each row. As our example, we use the `Sales` database with five tables. The `Customer` table has `CustomerID` as its key. The `Orders` table has `OrderNumber` as its key, but also includes the foreign keys `CustomerID` and `SalespersonID` which refer to entries in the `Customer` and `Salesperson` tables so the information does not have to be duplicated in the `Orders` table. The `OrderItem` table has a compound key `(OrderNumber, ItemNumber)`; we need both values to identify an order item.
- Structured Query Language (SQL) provides an interface to database systems from different vendors. Users can write statements that each database will translate to process the desired request. In this text, we use the `CREATE`, `INSERT`, `UPDATE`, `DELETE`, and `SELECT` statements. The `CREATE` statement defines data in a table. This statement may use data types that are valid in a particular database system. In this text, we use `VARCHAR(N)`, a variable size character string of maximum size `N`, `INTEGER`, and `DATE`, all of which are standard, and `CURRENCY` which is used in Microsoft Access.

- To use the JDBC we need a driver to translate from the JDBC interface to the commands used by the database system, which may reside on the user's machine or at a remote site. Loading the driver, using the **new** operator, or the `forName` method, causes it to register with `DriverManager`. The `getConnection` method connects to the database using a URL to specify the location of the database. In this text we use the `jdbc:odbc:Sales` URL because we use the `JdbcOdbcDriver` to translate to the older ODBC commands, which then use the ODBC driver for the Microsoft Access database system. `Sales` is the name of our ODBC database. Other database system will provide the URL's needed to access them. In this text, we do not discuss the other types of JDBC drivers available.
- Once connected to the database, we use the `createStatement` method to create a statement, whose `executeUpdate` method we can use to execute SQL statements to create a new table or to insert values into a table. We could also create and populate tables using the database system, outside of Java.
- To retrieve information from the database, we use the `executeQuery` method, which returns a `ResultSet`, to execute SQL `SELECT` statements. The `ResultSet` contains the rows that satisfy the query. To get the fields in a row, we use the `getXXX` method, where `XXX` is the type of the data, so we use `getInt` for an `INTEGER` field and `getString` for a `VARCHAR` field. We pass either the column number of the field or its name, so we could use `getString(1)` or `getString("CustomerName")` if `CustomerName` is the first column of the result set.
- The `SELECT` statement has various options, including a `WHERE` clause to add conditions, `SELECT DISTINCT` to remove duplicates, and `ORDER BY` to sort the result. A `SELECT` statement may refer to one table or may join information from several tables.
- Metadata describes data. The `DatabaseMetaData` class provides many methods which give information about the database. We can find the data types in uses, the names of its tables, and the names and types of the columns of each table. We use the `ResultSetMetaData` class to find the number of columns in a result set and the names and types of each column.
- Aggregate functions compute values using all the rows of the table. We use `SUM`, `MAX`, `MIN`, `AVG`, and `COUNT` in our examples. Prepared statements allow us to pass arguments to a statement to reuse it without having to repeat its translation to an efficient implementation in the database system. Transactions permit us to rollback SQL commands in the event the whole sequence did not complete successfully. The default is to commit each command as soon as it is executed, but we can change the default and use the `commit` statement to make the changes permanent only when appropriate.
- Our case study builds a graphical user interface for the `Sales` database, allowing users to specify various parts of a `SELECT` statement and execute it.

Program Modification Exercises

1. Modify Example 17.3 to pass the JDBC driver and the database URL as program arguments.
2. Modify Example 17.4 to pass the JDBC driver and the database URL as program arguments.
3. Modify Example 17.2 to read the data from a file to insert into the tables.
4. Modify Example 17.6 to use the most appropriate `getXXX` method rather than the `getString` method referred to in Note 21.
5. Modify Example 17.6 to allow >=, <=, >, and < operators in addition to =.
6. Modify Example 17.6 to check that exactly two columns, from different tables, have been selected when the user presses the *Join* button.
7. Modify Example 17.6 to add a checkbox to require that the query remove duplicates from the result.
8. Modify Example 17.6 to check that exactly one column has been selected when the user presses the *Enter Value* button.
9. Modify Example 17.6 to add column headings in the output.
10. Modify Example 17.6 to allow the user to keep executing queries.
11. Modify Example 17.2 to create a `Sales1` database that is like `Sales` except it has `LastName` and `FirstName` fields, instead of `CustomerName`, in the `Customer` table.

Program Design Exercises

12. Write a graphical user interface for the `Sales` database which lists all customer names in one *Choice* box and all products in another. When the user selects a customer name and a product, and presses the *Submit* button, display a list with the customer name, product, quantity, and date of orders by customers with that name for that product. Use prepared statements wherever possible.
13. Write a graphical user interface for a salesperson using the `Sales` database. The salesperson should be able to enter new orders. Rollback the order, if, after part of an order has been entered, a part of the order cannot be filled because of insufficient quantity of a product.
14. Develop an `Account` database to use with an electronic banking system. provide a user interface for a client to transfer funds from one account to another. The user should be able to select the source and target accounts, and enter an amount to transfer.

15. Design and populate a database for a car rental system. Allow the client to check availability of a category of car, and to make reservations.
16. Design and populate a database for a record collection. Provide a screen for the collection's owner to add and remove items, to change entries, and to search.
17. Design and populate a database for sports records. Use an almanac or search the Web for sample data. Provide a screen for the user to add and remove items, to change entries, and to search.

CHAPTER

18 Servlets and JavaServer Pages™

OUTLINE

Introduction

Servlets add functionality to web servers. In contrast to applets, which we download and execute on the client, servlets execute on the server where they may connect to database servers and process information returning results in a web page to the client. Some web servers are able to include servlets, while others use a third-party tool to run them. We use the `JRun` tool, free from `allaire.com`, which includes a web server that we will use to test our servlets.*

HTML forms can pass information to servlets which process it and send results back to the client. In this approach the servlet includes sends a web page back to the client which includes presentation and content. By using server-side includes or JavaServer Pages the web page designer can focus on the presentation while the programmer handles the content.

* The free Apache web server for Unix or NT is available from `www.apache.org`. Setting up a web server is beyond the scope of this text.

With a three-tiered architecture, the client communicates with a servlet on the middle-tier which in turn connects with a database server on the third-tier. In this way clients do not have to connect directly to a database.

HTML connections are stateless, meaning that when a client connects again there is no record of previous connections. Session-tracking allows servers to maintain client information from one connection to the next, an essential feature needed for many web applications including web commerce.

OBJECTIVES:

- Use `JRun` to test servlets and JavaServer Pages
- Interact with servlets from HTML forms
- Use server-side includes to embed servlets in web pages
- Send the output of one servlet to another in a servlet chain
- Add database connectivity in a three-tiered architecture
- Use session-tracking to maintain user information
- Use JavaServer Pages to separate content from presentation

18.1 A First Servlet

We start with a simple servlet that just prints a welcome message, testing our servlet engine installation.

Servlets with the `JSWDK` or `JRun`

The servlet API (Application Programming Interface) is not part of the core Java packages, but rather one of the standard extensions using the package prefix, `javax`. We find it in the packages `javax.servlet`, `javax.servlet.http`, and `javax.servlet.jsp`. We obtain the servlet API with the JavaServer™ Web Development Kit (JSWDK) from Sun Microsystems, `http://java.sun.com/products/jsp/download.html`, or with `JRun` from Allaire Corp., `http://www.allaire.com/`. Both products include a web server to handle client requests and a servlet engine to run the servlets, but only `JRun` handles all the examples in this chapter. We use `JRun`, but will indicate how to use the `JSWDK`.

The simplest way to get started is to add our servlets in the default directory containing the tool's sample servlets. For the `JSWDK` the default directory is `JSWDK_HOME\examples\Web-inf\servlets` where `JSWDK_HOME` is the directory in which the `JSWDK` is installed. On Windows systems, executing `startserver.bat` in the `JSWDK_HOME` directory will start the `JSWDK` server and its servlet engine. (The `startserver` file works for Unix systems.)

For `JRun`, the default location for servlets is

```
JRUN_HOME\servers\default\default-app\web-inf\classes
```

where JRUN_HOME is the directory in which JRun is installed. Clicking *Start, JRun 3.0, Default server* the *Start* menu will start the JRun web server, which runs on port 8100, and the servlet engine.

Web server configurations specify the URL for servlet access. For example, in Example 18.1 we create a servlet, Welcome.java, compile it, and put Welcome.class in the default servlet directory for the tool we are using. Using the JSWDK web server, the URL to access the Welcome servlet is

```
http://localhost:8080/examples/servlet/Welcome
```

while using JRun the correct URL is

```
http://localhost:8100/servlet/Welcome
```

Generic Servlets

The GenericServlet class, in javax.servlet, defines a protocol-independent servlet. It handles the starting, stopping, and configuration of a servlet. The only method we need to override is

```
public abstract void service(ServletRequest req, ServletResponse res)
  throws ServletException, java.io.IOException
```

which handles a request from a client. The ServletRequest interface encapsulates the parameters sent from the client, while ServletResponse includes methods to access the properties of the server's response. The service method throws exceptions of types ServletException and IOException to its caller, so that we do not need to handle them inside the service body.

Our first servlet example, Welcome, just displays a welcome message, not processing any data from the client. Figure 18.1 shows the result when connecting from a browser using the JRun web server with the URL

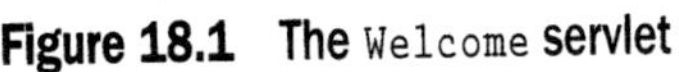
Figure 18.1 The Welcome servlet

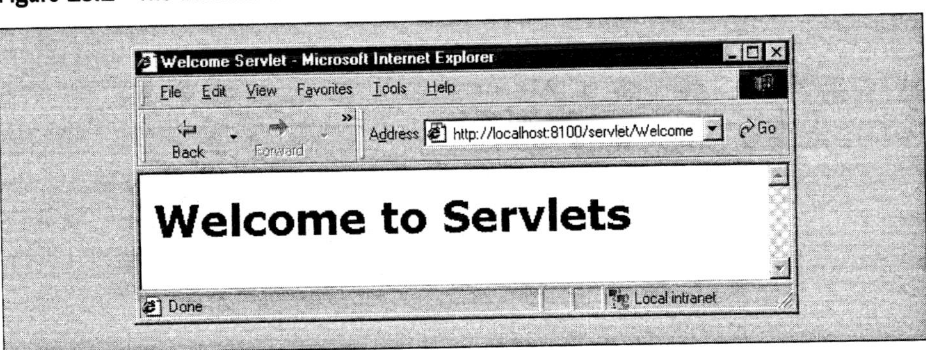


```
http://localhost:8100/servlet/Welcome
```

Naturally, if the server were on another machine we would have used its IP address instead of localhost. The JRun web server by default invokes a servlet when we specify the /servlet path in the URL. This configuration is independent of the directory name where the servlet is stored. The servlet is a Java program, `Welcome.java`, which we compile in the usual way.

TIP

To make the servlet library available to the compiler we can include the JAR files in the classpath. Using JRun, we could add

```
JRUN_HOME\lib\ext\servlet.jar
```

to the classpath or compile and run using the option

```
-classpath .;JRUN_HOME\lib\ext\servlet.jar.
```

We could also connect to the server using another client such as our `VerySimpleBrowser` with the command

```
java VerySimpleBrowser localhost 8100 /servlet/Welcome
```

which returns the uninterpreted HTML file, since our browser is very feeble.

EXAMPLE 18.1 Welcome.java

```
/* A simple servlet which uses no data from the client */

import java.io.*;
import javax.servlet.*;

public class Welcome extends GenericServlet {
  public void service(ServletRequest req, ServletResponse resp)
                              throws ServletException, IOException {
    resp.setContentType("text/html");                              // Note 1
    PrintWriter out = resp.getWriter();                            // Note 2
    String message = "Welcome to Servlets";
    out.println("<html>");                                         // Note 3
    out.println("<head><title>Welcome Servlet</title></head>");
    out.println("<body><h1><strong>"+message+"</strong></h1></body>");
    out.println("</html>");
    out.close();
  }
}
```

Output using Internet Explorer (See Figure 18.1)

Output using java VerySimpleBrowser localhost 8100 /servlet/Welcome

```
<html>
<head><title>Welcome Servlet</title></head>
<body><h1><strong>Welcome to Servlets</strong></h1></body>
</html>
```

Note 1: We use the setContentType method to indicate the MIME type for the response. We could have also used the setContentLength method to specify the length of the response.

Note 2: The getWriter method conveniently encapsulates the details of creating a PrintWriter.

Note 3: We send several lines encoded with HTML, containing the response, to the client.

Using the Web Server

While we use the JSWDK and the JRun web servers in conjunction with their corresponding servlet engines to execute servlets, they can serve other files. Using JRun

```
JRUN_HOME\servers\default\default-app
```

is the default directory for the JRun web server. If we copy jrunlogo.gif from JRUN.HOME\servers\default\demo-app to this directory, browsing with the URL

```
http://localhost:8100/jrunlogo.gif
```

will return the image for JRun's logo. Using JSWDK the default directory for the web server is

```
JSWDK_HOME\webpages
```

Browsing with the URL

```
http://localhost:8080/FAQ.html
```

returns a frequently asked questions page for the JSWDK.

TIP ☛

Instead of entering the servlet URL in our browser, we can enter it in an anchor tag in an HTML file. For example, pointing a browser to TryServlet.html given by

```
<html>
<head><title>Try a Servlet</title></head>
<body><h3>The Welcome servlet displays a message</h3>
<p><h5><a href="http://localhost:8100/servlet/Welcome">
Try a servlet </a></h5>
</body></html>
```

will show a link to the Welcome servlet. Clicking on the link produces the result shown in Figure 18.1.

THE BIG PICTURE

Servlets add the power of Java programming to a web server. The servlet API is a standard Java extension, but not part of the core. Tools such as JRun enable web servers to use servlets and have their own servers for testing servlets. The generic servlet defines a protocol-independent servlet which we can use if we do not use details specific to HTTP requests and responses.

TEST YOUR UNDERSTANDING

TRY IT YOURSELF 1. Put `Welcome.class` in the default servlet directory and enter the appropriate URL in a browser to execute the `Welcome` servlet.

TRY IT YOURSELF 2. Point any browser to `TryServlet.html` and click on the link to execute the `Welcome` servlet. If not using `JRun`, modify the URL in `TryServlet` to the one need for the web server used.

TRY IT YOURSELF 3. Put a file in the default directory for the web server you are using. Enter the appropriate URL for that file in a browser to see that the web server does serve files.

18.2 HTML Forms

The easy to use HTML has helped the World Wide Web to become a primary computing platform. HTML forms let the user submit information to a remote site. The HTTP protocol defines how web servers and clients communicate. A client sends `GET` and `POST` requests which may include data entered in forms. In fulfilling requests the server may have the servlet engine execute servlets. With `GET` we send any data as part of the `GET` command, while with `POST` we send the data separately. `GET` is useful for small amounts of data, while `POST` is more suitable when we need to send more data.

GET Requests

Extending the `HttpServlet` class, in the `javax.servlet.http` package, allows a servlet to use properties specific to HTTP requests and responses. To handle a `GET` request the `HttpServlet` class provides a `doGet` method

```
public void doGet (HttpServletRequest req, HttpServletResponse resp)
  throws ServletException, IOException;
```

to handle `GET` requests from a client. The first argument, an `HttpServletRequest` object, encapsulates the data sent by the client, while the second argument, of type `HttpServletResponse`, encapsulates the response information from the server. The `doGet` method throws exceptions of types `ServletException` and `IOException` to its caller, so that we do not need to handle them inside the `doGet` body.
When sending data in a `GET` request we can either append it to the URL or include it in the HTML file, letting the browser append it to the URL. In Example 18.2, we will send an order to the server, which will invoke our `GetOrder` servlet to respond. The first way to send our order when, for example, requesting food and drink, is:

```
http://localhost:8100/servlet/GetOrder?Order=Food and Drink
```

which gives the response shown in Figure 18.2. We use a question mark, ?, to begin the data. Since HTTP does not allow spaces in a `GET` request, the browser replaces the space by its ASCII value, hexadecimal `20`, prefixed by the escape character, `%`, so that the `GET` request becomes

```
http://localhost:8100/servlet/GetOrder?Order=Food%20and%20Drink
```

We send `GET` data in the form of parameter values. In this example, we use an `Order` parameter, giving its value as `Food and Drink`. A variant of this approach includes the servlet URL in an anchor tag

```
<a href= "http://localhost:8100/servlet/GetOrder?Order=Food+and+Drink">
```

Figure 18.2 **The `GetOrder` servlet**

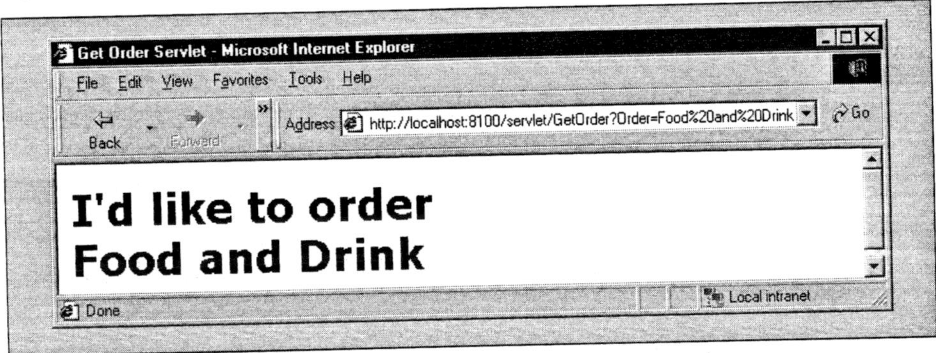

To explicitly use the `GET` command in our HTML file we use the `form` tag. Figure 18.3 shows an HTML file we can use for our `GetOrder` example.

Figure 18.3 `GetOrder.html`

```
<html>
<head><title>Get Order</title></head>
<body>
<h3>Enter an order</h3>
<form action="http://localhost:8100/servlet/GetOrder" method=GET>
Order: <input type=text name=Order size=20>
</form></body></html>
```

In the `form` tag we indicate the `action` we wish the server to apply to our data; in this example, the `action` is the `URL` for the `GetOrder` servlet. We fill in `GET` as the request method to use in the `method` attribute of the `form` tag. To make the form we can use `input` tags of various types. Here we use one `input` tag of type `text`, meaning a text field input, for the user to enter the order. We name it `Order`, by which the servlet will find it, and give it a size of 20 characters. Pointing our browser to `GetOrder.html` gives the web page of Figure 18.4. Filling in `Food and Drink` in the text field and hitting `Enter` will result in the same response as in Figure 18.2, except that Communicator replaces the spaces with + characters, using the URL

```
http://localhost:8100/servlet/GetOrder?Order=Food+and+Drink
```

Figure 18.4 An HTML form

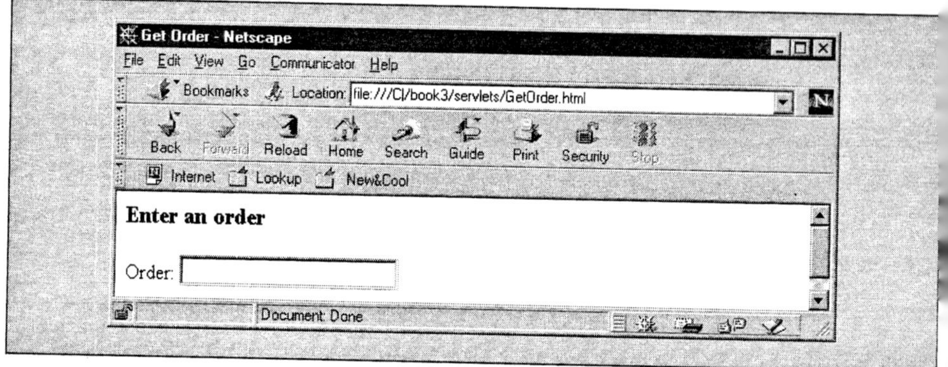

EXAMPLE 18.2 GetOrder.java

```
/* Echoes the user's order made in a GET request */

import java.io.*;
import javax.servlet.*;
import javax.servlet.http.*;

public class GetOrder extends HttpServlet {
   public void doGet(HttpServletRequest req, HttpServletResponse resp)
                throws ServletException, IOException {
   resp.setContentType("text/html");
   PrintWriter out = resp.getWriter();
   String message = req.getParameter("Order");                    // Note 1
   out.println("<html>");
   out.println("<head><title>Get Order Servlet</title></head>");
   out.println("<body><h1><strong>I'd like to order<br>");
   out.println(message+"</strong></h1></body>");                  // Note 2
   out.println("</html>");
   out.close();
  }
}
```

Note 1: The `getParameter` method returns the parameter entered in an `HTML` form or appended directly to a URL.

Note 2: Here we just echo the order back to the user.

POST requests

To include more data in our request we use the `POST` request, making a more extensive form for user input. Before going on we revise Example 18.2 to allow the user to submit an order either with a GET or a POST request. To use a POST request, we create PostOrGetOrder.html by changing the method in the GetOrder.html file of Figure 18.3 to POST. The HttpServlet class has a doPost method to handle POST requests. Since we are simply recreating Example 18.2, we delegate any POST requests to the doGet method, as shown in Example 18.3.

XAMPLE 18.3 PostOrGetOrder.java

```
/* Revises Example 18.2 to allow the user to order with
 * a POST request as well as a GET request
 */

import java.io.*;
import javax.servlet.*;
import javax.servlet.http.*;

public class PostOrGetOrder extends HttpServlet {

  // the doGet method is the same as in Example 2


  public void doPost(HttpServletRequest req, HttpServletResponse resp)
                    throws ServletException, IOException {
    doGet(req,resp);
  }
}
```

In Figure 18.5 we see that the browser does not include the data with the POST request. Thus using POST rather than GET is essential to keep the data sent private. Data set with a GET request is appended to the URL and displayed in the browser's address field.

Figure 18.5 PostOrGetOrder.html

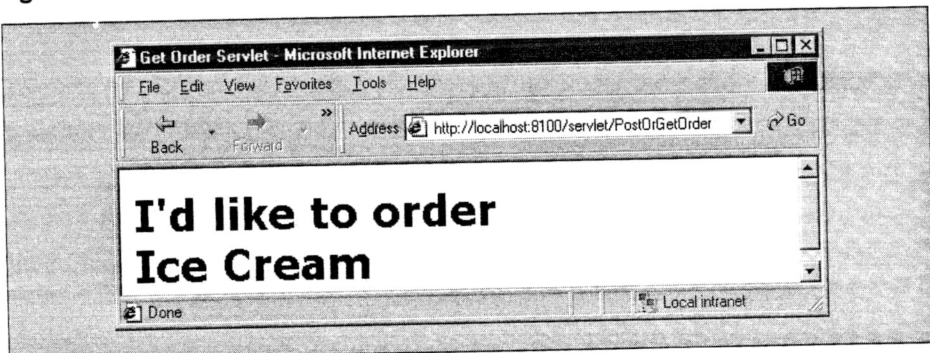

To send a more detailed order for an ice cream sundae, we add additional elements to an HTML form. Figure 18.6 shows the HTML file, while Figure 18.7 shows the form in a browser.

Figure 18.6 The `PostOrder.html` file

```
<html>
<head><title>Post Order</title></head>
<body>
<form action="http://localhost:8100/servlet/PostOrder" method=POST>
  <strong>Name:</strong>
    <input type=text name=name size=20><br>
  <strong>Password:</strong>
    <input type=password name=password size=12><p>
  <strong>Flavor:</strong>
    <select name=flavor size=3>
      <option>Vanilla
      <option>Chocolate
      <option>Strawberry
    </select><p>
  <strong>Toppings:</strong>
    <input type=checkbox name=toppings value="Hot Fudge">  Hot Fudge
    <input type=checkbox name=toppings value="Butterscotch"> Butterscotch
    <input type=checkbox name=toppings value="Nuts">    Nuts
    <input type=checkbox name=toppings
      value="Whipped Cream">Whipped Cream <p>
    <input type=radio name=place value="Eat here"> Eat here
    <input type=radio name=place value="Take out"> Take out<p>
    <input type=submit value="Order">
    <input type=reset>
</form></body></html>
```

This form uses a text field to enter the customer's name. An `input` tag of type `password` is like a text field, but it hides the input. We use the `select` tag to get the `list` box for the ice cream flavors. Each `option` tag within the `select` tag specifies an item in the list. We can only select one flavor from the list. To enable multiple selections we could add the attribute `multiple` to the `select` tag.

We use the `input` tag of type `checkbox` to allow multiple selections for toppings. We use the `radio` type to allow only one choice of where to eat. The `submit` type creates a button to allow the user to submit the data to the server. The `value` attribute allows us to choose a name for the button. The `reset` type provides a button to allow the user to reset the form.

Figure 18.7 `PostOrder.html` **displayed in a browser**

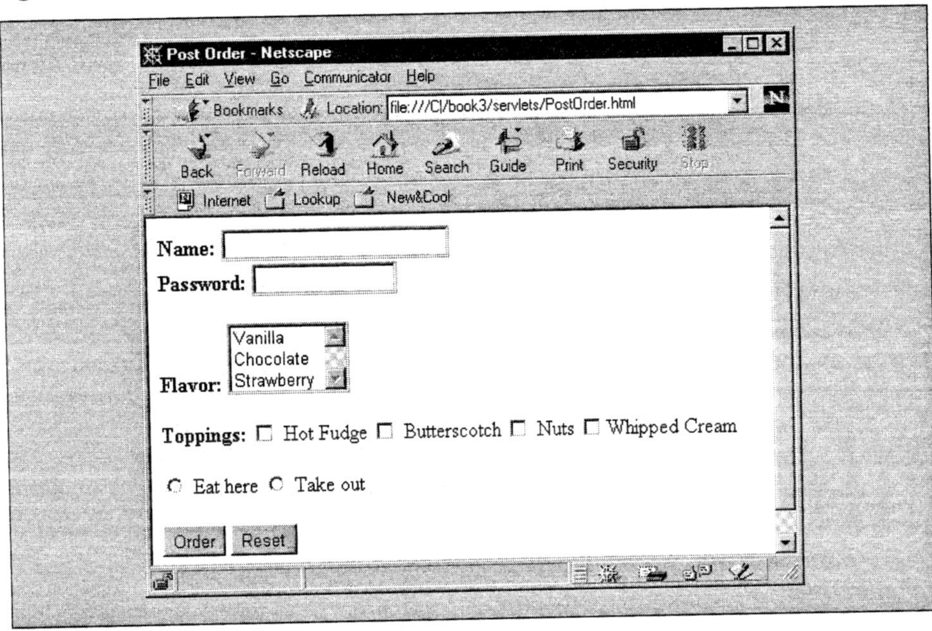

Filling in the form and pressing the *Order* button produces the result shown in Figure 18.8.

Figure 18.8 **The** `PostOrder` **servlet**

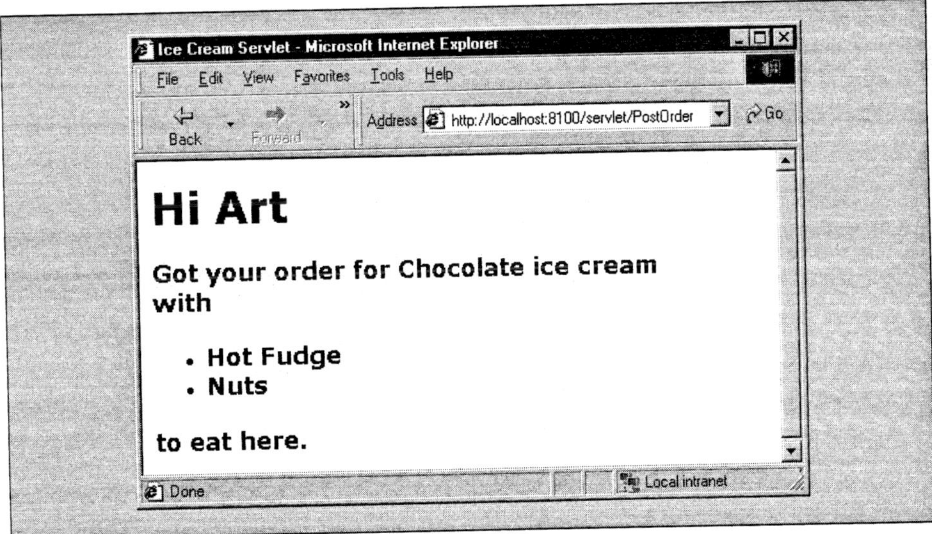

In the `PostOrder` servlet we get the values of the parameters submitted by the customer and send that information back to the client.

EXAMPLE 18.4 PostOrder.java

```
/* Echoes the user's order made in a POST request. */

import java.io.*;
import javax.servlet.*;
import javax.servlet.http.*;

public class PostOrder extends HttpServlet {
  public void doPost(HttpServletRequest req, HttpServletResponse resp)
                              throws ServletException, IOException{
    resp.setContentType("text/html");
    PrintWriter out = resp.getWriter();
    String message = req.getParameter("name");
    String result = req.getParameter("password");                    // Note 1
    out.println("<html>");
    out.println("<head><title>Ice Cream Servlet</title></head>");
    out.println("<body><h1><strong>Hi " + message);
    out.println("</strong></h1><h3>");
    result = req.getParameter("flavor");
    out.println("Got your order for "+result+" ice cream<br>");
    String[] kinds = req.getParameterValues("toppings");             // Note 2
    if (kinds==null) out.println("with no toppings");
    else {
      out.println("with <ul>");
      for(int i=0; i<kinds.length; i++)
        out.println("<li>" + kinds[i]);
      out.println("</ul>");
    }
    result = req.getParameter("place");
    if (result.equals("Eat here"))
      out.println("to eat here.");
    else
      out.println("to go");
    out.println("</h3></body></html>");
    out.close();
  }
}
```

Note 1: We get the password but make no use of it in this example.

Note 2: Whenever a parameter can have more than one value we use the `getParameterValues` method which returns an array of `String`. We could use it instead of the `getParameter` method even when a parameter has only one value.

THE BIG PICTURE

HTML forms let users communicate with a web server. A `GET` request appends data to the URL, while a `POST` request sends data separately. The form tag has an action attribute that specifies the program on the server that will handle the form data, and a method attribute to specify the type of request. A form may include various input tags including `text`, `password`, `checkbox`, `radio`, `submit`, and `reset` types. We use the `select` tag to add a `list`. Servlets use the `getParameter` method to obtain the form data, and respond by sending an HTML page to the client.

TEST YOUR UNDERSTANDING

4. What change to Example 18.2 would we have to make if we change the name attribute in the HTML file of Figure 18.3 from `Order` to `Choices`?
5. In addition to modifying the HTML file of Figure 18.3 to use a `POST` request instead of `GET`, what other change do we need to make to it in order to use the servlet of Example 18.3?

TRY IT YOURSELF

6. Omit the `value` attribute of the `submit` type in the `input` tag of the HTML file of Figure 18.6. How will Figure 18.7 change as a consequence of this change?

18.3 Server-Side Includes and Servlet Chaining

In our previous examples clients communicated with servlets which sent entire HTML pages back to them. Thus the servlet writer had to handle the application's content and the HTML presentation to return to the client. Using a server-side include, we can embed the servlet response in a web page, so the servlet can focus on content. Servlet chaining lets us send the output of one servlet to another before presenting the results to the client.

The `JSWDK` server does not support server-side includes or servlet chaining, but it does handle JavaServer Pages which we cover later in this chapter. JavaServer pages can replace server-side includes, so this section may be omitted.

Server-Side Includes

Using server-side includes (SSI) we can embed servlets in web pages using the `<servlet>` tag. The web server which handles server-side includes serves the file in the usual manner, and in addition calls a special servlet to process the `<servlet>` tag. To alert the server, we use a special file extension such as `.shtml` to denote an `HTML` file which contains the `<servlet>` tag.

The default configuration for the `JRun` server uses this `.shtml` extension for server-side includes. We put `.shtml` files in the directory

```
JRUN_HOME\servers\default\default-app
```

when using the default web server included with JRun, and users can request these files via the URL `http://localhost:8100/file_name.shtml`

The path `/servlet/` indicates a call by the server to the `invoker` servlet to execute a servlet. We have been using this path in our examples.

As an example we use a server-side include to call a servlet that tallies how many times a user has requested pages with a given subject. Figure 18.9 shows the `.shtml` file

Figure 18.9 `TallyTest.shtml`

```
<html>
<head><title>Tally Test</title></head>
<body>
<h2>Testing the Tally servlet</h2>
<servlet code=Tally codebase="http://localhost:8100/servlet/">
<param name=size value=3>
<param name=subject value=Test>
This server does not support server side includes.
</servlet>
</body></html>
```

The `<servlet>` tag uses the `code` attribute to specify the servlet to execute and the `codebase` to specify its URL. The `Tally` servlet will use the `size` and `subject` parameters specified using the `<param>` tag as in applets. The `size` parameter represents the size of the heading used to output the message, while the `subject` parameter represents a subject reflecting a type of request. We add a message after the param tag that displays only if the server does not support server-side includes. Our servlet will keep a separate tally of connections for each subject from clients who connect with that subject value. Figure 18.10 shows a client connecting using the subject `Test`.

Figure 18.10 Using a server-side include

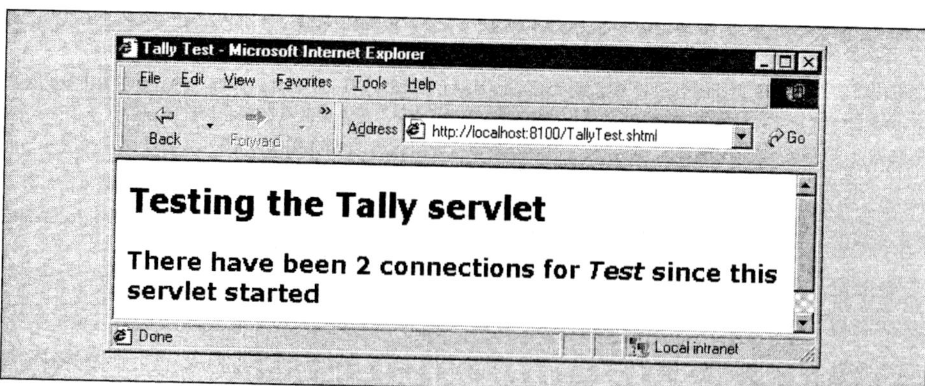

We can add a server-side include to any HTML file. Our tally servlet tells us the number of connections. We can have several pages active at once, and the servlet will report connections according to subject. For example, we add the code

```
<servlet code=Tally codebase="http://localhost:8100/servlet/">
<param name=size value=3>
<param name=subject value=Order>
This server does not support server side includes.
</servlet>
```

to the `PostOrder.html` file of Figure 18.6 to create the `TallyOrder.shtml` file. Pointing our browser to the URL

```
http://localhost:8100/TallyOrders.shtml
```

will return the form of Figure 18.7, with the additional line

```
There has been 1 connection for Order since this servlet started.
```

Repeated connections to this URL will increase the count for the subject `Order`, each time. This will be distinct from the count for the `Test` subject shown in Figure 18.10.

The `Tally` servlet extends `GenericServlet` rather than its subclass `HttpServlet`, since it is not responding to `GET` or `POST` requests. We use a hash table to keep track of the number of connections from a given subject. In contrast to an array, which uses integer indices to find its elements, a hash table uses the data itself. In our example, we have a simple table

Subject	Number of connections
`Order`	1
`Test`	3

Using additional subjects would add entries to the table.

We create a hash table using the constructor

```
Hashtable table = new Hashtable();
```

for the `Hashtable` class in the `java.util` package. To make an entry we call

```
table.put("Order", new Integer(1));
```

for example, where we wrap the value `1` as an `Integer` object.. To retrieve an entry we call

```
Object o = table.get("Order");
```

which returns the value associated with `Order`.

EXAMPLE 18.5 Tally.java

```
/* Uses a hash table to keep track of the number of
 * connections regarding a particular subject.
 */

import java.io.*;
import javax.servlet.*;
import javax.servlet.http.*;
import java.util.*;

public class Tally extends GenericServlet {
  int count;
  Hashtable table = new Hashtable();

  public void service(ServletRequest req, ServletResponse resp)
                    throws ServletException, IOException {
    resp.setContentType("text/html");
    String subject = req.getParameter("subject");
    Object o = table.get(subject);
    if (o==null)                                                  // Note 1
    count = 0;
    else
    count = ((Integer)o).intValue();
    table.put(subject, new Integer(++count));                     // Note 2
    PrintWriter out = resp.getWriter();
    String size = req.getParameter("size");
    String have = count==1?"has":"have";                          // Note 3
    String suffix = count==1?"":"s";
    out.println("<h" + size + "> There " + have + " been " + count   // Note 4
        + " connection" + suffix + " for <em>" + subject
        + "</em> since this servlet started </h" + size + '>');
    out.close();
  }
}
```

Note 1: A **null** value from the hash table for a given subject means that there is no entry for that subject and we set count to `0`. Otherwise, we cast the value to `Integer` and use the `intValue` method to get the **int** value of count.

Note 2: We update the hash table, increasing `count` to reflect the current connection. We must wrap the **int** value in an `Integer` object, since the `put` method uses `Object` values.

Note 3: We use the Java conditional expression to help us with grammar. When `count` is 1 we want to use has and to use have otherwise. A conditional expression of the form

```
condition ? true_value : false_value
```

has the value `true_value` if the condition is **true**, and `false_value` if the condition is **false**. The conditional expression is a short form of the **if-else** statement.

Note 4: We use the `size` parameter to specify the size of the header tag in the `HTML` response.

Servlet Chaining

We can use servlet chaining to pass the output of one servlet as the input to another. As an example, we devise our own HTML tag, `<lucky>`. When this tag occurs in an HTML file we want the user to receive six lucky numbers. Since the `<lucky>` tag is not part of standard HTML, we use the `LuckyTag` servlet to process an HTML file, replacing the `<lucky>` tag by the six lucky numbers.

Two different methods will allow us to implement servlet chaining. The first chains the servlets in the URL; for example

```
http://localhost:8100/servlet/LuckyWelcome,LuckyTag
```

Figure 18.11 shows this approach.

Figure 18.11 Servlet chaining in the URL

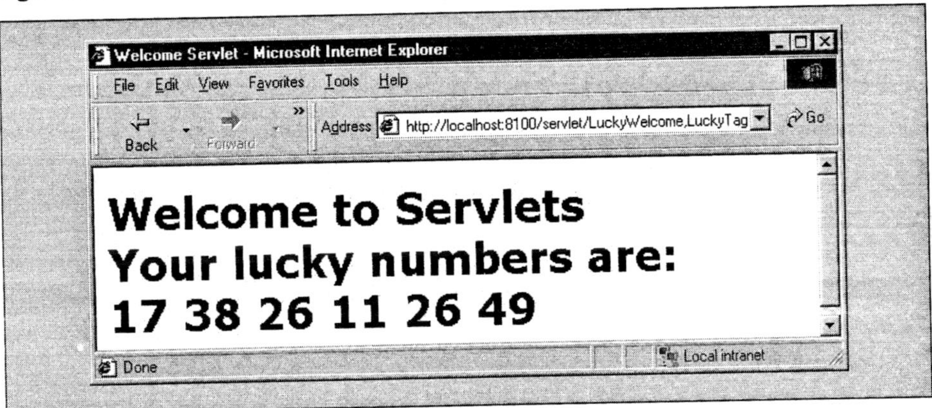

The second approach uses a MIME (Multipurpose Internet Mail Extensions) filter. We configure the web server to pass servlet output with a specified MIME content type to another servlet for further processing. We create a custom MIME type called `custom/lucky`. The LuckyWelcome servlet sets the content type to `custom/lucky` to signify that it is sending output that contains the `<lucky>` tag. In our example, we will configure the JRun default web server to pass output whose content is `custom/lucky` to the `LuckyTag` servlet, which will check for the `<lucky>` tag.

To configure JRun, we use the JRun Management Console (JMC). We must first start the web server, which is different than the default server, by clicking on *`Start`*, *`JRun Admin Server`*. Entering the URL

```
http://localhost:8000
```

in the browser brings up the JMC. A user login box appears in which we enter the user name and password used during the JRun install. The default user name is `admin`.

Once logged in, we open the *`JRun Default Server`* entry in the left frame in the browser. Next, we open the *`Web Applications`* entry, and within that, the *`Default User Application Entry`*. Clicking on *`MIME Type Chaining`* brings up the frame of Figure 18.12

Figure 18.12 Using the `JRun` Management Console

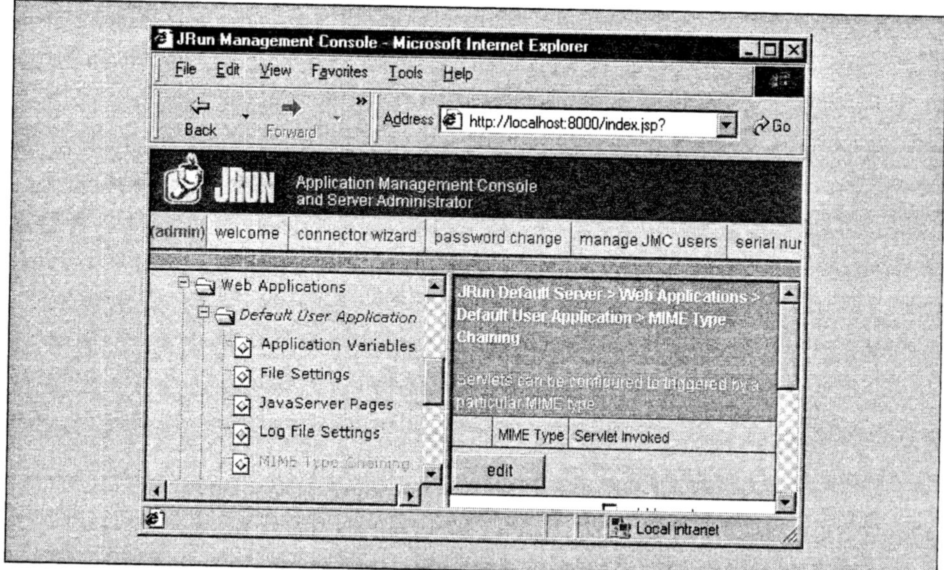

Clicking the *`Edit`* button brings up a window that allows us to associate the `LuckyTag` servlet with the MIME type `custom/lucky`. Any servlet whose output has content type `custom/lucky` will have that output filtered through the `LuckyTag` servlet. We enter `custom/lucky` as the MIME type and `LuckyTag` as the servlet invoked in Figure 18.13, and click on `Update`.

Figure 18.13 Configureing `JRun` to use a MIME filter

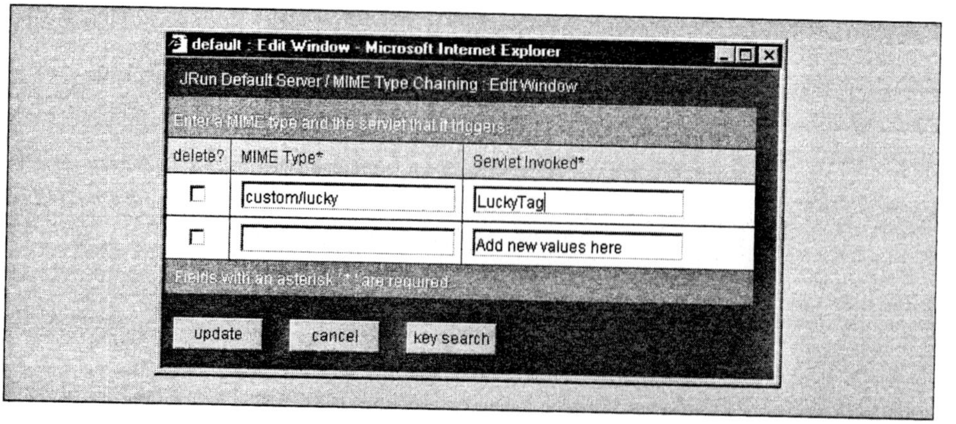

When we change the configuration, we must stop and restart the default server to use the new configuration.Since `LuckyWelcome` outputs an HTML file, the MIME filter will send it to the `LuckyTag` servlet to add the lucky numbers.

Figure 18.14 Using a MIME filter

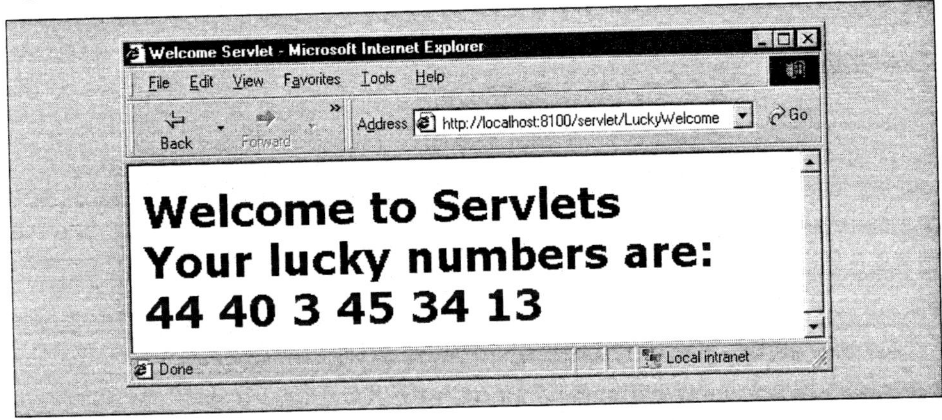

EXAMPLE 18.6 **LuckyWelcome.java**

```
/* Includes the <lucky> tag which the LuckyTag servlet
 * interprets in a servlet chain or as a MIME filter
 */

import java.io.*;
import javax.servlet.*;
import javax.servlet.http.*;

public class LuckyWelcome extends HttpServlet {
  public void doGet(HttpServletRequest req, HttpServletResponse resp)
                               throws ServletException, IOException {
    resp.setContentType("custom/lucky");
    PrintWriter out = resp.getWriter();
    String message = "Welcome to Servlets";
    out.println("<html>");
    out.println("<head><title>Welcome Servlet</title></head>");
    out.println("<body><h1><strong>" + message + "<br>");
    out.println("<lucky></strong></h1></body>");                // Note 1
    out.println("</html>");
    out.close();
  }
}
```

Note 1: The `<lucky>` tag is not standard HTML. The `custom/lucky` content must be sent to the `LuckyTag` servlet, either in a servlet chain, or using a MIME filter, to replace the `<lucky>` tag by a message with six random numbers.

EXAMPLE 18.7 LuckyTag.java

```
/* Replaces the <lucky> tag by a message
 * with six random numbers.
 */

import java.io.*;
import javax.servlet.*;
import javax.servlet.http.*;

public class LuckyTag extends GenericServlet {

  public void service(ServletRequest req, ServletResponse resp)
                              throws ServletException, IOException {
    resp.setContentType("text/html");
    BufferedReader in = req.getReader();
    PrintWriter out = resp.getWriter();
    String line;
    int index;
    while((line=in.readLine())!=null) {
      index = line.toUpperCase().indexOf("<LUCKY>");                    // Note 1
    if(index == -1)                                                     // Note 2
        out.println(line);
      else {
        out.println("<strong>Your lucky numbers are: <br>");
        for(int i=0; i<6; i++)
          out.println((int)(51*Math.random()+1)+ " ");
        out.println("<br>");
      }
    }
    in.close();
    out.close();
  }
}
```

Note 1: Tags are not case sensitive, so we convert the line to upper-case before searching for the `<lucky>` tag.

Note 2: We output lines unchanged which do not contain the `<lucky>` tag, but replace lines with the tag by a message with six random numbers. We leave it as an exercise to just replace the `<lucky>` tag by random number rather than the whole line containing it.

THE BIG PICTURE

Server-side includes use the `<servlet>` tag to include a call to a servlet in an HTML file. The servlet returns HTML lines which fit within the page rather than as a separate page.

Using servlet chaining we can pipe the output of one servlet to another before sending results back to the client. One way to chain is to include both servlets in the URL. Another is to use a MIME filter. We configure the servlet engine to pipe the output of a servlet which outputs a particular MIME type, such as text/html, to another servlet. We use the second servlet to filter the output of the first before presenting it to the client.

TEST YOUR UNDERSTANDING

TRY IT YOURSELF 7. Browse `TallyTest.shtml` several times, either using different browsers, or pressing the *Reload* or *Refresh* button. Also browse `TallyOrders.shtml`. Describe the results.

8. Why do we need use the .shtml extension for HTML files which include the servlet tag?

TRY IT YOURSELF 9. Try to execute a servlet chain with the URL

```
http://localhost:8000/servlet/LuckyWelcome, LuckyTag
```

which includes a space between the two servlet names. Describe the result.

TRY IT YOURSELF 10. Write an HTML file with an anchor tag to use servlet chaining, rather than entering the URL directly in the browser.

18.4 Three-tiered Architectures

In a two-tiered client-server application, the client connects directly to a database server. The client handles the business logic, the code needed to implement the business model, as well as the presentation of the data. The inevitably frequent changes in business logic require changes to the programs running on each client. Adding a middle tier to handle business logic simplifies maintenance and does not require as much computational power on client machines.

Using a Database in a Three-tiered Architecture

We can use a servlet to access a database. In a three-tiered architecture, the client tier contains a user interface. The client connects to a middle-tier server that processes the client's request, accessing a database server in the third tier to store and receive information. In this way the business logic resides in middleware and can be changed without reconfiguring the various clients.

Our `SalesServlet` simply executes the client's SQL query. We leave it to the exercises to design a servlet to create a query from form information supplied by the client. In this example we provide a form with a text area for the user to enter a SQL query which the servlet executes.

Figure 18.15 Sales.html

```
<html>
<head><title>Sales</title></head>
<body>
<form action="http://localhost:8100/servlet/SalesServlet" method=POST>
<strong>Select:</strong>
<textarea cols=50 rows=8 name=select></textarea><p>
<input type=submit value="Query">
<input type=reset>
</form></body></html>
```

Figure 18.16 The `Sales` query form

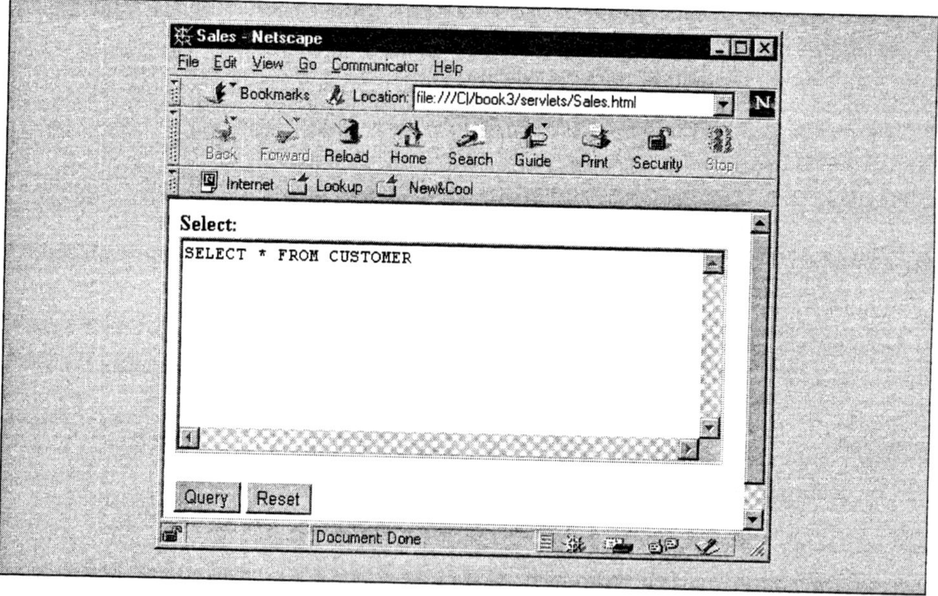

In `SalesServlet`, we use the `init` method to connect to the database. Once we initialize the servlet, the connection to the database will remain while the servlet is active. Connecting to the database in the `doGet` method would require a new connection for each client request.

Figure 18.17 Result from the `Sales` query

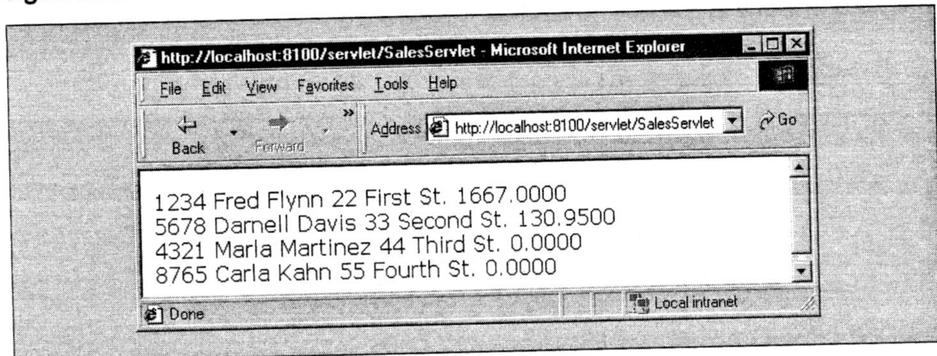

EXAMPLE 18.8 SalesServlet.java

```
/* Queries the Sales database. Needs to be modified
 * to use metadata to correctly output the result set.
 */

import java.io.*;
import javax.servlet.*;
import javax.servlet.http.*;
import java.sql.*;
import sun.jdbc.odbc.JdbcOdbcDriver;

public class SalesServlet extends HttpServlet {
  Connection con;
  Statement stmt;

  public void init(ServletConfig sc) throws ServletException {   // Note 1
    super.init(sc);
    try{
      new JdbcOdbcDriver();
      String url = "jdbc:odbc:Sales";
      String user = "";
      String password = "";
      con = DriverManager.getConnection(url, user, password);
      stmt = con.createStatement();
    }catch (Exception e) {
      e.printStackTrace();
      System.exit(1);
    }
  }
  public void doGet(HttpServletRequest req, HttpServletResponse resp)
                            throws ServletException, IOException {
    resp.setContentType("text/html");
    PrintWriter out = resp.getWriter();
    try{
      String query = req.getParameter("select");
      ResultSet rs = stmt.executeQuery(query);
```

```
        ResultSetMetaData rsMetaData = rs.getMetaData();
        int cols = rsMetaData.getColumnCount();
        while(rs.next()) {
          String s = "";
          for(int i=1; i<=cols; i++)
            s += rs.getString(i) + ' ';
          s += "<br>";
          out.println(s);
        }
      }catch(Exception e) {
        e.printStackTrace();
      }
      out.close();
    }
    public void doPost(HttpServletRequest req, HttpServletResponse resp)
                      throws ServletException, IOException {
      doGet(req,resp);
    }
  }
```

Note 1: Always call the `super.init` method when overriding `init`.

THE BIG PICTURE

A three-tiered architecture configures business logic on a middle tier. The client handles the graphic presentation and communicates with the middle tier which handles the content. The middle tier stores and retrieves data from a database server on the third tier. This architecture keeps business logic in a central location making it easier and cheaper to perform updates. Powerful middle tier application servers can scale to meet the demands of serving many clients.

TEST YOUR UNDERSTANDING

TRY IT YOURSELF 11. Change the method in `Sales.html` in Figure 15 from POST to GET. Does the servlet still function properly? Why or why not?

TRY IT YOURSELF 12. Point a browser to `Sales.html` and enter a query to find the names of all the salespersons. Describe the result.

18.5 Session Tracking

Internet commerce will continue growing in importance. The HTTP protocol does not automatically maintain a connection, so that if a customer selects an item and moves to another page, perhaps for an additional item, the connection is lost. The vendor would like to keep the customer's information, including the items ordered, so that the customer can add items to the order and complete the purchase. The session tracking API lets a servlet keep track of clients from one connection to the next. Session tracking may be implemented using cookies which are bits of information sent by the web server to the client, which the client sends back to the browser when it accesses that page again. A cookie uniquely identifies a client.

We will use an `HttpSession` object to allow a servlet to maintain a session with each client. With an `HttpSession` object, we can store values using the `putValue` method and retrieve them using the `getValue` method. The HTML form of Figure 18.18 defines a form for the client to place an order.

Figure 18.18 `SessionOrder.html`

```
<html>
<head><title>Session Order</title></head>
<body>
<form action="http://localhost:8100/servlet/SessionOrder" method=GET>
<strong><h3>Choose the items you would like to order.</h3></strong><p>
<input type=checkbox name=Order value="Java Book"> Java Book        <br>
<input type=checkbox name=Order value="Baseball">  Baseball         <br>
<input type=checkbox name=Order value="Bicycle">   Bicycle          <br>
<input type=checkbox name=Order value="Dress">     Dress            <br>
<input type=checkbox name=Order value="Shirt">     Shirt            <br>
<input type=checkbox name=Order value="Shoes">     Shoes            <br>
<input type=checkbox name=Order value="Theater tickets">
                                                   Theater tickets  <br>
<input type=checkbox name=Order value="Compact disk">
                                                   Compact disk     <br>
<input type=checkbox name=Order value="Cellular phone">
                                                   Cellular phone   <br>
<input type=checkbox name=Order value="Computer">  Computer         <p>
<input type=submit value="Order">
<input type=reset>
</form></body></html>
```

Figure 18.19 shows the order form. Submitting an order sends the user's choices to the `SessionOrder` servlet. The servlet sends back a list of all items ordered so far and the user's session id as Figure 18.20 shows.

Figure 18.19 An order form

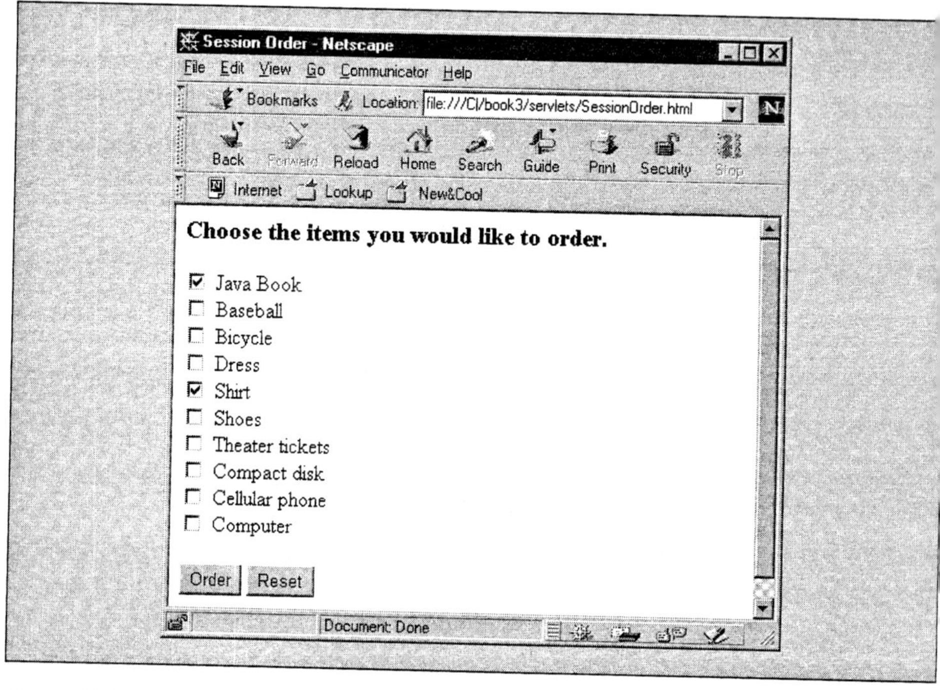

Figure 18.20 The response to an order

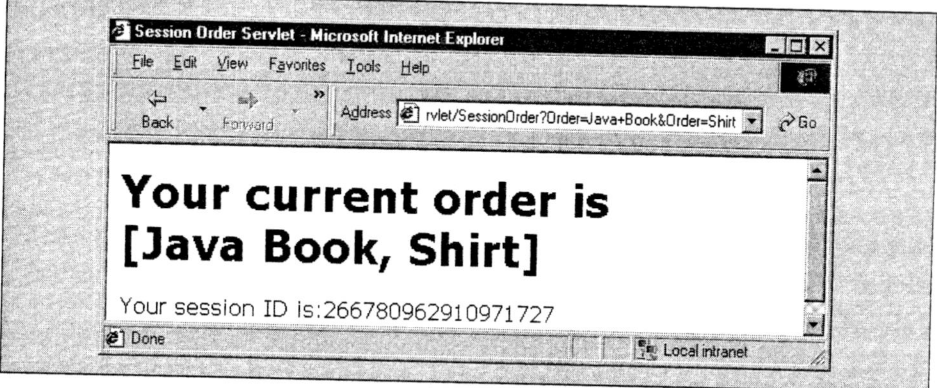

The `SessionOrder` servlet returns a list of the items ordered, and also displays the client's session ID. Since we use a `GET` request, the browser appends the items requested to the URL, in making the request.

Figure 18.21 shows the request from another customer and Figure 18.22 shows the servlet's response.

Figure 18.21 An order from another customer

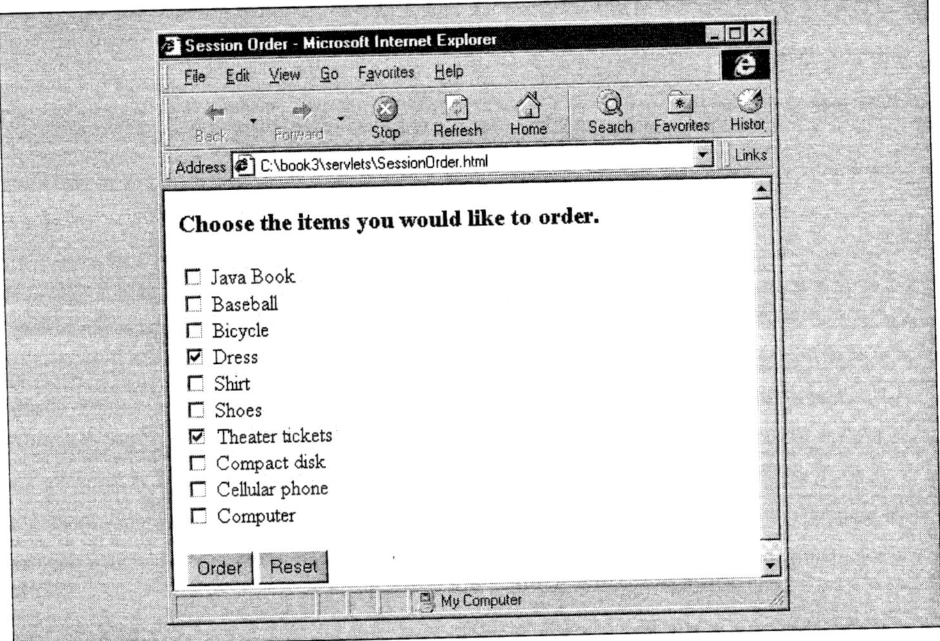

Figure 18.22 The servlet's response to the second customer

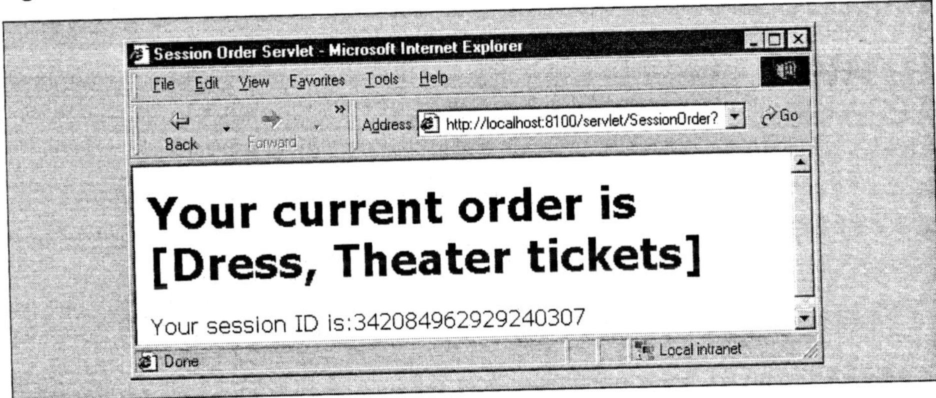

The servlet still remembers the order from the first customer. Figure 18.23 shows the response when that customer connects again, ordering shoes and a compact disk.

The `SessionOrder` servlet adds the new items maintaining all the items ordered by the first customer.

Figure 18.23 The response to an additional order

EXAMPLE 18.9 SessionOrder.java

```
/* Uses session tracking to maintain a customer's
 * information over multiple connections.
 */

import java.io.*;
import javax.servlet.*;
import javax.servlet.http.*;
import java.util.*;

public class SessionOrder extends HttpServlet {
  public void doGet(HttpServletRequest req, HttpServletResponse resp)
                             throws ServletException, IOException {
    resp.setContentType("text/html");
    PrintWriter out = resp.getWriter();
    HttpSession session = req.getSession(true);                       // Note 1
    String[] newItems = req.getParameterValues("Order");
    Vector items = (Vector)session.getValue("items");                 // Note 2
    if(items==null)                                                   // Note 3
      items = new Vector();
    for(int i=0; i<newItems.length; i++)
      items.addElement(newItems[i]);                                  // Note 4
    session.putValue("items",items);                                  // Note 5
    out.println("<html>");
    out.println("<head><title>Session Order Servlet</title></head>");
    out.println("<body><h1><strong>Your current order is<br>");
    out.println(items + "</strong></h1><p>");
    out.println("Your session ID is:" + session.getId() + "<br>");
    out.println("</body></html>");
    out.close();
  }
}
```

Note 1: The `getSession` method returns the current session. If the argument is **true**, it creates a new session if there is no current session.

Note 2: The `getValue` method returns the `Object` associated with the argument `"items"`. We cast it to a `Vector` which is what we are using in this example.

Note 3: If `items` is **null** we have just begun a session and need to create a new `Vector` to hold the orders.

Note 4: We add the newly chosen items to the `Vector` containing the previous choices.

Note 5: Having updated items, we use the `putValue` method to save it, associated with the name `"items"`.

THE BIG PICTURE

Session tracking allows the server to keep track of a client during multiple connections. Information the client sent will be saved so that the server can read it the next time the client connects. Using HTTP each client request requires a separate connection, so session tracking is essential for e-commerce applications. Session tracking may use cookies, bits of stored information, to save the data for later recall.

TEST YOUR UNDERSTANDING

TRY IT YOURSELF 13. Browse `SessionOrder.html` repeatedly, returning this page several times and making various choices of items. Describe the results.

TRY IT YOURSELF 14. Browse `SessionOrder.html` placing an order, and then open a new copy of the browser and browse `SessionOrder.html` again. Compare the results to those of Exercise 18.13.

18.6 JavaServer Pages (JSP)

JavaServer Pages make using servlets even simpler. JSP provides script tags to include Java code in a web page to create dynamic content. It automatically creates a servlet from the JSP page. We can call JavaBeans component methods to more cleanly separate application logic from web page presentation.

Getting Started with JSP

We use the JSP in place of the servlet of Example 18.2, in order to compare the two approaches to adding dynamic content to a web page. Using JSP, rather than writing a separate servlet class we add Java code directly in the web page returned to the client.

In writing a servlet we use an `HttpServletRequest` object to get parameters from the client and a `PrintWriter` to send a response. Both these objects are implicitly available in a JSP page, as `request` and `out` respectively.

JSP tags are case sensitive. In Example 18.10 we include a Java code fragment using

```
<% code fragment %>
```

In place of the servlet of Example 18.2, we write a JSP page, giving it a `.jsp` extension. We replace the action in the HTML file of Figure 18.3, which refers to the servlet of Example 18.2, by a reference to our JSP page. Figure 18.24 shows the revised HTML. We use a relative URL for the action, indicating that `GetOrder.jsp` can be found in the same directory as the HTML file. Browsing `GetJspOrder.html` will bring up the screen of Figure 18.4.

Figure 18.24 `GetJspOrder.html`

```
<html>
<head><title>Get Jsp Order</title></head>
<body>
<h3>Enter an order</h3>
<form action = GetOrder.jsp method=GET>
 Order: <input type=text name="Order" size=20>
    <input type=submit>
</form>
</body></html>
```

In Example 18.10 we write the web page we want to return in response to the client's request. We insert only one Java line in the response

```
<% out.println(" " + request.getParameter("Order")); %>
```

which says to echo the order the customer requested. When the user browses `GetJspOrder.html` and submits an order, the output will be the same as that of Figure 18.2 that resulted from using the servlet of Example 18.2.

EXAMPLE 18.10 GetOrder.jsp

```
<%-- JSP version of the servlet of Example 2 --%>                  // Note 1

<html>
<head><title>Get Jsp Order Results</title></head>
<body>
<h1><strong>

I'd like to order<br>

<%
 out.println(" " + request.getParameter("Order"));
%>

</strong></h1>
</body></html>
```

Note 1: We use the <%-- comment --%> tag to insert a hidden comment that documents the file but is not sent to the client.

Comparing Example 18.10 to Example 18.2, we see how much simpler a JSP page can be to write. We do not have to send HTML formatting from a servlet, but rather augment the HTML page with Java code and let the servlet engine create the servlet.

To execute JavaServer Pages, we put the file GetJspOrder.html of Figure 18.24 and GetOrder.jsp of Example 18.10 in the JRUN_HOME\servers\default\default-app directory, where JRUN_HOME is in the directory in which JRUN is installed. We browse the URL.

```
http://localhost:8100/GetJspOrder.html
```

when using a local machine, but replace localhost with the IP address of a remote site if we are connecting to it.

Two stages occur in the processing. At HTML translation the JSP source file is compiled to a servlet, using a Java compiler associated with the servlet engine. When the client submits a request the servlet is executed.

A JSP Response to a Form

The simple form produced by the page of Figure 18.24 was easy to handle. For a more complex example, we respond to the POST command of Figure 18.6, whose form is shown in Figure 18.7, using JSP rather than the servlet of Example 18.4. The result of processing the form by the JSP will be the same, shown in Figure 18.8. The PostJspOrder.html file of Figure 18.25 is the same as the PostOrder.html file of Figure 18.6 except that the action is now a JSP rather than a servlet.

In the JSP of Example 18.11, we use an expression tag

```
<%= expression %>
```

where the expression can be any valid Java expression. We interleave Java code inside scriptlet tags with HTML code. For example, the fragment

```
<% if (kinds==null) %>
with no toppings.
<% else { %>
with <ul>
<% for(i=0; i<kinds.length; i++) { %>
<li> <%= kinds[i] %>
<% } %>
</ul>
```

uses Java code to generate a web page. If the user did not choose any toppings, we display "with no toppings." Otherwise, we create an unordered list and display each kind of topping as a list item. The Java code, including braces, goes in scriptlet tags, <% %>. We put the Java variable, kinds[i], in an expression tag which we can insert directly into the HTML.

Figure 18.25 PostJspOrder.html

```
<html>
<head><title>Post Order</title></head>
<body>
<form action="PostOrder.jsp" method=POST>
<strong>Name:</strong>    <input type=text name=name size=20><br>
<strong>Password:</strong> <input type=password name=password size=12><p>
<strong>Flavor:</strong>
<select name=flavor size=3>
<option>Vanilla
<option>Chocolate
<option>Strawberry
</select><p>
<strong>Toppings:</strong>
  <input type=checkbox name=toppings value="Hot Fudge">      Hot Fudge
  <input type=checkbox name=toppings value="Butterscotch"> Butterscotch
  <input type=checkbox name=toppings value="Nuts">           Nuts
  <input type=checkbox name=toppings value="Whipped Cream"> Whipped Cream<p>
  <input type=radio name=place value="Eat here"> Eat here
  <input type=radio name=place value="Take out"> Take out<p>
  <input type=submit value="Order">
  <input type=reset>
</form></body></html>
```

EXAMPLE 18.11 PostOrder.jsp

```
<!-- Echoes the user's order made in a POST request. -->
<% String message = request.getParameter("name");                  // Note 1
String result = request.getParameter("flavor");                    // Note 2
String[] kinds = request.getParameterValues("toppings");
int i;
%>
<html>
<head><title>Ice Cream Servlet</title></head>
<body><h1><strong>Hi <%= message %>
</strong></h1><h3>                                                 // Note 3

Got your order for <%= result %> ice cream<br>

<% if (kinds==null) %>
with no toppings.
<% else { %>
with <ul>
<% for(i=0; i<kinds.length; i++) { %>
<li> <%= kinds[i] %>
<% } %>
</ul>                                                              // Note 4
```

```
<% }
result = request.getParameter("place");
if (result.equals("Eat here"))
%>
to eat here.
<% else %>
to go.
</h3></body></html>
```

Note 1: This comment is sent to the client in the page source, and not hidden.

Note 2: The `request` object is implicitly available. It represent the `POST` request that the user made.

Note 3: We use the `expression` tag to embed the value of the expression in the HTML file. In this case the `message` string represents the user's name entered in the form. The form includes a password field, but we do not use it to restrict access, leaving that improvement for the exercises.

Note 4: The closing brace, }, is part of the Java code and not the HTML file, so we must enclose it in a scriptlet tag.

TIP To import a package, use the page directive, as for example

```
<%@ page import="java.io.*" %>
```

JSP and JavaBeans Components

To further separate the content of a response from its presentation in HTML we can use the JavaBeans components that we will cover in a later chapter. For this section, all we need to know about JavaBeans is that they are Java programs which allow us to store and retrieve values using get and set methods. For example to store a name we use `setName("George")`, while to retrieve it we use `getName()`.

Example 18.12 shows the bean we will use. It contains methods to set and get the values associated with the sundae ordering of Example 18.11 which we will redo using this bean. We could add additional methods if desired.

EXAMPLE 18.12 OrderBean.java

```
/* A JavaBean to hold values from a form request
 */

package order;

  public class OrderBean {                                    // Note 1
  private String name = "Name";
  private String password = "Password";
  private String flavor = "Flavor" ;
  private String[] toppings = {"Toppings"};
```

```
    private String place = "Place";

    public void setName(String n) {                              // Note 2
      name = n;
    }
    public String getName() {                                    // Note 3
      return name;
    }
    public void setPassword(String p) {
      password = p;
    }
    public String getPassword() {
      return password;
    }
    public void setToppings(String[] t) {
      toppings = t;
    }
    public String[] getToppings() {
      return toppings;
    }
    public void setFlavor(String f) {
      flavor = f;
    }
    public String getFlavor() {
      return flavor;
    }
    public void setPlace(String p) {
      place = p;
    }
    public String getPlace() {
      return place;
    }
}
```

Note 1: We declare one variable for each form value.

Note 2: We declare one set method for each value we wish to set.

Note 3: We declare one get method for each value we wish to retrieve. To retrieve a value there must be a corresponding set method to set the value.

The `PostJspOrderBean.html` file that we use to define our form is the same as Figure 18.25 except that the action is `PostOrderBean.jsp`. In that JSP file we introduce tags to use bean values.

To use a bean we use a `<jsp:useBean>` tag which may include various attributes. In our example we use the `id` attribute to refer to our bean, and the `class` attribute to specify its class file.

```
<jsp:useBean id="sundae" class="order.OrderBean" />
```

With the <jsp:setProperty> tag we can set some or all of the bean values sent by the client in the POST request. In our example, we set all the values using

```
<jsp:setProperty name="sundae" property="*" />
```

The name attribute gives the name of the bean, while the property attribute states which property to set. In this tag, the * value represents a wildcard that matches all properties, so all values sent by the client will be set in the bean.

We can retrieve bean values using the <jsp:getProperty> tag. For example, the tag

```
<jsp:getProperty name="sundae" property="name" />
```

retrieves the name property. We embed the returned value in the HTML code.

Inside the scriptlet tag we can call bean methods directly. In Example 18.13, we call

```
sundae.getToppings()
```

to retrieve the kinds of topping the client selected.

EXAMPLE 18.13 PostOrderBean.jsp

```
<!-- Echoes the user's order made in a POST request. -->

<jsp:useBean id="sundae" class="order.OrderBean" />
<jsp:setProperty name="sundae" property="*" />

<%
  String[] kinds;
  int i;
  %>
<html>
<head><title>Ice Cream Servlet</title></head>
<body><h1><strong>Hi <jsp:getProperty name="sundae" property="name" />
</strong></h1><h3>

Got your order for <jsp:getProperty name="sundae"
                              property="flavor" /> ice cream<br>
   <% kinds = sundae.getToppings();
   if (kinds==null) %>
 with no toppings.
   <% else { %>
 with <ul>
   <% for(i=0; i<kinds.length; i++) { %>
     <li> <%= kinds[i] %>
   <% } %>
 </ul>
   <% }
     String result = sundae.getPlace();
     if (result.equals("Eat here"))
   %>
 to eat here.
```

```
  <% else %>
to go
</h3></body></html>
```

To execute this example using the JRUN

- Place PostJspOrderBean.html and PostOrderBean.jsp in the JRUN_HOME\servers\default\default-app directory.
- Create an order subdirectory of JRUN_HOME\servers\default\default-app\web-inf\classes.
- Compile OrderBean.java and place OrderBean.class in this directory.
- Browse http://localhost:8100/PostJspOrderBean.html.

THE BIG PICTURE

JSP allows the easy creation of server side HTML pages. JSP uses Java as a scripting language. Both JRun and the JSWDK have a server that handles JSP. JSP commands augment HTML to add dynamic content. A JSP page is compiled to a servlet which is executed when the client submits a request. JavaServer Pages can use JavaBeans components to respond to client requests.

TEST YOUR UNDERSTANDING

TRY IT YOURSELF 15. Modify GetJspOrder of Figure 18.24 to use a POST request instead of GET. What differences if any do you observe when sending an order?

TRY IT YOURSELF 16. What difference do you observe in effect of the comments between Example 18.10 and Example 18.11?

17. In Example 18.13, what is the difference in usage between a bean method call and the <jsp:getProperty> tag?

SUMMARY

- Servlets extend the functionality of a web server. They can respond to GET and POST requests from web clients. A servlet can extend GenericServlet, using the service method to handle request, or extend HttpServlet and use the doGet or doPost methods to handle requests. A servlet has access to request and response objects to communicate with the client. Servlets may output HTML code to the client. HTML forms include various types of input including text fields, lists, checkboxes, radio buttons, and buttons.
- Server-side includes allow us to embed a servlet in a web page using a <servlet> tag. The server-side include response will be included with the response to the rest of the page. For example, we could add a server-side include to each page to display the date and time and other current information.
- Servlet chaining lets us direct the output of one servlet to another servlet to filter the output before sending it back to the client. We can chain two servlets in a URL,

or configure the server to use a MIME filter, sending every file of a certain type to the servlet filter.

- Three-tiered architecture allows the client to concentrate on presentation, connecting to a middle-tier executing a servlet to implement the business logic and connect to a database on the third tier.
- Session tracking lets the server keep track of a client who makes multiple requests. Since HTTP is a stateless protocol, not saving information about the client, session-tracking is essential to enable electronic commerce applications.
- JavaServer Pages (JSP) add dynamic content to web pages. They use scripting to enhance HTML code. The resulting JSP page gets compiled to a servlet which executes when the client submits a request.

Program Modification Exercises

1. Modify the servlet of Example 18.1 to extend `HttpServlet` and to handle a `GET` request.
2. Modify Examples 18.6 and 18.7, so that the `<lucky>` tag does not have to be on a separate line.
3. Modify Example 18.7 so that it always returns distinct random numbers.
4. Modify Figure 18.15 and Example 18.8 to pass the JDBC driver name and the database URL from the HTML form to the servlet.
5. Modify Example 18.9 to allow the customer to delete items from an order.
6. **PUTTING IT ALL TOGETHER** Use the `SearchSales` program, Example 3.6, to create the query to send to the `SalesServlet` of Example 18.8.
7. Modify Example 18.8 to create an SQL query from a form the user fills in, rather than having the user enter the query directly.
8. Modify Example 18.6 to add a `doPost` method to handle `POST` requests.
9. Modify Example 18.9 to add a `doPost` method to handle `POST` requests. Modify `SessionOrder.html` and browse it to test the revised servlet.
10. Modify Example 18.10 to use a JavaBean.

Program Design Exercises

11. Write a server-side include that displays the current date. Use the `Date` class to get the date. Add it to `GetOrder.html` so the output from the server will show the date.

12. Write a servlet filter that outputs the date in place of a `<date>` tag. Create an HTML page which includes a `<date>` tag and use a servlet chain to let the filter process it to ouput the date in the web page.

PUTTING IT ALL TOGETHER

13. Write an HTML page with a form for the user to select a favorite food. Write a servlet to save the client's response in a database, and output the number of clients who prefer each food.
14. Write an HTML page with a form for the user to select a favorite sport. Write a servlet to save the client's response in a hashtable, and output the number of clients who prefer each sport.
15. Write an HTML page with a form for the user to order a pizza with either thick or thin crust and a choice of toppings. Write a JSP page to echo this request back to the client.
16. Write an HTML page with a form for the user to order a pizza with either thick or thin crust and a choice of toppings. Write a JSP page which uses a JavaBean to echo this request back to the client.

CHAPTER

19 Java Beans

OUTLINE

Introduction

Java Beans provide a platform-independent component technology that makes it easier to build Java programs. Hardware designers commonly integrate various components in building a new system. For example, a computer manufacturer uses available memory chips and hard drives, rather than designing them again. Unfortunately many software systems create the whole application from scratch even though many parts of it may be familiar from previously developed systems.

With Java Beans, software developers can integrate components obtained from various sources. For example, a reservation system might want to make a calendar available to the user. The developer might obtain a calendar bean which helps the user make a reservation. When the user enters a date in a text field, the calendar for the three months nearest that date appears.

We first show how to use beans to build an application and then show how to write our own beans. Most commonly, developers use a visual tool to create applications using beans, but as we shall see they may also include beans directly in Java programs.

OBJECTIVES

- Use the **BeanBox** to build an applet from `Bean` components.
- Show how to use beans with bound and constrained properties.
- Write a simple Java Bean.
- Package a Java Bean in a JAR (Java Archive) file.
- Write beans that have bound properties.
- Introduce anonymous inner classes.
- Use `BeanInfo` to make beans more user friendly.
- Use beans in a Java program.

19.1 Building with Beans

Typically developers use a visual tool to build applets from Java Bean **components**. Our example demonstrates this process, using beans from the `demo` directory included with the Bean Development Kit.

Several vendors provide visual tools with which to develop applications using Java Beans. Sun offers the Beans Development Kit (BDK) as a free download from its web site, `java.sun.com`. The **BDK** contains a simple development environment, the **BeanBox**, which is available for learning and testing, much as the applet viewer is a simple tool for testing applets, rather than a full browser.

Figure 19.1 Running the `BeanBox`

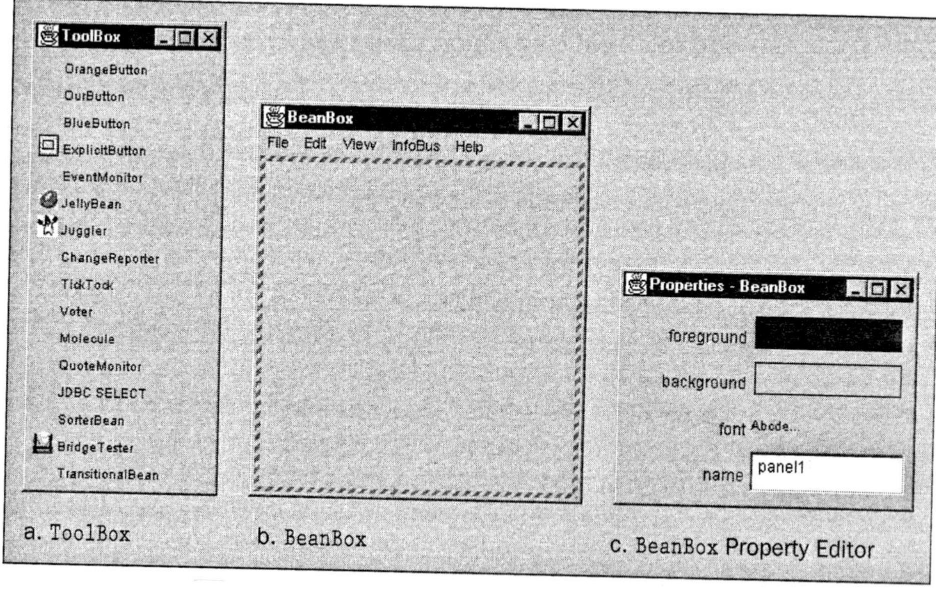

Starting the BeanBox

Once the BDK has been installed, we can start the **BeanBox** by executing the `run` command from the command prompt in the `C:\BDK\beanbox` directory on Windows systems, where `C:\BDK` is the directory in which the BDK is installed. The three windows shown in Figure 19.1 will pop up. Figure 19.1a, the **ToolBox**, contains a list of beans we can drag into the **BeanBox**, Figure 19.1b. The border inside the **BeanBox** surrounds the currently selected bean, in this case the **BeanBox** itself. Every bean is configurable, meaning that we can change its properties.

Figure 19.1c shows the four properties of the **BeanBox** that we can change, its foreground and background colors, font, and name. Clicking on the gray rectangle, showing the current light-gray background, will pop up the color editor shown in Figure 19.2, in which the rectangle on the left shows the current background, the numbers 192,192,192 in the center text field are the red, green, and blue components of light gray, and the Choice box lists other colors from which to select. We can either enter new RGB values or select another color, such as yellow, from the Choice box. Doing so will immediately change the **BeanBox** to have the chosen background color.

Figure 19.2 The color editor for the `BeanBox` background

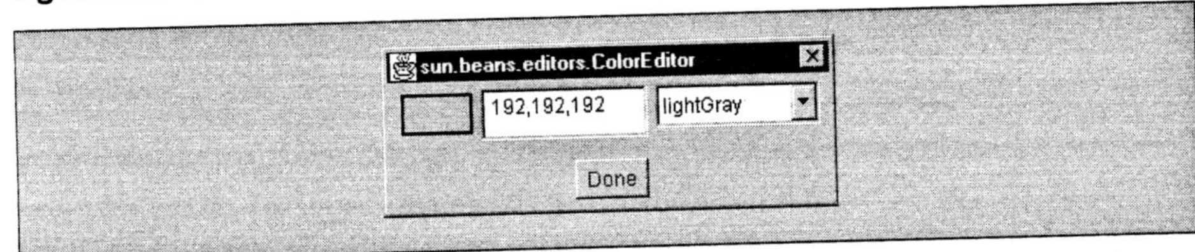

Figure 19.3 The `Juggler` and `ExplicitButton` beans

Building an Applet with Beans

To use the **BeanBox** to build an applet, we drag beans from the **ToolBox** to the **BeanBox**, customize the beans using the property editors from the **Properties** window, and connect the beans using hookup classes generated by the **BeanBox**.

For example, we drag the `Juggler` bean and the `ExplicitButton` bean into the **BeanBox**, each time clicking the mouse where we want to position the bean. Figure 19.3 shows the **BeanBox**, with the `ExplicitButton` selected. In color, the **BeanBox** background would appear yellow, and when run on the computer the `Juggler` is actually juggling the beans. Because we selected `ExplicitButton`, the **Properties** window in Figure 19.4 shows its properties that we can change. By typing `Stop` instead of press in the text field for the label property and pressing the *`Enter`* key, the button will have "Stop" as its label.

Figure 19.4 Changeable properties of an `ExplicitButton`

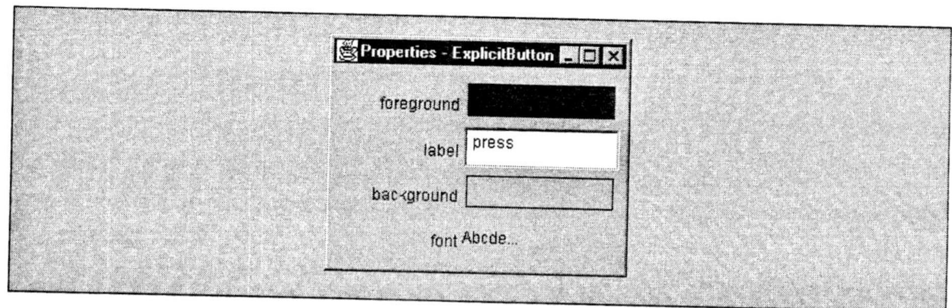

When the user presses the *`Stop`* button, Java generates an `ActionEvent`, passing it to the `actionPerformed` method of an object registered with the button as an `ActionListener`. The code inside the `actionPerformed` method implements the behavior desired when the user presses the button. We might call the class containing the `actionPerformed` method the **hookup** (or **adapter**) **class** because it connects the source of the action event with the target.

When we write our own applets we implement all these steps to make button presses have the desired effects. Using Java Beans, the **BeanBox** (or other bean development tool) creates the hookup class for us, generating the `actionPerformed` method. In our example, we would like the `Stop` button to cause the `Juggler` to stop juggling. We highlight the *`Stop`* button, click on the *`Edit`* menu, then *`Events`*, then *`button push`*, then *`actionPerformed`*, as Figure 19.5 shows.

Clicking on the *`actionPerformed`* item causes a red line to emanate from the *`Stop`* button (Figure 19.6). We drag the line to the target object, Juggler in this example, and click the mouse. The mouse click brings up the `EventTargetDialog` (Figure 19.7), which asks us to select the method that will be invoked by the `actionPerformed` method when the user presses the *`Stop`* button.

We select the `stopJuggling` method and click OK, receiving the message that the **BeanBox** is generating and compiling an adapter class to hookup the *`Stop`* button source to the `Juggler` target. Now, pressing the *`Stop`* button will cause the `Juggler` to stop juggling.

Figure 19.5 Connecting the `Stop` button

BeanBox
File
Edit
View
InfoBus
Help
Cut
Copy
Paste
Report...
Customize...
Events
Bind property...
button push
bound property change
actionPerformed
Stop

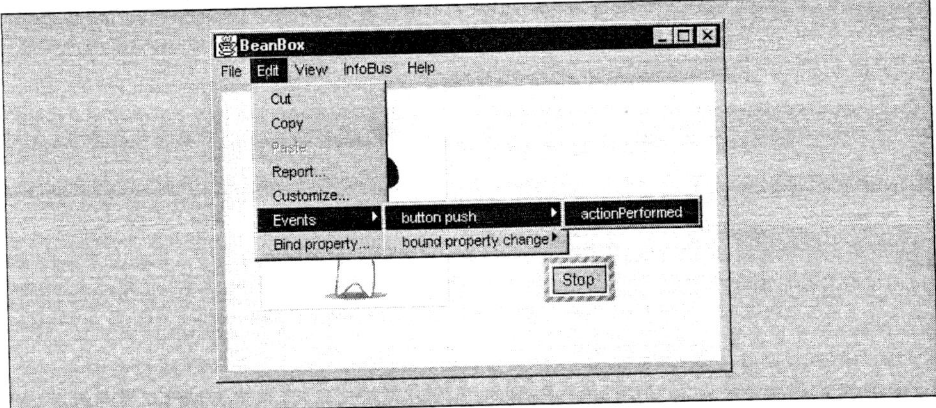

Figure 19.6 Connecting the source to the target

BeanBox
File
Edit
View
InfoBus
Help
Stop

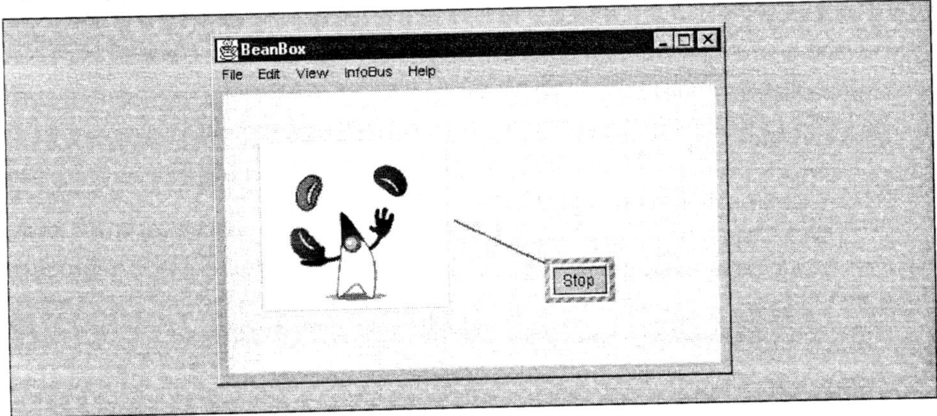

Figure 19.7 The target methods

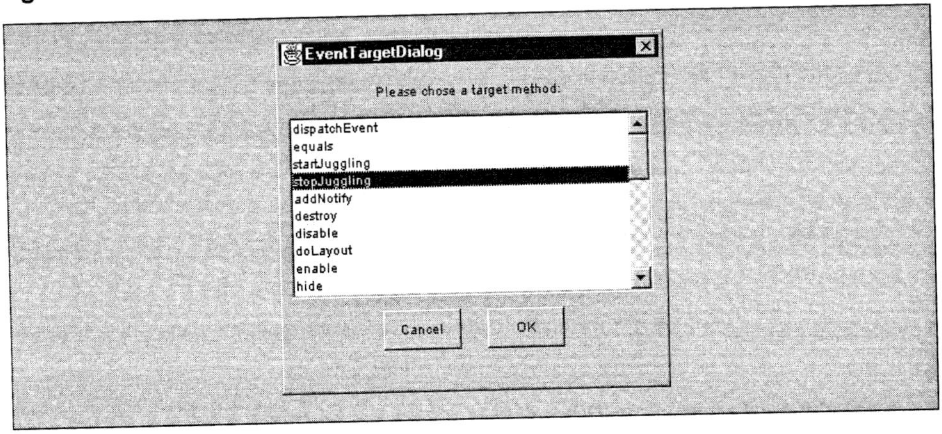

EventTargetDialog
Please chose a target method:
dispatchEvent
equals
startJuggling
stopJuggling
addNotify
destroy
disable
doLayout
enable
hide
Cancel
OK

To be able to start the `Juggler` juggling again we add another button to the **BeanBox**. This time we drag an `OurButton` rather than an `ExplicitButton` to the **BeanBox**, changing its label to `Start` (See Figure 19.8).

Figure 19.8 Adding a Start button

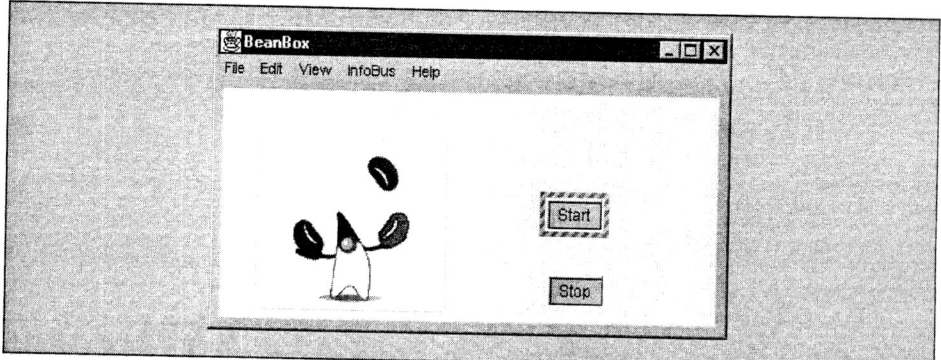

When we select the *Start* button, click on *Edit*, and click on *Events*, we get a different list of events, shown in Figure 19.9, than we got for the *Stop* button. We will explain the reason for this difference later in the chapter.

Figure 19.9 Connecting the *Start* button

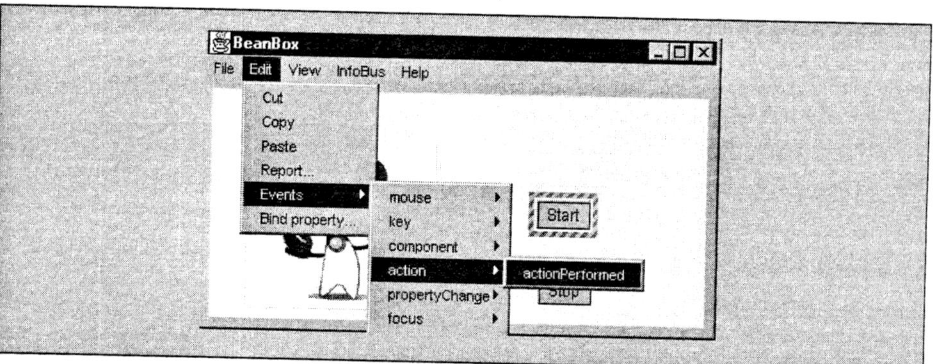

Continuing, we connect the *Start* button to the Juggler. The **BeanBox** then generates the hookup class that will cause the `startJuggling` method of the `Juggler` to execute when the user presses the *Start* button.

The **BeanBox** is a tool we can use to build an applet from beans. We have customized the **BeanBox** to have a yellow background and the buttons to have `Start` and `Stop` labels. We let the **BeanBox** create hookup classes which implement the actions for the events the buttons generate. Now we click on *File, Make Applet* to let the **BeanBox** make this creation into an applet.

We will discuss JAR (Java Archive) files later in this chapter. In the Make an Applet window we change the default `myApplet` name to `ButtonJuggle` in both text

Figure 19.10 Making an applet

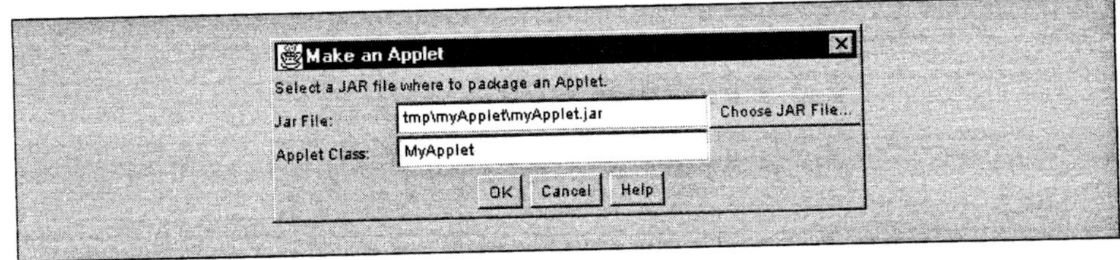

fields and click OK. We get a sequence of messages listing the steps the **BeanBox** is taking to create the applet. The **BeanBox** puts all the files for the `ButtonJuggle` applet in the directory `c:\BDK\beanbox\tmp\ButtonJuggle`. We can test the applet using the applet viewer with the `ButtonJuggle.html` file or we can run it using the Internet Explorer browser.

THE BIG PICTURE

The JavaBean component technology allows us to build applets by customizing and connecting bean components, without doing any programming. The **BeanBox** is a simple visual tool for building with beans. Each bean has a property list providing editors to change each property. We can connect a source event in one bean to a target method in another. The **BeanBox** will create the hookup class which will call the target method when the source event occurs. The bean developer writes beans which the applet designer uses to make an applet run by the end user.

TEST YOUR UNDERSTANDING

TRY IT YOURSELF 1. Start the **BeanBox**. Change its background color to orange.

TRY IT YOURSELF 2. Following the steps in the text, use the **BeanBox** to create the `ButtonJuggle` applet, additionally changing the background color of the *Start* and *Stop* buttons to blue and the foreground color to white.

19.2 Bound and Constrained Properties

With **bound properties**, beans can use Java events to notify other components of changes in property values. **Constrained properties** allow those components to veto the changes.

In building the `ButtonJuggle` applet, we used the **BeanBox** to hookup the *Start* button source of an `ActionEvent` with the `Juggler` target, so the `Juggler` will start juggling when the user presses the *Start* button. In this section, we show how the **BeanBox** can hookup sources and targets of property changes and vetoable changes.

Simple Properties

Java objects may have various properties that we can change. For example, every component, such as a `Button`, has foreground and background properties that we can change using the `setForeground` or `setBackground` methods in a Java program. When using a tool such as the **BeanBox**, we often want to change some properties of beans before we incorporate them into an applet. In building the `ButtonJuggle` applet, we changed the labels on the buttons, for example.

By using the **BeanBox** we avoid the details of calling the `setLabel` method in a program, using instead the property editor for the label in the **Properties** window. The **Properties** window, shown in Figure 19.4, lets us change the `foreground`, `label`, `background`, and `font` properties of an `ExplicitButton`.

Bound Properties

A bound property lets other components know when it is changed. We can use the **BeanBox** to connect beans so changing the color, for example, of the source bean will notify the target bean to change its color also. If a bean has any bound properties there will be a *`Bind Property`* item in its *`Edit`* menu. Not all beans have any bound properties; the `Juggler` has no *`Bind Property`* item on its *`Edit`* menu.

For example, let us drag an `ExplicitButton` and a `JellyBean` into the **BeanBox**. Selecting the `Explicit Button` and clicking *`Edit, Bind Property`* pops up the window of Figure 19.11a to let us choose the property whose changes we want to transmit to other beans. If we choose the background property and click OK a red line will appear which we can drag, clicking on the JellyBean, popping up the list of properties shown in Figure 19.11b.

Figure 19.11 **Bound Properties**

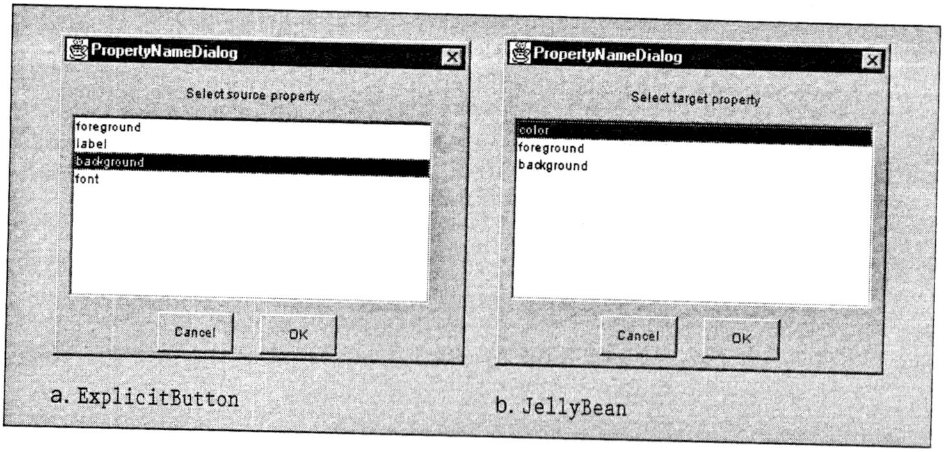

a. `ExplicitButton`

b. `JellyBean`

Selecting color and clicking OK, binds the background of the `ExplicitButton` to the color of the `JellyBean`. Before binding the two beans in this way, changing the background of the `ExplicitButton` to red leaves the `JellyBean` orange (Figure 19.12a)

. After binding, changing the background of the `ExplicitButton` to red also changes the color of the `JellyBean` to red (Figure 19.12b).

Figure 19.12

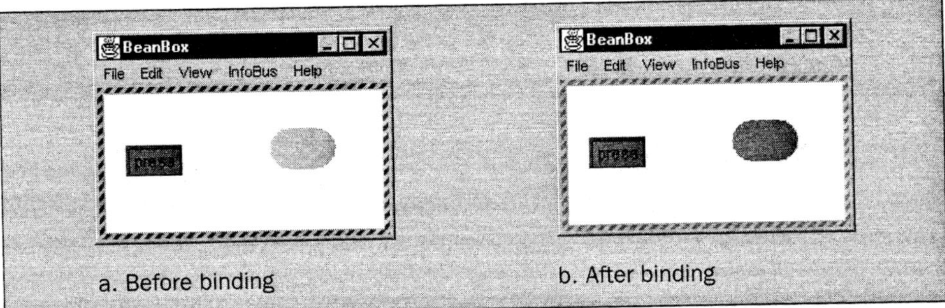

a. Before binding b. After binding

TIP We must distinguish between the applet designer and the applet user. Using the **BeanBox**, we are functioning as the applet designer. We did not make an applet out of the bound property example above, because the applet user would have no way to change the background color of the button. If the user could change that background color, then the `JellyBean`'s color would also change. As the applet designer we have the property editors in the **Properties** window to use to change the background color of the `ExplicitButton`, to show how bound properties work. Later we will design an applet that uses bound properties effectively.

Constrained Properties

Simple properties change without affecting properties of other beans. Changes in bound properties may change properties of other beans. Constrained properties give other beans the chance to veto the change before it takes effect. For example, the `priceInCents` property of the `JellyBean` is vetoable. The `Voter` bean, in the **ToolBox**, normally vetoes every change presented to it.

To see how constrained properties work, we drag the `JellyBean` and the `Voter` bean into the **BeanBox**. Selecting the `JellyBean`, we show in Figure 19.13 the *`Edit, Events, vetoableChange, vetoableChange`* menu items. The `JellyBean` can generate a `VetoableChange` event which is handled by the `vetoableChange` method. The bean at the right of Figure 19.13 displays a large "**No**" signifying that it will veto every property change presented to it.

Clicking on the *`vetoableChange`* item will cause the red line to appear, which we drag and click on the `Voter` bean popping up the list of Figure 19.14. Selecting `vetoableChange` and clicking OK will cause the **BeanBox** to hookup the `JellyBean` source to the `Voter` target. Highlighting the `JellyBean` and trying to use the property editor to change its `priceInCents` to `3` will cause the message

```
WARNING: Vetoed; reason is: NO!
```

Figure 19.13 A vetoable change event

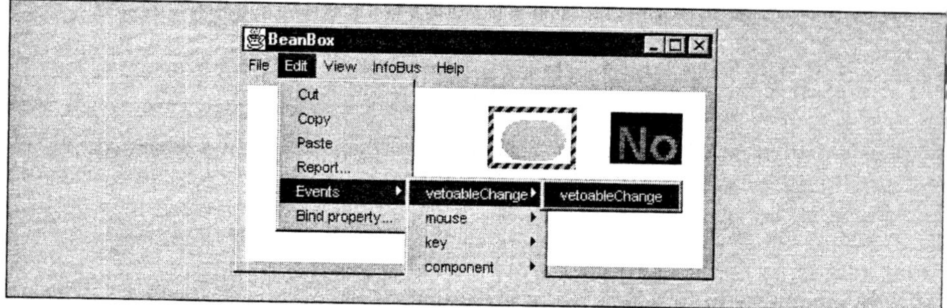

to appear on the console screen. The `priceInCents` remains `2`, as the `Voter` bean has vetoed the change. If we change the `vetoAll` property of the `Voter` bean from **true** to **false**, then the `Voter` bean will display a large "**Yes**" instead of "**No**," and will allow the change to `priceInCents` to proceed.

> **THE BIG PICTURE**
>
> In the **BeanBox**, or similar tool, we can bind a bound property of one bean to a property of the same type of another bean. When the source bean's bound property changes value so will the target's. A constrained property is like a bound property with the additional feature that a target bean may veto the change, forcing the source bean to withdraw it.

Figure 19.14 Choosing a target method `vetoableChange`

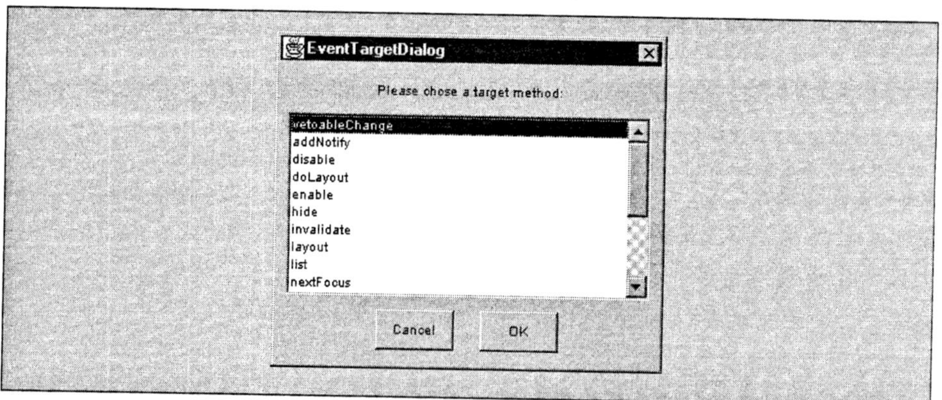

TEST YOUR UNDERSTANDING

TRY IT YOURSELF

3. Use the **BeanBox** to bind the `priceInCents` of the `JellyBean` to the `animationRate` of the `Juggler`. Enter different values in the **Properties** window editor for the `priceInCents` and observe the change in the `animationRate`.

TRY IT YOURSELF 4. Use the **BeanBox** to bind the foreground color of an `ExplicitButton` to the color of a `JellyBean` and to the background color of an `OurButton`. Change the foreground color of the `ExplicitButton` several times, using the **Properties** window color editor, and observe the effect.

TRY IT YOURSELF 5. Use the BeanBox to bind the `priceInCents` of the JellyBean to the `animationRate` of the Juggler. Also hookup the `vetoableChange` event from the JellyBean source to the `vetoableChange` handler method of the Voter bean. Try to change the `priceInCents`, using the **Properties** window editor, and observe what happens.

19.3 Writing and Packaging a Bean

Now that we have used the **BeanBox** to build an applet with the demo beans provided by Sun, we will learn to write our own beans and add them to the **BeanBox**. We package beans in JAR (Java Archive) files that combine individual files to avoid multiple connections when downloading a bean, and compress files to save space and time. We use anonymous inner classes to conveniently define event handlers.

A Simple Bean

A bean is just a Java program. Our first example, `TextBean`, has just a constructor and two methods, `setNumber` and `getNumber`, to set and get a single integer value. It extends `TextField` to provide a display for an integer value. Using the standard prefixes `set` and `get`, followed by the property name, as in `setNumber` and `getNumber`, allows the **BeanBox** to add these properties in the **Properties** window.

Example 19.1 has no `main` method because we will use it in the **BeanBox**, rather than as a standalone program. Adding a `main` method would allow it to run as a standalone application as well as to be used as a bean in the **BeanBox**. All programs to be used as beans should extend the `Serializable` interface, because Java uses object serialization to save the designer's customizations which can be reloaded and used in their customized state.

EXAMPLE 19.1 TextBean.java

```
/* A simple program to use
 * as a bean.
 */

import java.awt.*;
import java.awt.event.*;
import java.io.*;

public class TextBean extends TextField
                      implements Serializable {
```

```
  int myNumber = 10; // Value to set and get
  public TextBean() {
    super(5);                                      // Note 1
    setBackground(Color.white);                    // Note 2
  }
  public void setNumber(int x) {
    myNumber = x;
    setText("" + x);                               // Note 3
  }
  public int getNumber() {
    return myNumber;
  }
}
```

Note 1: We call the constructor of the superclass, `TextField`, to set the width of the text field to 5.

Note 2: Setting the background of the text field to white helps it to standout from the background of the **BeanBox**.

Note 3: The `setText` method displays the text in the text field. Binding another bean, such as the `JellyBean`, to set the `number` property when its `priceInCents` is changed, will cause the `priceInCents` to be displayed.

JAR Files

JAR (Java Archive) **files** allow us to package several files—class files, images, and sounds—together as one file. We will use them here to package our beans, but another important use is to package the files needed for an applet. When we download an applet from a web site, we must make a separate connection to download each of the files used by the applet. Packaging all the files in a JAR file allows the applet to be downloaded with one connection saving much time. The JAR file may also compress the files, further reducing the download time.

We can use the jar utility program to create JAR files. For Java Beans we should always include a **manifest** file which describes the contents of the JAR file, indicating which files are beans. To package our `TextBean`, we first create the manifest file, `TextBean.mf`, containing just two lines.

```
Name: TextBean.class
Java-Bean: True
```

The jar command, given at the command prompt, is

```
jar cfm TextBean.jar TextBean.mf TextBean.class
```

where the options are

`c` create a new archive

`f` archive name is the first file on the list (`TextBean.jar` here)

`m` manifest file is the second file on the list (`TextBean.mf` here)

Executing this jar command will create the JAR file `TextBean.jar`. To put this JAR file into the **BeanBox**, we copy it to `c:\BDK\jars` which already contains the Sun demo beans. Starting the **BeanBox** shows the `TextBean` in the **ToolBox** (Figure 19.15a). Dragging the `TextBean` and the `JellyBean` into the **BeanBox** (Figure 19.15b) and selecting the `TextBean` shows the number property appears in the **Properties** window (Figure 19.15c).

Figure 19.15 The `BeanBox` with the `TextBean`

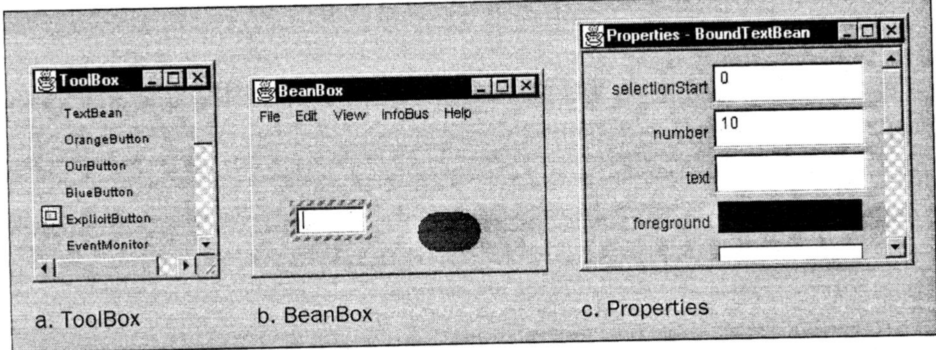

We will configure these beans so when the `priceInCents` of the `JellyBean` changes the new value will appear in the `TextBean`. Selecting the `JellyBean` and clicking on *`Edit, Bind Property`* pops up the *`PropertyNameDialog`*. Selecting `priceInCents`, and clicking OK produces the red line that we drag to the `TextBean`. Clicking on the `TextBean` pops up the *`PropertyNameDialog`* for the target property shown in Figure 19.16. Selecting the number property and clicking *`OK`* will complete the binding.

Figure 19.16 Selecting the target property in the `TextBean`

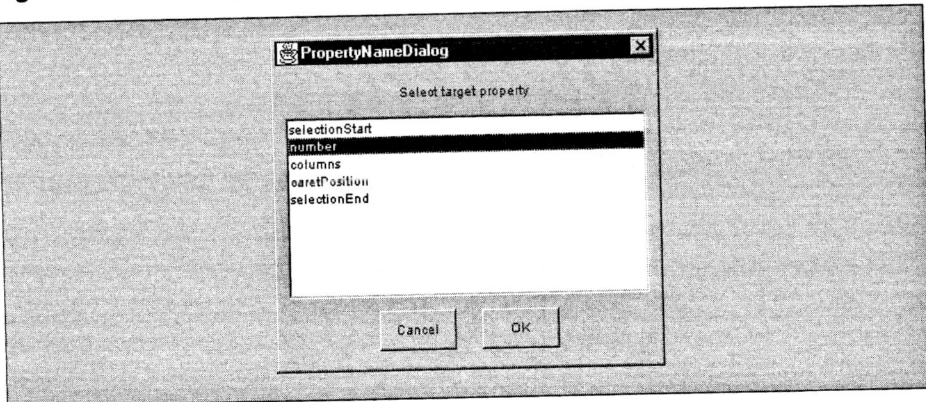

Selecting the `JellyBean` and entering `5` for its `priceInCents` will now cause the value `5` to be displayed in the text field of the `TextBean` (Figure 19.17).

Figure 19.17 TextBean displaying `priceInCents`

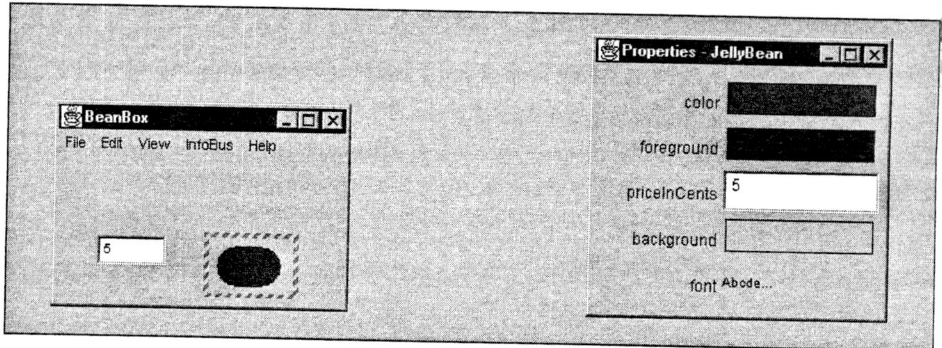

A Bean with a Bound Property

Next we make the number property a bound property with the capability to notify property change listeners when `myNumber` is changed. We will use this `BoundTextBean` later in building an applet.

The `java.beans` package has a `PropertyChangeEvent` class. The `PropertyChangeListener` interface has one method,

```
public void propertyChange(PropertyChangeEvent e)
```

which Java calls when a property value changes. We use the `PropertyChangeSupport` methods to do most of the work implementing bound properties. Instead of managing a vector of `PropertyChangeListeners` ourselves, we delegate that to the `addPropertyChangeListener` and `removePropertyChangeListener` methods. Instead of creating a `PropertyChangeEvent` and sending it to each listener we can just call the `firePropertyChange` method of the `PropertyChangeSupport` class. Example 19.2 shows these additions to Example 19.1.

EXAMPLE 19.2 BoundTextBean.java

```
/* Makes the number property a bound property.
 * Notifies PropertyChangeListeners when
 * myNumber changes.
 */

import java.awt.*;
import java.awt.event.*;
import java.io.*;
import java.beans.*;

public class BoundTextBean extends TextField
        implements Serializable, ActionListener {
  private int myNumber = 10;
  private PropertyChangeSupport pChange
        = new PropertyChangeSupport(this);                // Note 1
```

```
public BoundTextBean(){
  super(5);
  setBackground(Color.white);
  addActionListener(this);
}
public void setNumber(int x) {
  Integer oldVal = new Integer(myNumber);                         // Note 2
  Integer newVal = new Integer(x);
  myNumber = x;
  setText("" + x);
  pChange.firePropertyChange("number",oldVal,newVal);             // Note 3
}
public int getNumber() {
  return myNumber;
}
public void actionPerformed(ActionEvent e) {
  setNumber(Integer.parseInt(getText()));                         // Note 4
}
public void addPropertyChangeListener(PropertyChangeListener l) { // Note 5
  pChange.addPropertyChangeListener(l);
}
public void removePropertyChangeListener(PropertyChangeListener l) {
  pChange.removePropertyChangeListener(l);
}
}
```

Note 1: We create a PropertyChangeSupport object to manage registering PropertyChangeListener objects, and sending a PropertyChangeEvent to them.

Note 2: The firePropertyChange method, which notifies property change listeners when a property changes, takes Object arguments for the old and new values of the changing property. Because myNumber is a primitive **int** value we need to wrap it in an Integer object to pass as an argument to firePropertyChange.

Note 3: Our PropertyChangeSupport object, pChange, notifies each registered PropertyChangeListener of the change to myNumber, using the firePropertyChange method. The three arguments are a string with the name of the property; number is the name we used in the setNumber method, but with lowercase, that is, "number" not "Number." The second argument is the old value of the property, wrapped as an object if necessary, while the third argument is the new value of the property, also wrapped as an object.

Note 4: We want to enter the value of myNumber in the text field. When the user presses the *Enter* key, Java generates an ActionEvent which we handle in the actionPerformed method by calling the setNumber method to change myNumber to the value entered.

Note 5: Using the **BeanBox**, we can connect other beans who want to be notified when `myNumber` changes. These beans call the `addPropertyChangeListener` method to register to receive notification of changes. Rather than keep a vector of these listeners ourselves, we let `pChange` keep them for us and inform them of changes using the `firePropertyChange` method.

Smiley Bean

To illustrate a bean with additional features, we create `Smiley` bean with a happy face; pressing its nose generates an `ActionEvent`. `Smiley`'s age is a bound property. Before discussing the code for `Smiley`, we use it in the **BeanBox**. Figure 19.18 shows the **BeanBox** containing our `BoundTextBean` from Example 19.2, an `Explicit Button`, `Smiley`, and a `Juggler`.

Figure 19.18 Using `Smiley` in an applet

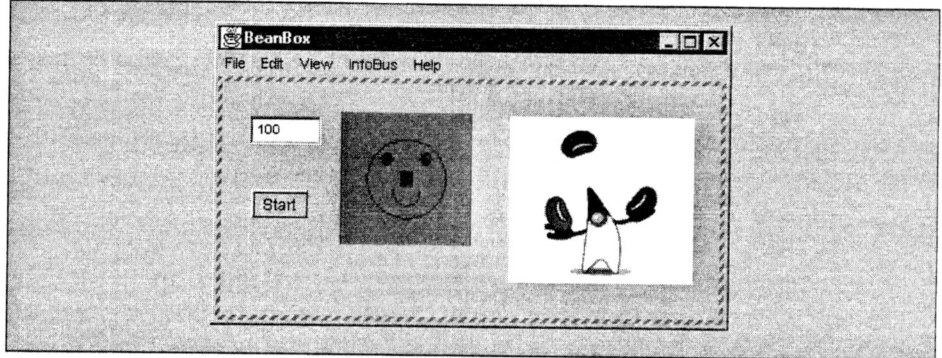

We customized the `ExplicitButton` to have the label "Start" and the `Smiley` bean to have a red background color. We bound the number property of the `BoundTextBean` to the `Smiley`'s age, so when we enter a value in the `BoundTextBean`, `Smiley`'s age will also have that value. We bound `Smiley`'s age to the animation rate of the `Juggler`, so entering a value in the `BoundTextBean` will actually change the `Juggler`'s animation rate.

Using the **BeanBox**, we hooked up `Smiley` to the `Juggler`, so when the user clicks on `Smiley`'s nose, generating an `ActionEvent`, the `Juggler` stops juggling. The *`Start`* button starts the `Juggler` juggling. Figure 19.19 shows Internet Explorer running the `SmileApplet` applet made in the **BeanBox** by clicking on the *`File, Make Applet`* menu item.
Now that we have used `Smiley` as part of `SmileApplet`, we discuss its implementation. Implementing the age property follows the same steps used for the number property in Example 19.2. Smiley generates an `ActionEvent` when the user presses its nose. We use the `mousePressed` method to detect when the mouse is over `Smiley`'s nose. We are making `Smiley`'s nose function like a button, and like a button we generate an `ActionEvent` and call the `actionPerformed` method of all listeners.

`Smiley` implements the `addActionListener` and `removeActionListener` methods to allow objects to register to be notified when the user presses `Smiley`'s nose. A vector

Figure 19.19 Running `SmileApplet`

holds these listeners. When the user presses `Smiley`'s nose, the `fireAction` method calls the `actionPerformed` method of all the registered listeners.

Anonymous Inner Classes

Sometimes we use an inner class just once, perhaps to define an event handler. Our `Smiley` example uses an inner class that overrides `MouseAdapter` to handle the `MOUSE_PRESSED` event. We could have named it, for example, as

```
class MousePress extends MouseAdapter {
  public void mousePressed(MouseEvent e) {
    // code to handle mouse press goes here
  }
}
```

and registered it using

```
addMouseListener(new MousePress());
```

Because we only use the `MousePress` class once, we do not need to give it a name. Java lets us use it anonymously, as in

```
addMouseListener(new MouseAdapter() {
  public void mousePressed(MouseEvent e) {
    // code to handle mouse press goes here
  }
} );
```

which uses an extension of the **new** operator for the syntax. Writing `'new MouseAdapter()'` signifies an anonymous inner class that extends `MouseAdapter`. The class definition follows, as usual, between curly braces. An **anonymous inner class** is an unnamed class defined within a block of code.

While we do not name an anonymous class, Java does name it. Looking in the package `smiley`, after compiling `Smiley.java`, we find the class file, `Smiley$1.class`, containing the byte code for the anonymous extension to `MouseAdapter`. We include the `Smiley$1.class` file in the manifest with an entry

```
Name: smiley/Smiley$1.class
```

and add it to the list of files to include in the JAR file for `Smiley`.

EXAMPLE 19.3 Smiley.java

```
/* A bean with a smiley face. Pressing its nose
 * generates an ActionEvent. Smiley's age is a
 * bound property.
 */

package smiley;                                                    // Note 1
import java.awt.*;
import java.awt.event.*;
import java.beans.*;
import java.io.Serializable;
import java.util.Vector;

public class Smiley extends Canvas
  implements Serializable {
  private int age = 10;
  private PropertyChangeSupport changes = new PropertyChangeSupport(this);
  private Vector listeners = new Vector();
  public Smiley() {
    setSize(new Dimension(100,100));
    addMouseListener(new MouseAdapter () {                         // Note 2
      public void mousePressed(MouseEvent evt) {
        int x = evt.getX();
        int y = evt.getY();
        if( x >= 45 && x <= 55 && y >= 45 && y <= 55)
          if(listeners != null) fireAction();                      // Note 3
      }
  } );
}
public void paint(Graphics g) {
  g.drawOval(20,20,60,60);
  g.fillOval(30,30,10,10);
  g.fillOval(60,30,10,10);
  g.fillRect(45,45,10,10);
  g.drawArc(40,50,20,20,170,200);
}
```

```
public void fireAction() {
    ActionEvent e = new ActionEvent(this, 0, null);                // Note 4
    for (int i = 0; i < listeners.size(); i++)
      ((ActionListener)listeners.elementAt(i)).actionPerformed(e);   // Note 5
}
public void setAge(int a) {
    Integer oldage = new Integer(age);
    age = a;
    Integer newage = new Integer(a);
    changes.firePropertyChange("age", oldage, newage);
  }
  public int getAge() {
    return age;
  }
  public void addActionListener(ActionListener l) {                // Note 6
    listeners.addElement(l);
  }
  public void removeActionListener(ActionListener l) {
    listeners.removeElement(l);
  }
  public void addPropertyChangeListener(PropertyChangeListener l) {
    changes.addPropertyChangeListener(l);
  }
  public void removePropertyChangeListener(PropertyChangeListener l) {
    changes.removePropertyChangeListener(l);
  }
}
```

Note 1: We put `Smiley` in a package to keep all its files together. In the manifest file we use the forward slash, /, to name files, as in

```
smiley/Smiley.class
```

even on Windows systems. Executing the `jar` command from the command prompt in the directory containing the `smiley` package directory, we include the package name when naming files, as in

```
jar cfm smiley\Smiley.jar smiley\Smiley.mf
smiley\Smiley.class smiley\Smiley$1.class
```

on Windows systems.

Note 2: This is an anonymous inner class. We define it right where it is used. Defining a named class `MousePress` would be fine too, but anonymous inner classes are often used to provide adapter classes for event handling as we do here.

Note 3: If the coordinates where the user pressed the mouse are within the rectangle defining `Smiley`'s nose, and if there are any listeners waiting to be notified, we call the `fireAction` method to notify them.

Note 4: We create an `ActionEvent` to send to registered listeners. The first argument is the source of the event; we pass this representing `Smiley`. The second argument, of type **int**, is an ID for the type of event. We do not use the ID and arbitrarily pass `0`. The AWT passes `ActionEvent.ACTION_PERFORMED` when it generates an `ActionEvent`, and we could alternatively have passed that value. The third argument, of type `String`, is the command; for example, a label for a button. We do not use this argument and pass **null** instead.

Note 5: We cast each listener in the listener's vector to an `ActionListener` (we added only action listeners to listeners so this cast is valid), and call its `actionPerformed` method which specifies how that listener wants to handle the nose press. In the `SmileApplet`, the **BeanBox** has hooked up the `Juggler` to respond to this action by stopping juggling.

Note 6: `public void addActionListener(ActionListener l)`
We implement the `addActionListener` method to save listeners in a vector. They will be notified when the user presses `Smiley`'s nose.

A LITTLE EXTRA

The `SmileApplet` uses four beans, each with its own JAR file composed of files needed to implement that bean. The `archive` attribute allows us to list JAR files in the applet tag of an HTML file. The browser or applet viewer will search these JAR files for the classes needed to load an applet. We use the `archive` attribute in addition to the `code` attribute which still specifies the applet's class file. For example the **BeanBox** generated the applet tag

```
<applet
  archive="./SmileApplet.jar,./support.jar
    ,./juggler.jar,./Smiley.jar,./buttons.jar
    ,./BoundTextBean.jar"
  code="SmileApplet" width=382 height=173>
```

for `SmileApplet`.

THE BIG PICTURE

In writing a bean we include `set` and `get` methods for each property. The `PropertyChangeSupport` object helps us manage property change listeners, but we still need to include `addPropertyChangeListener` and `removePropertyChangeListener` methods if we have bound properties. We call the `firePropertyChange` method when the property value changes. If our bean generates an `ActionEvent` we call the `actionPerformed` method for all listeners, and include `addActionListener` and `removeActionListener` methods. We use the `jar` command to package our bean in a JAR file; the manifest indicates which files are beans.

TEST YOUR UNDERSTANDING

TRY IT YOURSELF 6. Modify `TextBean` by changing the name of the `setNumber` method to `numberSet` and `getNumber` to `numberGet`. Create the JAR file and add it to the **BeanBox**. When you drag the modified `TextBean` into the **BeanBox** does the number property appear in the **Properties** window?

TRY IT YOURSELF 7. Using the **BeanBox**, bind the number property of the `BoundTextBean` to the `priceInCents` of the `JellyBean`. In the **BeanBox**, change the number and check the **Properties** window of the `JellyBean` to see that its `priceInCents` changes to that same value.

8. An anonymous inner class can implement an interface as well as extend a class. Write the argument to the `addActionListener` method, called in the `BoundTextBean` of Example 19.2, as an anonymous inner class. Its start is `new ActionListener() {`

TRY IT YOURSELF 9. Modify Example 19.3 not to implement `Serializable`. Follow the steps to create the `SmileApplet`. What happens?

19.4 Using BeanInfo

In the absence of a **BeanInfo class** for a bean, Java uses its reflection facility to inspect the bean's code and determine its characteristics. By adding a `BeanInfo` class, the bean creator can configure the bean to present its properties in a more user friendly form than would result from letting Java figure them out by itself.

What Is `BeanInfo`?

The two **BeanBox** demo beans, `ExplicitButton` and `OurButton`, are very similar. `ExplicitButton` is just an `OurButton` with an `ExplicitButtonBeanInfo` class used to make the `ExplicitButton` more user friendly.*

The *`Events`* menu for the `OurButton`, shown in Figure 19.9, lists six event types, mouse, key, component, action, propertyChange, and focus, some of which are solely used internally by `OurButton` or its superclass, `Component`. By contrast, the *`Events`* menu for the `ExplicitButton`, shown in Figure 19.5, lists just `button push` (renamed from action to be more informative) and `bound property change` (renamed from `propertyChange`). The other event types, not meant for the end user, have been omitted.

The **Properties** window for an `ExplicitButton` (Figure 19.4) shows four properties; we leave it as an exercise to check that the similar window for an `OurButton` shows seven.

The **BeanBox** uses a `BeanInfo` class, if provided by the bean developer, to determine how to present that bean to the **BeanBox** user. If no `BeanInfo` class is available, the **BeanBox** uses the facilities of the `java.lang.reflect` package to analyze the code for the bean to determine its features to present to the **BeanBox** user. As users of

* We can read the `BeanBox` demo source files in the directory `c:\BDK\demo\sunw\demo`.

beans, rather than developers of tools such as the **BeanBox**, we do not need to explore Java's reflection facilities in this text.

`BeanInfo` is an interface in the `java.beans` package containing eight methods. The `SimpleBeanInfo` class provides default implementations of the `BeanInfo` interface methods, so by extending `SimpleBeanInfo` we only have to override those methods of interest to us.

To illustrate the use of `BeanInfo`, we will make our `Smiley` bean more user friendly.

Friendly Bean

`Friendly` bean is just a `Smiley` bean with a `BeanInfo` class. Its code is

```
package smiley;
public class Friendly extends Smiley {
}
```

To make `Friendly` more user friendly, we specify that the only properties we want to display in the **Properties** window are background, foreground, and age. Figure 19.20 shows the simplification.

Figure 19.20 Comparing Properties windows

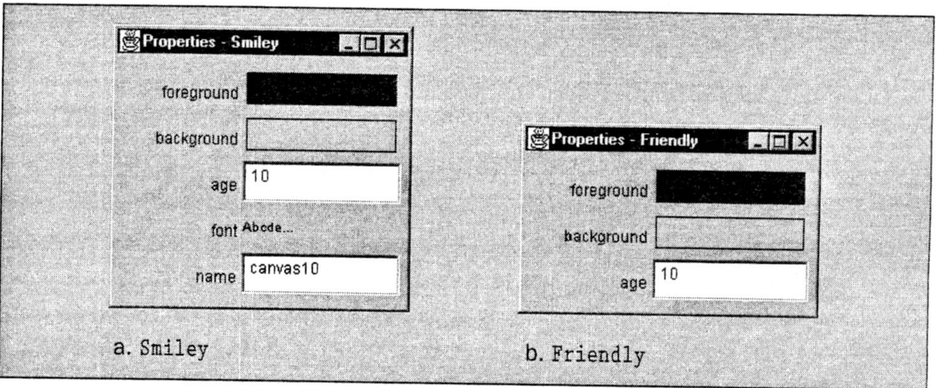

We will further specify that the only source events we want to display are `nosePress` and `ageChange`. Figure 19.21 shows the contrast.

The third feature we make more user friendly is the list of target methods that the hookup class can call when handling a source event. When using the **BeanBox** to hookup a `Friendly nosePress` to a `Smiley` target method, Figure 19.22a shows that `Smiley` has many methods with no arguments (20 in all) inherited from its various superclasses. By contrast, when using the **BeanBox** to hookup a `Smiley` action event to a `Friendly` target method, Figure 19.22b shows that `Friendly` has only one method, `fireAction`, available. We have hidden the other 19 inherited methods, for which we have no use.

Figure 19.21 Comparing source events

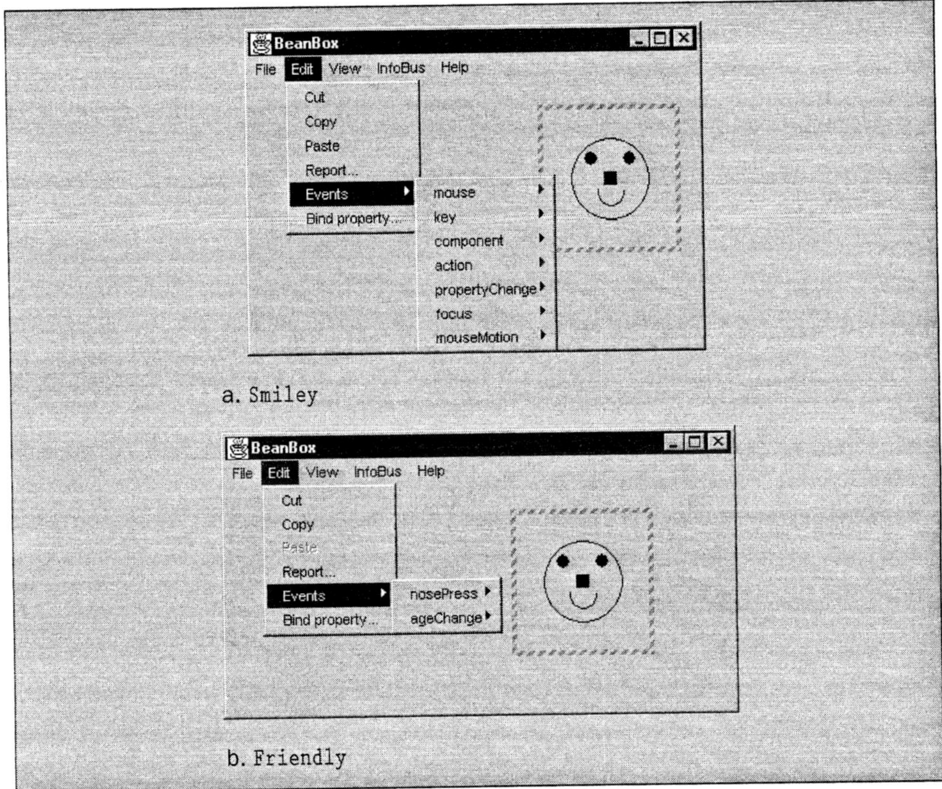

Figure 19.22 Comparing target methods

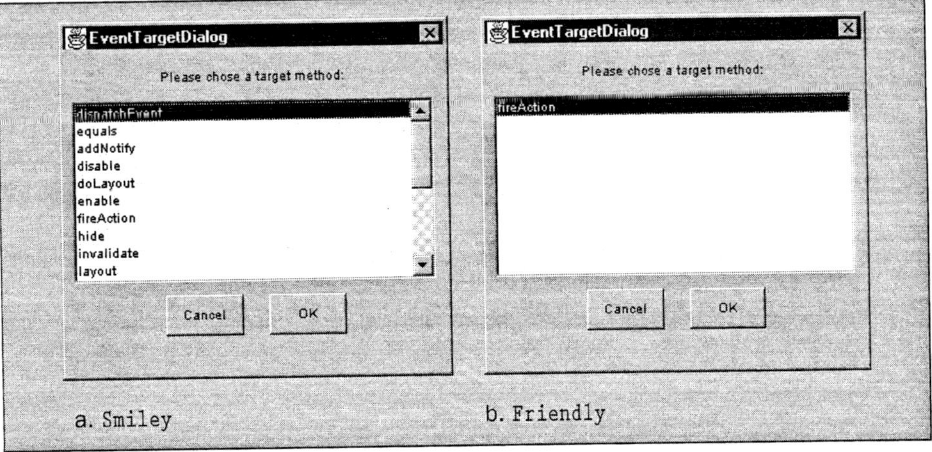

BeanInfo for Friendly

The `FriendlyBeanInfo` class makes `Friendly` more user friendly than `Smiley`. By creating `PropertyDescriptor`, `EventSetDescriptor`, and `MethodDescriptor` objects, we can get the **BeanBox** to create the friendlier display in Figures 19.20b, 19.21b, and 19.22b.

To specify the properties to display in the **Properties** window we override the `getPropertyDescriptors` method of `SimpleBeanInfo`. We create a `PropertyDescriptor` for each property we want to display, as, for example

```
PropertyDescriptor age = new PropertyDescriptor("age", Friendly.class);
```

where the first argument, `age`, is the name of the property, and the second argument is the bean class. Writing `Friendly.class` specifies the `Class` object for the `Friendly` class. Because `age` is a bound property we invoke

```
age.setBound(true);
```

so the **BeanBox** will list `age` as an item in the *Edit, Bind Property* menu.

To expose the `background` and `foreground` properties to the designer, we create a `PropertyDescriptor` for each. The return value for the `getPropertyDescriptor` method is a `PropertyDescriptor` array containing, in this case, the three property descriptors we created

```
PropertyDescriptor[] pd = {age,background,foreground};
```

The **Properties** window for `Friendly` displays these three properties in Figure 19.20b.

The `getEventSetDescriptors` method lets us simplify the *Edit, Events* menu in the **BeanBox**, describing the source events available to the designer. We create an `EventSetDescriptor` for each event we want the designer to see. For the `ActionEvent` generated by pressing `Friendly`'s nose, we have

```
EventSetDescriptor nosePress =
      new EventSetDescriptor(Friendly.class, "nosePress",
            ActionListener.class, "actionPerformed");
```

where the arguments are:

Type	Meaning
`Class`	the bean class
`String`	the name for our event
`Class`	the listener type for that event
`String`	the listener method name to handle the event

In all, we expose two events for `Friendly`, the `nosePress` and the `PropertyChangeEvent`, created in response to age changes. Letting the `getEventSetDescriptors` method return the array

```
EventSetDescriptor[] esd = {ageChange, nosePress};
```

produces the shorter and more informative *Event* menu of Figure 19.21b.

Using BeanInfo can dramatically shorten the list of target methods displayed to the designer. We implement `getMethodDescriptors` to return just one method descriptor so we get the one-item list of Figure 19.22b rather than the 20-item list shown in Figure 19.22a for `Smiley`.

To create a `MethodDescriptor`, we need a `Method` object. `Friendly.class` is a class of type `Class`. We call its `getMethod` method, as

```
Method m = Friendly.class.getMethod("fireAction", null);
```

The first argument names the method. The second is of type `Class[]` which gives the types of the arguments to the method and gives us the `Method` object we need. The `fireAction` method in `Smiley`, which `Friendly` inherits, generates and sends an `ActionEvent`. This event will be handled by the `actionPerformed` method of listeners. We pass **null** for the second arguement since `fireAction` has no arguments.

The **ToolBox** of Figure 19.1a shows some of the buttons with icons at their left. We use the `getIcon` method to return an image of the very friendly author to serve as an icon for `Friendly`.

EXAMPLE 19.4 FriendlyBeanInfo.java

```
/* Uses a BeanInfo class to make a more
 * user friendly version of Smiley.
 */

package smiley;
import java.beans.*;
import java.awt.*;
import java.awt.event.*;
import java.lang.reflect.*;                                    // Note 1

public class FriendlyBeanInfo extends SimpleBeanInfo {
  public PropertyDescriptor[] getPropertyDescriptors() {
    try {
      PropertyDescriptor age =
        new PropertyDescriptor("age", Friendly.class);
      PropertyDescriptor background =
        new PropertyDescriptor("background", Friendly.class);  // Note 2
      PropertyDescriptor foreground =
        new PropertyDescriptor("foreground", Friendly.class);
      age.setBound(true);
      PropertyDescriptor[] pd = {age,background,foreground};
      return pd;
    } catch (IntrospectionException e) {                       // Note 3
      return null;
    }
  }
  public EventSetDescriptor[] getEventSetDescriptors() {
```

```
    try {
      EventSetDescriptor nosePress = new EventSetDescriptor(Friendly.class,
        "nosePress", ActionListener.class, "actionPerformed");
      EventSetDescriptor ageChange = new EventSetDescriptor(Friendly.class,
            "propertyChange", PropertyChangeListener.class,           // Note 4
            "propertyChange");
      EventSetDescriptor[] esd = {ageChange, nosePress};
      ageChange.setDisplayName("ageChange");                          // Note 5
      return esd;
    } catch (IntrospectionException e) {
      return null;
    }
  }
  public MethodDescriptor[] getMethodDescriptors() {
    try {
      Method m = Friendly.class.getMethod("fireAction", null);
      MethodDescriptor fireAction = new MethodDescriptor(m);          // Note 6
      MethodDescriptor[] md = {fireAction};
      return md;
    } catch(Exception e) {                                            // Note 7
      return null;
    }
  }
  public Image getIcon(int iconKind) {                                // Note 8
    return loadImage("gittleman.gif");
  }
}
```

Note 1: The `java.lang.reflect` package lets development tools, such as the **BeanBox**, find the fields and methods of a class. We use its `Method` class in this program.

Note 2: Creating a `PropertyDescriptor` for the background will cause the background property to appear in the **Properties** window. The designer will be able to change `Friendly`'s background color. Unlike in the `ExplicitButton`, the background property is not bound.

Note 3: The `PropertyDescriptor` constructor may throw an `IntrospectionException`, meaning an error occurred when Java was gathering information about a program. Returning **null** tells the **BeanBox** not to use property descriptors, but rather to use reflection to find all the properties as it would if there were no `BeanInfo` class.

Note 4: For the `nosePress` `EventSetDescriptor` we were able to choose our own name, `nosePress`, for the event, which we passed as the second argument. For the `ageChange` `EventDescriptor`, we must use the "`propertyChange`" name to show the bean generates property change events so the **BeanBox**

will add the *Bind Property* menu item. We use the `setDisplayName` method to make name `propertyChange` more user friendly (`ageChange`).

Note 5: The `setDisplayName` method displays its argument, `ageChange`, in the event list instead of the name in the second argument of the `EventSetDescriptor`, `propertyChange`.

Note 6: `MethodDescriptor fireAction = new MethodDescriptor(m);`
We only want to make one target method available to the designer, the `fireAction` method. The `MethodDescriptor` constructor takes a `Method` object as its argument.

Note 7: `} catch(Exception e) {`
The `getMethod` method may throw `NoSuchMethodException` or `SecurityException` exceptions. We handle them generically with the superclass `Exception`, again returning **null** to let the **BeanBox** use its default process for finding methods, as if there were no `BeanInfo` class.

Note 8: `public Image getIcon(int iconKind) {`
The `BeanInfo` class has four constants for different icon types. We ignore this argument, using the `loadImage` method from the `SimpleBeanInfo` class to always return the same image.

Packaging Friendly

Because `Friendly` is just a `Smiley` bean with `BeanInfo`, we put it in the `smiley` package. We package both `Smiley` and `Friendly` in the same JAR file so the manifest file, `Happy.mf`, is

```
Name: smiley/Smiley.class
Java-Bean: True

Name: smiley/Friendly.class
Java-Bean: True

Name: smiley/Smiley$1.class

Name: smiley/FriendlyBeanInfo.class

Name: smiley/gittleman.gif
```

We package all files used in `Smiley` and `Friendly` into a JAR file, `Happy.jar`, using the command

```
jar cfm smiley\Happy.jar smiley\Happy.mf
smiley\Smiley.class smiley\Smiley$1.class
smiley\Friendly.class smiley\FriendlyBeanInfo.class
smiley\gittleman.gif
```

THE BIG PICTURE

We add a `BeanInfo` class for a bean to make it more friendly. The `getPropertyDescriptors` method returns a property descriptor for each property we wish to display in the **Properties** window. The `getEventSetDescriptors` method returns an event set descriptor for each source event we wish to display in the menu. The `getMethodDescriptors` method returns a method descriptor for each target method we wish to display. The `getIcon` method lets us choose an icon to represent the bean. We name our `BeanInfo` class `cnameBeanInfo`, where `cname` is the name of the bean class. By overriding `SimpleBeanInfo` we only have to implement those methods of the `BeanInfo` interface in which we are interested.

TEST YOUR UNDERSTANDING

TRY IT YOURSELF 10. Compare the **Properties** window for the `OurButton`, which does not have a `BeanInfo` class, with that for `ExplicitButton`, which is an `OurButton` with a `BeanInfo` class.

TRY IT YOURSELF 11. Use the **BeanBox** to make an applet using one `Friendly` bean to start the `Juggler` juggling and another to stop the juggling.

TRY IT YOURSELF 12. Modify Example 19.4 to omit the `getEventSetDescriptors` method. How does this effect how `Friendly` is presented in the **BeanBox**?

19.5 Programming with Beans

Java Beans are meant to be used with visual development tools, of which the **BeanBox** is a rudimentary example. Nevertheless beans are just Java programs, and we are free to use them in hand-coded programs developed without the use of any visual tools. In doing so, we use the event-handling techniques covered earlier in the text.

Using Beans in an Applet

Our example is similar to the `SmileApplet`, developed in Section 19.3 using the **BeanBox**. We write our program favoring the style of the **BeanBox**, creating a separate hookup class to handle each event. Figure 19.23 shows the `SmileyJug` applet. Pressing `Smiley`'s nose alternately stops and starts the `Juggler` juggling. Entering a value for `Smiley`'s age changes the animation rate of the `Juggler`.

To create beans we use the **new** operator, as in

```
private Smiley smile = new Smiley();
```

The `Juggler` is an applet, so after we construct it we need to call its `init` and `start` methods. Each hookup class handles a single connection from a source of the event to its target.

Bound properties generate a `PropertyChangeEvent` when they are changed. The `PropertyChangeListener` interface specifies the method

```
public void propertyChange(PropertyChangeEvent evt)
```

Figure 19.23 The `SmileyJug` applet

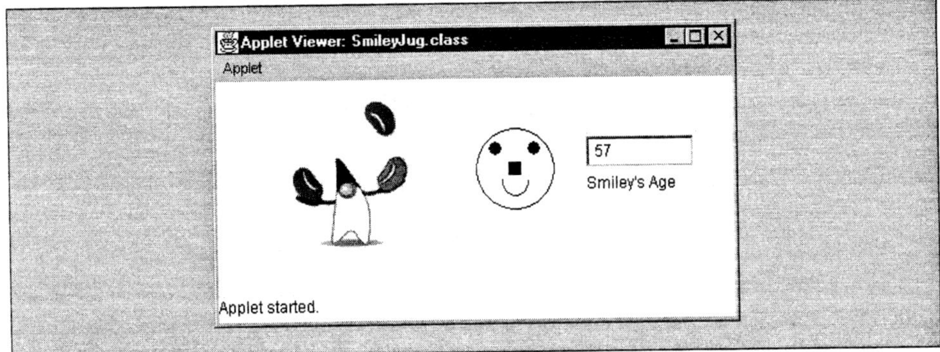

to handle property change events.

EXAMPLE 19.5 SmileyJug.java

```
/* Uses Juggler, Smiley, and BoundTextBean in a
 * Java program. Entering Smiley's age changes the
 * Juggler's animation rate. Clicking on Smiley's nose
 * stops and starts the Juggler.
 */

import sunw.demo.juggler.*;                                    // Note 1
import smiley.*;
import java.applet.*;
import java.awt.event.*;
import java.awt.*;
import java.beans.*;

public class SmileyJug extends Applet {
  private Juggler jug = new Juggler();
  private Smiley smile = new Smiley();
  private BoundTextBean text = new BoundTextBean();
  private Label label = new Label("Smiley's Age");
  private boolean on = true;                   // Is Juggler juggling?
  public void init() {
    add(jug);
    add(smile);
    Panel p = new Panel();
    p.setLayout(new GridLayout(2,1));
    p.add(text);
    p.add(label);
    add(p);
    jug.init();
    jug.start();
    smile.addPropertyChangeListener
            (new HookupAgeToAnimationRate());                  // Note 2
    smile.addActionListener(new HookupNosePress());
```

```
      text.addPropertyChangeListener(new HookupNumberToAge());
      }
      class HookupNosePress implements ActionListener {
        public void actionPerformed(ActionEvent e) {
          if (on){                                                // Note 3
          jug.stopJuggling();
          on = false;
        }
        else {
          jug.startJuggling();
          on = true;
        }
      }
    }
    class HookupNumberToAge implements PropertyChangeListener {       // Note 4
      public void propertyChange(PropertyChangeEvent evt) {
        Object object = evt.getNewValue();
        int a = ((Integer)object).intValue();
        smile.setAge(a);
      }
  }
  class HookupAgeToAnimationRate
                implements PropertyChangeListener {                   // Note 5
      public void propertyChange(PropertyChangeEvent evt) {
        Object object = evt.getNewValue();
        int a = ((Integer)object).intValue();
        jug.setAnimationRate(a);
      }
    }
  }
```

Note 1: The `Juggler` is in the `sunw.demo.juggler` package. We also need to make sure this directory is on the classpath. In Windows we can add its parent directory `C:\BDK\demo` to the classpath using the command

```
set classpath=c:\BDK\demo;%classpath%
```

where `%classpath%` is the old classpath, which for the JDK1.1 must include the current directory, the path to user packages, and the path to the system packages. When using Java 2 it works best to copy the `BDK\demo\sunw\demo\juggler` directory to a `sunw\demo\juggler` subdirectory of the directory containing this program.

Note 2: We could have let `SmileyJug` implement `ActionListener` and `PropertyChangeListener` to handle these events, but we use hookup classes to more closely follow the technique of visual tools building applets from components. For simplicity, our hookup classes are inner classes. The **BeanBox** would make each a public class on a separate file.

Note 3: The variable `on` is **true** when the `Juggler` is juggling and **false** when not. This differs from the `SmileApplet` of Section 19.3 where `Smiley` stopped the `Juggler` and an `ExplicitButton` started it. The **BeanBox** connects an event, such as a `nosePress`, unconditionally to a single target method. Here we alternately choose the `stopJuggling` and `startJuggling` methods.

Note 4: When the user enters a desired value for `Smiley`'s age in the `BoundTextBean`, that bean sets its number property which generates a `PropertyChangeEvent` that we handle here by calling the `setAge` method to change `Smiley`'s age to the desired value.

Note 5: When `Smiley`'s age changes it generates a `PropertyChangeEvent` which we handle here by changing the `Juggler`'s animation rate.

Customizing Beans

Inside a tool such as the **BeanBox** we use property editors available in the **Properties** window to change properties of our beans as we build an applet with them. We can also write a Java program to change a bean's properties, saving the changed bean which we can use in its new configuration to build applets.

For example, suppose we would like an alternate version of `Smiley` bean with a red background. We can create a new `Smiley` in our program, set its background to red,

```
smile.setBackgound(Color.red);
```

and save the red `Smiley`.

Because `Smiley` implements `Serializable` we can save it using the `writeObject` method. We save it in the file `smiley/Smiley.ser`, where the `.ser` extension represents a serialized Java file.

EXAMPLE 19.6 SaveSmiley.java

```
/* Saves a red Smiley in the
 * smiley/Smiley.ser file.
 */

import java.awt.*;
import java.io.*;
import smiley.*;

public class SaveSmiley {
  public static void main(String[] args) {
    Smiley smile = new Smiley();
    smile.setBackground(Color.red);
    try {
        FileOutputStream f = new FileOutputStream("smiley/Smiley.ser"); // Note 1
        ObjectOutputStream out = new ObjectOutputStream(f);
        out.writeObject(smile);
        out.flush();
```

```
    }catch(Exception e) {
      e.printStackTrace();
    }
  }
}
```

Note 1: We save `smile` in `smiley/Smiley.ser`, where the `smiley` directory is contained in the directory containing `SaveSmiley.class`. We could have used a program argument to specify the directory in which to save `smile`.

To use the customized version of `Smiley` in an applet we cannot just call its constructor. Calling `new Smiley()` would give us the original unmodified `Smiley`. The `Beans` class provides the `instantiate` method to load a class from a `.ser` file. In our `RedSmiley` applet, we use

```
smile=(Smiley)Beans.instantiate(null,"smiley.Smiley");
```

where the first argument specifies the class loader to use to load the class, and the second is the name of the bean. Passing **null** for the first argument lets Java use the standard system loader. The second argument, `smiley.Smiley`, tells Java to look first for a file `Smiley.ser` in the `smiley` directory (on the classpath) and if it cannot find it to look for `Smiley.class`, the original `Smiley`. Because `instantiate` returns an object, we cast the return value to have type `Smiley`.

Example 19.7 shows the changes to Example 19.5 needed to use the red `Smiley`. The complete code is on the disk included with this text. Running the `RedSmiley` applet shows a screen like that of Figure 19.23 except `Smiley`'s background is red.

EXAMPLE 19.7 RedSmiley.java

```
/* Modifies Example 19.5 to use a serialized
 * red Smiley instead of the original.
 */

// rest of code same as Example 19.5
public class RedSmiley extends Applet {
  public void init() {
    try {
      smile=(Smiley)Beans.instantiate(null,"smiley.Smiley");
    } catch (Exception e) {                                  // Note 1
      e.printStackTrace();
    }
    ....
  }
}
```

Note 1: The `instantiate` method may throw an `IOException` or a `ClassNotFoundException`. We catch both with the superclass `Exception`.

THE BIG PICTURE

When using beans in our own Java program, we have to create the hookup classes that the **BeanBox** created. By using `set` methods, we can customize a bean in a program and write it, using object serialization, to a `.ser` file. This assumes that our bean class implements the `Serializable` interface. The `instantiate` method lets us load the customized bean and use it in our program.

TEST YOUR UNDERSTANDING

13. What additional capability does the `instantiate` method give, compared to the **new** operator for loading a bean into a program.

TRY IT YOURSELF 14. Modify Example 19.6 to use the `instantiate` method, instead of the **new** operator, to create the Juggler.

TRY IT YOURSELF 15. Modify Example 19.5 to omit the call `jug.start()`. What is the effect of this change?

SUMMARY

- Java Beans are components we can use to build programs. Typically designers use a visual tool to build with beans. We illustrate this with the simple BeanBox provided by Sun to test beans. The **ToolBox** window contains a list of beans which the designer can drag into the **BeanBox** window. The **Properties** window lists properties of the selected bean, and provides editors for the designer to change these properties, customizing the bean for use in an applet.
- Each bean shows three aspects of itself to interface with the **BeanBox**. In addition to its properties, a bean shows the events it can generate, which can be connected, using the **BeanBox**, to methods in a target bean. The event occurring in the source bean causes the chosen method to execute in the target bean. For example, we connected a button so pressing the button caused the `Juggler` to stop juggling. The **BeanBox** wrote the code to hookup the source event with the target action. The third feature a bean shows is the list of methods it can execute as the target of an event in a source bean.
- Beans use standard syntax for properties, for example using a `getBackground` method to get its background color, and a `setBackground` method to set it. For a custom property such as age, the bean uses `getAge` and `setAge` methods. Properties can be bound or constrained. Using the **BeanBox**, the *`Bind Property`* menu allows the designer to bind a property of the source bean to a property of the same type in the target bean. When the value of that property changes in the source, it automatically changes in the target also. A constrained property allows the target to veto the change in the value of the source property.
- A bean is a Java program. Our simple `TextBean` has a number property that we can get and set. We package a bean in a JAR file which includes all files needed by the bean so it may be downloaded or otherwise distributed as a component to use in

building Java programs. We include a manifest file stating which of the files in the JAR file are beans.

- A bean with a bound property calls the `firePropertyChange` method when that property is changed. A `PropertyChangeSupport` object handles the details of notifying property change listeners, which register using the `addPropertyChangeListener` method.
- Our `Smiley` bean creates its own `ActionEvent` when the user presses the nose. This bean uses a vector to keep track of action listeners and notifies them when an action event occurs. It uses an anonymous inner class, defining the unnamed class right where it is used, as a method argument. We often use anonymous inner classes in this way, defining them while registering them as event handlers.
- By including a `BeanInfo` class with a bean, the bean developer can customize the list of properties, source events, and target methods that the bean designer sees when using a tool such as the **BeanBox**, making that bean easier to use.
- Although visual tools are the intended way to develop programs using beans, we can use beans in hand-coded programs. Just as the **BeanBox** allows us to customize beans, we can write programs to customize beans and save the modified beans which can be reloaded in their changed state.
- Component technology will have an increasingly important role in economically producing robust software.

Program Modification Exercises

1. Modify Example 19.2 to use an anonymous inner class to handle the `ActionEvent` generated.
2. Modify Example 19.3 to generate an `ActionEvent` when the user releases the mouse on `Smiley`'s nose, rather than when the user presses it.
3. Modify Example 19.2 to make the background a bound property.
4. Modify Example 19.2 to catch the `NumberFormatException` thrown when the user enters an invalid value in the text field. Handle the exception by erasing the invalid value and leaving the focus in the text field so the user must enter another value.
5. Modify Example 19.5 to let `SmileyJug` handle the events it generates, rather than using hookup classes.
6. Modify Example 19.6 to save `Smiley` with a red background and an age of `50`.

Program Design Exercises

7. Write an `InsertSort` bean which has a value property. When value is set, it should add the new value to an array of integers and display the array in sorted order in a bar chart, using rectangles in alternating colors. Assume the values range from 0 to 100. Package this bean and add it to the **BeanBox**. Add a `BoundTextBean` to the **BeanBox**. Configure the beans so when the user enters a value in the `BoundTextBean` it is displayed in sorted order in `InsertSort`. Make an applet from this configuration.
8. Write a Java program to make an applet, as described in Exercise 19.7, from a `BoundTextBean` and an `InsertSort` bean.
9. Write a `NewBoundTextBeanBeanInfo` class for the `NewBoundTextBean` which is like the `BoundTextBean` of Example 19.2, but which uses `BeanInfo`. Repackage `NewBoundTextBean` with its `BeanInfo` class and drag it into the **BeanBox** to test it.
10. Write a `Boss` bean that generates an `ActionEvent` when the user clicks its left eye and an `ItemEvent` when the user clicks its right eye. Construct an item event using

    ```
    new ItemEvent (new Choice(),0,null,ItemEvent.ITEM_STATE_CHANGED)
    ```

    Write a `Worker` bean that has methods `payRaised` and `payCut`. The `payRaised` method displays a drawing of a happy face whenever it is called while the `payCut` method displays a sad face. Use the **BeanBox** to create an applet in which clicking the boss's left eye causes a pay raise for the worker, while clicking the right eye causes a pay cut.
11. Using Exercise 19.10, write a Java program to make an applet from a `Boss` bean and a `Worker` bean.
12. Create a `Calculator` bean from various bean components such as button beans and text field beans. You may use beans without any visible representation to hold intermediate values.
13. Create a `Calendar` bean which displays the days of the month which the user enters or selects.
14. Create a `BarChart` bean which displays data entered by the user in a bar chart.
15. Create a `Database` bean that uses JDBC to connect to the database specified by the user, using the driver specified, and execute an SQL query.

HAPTER

20 XML (Extensible Markup Language)

OUTLINE

20.1 XML and Information
20.2 SAX (Simple API for XML) Processing
20.3 DOM (Document Object Model) Processing
20.4 XSLT (Extensible Stylesheet Language for Transformations)
20.5 SOAP (Simple Object Access Protocol)

Introduction

Web pages use HTML to indicate formatting to a browser. The web has become very popular in part because HTML is relatively simple and easy to use. But HTML focuses on presentation making it hard to determine the information on a page. XML (Extensible Markup Language) lets us devise our own tags to reflect the information content. We can pass these standard XML files among various applications to transfer information from one program to another. Java makes programs platform independent and XML makes data platform independent.

OBJECTIVES:

- Learn XML syntax.
- Use a DTD (Document Type Definition) to specify a valid XML type.

- Try a SAX (Simple API for XML) parser for processing XML files.
- Try DOM (Document Object Model) for processing XML files.
- Use XSLT to transform XML to other representations.
- Make SOAP XML remote procedure call requests.

20.1 XML and Information

We first illustrate the limitations of HTML for representing content and then introduce XML.

The Limitations of HTML

With HTML we can easily format data for display, but the content is not easy to retrieve. Figure 20.1 shows the web page displayed by the Internet Explorer browser given the HTML file of Figure 20.2.

Figure 20.1 Listing the author's books

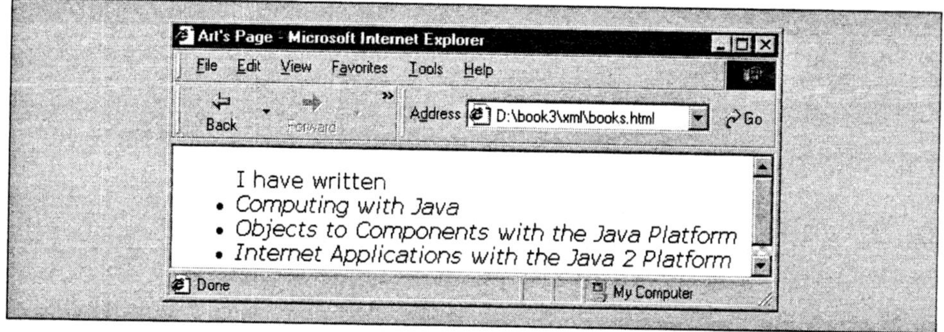

Figure 20.2 The `author.html` file for the web page of Figure 20.1

```
<html>
<title>Art's Page</title>
<ul>I have written
  <li> <em>Computing with Java</em>
  <li> <em>Objects to Components with the Java Platform</em>
  <li> <em>Internet Applications with the Java 2 Platform</em>
</html>
```

Most of the tags in Figure 20.2 refer to the display of the file. `<ul>` indicates and unordered list, while `<li>` specifies a list item. A human reader might deduce quickly that a person name Art is listing books he has written, but the word "books" is never used. A program processing this file would find it very difficult to determine its content.

Moreover browsers accept many variations in HTML syntax. In Figure 20.2 the end tag `</ul>` for the unordered list does not appear, and none of the list items have end tags `</li>`. We could have omitted the `<html>` and `</html>` tags. Permitting such variations in syntax makes it hard for programs to extract information from HTML files.

XML Syntax*

We can define our own XML tags to indicate the content. For example we might rewrite (and expand) the HTML file of Figure 20.2 as the XML file of Figure 20.3.

Figure 20.3 The `author.xml` file

```
<?xml version="1.0"?>
<!-- Books written by an author -->
<author>
  <name>
    <first> Art </first>
    <last> Gittleman </last>
  </name>
  <age> 39+   </age>
  <books>
     <book type="text">
        <title full="false">Computing with Java</title>
        <edition> second </edition>
        <copyright> 1998, 2001 </copyright>
        <isbn> 1-57676-023-5 </isbn>
     </book>
     <book type="text">
        <title>Objects to Components with the Java Platform</title>
        <edition> first </edition>
        <copyright> 2000 </copyright>
        <isbn> 1-57676-035-9 </isbn>
     </book>
     <book type="text">
        <title>Internet Applications with the Java 2 Platform</title>
        <edition> first </edition>
        <copyright> 2001 </copyright>
        <isbn> 1-57676-052-9 </isbn>
     </book>
  </books>
</author>
```

Notice that the `author.xml` file of Figure 20.3 has content tags such as `<author>` and `<book>`, rather than formatting tags such as `<li>` and `<em>`. The human reader finds it easy to read, and understandable. More importantly, programs can easily find relevant information such as the copyright date or the ISBN number.

Each XML file starts with an optional prolog, which in Figure 13 is

```
<?xml version="1.0"?>
```

XML comments use the same HTML syntax, as in

```
<!-- Comments go here. -->
```

Tags may have attributes. For example the `<book>` tag in Figure 20.3 has the `type` attribute with value "`text`." Attributes may be optional. For example, the `<title>` tag has a `full` attribute that appears in one title, but not in others.

---

* See `http://www.w3.org/XML` for the XML specification.

In order for programs to easily process XML the syntax rules are precise.

- Each tag must have an end tag.

  For example, the `<book>` tag must have a `</book>` tag to mark the end of the `<book>` element. We place the content between the start and the end tags. A tag may be empty, meaning it has no content. For example in Figure 20.3 we might have use a `<softcover>` tag to indicate that a book has a soft cover. The correct form would be

  ```
  <softcover></softcover>
  ```

  which may be abbreviated as

  ```
  <softcover/>
  ```

- Tags must be nested.

  For example, If the start tag `<title>` occurs between `<book>` and `</book>` then its end tag `</title>` must occur before `</book>`. Correct: `<book>` … `<title>` … `</title>` … `</book>` Incorrect: `<book>` … `<title>` … `</book>` … `</title>`

- Attribute values must be enclosed in quotes.

  Correct: `type = "text"`

  Incorrect `type = text`

A Document Type Definition

A well-formed XML document uses correct XML syntax. A document that had an `<author>` tag without an `</author>` tag would not be well-formed. However a well-formed document may not make sense. For example the fragment

```
<name>
   <first> George </first>
   <first> John </first>
   <first> Mary </first>
</name>
```

uses correct syntax, but not look appropriate. A name has three `first` entries and no `last`.

We can use a Document Type Definition (DTD) to specify the form of a valid type of XML document. A DTD specifies a markup language. Various groups are developing standard markup languages for specialized applications. Examples include Synchronized Multimedia Integration Language (SMIL), Mathematical Markup Language (MathML), and Scalable Vector Graphics (SVG).

Figure 20.4 shows a DTD for the author type.

Figure 20.4 The `author.dtd` DTD

```
<!ELEMENT author (name, age?, books)>
<!ELEMENT name (first, last)>
<!ELEMENT first (#PCDATA)>
<!ELEMENT last (#PCDATA)>
<!ELEMENT age (#PCDATA)>
<!ELEMENT books (book+)>
<!ELEMENT book (title, edition?, copyright?, isbn?)>
<!ATTLIST book
   type (text|trade) "text">
<!ELEMENT title (#PCDATA)>
<!ATTLIST title
   full (true|false) "true">
<!ELEMENT edition (#PCDATA)>
<!ELEMENT copyright (#PCDATA)>
<!ELEMENT isbn (#PCDATA)>
```

Before we look at the DTD syntax, we show the tree structure of the author type in Figure 20.5. Because XML tags must nest, we can always diagram XML document structure in tree form.

Figure 20.5 The tree structure of the author document type

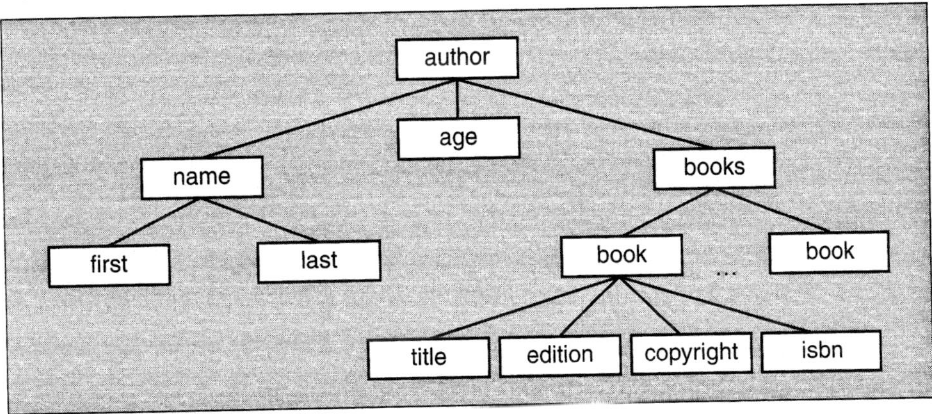

The `ELEMENT` declaration defines the structure of a tag. The `author` type defines the author, name, first, last, age, books, book, title, edition, copyright, and isbn tags. A tag may have nested tags, which we list, separated by commas, between parentheses. The following symbols may be used

Symbol	Meaning
?	Zero or one occurrence
*	Zero or more occurrences
+	One or more occurrences

The declaration

```
<!ELEMENT name (first, last)>
```

states that the `name` tag contains a `first` tag followed by a `last` tag. The declaration

```
<!ELEMENT author (name, age?, books)>
```

states that the `author` tag contains a `name` tag followed optionally by an `age` tag and then a `books` tag. The declaration

```
<!ELEMENT books (book+)>
```

states that the `books` tag contains one or more `book` tags.

Some tags do not use any of the other tags of the author type. For example,

```
<!ELEMENT first (#PCDATA)>
```

states that the first tag consists of character data.

We used enumerations for the attribute values in the DTD of Figure 20.4. The declaration

```
<!ATTLIST book type (text|trade) "text">
```

specifies an attribute for the `book` element. We could specify more than one in the same declaration. The attribute name is `type` and its values must be chosen from `text` or `trade`. The default is `text`. We could have used the declaration

```
<!ATTLIST book type CDATA "text">
```

which states that the attribute values are character data and the default is `text`, but that would allow any value for the attribute, rather than just `text` or `trade`.

Valid Documents

A valid XML documents follows the rules given in its DTD. A document can be well-formed without being valid. For example, the fragment

```
<name>
   <first> George </first>
   <first> John </first>
   <first> Mary </first>
</name>
```

is not valid. The rule for `<name>` specifies a single `<first>` followed by a single `<last>`.

We now turn to the processing of XML documents.

> **THE BIG PICTURE**
>
> XML allows us to define a language to represent data. We define tags and their structure. Well-formed XML follows precise rules to make it easier to transfer XML documents between programs. A DTD defines the language so that we can determine is an XML document is valid, in that it follows the rules of that language.

TEST YOUR UNDERSTANDING

1. Which of the following are well-formed XML documents?

a.
```
<author>
<name>
<first> Art </first>
<last> Gittleman </last>
</name>
</author>
```

b.
```
<author>
<name/>
<first> Art </first>
<last> Gittleman </last>
</author>
```

c.
```
<author/>
```

2. Which of the following are valid XML documents with respect to the DTD of Figure 20.4?

a.
```
<author>
   <name>
      <first> Art </first>
      <last> Gittleman </last>
</name>
   <books>
     <book>
        <title>Objects to Components with the Java
               Platform
        </title>
     </book>
   </books>
</author>
```

b.
```
<author>
   <name>
      <last> Gittleman </last>
   </name>
   <age> 39++ </age>
   <books>
      <book>
      <title>Objects to Components with the
             Java Platform</title>
      </book>
   </books>
</author>
```

3. Write an XML document for a record collection.

4. Write a DTD to define the type used in Exercise 3.

20.2 SAX (Simple API for XML) Processing

SAX, Simple API for XML, lets us parse an XML document using an event model. As the parser finds various portions of the document it calls specific methods. In comparison with DOM, which we will study in the next section, it is more efficient because it does not build a memory representation of the document. However, it traverses the document sequentially, not providing random access to elements. The user may have to store earlier results to use when accessing later parts of the document, which can make programming more cumbersome than with DOM.

The `ContentHandler` interface contains the methods that a SAX parser calls as it parses an XML document. The ones we use are

Method name	Description
startDocument	signals the start of the document
endDocument	signals the end of the document
startElement	signals the start of a tag
endElement	signals the end of a tag
characters	signals the occurrence of text

To avoid having to implement all of the `ContentHandler` methods, we will extend the `DefaultHandler` adapter that implements the `ContentHandler` methods with empty bodies. We only need to override the five methods we use.

Using a SAX Parser

A parser can be validating or non-validating. A non-validating parser checks for well-formed XML, but not for valid XML. It does not need a DTD. A validating parser uses the DTD to determine whether or not the document follows the rules the DTD specifies. Of course, it also checks that the document is well-formed.

For simplicity we shorten the `author.xml` file of Figure 20.3 to `authorSimple.xml` shown in Figure 20.6. The `<name>` element adds a `<gender>` attribute to show attribute processing.

Figure 20.6 `authorSimple.xml`

```
<?xml version="1.0"?>
<!-- An author -->
<author>
  <name  gender = "male">
    <first> Art </first>
    <last> Gittleman </last>
  </name>
</author>
```

Example 20.1 will use the SAX parser to identify the parts of an XML file. Later we will use that information in more complex applications. We will allow the user to choose whether to use a validating parser. We use the parser provided by Sun, in the jaxp1.1 release. This release supports SAX 2.0, which adds to SAX 1.0 to allow the use of namespaces.* Java deprecated some of the earlier API so we will use the newer version even though we are not using namespaces.

Because authorSimple.xml does not use a DTD, we will test it with a non-validating parser. When compiling, we must include the XML and parser classes in the classpath. We use the command

```
javac -classpath
.;%JAXP_HOME%\jaxp.jar;%JAXP_HOME%\crimson.jar  Sax.java
```

to compile, and

```
java -classpath
.;%JAXP_HOME%\jaxp.jar;%JAXP_HOME%\crimson.jar
Sax authorSimple.xml false
```

to run, where JAXP_HOME is the directory in which JAXP is installed. The argument false selects a non-validating parser. Figure 20.7 shows the result.

Figure 20.7 The output from Example 20.1 on a well-formed XML file

```
Start d:\book3\xml\authorSimple.xml
  Start element author
    Start element name
      Attributes gender male
       Start element first
         Art
       End element first
       Start element last
         Gittleman
       End element last
    End element name
  End element author
End d:\book3\xml\authorSimple.xml
```

To show how the parser checks for a well-formed document, we omit the end tag </first> in the authorSimple.xml file of Figure 20.6 to form the authorSimpleError.xml file. Figure 20.8 shows the result of parsing this file.

EXAMPLE 20.1 Sax.java

```
/* Uses a SAX parser to identify the parts of an XML
 * file. The user specifies whether to use a validating parser.
 */
```

* See http://www.megginson.com/SAX/index.html for SAX information including the changes from the 1.0 to the 2.0 versions.

Figure 20.8 The output from Example 20.1 on `authorSimpleError.xml`

```
Start d:\book3\xml\authorSimpleError.xml
   Start element author
      Start element name
        Attributes gender male
         Start element first
            Art
            Start element last
                Gittleman
            End element last
org.xml.sax.SAXParseException: Expected "</first>" to terminate element
starting on line 5.
   at org.apache.crimson.parser.Parser2.fatal(Parser2.java:3030)
   at org.apache.crimson.parser.Parser2.fatal(Parser2.java:3024)
   at org.apache.crimson.parser.Parser2.maybeElement(Parser2.java:1467)
   at org.apache.crimson.parser.Parser2.content(Parser2.java:1695)
   at org.apache.crimson.parser.Parser2.maybeElement(Parser2.java:1461)
   at org.apache.crimson.parser.Parser2.content(Parser2.java:1695)
   at org.apache.crimson.parser.Parser2.maybeElement(Parser2.java:1461)
   at org.apache.crimson.parser.Parser2.parseInternal(Parser2.java:499)
   at org.apache.crimson.parser.Parser2.parse(Parser2.java:304)
   at org.apache.crimson.parser.XMLReaderImpl.parse
                                            (XMLReaderImpl.java:433)
     at Sax.main(Sax.java:52)
```

```
import org.xml.sax.Attributes;                                    // Note 1
import org.xml.sax.helpers.DefaultHandler;
import org.xml.sax.XMLReader;
import javax.xml.parsers.SAXParserFactory;
import javax.xml.parsers.SAXParser;
import org.xml.sax.InputSource;
import java.io.FileReader;

public class Sax extends DefaultHandler {
  private int level = 0;                                          // Note 2
  private String spaces = "              ";                       // Note 3
  private String docName;

  public void characters(char[] ch, int start, int length){       // Note 4
    String s = new String(ch,start,length);
    s = s.trim();                                                 // Note 5
    if (!s.equals(""))
      System.out.println
           (spaces.substring(0,level*3+2) + s);                   // Note 6
  }
  public void endDocument() {
    System.out.println("End " + docName);
  }
  public void endElement
       (String uri, String localName, String qName) {             // Note 7
    System.out.print(spaces.substring(0,level*3));
    level--;
```

```
    System.out.println("End element " + localName);
  }
  public void startDocument() {
    System.out.println("Start " + docName);
  }
  public void startElement(String uri, String localName,
                 String qName, Attributes attributes){          // Note 8
    level++;
    System.out.print(spaces.substring(0,level*3));
    System.out.println("Start element " + localName);
    for (int i = 0; i < attributes.getLength(); i++)
      System.out.println(spaces.substring(0,level*3+1)
           + " Attributes " + attributes.getLocalName(i)
           + ' ' + attributes.getValue(i));
  }
  public static void main(String[] args) {
    Sax sax = new Sax();
    sax.docName = args[0];                                      // Note 9
    try {
      SAXParserFactory factory
              = SAXParserFactory.newInstance();                 // Note 10
      boolean validate =
              args[1].equals("true")?true:false;                // Note 11
      factory.setValidating(validate);                          // Note 12
      SAXParser parser = factory.newSAXParser();                // Note 13
      XMLReader reader = parser.getXMLReader();                 // Note 14
      reader.setContentHandler(sax);                            // Note 15
      reader.parse
              (new InputSource(new FileReader(args[0])));       // Note 16
    }catch (Exception e) {
      e.printStackTrace();
    }
  }
}
```

Output

See Figures 20.7 and 20.8

Note 1: We use XML related classes from the packages `org.xml.sax`, `org.xml.sax.helpers`, and `javax.xml.parsers`. We list each class by name to indicate where each is found.

Note 2: `level` represents the level of nesting of tags. We use in to display nicely.

Note 3: We prefix output with substrings of this string of blanks. We choose the length of the substring so that the display is indented according to its level of nesting.

Note 4: The parser calls the characters method when it encounters text. We display text that is not whitespace.

Note 5: The `trim` method removes whitespace from either end of the string.

Note 6:
```
System.out.println
     (spaces.substring(0,level*3+2) + s);
```
Because we indent the tag by three spaces for each level of nesting, we indent the text by an additional two spaces. The prefix string of blanks has `level*3 + 2` characters.

Note 7:
```
public void endElement
     (String uri, String localName, String qName) {
```
We display a message, indented according to the nesting level. We do not use the first or third arguments. The first gives the Uniform Resource Identifier for the namespace, and the third gives the fully qualified element name relative to that namespace. We only need to local name which is the name of the tag. The purpose of namespaces is to keep tag names localized so that they do not conflict with those in other documents.

Note 8:
```
public void startElement(String uri, String
     localName, String qName, Attributes attributes){
```
We display the tag, indented according to its level, and then any attributes, indented just under the corresponding tag. The Attributes class has methods `getLocalName` and `getValue` to get the name and value of each attribute.

Note 9:
```
sax.docName = args[0];
```
We save the file name of the document to use in the display.

Note 10:
```
SAXParserFactory factory =
        SAXParserFactory.newInstance();
```
A parser factory hides the names of the concrete parser classes. We set the desired parser properties in the factory and ask it to produce an appropriate parser.

Note 11:
```
boolean validate = args[1].equals("true")?true:false;
```
The second command line argument, `args[1]` indicates whether to use a validating parser. We use the conditional expression to set a `boolean` flag. Its form is `condition ? true-part : false-part` The value of the expression is `true-part` if the condition is true and `false-part` otherwise.

Note 12:
```
factory.setValidating(validate);
```
We specify validating or non-validating according to the user's choice.

Note 13:
```
SAXParser parser = factory.newSAXParser();
```
`SAXParser` is an abstract class. The factory returns a concrete implementation with the specified properties.

Note 14:
```
XMLReader reader = parser.getXMLReader();
```
`XMLReader` is an interface for reading an XML document using callbacks as we are doing in this example.

Note 15: `reader.setContentHandler(sax);`
We must pass an argument that implements the `ContentHandler` interface. `Sax` extends `DefaultHandler` which implements `ContentHandler`. The `set-ContentHandler` method registers the content handler with the reader.

Note 16:
```
reader.parse
    (new InputSource(new FileReader(args[0])));
```
The `InputSource` encapsulates information about the XML source. The reader will accept a character stream or bytes or a URI. A URI (Uniform Resource Identifier) is a name or address used to identify a resource. One example is a URL.

Using a Validating Parser

A validating parser checks that an XML document satisfies the rules in the DTD. Figure 20.9 shows a DTD that we will use with `authorSimple.xml` of Figure 20.6. The `#REQUIRED` field indicates that the gender attribute is required.

Figure 20.9 A simple DTD for `<author>`

```
<!ELEMENT author (name)>
<!ELEMENT name (first, last)>
<!ATTLIST name
   gender (male|female) #REQUIRED>
<!ELEMENT first (#PCDATA)>
<!ELEMENT last (#PCDATA)>
```

We can use this DTD either internally, in the same file as the XML document, or externally. Figure 20.10 shows the DTD internal to the XML file

Figure 20.10 `authorSimpleInternal.xml`

```
<?xml version="1.0"?>
<!-- An author -->
<!DOCTYPE author [
<!ELEMENT author (name)>
<!ELEMENT name (first, last)>
<!ATTLIST name
   gender (male|female) #REQUIRED>
<!ELEMENT first (#PCDATA)>
<!ELEMENT last (#PCDATA)>
]>
<author>
  <name gender = "male">
    <first> Art </first>
    <last> Gittleman </last>
  </name>
</author>
```

The DTD declaration in Figure 20.10 follows the format

```
<!DOCTYPE author [  DTD  ]>
```

Running Example 1 with command line arguments `authorSimpleInternal.xml` and `true` produces the output of Figure 20.7. If we change Figure 20.7 to add an extra line

```
<middle> Paul </middle>
```

between the `<first>` and `<last>` lines, the document will be well-formed but invalid. Figure 20.11 show the result of processing using the command

Figure 20.11 Processing an invalid XML file

```
java -classpath
        .;..\..\jaxp.jar;..\..\crimson.jar;d:\book3\xml
        Sax
                d:\book3\xml\authorSimpleInternalError.xml
        true

Start d:\book3\xml\authorSimpleInternalError.xml
   Start element author
      Start element name
        Attributes gender male
         Start element first
           Art
         End element first
org.xml.sax.SAXParseException: Element "name" does not allow "middle" here.
  at org.apache.crimson.parser.Parser2.error(Parser2.java:3008)
  at org.apache.crimson.parser.ValidatingParser$ChildrenValidator

       .consume(ValidatingParser.java:349)
  at org.apache.crimson.parser.Parser2.maybeElement(Parser2.java:1298)
  at org.apache.crimson.parser.Parser2.content(Parser2.java:1695)
  at org.apache.crimson.parser.Parser2.maybeElement(Parser2.java:1461)
  at org.apache.crimson.parser.Parser2.content(Parser2.java:1695)
  at org.apache.crimson.parser.Parser2.maybeElement(Parser2.java:1461)
  at org.apache.crimson.parser.Parser2.parseInternal(Parser2.java:499)
  at org.apache.crimson.parser.Parser2.parse(Parser2.java:304)
  at org.apache.crimson.parser.XMLReaderImpl
                                          .parse(XMLReaderImpl.java:433)
  at Sax.main(Sax.java:57)
```

Figure 20.12 shows how to use the DTD externally. The DTD declaration refers to the file containing the DTD. Figure 20.9 shows `authorSimple.dtd`.

Running Example 20.1 with the arguments `authorSimpleExternal.xml` and `true` produces the output of Figure 20.7

Figure 20.12 `authorSimpleExternal.xml`

```
<?xml version="1.0"?>
<!-- An author -->
<!DOCTYPE author SYSTEM "file:///d:/book3/xml/authorSimple.dtd">
<author>
  <name gender = "male">
    <first> Art </first>
    <last> Gittleman </last>
  </name>
</author>
```

THE BIG PICTURE

The Simple API for XML (SAX) uses an event handling approach. It calls specific methods to signal the occurrence of particular pieces of the XML document. A non-validating parser will identify XML that is not well-formed. A validating parser will, in addition, identity XML that does not follow the Document Type Definition (DTD).

TEST YOUR UNDERSTANDING

5. Which method should we implement to respond to the occurrence of the `<first>` tag?
6. What is the advantage of extending the `DefaultHandler` class in Example 20.1?
7. Use an if-else statement to write code equivalent to the line `boolean validate = args[1].equals("true")?true:false;` from Example 20.1.

20.3 DOM (Document Object Model) Processing

The DOM (Document Object Model) API supports the reading of the entire document to make a tree model in memory. We can access nodes of the tree to locate information contained in the XML document. Having the tree facilitates processing compared to a SAX parser, which has to save any information it, might need. But the DOM tree requires internal memory. Performance may suffer due to the creation of objects for each node.

We use the following interfaces from the `org.w3c.com` package.

Interface	Description
Document	Represents the entire XML document.
Element	Represents an element in an XML document.
Node	A superinterface for each node of the DOM tree.
NodeList	A collection of nodes.
Attr	An attribute of an element.
Text	The text of an element or attribute.

TIP

Check the documentation for the `org.w3c.com` package to see descriptions of each of the methods of these interfaces, and for the complete list of interfaces.

Building a DOM Tree from an XML File

Example 20.2 produces a DOM tree from an XML file. For example, it will produce a tree with structure like Figure 20.5 from the `author.xml` file of Figure 20.3. We then find all `<title>` elements and read the `full` attribute to determine whether or not each is the full title. We compile using the command

```
javac -classpath .;%JAXP_HOME%\jaxp.jar;%JAXP_HOME%\crimson.jar Dom.java
```

and run using

```
java -classpath .;%JAXP_HOME%\jaxp.jar;%JAXP_HOME%\crimson.jar
Dom author.xml false
```

EXAMPLE 20.2 Dom.java

```
/* Uses a DOM parser to identify the parts of an XML
 * document. The user specifies whether to use a
 * validating parser.
 */

import org.w3c.dom.Document;
import org.w3c.dom.Element;
import org.w3c.dom.NodeList;
import org.w3c.dom.Text;
import javax.xml.parsers.DocumentBuilder;
import javax.xml.parsers.DocumentBuilderFactory;
import java.io.*;

public class Dom {
  public static void main(String[] args) {
    try {
      DocumentBuilderFactory factory =
             DocumentBuilderFactory.newInstance();                // Note 1
      boolean validate = args[1].equals("true")?true:false;
      factory.setValidating(validate);
      DocumentBuilder builder = factory.newDocumentBuilder();
      Document document = builder.parse(new File(args[0]));      // Note 2
      Element root = document.getDocumentElement();              // Note 3
      root.normalize();                                          // Note 4
      NodeList titles = root.getElementsByTagName("title");      // Note 5
      for (int i=0; i < titles.getLength(); i++) {
         Element title = (Element)titles.item(i);                // Note 6
         String full = title.getAttribute("full");               // Note 7
         Text text = (Text)title.getFirstChild();                // Note 8
```

```
        String result =
                full.equals("false") ? : is not" : " is";
        System.out.println(text.getNodeValue()
                + result + " the full title.");              // Note 9
      }
    }catch (Exception e) {
      e.printStackTrace();
    }
  }
}
```

Output

```
Computing with Java is not the full title.
Objects to Components with the Java Platform is the full title.
Internet Applications with the Java 2 Platform is the full title.
```

Note 1: We use `DocumentBuilderFactory` rather than the `SAXParserFactory` we used for SAX processing in Example 20.1.

Note 2: `args[0]` is the XML file from which we build the DOM tree.

Note 3: The `getDocumentElement` method returns the `Element` that is the root of the document. It is a child node of the `Document` node that is the root of the DOM tree.

Note 4: The `normalize` method combines adjacent `Text` nodes into one `Text` node. Otherwise the parser may produce nodes representing whitespace only.

Note 5: The `getElementsByTagName` method returns a `NodeList` of all descendant elements with the name passed to it.

Note 6: `Element title = (Element)titles.item(i);`
The item method returns the `Node` with the specified index in the `NodeList`. We cast it to `Element`.

Note 7: `String full = title.getAttribute("full");`
The `getAttribute` method returns the value of the attribute with the specified name. Attributes are not represented as separate nodes in the DOM tree. They are associated with an `Element` node.

Note 8: `Text text = (Text)title.getFirstChild();`
The text in an `Element` is a `Text` node that is a child, in the DOM tree, of the containing `Element`.

Note 9: `System.out.println(text.getNodeValue() + result`
`+ " the full title.");`
The `getNodeValue` method returns the text in a `Text` node.

Checking for Well-Formed and Valid Documents

Running Example 20.2 using the command

```
javac -classpath .;%JAXP_HOME%\jaxp.jar;%JAXP_HOME%\crimson.jar
Dom authorSimpleError.xml false
```

with the non well-formed file `authorSimpleError.xml`, which omits the `</first>` tag, produces

```
org.xml.sax.SAXParseException: Expected "</first>" to terminate element start-
ing on line 5.
  at org.apache.crimson.parser.Parser2.fatal(Parser2.java:3030)
  at org.apache.crimson.parser.Parser2.fatal(Parser2.java:3024)
  at org.apache.crimson.parser.Parser2.maybeElement(Parser2.java:1467)
  at org.apache.crimson.parser.Parser2.content(Parser2.java:1695)
  at org.apache.crimson.parser.Parser2.maybeElement(Parser2.java:1461)
  at org.apache.crimson.parser.Parser2.content(Parser2.java:1695)
  at org.apache.crimson.parser.Parser2.maybeElement(Parser2.java:1461)
  at org.apache.crimson.parser.Parser2.parseInternal(Parser2.java:499)
  at org.apache.crimson.parser.Parser2.parse(Parser2.java:304)
    at org.apache.crimson.parser.XMLReaderImpl
                .parse(XMLReaderImpl.java:433)
  at org.apache.crimson.jaxp.DocumentBuilderImpl
                       .parse(DocumentBuilderImpl.java:171)
  at javax.xml.parsers.DocumentBuilder.parse(DocumentBuilder.java:134)
  at Dom.main(Dom.java:22)
```

We did not need to use a validating parser to detect a document that is not well-formed. Nor is a DTD necessary.

The invalid document `authorSimpleInternalError.xml` includes a DTD which does not specify a `<middle>` tag, yet it uses one. Checking with a nonvalidating parser using the command

```
java -classpath .;%JAXP_HOME%\jaxp.jar;%JAXP_HOME%\crimson.jar
Dom authorSimpleInternalError.xml false
```

produces no errors. Checking with a validating parser using the command

```
java -classpath .;%JAXP_HOME%\jaxp.jar;%JAXP_HOME%\crimson.jar
Dom authorSimpleInternalError.xml true
```

results in the output

```
org.xml.sax.SAXParseException: Element "name" does not allow "middle" here.
  at org.apache.crimson.parser.Parser2.error(Parser2.java:3008)
  at org.apache.crimson.parser.ValidatingParser$ChildrenValidator
                        .consume(ValidatingParser.java:349)
  at org.apache.crimson.parser.Parser2.maybeElement(Parser2.java:1298)
  at org.apache.crimson.parser.Parser2.content(Parser2.java:1695)
  at org.apache.crimson.parser.Parser2.maybeElement(Parser2.java:1461)
  at org.apache.crimson.parser.Parser2.content(Parser2.java:1695)
```

```
at org.apache.crimson.parser.Parser2.maybeElement(Parser2.java:1461)
at org.apache.crimson.parser.Parser2.parseInternal(Parser2.java:499)
at org.apache.crimson.parser.Parser2.parse(Parser2.java:304)
at org.apache.crimson.parser.XMLReaderImpl
                    .parse(XMLReaderImpl.java:433)
at org.apache.crimson.jaxp.DocumentBuilderImpl
                    .parse(DocumentBuilderImpl.java:171)
at javax.xml.parsers.DocumentBuilder.parse(DocumentBuilder.java:134)
at Dom.main(Dom.java:23)
```

Building a DOM Tree from Data

In Example 20.3 we will build a DOM tree from the customer data in the `Sales` database we created in Chapter 3. We leave the more interesting problem of representing data from several of the `Sales` tables in an XML document for the exercises. Figure 20.13 shows the DTD for the XML document we build.

Figure 20.13 A `customers` DTD

```
<!ELEMENT customers (customer*)>
<!ELEMENT customer (name, address, balance)>
<!ELEMENT name (#PCDATA)>
<!ELEMENT address (#PCDATA)>
<!ELEMENT balance (#PCDATA)>
```

The `Document` class includes the following methods to create nodes.

```
Attr createAttribute(String name)
Comment createComment(String data)
Element createElement(String tagName)
Text createTextNode(String data)
```

The various subinterfaces of `Node` inherit the

```
Node appendChild(Node newChild)
```

method to append a new node to the tree.

EXAMPLE 20.3 MakeXml.java

```
/* Uses the DOM API to create an XML document from
 * Sales database information.
 */

import org.w3c.dom.Document;
import org.w3c.dom.Element;
import javax.xml.parsers.DocumentBuilder;
import javax.xml.parsers.DocumentBuilderFactory;
import java.io.*;
import java.sql.*;
import sun.jdbc.odbc.*;
```

```
import java.math.BigDecimal;
import java.text.NumberFormat;

public class MakeXml {
  public static void main(String[] args) {
    try{
      new JdbcOdbcDriver();
      String url = "jdbc:odbc:Sales";
      Connection con = DriverManager.getConnection(url);
      Statement stmt = con.createStatement();

      DocumentBuilderFactory factory =
                         DocumentBuilderFactory.newInstance();
      DocumentBuilder builder = factory.newDocumentBuilder();
      Document document = builder.newDocument();                    // Note 1
      Element customers = document.createElement("customers");     // Note 2
      document.appendChild(customers);                              // Note 3
      String query = "SELECT * FROM Customer";
      ResultSet rs = stmt.executeQuery(query);                      // Note 4
      while (rs.next()) {
        Element customer = document.createElement("customer");
        customers.appendChild(customer);
        Element name = document.createElement("name");
        customer.appendChild(name);
        name.appendChild(document.createTextNode
                  (rs.getString("CustomerName")));                  // Note 5
        Element address = document.createElement("address");
        customer.appendChild(address);
        address.appendChild
          (document.createTextNode(rs.getString("Address")));
        Element balance = document.createElement("balance");
        customer.appendChild(balance);
        BigDecimal b = rs.getBigDecimal("BalanceDue");
        NumberFormat nf = NumberFormat.getCurrencyInstance();
        balance.appendChild
           (document.createTextNode(nf.format(b)));                 // Note 6
      }
      System.out.println(customers);
    }catch (Exception e) {
      e.printStackTrace();
    }
  }
}
```

Output

```
<customers><customer><name>Fred Flynn</name><address>22 First St.
</address><balance>1667.00</balance></customer> <customer><name>Darnell Davis
</name><address>33SecondSt. </address><balance>130.95 </balance>
</customer><customer> <name>Marla Martinez</name><address>44 Third St.
</address> <balance>0.00</balance></customer><customer> <name>Carla Kahn
```

```
</name><address>55 FourthSt.</address><balance> 0.00 </balance></customer>
</customers>
```

Note 1: The `newDocument` method returns the `Document` to represent the DOM tree.

Note 2: The `customers` node represents the `<customers>` tag.

Note 3: The `customers` node will be the only child of the `document` node.

Note 4: The result set contains one entry for each row of the `Customer` table.

Note 5: We create the `Text` node and append it without bothering to declare a variable to refer to it.

Note 6:
```
balance.appendChild
      (document.createTextNode(nf.format(b)));
```
The default `BigDecimal` format uses four decimal places. We use a currency instance to format the balance due according to the currency format of the default locale.

THE BIG PICTURE

The Document Object Model (DOM) builds a tree representing the XML document. The Node interface represents a single node in the tree. Subinterfaces identify the components of an XML document. Methods allow us random access to nodes. We can create a DOM tree from an XML document or construct it from data.

TEST YOUR UNDERSTANDING

8. Draw the tree represented by the DTD of Figure 20.13.
9. Which method, from which class, returns the root element of an XML document?
10. Which is represented as a separate node in the DOM tree, an attribute of an element or the text between the start and end tags of an element?

20.4 XSLT (Extensible Stylesheet Language for Transformations)

XSL (Extensible Stylesheet Language) has two parts, one for formatting and the other for transformations. The transformation part, XSLT (Extensible Stylesheet Language for Transformations), has been developed first. It allows us to transform one document to another. We can transform an XML document to another XML document or to HTML for display in a browser.

Stylesheets

We specify the transformations in a stylesheet. The stylesheet follows XML syntax. The transformations use templates that a processor matches against the tags in a XML file. Figure 20.14 shows a stylesheet for the `authorSimple.xml` file of Figure 20.6.

Figure 20.14 `authorSimple.xsl`

```
<?xml version="1.0"?>
<xsl:stylesheet version="1.0"
    xmlns:xsl="http://www.w3.org/1999/XSL/Transform">

   <xsl:template match="/">
      <html>
        <head>
          <title> An author </title>
        </head>
        <body>
          <xsl:apply-templates />
        </body>
      </html>
   </xsl:template>

   <xsl:template match="name">
      <h1>
        First: <xsl:value-of select="first"/><br/>
        Last: <xsl:value-of select="last"/><br/>
      </h1>

   </xsl:template>
</xsl:stylesheet>
```

We use the `.xsl` extension for stylesheets. Figure 20.15 shows the HTML file produces when we use Example 20.4 to apply this stylesheet to `authorSimple.xml`, and Figure 20.16 shows the resulting web page

Figure 20.15 The `authorSimple.html` web page

```
<html>
<head>
<title> An author </title>
</head>
<body>
  <h1>
          First:  Art <br>
          Last:  Gittleman <br>
</h1>
</body>
</html>
```

As with other XML files we start the stylesheet with the processing instruction

```
<?xml version="1.0"?>
```

Processing instructions occur between `<?` and `?>`. XSLT stylesheets use the XSLT namespace to provide a context for the XSLT commands. Each command uses a tag with the `xsl` prefix, as in `xsl:template`. The `xsl:stylesheet` tag

Figure 20.16 authorSimple.html

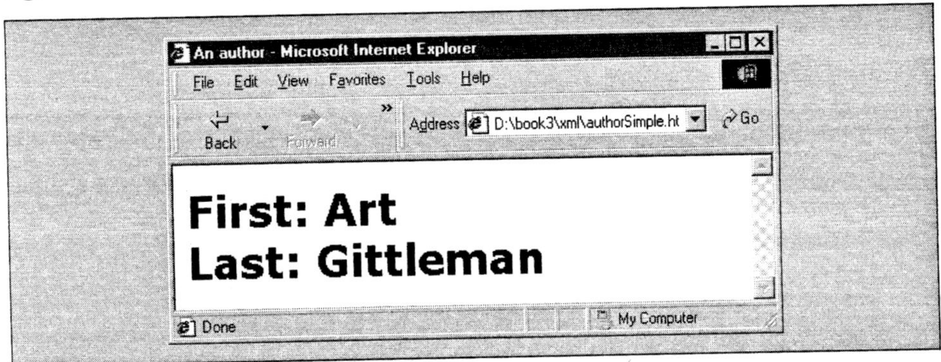


```
<xsl:stylesheet version="1.0"
xmlns:xsl="http://www.w3.org/1999/XSL/Transform">
```

indicates the version, 1.0. The xmlns:xsl attribute states that the namespace name is xsl and gives the URL where that namespace is defined. As with all XML tags, the xsl:stylesheet tag has a closing tag at the end of the stlyesheet.

The stylesheet of Figure 20.14 uses two xsl:template tags. The first

```
<xsl:template match="/">
```

include a match attribute with the value "/," which matches the root tag of the XML file, <author> in Figure 20.6. We could have used the tag

```
<xsl:template match="author">
```

When the XSLT processor applies the template to authorSimple.xml, it finds a match with the <author> tag and outputs its body

```
<html>
  <head>
    <title> An author </title>
  </head>
  <body>
    <xsl:apply-templates />
  </body>
</html>
```

The <xsl:apply-templates /> tag applies the templates of the stylesheet to tags nested within the <author> tag. Because it is an empty tag, we use the short form, closing it with a forward slash.

Next the XSLT processor finds a match with the <name> tag, so it fills in its body in the output giving

```
<html>
  <head>
    <title> An author </title>
  </head>
  <body>
    <h1>
      First: <xsl:value-of select="first"/><br/>
      Last: <xsl:value-of select="last"/><br/>
    </h1>
  </body>
</html>
```

Finally the `<xsl:value-of select="first"/>` tag returns the text body of the `<first>` tag as a `String`.

Example 20.4 is quite short. The Sun JAXP release includes the Xalan XSLT processor. We add `xalan.jar` to the class, compiling Example 20.4 with

```
javac -classpath .;%JAXP_HOME%\jaxp.jar;%JAXP_HOME%\crimson.jar
;d:\jaxp-1.1ea\xalan.jar XmlToHtml.java
```

and running it using

```
java -classpath .;%JAXP_HOME%\jaxp.jar;%JAXP_HOME%\crimson.jar;
%JAXP_HOME%\xalan.jar XmlToHtml authorSimple.xml authorSimple.xsl
authorSimple.html
```

EXAMPLE 20.4 XmlToHtml.java

```
/* Converts the XML file of args[0] to that of args[2]
 * using the XSL stylesheet of args[1].
 */

import javax.xml.transform.*;
import javax.xml.transform.stream.*;
import java.io.File;

public class XmlToHtml {
  public static void main(String[] args) {
    try {
      TransformerFactory factory
                  = TransformerFactory.newInstance();              // Note 1
      Transformer translate = factory.newTransformer(
                    new StreamSource(new File(args[1])));          // Note 2
      translate.transform(new StreamSource(new File(args[0])),
                    new StreamResult(new File(args[2])));          // Note 3
    }catch (Exception e) {
      e.printStackTrace();
    }
  }
}
```

Output

See Figures 20.15 and 20.16

Note 1: The `TransformerFactory` provides us with a `Transformer`.

Note 2: Implements a transform based on the stylesheet passed as its argument. The `StreamSource` handles the input of XML.

Note 3: Applies the stylesheet transform to the file of `args[0]` outputting to the file of `args[2]`. The `StreamResult` may use instructions in the transformer to handle the output encoding.

A Stylesheet for the Author Document

Now that we have seen how XSLT works, we will process the full `author.xml` document of Figure 20.3. Figure 20.17 shows the stylesheet we will apply. Figure 20.18 shows the resulting HTML file, and Figure 20.19 the web page.

Figure 20.17 `author.xsl`

```
<?xml version="1.0"?>
<xsl:stylesheet version="1.0"
    xmlns:xsl="http://www.w3.org/1999/XSL/Transform">

  <xsl:template match="/">
    <html>
      <head>
        <title> Book written by an author </title>
      </head>
      <body>
        <xsl:apply-templates />
      </body>
    </html>
  </xsl:template>

  <xsl:template match="name">
    <h3>
       Author: <xsl:value-of select="first"/>
         <xsl:value-of select="last"/><br/>
    </h3>
  </xsl:template>
  <xsl:template match="age">
    <h4>
       Age: <xsl:value-of select="." />
    </h4>
    <hr/>
</xsl:template>
<xsl:template match="books">
    <xsl:apply-templates />
  </xsl:template>
```

(program continues)

Figure 20.17 author.xsl (Continued)

```
<xsl:template match="book">
     <h4><strong>
          <xsl:value-of select="title"/>
     </strong></h4>
     <table>
       <th>Edition</th>
       <th>Copyright</th>
       <th>ISBN</th>
       <tr>
         <td><xsl:value-of select="edition"/></td>
         <td><xsl:value-of select="copyright"/></td>
         <td><xsl:value-of select="isbn"/></td>
      </tr>
     </table>
     <hr/>
  </xsl:template>
</xsl:stylesheet>
```

Figure 20.18 author1.html

```
<html>
<head>
<title> Book written by an author </title>
</head>
<body>
  <h3>
         Author:  Art  Gittleman <br>
</h3>
  <h4>
         Age:  39+   </h4>
<hr>

     <h4>
       <strong>Computing with Java</strong>
</h4>
<table>
<th>Edition</th><th>Copyright</th><th>ISBN</th>
<tr>
<td> second </td><td> 1998, 2001 </td>
     <td> 1-57676-023-5 </td>
</tr>
</table>
<hr>
     <h4>
       <strong>Objects to Components with the Java Platform
       </strong>
</h4>
<table>
<th>Edition</th><th>Copyright</th><th>ISBN</th>
<tr>
<td> first </td><td> 2000 </td><td> 1-57676-035-9 </td>
</tr>
</table>
```

(program continues)

Figure 20.18 `author1.html (Continued)`

```
<hr>
    <h4>
        <strong>Internet Applications with the Java 2
                Platform
        </strong>
</h4>
<table>
<th>Edition</th><th>Copyright</th><th>ISBN</th>
<tr>
<td> first </td><td> 2001 </td><td> 1-57676-052-9 </td>
</tr>
</table>
<hr>

</body>
</html>
```

Figure 20.19 The `author1.html` web page

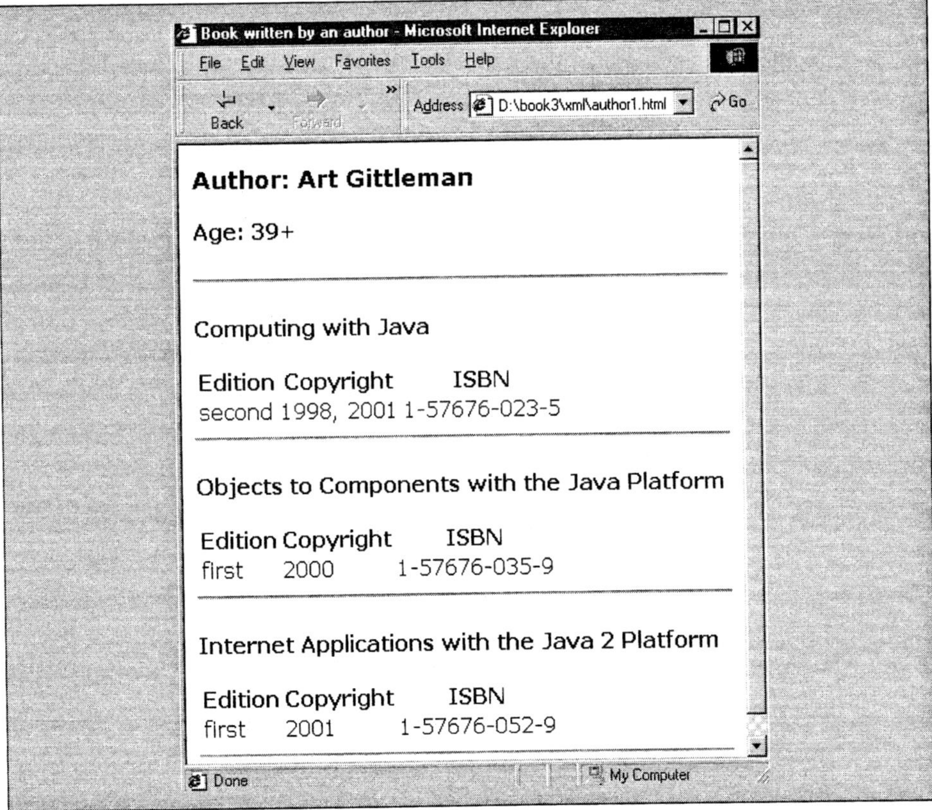

The `author.xsl` stylesheet uses the `<xsl:value-of select="." />` tag inside the `age` match. The "." in the `select` attribute refers to the tag of the match containing the `value-of` command, which in this case is the `age` tag. Thus the `value-of` command returns the text of the `age` tag, which is `39+`.

The match for the `<books>` tag does not directly add any new HTML code, but it specifies the `<xsl:apply-templates />` command which causes the XSLT processor to apply the templates to the tags nested within `<books>`. When matching `<book>` we display the title followed by a table containing the book information. The `<th>` tag indicates a table header, while `<tr>` specifies a table row, and `<td>` represents the table data in one cell. We follow each table with the empty `<hr/>` tag to insert a horizontal rule.

We use the command

```
java -classpath .;%JAXP_HOME%\jaxp.jar;%JAXP_HOME%\crimson.jar;
%JAXP_HOME%\xalan.jar XmlToHtml author.xml author.xsl author1.html
```

to run the XSLT processor.

Using a Stylesheet

Example 20.2 created a DOM tree from an XML file and then processed it to the find the book titles and indicated whether each was the full title. We can use a stylesheet to transform the XML file to give the desired information as a web page. Figure 20.20 shows the stylesheet, Figure 20.21 the resulting HTML file, and Figure 20.22 its corresponding web page.

Figure 20.20 `titles.xsl`

```
<?xml version="1.0"?>
<xsl:stylesheet version="1.0"
    xmlns:xsl="http://www.w3.org/1999/XSL/Transform">

   <xsl:template match="/">
      <html>
        <head>
          <title> Book titles </title>
        </head>
        <body>
          <xsl:apply-templates />
        </body>
      </html>
   </xsl:template>
   <xsl:template match="age">
   </xsl:template>
   <xsl:template match="name">
      <h3>
         Author: <xsl:value-of select="first"/>
           <xsl:value-of select="last"/><br/>
      </h3>
   </xsl:template>
   <xsl:template match="books">
      <xsl:apply-templates />
   </xsl:template>
```

(program continues)

Figure 20.20 titles.xsl (Continued)

```
  <xsl:template match="book">
      <xsl:apply-templates select="title"/>
  </xsl:template>

  <xsl:template match="title[@full='false']">
    <h4><strong>
      <xsl:value-of select="."/>
    </strong></h4> is not the full title.
    <hr/>
  </xsl:template>
  <xsl:template match="title">
    <h4><strong>
      <xsl:value-of select="."/>
    </strong></h4> is the full title.
    <hr/>
  </xsl:template>

</xsl:stylesheet>
```

Figure 20.21 titles.html

```
<html>
<head>
<title> Book titles </title>
</head>
<body>
  <h3>
         Author:  Art  Gittleman <br>
</h3>


     <h4>
<strong>Computing with Java</strong>
</h4>
 is not the full title.
     <hr>
     <h4>
<strong>Objects to Components with the Java Platform</strong>
</h4>
   is the full title.
     <hr>
     <h4>
<strong>Internet Applications with the Java 2 Platform</strong>
</h4>
   is the full title.
     <hr>

</body>
</html>
```

Figure 20.22 The `titles.html` web page

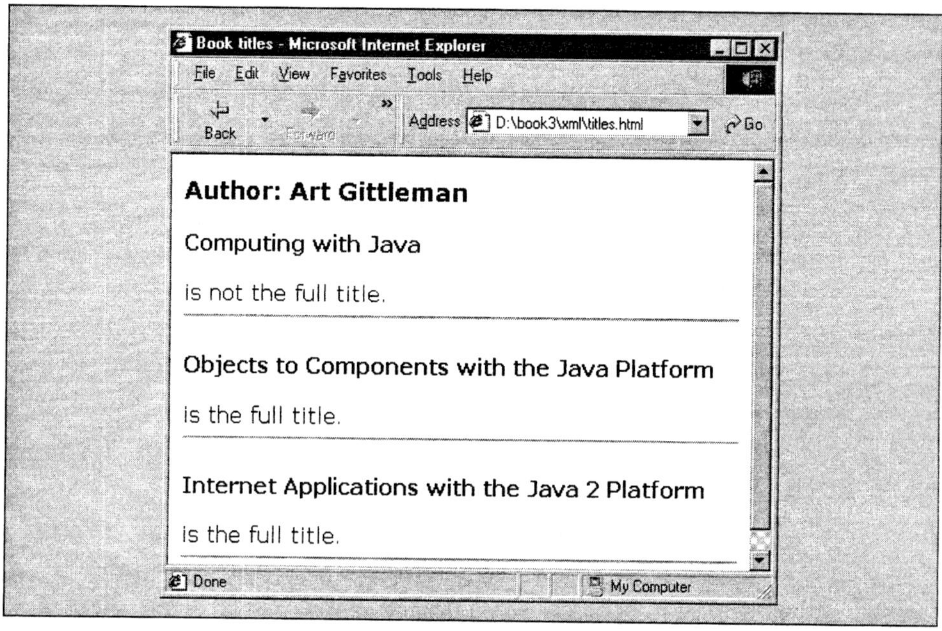

We use the command

```
java -classpath .;%JAXP_HOME%\jaxp.jar;%JAXP_HOME%\crimson.jar;
%JAXP_HOME%\xalan.jar XmlToHtml author.xml titles.xsl titles.html
```

to do the processing.

We do not want to list the author's age in the output. The `<xsl:apply-templates />` command in the root template will apply to all the nested tags including `<age>`. If we omit an "`age`" match, the default will be to include the text of the `<age>` tag. To prevent this we include an "`age`" match with an empty body, so no code will be added to the HTML output.

The `<xsl:apply-templates select="title"/>` command will only apply templates to the `<title>` tag, and will ignore the `<edition>`, `<copyright>`, and `<isbn>` tags. When matching the title we want to distinguish full titles from the others. We use the `full` attribute to indicate which are full titles. It has a default value of "`true`" so it only appears explicitly when its value is "`false`."

We match on titles with the `full` attribute set to `false` using the command

```
<xsl:template match="title[@full='false']">
```

The `@` symbol indicates an attribute. We also include a default match for "`title`" that will apply to the `<title>` tags not matched by the previous command when the attribute is `false`. This will cover the cases when the title is the full title.

THE BIG PICTURE

Extensible Stylesheet Language for Transformations (XSLT) allows us to transform an XML document. It is itself an XML file that uses the xsl namespace with stylesheet commands. The `template` command matches document tags, building the transformed document with its included code. One application is to transform an XML document, which expresses content, to an HTML document for presentation.

TEST YOUR UNDERSTANDING

11. Write the unabbreviated equivalent of the `<xsl:apply-templates />` tag.
12. Figure 20.20 includes the `<xsl:apply-templates select="title"/>` tag. Explain the difference between this tag and the tag `<xsl:apply-templates />`.
13. How would we have to change the tag `<xsl:template match="book">` in Figure 20.17 to match only textbooks?

20.5 SOAP (Simple Object Access Protocol)

SOAP provides a simple mechanism for making remote procedure calls and other exchanges using XML.* Using SOAP with HTTP makes it readily available. The Apache Software Foundation provides an API for writing SOAP clients and servers in Java.† The XMethods site (`www.xmethods.com`) contains many SOAP servers to which we shall connect.

A SOAP Message

A SOAP message is an XML document that contains a mandatory SOAP envelope, an optional SOAP header, and a mandatory SOAP body. For example the XMethods site has an ITime server which returns the Internet time as defined by Swatch. A day is divided into 1000 beats. Beat 0 starts at midnight in Biel, Switzerland. Everyone in the world uses the same Internet time.

Figure 20.23 shows the SOAP message we use to obtain Internet time.

Figure 20.23 A SOAP message

```
<SOAP-ENV:Envelope
    xmlns:SOAP-ENV="http://schemas.xmlsoap.org/soap/envelope">
  <SOAP-ENV:Body>
   <ns1:getInternetTime xmlns:ns1="urn:lemurlabs-ITimeService"
    SOAP-ENV:encodingStyle="http://schemas.xmlsoap.org/soap/encoding/">
   </ns1:getInternetTime>
  </SOAP-ENV:Body>
</SOAP-ENV:Envelope>
```

* See `http://www.w3c.org/TR/SOAP` for the SOAP specification.

† See `http://xml.apache.org` for SOAP and other XML materials.

The ITime entry on the XMethods site gives us the information we need to write Figure 20.23. We call the `getInternetTime` method. The object on the server is `urn:lemurlabs-TimeService`. We must have the `Envelope` tag. We specify a `SOAP-ENV` namespace with the SOAP URI

```
http://schemas.xmlsoap.org/soap/envelope
```

For the `getInternetTime` tag we declare the `ns1` namespace referring to the object on the server. `getInternetTime` has no arguments.

The ITime service is a servlet that we must connect to with a POST request. Example 20.5 will send the XML SOAP request of Figure 20.23. We find from the ITime entry on the XMethods site that

```
http://www.lemurlabs.com/rpcrouter
```

is the resource we need to connect to on the server. We execute Example 20.5 using the command

```
java TrySoapTime www.lemurlabs.com 80 /rpcrouter
```

We ran this program at about 10 am in California. The time of 749 beats shows that three-quarters of the day had passed in Switzerland. Using beats everyone around the world can use the same time. It is 749 beats at the same time everywhere in the world.

EXAMPLE 20.5 TrySoapTime.java

```
/* Connects to an ITime server to get the Internet
 * time (beats).
 */

import java.net.*;
import java.io.*;

public class TrySoapTime {
  public static void main(String [] args) {
    String s;
    if (args.length != 3){
      System.out.println("Usage: java TrySoapTime host port file");
      System.exit(1);
    }
    try {
      int port = Integer.parseInt(args[1]);
      Socket server = new Socket(args[0],port);
      System.out.println("Connected to host "
                            + server.getInetAddress());
      BufferedReader fromServer = new BufferedReader
         (new InputStreamReader(server.getInputStream()));
```

```
    PrintWriter toServer = new PrintWriter
                 (server.getOutputStream(),true);
    toServer.println("POST " + args[2] + " HTTP/1.0");            // Note 1
    toServer.println("Host: " + args[0]+ ':' + args[1]);
    toServer.println("Content-Type: text/xml");                   // Note 2

    String request =
       "<SOAP-ENV:Envelope xmlns:SOAP-ENV="
           + "\"http://schemas.xmlsoap.org/soap/envelope/\">"
        + " <SOAP-ENV:Body>"
         + " <ns1:getInternetTime "
             + "xmlns:ns1=\"urn:lemurlabs-ITimeService\""
             + " SOAP-ENV:encodingStyle"
             + "=\"http://schemas.xmlsoap.org/soap/encoding/\">"
         + " </ns1:getInternetTime> "
        + " </SOAP-ENV:Body> "
     + "</SOAP-ENV:Envelope>";
    toServer.println("Content-Length: " + request.length());      // Note 3
    toServer.println();                                           // Note 4
    toServer.println(request);                                    // Note 5
    while (!(s=fromServer.readLine()).equals(""))                 // Note 6
      System.out.println(s);
    while ((s=fromServer.readLine()) != null)                     // Note 7
      System.out.println(s);
    fromServer.close();
    toServer.close();
    server.close();
   }catch(Exception e) {
    e.printStackTrace();
   }
  }
}
```

Output

```
Connected to host www.lemurlabs.com/208.192.176.221
HTTP/1.1 200 OK
Date: Tue, 10 Apr 2001 16:59:25 GMT
Server: Orion/1.4.7
Content-Length: 438
Set-Cookie: JSESSIONID=DMGJKBIFONLH; Path=/
Cache-Control: private
Connection: Close
Content-Type: text/xml; charset=UTF-8
<SOAP-ENV:Envelope
 xmlns:SOAP-ENV="http://schemas.xmlsoap.org/soap/envelope/"
 xmlns:xsi="http://www.w3.org/1999/XMLSchema-instance"
 xmlns:xsd="http://www.w3.org/1999/XMLSchema">
<SOAP-ENV:Body>
```

```
    <nsl:getInternetTimeResponse
       xmlns:nsl="urn:lemurlabs-ITimeService"
       SOAP-ENV:encodingStyle=
             "http://schemas.xmlsoap.org/soap/encoding/">
    <return xsi:type="xsd:int">749</return>
   </nsl:getInternetTimeResponse>
</SOAP-ENV:Body>
</SOAP-ENV:Envelope>
```

Note 1: We must use a POST request to connect to the `rpcrouter` servlet.

Note 2: The content type describes the XML message we send.

Note 3: We must send the length of the message.

Note 4: The blank line terminates the request headers, according to HTTP.

Note 5: We send the SOAP request.

Note 6: `while (!(s=fromServer.readLine()).equals(""))`
We read and display the status line and the response headers.

Note 7: `while ((s=fromServer.readLine()) != null)`
We read the SOAP response.

Calling a Method with Arguments

The ITime service does not require arguments. The Barnes and Noble Price Quote service on the XMethods site returns the price of a book at BN,com given its ISBN number. Figure 20.24 shows the SOAP XML request.

Figure 20.24 The SOAP request for the Price Quote service

```
<SOAP-ENV:Envelope
     xmlns:SOAP-ENV="http://schemas.xmlsoap.org/soap/envelope/"
     xmlns:xsi="http://www.w3.org/1999/XMLSchema-instance"
     xmlns:xsd="http://www.w3.org/1999/XMLSchema">
 <SOAP-ENV:Body>
   <nsl:getPrice xmlns:nsl="urn:xmethods-BNPriceCheck"
           SOAP-ENV:encodingStyle=
              "http://schemas.xmlsoap.org/soap/encoding/">
     <isbn xsi:type="xsd:string">1576760235</isbn>
   </nsl:getPrice>
 </SOAP-ENV:Body>
</SOAP-ENV:Envelope>
```

We include two extra namespace declarations used in the argument tag.Example 20.6 sends the SOAP XML request to the server. We execute it using the command

```
java GetPrice services.xmethods.net 80 /soap/servlet/rpcrouter 1576760235
```

EXAMPLE 20.6 GetPrice.java

```
/* Connects to a SOAP Service to returns the price of a
 * book at BN.com given its ISBN number.
 */

import java.net.*;
import java.io.*;

public class GetPrice {
  public static void main(String [] args) {
    String s;
    if (args.length != 4){
      System.out.println("Usage: java GetPrice host port file ISBN");
      System.exit(1);
    }
    try {
      int port = Integer.parseInt(args[1]);
      Socket server = new Socket(args[0],port);
      System.out.println("Connected to host "
                        + server.getInetAddress());
      BufferedReader fromServer = new BufferedReader
         (new InputStreamReader(server.getInputStream()));
      PrintWriter toServer = new PrintWriter
                  (server.getOutputStream(),true);
      toServer.println("POST " + args[2] + " HTTP/1.0");
      toServer.println("Host: " + args[0]+ ':' + args[1]);
      toServer.println("Content-Type: text/xml");
      toServer.println
         ("SOAPMethodName: urn:xmethods-BNPriceCheck#getPrice");

      String request =
       "<SOAP-ENV:Envelope"+
           " xmlns:SOAP-ENV="
               + "\"http://schemas.xmlsoap.org/soap/envelope/\""
          +" xmlns:xsi="
               + "\"http://www.w3.org/1999/XMLSchema-instance\""
          +" xmlns:xsd="
               + "\"http://www.w3.org/1999/XMLSchema\">"
      +" <SOAP-ENV:Body>"
        +" <ns1:getPrice xmlns:ns1=\"urn:xmethods-BNPriceCheck\""
               +" SOAP-ENV:encodingStyle"
 +"=\"http://schemas.xmlsoap.org/soap/encoding/\">"
          +" <isbn xsi:type=\"xsd:string\">"+args[3]+"</isbn>"       // Note 1
        +" </ns1:getPrice> "
      + " </SOAP-ENV:Body> "
      + "</SOAP-ENV:Envelope>";
       toServer.println("Content-Length: " + request.length());
       toServer.println();
       toServer.println(request);
```

```
      while (!(s=fromServer.readLine()).equals(""))
        System.out.println(s);
      while ((s=fromServer.readLine()) != null)
        System.out.println(s);
      fromServer.close();
      toServer.close();
      server.close();
    }catch(Exception e) {
      e.printStackTrace();
    }
  }
}
```

Output

```
Connected to host services.xmethods.net/206.135.115.105
HTTP/1.1 200 OK
Date: Tue, 10 Apr 2001 22:38:49 GMT
Status: 200
Set-Cookie2: JSESSIONID=To10904mC22528739702399958At;Version=1;Discard;
Path="/soap"
Servlet-Engine: Tomcat Web Server/3.1 (JSP 1.1; Servlet 2.2;
Java 1.3.0; SunOS 5.8 sparc; java.vendor=Sun Microsystems Inc.)
Set-Cookie: JSESSIONID=To10904mC22528739702399958At;Path=/soap
Content-Type: text/xml; charset=utf-8
Content-Length: 469
Content-Language: en
Server: Electric/1.0
Electric-Routing: true
<?xml version='1.0' encoding='UTF-8'?>
<SOAP-ENV:Envelope
     xmlns:SOAP-ENV="http://schemas.xmlsoap.org/soap/envelope/"
     xmlns:xsi="http://www.w3.org/1999/XMLSchema-instance"
     xmlns:xsd="http://www.w3.org/1999/XMLSchema">
  <SOAP-ENV:Body>
    <ns1:getPriceResponse xmlns:ns1="urn:xmethods-BNPriceCheck"
         SOAP-ENV:encodingStyle=
                "http://schemas.xmlsoap.org/soap/encoding/">
      <return xsi:type="xsd:float">62.75</return>
    </ns1:getPriceResponse>
  </SOAP-ENV:Body>
</SOAP-ENV:Envelope>
```

Note 1: We specify the string type for ISBN argument and give its value.

Using the SOAP API

We can download the SOAP API from the `xml.apache.org` site. These packages allow us to write SOAP clients without having to write the XML request explicitly. We can also write SOAP servers although we do not do that here.* Example 20.7 connects to the Barnes and Noble Price Quote service using the SOAP API. We compile it using the command

```
javac -classpath .;%SOAP_HOME%\lib\soap.jar GetJavaPrice.java
```

where SOAP_HOME is the path to the SOAP API, and run using

```
java -classpath .;%SOAP_HOME%\lib\soap.jar;
%SOAP_HOME%\lib\xerces.jar;%SOAP_HOME%\lib\mail.jar;
%SOAP_HOME%\lib\activation.jar GetJavaPrice 1576760235
```

EXAMPLE 20.7 GetJavaPrice.java

```
/* Uses the SOAP API to connect to the Barnes and Noble
 * Price Quote Service.
 */

import java.net.*;
import org.apache.soap.util.xml.*;
import org.apache.soap.*;
import org.apache.soap.rpc.*;
import java.util.*;

public class GetJavaPrice {
  public static void main(String[] args) {
   try {
    Call call = new Call();                                     // Note 1
    call.setEncodingStyleURI(Constants.NS_URI_SOAP_ENC);        // Note 2
    call.setTargetObjectURI("urn:xmethods-BNPriceCheck");       // Note 3
    call.setMethodName("getPrice");
    Vector params = new Vector();
    params.addElement
      (new Parameter("isbn",String.class,args[0],null));        // Note 4
    call.setParams(params);
    URL url = new URL
      ("http://services.xmethods.com/soap/servlet/rpcrouter");  // Note 5
    Response resp = call.invoke(url, "");                       // Note 6
    if (resp.generatedFault()) {
      Fault fault = resp.getFault();
      System.out.println(" Fault code: " + fault.getFaultCode());
      System.out.println(" Fault string: " + fault.getFaultString());
    }
```

* The `RPCRouter` servlet used to manage SOAP services is included with the SOAP API.

```
      else{
        Parameter result = resp.getReturnValue();                    // Note 7
        System.out.println(result.getValue());
      }
    }catch (Exception e) {
      e.printStackTrace();
    }
  }
}
```

Output

```
62.75
```

Note 1: The Call object represents a remote procedure call.

Note 2: We set the encoding style to indicate the serialization rules used in a SOAP message.

Note 3: We specify the target object on the server.

Note 4: The four arguments are the parameter name, the parameter type, the parameter value, and the encoding to use to serialize it. Passing `null` for the last argument indicates the default encoding.

Note 5: This is the URL for the service.

Note 6: `Response resp = call.invoke(url, "");`
We invoke the method. The last argument is an action that we do not use.

Note 7: `Parameter result = resp.getReturnValue();`
We get the value returned by the `getPrice` method invoked on the server.

TEST YOUR UNDERSTANDING

14. What parts of a SOAP message are mandatory?
15. What method will be invoked using the SOAP message of Figure 20.23?

SUMMARY

- HTML tags support the presentation of data. XML tags make it easier to identify the content of a document. The optional prolog

  `<?xml version="1.0"?>`

  is a `processing instruction` tag. Tags may have attributes. XML follows precise syntactical rules to facilitate machine processing of XML files. For example, each tag must have an end tag. Tags must nest properly, and attributes must be enclosed in quotes.

- A Data Type Definition (DTD) defines the valid syntax for a document type. Its rules for elements occur in `<!ELEMENT>` tags and its rules for attributes occur in `<!ATTLIST>` tags. A well-formed document conforms to the XML syntax. In addition, a valid document conforms to its DTD.
- The Simple API for XML (SAX) uses an event handling model. It generates callbacks corresponding to the pieces of the document it encounters. The callback methods are part of the `ContentHandler` interface. We use `startElement`, `endElement`, `startDocument`, `endDocument`, and `characters`. We override the `DefaultHandler` which provides default implementations of `ContentHandler` methods.
- The Document Object Model (DOM) builds a tree representation of the XML document in memory. The parse method builds a DOM tree from an XML file. Methods such as `getElementsByTagName` let us directly access nodes of the tree. Methods such as `createElement` and `appendChild` let us build a DOM tree from data.
- The Extensible Stylesheet Language for Transformations lets us transform XML documents. For example, we can transform an XML document, which focuses on content, to an HTML document for presentation. We could transform the content to an XML document suitable for a different application. The `xsl` namespace includes commands that implement the transformations. A `template` command matches pieces of the XML documents and specifies the transformed code to use when a match is found. Other commands include `apply-templates` and `value-of`.
- The Simple Object Access Protocol allows us to execute remote procedure calls. HTTP provides wide access and ease of use. An XML message specifies the object on the server, the method to call, and any arguments to that method. The server returns a SOAP XML response. The Apache Software Foundation provides a SOAP API to program clients and servers handling the XML details.

Program Modification Exercises

1. Modify Example 20.2 to write the output as an HTML file. Write it to the external file `Dom.html`.
2. Modify Example 20.3 to create an XML document with the customer's name and the dates on which that customer placed orders.
3. Modify Example 20.2 to list those titles that contain a word entered on the command line.

Program Design Exercises

4. a. Using data from the Sales database of Chapter 3, write a program to create a DOM tree which for each salesperson lists the order number and date of each order handled by that salesperson.

   b. Write a stylesheet to transform the XML document of part a to an HTML file to display the results. Execute Example 20.4 to obtain the HTML file.

5. Write a stylesheet to produce an HTML file from `author.xml`, using Example 20.4, that displays the title and ISBN of each book.

6. Write a stylesheet to produce an HTML file from `author.xml`, using Example 20.4, that displays the author's name and the copyright date of each book.

7 Write a program that uses a SAX parser on `author.xml` to output the title of each book.

8. Write a program that reads the SOAP XML message from a file and connects to a SOAP server to execute a remote procedure call. Test it with the SOAP messages used in examples 20.5 and 20.6.

9. Write a stylesheet to transform the XML document created by Example 20.3 to an HTML file to display the results Execute Example 20.4 to obtain the HTML file.

10. Pick a service from the www.xmethods.com site and write a SOAP client to access that service. Create the SOAP XML message explicitly.

Appendix A—Binary and Hexadecimal Numbers

Our familiar decimal number system uses ten digits, 0, 1, 2, 3, 4, 5, 6, 7, 8, and 9, to represent numbers. We can only represent numbers up to nine with one digit. To write the number ten, we use two digits, 10, with the idea that the one in the ten's place represents ten. The number 387 represents 3x100 + 8x10 + 7 since the three is in the hundred's place, and the eight is in the ten's place. We call this the base ten system because each place represents a power of ten. The unit's place is 100 = 1, the ten's place is 101 = 10, the hundred's place is 102 = 100, and so on.

In the **binary** number system we use two digits, 0 and 1 to represent integers. This is particularly suitable for computers where each hardware memory **bit** (binary digit) can represent a 0 or a 1. Using only two digits, the largest number we can represent in one digit is one. The first few binary numbers are

binary	decimal equivalent
0	0
1	1
10	2 = 1x2 + 0
11	3 = 1x2 + 1
100	4 = 1x4 + 0x2 + 0x1
101	5 = 1x4 + 0x2 + 1x1
110	6 = 1x4 + 1x2 + 0x1
111	7 = 1x4 + 1x2 + 1x1
1000	8 = 1x8 + 0x4 + 0x2 + 0x1
1001	9 = 1x8 + 0x4 + 0x2 + 1x1
1010	10 = 1x8 + 0x4 + 1x2 + 0x1

Just as the decimal system is base 10, the binary system is in base 2, and has a unit's place, a two's place, a four's place, an eight's place, and so on as given by the sequence `20 = 1, 21 = 2, 22 = 4, 23 =8`, and so on.

While the computer hardware uses binary digits, it is hard for human readers to grasp say 16 bits of binary, as for example

```
0010110100110110
```

If we group the bits by fours, as in,

```
0010 1101 0011 0110
```

it's a bit easier to read but still cumbersome. Each group of four represents a number from 0 to 15 in the binary system. If we had a system with 16 digits, we could replace each group of four bits by a single digit. The **hexadecimal** system uses the digits `0,1,2,3,4,5,6,7,8,9,a,b,c,d,e`, and `f`, where `a=10`, `b=11`, `c=12`, `d=13`, `e=14`, and `f=15`. We can use either lower or uppercase letters `A, B, C, D, E`, and `F`. To write the above 16-bit number in hexadecimal replace each group of four by its corresponding hexadecimal digit, giving

```
binary                  0010 1101 0011 0110
hexadecimal               2    d    3    6
```

We can specify hexadecimal constants in Java using `0x` or `0X` to prefix the number as, for example, `0x2d36`.

The first 10 hexadecimal digits are the same as the decimal digits. The remaining six have the following binary and decimal equivalents.

Hexadecimal	Binary	Decimal
a or A	1010	10
b or B	1011	11
c or C	1100	12
d or D	1101	13
e or E	1110	14
f or F	1111	15

The main use of hexadecimal numbers is to give a shorter representation for binary numbers which, using only two digits, tend to get long. We could of course convert the binary number to base ten but that takes more work. If you are curious, `0010 1101 0011 0110` converts to

```
8192 + 2048 + 1024 + 256 + 32 + 16 + 4 + 2 = 11,574
```

in base 10.

LITTLE EXTRA—CONVERTING BETWEEN BASE 10 AND BINARY

As we have just seen, to convert a binary number to decimal, just add the powers of two corresponding to the positions of the 1's in the number. Converting `11001` we add `16+8+1 = 25` because the `11001` has a one in the sixteen's place, the eight's place, and the one's place.

To convert a base 10 number to binary we use division to get the digits from right to left, starting with the one's digit. To convert 25, divide by two, and the remainder will be the one's digit. Divide the quotient, 12, by two, and the remainder will be the two's digit. Repeat this process until the quotient is zero. The example below shows how the base ten number 25 converts to the base two number `11001`.

`25 ÷ 2 = 12 r. 1` so the 1's digit is 1.

`12 ÷ 2 =  6 r. 0` so the 2's digit is 0.

` 6 ÷ 2 =  3 r. 0` so the 4's digit is 0.

` 3 ÷ 2 =  1 r. 1` so the 8's digit is 1.

` 1 ÷ 2 =  0 r. 1` so the 16's digit is 1.

TEST YOUR UNDERSTANDING

1. Express the value of each base 10 number using powers of 10. For example, 254 has the value `2x100 + 5x10 + 4`.

   a. 38 b. 4179 c. 562 d. 94531 e. 306

2. Express the value of each base 2 number using powers of 2. For example, 101 has the value `1x4 + 0x2 + 1x1`.

   a. 11 b. 1101 c. 101100 d. 11011 e. 11101010

3. Give the base 10 value for each of the binary numbers in Exercise 2.

4. Write each of the binary numbers in Exercise 2 in hexadecimal. (Hint: Group by fours, and add zeros in front if necessary. For example, `111010` would group as `0011 1010` and convert to `3a`.)

A LITTLE EXTRA

5. Convert each of the following base 10 numbers to binary.

   a. 17 b. 23 c. 38 d. 86 e. 160 f. 235 g. 4444

Appendix B— Bitwise and Shift Operators

We typically use base 10 integers in our program which are represented internally as binary numbers. Java requires that **int** values always use 32 bits. Thus Java represents the number 25 internally as

```
0000 0000 0000 0000 0000 0000 0001 1001
```

Bitwise Operators

Java has several **bitwise** operators that operate on each bit of an **int** value.

&	bitwise AND
|	bitwise OR
^	bitwise XOR (exclusive or)
~	bitwise complement

Figure B.1 shows the effect of these operations on corresponding bits of each operand.

Figure B.1 The effect of bitwise operators

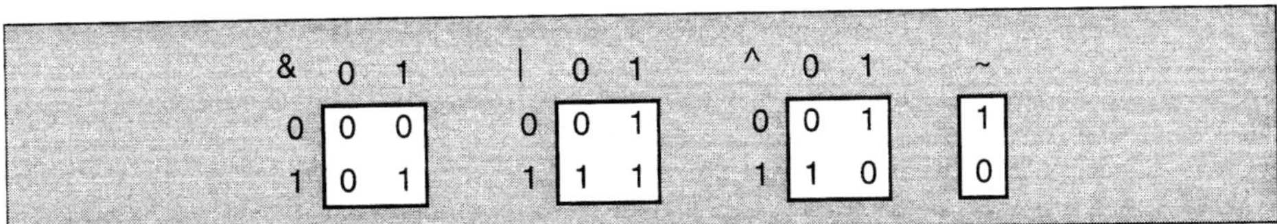

&	0	1
0	0	0
1	0	1

|	0	1
0	0	1
1	1	1

^	0	1
0	0	1
1	1	0

~
1
0

To illustrate these operators we use four bit values for simplicity, rather than work with the much longer 32-bit **int** values. To evaluate `1010 & 0011` we apply the & operator to the bits in corresponding positions in the left and right operands, according to the table in Figure B.1. Using the & operator on each pair of corresponding bits gives

```
1 & 0 = 0
```
for the leftmost bits of 1010 and 0011,
```
0 & 0 = 0
```
for the corresponding bits in the next position,
```
1 & 1 = 1
```
for the next bits,

and
```
0 & 1 = 0
```
for the rightmost bits,

so that the result is `0010`.

Similarly using the tables in Figure B.1 we see that

```
1010 | 0011 = 1011
1010 ^ 0011 = 1001
~ 1010      = 0101
```

We can apply the bitwise operators to variables. For example, if

```
int a = 10;
int b =  3;
```

then the 32-bit representations of `a` and `b` are

```
    0000 0000 0000 0000 0000 0000 0000 1010 for a
and 0000 0000 0000 0000 0000 0000 0000 0011 for b
```

so that

```
a & b =  2  (0010 in binary)
a | b = 11  (1011 in binary)
a ^ b =  9  (1001 in binary)
```

Logical Operators

The operators `&`, `|`, and `^` can also operate on boolean values. The `&` and `|` operators are like the `&&` and `||` operators, except that the logical operators `&` and `|` always evaluate both operands, while the conditional operators `&&` and `||` evaluate both operands only when necessary.

Shift Operators

The Java **shift** operators are:

`<<` Shift bits left, filling with zero bits on the right-hand side

`>>` Shift bits right, filling with the high bit on the left-hand side

`>>>` Shift bits right, filling with zero bits on the left-hand side

Using 8-bit numbers, rather than 32-bit, to illustrate

`10101010 << 3` evaluates to `01010000`

`10101010 >> 3` evaluates to `11110101`
`10101010 >>> 3` evaluates to `00010101`

where the left-hand operand is the number to shift, and the right-hand operand is the number of positions to shift. In evaluating `10101010 << 3`, when we shift `10101010` three positions to the left, the rightmost three bits disappear and we replace the left-most three bits with zeros.

We can use the shift operator with **int** variables. For example given

```
int a = 0x00003A7D;
```

evaluating `a << 7` will give `0x001D3E80` since `0x00003A7D` in binary is

```
0000 0000 0000 0000 0011 1010 0111 1101
```

and shifting seven positions to the left gives

```
0000 0000 0001 1101 0011 1110 1000 0000
```

in binary, or `0x001D3E80` in hex.

TEST YOUR UNDERSTANDING

1. Find

   a. `1100 & 0011` b. `1111 & 0101` c. `0000 & 1010`

2. Find

   a. `1100 | 0011` b. `1111 | 0101` c. `0000 | 1010`

3. Find

   a. `1100 ^ 0011` b. `1111 ^ 0101` c. `0000 ^ 1010`

4. Find

   a. `~0010` b. `~1011`

5. Given

   ```
   int a = 27;
   int b = 53;
   ```

   find

   a. `a & b` b. `a | b` c. `a ^ b` d. `~a`

6. Evaluate, using 8-bit numbers

   a. `11001011 << 5` b. `11001011 >> 4` c. `11001011 >>> 4`

Appendix C— Operator Precedence Table

Highest

<table>
<tr><td>Postfix Operators</td><td>[ ] . () ++ --</td></tr>
<tr><td>Unary Operators</td><td>++ (prefix) -- (prefix) + - ~ !</td></tr>
<tr><td>Cast, Allocation</td><td>() new</td></tr>
<tr><td>Multiplicative</td><td>* / %</td></tr>
<tr><td>Additive</td><td>+ -</td></tr>
<tr><td>Shift</td><td><< >> >>></td></tr>
<tr><td>Relational</td><td>< > <= >= instanceof</td></tr>
<tr><td>Equality</td><td>== !=</td></tr>
<tr><td>Bitwise, Logical AND</td><td>&</td></tr>
<tr><td>Bitwise, Logical XOR</td><td>^</td></tr>
<tr><td>Bitwise, Logical OR</td><td>|</td></tr>
<tr><td>Conditional AND</td><td>&&</td></tr>
<tr><td>Conditional OR</td><td>||</td></tr>
<tr><td>Conditional</td><td>?:</td></tr>
<tr><td>Assignment</td><td>= += -= *= /= %= >>= <<= >>>= &= ^= |=</td></tr>
</table>

Lowest

Appendix D—The ASCII Character Set

The first 32 characters and the last are control characters. We label those control characters we use in the text.

<table>
<tr><td>0</td><td></td><td>32</td><td>blank</td><td>64</td><td>@</td><td>96</td><td>`</td></tr>
<tr><td>1</td><td></td><td>33</td><td>!</td><td>65</td><td>A</td><td>97</td><td>a</td></tr>
<tr><td>2</td><td></td><td>34</td><td>"</td><td>66</td><td>B</td><td>98</td><td>b</td></tr>
<tr><td>3</td><td></td><td>35</td><td>#</td><td>67</td><td>C</td><td>99</td><td>c</td></tr>
<tr><td>4</td><td></td><td>36</td><td>$</td><td>68</td><td>D</td><td>100</td><td>d</td></tr>
<tr><td>5</td><td></td><td>37</td><td>%</td><td>69</td><td>E</td><td>101</td><td>e</td></tr>
<tr><td>6</td><td></td><td>38</td><td>&</td><td>70</td><td>F</td><td>102</td><td>f</td></tr>
<tr><td>7</td><td></td><td>39</td><td>'</td><td>71</td><td>G</td><td>103</td><td>g</td></tr>
<tr><td>8</td><td>\b</td><td>40</td><td>(</td><td>72</td><td>H</td><td>104</td><td>h</td></tr>
<tr><td>9</td><td>\t</td><td>41</td><td>)</td><td>73</td><td>I</td><td>105</td><td>i</td></tr>
<tr><td>10</td><td>\n</td><td>42</td><td>*</td><td>74</td><td>J</td><td>106</td><td>j</td></tr>
<tr><td>11</td><td></td><td>43</td><td>+</td><td>75</td><td>K</td><td>107</td><td>k</td></tr>
<tr><td>12</td><td></td><td>44</td><td>,</td><td>76</td><td>L</td><td>108</td><td>l</td></tr>
<tr><td>13</td><td>\r</td><td>45</td><td>-</td><td>77</td><td>M</td><td>109</td><td>m</td></tr>
<tr><td>14</td><td></td><td>46</td><td>.</td><td>78</td><td>N</td><td>110</td><td>n</td></tr>
<tr><td>15</td><td></td><td>47</td><td>/</td><td>79</td><td>O</td><td>111</td><td>o</td></tr>
<tr><td>16</td><td></td><td>48</td><td>0</td><td>80</td><td>P</td><td>112</td><td>p</td></tr>
<tr><td>17</td><td></td><td>49</td><td>1</td><td>81</td><td>Q</td><td>113</td><td>q</td></tr>
<tr><td>18</td><td></td><td>50</td><td>2</td><td>82</td><td>R</td><td>114</td><td>r</td></tr>
<tr><td>19</td><td></td><td>51</td><td>3</td><td>83</td><td>S</td><td>115</td><td>s</td></tr>
<tr><td>20</td><td></td><td>52</td><td>4</td><td>84</td><td>T</td><td>116</td><td>t</td></tr>
<tr><td>21</td><td></td><td>53</td><td>5</td><td>85</td><td>U</td><td>117</td><td>u</td></tr>
<tr><td>22</td><td></td><td>54</td><td>6</td><td>86</td><td>V</td><td>118</td><td>v</td></tr>
<tr><td>23</td><td></td><td>55</td><td>7</td><td>87</td><td>W</td><td>119</td><td>w</td></tr>
<tr><td>24</td><td></td><td>56</td><td>8</td><td>88</td><td>X</td><td>120</td><td>x</td></tr>
<tr><td>25</td><td></td><td>57</td><td>9</td><td>89</td><td>Y</td><td>121</td><td>y</td></tr>
<tr><td>26</td><td></td><td>58</td><td>:</td><td>90</td><td>Z</td><td>122</td><td>z</td></tr>
<tr><td>27</td><td></td><td>59</td><td>;</td><td>91</td><td>[</td><td>123</td><td>{</td></tr>
<tr><td>28</td><td></td><td>60</td><td><</td><td>92</td><td>\</td><td>124</td><td>|</td></tr>
<tr><td>29</td><td></td><td>61</td><td>=</td><td>93</td><td>]</td><td>125</td><td>}</td></tr>
<tr><td>30</td><td></td><td>62</td><td>></td><td>94</td><td>^</td><td>126</td><td>~</td></tr>
<tr><td>31</td><td></td><td>63</td><td>?</td><td>95</td><td>_</td><td>127</td><td></td></tr>
</table>

Appendix E—Using Java in Various Environments

We show how to compile and run the programs in this text using:

Java Development Kit	Sun Microsystems, Inc.
JBuilder	Borland International, Inc.

Consult the documentation that comes with these or other environments for more complete information on their use.

JBuilder

We used the **JBuilder Foundation version 3.5**. Check `www.borland.com` for further information and free downloading.

Creating the Project in JBuilder

After opening **JBuilder**, click on the *`File`* menu and then *`New Project`* to create a project which will contain all the files used in the given applet or application. Enter a file name for the project in the *`Project File`* field and click *`Finish`*. We demonstrate with Example 1.1, so we will call our project `ex1_1`, and enter `d:\ex1_1\ex1_1.jpr`. All files for the project will be in the `D:\ex1_1` directory.If the project files are in a package, use the package name as the directory name.

The left pane shows the files in the project. **JBuilder** includes a default HTML file, `ex1_1.html`. Since our first program is an application, remove this HTML file by highlighting it and clicking the `minus (-)` button just above the file list.

Adding a Program to the Project in JBuilder

To add the `Hello.java` program of Example 1.1 to the project:

- Click on the `plus (+)` button above the left pane, which pops up a file dialog.
- Browse in the file dialog to find `Hello.java`, and open it.

To compile `Hello.java`:

- Click on *`File`*, *`Project`*, *`Project Properties`* tab.
- Click on the `Add` button to select the directory containing the `Hello.java` and click `OK`. This allows the compiler to find the source file.
- Click on the *`Project`*, *`Make Project "ex1_1.jpr"`* menu item.

Running the project in JBuilder

To run the program:

- Click on the *`Run`*, *`Debug project`* menu item.
- The first time we run the program a `Runtime properties` window pops up. Press the *`Set`* button to choose the class file containing the `main` method. In this example we choose `Hello`. Click *`OK`*. The output appears in the text area.

Applets in JBuilder

We use Example 1.2 `HelloApplet.java` to illustrate running an applet in **JBuilder**.

- Make a project, say `ex1_2.jpr`, as shown above for `ex1_1`.
- Remove `ex1_2.html` from the project by clicking on it and clicking the `minus (-)` button.
- Add `HelloApplet.java` to the project as shown above for `Hello.java`.
- Compile `HelloApplet.java` as shown above for `Hello.java`.
- Click on `Run, Debug project.` The first time we run the program a `Runtime properties` window pops up. Click on the *`Applet`* tab and press the *`Set`* button to choose the class file for the applet. In this example we choose `HelloApplet`. Enter the height and width. Click OK.

The applet screen appears.

Importing User-Defined Packages in JBuilder

The `Project Properties` defaults are set to allow the compiler to find the standard Java classes. To run programs such as Example 1.5 `AtmScreen.java` that use our own packages from the text follow the instructions for compiling. Add the directories containing each of the packages to the source:

- Click on *`Project`*, *`ProjectProperties`*, *`Paths`*, *`Required Libraries`* tab.
- Click on the `Add` button, and the *`New`* button. In the `Edit` window that pops up, click on the *`Add`* button, selecting the directory that contains the package directory (not the package directory itself).

- Enter the package name in the `Name` field and click `OK`. Click `OK`.
- Click `OK`.
- Repeat these steps for each user-defined package used. For the `AtmScreen` example we need the `personData` package, and add the directory which contains the `personData` directory.

Passing Program Arguments in JBuilder

To run a program such as Example 11.1, `PassArguments.java`, which uses program arguments, follow the steps for a console application, and to pass the arguments to the program:

- Click on `Project, Project Properties, Run tab.`
- Add the arguments in the `Application Parameters` field and click `OK`.

Creating a New Program in JBuilder

Follow the steps for working with an existing program, but in the file dialog that pops up after clicking on the `plus (+)` button to add a file to the project:

- Enter the file name of the file to be created in the `File name` field and click on `Open`.

Java Development Kit*

We used **JDK 1.2** and **JDK 1.3**. These are versions of the Java 2 Platform Standard Edition. See

```
java.sun.com
```

to download the Java 2 Platform Standard Edition. The documentation requires a separate download.

Compiling using the JDK

- If using Windows, use the `Start` button to get a command (MS-DOS) prompt.
- Enter the command

  ```
  javac Hello.java
  ```

  to compile the `Hello.java` file.

Running a console application using the JDK

- Enter the command

  ```
  java Hello
  ```

  to run the `Hello` application.

* We have also included instructions for using the JDK in the text.

Applets using the JDK

- Compile using the command

  ```
  javac HelloApplet.java
  ```

- Run using the command

  ```
  appletviewer HelloApplet.html
  ```

Importing User-Defined Packages using the JDK

The default classpath allows the compiler to find the system classes. When using own packages we need to augment the classpath. One method is to use the `-classp` option. For example, using the Java 2 Platform (in Windows) we compile with

```
javac -classpath .;c:\gittleman AtmScreen.java
```

This class path has two directories, dot (`.`), representing the current directory, a `c:\gittleman` denoting the directory which contains the `personData` subdirect containing the package used in the `AtmScreen` example.

Using Java 1.1 we include the directory for the system classes in the classpa compiling with

```
javac -classpath .;c:\JAVA\lib\classes.zip;c:\gittleman
```

`AtmScreen.java` where `JAVA` is replaced by the directory in which the JDK is install This class path has three directories, dot (`.`), representing the current directo `c:\JAVA\lib\classes.zip` containing the system classes, and `c:\gittleman` denoti the directory which contains the `personData` subdirectory containing the packa used in the `AtmScreen` example. On UNIX systems the classpath directories are sep rated by colons instead of semicolons, and would be different. When running t program add the same classpath option used with the compiler.

Another approach changes the `CLASSPATH` environment variable. In Windows, the command prompt enter

```
set CLASSPATH=.;c:\JAVA\lib\classes.zip;c:\gittleman
```

if using the JDK 1.1 and

```
set CLASSPATH=.;c:\gittleman
```

if using the Java 2 platform where `JAVA` is replaced by the directory in which the JD is installed.Unless you include this `set` command as part of the system startup yo will need to execute it each time you open a command prompt window. To make th `set` command part of the system startup, on Windows 95 or 98 add it to th `autoexec.bat` file. On Windows NT, click on the `Start` button, then on `Settings` then on `Control Panel`, then on the `System` icon, then on the `Environment` tab. Fill i `CLASSPATH` as the variable, fill in

```
.;c:\gittleman,
```

if using Java 2, or

```
.;c:\JAVA\lib\classes.zip;c:\gittleman
```

if using Java 1.1, as the value, and click the `set` button.

Passing Program Arguments using the JDK

- Add the program arguments to the end of the command, as in

  ```
  java ReadFileLines ReadFileLines.java 5
  ```

  which will display the first five lines of the file `ReadFileLines.java`.

Creating a New Program Using the JDK

Use a simple editor such as Notepad on Windows to create the `.java` and `.html` files.

Browsers

Microsoft's Internet Explorer 4.0 and later support Java version 1.1.

Netscape's Communicator 4.5 and later for Windows NT/95/98 support Java version 1.1.

To run applets that use any features of the Java 2 Platform, not included in version 1.1, we need to use the Java Plugin, which diverts the browser to use the Java Runtime Environment (JRE) from the Java 2 Platform instead of the JRE from the browser. It will offer to download a current JRE to users who do not have one installed.

To make an applet that will use the Java Plugin, run the HTML Converter program found in the `JAVA_HOME\plugin\converter\classes` directory, where `JAVA_HOME` is the directory in which the JDK is installed. A GUI will appear. Enter the directory containing the HTML file for the applet in *`All Files in Folder`* text field. Enter the HTML file name in the *`Matching File Names`* field. Click on *`Convert`*. Deploy the converted HTML file.

Appendix F—Javadoc

The javadoc utility produced the Java documentation, and we can use it to document our programs. The documentation for the Java 2 Platform Standard Edition may be viewed or downloaded from http://java.sun.com/. This HTML documentation describes each class, including fields, constructors, and methods.

We download the documentation ZIP file, which unzips in the docs directory. To find, for example, the documentation for the String class we go to the docs\api\java\lang directory and open String.html. Figure F.1 shows part of this file.

Figure F.1 String.html

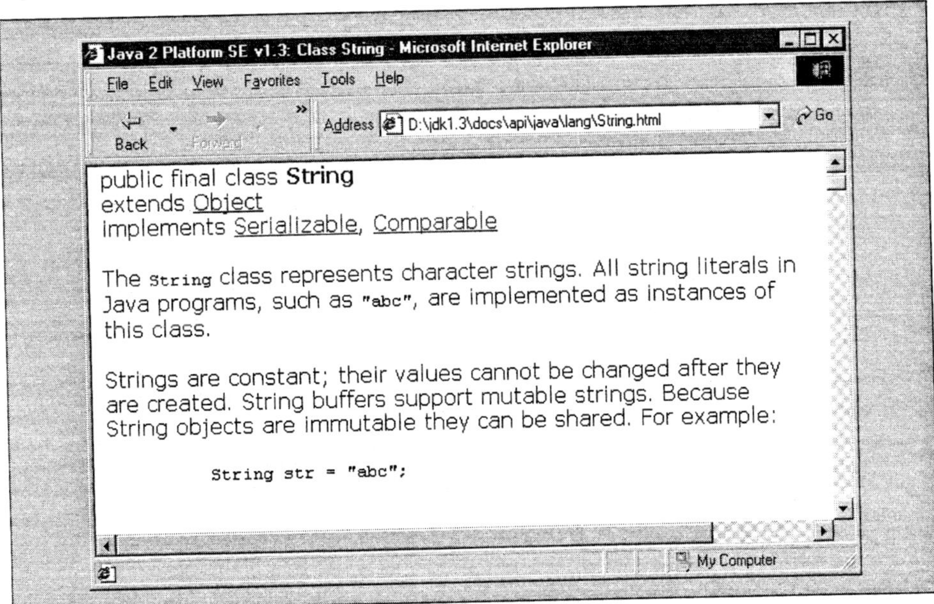

Figure F.2 shows the documentation for the `indexOf(String str)` method. It describes the method, the argument, the return value, and the exception it throws. The `javadoc` utility produced this documentation from a special kind of comment in the source code for the `String` class.

To create comments that javadoc will recognize, use the syntax

```
/**  This is a javadoc comment.
*/
```

with two asterisks after the initial forward slash. Inside the comment use tags that start with the `@` character, such as

`@author`	list author here
`@param`	describe parameters here
`@return`	describe return value here

Figure F.2 The documentation for `indexOf(String str)`

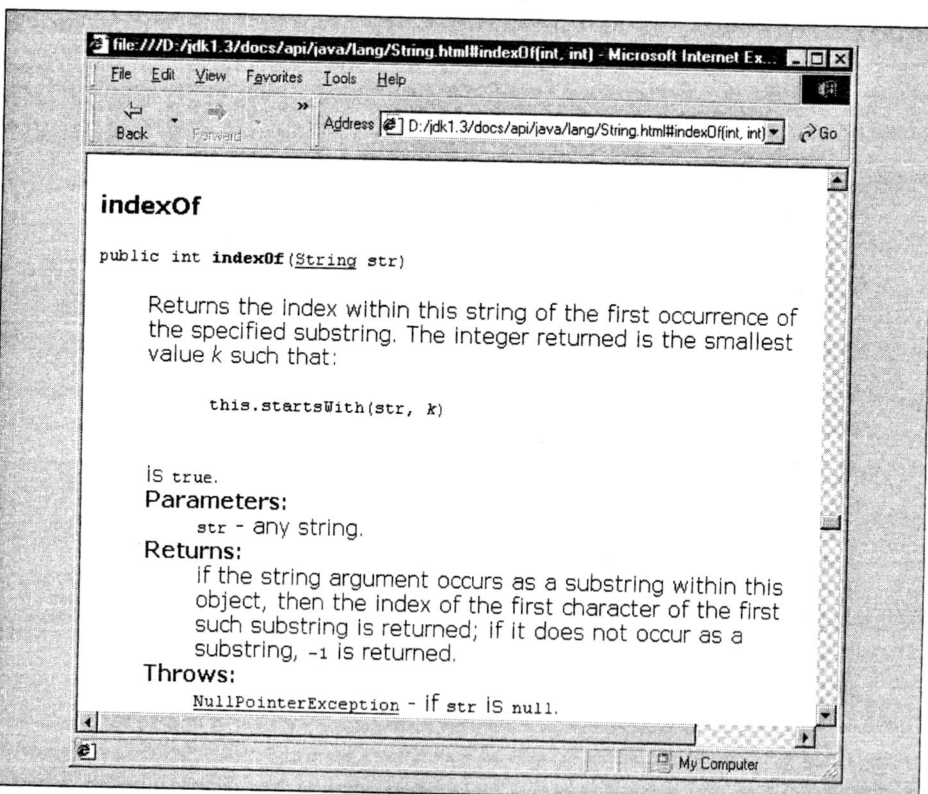

We illustrate the use of `javadoc` with Example 2.10 `PassByValue.java`. Example F.1 shows the annotated version.

```
/**  Illustrates pass by value
     @author  Art Gittleman
 */
```

```
public class PassByValue {

  /** Computes the cube of its argument.  Changes the argument.
   *  @param aNumber the number to cube
   *  @return the cube of the argument
   */
  public static int cube(int aNumber) {
    int result = aNumber*aNumber*aNumber;
    aNumber += 5;
    return result;
  }
  /** Test with the input 12.  Shows that the input is unchanged
   *  even though the argument changes inside the cube method.
   *  @param command-line arguments, not used in this example
   */
  public static void main(String [ ] args) {
    int x = 12, value = 0;
    value = cube(x);
    System.out.println("The cube of " + x + " is " + value);
    System.out.println("The value of x is still " + x);
  }
}
```

We use the command

```
javadoc PassByValue.java
```

to produce the `PassByValue.html` documentation file. Figures F.3 and F.4 show part of it.

Figure F.3 Part of `PassByValue.html`

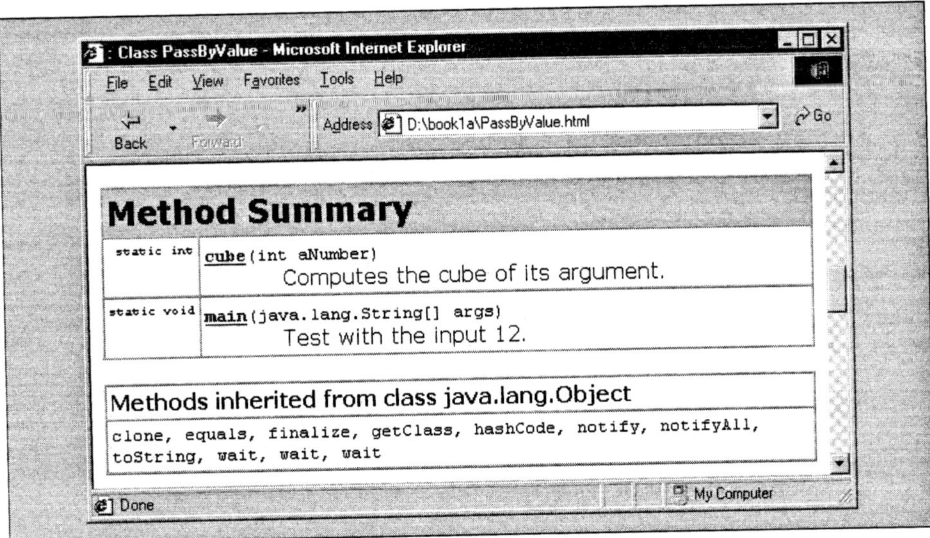

Figure F.4 Another part of `PassByValue.html`

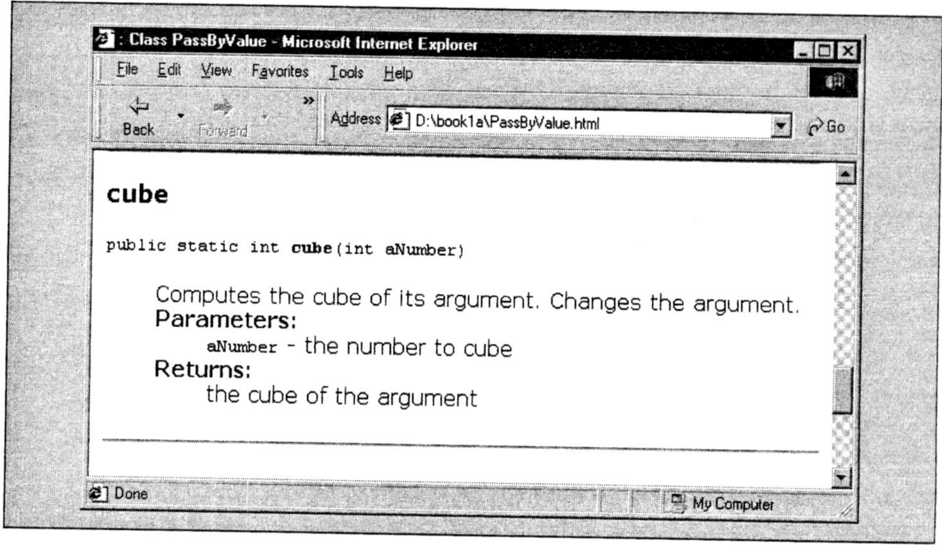

Appendix G—Listing of Packages, Classes and Methods

All Packages in the Java 2™ Platform Standard Edition version 1.3

(Boldface indicates a package used in the text.)

java.applet **java.awt** java.awt.color java.awt.datatransfer java.awt.dnd **java.awt.event** java.awt.font java.awt.geom java.awt.im java.awt.im.spi java.awt.image java.awt.image.renderable java.awt.print **java.beans** java.beans.beancontext **java.io** **java.lang** java.lang.ref **java.lang.reflect** **java.math** **java.net** **java.rmi** java.rmi.activation java.rmi.dgc java.rmi.registry **java.rmi.server** java.security java.security.acl java.security.cert java.security.interfaces java.security.spec **java.sql** **java.text** **java.util** java.util.jar java.util.zip javax.accessibility javax.naming javax.naming.directory javax.naming.event javax.naming.ldap javax.naming.spi javax.rmi javax.rmi.CORBA javax.sound.midi javax.sound.midi.spi javax.sound.sampled javax.sound.sampled.spi **javax.swing** javax.swing.border javax.swing.colorchooser **javax.swing.event** javax.swing.filechooser javax.swing.plaf javax.swing.plaf.basic javax.swing.plaf.metal javax.swing.plaf.multi **javax.swing.table** javax.swing.text javax.swing.text.html javax.swing.text.html.parser javax.swing.text.rtf javax.swing.tree javax.swing.undo javax.transaction org.omg.CORBA org.omg.CORBA_2_3 org.omg.CORBA_2_3.portable org.omg.CORBA.DynAnyPackage org.omg.CORBA.ORBPackage org.omg.CORBA.portable org.omg.CORBA.TypeCodePackage org.omg.CosNaming org.omg.CosNaming.NamingContextPackage org.omg.SendingContext org.omg.stub.java.rmi

Packages in Standard Extensions and Others Used in this Text

javax.media javax.servlet javax.servlet.http javax.xml.parsers javax.xml.transform javax.xml.transform.stream org.apache.soap org.apache.soap.rpc org.apache.soap.util.xml org.xml.sax org.xml.sax.helpers org.w3c.dom sun.jdbc.odbc

All Classes in the Java 2™ Platform Standard Edition version 1.3

(Boldface indicates a class or interface used in the text. Italics indicates an interface.)

AbstractAction AbstractBorder **AbstractButton** AbstractCellEditor AbstractCollection AbstractColorChooserPanel AbstractDocument *AbstractDocument.AttributeContext* *AbstractDocument.Content* AbstractDocument.ElementEdit AbstractLayoutCache AbstractLayoutCache.NodeDimensions AbstractList AbstractListModel AbstractMap AbstractMethodError AbstractSequentialList AbstractSet **AbstractTableModel** AbstractUndoableEdit AbstractWriter AccessControlContext AccessControlException AccessController AccessException *Accessible* *AccessibleAction* AccessibleBundle *AccessibleComponent* AccessibleContext AccessibleHyperlink *AccessibleHypertext* *AccessibleIcon* AccessibleObject AccessibleRelation AccessibleRelationSet AccessibleResourceBundle AccessibleRole *AccessibleSelection* AccessibleState AccessibleStateSet *AccessibleTable* *AccessibleTableModelChange* *AccessibleText* *AccessibleValue* *Acl* *AclEntry* AclNotFoundException *Action* **ActionEvent** ***ActionListener*** ActionMap ActionMapUIResource Activatable ActivateFailedException ActivationDesc ActivationException ActivationGroup ActivationGroupDesc ActivationGroupDesc.CommandEnvironment ActivationGroupID ActivationID *ActivationInstantiator* *ActivationMonitor* *ActivationSystem* *Activator* *ActiveEvent* *Adjustable* AdjustmentEvent *AdjustmentListener* Adler32 AffineTransform AffineTransformOp AlgorithmParameterGenerator AlgorithmParameterGeneratorSpi AlgorithmParameters *AlgorithmParameterSpec* AlgorithmParametersSpi AllPermission AlphaComposite AlreadyBound AlreadyBoundException AlreadyBoundHelper AlreadyBoundHolder AncestorEvent *AncestorListener* Annotation Any AnyHolder AnySeqHelper AnySeqHolder **Applet** ***AppletContext*** *AppletInitializer* *AppletStub* ApplicationException Arc2D Arc2D.Double Arc2D.Float Area AreaAveragingScaleFilter *ARG_IN* *ARG_INOUT* *ARG_OUT* ArithmeticException Array *Array* **ArrayIndexOutOfBoundsException** **ArrayList** Arrays ArrayStoreException AsyncBoxView *Attribute* *AttributedCharacterIterator* AttributedCharacterIterator.Attribute AttributedString AttributeInUseException AttributeList AttributeModificationException Attributes *Attributes* Attributes.Name *AttributeSet* *AttributeSet.CharacterAttribute* *AttributeSet.ColorAttribute* *AttributeSet.FontAttribute* *AttributeSet.ParagraphAttribute* ***AudioClip*** AudioFileFormat AudioFileFormat.Type AudioFileReader AudioFileWriter

AudioFormat AudioFormat.Encoding AudioInputStream AudioPermission AudioSystem AuthenticationException AuthenticationNotSupportedException Authenticator *Autoscroll* AWTError AWTEvent *AWTEventListener* AWTEventMulticaster AWTException AWTPermission BAD_CONTEXT BAD_INV_ORDER BAD_OPERATION BAD_PARAM *BAD_POLICY* *BAD_POLICY_TYPE* *BAD_POLICY_VALUE* BAD_TYPECODE BadKind BadLocationException BandCombineOp BandedSampleModel BasicArrowButton BasicAttribute BasicAttributes BasicBorders BasicBorders.ButtonBorder BasicBorders.FieldBorder BasicBorders.MarginBorder BasicBorders.MenuBarBorder BasicBorders.RadioButtonBorder BasicBorders.SplitPaneBorder BasicBorders.ToggleButtonBorder BasicButtonListener BasicButtonUI BasicCheckBoxMenuItemUI BasicCheckBoxUI BasicColorChooserUI BasicComboBoxEditor BasicComboBoxEditor.UIResource BasicComboBoxRenderer BasicComboBoxRenderer.UIResource BasicComboBoxUI BasicComboPopup BasicDesktopIconUI BasicDesktopPaneUI BasicDirectoryModel BasicEditorPaneUI BasicFileChooserUI BasicGraphicsUtils BasicHTML BasicIconFactory BasicInternalFrameTitlePane BasicInternalFrameUI BasicLabelUI BasicListUI BasicLookAndFeel BasicMenuBarUI BasicMenuItemUI BasicMenuUI BasicOptionPaneUI BasicOptionPaneUI.ButtonAreaLayout BasicPanelUI BasicPasswordFieldUI BasicPermission BasicPopupMenuSeparatorUI BasicPopupMenuUI BasicProgressBarUI BasicRadioButtonMenuItemUI BasicRadioButtonUI BasicRootPaneUI BasicScrollBarUI BasicScrollPaneUI BasicSeparatorUI BasicSliderUI BasicSplitPaneDivider BasicSplitPaneUI BasicStroke BasicTabbedPaneUI BasicTableHeaderUI BasicTableUI BasicTextAreaUI BasicTextFieldUI BasicTextPaneUI BasicTextUI BasicTextUI.BasicCaret BasicTextUI.BasicHighlighter BasicToggleButtonUI BasicToolBarSeparatorUI BasicToolBarUI BasicToolTipUI BasicTreeUI BasicViewportUI BatchUpdateException *BeanContext* *BeanContextChild* *BeanContextChildComponentProxy* BeanContextChildSupport *BeanContextContainerProxy* BeanContextEvent BeanContextMembershipEvent *BeanContextMembershipListener* *BeanContextProxy* BeanContextServiceAvailableEvent *BeanContextServiceProvider* *BeanContextServiceProviderBeanInfo* BeanContextServiceRevokedEvent *BeanContextServiceRevokedListener* *BeanContextServices* *BeanContextServicesListener* BeanContextServicesSupport BeanContextServicesSupport.BCSSServiceProvider BeanContextSupport BeanContextSupport.BCSIterator BeanDescriptor *BeanInfo* Beans BevelBorder BigDecimal **BigInteger** BinaryRefAddr BindException Binding Binding BindingHelper BindingHolder *BindingIterator* BindingIteratorHelper BindingIteratorHolder *BindingIteratorOperations* BindingListHelper BindingListHolder BindingType BindingTypeHelper BindingTypeHolder BitSet *Blob* BlockView Book Boolean BooleanControl BooleanControl.Type BooleanHolder BooleanSeqHelper BooleanSeqHolder *Border* BorderFactory **BorderLayout** BorderUIResource BorderUIResource.BevelBorderUIResource BorderUIResource.CompoundBorderUIResource BorderUIResource.EmptyBorderUIResource BorderUIResource.EtchedBorderUIResource BorderUIResource.LineBorderUIResource

BorderUIResource.MatteBorderUIResource
BorderUIResource.TitledBorderUIResource *BoundedRangeModel* Bounds Bounds
Box Box.Filler *BoxedValueHelper* BoxLayout BoxView BreakIterator
BufferedImage BufferedImageFilter *BufferedImageOp* **BufferedInputStream**
BufferedOutputStream **BufferedReader** BufferedWriter **Button** **ButtonGroup**
ButtonModel ButtonUI Byte ByteArrayInputStream ByteArrayOutputStream
ByteHolder ByteLookupTable Calendar *CallableStatement* CannotProceed
CannotProceedException CannotProceedHelper CannotProceedHolder
CannotRedoException CannotUndoException **Canvas** CardLayout *Caret*
CaretEvent *CaretListener* *CellEditor* *CellEditorListener* CellRendererPane
Certificate Certificate Certificate.CertificateRep
CertificateEncodingException CertificateException
CertificateExpiredException CertificateFactory CertificateFactorySpi
CertificateNotYetValidException CertificateParsingException
ChangedCharSetException ChangeEvent *ChangeListener* Character
Character.Subset Character.UnicodeBlock *CharacterIterator*
CharArrayReader CharArrayWriter CharConversionException CharHolder
CharSeqHelper CharSeqHolder **Checkbox** **CheckboxGroup** CheckboxMenuItem
CheckedInputStream CheckedOutputStream *Checksum* **Choice** ChoiceFormat
Class ClassCastException ClassCircularityError ClassDesc
ClassFormatError ClassLoader ClassNotFoundException *Clip* Clipboard
ClipboardOwner *Clob* *Cloneable* CloneNotSupportedException CMMException
CodeSource CollationElementIterator CollationKey Collator ***Collection***
Collections **Color** ColorChooserComponentFactory ColorChooserUI
ColorConvertOp ColorModel *ColorSelectionModel* ColorSpace ColorUIResource
ComboBoxEditor *ComboBoxModel* ComboBoxUI *ComboPopup* COMM_FAILURE
CommunicationException ***Comparable*** *Comparator* Compiler CompletionStatus
CompletionStatusHelper **Component** ComponentAdapter ComponentColorModel
ComponentEvent ComponentInputMap ComponentInputMapUIResource
ComponentListener ComponentOrientation ComponentSampleModel ComponentUI
ComponentView *Composite* *CompositeContext* CompositeName CompositeView
CompoundBorder CompoundControl CompoundControl.Type CompoundEdit
CompoundName ConcurrentModificationException ConfigurationException
ConnectException ConnectException ConnectIOException ***Connection***
Constructor **Container** ContainerAdapter ContainerEvent *ContainerListener*
ContentHandler *ContentHandlerFactory* ContentModel *Context* Context
ContextList ContextNotEmptyException *ContextualRenderedImageFactory*
Control *Control* Control.Type ControlFactory *ControllerEventListener*
ConvolveOp CRC32 CRL CRLException CropImageFilter CSS CSS.Attribute
CTX_RESTRICT_SCOPE CubicCurve2D CubicCurve2D.Double CubicCurve2D.Float
Current CurrentHelper CurrentHolder *CurrentOperations* Cursor *Customizer*
CustomMarshal *CustomValue* DATA_CONVERSION ***DatabaseMetaData*** DataBuffer
DataBufferByte DataBufferInt DataBufferShort DataBufferUShort DataFlavor
DataFormatException DatagramPacket DatagramSocket DatagramSocketImpl
DatagramSocketImplFactory *DataInput* **DataInputStream** *DataInputStream*
DataLine DataLine.Info *DataOutput* **DataOutputStream** *DataOutputStream*
DataTruncation **Date** **Date** DateFormat DateFormatSymbols DebugGraphics
DecimalFormat DecimalFormatSymbols DefaultBoundedRangeModel
DefaultButtonModel DefaultCaret DefaultCellEditor

DefaultColorSelectionModel DefaultComboBoxModel DefaultDesktopManager DefaultEditorKit DefaultEditorKit.BeepAction DefaultEditorKit.CopyAction DefaultEditorKit.CutAction DefaultEditorKit.DefaultKeyTypedAction DefaultEditorKit.InsertBreakAction DefaultEditorKit.InsertContentAction DefaultEditorKit.InsertTabAction DefaultEditorKit.PasteAction DefaultFocusManager DefaultHighlighter DefaultHighlighter.DefaultHighlightPainter DefaultListCellRenderer DefaultListCellRenderer.UIResource DefaultListModel DefaultListSelectionModel DefaultMenuLayout DefaultMetalTheme DefaultMutableTreeNode DefaultSingleSelectionModel DefaultStyledDocument DefaultStyledDocument.AttributeUndoableEdit DefaultStyledDocument.ElementSpec DefaultTableCellRenderer DefaultTableCellRenderer.UIResource DefaultTableColumnModel DefaultTableModel DefaultTextUI DefaultTreeCellEditor DefaultTreeCellRenderer DefaultTreeModel DefaultTreeSelectionModel DefinitionKind DefinitionKindHelper Deflater DeflaterOutputStream Delegate Delegate *DesignMode* DesktopIconUI *DesktopManager* DesktopPaneUI *DGC* Dialog Dictionary DigestException DigestInputStream DigestOutputStream **Dimension** Dimension2D DimensionUIResource *DirContext* DirectColorModel DirectoryManager *DirObjectFactory* *DirStateFactory* DirStateFactory.Result DnDConstants *Document* *DocumentEvent* *DocumentEvent.ElementChange* DocumentEvent.EventType *DocumentListener* DocumentParser *DomainCombiner* *DomainManager* *DomainManagerOperations* **Double** DoubleHolder DoubleSeqHelper DoubleSeqHolder DragGestureEvent *DragGestureListener* DragGestureRecognizer DragSource DragSourceContext DragSourceDragEvent DragSourceDropEvent DragSourceEvent *DragSourceListener* *Driver* **DriverManager** DriverPropertyInfo DropTarget DropTarget.DropTargetAutoScroller DropTargetContext DropTargetDragEvent DropTargetDropEvent DropTargetEvent *DropTargetListener* *DSAKey* *DSAKeyPairGenerator* DSAParameterSpec *DSAParams* *DSAPrivateKey* DSAPrivateKeySpec *DSAPublicKey* DSAPublicKeySpec DTD *DTDConstants* DynamicImplementation *DynAny* *DynArray* *DynEnum* *DynFixed* *DynSequence* *DynStruct* *DynUnion* *DynValue* EditorKit *Element* Element ElementIterator Ellipse2D Ellipse2D.Double Ellipse2D.Float EmptyBorder EmptyStackException EncodedKeySpec Entity EnumControl EnumControl.Type ***Enumeration*** Environment EOFException Error EtchedBorder Event *EventContext* *EventDirContext* *EventListener* EventListenerList EventObject EventQueue EventSetDescriptor **Exception** ExceptionInInitializerError ExceptionList ExpandVetoException ExportException *ExtendedRequest* *ExtendedResponse* *Externalizable* FeatureDescriptor Field FieldNameHelper FieldPosition FieldView **File** FileChooserUI FileDescriptor FileDialog *FileFilter* FileFilter **FileInputStream** *FilenameFilter* *FileNameMap* **FileNotFoundException** **FileOutputStream** FilePermission **FileReader** FileSystemView FileView **FileWriter** FilteredImageSource FilterInputStream FilterOutputStream FilterReader FilterWriter FixedHeightLayoutCache FixedHolder FlatteningPathIterator *FlavorMap* Float FloatControl FloatControl.Type FloatHolder FloatSeqHelper FloatSeqHolder **FlowLayout** FlowView FlowView.FlowStrategy FocusAdapter FocusEvent *FocusListener* FocusManager **Font** FontFormatException **FontMetrics** FontRenderContext

FontUIResource Format FormatConversionProvider FormView **Frame** FREE_MEM GapContent GeneralPath GeneralSecurityException GlyphJustificationInfo GlyphMetrics GlyphVector GlyphView GlyphView.GlyphPainter GradientPaint GraphicAttribute **Graphics** Graphics2D GraphicsConfigTemplate GraphicsConfiguration GraphicsDevice GraphicsEnvironment GrayFilter GregorianCalendar **GridBagConstraints** **GridBagLayout** **GridLayout** *Group* *Guard* GuardedObject GZIPInputStream GZIPOutputStream *HasControls* **HashMap** **HashSet** **Hashtable** HierarchyBoundsAdapter *HierarchyBoundsListener* HierarchyEvent *HierarchyListener* *Highlighter* *Highlighter.Highlight* *Highlighter.HighlightPainter* HTML HTML.Attribute HTML.Tag HTML.UnknownTag HTMLDocument HTMLDocument.Iterator HTMLEditorKit HTMLEditorKit.HTMLFactory HTMLEditorKit.HTMLTextAction HTMLEditorKit.InsertHTMLTextAction HTMLEditorKit.LinkController HTMLEditorKit.Parser HTMLEditorKit.ParserCallback HTMLFrameHyperlinkEvent HTMLWriter HttpURLConnection HyperlinkEvent HyperlinkEvent.EventType *HyperlinkListener* ICC_ColorSpace ICC_Profile ICC_ProfileGray ICC_ProfileRGB ***Icon*** IconUIResource IconView IdentifierHelper Identity IdentityScope *IDLEntity* *IDLType* IDLTypeHelper *IDLTypeOperations* IllegalAccessError IllegalAccessException IllegalArgumentException IllegalComponentStateException IllegalMonitorStateException IllegalPathStateException IllegalStateException IllegalThreadStateException **Image** *ImageConsumer* ImageFilter ImageGraphicAttribute **ImageIcon** *ImageObserver* *ImageProducer* ImagingOpException IMP_LIMIT IncompatibleClassChangeError InconsistentTypeCode IndexColorModel IndexedPropertyDescriptor IndexOutOfBoundsException IndirectionException InetAddress Inflater InflaterInputStream InheritableThreadLocal InitialContext *InitialContextFactory* *InitialContextFactoryBuilder* InitialDirContext INITIALIZE Initializer InitialLdapContext InlineView InputContext InputEvent InputMap InputMapUIResource *InputMethod* *InputMethodContext* *InputMethodDescriptor* InputMethodEvent InputMethodHighlight *InputMethodListener* *InputMethodRequests* **InputStream** InputStream InputStream **InputStreamReader** InputSubset InputVerifier Insets InsetsUIResource InstantiationError InstantiationException Instrument InsufficientResourcesException **Integer** INTERNAL InternalError InternalFrameAdapter InternalFrameEvent *InternalFrameListener* InternalFrameUI **InterruptedException** InterruptedIOException InterruptedNamingException INTF_REPOS IntHolder IntrospectionException Introspector INV_FLAG INV_IDENT INV_OBJREF INV_POLICY Invalid INVALID_TRANSACTION InvalidAlgorithmParameterException InvalidAttributeIdentifierException InvalidAttributesException InvalidAttributeValueException InvalidClassException InvalidDnDOperationException InvalidKeyException InvalidKeySpecException InvalidMidiDataException InvalidName InvalidName InvalidNameException InvalidNameHelper InvalidNameHolder InvalidObjectException InvalidParameterException InvalidParameterSpecException InvalidSearchControlsException InvalidSearchFilterException InvalidSeq InvalidTransactionException InvalidValue InvocationEvent *InvocationHandler* InvocationTargetException *InvokeHandler* **IOException**

IRObject *IRObjectOperations* IstringHelper **ItemEvent** *ItemListener* *ItemSelectable* ***Iterator*** **JApplet** JarEntry JarException JarFile JarInputStream JarOutputStream JarURLConnection **JButton** **JCheckBox** JCheckBoxMenuItem **JColorChooser** **JComboBox** *JComboBox.KeySelectionManager* **JComponent** JDesktopPane JDialog JEditorPane **JFileChooser** **JFrame** JInternalFrame JInternalFrame.JDesktopIcon **JLabel** JLayeredPane **JList** **JMenu** **JMenuBar** **JMenuItem** JobAttributes JobAttributes.DefaultSelectionType JobAttributes.DestinationType JobAttributes.DialogType JobAttributes.MultipleDocumentHandlingType JobAttributes.SidesType **JOptionPane** **JPanel** JPasswordField JPopupMenu JPopupMenu.Separator JProgressBar **JRadioButton** JRadioButtonMenuItem JRootPane JScrollBar **JScrollPane** JSeparator JSlider JSplitPane **JTabbedPane** **JTable** JTableHeader **JTextArea** **JTextComponent** JTextComponent.KeyBinding **JTextField** JTextPane **JToggleButton** JToggleButton.ToggleButtonModel JToolBar JToolBar.Separator JToolTip JTree JTree.DynamicUtilTreeNode JTree.EmptySelectionModel JViewport JWindow Kernel *Key* **KeyAdapter** **KeyEvent** KeyException KeyFactory KeyFactorySpi ***KeyListener*** KeyManagementException *Keymap* KeyPair KeyPairGenerator KeyPairGeneratorSpi *KeySpec* KeyStore KeyStoreException KeyStoreSpi KeyStroke **Label** LabelUI LabelView LastOwnerException LayeredHighlighter LayeredHighlighter.LayerPainter *LayoutManager* *LayoutManager2* LayoutQueue *LdapContext* LdapReferralException Lease LimitExceededException *Line* Line.Info Line2D Line2D.Double Line2D.Float LineBorder LineBreakMeasurer LineEvent LineEvent.Type *LineListener* LineMetrics LineNumberInputStream LineNumberReader LineUnavailableException LinkageError **LinkedList** LinkException LinkLoopException LinkRef **List** ***List*** *ListCellRenderer* ListDataEvent *ListDataListener* ***ListIterator*** *ListModel* ListResourceBundle **ListSelectionEvent** ***ListSelectionListener*** ***ListSelectionModel*** ListUI ListView *LoaderHandler* Locale LocateRegistry LogStream Long LongHolder LongLongSeqHelper LongLongSeqHolder LongSeqHelper LongSeqHolder LookAndFeel LookupOp LookupTable MalformedLinkException **MalformedURLException** Manifest ***Map*** ***Map.Entry*** MARSHAL MarshalException MarshalledObject Math MatteBorder **MediaTracker** *Member* MemoryImageSource Menu MenuBar MenuBarUI MenuComponent *MenuContainer* MenuDragMouseEvent *MenuDragMouseListener* *MenuElement* MenuEvent MenuItem MenuItemUI MenuKeyEvent *MenuKeyListener* *MenuListener* MenuSelectionManager MenuShortcut MessageDigest MessageDigestSpi MessageFormat *MetaEventListener* MetalBorders MetalBorders.ButtonBorder MetalBorders.Flush3DBorder MetalBorders.InternalFrameBorder MetalBorders.MenuBarBorder MetalBorders.MenuItemBorder MetalBorders.OptionDialogBorder MetalBorders.PaletteBorder MetalBorders.PopupMenuBorder MetalBorders.RolloverButtonBorder MetalBorders.ScrollPaneBorder MetalBorders.TableHeaderBorder MetalBorders.TextFieldBorder MetalBorders.ToggleButtonBorder MetalBorders.ToolBarBorder MetalButtonUI MetalCheckBoxIcon MetalCheckBoxUI MetalComboBoxButton MetalComboBoxEditor MetalComboBoxEditor.UIResource MetalComboBoxIcon MetalComboBoxUI MetalDesktopIconUI MetalFileChooserUI MetalIconFactory

MetalIconFactory.FileIcon16 MetalIconFactory.FolderIcon16 MetalIconFactory.PaletteCloseIcon MetalIconFactory.TreeControlIcon MetalIconFactory.TreeFolderIcon MetalIconFactory.TreeLeafIcon MetalInternalFrameTitlePane MetalInternalFrameUI MetalLabelUI MetalLookAndFeel MetalPopupMenuSeparatorUI MetalProgressBarUI MetalRadioButtonUI MetalScrollBarUI MetalScrollButton MetalScrollPaneUI MetalSeparatorUI MetalSliderUI MetalSplitPaneUI MetalTabbedPaneUI MetalTextFieldUI MetalTheme MetalToggleButtonUI MetalToolBarUI MetalToolTipUI MetalTreeUI MetaMessage Method MethodDescriptor *MidiChannel* *MidiDevice* MidiDevice.Info MidiDeviceProvider MidiEvent MidiFileFormat MidiFileReader MidiFileWriter MidiMessage MidiSystem MidiUnavailableException MimeTypeParseException MinimalHTMLWriter MissingResourceException *Mixer* Mixer.Info MixerProvider ModificationItem Modifier **MouseAdapter** MouseDragGestureRecognizer MouseEvent MouseInputAdapter *MouseInputListener* ***MouseListener*** **MouseMotionAdapter** ***MouseMotionListener*** MultiButtonUI MulticastSocket MultiColorChooserUI MultiComboBoxUI MultiDesktopIconUI MultiDesktopPaneUI MultiFileChooserUI MultiInternalFrameUI MultiLabelUI MultiListUI MultiLookAndFeel MultiMenuBarUI MultiMenuItemUI MultiOptionPaneUI MultiPanelUI MultiPixelPackedSampleModel *MultipleMaster* MultiPopupMenuUI MultiProgressBarUI MultiScrollBarUI MultiScrollPaneUI MultiSeparatorUI MultiSliderUI MultiSplitPaneUI MultiTabbedPaneUI MultiTableHeaderUI MultiTableUI MultiTextUI MultiToolBarUI MultiToolTipUI MultiTreeUI MultiViewportUI *MutableAttributeSet* *MutableComboBoxModel* *MutableTreeNode* *Name* NameAlreadyBoundException NameClassPair NameComponent NameComponentHelper NameComponentHolder NamedValue NameHelper NameHolder NameNotFoundException *NameParser* *NamespaceChangeListener* NameValuePair NameValuePairHelper **Naming** *NamingContext* NamingContextHelper NamingContextHolder *NamingContextOperations* *NamingEnumeration* NamingEvent NamingException NamingExceptionEvent *NamingListener* NamingManager NamingSecurityException NegativeArraySizeException NetPermission NO_IMPLEMENT NO_MEMORY NO_PERMISSION NO_RESOURCES NO_RESPONSE NoClassDefFoundError NoInitialContextException NoninvertibleTransformException NoPermissionException NoRouteToHostException NoSuchAlgorithmException NoSuchAttributeException NoSuchElementException NoSuchFieldError NoSuchFieldException NoSuchMethodError NoSuchMethodException NoSuchObjectException NoSuchProviderException NotActiveException NotBoundException NotContextException NotEmpty NotEmptyHelper NotEmptyHolder NotFound NotFoundHelper NotFoundHolder NotFoundReason NotFoundReasonHelper NotFoundReasonHolder NotOwnerException NotSerializableException NullPointerException Number **NumberFormat** **NumberFormatException** NVList OBJ_ADAPTER **Object** *Object* OBJECT_NOT_EXIST *ObjectChangeListener* *ObjectFactory* *ObjectFactoryBuilder* ObjectHelper ObjectHolder ObjectImpl ObjectImpl *ObjectInput* **ObjectInputStream** ObjectInputStream.GetField *ObjectInputValidation* *ObjectOutput* **ObjectOutputStream** ObjectOutputStream.PutField ObjectStreamClass *ObjectStreamConstants* ObjectStreamException ObjectStreamField ObjectView ObjID Observable *Observer* OctetSeqHelper OctetSeqHolder *OMGVMCID* *OpenType* Operation

OperationNotSupportedException Option OptionalDataException OptionPaneUI ORB ORB **OutOfMemoryError** OutputStream OutputStream OutputStream OutputStreamWriter OverlayLayout *Owner* Package PackedColorModel *Pageable* PageAttributes PageAttributes.ColorType PageAttributes.MediaType PageAttributes.OrientationRequestedType PageAttributes.OriginType PageAttributes.PrintQualityType PageFormat *Paint* *PaintContext* PaintEvent **Panel** PanelUI Paper ParagraphView ParagraphView ParameterBlock ParameterDescriptor ParseException ParsePosition Parser ParserDelegator PartialResultException PasswordAuthentication PasswordView Patch *PathIterator* Permission *Permission* PermissionCollection Permissions PERSIST_STORE PhantomReference PipedInputStream PipedOutputStream PipedReader PipedWriter PixelGrabber PixelInterleavedSampleModel PKCS8EncodedKeySpec PlainDocument PlainView **Point** Point2D Point2D.Double Point2D.Float Policy *Policy* PolicyError PolicyHelper PolicyHolder PolicyListHelper PolicyListHolder *PolicyOperations* PolicyTypeHelper **Polygon** PopupMenu PopupMenuEvent *PopupMenuListener* PopupMenuUI *Port* Port.Info PortableRemoteObject *PortableRemoteObjectDelegate* *Position* Position.Bias ***PreparedStatement*** *Principal* Principal PrincipalHolder *Printable* PrinterAbortException PrinterException *PrinterGraphics* PrinterIOException PrinterJob *PrintGraphics* PrintJob PrintStream **PrintWriter** *PRIVATE_MEMBER* *PrivateKey* *PrivilegedAction* PrivilegedActionException *PrivilegedExceptionAction* Process ProfileDataException ProgressBarUI ProgressMonitor ProgressMonitorInputStream Properties PropertyChangeEvent *PropertyChangeListener* PropertyChangeSupport PropertyDescriptor *PropertyEditor* PropertyEditorManager PropertyEditorSupport PropertyPermission PropertyResourceBundle PropertyVetoException ProtectionDomain ProtocolException Provider ProviderException Proxy *PUBLIC_MEMBER* *PublicKey* PushbackInputStream PushbackReader QuadCurve2D QuadCurve2D.Double QuadCurve2D.Float **Random** **RandomAccessFile** Raster RasterFormatException *RasterOp* Reader *Receiver* Rectangle Rectangle2D Rectangle2D.Double Rectangle2D.Float RectangularShape *Ref* RefAddr Reference Reference *Referenceable* ReferenceQueue ReferralException ReflectPermission *Registry* *RegistryHandler* RemarshalException ***Remote*** *RemoteCall* **RemoteException** RemoteObject *RemoteRef* RemoteServer RemoteStub *RenderableImage* RenderableImageOp RenderableImageProducer RenderContext *RenderedImage* *RenderedImageFactory* *Renderer* RenderingHints RenderingHints.Key RepaintManager ReplicateScaleFilter *Repository* RepositoryIdHelper Request RescaleOp *Resolver* ResolveResult ResourceBundle *ResponseHandler* ***ResultSet*** ***ResultSetMetaData*** ReverbType RGBImageFilter RMIClassLoader *RMIClientSocketFactory* *RMIFailureHandler* RMISecurityException RMISecurityManager *RMIServerSocketFactory* RMISocketFactory Robot *RootPaneContainer* RootPaneUI RoundRectangle2D RoundRectangle2D.Double RoundRectangle2D.Float *RowMapper* *RSAKey* RSAKeyGenParameterSpec *RSAPrivateCrtKey* RSAPrivateCrtKeySpec *RSAPrivateKey* RSAPrivateKeySpec *RSAPublicKey* RSAPublicKeySpec RTFEditorKit RuleBasedCollator ***Runnable*** Runtime *RunTime* **RuntimeException** *RunTimeOperations* RuntimePermission SampleModel

SchemaViolationException ***Scrollable*** Scrollbar ScrollBarUI ScrollPane *ScrollPaneConstants* ScrollPaneLayout ScrollPaneLayout.UIResource ScrollPaneUI SearchControls SearchResult SecureClassLoader SecureRandom SecureRandomSpi Security SecurityException SecurityManager SecurityPermission Segment SeparatorUI Sequence SequenceInputStream *Sequencer* Sequencer.SyncMode ***Serializable*** SerializablePermission ServantObject ServerCloneException ServerError ServerException ServerNotActiveException *ServerRef* ServerRequest ServerRuntimeException **ServerSocket** ServiceDetail ServiceDetailHelper ServiceInformation ServiceInformationHelper ServiceInformationHolder ServiceUnavailableException *Set* SetOverrideType SetOverrideTypeHelper *Shape* ShapeGraphicAttribute Short ShortHolder ShortLookupTable ShortMessage ShortSeqHelper ShortSeqHolder Signature SignatureException SignatureSpi SignedObject Signer SimpleAttributeSet SimpleBeanInfo SimpleDateFormat SimpleTimeZone SinglePixelPackedSampleModel *SingleSelectionModel* SizeLimitExceededException SizeRequirements SizeSequence *Skeleton* SkeletonMismatchException SkeletonNotFoundException SliderUI **Socket** SocketException SocketImpl *SocketImplFactory* *SocketOptions* SocketPermission SocketSecurityException SoftBevelBorder SoftReference ***SortedMap*** ***SortedSet*** *Soundbank* SoundbankReader SoundbankResource *SourceDataLine* SplitPaneUI *SQLData* SQLException *SQLInput* *SQLOutput* SQLPermission SQLWarning Stack StackOverflowError StateEdit *StateEditable* *StateFactory* ***Statement*** *Streamable* *StreamableValue* StreamCorruptedException StreamTokenizer StrictMath **String** **StringBuffer** StringBufferInputStream StringCharacterIterator StringContent StringHolder StringIndexOutOfBoundsException StringReader StringRefAddr StringSelection **StringTokenizer** StringValueHelper StringWriter *Stroke* *Struct* StructMember StructMemberHelper Stub *StubDelegate* StubNotFoundException *Style* StyleConstants StyleConstants.CharacterConstants StyleConstants.ColorConstants StyleConstants.FontConstants StyleConstants.ParagraphConstants StyleContext *StyledDocument* StyledEditorKit StyledEditorKit.AlignmentAction StyledEditorKit.BoldAction StyledEditorKit.FontFamilyAction StyledEditorKit.FontSizeAction StyledEditorKit.ForegroundAction StyledEditorKit.ItalicAction StyledEditorKit.StyledTextAction StyledEditorKit.UnderlineAction StyleSheet StyleSheet.BoxPainter StyleSheet.ListPainter ***SwingConstants*** SwingPropertyChangeSupport SwingUtilities SyncFailedException *Synthesizer* SysexMessage **System** SystemColor SystemException SystemFlavorMap *TabableView* TabbedPaneUI *TabExpander* *TableCellEditor* *TableCellRenderer* TableColumn *TableColumnModel* TableColumnModelEvent *TableColumnModelListener* TableHeaderUI ***TableModel*** TableModelEvent *TableModelListener* TableUI TableView TabSet TabStop TagElement *TargetDataLine* TCKind TextAction **TextArea** TextAttribute **TextComponent** TextEvent **TextField** TextHitInfo TextLayout TextLayout.CaretPolicy

TextListener TextMeasurer TextUI TexturePaint **Thread** ThreadDeath ThreadGroup ThreadLocal **Throwable** *Tie* *TileObserver* Time TimeLimitExceededException Timer Timer TimerTask Timestamp TimeZone TitledBorder ToolBarUI Toolkit ToolTipManager ToolTipUI TooManyListenersException Track TRANSACTION_REQUIRED TRANSACTION_ROLLEDBACK TransactionRequiredException TransactionRolledbackException *Transferable* TransformAttribute TRANSIENT *Transmitter* *Transparency* *TreeCellEditor* *TreeCellRenderer* TreeExpansionEvent *TreeExpansionListener* **TreeMap** *TreeModel* TreeModelEvent *TreeModelListener* *TreeNode* TreePath TreeSelectionEvent *TreeSelectionListener* *TreeSelectionModel* **TreeSet** TreeUI *TreeWillExpandListener* TypeCode TypeCodeHolder TypeMismatch Types UID UIDefaults *UIDefaults.ActiveValue* UIDefaults.LazyInputMap *UIDefaults.LazyValue* UIDefaults.ProxyLazyValue **UIManager** **UIManager.LookAndFeelInfo** *UIResource* ULongLongSeqHelper ULongLongSeqHolder ULongSeqHelper ULongSeqHolder UndeclaredThrowableException *UndoableEdit* UndoableEditEvent *UndoableEditListener* UndoableEditSupport UndoManager UnexpectedException **UnicastRemoteObject** UnionMember UnionMemberHelper UNKNOWN UnknownError UnknownException UnknownGroupException UnknownHostException UnknownHostException UnknownObjectException UnknownServiceException UnknownUserException UnmarshalException UnrecoverableKeyException *Unreferenced* UnresolvedPermission UnsatisfiedLinkError *UnsolicitedNotification* UnsolicitedNotificationEvent *UnsolicitedNotificationListener* *UNSUPPORTED_POLICY* *UNSUPPORTED_POLICY_VALUE* UnsupportedAudioFileException UnsupportedClassVersionError UnsupportedEncodingException UnsupportedFlavorException UnsupportedLookAndFeelException UnsupportedOperationException **URL** URLClassLoader **URLConnection** URLDecoder URLEncoder URLStreamHandler *URLStreamHandlerFactory* UserException UShortSeqHelper UShortSeqHolder UTFDataFormatException Util *UtilDelegate* Utilities *ValueBase* ValueBaseHelper ValueBaseHolder *ValueFactory* *ValueHandler* ValueMember ValueMemberHelper VariableHeightLayoutCache **Vector** VerifyError VersionSpecHelper *VetoableChangeListener* VetoableChangeSupport View *ViewFactory* ViewportLayout ViewportUI VirtualMachineError *Visibility* VisibilityHelper *VM_ABSTRACT* *VM_CUSTOM* *VM_NONE* *VM_TRUNCATABLE* VMID VoiceStatus Void WCharSeqHelper WCharSeqHolder WeakHashMap WeakReference **Window** **WindowAdapter** *WindowConstants* **WindowEvent** ***WindowListener*** WrappedPlainView WritableRaster *WritableRenderedImage* WriteAbortedException Writer WrongTransaction WStringValueHelper X509Certificate X509CRL X509CRLEntry X509EncodedKeySpec *X509Extension* ZipEntry ZipException ZipFile ZipInputStream ZipOutputStream ZoneView _BindingIteratorImplBase _BindingIteratorStub _IDLTypeStub _NamingContextImplBase _NamingContextStub _PolicyStub _Remote_Stub

Constructors and Methods Used in the Text

(Grouped by package and class or interface)

java.applet

AppletContext

```
void showDocument(URL url)
```

AudioClip

```
void loop()
```

Applet (extends Panel)

```
AppletContext getAppletContext()
AudioClip getAudioClip(URL url)
Image getImage(URL url)
String getParameter(String name)
void init()
void play(URL url)
void start()
void stop()
```

java.awt

AWTEvent (extends java.util.EventObject)

BorderLayout

```
BorderLayout()
```

Button (extends Component)

```
Button(String label)
void addActionListener(ActionListener l)
String getActionCommand()
void setLabel(String label)
```

Canvas (extends Component)

```
void paint(Graphics g)
```

Checkbox (extends Component)

```
Checkbox(String label)
Checkbox(String label, boolean state, CheckboxGroup group)
void addItemListener(ItemListener l)
boolean getState()
```

CheckboxGroup

```
CheckboxGroup()
```

Choice (extends Component)

```
Choice()
void add(String item)
void addItemListener(ItemListener l)
int getSelectedIndex()
String getSelectedItem()
void select (int pos)
void select(String str)
```

Color

```
Color(int r, int g, int b)
Color(float r, float g, float b)
Color brighter()
Color darker()
int getBlue()
int getGreen()
int getRed()
```

Component

```
void addKeyListener(KeyListener l)
void add MouseListener(MouseListener l)
void add MouseMotionListener(MouseMotionListener l)
boolean contains(int x, int y)
boolean contains(Point p)
Image createImage(int  width, int height)
Color getBackground()
FontMetrics getFontMetrics(Font f)
Color getForeground()
Graphics getGraphics()
int getHeight()
Dimension getSize()
int getWidth()
boolean hasFocus()
void paint(Graphics g)
void paintAll(Graphics g)
void repaint()
void repaint(int x, int y, int width, int height)
void requestFocus()
void setBackground(Color c)
void setBounds(int x, int y, int width, int height)
void setEnabled(boolean b)
void setFont(Font f)
void setForeground(Color c)
void setLocation(int x, int y)
void setSize(int width, int height)
void setVisible(boolean b)
void update(graphics g)
```

Container (extends Component)

```
Component add(Component c)
void paint(Graphics g)
void setFont(Font f)
void setLayout(LayoutManager ,gr)
void update(Graphics g)
```

Dimension (extends java.awt.geom.Dimension2D)

```
int height
int width
```

FlowLayout

```
FlowLayout()
```

Font

```
Font(String name, int style, int size)
String getFontName()
String getName()
```

FontMetrics

```
int getHeight()
int stringWidth(String s)
```

Frame (extends Container)

```
Frame(String title)
```

Graphics

```
abstract void clearRect(int x, int y, int width, int height)
abstract void draw3DRect
    (int x, int y, int width, int height. boolean raised)
abstract void drawArc(int x, int y, int width, int height,
    int startAngle, int arcAngle)
abstract boolean drawImage
    (Image img, int x, int y, ImageObserver o)
abstract boolean drawImage(Image img, int x, int y,
    int width, int height, ImageObserver o)
abstract void drawLine(int x1, int y1, int x2, int y2)
abstract void drawOval(int x, int y, int width, int height)
abstract void drawPolygon(int[] xPoints, int[] yPoints,
    int nPoints)
void drawPolygon(Polygon p)
void drawRect(int x, int y, int width, int height)
abstract void drawRoundRect(int x, int y, int width,
    int height, int xdi, int ydi)
abstract void drawString(String str, int x, int y)
abstract void fill3DRect
    (int x, int y, int width, int height. boolean raised)
abstract void fillArc(int x, int y, int width, int height,
    int startAngle, int arcAngle)
```

```
abstract void fillOval(int x, int y, int width, int height)
abstract void fillPolygon(int[] xPoints, int[] yPoints,
  int nPoints)
void fillPolygon(Polygon p)
void fillRect(int x, int y, int width, int height)
abstract void fillRoundRect(int x, int y, int width,
int height, int xdi, int ydi)
abstract Color getColor()
FontMetrics getFontMetrics(Font f)
abstract void setColor(Color c)
abstract void setFont(Font f)
```

GridBagConstraints

```
int anchor
int BOTH
static int CENTER
static int EAST
int fill
int gridheight
int gridwidth
int gridx
int gridy
static int HORIZONTAL
Insets insets
int ipadx
int ipady
static int NONE
static int NORTH
static int NORTHEAST
static int NORTHWEST
int RELATIVE
static int REMAINDER
static int SOUTH
static int SOUTHEAST
static int SOUTHWEST
static int VERTICAL
double weightx
double weighty
static int WEST
GridBagConstraints()
```

GridBagLayout

```
GridBagLayout()
void setConstraints(Component comp, GridBagConstraints gbc)
```

GridLayout

```
GridLayout(int rows, int cols)
```

Image

```
abstract Graphics getGraphics()
abstract int getHeight(ImageObserver o)
abstract int getWidth(ImageObserver o)
```

Label (extends Component)

```
Label(String text)
String getText()
void setText(String text)
```

List

```
List()
List(int rows)
void add(String item)
void addActionListener(ActionListener l)
void addItemListener(ItemListener l)
void deselect(int index)
String getItem(int index)
int getItemCount()
String[] getItems()
int getSelectedIndex()
int[] getSelectedIndexes()
String getSelectedItem()
String[] getSelectedItems()
boolean isMultipleMode()
void select(int index)
void setMultipleMode(boolean b)
```

MediaTracker

```
MediaTracker(Component comp)
void addImage(Image image, int id)
void waitForID(int id)
```

Panel (extends Container)

```
Panel()
```

Point (extends java.awt.geom.Point2D)

```
Point(int x, int y)
void move(int x, int y)
void translate(int deltaX, int deltaY)
```

Polygon

```
Polygon(int[] xpoints, int[] ypoints, int npoints)
boolean contains(double x, double y)
boolean contains(int x, int y)
boolean contains(Point p)
void translate(int deltaX, int deltaY)
```

TextArea (extends TextComponent)

```
TextArea()
TextArea(int rows, int cols)
TextArea(String text, int rows, int cols)
void append(String str)
void insert(String str, int pos)
```

TextComponent (extends Component)

```
String getSelectedText()
String getText()
void setText(String text)
```

TextField (extends TextComponent)

```
TextField()
TextField(int cols)
TextField(String str, int cols)
void addActionListener(ActionListener l)
void setText(String text)
```

Window (extends Container)

```
void addWindowListener(WindowListener l)
void dispose()
void hide()
void pack()
void show()
```

java.awt.event

ActionListener (extends EventListener)

```
void actionPerformed(ActionEvent e)
```

ItemListener (extends EventListener)

```
void itemStateChanged(ItemEvent e)
```

KeyListener (extends EventListener)

```
void keyPressed(KeyEvent e)
void keyReleased(KeyEvent e)
void keyTyped(KeyEvent e)
```

MouseListener (extends EventListener)

```
void mouseClicked(MouseEvent e)
void mouseEntered(MouseEvent e)
void mouseExitedMouseEvent e)
void mousePressed(MouseEvent e)
void mouseReleased(MouseEvent e)
```

MouseMotionListener (extends EventListener)

```
void mouseDragged(MouseEvent e)
void mouseMoved(MouseEvent e)
```

WindowListener (extends EventListener)

```
void windowActivated(WindowEvent e)
void windowClosed(WindowEvent e)
void windowClosing(WindowEvent e)
void windowDeactivated(WindowEvent e)
void windowDeiconified(WindowEvent e)
void windowIconified(WindowEvent e)
void windowOpened(WindowEvent e)
```

ActionEvent (extends java.awt.AWTEvent)

```
String getActionCommand()
```

ComponentEvent (extends java.awt.Event)

InputEvent (extends ComponentEvent)

ItemEvent (extends java.awt.AWTEvent)

```
Object getItem()
int getStateChange()
```

KeyAdapter

```
void keyPressed(KeyEvent e)
void keyReleased(KeyEvent e)
void keyTyped(KeyEvent e)
```

KeyEvent (extends InputEvent)

```
char getKeyChar()
int  getKeyCode()
```

MouseAdapter

```
void mouseClicked(MouseEvent e)
void mouseEntered(MouseEvent e)
void mouseExitedMouseEvent e)
void mousePressed(MouseEvent e)
void mouseReleased(MouseEvent e)
```

MouseEvent (extends InputEvent)

```
int getClickCount()
int getX()
int getY()
```

MouseMotionAdapter

```
void mouseDragged(MouseEvent e)
void mouseMoved(MouseEvent e)
```

WindowAdapter

```
void windowActivated(WindowEvent e)
void windowClosed(WindowEvent e)
void windowClosing(WindowEvent e)
void windowDeactivated(WindowEvent e)
void windowDeiconified(WindowEvent e)
void windowIconified(WindowEvent e)
void windowOpened(WindowEvent e)
```

WindowEvent (extends ComponentEvent)

ava.io

Serializable

BufferedInputStream (extends FilterInputStream)

```
BufferedInputStream(InputStream in)
int read()
int read(byte[] b, int off, int len)
```

BufferedOutputStream (extends FilterOutputStream)

```
BufferedOutputStream(OutputStream out)
void flush()
void write()
void write(byte[] b, int off, int len)
```

BufferedReader (extends Reader)

```
BufferedReader(Reader in)
void close()
int read()
int read(char[] c, int off, int len)
String readLine()
```

DataInputStream (extends FilterInputStream)

```
DataInputStream(InputStream in)
int read(byte[] b)
int read(byte[] b, int off, int len)
double readDouble()
int readInt()
```

DataOutputStream (extends FilterOutputStream)

```
void flush()
void write()
void write(byte[] b, int off, int len)
void writeDouble(double d)
void writeInt(int i)
```

File

```
File(String name)
String getName()
String getParent()
String getPath()
boolean isDirectory()
long lastModified()
long length()
```

FileInputStream (extends InputStream)

```
FileInputStream(File f)
FileInputStream(String s)
void close()
void read()
void read(byte[] b)
void read(byte[] b, int off, int len)
```

FileOutputStream (extends OutputStream)

```
FileOutputStream(File f)
FileOutputStream(String name)
void close()
void write(byte[] b)
void write(byte[] b, int off, int len)
void write(int b)
```

FileReader (extends InputStreamReader)

```
FileReader(File f)
FileReader(String name)
```

FileWriter (extends OutputStreamWriter)

```
FileWriter(File f)
FileWriter(String name)
```

InputStream

```
void close()
int read()
int read(byte[] b)
int read(byte[] b, int off, int len)
```

InputStreamReader (extends Reader)

```
InputStreamReader(InputStream in)
void close()
int read()
int read(char[] c, int off, int len)
```

ObjectInputStream (extends InputStream)

```
ObjectInputStream(InputStream in)
void close()
int read()
int read(byte[] b, int off, int len)
double readDouble()
int readInt()
Object readObject()
```

ObjectOutputStream (extends OutputStream)

```
ObjectOutputStream(OutputStream out)
void close()
void write(byte[] b)
void write(byte[] b, int off, int len)
void write(int data)
void writeDuble(double data)
void writeInt(int data)
void writeObject(Object obj)
```

PrintStream (extends FilterOutputStream)

```
PrintStream(OutputStream out)
void close()
void flush()
void print(boolean b)
void print(char c)
void print(char[] s)
void print(double d)
void print(float f)
void print(int i)
void print(long l)
void print(Object obj)
void print(String s)
void println(boolean b)
void println(char c)
void println(char[] s)
void println(double d)
void println(float f)
void println(int i)
void println(long l)
void println(Object obj)
void println(String s)
void write(byte[] b, int off, int len)
void write(int b)
```

PrintWriter (extends Writer)

```
PrintWriter(OutputStream out)
PrintWriter(OutputStream out, boolean autoFlush)
PrintWriter(Writer out)
PrintWriter(Writer out, boolean autoFlush)
void close()
void flush()
void print(boolean b)
void print(char c)
void print(char[] s)
void print(double d)
void print(float f)
void print(int i)
void print(long l)
void print(Object obj)
void print(String s)
void println(boolean b)
void println(char c)
void println(char[] s)
void println(double d)
void println(float f)
void println(int i)
void println(long l)
void println(Object obj)
void println(String s)
void write(char[] buf)
void write(char[] buf, int off, int len)
void write(int c)
void write(String s)
void write(String buf, int off, int len)
```

RandomAccessFile

```
RandomAccessFile(File file, String mode)
RandomAccessFile(String name, String mode)
void close()
long length()
int read()
int read(byte[] b)
int read(byte[] b, int off, int len)
double readDouble()
int readInt()
void seek(long pos)
void write(byte[] b)
void write(byte[] b, int off, int len)
void write(int b)
void wrtieDouble(double d)
void writeInt(int i)
```

FileNotFoundException (extends IOException)

```
FileNotFoundException(String s)
```

IOException (extends java.lang.Exception)

```
IOException(String s)
```

java.beans

BeanInfo

```
EventSetDescriptor[] getEventSetDescriptors()
Image getIcon(int iconKind)
MethodDescriptor[] getMethodDescriptors()
PropertyDescriptor[] getPropertyDescriptors()
```

PropertyChangeListener

```
void propertyChange(PropertyChangeEvent evt)
```

EventSetDescriptor

```
EventSetDescriptor(Class sourceClass,
  String eventSetName, Class listenerType,
  String listenerMethodName)
```

FeatureDescriptor

```
void setDisplayName(String displayName)
```

MethodDescriptor

```
MethodDescriptor(Method method)
```

PropertyChangeEvent

```
Object getNewValue()
```

PropertyChangeSupport

```
void firePropertyChange(String propertyName, int
  oldValue, int newValue)
void firePropertyChange(String propertyName,
  Object oldValue, Object newValue)
```

PropertyDescriptor

```
PropertyDescriptor
  (String propertyName, Class beanClass)
```

SimpleBeanInfo

```
EventSetDescriptor[] getEventSetDescriptors()
Image getIcon(int iconKind)
MethodDescriptor[] getMethodDescriptors()
PropertyDescriptor[] getPropertyDescriptors()
```

java.lang

Comparable

```
int compareTo(Object o)
```

Runnable

```
void run()
```

Class

```
Method getMethod(Stringname, class[] parameterTypes
```

Double (extends Number)

```
Double(double d)
Double(String s)
double doubleValue()
static double parseDouble(String s)
static Double valueOf(String s)
```

Integer (extends Number)

```
Integer(int value)
Integer(String s)
int intValue()
static int parseInt(String s)
static int parseInt(String s, int radix)
static String toBinaryString(int i)
static String toHexString(int i)
static String toOctalString(int i)
static Integer valueOf(String s)
static Integer valueOf(String s, int radix)
```

Math

```
static double abs(double a)
static float abs(float a)
static int abs(int a)
static long abs(long a)
static double ceil(double a)
static double cos(double a)
static double exp(double a)
static double floor(double a)
static double log(double a)
static double max(double a, double b)
static float max(float a, float b)
static int max(int a, int b)
static long max(long a, long b)
static double min(double a, double b)
static float min(float a, float b)
static int min(int a, int b)
static long min(long a, long b)
static double pow(double a, double b)
```

```
static double random()
static long round(double a)
static int round(float a)
static double sin(double a)
static double sqrt(double a)
static double tan(double a)
static double toDegrees(double angrad)
static double toRadians(double angdeg)
```

Object

```
boolean equals(Object obj)
int hashCode()
void notify()
void notifyAll()
String toString()
void wait()
```

String

```
String()
String(bytes[] b)
String(char[] c)
String(String s)
String(StringBuffer sb)
char charAt(int index)
int compareTo(Object o)
int compareTo(String anotherString)
int compareToIgnoreCase(String str)
String concat(String str)
static String copyValueOf(char[] data)
static String copyValueOf(char[] data, int offset, int count)
boolean endsWith(String suffix)
boolean equals(Object anObject)
boolean equalsIgnoreCase(String anotherString)
byte[] getBytes()
void getBytes
   (int srcBegin, int srcEnd, byte[] dst, int dstBegin)
byte[] getBytes(String enc)
void getChars
   (int srcBegin, int srcEnd, char[] dst, int dstBegin)
int hashCode()
int indexOf(int ch)
int indexOf(int ch, int fromIndex)
int indexOf(String str)
int indexOf(String str, int fromIndex)
int lastIndexOf(int ch)
int lastIndexOf(int ch, int fromIndex)
int lastIndexOf(String str)
int lastIndexOf(String str, int fromIndex)
int length()
```

```
String replace(char oldChar, char newChar)
boolean startsWith(String prefix)
boolean startsWith(String prefix, int toffset)
String substring(int beginIndex)
String substring(int beginIndex, int endIndex)
char[] toCharArray()
String toLowerCase()
String toString()
String toUpperCase()
String trim()
static String valueOf(boolean b)
static String valueOf(char c)
static String valueOf(char[] data)
static String valueOf(char[] data, int offset, int count)
static String valueOf(double d)
static String valueOf(float f)
static String valueOf(int i)
static String valueOf(long l)
static String valueOf(Object obj)
```

StringBuffer

```
StringBuffer()
StringBuffer(int len)
StringBuffer(String s)
StringBuffer append(boolean b)
StringBuffer append(char c)
StringBuffer append(char[] str)
StringBuffer append(char[] str, int offset, int len)
StringBuffer append(double d)
StringBuffer append(float f)
StringBuffer append(int i)
StringBuffer append(long l)
StringBuffer append(Object obj)
StringBuffer append(String str)
int capacity()
char charAt(int index)
StringBuffer delete(int start, int end)
StringBuffer deleteCharAt(int index)
void ensureCapacity(int minimumCapacity)
void getChars
   (int srcBegin, int srcEnd, char[] dst, int dstBegin)
StringBuffer insert(int offset, boolean b)
StringBuffer insert(int offset, char c)
StringBuffer insert(int offset, char[] str)
StringBuffer insert
   (int index, char[] str, int offset, int len)
StringBuffer insert(int offset, double d)
StringBuffer insert(int offset, float f)
StringBuffer insert(int offset, int i)
```

```
StringBuffer insert(int offset, long l)
StringBuffer insert(int offset, Object obj)
StringBuffer insert(int offset, String str)
int length()
StringBuffer replace(int start, int end, String str)
StringBuffer reverse()
void setCharAt(int index, char ch)
void setLength(int newLength)
String substring(int start)
String substring(int start, int end)
String toString()
```

System

```
static PrintStream err
static InputStream in
static PrintStream out
static void arraycopy
  (Object src, int src_pos, Object dst, int dst_pos)
static long currentTimeMillis()
static void exit(int status)
static void setSecutityManager(SecurityManager s)
```

Thread

```
Thread()
Thread(Runnable target)
Thread(Runnable target, String name)
Thread(String name)
static Thread currentThread()
String getName()
static void sleep(long millis)
static void sleep(long millis, int nanos)
void start()
```

Throwable

```
Throwable(String message)
String getMessage()
void printStackTrace()
```

ArrayIndexOutOfBoundsException (extends java.lang.IndexOutOfBoundsException)

```
ArrayIndexOutOfBounds(String message)
```

Exception (extends Throwable)

```
Exception(String message)
```

InterruptedException (extends Exception)

```
InterruptedException(String message)
```

NumberFormatException (extends java.lang.IllegalArgumentException)

```
NumberFormatException(String message)
```

RuntimeException (extends Exception)

```
RuntimeException(String message)
```

Error (extends Throwable)

```
Error(String message)
```

OutOfMemoryError (extends java.lang.VirtualMemoryError)

```
OutOfMemoryError(String message)
```

java.lang.reflect

Method

java.math

BigInteger (extends java.lang.Number)

```
BigInteger(String value)
BigInteger add(BigInteger value)
BigInteger divide(BigInteger value)
BigInteger gcd(BigInteger value)
BigInteger multiply(BigInteger value)
BigInteger remainder(BigInteger value)
BigInteger subtract(BigInteger value)
```

BigDecimal

java.net

ServerSocket

```
ServerSocket(int port)
Socket accept()
void close()
InetAddress getInetAddress()
```

Socket

```
Socket(String host, int port)
void close()
InetAddress getInetAddress()
InputStream getInputStream()
OutputStream getOutputStream()
```

URL

```
URL(String s)
String getHost()
String getPath()
int getPort()
String getProtocol()
URLConnection openConnection()
InputStream openStream()
```

URLConnection

```
int getContentLength()
String getContentType()
String getHeaderField(int n)
String getHeaderField(String name)
String getHeaderFieldKey(int n)
InputStream getInputStream()
String getRequestProperty(String key)
void setRequestProperty(String key, int value)
```

MalformedURLException (extends java.io.IOException)

```
MalformedURLException(String message)
```

ava.rmi

Remote

Naming

```
static Remote lookup(String name)
static void rebind(String name, Remote obj)
```

RMISecurityManager (extends java.lang.SecurityManager)

```
RMISecurityManager()
```

RemoteException (extends java.io.IOException)

```
String getMessage()
void printStackTrace()
```

java.rmi.server

UnicastRemoteObject (extends RemoteServer)

java.sql

Connection

```
void close()
void commit()
Statement createStatement()
DatabaseMetaData getMetaData()
PreparedStatement prepareStatement(String sql)
void rollback()
void setAutoCommit(boolean autoCommit)
```

DatabaseMetaData

```
ResultSet getColumns(String catalog, String schemaPattern,
String tableNamePattern, String columnNamePattern)
String getIdentifierQuoteString()
ResultSet getTables(String catalog, String schemaPattern,
String tableNamePattern, String[] types)
```

```
ResultSet getTypeInfo()
boolean supportsANSI92EntryLevelSQL()
boolean supportsANSI92FullSQL()
boolean supportsANSI92IntermediateSQL()
boolean supportsStoredProcedures()
boolean supportsTransactions()
```

PreparedStatement

```
ResultSet exceuteQuery()
int executeUpdate()
void setBigDecimal(int index, BigDecimal x)
void setDate(int index, Date x)
void setDouble(int index, double x)
void setInt(int index, int x)
void setString(int index, String x)
```

ResultSet

```
void close()
BigDecimal getBigDecimal(int columnIndex)
BigDecimal getBigDecimal(int columnIndex, int dig)
BigDecimal getBigDecimal(String columnName)
BigDecimal getBigDecimal(String columnName, int dg)
Date getDate(int columnIndex)
Date getDate(String columnName)
Date getDouble(int columnIndex)
Date getDouble(String columnName)
Date getInt(int columnIndex)
Date getInt(String columnName)
ResultSetMetaData getMetaData()
Date getString(int columnIndex)
Date getString(String columnName)
boolean next()
```

ResultSetMetaData

```
int getColumnCount()
String getColumnLabel(int column)
String getColumnName(int column)
String getColumnType(int column)
String getColumnTypeName(int column)
```

Statement

```
void close()
ResultSet exceuteQuery(String sql)
int executeUpdate(String sql)
```

Date (extends java.util.Date)

```
static Date valueOf(String s
```

DriverManager

```
static Connection getConnection(String url)
static Connection
getConnection(String url, String user, String password)
```

java.text

NumberFormat (extends java.text.Format)

```
String format(double number)
String format(long number)
static NumberFormat getCurrencyInstance()
static NumberFormat getInstance()
static NumberFormat getNumberInstance()
static NumberFormat getPercentInstance()
void setMaximumFractionDigits(int newValue)
void setMinimumFractionDigits(int newValue)
```

java.util

Collection

```
boolean add(Object o)
boolean addAll(Collection c)
void clear()
boolean contains(Object o)
boolean containsAll(Collection c)
boolean equals(Object o)
int hashCode()
boolean isEmpty()
Iterator iterator()
boolean remove(Object o)
boolean removeAll(Collection c)
boolean retainAll(Collection c)
int size()
Object[] toArray()
Object[] toArray(Object[] a)
```

Enumeration

```
boolean hasMoreElements()
Object nextElement()
```

Iterator

```
boolean hasNext()
Object next()
void remove()
```

List (extends Collection)

```
void add(int index, Object o)
boolean add(Object element)
boolean addAll(Collection c)
```

```
boolean addAll(int index, Collection c)
void clear()
boolean contains(Object o)
boolean containsAll(Collection c)
boolean equals(Object o)
Object get(int index)
int hashCode()
int indexOf(Object o)
boolean isEmpty()
Iterator iterator()
int lastIndexOf(Object o)
ListIterator listIterator()
ListIterator listIterator(int index)
Object remove(int index)
boolean remove(Object o)
boolean removeAll(Collection c)
boolean retainAll(Collection c)
Object set(int index, Object element)
int size()
List subList(int fromIndex, int toIndex)
Object[] toArray()
Object[] toArray(Object[] a)
```

ListIterator (extends Iterator)

```
void add(Object o)
boolean hasNext()
boolean hasPrevious()
Object next()
int nextIndex()
Object previous()
void remove()
void set(Object o)
```

Map

```
void clear()
boolean containsKey(Object key)
boolean containsValue(Object value)
Set entrySet()
boolean equals(Object o)
Object get(Object key)
int hashCode()
boolean isEmpty()
Set keySet()
Object put(Object key, Object value)
void putAll(Map t)
Object remove(Object key)
int size()
Collection values()
```

Map.Entry

```
boolean equals(Object o)
Object getKey()
Object getValue()
int hashCode()
Object setValue(Object value)
```

Set (extends Collection)

```
boolean add(Object o)
boolean addAll(Collection c)
void clear()
boolean contains(Object o)
boolean containsAll(Collection c)
boolean equals(Object o)
int hashCode()
boolean isEmpty()
Iterator iterator()
boolean remove(Object o)
boolean removeAll(Collection c)
boolean retainAll(Collection c)
int size()
Object[] toArray()
Object[] toArray(Object[] a)
```

SortedMap (extends Map)

```
Comparator comparator()
Object firstKey()
SortedMap headMap(Object toKey)
Object lastKey()
SortedMap subMap(Object fromKey, Object toKey)
SortedMap tailMap(Object fromKey)
```

SortedSet (extends Set)

```
Comparator comparator()
Object first()
SortedSet headSet(Object toElement)
Object last()
SortedSet subSet(Object fromElement, Object toElement)
SortedSet tailSet(Object fromElement)
```

ArrayList (extends java.util.AbstractList)

```
ArrayList()
ArrayList(Collection c)
ArrayList(int initialCapacity)
void add(int index, Object o)
boolean add(Object element)
boolean addAll(Collection c)
```

```
boolean addAll(int index, Collection c)
void clear()
Object clone()
boolean contains(Object o)
void ensureCapacity(int minCapacity)
Object get(int index)
int indexOf(Object o)
boolean isEmpty()
int lastIndexOf(Object o)
Object remove(int index)
Object set(int index, Object element)
int size()
Object[] toArray()
Object[] toArray(Object[] a)
void trimToSize()
```

Collections

```
static int binarySearch(List list, Object key)
static int binarySearch(List list, Object key, Comparator c)
static void copy(List dest, List src)
static Enumeration enumeration(Collection c)
static void fill(List list, Object o)
static Object max(Collection coll)
static Object max(Collection coll, Comparator comp)
static Object min(Collection coll)
static Object min(Collection coll, Comparator comp)
static List nCopies(int n, Object o)
static void reverse(List l)
static Comparator reverseOrder()
static void shuffle(List list)
static void shuffle(List list, Random rnd)
static void sort(List list)
static void sort(List list, Comparator c)
```

Date

```
Date()
```

Event Object

```
Object getSource()
```

HashMap (extends AbstractMap)

```
HashMap()
HashMap(int initialCapacity)
HashMap(int initialCapacity, float loadFactor)
HashMap(Map m)
void clear()
Object clone()
boolean containsKey(Object key)
boolean containsValue(Object value)
Set entrySet()
```

```
Object get(Object key)
boolean isEmpty()
Set keySet()
Object put(Object key, Object value)
void putAll(Map t)
Object remove(Object key)
int size()
Collection values()
```

HashSet (extends AbstractSet)

```
HashSet()
HashSet(Collection c)
HashSet(int initialCapacity)
HashSet(int initialCapacity, float loadFactor)
boolean add(Object o)
void clear()
Object clone()
boolean contains(Object o)
boolean isEmpty()
Iterator iterator()
boolean remove(Object o)
int size()
```

Hashtable (extends java.util.Dictionary)

```
Hashtable()
Hashtable(int initialCapacity)
Hashtable(int initialCapacity, float loadFactor)
Hashtable(Map m)
void clear()
Object clone()
boolean contains(Object value)
boolean containsKey(Object key)
boolean containsValue(Object value)
Enumeration elements()
Set entrySet()
boolean equals(Object o)
Object get(Object key)
int hashCode()
boolean isEmpty()
Enumeration keys()
Set keySet()
Object put(Object key, Object value)
void putAll(Map t)
Object remove(Object key)
int size()
Collection values()
```

LinkedList (extends java.util.AbstractSequentialList)

```
LinkedList()
LinkedList(Collection c)
```

```
void add(int index, Object o)
boolean add(Object element)
boolean addAll(Collection c)
boolean addAll(int index, Collection c)
void addFirst(Object o)
void addLast(Object o)
void clear()
Object clone()
boolean contains(Object o)
Object get(int index)
Object getFirst()
Object getLast()
int indexOf(Object o
int lastIndexOf(Object o)
ListIterator listIterator(int index)
Object remove(int index)
boolean remove(Object o)
Object removeFirst()
Object removeLast()
Object set(int index, Object element)
int size()
Object[] toArray()
Object[] toArray(Object[] a)
```

Random

```
Random()
int nextInt(int n)
```

StringTokenizer

```
StringTokenizer(String str)
StringTokenizer(String str, String delim)
int countTokens()
boolean hasMoreElements()
boolean hasMoreTokens()
Object nextElement()
String nextToken()
String nextToken(String delim)
```

TreeMap (implements AbstractMap)

```
TreeMap()
TreeMap(Map m)
TreeMap(SortedMap m)
void clear()
Object clone()
boolean containsKey(Object key)
boolean containsValue(Object value)
Set entrySet()
Object firstKey()
Object get(Object key)
```

```
SortedMap headMap(Object toKey)
Set keySet()
Object lastKey()
Object put(Object key, Object value)
void putAll(Map t)
Object remove(Object key)
int size()
SortedMap subMap(Object fromKey, Object toKey)
SortedMap tailMap(Object fromKey)
Collection values()
```

TreeSet (extends AbstractSet)

```
TreeSet()
TreeSet(Collection m)
TreeSet(SortedSet m)
boolean add(Object o)
boolean addAll(Collection c)
void clear()
Object clone()
Comparator comparator()
boolean contains(Object o)
Object first()
SortedSet headSet(Object toElement)
boolean isEmpty()
Iterator iterator()
Object last()
boolean remove(Object o)
int size()
SortedSet subSet(Object fromElement, Object toElement)
SortedSet tailSet(Object fromElement)
```

Vector (extends AbstractList)

```
Vector()
Vector(Collection c)
Vector(int initialCapacity)
Vector(int initialCapacity, int capacityIncrement)
void add(int index, Object element)
boolean add(Object o)
boolean addAll(Collection c)
boolean addAll(int index, Collection c)
void addElement(Object obj)
int capacity()
void clear()
Object clone()
boolean contains(Object elem)
boolean containsAll(Collection c)
void copyInto(Object[] anArray)
Object elementAt(int index)
Enumeration elements()
void ensureCapacity(int minCapacity)
```

```
boolean equals(Object o)
Object firstElement()
Object get(int index)
int hashCode()
int indexOf(Object elem)
int indexOf(Object elem, int index)
void insertElementAt(Object obj, int index)
boolean isEmpty()
Object lastElement()
int lastIndexOf(Object elem)
int lastIndexOf(Object elem, int index)
Object remove(int index)
boolean remove(Object o)
boolean removeAll(Collection c)
void removeAllElements()
boolean removeElement(Object obj)
void removeElementAt(int index)
boolean retainAll(Collection c)
Object set(int index, Object element)
void setElementAt(Object obj, int index)
void setSize(int newSize)
int size()
List subList(int fromIndex, int toIndex)
Object[] toArray()
Object[] toArray(Object[] a)
String toString()
void trimToSize()
```

javax.media

Clock

```
void setMediaTime(Time now)
void stop()
```

Controller (extends Clock, javax.media.Duration)

```
void addControllerListener(ControllerListener l)
void close()
void deallocate()
```

ControllerListener

```
void controllerUpdate(ControllerEvent e)
```

Player (extends javax.media.MediaHandler, Controller)

```
Component getControlPanelComponent()
Component getVisualComponent()
void start()
```

ControllerEvent (extends javax.media.MediaEvent)

EndOfMediaEvent (extends javax.media.StopEvent)

Manager

```
static Player createPlayer(URL sourceURL)
```

RealizeCompleteEvent (extends java.media.TransitionEvent)

Time

```
Time(double seconds)
Time(long nanoseconds)
```

avax.servlet

ServletRequest

```
String getParameter(String name)
String[] getParameterValues(String name)
```

ServletResponse

```
PrintWriter getWriter()
void setContentType(String type)
```

GenericServlet

```
void init()
abstract void
service(ServletRequest req, ServletResponse res)
```

ServletException (extends java.lang.Exception)

javax.servlet.http

HttpServletRequest (extends javax.servlet.ServletRequest)

```
HttpSession getSession(boolean create)
```

HttpServletResponse (extends javax.servlet.ServletResponse)

HttpSession

```
Object getAttribute(String name)
Object getValue(String name)
void putValue(String name, Object value)
void setAttribute(String name, Object value)
```

HttpServlet (extends javax.servlet.GenericServlet)

```
void init()
void doGet(HttpServletRequest req, HttpServletResponse res)
void doPost(HttpServletRequest req, HttpServletResponse res)
```

javax.swing

Icon

```
int getIconHeight()
int getIconWidth()
void paintIcon(Component c, Graphics g, int x, int y)
```

ListSelectionModel

```
static int MULTIPLE_INTERVAL_SELECTION
static int SINGLE_INTERVAL_SELECTION
static int SINGLE_SELECTION
void addListSelectionListener(addListSelectionListener l)
int getMinSelectionIndex()
boolean getValueIsAdjusting()
void setSelectionMode(int selectionMode)
```

AbstractButton (extends JComponent)

```
void addActionListener(ActionListener l)
void addItemListener(ItemListener l)
String getActionCommand()
String getText()
void setActionCommand(String actionCommand)
void setEnabled(boolean b)
void setMnemonic(int mnemonic)
void setPressedIcon(Icon pressedIcon)
void setRolloverIcon(Icon rolloverIcon)
void setText(String selectedText)
```

ButtonGroup

```
ButtonGroup()
void add(AbstractButton b)
```

ImageIcon

```
ImageIcon(Image image)
ImageIcon(String filename)
ImageIcon(URL location)
int getIconHeight()
int getIconWidth()
Image getImage()
void paintIcon(Component c, Graphics g, int x, int y)
```

JApplet (extends JPanel)

```
Container getContentPane()
void setJMenuBar(JMenuBar bar)
void setLayout(LayoutManager manager)
void update(Graphics g)
```

JButton (extends AbstractButton)

```
JButton()
JButton(Icon icon)
JButton(String text)
JButton(String text, Icon icon)
```

JCheckBox (extends JToggleButton)

```
JCheckBox()
JCheckBox(Icon icon)
JCheckBox(Icon icon, boolean selected)
JCheckBox(String text)
JCheckBox(String text, boolean selected)
JCheckBox(String text, Icon icon)
JCheckBox(String text, Icon icon, boolean selected)
```

JColorChooser (extends JComponent)

```
JColorChooser()
JColorChooser(Color initialColor)
Color getColor()
```

JComboBox (extends JComponent)

```
JComboBox()
JComboBox(Object[] items)
JComboBox(Vector items)
void addActionListenr(ActionListener l)
void addItem(Object o)
void addItemListenr(ItemListener l)
String getActionCommand()
int getItemCount()
int getSelectedIndex()
int getSelectedItem()
void setSelectedIndex(int index)
```

JComponent (extends java.awt.Container)

```
Graphics getGraphics()
int getHeight()
int getWidth()
void paint(Graphics g)
protected void paintComponent(Graphics g)
void requestFocus()
void setBackground(Color c)
void setEnabled(boolean enabled)
void setFont(Font font)
void setForeground(Color c)
void setPreferredSize(Dimension d)
void setToolTipText(String text)
void setVisible(boolean b)
void update(Graphics g)
```

JFileChooser (extends JComponent)

```
static int APPROVE_OPTION
static int CANCEL_OPTION
JFileChooser()
JFileChooser(String directoryPath)
void addActionListenr(ActionListener l)
void approveSelection()
void cancelSelection()
File getSelectedFile()
```

JFrame (extends java.awt.Frame)

```
JFrame(String title)
Container getContentPane()
void setMenuBar(JMenuBar bar)
void setLayout(LayoutManager manager)
void update(Graphics g)
```

JLabel (extends JComponent)

```
JLabel(Icon icon)
JLabel(String text)
```

JList (extends JComponent)

```
JList()
JList(Object[] listData)
JList(Vector listData)
void addListSelectionListener(ListSelectionListener l)
int getSelectedIndex()
int[] getSlelectedIndices()
Object getSelectedValue()
Object[] getSelectedValues()
boolean getValueIs Adjusting()
void setSelectedIndex(int index)
void setSelectedMode(int selectionMode)
```

JMenu (extends JMenuItem)

```
JMenu(String s)
Component add(Component c)
JMenuItem add(JMenuItem menuItem)
JMenuItem getItem(int pos)
int getItemCount()
JMenuItem insert(JMenuItem menuItem, int pos)
```

JMenuBar (extends JComponent)

```
JMenuBar()
JMenu add(JMenu menu)
```

JMenuItem (extends AbstractButton)

```
JMenuItem()
JMenuItem(Icon icon)
```

```
JMenuItem(String text)
JMenuItem(String text, Icon icon)
JMenuItem(String text, int mnemonic)
void setEnabled(boolean b)
```

JOptionPane (extends JComponent)

```
static int CANCEL_OPTION
static int ERROR_MESSAGE
static int INFORMATION_MESSAGE
static int NO_OPTION
static int OK_CANCEL_OPTION
static int OK_OPTION
static int QUESTION_MESSAGE
static int WARNING_MESSAGE
static int YES_NO_CANCEL_OPTION
static int YES_NO_OPTION
static int YES_OPTION
static int showConfirmDialog(Component parent, Object msg)
static int showInputDialog(Component parent, Object msg)
static int showConfirmDialog(Object msg)
static int showMessageDialog(Component parent, Object msg)
static int showOptionDialog(Component parentComponent,
Object message, String title, int optionType,
int messageType, Icon icon, Object[] options,
Object initialValue)
```

JPanel (extends JComponent)

```
JPanel()
```

JRadioButton (extends JToggleButton)

```
JRadioButton()
JRadioButton(Icon icon)
JRadioButton(Icon icon, boolean selected)
JRadioButton(String text)
JRadioButton(String text, boolean selected)
JRadioButton(String text, Icon icon)
JRadioButton(String text, Icon icon, boolean selected)
```

JScrollPane (extends JComponent)

```
JScrollPane(Component view)
```

JTabbedPane (extends JComponent)

```
JTabbedPane()
void addTab(String title, Component component)
void addTab(String title, Icon icon, Component component)
void addTab
(String title, Icon icon, Component component, String tip)
```

JTable (extends JComponent)

```
JTable(Object[][] rowData, Object[] columnNames)
JTable(TableModel model)
JTable(Vector rowData, Vector columnNames)
void setValueAt(Object value, int row, int col)
```

JTextArea (extends JTextComponent)

```
JTextArea()
JTextArea(int rows, int columns)
JTextArea(String text)
JTextArea(String text, int rows, int columns)
void append(String text)
void insert(String text, int position)
void setFont(Font f)
```

JTextField (extends JTextComponent)

```
JTextField()
JTextField(int columns)
JTextField(String text)
JTextField(String text, int columns)
void addActionListener(ActionListener l)
void setActionCommand(String command)
void setFont(Font f)
```

JToggleButton (extends AbstractButton)

UIManager

```
static UIManager.LookAndFeelInfo[] getInstalledLookAndFeels()
static void setLookAndFeel(String className)
```

UIManager.LookAndFeelInfo

```
String getClassName()
String getName()
```

javax.swing.event

ListSelectionListener

```
void valueChanged(ListSelectionEvent e)
```

ListSelectionEvent (extends java.util.EventObject)

```
boolean getValueIsAdjusting()
```

javax.swing.table

TableModel

```
void addTableModelListener(TableModelListener l)
Class getColumnClass(int columnIndex)
int getColumnCount()
String getColumnName(int columnIndex)
```

```
int getRowCount()
Object getValueAt(int rowIndex, int columnIndex)
boolean isCellEditable(int rowIndex, int columnIndex)
void removeTableModelListener(TableModelListener l)
void setValueAt(Object aValue, int rowIndex, int columnIndex)
```

AbstractTableModel

```
String getColumnName(int column)
void setValueAt(Object aValue, int rowIndex, int columnIndex)
```

javax.xml.parsers

DocumentBuilder

```
Document parse(File f)
```

DocumentBuilderFactory

```
abstract DocumentBuilder newDocumentBuilder ()
static DocumentBuilderFactory newInstance()
void setValidating(boolean validating)
```

SAXParser

```
abstract XMLReader getXMLReader()
```

SAXParserFactory

```
static SAXParserFactory newInstance()
abstract SAXParser newSAXParser()
void setValidating(boolean validating)
```

javax.xml.transform

Transformer

```
abstract void transform
(StreamSource xml source, StreamResult outputTarget)
```

TransformerFactory

```
static TransformerFactory newInstance()
abstract Transformer newTransformer(Source source)
```

javax.xml.transform.stream

StreamResult

```
StreamResult(File f)
```

StreamSource

```
StreamSource(File f)
```

org.apache.soap

Fault

```
String getFaultCode()
String getFaultString()
```

org.apache.soap.rpc

Call (extends RPCMessage)

```
Call()
Response invoke(URL url, String SOAPActionURI)
```

Parameter

```
Parameter(String name, Class type,
Object value, String encodingStyleURI)
Object getValue()
```

Response (extends RPCMessage)

```
boolean generatedFault()
Fault getFault()
Parameter getReturnValue()
```

RPCMessage

```
String setEncodingStyleURI(String uri)
void setMethodName(String name)
void setParams(Vector params)
void setTargetObjectURI(String uri)
```

org.xml.sax

Attributes

```
int getLength()
String getLocalName(int index)
String getValue(int index)
```

XMLReader

```
parse
setContentHandler
```

InputSource

```
InputSource(Reader characterStream)
```

org.xml.sax.helpers

DefaultHandler

```
void characters(char[] ch, int start, int length)
void endDocument()
void endElement(String uri, String localName, String qName)
void startDocument()
void startElement(String uri, String localName,
String qName, Attributes attributes)
```

org.w3c.dom

Document (extends org.w3c.dom.Node)

```
Element createElement(String name)
Text createTextNode(String data)
Element getDocumentElement()
```

Element (extends org.w3c.dom.Node)

```
String getAttribute(String name)
NodeList getElementsByTagName(String name)
```

Node

```
Node appendChild(Node child)
Node getFirstChild()
String getNodeValue()
void normalize()
```

NodeList

```
int getLength()
Node item(int index)
```

Text (extends org.w3c.dom.CharacterData)

```
sun.jdbc.odbc
```

JdbcOdbcDriver

```
JdbcOdbcDriver()
```

Answers to Selected Exercises

Test Your Understanding Exercises

Chapter 1

3. 20 3500
   21 4200
   22 2300
4. 15 3950 5600 1234
5. A compiler.
6. An interpreter.
7. C (and C++)
9. The Java Virtual Machine
10. Byte code can run on any machine that has a Java Virtual Machine.
14. Many answers are possible. Each represents a step-by-step procedure. For example,

    Use a hose to rinse the car.
    Put some car wash liquid in a bucket.
    Fill the bucket with water.
    Repeatedly dip a soft cloth in the water and use it to wash a portion of the car.
    Rinse off the car.
    Use clean cloths to dry the car.
    Polish the trim and hub caps.
    Clean up.

15. Many answers are possible. Each represents responses to external events as well as internally generated chores. For example,

    !!! It's late.
    Go to sleep.
    !!! Alarm rings signaling a fire.
    Throw on some clothes.
    Slide down the fire pole.
    Drive fire engines to the fire.
    Execute put out fire procedure.
    Return to station.
    !!! It's time for breakfast.
    Execute make breakfast procedure.
    !!! Alarm rings signaling a medical emergency.
    Drive paramedic truck to the scene of the emergency.
    Execute paramedic procedures.
    Return to station.

17. A puppet show is more analogous to procedural programming. The puppeteer controls all the actions and speech of the puppets, the way that the procedural logic manipulates the data. In contrast, in a stage play each is responsible for his or her own lines, just as objects contain their own methods to meet their responsibilities, acting on their private data.

19. One possibility is:

    The agent asks the customer to select a car.
    The customer asks the agent to provide a mid-size convertible.
    The agent asks the customer to specify a rental period.
    The customer tells the agent that the rental is for one week.
    The agent checks the computer system for a mid-size convertible.
    The computer checks the inventory for a mid-size convertible.
    The inventory shows a mid-size convertible is available.
    The computer system checks the reservations for a conflict.
    The reservations indicates no conflict.
    The database tells the agent that such a car is available.
    The agent requests a license and credit card from the customer.
    The customer provides a license and a credit card.
    The agent updates the system.
    The system updates the inventory.
    The agent provides the car to the customer.

    Agent
    Accept request for car.
    Accept result of inquiry to system.

Customer
  Provide rental type.
  Provide license and credit card. System
  Accept request for rental.
  Accept update.
Inventory
  Accept request for car availability.
  Accept update.
Reservation List
  Accept request for conflict check

Chapter 2

1. a, b, f, g, j, and k are valid. c, d, e use invalid characters. h starts with a digit, i is a keyword.

3.
```
public Vending1() {
    quarters =10;
    candyBars = 10;
}
```

5. a. `Vending1 v = new Vending1(30,20);`
   b. `String result = v.selectCandy();`

7. Inside a method or a block (enclosed in curly braces { })

9. Numbers 12 and 5

```
a + b = 17        a - b = 7
a * b = 60        a / b = 2        a % b = 2
```

10. a. 5 b. 3 c. 4 d. -4 e. -305 f. 15 g. -1 h. -1

11. a + b = 176 is the output because Java concatenates "a + b = " and "17" and then concatenates "6".

13.
```
a+7*b = 28
c/a + 4 = 4
c-a % b-a = -10

a+(7*b) = 28
(c/a) + 4 = 4
(c-(a%b))-a = -10

(a+7)*b = 42
c/(a + 4) = 0
(c-a) % (b-a) = -1
```

14. a. 4 b. -19 c. 4 d. 9 e. -2 f. 0 g. 8 h. -3 i. 1

15. a. `x+(w/2)` c. `y+(w%2)` e. `(x*z)/y` g. `(y*z)-(z/x)` i. `(14%w)%y`

17. a. 38 b. -44 c. 8 d. 4 e. -2

19. a. 5 b. 13 c. 28 d. 1 e. 2 f. 12

21. `java vend.Vending2`

23. a. `myAgeIs` b. **int** c. `myAge` d. **int**
e. `int myAge = myAgeIs(55);`

25. Replace the `main` method code with:

```
Precedence test = new Precedence();
String input = JOptionPane.showInputDialog("Enter a");
int a = Integer.parseInt(input);
input = JOptionPane.showInputDialog("Enter b");
int b = Integer.parseInt(input);
input = JOptionPane.showInputDialog("Enter c");
int c = Integer.parseInt(input);
test.noParen(a,b,c);
test.sameParen(a,b,c);
test.changeParen(a,b,c);
```

27. `worker.washCar(myCar)`

28. `public void paint(Graphics g)`

Chapter 3

1. a. `234 < 52` b. `435 != 87` c. `-12 == -12` d. `76 >= 54`
2. a. true b. true c. false
3. The left operand is a boolean value.
4. a. true b. true c. false d. true
5. `x=5` assigns 5 to x. `x==5` tests whether x is equal to 5.
6. There must be no space between the two characters in the `>=` operator.
7. a, b, and c. `if (x == 12) y += 7;`
8. a. block `{z=7; z=5}` b. parentheses `(y>5)` c. braces `{s=y+7; z=s-2;}`
9. a. Indent `z += 5;` several spaces.
10. a.

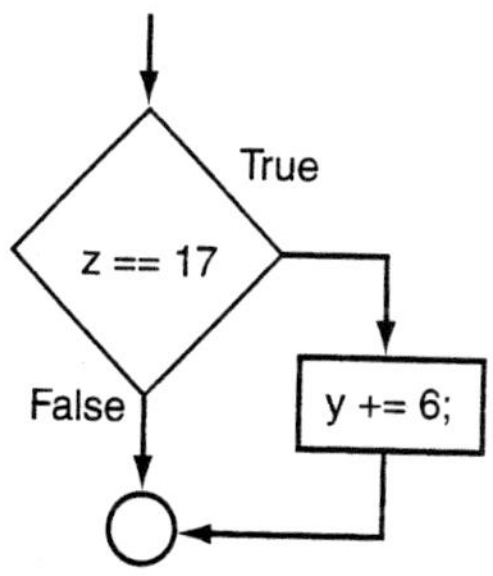

11. a.

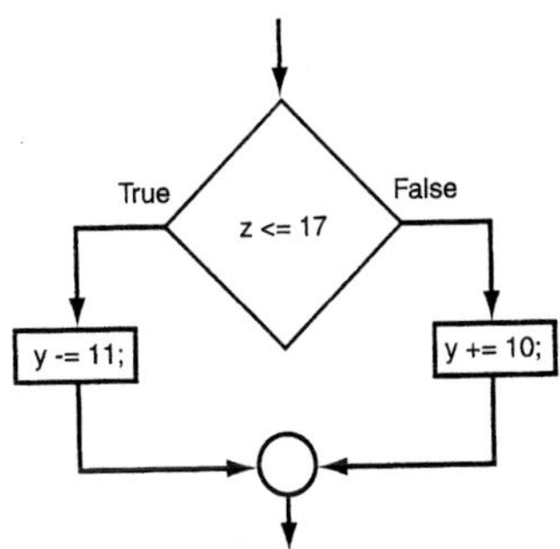

13. a. `3.4522` b. `-29876.5` c. `9876.5` d. `4.35`
14. a. `8.93454e2` b. `3.45722e-4` c. `9.8761234e7` d. `9.0909e-2`
15. `a` and `c`
16. a. `2.5` b. `2`
17. a. `3456.789` b. `2.3456E-6` c. `.09876543`
    d. `1.234567890987E9` e. `-234567.765432`
18. a. correct b. correct c. incorrect
19. a. `(double)72+37.5` b. `23.28/(double)7` c. `double d = (double)874;`
20. a. `2` b. `0` c. `4`
21. a. `}` should be `)` b. test condition must be `boolean` valued
    c. `=!` should be `!=`
22. a. total = 0, count = 0, quantity = 4, `0<4` is true, score = 95, total = 95, count = 1, `1<4` is true, score = 46, total = 139, count = 2, `2<4` is true, score = 68, total = 207, count = 3, `3<4` is true, score = 79, total = 286, count = 4, `4<4` is false. The total of 4 scores is 286.
23. a. does not terminate b. terminates
24. a.

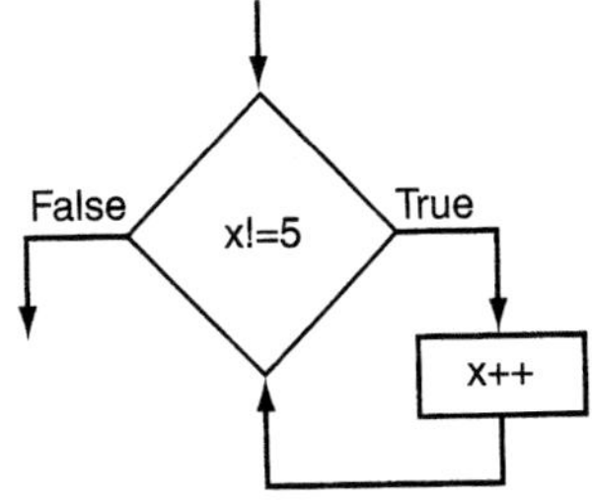

25. Look up a number in the telephone directory. (Item 1)

 Refining Item 1.
 Set start to first page.
 Set end to last page.
 while(listing not found and start <= end) {
 Open the directory to a page between start and end.
 Check for listing. (Item 2)
 }

 Refining Item 2.
 if (listing after current page){
 set start to the page after the current page
 else if (listing before current page)
 set end to the page before the current page
 else display listing

27. Read 49.23, max = 49.23, 49.23 is nonnegative, read 16.789, `16.789 < 49.23`, 16.789 is non-negative, read 92.145, `92.145 > 49.23`, max = 92.145, 92.145 is nonnegative. read 32.7, `32.7< 92.145`, 32.7 is nonnegative, read -1, `-1 < 92.145`, -1 is negative, The max is 92.145.

29 . Find the maximum and the minimum of numbers input by the user. (Item 1)

 Refining item 1.
 Read the quantity of numbers.
 Read first number.
 Set max to first number.
 Set min to first number.
 Set count to one.
 while (count < quantity)
 Process the rest of the numbers. (Item 2)
 Display the maximum and minimum.

 Refining Item 2.
 Read the next number.
 if (next number < min) set min to next number
 else if (next number > max) set max to next number.

31. 1860

33. `g.drawLine(3,5,15,5);`

35. `g.drawRect(30,60,50,50);`

37. `g.drawArc(100,50,200,100,90,120);`

Chapter 4

1. Many correct answers are possible, for example
 a. `x=2, y=7` b. `x=0, y = any integer`
 c. `x = 20, y = any integer` d. `x=11, y =0`

3. Many correct answer are possible, for example
   a. 3,false b. 3,true c. 13,true d. 3,false

5. Many correct answers are possible, for example
   a. 3 b. 12 c. 3 d. 3

7. a. `a>1 || c==5` b. `x<y+5 && y>2` c. `!(x>2 || y!=8)`

9.
```
if (amount >= 1 && amount <= 99) System.out.println("Thanks Contributor");
else if (amount >+ 100 && amount < 499)
  System.out.println("Thanks Supporter");
else if (amount >= 500 && amount <= 999)
  System.out.println("Thanks Patron");
else if (amount >= 1000) System.out.println("Thanks Benefactor");
else System.out.println("Please contribute to out charity");
```

11. a. 8 b. 7 c. 6 d. 7

13. a. 9 b. 6 c. 7 d. 9 e. 8 f. 9 g. 9

15. a. 9 b. 7 c. 9 d. 7 e. 9 f. 9 g. 9

17. `for(int i = 1; i <= 10; i++) System.out.println(i);`

19. `for(int i=9; i>=3; i--) System.out.println(i);`

21. 28 23. 26 25. 55 27. 0 29. 72

31. a. I like

    to write Java programs.

    b. Ali Baba said, "Open, Sesame!"

    c. 67845

    d. Find 3\4 of 24

33. 31

35. a. `Math.pow(7,4)` b. `Math.sqrt(43.0)`
    c. `Math.max(476.22,-608.90)` d. `Math.min(58.43,6.32*8.87)`
    e. `Math.abs(-65.234)` f. `Math.floor(-43.99)`

37. `Math.PI * r * r`

39. Compute `Math.floor(1 + 6*Math.random())` to get a random integer from 1 to 6.

41.
```
do {
  System.out.println();
  System.out.println("Choose from the following list");
  System.out.println("1. Convert from British pounds to US dollars");
  System.out.println("2. Convert from US dollars to British pounds");
  System.out.println("3. Quit");
  int choice = Io.readInt("Enter your choice, 1, 2 or 3");
    switch (choice) {
```

```
        case 1:
          PoundsToDollars();
          break;
        case 2:
          DollarsToPounds();
          break;
        case 3: System.out.println("Bye, Have a nice day");
      }
    } while (choice != 3);
```

43.
```
public class ConvertMoney {
  public static void DollarsToPounds {
    System.out.println("Converting from US dollars to British pounds.");
  }
  public static void PoundsToDollars {
    System.out.println("Converting from British pounds to US dollars");
  }
  public static void main(String [] args) {
    int choice;
      do {
        System.out.println();
        System.out.println("Choose from the following list");
        System.out.println("1. Convert from British pounds to US dollars");
        System.out.println("2. Convert from US dollars to British pounds");
        System.out.println("3. Quit");
        choice = Io.readInt("Enter your choice, 1, 2 or 3");     // Note 3
        switch (choice) {
          case 1:
            DollarsToPounds();
            break;
          case 2:
            PoundsToDollars();
            break;
          case 3: System.out.println("Bye, Have a nice day");
        }
      } while (choice != 3);
  }
}
```

Chapter 5

1. a. 27 b. h c. 2 d. 10 e. three f. THE THREE DID FEED THE DEER
3. a. negative b. positive c. zero
5. We declare instance variables outside of any method. Example 2.9 uses the instance variable `balance`.
7. `null`
9. The `BankAccount` constructor with no arguments.
11. `TestBankAccount.java`:12: Variable balance in class `BankAccount` not accessible from class `TestBankAccount`.

13. Not allowed, since there is already a constructor with no arguments.

15. After the `serve burger` arrow add a `take burger` arrow from `aWaiter` to `aCustomer`. Similarly, add a `take soda` arrow after `serve soda`, and add a `take fries` arrow after `serve fries`.

17. Address myAddress = new Address(street, city, state, zip) where

    String street = 123 Main St.
    String city = Hometown
    String state = CA
    String zip = 12345

Chapter 6

1. Hypertext Transer Protocol (HTTP)

3. Hypertext Markup Language (HTML)

5. To link to another document.

9. The upper left corner.

11. Font f = new Font("Monospaced", Font.ITALIC, 30);

13. `g.drawString(s,175,h)` where h is the vertical position of the string.

15. `new Color(0,0,255);`

17.
```
int red = Color.black.getRed();
int green = Color.black.getGreen();
int blue = Color.black.getBlue();
```

19.
```
public void aroundBlock(Drivable d) {
    d.start();
    d.accelerate();
    d.turn(Drivable.RIGHT);
    d.turn(Drivable.RIGHT);
    d.turn(Drivable.RIGHT);
    d.turn(Drivable.RIGHT);
    d.decelerate();
    d.stop();
}
```

21. Each customer implements the TicketListener interface which contains the `concertComng` method.

23. java.awt.Component

25. Every user-defined applet extends Applet, found in the `java.applet` package.

27. Component, Button, List, Checkbox, Container, Panel, and Applet.

Chapter 7

1. From left to right and top to bottom. By default components are centered when they do not fill the entire last row.

3. The canvas has a default size of `0x0` so we do not see it.

5. The extension is:

   The user presses the `Clear` button.
   The `Clear` button sends an action event as an argument to the canvas' `actionPerformed` method.
   The canvas' `actionPerformed` method saves the label of the button which the user pressed.
   The canvas' `actionPerformed` method calls the `repaint` method, which asks Java to schedule a call the `update` method to redraw the canvas.
   Java calls the `update` method of the canvas.
   The canvas' `update` method clears the screen and calls the `paint` method.
   The canvas' `paint` method uses the button's label to determine that the `Clear` button was pressed, and returns, taking no action.

7. The applet registers the canvas to listen for presses of the `Draw` button.

   The user selects the color green.
   The user selects the square shape.
   The user presses the `Draw` button.
   The `Draw` button sends an action event as an argument to the canvas' `actionPerformed` method.
   The canvas' `actionPerformed` method calls the `repaint` method, which asks Java to schedule a call the `update` method to redraw the canvas.
   The `update` method (inherited from `Component`) clears the screen and calls the `paint` method.
   The `paint` method sets the color to the selected color, green, and draws the selected square shape.

9. Change the arrays `colorName` and `theColor` to include the four additional colors.

11. The flow layout always respects the preferred sizes of the components it is laying out. The grid layout never respects the preferred sizes of its components. It always makes the component fill the entire cell it is in.

13. String is immutable but a StringBuffer object may change.

15. A TextField hold a single line of text while a TextArea

17. The result is the same. The overall row weight is the maximum of the weights for each component in that row, so giving b1 a `weighty` of 1.0 and b2 a `weighty` of 0.0 is the same as the original in which these weights were reversed.

19. Because `gridx` remains equal to 1, the remaining buttons appear in the same column, below b4. Since b6 has a `weightx` of 1.0 and the other buttons have a `weightx` of 0.0, the second column, containing b6, gets all the extra space.

Chapter 8

1.
```
int[] intArray = {37,44,68,-12};
intArray[1] = 55;
```

3.
```
char[] charArray = {'s','y','t','c','v','w'};
```

5.
```
21 31 41 51 61 71
L              R
71 31 41 51 61 21
   L        R
71 61 41 51 31 21
      L  R
72 61 51 41 31 21
      R  L
```

7. a. `intArray`

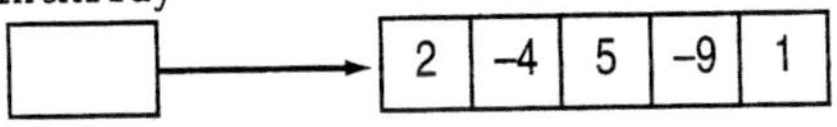

2	–4	5	–9	1

b. 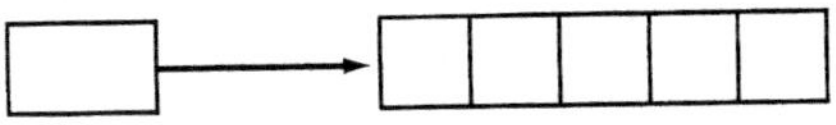 `charArray`

c. `doubleArray` → null

9.
```
int[] b = new int[a.length];
for(int i=0; i<a.length, i++)b[i]=a[i];
```

11. `display(myArray);`

13. `reverse(myArray);`

15. `(int)(450*Math.random()) + 50;`

17. `int[][] results = {{55,66,87,76},{86,92,88,95}};`

19. a. b b. x c. w d. c

21. loop, stopping when item i >= item i-1 or index = 0 {
interchange item i and item i-1;
decrease i by 1;
}

23.
```
                52 38  6 97  3 41 67 44 15
Insert   38     38 52  6 97  3 41 67 44 15
Insert   6      38  6 52 97  3 41 67 44 15
                 6 38 52 97  3 41 67 44 15
Insert   97
Insert   3       6 38 52  3 97 41 67 44 15
                 6 38  3 53 97 41 67 44 15
                 6  3 38 53 97 41 67 44 15
                 3  6 38 53 97 41 67 44 15
Insert   41      3  6 38 53 41 97 67 44 15
                 3  6 38 41 53 97 67 44 15
Insert   67      3  6 38 41 53 67 97 44 15
Insert   44      3  6 38 41 53 67 44 97 15
                 3  6 38 41 53 44 67 97 15
                 3  6 38 41 44 53 67 97 15
```

```
Insert      15     3  6 38 41 44 53 67 15 97
                   3  6 38 41 44 53 15 67 97
                   3  6 38 41 44 15 53 67 97
                   3  6 38 41 15 44 53 67 97
                   3  6 38 15 41 44 53 67 97
                   3  6 15 38 41 44 53 67 97
```

Chapter 9

1. a. BankAccount b. Object c. Object d. Object e. BankAccount
3. CheckingAccount c = new CheckingAccount(1500.0, 0.35);
5. Overloading. To override, the method must have exactly the same parameters as the method of the same name in the superclass. Here we added a boolean parameter not present in the superclass method.
7. c
9. Yes, because the class is still declared using the abstract keyword.
11. `package stuff;`
13. Call `stuff.GoodStuff.doStuff();`
15. It must be public, because we use it outside of the `java.awt` package. A non-public class would be available only within `java.awt`.
17. We can only use `get4()` in the class `A` in which it is declared. We can use `get2()` anywhere in the package `visibility`.
19. The user asks the teller to accept an ATM card.
    The teller asks the user to enter a PIN.
    The user asks the teller to accept a PIN.
    The teller asks the user to select a transaction type.
    The user asks the teller to accept a withdraw.
    The teller asks the user to select an account type.
    The user asks the teller to accept a savings account type.
    The teller asks the bank to find the account of the chosen type for the user with the specified PIN. The bank gives the teller a reference to the account.
    The teller asks the user to specify an amount.
    The user asks the teller to accept an amount.
    The teller asks the account to withdraw the specified amount.
    The teller asks the user to select another transaction, ...
21. The user asks the teller to accept an ATM card.
    The user asks the teller to accept a PIN.
    The teller asks the user to select a transaction type.
    The user asks the teller to accept a deposit.
    The teller asks the user to select an account type.
    The user asks the teller to accept a cancellation.

Chapter 10

1. A compiler error results since the `WindowListener` interface is not fully implemented.

3. Closing the frame does not work, and no event terminates the program. The user must abort pressing `Control C` while the console window is selected.

5. The applet registers as a mouse listener with the polygon.
   The user presses the mouse inside the polygon.
   The applet (the component in which the user pressed the mouse)
   passes a mouse event describing the mouse press to the applet's
   `mousePressed` method.
   The applet's `mousePressed` method does nothing since the user pressed
   the mouse outside of the polygon.
   The user releases the mouse inside the polygon.
   The applet (the component in which the user pressed the mouse) passes a
   mouse event describing the mouse release to the applet's
   `mouseReleased` method.
   The applet's `mouseReleased` method changes the foreground color to blue
   and asks Java to redraw it.
   Java calls the applet's `update` method which clears the screen and calls the
   `paint` method which fills the polygon in blue.

9. For `r` : pressed, typed, released.
   For `R` : pressed, pressed, typed, released, released

13. The polygon in which the mouse was last pressed will rotate around the point at which the mouse was last released which may be far away from the polygon. This is not what we need to solve the tangram puzzle.

Chapter 11

1. `new Double(String s.doubleValue()`

3. In Example 11.5 the output is `value=8`, the value set in the `catch` block when an exception occurs. Example 11.6 also prints the stack trace to show explicitly the error that has occurred.

5.
```
public class ArrayTest {
public static void main(String[] args) {
  Object[] objectArray = new Object[3];
  objectArray[0] = new Integer(12);
  objectArray[1] = new Double(4.5);
// objectArray[2] = 7; Compiler error
}
}
```

7. Using the prices.data file
   Milk 3 2.10
   Coffee 2.5 3.39
   Bread 3 1.89

   will cause the program to abort after the output of the total price for milk. The quantity `2.5` for coffee causes Java to throw a `NumberFormatException`. We could modify the program to handle the exception and continue executing good lines in the data file.

9. The program ignores the line containing the item ice cream because the number of tokens on the line is now four and it fails the test `strings.countTokens()==3`.

11.
```
import java.io.*;
public class FileCopy {
  public static void main(String [] args) {
    FileInputStream fis = null;
    FileOutputStream fos = null;
    try {
      File f = new File(args[0]);
      fis = new FileInputStream(f);
      fos = new FileOutputStream(args[1]);
      int length = (int)f.length();
      byte [] data = new byte[length];
      fis.read(data);
      fos.write(data);
    }catch (IOException e) {
      e.printStackTrace();
    }finally {
      try {
        fis.close();fos.close();
      }catch(IOException e) {
        e.printStackTrace();
      }
    }
  }
}
```

13. The changed part is:

```
for (int i=0; i<10; i++)
  raf.writeDouble(i);
raf.seek(40);
double number = raf.readDouble();
System.out.println("The number starting at byte 40 is " + number);
raf.seek(8);
number = raf.readDouble();
System.out.println("The number starting at byte 8 is " + number);
```

Chapter 12

1. There is no difference between the commented and the uncommented version.
3. Use the command `java GrowthFrameSwing 2`.
5. Create

```
ImageIcon lady = new ImageIcon(
    new URL("http://www.nga.gov/thumb-s/a0000d/a0000dee.jpg");
  //or use another image file
JButton print = new JButton("Print", lady);
```

7. We can select multiple colors from the list. The selected color with the lowest index becomes the drawing color.
9. We can select both the square and the circle, or neither. The last shape selected or deselected is drawn.
11. The dialog gives the choices Yes or No, which are not appropriate answers for the question, How are your studies progressing?
13. Change the `setSelecteIndex` statement to `tabPane.setSelectedIndex(1);`
15. Add another entry, such as `{"326", "Operating Systems"}`, to the courses array.

Chapter 13

1.
```
int[] data = {8,5,2,7,10,9,3,4};
mergeSort(data,1,8);
  mergeSort(data,1,4);
    mergeSort(data,1,2);
      mergeSort(data,1,1);
      mergeSort(data,2,2);
      merge(data,1,1,2,2); result {5,8}
    mergeSort(data,3,4);
      mergeSort(data,3,3);
      mergeSort(data,4,4);
      merge(data,3,3,4,4); result {2,7}
    merge(data,1,2,3,4); result {2,5,7,8}
  mergeSort(data,5,8);
    mergeSort(data,5,6);
      mergeSort(data,5,5);
      mergeSort(data,6,6);
      merge(data,5,5,6,6); result {9,10}
    mergeSort(data,7,8);
      mergeSort(data,7,7);
      mergeSort(data,8,8);
      merge(data,7,7,8,8); result {3,4}
    merge(data,5,6,7,8); result {3,4,9,10}
  merge(data,1,4,5,8); result {2,3,4,5,7,8,9,10}
```

3. Try each list operation with a null list. Try the operations in various orders with a list of length one, and with a list of length greater than one.
7. The stack will be the same. The push operation is the inverse pop.

11. `Vector v = new Vector(25,7);`

13. Running with different data

```
  potato -982438873 9
  fish 3143256 7
  steak 109760846 16
  lettuce 68393790 1
  pizza 106683528 6
  hamburger -871931895 14
  hot dog 1097119465 7
  pie 110988 13
  tuna 3571700 7
  candy 94427237 1
  cake 3045944 8
  ice cream 389990061 14
gives more collisions.
  Using randomly generated data
    cnxzcatj -1163064959 7
    xtzarjex 2140893838 18
    vbrtwqve -351254025 20
    unpeecjk -105615955 22
    rdtbkknp -1212249278 15
    njkticlb 1195392437 5
    punojpcj 1639963571 22
    jxslnhen -1718933366 16
    onoxuyfp -1983127946 19
    etlnjisf -1296772669 14
    pizwwcut -68832671 4
    payotnwn 1384976408 13
gives less.
```

Chapter 14

1. The conditions on implementations of Set methods may be more stringent. The `add` method must check for duplicates in a Set but not generally in a Collection.

3. Not directly, because the element type is Object. Primitive types need to be wrapped in wrapper classes such as Integer.

5. The punctuation is included, giving words like "detract.," and "us--that."

7. The List methods specify the position at which to insert or update. The ListIterator does not need this argument because it always inserts or updates at the current position of the iteration.

9. Change the argument in the line `linkImp.get(5000);` to get the time for 10,000 gets. The actual time will vary depending on the system used. Relatively, the time taken increases as the element index increases.

11. The time decreases.

13. It is much easier to find a range of words near the word for which one is searching to provide possible correct spellings.
15. Java throws a ClassCastException because the String cannot be cast to a NewOrderedName. The `compareTo` method for NewOrderedName checks first name, last name, and middle initial and does not work with strings. We could add a constructor to create a NewOrderedName from a String.
17. The algorithms that require the data to be ordered specify a List parameter.

Chapter 15

1. main 1, Bonnie 1, Clyde 1, Clyde 2, Bonnie 2, Clyde 3, Bonnie 3, Clyde 4, Clyde 5, Bonnie 4, main 2, Bonnie 5, main 3, main 4, main 5
3. Main will print its name five times followed first by five Bonnies then by five Clydes. Each thread has more than enough time to print its name five times when it has the processor.
5. Yes, we can edit another program while the animation is running and open another console window to run another Java program.
7. The image starts at a much smaller size and reaches a smaller final size because `imageWidth` and `imageHeight` each get the value `-1` since they are called before the image has finished loading. By executing the `waitForID(0)`we get the correct values of `imageWidth` and `imageHeight`.
9. Omitting the call to `clearRect` causes parts of the image that were drawn in a previous frame to remain on the screen when the new image is drawn.
11. If we stop the applet, the whistle continues to play until we terminate the applet.
13. The frame pops up but does not display the media file.
15. For example, with `java PutGet 100 500`, the buffer becomes full six times, while with `java PutGet 500 100`, the buffer becomes empty nine times.

Chapter 16

1. Using the applet viewer shows a blank screen because the applet viewer does not display HTML documents but only runs applets embedded in those documents.
3. The program displays the HTML file, index.html, with all the HTML tags.
5. The changes are:

```
URLConnection c = url.openConnection();
input = new BufferedReader
          (new InputStreamReader(c.getInputStream()));
```

7. The change is:

```
System.out.println("Content type: " + c.getHeaderField("Content-type"));
```

9. The output includes part of the request headers, which should be informational only to the client.

11. The client receives a message that it is connected, but no data because only headers were requested. We could use this to inspect the headers if we modified the program.
13. Clients will be active simultaneously, and will alternately receive data.
15. The port 3000 overrides the default port of 1099.

Chapter 17

1. The ID is unique, but the name may be duplicated.
3. INSERT INTO Salesperson VALUES ('12', 'Peter Patterson', '66 FifthSt.')
   INSERT INTO Salesperson VALUES ('98','Donna Dubarian', '77 Sixth St.')
5. DELETE FROM OrderItem
   WHERE OrderNumber = '5' AND ItemNumber = '444444'
7. SELECT OrderNumber FROM Orders, Salesperson
   WHERE Orders.SalesPersonID = Salesperson.SalesPersonID
   AND SalespersonName = 'Peter Patterson'
9. Changes are:

   `Class.forName(args[0]);` (instead of `new JdbcOdbcDriver()`)
   `Connection con = DriverManger.getConnection(args[1], user, password);`
11. SELECT DISTINCT SalespersonName, CustomerName
    FROM Salesperson, Customer, Orders
    WHERE Orders.CustomerID = Customer.CustomerID
    AND Orders.SalesPersonID = Salesperson.SalesPersonID
13. Change `rs.getString("CustomerName")` to `rs.getString(1)` in two places and change `rs.getString("OrderNumber")` to `rs.getString(1)`
15. SELECT DISTINCT CustomerName, CustomerAddress
    FROM Customer, Salesperson, Orders
    WHERE Customer.CustomerID = Orders.CustomerID
    AND Salesperson.SalesPersonID = Orders.SalesPersonID
    AND SalespersonName = 'Peter Patterson'
17. Use `dbMetaData.getTables(null, null, "Order%", tables);`
19. Add
    `displayStrings("Type Info Column Names and Types", colNamesTypes(rs));`
    after `getTypeInfo()`.
21. java.sql.SQLException: [Microsoft][ODBC Microsoft Access 97 Driver]Invalid cursor state
25. After pressing the Display button, the new labels are truncated to have the same size as the generic table labels they are to replace.

27. The `fieldValue` text field remains 12 character wide, centered in its two- column field, rather than expanding to fill the two columns.

Chapter 18

1. Using JRun, `Welcome.class` belongs in the JRUN_HOME\servers\default\default-app\web-inf\classes directory. The URL is `http://localhost:8100/servlet/Welcome`. JRun must be started first.
3. Use `Welcome.java` for an entertaining example. Using JRun, put the

   `Welcome.java` in `JRUN_HOME\servers\default\default-app`.

   Enter the URL http://localhost:8100/Welcome.java. Be sure to start JRun.
5. Change the action to
   `http://localhost:8100/servlet/PostOrGetOrder`
7. Every time we press the refresh button or use another copy of the browser to connect, the display increases the connection count.
9. The browser cannot display the page.
11. The servlet still functions properly because it has a `doGet` method to respond to GET requests.
13. The order will be updated and the same session ID will be listed for this session.
15. With GET the client appends the data to the URL `http://localhost:8100/GetOrder.jsp?Order=ice+cream` while with POST it is sent separately.
17. We call bean methods inside a <% %> tag. There may be other bean methods besides those that retrieve property values.

Chapter 19

1. Click on the background entry in the Properties window and choose orange in the color editor that pops up.
3. Bind using the Bind Properties item of the Edit menu. Higher prices make the juggler go slower.
5. The change is vetoed.
7. Bind using the Bind Properties item of the Edit menu.
9. The BeanBox cannot load `Smiley.jar` if `Smiley` does not implement `Serializable`.
11. Use the Events, nosePress item in the Edit menu to hookup one Friendly to the `startJuggling` method of the Juggler, and another to the `stopJuggling` method.
13. The `instantiate` method allows us to load a `.ser` file for a serialized bean whose state we changed by configuring in a tool such as the BeanBox.

    Using **new** loads only the original version of the bean.
15. The Juggler does not appear in the applet.

Chapter 20

1. They are all well-formed.

3.
```
<cds>
    <cd>
        <title>Beethoven Violin Concerto</title>
        <artist>Itzhak Perlman</artist>
        <artist>Daniel Barenboim</artist>
        <tracks>5</tracks>
    </cd>
    <cd>
        <title>from broken hearts to blue skies</title>
        <artist>Susannah McCorkle</artist>
        <tracks>14</tacks>
    </cd>
</cds>
```

5. `startElement`

7.
```
if (args[1].equals(true))
   validate = true;
else
   validate = false;
```

9. `getDocumentElement()` from the class that implements the Document interface.

11. `<xsl:apply-templates></xsl:apply-templates>`

13. `<xsl:template match="book[@type='text']">`

15. `getInternetTime`

Appendix A

1. a. 3 x 10 + 8 c. 5 x 100 + 6 x 10 + 2 e. 3 x 100 + 6

3. a. 3 b. 13 c. 44 d. 27 e. 234

5. a.10001 b. 10111 c. 100110 d. 1010110 e. 10100000 f. 11101011 g. 1000101011100

Appendix B

1. a. 0000 b. 0101 c. 0000

3. a. 1111 b. 1010 c. 1010

5. a. 17 b. 63 c. 46 d. 4

Answers to Skill Builder and Critical Thinking Exercises

Chapter 2

1. a. int x;
   b. public static void main (String [] args) { // code goes here }
   c. z+y cannot occur on the left side of an assignment.
   d. public class MyClass { // put code here }

2. 64

3. a. ii b. iii c. iv d. i

4. b and c 5. a and c 6. a. 3, 4 b. 2, 3 7. d

Chapter 3

1. 2

2. a. v b. i c. iv

3. a.
```
if (x > y) System.out.println("x > y")
else System.out.println("y >= x");
```
   b.
```
while (x > 10) x -=2;
```

4. c 5. d 6. b 7. e

Chapter 4

1.
```
if (i == 1) j += 2;
else if (i == 3) j-= 5;
else if (i==7 || i==10) j *= 17;
else j = 0;
```

2.
```
int i = 0;
while (i <= 20) {
  sum += i * i;
  i++;
}
```

3.
```
int sum = 0, i;
do {
  String input = JOptionPane.showInputDialog("Enter an integer");
  i = Integer.parseInt(input);
  sum += i;
} while (sum < 100);
```

4. c 5. b 6. d 7. b

Chapter 5

1. a. iii b. i c. iv d. ii

2. value, reference

3. hack

4. a 5. e 6. e 7. c

Chapter 6

1. a. iv b. v c. i d. iii e. ii
2. The applet displays a centered rectangle whose dimensions are half those of the applet.
3. <applet code=DrawFill.class width=500 height=320>
4. c 5. a 6. c 7. d

Chapter 7

1. Action, Item, Item, Action
2. a. ii b. i c. iii
3. implements, ActionListener, actionPerformed, implements, ItemListener, itemStateChanged
4. b 5. c 6. b 7. c

Chapter 8

1. `split(0,7) returns 4, nums = { 3, 23, 12, 11, 45, 88, 67, 77}`
2. `{{21, 21, 21, 21}, {21, 21, 21, 21} {21, 21, 21, 21}}`
3. `{{34}, {34, 34}, {34, 34, 34}, {34, 34, 34, 34}, {34, 34, 34, 34, 34}}`
4. a. i b. iv c. ii d. iii 5. c 6. c 7. b

Chapter 9

1. class, interface, abstract, methods, overriding, class
2. a. no modifier b. protected c. public d. private
3. 4, 25
4. b 5. a 6. d 7. d

Chapter 10

1. `KEY_PRESSED, KEY_PRESSED, KEY_TYPED, KEY_RELEASED,KEY_RELEASED`
2.
```
import java.awt.*;
import java.awt.event.*;
import java.applet.Applet;
public class MouseClickRed extends Applet {
  int x = 25, y = 25;
  public void init() {
    setForeground(Color.red);
    addMouseListener(new MouseHandler());
  }
```

```
    public void paint(Graphics g) {
      g.fillOval(x-25,y-25,50,50);
    } class MouseHandler extends MouseAdapter {
      public void mouseClicked(MouseEvent e) {
        x = e.getX();
        y = e.getY();
        repaint();
      }
    }
  }
```

3.
```
import java.awt.*;
import java.awt.event.*;
public class MouseClickRedAlone extends Frame {
  int x = 25, y = 25;
  public MouseClickRedAlone() {
    setForeground(Color.red);
    addMouseListener(new MouseHandler());
    addWindowListener(new WindowClose());
    } public void paint(Graphics g) {
      g.fillOval(x-25,y-25,50,50);
    }
    class MouseHandler extends MouseAdapter {
      public void mouseClicked(MouseEvent e) {
        x = e.getX();
        y = e.getY();
        repaint();
      }
    }
    class WindowClose extends WindowAdapter { public void
    windowClosing(WindowEvent e) {
      System.exit(0);
    }
  }
  public static void main(String[] args) {
    MouseClickRedAlone m = new MouseClickRedAlone();
    m.setSize(300,200);
    m.show();
  }
}
```

4. a   5. c   6. d   7. b

Chapter 11

1. a. iii   b. i   c. ii   d. iii
2. BufferedReader, FileReader, "text.data"
3. PrintWriter, FileWriter, "text.out"
4. d   5. a   6. b   7. b

Chapter 12

1. JMenuBar, JMenu, JMenuItem
2. ListSelectionListener, valueChanged
3. getRowCount, getColumnCount, getValueAt
4. b 5. d 6. a 7. e

Chapter 13

1. 13
2. 243
3. a. ii b. iv c. i d. iii
4. c 5. a 6. d 7. d

Chapter 14

1. a. HashSet b. TreeSet c. ArrayList or LinkedList d. HashMap e. TreeMap
2. equals, hashCode
3. Comparable, compareTo
4. a 5. b 6. e 7. a

Chapter 15

1. a. iii b. ii c. i d. ii
2. a. ii b. iii c. ii d. i
3. a. ii b. iv c. i d. iii
4. c 5. e 6. d 7. a

Index

Note: The boldface entries refer to example programs in the text which are also found on the included disk.

G

H

Interfaces (See pages 269–277)

Specify behavior but omit implementation.

May contain constants and method declarations (no method bodies).

Users of an interface do not know how the methods are implemented. (See page 270)

Code that uses an interface will run invoking implementations written at different times and places.

Classes (See pages 36–42 and 215–229)

Define a type.

May include instance variables that hold state data.

May include instance methods that implement behavior.

May include constructors that create the object.

May include class variables and methods shared by all instances.

Objects (See pages 23–24, 42–48, 206–214, 221–225)

An object is an instance of a class.

The `new` operator creates an object.

An object variable refers to an object.

An object variable has the value `null` when no object is assigned to it.

An object invokes its methods, which may have arguments.

`this` refers to the current object.

Layout Managers

Arrange components in a user interface.

Adjust the layout when required by resizing.

Flow Layout is the default for panels and applets.

- Always respects the preferred sizes of components.
- Enters components in rows.

Border Layout is the default for windows and frames.

- Alters components vertically in East and West.
- Alters components horizontally in North and South.
- Alters components in both directions in the Center region.
- Enters up to one component in each of five regions.

Grid Layout

- Never respects preferred sizes of components.
- Enter components in an m by n grid, across rows first.

Event-Driven Programming (Overview)

Paint events

- Handle in the paint method (See page 257)

More Quick Computing with Java™

Other events

- Register an event listener with the source of the event.
- Implement an event listener.
  - The user interface class implements the listener (See page 296)
  - or, a separate class implements the listener (See page 298)
  - or, an inner class implements the listener. (See pages 307–308)

ActionEvent (Button, TextField, List sources) (See page 296, page 302, and page 322)

Invoke `addActionListener` to register an ActionListener.

The ActionListener implements

```
public void actionPerformed(ActionEvent e)
```

which specifies the effect of the event.

Find out about the event

- `e.getSource()` returns the Object event source
- `e.getActionCommand()` returns the String action associated with the event.

Use source methods.

- `getText` or `setText` for a TextField
- `getSelectedItems` or `getSelectedItem` for a List

ItemEvent (Checkbox, Choice, List sources) (See page 311 and page 322)

Invoke `addItemListener` to register an ItemListener.

The ItemListener implements

```
public void itemStateChanged(ItemEvent e)
```

which specifies the effect of the event.

Find out about the event

- `e.getSource()` returns the Object event source
- `e.getItem()` returns an object associated with the event.
  - the label of a Checkbox
  - the item selected in the Choice box
- `e.getStateChange()` returns ItemEvent.SELECTED or Item.EventDESELECTED.

Use source methods.

- `getSelectedItem()` for a Choice box or a List.
- `getState()` for a Checkbox

Inheritance

A subclass extends a superclass. (See page 401

A subclass inherits methods from its superclass. (See page 402)

A subclass constructor calls a superclass constructor explicitly (See page 403)

A subclass constructor calls a superclass constructor implicitly (See page 401)

A subclass adds variables and methods. (See page 404)

A subclass overrides methods. (See page 408)

Polymorphism (many structures)

A superclass method may have different implementations in each subclass (See page 414)

Java determines an object's type at runtime and calls the correct implementation. (See page 415)

Abstract classes have no instances. (See page 423)

An abstract class may have abstract methods. (See page 423)

Concrete subclasses of an abstract class must implement its abstract methods. (See page 426)

Modifiers (See pages 428–437)

Classes and Interfaces

`public`	Visible everywhere.
`(No modifier)`	Visible within its package.

Data Fields and Methods

`public`	Accessible anywhere the class name is accessible.
`protected`	Accessible in the package that contains the class in which the data field or method is declared, and in any subclass thereof.
`(No modifier)`	Accessible in the package that contains the class in which the data field or method is declared.
`private`	Accessible only in the class in which the data field or method is declared.

Packages

Every Java class is contained in a package.

The default package is the current directory (when no package statement appears.)

A package statement at the top of the program put that code into that named package. (See page 40)

A package corresponds to a directory in the file system.

Code that wishes to use a class in another package uses an import statement to declare which package that class is in. (See page 47)

Compile using the -classpath option to indicate the location of a package directory. (See page 430)

Include the current directory in the classpath. (See page 430)

Arrays

An array variable refers to an array. (See page 348)

The value of an array variable is `null` until an array is assigned to it. (See page 349)

An array variable may be initialized to refer to an array. (See page 353)

The new operator creates an array. (See page 353)

Arrays may be passed as arguments to methods or returned from methods. (See page 360)

Creating an array of objects produces an array of references. The objects they refer to must be created separately.

WindowEvent (Frame) (See pages 458–464)

Invoke `addWindowListener` to register a WindowListener.

The WindowListener implements

`windowActivated`	Window gets the focus.
`windowDeactivated`	Window loses the focus.
`windowOpened`	Window is opened.
`windowClosed`	Window is closed.
`windowClosing`	The user asks to close window.
`windowIconified`	Window is minimized as an icon.
`windowDeiconified`	Window is restored from an icon to handle seven window events.

The WindowAdapter class implements the WindowListener interface, giving each method an empty body.

A window listener can either implement the WindowListener interface and implement all seven methods (See pp. 460–461) OR it can extend WindowAdapter and only override methods to handle the window events of interest. (See pp. 463–464).

Exceptions

A Java class defines each exception. (See page 514)

Exceptions that are subclasses of Error and RuntimeException are unchecked and may be ignored.

All other exceptions are checked and must be handled or the compiler will report an error.

A `try` block contains code that may throw an exception. (See page 517)

A `catch` block contains code that handles an exception. (See page 517)

A Reference Guide

Quick Computing with Java™

Writing a Stand-alone Program

Declare a class that includes a `main` method. (See page 47)

Put the code to start execution in the `main` method.

The class may have other class methods. (See page 51)

The code may create objects using classes in the Java library. (See page 469)

The code may create objects using our own classes. (See page 235)

The code may start objects interacting. (See page 235)

The code may use graphics. (See pages 468–470)

Writing an Applet

Import `java.applet.Applet.`

Declare a class that extends Applet.

(If no components added) Override the applet's `paint` method. (See page 269)

(If components added) Add a component to draw on. (See pages 298–299)

Declare a class that extends Canvas.

Override the canvas' paint method.

Stepwise Refinement (Top-down Design)

```
State the problem clearly;
while (more subproblems to refine) {
    Pick a subproblem that needs to be refined;
    Replace the subproblem by a refinement which
        uses the sequence, if-else, or while structures;
}
Trace the pseudocode with sample data for several cases;
Convert the pseudocode to a Java program;
```

Object-Oriented Design

Define a use case for each intended use of the system.

Write scenarios for each use. (See page 25)

For the typical successful use.

For error cases.

Identify the classes and their responsibilities from the scenarios. (See page 27)

Diagram the class associations in a class diagram. (See page 231)

Diagram the object interactions in a sequence diagram. (See page 232)

Continued inside the back cover ...